Western Canada & Alaska

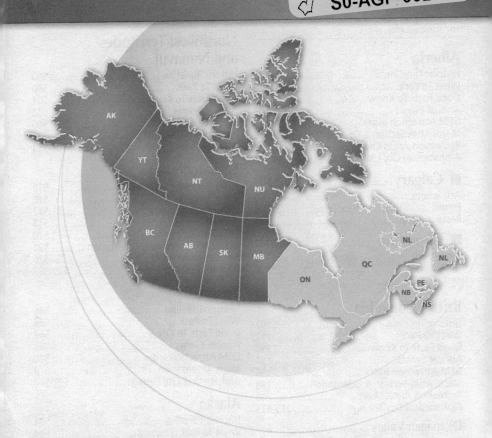

Published by AAA Publishing
1000 AAA Drive, Heathrow, FL 32746-5063
Copyright AAA 2013, All rights reserved

Advertising Rate and Circulation Information: (407) 444-8280

Printed in the USA by Quad/Graphics

This book is printed on paper certified by third-party standards for sustainably managed forestry and production.

Printed on recyclable paper.
Please recycle whenever possible.

Stock #4601

CONTENTS

Attractions, hotels, restaurants and other travel experience information are all grouped under the alphabetical listing of the city in which those experiences are physically located—or the nearest recognized city.

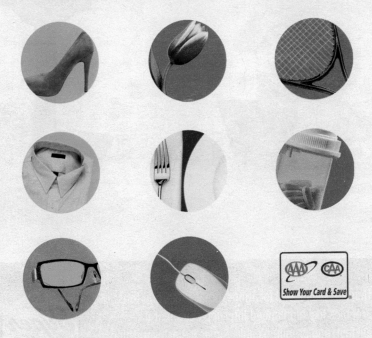

**Great rates and free breakfast.
It's not business,
IT'S PERSONAL**

With more than 2,200 locations, great rates, and tons
of freebies like high-speed Internet, continental
breakfast, and premium cable, Super 8® has everything
you need to make it your hotel of choice when on the
road for business.

Destination Super®

Highlights

Enjoy the trimmer, more colorful, reorganized
TourBook® format introduced to make the
series richer and easier to use.

Plus, find even more of the visuals,
expert recommendations and special
extras you value most for reliable travel
planning and decision making.

Colorful visuals
- More attraction photos
- *New!* Destination area maps
  for seven national parks

Travel recommendations
- More *Must Do: AAA Editor's
  Picks* and *1-Day Itineraries*
- *New! Top Picks for Kids*
  for 19 destination cities

Special extras
- Mass transit information for six
  metropolitan areas
- *New!* Electric vehicle charging
  station locations

**See for yourself. Travel better
with AAA TourBook® guides.**

A to Z City Listings

Cities and places are listed alphabetically within each state or province. Attractions, hotels and restaurants are listed once — under the city in which they are physically located.

Cities that are considered part of a larger destination city or area have an expanded city header. The header identifies the larger region and cross-references pages that contain shared trip planning resources:

- Destination map – outline map of the cities that comprise a destination city or area
- Attraction spotting map – regional street map marked with attraction locations
- Hotel/restaurant spotting map and index – regional street map numbered with hotel and restaurant locations identified in an accompanying index

Cities that are not considered part of a larger destination city or area but have a significant number of listings may have these resources within the individual city section:

- Attraction spotting map
- Hotel/restaurant spotting map and index

About Listed Establishments

AAA/CAA Approved attractions, hotels and restaurants are listed on the basis of merit alone after careful evaluation and approval by full-time, professionally trained AAA/CAA inspectors. An establishment's decision to advertise in the TourBook guide has no bearing on its evaluation or rating; nor does inclusion of advertising imply AAA endorsement of products and services.

Information in this guide was believed accurate at the time of publication. However, since changes inevitably occur between annual editions, please contact your AAA travel professional or visit AAA.com to confirm prices and schedules.

Location Abbreviations

Directions are from the center of town unless otherwise specified, using these highway abbreviations:

Bus. Rte.=business route
CR=county road
FM=farm to market

FR=forest road
Hwy.=Canadian highway
I=interstate highway
LR=legislative route
R.R.=rural route
SR/PR=state or provincial route
US=federal highway

Atlas Section

The Atlas Section provides navigable road maps from the AAA Road Atlas series. The overview map displays the entire coverage area. Corresponding, numbered detail maps offer a closer view for route planning and navigation.

Mobile Tags

Look for Microsoft Tags or QR codes throughout the TourBook guide and scan them with your smartphone to access special online offers, menus, videos and more.

To scan Microsoft Tags or QR codes:

- Download AAA's recommended scanning app to your smartphone at http://gettag.mobi.
- Start scanning Tags or QR codes.
- Link to featured content.

Some advertisers may use bar codes other than Microsoft Tags or QR codes. In those cases, please note any accompanying text that indicates where to download the required reader.

Attraction Listings

> **SAVE** **ATTRACTION NAME,** 3 mi. n. off SR 20A (Main Ave.), consists of 250 acres with Olmsted-designed gardens, a 205-foot marble and coquina bell tower and a Mediterranean-style mansion. One of the state's oldest attractions, the tower and gardens were dedicated to the American people in 1929 by President Calvin Coolidge on behalf of their founder, a Dutch immigrant.
>
> Other features include daily concerts from the 60-bell carillon, a nature observatory and Nature Preserve Trail. The visitor center presents art exhibits, an orientation film and exhibits about the family legacy, the carillon and endangered plants and animals found on the property.
>
> **Hours:** Gardens daily 8-6. Last admission 1 hour before closing. Visitor center daily 9-5. Estate tours are given at noon and 2. Carillon concerts are given at 1 and 3. Phone ahead to confirm schedule. **Cost:** $10; $3 (ages 5-12). Gardens and estate $16; $8 (ages 5-12). **Phone:** (555) 555-5555.
> 🔌 🍽 🎀 🚆 Dupont Circle, 13

AAA/CAA inspectors may designate an attraction of exceptional interest and quality as a AAA GEM — a *Great Experience for Members®.* See GEM Attraction Index (listed on CONTENTS page) for complete list of locations.

Adventure Travel

Activities such as air tours, hiking, skiing and white-water rafting are listed to provide member information and do not imply AAA/CAA endorsement. For your safety, be aware of inherent risks and adhere to all safety instructions.

Cost

Prices are quoted without sales tax in the local currency (U.S. or Canadian dollars). Children under the lowest age specified are admitted free when accompanied by an adult. Most establishments accept credit cards, but a small number require cash, so please call ahead to verify.

Icons

SAVE Show Your Card & Save® member discount

🔌 Electric vehicle charging station on premises. Station locations are provided by Department of Energy.

🅰 Camping facilities

🍽 Food on premises

🎯 Recreational activities

🎀 Pets on leash allowed

🚆 Picnicking allowed

In select cities only:

🚆 Mass transit station within 1 mile. Icon is followed by station name and AAA/CAA designated station number within listing.

Information-Only Attraction Listings

Bulleted listings, which include the following categories, are listed for informational purposes as a service to members:

- **Gambling establishments** (even if located in a AAA/CAA Approved hotel)
- **Guided food tours**
- **Participatory recreational activities** (those requiring physical exertion or special skills)
- **Wineries that offer tours and tastings**

Hotel and Restaurant Listings

1 Diamond Rating – AAA/CAA Approved hotels and restaurants are assigned a rating of one to five Diamonds. Red Diamonds distinguish establishments that participate in the AAA/CAA logo licensing program. For details, see p. 11 or AAA.com/Diamonds.

[fyi] indicates hotels and restaurants that are not AAA/CAA Approved and Diamond Rated but are listed to provide additional choices for members:

- **Hotels** may be unrated if they are: too new to rate, under construction, under major renovation, not evaluated, do not meet all AAA requirements. Hotels that do not meet all AAA requirements may be included if they offer member value or are the only option; details are noted in the listing.
- **Restaurants** may be unrated if they have not yet been evaluated by AAA.

2 Classification or Cuisine Type – Noted after the Diamond Rating.

- **Hotel Classifications** indicate the style of operation, overall concept and service level. Subclassifications may also be added. (See p. 12 list.)
- **Restaurant Cuisine Types** identify the food concept from more than 100 categories. If applicable, a classification may also be added. (See p. 13 list.)

3 Dollar Amounts – Quoted without sales tax in the local currency (U.S. or Canadian dollars), rounded up to the nearest dollar. Most establishments accept credit cards, but a small number require cash, so please call ahead to verify.

- **Hotel Rates** indicate the publicly available two-person rate or rate range for a standard room, applicable all year.
- **Restaurant Prices** represent the minimum and maximum entrée cost per person. Exceptions may include one-of-a-kind or special market priced items.

4 Spotting Symbol – Ovals containing numbers correspond with numbered location markings on hotel and restaurant spotting maps.

5 Parking – Unless otherwise noted, parking is free, on-site self parking.

6 Hotel Value Nationwide – Blue boxes highlight member benefits available at all AAA/CAA Approved locations across a hotel chain. (See Just For Members section for details.)

7 Hotel Unit Limited Availability – Unit types, amenities and room features preceded by "some" are available on a limited basis, potentially as few as one.

8 Hotel Terms – Cancellation and minimum stay policies are listed. Unless otherwise noted, most properties offer a full deposit refund with cancellations received at least 48 hours before standard check-in. Properties that require advance payment may not refund the difference for early departures. "Resort fee" indicates a charge may apply above and beyond the quoted room rate.

9 Hotel Check-in/Check-out – Unless otherwise noted, check-in is after 3 p.m. and check-out is before 10 a.m.

10 Restaurant Dress Code – Unless otherwise noted, dress is casual or dressy casual.

11 Restaurant Menu – Where indicated, menus may be viewed in a secure online environment at AAA.com or, if a mobile tag is provided, via the restaurant's website.

12 Hotel Icons – May be preceded by CALL, FEE and/or SOME UNITS.

Member Information:

[SAVE] Rate guarantee: discounted standard room rate or lowest public rate available at time of booking for dates of stay.

[ECO] Eco-certified by government or private organization. Visit AAA.com/eco for details.

[EV] Electric vehicle charging station on premises. Station locations are provided by Department of Energy.

[X] Smoke-free premises

In select cities only:

[🚇] Mass transit station within 1 mile. Icon is followed by station name and AAA/CAA designated station number within listing.

Services:

[📶] Wireless Internet service on premises

[✈] Airport transportation

[🐾] Pets allowed (Call property for restrictions and fees.)

HOTEL LISTING

RESTAURANT LISTING

| | Restaurant on premises
| | Restaurant off premises
| | Room service for 2 or more meals
| | Full bar
| | Child care
BIZ Business services
| | Accessible features (Call property for available services and amenities.)

Activities:

| | Full-service casino
| | Pool
| | Health club on premises
| | Health club off premises

In-Room Amenities:

| | Pay movies
| | Refrigerator
| | Microwave
| | Coffee maker
| | No air conditioning
| | No TV
| | No telephones

13 Restaurant Icons

SAVE Show Your Card & Save® member discount

ECO Eco-certified by government or private organization. Visit AAA.com/eco for details.

| | Electric vehicle charging station on premises. Station locations are provided by Department of Energy.

| | No air conditioning

| | Accessible features (Call property for available services and amenities.)

| | Designated smoking section

B Breakfast

L Lunch

D Dinner

24 Open 24 hours

LATE Open after 11 p.m.

In select cities only:

| | Mass transit station within 1 mile. Icon is followed by station name and AAA/CAA designated station number within listing.

We Do Everything But Jump On The Beds

AAA backs the Diamond Ratings with expert, in-person evaluations – whether the hotel or restaurant is no-frills, moderate or upscale.

▶ AAA/CAA inspections are unannounced to ensure our experience is comparable to yours.

▶ Only hotels and restaurants that meet AAA standards and member expectations are Approved.

▶ The Diamond Rating, from One to Five, describes the type of experience you can expect.

 Learn more at AAA.com/Diamonds

Just For Members

Understanding the Diamond Ratings

Hotel and restaurant evaluations are unscheduled to ensure our professionally trained inspectors encounter the same experience members do.

- When an establishment is Diamond Rated, it means members can expect a good fit with their needs. The inspector assigns a rating that indicates the type of experience to expect.
- While establishments at high levels must offer increasingly complex personalized services, establishments at every level are subject to the same basic requirements for cleanliness, comfort and hospitality. Learn more at AAA.com/Diamonds.

Hotels

Budget-oriented, offering basic comfort and hospitality.

Affordable, with modestly enhanced facilities, décor and amenities.

Distinguished, multi-faceted with enhanced physical attributes, amenities and guest comforts.

Refined, stylish with upscale physical attributes, extensive amenities and high degree of hospitality, service and attention to detail.

Ultimate luxury, sophistication and comfort with extraordinary physical attributes, meticulous personalized service, extensive amenities and impeccable standards of excellence.

Restaurants

Simple, familiar specialty food at an economical price. Often self-service, basic surroundings.

Familiar, family-oriented experience. Home-style foods and family favorites, often cooked to order, modestly enhanced and reasonably priced. Relaxed service, casual surroundings.

Fine dining, often adult-oriented. Latest cooking trends and/or traditional cuisine, expanded beverage offerings. Professional service staff and comfortable, well-coordinated ambience.

Distinctive fine-dining, typically expensive. Highly creative chefs, imaginative presentations and fresh, top-quality ingredients. Proficient service staff, upscale surroundings. Wine steward may offer menu-specific knowledge.

Luxurious and consistently world-class. Highly acclaimed chefs, artistic and imaginative menu selections using the finest ingredients. Maitre d' and unobtrusive, expert service staff.

What's the difference?

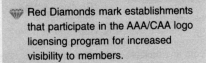

Red Diamonds mark establishments that participate in the AAA/CAA logo licensing program for increased visibility to members.

Black Diamonds identify all other AAA/CAA Approved and Diamond Rated establishments.

Hotel Classifications

Quality and comfort are usually consistent across each Diamond Rating level, but décor, facilities and service levels vary by classification.

1884 Paxton House Inn
Thomasville, GA

Bed & Breakfast – Typically small-scale, emphasizing personal touches. Individually decorated units may not include televisions, telephones or private bathrooms. Usually a common room and continental or full, hot breakfast.

Barkwells
Mills River, NC

Cabin – Vacation-oriented, typically small-scale, free-standing units with simple construction and basic décor. Often in wooded, rural or waterfront location. Cleaning supplies, utensils and bath linens provided. Check-in may be off site.

Camelot by the Sea
Myrtle Beach, SC

Condominium – Vacation-oriented, commonly for extended stays. Routinely rented through a management company. Generally one or more bedrooms, living room, full kitchen and eating area. Studio units combine sleeping and living areas. Cleaning supplies, utensils and linens provided. Check-in may be off site.

The Dunes on the Waterfront
Ogunquit, ME

Cottage – Vacation-oriented, typically small-scale, freestanding units with homey design and décor. Often in wooded, rural or waterfront location. Cleaning supplies, utensils and linens provided. Check-in may be off site.

The Lodge at Moosehead Lake, Greenville, ME

Country Inn – Similar to bed and breakfasts but larger scale with spacious public areas and dining facility that serves, at a minimum, breakfast and dinner.

The Grand America Hotel
Salt Lake City, UT

Hotel – Commonly multistory with interior room entrances. Unit styles vary. Public areas determined by overall theme, location and service level, but may include restaurant, shops, fitness center, spa, business center and meeting rooms.

Best Western Plus Sea Island Inn, Beaufort, SC

Motel – Commonly one- or two-story with exterior room entrances and drive-up parking. Typically one bedroom with bathroom. Limited public areas and facilities.

Lost Valley Ranch
Deckers, CO

Ranch – Typically a working ranch with rustic, Western theme, equestrian activities and various unit styles.

Indian Creek-Alexander Holiday Homes
Kissimmee, FL

Vacation Rental House – Commonly for extended stays. Typically large scale, freestanding and of varying design. Routinely rented through a management company. Often two or more bedrooms, living room, full kitchen, dining room and multiple bathrooms. Cleaning supplies, utensils and linens supplied. Check-in may be off site.

Hotel Subclassifications

These additional descriptives may be added to the classification for more information:

- **Boutique** – Often thematic and informal, highly personalized experience. May have fashionable, luxurious or quirky style.
- **Casino** – (Identified by listing icon) Extensive gambling facilities such as blackjack, craps, keno and slot machines.
- **Classic** – Landmark property, older than 50 years, renowned style and ambience.
- **Contemporary** – Design and theme reflective of current mainstream tastes and style.
- **Extended Stay** – Predominantly long-term units with full-service kitchens.
- **Historic** – Typically 75 years or older with historic architecture, design, furnishings, public record or acclaim and at least one of the following: maintains integrity of the historical nature, listed on the National Register of Historic Places, designated a National Historic Landmark or located in a National Register Historic District.
- **Resort** – Recreation-oriented, geared to a specific destination experience. Typically offer travel packages, meal plans, themed entertainment and social and recreational programs. Extensive recreational facilities may include spa treatments, golf, tennis,

skiing, fishing or water sports. Larger resorts may offer a variety of unit types.

- **Retro** – Contemporary design and theme that reinterpret styles of a bygone era.
- **Vacation Rental** – Typically a house, condo, cottage or cabin offering space, value and conveniences such as full kitchens and washers/dryers. Located in a resort or popular destination area near major points of interest. May require reservations and off-site check-in. Limited housekeeping services.
- **Vintage** – Design and theme reflective of a bygone era.

Restaurant Classifications

If applicable, in addition to the cuisine type noted under the Diamond Rating, restaurant listings may also include one or both classifications:

- **Classic** – Renowned and landmark operation in business for 25 plus years; unique style and ambience.
- **Historic** – Meets one of the following: Listed on National Register of Historic Places, designated a National Historic Landmark or located in a National Register Historic District.

Service Animals

Under the Americans with Disabilities Act (ADA), U.S. businesses that serve the public must allow people with disabilities to bring their service animals into all areas of the facility where customers are normally allowed to go.

Businesses may ask if an animal is a service animal and what tasks the animal has been trained to perform. Businesses may not ask about the person's disability, require special identification for the animal or request removal of the animal from the premises except in limited cases that require alternate assistance. Businesses may not charge extra fees for service animals, including standard pet fees, but may charge for damage caused by service animals if guests are normally charged for damage they cause.

Call the U.S. Department of Justice ADA Information Line: (800) 514-0301 or TTY (800) 514-0383, or visit ada.gov. Regulations may differ in Canada.

AAA/CAA Approved Hotels

For members, AAA/CAA Approved means quality assured.

- Only properties that meet basic requirements for cleanliness, comfort and hospitality pass inspection.
- Approved hotels receive a Diamond Rating that tells members the type of experience to expect.

Guest Safety

Inspectors view a sampling of rooms during evaluations and, therefore, AAA/CAA cannot guarantee the presence of working locks and operational fire safety equipment in every guest unit.

Member Rates

AAA/CAA members can generally expect to pay no more than the maximum TourBook listed rate for a standard room. Member discounts apply to rates quoted within the rate range and are applicable at the time of booking. Listed rates are usually based on last standard room availability. Within the range, rates may vary by season and room type. Obtain current AAA/CAA member rates and make reservations at AAA.com.

Exceptions

- Rates for properties operating as concessionaires for the U.S. National Park Service are not guaranteed due to governing regulations.
- Special advertised rates and short-term promotional rates below the rate range are not subject to additional member discounts.
- During special events, hotels may temporarily increase room rates, not recognize discounts or modify pricing policies. Special events may include Mardi Gras, the Kentucky Derby (including pre-Derby events), college football games, holidays, holiday periods and state fairs. Although some special events are listed in the TourBook guides and on AAA.com, it's always wise to check in advance with AAA travel professionals for specific dates.

If you are charged more than the maximum TourBook listed rate, question the additional charge. If an exception is not in effect and management refuses to adhere to the published rate, pay for the room and contact AAA/CAA. The amount paid above the stated maximum will be refunded if our investigation indicates an unjustified charge.

Reservations and Cancellations

When making your reservation, identify yourself as a AAA/CAA member and request written confirmation of your room type, rate, dates of stay, and cancellation and refund policies. At registration, show your membership card.

To cancel, contact the hotel or your AAA/CAA club office, depending on how you booked your reservation. Request a cancellation number or proof of cancellation.

If your room is not as specified and you have written confirmation of your reservation for a specific room type, you should be given the option of choosing a different room or receiving a refund. If management refuses to issue a refund, contact AAA/CAA.

Contacting AAA/CAA About Approved Properties

If your visit to a AAA/CAA Approved attraction, hotel or restaurant doesn't meet your expectations, please tell us about it — *during your visit or within 30 days*. Be sure to save your receipts and other documentation for reference.

Use the easy online form at AAA.com/TourBookComments to send us the details.

Alternatively, you can email your comments to:
memberrelations@national.aaa.com
or submit them via postal mail to:
AAA Member Comments, 1000 AAA Dr., Box 61, Heathrow, FL 32746.

AAA/CAA Preferred Hotels

All AAA/CAA Approved hotels are committed to providing quality, value and member service. In addition, those designated as AAA/CAA Preferred Hotels also offer these extra values at Approved locations nationwide. Valid AAA/CAA membership required.

- **Best AAA/CAA member rates for your dates of stay.**
- **Seasonal promotions and special member offers.** Visit AAA.com to view current offers.
- **Member benefit.** Look for the blue boxes in the TourBook listings to find values offered at AAA/CAA Approved locations nationwide. Chains and offers valid at time of publication may change without notice.

- **Total satisfaction guarantee.** If you book your stay with AAA/CAA Travel and your stay fails to meet your expectations, you can apply for a full refund. Bring the complaint to the hotel's attention during the stay and request resolution; if the complaint is not resolved by the hotel, ask your AAA/CAA travel agent to request resolution through the AAA/CAA Assured Stay program.

Show Your Card & Save

Preferred Hotels

ASSURED STAY

Total Satisfaction Guarantee

Best Western, Best Western Plus and Best Western Premier

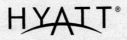

Conrad Hotels & Resorts, DoubleTree by Hilton, Embassy Suites, Hampton Inns & Suites, Hilton Hotels & Resorts, Hilton Garden Inns, Hilton Grand Vacations, Home2 Suites, Homewood Suites, and Waldorf Astoria

ANdAZ, Grand Hyatt, Hyatt Hotels & Resorts, Hyatt House, Hyatt Place, Hyatt Regency and Park Hyatt

Autograph Collection, Courtyard, EDITION, Fairfield Inn & Suites, JW Marriott, Marriott Hotels & Resorts, Renaissance Hotels, Residence Inn, The Ritz-Carlton, SpringHill Suites and TownePlace Suites

Aloft, Element, Four Points, Le Meridien, Sheraton, St. Regis Hotels & Resorts, The Luxury Collection, Westin and W Hotels

Show Your Card & Save® Member Discounts

Visit AAA.com/Discounts to find local Show Your Card & Save discounts. Your AAA/CAA club may offer even greater discounts on theme park tickets. Amtrak, Gray Line and theme park discounts may be used for up to six tickets; restaurant savings may be used for up to six patrons. Other restrictions may apply. All offers subject to change. For complete restrictions visit your AAA office or AAA.com/restrictions.

ATTRACTIONS

SeaWorld, Busch Gardens, Sesame Place

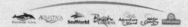

- Save on admission at the gate, participating AAA/CAA offices or AAA.com/SeaWorld.
- Save 10% on up-close dining; visit Guest Relations for details.

Six Flags

- Save on admission at the gate, participating AAA/CAA offices or AAA.com/SixFlags.
- Save 10% on merchandise of $15 or more at in-park stores.

Universal Orlando Resort and Universal Studios Hollywood

- Save on admission at the gate, participating AAA/CAA offices or AAA.com/Universal.
- Save at select food and merchandise venues in-park and at Universal CityWalk®.

The Entertainment Capital of L.A.®

DINING & SHOPPING

Hard Rock Cafe

- Save 10% on food, nonalcoholic beverages and merchandise at all U.S., Canadian and select international locations.

Landry's Seafood House, The Crab House, Chart House, Oceanaire, Saltgrass Steak House, Muer Seafood Restaurants and Aquarium Restaurants

- Save 10% on food and nonalcoholic beverages at all of the above restaurants.
- Save 10% on merchandise at Aquarium and Downtown Aquarium restaurants.
- Location information: AAA.com/Discounts.

Tanger Outlet Centers

- Save up to 20% on total purchase at select merchants with FREE coupon booklet available with registration at AAA/CAA customer service desk.
- Location information: tangeroutlet.com.

TRANSPORTATION & TOURS

Amtrak

- Save 10% on rail fare booked at least 3 days in advance of travel date at AAA.com/Amtrak.

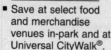

Gray Line

- Save 10% on sightseeing tours of 1 day or less worldwide at AAA.com/GrayLine.

Hertz

- Save on daily, weekend, weekly and monthly rentals at AAA.com/hertz or 1-800-654-3080.

Banff National Park

Alberta

**Alberta is the great outdoors personi-
fied. Mirror images of mountain peaks
are reflected on the surface of glacially fed, brilliantly blue lakes. The
twinkling, shimmering dance of lights
known as aurora borealis provides a
surreal sky show. Golden wheat and
the bright yellow flowers of the canola
plant create blankets of color across
endlessly rolling countryside. Is this
your typical version of the Wild West?
Hardly—but Alberta urges you to
stretch the definition of what the Canadian West is all about.**

Plenty in Canada's fourth-largest province
does fit neatly into the Western mold. Take
Calgary, for instance. This former cow town's
earliest roots were in ranching and meatpacking. Even the roof of the Scotiabank
Saddledome is in the shape of you know
what. The home of the National Hockey
League's Calgary Flames, the Western
Hockey League's Calgary Hitmen and the

The surreal aurora borealis

National Lacrosse League's Calgary Roughnecks also is the venue of choice for everyone from country superstar Kenny Chesney
to the Dalai Lama of Tibet, who visited the
city in 2009.

Thousands of folks decked out in cowboy
boots and ten-gallon hats gather at Stampede Park every July to watch bull ridin',
barrel racin' and other rough-and-tumble rodeo events at the Calgary Stampede, which
celebrated its centennial in 2012. The city
wears its Western heritage proudly, but Calgary also prides itself on being remarkably
well-rounded.

Take the XV Olympic Winter Games in
1988, for instance. Besides showcasing the
world's best athletes—including the memorable "Battle of the Brians" between Brian
Boitano of the United States and Brian Orser
of Canada—the city was in the glare of the
world spotlight. Not to worry; five world-class
facilities were built, and a concerted grass-
roots effort enlisted more than 10,000 resident volunteers to help stage the games.

From grizzly bears to wood bison, the Calgary Zoo, Botanical Garden & Prehistoric Park
offers outstanding opportunities to view native
wildlife. It also is home to more than 4,000
plants and a collection of life-size replicas of
dinosaurs in a simulated Mesozoic landscape.
In futuristic contrast are the elevated "pedways" that link many downtown buildings.

Such dichotomies are commonplace in this vast province. Hikers in Cypress Hills Interprovincial Park might catch the scent of pine and the subtle fragrance of wild orchids. But just to the northwest, Medicine Hat harnesses an extensive reserve of natural gas that once prompted Rudyard Kipling to describe the city, in an olfactory sense, as having "all hell for a basement."

Rafters steel themselves against the raging rapids of the Elbow, Highwood and Kananaskis rivers in Kananaskis Country. Turbulent rushes of water sweeping over rock at Athabasca and Sunwapta falls become imposing frozen challenges for ice climbers who chink away at them in winter. In serene contrast, canoeists play the placid, emerald waters of Banff National Park's Moraine Lake on still summer mornings, gazing at a backdrop of unspoiled wilderness.

A Canadian Melting Pot

Alberta's ethnic diversity is on display at places like the Ukrainian Cultural Heritage Village east of Edmonton, where costumed interpreters demonstrate what life was like for settlers from the 1890s to 1930. In Vegreville, the design of a famed bronze, gold and silver pysanka, or Ukrainian Easter egg, depicts the people's faith and commemorates the protection provided to them by the Royal Canadian Mounted Police. The Basilian Fathers Museum in Mundare chronicles the order's work in eastern Alberta and holds a collection of Canadian and Ukrainian religious and folk artifacts.

The history of native cultures comes alive at the Head-Smashed-In Buffalo Jump Interpretive Centre near Fort Macleod and in the petroglyphs and pictographs at Writing-on-Stone Provincial Park, near Milk River. Indian Battle Park in Lethbridge details a dust-up between the Cree and Blackfoot Indians, the last intertribal conflict in North America.

And let's not forget dinosaurs. They left their mark on the Red Deer Valley by way of fossils buried in walls of sediment. Drumheller pays tribute to that bygone age along the Dinosaur Trail (hwys. 838 and 837). To the southeast, a fertile fossil bed at Dinosaur Provincial Park, near Patricia, contains the remains of 39 species of extinct reptiles.

Recreation

Nature and outdoor lovers need only look to Alberta's five national parks. In fact Banff is Canada's first national park. Elk Island is an oasis for rare and endangered species. Jasper is a feast of glaciers. The Rockies and the prairie meet at Waterton Lakes. And Wood Buffalo reaches north into neighboring Northwest Territories.

But they're not the only popular outdoor destinations in untamed Alberta. Experienced guides lead trail riding expeditions through the Elbow and Sheep valleys in the Kananaskis high country, west of Calgary. Hiking, mountain climbing and mountain biking are ways to experience the challenging peaks of the Rockies.

White-water rafting fans gravitate to the Athabasca, Elbow, Highwood, Kananaskis, Kicking Horse, Red Deer and Sunwapta rivers. The Blackstone River, a hot spot for kayaking in inflatable boats, cuts through the foothills of the Rockies.

Or take advantage of one of North America's longest ski seasons. Some of the best downhill skiing and snowboarding Alberta has to offer is at Marmot Basin, south of Jasper; Lake Louise, northwest of Banff; Sunshine Village and Banff Mount Norquay, both within 15 minutes of Banff; Fortress Mountain, in Kananaskis Country; and Nakiska, west of Calgary.

Plus, there are opportunities galore for fishing. The Bow River offers exceptional trout fly-fishing, while notable fly-in trophy lakes are Gardiner and Namur, northwest of Fort McMurray, and Winefred, northeast of Lac La Biche.

Angel Glacier, Jasper National Park

Historic Timeline

1670	The Hudson's Bay Co. obtains fur-trading rights to a portion of what is now Alberta.
1754	Englishman Anthony Henday is one of the first Europeans to explore the territory.
1795	Fort Edmonton is founded as a Hudson's Bay trading post.
1875	Calgary is designated a North West Mounted Police fort.
1883	The Canadian Pacific Railway reaches Calgary.
1905	The province of Alberta is created.
1930	Jasper National Park is established.
1967	The Great Canadian Oil Sands Co. in Fort McMurray begins producing synthetic crude oil from large deposits of oil sands.
1981	West Edmonton Mall—now one of the world's largest shopping centers following three expansions—opens.
1988	Calgary hosts the XV Olympic Winter Games.
2005	Alberta celebrates its centennial.

What To Pack

Temperature Averages Maximum/Minimum (Celsius)	JANUARY	FEBRUARY	MARCH	APRIL	MAY	JUNE	JULY	AUGUST	SEPTEMBER	OCTOBER	NOVEMBER	DECEMBER
Banff NP	-5 / -15	0 / -11	4 / -8	9 / -3	14 / 2	19 / 6	22 / 7	22 / 7	16 / 3	10 / -1	1 / -8	-5 / -14
Calgary	-3 / -16	-1 / -12	3 / -8	11 / -2	17 / 3	21 / 7	23 / 9	23 / 9	17 / 4	13 / -1	3 / -9	-2 / -14
Edmonton	-8 / -17	-4 / -14	1 / -9	10 / -1	17 / 6	21 / 9	23 / 12	22 / 11	16 / 6	11 / 1	-1 / -9	-7 / -15
Fort McMurray	-15 / -25	-9 / -21	-1 / -15	9 / -4	17 / 3	21 / 7	23 / 10	22 / 8	15 / 3	8 / -2	-5 / -14	-13 / -22
Grande Prairie	-10 / -21	-6 / -18	-1 / -12	9 / -3	16 / 3	20 / 8	22 / 9	21 / 8	16 / 3	10 / -2	-2 / -12	-8 / -19
Jasper NP	-6 / -16	-1 / -12	4 / -8	10 / -3	15 / 2	19 / 6	22 / 8	22 / 7	16 / 3	10 / -1	0 / -9	-6 / -14

From the records of The Weather Channel Interactive, Inc.

Good Facts To Know

ABOUT THE PROVINCE

POPULATION: 3,645,257.

AREA: 640,045 sq km (247,123 sq mi.); ranks 6th.

CAPITAL: Edmonton.

HIGHEST POINT: 3,747 m (12,293 ft.), Mount Columbia.

LOWEST POINT: 152 m (499 ft.), Salt River at border with the Northwest Territories.

TIME ZONE(S): Mountain. DST.

GAMBLING

MINIMUM AGE FOR GAMBLING: 18.

REGULATIONS

TEEN DRIVING LAWS: For probationary licensees, driving is not permitted daily midnight-5 a.m. The minimum age for an unrestricted driver's license is 18. Phone (780) 422-8839 for more information about Alberta driver's license regulations.

SEAT BELT/CHILD RESTRAINT LAWS: Seat belts are required for driver and all passengers ages 16 and older. Children ages 6-15 and 18 kilograms (40 lbs.) and over are required to be in a child restraint or seat belt. Child restraints are required for those under age 6 and under 18 kilograms (40 lbs.).

CELL PHONE RESTRICTIONS: The use of handheld cell phones and text messaging while driving are prohibited.

HELMETS FOR MOTORCYCLISTS: Required for all riders.

RADAR DETECTORS: Permitted.

MOVE OVER LAW: A motorist may not drive more than 60 kph (37 mph) or the maximum speed limit, whichever is lower, if traveling in the same direction in the lane immediately adjacent and passing a stopped emergency vehicle or tow truck using flashing signals.

FIREARMS LAWS: By federal law, all nonresidents entering Canada with a firearm must declare their weapon in writing and pay a fee of $25 (Canadian). Contact the Canadian Firearms Centre at (800) 731-4000 to receive a declaration form or for additional information.

ALCOHOL CONSUMPTION: Legal age 18.

HOLIDAYS

HOLIDAYS: Jan. 1 ▪ Family Day, Feb. (3rd Mon.) ▪ Good Friday ▪ Easter Monday ▪ Victoria Day, May 24 (if a Mon.) or the closest prior Mon. ▪ Canada Day, July 1 ▪ Heritage Day, Aug. (1st Mon.) ▪ Labour Day, Sept. (1st Mon.) ▪ Thanksgiving, Oct. (2nd Mon.) ▪ Remembrance Day, Nov. 11 ▪ Christmas, Dec. 25 ▪ Boxing Day, Dec. 26.

MONEY

TAXES: Alberta has no provincial sales tax. However, there is a 4 percent hotel tax, plus a 1-2 percent tourism levy in some areas. In addition there is a 5 percent national Goods and Service Tax (GST).

VISITOR INFORMATION

INFORMATION CENTERS: Travel Alberta Visitor Centres provide information about accommodations and campgrounds as well as maps. They are located at Canmore on Hwy. 1 ▪ Crowsnest Pass on Hwy. 3 ▪ Field, British Columbia, on Hwy. 1 ▪ Grande Prairie on 106th St. ▪ Hinton on Hwy. 16 ▪ Lloydminster on Hwy. 16 ▪ Milk River on Hwy. 4 ▪ Oyen at the junction of hwys. 9 and 41 ▪ Walsh on Hwy. 1 ▪ and West Glacier, Mont., at the junction of Hwy. 2 and Going-to-the-Sun Road. Most centers are open daily 9-6, mid-May through Labour Day. A tourism office is open year-round in Canmore.

FURTHER INFORMATION FOR VISITORS:
Travel Alberta
P.O. Box 2500
Edmonton, AB T5J 2Z4
Canada
(780) 427-4321
(800) 252-3782

FISHING AND HUNTING REGULATIONS:
Sustainable Resource Development Information Centre
9920 108th St., Main Floor
Edmonton, AB T5K 2M4
Canada
(780) 944-0313
(877) 944-0313 (in Alberta)

RECREATION INFORMATION:
Alberta Tourism, Parks and Recreation
Parks & Protected Areas
9820 106th St., 2nd Floor
Edmonton, AB T5K 2J6
Canada
(866) 427-3582

Alberta Annual Events

Please call ahead to confirm event details.

JANUARY

- Jasper in January / Jasper
  780-852-3858
- Ice Magic Festival
  International Ice Sculpture
  Competition / Lake Louise
  403-762-0270
- Ice on Whyte Festival
  Edmonton
  780-439-9166

FEBRUARY

- Calgary Home and Garden
  Show / Calgary
  403-253-1177
- Silver Skate Festival
  Edmonton
  780-496-4000
- Canadian Birkebeiner Ski
  Festival / Edmonton
  780-430-7153

MARCH

- Edmonton Home and
  Garden Show / Edmonton
  780-459-2008
- Outdoor Adventure Sports
  Show / Calgary
  403-261-0101
- Camrose Spring Classic
  Pro Rodeo / Camrose
  780-672-3640

APRIL

- Edmonton Kiwanis Music
  Festival / Edmonton
  780-488-3498
- Aggie Days Family Fun
  Days / Calgary
  403-261-0162
- Red Deer Festival of the
  Performing Arts / Red Deer
  403-342-3504

MAY

- Grande Prairie Stompede
  Grande Prairie
  780-532-4646
- Calgary International
  Children's Festival / Calgary
  403-294-7414
- Lilac Festival at 4th Street
  Calgary
  403-229-0902

JUNE

- Edmonton International
  Jazz Festival / Edmonton
  780-990-0222
- International Children's
  Festival / St. Albert
  780-459-1542
- Grande Prairie Highland
  Games / Grande Prairie
  780-513-2492

JULY

- Edmonton's K-Days
  Edmonton
  780-471-7210
- Medicine Hat Exhibition and
  Stampede / Medicine Hat
  403-527-1234
- Calgary Stampede / Calgary
  403-261-0172

AUGUST

- Taste of Calgary / Calgary
  403-293-2888
- Edmonton International
  Fringe Theatre Festival
  Edmonton
  780-448-9000
- Edmonton Folk Music
  Festival / Edmonton
  780-429-1899

SEPTEMBER

- Canmore Highland Games
  Canmore
  403-678-9454
- Edmonton International
  Film Festival / Edmonton
  780-423-0844
- Masters Tournament
  Calgary
  403-974-4200

OCTOBER

- Rocky Mountain Wine and
  Food Festival / Calgary
  403-261-0101
- Great White North Pumpkin
  Fair and Weigh-Off
  Smoky Lake
  780-656-3674
- Grande Prairie Museum
  Lantern Tours
  Grande Prairie
  780-830-7090

NOVEMBER

- Spruce Meadows
  International Christmas
  Market / Calgary
  403-974-4200
- Banff Mountain Film and
  Book Festival / Banff
  800-413-8368
- Canadian Finals Rodeo
  Edmonton
  888-800-7275

DECEMBER

- Jingle On Indoor Santa
  Claus Parade / Edmonton
  780-424-4085
- A Traditional Christmas
  Calgary
  403-571-0849
- Once Upon a Christmas at
  Heritage Park / Calgary
  403-268-8500

Saamis Teepee, Medicine Hat

Chinese Cultural Centre
Museum, Calgary

Ride the Jasper Tramway,
Jasper

Bighorn sheep, Jasper National Park

Moraine Lake, Banff National Park

Index: Great Experience for Members

AAA editor's picks of exceptional note

Dinosaur Provincial Park

Frank Slide Interpretive Centre

Muttart Conservatory

Nikka Yuko Japanese Garden

Alberta Atlas Section

ROADS/HIGHWAYS

- INTERSTATE
- CONTROLLED ACCESS
- CONTROLLED ACCESS TOLL
- TOLL ROAD
- PRIMARY DIVIDED
- PRIMARY UNDIVIDED
- SECONDARY DIVIDED
- SECONDARY UNDIVIDED
- LOCAL DIVIDED
- LOCAL UNDIVIDED
- UNPAVED ROAD
- UNDER CONSTRUCTION
- TUNNEL
- PEDESTRIAN ONLY
- AUTO FERRY
- PASSENGER FERRY
- SCENIC BYWAY
- **10** DISTANCE BETWEEN MARKERS
- EXIT NUMBER-FREE/TOLL
- INTERCHANGE FULL/PARTIAL
- WELCOME CENTER
- REST AREA/ SERVICE CENTER

BOUNDARIES

- INTERNATIONAL
- STATE
- COUNTY
- TIME ZONE
- CONTINENTAL DIVIDE

ROAD SHIELDS

- INTERSTATE/BUSINESS
- U.S./STATE/COUNTY
- FOREST/INDIAN
- TRANS-CANADA
- PROVINCIAL AUTOROUTE
- MEXICO
- HISTORIC ROUTE 66
- **VT 41** REFERENCE PAGE INDICATOR

AREAS OF INTEREST

- INDIAN
- MILITARY
- PARK
- FOREST
- GRASSLANDS
- HISTORIC
- INT'L/REGIONAL AIRPORT
- INCORPORATED CITY

POINTS OF INTEREST

- TOWN
- NATIONAL CAPITAL
- STATE/PROVINCIAL CAPITAL
- AAA/CAA CLUB LOCATION
- FEATURE OF INTEREST
- COLLEGE/UNIVERSITY
- CAMPGROUND INFORMATION PROVIDED BY WOODALL'S®
- CUSTOMS STATION
- HISTORIC
- LIGHTHOUSE
- MONUMENT/MEMORIAL
- STATE/PROVINCIAL PARK
- NATIONAL WILDLIFE REFUGE
- SKI AREA
- SPORTS COMPLEX
- DAM

CITIES/TOWNS are color-coded by size, showing where to find AAA Approved and Diamond rated lodgings or restaurants listed in the AAA TourBook guides and on AAA.com:

- Red - major destinations and capitals; many listings
- Black - destinations; some listings
- Grey - no listings

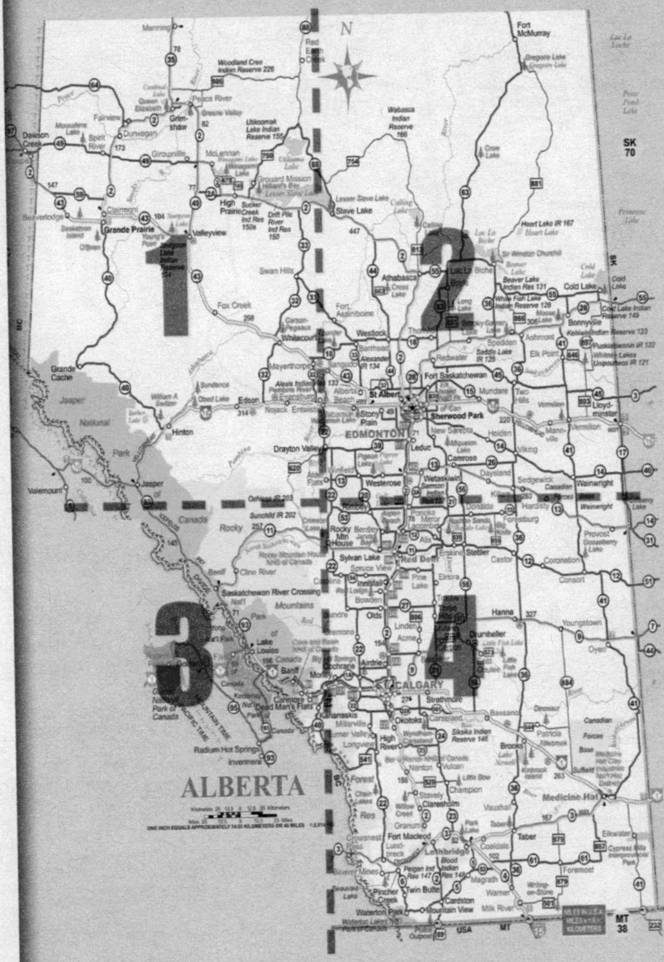

ALBERTA

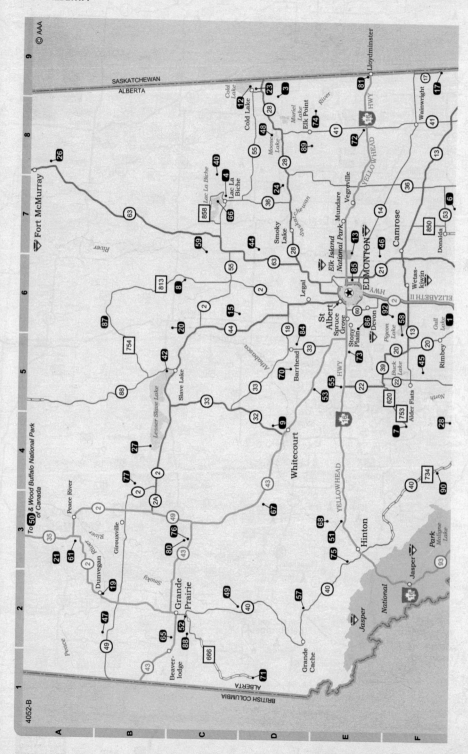

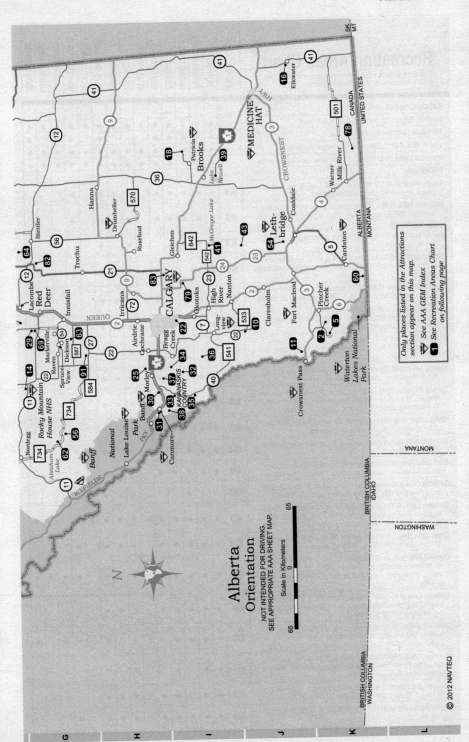

Alberta
Orientation

NOT INTENDED FOR DRIVING.
SEE APPROPRIATE AAA SHEET MAP.

Scale in Kilometers

65   0   65

Only places listed in the Attractions
section appear on this map.

11 See AAA GEM Index

1 See Recreation Areas Chart
on following page

© 2012 NAVTEQ

Recreation Areas Chart

The map location numerals in column 2 show an area's location on the preceding map.

	MAP LOCATION	CAMPING	PICNICKING	HIKING TRAILS	BOATING	BOAT RAMP	BOAT RENTAL	FISHING	SWIMMING	PETS ON LEASH	BICYCLE TRAILS	WINTER SPORTS	VISITOR CENTER	LODGE/CABINS	FOOD SERVICE
NATIONAL PARKS *(See place listings.)*															
Banff (G-5) 6,641 square kilometres. Horse rental.		•	•	•	•	•	•	•	•	•	•	•	•	•	•
Elk Island (D-7) 194 square kilometres.		•	•	•					•	•			•		•
Jasper (E-2, F-2) 11,228 square kilometres. Horse rental.		•	•	•	•	•	•	•	•	•	•	•	•	•	•
Waterton Lakes (K-5) 505 square kilometres. Golf; horse rental.		•	•	•	•	•	•	•	•	•	•	•	•	•	•
PROVINCIAL															
Aspen Beach (F-6) 214 hectares on Gull Lake, 17 km w. of Lacombe on Hwy. 12. *(See Lacombe p. 163.)*	①	•	•	•	•	•			•	•	•				
Beauvais Lake (K-5) 1,160 hectares 11 km w. of Pincher Creek on Hwy. 507, then 8 km s. on Hwy. 775. Canoeing, kayaking, sailing, windsurfing.	②	•	•	•	•	•			•	•					
Beaverdam (D-9) 110 hectares 5 km e. of Nordegg on Hwy. 11. Canoeing, kayaking.	③	•	•	•				•		•					
Beaver Lake (C-8) 96 hectares 6 km s.e. of Lac La Biche off Hwy. 36, on the n.e. shore of Beaver Lake. Bird-watching, canoeing, kayaking.	④	•		•	•	•		•	•	•					
Beaver Mines Lake (K-6) 118 hectares 20 km w. of Pincher Creek on Hwy. 507, 10 km s.w. on Hwy. 774, then 5 km s. on access road.	⑤	•	•	•	•	•		•		•					
Big Knife (F-7) 295 hectares 8 km w. and 13 km s. of Forestburg on Hwy. 855. Canoeing, kayaking.	⑥	•	•	•	•			•	•	•					
Brazeau Reservoir (F-4) 130 hectares 60 km s.w. of Drayton Valley along Hwy. 620. Bird-watching, canoeing, kayaking, sailing, windsurfing.	⑦	•			•	•		•		•					
Calling Lake (C-6) 738 hectares 55 km n. of Athabasca on Hwy. 813. Bird-watching, canoeing, kayaking.	⑧	•	•	•	•	•		•	•	•					
Carson-Pegasus (D-4) 1,209 hectares 6 km w. of Whitecourt on Hwy. 43, 11 km n. on Hwy. 32, then 5 km e. on access road. Bird-watching, canoeing, kayaking, wildlife observation.	⑨	•	•		•	•	•	•		•			•		•
Chain Lakes (J-6) 409 hectares 38 km s.w. of Nanton on Hwy. 533. Canoeing, kayaking, sailing, windsurfing.	⑩	•	•		•	•		•		•					
Chinook (J-5) 48 hectares 8 km w. of Crowsnest Pass off Hwy. 3. Canoeing, kayaking.	⑪	•	•	•				•		•	•	•			
Cold Lake (C-8) 5,849 hectares 3 km n.e. of Cold Lake off Hwy. 28. Bird-watching, canoeing, kayaking, sailing, windsurfing.	⑫	•	•		•	•		•	•	•		•			
Cooking Lake-Blackfoot (E-7) 9,700 hectares 24 km e. of Sherwood Park s. of Hwy. 16. Bird-watching, canoeing, kayaking.	⑬		•	•				•		•	•	•			
Crimson Lake (G-5) 3,209 hectares 14 km w. of Rocky Mountain House on Hwy. 11, then 6 km n. on Hwy. 756. Bird-watching, canoeing, kayaking; interpretive programs.	⑭	•	•	•	•	•		•	•	•	•	•			•
Cross Lake (C-6) 2,076 hectares 8 km n. and 19 km n.e. of Jarvie off Hwy. 663. Bird-watching, canoeing, kayaking.	⑮	•	•	•	•	•		•	•	•		•			
Cypress Hills (J-9) 20,451 hectares 1.5 km s. of Elkwater on Hwy. 41. Historic. Canoeing, cross-country skiing, golf, kayaking, sailing, windsurfing; interpretive programs. *(See Elkwater p. 142.)*	⑯	•	•	•	•	•		•	•	•		•	•	•	•
Dillberry Lake (F-9) 1,205 hectares 15 km s.e. of Chauvin on Hwy. 17 at Alberta/Saskatchewan border. Bird-watching, canoeing, kayaking, sailing, windsurfing.	⑰	•	•	•	•	•		•	•	•		•			
Dinosaur (I-8) 8,085 hectares 13 km n.e. of Patricia via Hwy. 210. Historic. Bird-watching, canoeing, kayaking; interpretive programs. *(See Patricia p. 174.)*	⑱	•	•					•		•		•	•		•
Dunvegan (B-2) 9 hectares off Queen Elizabeth II Hwy. on the n. side of the Peace River beside Dunvegan Suspension Bridge. Historic. *(See Dunvegan p. 107.)*	⑲	•	•		•			•		•			•		
Fawcett Lake (West) (C-6) 48 hectares 55 km s.e. of Slave Lake on Hwy. 2, 20 km n. on Hwy. 2A, then 18 km n. on access road.	⑳	•	•		•	•		•	•	•					
Figure Eight Lake (A-3) 90 hectares 25 km w. of Peace River off Hwy. 35.	㉑	•	•	•	•	•		•	•	•		•			

Recreation Areas Chart

The map location numerals in column 2 show an area's location on the preceding map.

	MAP LOCATION	CAMPING	PICNICKING	HIKING TRAILS	BOATING	BOAT RAMP	BOAT RENTAL	FISHING	SWIMMING	PETS ON LEASH	BICYCLE TRAILS	WINTER SPORTS	VISITOR CENTER	LODGE/CABINS	FOOD SERVICE
Fish Creek (I-6) 1,355 hectares in Calgary between 37th St. S.W. and the Bow River. Bird-watching, golf; interpretive programs.	22		•	•				•	•	•	•		•		•
French Bay (D-9) 449 hectares 11 km e. and 3 km n. of Cold Lake off Hwy. 55. Canoeing, kayaking, sailing, windsurfing.	23	•			•	•		•	•	•					
Garner Lake (D-7) 74 hectares 5 km n. of Spedden off Hwy. 28. Canoeing, kayaking.	24	•	•	•	•	•		•	•	•			•		
Ghost Reservoir (H-5) 24 hectares 18 km w. of Cochrane on Hwy. 1A. Sailing, windsurfing.	25	•	•		•	•	•	•		•			•		
Gregoire Lake (A-8) 696 hectares 19 km s. of Fort McMurray on Hwy. 63, then 10 km e. on Hwy. 881.	26	•	•		•	•		•	•	•					
Hilliard's Bay (B-4) 2,323 hectares 10 km e. of Grouard off Hwy. 750. Canoeing, kayaking, sailing, windsurfing.	27	•		•	•	•		•	•						
Jackfish Lake (F-4) 203 hectares 50 km w. of Rocky Mountain House on Hwy. 11, then 2 km n. on access road. Pier.	28	•				•		•		•	•	•			
Jarvis Bay (G-5) 86 hectares 4 km n. of Sylvan Lake townsite on Hwy. 20.	29	•		•						•	•				
Kananaskis Country (I-4) *(See place listing p. 162.)*															
Bow Valley (H-5) 3,129 hectares 25 km e. of Canmore on Hwy. 1 and .5 km n. on Hwy. 1X. Canoeing, kayaking; bicycle rental, interpretive programs.	30	•	•	•				•	•	•	•	•	•		
Canmore Nordic Centre (H-4) 804 hectares 3 km s. of Canmore on Spray Lakes Rd.	31		•	•						•	•	•	•		•
Elbow River (I-5) 245 hectares 20 km w. of Bragg Creek on Hwy. 66. Interpretive programs.	32	•	•	•				•		•	•	•			
Evan-Thomas (I-5) 2,571 hectares 30 km e. of Canmore on Spray Lakes Rd.	33	•	•	•				•		•		•	•	•	
McLean Creek (I-5) 238 hectares 12 km w. of Bragg Creek on Hwy. 66, then 1.3 km s. on McLean Creek Trail.	34	•	•					•		•		•			
Peter Lougheed (I-5) 50,142 hectares 43 km s.e. of Canmore on Hwy. 40. Canoeing, kayaking; interpretive programs.	35	•	•	•	•	•		•	•	•		•	•	•	•
Sheep River (I-5) 6,191 hectares 25 km w. of Turner Valley on Hwy. 546. Horseback riding.	36	•	•					•		•		•			
Sibbald Lake (I-5) 79 hectares 30 km e. of Canmore on Hwy. 1, 6 km s. on Hwy. 40, then 12 km e. on Hwy. 68. Canoeing, kayaking; amphitheater, interpretive programs.	37	•	•	•	•			•		•		•			
Spray Valley (I-5) 27,471 hectares s.w. of Canmore, surrounding the Spray Lakes Reservoir. Golf.	38	•	•	•				•		•		•			
Kinbrook Island (I-8) 540 hectares 13 km s. of Brooks off Hwy. 873. Bird-watching, canoeing, kayaking, sailing, windsurfing.	39	•	•		•	•		•	•	•					•
Lakeland (C-8) 59,030 hectares 13 km e. of Lac La Biche off Hwy. 663. Bird-watching, canoeing, kayaking. *(See Lac La Biche p. 163.)*	40	•	•	•	•			•	•	•		•			
Lake McGregor (I-7) 140 hectares 20 km n. of Vulcan on Hwy. 23, then 25 km e. on Hwy. 542. Canoeing, kayaking, sailing, windsurfing.	41	•	•		•	•		•	•						
Lesser Slave Lake (B-5) 7,566 hectares 6 km n. of Slave Lake on Hwy. 88. Interpretive programs. *(See Slave Lake p. 181.)*	42	•	•	•	•			•	•	•		•	•		
Little Bow (J-7) 110 hectares 20 km s. of Vulcan on Hwy. 23, 16 km e. on Hwy. 529, then 1 km s. on access road. Bird-watching, canoeing, kayaking.	43	•	•		•	•	•	•	•	•					
Long Lake (D-7) 769 hectares 20 km s. of Boyle on Hwy. 831, then 2 km n.e. on access road. Golf (adjacent to park).	44	•	•		•	•		•	•	•			•	•	
Medicine Lake (F-5) 24 hectares 47 km n. of Rocky Mountain House on Hwy. 22, then 8 km s.e. on access road. Canoeing, kayaking.	45	•	•					•	•	•					
Miquelon Lake (E-7) 1,299 hectares 3 km s. of New Sarepta on Hwy. 21, then 20 km e. on Hwy. 623. Bird-watching, canoeing, golf (adjacent to park), kayaking, sailing, windsurfing; interpretive programs.	46	•	•	•				•	•		•	•		•	•

Recreation Areas Chart

The map location numerals in column 2 show an area's location on the preceding map.

Area	MAP LOCATION	CAMPING	PICNICKING	HIKING TRAILS	BOATING	BOAT RAMP	BOAT RENTAL	FISHING	SWIMMING	PETS ON LEASH	BICYCLE TRAILS	WINTER SPORTS	VISITOR CENTER	LODGE/CABINS	FOOD SERVICE
Moonshine Lake (B-2) 1,103 hectares 27 km w. of Spirit River on Hwy. 49, then 7 km n. on Hwy. 725.	47	•	•	•	•	•		•	•	•		•			
Moose Lake (D-8) 736 hectares 5 km n. of Bonnyville on Hwy. 41, 10 km w. on Hwy. 660, then 2 km s. on access road. Canoeing, kayaking, sailing, windsurfing.	48	•	•	•	•	•		•	•	•					
Musreau Lake (C-2) 1,803 hectares 80 km s. of Grande Prairie on Hwy. 40, then 2 km e. on access road. Canoeing, kayaking.	49	•	•	•	•	•		•		•					
Notikewin (A-3) 9,697 hectares 37 km n. of Manning via Hwy. 35, then 30 km e. on Hwy. 692. Bird-watching, canoeing, golf, kayaking.	50	•	•	•	•			•		•					
Obed Lake (E-3) 3,402 hectares 55 km w. of Edson off Hwy. 16. Canoeing, kayaking.	51	•	•		•			•							
O'Brien (C-2) 65 hectares 10 km s. of Grande Prairie on Hwy. 40. Canoeing, kayaking.	52		•	•				•	•	•		•			
Paddle River Dam (E-5) 70 hectares 10 km n.w. of Sangudo on Hwy. 43. Canoeing, kayaking.	53	•	•		•	•		•							
Park Lake (J-7) 224 hectares 17 km n.w. of Lethbridge on Hwy. 25, then 5 km n.w. on Hwy. 101. Canoeing, kayaking, sailing.	54	•	•	•	•	•		•	•	•					
Pembina River (E-5) 167 hectares 2 km n.e. of Entwistle on Hwy. 16A. Canoeing, kayaking; interpretive trails.	55	•	•	•				•	•	•					
Peppers Lake (G-4) 18 hectares 84 km s.e. of Nordegg on Forestry Trunk Rd. (Hwy. 734). Canoeing, horseback riding, kayaking.	56		•		•			•		•					
Pierre Grey's Lakes (D-2) 633 hectares 37 km s. of Grande Cache off Hwy. 40 on access road. Historic.	57	•	•	•	•			•		•		•			
Pigeon Lake (F-6) 443 hectares 5 km w. and 10 km n. of Westerose off Hwy. 771.	58	•	•	•	•	•		•	•	•	•	•			
Poachers' Landing (C-7) 1,518 hectares 35 km n.e. of Athabasca on Hwy. 55, then 25 km n. on access road. Horseback riding.	59	•	•		•			•		•					
Police Outpost (K-6) 223 hectares 10 km s. and 23 km w. of Cardston on Queen Elizabeth II Hwy. Canoeing, kayaking.	60	•	•	•	•	•		•		•					
Queen Elizabeth (A-3) 86 hectares 3 km n. and 5 km w. of Grimshaw off Hwy. 35. Bird-watching, canoeing, kayaking, sailing.	61	•	•		•				•						
Ram Falls (G-4) 409 hectares 64 km s. of Nordegg on Forestry Trunk Rd. (Hwy. 734).	62	•	•	•				•		•					
Red Lodge (G-6) 129 hectares 15 km w. of Bowden on Hwy. 587. Canoeing, kayaking.	63	•	•					•	•	•					
Rochon Sands (G-7) 119 hectares 12 km w. of Stettler on Hwy. 12, then 16 km n. on Hwy. 835. Canoeing, kayaking, sailing, windsurfing.	64	•	•		•	•		•							
Saskatoon Island (B-2) 101 hectares 21 km w. of Grande Prairie on Hwy. 43, then 4 km n. on an access road. Bird-watching, water sports; interpretive programs.	65	•	•	•	•	•				•	•	•			
Sir Winston Churchill (C-7) 662 hectares 11 km n.e. of Lac La Biche off Hwy. 881. Bird-watching, canoeing, kayaking. *(See Lac La Biche p. 163.)*	66	•	•	•	•			•	•	•		•			
Smoke Lake (D-3) 102 hectares 9 km s.w. of Fox Creek off Hwy. 43. Canoeing, kayaking.	67	•	•		•			•	•	•					
Sundance (E-3) 151 hectares 56 km n.e. of Hinton on Emerson Creek Rd. Canoeing, kayaking.	68	•	•	•				•		•	•				
Sylvan Lake (G-5) 67 hectares 18 km n.w. of Red Deer on Hwy. 11 in the town of Sylvan Lake. Canoeing, golf, kayaking, sailing, windsurfing. *(See Red Deer p. 175.)*	69		•	•				•	•	•				•	
Thunder Lake (D-5) 208 hectares 21 km w. of Barrhead on Hwy. 18.	70	•	•		•	•		•	•	•					•
Two Lakes (D-1) 1,566 hectares 130 km s.w. of Grande Prairie on Two Lakes Rd. Canoeing, kayaking.	71	•		•	•	•		•		•					
Vermilion (E-8) 759 hectares 1.5 km n. of Vermilion on Hwy. 41 from jct. Hwy. 16, then w. on 50th Ave. following signs. Canoeing, golf, kayaking.	72	•	•	•				•		•					

Recreation Areas Chart

The map location numerals in column 2 show an area's location on the preceding map.

	MAP LOCATION	CAMPING	PICNICKING	HIKING TRAILS	BOATING	BOAT RAMP	BOAT RENTAL	FISHING	SWIMMING	PETS ON LEASH	BICYCLE TRAILS	WINTER SPORTS	VISITOR CENTER	LODGE/CABINS	FOOD SERVICE
Wabamun Lake (E-5) 231 hectares 3 km e. and 1 km s. of Wabamun off Hwy. 16A. Bird-watching, golf (adjacent to park), kayaking, sailing, windsurfing.	73	•	•	•	•	•		•	•	•					
Whitney Lakes (D-8) 1,489 hectares 24 km e. of Elk Point off Hwy. 646. Historic. Bird-watching, canoeing, kayaking, sailing, windsurfing.	74	•	•	•	•	•		•	•	•	•		•		
William A. Switzer (E-3) 6,268 hectares 3 km w. of Hinton on Hwy. 16, then 19 km n. on Hwy. 40. Historic. Bird-watching, canoeing, kayaking; interpretive programs.	75	•	•	•	•	•	•	•	•	•	•	•	•	•	
Williamson (C-3) 17 hectares 17 km w. of Valleyview on Hwy. 43, then 2 km n. on an access road. Canoeing, kayaking, sailing, windsurfing.	76	•	•	•	•	•		•	•				•		
Winagami Lake (B-4) 6,542 hectares 20 km n. of High Prairie on Hwy. 749, 10 km w. on Hwy. 679, then 7 km n. on access road. Bird-watching, canoeing, kayaking.	77	•	•	•	•	•		•	•	•			•		
Writing-on-Stone (K-8) 1,718 hectares 35 km e. of Milk River off Hwy. 501. Historic. Bird-watching, canoeing, kayaking; interpretive programs. *(See Milk River p. 172.)*	78	•	•	•	•			•	•	•				•	
Wyndham-Carseland (I-6) 178 hectares 2 km e. and 2 km s. of Carseland on Hwy. 24. Canoeing, kayaking.	79	•	•	•	•	•		•		•			•		
Young's Point (B-3) 3,072 hectares 26 km w. of Valleyview on Hwy. 43, then 10 km n.e. on an access road. Water sports.	80	•	•	•	•	•		•	•	•			•		
OTHER															
Bud Miller All Seasons Park (E-9) 81 hectares at 2902 59th Ave. in Lloydminster. Bird-watching, lawn bowling, miniature golf, soccer, tennis, volleyball; aquatic complex, interpretive trails, playgrounds, skateboard park. *(See Lloydminster p. 169.)*	81		•	•					•	•			•		
Content Bridge (G-6) 12 hectares 6 km s. of Nevis on Hwy. 21. Canoeing, kayaking.	82	•	•		•			•		•					
Eagle Lake Park (H-6) 7 km e. and 6 km s. of Strathmore via Hwy. 1.	83	•	•			•	•	•		•					•
Elks Beach (D-6) 14 km s. of Barrhead on Hwy. 33, then e. on Hwy. 651.	84	•	•		•	•		•		•					•
Half Moon Lake (E-6) 4 hectares 3 km e. of Sherwood Park on Hwy. 630. Canoeing, kayaking; horse rental.	85	•	•	•	•	•	•	•	•	•					•
Hasse Lake (E-6) 81 hectares 5 km w. and 10 km s. of Stony Plain on Hwy. 16.	86		•	•				•	•	•			•		
North Wabasca (B-6) 77 hectares 38 km n. of Slave Lake on Hwy. 88, 100 km n.e. on Hwy. 754, then 7 km. n. on access road.	87	•	•		•	•		•	•	•					
Pipestone Creek (C-2) 15 km s. of Wembley. Interpretive trails.	88	•	•	•				•		•			•		
Stony Lake (D-8) 158 hectares on Stony Lake, 16 km s.w. of Elk Point off Hwy. 646.	89	•	•		•	•		•		•					
Upper Shunda Creek (F-4) 47 hectares 3 km w. of Nordegg off Hwy. 11.	90	•		•				•					•	•	
Westward Ho (G-5) 8 km e. of Sundre on Hwy. 27. Canoeing, kayaking.	91	•	•		•			•	•	•			•		
Wizard Lake (E-6) 33 hectares 19 km s. of Calmar on Hwy. 795.	92	•	•		•	•		•	•	•					•

AIRDRIE (H-6) pop. 42,564, elev. 1,077m/3,533'
• Part of Calgary area — see map p. 54

NOSE CREEK VALLEY MUSEUM is just w. off Hwy. 2 Big Hill Springs Rd. exit, then 1 km (.6 mi.) n. to 1701 Main St. S. Located in Nose Creek Park's visitor center, this museum contains exhibits about early farming and ranching, wildlife, military history and native peoples. A topographical map, replicas of a pioneer house and a blacksmith shop, and antique vehicles are on display. Also included is an extensive collection of Indian artifacts and crafts.

Time: Allow 30 minutes minimum. **Hours:** Mon.-Fri. 10-5, Sat.-Sun. 1-4:30, June-Aug.; Mon.-Fri. 1-5, Sat.-Sun. 1-4:30, rest of year. Closed Easter, Thanksgiving and Christmas. **Cost:** $2; free (ages 0-11). **Phone:** (403) 948-6685.

BEST WESTERN REGENCY INN (403)948-3838

Hotel
$130-$200

AAA Benefit: Members save up to 20%, plus 10% bonus points with Best Western Rewards®.

Address: 121 Edmonton Tr SE T4B 1S2 **Location:** Hwy 2 exit Airdrie/Irricana, just w., then 0.5 mi (0.9 km) s. **Facility:** 60 units. 3 stories, interior/exterior corridors. **Parking:** winter plug-ins. **Activities:** whirlpool, exercise room. **Guest Services:** coin laundry. **Free Special Amenities:** full breakfast and high-speed Internet.

COMFORT INN & SUITES AIRDRIE (403)948-3411

Hotel
$129-$149

Address: 133 Sierra Springs Dr SE T4B 3G6 **Location:** Hwy 2 exit 282 (Yankee Valley Blvd), just w. **Facility:** 103 units. 4 stories, interior corridors. **Parking:** winter plug-ins. **Terms:** check-in 4 pm. **Amenities:** high-speed Internet. **Pool(s):** heated indoor. **Activities:** exercise room. **Guest Services:** valet and coin laundry. **Free Special Amenities:** full breakfast and high-speed Internet.

HOLIDAY INN EXPRESS & SUITES AIRDRIE-CALGARY NORTH (403)912-1952

Hotel $129-$169 **Address:** 64 E Lake Ave NE T4A 2G8 **Location:** Hwy 2 exit E Airdrie, 0.6 mi (1 km) n. Located in an industrial area. **Facility:** 79 units. 4 stories, interior corridors. **Parking:** winter plug-ins. **Terms:** cancellation fee imposed. **Amenities:** high-speed Internet. **Pool(s):** heated indoor. **Activities:** whirlpool, waterslide, exercise room. **Guest Services:** coin laundry.

RAMADA INN & SUITES (403)945-1288

Hotel $140-$220 **Address:** 191 E Lake Crescent T4A 2H7 **Location:** Hwy 2 exit E Airdrie. Located in an industrial area. **Facility:** 59 units, some two bedrooms and kitchens. 4 stories, interior corridors. **Parking:** winter plug-ins. **Amenities:** high-speed Internet. **Dining:** Smitty's, see separate listing. **Pool(s):** heated indoor. **Activities:** whirlpool, waterslide, exercise room. **Guest Services:** coin laundry.

SUPER 8 AIRDRIE (403)948-4188

Hotel $125-$140 **Address:** 815 E Lake Blvd T4A 2G4 **Location:** Hwy 2 exit E Airdrie, just e. Located in an industrial area. **Facility:** 49 units, some two bedrooms. 3 stories, interior corridors. **Parking:** winter plug-ins. **Guest Services:** coin laundry.

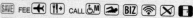
WHERE TO EAT

SMITTY'S 403/945-1225

International
Family Dining
$7-S20

AAA Inspector Notes: The family-oriented restaurant satisfies patrons with its ever-popular all-day breakfast items, as well as tasty and wholesome soups and salads at lunchtime. A relaxed mood characterizes the dining space. **Address:** 191 E Lake Crescent T4A 1H3 **Location:** Hwy 2 exit E Airdrie; in Ramada Inn & Suites. **B L D** CALL

All your favorites all day long & great weekend buffet

ALDER FLATS (F-5) pop. 152, elev. 953m/3,125'

EM-TE TOWN is 3 km (1.9 mi.) s. of jct. hwys. 13 and 22, then 10 km (6.2 mi.) w. on a gravel road following signs. This replica of an 1880s Western ghost town has 27 buildings including a saloon, gazebo, church, blacksmith shop, school, emporium, jail and restaurant. **Time:** Allow 1 hour minimum. **Hours:** Town open Thurs.-Sat. 9-9, Sun. 9-7. **Cost:** $7; $5 (ages 13-17 and 65+); $4 (ages 8-12). Prices may vary; phone ahead. **Phone:** (780) 388-2166.

ATHABASCA pop. 2,990

DAYS INN ATHABASCA (780)675-7020

Hotel $139-$149 **Address:** 2805 48th Ave T9S 0A4 **Location:** Jct Hwy 2 and 55, 1.6 mi (2.7 km) e.; east end of town. **Facility:** 69 units, some kitchens. 4 stories, interior corridors. **Parking:** winter plug-ins. **Amenities:** high-speed Internet. **Activities:** exercise room. **Guest Services:** coin laundry.

WHERE TO EAT

THE 49TH STREET GRILL 780/675-5418

International. Casual Dining. $12-$31 **AAA Inspector Notes:** A favored spot to dine, guests can find well-prepared, uncomplicated fare with an accent on Greek dishes including calamari, Greek salad and souvlaki. Also on the menu is pizza, simple Italian pasta and entrées of steak, chicken, salmon and lamb. **Bar:** full bar. **Address:** 4901 49th St T9S 1C5 **Location:** Just e of Hwy 2 (50th St); corner of 49th Ave. **Parking:** street only. **L D** CALL

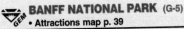

BANFF NATIONAL PARK (G-5)
 • Attractions map p. 39

Elevations in the park range from 1,326 metres (4,350 ft.) around the Bow River to 3,612 metres (11,851 ft.) at Mount Forbes. Refer to CAA/AAA maps for additional elevation information.

Banff National Park sprawls across the jagged backs of the Rocky Mountains, offering some of the most beautiful alpine scenery in the world. It is a land of breathtaking vistas no photo can do justice to—no matter how gifted the photographer. Craggy, snow-capped peaks encircle forested valleys and glacier-fed lakes. Sheltered meadows wear a glorious mantle of wildflowers, vibrant with fireweed, Indian paintbrush, columbine and anemone. Rushing streams sparkle in the crisp mountain air, flowing through forests of lodgepole pine and Douglas fir.

Banff was established in 1885, 2 years after railway workers discovered a misty cave containing thermal springs, a find that led to a legal battle over who would develop the springs as a bathing resort. The conflict was resolved when the Canadian government set aside the rugged land for the benefit of all its citizens, creating what would become the country's first national park. Although bathing in these mineral springs is no longer permitted, you can still see the natural grotto where it all began at Cave and Basin National Historic Site *(see attraction listing p. 41).*

To attract wealthy tourists, the Canadian Pacific Railway built the luxurious Banff Springs Hotel in 1888. The castle-like stone-and-concrete building you see today replaced the original wooden hotel after it burned in 1926, but the idea of providing guests with opulent accommodations while they enjoy the area's scenic beauty remains unchanged. The image of the hotel's stately, high-peaked roofline rising above the surrounding evergreens is a fixture on postcards.

Known today as The Fairmont Banff Springs, the hotel stands on the outskirts of the charming resort

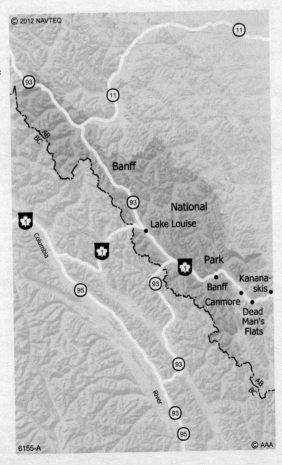

This map shows cities in Banff National Park where you will find attractions, hotels and restaurants. Cities are listed alphabetically in this book on the following pages.

6155-A

© AAA

town of Banff *(see place listing p. 40)*, where most development within the park is focused and where you'll find the largest number of hotels. Rustic mountain lodge-style buildings house boutiques, sporting goods stores, gift shops and restaurants. In spring and summer the sidewalks—radiant with colorful annuals planted in window boxes and hanging baskets—are crowded with visitors; in winter the streets in the town center can be just as packed as in warm-weather months with the difference being roof racks now carry skis and winter gear instead of canoes and kayaks.

Lake Louise *(see place listing p. 163)* is the park's second most developed area, where you'll find a small shopping center, cafes, hotels and a ski resort. The community takes its name from the beautiful lake nearby, which is fed by meltwater from Victoria Glacier. The runoff carries finely ground rock flour that gives the lake a striking milky turquoise color you'll see in the area's other glacially fed lakes. Facing the glacier on the opposite shore is The Fairmont Chateau Lake Louise, a grand hotel with more than 500 rooms. The hotel, lake and glacier together create one of the most photographed settings in the park.

Another highlight of Banff National Park is Bow Valley Parkway *(see attraction listing)*, a scenic byway that parallels Trans-Canada Highway (Hwy. 1), connecting the towns of Banff and Lake Louise. Nestled in Valley of the Ten Peaks, Moraine Lake *(see attraction listing p. 40)* dazzles visitors with its sparkling blue waters, earning it the nickname, "Jewel of the Rockies."

Other sights for which the park is famous: Johnston Canyon *(see attraction listing p. 40)*, Crow Foot Glacier, the sawtooth profile of Mount Rundle reflected in the clear waters of Vermilion Lakes—aptly named Castle Mountain—and, in winter, the frozen waterfall known as Weeping Wall. And while you make your way among these scenic points, you'll likely encounter Banff's abundant wildlife, especially visible in the fall. Elk, deer and bighorn sheep are most common, and if you have binoculars you may catch sight of mountain goats and moose in the distance. If you should spot them, you may want to steer clear of the area's predators: bears, wolves, coyotes and lynx, but odds are they'll want to keep their distance from you, too.

General Information and Activities

The park, which is open all year, has about 354 kilometres (219 mi.) of scenic roads. Hwy. 1 to Vancouver and Hwy. 93S (Banff-Windermere Hwy.) are open year-round, as is the northern end of Hwy. 93N (Icefields Parkway) from Lake Louise to Jasper; check locally for road conditions. One- or multiple-day bus tours of the park's major points of interest also are available.

More than 1,300 kilometres (800 mi.) of trails traverse the park. All activities involving an overnight stay in the backcountry require a wilderness permit offered at information centers and park warden offices in the Banff and Lake Louise townsites. Public campgrounds in the park are available by reservation, with some sites set aside on a first-come, first-served basis; phone (877) 737-3783, or TTY (866) 787-6221 in Canada.

If such potentially risky activities as mountain climbing or hiking away from designated trails are planned, visitors should register their trips in person at a park warden office or information center. Upon return, notify the warden office or information center in person or by phone. Phone (403) 762-1550 for backcountry travel information, including weather and avalanche bulletins.

Lake Louise's waters, about 4 C (39 F), are too cold for swimming but are ideal for boating. Motors are not permitted; motorboats may be used only on Lake Minnewanka. Cruises on Lake Minnewanka are offered during the summer. Skating, skiing, curling and hockey are available in the park in winter.

Park naturalists conduct interpretive programs at major campgrounds most evenings and at key attractions daily throughout the summer. Bankhead, a once-booming mining town 4.8 kilometres (3 mi.) northeast of Banff, has a self-guiding trail with explanatory signs and a mining exhibit. The trail is open daily 24 hours.

Special events include the Banff Mountain Film and Book Festival, held late October through early November. From May through August, The Banff Centre, a performing arts venue off Tunnel Mountain Drive in the town of Banff, hosts the ▼Banff Summer Arts Festival.

Throughout the summer guides and outfitters offer fishing, hiking and float trips. Saddle horses are available for treks through the mountains to glacier-fed lakes. White-water rafting trips and helicopter tours can be arranged outside the park boundaries in Canmore and in Golden, British Columbia *(see place listings p. 96 and p. 243)*.

Information, interpretive program schedules and backcountry trail tips are available at Banff Visitor Information Centre, (403) 762-1550, 224 Banff Ave., and Lake Louise Visitor Information Centre, (403) 522-3833, 201 Village Rd.; topographical maps and trail guides are sold at both locations. The Banff center is open daily 8-8, late June-early Sept.; hours vary rest of year. The Lake Louise center is open daily 8:30-7, mid-June to early Sept.; hours vary rest of year. GPS Audio Tours are available at The Bear & The Butterfly, a retail outlet at 214 Banff Ave.; phone (403) 760-5332.

Fishing is permitted; national park fishing permits are sold at park information, administration and warden offices as well as at some boat concessionaires and tackle shops. Check at information centers in Banff or Lake Louise for a summary of park fishing regulations.

Note: Hunting is strictly prohibited; visitors entering the area must have firearms dismantled. Night travelers should be alert for animals on the highways. It is not only dangerous but also against park regulations to feed, molest, touch or tease the animals. *See Recreation Areas Chart.*

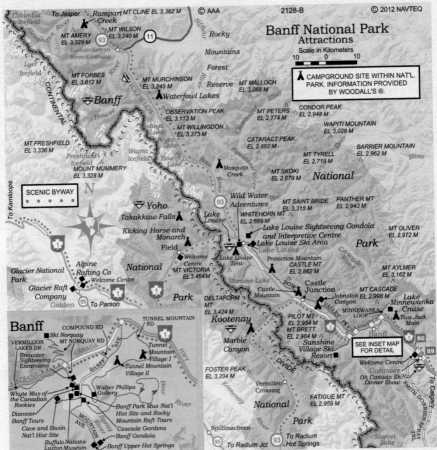

Banff National Park
Attractions

Scale in Kilometers

CAMPGROUND SITE WITHIN NAT'L. PARK. INFORMATION PROVIDED BY WOODALL'S ®.

ADMISSION to the park is $19.60 per private vehicle (two to seven persons). Otherwise admission per person is $9.80; $8.30 (ages 65+); $4.90 (ages 6-16). An annual pass, valid at all Canadian national parks, is available. **Cards:** AX, MC, VI.

PETS are allowed in the park but must be leashed, crated or physically restrained.

ADDRESS inquiries to the Superintendent, Banff National Park, P.O. Box 900, Banff, AB, Canada T1L 1K2; phone (403) 762-1550.

BOW VALLEY PARKWAY (HWY. 1A) is 5 km (3 mi.) w. of the town of Banff off Hwy. 1. The parkway, the original road between the villages of Banff and Lake Louise, runs along the Bow River parallel to the Trans-Canada Hwy. The parkway's speed limit of 60 kph (37 mph) provides a slower, more scenic alternative to Hwy. 1. Each curve in the road brings postcard-like images of snow-capped mountains, glaciers and ice fields.

There are frequent pull-offs with viewpoints, interpretive panels, picnic sites and trailheads. Wildlife such as bears, bighorn sheep, elks and deer can frequently be spotted. **Note:** In order to help protect wildlife, there is a voluntary restriction on driving the section of the parkway between Banff and Johnston Canyon daily 6-9 p.m., Mar. 1-June 25. Use Hwy. 1 instead.

ICEFIELDS PARKWAY (HWY. 93) crosses Banff and Jasper national parks. The scenic highway parallels the Continental Divide for 230 kilometres (143 mi.) between Lake Louise and the town of Jasper, passing through a breathtaking landscape of snowcapped mountains, waterfalls, lakes and rivers. The park's most visited sights are either along the parkway or just a short distance from it. Driving this spectacular route—roughly a 4-hour trip one way—is an experience you shouldn't miss.

The parkway gets its chilly name from the vast bodies of ice you can see along its length, the most impressive being the massive Columbia Icefield *(see attraction listing p. 152)*, source of eight glaciers including the Athabasca Glacier, which reaches to within walking distance of the parkway just inside Jasper National Park *(see place listing p.*

151). For an up-close look at the glacier, climb aboard a specially designed snowcoach departing from the Columbia Icefield Centre *(see attraction listing p. 152)* for a narrated excursion and walk out onto the glacier's frozen surface.

There are too many scenic overlooks and turnouts along the parkway to name, but some of the most outstanding include Bow Glacier, Chephren Lake, Peyto Lake at the Bow Summit area and the Saskatchewan River Crossing, where several display panels explain history of the Howse Pass and the fur trade. Farther north are viewpoints taking in the Weeping Wall, Bridal Veil Falls and Cirrus Mountain.

Many turnouts also serve as trailheads for day hikes to even more panoramas. One of the best: Parker Ridge just south of Banff's northern boundary. The trail leads up to a fantastic vista encompassing a narrow river valley with the Saskatchewan Glacier at one end. In Jasper National Park, you can enjoy amazing views of the Stutfield Glacier and Tangle Falls right from the parkway, and both Sunwapta and Athabasca falls are a short drive off the main road.

Note: Drivers should be alert for slow or stopped vehicles and animals. Snow tires and/or chains are recommended in winter; check for weather and road conditions. **Cost:** Parkway free; drivers must pay the national park entrance fee regardless of whether they stop inside the park. **Phone:** (403) 762-2088 for weather information, or (403) 762-1450 for road condition information.

JOHNSTON CANYON is 18 km (11 mi.) w. of the town of Banff on the Bow Valley Pkwy. (Hwy. 1A). An uphill hike to one or both of the two waterfalls at this canyon follows a paved pathway through a wooded area along Johnston Creek. Observation points along the way allow for scenic views of the rushing water. The pathway soon becomes more of a catwalk that is literally attached to the canyon wall.

The Lower Falls are reached after a hike of about 1.1 kilometres (.7 mi.); the trail continues another 1.7 kilometres (1 mi.) to the Upper Falls. **Note:** This is a popular day-use area, and the parking lot can become crowded.

 LAKE LOUISE—see Lake Louise p. 163.

LAKE MINNEWANKA CRUISE is on Lake Minnewanka, 8 km (5 mi.) n.e. of the town of Banff on Hwy. 1, then n. 7 km (4 mi.) from the beginning of Lake Minnewanka Loop. The interpretive sightseeing cruises, in glass-enclosed, heated boats, last 1 hour, 30 minutes. Rental motorboats and charter fishing tours also are available. Visitors should arrive at least 30 minutes prior to departure time. **Hours:** Sightseeing cruises depart daily on the hour 10-6, early June to mid-Sept.; Mon.-Fri. at 10, noon, 2, 4 and 6, Sat.-Sun. on the hour 10-6, mid-May to early June; daily at noon, 2 and 5, mid-Sept. to early Oct. **Cost:** Sightseeing cruise $45; $20 (ages 6-15). **Phone:** (403) 762-3473.

MORAINE LAKE is about 14 km (8.7 mi.) s. of the Lake Louise townsite and about 71 km (44 mi.) n.w. of the town of Banff. Though roughly half the size of better-known nearby Lake Louise, many believe blue-green Moraine Lake is equally beautiful. Known as "the jewel of the Rockies," the lake is in the Valley of the Ten Peaks, which provides the ten saw-toothed ridges that rise dramatically from the lakeshore. A short hike to the top of a rockslide leads to panoramic views of the lake and valley. A number of hikes begin at the lake, and canoe rentals are available. **Phone:** (403) 522-3833 for the Lake Louise Visitor Information Centre.

RECREATIONAL ACTIVITIES
Skiing
- **Sunshine Village Ski Resort** is just off Sunshine Road, 20 km (12.4 mi.) w. of the town of Banff via Hwy. 1. **Hours:** Daily 9-4, mid-Nov. to late May. **Phone:** (403) 762-6500 or (877) 542-2633.

BANFF (H-4) pop. 7,584
- Hotels p. 44 • Restaurants p. 48
- Hotels & Restaurants map & index p. 42
- Part of Banff National Park area — see map p. 37

BANFF GONDOLA is 3.2 km (2 mi.) s. on Mountain Ave. (lower terminal next to the Upper Hot Springs). An enclosed gondola journeys along the eastern slope of Sulphur Mountain. The lift rises 698 metres (2,290 ft.) from the 1,583-metre (5,194-ft.) level to the 2,281-metre (7,484-ft.) summit ridge in 8 minutes. An open-air observation deck affords spectacular views of Banff and the surrounding mountains. A self-guiding nature walk affords other panoramic views and leads to a historic cosmic ray station and an old weather observatory.

Time: Allow 1 hour, 30 minutes minimum. **Hours:** Daily 8 a.m.-9 p.m., early May-day before Labour Day; otherwise varies. Closed 12 days in January for maintenance and Christmas. **Cost:** Round-trip fare $33.95; $14.95 (ages 6-15). **Phone:** (403) 762-2523. ⓕ

BANFF PARK MUSEUM NATIONAL HISTORIC SITE is at 91 Banff Ave. Established in 1895, the collection moved to its present building in 1903. The museum depicts the way natural history exhibits were presented and interpreted at the beginning of the 20th century. Exhibits include mounted animals and mineral specimens. **Time:** Allow 30 minutes minimum. **Hours:** Daily 10-6, mid-May to early Oct.; 1-5, rest of year. Guided tours are given daily at 11 and 3. Closed Christmas. **Cost:** $3.90; $3.40 (ages 65+); $1.90 (ages 7-18); $9.80 (family). **Phone:** (403) 762-1558.

BANFF UPPER HOT SPRINGS is 4 km (2.5 mi.) s. via Mountain Ave. Natural hot springs feed this bathing pool with temperatures ranging between 34 C (93 F) and 42 C (108 F). A day spa is on the premises. Swimsuit, towel and locker rentals are available. **Time:** Allow 1 hour minimum. **Hours:** Daily 9 a.m.-11 p.m., mid-May to early Oct.; 10-10 (also Fri.-Sat. 10-11 p.m.), rest of year. **Cost:** $7.30; $6.30 (ages 3-17 and 65+); $22.50

(See map & index p. 42.)

(family, two adults and two children, $3.40 for each additional child). Prices may vary; phone ahead. **Phone:** (403) 762-1515 or (800) 767-1611. Ⓣ

SAVE **BREWSTER SIGHTSEEING EXCURSIONS** departs from several area hotels. Guides discuss local history during the 3-hour Discover Banff tour, which offers views of wildlife and such points of interest as the Banff Gondola and Lake Minnewanka. A variety of full- and half-day narrated excursions of and from Banff to Lake Louise, the Columbia Icefield and Jasper also are offered. **Time:** Allow 3 hours, 30 minutes minimum. **Hours:** Tours are offered daily, May 1 to mid-Oct. Departure times vary; phone ahead. **Cost:** Explore Banff tour $50; $25 (children). **Phone:** (403) 762-6700 or (866) 606-6700.

BUFFALO NATIONS LUXTON MUSEUM is just w. of Banff Ave. at 1 Birch Ave. This log-fort museum re-creates the era when Europeans first arrived on the Plains to find a culture rich in ceremonies, songs and legends. Arts, crafts, dioramas and displays showcase the historical journey of the Northern Plains people, their culture and the flora and fauna of the surrounding area.

Tours: Guided tours are available. **Time:** Allow 30 minutes minimum. **Hours:** Daily 11-6, mid-May to early Oct.; 1-5, rest of year. Closed Christmas. **Cost:** $6; $4 (ages 65+ and students with ID); $2.50 (ages 6-12); $13 (family). **Phone:** (403) 762-2388.

CASCADE GARDENS encircle the Banff National Park administration building at 101 Mountain Ave. These gardens are built in a series of rock terraces connected by small cascades that highlight flowers, plants and shrubs, rustic bridges, pavilions and flagged walks. Traditional dancing and drumming performances are held on the grounds at the Siksika Nation Interpretive Centre. **Time:** Allow 30 minutes minimum. **Hours:** Gardens daily dawn-dusk, June-Sept. **Cost:** Free. **Phone:** (403) 760-1338. 🎫

CAVE AND BASIN NATIONAL HISTORIC SITE is at 311 Cave Ave. The beginnings of Canada's national park system are founded on a cave and hot springs discovered in 1883 by three Canadian Pacific Railway workers. Disputes over the ownership of the area prompted the Canadian government to declare the area a national reserve 2 years later. The site consists of naturally occurring warm mineral springs inside the cave and an emerald-colored basin outside. Exhibits, interpretive trails and a 30-minute video presentation explain the history of the springs and the development of Banff National Park.

Note: A major renovation project will be underway at the national historic site until December 2012. Although some portions of the park will remain accessible, visitors should phone ahead for parking information, construction updates, and to confirm hours and prices. **Time:** Allow 1 hour minimum. **Hours:** Daily 9-6, mid-May through Sept. 30; Mon.-Fri. 11-4, Sat.-Sun. 9:30-5, rest of year. Guided tours are given daily at 11, 2 and 4, mid-May through

Sept. 30; Sat.-Sun. at 11, rest of year. Closed Jan. 1, Christmas and day after Christmas. **Cost:** $3.90; $3.40 (ages 65+); $1.90 (ages 6-18); $9.80 (family). **Phone:** (403) 762-1566.

DISCOVER BANFF TOURS is at 215 Banff Ave. in the Sundance Mall. Passengers also are picked up at area hotels. Various year-round guided tours are offered, including ice walks, snowshoe treks, dog sled trips, sleigh rides, mountain hikes, wildlife safaris, horseback riding, white-water rafting and nature walks. Some tours include lunch. Canoe rentals and self-guiding tours also are available.

Inquire about cancellation policies. Allow 3-9 hours minimum, depending on tour. **Hours:** Tours depart daily (weather permitting) 7:30 a.m.-10 p.m. Tour times vary; phone ahead. **Cost:** Fees vary, depending on activity. **Phone:** (403) 760-5007 or (877) 565-9372.

ROCKY MOUNTAIN RAFT TOURS launch point meeting area below Bow Falls is reached by buses departing the Banff Park Lodge Resort Hotel & Conference Centre and The Fairmont Banff Springs. Tickets are available at The Fairmont Banff Springs concierge desk and at the launch point. Scenic 1-hour guided raft tours travel the river in the section of the Bow Valley below Tunnel and Rundle mountains. **Hours:** Raft trips depart daily at 9:20, 11:20, 1:20, 3:20 and 5:20, mid-May to late Sept. **Cost:** $45; $20 (ages 0-15). **Phone:** (403) 762-3632.

WALTER PHILLIPS GALLERY is in Glyde Hall at The Banff Centre, 107 Tunnel Mountain Dr. Exhibits contain international and Canadian contemporary art. Media include painting, sculpture, printmaking, textiles, ceramics, photography, video and performance art. Works by established and emerging artists are featured. **Hours:** Wed.-Sun. 12:30-5 (also Thurs. 5-8). Closed holidays and between exhibitions. **Cost:** Donations. **Phone:** (403) 762-6281.

SAVE **WHYTE MUSEUM OF THE CANADIAN ROCKIES**, 111 Bear St., presents the heritage of the region through four galleries exhibiting cultural and natural history displays and artwork. Docents also lead visitors through several historic houses on-site, including the former residence of the museum's founders, Peter and Catharine Whyte. **Time:** Allow 30 minutes minimum. **Hours:** Museum daily 10-5. Heritage Homes Tour is given daily on the half-hour 10:30-3:30, June 1-Labour Day; Sun. at 2:30, rest of year. Luxton Open House Fri.-Sun. 11-3, June 1-Labour Day. Closed Jan. 1 and Christmas. **Cost:** $8; $5 (ages 65+ and students with ID); free (ages 0-6); $20 (family, two adults and two children). Guided house tours $8-$13. **Phone:** (403) 762-2291.

RECREATIONAL ACTIVITIES
Skiing
- **Ski Norquay** is 6 km (4 mi.) n. via the Mount Norquay access road. **Hours:** Daily 9-4, early Dec. to mid-Apr. (also Fri. 4-9, Jan.-Mar.). **Phone:** (403) 762-4421.

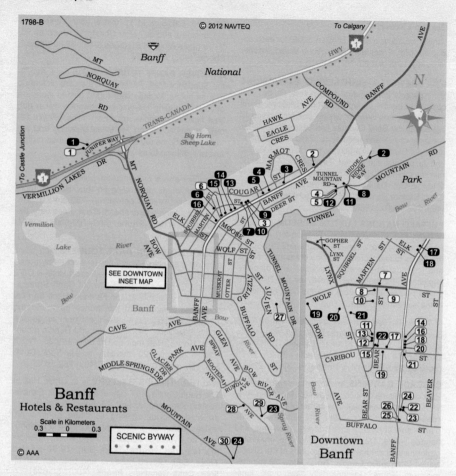

Banff
Hotels & Restaurants

Banff

This index helps you "spot" where approved hotels and restaurants are located on the corresponding detailed maps. Hotel daily rate range is for comparison only. Restaurant price range is a combination of lunch and/or dinner. Turn to the listing page for more detailed rate and price information and consult display ads for special promotions.

BANFF

Map Page	Hotels	Diamond Rated	Rate Range	Page
1 this page	The Juniper	▽▽▽	Rates not provided	47
2 this page	Hidden Ridge Resort	▽▽▽	$129-$249	47
3 this page	**Rundlestone Lodge**	▽▽▽	$115-$300 SAVE	48
4 this page	Banff Caribou Lodge	▽▽▽	$109-$219	44
5 this page	Charlton's Cedar Court (See ad p. 46.)	▽▽▽	$110-$269	46
6 this page	Buffaloberry Bed and Breakfast	▽▽▽	$260-$335	45
7 this page	**BEST WESTERN PLUS Siding 29 Lodge**	▽▽▽	$100-$221 SAVE	45
8 this page	Tunnel Mountain Resort	▽▽	$195-$294	48
9 this page	The Fox Hotel & Suites	▽▽▽	Rates not provided	47
10 this page	Delta Banff Royal Canadian Lodge (See ad p. 46.)	▽▽▽	$168-$345	46

BANFF (cont'd)

Map Page	Hotels (cont'd)	Diamond Rated	Rate Range	Page
11 p. 42	**Douglas Fir Resort & Chalets**	◆◆◆	$125-$475 SAVE	47
12 p. 42	Buffalo Mountain Lodge	◆◆◆	$179-$349	45
13 p. 42	**Irwin's Mountain Inn**	◆◆	$119-$219 SAVE	47
14 p. 42	**Red Carpet Inn**	◆◆	$89-$189 SAVE	47
15 p. 42	**High Country Inn**	◆◆◆	$99-$299 SAVE	47
16 p. 42	**Banff Aspen Lodge**	◆◆◆	$128-$230 SAVE	44
17 p. 42	Banff Ptarmigan Inn	◆◆	Rates not provided	44
18 p. 42	Banff International Hotel	◆◆◆	$145-$245	44
19 p. 42	Bow View Lodge	◆◆	$89-$299	45
20 p. 42	Banff Park Lodge Resort Hotel & Conference Centre *(See ad p. 44.)*	◆◆◆	$149-$399	44
21 p. 42	Homestead Inn	◆	$99-$149	47
22 p. 42	**Brewster's Mountain Lodge**	◆◆	$109-$401 SAVE	45
23 p. 42	**The Fairmont Banff Springs**	◆◆◆◆	$250-$593 SAVE	47
24 p. 42	**The Rimrock Resort Hotel**	◆◆◆◆	$218-$395 SAVE	48

Map Page	Restaurants	Diamond Rated	Cuisine	Price Range	Page
1 p. 42	Juniper Bistro	◆◆	Canadian	$13-$37	50
2 p. 42	Bumper's The Beef House	◆◆	Steak	$13-$40	49
3 p. 42	The Evergreen *(See ad p. 46.)*	◆◆◆	Continental	$14-$37	49
4 p. 42	Sleeping Buffalo Lounge	◆◆◆	Regional Canadian	$14-$40	50
5 p. 42	Cilantro Mountain Cafe	◆◆	New Canadian	$14-$20	49
6 p. 42	Ticino Swiss-Italian Restaurant	◆◆◆	International	$19-$37	50
7 p. 42	Timbers Food Company	◆◆	Italian	$10-$27	51
8 p. 42	Masala Authentic Indian Cuisine	◆◆	Indian	$15-$20	50
9 p. 42	St. James's Gate Olde Irish Pub	◆◆	Irish	$10-$25	50
10 p. 42	The Bear Street Tavern	◆◆	Pizza	$11-$18	49
11 p. 42	Saltlik A Rare Steakhouse	◆◆◆	Steak	$14-$36	50
12 p. 42	Wild Flour Bakery Cafe	◆	Natural/Organic	$6-$8	51
13 p. 42	The Bison Restaurant & Terrace	◆◆◆	Regional Canadian	$18-$40	49
14 p. 42	Giorgio's Trattoria	◆◆	Italian	$15-$40	49
15 p. 42	Sushi Bistro	◆◆	Sushi	$12-$24	50
16 p. 42	**Silver Dragon Restaurant Banff**	◆◆	Chinese	$10-$24	50
17 p. 42	Coyotes Deli & Grill	◆◆	New Southwestern	$8-$29	49
18 p. 42	Grizzly House	◆◆	Fondue	$15-$64	50
19 p. 42	The Eddie Burger + Bar	◆◆	Burgers	$14-$20	49
20 p. 42	Shakes	◆	American	$4-$6	50
21 p. 42	The Maple Leaf Grille & Spirits	◆◆◆	Canadian	$12-$50	50
22 p. 42	Tommy's Neighbourhood Pub	◆◆	American	$7-$13	51
23 p. 42	Banff Ave Brewing Co	◆◆	American	$11-$27	48
24 p. 42	Balkan The Greek Restaurant	◆◆	Greek	$10-$33	48

Map Page	Restaurants (cont'd)	Diamond Rated	Cuisine	Price Range	Page
25 p. 42	Le Beaujolais	▽▽▽	French	$22-$40	50
26 p. 42	Bistro "Cafe de Paris"	▽▽▽	French	$15-$29	49
27 p. 42	Three Ravens Restaurant & Wine Bar	▽▽▽	New American	$28-$39	50
28 p. 42	Grapes Wine Bar	▽▽▽	American	$20-$44	49
29 p. 42	The Banffshire Club	▽▽▽	New Canadian	$32-$47	49
30 p. 42	Eden	▽▽▽▽	French	$64-$197	49

BANFF ASPEN LODGE (403)762-4401 **16**
▽▽▽
Hotel
$128-$230

Address: 401 Banff Ave T1L 1A9 **Location:** Between Moose and Rabbit sts. **Facility:** 89 units. 3 stories, interior/exterior corridors. **Parking:** winter plug-ins. **Terms:** 2 night minimum stay - seasonal and/or weekends, cancellation fee imposed. **Activities:** sauna, whirlpools, steamroom. **Guest Services:** valet and coin laundry, area transportation (fee)-ski area. **Free Special Amenities: continental breakfast and high-speed Internet.**

SAVE ECO ▮▶ BIZ 📶 ✕ 🎦 🅱 🖥

BANFF CARIBOU LODGE (403)762-5887 **4**
▽▽▽ **Hotel** $109-$219 **Address:** 521 Banff Ave T1L 1A4 **Location:** Trans-Canada Hwy 1 exit Banff Ave (Minnewanka Loop), 2.1 mi (3.5 km) sw. Opposite Rotary Park. **Facility:** 195 units. 4 stories, interior corridors. **Terms:** check-in 4 pm, 3 day cancellation notice-fee imposed. **Amenities:** safes. **Activities:** whirlpool, steamroom, exercise room, spa. **Guest Services:** valet and coin laundry, area transportation-public transit.

▮▮ 🍽 CALL 🅼 BIZ 📶 ✕ 🎦 🅱 🖥

BANFF INTERNATIONAL HOTEL (403)762-5666 **18**
▽▽▽ **Hotel** $145-$245 **Address:** 333 Banff Ave T1L 1B1 **Location:** Corner of Elk St; center. **Facility:** 162 units. 3 stories, interior corridors. **Parking:** winter plug-ins. **Terms:** check-in 4 pm, cancellation fee imposed. **Activities:** sauna, whirlpool, steamroom, exercise room. **Guest Services:** valet and coin laundry.

▮▮ 🍽 📶 ✕ 🎦 🅱 🖥 / SOME UNITS FEE 🐾 🖥

BANFF PARK LODGE RESORT HOTEL & CONFERENCE CENTRE (403)762-4433 **20**

▽▽▽ **Hotel** $149-$399 **Address:** 222 Lynx St T1L 1K5 **Location:** Between Caribou and Wolf sts; downtown. **Facility:** 211 units. 3 stories, interior corridors. **Parking:** check-in 4 pm (fee) and valet. **Terms:** check-in 4 pm, 3 day cancellation notice-fee imposed. *Some:* high-speed Internet (fee). **Dining:** 2 restaurants. **Activities:** whirlpool, steamroom, hiking trails, limited exercise equipment. **Guest Services:** valet and coin laundry, area transportation (fee)-ski area. *(See ad this page.)*

ECO FEE 🚭 ▮▮ 🍽 CALL 🅼 🛬 BIZ 📶 ✕ 🎦 🅱 🖥 / SOME UNITS 🖥

BANFF PTARMIGAN INN 403/762-2207 **17**
▽▽▽ **Hotel.** Rates not provided. **Address:** 337 Banff Ave T1L 1B1 **Location:** Between Moose and Elk sts. **Facility:** 134 units. 2-3 stories, interior corridors. **Parking:** winter plug-ins. **Terms:** check-in 4 pm. **Activities:** sauna, whirlpools, steamroom, limited exercise equipment. **Fee:** massage. **Guest Services:** valet laundry, area transportation (fee)-ski area.

▮▮ 🍽 BIZ 📶 ✕ 🎦 🖥 / SOME UNITS FEE 🐾 🅱

Download eTourBook guides for top destinations at AAA.com/ebooks

▼ See AAA listing this page ▼

(See map & index p. 42.)

BANFF ROCKY MOUNTAIN RESORT   (403)762-5531

 Resort Condominium $99-$219 **Address:** 1029 Banff Ave T1L 1A2 **Location:** Banff Ave and Tunnel Mountain Rd; just s of Trans-Canada Hwy 1. **Facility:** Just outside of downtown, this resort is nestled at the base of the Rundle and Cascade mountains. All rooms have a gas or wood-burning fireplace. 171 condominiums. 2 stories (no elevator), exterior corridors. **Parking:** winter plug-ins. **Terms:** check-in 4 pm, 3 day cancellation notice-fee imposed. **Amenities:** *Fee:* video games, high-speed Internet. **Dining:** 2 restaurants. **Pool(s):** heated indoor. **Activities:** sauna, whirlpools, 2 tennis courts, ice skating, recreation programs, rental bicycles, playground, basketball, horseshoes, shuffleboard, volleyball, exercise room. **Guest Services:** valet and coin laundry, area transportation-public transit.

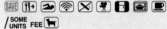

BEST WESTERN PLUS SIDING 29 LODGE
(403)762-5575

Hotel
$100-$221

AAA Benefit: Members save up to 20%, plus 10% bonus points with Best Western Rewards®.

Address: 453 Marten St T1L 1B3 **Location:** 0.6 mi (1 km) ne, just off Banff Ave. Located in a residential area. **Facility:** 56 units, some kitchens. 3 stories, interior corridors. **Terms:** 2 night minimum stay - seasonal. **Amenities:** high-speed Internet. **Pool(s):** heated indoor. **Activities:** whirlpool. **Guest Services:** valet laundry. **Free Special Amenities:** full breakfast and local telephone calls.

BOW VIEW LODGE   (403)762-2261 [19]

 Motel $89-$299 **Address:** 228 Bow Ave T1L 1A5 **Location:** Between Lynx St and Bow Ave, on Wolf St. **Facility:** 58 units, some two bedrooms. 3 stories, interior corridors. **Parking:** winter plug-ins. **Terms:** check-in 4 pm, 3 day cancellation notice-fee imposed. **Guest Services:** valet laundry, area transportation (fee)-ski area.

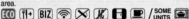

BREWSTER'S MOUNTAIN LODGE   (403)762-2900 [22]

Hotel
$109-$401

Address: 208 Caribou St T1L 1C1 **Location:** Just w off Banff Ave; downtown. **Facility:** 77 units. 3 stories, interior corridors. **Parking:** on-site (fee). **Terms:** check-in 4 pm, 3 day cancellation notice-fee imposed. **Dining:** Sushi Bistro, see separate listing. **Activities:** sauna, whirlpool, limited exercise equipment. **Guest Services:** valet and coin laundry.

BUFFALOBERRY BED AND BREAKFAST   (403)762-3750 [6]

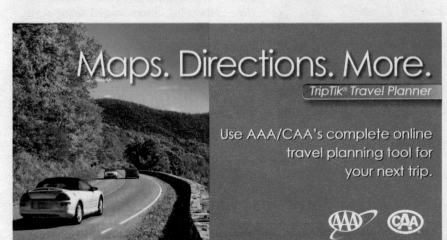 **Bed & Breakfast** $260-$335 **Address:** 417 Marten St T1L 1G5 **Location:** Just e of jct Rabbit St. Located in a residential area. **Facility:** Stay on a quiet street near the downtown core at this B&B, which offers a rustic yet contemporary flair. Each room boasts its own unique, attractive décor. Secure underground parking is available. 4 units. 2 stories, interior corridors. **Terms:** check-in 4 pm, 21 day cancellation notice-fee imposed. **Amenities:** high-speed Internet.

BUFFALO MOUNTAIN LODGE   (403)762-2400 [12]

Hotel $179-$349 **Address:** 700 Tunnel Mountain Rd T1L 1B3 **Location:** Jct Banff Ave and Wolf St, 1 mi (1.6 km) ne. Located in a secluded area. **Facility:** 108 units, some efficiencies. 2 stories (no elevator), exterior corridors. **Parking:** winter plug-ins. **Terms:** check-in 4 pm, 3 day cancellation notice-fee imposed. **Amenities:** high-speed Internet. **Dining:** Cilantro Mountain Cafe, Sleeping Buffalo Lounge, see separate listings. **Activities:** whirlpool, steamroom, exercise room. **Guest Services:** valet laundry.

CASTLE MOUNTAIN CHALETS   (403)762-3868

Cabin $149-$349 **Address:** Bow Valley Pkwy (Hwy 1A) & Hwy 93 S T1L 1B5 **Location:** 20 mi (32 km) w on Trans-Canada Hwy 1, jct Castle, 0.6 mi (1 km) ne on Hwy 1A (Bow Valley Pkwy). **Facility:** 22 cabins. 1 story, exterior corridors. **Parking:** winter plug-ins. **Terms:** check-in 4 pm, 2-3 night minimum stay - seasonal and/or weekends, 14 day cancellation notice-fee imposed. **Activities:** whirlpool, cross country skiing, rental bicycles, limited exercise equipment. *Fee:* game room. **Guest Services:** coin laundry.

(See map & index p. 42.)

CHARLTON'S CEDAR COURT   (403)762-4485   **5**

🔶🔶 **Motel** $110-$269 **Address:** 513 Banff Ave T1L 1B4 **Location:** Just w of Marmot Crescent. **Facility:** 57 units, some efficiencies. 2-3 stories, exterior corridors. **Parking:** winter plug-ins. **Terms:** check-in 4 pm, 3 day cancellation notice-fee imposed. **Pool(s):** heated indoor. **Activities:** whirlpool, steamroom. **Guest Services:** valet laundry. *(See ad this page.)*

ECO 🍴 🏊 BIZ 📶 ✕ 🔌 💻 / SOME UNITS 🔳

DELTA BANFF ROYAL CANADIAN LODGE
(403)762-3307   **10**

🔶🔶🔶 **Hotel** $168-$345 **Address:** 459 Banff Ave T1L 1B4 **Location:** 0.6 mi (1 km) ne. **Facility:** 99 units. 3 stories, interior corridors. **Parking:** on-site (fee) and valet. **Terms:** check-in 4 pm, cancellation fee imposed. **Amenities:** high-speed Internet, safes. **Dining:** The Evergreen, see separate listing. **Pool(s):** heated indoor. **Activities:** whirlpool, steamroom, exercise room. *Fee:* massage. **Guest Services:** valet laundry. *(See ad this page.)*

ECO 🍴 🍸 🏊 BIZ 📶 ✕ 🔌 💻

▼ *See AAA listing this page* ▼

Charlton's
CEDAR COURT
BANFF NATIONAL PARK

Free continental breakfast, internet and parking

513 Banff Ave., Banff, Alberta

www.charltonresorts.com • toll-free: 1.800.661.1225

▼ *See AAA listing this page* ▼

- Located in downtown Banff, conveniently close to shopping, attractions and dining along Banff Avenue.

- Offering luxurious junior suites with a comfortable king bed, romantic gas fireplace and relaxing soaker tub.

- Amenities include an indoor pool and hot tub, The Grotto Spa, fitness centre, Evergreen Restaurant, valet parking and complimentary wireless Internet.

My

DELTA
BANFF ROYAL CANADIAN LODGE

459 Banff Avenue, Banff, AB T1L 1B4 1-800-661-1379 www.deltabanff.com

Learn about inspections and Diamond Ratings at AAA.com/Diamonds

(See map & index p. 42.)

DOUGLAS FIR RESORT & CHALETS

(403)762-5591 **11**

Condominium
$125-$475

Address: 525 Tunnel Mountain Rd T1L 1B2 **Location:** Jct Banff Ave and Wolf St, 1 mi (1.6 km) ne. Located in a secluded area. **Facility:** On a wooded hillside with scenic mountain views, the resort offers a mix of chalets and condos designed for longer visits. 130 units, some cottages and condominiums. 2-3 stories, interior/exterior corridors. **Parking:** winter plug-ins. **Terms:** check-in 4 pm, cancellation fee imposed. **Amenities:** safes. **Pool(s):** heated indoor. **Activities:** saunas, whirlpools, steamroom, waterslide, exercise room. **Fee:** game room. **Guest Services:** coin laundry, area transportation-downtown.

THE FAIRMONT BANFF SPRINGS

(403)762-2211 **23**

Historic
Resort Hotel
$250-$593

Address: 405 Spray Ave T1L 1J4 **Location:** Just s on Banff Ave over the bridge, 0.3 mi (0.5 km) e. **Facility:** You'll never get tired of visiting this majestic hotel, which puts to mind a magnificent castle. This historic jewel offers boundless possibilities for exploring the nearby Canadian Rockies. 768 units. 3-9 stories, interior corridors. **Parking:** on-site (fee) and valet, winter plug-ins. **Terms:** check-in 4 pm, 3-5 night minimum stay - seasonal, 3 day cancellation notice-fee imposed, resort fee. **Amenities:** high-speed Internet (fees), safes. *Some:* video games. **Dining:** 8 restaurants, also, The Banffshire Club, Grapes Wine Bar, see separate listings. **Pool(s):** heated outdoor, heated indoor. **Activities:** saunas, whirlpools, steamrooms, 5 tennis courts, ice skating, tobogganing, recreation programs, rental bicycles, hiking trails, jogging, spa. **Fee:** golf-27 holes, horseback riding, game room. **Guest Services:** valet laundry.

Fairmont BANFF SPRINGS
Few hotels in the world rival the majesty, hospitality and grandeur of The Fairmont Banff Springs.

THE FOX HOTEL & SUITES

403/760-8500 **9**

Hotel. Rates not provided. **Address:** 461 Banff Ave T1L 1B1 **Location:** Just w of Fox St. **Facility:** 116 units, some two bedrooms. 4 stories, exterior corridors. **Terms:** check-in 4 pm. **Amenities:** high-speed Internet, safes. **Activities:** whirlpool, limited exercise equipment. **Guest Services:** valet and coin laundry.

HIDDEN RIDGE RESORT

(403)762-3544 **2**

Condominium $129-$249 **Address:** 901 Hidden Ridge Way T1L 1B7 **Location:** 1.5 mi (2.4 km) ne at Tunnel Mountain Rd. **Facility:** Set above Banff, between downtown and the Hoodoos, property guests will enjoy renovated rooms and an inviting hot tub. 107 condominiums. 2-4 stories (no elevator), exterior corridors. **Parking:** winter plug-ins. **Terms:** check-in 4 pm, 3 day cancellation notice-fee imposed. **Amenities:** *Some:* video games. **Activities:** sauna, whirlpools, playground. **Guest Services:** coin laundry.

HIGH COUNTRY INN

(403)762-2236 **15**

Hotel
$99-$299

Address: 419 Banff Ave T1L 1A7 **Location:** Between Beaver and Rabbit sts. **Facility:** 70 units, some two bedrooms. 3 stories, interior corridors. **Parking:** winter plug-ins. **Terms:** check-in 4 pm, cancellation fee imposed. **Dining:** Ticino Swiss-Italian Restaurant, see separate listing. **Pool(s):** heated indoor. **Activities:** sauna, whirlpools. **Guest Services:** coin laundry. **Free Special Amenities:** expanded continental breakfast and high-speed Internet.

HOMESTEAD INN

(403)762-4471 **21**

Motel $99-$149 **Address:** 217 Lynx St T1L 1A7 **Location:** Banff Ave, just w on Caribou St, then just n; downtown. **Facility:** 27 units. 3 stories (no elevator), exterior corridors. **Parking:** winter plug-ins. **Terms:** check-in 4 pm, 3 day cancellation notice-fee imposed. **Guest Services:** valet laundry, area transportation (fee)-ski area.

IRWIN'S MOUNTAIN INN

(403)762-4566 **13**

Hotel
$119-$219

Address: 429 Banff Ave T1L 1B2 **Location:** North of Rabbit St. **Facility:** 65 units, some two bedrooms. 3 stories, interior corridors. **Parking:** winter plug-ins. **Terms:** check-in 4 pm, cancellation fee imposed. **Activities:** sauna, whirlpool, exercise room. **Guest Services:** valet and coin laundry. **Free Special Amenities:** local telephone calls and high-speed Internet.

JOHNSTON CANYON RESORT

(403)762-2971

Cabin
$149-$314

Address: Hwy 1A T1L 1A9 **Location:** 15 mi (24 km) nw on Hwy 1A (Bow Valley Pkwy). Located at Johnston Canyon. **Facility:** 42 cabins. 1 story, exterior corridors. **Terms:** closed 10/8-5/16, check-in 4 pm. **Dining:** 2 restaurants. **Activities:** tennis court, hiking trails.

7 spectacular waterfalls. Scenic and wildlife photo opportunities all located at your doorstep.

THE JUNIPER

403/762-2281 **1**

Hotel. Rates not provided. **Address:** 1 Mt. Norquay Rd T1L 1E1 **Location:** Trans-Canada Hwy 1 exit Mt. Norquay Rd, just n. **Facility:** 52 units, some kitchens and cabins. 3 stories (no elevator), interior corridors. **Parking:** winter plug-ins. **Terms:** check-in 4 pm. **Amenities:** *Some:* high-speed Internet, safes. **Dining:** Juniper Bistro, see separate listing. **Activities:** whirlpool.

RED CARPET INN

(403)762-4184 **14**

Hotel
$89-$189

Address: 425 Banff Ave T1L 1B6 **Location:** Between Beaver and Rabbit sts. **Facility:** 52 units. 3 stories, interior/exterior corridors. **Parking:** winter plug-ins. **Terms:** check-in 4 pm. **Amenities:** safes. **Activities:** whirlpool. **Free Special Amenities:** local telephone calls and high-speed Internet.

(See map & index p. 42.)

THE RIMROCK RESORT HOTEL   (403)762-3356 24

Resort Hotel
$218-$395

Address: 300 Mountain Ave T1L 1J2 **Location:** 2.4 mi (4 km) s via Sulphur Mountain Rd; adjacent to Upper Hot Springs Pool. Located in a quiet secluded area. **Facility:** Tucked in the mountains on the outskirts of town, this luxurious resort hotel features elegant rooms and upscale dining. 346 units. 9 stories, interior corridors. **Parking:** on-site (fee) and valet, winter plug-ins. **Terms:** check-in 4 pm, 3 day cancellation notice-fee imposed. **Amenities:** video games (fee). *Some:* safes. **Dining:** Eden, see separate listing. **Pool(s):** heated indoor. **Activities:** sauna, whirlpool, steamrooms, ice skating, hiking trails, sports court, spa. **Guest Services:** valet laundry, area transportation-downtown. **Free Special Amenities:** local telephone calls and local transportation.

SAVE [TI] [symbols] CALL [symbols] BIZ [symbols] / SOME UNITS FEE [symbol]

RUNDLESTONE LODGE   (403)762-2201 3

Hotel
$115-$300

Address: 537 Banff Ave T1L 1A6 **Location:** Trans-Canada Hwy 1 exit Banff/Minnewanka Loop, 2 mi (3.2 km) sw. **Facility:** 96 units, some two bedrooms, efficiencies and kitchens. 3 stories, interior corridors. **Terms:** check-in 4 pm, cancellation fee imposed. **Pool(s):** heated indoor. **Activities:** whirlpool, bicycles, exercise room. **Guest Services:** valet and coin laundry. **Free Special Amenities:** local telephone calls and high-speed Internet.

SAVE [TI] [symbols] BIZ [symbols] / SOME UNITS [symbols]

SUNSHINE MOUNTAIN LODGE   (403)762-6500

Resort Hotel $299-$395 **Address:** 1 Sunshine Access Rd T1L 1J5 **Location:** 4.2 mi (7 km) w on Trans-Canada Hwy 1 exit Sunshine Village, then 4.2 mi (7 km) s. **Facility:** This first-class hotel is located in Sunshine Village surrounded by a plethora of activities and restaurants; guests arrive by gondola. 84 units. 2-5 stories, interior corridors. **Terms:** closed 5/20-11/9, check-in 4 pm, 14 day cancellation notice-fee imposed. **Dining:** 7 restaurants. **Activities:** sauna, whirlpool, cross country skiing, tobogganing, recreation programs, hiking trails, exercise room. *Fee:* downhill skiing, snowmobiling, game room, massage. **Guest Services:** valet laundry, area transportation-downtown.

[symbols]

TUNNEL MOUNTAIN RESORT   (403)762-4515 8

Condominium $195-$294 **Address:** 502 Tunnel Mountain Rd T1L 1B1 **Location:** Jct Banff Ave and Wolf St, 1 mi (1.6 km) ne. Located in a secluded area. **Facility:** 94 condominiums. 2 stories (no elevator), exterior corridors. **Parking:** winter plug-ins. **Terms:** check-in 4 pm, 3 day cancellation notice-fee imposed. **Amenities:** *Some:* safes. **Pool(s):** heated indoor. **Activities:** sauna, whirlpools, steamroom, playground, exercise room. **Guest Services:** valet and coin laundry.

ECO [symbols] BIZ [symbols] / SOME UNITS [symbols]

WHERE TO EAT

BALKAN THE GREEK RESTAURANT   403/762-3454 24

Greek. Casual Dining. $10-$33 **AAA Inspector Notes:** This long-established restaurant has traded in the typical blue and white décor for a new striking and upscale Greek ambience. The wonderful menu still has a very good range including all of the favorites including saganaki or spanakopita, a variety of dips and pita, roast lamb and other grilled meat and fish dishes. The baklava cheesecake always is worth saving room for. Greek nights on Tuesday and Thursday are extra fun with belly dancing followed by Greek dancing and plate smashing. **Bar:** full bar. **Reservations:** suggested. **Address:** 120 Banff Ave T1L 1A4 **Location:** Between Buffalo and Caribou sts; center. **Parking:** street only. L D

BANFF AVE BREWING CO   403/762-1003 23

American. Gastropub. $11-$27 **AAA Inspector Notes:** This bright and modern pub does not offer the average pub grub, they offer dishes made with quality ingredients and innovative twists. Appetizers include crispy wok-fried lobster rolls and monkey fingers (banana chip breaded chicken), while entrées feature banana and panko crusted chicken served with mango curry sauce or grilled AAA beef salad with organic greens and roasted beets. A nice wine list, great cocktails and hand-crafted beers round out the menu. **Bar:** full bar. **Address:** 110 Banff Ave T1L 1C9 **Location:** Center; in Clock Tower Village Mall, 2nd Floor. **Parking:** street only. L D LATE

Enjoy exclusive member discounts
and benefits from Hertz

▼ See AAA listing p. 99 ▼

(See map & index p. 42.)

THE BANFFSHIRE CLUB
403/762-6860 **29**

New
Canadian
Fine Dining
$32-$47

AAA Inspector Notes: Reminiscent of a castle dining room, this restaurant is beautiful and elegant, complete with a stone fireplace, original stone walls and dark wood accents. Accomplished servers provide a wonderful dining experience, and a talented team of chefs serve up highly-creative offerings with a very good seasonal variety of local and regional menu ingredients. Guests can choose from fantastic and extensive wine cellar choices. **Bar:** full bar. **Reservations:** required. **Address:** 405 Spray Ave T1L 1J4 **Location:** Just s on Banff Ave over the bridge, 0.3 mi (0.5 km) e; in The Fairmont Banff Springs. **Parking:** on-site and valet. D

THE BEAR STREET TAVERN
403/762-5550 **10**

Pizza. Gastropub. $11-$18 **AAA Inspector Notes:** Excellent gourmet pizza made with high-quality ingredients is found at this casual and hip spot. Such creative combinations as smoked bison with caramelized onion and edamame beans is just one example. Interestingly, they serve them with bottles of honey and chili oil to add zing of your own making—it really seems to work. There also are a few appetizers and skillet options including baked enchiladas. Add some great beer, cocktails, a nice wine list and guests are all set. **Bar:** full bar. **Reservations:** suggested. **Address:** 211 Bear St T1L 1E4 **Location:** Just n of Caribou St; center. **Parking:** street only.

L D CALL M

THE BISON RESTAURANT & TERRACE
403/762-5550 **13**

Regional Canadian. Casual Dining. $18-$40 **AAA Inspector Notes:** Up the curving staircase to the second floor is a warm and inviting room where fine service and exceptional food await. The delicious and distinctive menu leans heavily toward local Alberta products and specialty cheeses. This is a challenging and creative menu with fabulous ingredients where one might recognize items on the menu, but the interesting twists make the dishes irresistible. Quality gourmet sandwiches, fondue and pizza are offered daily. **Bar:** full bar. **Reservations:** suggested. **Address:** 211 Bear St T1L 1E4 **Location:** Just n of Caribou St; center; on 2nd level. **Parking:** street only. D CALL M

BISTRO "CAFE DE PARIS"
403/762-5365 **26**

French
Casual Dining
$15-$29

AAA Inspector Notes: Attached to Le Beaujolais, this casual dining room offers such authentic French bistro fare as house pate, Coquille St. Jacques, French onion soup, bouillabaisse, coq au vin and duck cassoulet. Their specialty is entrecote AAA beef finished tableside with café de Paris butter and pommes frites. **Bar:** full bar. **Address:** 212 Buffalo St T1L 1B5 **Location:** Northwest corner of Banff Ave and Buffalo St; upstairs; near bridge. **Parking:** street only. D

BUMPER'S THE BEEF HOUSE
403/762-2622 **2**

Steak. Family Dining. $13-$40 **AAA Inspector Notes:** Established in 1975, this restaurant occupies an A-frame building. The decor is a blend of the Old West and a mountain chalet, with the loft-lounge overlooking the dining room. Patrons can enjoy the all-you-can-eat salad bar with each entree. Although the succulent hamburgers are a favorite, the menu also features prime rib and steak, all served by the friendly staff. **Bar:** full bar. **Address:** 603 Banff Ave T1L 1A9 **Location:** 0.8 mi (1.2 km) ne on Banff Ave; at Marmot's Inn. D

CILANTRO MOUNTAIN CAFE
403/760-4488 **5**

New Canadian. Casual Dining. $14-$20 **AAA Inspector Notes:** This seasonal restaurant treats patrons to fine, friendly service in a casual atmosphere. However, the food is anything but casual and includes an eclectic mix of gourmet salads, designer wood-fired pizza, homemade terrines, house-cured meats, pasta dishes, cheeses and fantastic desserts—all relying heavily on regional ingredients. **Bar:** beer & wine. **Address:** 700 Tunnel Mountain Rd T1L 1B3 **Location:** Jct Banff Ave and Wolf St, 1 mi (1.6 km) ne; in Buffalo Mountain Lodge. D

COYOTES DELI & GRILL
403/762-3963 **17**

New Southwestern. Casual Dining. $8-$29 **AAA Inspector Notes:** Set in a relaxed yet lively deli-bistro, this eatery focuses on contemporary Southwest cuisine with an accent on creativity and color. A large open kitchen allows guests to watch as food is being prepared. The menu features predominately Southwestern food with a Pacific flair and Asian influences. The colors of Santa Fe feature predominately in this open kitchen deli-bistro. Polite and friendly service. **Bar:** full bar. **Reservations:** suggested, for dinner. **Address:** 206 Caribou St T1L 1A2 **Location:** Just w of Banff Ave; center. **Parking:** street only. B L D

THE EDDIE BURGER + BAR
403/762-2230 **19**

Burgers. Gastropub. $14-$20 **AAA Inspector Notes:** This hip burger bar, with a funky decor, makes their own burgers with top-quality ingredients like AAA Alberta beef, Wagyu Canada Kobe beef, organic beef, bison, spicy pork sausage and lamb. Eclectic gourmet combinations include the Aussie burger with grilled pineapple, beet and fried egg or the Greek lamb burger with feta cheese and tzatziki or choose the build-your own burger option. They also make their own house-cut fries and onions rings. For dessert, only local Mackay ice cream is served. **Bar:** full bar. **Reservations:** suggested. **Address:** 137 Banff Ave, #6 T1L 1B7 **Location:** Just w on Caribou St. **Parking:** street only.

L D LATE

EDEN
403/762-1840 **30**

French
Fine Dining
$64-$197

AAA Inspector Notes: Tastes, textures, creativity and imagination mingle to produce an exquisite meal from beginning to end. A touch of something magical is evident at the intimate restaurant, where hours pass unnoticed as diners unwind in plush wingback chairs, gazing out at the spectacular Rocky Mountains. A team of professional and engaging servers provide attentive and knowledgeable service with a most impressive food delivery where entrées arrive in a perfectly synchronized fashion. **Bar:** full bar. **Reservations:** suggested. **Address:** 300 Mountain Ave T1L 1J2 **Location:** 2.4 mi (4 km) s via Sulphur Mountain Rd; adjacent to Upper Hot Springs Pool; in The Rimrock Resort Hotel. **Parking:** on-site and valet. *Menu on AAA.com* D

THE EVERGREEN
403/762-3307 **3**

Continental. Fine Dining. $14-$37 **AAA Inspector Notes:** An open-concept kitchen, innovative Continental menu and comfortable yet elegant ambience make the restaurant a popular choice. Dishes highlight fresh local and regional ingredients. This place is within easy walking distance of the town center. **Bar:** full bar. **Reservations:** suggested. **Address:** 459 Banff Ave T1L 1B4 **Location:** 0.6 mi (1 km) ne; in Delta Banff Royal Canadian Lodge. **Parking:** valet and street only. *(See ad p. 46.)*

B L D CALL M

GIORGIO'S TRATTORIA
403/762-5114 **14**

Italian. Casual Dining. $15-$40 **AAA Inspector Notes:** Southern and Mediterranean décor provides a warm, relaxed ambience at this downtown spot. Settle in and study a menu offering fresh, made-in-house pasta, meat and seafood specialties, and pizza cooked in a traditional wood-burning oven. It's closed for lunch in the off season. **Bar:** full bar. **Reservations:** suggested. **Address:** 219 Banff Ave T0L 0C0 **Location:** Center. **Parking:** street only.

L D

GRAPES WINE BAR
403/762-6860 **28**

American
Casual Dining
$20-$44

AAA Inspector Notes: During some renovation work in the 1980s a carved grape ceiling trim was discovered dating from 1926 and thus this wine bar was born. The intimate little spot, with dark wood and stone work, offers a nice menu made with quality ingredients including some lovely soups and salads as well as sharing starters. Fondues are feature on the menu as well as such finely prepared entrées as rack of lamb or stuffed roast chicken. Reservations are not accepted. **Bar:** full bar. **Address:** 405 Spray Ave T1L 1J4 **Location:** Just s on Banff Ave over the bridge, 0.3 mi (0.5 km) e; in The Fairmont Banff Springs. **Parking:** on-site (fee) and valet. D

(See map & index p. 42.)

GRIZZLY HOUSE
403/762-4055 (18)

▼▼ Fondue. Casual Dining. $15-$64 **AAA Inspector Notes:** The eclectic, rustic downtown restaurant treats patrons to a distinctive fondue experience. Hot rock fondues are particularly memorable, and beef, buffalo, chicken, ostrich, rattlesnake, lobster and shark are among meats available for dipping. Finish the meal with a decadent chocolate fondue. The bustling atmosphere is fun and lively, and there are phones at every table. **Bar:** full bar. **Reservations:** suggested. **Address:** 207 Banff Ave T1L 1B4 **Location:** Between Caribou and Wolf sts. **Parking:** street only.

L D ⚿

JUNIPER BISTRO
403/763-6205 (1)

▼▼ Canadian. Casual Dining. $13-$37 **AAA Inspector Notes:** Offering an unparalleled view of Mount Rundle, the Vermilion Lakes and Banff, this upscale restaurant, with its semi-open kitchen, features a menu of fine ingredients sourced mainly in Western Canada. Depending on the season diners might find nice preparations of Tofino spring salmon or Alberta bison among the offerings. **Bar:** full bar. **Reservations:** suggested. **Address:** 1 Mt. Norquay Rd T1L 1E1 **Location:** Trans-Canada Hwy 1 exit Mt. Norquay Rd, just n; in The Juniper.

B L D CALL ♿ M

LE BEAUJOLAIS
403/762-2712 (25)

French Fine Dining $22-$40

AAA Inspector Notes: Guests ascend the stairs to this elegant dining room, which overlooks the first major intersection North of the Bow River. The restaurant offers an experience, not just a meal. Professional servers ensure a memorable event from beginning to end. The cuisine, a harmony of traditional elements prepared with a contemporary flair, is available as a prix fixe menu or a la carte. The wine list is among the most impressive in town. **Bar:** full bar. **Reservations:** suggested. **Address:** 212 Buffalo St T1L 1B5 **Location:** Northwest corner of Banff Ave and Buffalo St; upstairs; near bridge. **Parking:** street only. *Menu on AAA.com*

D

THE MAPLE LEAF GRILLE & SPIRITS
403/760-7680 (21)

▼▼▼ Canadian. Casual Dining. $12-$50 **AAA Inspector Notes:** The restaurant is a favorite for a truly Canadian experience, both in food and decor. The cozy, rock-and-wood interior displays Canadian art, as well as a canoe on the ceiling and snowshoes on the walls. The chef creates artistic regional dishes, using organic, free-range, locally grown ingredients when possible. Among selections are preparations of elk, venison, salmon and char, all made to complement the season. **Bar:** full bar. **Reservations:** suggested. **Address:** 137 Banff Ave T1L 1C8 **Location:** Corner of Banff Ave and Caribou St. **Parking:** street only.

L D CALL ♿ M

MASALA AUTHENTIC INDIAN CUISINE
403/760-6612 (8)

▼▼ Indian. Casual Dining. $15-$20 **AAA Inspector Notes:** This popular spot has delicious authentic biryanis, masalas, vindaloos, curries and vegetarian dishes as well as some tandoori clay oven options, all of which can be spiced to order. The amritsari fish appetizer is surprisingly light and flavorful. The décor has a simple Indian flair with windows overlooking the street. A buffet is offered at lunch. **Bar:** full bar. **Reservations:** suggested. **Address:** 229 Bear St T1L 1B7 **Location:** Corner of Wolf St; center. **Parking:** street only.

L D

ST. JAMES'S GATE OLDE IRISH PUB
403/762-9355 (9)

▼ Irish. Casual Dining. $10-$25 **AAA Inspector Notes:** For a casual place to kick back in the typical Irish way, look no further. This modern-day version of a rustic pub serves traditional food, such as shepherd's pie, steak and Guinness pie. Lamb stew is a fantastic, hearty choice, served with a chunk of soda bread. Guests can savor a pint of locally brewed beer or try some of the ales from overseas. Also on hand is an impressive selection of single-malt scotches as well as local and imported draft beers. **Bar:** full bar. **Address:** 207 Wolf St T1L 1C2 **Location:** Just w of Banff Ave; center. **Parking:** street only.

L D

SALTLIK A RARE STEAKHOUSE
403/762-2467 (11)

▼▼▼ Steak. Casual Dining. $14-$36 **AAA Inspector Notes:** True to its name, the restaurant truly is a "rare steak house" and a superb place. From the moment guests ascend the stairs to the upscale, contemporary dining room, they're impressed by the atmosphere. Also praiseworthy are the incredibly friendly, attentive servers, who take the time to explain the different cuts of meat and accompanying sauces. All entrees are a la carte, and the side orders are large enough to share. **Bar:** full bar. **Reservations:** suggested. **Address:** 221 Bear St T1L 1B3 **Location:** Just s of Wolf St; center. **Parking:** street only.

L D CALL ♿ M

SHAKES
403/762-9148 (20)

▼ American. Quick Serve. $4-$6 **AAA Inspector Notes:** This is a super stop for a quick lunch or snack. The milk shakes are delicious with quality ice cream and flavorings. Also great is the variety of bubble teas—a refreshing drink made with fresh, in-house tapioca pearls. Soup, chili, fries, Nathan's hot dogs and tasty chicken or beef Vietnamese subs make up the rest of the menu. Most folk get it to go, but some limited counter seating is available. **Address:** 201 Banff Ave, #5 T1L 1C5 **Location:** Just w off Banff Ave. **Parking:** street only.

L D

SILVER DRAGON RESTAURANT BANFF
403/762-3939 (16)

Chinese Casual Dining $10-$24

AAA Inspector Notes: Two flights up from street level, this restaurant is a definite stop for those who crave Chinese food. Dishes of seafood, pork, noodles and beef are certain to satisfy any appetite. Patrons discover a contemporary decor, complete with a fish tank that the kids will enjoy. **Bar:** full bar. **Reservations:** suggested. **Address:** 211 Banff Ave T1L 1E4 **Location:** Center; on Third Floor. **Parking:** street only.

L D CALL ♿ M

SLEEPING BUFFALO LOUNGE
403/760-4484 (4)

▼▼▼ Regional Canadian. Casual Dining. $14-$40 **AAA Inspector Notes:** Diners can appreciate the casual elegance in this restaurant's mountain setting. Its Rocky Mountain cuisine features wild-game meat, robust flavors and an excellent wine list. After-dinner drinks are offered fireside in the lounge. Friendly and attentive service is offered. **Bar:** full bar. **Reservations:** suggested. **Address:** 700 Tunnel Mountain Rd T1L 1B3 **Location:** Jct Banff Ave and Wolf St, 1 mi (1.6 km) ne; in Buffalo Mountain Lodge.

B L D ⚿

SUSHI BISTRO
403/762-4000 (15)

▼▼ Sushi. Casual Dining. $12-$24 **AAA Inspector Notes:** This is a simple and bright little spot with an uncomplicated, but good, sushi menu. A few other items on the menu include sunomono salad, gyoza and teriyaki bites. **Bar:** beer & wine. **Address:** 208 Caribou St T1L 1B4 **Location:** Just w off Banff Ave; downtown; in Brewster's Mountain Lodge. **Parking:** street only.

L D

THREE RAVENS RESTAURANT & WINE BAR
403/762-6300 (27)

▼▼▼ New American. Casual Dining. $28-$39 **AAA Inspector Notes:** Imagine the views from this glassed in aerie perched on the top floor of the Sally Borden Building. The chef utilizes high quality ingredients and creates a fabulous seasonal menu. A sample menu might start with Qualicum Bay scallops with beluga lentil ragout and lemon grass emulsion followed by pomegranate glazed local free range duck with wild rice risotto, sun-dried cranberries and rye and walnut sauce, finishing with a mocha pot de crème or artisan cheeses. **Bar:** full bar. **Reservations:** suggested. **Address:** 107 Tunnel Mountain Dr T1L 1H5 **Location:** From Tunnel Mountain Dr, just n on St Julien Rd; at Banff Centre.

D CALL ♿ M

TICINO SWISS-ITALIAN RESTAURANT
403/762-3848 (6)

▼▼▼ International. Fine Dining. $19-$37 **AAA Inspector Notes:** Set among the spectacular mountain peaks of Banff, this Swiss restaurant, which has been serving customers for over 30 years, has produced a solid reputation with locals and repeat visitors alike for its contemporary cucina nostrana. Using local ingredients, whenever possible, the restaurant also features a number of traditional Swiss dishes including medallions of venison, roasted duck breasts and their famous fondues including a superb chocolate fondue for dessert. **Bar:** full bar. **Reservations:** suggested. **Address:** 415 Banff Ave T1L 1B5 **Location:** Between Beaver and Rabbit sts; in High Country Inn.

D

(See map & index p. 42.)

TIMBERS FOOD COMPANY 403/762-8987 (7)

▼▼▼ Italian. Casual Dining. $10-$27 **AAA Inspector Notes:** This simple and casual spot focuses on Italian fare at dinner. They have a small selection of appetizers and some fresh salads and soups to start followed by interchangeable pastas and more complex entrées. Favorites include orange-infused salmon or AAA Alberta beef tenderloin with leek and mushroom duxelle. The daily varieties of Italian style crème brûlée are worth saving room for. Lunch is simpler with limited pastas, burgers and sandwiches as main courses. **Bar:** full bar. **Address:** 204 Wolf St T1L 1A9 **Location:** Jct Bear St; center. **Parking:** street only. [L] [D] CALL ♿ⓜ

TOMMY'S NEIGHBOURHOOD PUB 403/762-8888 (22)

▼▼▼ American. Casual Dining. $7-$13 **AAA Inspector Notes:** After a day on the ski hills or hiking in the mountains, this is a good stop for a pint of ale and a great burger with various toppings in a choice of beef, elk, buffalo, salmon or veggie patties. Locals frequent this eatery not only for its food but also for its casual, pub-style atmosphere. Menu offerings also include soup, salad, panini, quesadillas, stew and fish and chips. Guests can settle into a booth or table or just belly up to the bar for great conversations and good times. **Bar:** full bar. **Address:** 120 Banff Ave T1L 1A4 **Location:** Downtown. **Parking:** street only. [L] [D] [LATE]

WILD FLOUR BAKERY CAFE 403/760-5074 (12)

▼ Natural/Organic Breads/Pastries. Quick Serve. $6-$8 **AAA Inspector Notes:** Look no further than this trendy little café for a healthy start to a mountain adventure day. Healthy all-day breakfasts include whole wheat flax seed waffles, the Wild Flour granola bowl and Bircher muesli. Lunch items include grilled sandwiches, soups and salads and there is a host of goodies to choose from which include croissants, squares, muffins, loaves, pies and cookies. Pick up a packed lunch or a loaf of organic bread to go. **Address:** 211 Bear St, #101 T1L 1E8 **Location:** Just n of Caribou St; center. **Parking:** street only. [B] [L] CALL ♿ⓜ

BARRHEAD (D-5) pop. 4,432, elev. 648m/2,125'

BARRHEAD CENTENNIAL MUSEUM is at 5629 49th St. Displays depict early area history. Exhibits include farm equipment, pioneer furniture, tools, woodcrafts, a wildlife display, Native artifacts and a collection of African trophies. The museum also serves as a visitor information center. **Time:** Allow 1 hour minimum. **Hours:** Tues.-Sat. 10-5, May-Sept.; by appointment rest of year. **Cost:** Donations. **Phone:** (780) 674-5203.

BEAVERLODGE (C-1) pop. 2,365

First settled in 1908, Beaverlodge derives its name from the Beaver Indians who made their temporary home, or lodge, in the area. With the arrival of the railway in 1928, a new townsite was created about 1.6 kilometres (1 mi.) northwest of the original hamlet; many original buildings were moved. In the Beaverlodge Valley, the town serves as a gateway to Monkman Pass and is a large agricultural center.

Beaverlodge & District Chamber of Commerce: P.O. Box 303, Beaverlodge, AB, Canada T0H 0C0. **Phone:** (780) 354-8785.

SOUTH PEACE CENTENNIAL MUSEUM is 3 km (1.9 mi.) n.w. on Hwy. 43. Pioneer items, equipment and furnishings used in the early 1900s are displayed. A 1928 pioneer house is furnished in period.

Other exhibits include a trading post, a general store, a flour mill, a schoolhouse, an Anglican church, a railway caboose, antique steam engines, vintage cars and trucks, and 48 antique tractors. **Hours:** Daily 10-6, mid-May to early Sept. **Cost:** $5; free (ages 0-10). **Phone:** (780) 354-8869.

BONNYVILLE pop. 6,216

BEST WESTERN BONNYVILLE INN & SUITES
(780)826-6226

Hotel
$145-$150

AAA Benefit: Members save up to 20%, plus 10% bonus points with Best Western Rewards®.

Address: 5401 43rd St T9N 0H3 **Location:** Hwy 28, just n at 44th St. **Facility:** 98 units. 4 stories, interior corridors. **Parking:** winter plug-ins. **Terms:** check-in 4 pm. **Activities:** whirlpool, exercise room. **Guest Services:** valet and coin laundry. **Free Special Amenities:** expanded continental breakfast and high-speed Internet.

AAA Travel Information

In Print
TourBook® Guides
Available at AAA and CAA offices

Online
Travel Guides | TripTik® Travel Planner
AAA.com and CAA.ca

On The Go
eTourBook® Guides
AAA.com/ebooks

AAA or CAA App
iTunes Store or Google Play

Products and services are available through participating AAA and CAA clubs. Selections vary by location. Mobile Services: Not all features may be available on all devices or in all areas.

BRAGG CREEK (I-5) pop. 595
• Part of Calgary area — see map p. 54

Bragg Creek, 40 kilometres (25 mi.) southwest of Calgary on Hwy. 22, was named after Albert Bragg, a rancher who settled in the area in 1894. Known as the "Gateway to the Kananaskis" for its proximity to the Northern Rockies, the town has been a popular weekend getaway and year-round recreation area since the 1920s. Bragg Creek offers picnic areas, hiking trails, cross-country skiing, campgrounds and scenic Elbow Falls. The area has evolved as an artist's community with sculptors, potters, weavers, painters and other artisans practicing their crafts.

Bragg Creek Chamber of Commerce: P.O. Box 216, Bragg Creek, AB, Canada T0L 0K0. **Phone:** (403) 949-0004.

BROOKS (I-8) pop. 13,676

Brooks is surrounded by 105,222 hectares (260,000 acres) of irrigated farmland and more than 404,700 hectares (1 million acres) of rangeland used for cattle grazing. This semiarid shortgrass section of the province is the setting for wildlife and horticultural research centers.

Brooks Visitor Information Centre: 568 Sutherland Dr. E., Brooks, AB, Canada T1R 1C7. **Phone:** (403) 362-5073.

BROOKS AQUEDUCT is 2 km (1 mi.) s.e. of Hwy. 1 exit Cassils Rd. (Hwy. 542), then 3 km (2 mi.) s. on a gravel road, following signs. Hailed as an engineering marvel when it was built in the early 1900s, the concrete aqueduct carried water to farmers and ranchers who settled in the region following the arrival of the Canadian Pacific Railway.

Operational until 1979, it has been preserved as a monument to the engineers and agriculturalists who developed the region. Signage and brochures offer information for self-guiding tours. **Tours:** Guided tours are available. **Time:** Allow 30 minutes minimum. **Hours:** Daily 10-5, May 15-Labour Day. **Cost:** Donations. **Phone:** (403) 362-4451.

BROOKS AND DISTRICT MUSEUM is .4 km (.2 mi.) w. of Trans-Canada Hwy. at 568 Southerland Dr. E. Exhibits about early ranchers, homesteaders, the Royal Canadian Mounted Police, railroading and irrigation trace local history from the late 19th and early 20th centuries. Seventeen buildings, including a log cabin, a schoolhouse and a church, are on the grounds. **Time:** Allow 1 hour, 30 minutes minimum. **Hours:** Daily 9-5, Victoria Day weekend-Labour Day; by appointment rest of year. **Cost:** Donations. **Phone:** (403) 362-5073.

 DINOSAUR PROVINCIAL PARK—see Patricia p. 174.

HERITAGE INN & SUITES   (403)362-8688
Hotel $137-$227 **Address:** 1239 2nd St W T1R 1P7 **Location:** Trans-Canada Hwy 1 exit Hwy 873, 0.5 mi (0.8 km) s. **Facility:** 61 units, some two bedrooms and efficiencies. 3 stories, interior corridors. **Parking:** winter plug-ins. **Terms:** cancellation fee imposed. **Amenities:** high-speed Internet. **Pool(s):** heated indoor. **Activities:** whirlpool, exercise room. **Guest Services:** valet and coin laundry.

HERITAGE INN HOTEL & CONVENTION CENTRE   (403)362-6666
Hotel $116-$177 **Address:** 1217 2nd St W T1R 1P7 **Location:** Trans-Canada Hwy 1 exit Hwy 873, 0.5 mi (0.8 km) s. **Facility:** 106 units, some efficiencies. 2 stories (no elevator), interior corridors. **Parking:** winter plug-ins. **Terms:** cancellation fee imposed. **Dining:** nightclub. **Activities:** whirlpool. **Guest Services:** valet and coin laundry.

LAKEVIEW INNS & SUITES   403/362-7440
Hotel
Rates not provided
Address: 1307 2nd St W T1R 1P7 **Location:** Trans-Canada Hwy 1 exit Hwy 873, 0.5 mi (0.8 km) s. **Facility:** 77 units. 3 stories, interior corridors. **Parking:** winter plug-ins. **Pool(s):** heated indoor. **Activities:** whirlpool, exercise room. **Guest Services:** valet and coin laundry. **Free Special Amenities:** expanded continental breakfast and high-speed Internet.

RAMADA BROOKS   (403)362-6440
Hotel $140-$219 **Address:** 1319 2nd St W T1R 1P7 **Location:** Trans-Canada Hwy 1 exit Hwy 873, 0.5 mi (0.8 km) s. **Facility:** 101 units, some efficiencies. 4 stories, interior/exterior corridors. **Parking:** winter plug-ins. **Amenities:** high-speed Internet. **Pool(s):** heated indoor. **Activities:** whirlpool, steamroom, waterslide, exercise room. **Guest Services:** valet and coin laundry.

SUPER 8 BROOKS   (403)363-0080
Hotel
$120-$130
Address: 115 15th Ave W T1R 1C4 **Location:** Just s off Trans-Canada Hwy 1. **Facility:** 94 units, some efficiencies. 3 stories, interior/exterior corridors. **Parking:** winter plug-ins. **Amenities:** high-speed Internet. *Some:* video games, safes. **Dining:** O'Shea's Eatery & Ale House, see separate listing. **Pool(s):** heated indoor. **Activities:** whirlpool, waterslide, exercise room. **Guest Services:** coin laundry.

WHERE TO EAT

O'SHEA'S EATERY & ALE HOUSE   403/501-5656
American. Casual Dining. $10-$25 **AAA Inspector Notes:** This attractive, Irish theme restaurant offers up an expanded pub menu as well as a good variety of salads, pastas, chicken, ribs, fish and steaks. The kitchen also cooks up such classic Irish favorites as fish and chips, shepherd's pie and Guinness beef stew. **Bar:** full bar. **Address:** 119 15th Ave W T1R 1C3 **Location:** Just s off Trans-Canada Hwy 1; in Super 8 Brooks. L D

Calgary

Then & Now

Calgary, once considered a cow town, now is one of Canada's fastest-growing cities, with skyscrapers, light-rail transit, shopping complexes and contemporary houses. The city's economy began with—and still includes—ranching and the subsequent meatpacking industry, but the discovery of oil just south of the city in 1914 and just north in 1947 fueled a spurt of growth that turned an agricultural community into a metropolis.

Calgary today boasts a high concentration of corporate offices, the second largest in Canada. Energy, agriculture, tourism, manufacturing, research and development, and advanced technology comprise Calgary's industrial base.

The city's modern skyline, jagged with skyscrapers, makes a dramatic appearance on the vast expanse of Alberta prairie. To the west, almost mirroring Calgary's silhouette, are the Ca-

nadian Rockies, jutting into the sky just over an hour's drive away. The Trans-Canada Highway, a major national east-west roadway, runs through the heart of the city; in Calgary the highway also is known as 16th Avenue.

The region's history of human habitation began almost 10,000 years before the first 19th-century fur and whiskey traders arrived. Indian tribes chose the confluence of the Bow and Elbow rivers as a campsite; emerging as the dominant tribe was the Blackfoot. Their acquisition of horses allowed them to hunt buffalo and fight almost every other prairie tribe with great success. As European settlement increased, so did the friction between the natives and the newcomers.

The Calgary Stampede

An 1877 treaty calmed the rough waters, and relative peace among all factions has existed since. Several reservations, including the Tsuu T'ina Reserve south of the city, are near Calgary. Native North Americans have sought to assimilate themselves into Canadian culture while retaining their native heritage.

Chinese were recruited abroad in the early 1900s to build railroads; once the trains were running, however, immigration was restricted. Oil and money lured Americans who brought technology and investment funds needed to get Calgary's petroleum industry started. But many of those who came for the money enjoyed the area and stayed, becoming Canadian citizens.

Calgary's modern sophistication is offset by a romantic perception of the past—a past in which the city was established as a North West Mounted Police fort in 1875. The Calgary Stampede, a 10-day Western wingding that celebrated its centennial in 2012, is attended by more than a million residents and visitors who

(Continued on p. 55.)

Destination Calgary

Airdrie

Cochrane

(22)

(201)

✈ (YYC)

(1A)

Strathmore

(22)

Bragg Creek

Calgary

(2A)

(2A)

Okotoks

(2)

6053-B

This map shows cities in the Calgary vicinity where you will find attractions, hotels and restaurants. Cities are listed alphabetically in this book on the following pages.

Fast Facts

ABOUT THE CITY

POP: 1,096,833 ■ **ELEV:** 1,048 m/3,440 ft.

MONEY

SALES TAX: The federal Goods and Service Tax is 5 percent and applies to most goods, food/beverages and services, including lodgings. Alberta does not have a provincial sales tax but does impose a 4 percent hotel tax. A 1-2 percent tourism levy also is charged in some areas.

WHOM TO CALL

EMERGENCY: 911

POLICE (non-emergency): (403) 266-1234

FIRE (non-emergency): (403) 287-4299

TEMPERATURE: (403) 299-7878

ROAD CONDITIONS: (877) 262-4997

HOSPITALS: Foothills Medical Centre, (403) 944-1110 ■ Peter Lougheed Centre, (403) 943-4555 ■ Rockyview General Hospital, (403) 943-3000.

WHERE TO LOOK AND LISTEN

NEWSPAPERS: Calgary's daily newspapers are the *Calgary Herald* and the *Calgary Sun,* both morning papers. The national newspapers are *The Globe and Mail* and the *National Post.*

RADIO: Calgary radio station CBC (1010 AM) is a member of the Canadian Broadcasting Corp.

VISITOR INFORMATION

Tourism Calgary: 238 11th Ave. S.E., Room 200, Calgary, AB, Canada T2G 0X8. **Phone:** (403) 263-8510 or (800) 661-1678.

Visitor information also is available at the Calgary International Airport on the arrivals level and at the Riley & McCormick Western Store at 220 Stephen Ave. in the Eau Claire Market.

TRANSPORTATION

AIR TRAVEL: Calgary International Airport (YYC) is northeast of downtown off Hwy. 2 exit 266. Public bus transportation to and from the airport is offered by Calgary Transit via Route 300, with service to and from downtown. Taxi service between the airport and downtown typically costs $40-$45. Many hotels also offer free shuttle service for their guests.

RENTAL CARS: Hertz, downtown or at the airport, offers discounts to CAA and AAA members; phone (403) 221-1676, (800) 263-0600 in Canada, or (800) 654-3080 outside of Canada.

RAIL SERVICE: The nearest VIA Rail stations are in Jasper and Edmonton; phone (506) 857-9830 or (888) 842-7245.

BUSES: Greyhound Lines Inc. operates from the depot at 850 16th St. S.W.; phone (800) 661-8747. Red Arrow Express operates luxury motor coaches between Calgary, Red Deer, Edmonton and Fort McMurray; phone (403) 531-0350 or (800) 232-1958.

TAXIS: Taxi companies include Association Cab, (403) 299-1111 ■ Checker Yellow Cab, (403) 299-9999 ■ Mayfair Taxi, (403) 255-6555 ■ and Prestige Limousine, (403) 975-8233. Rates begin at $3.40 for the first 135 metres (about 1/12 mi.) or portion thereof, plus 20c for each additional 135 metres (about 1/12 mi.) or portion thereof. Cabs can be hailed on the street, but phoning ahead is recommended.

PUBLIC TRANSPORTATION: Calgary has both bus and light-rail transit (LRT) service; the latter is free in the downtown core. Calgary Transit's office, 224 7th Ave. S.W., has schedules and maps and sells transit passes. Fare is $2.75; $1.75 (ages 6-14). A 1-day pass is $8.25; $5.25 (ages 6-14). Phone (403) 262-1000.

(Continued from p. 53.)

relive the days of chuck wagons and lassos. Those days existed more than a century ago, after the North West Mounted Police—the forerunner of today's Royal Canadian Mounted Police—and the railroad brought law, order and homesteaders to a region previously settled by trappers, buffalo hunters and whiskey traders. The festival, held each year since 1912, takes place in July.

Although Calgary's growth has been rapid, it has been practical. The bustling downtown district was designed to accommodate a large amount of activity, even during winter when below-freezing temperatures normally would inhibit commerce. Enclosed walkways called "plus-15s" (since they are 15 feet above street level) connect almost half the downtown buildings, making it possible to eat, work, shop or visit neighbors without donning so much as a mitten.

The Stephen Avenue Walk, a brick pedestrian mall in the city center lined with restored late 19th- and early 20th-century buildings, trees, statues, benches and fountains, is an urban refuge from traffic as well as a nice place to people watch and enjoy lunch or a stroll in warm weather.

Nearby is Olympic Plaza, the site of the awards ceremonies during the 15th Olympic Winter Games, held in Calgary in 1988, and now a popular venue for events and festivals.

Must Do: AAA Editor's Picks

- Trek back through time to the age of the dinosaurs at the 🚏 **Calgary Zoo, Botanical Garden & Prehistoric Park,** home to a collection of fierce-looking dinosaur replicas, to say nothing of the even more impressive collection of living, breathing animals from all over the world. Grizzly bears and wolves, giraffes and gorillas, spider monkeys and marmosets all thrive within their particular re-created habitats.

- Zip to the top of 🚏 **Calgary Tower** via high-speed elevator to take in a fantastic 360-degree view of the city, a great way to get your bearings. Built to commemorate Canada's centennial, the tower has been a distinctive city landmark since 1968, and since 2005 it has dared brave visitors to step onto the glass floor of its observation deck.

- Pull on a pair of cowboy boots and celebrate all things wild and western during the 🚏 **Calgary Stampede,** a rodeo-centered event attended by more than a million people. For 10 days every July, the Stampede puts on a tremendous show that not only includes barrel racing, bull riding and chuck wagon races, but also fireworks, parades, street parties, a carnival midway and a huge outdoor music festival.

- Walk in the footsteps of Olympic greats from the 1988 Winter Games at 🚏 **Canada Olympic Park,** a year-round sports complex offering miniature golf, a zipline and bobsleigh runs in summer and skiing, snowboarding and luge rides in winter. And from the Ski Jump Tower's observation level you'll have a spectacular view of the Rocky Mountains and Calgary's skyline.

- Hop aboard a steam train or ride in a horse-drawn wagon as you explore nearly a century's worth of local history at 🚏 **Heritage Park Historical Village.** You'll get a feel for life in the isolated prairie settlement that Calgary once was when you tour the historic buildings relocated to the park and chat with the costumed "townspeople" inside.

- Listen to birdsong as you wander through the **Inglewood Bird Sanctuary,** a lovely bit of wooded parkland just minutes from downtown Calgary. And once your inner peace has been restored, explore nearby Inglewood, one of the city's oldest neighborhoods. It's a place known for boutiques, art galleries and antique stores, especially along 9th Avenue S.E.

- Get answers at 🚏 **TELUS Spark** to such weighty questions as: What does it mean to be human? What natural forces have shaped our world? How can we harness energy for our use? Having opened in its latest location in 2011, the science center is filled with state-of-the-art interactive exhibits and high-tech displays that engage both children and adults.

- Discover the bravery of Canada's military heroes at 🚏 **The Military Museums,** showcasing the nation's army, navy and air force as well as four army regiments. Tanks and a fighter jet seem poised for battle outside the museum, while inside dramatic dioramas and displays of weaponry, medals and photographs bring Canada's military history to life.

- Flip, fly and fall courtesy of thrill rides at **Calaway Park,** where the amusements range from tame to terrifying. The Adrenaline Test Zone, Chaos and the Vortex roller coaster are in the latter group, but there are plenty of rides designed for smaller children as well.

- Imagine rubbing elbows with one of 19th-century Calgary's wealthiest and most influential families when you enter **Lougheed House,** their imposing sandstone mansion. Stroll through the formal gardens and you'll understand why the estate was named Beaulieu, French for "beautiful place."

Calgary Tower

Calgary 1-day Itinerary

AAA editors suggest these activities for a great short vacation experience.

Morning

- Start your day out and about in Calgary with breakfast at **Diner Deluxe,** 804 Edmonton Tr. N.E. This fun, 1950s retro-cool eatery serves classic eggs-and-toast breakfasts along with French toast stuffed with gouda and Canadian bacon and a French-Canadian twist on hash browns involving cheese curds and hollandaise sauce.
- Diner Deluxe makes a good starting point not just for the hearty food or the mid-century modern ambience (picture Formica countertops and vinyl chairs) but also because it's just a few minutes from the ⟿**Calgary Zoo, Botanical Garden & Prehistoric Park,** your next stop.
- Grizzly bears and wolves thrive in the zoo's Canadian Wilds section, while massive elephants lumber about the Eurasia area. Visit Destination Africa to see gorillas and giraffes, the South American pavilion for spider monkeys and marmosets, Penguin Plunge to witness four species of penguins waddling and shaking their tail feathers in an indoor-outdoor exhibit complete with a waterfall, and the Botanical Gardens to wander among a treasure trove of plants—both tropical exotics and hardy locals.

Afternoon

- You'll probably want to spend a few hours exploring the zoo's carefully designed animal enclosures, so when hunger strikes, you fortunately have several options within the park. Among them are Kitamba Café, a cafeteria with an adjacent coffee shop, or Tusk N' Grill, which serves hamburgers and hot dogs.
- Cross the river into downtown to arrive at the ⟿**Glenbow Museum,** a complex that includes both a history museum housing more than a million artifacts and an art gallery with thousands of works of art. Although the culture and heritage of Western Canada is the focus here, you'll also find cultures outside of Canada represented, for example, in the Asian Gallery and within an exhibition of West African cultural artifacts. There's also an extensive mineral collection with a dazzling assortment of sparkling gemstones.
- Across from the museum is ⟿**Calgary Tower,** the place to go for stunning views of the city and on the horizon, the Rocky Mountains. The wraparound observation deck not only allows 360-degree panorama, but a glass-floored section lets you step out over a sheer drop to the street. The tower's restaurant, **Sky 360,** rotates once an hour, giving diners a complete tour of the scenery from the comfort of their table.
- Just a block north from the tower is Stephen Avenue Walk, a portion of 8th Avenue S.W. closed to car traffic 6 a.m.-6 p.m. The many examples of public art you'll see here include the towering steel tree sculptures that serve both to beautify and reduce gusting winds.

Red panda, Calgary Zoo, Botanical Garden & Prehistoric Park

Boutiques, bars, restaurants, shopping centers and historic buildings line the pedestrian mall, and during warm weather months, street performers entertain the crowds.

- As you stroll along Stephen Avenue, you'll notice pedestrian bridges spanning the street. These are part of the +15 Walkway System, so-called because they are generally 15 feet (4.6 metres) above street level. The network of enclosed walkways allows people to reach office buildings and shopping malls throughout a 50-block area in climate-controlled comfort, something Calgarians appreciate in the freezing cold of winter.

Evening

- Of course, dinner up in the air at the Calgary Tower's Sky 360 restaurant would be a spectacular conclusion to your day, but now that you've already seen Calgary from a bird's-eye perspective, head to the River Café on Prince's Island Park for a totally different but equally beautiful city view.
- Prince's Island Park is adjacent to the Eau Claire neighborhood and the downtown business district. It's a lush urban oasis in the Bow River and the frequent site of summer picnics, music festivals and holiday celebrations.
- Park at the Eau Claire Market and take the Jaipur footbridge across to the island. The **River Café** occupies a rustic wood-and-stone building that evokes a cabin deep in the woods, yet looking out over the river from its patio, you see downtown's office towers. Make reservations because the café's lovely setting and fabulous dishes specializing in wild game and fish make it a popular dinner spot highly sought-after by both locals and visitors.

Arriving
By Car

Two major highways pass through Calgary. Queen Elizabeth II Hwy. runs north and south through the city; Trans-Canada Hwy. provides access from the east and west. Hwy. 1A, which connects Calgary and Cochrane, also serves as an alternate route between Calgary and the towns of Canmore and Banff. Hwy. 8 connects Calgary with Bragg Creek.

Getting Around
Street System

Calgary is divided into quadrants, with Centre Street separating the east and west sectors and the Bow River and Memorial Drive delineating north and south. Streets run north and south, avenues east and west. All are numbered from the intersection of Centre Street and Centre Avenue, just north of downtown. Roads in suburban areas are numbered where they form grids and named where they do not.

The speed limit is 50 kilometres per hour (30 mph) or as posted. A right turn on red after stopping is permitted unless otherwise posted; U-turns are not. Other restrictions apply during rush hours in certain areas; be aware of signs, especially in school and playground zones. Pedestrian crosswalks are designated by "X" signs, and motorists must yield to pedestrians.

Parking

Parking is not permitted on major roads in the downtown core during rush hours, between 6:30 and 9 a.m. and 3:30 and 6 p.m. Downtown metered street parking usually is limited to 2 hours at a maximum cost of $5 per hour. Pay parking for extended periods is available at numerous locations. Rates for downtown parking lots range from $1.75-$3.50 per half-hour during the day.

Shopping

Stephen Avenue Walk, a downtown pedestrian mall, extends from Bankers Hall to the city municipal buildings. This popular spot for people watching features shops, galleries and restaurants housed within historic buildings. Also downtown, a five-block shopping complex linked by an indoor walkway includes the more than 200 boutiques, department stores and retail chains of **Calgary Eaton Centre/TD Square, Bankers Hall** and **Scotia Centre.**

Unique specialty shops, kiosks and restaurants are the draw at **Eau Claire Market,** adjacent to the Bow River and Prince's Island Park at 2nd Avenue and 2nd Street S.W.

The trendy **Uptown 17th Avenue,** a scenic neighborhood and upscale shopping district, features stylish fashion shops, antiques stores and eclectic craft boutiques. The avenue also is home to the exclusive shops at **Mount Royal Village.** The **Kensington district** features smaller stores in new and old buildings. Originally Atlantic Avenue, **Ninth Avenue S.E.** now is lined with antiques and home-furnishings stores, bookstores and cappuccino bars.

Major department stores and a wide variety of chain and specialty stores occupy the city's shopping centers: **Chinook Centre** at 6455 Macleod Tr. S.W., **Deerfoot Outlet Mall** at 901 64th Ave. N.E., **Market Mall** at 3625 Shaganappi Tr. N.W., **North Hill Mall** at 1632 14th Ave. N.W., **Northland Village Shoppes** at 5111 Northland Dr. N.W., **Shawnessy Centre** at 162nd Avenue and Macleod Trail, **Southcentre Mall** at Macleod Trail and Anderson Road S.E., **Sunridge Mall** at 2525 36th St. N.E., **Westhills Towne Centre** at Stewart Green S.W. off Richmond Road and Sarcee Trail S.W. and **Willow Park Village** on Macleod Trail S.

Big Events

To celebrate the season and showcase local arts, culture and sports, **Calgary Winter Festival** takes place for 11 days in February. The festival, which takes advantage of the venues from the 1988 Winter Olympics, features dog sledding, snowboarding and the Winter Village.

Calgary International Children's Festival, which begins the third Wednesday in May and continues for 5 days, draws performers from such locales as Peru, Germany, Russia and Zimbabwe. The festival's many offerings include music, puppetry, dance and storytelling.

Despite a focus on the modern oil and gas industry, Calgary citizens recall their past with the ☙ **Calgary Stampede,** held in July. This 10-day Wild West exhibition features a rodeo, chuck wagon races, livestock shows, a re-creation of a Plains Indian village, beach-themed attractions, educational displays, shopping, extreme sports events and a

Shop the boutiques of Stephen Avenue Walk

midway. Parades, fireworks, street dancing, pancake breakfasts and other activities create a carnival-like atmosphere. Families enjoy the cultural and musical events that take place during the ⚑ **Calgary Folk Music Festival,** held over 4 days in late July.

GlobalFest takes place in August and features such events as an international fireworks competition and a multicultural celebration. **Afrikadey!** celebrates African culture through traditional and contemporary music, crafts, food and special scheduled events. Venues for the popular mid-August event are found throughout the area, with festivities concluding at **Prince's Island Park.** Visitors can sample fine foods and beverages at the **Eau Claire Market** during ⚑ **Taste of Calgary,** which also occurs in mid-August.

During Labour Day weekend **BBQ on the Bow** offers a barbecue competition, live performances by local bands, a children's craft tent, and vendors selling food samples and take-home goods. The **Masters Tournament** takes place in September at the **Spruce Meadows** outdoor equestrian center, off Hwy. 22X (Spruce Meadows Trail) and Macleod Trail. Other racing and dressage events are held at the center throughout the year.

Sports & Rec

Calgary was an appropriate choice as host of the 1988 Winter Olympic Games—opportunities for indoor and outdoor recreation abound. For information about recreational activities, programs and facilities visitors can phone the city's recreation department by dialing 311 in Calgary or (403) 268-2489.

In winter public **skiing** facilities at **Canada Olympic Park** *(see attraction listing p. 62)* and in numerous areas nearby are available. Canada Olympic Park also is where to go for other **winter sports,** such as bobsledding, luge, ski jumping and snowboarding.

At **Talisman Centre,** 2225 Macleod Tr. S., **swimming, track events** and **weight lifting** are among the popular activities; phone (403) 233-8393. Similar facilities are offered at the following leisure centers: **Eau Claire YMCA,** 101 3rd St. S.W.; **YWCA,** 320 5th Ave. S.E.; **Southland Leisure Center,** 2000 Southland Dr. S.W.; and **Village Square Leisure Center,** 2623 56th St. N.E. The latter two offer wave pools.

Ice-skating is featured during the winter at Olympic Plaza as well as year-round at more than two dozen other locations. The **Olympic Oval,** at 2500 University Dr. N.W., is the site of the 1988 Olympic speed-skating events; skate rentals are available.

Several parks are in the city, particularly along the **Bow River. Fish Creek Provincial Park** *(see Recreation Areas Chart)* has a visitor center and a small lake providing swimming in summer and ice-skating in winter. Joggers and bicyclists use the park's extensive trail system. Other recreation sites include **Bowness, Edworthy** and **Riley** parks in northwest

Spend a day snowboarding

Calgary and **Prince's Island Park** in the city center. The 145-hectare (360-acre) **Glenmore Reservoir** provides ample space for **sailing** and **canoeing;** the Dragon Boat races are held in late July.

With spectacular natural areas nearby, many visitors to Calgary will be lured to the wilds to enjoy canoeing, **camping, rafting, hiking** and other outdoor pursuits. **Walking** and **bicycling** trails meander through these regions, as do **cross-country skiing** routes. **Tennis** and swimming enthusiasts will find courts and pools throughout Calgary.

Golf lovers can play at more than 40 local courses, including 18 holes at **Maple Ridge,** 1240 Mapleglade Dr. S.E.; **McCall Lake,** 1600 32nd Ave. N.E.; **McKenzie Meadows,** 17215 McKenzie Meadows Dr. S.E.; and **Shaganappi Point,** 1200 26th St. S.W. Nine-hole courses are at **Confederation,** 3204 Collingwood Dr. N.W.; **Lakeview,** 5840 19th St. S.W.; and **Richmond Green,** 2539 33rd Ave. S.W. Some private courses accept visiting golfers; check locally for greens fees and restrictions.

With names like Flames, Stampeders **Roughnecks** and **Hitmen,** Calgary's major sports teams cannot help but be exciting. The **Flames** play **ice hockey** at **Scotiabank Saddledome,** 555 Saddledome Rise S.E. in Stampede Park; phone (403) 777-2177 or (407) 777-4646.

The local Canadian **Football** League team, the **Calgary Stampeders,** pounds the turf at **McMahon Stadium,** off 16th Avenue at 1817 Crowchild Tr. N.W. Tickets can be obtained by phoning the box office at (403) 289-0258. Ticket prices are $30-$102.

Spruce Meadows, an outdoor equestrian center and show jumping venue 3 kilometres (2 mi.) west on Hwy. 22X (Spruce Meadows Trail) from Macleod Trail at 18011 Spruce Meadows Way S.W., has world-class programs, including international show jumping events. On days when no shows are scheduled the grounds are open free to the public, daily 9-6. Visitors are invited to wander the grounds, picnic and view horses in the stables; phone (403) 974-4200 for a schedule of Spruce Meadows events.

Performing Arts

Four of Calgary's most illustrious theater and music companies perform in the **Epcor Centre for the Performing Arts** at 205 8th Ave. S.E. The center is shared by **Alberta Theatre Projects, Theatre Calgary, One Yellow Rabbit Theatre Company** and **Calgary Philharmonic Orchestra.** In addition to four theaters and a concert hall, it contains shops, a restaurant and a coffee bar. For information about performance schedules and ticket sales phone Ticketmaster at (855) 985-5000.

Southern Alberta Jubilee Auditorium, 1415 14th Ave. N.W., stages a variety of performing arts, including touring companies of Broadway musicals and presentations by **Calgary Opera;** for details phone the opera company at (403) 262-7286 or the auditorium at (403) 297-8000.

Loose Moose Theatre Company, 1235 26th Ave. S.E., performs adult comedy and drama as well as children's theater; phone (403) 265-5682. **Pumphouse Theatre,** 2140 Pumphouse Ave. S.W., gets its name from the 1913 former pumphouse that the

Spend an evening at the orchestra while in town

city converted into two theaters; phone (403) 263-0079 for schedule and ticket information. Midday performances take place in the aptly named **Lunchbox Theatre,** at the base of Calgary Tower at 160 9th Ave. S.E.; phone (403) 265-4292.

A popular dinner theater that often showcases well-known performers in its productions is **Stage West,** 727 42nd Ave. S.E.; phone (403) 243-6642. Other theater, dance and music companies operate locally; check newspapers for performance schedules.

ATTRACTIONS

AERO SPACE MUSEUM OF CALGARY is at 4629 McCall Way N.E. In a former Royal Air Force drill hall, the museum contains exhibits about western Canada's aviation history. Aircraft displayed include an F86 Sabre jet, a Bell 47G helicopter and one of the few remaining World War I Sopwith Triplanes. Also featured are piston and jet aircraft engines, aviation artwork and a Martin Baker ejection seat.

Time: Allow 30 minutes minimum. **Hours:** Daily 10-4. Closed Jan. 1, Good Friday, Easter, Christmas Eve, Christmas and day after Christmas. **Cost:** $10; $7 (ages 60+ and students with ID); $5 (ages 6-11); $25 (family). **Phone:** (403) 250-3752.

ART GALLERY OF CALGARY is at 117 8th Ave. S.W. Housed in two joined, historic buildings, the art gallery presents four to five exhibitions of contemporary work each year. Such mediums as painting, photography and sculpture are represented, with pieces from both emerging and established artists displayed. **Time:** Allow 30 minutes minimum. **Hours:** Tues.-Sat. 10-5 (also first Thurs. of the month 5-9, July-Aug.). Closed major holidays. **Cost:** Donations. **Phone:** (403) 770-1350.

BOW HABITAT STATION is at 1440 17A St. S.E. in Pearce Estate City Park. Located along the Bow River, the center educates visitors about fish management, water future and Alberta's wetlands through both interactive exhibits and aquariums that shelter a variety of marine species. Highlights include a large model outlining the anatomy of a fish, an exhibit that explores the cycle of water and the 40-minute film "Wet Alberta." Interpretive trails allow for exploration of the outdoor Pearce Estate Park Wetland. Guided tours of the Sam Livingston Fish Hatchery, one of the largest fish hatcheries in North America, last between 45 and 60 minutes.

Time: Allow 2 hours minimum. **Hours:** Tues.-Sat. 11-4 (also Thurs. 4-8), July-Aug.; otherwise varies. Closed major holidays. **Cost:** Bow Habitat Station and Sam Livingston Fish Hatchery $14; $12 (ages 65+ and students with ID); $8 (ages 5-17); $45 (family). Bow Habitat Station only $10; $8 (ages 65+ and students with ID); $6 (ages 5-17); $30 (family). Reservations are required for guided tours of the Sam Livingston Fish Hatchery. **Phone:** (403) 297-6561.

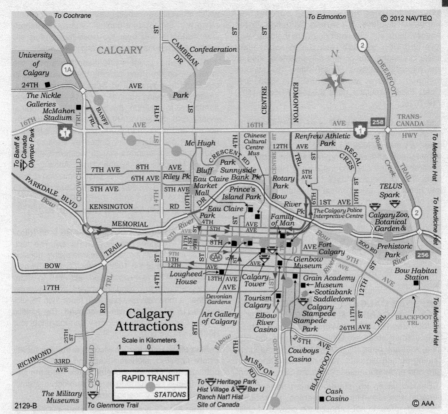

© 2012 NAVTEQ

Calgary Attractions

Scale in Kilometers

RAPID TRANSIT STATIONS

2129-B

© AAA

BUTTERFIELD ACRES CHILDREN'S FARM is 3 km (1.9 mi.) n. of Crowchild Tr. at 254077 Rocky Ridge Rd. At this whimsical, educational farm, visitors can meet and interact with such animals as calves, chicks, llamas, pigs, rabbits and sheep. In addition to interactive displays and pony and wagon rides, children also can learn how to milk a goat, walk on farm stilts or climb aboard an old farm tractor.

Note: Closed footwear with socks is required. Pets are not permitted. **Time:** Allow 2 hours minimum. **Hours:** Daily 10-4, July-Aug.; Mon.-Fri. 10-2, Sat.-Sun. 11-6, Apr.-June and in Sept. **Cost:** $13.99; $11.99 (ages 65+); $10.99 (ages 1-17). Pony ride $1. **Phone:** (403) 547-3595 or (403) 239-0638.

CALAWAY PARK, 10 km (6 mi.) w. off Trans-Canada Hwy. Springbank Rd. exit, is said to be western Canada's largest outdoor amusement park. It features 34 rides, including a roller coaster, a log ride, bumper boats and skill games. Live stage shows are presented daily. The landscaped grounds also include an interactive maze, a miniature golf course and a fishing hole.

Kennel, stroller and wheelchair rentals are available. **Time:** Allow 4 hours minimum. **Hours:** Daily 10-7, July 1-Labour Day; Fri. 5-9 p.m., Sat.-Sun. and Mon. holidays 10-7, Victoria Day weekend-June 30; Sat.-Sun. and Mon. holidays 10-6, day after Labour Day-late Nov. **Cost:** $33.95; $27 (ages 3-6); $25 (ages 50+); $89 (family). After 2 p.m. $18.95; free (ages 0-2). Admission includes unlimited rides; prices for individual games, the maze, fishing and miniature golf vary. Phone ahead to confirm schedule and prices. **Phone:** (403) 240-3822. *(See ad p. 62.)*

THE CALGARY POLICE INTERPRETIVE CENTRE is on the second floor of the Police Administration Building at 316 7th Ave. S.E. Interactive displays help children to understand the role of police officers in society. Exhibit galleries detail the early days of police work through artifacts and photos. Visitors also learn how to deal with serious issues facing society today, including substance abuse and domestic violence.

Time: Allow 45 minutes minimum. **Hours:** Mon.-Fri. 10-4. Closed major holidays. Phone ahead to confirm schedule. **Cost:** $5; free (ages 0-17). Under 13 must be with an adult. **Phone:** (403) 206-4566.

THE CALGARY SPACEPORT is on the third floor of the Calgary International Airport off Hwy. 2 (Deerfoot Tr. N.E.). The entertaining educational facility offers exhibits focusing on space and aeronautics. Hands-on displays, NASA and Canadian Space Agency items and simulator rides are featured. Visitors can view a moon rock, learn about flight tracking systems and control a live camera used on the airport's runways. **Time:** Allow 30 minutes minimum. **Hours:** Mon.-Fri. 9-9, Sat.-Sun. 9-5. **Cost:** Free. Simulator rides $3-$14. **Phone:** (403) 717-7678.

CALGARY TOWER is in Tower Centre at 101 9th Ave. S.W. at Centre St. S. The tower rises 191 metres (626 ft.) above the city. An observation deck and revolving restaurant provide a panorama of the city and the nearby Rocky Mountains. The observation deck features a glass floor and glass walls, which create in visitors the sensation of floating high above the city.

A torch atop the tower burned nonstop during the 1988 Olympic Games; it is illuminated on special occasions. **Hours:** Daily 9 a.m.-10 p.m., July-Aug.; 9-9, rest of year. Hours may vary Oct.-May; phone ahead. **Cost:** $15.24; $13.33 (ages 65+); $10.48 (ages 13-17); $6.67 (ages 4-12). **Phone:** (403) 266-7171.

CALGARY ZOO, BOTANICAL GARDEN & PREHISTORIC PARK is at 1300 Zoo Rd. N.E. at Memorial Dr. and 12th St. E. In themed areas like Destination Africa and Eurasia, visitors observe nearly 1,500 animals, including purring big cats, yawning hippos and such rare and endangered species as the Siberian tiger.

Basking in an icy, state-of-the-art habitat, four penguin species—Humboldt, gentoo, rockhopper and king—pretend not to notice the crowds of chilly onlookers drawn to the zoo's most recent addition, Penguin Plunge. On the other hand, sharp-eyed lemurs, nestled in the trees of an African rain forest,

watch inquisitively as bold guests thump their chests along with the resident gorillas. Nearby, apprehensive visitors shiver over too-close-for-comfort encounters with boas, crocodiles and giant snails.

Black bears, cougars and bison are among the creatures children and parents can learn about in the Canadian Wilds. The South America exhibit shelters fruit-loving squirrel monkeys and preening flamingos. In addition, the zoo features a tropical aviary and conservatory containing a butterfly garden and more than 4,000 plants. A 2.6-hectare (6.5-acre) prehistoric park dotted by life-size dinosaur replicas transports you to western Canada's bygone Mesozoic landscape. **Time:** Allow 3 hours minimum. **Hours:** Daily 9-6. Last admission 1 hour before closing. Closed Christmas. **Cost:** $21; $19 (ages 60+); $13 (ages 3-15). **Phone:** (403) 232-9300 or (800) 588-9993. *(See ad p. 63.)*

CANADA OLYMPIC PARK is off Trans-Canada Hwy. Bowfort Rd. exit. The park, the host area for ski jumping, freestyle skiing, bobsled and luge events at the 1988 Winter Olympic Games, remains a site for year-round sports activities. In winter visitors can learn to ski and snowboard, and in warmer weather, a mountain bike park with more than 25 kilometres (15 mi.) of trails can be enjoyed. The Athletic and Ice Complex, home to Hockey Canada, offers four North American rinks.

Also on-site are the Ice House, a training facility where bobsled, skeleton-sled and luge athletes practice; the Olympic bobsled track; and the 90-metre (295-ft.) ski-jump tower. In summer, a chairlift offers breathtaking scenic views.

Time: Allow 2 hours minimum. **Hours:** Daily 9-5, July-Aug.; 10-4, rest of year. **Cost:** Prices for activities and rides vary; phone ahead. **Phone:** (403) 247-5452.

▼ *See AAA listing p. 61* ▼

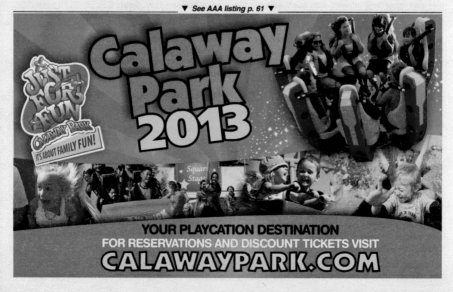

Canada's Sports Hall of Fame, 169 Canada Olympic Rd. S.W., highlights the inspiring achievements of 520 inducted athletes. Twelve hands-on areas—including the Motion, Bounce and Olympic & Paralympic galleries—house 50 interactive exhibits and a collection of more than 95,000 relics. Among the items on display are Olympic gold medalist skeleton racer Jon Montgomery's skin suit and golf clubs and trophies belonging to Sandra Post, one of the youngest players to ever win the LPGA Championship.

Also on-site are the Education and Resource Centre, which chronicles the history and impact of sports in Canada, and the 120-seat Riddell Family Theatre. **Hours:** Tues.-Sun. 10-5. **Cost:** $12; $10 (ages 65+); $8 (ages 4-18); $35 (family, two adults and two children). **Phone:** (403) 776-1040.

CHINESE CULTURAL CENTRE MUSEUM is at 197 1st St. S.W. Exhibits represent Chinese culture and history and include sculptures, ceramics and other artifacts dating back thousands of years. Permanently displayed is a replica of the army of terra-cotta soldiers found during a 1974 excavation at Mount Li in China. The clay archers, bowmen, cavalry, chariots and saddled cavalry horses were found in battle-ready formation guarding the Tomb of Qin Shihuang; each figure is unique. **Hours:** Cultural center daily 9-9. Museum daily 11-5. Closed major holidays. **Cost:** $4; $2 (ages 6-12 and 65+); free (ages 0-5 and students with ID). **Phone:** (403) 262-5071.

DEVONIAN GARDENS is on the fourth level of Toronto Dominion Square, 324 8th Ave. S.W. These 1-hectare (2.5-acre) glassed-in, indoor gardens contain 15,700 subtropical trees, plants, fish and turtles as well as waterfalls, fountains and a reflecting pool. Monthly exhibits display works by local artists. A 100-seat amphitheater occasionally hosts shows at noon. **Hours:** Daily 9-9. **Cost:** Free. **Phone:** (403) 268-3830.

FAMILY OF MAN is outside the Calgary Board of Education Building at 515 Macleod Tr. S.E. This grouping of sculpted metal figures stands 6.5 metres (21 ft.) tall. Originally commissioned as part of Great Britain's exhibit for Expo 67, the statues were created by Mario Armengol. Nude and lacking a discernible race, the figures extend their arms and hands in gestures of goodwill and friendship. **Hours:** Daily 24 hours. **Cost:** Free. **Phone:** (403) 268-2489.

[SAVE] **FORT CALGARY** is at 750 9th Ave. S.E. The 16-hectare (40-acre) riverside park contains a reconstruction of an 1875 North West Mounted Police fort and its 1888 barracks and the Deane House Historic Site, the last remaining building from the site's days as a garrison. Interactive exhibits, costumed interpreters, hands-on activities and audiovisual presentations tell the story of the site, the settlement and the people of Calgary.

Hours: Daily 9-5. Closed Jan. 1, Good Friday, Christmas Eve, Christmas and Dec. 31. **Cost:** $12;

▼ *See AAA listing p. 62* ▼

$11 (ages 65+ and college students with ID); $7 (ages 7-17); $5 (ages 3-6). Prices may vary; phone ahead. **Phone:** (403) 290-1875. ⑪

GLENBOW MUSEUM is at 130 9th Ave. S.E., across from the Calgary Tower. The complex includes a museum, an art gallery, a library and archives. Fascinating men and women who contributed to the development of the province are highlighted in Mavericks: An Incorrigible History of Alberta. Niitsitapiisinni: Our Way of Life features artifacts and interactive displays illustrating Blackfoot traditions and values.

Other galleries feature exhibits about warriors, gemstones and West Africa. An Asian sculpture gallery and a hands-on art studio also are on-site. **Time:** Allow 2 hours minimum. **Hours:** Mon.-Sat. 9-5, Sun. noon-5. Closed Christmas. **Cost:** $14; $10 (ages 65+); $9 (ages 7-17 and college students with ID); $32 (family, two adults and four children). **Phone:** (403) 268-4100. ⑪

GRAIN ACADEMY MUSEUM is at Stampede Park off 4th St. S.E. on the second level of Round Up Centre. Visitors can learn about the processes of bringing grain from the field to the table. Highlights include a miniature grain elevator and a working model train that depicts the transportation of grain from the prairie to the Pacific coast. A movie theater and displays describing the history of grain also are featured. **Time:** Allow 1 hour minimum. **Hours:** Mon.-Fri. 10-4. Closed major holidays. **Cost:** Donations. **Parking:** $13. **Phone:** (403) 263-4594.

HERITAGE PARK HISTORICAL VILLAGE is 2.5 km (1.5 mi.) w. off Queen Elizabeth II Hwy. to 1900 Heritage Dr. S.W. The re-created pre-1914 village reflects the fur trade of the 1860s, the pre-railway settlements of the 1880s and businesses and residences 1900-14. Among the park's more than 150 exhibits are a general store, an antique midway, pioneer farm machinery and a Hudson's Bay Co. trading post. Most of the buildings are originals that have been moved to the 27-hectare (66-acre) site.

An antique steam train circles the park, and a 200-passenger stern-wheeler cruises Glenmore Reservoir. The Gasoline Alley Museum features interactive displays and a collection of vintage vehicles. Representing the 1930s, '40s and '50s, Heritage Town Square depicts the prairie's urban enclaves.

Hours: Historical village daily 9:30-5, late May-Labour Day; Sat.-Sun. 9:30-5, day after Labour Day to mid-Oct. Heritage Town Square and Gasoline Alley Museum daily 9:30-4, year-round. **Cost:** May-Sept. $19.99; $15.99 (senior citizens); $14.99 (ages 3-17). Rest of year $9.99; $7.99 (senior citizens);

$4.89 (ages 3-17). Unlimited rides pass $10. Individual ride $3. Prices may vary; phone ahead. **Phone:** (403) 268-8500. *(See ad p. 65.)*

INGLEWOOD BIRD SANCTUARY is at 2425 9th Ave. S.E. on the Bow River. Self-guiding trails wind throughout the forest, where some 280 species of birds and various mammals have been sighted. Natural history programs and guided nature walks also are offered. **Time:** Allow 1 hour minimum. **Hours:** Trails daily dawn-dusk. Visitor center daily 10-4. Closed Jan. 1, Easter, Nov. 11, Christmas Eve, Christmas and day after Christmas. **Cost:** Donations. **Phone:** (403) 268-2489.

LOUGHEED HOUSE is at 707 13th Ave. S.W. Built in 1891 and enlarged in 1907, the sandstone mansion was the residence of Sir James Alexander Lougheed, a cabinet minister and party leader in the Senate, and his family. It later served as a barracks for the Canadian Women's Army Corps and as a blood donor clinic and dormitory for the Canadian Red Cross Society; today it houses interpretive exhibits detailing the structure's history and architecture.

The lovely 1.1-hectare (2.8-acre) estate includes the formal Beaulieu Gardens. Redesigned every year, the green space dazzles onlookers with such flora as yellow cannas and marigolds, red dahlias, and white and pink peonies. **Tours:** Guided tours are available. **Time:** Allow 30 minutes minimum. **Hours:** House Wed.-Fri. 11-4, Sat.-Sun. 10-4. Gardens daily 7 a.m.-dusk. Closed major holidays. **Cost:** House $8.50; $6.50 (students with ID and senior citizens); $5 (ages 6-12); $25 (family). Gardens free. **Phone:** (403) 244-6333. ⑪

THE MILITARY MUSEUMS, 4520 Crowchild Tr. S.W., off Flanders Ave. exit, is home to seven museums detailing the history of the Canadian Forces. On-site are the Naval Museum of Alberta, the Army Museum of Alberta and the Air Force Museum of Alberta as well as museums highlighting Lord Strathcona's Horse Regiment—the Royal Canadians, Princess Patricia's Canadian Light Infantry, The King's Own Calgary Regiment and The Calgary Highlanders.

Galleries re-create battle scenes and specific acts of heroism with audio and artifacts. Featured are an impressive collection of weapons, including guns, cannons and torpedoes; a Banshee Naval jet fighter; a submarine exhibit; and other equipment relating to life in the military. In addition, short videos are shown in two unique theaters: one a to-scale interior model of a C-130 Hercules transport aircraft and the other a period Nissen hut.

Visitors also can view a huge mural in the Queen Elizabeth II Atrium entry hall; videos explain what each mosaic piece represents. Outside, vintage tanks and carriers dot the landscaped grounds.

Time: Allow 3 hours minimum. **Hours:** Mon.-Fri. 9-5, Sat.-Sun. and holidays 9:30-4. Closed Jan. 1 and Christmas. **Cost:** $10; $5 (senior citizens); $4 (ages 7-17); free (ages 0-6 and veterans and active military with ID); $20 (family). **Phone:** (403) 974-2850.

THE NICKLE GALLERIES is on the University of Calgary campus in the Taylor Family Digital Library at 410 University Ct. N.W. Three galleries present changing exhibits of contemporary art, textiles and numismatic collections. Lectures, gallery talks and other events are offered throughout the year. **Time:** Allow 1 hour minimum. **Hours:** Mon.-Sat. 10-5 (also Thurs. 5-8), Sept.-May; Mon.-Fri. 10-5, rest of year. Closed major holidays. Phone ahead to confirm schedule. **Cost:** Free. **Phone:** (403) 220-7234.

TELUS SPARK is at 220 St. George's Dr. N.E. Science is at the core of this educational feast for the senses with more than 100 interactive displays. In Energy & Innovation, you can inspect a wind turbine and see how much energy your household electronics use. Create snowflakes or view distant galaxies in the Earth & Sky gallery. Check your mood on a special camera or monitor your reaction time in the Being Human exhibit area. In the Open Studio, you can build an invention using toothpicks, take apart a machine or digitally animate a story.

High-definition films and live planetarium shows are the highlight of the HD Digital Dome Theatre.

▼ See AAA listing p. 64 ▼

The Creative Kids Museum offers hands-on activities geared toward children under age 9. Educational programs and performances connecting science and the arts take place in the 164-seat Presentation Theatre.

Time: Allow 3 hours minimum. **Hours:** Sun.-Wed. and Fri. 9-6, Sat. 9-5, Thurs. 9-9 (except second Thurs. of the month during Adults Only Night). Closed Christmas. **Cost:** $19.95; $17.95 (ages 65+); $15.95 (ages 13-17); $12.95 (ages 3-12). **Parking:** $5. **Phone:** (403) 817-6800. 🍴

GAMBLING ESTABLISHMENTS

- **Cash Casino** is at 4040 Blackfoot Tr. S.E. **Hours:** Daily 9:30 a.m.-3 a.m. Closed Christmas. **Phone:** (403) 287-1635.
- **Casino Calgary** is at 1420 Meridian Rd. N.E. **Hours:** Casino open daily 9:30 a.m.-3 a.m. Poker daily 24 hours. Closed Christmas. **Phone:** (403) 248-9467.
- **Century Casino** is at 1010 42nd Ave. S.E. **Hours:** Casino open daily 9:30 a.m.-3 a.m. Slot machines daily 10 a.m.-3 a.m. Table games daily noon-3 a.m. Closed Christmas. **Phone:** (403) 287-1183.
- **Cowboys Casino** is at 421 12th Ave. S.E. in the Big Four Building in Stampede Park. **Hours:** Casino open daily 9:30 a.m.-3 a.m. A 24-hour poker room is available. Closed Christmas. **Phone:** (403) 514-0100.
- **Elbow River Casino** is at 218 18th Ave. S.E. **Hours:** Slot machines 10 a.m.-3 a.m. Table games daily noon-2 a.m. Poker daily 24 hours. Closed Christmas. **Phone:** (403) 289-8880.

Sightseeing
Bus, Train and Van Tours

Brewster Transportation and Tours offers a 4-hour bus tour of Calgary's attractions as well as trips to Banff, Lake Louise, Jasper and the Columbia Icefield; phone (403) 221-8242 for schedules and fares.

Rocky Mountaineer Vacations offers scenic vacation packages, including the Rocky Mountaineer, a 2-day, all-daylight, narrated rail tour between Canada's west and the Canadian Rockies. The Rocky Mountaineer tour departs mid-April to mid-October, with winter rail trips available in December; phone (604) 606-7245 or (877) 460-3200.

Walking Tours

Free pamphlets detailing a self-guiding tour of Stephen Avenue, a heavily trafficked commercial thoroughfare, are available from the Calgary Downtown Association, 304 8th Ave. S.W., (403) 215-1570. A showcase for historical buildings, murals and sculptures, the mall extends along 8th Avenue S.W. between 1st Street S.E. and 4th Street S.W. and is open to pedestrians only from 6 a.m. to 6 p.m.

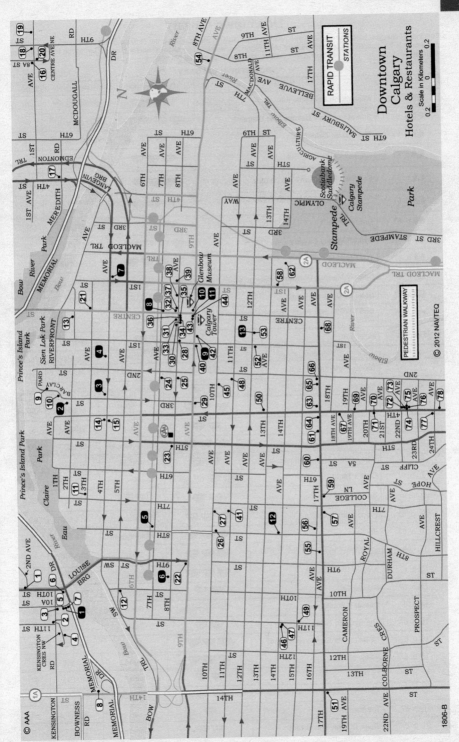

Downtown
Calgary
Hotels & Restaurants

RAPID TRANSIT
STATIONS

PEDESTRIAN WALKWAY

Scale in Kilometers

© 2012 NAVTEQ

1806-B

Downtown Calgary

This index helps you "spot" where approved hotels and restaurants are located on the corresponding detailed maps. Hotel daily rate range is for comparison only. Restaurant price range is a combination of lunch and/or dinner. Turn to the listing page for more detailed rate and price information and consult display ads for special promotions.

DOWNTOWN CALGARY

Map Page	Hotels	Diamond Rated	Rate Range	Page
1 p. 67	**Kensington Riverside Inn**	◇◇◇	$229-$549 SAVE	78
2 p. 67	**Sheraton Suites Calgary Eau Claire**	◇◇◇	$149-$549 SAVE	78
3 p. 67	**The Westin Calgary**	◇◇◇	$139-$519 SAVE	78
4 p. 67	International Hotel of Calgary	◇◇◇	Rates not provided	78
5 p. 67	Sandman Hotel Downtown Calgary	◇◇◇	Rates not provided	78
6 p. 67	Holiday Inn Express Hotel & Suites Calgary Downtown	◇◇◇	Rates not provided	78
7 p. 67	Delta Bow Valley	◇◇◇	$109-$409	76
8 p. 67	**Hyatt Regency Calgary**	◇◇◇◇	$129-$549 SAVE	78
9 p. 67	The Fairmont Palliser	◇◇◇◇	$179-$709	78
10 p. 67	**Calgary Marriott Downtown** (See ad p. 77.)	◇◇◇◇	$139-$599 SAVE	76
11 p. 67	**Hotel Le Germain Calgary**	◇◇◇◇	$199-$539 SAVE	78
12 p. 67	**BEST WESTERN PLUS Suites Downtown** (See ad p. 77.)	◇◇◇	$170-$300 SAVE	76
13 p. 67	Hotel Arts	◇◇◇	$139-$299	78

Map Page	Restaurants	Diamond Rated	Cuisine	Price Range	Page
1 p. 67	Broken Plate Kitchen & Bar	◇◇	Greek	$12-$35	79
2 p. 67	Maurya	◇◇	Eastern Indian	$14-$16	82
3 p. 67	Winebar Kensington	◇◇◇	Provincial American	$12-$18	85
4 p. 67	Pulcinella	◇◇	Pizza	$13-$30	83
5 p. 67	Muse Restaurant & Lounge	◇◇◇	New American	$28-$37	83
6 p. 67	Julio's Barrio Mexican Restaurant	◇◇	Mexican	$10-$22	81
7 p. 67	**Chef's Table**	◇◇◇◇	New American	$26-$40	80
8 p. 67	Sultan's Tent	◇◇	Traditional Moroccan	$18-$27	84
9 p. 67	Prego Cucina Italiana	◇◇◇	Italian	$16-$34	83
10 p. 67	Barclay's	◇◇◇	International	$12-$35	79
11 p. 67	Buchanan's Chop House & Whisky Bar	◇◇◇	Steak	$15-$40	79
12 p. 67	Anju	◇◇◇	Korean	$15-$24	79
13 p. 67	Sakana Grill	◇◇	Japanese	$13-$20	84
14 p. 67	**Caesar's Steakhouse**	◇◇◇	Steak	$15-$52	80
15 p. 67	The Glory Of India	◇◇	Indian	$17-$32	81
16 p. 67	La Dolce Vita Ristorante Italiano	◇◇◇	Italian	$9-$40	82
17 p. 67	Il Sogno	◇◇	Italian	$13-$32	81
18 p. 67	La Brezza	◇◇	Italian	$10-$45	82
19 p. 67	Sushi Bar Zipang	◇◇	Japanese	$15-$25	84
20 p. 67	The Main Dish	◇	Deli	$8-$20	82
21 p. 67	**Silver Dragon Restaurant**	◇◇	Chinese	$9-$19	84

Map Page	Restaurants (cont'd)	Diamond Rated	Cuisine	Price Range	Page
22 p. 67	Atlas Specialty Supermarket & Persian Cuisine	◆◆	Persian	$8-$29	79
23 p. 67	Chicago Chophouse	◆◆◆	Steak	$17-$49	80
24 p. 67	Metropolitan Grill	◆◆◆	American	$15-$38	82
25 p. 67	The Orchid Room Fusion Cuisine	◆◆	Vietnamese	$17-$24	83
26 p. 67	Bonterra Trattoria	◆◆	New Italian	$15-$36	79
27 p. 67	The Holy Grill	◆	American	$8-$13	81
28 p. 67	Murrieta's Westcoast Grill	◆◆◆	Western Pacific Rim	$12-$39	83
29 p. 67	Oriental Phoenix	◆◆	Vietnamese	$10-$19	83
30 p. 67	TRIB Steakhouse	◆◆	Steak	$12-$40	85
31 p. 67	Blink Restaurant & Bar	◆◆◆	New World	$15-$38	79
32 p. 67	**Catch Restaurant**	◆◆◆◆	Seafood	$16-$45	80
33 p. 67	Divino Wine & Cheese Bistro	◆◆	New Canadian	$17-$37	81
34 p. 67	The Belvedere	◆◆◆	New Canadian	$13-$52	79
35 p. 67	Catch Oyster Bar	◆◆	Seafood	$18-$28	80
36 p. 67	Saltlik, A Rare Steakhouse	◆◆	Steak	$12-$40	84
37 p. 67	Thomson's Restaurant	◆◆◆	American	$14-$28	85
38 p. 67	**Centini Restaurant and Lounge**	◆◆◆	Italian	$18-$54	80
39 p. 67	Teatro	◆◆◆	New Italian	$15-$52	85
40 p. 67	Rush	◆◆◆	New American	$14-$36	84
41 p. 67	The King & I	◆◆◆	Thai	$12-$32	82
42 p. 67	The Rimrock Dining Room	◆◆◆	New Canadian	$12-$55	84
43 p. 67	Sky 360	◆◆◆	American	$16-$45	84
44 p. 67	CHARCUT Roast House	◆◆◆	Canadian	$14-$29	80
45 p. 67	Thai Sa-On Restaurant	◆◆	Thai	$15-$20	85
46 p. 67	Galaxie Diner	◆	American	$8-$15	81
47 p. 67	Myhre's Deli	◆	Sandwiches	$10-$12	83
48 p. 67	Vintage Chophouse & Tavern	◆◆◆	Steak	$12-$39	85
49 p. 67	Good Earth Coffeehouse & Bakery	◆	Breads/Pastries	$5-$8	81
50 p. 67	Boxwood Cafe	◆◆◆	Canadian	$10-$17	79
51 p. 67	Moti Mahal	◆◆	Northern Indian	$11-$17	83
52 p. 67	Kickers Smoked Meat & Deli	◆	Specialty	$10-$12	81
53 p. 67	Taste	◆◆◆	Small Plates	$12-$30	84
54 p. 67	Deane House Historic Site Restaurant at Fort Calgary	◆◆	American	$13-$19	80
55 p. 67	The Coup + Meet	◆◆	Vegetarian	$11-$18	80
56 p. 67	Steeps The Urban Teahouse	◆	Coffee/Tea	$5-$6	84
57 p. 67	Manies Greek Cuisine	◆◆	Greek	$13-$25	82
58 p. 67	Manuel Latruwe Belgian Patisserie & Bread Shop	◆◆	Breads/Pastries	$7-$13	82
59 p. 67	Brava Bistro	◆◆◆	Canadian	$14-$32	79
60 p. 67	Una Pizza + Wine	◆◆◆	Mediterranean	$10-$21	85

Map Page	Restaurants (cont'd)	Diamond Rated	Cuisine	Price Range	Page
61 p. 67	Ox and Angela	◆◆◆	Spanish	$9-$28	83
62 p. 67	loungeburger	◆◆	Burgers	$13-$23	82
63 p. 67	Petite Bistro & Wine Bar	◆◆◆	New French	$18-$30	83
64 p. 67	The Living Room	◆◆◆	Canadian	$14-$42	82
65 p. 67	Cilantro	◆◆◆	California	$14-$44	80
66 p. 67	Model Milk	◆◆◆	New World	$18-$29	82
67 p. 67	Hana Sushi	◆◆	Japanese	$7-$20	81
68 p. 67	**La Chaumiere Restaurant**	◆◆◆◆	French	$13-$37	82
69 p. 67	Peking Dragon	◆◆	Chinese	$10-$20	83
70 p. 67	Fat City Franks	◆	Hot Dogs	$6-$8	81
71 p. 67	Fleur de Sel	◆◆	New French	$15-$39	81
72 p. 67	Sushi Kawa	◆◆	Japanese	$10-$20	84
73 p. 67	Aida's	◆◆	Lebanese	$5-$21	79
74 p. 67	Purple Perk	◆	Coffee/Tea	$9-$13	83
75 p. 67	**Bistro 2210**	◆◆◆	French	$12-$31	79
76 p. 67	Mercato	◆◆◆	Italian	$15-$43	82
77 p. 67	The Joyce on 4th Irish Pub	◆◆	Irish	$13-$17	81
78 p. 67	Rajdoot	◆◆	Indian	$11-$17	83
79 p. 67	Candela Lounge	◆◆◆	Latin American	$18-$30	91

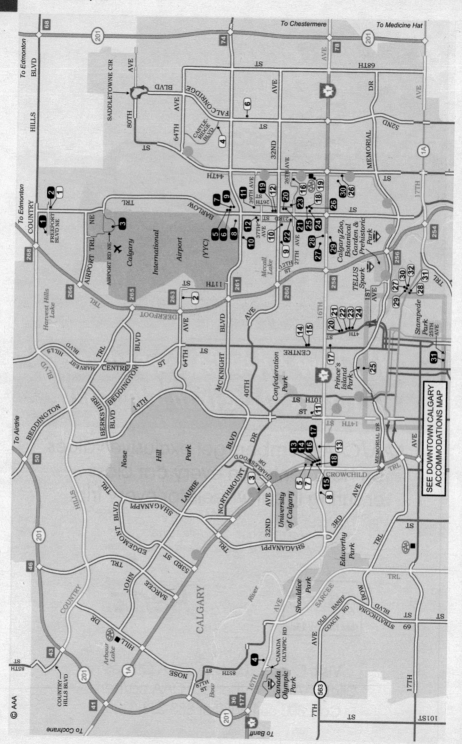

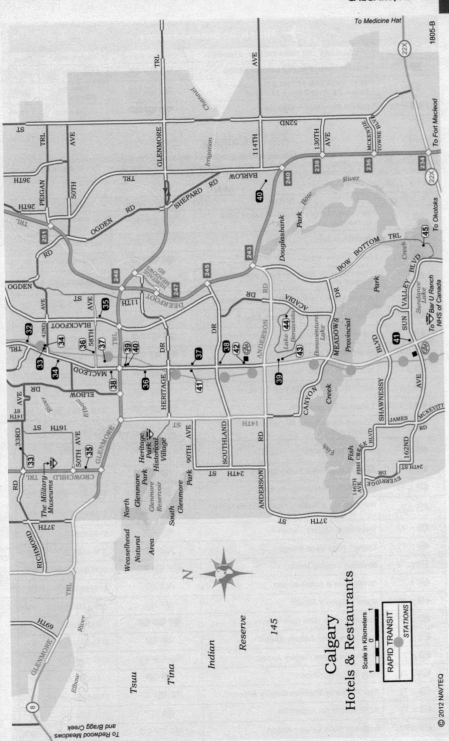

Calgary
Hotels & Restaurants

© 2012 NAVTEQ

✈ Airport Accommodations

Map Page	CALGARY INTERNATIONAL AIRPORT	Diamond Rated	Rate Range	Page
2 p. 72	Acclaim Hotel, 2 mi (3.3 km) n of airport	◈◈◈	$185-$195 SAVE	85
1 p. 72	BEST WESTERN PREMIER Freeport Inn & Suites, 2.2 mi (3.7 km) n of airport	◈◈◈	Rates not provided SAVE	86
3 p. 72	Delta Calgary Airport, at airport	◈◈◈	$149-$409	87

Calgary

This index helps you "spot" where approved hotels and restaurants are located on the corresponding detailed maps. Hotel daily rate range is for comparison only. Restaurant price range is a combination of lunch and/or dinner. Turn to the listing page for more detailed rate and price information and consult display ads for special promotions.

CALGARY

Map Page	Hotels	Diamond Rated	Rate Range	Page
1 p. 72	BEST WESTERN PREMIER Freeport Inn & Suites (See ad p. 86.)	◈◈◈	Rates not provided SAVE	86
2 p. 72	Acclaim Hotel	◈◈◈	$185-$195 SAVE	85
3 p. 72	Delta Calgary Airport	◈◈◈	$149-$409	87
4 p. 72	Four Points by Sheraton Hotel and Suites, Calgary West	◈◈◈	$159-$429 SAVE	88
5 p. 72	Residence Inn by Marriott Calgary Airport	◈◈◈	$139-$419 SAVE	90
6 p. 72	Courtyard by Marriott Calgary Airport	◈◈◈	$129-$409 SAVE	87
7 p. 72	Sandman Hotel Suites & Spa Calgary Airport	◈◈◈	$129-$219	90
8 p. 72	Hilton Garden Inn-Calgary Airport	◈◈◈	$129-$209	88
9 p. 72	Holiday Inn Express Airport Calgary	◈◈◈	$115-$155	88
10 p. 72	BEST WESTERN PLUS Port O'Call Hotel	◈◈◈	$129-$199 SAVE	86
11 p. 72	Lakeview Signature Inn	◈◈◈	$140-$310 SAVE	88
12 p. 72	Country Inn & Suites By Carlson, Calgary-Airport	◈◈◈	$139-$249 SAVE	87
13 p. 72	Quality Inn University	[fyi]	Rates not provided	89
14 p. 72	Econo Lodge Inn & Suites University	◈◈	$89-$199 SAVE	87
15 p. 72	BEST WESTERN Village Park Inn	◈◈	$119-$199 SAVE	86
16 p. 72	Hampton Inn & Suites Calgary University NW (See ad p. 89.)	◈◈◈	$129-$319 SAVE	88
17 p. 72	Travelodge Calgary University	◈◈	$109-$199 SAVE	90
18 p. 72	Econo Lodge Motel Village	◈◈	$70-$109 SAVE	87
19 p. 72	Sheraton Cavalier Hotel	◈◈◈	$139-$469 SAVE	90
20 p. 72	Comfort Inn & Suites-Airport	◈◈	$100-$200 SAVE	87
21 p. 72	Super 8 Calgary Airport	◈◈	$99-$219 SAVE	90
22 p. 72	Executive Royal Hotel North Calgary	◈◈◈	$104-$220	87
23 p. 72	Travelodge Hotel Calgary Airport	◈◈	$113-$300 SAVE	90
24 p. 72	Staybridge Suites Calgary Airport	◈◈◈	$169-$269 SAVE	90
25 p. 72	Days Inn Calgary Airport	◈◈	$140-$220	87
26 p. 72	Four Points by Sheraton Calgary Airport	◈◈◈	$119-$299 SAVE	88
27 p. 72	BEST WESTERN Airport Inn	◈◈	$126-$220 SAVE	85
28 p. 72	Radisson Hotel Calgary Airport	◈◈◈	$129-$299 SAVE	89

CALGARY (cont'd)

Map Page	Hotels (cont'd)	Diamond Rated	Rate Range	Page
29 p. 72	Holiday Inn Calgary-Airport	▽▽▽	$120-$160	88
30 p. 72	Coast Plaza Hotel & Conference Centre	▽▽▽	$99-$399	87
31 p. 72	Calgary Westways Guest House	▽▽▽	$109-$180	86
32 p. 72	**BEST WESTERN PLUS Calgary Centre Inn**	▽▽▽	$139-$279 SAVE	85
33 p. 72	**Holiday Inn Calgary-Macleod Trail South**	▽▽▽	$119-$269 SAVE	88
34 p. 72	**Comfort Inn & Suites-South**	▽▽▽	$110-$190 SAVE	87
35 p. 72	Hotel Blackfoot	▽▽▽	$119-$289	88
36 p. 72	**Econo Lodge South**	▽▽	$90-$130 SAVE	87
37 p. 72	**Carriage House Inn**	▽▽▽	$135-$249 SAVE	86
38 p. 72	Delta Calgary South	▽▽▽	$109-$429	87
39 p. 72	Holiday Inn Express Hotel & Suites Calgary-South	▽▽▽	$139-$259	88
40 p. 72	**Service Plus Inn & Suites Calgary**	▽▽▽	$129-$149 SAVE	90
41 p. 72	Wingate by Wyndham Calgary	▽▽▽	$129-$309	90

Map Page	Restaurants	Diamond Rated	Cuisine	Price Range	Page
1 p. 72	Pacini Pasta & Grill Ristorante	▽▽▽	Italian	$10-$29	93
2 p. 72	Buffet Yangtze	▽	Chinese	$11-$19	91
3 p. 72	Jamesons Pub	▽▽	American	$10-$19	92
4 p. 72	Captain Scott's Fish & Chips	▽	Seafood	$7-$15	91
5 p. 72	Nick's Steakhouse & Pizza	▽▽	Steak	$12-$46	93
6 p. 72	Alberta King of Subs	▽	Canadian	$5-$14	90
7 p. 72	Big T's BBQ	▽▽	Barbecue	$8-$29	91
8 p. 72	Gus's Cafe & Pizzeria	▽▽	Pizza	$8-$16	92
9 p. 72	Misai Japanese Restaurant	▽▽	Japanese	$10-$16	93
10 p. 72	Thai Boat	▽▽	Thai	$8-$13	94
11 p. 72	Jimmy's A & A Deli	▽	Mediterranean	$7-$12	92
12 p. 72	Carver's Steakhouse	▽▽▽	Steak	$28-$47	92
13 p. 72	Juree's Thai Place Restaurant	▽▽	Thai	$10-$18	93
14 p. 72	Boccavino Lounge & Grill	▽▽	Italian	$10-$23	91
15 p. 72	Lina's Italian Market	▽	Deli	$5-$10	93
16 p. 72	Samosa Grill	▽▽	Eastern Indian	$11-$17	94
17 p. 72	Santorini Greek Taverna	▽▽	Greek	$13-$30	94
18 p. 72	Ric's Lounge & Grill	▽▽	American	$11-$35	94
19 p. 72	Jamesons Irish Pub	▽▽	Irish	$8-$15	92
20 p. 72	Open Range Steaks & Chops	▽▽▽	New American	$14-$36	93
21 p. 72	Big Fish	▽▽▽	Seafood	$14-$30	91
22 p. 72	Boogie's Burgers	▽	Burgers	$5-$16	91
23 p. 72	Oeb Breakfast Co.	▽▽	Breakfast	$13-$19	93
24 p. 72	Diner Deluxe	▽▽	American	$10-$20	92

Map Page	Restaurants (cont'd)	Diamond Rated	Cuisine	Price Range	Page
25 p. 72	River Cafe	◆◆◆	Regional Canadian	$16-$49	94
26 p. 72	Forbidden City Seafood & Dim Sum Restaurant	◆◆	Chinese	$4-$20	92
27 p. 72	Rouge	◆◆◆	French	$16-$40	94
28 p. 72	Kane's Harley Diner	◆◆	Comfort Food	$7-$22	93
29 p. 72	Without Papers Pizza	◆◆	Pizza	$14-$22	95
30 p. 72	Sugo Caffe Italia	◆◆◆	Italian	$15-$39	94
31 p. 72	Jacqueline Suzanne's Bistro & Antiquities	◆◆	International	$13-$40	92
32 p. 72	Spolumbo's Deli	◆	Deli	$6-$10	94
33 p. 72	Belmont Diner	◆	Canadian	$9-$15	91
34 p. 72	Alloy	◆◆◆	New International	$14-$35	91
35 p. 72	**Pfanntastic Pannenkoek Haus**	◆◆	Dutch	$7-$15	94
36 p. 72	Oriental Phoenix	◆◆◆	Vietnamese	$10-$18	93
37 p. 72	Bagolac Saigon Restaurant	◆◆	Vietnamese	$9-$22	91
38 p. 72	Globefish Sushi & Izakaya	◆◆	Sushi	$15-$25	92
39 p. 72	Open Sesame	◆◆	Asian	$9-$23	93
40 p. 72	Smuggler's Inn	◆◆	Steak	$9-$36	94
41 p. 72	**Redwater Rustic Grille**	◆◆	American	$11-$38	94
42 p. 72	Broken Plate Kitchen & Bar	◆◆	Greek	$10-$32	91
43 p. 72	Fire Kirin	◆◆	Asian	$9-$22	92
44 p. 72	Newport Grill on Lake Bonavista	◆◆◆	Continental	$12-$38	93
45 p. 72	The Ranche Restaurant	◆◆◆	Regional Canadian	$15-$39	94

DOWNTOWN CALGARY
• Restaurants p. 79
• Hotels & Restaurants map & index p. 67

BEST WESTERN PLUS SUITES DOWNTOWN
(403)228-6900 **12**

 Hotel $170-$300

AAA Benefit: Members save up to 20%, plus 10% bonus points with Best Western Rewards®.

Address: 1330 8th St SW T2R 1B6 **Location:** Corner of 8th St and 13th Ave SW. **Facility:** 124 units, some two bedrooms, efficiencies and kitchens. 16 stories, interior corridors. **Parking:** winter plug-ins. **Terms:** 30 day cancellation notice-fee imposed. **Amenities:** high-speed Internet. **Activities:** sauna, exercise room. **Guest Services:** valet and coin laundry. **Free Special Amenities:** full breakfast and high-speed Internet. *(See ad p. 77.)*

CALGARY MARRIOTT DOWNTOWN
(403)266-7331 **10**

Hotel $139-$599

Marriott HOTELS & RESORTS **AAA Benefit:** AAA hotel discounts of 5% or more.

Address: 110 9th Ave SE T2G 5A6 **Location:** Jct 9th Ave and Centre St; adjacent to TELUS Convention Centre. Across from Calgary Tower. **Facility:** The downtown property features spacious and upscale rooms, attentive service and great views of the city. 384 units. 22 stories, interior corridors. **Parking:** valet only. **Pool(s):** heated indoor. **Activities:** whirlpool, exercise room. **Guest Services:** valet laundry. *(See ad p. 77.)*

DELTA BOW VALLEY
(403)266-1980 **7**
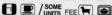Hotel $109-$409 **Address:** 209 4th Ave SE T2G 0C6 **Location:** 1st St SE and 4th Ave SE. **Facility:** 394 units. 25 stories, interior corridors. **Parking:** on-site (fee) and valet. **Terms:** 3 day cancellation notice-fee imposed. **Amenities:** Fee: video games, high-speed Internet. **Pool(s):** heated indoor. **Activities:** saunas, whirlpool, exercise room. **Guest Services:** valet laundry.

Be a better driver.
Keep your mind on the road.

▼ *See AAA listing p. 76* ▼

For business or leisure, we're thoughtfully designed for every type of trip.

Scan this tag on your smartphone for more information

Get the free mobile app at
http://gettag.mobi

BEST WESTERN PLUS Suites Downtown
1330 8th Street SW • Calgary, AB T2R 1B6
403-228-6900   1-800-981-2555
bestwestern.com/aaa

· AAA/CAA Preferred hotel
· Minimum 10% discount off published rates
· FREE Best Western Rewards® program
· Complimentary full, hot breakfast
· Fitness centre, sauna and business centre
· Dataports and HSIA available in all rooms
· Refrigerators in all rooms

Show Your Card & Save
Preferred Hotel

▼ *See AAA listing p. 76* ▼

CALGARY MARRIOTT DOWNTOWN. FRONT ROW SEATS TO THE CANADIAN ROCKIES.

Four Diamond Award

$139 - $499*
single/double

For information or to make reservations, call **1.800.896.6878** or visit
www.marriott.com/yycdt.

CALGARY MARRIOTT DOWNTOWN
110 9th Ave SE
Calgary, AB T2G 5A6
Phone 403. 266.7331
www.marriott.com/yycdt

Scan to make a reservation today!

Get the free mobile app at
http://gettag.mobi

* Based on Availability

Keep seasonal vehicles travel-ready

with a AAA/CAA Battery Tender®

(See map & index p. 67.)

THE FAIRMONT PALLISER (403)262-1234 **9**

▼▼▼▼ ▼▼▼▼ **Historic Hotel** $179-$709 **Address:** 133 9th Ave SW T2P 2M3 **Location:** 9th Ave SW and 1st St SW. **Facility:** A sense of history and nostalgia reigns at this grand hotel, which features an imperial theme throughout the spacious and comfortable public areas. Most guest rooms have been renovated. 407 units. 12 stories, interior corridors. **Parking:** on-site (fee) and valet, winter plug-ins. **Terms:** check-in 4 pm, cancellation fee imposed. **Amenities:** *Fee:* video games, high-speed Internet. *Some:* safes. **Dining:** The Rimrock Dining Room, see separate listing. **Pool(s):** heated indoor. **Activities:** whirlpool, steamroom, spa. **Guest Services:** valet laundry.

[ECO] [icons] CALL [icons] BIZ [icons] / SOME UNITS FEE [icon]

HOLIDAY INN EXPRESS HOTEL & SUITES CALGARY DOWNTOWN 403/269-8262 **6**

▼▼▼ **Hotel.** Rates not provided. **Address:** 1020 8th Ave SW T2P 1J2 **Location:** At 10th St SW. **Facility:** 56 units. 9 stories, interior corridors. **Parking:** winter plug-ins. **Amenities:** high-speed Internet. **Activities:** exercise room. **Guest Services:** valet and coin laundry.

[icons] BIZ [icons] / SOME UNITS FEE [icon]

HOTEL ARTS (403)266-4611 **13**

▼▼▼ **Hotel** $139-$299 **Address:** 119 12th Ave SW T2R 0G8 **Location:** At 1st St SW; center. **Facility:** 185 units. 11 stories, interior corridors. **Parking:** on-site (fee). **Terms:** cancellation fee imposed. **Amenities:** high-speed Internet (fee). **Pool(s):** heated outdoor. **Activities:** exercise room. **Guest Services:** valet laundry.

[icons] CALL [icons] BIZ [icons] / SOME UNITS FEE [icons]

HOTEL LE GERMAIN CALGARY (403)264-8990 **11**

▼▼▼ ▼▼▼ Boutique Contemporary Hotel $199-$539

Address: 899 Centre St SW T2G 1B8 **Location:** Corner of 1st St SW and 9th Ave SW; center. **Facility:** This sleek, downtown property offers ultra modern guest rooms with luxurious bedding, huge desk space, an oversize LCD television and a separate sitting area. 143 units. 12 stories, interior corridors. **Parking:** on-site (fee) and valet. **Terms:** cancellation fee imposed. **Amenities:** high-speed Internet, safes. **Dining:** CHARCUT Roast House, see separate listing. **Activities:** saunas, exercise room. **Guest Services:** valet laundry, area transportation-downtown. **Free Special Amenities:** continental breakfast and high-speed Internet.

[SAVE] [icons] BIZ [icons] / SOME UNITS FEE [icon]

HYATT REGENCY CALGARY (403)717-1234 **8**

▼▼▼ ▼▼▼ Hotel $129-$549

HYATT® **AAA Benefit:** Members save 10% or more everyday.

Address: 700 Centre St SE T2G 5P6 **Location:** Corner of Centre St and 7th Ave SW. Adjacent to TELUS Convention Centre. **Facility:** Featuring a Canadian theme throughout, this downtown hotel with a luxurious ambiance offers attentive service and upscale rooms. 355 units. 22 stories, interior corridors. **Parking:** on-site (fee) and valet. **Terms:** cancellation fee imposed. **Amenities:** high-speed Internet (fee), safes. **Dining:** Catch Oyster Bar, Catch Restaurant, Thomson's Restaurant, see separate listings. **Pool(s):** heated indoor. **Activities:** whirlpool, steamroom, exercise room, spa. **Guest Services:** valet laundry.

[SAVE] [icons] BIZ [icons] / SOME UNITS FEE [icon]

INTERNATIONAL HOTEL OF CALGARY 403/265-9600 **4**

▼▼▼ ▼▼▼ **Hotel.** Rates not provided. **Address:** 220 4th Ave SW T2P 0H5 **Location:** Corner of 4th Ave and 2nd St SW. **Facility:** 248 units, some two bedrooms. 35 stories, interior corridors. **Parking:** on-site (fee) and valet. **Amenities:** high-speed Internet, safes. **Pool(s):** heated indoor. **Activities:** whirlpool, exercise room. *Fee:* massage. **Guest Services:** complimentary and valet laundry, area transportation-downtown.

[icons] CALL [icons] BIZ [icons] [icons]

KENSINGTON RIVERSIDE INN (403)228-4442 **1**

▼▼▼ ▼▼▼ Boutique Hotel $229-$549

Address: 1126 Memorial Dr NW T2N 3E3 **Location:** Just w of 10th St NW. Located in Kensington area. **Facility:** Upscale and exquisite, the inn features original artwork, gourmet breakfasts and a convenient location near several shops. 19 units. 2 stories, interior corridors. **Parking:** on-site (fee). **Terms:** cancellation fee imposed. **Amenities:** high-speed Internet. **Dining:** Chef's Table, see separate listing. **Activities:** jogging. **Guest Services:** valet laundry. **Free Special Amenities:** full breakfast and high-speed Internet. [SAVE] [icons]

SANDMAN HOTEL DOWNTOWN CALGARY 403/237-8626 **5**

▼▼▼ ▼▼▼ **Hotel.** Rates not provided. **Address:** 888 7th Ave SW T2P 3J3 **Location:** Corner of 7th Ave SW and 8th St SW. **Facility:** 300 units. 23 stories, interior corridors. **Parking:** on-site (fee) and valet. **Terms:** check-in 4 pm. **Amenities:** video games (fee), high-speed Internet. **Dining:** Moxie's Classic Grill, see separate listing. **Pool(s):** heated indoor. **Activities:** whirlpool, exercise room. **Guest Services:** valet and coin laundry.

[ECO] [icons] BIZ [icons] / SOME UNITS FEE [icons]

SHERATON SUITES CALGARY EAU CLAIRE (403)266-7200 **2**

▼▼▼ ▼▼▼ Hotel $149-$549

Ⓢ Sheraton HOTELS & RESORTS **AAA Benefit:** Members get up to 20% off, plus Starwood Preferred Guest® bonuses.

Address: 255 Barclay Parade SW T2P 5C2 **Location:** At 3rd St SW and 2nd Ave SW. **Facility:** Set along the river's edge and with a prime location next to the Eau Claire market, this all-suite hotel offers upscale rooms and attentive service. 323 units, some two bedrooms. 15 stories, interior corridors. **Parking:** valet only. **Terms:** cancellation fee imposed. **Amenities:** high-speed Internet (fee). *Some:* safes. **Dining:** Barclay's, see separate listing. **Pool(s):** heated indoor. **Activities:** whirlpool, waterslide, jogging, exercise room. *Fee:* massage. **Guest Services:** valet and coin laundry.

[SAVE] [ECO] [icons] BIZ [icons] / SOME UNITS [icons]

THE WESTIN CALGARY (403)266-1611 **3**

▼▼▼ ▼▼▼ Hotel $139-$519

WESTIN® HOTELS & RESORTS **AAA Benefit:** Enjoy up to 20% off your next stay, plus Starwood Preferred Guest® bonuses.

Address: 320 4th Ave SW T2P 2S6 **Location:** Corner of 4th Ave SW and 3rd St. **Facility:** The upscale hotel's lobby is inviting with a contemporary refinement. Guest rooms offer a spacious desk area. 525 units. 20 stories, interior corridors. **Parking:** on-site (fee) and valet. **Terms:** cancellation fee imposed. **Amenities:** high-speed Internet (fee), safes. **Dining:** 2 restaurants. **Pool(s):** heated indoor. **Activities:** saunas, exercise room. *Fee:* massage. **Guest Services:** valet laundry.

[SAVE] [ECO] [icons] CALL [icons] BIZ [icons] / SOME UNITS [icons]

(See map & index p. 67.)

WHERE TO EAT

AIDA'S
403/541-1189 **73**

◆◆ Lebanese. Casual Dining. $5–$21 **AAA Inspector Notes:** Hearty portions of tasty, traditional Lebanese food await patrons of the cozy, bistro-style restaurant. A taste of Lebanon infuses such dishes as falafel and flavorful tabbouleh salad. Save room for dessert, particularly the delicious layali loubnan, a Lebanese version of tiramisu. **Bar:** full bar. **Reservations:** suggested, weekends. **Address:** 2208 4th St S T2S 1W9 **Location:** At 4th St and 23rd Ave. **Parking:** street only. L D CALL M

ANJU
403/532-9419 **12**

◆◆◆ Korean Small Plates. Casual Dining. $15–$24 **AAA Inspector Notes:** This converted house has a warm, contemporary feel with dining on two levels. The menu is quite challenging and changes frequently. It is best to come with friends so plates can be shared. Sample such items as honey garlic crispy anchovies and seaweed wafers with chili mustard oil. For the less adventurous, try the prawn tempura or calamari with Kaffir lime and citrus aioli. The hot stone rice bowl is a staple and comes with vegetables, a poached egg and a choice of meat or fish. **Bar:** full bar. **Reservations:** suggested. **Address:** 507 10th St SW T2P 2B8 **Location:** Between 5th and 6th sts SW. **Parking:** street only. D

ATLAS SPECIALTY SUPERMARKET & PERSIAN CUISINE
403/230-0990 **22**

◆◆ Persian. Casual Dining. $8–$29 **AAA Inspector Notes:** This family-run kebab house offers a hospitable welcome and is an excellent value. The feature here is the chicken or steak kebabs as well as the popular spiced ground beef and a variety of khoresht (slow roasted stew) served with flavorful and fluffy saffron rice which is just plain delicious. Also on the menu is a variety of dips served with pita, salads and wraps. Save a little room for the tasty saffron ice cream. Hard-to-find spices and a few groceries also are available. **Address:** 1000 9th Ave SW, #100 T2P 2Y6 **Location:** Just w of 9th St SW. **Parking:** street only. L D

BARCLAY'S
403/517-6666 **10**

◆◆◆ International. Casual Dining. $12–$35 **AAA Inspector Notes:** This bright and casual eatery offers a good mix of well prepared appetizers, nouveau pizza, pasta and such entrees as Alberta AAA beef with a variety of sauces, crab-crusted salmon and roast lamb loin. **Bar:** full bar. **Reservations:** suggested. **Address:** 255 Barclay Parade SW T2P 5C2 **Location:** At 3rd St SW and 2nd Ave SW; in Sheraton Suites Calgary Eau Claire. **Parking:** valet only. B L D

THE BELVEDERE
403/265-9595 **34**

◆◆◆◆ New Canadian. Fine Dining. $13–$52 **AAA Inspector Notes:** New York meets Calgary at the upscale, intimate restaurant, tucked amid the shops and restaurants of Stephen Avenue. The decor is all New York, a long, narrow space with exposed brick walls, mirrors, walnut trim and exposed lighting. The menu changes every few months but might list such innovative creations as gingered ahi tuna, venison and duck. The romantic setting is fitting for special occasions, and the plush lounge at the entrance is the perfect relaxing spot for an after-work cocktail. **Bar:** full bar. **Reservations:** suggested. **Address:** 107 8th Ave SW T2P 1B4 **Location:** Just e of 1st St SW. **Parking:** street only. L D CALL M

BISTRO 2210
403/228-4528 **75**

◆◆◆◆

French
Casual Dining
$12–$31

AAA Inspector Notes: On trendy Fourth Street, this modern little bistro integrates exposed brick and a century-old tin ceiling in the décor. Canadian influences and ingredients accent the contemporary French comfort food menu. Samples of the delicious menu may include such starters as duck confit poutine or a house terrine followed with entrées of risotto aux coquilles St. Jacques or steak frites with AAA Alberta beef. Wine and cocktails follow very much in the French theme and the service is friendly and casual. **Bar:** full bar. **Address:** 2210 4th St SW T2S 1W9 **Location:** Just n of 22nd Ave SW. **Parking:** street only. L D CALL M

BLINK RESTAURANT & BAR
403/263-5330 **31**

◆◆◆ New World. Casual Dining. $15–$38 **AAA Inspector Notes:** This is a stylish room with exposed brick walls and an open kitchen where high-quality ingredients are sourced from a variety of producers and farms in the area. The menu changes frequently and beautiful clean flavors are reflected in such items as albacore tuna tartare with salt-baked golden beets and chioggia beets for an appetizer or rabbit with fresh pappardelle pasta and wild mushrooms. Service is suggested but can get a bit hectic at prime dining times. **Bar:** full bar. **Reservations:** suggested. **Address:** 111 8th Ave SW T2B 1B4 **Location:** On Stephen Ave, just e of Centre St S. **Parking:** street only. L D CALL M

BONTERRA TRATTORIA
403/262-8480 **26**

◆◆◆ New Italian. Casual Dining. $15–$36 **AAA Inspector Notes:** For an upscale Italian dining experience, look no further than this restaurant. Sumptuous smells waft from the open concept kitchen, where contemporary Italian dishes are created. The romantic dining room is a great place for a special occasion, and in the summer a garden oasis patio awaits in the back. With an extensive wine list, and superb professional service, this is one fine place for a great meal. **Bar:** full bar. **Reservations:** suggested. **Address:** 1016 8th St SW T2R 1K2 **Location:** 10th Ave and 8th St SW. L D

BOXWOOD CAFE
403/265-4006 **50**

◆◆◆ Canadian. Casual Dining. $10–$17 **AAA Inspector Notes:** A strong focus on sustainable and local products, all prepared with a light hand so the freshness shines through, can be found at this café overlooking the park. The menu revolves around rotisserie meats, mostly porchetta (pork) and chicken, with one revolving item. Guests can share a variety of appetizers such as lamb meatballs and red lentil hummus. Side dishes paired with the meats include chickpea and roast tomato stew with ricotta or roasted organic potatoes with parsley and lemon. **Bar:** beer & wine. **Address:** 340 13th Ave SW T2R 0W9 **Location:** Jct Macleod Tr SE, 0.5 mi (0.9 km) w; in Central Memorial Park (southwest corner). **Parking:** street only. L D CALL M

BRAVA BISTRO
403/228-1854 **59**

◆◆◆ Canadian. Fine Dining. $14–$32 **AAA Inspector Notes:** Old World inspiration combines with New World ingredients at this upscale, trendy dining option on 17th Avenue. The bistro is an ideal place for a first date or special occasion. Artistic and creative dishes emphasize freshness, simplicity and seasonality. Diners can complete their meal with a selection from the award-winning wine list. Popular with the local crowd, diners can make reservations to shorten their wait. **Bar:** full bar. **Reservations:** suggested. **Address:** 723 17th Ave SW T2S 0B6 **Location:** Just e of 7th St. **Parking:** on-site and street. L D

BROKEN PLATE KITCHEN & BAR
403/283-6300 **1**

◆◆ Greek. Casual Dining. $12–$35 **AAA Inspector Notes:** On the main street of the trendy Kensington neighborhood, this small chain restaurant is one of three in the city. Offering a wide selection of Greek standards, the comfortable restaurant reflects plenty of blue and white accents and shows how its name came about via the occasional broken plate. **Bar:** full bar. **Reservations:** suggested. **Address:** 302 10th St NW T2N 1V8 **Location:** 0.6 mi (1 km) n of Memorial Dr. **Parking:** on-site and street. L D CALL M

BUCHANAN'S CHOP HOUSE & WHISKY BAR
403/261-4646 **11**

◆◆◆ Steak. Casual Dining. $15–$40 **AAA Inspector Notes:** This restaurant has an attractive historical feel. They pride themselves on scratch cooking and quality ingredients. Good examples to start would be Cajun seafood chowder or Dungeness crab cakes with pineapple-curry mayo and fruit salsa followed by fabulous preparations of Alberta Angus beef, fresh fish, house made pastas and chicken dishes. With over 200 kinds, they are known for one of the largest collections of malt whiskey outside Scotland. **Bar:** full bar. **Reservations:** suggested. **Address:** 738 3rd Ave SW T2P 0G7 **Location:** Corner of 7th St SW; center. **Parking:** street only. L D CALL M

(See map & index p. 67.)

CAESAR'S STEAKHOUSE
403/264-1222 (14)

Steak
Fine Dining
$15-$52

AAA Inspector Notes: One of the city's original steakhouses, the dark, dimly lit restaurant speaks to years gone by, with professionally dressed servers, intimate corners and a booming lunch business. A trip to the West is not complete without a stop at this popular restaurant. An extensive selection of AAA Alberta beef is prepared to the diner's liking from the glassed-in barbecue area. The place buzzes at lunch, as many corporate-types nosh on a Caesar alongside their steak. **Bar:** full bar. **Reservations:** suggested. **Address:** 512 4th Ave SW T2P 0J6 **Location:** Just e of 5th St SW. **Parking:** valet and street only. [L] [D]

CATCH OYSTER BAR
403/206-0000 (35)

Seafood. Casual Dining. $18-$28 **AAA Inspector Notes:** Down the stairs from Catch (which offers a more upscale experience), this oyster bar is more casual yet still offers a fine food experience. The bustling, nautical place prepares an extensive selection of fresh seafood, flown in each day. Guests can enjoy not only oysters but also other distinctive choices, including salmon, traditional fish and chips and the catch of the day. **Bar:** full bar. **Reservations:** suggested. **Address:** 100 8th Ave SE T2P 1B3 **Location:** Corner of Centre St and 7th Ave SW; in Hyatt Regency Calgary. **Parking:** street only. [L] [D]

CATCH RESTAURANT
403/206-0000 (32)

Seafood
Fine Dining
$16-$45

AAA Inspector Notes: On the second level above the oyster bar, this upscale and striking dining room, with lofty ceilings and exposed original stone, is where diners can enjoy a remarkable and changing range of meticulous and delicious preparations. Alaskan sable fish, Hawaiian yellowfin tuna, British Columbia Kusshi oysters, spot prawns, Nova Scotia lobster and wild British Columbia ling cod are some of the choices seafood lovers might find. **Bar:** full bar. **Reservations:** suggested. **Address:** 100 8th Ave SE T2P 1B3 **Location:** Corner of Centre St and 7th Ave SW; in Hyatt Regency Calgary. **Parking:** street only. [L] [D]

CENTINI RESTAURANT AND LOUNGE
403/269-1600 (38)

Italian
Fine Dining
$18-$54

AAA Inspector Notes: While the dining room at this eatery is decidedly upscale, the atmosphere remains quite informal. An excellent selection of wines, cognacs and aged scotches complements items on seasonal menus, which feature new Italian cuisines incorporating Asian and French influences combined with more local ingredients. Must-try entrees include the fresh Italian truffles, which find their way onto the menu in the fall. **Bar:** full bar. **Reservations:** suggested. **Address:** 160 8th Ave SE T2G 0K6 **Location:** Corner of 8th Ave SE (Stephen Ave) and 1st St SE; in TELUS Convention Centre. **Parking:** street only. [L] [D] CALL [M]

CHARCUT ROAST HOUSE
403/984-2180 (44)

Canadian. Casual Dining. $14-$29 **AAA Inspector Notes:** Not for the faint hearted, this contemporary eatery offers a menu focusing on local meat, including homemade sausage and cured meat. Appetizers run the gamut from slow-roasted heirloom beets and warm Quebec raclette cheese to bone marrow au gratin. Entrees include spit-roasted Spring Creek prime rib and fire grilled lamb legs as well as fish and pasta. An eclectic collection of wine, beer, freshly squeezed juices, cocktails and premium spirits is offered. Save room for the homemade desserts. **Bar:** full bar. **Reservations:** suggested. **Address:** 899 Centre St SW T2G 1B8 **Location:** Corner of 1st St SW and 9th Ave SW; center; in Hotel Le Germain Calgary. **Parking:** on-site (fee) and valet. [L] [D] CALL [M]

CHEF'S TABLE
403/228-4442 (7)

New
American
Fine Dining
$26-$40

AAA Inspector Notes: Located in the heart of trendy Kensington, the tiny, intimate restaurant is new to the Calgary dining scene. The open-kitchen concept gives some real insight into the inner workings of the kitchen. Meals are impeccably presented, not to mention delicious. The chef's five-course tasting menu changes bi-weekly, and a la carte offerings feature house-smoked organic salmon and Black Angus beef. Guests can relax in a contemporary lounge to enjoy a fireplace and original artwork. **Bar:** full bar. **Reservations:** suggested. **Address:** 1126 Memorial Dr NW T2N 3E3 **Location:** Just w of 10th St NW; in Kensington Riverside Inn. **Parking:** street only. [B] [D] CALL [M]

Elegant cuisine, award winning with open kitchen design

CHICAGO CHOPHOUSE
403/265-3000 (23)

Steak. Casual Dining. $17-$49 **AAA Inspector Notes:** Guests can see and be seen at this ultra-modern, contemporary steakhouse, in the heart of the city. Efficient, professional servers help make this place popular with the business crowd at lunchtime. The menu blends a wide selection of top-quality cuts of beef with sandwiches and meal-size salads. The chic, lofty interior has an open-concept kitchen, and the selection of by-the-glass wines is one of the best in the city. **Bar:** full bar. **Reservations:** suggested. **Address:** 604 8th Ave SW T2P 1G4 **Location:** Corner of 8th Ave SW and 5th St SW. **Parking:** street only. [L] [D] CALL [M]

CILANTRO
403/229-1177 (65)

California. Casual Dining. $14-$44 **AAA Inspector Notes:** The dark wood interior and lovely stained-glass windows combine to create an intimate atmosphere in the small dining room, where guests can enjoy an interesting selection of California-inspired cuisine. Good choices include melt-in-the-mouth sea bass, various pastas and salads and any of the delectable desserts. Service is professional and friendly. **Bar:** full bar. **Reservations:** suggested. **Address:** 338 17th Ave SW T2S 0A8 **Location:** Just e of 4th St SW. **Parking:** on-site and street. [L] [D] [M]

THE COUP + MEET
403/541-1041 (55)

Vegetarian. Casual Dining. $11-$18 **AAA Inspector Notes:** In Alberta beef land, this popular vegetarian restaurant is holding its own. Not surprisingly, the chef supports local and organic producers and they recycle and compost as much as possible. Interesting dips and spreads, salads and a variety of sandwiches are offered at lunch. At dinner the menu features a nice range of appetizers while the entrées are a little heartier. Quite a few vegan and gluten-free items are available. They also are open for breakfast on Saturday and Sunday. **Bar:** full bar. **Address:** 924 B 17th Ave SW T2T 0A2 **Location:** Between 8th and 9th sts SW. **Parking:** street only. [L] [D]

DEANE HOUSE HISTORIC SITE RESTAURANT AT FORT CALGARY
403/269-7747 (54)

American. Casual Dining. $13-$19 **AAA Inspector Notes:** *Historic.* The glassed-in, veranda dining room offers a lovely view of the Elbow River. Menu offerings utilize organic items and super fresh ingredients, some from their own garden. Highlights include fresh scones, homemade soup, lovely salads, gourmet sandwiches and burgers and homemade desserts. A table d'hôte menu offers more complex entrées. Friendly servers work quickly. On select evenings, the Mystery from History dinner theater takes the stage. **Bar:** full bar. **Reservations:** suggested. **Address:** 806 9th Ave SE T2P 2M5 **Location:** Corner of 8th St. [L] CALL [M]

(See map & index p. 67.)

DIVINO WINE & CHEESE BISTRO 403/410-5555 33
New Canadian. Fine Dining. $17-$37 **AAA Inspector Notes:** There is more than just wine and cheese at this upscale bistro, and the variety makes it a good reason to come. Cheese from around the world, including Alberta varieties, is paired with fresh artisan bread. Those in the mood for something more can expect decadent, beautiful food, ranging from grilled rabbit appetizers and British Columbia salmon to bison and elk from their own ranch. Professional service completes the experience. Closed for lunch on Saturday. **Bar:** full bar. **Reservations:** suggested. **Address:** 113 8th Ave SW T2P 1B4 **Location:** Just w of Center St S. **Parking:** street only.
L D CALL M

EARLS RESTAURANT
American. Casual Dining. $10-$35 **AAA Inspector Notes:** Offering an experience that falls between fast food and fine dining, the fun, relaxed restaurant prepares great food at a great price. Choices range from juicy burgers, hearty sandwiches, fresh salads, wings and pizza to full entrees of steak, chops and seafood. Made-from-scratch soups and assorted breads, as well as a nice choice of wines and beers, round out the offerings. This is a fitting spot for impromptu get-togethers and festive occasions. **Bar:** full bar.
L D LATE CALL M
For additional information, visit AAA.com
LOCATIONS:
Address: 2401 4th St SW T2S 1X5 **Location:** Corner of 4th St SW and 24th Ave. **Phone:** 403/228-4141
Address: 315 8th Ave SW T2P 1C4 **Location:** Between 2nd and 3rd sts SW; in Bankers Hall. **Phone:** 403/265-3275

FAT CITY FRANKS 403/229-3641 70
Hot Dogs. Quick Serve. $6-$8 **AAA Inspector Notes:** Stop in for a gourmet hot dog, the likes of which could be Chilean, Mexican, French, Mediterranean, Italian or Ukrainian. This quick-serve joint has more dog varieties than the local paw park. **Address:** 2015 4th St SW, #3 T2S 1W6 **Location:** Jct 20th Ave. **Parking:** street only.
L D

FLEUR DE SEL 403/228-9764 71
New French. Casual Dining. $15-$39 **AAA Inspector Notes:** Elegantly funky is a good description of the atmosphere at this small brasserie. A favorite with locals, this spot serves nouveau French cuisine and fine wines. A memorable experience encompasses more than just creative, sophisticated food. Jazz music fills the dining room, and the open concept warehouse pipes have been boldly painted in primary colors to contrast with a red brick accent wall. Efficient, friendly service awaits, and the owner often appears to chat with guests. **Bar:** full bar. **Reservations:** suggested. **Address:** 2015 4th St SW, #2 T2S 1W6 **Location:** 4th St and 21st Ave SW; in Tivoli Theatre Building. **Parking:** street only. L D

GALAXIE DINER 403/228-0001 46
American. Family Dining. $8-$15 **AAA Inspector Notes:** Decorated with a few Elvis posters, the unassuming diner often has locals waiting in lengthy lines on the weekend, all vying for a spot at one of the few crowded tiny tables. It would be fair to say the atmosphere is intimate, very intimate, but it's the simple, uncomplicated and uncluttered home cooking and comfort foods that pack customers in. All-day breakfasts along with burgers, sandwiches and thick milkshakes complete the menu. **Address:** 1314 11th St SW T3C 0M9 **Location:** Just n of 17th Ave SW. **Parking:** street only.
B L

THE GLORY OF INDIA 403/263-8804 15
Indian. Casual Dining. $17-$32 **AAA Inspector Notes:** This casual Indian restaurant serves tasty portions of traditional Indian cuisine. The lunch buffet is popular, and reservations are recommended. A la carte dinner items are best enjoyed with several people to allow for sampling of the varied dishes, including alu goobi, lamb and beef curries and chicken tikka. **Bar:** full bar. **Reservations:** suggested. **Address:** 515 4th Ave SW T2P 0J8 **Location:** Jct 5th St and 4th Ave SW; on ground floor of apartment building. **Parking:** street only. L D

GOOD EARTH COFFEEHOUSE & BAKERY 403/228-9543 49
Breads/Pastries Sandwiches. Quick Serve. $5-$8 **AAA Inspector Notes:** One of several locations in Calgary, the casual restaurant offers a variety of take-out items, including garden salads and soups. Also on the menu are sweet and savory baked goods, freshly made sandwiches and a limited selection of hot entrées that can be enjoyed over a lingering cup of coffee at one of the comfortable tables. **Address:** 1502 11th St SW T2R 1G9 **Location:** Just n of 17th Ave SW. **Parking:** street only. B L D

HANA SUSHI 403/229-1499 67
Japanese. Casual Dining. $7-$20 **AAA Inspector Notes:** The small, traditional restaurant is a great spot for good sushi at a great value. In addition to a wide variety of sushi and sashimi, the menu lists full dinners that also include miso soup and salad. **Bar:** full bar. **Reservations:** suggested. **Address:** 1803 4th St SW T2S 1W2 **Location:** Corner of 18th Ave SW. **Parking:** street only.
L D

THE HOLY GRILL 403/261-9759 27
American. Quick Serve. $8-$13 **AAA Inspector Notes:** This casual restaurant serves exciting and interesting soups, panini, burgers and salads that are made to order while guests wait. Same goes for breakfast with a variety of eggs Benedict and breakfast sandwiches. **Address:** 827 10th Ave SW T2R 0B4 **Location:** Jct 8th St SW; across from Mountain Equipment Co-op. **Parking:** on-site and street. B L

IL SOGNO 403/232-8901 17
Historic. Italian. Fine Dining. $13-$32 **AAA Inspector Notes:** Italian for "the dream," Il Sogno is a simply elegant restaurant with an upscale decor and sumptuous Italian food. Classically prepared and beautifully presented dishes on the seasonally inspired menu incorporate the finest regional and imported Italian products, including exotic house-made pasta, Alberta rabbit, Quebec foie gras, Alberta beef and fresh fish and other seafood. The building originally was a rooming house, and the owners have maintained the history and integrity in the decor. Closed for lunch on Saturday. **Bar:** full bar. **Reservations:** suggested. **Address:** 24 4th St NE T2E 3R7 **Location:** Just n of Memorial Dr; at Meredith Rd and 4th St NE.
L D CALL M

JOEY RESTAURANTS 403/263-6336
American. Casual Dining. $13-$33 **AAA Inspector Notes:** The cuisine blends Mediterranean and Asian cooking styles and emphasizes finger foods for sharing. Those who aren't big fans of tapas can consider full meal offerings centered on steaks and chops. **Bar:** full bar. **Address:** 200 Barclay Parade SW T2P 4R5 **Location:** At 208 Eau Claire Market. L D LATE

THE JOYCE ON 4TH IRISH PUB 403/541-9168 77
Irish. Casual Dining. $13-$17 **AAA Inspector Notes:** A wide selection of ales and whiskeys complements traditional fare, including boxty, an Irish dish made with a potato pancake and various fillings, and Guinness and beef pie. Saturday visitors can expect live music and Celtic dancers. The rich decor incorporates oversized couches and a long bar. The mood is lively and upbeat. **Bar:** full bar. **Address:** 506 24th Ave SW T2S 0K4 **Location:** Jct 24th Ave SW and 4th St SW. L D LATE

JULIO'S BARRIO MEXICAN RESTAURANT 403/203-3066 6
Mexican. Casual Dining. $10-$22 **AAA Inspector Notes:** This upbeat, casual and boisterous restaurant is a fun place to visit for hearty helpings of Mexican cuisine. **Bar:** full bar. **Reservations:** suggested. **Address:** 101 10th St NW T2N 1V4 **Location:** Corner of Memorial Dr. **Parking:** on-site (fee) and street. L D CALL M

KICKERS SMOKED MEAT & DELI 403/288-8860 52
Specialty Sandwiches. Quick Serve. $10-$12 **AAA Inspector Notes:** It was a little surprising to walk into a sandwich joint and find a gorgeous chandelier but this used to be the lobby in the historic Radio Block back in the day and the owner has renovated the space keeping the original exposed brick with some added contemporary touches. Specializing in Montreal smoked meat sandwiches and keeping with the Canadian theme they also serve other creative sandwiches named after Canadian cities utilizing quality ingredients like smoked salmon. **Bar:** beer & wine. **Address:** 1215 1st St SW, Unit 100 T2R 0V3 **Location:** Between 12th and 13th aves SW. **Parking:** on-site (fee). B L CALL M

(See map & index p. 67.)

THE KING & I
403/264-7241 (41)

▼▼▼ Thai. Casual Dining. $12-$32 **AAA Inspector Notes:** Experience a taste of Thailand in an upscale, contemporary atmosphere. Here, modern furnishings and decor set the scene for authentic, tasty Thai dishes. The chef utilizes excellent quality ingredients from the fresh herbs and vegetables to fine seafood and cuts of meat. The menu is extensive and features a wide variety of items from appetizers, salads, soups and all the entrées expected in a Thai restaurant as well as some not expected. Closed for lunch on Saturday and Sunday. **Bar:** full bar. **Reservations:** suggested. **Address:** 822 11th Ave SW T2R 0E5 **Location:** Corner of 11th Ave SW and 8th St SW. **Parking:** street only.

[L] [D] CALL [&][M]

LA BREZZA
403/262-6230 (18)

▼▼ Italian. Casual Dining. $10-$45 **AAA Inspector Notes:** In a small house, the setting enhances a warm, relaxed atmosphere, topped by funky lighting crisscrossing the ceiling. Whether for a first date or reunion with old friends, the restaurant's eclectic atmosphere, refined service and creative Italian cuisine create a lingering memory. **Bar:** full bar. **Reservations:** suggested. **Address:** 990 1st Ave NE T2E 4J9 **Location:** At 9th St NE; in Bridgeland. [L] [D]

LA CHAUMIERE RESTAURANT
403/228-5690 (68)

▼▼▼▼

French
Fine Dining
$13-$37

AAA Inspector Notes: This upscale restaurant's impressive, almost château-like building has a peaked roof and elegant exterior, making it an ideal spot for fine French dining. From the moment patrons cross the threshold over polished granite floors into an exquisitely appointed dining room, they will experience professional service. Donned in black and white, servers begin by pulling out chairs and end with a polite adieu. A French accent can be heard in the dining room. Semiformal attire. **Bar:** full bar. **Reservations:** suggested. **Address:** 139 17th Ave SW T2S 0A1 **Location:** Corner of 1st St SW and 17th Ave SW. [L] [D]

LA DOLCE VITA RISTORANTE ITALIANO
403/263-3445 (16)

▼▼▼ Italian. Casual Dining. $9-$40 **AAA Inspector Notes:** In the city's Little Italy area, this restaurant boasts yellow walls, hardwood floors and colorful art upstairs amid an upbeat ambience. Downstairs is more intimate, with formal table settings. The menu features large appetizers, including sumptuous salmon salad, mussels and scampi. Mouthwatering veal options as well as homemade pasta satisfy hearty appetites. Formally attired servers provide brisk service during the lunch rush but are more attentive at dinner. Open for dinner only on Saturday. **Bar:** full bar. **Reservations:** suggested. **Address:** 916 1st Ave NE T2E 0C5 **Location:** At 9th St NE; in Bridgeland. **Parking:** street only. [L] [D]

THE LIVING ROOM
403/228-9830 (64)

▼▼▼ Canadian. Casual Dining. $14-$42 **AAA Inspector Notes:** This contemporary restaurant serves imaginative Canadian fare, including a five-course menu surprise. As the name suggests, the décor includes oversize, couch-like chairs which contribute to a cozy and comfortable dining environment. **Bar:** full bar. **Reservations:** suggested. **Address:** 514 17th Ave SW T5W 4X6 **Location:** Just e of 5th St SW. **Parking:** on-site and street.

[L] [D] [LATE]

LOUNGEBURGER
403/250-2747 (62)

▼ Burgers. Casual Dining. $13-$23 **AAA Inspector Notes:** Across from the Saddledome, this smart yet casual spot can get really busy before or after the game. But you can also enjoy the game here on one of the many TVs in the lounge; the restaurant sports a couple of big screens, too. Delicious designer burgers run the gamut from bison and Kobe beef to turkey, shrimp and pulled pork. Or if you prefer, build your own favorite burger. Rounding out the menu are great appetizers, salads, soups and house desserts. **Bar:** full bar. **Reservations:** suggested. **Address:** 270 14th Ave SE T2G 0L3 **Location:** Just w of Macleod Tr SE. **Parking:** on-site (fee) and street.

[L] [D] [LATE] CALL [&][M]

THE MAIN DISH
403/265-3474 (20)

▼ Deli. Casual Dining. $8-$20 **AAA Inspector Notes:** Contemporary space and creative concoctions are in store for diners at this little café. Order freshly prepared gourmet burgers, sandwiches, pasta and stir-fries from the hot counter or grilled items at dinner. Deluxe breakfast and brunch items are offered in the mornings. Another counter has delicious sandwiches, salads, soup and a selection of ready-to-take-home items that are available in the central display case. After paying, guests can wait at lovely copper-top tables for orders to arrive. **Bar:** beer & wine. **Address:** 903 General Ave NE T2E 9E1 **Location:** From Memorial Dr NE, just n on Edmonton Tr NE, then 0.4 mi (0.6 km) e on 1st Ave NE. **Parking:** street only.

[B] [L] [D] CALL [&][M]

MANIES GREEK CUISINE
403/228-9207 (57)

▼▼ Greek. Casual Dining. $13-$25 **AAA Inspector Notes:** Attractive framed photographs of Greece adorn the walls of this casual, family-run restaurant. Friendly staff circulate through the dining room with plates of traditional Greek food, such as the souvlaki pita, lamb chops and moussaka, as well as oven-baked thick-crust pizzas. **Bar:** full bar. **Address:** 819 17th Ave SW T2T 0A1 **Location:** Between 8th and 7th sts SW. **Parking:** street only. [L] [D]

MANUEL LATRUWE BELGIAN PATISSERIE & BREAD SHOP
403/261-1092 (58)

▼▼ Breads/Pastries. Quick Serve. $7-$13 **AAA Inspector Notes:** Elegance and refinement characterize this upscale bakery, which features the divine dessert creations of Manuel Latruwe. The display case is filled with gorgeous mousses, cheesecakes, tarts and pastries, as well as artisan breads. Delicious soup, daily creamy quiche, pâté, house-smoked salmon and such gourmet sandwiches as croque Monsieur (a decadent ham and cheese sandwich with béchamel) are offered to sustain diners' before diving into one of the tempting desserts. **Address:** 1333 1st St SE T2G 5L1 **Location:** At 13th Ave. [B] [L] CALL [&][M]

MAURYA
403/270-3133 (2)

▼▼ Eastern Indian. Casual Dining. $14-$16 **AAA Inspector Notes:** Diners find excellent, tasty East Indian cuisine at this spot, tucked away in a shopping area in trendy Kensington. The menu specializes in tandoori and includes many vegetarian dishes. Mint or coriander sauces tease the taste buds when served atop crispy pakoras and samosas. An extensive lunch buffet has more than a dozen items, and guests can spend hours dining in this relaxing, simple ambience if lingering between courses. Efficient servers ensure glasses stay full. **Bar:** full bar. **Reservations:** suggested. **Address:** 1204 Kensington Rd NW T2N 3P5 **Location:** At 12th St NW. **Parking:** street only. [L] [D]

MERCATO
403/263-5535 (76)

▼▼▼ Italian. Casual Dining. $15-$43 **AAA Inspector Notes:** Hugely popular, this is a boisterous and often chaotic spot, with heady aromas making your mouth water as you watch the action in the open kitchen or nibble olives from a small bowl while sipping on a great Italian wine. Peruse the menu for flavorful and creative choices including the popular bistecca, a thick Fiorentina-style rib-eye steak with grilled lemons and first-press Fontodi olive oil. The high-quality ingredients are found right there in the on-site, high-end Italian retail market. **Bar:** full bar. **Reservations:** suggested. **Address:** 2224 4th St SW T2S 1W9 **Location:** Corner of 22nd Ave SW. **Parking:** street only. [L] [D] CALL [&][M]

METROPOLITAN GRILL
403/263-5432 (24)

▼▼▼ American. Casual Dining. $15-$38 **AAA Inspector Notes:** Across from Banker's Hall, this Stephen Avenue location is the place to be for a power lunch. The upscale restaurant is known for its creative takes on classic comfort food, ranging from lobster macaroni and cheese to great AAA Alberta steaks. **Bar:** full bar. **Reservations:** suggested. **Address:** 317 8th Ave S, Suite 150 T2P 1C4 **Location:** In TD Square. **Parking:** street only. [L] [D]

MODEL MILK
403/265-7343 (66)

▼▼▼ New World. Casual Dining. $18-$29 **AAA Inspector Notes:** Getting its name from the restored 1930s Model Milk Dairy building it is located in, this spot has a funky and open space which can get pretty boisterous. The inventive menu is small but changes about every two weeks so it never gets dull. Creamy shrimp and grits with ham hock appetizer and entrées of British Columbia Ling cod with clams and soy broth or smoked pork tenderloin wrapped in sausage and bacon are good choices. Super selections of interesting wines also are up for tasting. **Bar:** full bar. **Address:** 308 17th Ave SW T2S 0A8 **Location:** Just w of 2nd St SW. **Parking:** on-site and street. [D] CALL [&][M]

(See map & index p. 67.)

MOTI MAHAL 403/228-9990 51

▼▼ Northern Indian. Casual Dining. $11-$17 **AAA Inspector Notes:** Tapestries hung around the dining room create a royal environment at this restaurant known for its Northern Indian cuisine. Peruse a varied menu to find such dishes as buttery masalas, curries and the specialty chicken tikka, served with spicy yogurt and tomato sauce. It's closed for lunch on Saturday. **Bar:** full bar. **Reservations:** suggested. **Address:** 1805 14th St SW T2T 3P1 **Location:** Just s of jct 17th Ave SW and 14th St SW; in small strip mall.

L D CALL &M

MOXIE'S CLASSIC GRILL 403/234-7507

▼▼ American. Casual Dining. $10-$29 **AAA Inspector Notes:** This sleek, funky and popular restaurant presents an extensive menu of creatively prepared dishes, including pizza, pasta, rice, noodles, signature salads and burgers. Other menus include one for children and one for Sunday brunch. Lending to the upbeat, stylish decor are dark wood appointments and river rock fireplaces. **Bar:** full bar. **Address:** 888 7th Ave SW T2P 3J3 **Location:** Corner of 7th Ave SW and 8th St SW; in Sandman Hotel Downtown Calgary. **Parking:** on-site (fee).

B L D LATE

MURRIETA'S WESTCOAST GRILL 403/269-7707 28

▼▼▼ Western Pacific Rim. Casual Dining. $12-$39 **AAA Inspector Notes:** The lively, airy dining room buzzes with sounds from the open-concept kitchen amid animated conversations. The bustling restaurant has an energy and liveliness that makes it a popular spot for a gathering of friends. For a more intimate experience, smaller areas are tucked away from the main dining room. Among offerings are mussels, ahi tuna, salmon and various pasta dishes. **Bar:** full bar. **Reservations:** suggested. **Address:** 200-808 1st St SW T2P 1M9 **Location:** Corner of 8th Ave SW and 1st St SW; 2nd Floor. **Parking:** street only.

L D CALL &M

MUSE RESTAURANT & LOUNGE 403/670-6873 5

▼▼▼ New American. Fine Dining. $28-$37 **AAA Inspector Notes:** This establishment presents a dazzling, innovative menu. The decor sets the scene for an upscale evening. The chef emphasizes regional items in the imaginative dishes. Desserts are delicious. **Bar:** full bar. **Reservations:** suggested. **Address:** 107-10A St NW T2N 4M7 **Location:** From Memorial Dr, just n on 10th St, just w on Kensington Rd, then just s. **Parking:** street only.

D

MYHRE'S DELI 403/244-6602 47

▼ Sandwiches. Quick Serve. $10-$12 **AAA Inspector Notes:** The funky, table-free eatery takes its name from a restaurant that stood in downtown Calgary from 1920 to the mid-'60s. A true gem, this place specializes in Montreal-style bagels, creamy milkshakes and hand-sliced, stacked Montreal smoked meat sandwiches on Winnipeg rye. Check out the original mahogany paneling and benches, which give the restaurant an antique feel. Open until 7 pm during the week and until 4 pm on the weekend. **Address:** 1411 11th St SW T2R 1G7 **Location:** Just n of 17th Ave SW. **Parking:** only.

L D K

THE ORCHID ROOM FUSION CUISINE 403/263-4457 25

▼ Vietnamese. Casual Dining. $17-$24 **AAA Inspector Notes:** A combination of Vietnamese and French cuisine makes for an eclectic menu with an accent on healthy choices. Colorful plate presentations include banana leaves, yellow daisies and orchids. Among choices are many unusual vegan dishes. The cozy setting has an open atmosphere. **Bar:** full bar. **Reservations:** suggested. **Address:** 315 8th Ave SW T2P 4K1 **Location:** Corner of 2nd St SW; in Bankers Hall, 2nd Floor. **Parking:** on-site (fee) and street.

L

ORIENTAL PHOENIX 403/262-3633 29

▼▼▼ Vietnamese. Casual Dining. $10-$19 **AAA Inspector Notes:** Traditional Vietnamese food is served simply, but the service and decor is anything but. Upscale and sleek, the modern dining room is a busy place at lunch and around the dinner hour. Guests can sample tasty food in fine surroundings characterized by bold, contemporary colors and art. Among the varied choices are salad rolls, rice vermicelli dishes and noodle soups. **Bar:** full bar. **Address:** 401 9th Ave S, Unit 105 T2P 3C5 **Location:** Jct 4th St SW; in Gulf Canada Square. **Parking:** street only.

L D CALL &M

OX AND ANGELA 403/457-1432 61

▼▼▼ Spanish. Casual Dining. $9-$28 **AAA Inspector Notes:** Spanish shrine and contemporary pieces accent this tiny modern restaurant. Choose from nibbles of Turkish olives, candied nuts or daily pintxos to keep your appetite at bay while perusing the enticing menu. A range of tapas and entrées are made with such quality ingredients as Serrano ham, wild British Columbia mushrooms, Manchego cheese, West coast scallops, pomegranates, smoked paprika, Brome Lake duck or Carmen Creek Farms beef. Eclectic cocktails and great wines complement the menu. **Bar:** full bar. **Reservations:** suggested. **Address:** 528 17th Ave SW T2S 0A9 **Location:** Just e of 5th St SW. **Parking:** on-site (fee) and street.

L D CALL &M

PEKING DRAGON 403/228-1205 69

▼▼ Chinese. Casual Dining. $10-$20 **AAA Inspector Notes:** A popular spot with the locals, this casual Chinese restaurant prepares traditional selections and offers fine, friendly service. Among choices are egg rolls, Peking duck and egg foo yong. Closed for lunch on Saturday and Sunday. **Bar:** full bar. **Address:** 1904 4th St SW T2S 1W3 **Location:** At 19th Ave SW.

L D CALL &M

PETITE BISTRO & WINE BAR 403/452-5350 63

▼▼▼ New French. Casual Dining. $18-$30 **AAA Inspector Notes:** Casual sophistication leads the way at this smartly decorated spot. The talented chef uses fine ingredients and creates a delicious modern menu with some distinct flavor profiles. Servers are helpful and are not afraid to recommend items on the menu for those having a difficult time choosing. In good weather the patio is prime for people watching. **Bar:** full bar. **Reservations:** suggested. **Address:** 344 17th Ave SW T2S 0A8 **Location:** Corner of 4th St. **Parking:** street only.

L D CALL &M

PREGO CUCINA ITALIANA 403/233-7885 9

▼▼▼ Italian. Casual Dining. $16-$34 **AAA Inspector Notes:** One of the long-standing tenants of Eau Claire Market, this is a well-loved spot for business folk, shoppers and locals. Start with the tender calamari served with flavorful tomato sauce. Follow with lovely classic and house-created pasta, gnocchi and risotto as well as such tantalizing entrées as chicken with mushrooms, spinach and blue cheese cream sauce or grilled veal with arugula and tiger prawns. Service is professional with a casual flair. **Reservations:** suggested. **Address:** 200 Barclay Parade SW, #218 T2P 4R5 **Location:** Just n of 2nd Ave SW; in Eau Claire Market on Second Level. **Parking:** street only.

L D CALL &M

PULCINELLA 403/283-1166 4

▼▼ Pizza. Casual Dining. $13-$30 **AAA Inspector Notes:** The restaurant is a member of an Italian organization dedicated to preserving Naples-style pizza. An apple wood-burning oven imported from Italy cooks the 18 varieties of thin-crust pizza, in addition to a few additional choices, such as polenta lasagna and arancini rice balls stuffed with mozzarella and tomato sauce. The cheerful spot displays an impressive number of white mosaic tiles and back-lit black and white photographs featuring street scenes around a Naples pizzeria. **Bar:** full bar. **Reservations:** suggested. **Address:** 1147 Kensington Crescent NW T2N 1X7 **Location:** 0.3 mi (0.4 km) e of jct 14th St NW. **Parking:** street only.

L D CALL &M

PURPLE PERK 403/244-1300 74

▼ Coffee/Tea. Quick Serve. $9-$13 **AAA Inspector Notes:** This is more than just a coffee shop. In addition to great coffee, guests will find a variety of freshly made wraps and panini, soup, salads and such pastas as lasagna and macaroni and cheese. Delicious homemade squares, cookies, muffins and other desserts round out the choices. Seats are inside or streetside, where diners can watch the action along trendy 4th Street. **Address:** 2212 4th St SW T2S 1W9 **Location:** Between 22nd and 23rd aves SW. **Parking:** street only.

B L D

RAJDOOT 403/245-0181 78

▼▼ Indian. Casual Dining. $11-$17 **AAA Inspector Notes:** The casual Indian restaurant lures locals and celebrities alike for its fantastic all-you-can-eat lunch buffet. **Bar:** full bar. **Reservations:** suggested. **Address:** 2424 4th St SW T2S 2T4 **Location:** 4th St at 24th Ave SW. **Parking:** on-site and street.

L D

(See map & index p. 67.)

RIC'S GRILL
403/269-7427

🍷🍷 Steak. Casual Dining. $13-$35 **AAA Inspector Notes:** "Funky and modern" describes the decor and the food at the upscale steakhouse, which bustles with activity. Steaks are well worth it, but then again, so are the salmon, chicken and pasta dishes. A wide variety of distinctive appetizers rounds out the menu. Servers are friendly and attentive. **Bar:** full bar. **Reservations:** suggested. **Address:** 1436 8th St SW T2R 1R7 **Location:** Jct Trans-Canada Hwy 1 and Barlow Tr NE, 0.6 mi (1 km) n, then just e. **Parking:** on-site (fee) and street. 🇱 🇩

THE RIMROCK DINING ROOM
403/260-1219 ㊷

🍷🍷🍷 New Canadian. Fine Dining. $12-$55 **AAA Inspector Notes:** The fine dining room has an upscale and elegant Western flair complete with an original wall mural, leather tooled pillars and a heritage fireplace. The establishment has a reputation for delivering high-quality, locally farmed, organic beef and bison as well as delicious fish, pork, lamb and chicken choices. Patrons celebrating anniversaries or other special occasions are treated by attentive servers. **Bar:** full bar. **Reservations:** suggested. **Address:** 133 9th Ave SW T2P 2M3 **Location:** 9th Ave SW and 1st St SW; in The Fairmont Palliser. **Parking:** on-site (fee) and valet. 🇧 🇱 🇩

RUSH
403/271-7874 ㊵

🍷🍷🍷 New American. Fine Dining. $14-$36 **AAA Inspector Notes:** Diners will not want to hurry at this upscale dining room and lounge which has a striking contemporary décor, starting with the beautiful glassed-in wine cellar at the entry. The food captures some of the current trends with the chef sourcing high-quality local ingredients and crafting an alluring menu which is both creative and delicious. Upon arrival, guests are well-taken care of, and as expected, they have a super wine list to complement the menu. **Bar:** full bar. **Reservations:** suggested. **Address:** 207 9th Ave SW, #100 T2P 1K3 **Location:** Corner of 1st St SW. **Parking:** street only.
🇱 🇩 CALL 🖒M

SAKANA GRILL
403/290-1118 ⑬

🍷🍷 Japanese. Casual Dining. $13-$20 **AAA Inspector Notes:** Near the Eau Claire market, this bustling Japanese restaurant has many distinctive features, including a sushi bar, teppanyaki grill and private dining rooms. Business folks frequent the place at lunch time, grabbing seats at the sushi bar and making selections from the boat that floats by. Fantastic sushi and sashimi options offer exceptional value for the dollar. **Bar:** full bar. **Reservations:** suggested. **Address:** 116 2nd Ave SW T2P 0B9 **Location:** Corner of 1st St and 2nd Ave SW; in Chinatown. **Parking:** on-site (fee) and street.

SALTLIK, A RARE STEAKHOUSE
403/537-1160 ㊱

🍷🍷🍷 Steak. Fine Dining. $12-$40 **AAA Inspector Notes:** True to its name, this restaurant truly is a "rare steak house" and a superb place. From the moment guests ascend the stairs to the upscale, contemporary dining room, they are impressed by the atmosphere. Also praiseworthy are the incredibly friendly, attentive servers, who take the time to explain the different cuts of meat and accompanying sauces. All entrées are a la carte, and the side orders are large enough to share. **Bar:** full bar. **Reservations:** suggested. **Address:** 101 8th Ave SW T6E 1H1 **Location:** Corner of 8th Ave SW and 1st St SW. **Parking:** street only. 🇱 🇩 CALL 🖒M

SILVER DRAGON RESTAURANT
403/264-5326 ㉑

Chinese
Casual Dining
$9-$19

AAA Inspector Notes: This restaurant specializes in Cantonese and Szechuan cuisine, including excellent ginger beef. A delicious dim sum selection is served each day. The contemporary decor comprises nouveau Oriental artwork. Servers are cordial. **Bar:** full bar. **Reservations:** suggested. **Address:** 106 3rd Ave SE T2G 0B6 **Location:** In Chinatown. **Parking:** street only. *Menu on AAA.com*
🇱 🇩

SKY 360
403/532-7966 ㊸

🍷🍷🍷🍷 American. Fine Dining. $16-$45 **AAA Inspector Notes:** Expect contemporary elegance and stunning views at the top of Calgary Tower where this restaurant revolves. Utilizing the freshest local foods, the talented chef produces a menu sure to please. Exotic mushroom chowder, panko calamari, spinach and goat cheese penne pasta, Sturgeon Valley pork loin and tender AAA Alberta steaks are just a sample of the specialties. Service is informed and polished. Elevation fees are waived for guests with reservations and the purchase of an entree. **Bar:** full bar. **Reservations:** suggested. **Address:** 101 9th Ave SW T2P 1J9 **Location:** Jct 9th Ave SW and Centre St S; top of Calgary Tower. **Parking:** street only.
🇱 🇩 CALL 🖒M

STEEPS THE URBAN TEAHOUSE
403/209-0076 ㊶

🍷 Coffee/Tea. Quick Serve. $5-$6 **AAA Inspector Notes:** The teahouse lures those who yearn for a pot of tea. It's a little-known fact that the Americanization of tea involved the creation of the tea bag, but loose teas--150 types, ranging from the rare and exotic to more common varieties--are the preference at the urban spot. Guests can take their time choosing from one of the many tins, which can be paired with soup and a sandwich, a samosa or wrap or one of the homemade desserts. **Address:** 880 16th Ave SW T2T 0A3 **Location:** At 8th St SW; in Mount Royal Shops. **Parking:** street only.
🇧 🇱 🇩 CALL 🖒M

SULTAN'S TENT
403/244-2333 ⑧

🍷🍷 Traditional Moroccan. Casual Dining. $18-$27 **AAA Inspector Notes:** Eating is a communal event at this cozy Moroccan restaurant. Representative of the food are such delicacies as couscous, merguez, lamb, a five-course sultan's feast and other traditional dishes. And the traditional method of eating such creations is with the hands. The decor, inspired by the Berber culture of North Africa, offers intimate, tent-style seating. **Bar:** full bar. **Reservations:** suggested. **Address:** 4 14th St NW T2N 1Z4 **Location:** Just n of Kensington Rd NW. 🇩

SUSHI BAR ZIPANG
403/262-1888 ⑲

🍷🍷 Japanese. Casual Dining. $15-$25 **AAA Inspector Notes:** This little spot has a simple, yet smart, décor offering a little bit of everything to suit many palates. The traditional style menu features beautiful quality sushi and sashimi along with a range of such appetizers as lovely tempura or yakitori (teriyaki chicken), salads, noodle dishes and a few interesting cooked entrées including pork in ginger sauce and steak with sansho herbs. **Bar:** full bar. **Reservations:** suggested. **Address:** 1010 1 Ave NE T2E 7W7 **Location:** Just e of 9th St NE; in Bridgeland. **Parking:** street only. 🇱 🇩

SUSHI KAWA
403/802-0058 ㊷²

🍷🍷 Japanese. Casual Dining. $10-$20 **AAA Inspector Notes:** Fourth Street is a popular area for sushi restaurants, but what sets this one apart is the incredible and imaginative variety of appetizers and sushi platters. Patrons can try a vegetable sushi bowl—fresh vegetables atop sushi rice. Sushi pizza, vegetable gyozas and an incredible variety of other appetizers are pictured on the colorful menu, making decisions difficult. Sumo wrestling often is shown on the flat-screen TV and the décor is simple and contemporary. **Bar:** full bar. **Reservations:** suggested. **Address:** 2204 4th St SW T2S 1W9 **Location:** Jct 4th St SW and 22nd Ave. **Parking:** street only.
🇱 🇩

TASTE
403/233-7730 ㊼

🍷🍷🍷 Small Plates. Casual Dining. $12-$30 **AAA Inspector Notes:** This tiny and trendy spot utilizes very fine ingredients to prepare a delicious menu meant for sharing, so bring a friend or two. Each dish has a nifty presentation and changing choices could run from creamy chicken liver parfait, scallops with crunchy pancetta or daily meat, seafood and cheese platters. Service is casually competent and the small room means tight spacing so you might end up sharing one of the larger high tops. Lunch is more traditional but still with gourmet flair. **Bar:** full bar. **Address:** 1210 1st St SW T2R 0V4 **Location:** Between 12th and 13th aves SW. **Parking:** street only.
🇱 🇩 CALL 🖒M

(See map & index p. 67.)

TEATRO 403/290-1012 **39**

▼▼▼ New Italian. Fine Dining. $15-$52 **AAA Inspector Notes:** Located in the theater district, this upscale Italian trattoria is a great place to dine before a show, and many patrons consider it a top choice for a special event or first date. Featured several times on the Food Network, the chef will surprise and delight with many inventive creations. Whether diners are in the mood for seafood, pasta or meat dishes, they will find something exquisite to satisfy their appetite. **Bar:** full bar. **Reservations:** suggested. **Address:** 200 8th Ave SE T2G 0K7 **Location:** Corner of 8th Ave SE and 1st St SE. **Parking:** street only. ⃞L ⃞D CALL ⃞&M

THAI SA-ON RESTAURANT 403/264-3526 **45**

◆◆ Thai. Casual Dining. $15-$20 **AAA Inspector Notes:** Decorative presentation and good use of spices and condiments characterize offerings of well-prepared cuisine, including many vegetarian items. The quiet, casual ambience is enhanced by music and artwork from Thailand. **Bar:** full bar. **Reservations:** suggested. **Address:** 351 10th Ave SW T2R 0A5 **Location:** At 4th St SW; behind Gulf Canada Parkade. **Parking:** street only. ⃞L ⃞D

THOMSON'S RESTAURANT 403/537-4449 **37**

▼▼▼ American. Casual Dining. $14-$28 **AAA Inspector Notes:** The restaurant presents a varied menu of seafood, steaks and other regional meats. Guests can expect casual yet attentive service in the upscale dining room. A sumptuous breakfast buffet in addition to an a la carte menu is offered along with a Sunday brunch. **Bar:** full bar. **Reservations:** suggested. **Address:** 700 Centre St SE T2G 5P6 **Location:** Corner of Centre St and 7th Ave SW; in Hyatt Regency Calgary. ⃞B ⃞L ⃞D CALL ⃞&M

TRIB STEAKHOUSE 403/269-3160 **30**

▼▼▼ Steak. Casual Dining. $12-$40 **AAA Inspector Notes:** It is easy to walk right by this upscale restaurant so it is wise to keep focused to find the entrance. The kitchen showcases a good and creative variety of appetizers and salads with a focus on meats including AAA Alberta beef, double-cut pork chops, chicken and the specialty roasts which are great for sharing. Lighter fare includes seafood and pasta dishes. Service is proficient and professional. **Bar:** full bar. **Reservations:** suggested. **Address:** 118 8th Ave SW (Stephen Ave) T2E 0P5 **Location:** Just w of Centre Ave; center. **Parking:** street only. ⃞L ⃞D CALL ⃞&M

UNA PIZZA + WINE 403/453-1183 **60**

▼▼▼ Mediterranean Small Plates Pizza. Casual Dining. $10-$21 **AAA Inspector Notes:** This super trendy spot offers an inspired menu starting with walnut-stuffed dates wrapped in prosciutto or daily pintxo (a type of Spanish tapas). Larger portions include shrimp with chilies and Sambuca. The main events are the fabulous pizza creations like the fennel sausage, wilted radicchio, roasted garlic and provolone piccante along with a great selection of wine. Sorry, no reservations are accepted, but they will tweet your wait time on Twitter. **Bar:** full bar. **Address:** 618 17th Ave SW T2S 0B4 **Location:** Just w of 5th St SW. **Parking:** street only. ⃞L ⃞D ⃞LATE CALL ⃞&M

VINTAGE CHOPHOUSE & TAVERN 403/262-7262 **48**

▼▼▼ Steak. Fine Dining. $12-$39 **AAA Inspector Notes:** Set in a historic building, an upscale experience awaits with well-executed service by engaging servers at this fine steakhouse. Inside, the atmosphere is anything but historic with a large lounge catering to the after-work crowd while the dining room allows for a more leisurely meal. Well-prepared, hand-cut Prime Canadian steaks feature prominently on the menu, but diners also can find organic salmon or chicken, pasta dishes and a good range of seafood. Patrons must be 18 years old to enter. **Bar:** full bar. **Reservations:** suggested. **Address:** 322 11th Ave SW T2R 0C5 **Location:** Corner of 3rd St and 11th Ave SW. **Parking:** street only. ⃞L ⃞D CALL ⃞&M

WINEBAR KENSINGTON 403/457-1144 **3**

▼▼▼ Provincial American. Casual Dining. $12-$18 **AAA Inspector Notes:** This hip, unpretentious wine bar sits just below street level. Guests can sit at the bar of the open-concept kitchen and watch the chefs prepare tempting dishes. The knowledgeable staff can help choose from lovely cheeses, charcuterie and such creative items as sun-dried tomato-mascarpone ravioli and Spring Creek Ranch beef short ribs braised in espresso. Scrumptious desserts are worth the splurge. A carefully selected wine list is available. Reservations are not accepted. Must be 18 years old. **Bar:** full bar. **Address:** 1131 Kensington Rd NW T2N 3P4 **Location:** Just e of 10th St NW. **Parking:** street only. ⃞D ⃞LATE

CALGARY (H-6)
- **Restaurants p. 90**
- **Hotels & Restaurants map & index p. 72**

ACCLAIM HOTEL (403)291-8000 **2**

▼▼▼ Hotel $185-$195 **Address:** 123 Freeport Blvd NE T3N 0A3 **Location:** 1 mi (1.6 km) n of Calgary International Airport on Barlow Tr. **Facility:** 123 units. 4 stories, interior corridors. **Terms:** check-in 4 pm, cancellation fee imposed. **Amenities:** high-speed Internet, safes. **Dining:** Pacini Pasta & Grill Ristorante, see separate listing. **Activities:** whirlpools, exercise room. **Guest Services:** valet laundry. **Free Special Amenities:** high-speed Internet and airport transportation.

⃞SAVE ⃞ECO ⃞✈ ⃞¶¶ ⃞Ⓨ CALL ⃞&M ⃞BIZ ⃞🛜 ⃞✕ ⃞▭ / ⃞SOME UNITS ⃞🛏 ⃞🗄

BEST WESTERN AIRPORT INN (403)250-5015 **27**

◆◆ Hotel $126-$220 **AAA Benefit:** Members save up to 20%, plus 10% bonus points with Best Western Rewards®.

Address: 1947 18th Ave NE T2E 7T8 **Location:** 0.6 mi (1 km) e of jct Hwy 2 (Deerfoot Tr) and 16th Ave NE (Trans-Canada Hwy 1), just n on 19th St NE, then just w on 19th Ave NE. **Facility:** 76 units. 3 stories, interior corridors. **Parking:** winter plug-ins. **Amenities:** Some: high-speed Internet. **Pool(s):** heated indoor. **Activities:** whirlpool, exercise room. **Guest Services:** valet and coin laundry. **Free Special Amenities:** expanded continental breakfast and local telephone calls.

⃞SAVE ⃞ECO FEE⃞✈ ⃞¶¶ ⃞🏊 ⃞BIZ ⃞🛜 ⃞✕ ⃞📷 / ⃞SOME UNITS ⃞🛏 ⃞🗄

BEST WESTERN PLUS CALGARY CENTRE INN (403)287-3900 **32**

▼▼▼ Hotel $139-$279 **AAA Benefit:** Members save up to 20%, plus 10% bonus points with Best Western Rewards®.

Address: 3630 Macleod Tr S T2G 2P9 **Location:** East side of Hwy 2A (Macleod Tr) at 36th Ave SE. **Facility:** 71 units. 4 stories, interior corridors. **Parking:** winter plug-ins. **Amenities:** high-speed Internet. **Pool(s):** heated indoor. **Activities:** whirlpool, exercise room. **Guest Services:** valet and coin laundry. **Free Special Amenities:** full breakfast and room upgrade (subject to availability with advance reservations).

⃞SAVE ⃞🛖 ⃞BIZ ⃞🛜 ⃞▭ / ⃞SOME UNITS ⃞🛏 ⃞🗄

(See map & index p. 72.)

BEST WESTERN PLUS PORT O'CALL HOTEL
(403)291-4600

Hotel
$129-$199

AAA Benefit: Members save up to 20%, plus 10% bonus points with Best Western Rewards®.

Address: 1935 McKnight Blvd NE T2E 6V4 **Location:** 1.6 mi (2.5 km) ne of jct Hwy 2 (Deerfoot Tr); at 19th St NE. **Facility:** 201 units. 6-7 stories, interior corridors. **Amenities:** Some: high-speed Internet, safes. **Dining:** 2 restaurants. **Pool(s):** heated indoor. **Activities:** whirlpools, steamrooms, waterslide, exercise room. Fee: massage. **Guest Services:** valet laundry. **Free Special Amenities:** early check-in/late check-out and airport transportation.

BEST WESTERN PREMIER FREEPORT INN & SUITES
403/264-9650

Hotel
Rates not provided

AAA Benefit: Members save up to 20%, plus 10% bonus points with Best Western Rewards®.

Address: 86 Freeport Blvd NE T3J 5J9 **Location:** 1 mi (1.6 km) n of Calgary International Airport on Barlow Tr, just w. **Facility:** 97 units. 4 stories, interior corridors. **Parking:** winter plug-ins. **Amenities:** high-speed Internet, safes. **Pool(s):** heated indoor. **Activities:** whirlpool, waterslide, exercise room. **Guest Services:** valet and coin laundry. **Free Special Amenities: full breakfast and airport transportation.** (See ad this page.)

BEST WESTERN VILLAGE PARK INN
(403)289-0241

Hotel
$119-$199

AAA Benefit: Members save up to 20%, plus 10% bonus points with Best Western Rewards®.

Address: 1804 Crowchild Tr NW T2M 3Y7 **Location:** Just ne of jct Trans-Canada Hwy 1 and Crowchild Tr. Located in Motel Village. **Facility:** 160 units. 5 stories, interior corridors. **Terms:** cancellation fee imposed. **Amenities:** Some: safes. **Pool(s):** heated indoor. **Activities:** whirlpool, exercise room. **Guest Services:** valet and coin laundry. **Free Special Amenities:** local telephone calls and high-speed Internet.

CALGARY WESTWAYS GUEST HOUSE
(403)229-1758

Historic Bed & Breakfast $109-$180 **Address:** 216 25th Ave SW T2S 0L1 **Location:** 1.1 mi (1.7 km) s on Hwy 2A (Macleod Tr S), just w. Located in a residential area. **Facility:** This 1912 house has a third-floor addition where you will find original wood work in the living room and dining area. Room sizes vary with the top-floor units being the largest and most luxurious. 5 units. 3 stories (no elevator), interior corridors. **Parking:** winter plug-ins. **Terms:** 2 night minimum stay - seasonal, 4 day cancellation notice-fee imposed. **Amenities:** high-speed Internet. **Activities:** bicycles. **Guest Services:** complimentary laundry, area transportation (fee)-downtown.

CARRIAGE HOUSE INN
(403)253-1101

Hotel
$135-$249

Address: 9030 Macleod Tr S T2H 0M4 **Location:** On Hwy 2A (Macleod Tr); corner of 90th Ave SW. **Facility:** 157 units. 4-10 stories, interior corridors. **Parking:** winter plug-ins. **Amenities:** high-speed Internet. **Dining:** 3 restaurants. **Pool(s):** heated outdoor. **Activities:** saunas, whirlpool, exercise room. Fee: massage. **Guest Services:** valet laundry. **Free Special Amenities: full breakfast and high-speed Internet.**

▼ See AAA listing this page ▼

(See map & index p. 72.)

COAST PLAZA HOTEL & CONFERENCE CENTRE
(403)248-8888   **30**

▼▼▼▼ **Hotel** $99-$399 **Address:** 1316 33rd St NE T2A 6B6 **Location:** Just s of jct 16th Ave (Trans-Canada Hwy 1) and 36th St NE, just w on 12th Ave NE. Adjacent to Pacific Place Mall. **Facility:** 248 units. 6-12 stories, interior corridors. **Parking:** on-site and valet, winter plug-ins. **Terms:** cancellation fee imposed. **Amenities:** high-speed Internet. **Dining:** nightclub. **Pool(s):** heated indoor. **Activities:** sauna, whirlpool, exercise room. **Guest Services:** valet laundry.

COMFORT INN & SUITES-AIRPORT   (403)735-1966   **20**

Hotel
$100-$200

Address: 3111 26th St NE T1Y 7E4 **Location:** Just se of jct 32nd Ave NE and Barlow Tr NE. **Facility:** 74 units. 4 stories, interior corridors. **Parking:** winter plug-ins. **Terms:** cancellation fee imposed. **Amenities:** high-speed Internet, safes (fee). **Pool(s):** heated indoor. **Activities:** whirlpool, steamroom, waterslide, limited exercise equipment. **Guest Services:** valet and coin laundry. **Free Special Amenities: expanded continental breakfast and airport transportation.**

COMFORT INN & SUITES-SOUTH   (403)287-7070   **34**

▼▼▼ Hotel $110-$190

Address: 4611 Macleod Tr SW T2G 0A6 **Location:** Hwy 2A (Macleod Tr), w on 45th Ave. **Facility:** 93 units. 4 stories, interior corridors. **Parking:** winter plug-ins. **Terms:** cancellation fee imposed. **Amenities:** video games (fee), high-speed Internet, safes. **Pool(s):** heated indoor. **Activities:** whirlpool, waterslide, exercise room. **Guest Services:** valet and coin laundry. **Free Special Amenities: expanded continental breakfast and high-speed Internet.**

COUNTRY INN & SUITES BY CARLSON, CALGARY-AIRPORT   (403)250-1800   **12**

▼▼▼ Hotel $139-$249

Address: 2481 39th Ave NE T2E 8V8 **Location:** Barlow Tr and 39th Ave NE; access via 37th Ave. **Facility:** 106 units. 3 stories, interior corridors. **Parking:** winter plug-ins. **Amenities:** high-speed Internet. **Pool(s):** heated indoor. **Activities:** whirlpool, exercise room. **Guest Services:** valet and coin laundry. **Free Special Amenities: expanded continental breakfast and airport transportation.**

COURTYARD BY MARRIOTT CALGARY AIRPORT
(403)238-1000   **6**

▼▼▼ Hotel $129-$409

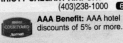
AAA Benefit: AAA hotel discounts of 5% or more.

Address: 2500 48th Ave NE T3J 4V8 **Location:** Just n of jct Barlow Tr NE and McKnight Blvd NE. **Facility:** 171 units. 6 stories, interior corridors. **Parking:** winter plug-ins. **Terms:** check-in 4 pm. **Amenities:** high-speed Internet, safes. **Pool(s):** heated indoor. **Activities:** exercise room. **Guest Services:** valet and coin laundry. **Free Special Amenities: high-speed Internet and airport transportation.**

DAYS INN CALGARY AIRPORT   (403)250-3297   **25**

▼▼▼ **Hotel** $140-$220 **Address:** 2799 Sunridge Way NE T1Y 7K7 **Location:** Barlow Tr, just e of Sunridge Way NE. **Facility:** 76 units. 4 stories, interior corridors. **Parking:** winter plug-ins. **Terms:** check-in 4 pm, 3 day cancellation notice-fee imposed. **Amenities:** Some: high-speed Internet. **Pool(s):** heated indoor. **Activities:** whirlpool, waterslide, exercise room. **Guest Services:** valet and coin laundry.

DELTA CALGARY AIRPORT   (403)291-2600   **3**

▼▼▼▼ **Hotel** $149-$409 **Address:** 2001 Airport Rd NE T2E 6Z8 **Location:** At Calgary International Airport. **Facility:** 296 units. 3-8 stories, interior corridors. **Parking:** on-site (fee) and valet. **Terms:** cancellation fee imposed. **Amenities:** Fee: video games, high-speed Internet. **Dining:** 2 restaurants. **Pool(s):** heated indoor. **Activities:** whirlpool, exercise room. **Guest Services:** valet laundry.

DELTA CALGARY SOUTH   (403)278-5050   **38**

▼▼▼▼ **Hotel** $109-$429 **Address:** 135 Southland Dr SE T2J 5X5 **Location:** On Hwy 2A (Macleod Tr); corner of Southland Dr. **Facility:** 252 units. 3-8 stories, interior corridors. **Parking:** winter plug-ins. **Terms:** cancellation fee imposed. **Dining:** 2 restaurants. **Pool(s):** 2 heated indoor. **Activities:** whirlpools, waterslide, exercise room. **Guest Services:** valet laundry.

ECONO LODGE INN & SUITES UNIVERSITY
(403)289-1921   **14**

▼▼▼ Motel $89-$199

Address: 2231 Banff Tr NW T2M 4L2 **Location:** Just n of jct 16th Ave NW (Trans-Canada Hwy 1) and Banff Tr NW. Located in Motel Village. **Facility:** 82 units, some two bedrooms, efficiencies and kitchens. 2-4 stories, interior/exterior corridors. **Parking:** winter plug-ins. **Terms:** cancellation fee imposed. **Pool(s):** heated indoor. **Activities:** whirlpool, exercise room. **Guest Services:** coin laundry. **Free Special Amenities: continental breakfast and high-speed Internet.**

ECONO LODGE MOTEL VILLAGE   (403)289-2561   **18**

▼▼▼ Motel $70-$109

Address: 2440 16th Ave NW T2M 0M5 **Location:** Jct 16th Ave NW (Trans-Canada Hwy 1) and Banff Tr NW. Located in Motel Village. **Facility:** 56 units, some two bedrooms and efficiencies. 2 stories (no elevator), interior/exterior corridors. **Parking:** winter plug-ins. **Terms:** cancellation fee imposed. **Activities:** sauna, limited exercise equipment. **Guest Services:** coin laundry. **Free Special Amenities: continental breakfast and high-speed Internet.**

ECONO LODGE SOUTH   (403)252-4401   **36**

▼▼▼ Motel $90-$130

Address: 7505 Macleod Tr SW T2H 0L8 **Location:** Corner of Hwy 2A (Macleod Tr) and 75th Ave. **Facility:** 73 units, some efficiencies and kitchens. 2 stories (no elevator), interior/exterior corridors. **Parking:** winter plug-ins. **Terms:** cancellation fee imposed. **Pool(s):** heated indoor. **Activities:** whirlpool, limited exercise equipment. **Guest Services:** coin laundry. **Free Special Amenities: continental breakfast and high-speed Internet.**

EXECUTIVE ROYAL HOTEL NORTH CALGARY
(403)291-2003   **22**

▼▼▼▼ **Hotel** $104-$220 **Address:** 2828 23rd St NE T2E 8T4 **Location:** Barlow Tr NE, just w; at 27th Ave NE. **Facility:** 200 units. 6 stories, interior corridors. **Parking:** winter plug-ins. **Terms:** check-in 4 pm, cancellation fee imposed. **Amenities:** high-speed Internet. **Activities:** whirlpools, steamrooms, exercise room. **Guest Services:** valet laundry.

(See map & index p. 72.)

FOUR POINTS BY SHERATON CALGARY AIRPORT
(403)648-3180 26

Hotel
$119-$299

AAA Benefit: Members get up to 20% off, plus Starwood Preferred Guest® bonuses.

Address: 2875 Sunridge Way NE T1Y 7K7 **Location:** Jct Trans-Canada Hwy 1 and Barlow Tr NE, 0.6 mi (1 km) n, then just e. **Facility:** 159 units, some two bedrooms. 7 stories, interior corridors. **Parking:** winter plug-ins. **Terms:** cancellation fee imposed. **Amenities:** high-speed Internet, safes. **Dining:** Ric's Lounge & Grill, see separate listing. **Pool(s):** heated indoor. **Activities:** sauna, whirlpool, steamroom, exercise room, spa. **Guest Services:** valet and coin laundry. **Free Special Amenities: high-speed Internet and airport transportation.**

FOUR POINTS BY SHERATON HOTEL AND SUITES, CALGARY WEST
(403)288-4441 4

Hotel
$159-$429

AAA Benefit: Members get up to 20% off, plus Starwood Preferred Guest® bonuses.

Address: 8220 Bowridge Crescent NW T3B 2V1 **Location:** Opposite Canada Olympic Park. **Facility:** 150 units. 4 stories, interior corridors. **Parking:** winter plug-ins. **Terms:** cancellation fee imposed. **Amenities:** high-speed Internet, safes. **Pool(s):** heated indoor. **Activities:** whirlpool, waterslide, exercise room, spa. **Guest Services:** valet and coin laundry. **Free Special Amenities: local telephone calls and high-speed Internet.**

HAMPTON INN & SUITES CALGARY UNIVERSITY NW
(403)289-9800 16

Hotel
$129-$319

AAA Benefit: Members save up to 10%!

Address: 2231 Banff Tr NW T2M 4L2 **Location:** Just n of jct 16th Ave NW (Trans-Canada Hwy 1). **Facility:** 96 units, some efficiencies. 4 stories, interior corridors. **Terms:** 1-7 night minimum stay, cancellation fee imposed. **Pool(s):** heated indoor. **Activities:** whirlpool, waterslide, exercise room. **Guest Services:** valet and coin laundry. **Free Special Amenities: expanded continental breakfast and high-speed Internet.** (See ad p. 89.)

HILTON GARDEN INN-CALGARY AIRPORT
(403)717-1999 8

Hotel $129-$209 **Address:** 2335 Pegasus Rd NE T2E 8C3 **Location:** Jct Barlow Tr and McKnight Blvd, just w, n on 19th St NE, then just e. **Facility:** 135 units. 5 stories, interior corridors. **Parking:** winter plug-ins. **Terms:** 1-7 night minimum stay, cancellation fee imposed. **Amenities:** high-speed Internet. **Pool(s):** heated indoor. **Activities:** whirlpool, exercise room. **Guest Services:** valet and coin laundry, area transportation-within 3 mi (4.8 km).

AAA Benefit: Unparalleled hospitality at a special Member rate.

HOLIDAY INN CALGARY-AIRPORT
(403)230-1999 29

Hotel $120-$160 **Address:** 1250 McKinnon Dr NE T2E 7T7 **Location:** 0.6 mi (1 km) e of jct Hwy 2 (Deerfoot Tr) and 16th Ave NE (Trans-Canada Hwy 1). **Facility:** 168 units. 5 stories, interior corridors. **Parking:** winter plug-ins. **Terms:** cancellation fee imposed, resort fee. **Amenities:** video games (fee), high-speed Internet. **Pool(s):** heated indoor. **Activities:** whirlpool, exercise room. **Guest Services:** valet and coin laundry.

HOLIDAY INN CALGARY-MACLEOD TRAIL SOUTH
(403)287-2700 33

Hotel $119-$269

Address: 4206 Macleod Tr S Tr S T2G 2R7 **Location:** Corner of 42nd Ave SW and Macleod Tr S. **Facility:** 151 units. 4 stories, interior corridors. **Parking:** winter plug-ins. **Terms:** cancellation fee imposed. **Amenities:** high-speed Internet. **Pool(s):** heated indoor. **Activities:** exercise room. **Guest Services:** valet and coin laundry.

HOLIDAY INN EXPRESS AIRPORT CALGARY
(403)769-1888 9

Hotel $115-$155 **Address:** 45 Hopewell Way NE T3J 4V7 **Location:** Jct Barlow Tr NE and McKnight Blvd NE, just n, then just e. Located in an industrial area. **Facility:** 101 units, some two bedrooms. 4 stories, interior corridors. **Parking:** winter plug-ins. **Terms:** check-in 4 pm, cancellation fee imposed. **Amenities:** high-speed Internet. **Pool(s):** heated indoor. **Activities:** whirlpool, waterslide, exercise room. **Guest Services:** valet and coin laundry.

HOLIDAY INN EXPRESS HOTEL & SUITES CALGARY-SOUTH
(403)225-3000 39

Hotel $139-$259 **Address:** 12025 Lake Fraser Dr SE (Macleod Tr S) T2J 7G5 **Location:** Hwy 2 (Deerfoot Tr) exit Anderson Rd W, just s on Macleod Tr, just e on Lake Fraser Gate, then 0.4 mi (0.7 km) n. **Facility:** 105 units. 4 stories, interior corridors. **Parking:** winter plug-ins. **Terms:** check-in 4 pm, cancellation fee imposed, resort fee. **Amenities:** video games (fee), high-speed Internet. **Pool(s):** heated indoor. **Activities:** whirlpool, waterslide, exercise room. **Guest Services:** valet and coin laundry.

HOTEL BLACKFOOT
(403)252-2253 35

Hotel $119-$289 **Address:** 5940 Blackfoot Tr SE T2H 2B5 **Location:** At 58th Ave SE. Access to property from 58th Ave only. **Facility:** 200 units. 7 stories, interior corridors. **Terms:** cancellation fee imposed. **Amenities:** Some: safes. **Dining:** 4 restaurants, nightclub. **Pool(s):** heated outdoor. **Activities:** whirlpool, steamroom, exercise room. **Guest Services:** valet laundry.

LAKEVIEW SIGNATURE INN
(403)735-3336 11

Hotel $140-$310

Address: 2622 39th Ave NE T1Y 7J9 **Location:** Barlow Tr NE, just e. **Facility:** 120 units, some two bedrooms, efficiencies and kitchens. 4 stories, interior corridors. **Parking:** winter plug-ins. **Amenities:** high-speed Internet. **Pool(s):** heated indoor. **Activities:** whirlpool, sports court, exercise room. **Guest Services:** valet and coin laundry, area transportation-within 2 mi (3.2 km). **Free Special Amenities: expanded continental breakfast and high-speed Internet.**

(See map & index p. 72.)

QUALITY INN UNIVERSITY 403/289-1973

fyi **Hotel.** Rates not provided. Under major renovation, scheduled to be completed February 2013. **Last Rated:** ♥♥♥ **Address:** 2359 Banff Tr NW T2M 4L2 **Location:** Just n of jct Trans-Canada Hwy 1 and Crowchild Tr. Located in Motel Village. **Facility:** 105 units. 2 stories, interior corridors. **Parking:** winter plug-ins. **Terms:** check-in 4 pm. **Amenities:** safes. **Pool(s):** heated indoor. **Activities:** exercise room, spa. *Fee:* game room. **Guest Services:** valet and coin laundry.

RADISSON HOTEL CALGARY AIRPORT
(403)291-4666

♥♥♥♥
Hotel
$129-$299

Address: 2120 16th Ave NE T2E 1L4 **Location:** Just e of jct 16th Ave NE (Trans-Canada Hwy 1) and Hwy 2 (Deerfoot Tr). **Facility:** 184 units. 10 stories, interior corridors. **Parking:** winter plug-ins. **Terms:** cancellation fee imposed. **Amenities:** high-speed Internet. **Pool(s):** heated indoor. **Activities:** whirlpool, exercise room. **Guest Services:** valet laundry. **Free Special Amenities:** local telephone calls and newspaper.

▼ See AAA listing p. 88 ▼

10% OFF
Published Rates

located at the intersection of good savings and great value.

No matter where you travel, there is always a clean and cozy Hampton in town.

Our strong partnership with AAA allows us to offer special rates* to all AAA members.

FREE
hot breakfast

clean and fresh
Hampton bed™

FREE high-speed
internet access

friendly
service

show your card
and save

Hampton Inn & Suites
Calgary University NW
2231 Banff Tr NW, Calgary AB T2M 4L2 CAN
(403) 289-9800 | 888-432-6777
www.hamptoncalgary.com

(See map & index p. 72.)

RESIDENCE INN BY MARRIOTT CALGARY AIRPORT
(403)278-1000

Extended Stay Hotel
$139-$419

AAA Benefit: AAA hotel discounts of 5% or more.

Address: 2530 48th Ave NE T3J 4V8 **Location:** Just n of jct Barlow Tr NE and McKnight Blvd NE. **Facility:** 157 units, some two bedrooms, efficiencies and kitchens. 6 stories, interior corridors. **Parking:** winter plug-ins. **Terms:** check-in 4 pm. **Amenities:** high-speed Internet, safes. **Pool(s):** heated indoor. **Activities:** exercise room. **Guest Services:** valet and coin laundry. **Free Special Amenities: full breakfast and high-speed Internet.**

SANDMAN HOTEL SUITES & SPA CALGARY AIRPORT
(403)219-2475

Hotel $129-$219 **Address:** 25 Hopewell Way NE T3J 4V7 **Location:** Just n of jct Barlow Tr and McKnight Blvd. **Facility:** 177 units. 4 stories (no elevator), interior corridors. **Parking:** winter plug-ins. **Terms:** check-in 4 pm. **Amenities:** high-speed Internet. **Pool(s):** heated indoor. **Activities:** whirlpool, exercise room. **Guest Services:** valet laundry.

SERVICE PLUS INN & SUITES CALGARY
(403)256-5352

Hotel $129-$149

Address: 3503 114th Ave SE T2Z 3X2 **Location:** South end of Barlow Tr, just w. Located in an industrial area. **Facility:** 139 units. 4 stories, interior corridors. **Parking:** winter plug-ins. **Terms:** cancellation fee imposed. **Amenities:** high-speed Internet. **Pool(s):** heated indoor. **Activities:** whirlpool, waterslide, exercise room. **Guest Services:** valet laundry, area transportation-Deerfoot Casino. **Free Special Amenities: full breakfast and manager's reception.**

SHERATON CAVALIER HOTEL
(403)291-0107

Hotel $139-$469

 Sheraton HOTELS & RESORTS

AAA Benefit: Members get up to 20% off, plus Starwood Preferred Guest® bonuses.

Address: 2620 32nd Ave NE T1Y 6B8 **Location:** Barlow Tr at 32nd Ave NE. **Facility:** 305 units. 7 stories, interior corridors. **Parking:** on-site and valet, winter plug-ins. **Terms:** cancellation fee imposed, resort fee. **Amenities:** high-speed Internet. Some: safes. **Dining:** 2 restaurants, also, Carver's Steakhouse, see separate listing. **Pool(s):** heated indoor. **Activities:** sauna, whirlpools, waterslide, exercise room. **Guest Services:** valet laundry. **Free Special Amenities: airport transportation.**

Traveling With Your Pet?
AAA.com/PetBook

STAYBRIDGE SUITES CALGARY AIRPORT
(403)204-7829

Extended Stay Hotel
$169-$269

Address: 2825 Sunridge Way NE T1Y 7K7 **Location:** Trans-Canada Hwy 1 exit Barlow Tr NE, just n, then just e. **Facility:** 96 efficiencies, some two bedrooms. 4 stories, interior corridors. **Parking:** winter plug-ins. **Terms:** resort fee. **Amenities:** high-speed Internet. **Pool(s):** heated indoor. **Activities:** whirlpool, waterslide, sports court, exercise room. **Guest Services:** complimentary and valet laundry. **Free Special Amenities: full breakfast and airport transportation.**

SUPER 8 CALGARY AIRPORT
(403)291-9888

Hotel $99-$219

Address: 3030 Barlow Tr NE T1Y 1A2 **Location:** Corner of 32nd Ave and Barlow Tr NE. **Facility:** 61 units. 4 stories, interior corridors. **Parking:** winter plug-ins. **Terms:** cancellation fee imposed. **Amenities:** safes (fee). **Guest Services:** valet and coin laundry. **Free Special Amenities: continental breakfast and airport transportation.**

TRAVELODGE CALGARY UNIVERSITY
(403)289-6600

Hotel $109-$199

Address: 2227 Banff Tr NW T2M 4L2 **Location:** 16th Ave NW (Trans-Canada Hwy 1) and Banff Tr NW. Located in Motel Village across from McMahon Stadium. **Facility:** 64 units. 3 stories, interior corridors. **Parking:** winter plug-ins. **Pool(s):** heated outdoor. **Activities:** exercise room. **Guest Services:** valet laundry. **Free Special Amenities: expanded continental breakfast and high-speed Internet.**

TRAVELODGE HOTEL CALGARY AIRPORT
(403)291-1260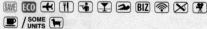

Hotel $113-$300

Address: 2750 Sunridge Blvd NE T1Y 3C2 **Location:** Just se of jct 32nd Ave NE and Barlow Tr NE. **Facility:** 203 units. 6 stories, interior corridors. **Parking:** winter plug-ins. **Amenities:** video games (fee), high-speed Internet. **Pool(s):** heated indoor. **Activities:** exercise room. **Guest Services:** valet and coin laundry.

WINGATE BY WYNDHAM CALGARY
(403)514-0099 ④1

Hotel $129-$309 **Address:** 400 Midpark Way SE T2X 3S4 **Location:** Hwy 2A (Macleod Tr), 0.3 mi (0.5 km) e on Sun Valley Blvd SE, just n on Midpark Blvd SE, then just s. **Facility:** 103 units. 4 stories, interior corridors. **Parking:** winter plug-ins. **Terms:** cancellation fee imposed. **Amenities:** video games (fee), high-speed Internet, safes. **Pool(s):** heated indoor. **Activities:** whirlpool, waterslide, exercise room. **Guest Services:** valet and coin laundry.

WHERE TO EAT

ALBERTA KING OF SUBS
403/293-5809 ⑥

Canadian. Quick Serve. $5-$14 **AAA Inspector Notes:** Montreal-style smoked-meat sandwiches and hot grilled subs are specialties at this strip mall eatery, which has only nine tables and a counter. French fries, poutine and coleslaw also are on the menu. Service is friendly and polite. **Bar:** beer only. **Address:** 7196 Temple Dr NE, #22 T1Y 4E8 **Location:** Jct McKnight Blvd and 52nd St NE, just s on 52nd St NE. L D

(See map & index p. 72.)

ALLOY
403/287-9255 **34**

▼▼▼ New International. Fine Dining. $14-$35 **AAA Inspector Notes:** Diners can expect proficient and attentive service at this fine dining spot. A creative Asian flair menu with Mediterranean and Latin twists from the combined backgrounds of the two owner/chefs is presented. The ultra fresh ingredients translate into such items as Mumbai vegetarian empanadas with mango-mint ceviche salad to start. Entrées might include a trio of lamb with pistachio pesto and vegetable ragout or wasabi crusted ahi tuna with carrot ginger mousse. Closed for lunch on the weekend. **Bar:** full bar. **Reservations:** suggested. **Address:** 220 42 Ave S T2G 1Y4 **Location:** Just e of Macleod Tr S. L D CALL &M

BAGOLAC SAIGON RESTAURANT
403/252-5588 **37**

▼▼ Vietnamese. Casual Dining. $9-$22 **AAA Inspector Notes:** Modern décor awaits at this Vietnamese restaurant, where a mixture of Thai and Vietnamese dishes coexist on the menu. The selection is so outstanding that diners may have a hard time selecting. It is best to order a variety of dishes to truly experience the tastes and flavors, starting with rice wrappers, green papaya salad or noodle soup. **Bar:** full bar. **Address:** 6130 1A St SW, #8 T2H 0G3 **Location:** Just e off Macleod Tr; near Chinook Centre. L D

BEARS DEN
403/241-7611

▼▼▼ Regional Canadian. Fine Dining. $30-$44 **AAA Inspector Notes:** A bit of a drive from downtown, this bunker-looking complex at the edge of the city limits offers a number of surprises. Following in the tradition of legendary steakhouses, this spot offers a rich and warmly luxurious set of dining rooms reminiscent of an old gentleman's club. Accents include dark wood paneling, hand-crafted murals and beautiful fireplaces. In addition to preparing some of the finest cuts of AAA Alberta beef, this place also puts together satisfying non-steak dishes. **Bar:** full bar. **Reservations:** suggested. **Address:** 254028 Bearspaw Rd NW T3L 2P7 **Location:** 1.2 mi (2 km) w of jct Stoney Tr; along Hwy 1A (Crowchild Tr). D CALL &M

BELMONT DINER
403/242-6782 **33**

▼ Canadian. Casual Dining. $9-$15 **AAA Inspector Notes:** Diners in search of a hearty breakfast need look no further than this Marda Loop diner. At lunchtime, sandwiches and milkshakes are popular choices. **Address:** 2008 33rd Ave SW T2T 1Z6 **Location:** At 33rd Ave and 20th St; in Marda Loop. **Parking:** street only.

B L CALL &M

BIG FISH
403/277-3403 **21**

▼▼▼ Seafood. Casual Dining. $14-$30 **AAA Inspector Notes:** Not a run of the mill seafood joint, the chef sources sustainable fish and seafood and supports local growers. A tasty menu covers starters like salt and pepper frog legs or green curry steamed mussels. Entrées include saffron seafood stew, Arctic char with blueberry barbecue sauce or New York steak with blue crab cake. An original lovely blue hued abstract piece is a focal point in the smart casual space. Service is both knowledgeable and complementary. **Bar:** full bar. **Reservations:** suggested. **Address:** 1112 Edmonton Tr NE T2E 3K4 **Location:** Jct Memorial Dr, 0.8 mi (1.3 km) n. **Parking:** on-site and valet. L D

BIG T'S BBQ
403/284-5959 **7**

▼▼ Barbecue. Casual Dining. $8-$29 **AAA Inspector Notes:** Southern barbecue at its messiest is the name of the game at this casual restaurant, where enormous portions will satisfy even the hungriest diner. **Bar:** full bar. **Address:** 2138 Crowchild Tr NW T2M 3Y7 **Location:** Jct 23 Ave NW; across from McMann Stadium.

L D CALL &M

BOCCAVINO LOUNGE & GRILL
403/276-2030 **14**

▼▼ Italian. Casual Dining. $10-$23 **AAA Inspector Notes:** An addition to the hugely popular Lina's Italian Market, this bistro like spot has an eclectic décor with a mix of sports memorabilia, Italian art and big screen TVs. While the focus is on good fresh Italian cuisine with your classic soups, salads, pastas, risottos, pizza, panini, steaks and veal, chicken and fish dishes they also dish up a few pub snack favorites. **Bar:** full bar. **Address:** 2220 Centre St NE T2E 2T5 **Location:** 0.3 mi (0.5 km) n of jct 16th Ave (Trans-Canada Hwy 1).

L D CALL &M

BOOGIE'S BURGERS
403/230-7070 **22**

▼ Burgers. Quick Serve. $5-$16 **AAA Inspector Notes:** A favorite neighborhood haunt, this burger joint whips up creamy milkshakes, huge burgers and crispy fries. Guests can grab a seat at the counter or, in the summer, enjoy a shake at a picnic table. Seating is at a premium at this popular diner, which features vintage photos and decor. Expect fast, friendly service from the South African owners, who holler out orders or prepare them in rapid time for take-out. Those with hearty appetites should try the half-pound, homemade, charbroiled burger. **Bar:** beer & wine. **Address:** 908 Edmonton Tr NE T2E 3K1 **Location:** Corner of 8th Ave NE. L D

BROKEN PLATE KITCHEN & BAR
403/225-9650 **42**

▼▼ Greek. Casual Dining. $10-$32 **AAA Inspector Notes:** While guests are not encouraged to actually throw plates on the ground after eating, it is not unusual to throw hands up in the air and shout "opa!" after enjoying Greek dishes made from fresh and authentic ingredients. This restaurant boasts a contemporary decor while offering all the classics, adding their own little twists. Fasolata salad with green beans, kalamata olives and fennel, "feta"ccini with Greek-style meatballs and Arctic char with spinach feta risotto are just a few specialties. **Bar:** full bar. **Address:** 590-10816 Macleod Tr SE T2J 5N8 **Location:** Just n of Anderson Rd; west side of Willow Park Shopping Plaza. L D CALL &M

BUFFET YANGTZE
403/275-3337 **2**

▼ Chinese. Cafeteria. $11-$19 **AAA Inspector Notes:** In the Deerfoot Crossing outlet mall, this unassuming restaurant is a bit of a drive from most hotels, especially during rush time. However, the navigation skills that come in handy on the Deerfoot Expressway also prove useful in negotiating the vast Chinese buffet. Food is refreshed regularly for the hungry patrons who loyally frequent this place. **Bar:** full bar. **Address:** 901 64th Ave NW T2E 7P4 **Location:** At north entrance of Deerfoot Mall. L D

CACTUS CLUB CAFE

▼▼▼ New American. Casual Dining. $11-$37 **AAA Inspector Notes:** This bustling, casual restaurant serves huge burgers, sandwiches, pasta, salads, soups, quesadillas, fajitas, vegetarian dishes, steak, ribs, chicken and fish. Featured are certified Angus beef and fresh wild British Columbia salmon. **Bar:** full bar.

L D LATE CALL &M

For additional information, visit AAA.com

LOCATIONS:

Address: 2612 39th Ave NE T1Y 7S9 **Location:** Barlow Tr at 39th Ave NE. **Phone:** 403/250-1120

Address: 7010 Macleod Tr SE T2H 0L3 **Location:** Jct Glenmore Tr SW, just s. **Phone:** 403/255-1088

CANDELA LOUNGE
403/719-0049

▼▼▼ Latin American Small Plates. Casual Dining. $18-$30 **AAA Inspector Notes:** This attractive restaurant offers a true tapas menu sticking strictly to a variety of imaginative small plates. The delicious and affordable cuisine has a definite slant toward South American influences which are reflected in the design featuring a green-and-white-pattern ceramic-tile floor. The open space conveys both an airiness and coziness making it a great spot to spend some time. The wine list is eclectic with some delicious good value glass pours to complement the food. **Bar:** full bar. **Address:** 1919 4th St SW T2S 1W4 **Location:** Corner of 20th Ave SW. **Parking:** on-site and street. L D LATE CALL &M

CAPTAIN SCOTT'S FISH & CHIPS
403/280-0009 **4**

▼ Seafood. Family Dining. $7-$15 **AAA Inspector Notes:** With its location in the far northeast of landlocked Calgary, this eatery does a pretty good imitation of an East Coast fish and chips shop. While the fish is not wrapped in newspaper for take-out, guests enjoy a good selection of deep-fried fish with a tasty batter in the modest, nautically themed restaurant. **Bar:** beer only. **Address:** 55 Castleridge Dr NE, #76 T3J 1Y9 **Location:** Jct 52nd St NE (Falconridge Blvd NE) and McKnight Blvd NE; in Castleridge Plaza.

L D

(See map & index p. 72.)

CARVER'S STEAKHOUSE
403/250-6327 12

▼▼▼ Steak. Fine Dining. $28-$47 **AAA Inspector Notes:** One of Calgary's finest steak houses, this is the place to go for aged AAA Alberta beef. In the contemporary, upscale dining room you'll feast on superb steak. On the menu you may also find bison, wild boar, salmon or halibut preparations, as well as decadent desserts. Tableside presentations include Châteaubriand and Caesar salad for two. **Bar:** full bar. **Reservations:** suggested. **Address:** 2620 32nd Ave NE T1Y 6B8 **Location:** Barlow Tr at 32nd Ave NE; in Sheraton Cavalier Hotel. **Parking:** on-site and valet. D

THE CHEESECAKE CAFE
403/255-7443

▼▼ American. Casual Dining. $12-$30 **AAA Inspector Notes:** As might be expected, cheesecake is the cafe's signature item, and lip-smacking varieties are made on the premises. A huge dessert display case greets guests upon arrival. Offerings on the extensive lunch and dinner menu range from sandwiches and entree salads to pasta, pizza and seafood selections. It takes a while to get through the menu. **Bar:** full bar. **Address:** 7600 Macleod Tr SE T2H 0L9 **Location:** Just s of jct Glenmore Tr. L D

THE CHEESECAKE CAFE
403/247-2407

▼▼ American. Casual Dining. $12-$30 **AAA Inspector Notes:** The signature items at The Cheesecake Cafe, not surprisingly, are the tempting homemade cheesecakes, which beckon from a display case near the entry. Expect to be overwhelmed by the lengthy menu, which lists lunch and dinner options ranging from sandwiches and entrée salads to pasta, pizza and seafood selections. **Bar:** full bar. **Address:** 5615 Northland Dr NW T2L 2J7 **Location:** Jct Shaganappi Tr NW, just s. L D CALL ⑤M

DINER DELUXE
403/276-5499 24

▼▼ American Comfort Food. Family Dining. $10-$20 **AAA Inspector Notes:** Everything old is new again, and such is the case at this funky retro diner, where all-day breakfasts are made with gourmet and specialty ingredients. The nostalgic atmosphere is complete with '50s-style Formica countertops, boldly colored vinyl chairs, tall milkshakes and hearty burgers. Friendly servers are quick and knowledgeable and offer great detail about the various dishes. **Bar:** full bar. **Address:** 804 Edmonton Tr NE T2E 3J6 **Location:** Corner of Edmonton Tr NE and 7th Ave NE. **Parking:** street only.
B L D

EARLS RESTAURANT

▼▼ American. Casual Dining. $10-$35 **AAA Inspector Notes:** Offering an experience that falls between fast food and fine dining, the fun, relaxed restaurant prepares great food at a great price. Choices range from juicy burgers, hearty sandwiches, fresh salads, wings and pizza to full entrees of steak, chops and seafood. Made-from-scratch soups and assorted breads, as well as a nice choice of wines and beers, round out the offerings. This is a fitting spot for impromptu get-togethers and festive occasions. **Bar:** full bar.
L D LATE

For additional information, visit AAA.com
LOCATIONS:
Address: 3030 23rd St NE T2E 8R7 **Location:** Jct 32nd Ave NE and Barlow Tr NE. **Phone:** 403/291-6700
Address: 1110 16th Ave NW T2M 0K8 **Location:** Jct 11th St NW. **Phone:** 403/289-2566

FIRE KIRIN
403/278-8018 43

▼▼▼ Asian. Casual Dining. $9-$22 **AAA Inspector Notes:** A modern design with comfortable booths and high-back, rattan-style chairs can be found here along with dishes from Vietnam, China, Korea, Japan and Thailand. Appetizers include tempura, lettuce wraps and such soups as coconut pumpkin and tom yum goong. Entrées run the gamut from rock and roll mussels with a choice of sauce and lemon grass chicken to white miso salmon and a variety of rice and noodle dishes. Expect items to be cooked to order and dished up by friendly servers. **Bar:** full bar. **Reservations:** suggested. **Address:** 12101 Lake Fraser Dr SE, #500 T2J 7G4 **Location:** Hwy 2 (Deerfoot Tr) exit Anderson Rd W, just s on Macleod Tr, just e on Lake Fraser Gate, then 0.4 mi (0.7 km) n. L D CALL ⑤M

FORBIDDEN CITY SEAFOOD & DIM SUM RESTAURANT
403/250-1848 26

▼▼▼ Chinese. Casual Dining. $4-$20 **AAA Inspector Notes:** The large, contemporary restaurant serves all the classic Chinese dishes, and lunch is extremely busy thanks to the dim sum offerings. Best enjoyed with a group of people, dim sum includes dozens of items, from steamed shrimp dumplings and crepes to fried rice dishes. Service is quick and efficient, and the atmosphere is bustling. **Bar:** full bar. **Address:** 220 Pacific Pl, 999 36th St NE T2A 7X6 **Location:** 16th Ave NE (Trans-Canada Hwy 1) exit 36th St E, just s; in Pacific Place Shopping Plaza. L D

GLOBEFISH SUSHI & IZAKAYA
403/457-1500 38

▼▼▼ Sushi. Casual Dining. $15-$25 **AAA Inspector Notes:** This is a small, modern design restaurant with cozy booth and banquette seating. The menu is great for a group of people since they have dozens of appetizers to enjoy ranging from gyoza, sunomono salad, miso butter mussels and wasabi beef to a nice selection of sushi and sashimi as well as some very creative rolls. Also available are some donburi rice and udon noodle dishes. **Bar:** full bar. **Address:** 6455 Macleod Tr SW, #0130 T2H 0K3 **Location:** At Chinook Centre Mall; next to Shoppers Drug Mart. L D

GUS'S CAFE & PIZZERIA
403/282-4005 8

▼▼▼ Pizza. Family Dining. $8-$16 **AAA Inspector Notes:** Stop at this family-run restaurant located just off Trans-Canada Highway 1 near the hospital. You'll be treated to simply good food. Although the specialty is pizza, you'll find a variety of other items on the menu, including soup, salads, quesadillas and pasta. Service is quick and prompt, and if you become a regular, don't be surprised if the owner sits and chats with you. **Bar:** full bar. **Address:** 1620 29th St NW, #180 T2W 4L7 **Location:** 16th Ave NW (Trans-Canada Hwy 1), just s at 29th St NW. L D CALL ⑤M

JACQUELINE SUZANNE'S BISTRO & ANTIQUITIES
403/266-1005 31

▼▼ International. Casual Dining. $13-$40 **AAA Inspector Notes:** Set in a 1912 building with original tin ceilings, there is a whimsical feel to the décor of this restaurant with lace fabric and damask linens. The menu is quite traditional with such starters as smoked salmon and escargot. Choose from an interesting selection of salads and entrées including seafood linguine, rack of lamb, jambalaya and beef tenderloin. Service is very hospitable and welcoming. An unusual note is the list of jewelry for sale on the back of the menu. **Bar:** full bar. **Reservations:** suggested. **Address:** 1219 9th Ave SE T2G 0S9 **Location:** Between 11th and 12th sts SE; in Inglewood. **Parking:** street only. L D

JAMESONS IRISH PUB
403/285-1608 19

▼▼ Irish. Casual Dining. $8-$15 **AAA Inspector Notes:** Just across from Sunridge Mall, this Irish pub welcomes travelers from around the globe. The restaurant offers a lively atmosphere, friendly service and live entertainment, as well as an extensive menu of both pub and Irish favorites. The selection of on-tap Irish beers is excellent. **Bar:** full bar. **Address:** 3575 20th Ave NE T1Y 6R3 **Location:** Jct 36th St NE; across from Sunridge Mall. L D LATE CALL ⑤M

JAMESONS PUB
403/220-9888 3

▼▼ American. Casual Dining. $10-$19 **AAA Inspector Notes:** This casual and lively restaurant and Irish pub presents a menu of comfort foods, including fish and chips, corned beef sandwiches, shepherd's pie, burgers, wraps and Philly cheese melts. Also offered are chicken teriyaki noodles, maple-glazed salmon, pasta dishes, steaks, baby back ribs, fried pickles, calamari and thin-crust pizzas. Guests may sit at tables in the center pub area or off to the sides in comfortable booths. Breakfast is served late on weekends. **Bar:** full bar. **Address:** 3790 Brentwood Rd NW T2L 1K8 **Location:** Just nw of Crowchild Tr and 32nd Ave NW; in Brentwood Village Mall. L D LATE

JIMMY'S A & A DELI
403/289-1400 11

▼ Mediterranean Deli. Quick Serve. $7-$12 **AAA Inspector Notes:** It is a little out of the way from some parts of the city, but this is, without a doubt, one of the best shawarmas and donair spots in Calgary and well worth a little drive for the flavorful and juicy sandwiches. There also is a great selection of samosas, fatyre, salads, dips and a super olive and feta bar. As if it could not get any better it also is the go-to spot for a very good variety of some of the best baklava ever. A steep set of stairs leads to a small table area. **Address:** 1401 20th Ave NW T2M 1G6 **Location:** Corner of 13th St NW. **Parking:** street only. L D 🅇

(See map & index p. 72.)

JOEY RESTAURANTS

WW American. Casual Dining. $13-$35 **AAA Inspector Notes:** The cuisine blends Mediterranean and Asian cooking styles and emphasizes finger foods for sharing. Those who aren't big fans of tapas can consider full meal offerings centered on steaks and chops. **Bar:** full bar. L D LATE

For additional information, visit AAA.com

LOCATIONS:

Address: 3026 23rd St NE T2E 8R7 **Location:** At Barlow Tr, just w of 26th St NE. **Phone:** 403/219-8465

Address: 50 Crowfoot Way NW T3G 4C8 **Location:** Just nw of Nose Hill Dr NW and Ranchlands Blvd NW. **Phone:** 403/547-5639

Address: 6455 Macleod Tr SW, #100A T2H 0K8 **Location:** At Chinook Centre Mall. **Phone:** 403/692-6626

JUREE'S THAI PLACE RESTAURANT 403/264-6477 13

WW Thai. Casual Dining. $10-$18 **AAA Inspector Notes:** Diners many think they have walked into an Asian tropical oasis upon entering this serene, charming spot with servers clad in traditional garb. Offering a well-made classic menu with several appetizers, a good starter to share is the combo plate with stuffed chicken, deep-fried spring rolls, satay and calamari. Follow that up with a tasty variety of curries, noodle dishes, stir-frys and fish dishes. Coconut lovers adore the ice cream. **Bar:** full bar. **Reservations:** suggested. **Address:** 2055 16th Ave NW T2M 0M3 **Location:** Just e of 19th St NW; in small retail complex. L D CALL M

KANE'S HARLEY DINER 403/269-7311 28

WW Comfort Food. Family Dining. $7-$22 **AAA Inspector Notes:** Orange and brown retro décor sets the scene at this popular diner in the heart of town. Guests seat themselves in booths and admire Harley motorcycles as they peruse the menu, which is laden with comfort foods. Among choices are grilled cheese and ham sandwiches, poutine, hearty hamburgers and even liver and onions. Breakfast is served all day, and service always comes with a smile. **Bar:** full bar. **Address:** 1209 9th Ave SE T2G 3E8 **Location:** 9th Ave SE at 12th St; in Inglewood. **Parking:** street only. B L CALL M

LINA'S ITALIAN MARKET 403/277-9166 15

W Deli. Quick Serve. $5-$10 **AAA Inspector Notes:** The family-owned, coffee bar-style restaurant has been an area landmark for many years. Inside, find eight tables and over-the-counter ordering. Big food comes at small prices. On the menu are homemade pizzas, pasta dishes, soups, salads and Italian pastries. Check out the family-size tiramisu in the cooler. Service is casual and friendly, and guests are often surprised to find that the polite person behind the counter is the owner. **Bar:** full bar. **Address:** 2202 Centre St N T2E 2T4 **Location:** 0.3 mi (0.5 km) n of jct 16th Ave N (Trans-Canada Hwy 1). L CALL M

MISAI JAPANESE RESTAURANT 403/250-1688 9

WW Japanese. Casual Dining. $10-$16 **AAA Inspector Notes:** Traditional décor awaits at the Northeast establishment, which is near many hotels and not far from the airport. The restaurant offers shuttle service to and from local hotels for large groups. Japanese art and dark wood decorate individual booths and rooms. The selection of sushi, sashimi, tempura and stir-fries offers good value for the dollar. **Bar:** full bar. **Reservations:** suggested. **Address:** 1915 32 Ave NE T2E 7C8 **Location:** From Barlow Tr, 0.6 mi (1 km) w at 32nd Ave. L D CALL M

MOXIE'S CLASSIC GRILL 403/291-4636

WW American. Casual Dining. $10-$30 **AAA Inspector Notes:** This swank, funky and popular restaurant presents an extensive menu of creatively prepared dishes, including pizza, pasta, rice, noodles, signature salads and burgers. Other menus include one for children and one for Sunday brunch. Lending to the upbeat, stylish decor are dark wood appointments and river rock fireplaces. **Bar:** full bar. **Address:** 29 Hopewell Way NE T3J 4V7 **Location:** Just n of jct Barlow Tr and McKnight Blvd; adjacent to Sandman Hotel Suites & Spa Calgary Airport. B L D LATE CALL M

NEWPORT GRILL ON LAKE BONAVISTA 403/271-6711 44

WWW Continental. Fine Dining. $12-$38 **AAA Inspector Notes:** Lovely views of Lake Bonavista can be had from almost every table at the upscale restaurant. Among interesting and eclectic entrees are preparations of salmon, linguine and buffalo. **Bar:** full bar. **Reservations:** suggested. **Address:** 205-747 Lake Bonavista Dr SE T2J 0N2 **Location:** 6.7 mi (11.2 km) se via Macleod Tr, 0.5 mi (0.8 km) e on Anderson Rd to Bonaventure Dr, just s to Lake Bonavista Dr, then 0.7 mi (1.2 km) e to Lake Bonavista Shopping Centre. L D CALL M

NICK'S STEAKHOUSE & PIZZA 403/282-9278 5

WW Steak. Family Dining. $12-$46 **AAA Inspector Notes:** A favorite with families, this restaurant has been a local fixture for more than 20 years. Steaks are grilled to perfection, along with a variety of chicken and veal dishes, pasta and pizza. The cozy decor and simple menu suit the tastes of all kinds of patrons, and the food is presented exactly as requested. **Bar:** full bar. **Address:** 2430 Crowchild Tr NW T2M 4N5 **Location:** Just nw of Motel Village. L D

OEB BREAKFAST CO. 403/278-3447 23

WW Breakfast. Casual Dining. $13-$19 **AAA Inspector Notes:** This trendy little diner is all about the eggs. At least 25 fabulous creations are made with eggs from their own flock of free-range chickens. Choices range from simple cracked eggs and crispy herb potatoes cooked in duck fat to North Pacific smoked cod and eggs scrambled with brown butter Hollandaise and vegetarian kelp caviar. Yummy waffles, pancakes and crepes are available. For those who do not eat eggs, there also are gourmet burgers, sandwiches and pasta. **Bar:** full bar. **Address:** 824 Edmonton Tr NE T2E 3J6 **Location:** Just s of 8th Ave NE. **Parking:** street only. B L CALL M

OPEN RANGE STEAKS & CHOPS 403/277-3408 20

WWW New American. Casual Dining. $14-$36 **AAA Inspector Notes:** This Western-theme restaurant evokes an elegant feel with some original contemporary artwork. The talented chef supports local producers and features a variety of flavorful meat dishes with a Southwestern theme running through the menu. Diners might find a beef rib chop with ancho chili rosemary butter, organic chicken with cranberry chipotle glaze or Alberta lamb with Mexican mole sauce. Such fish as Arctic char and steelhead trout comprise a lighter palate. **Bar:** full bar. **Reservations:** suggested. **Address:** 1114 Edmonton Tr NE T2E 3K4 **Location:** Jct Memorial Dr, 0.8 mi (1.3 km) n. **Parking:** on-site and street. D

OPEN SESAME 403/259-0123 39

WW Asian. Casual Dining. $9-$23 **AAA Inspector Notes:** Guests must descend the stairs to discover this restaurant's treasures. The Pan Asian noodle house features a do-it-yourself stir-fry station, as well as a full menu. Made-to-order dishes include sumptuous pot sticker appetizers and varied stir-fried noodle preparations. The rich decor of mahogany woods and dark, intimate corners sets the stage for a memorable meal. **Bar:** full bar. **Reservations:** suggested. **Address:** 6920 Macleod Tr S T2H 0L3 **Location:** Just s of Hwy 8 (Glenmore Tr). L D

ORIENTAL PHOENIX 403/253-8383 36

WWW Vietnamese. Casual Dining. $10-$18 **AAA Inspector Notes:** Traditional Vietnamese food is served simply, but the service and decor is anything but. Upscale and sleek, the modern dining room is a busy place at lunch and around the dinner hour. Guests can sample tasty food in fine surroundings characterized by bold, contemporary colors and art. Among the varied choices are salad rolls, rice vermicelli dishes and noodle soups. **Bar:** full bar. **Address:** 104 58th Ave SW, #80 T2H 0N7 **Location:** Jct Macleod Tr SW, just e. L D CALL M

PACINI PASTA & GRILL RISTORANTE 403/930-8080 1

WWW Italian. Casual Dining. $10-$29 **AAA Inspector Notes:** Fresh ingredients and modern twists on the menu at this ristorante include gourmet pizza and such house pasta as haddock pomodoro on linguine and penne bocconciutto featuring bocconcini wrapped in prosciutto. Classic pasta favorites also are offered as well as grilled entrées which are good paired with tasty Parmigiana fries. An all-you-can-eat bread bar, complimentary distilled and sparkling water and a taste of wine all are nice touches. **Bar:** full bar. **Reservations:** suggested. **Address:** 123 Freeport Blvd NE T3N 0A3 **Location:** 1 mi (1.6 km) n of Calgary International Airport on Barlow Tr; in Acclaim Hotel. B L D CALL M

(See map & index p. 72.)

PFANNTASTIC PANNENKOEK HAUS
403/243-7757 ㉟

Dutch
Family Dining
$7-$15

AAA Inspector Notes: This restaurant prepares 75 varieties of meal-size Dutch crepes served with various toppings. A savory selection for dinner and a sweet choice for dessert make for a tasty meal. Diners should come with an appetite since servings are huge. Soups and salads are also offered. Super friendly, efficient servers tend to recommend their favorite pannenkoek, and they also will help with pronunciation! **Bar:** full bar. **Address:** 2439 54th Ave SW T3E 1M4 **Location:** Just ne of jct Hwy 8 (Glenmore Tr) and Crowchild Tr; in small strip mall. *Menu on AAA.com*

B L D

THE RANCHE RESTAURANT
403/225-3939 ㊺

Regional Canadian. Fine Dining. $15-$39 **AAA Inspector Notes:** *Historic.* Originally built more than 100 years ago as a wealthy gent's mansion that lapsed into disuse, this house has been restored to its former grandeur. Creative, well-executed preparations draw on a variety of prairie ingredients and flavors. In a park in the southern part of Calgary, the restaurant offers a superb setting and experience. An a la carte brunch menu is offered on Sunday and they are closed for lunch on Saturday. **Bar:** full bar. **Reservations:** suggested. **Address:** 9005-15979 Bow Bottom Tr SE T2P 0Y8 **Location:** Off Bow Bottom Tr; in Fish Creek Provincial Park. L D

REDWATER RUSTIC GRILLE
403/253-4266 ㊶

American
Casual Dining
$11-$38

AAA Inspector Notes: A sleek and modern décor with very comfortable seating is found in this casually upscale dining room and lounge which circles around a spherical glass wine cellar. One of the nice aspects of the tasty menu is the gourmet salads and pasta which come in small or full sizes. Add that to the extensive selection of appetizers and there are some great opportunities for sharing. Fine meat and fish are expertly grilled and served with a choice of sauces and sides. **Bar:** full bar. **Reservations:** suggested. **Address:** 9223 Macleod Tr S T2J 0P6 **Location:** From Heritage Dr S, 0.4 mi (0.7 km) s. L D CALL &M

RICKY'S ALL DAY GRILL
403/571-3220

American. Family Dining. $11-$27 **AAA Inspector Notes:** The comfortable eatery, which employs friendly servers, presents a varied menu that includes pasta dishes, wraps, omelets, stir-fry preparations and burgers. Portions are generous. Children's and senior selections are offered. Guests can request seating in a booth or at a table. **Bar:** full bar. **Address:** 3321 20th Ave NE T1Y 7A8 **Location:** Just w of 36th St NE; across from Sunridge Mall.

B L D CALL &M

RIC'S LOUNGE & GRILL
403/668-9969 ⑱

American. Casual Dining. $11-$35 **AAA Inspector Notes:** Expect a modern décor here with comfortable seating circling the central bar which boasts a bank of TVs. The menu is extensive and made up off high-quality ingredients offering a good variety of trendy appetizers and gourmet thin-crust pizza. Choose from such entrées as linguine and Kobe beef meat sauce or coconut curry chicken as well as some Ocean Wise seafood and Sterling Silver beef. Service is brisk and friendly. **Bar:** full bar. **Reservations:** suggested. **Address:** 2875 Sunridge Way NE T1Y 7K7 **Location:** Jct Trans-Canada Hwy 1 and Barlow Tr NE, 0.6 mi (1 km) n, then just e; in Four Points by Sheraton Calgary Airport. B L D CALL &M

RIVER CAFE
403/261-7670 ㉕

Regional Canadian. Fine Dining. $16-$49 **AAA Inspector Notes:** One of the top restaurants in Calgary, the focus here is on Canadian Rocky Mountain cuisine with mainly local high-quality products. The chef has a knack for creating fabulous dishes where each component has a purpose, making for harmonious and flavorful foods. In the heart of Prince's Island Park, the enchanting, tree house-like restaurant features natural wood accents and a large fireplace. Service has a casual proficiency and during the summer, patio seating is a favorite choice. **Bar:** full bar. **Reservations:** suggested. **Address:** 25 Prince's Island Park T2P 0R1 **Location:** On Prince's Island; on Bow River. **Parking:** no self-parking. L D CALL &M

ROUGE
403/531-2767 ㉗

French. Fine Dining. $16-$40 **AAA Inspector Notes:** *Historic.* In a residential area near the zoo, this historic house has been converted into a quaint restaurant featuring contemporary French cuisine. Seasonally inspired dishes range from ricotta ravioli to salmon and specialty soups. Each dish is a work of art, and servers are highly attentive. The home maintains its historic roots with Victorian decor in each of its small dining rooms. Closed for lunch on Saturday. **Bar:** full bar. **Reservations:** suggested. **Address:** 1240 8th Ave SE T2G 0M7 **Location:** Corner of 12th St and 8th Ave SE.
L D CALL &M AC

SAMOSA GRILL
403/250-2515 ⑯

Eastern Indian. Casual Dining. $11-$17 **AAA Inspector Notes:** This second floor walk-up restaurant offers a unique mix of East Indian and East African dishes. Surrounded by lots of greenery and African tribal masks, diners will enjoy tasty and exotic dishes such as the house specialties of crispy samosas and tandoori chicken. The buffet offers a good value. **Bar:** full bar. **Address:** 210-3393 26th Ave NE T1Y 6L4 **Location:** Jct 36th St NE; across from Peter Longhead Hospital. L D

SANTORINI GREEK TAVERNA
403/276-8363 ⑰

Greek. Family Dining. $13-$30 **AAA Inspector Notes:** Hearty Greek food, friendly service and a bustling, festive atmosphere define the cozy taverna, which makes guests feel as though they've stepped into small town in Greece. The menu features traditional dishes, including mouthwatering moussaka, sumptuous souvlaki and spanakopita. Save some room for bougasta, a distinctive custard dessert. **Bar:** full bar. **Reservations:** suggested, weekends. **Address:** 1502 Centre St N T2E 2R9 **Location:** Just s of 16th Ave and Centre St N. L D

SMUGGLER'S INN
403/253-5355 ㊵

Steak. Casual Dining. $9-$36 **AAA Inspector Notes:** One of the city's oldest steak and prime rib houses, this place lets guests sample the all-you-can-eat soup and salad bar with any entree. The menu centers on steak, prime rib and chicken. The dark, cozy interior is a favorite with the business-lunch crowd. A brunch buffet is served on Saturdays and Sundays. **Bar:** full bar. **Reservations:** suggested. **Address:** 6920 Macleod Tr S T2H 0L3 **Location:** Just s of Glenmore Tr; attached to Open Sesame. L D

SPOLUMBO'S DELI
403/264-6452 ㉜

Deli. Quick Serve. $6-$10 **AAA Inspector Notes:** Owned by a group of former Canadian Football League Stampeders players, this bustling, energetic deli serves varied meats, including outstanding, high-quality sausage. This is a popular place at lunch, when patrons order at the counter and have their basket of food delivered to them. **Bar:** beer & wine. **Address:** 1308 9th Ave SE T2G 0T3 **Location:** Corner of 9th Ave SE and 13th St SE; in Inglewood.
L CALL &M

SUGO CAFFE ITALIA
403/263-1115 ㉚

Italian. Fine Dining. $15-$39 **AAA Inspector Notes:** In the funky Inglewood area, this upscale Italian eatery has a cozy decor to complement its innovative menu. Although the ingredients are not classically Italian, guests still can find daily selections of pasta and traditionally prepared food. The service is fine, and the atmosphere is casually elegant. Closed for lunch on Monday and Saturday. **Bar:** full bar. **Reservations:** suggested. **Address:** 1214 9th Ave SE T2G 0S9 **Location:** Between 11th and 12th sts SE; in Inglewood. **Parking:** street only. L D CALL &M

THAI BOAT
403/291-9887 ⑩

Thai. Casual Dining. $8-$13 **AAA Inspector Notes:** This restaurant is a must-stop for folks staying out by the airport. A sister property to Thai Sa-on downtown, this place displays casual Thai decor inside, but the food-an array of traditional items-is anything but casual. Thai salad rolls wow the taste buds. This place is affordable and enjoyable at lunch, and the service is friendly and efficient. Closed for lunch on Sunday. **Bar:** full bar. **Reservations:** suggested. **Address:** 2323 32nd Ave NE, #108 T2E 6Z3 **Location:** Just w of Barlow Tr at 32nd Ave. L D CALL &M

(See map & index p. 72.)

WHITE SPOT   403/278-8212

🔻🔻 ◆ American. Family Dining. $11-$22 **AAA Inspector Notes:**
Open for three meals a day, the popular casual restaurant prepares
offerings such as sandwiches and burgers, fresh salads, pastas and
stir-fries, fish and chips, chargrilled sirloin steaks and chicken, in addition to a selection of yummy desserts. **Bar:** full bar. **Address:**
10440 Macleod Tr SE T2J 0P8 **Location:** 0.3 mi (0.5 km) s of jct
Southland Dr SE. 🅱 🅛 🅓

WITHOUT PAPERS PIZZA   403/457-1154 (29)

🔻🔻 🔻🔻 Pizza. Casual Dining. $14-$22 **AAA Inspector Notes:** Between two Inglewood shops is where you'll find the inconspicuous
doorway to this pizzeria. Climb the stairs to reach a laid-back setting
with an open kitchen, where you can watch pizza dough being
tossed. Pick from pizzas made with wonderfully fresh ingredients like
free-range roasted chicken, wild boar bacon, fior di latte, pancetta,
wild mushrooms and truffle oil. Starters include enticing salads, olives
and cheese. Finish with a house-made ice cream or dessert pizza.
Bar: beer & wine. **Address:** 1216 9th Ave SE T2G 0T1 **Location:**
Between 11th and 12th sts SE; in Inglewood. **Parking:** street only.
🅛 🅓

ROCKY'S BURGERS   403/243-0405

[fyi] Not evaluated. Inside an old transit bus in an industrial section
of the city are some of the best hamburgers in the province. Handmade beef burgers, hand-cut fries and creamy milkshakes make this
spot popular and distinctive. Plus, the food is cheap. **Address:** 4645
12th St SE T3E 4R7 **Location:** From Blackfoot Tr SE, 0.5 mi (0.9 km)
e.

CAMROSE (F-7) pop. 17,286
• Restaurants p. 96

Camrose, first settled around 1900 as a trading
post, has a strong sense of its Scandinavian heritage. Known originally as the Hamlet of Sparling, its
name was changed to Camrose in 1906. Camrose
salutes country music during the 🔻 Big Valley
Jamboree, which typically begins in late July or early
August.

**Camrose Chamber of Commerce and Tourist In-
formation Centre:** 5402 48th Ave., Camrose, AB,
Canada T4V 0J7. **Phone:** (780) 672-4255.

**CAMROSE AND DISTRICT CENTENNIAL MU-
SEUM** is 2 blks. s. of Hwy. 13 at 4522 53rd St. at jct.
46th Ave. The museum houses items from Camrose's pioneer days. Buildings include a country
school; a fire hall; and a restored log pioneer house
and church, both furnished in period. A steam engine, a replica of the first newspaper building and a
working model of an early threshing machine are
displayed. **Hours:** Daily 10-5, Victoria Day-Labour
Day; by appointment rest of year. **Cost:** Donations.
Phone: (780) 672-3298.

BEST WESTERN PLUS CAMROSE RESORT CASINO
                                                780/679-2376

🔻🔻🔻 **AAA Benefit:** Members
Hotel   save up to 20%, plus 10%
Rates not provided   bonus points with Best
                             Western Rewards®.
Address: 3201 48 Ave T4V 0K9 **Location:** Hwy 13 (48th Ave),
just s of Correction Line Rd; eastern approach to city. **Facility:**
All modern and sparkles, the public spaces show off some contemporary crystal ball light fixtures as well as cool seating and art
pieces. Guest rooms also are lovely with a very nice design. 113
units, some efficiencies. 4 stories, interior corridors. **Parking:**
winter plug-ins. **Amenities:** high-speed Internet, safes. **Pool(s):**
heated indoor. **Activities:** whirlpool, waterslide, exercise room,
spa. **Guest Services:** valet and coin laundry. **Free Special
Amenities:** local telephone calls and high-speed Internet.

SAVE 🛜 🍽 🍸 CALL🅜 🕭 BIZ 🛜 ✉ ❢
🖼 📠 / SOME UNITS FEE 🐾

NORSEMEN INN   (780)672-9171

🔻🔻 Hotel $105-$199 **Address:** 6505 48th Ave T4V 3K3 **Location:** Hwy 13 (48th Ave) at 65th St; west end of town. **Facility:** 76
units. 4 stories, interior corridors. **Parking:** winter plug-ins. **Amenities:** high-speed Internet. **Dining:** 2 restaurants, nightclub. **Activities:** Fee: game room. **Guest Services:** valet laundry.

🍽 🍸 BIZ 🛜 ✉ ❢ 🖼 📠 / SOME UNITS FEE 🐾

Contact us about AAA/CAA Approved
properties at AAA.com/TourBookComments

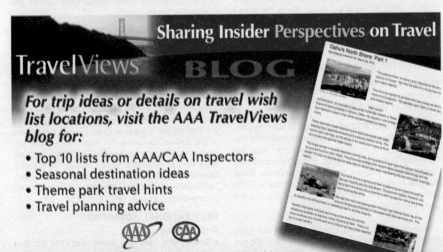

RAMADA INN & SUITES CAMROSE   (780)672-5220
▼▼▼ Hotel $145-$220 Address: 4702 73rd St T4V 0E5 Location: Hwy 13 (48th Ave), just s. Facility: 74 units. 4 stories, interior corridors. Parking: winter plug-ins. Amenities: high-speed Internet. Pool(s): heated indoor. Activities: whirlpool, waterslide, exercise room. Guest Services: coin laundry.

🏨 🛥 BIZ 🛜 ✕ 🖥 📷 💻 / SOME UNITS FEE 🐾

SUPER 8 CAMROSE   (780)672-7303
▼▼▼ Hotel $135-$200 Address: 4710 73rd St T4V 0E5 Location: Hwy 13 (48th Ave), just s. Facility: 78 units. 3 stories, interior corridors. Parking: winter plug-ins. Amenities: high-speed Internet. Pool(s): heated indoor. Activities: whirlpool, waterslide, exercise room. Guest Services: coin laundry.

🏨 🛥 BIZ 🛜 ✕ 🖥 📷 💻 / SOME UNITS FEE 🐾

WHERE TO EAT

MONTE CARLO RESTAURANT   780/672-1040
▼▼ American. Casual Dining. $11-$39 AAA Inspector Notes: One of the more popular places in town, this restaurant draws flocks of locals for lunch when the menu is based on soup, salads, sandwiches and burgers. Dinner choices expand to a good number of appetizers and entrées including salads, chicken Parmesan or cordon bleu, seafood, steaks, pizza and pasta dishes. Service is fast and friendly in a casual atmosphere. Bar: full bar. Address: 4907 48th Ave T4V 0J4 Location: Corner of 50th St and Hwy 13 (48th Ave).

L   D

CANMORE (H-5) pop. 12,288,
elev. 1,341m/4,400'
• Restaurants p. 99
• Attractions map p. 39
• Part of Banff National Park area — see map p. 37

Established in 1883 as a coal-mining center, Canmore was the first Canadian Pacific Railroad divisional point west of Calgary. The town also was the site of the biathlon and cross-country ski events of the 1988 Winter Olympics. Year-round recreational activities are abundant; fly fishing, rock climbing, snowshoeing and dog sledding are just a few activities visitors can enjoy. Hiking, mountain biking and cross-country skiing are popular along the area's numerous trails. The Canmore Highland Games in September also keeps sports enthusiasts entertained with a variety of athletic competitions. Scottish and Celtic dance and musical performances take place during the daylong festival as well.

Tourism Canmore: 907A 7th Ave., P.O. Box 8608, Canmore, AB, Canada T1W 3K1. Phone: (403) 678-1295 or (866) 226-6673.

ALPINE HELICOPTERS LTD. is off Hwy. 1 Canmore exit, following signs to Canmore Municipal Heliport at 91 Bow Valley Tr. Scenic flights over the Canadian Rockies are offered. Passengers can view alpine valleys, glaciers, the Continental Divide, Banff National Park and towering Mount Assiniboine—"the Matterhorn of the Canadian Rockies." Helicopters carry four to six passengers.

Hours: Sightseeing flights are offered daily (weather permitting). Departure times vary. Closed Jan. 1, Christmas and day after Christmas. Cost: Sightseeing flight $259 per passenger (30-minute tour); $229 per passenger (25-minute tour); $119

per passenger (12-minute tour). Reservations are required. Phone: (403) 678-4802.

CANADIAN ROCKIES RAFTING CO. departs from jct. Railway Ave. and Bow Valley Tr. S. The company offers a guided, 3-hour round-trip evening float trip along the Bow River. Several white-water rafting adventures along the Kananaskis River, Horseshoe Canyon on the Bow River and Kicking Horse River also are available.

Complimentary transportation from various Banff and Canmore locations is provided. Time: Allow 3 hours minimum. Hours: Departures require a minimum of six people. Float trips depart daily at 6 p.m., May-Sept. (weather permitting). Departure times vary; phone ahead. Cost: Float trip $55; $50 (ages 55+); $45 (ages 3-8 and students with ID). White-water rafting trip prices vary. Reservations are recommended. Phone: (403) 678-6535 or (877) 226-7625.

CANMORE MUSEUM AND GEOSCIENCE CENTRE is at 902B 7th Ave. Displays detail Canmore's past through photographs and coal-mining artifacts. The museum also presents a geology exhibit with fossils, rocks, photographs and videos. Time: Allow 30 minutes minimum. Hours: Mon.-Tues. noon-5, Wed.-Sun. 10-5, Victoria Day weekend-Labour Day; Mon.-Fri. noon-5, Sat.-Sun. 11-5, rest of year. Closed Jan. 1 and Christmas. Cost: $5; $3 (ages 65+ and students with ID); free (ages 0-7); $10 (family, two adults and two children). Phone: (403) 678-2462.

GEM OH CANADA EH?! DINNER SHOW is at 125 Kananaskis Way. The interactive show provides guests with a humorous take on Canadian culture and tradition. Singing Mounties, lumberjacks, a hockey player and other characters serve guests a family-style, traditional Canadian meal during the boisterous musical performance. Other shows are featured in the off-season.

Time: Allow 3 hours minimum. Hours: Shows are presented Fri.-Wed. at 6:15 p.m., Apr.-Oct.; otherwise varies. Cost: $75; $69 (senior citizens); $40 (ages 0-16). Ticket prices vary. Reservations are required. Phone: (403) 609-0004 or (800) 773-0004. 🅣

RAINBOW RIDERS ADVENTURE TOURS INC. departs from the Rafter Six Ranch Resort at Hwy. 1 and Hwy. 1X. The company offers a guided 3-hour round-trip float trip along the Bow River. Several white-water rafting adventures along the Kananaskis River and Horseshoe Canyon on the Bow River also are available. Hours: Float trips depart daily at 10, 2 and 6, May-Sept. (weather permitting). Cost: Float trip $49. White-water rafting trips $75-$89. Reservations are recommended. Phone: (403) 678-7238.

RECREATIONAL ACTIVITIES
Dog Sledding
• Snowy Owl Sled Dog Tours is at #104 602 Bow Valley Tr. Hours: Trips are offered daily, Nov.-Apr. (weather permitting). Departure times vary. Phone: (403) 678-4369 or (888) 311-6874.

White-water Rafting

- **Blast Adventures Inc.** is at 120 B Rundle Dr. **Hours:** Trips are offered daily, June 1 to mid-Sept. Departure times vary. **Phone:** (403) 609-2009, or (888) 802-5278 in Alberta and British Columbia.

- **Inside Out Experience** departs Fort Chiniki, just s. of Hwy. 1. Other activities are offered. **Hours:** Trips are offered daily, May 1-early Oct. Departure times vary. **Phone:** (403) 949-3305 or (877) 999-7238.

BANFF BOUNDARY LODGE   (403)678-9555

Condominium
$84-$189

Address: 1000 Harvie Heights Rd T1W 2W2 **Location:** Trans-Canada Hwy 1 exit 86, just n. **Facility:** 42 condominiums. 1-2 stories (no elevator), exterior corridors. **Parking:** winter plug-ins. **Terms:** check-in 4 pm, 3 day cancellation notice-fee imposed, resort fee. **Activities:** whirlpool. **Guest Services:** coin laundry. **Free Special Amenities:** high-speed Internet and use of on-premises laundry facilities.

BEST WESTERN PLUS POCATERRA INN
                                          (403)678-4334

Hotel
$110-$210

AAA Benefit:
Members save up to 20%, plus 10% bonus points with Best Western Rewards®.

Address: 1725 Mountain Ave T1W 2W1 **Location:** Trans-Canada Hwy 1 exit 86, 1.3 mi (2.1 km) e. **Facility:** 83 units. 4 stories, interior corridors. **Parking:** winter plug-ins. **Terms:** check-in 4 pm, cancellation fee imposed. **Pool(s):** heated indoor. **Activities:** sauna, whirlpool, steamroom, waterslide, game room, exercise room. **Guest Services:** valet and coin laundry. **Free Special Amenities:** local telephone calls and high-speed Internet.

Charming chateau-style hotel near Banff National Park. Free hot breakfast and pool with waterside.

BLACKSTONE MOUNTAIN LODGE   (403)609-8098
Hotel $139-$249 **Address:** 170 Kananaskis Way T1W 0A8 **Location:** Trans-Canada Hwy 1 exit 89, 1.2 mi (2 km) s. **Facility:** 126 units, some two bedrooms, three bedrooms and kitchens. 4 stories, interior corridors. **Terms:** check-in 4 pm, 2-3 night minimum stay - seasonal and/or weekends, cancellation fee imposed. **Amenities:** video games, high-speed Internet. **Pool(s):** heated outdoor. **Activities:** whirlpools, exercise room. **Fee:** massage. **Guest Services:** valet laundry.

BOW VALLEY MOTEL   403/678-5085
Motel $75-$110 **Address:** 610 8th St T1W 2B5 **Location:** Trans-Canada Hwy 1 exit 89, 1.1 mi (1.8 km) se. **Facility:** 25 units, some efficiencies. 1-3 stories (no elevator), exterior corridors. **Parking:** winter plug-ins. **Terms:** cancellation fee imposed. **Guest Services:** coin laundry.

CANADIAN ROCKIES CHALETS   (403)678-3799

Condominium
$89-$249

Address: 1206 Bow Valley Tr T1W 1N6 **Location:** Trans-Canada Hwy 1 exit 89, 0.9 mi (1.5 km) se. **Facility:** 40 condominiums. 3 stories (no elevator), exterior corridors. **Parking:** winter plug-ins. **Terms:** check-in 4 pm, 3 day cancellation notice-fee imposed. **Amenities:** high-speed Internet. **Activities:** whirlpool. **Free Special Amenities:** local telephone calls and high-speed Internet.

ECONO LODGE CANMORE   (403)678-5488

Hotel
$94-$150

Address: 1602 2nd Ave T1W 1M8 **Location:** Trans-Canada Hwy 1 exit 89, 1.3 mi (2.1 km) e. **Facility:** 60 units, some efficiencies. 2 stories (no elevator), interior corridors. **Parking:** winter plug-ins. **Terms:** check-in 4 pm, cancellation fee imposed. **Dining:** Chez Francois, see separate listing. **Activities:** exercise room.

Surrounded by beautiful Canadian Rocky Mountains, near many activities. Complimentary Breakfast.

FALCON CREST LODGE   (403)678-6150
Condominium
$122-$324

Address: 190 Kananaskis Way T1W 3K5 **Location:** Trans-Canada Hwy 1 exit 89, 1.2 mi (2 km) s. **Facility:** Units in this family-friendly property feature comfortable, contemporary décor and a fireplace. Some units include a laundry facility. 73 condominiums. 4 stories, interior corridors. **Terms:** check-in 4 pm, 2 night minimum stay - seasonal and/or weekends, cancellation fee imposed. **Dining:** Indochine, see separate listing. **Activities:** whirlpools, bicycles, hiking trails, jogging, exercise room. **Guest Services:** coin laundry. **Free Special Amenities:** high-speed Internet.

FIRE MOUNTAIN LODGE   (403)609-9949
Condominium $154-$319 **Address:** 121 Kananaskis Way T1W 2X2 **Location:** Trans-Canada Hwy 1 exit 89, 1 mi (1.6 km) s. **Facility:** This condominium property offers luxurious and spacious two- and three-bedroom suites with sleek and contemporary furnishings, full kitchens with granite-topped breakfast bars and leather stools. 21 condominiums. 2 stories (no elevator), exterior corridors. **Parking:** winter plug-ins. **Terms:** off-site registration, check-in 4 pm, 2 night minimum stay - seasonal and/or weekends, 7 day cancellation notice. **Activities:** whirlpool, limited exercise equipment. **Guest Services:** complimentary laundry.

THE GRANDE ROCKIES RESORT   (403)678-8880
Hotel $109-$425 **Address:** 901 Mountain St T1W 0C9 **Location:** Trans-Canada Hwy 1 exit 89, 1 mi (1.6 km) sw. **Facility:** 136 units, some two bedrooms. 4 stories, interior corridors. **Terms:** check-in 4 pm, 3 day cancellation notice-fee imposed, resort fee. **Amenities:** high-speed Internet, safes. **Dining:** Habitat Restaurant & Bar, see separate listing. **Pool(s):** heated indoor. **Activities:** whirlpool, waterslide, exercise room, spa. **Guest Services:** valet laundry.

HOLIDAY INN CANMORE
(403)609-4422

Hotel
$119-$249

Address: 1 Silver Tip Tr T1W 2Z7 **Location:** Trans-Canada Hwy 1 exit 89, just s. **Facility:** 99 units. 3 stories, interior corridors. **Parking:** winter plug-ins. **Terms:** cancellation fee imposed. **Amenities:** video games (fee). **Activities:** whirlpool, hiking trails, exercise room. **Guest Services:** valet and coin laundry. **Free Special Amenities:** early check-in/late check-out and high-speed Internet. *(See ad this page.)*

THE LADY MACDONALD COUNTRY INN
(403)678-3665

Country Inn
$125-$250

Address: 1201 Bow Valley Tr T1W 1P5 **Location:** Trans-Canada Hwy 1 exit 89, 1 mi (1.6 km) sw. **Facility:** A retreat-like ambiance enhances the upscale country inn, which features individually decorated rooms and a Victorian-style dining room. 10 units. 2 stories (no elevator), interior corridors. **Parking:** winter plug-ins.

      / SOME UNITS

MYSTIC SPRINGS CHALETS & HOT POOLS
403/609-0333

Condominium. Rates not provided. **Address:** 140 Kananaskis Way T1W 2X2 **Location:** Trans-Canada Hwy 1 exit 89, 1.1 mi (1.8 km) s. **Facility:** Featuring an outdoor saltwater pool, a barbecue area and upscale accommodations, this property offers amenities from martini glasses to DVD players. 44 condominiums. 2 stories (no elevator), exterior corridors. **Terms:** check-in 4 pm. **Amenities:** high-speed Internet. **Pool(s):** heated outdoor. **Activities:** whirlpool, limited exercise equipment. *Fee:* massage. **Guest Services:** valet and coin laundry.

QUALITY RESORT-CHATEAU CANMORE
(403)678-6699

Hotel
$89-$119

Address: 1720 Bow Valley Tr T1W 2X3 **Location:** Trans-Canada Hwy 1 exit 86, 0.5 mi (0.8 km) s. **Facility:** 93 units. 4 stories, interior corridors. **Parking:** winter plug-ins. **Terms:** check-in 4 pm, cancellation fee imposed. **Activities:** sauna, whirlpool, exercise room, spa. **Guest Services:** valet and coin laundry. **Free Special Amenities:** room upgrade (subject to availability with advance reservations) and high-speed Internet.

/ SOME UNITS FEE

Location, Location In the Heart of Canmore. A Spectacular Rocky Mountain setting.

RADISSON HOTEL & CONFERENCE CENTRE
(403)678-3625

Hotel
$99-$249

Address: 511 Bow Valley Tr T1W 1N7 **Location:** Trans-Canada Hwy 1 exit 89, 1.4 mi (2.2 km) s. **Facility:** 164 units. 2-3 stories, interior/exterior corridors. **Parking:** winter plug-ins. **Terms:** check-in 4 pm, 3 day cancellation notice-fee imposed. **Amenities:** high-speed Internet. *Some:* safes. **Pool(s):** heated indoor. **Activities:** whirlpool, exercise room. **Guest Services:** valet laundry. **Free Special Amenities:** local telephone calls and newspaper.

 / SOME UNITS FEE

▼ See AAA listing this page ▼

Save on theme park tickets at AAA.com/discounts

RAMADA INN & SUITES CANMORE (403)609-4656

 Hotel $79-$179 Address: 1402 Bow Valley Tr T1W 1N5 Location: Trans-Canada Hwy 1 exit 89, 1 mi (1.6 km) se. Next to railway tracks. Facility: 188 units, some two bedrooms. 3 stories, interior corridors. Parking: winter plug-ins. Terms: check-in 4 pm, cancellation fee imposed. Amenities: safes. Pool(s): heated indoor. Activities: whirlpool, waterslide, exercise room. Guest Services: coin laundry.

/SOME UNITS FEE

ROCKY MOUNTAIN SKI LODGE (403)678-5445
Motel
$119-$209

Address: 1711 Bow Valley Tr T1W 2T8 Location: Trans-Canada Hwy 1 exit 86, 0.5 mi (0.8 km) s. Located in a commercial area. Facility: 83 units, some two bedrooms and kitchens. 1-2 stories (no elevator), exterior corridors. Parking: winter plug-ins. Terms: cancellation fee imposed. Activities: sauna, whirlpool, playground. Guest Services: coin laundry. Free Special Amenities: newspaper and high-speed Internet.

/SOME UNITS FEE

 Minutes from Banff National Park, mountain views from all rooms, friendly and affordable in Canmore.

RUNDLE CLIFFS LODGE 403/678-5108
Condominium
Rates not provided

Address: 375 Spring Creek Dr T1W 1G9 Location: Trans-Canada Hwy 1 exit 89, 1.2 mi (2 km) s; in Spring Creek Village. Facility: Marvelous, modern one- to three-bedroom suites feature designer kitchens, balconies or decks with a grill and great bathrooms. In-floor heating throughout the units will be welcomed in the ski season. 15 condominiums. 4 stories, interior corridors. Terms: check-in 4 pm. Amenities: high-speed Internet. Activities: whirlpool, ice skating, bicycles, hiking trails, jogging, playground, game room, exercise room. Guest Services: complimentary laundry. Free Special Amenities: local telephone calls and children's activities.

SOLARA RESORT & SPA (403)609-3600

Condominium $159-$299 Address: 187 Kananaskis Way T1W 0A3 Location: Trans-Canada Hwy 1 exit 89, 1.2 mi (2 km) s. Facility: Units at this gorgeous all-suite property feature designer kitchens, comfortable living areas, spa-like bathrooms and a patio or deck. A theater and kids' playroom with a splash area is featured. 170 condominiums. 4 stories, interior corridors. Terms: check-in 4 pm, 2 night minimum stay - seasonal and/or weekends, cancellation fee imposed. Amenities: video games, safes. Activities: whirlpool, recreation programs in summer, rental bicycles, hiking trails, jogging, playground, spa. Guest Services: complimentary laundry.

/SOME UNITS FEE

AAA.com/ TourBook Comments

Tell Us How We're Doing

STONERIDGE MOUNTAIN RESORT CANMORE (403)675-5000

Condominium
$179-$399

Address: 30 Lincoln Park T1W 3E9 Location: Trans-Canada Hwy 1 exit 89, 1.3 mi (2.4 km) s. Facility: The upscale hotel offers spacious, full suites with granite counters, stainless steel appliances, washer and dryers, dining areas, breakfast bars with stools, fireplaces and balconies with grills. 105 condominiums. 4 stories, interior corridors. Terms: check-in 4 pm, cancellation fee imposed, resort fee. Amenities: safes. Pool(s): heated outdoor. Activities: whirlpool, exercise room. Guest Services: complimentary laundry. Free Special Amenities: early check-in/late check-out and high-speed Internet. (See ad p. 48.)

WINDTOWER LODGE & SUITES (403)609-6600

Condominium $119-$289 Address: 160 Kananaskis Way T1W 3E2 Location: Trans-Canada Hwy 1 exit 89, 1.1 mi (1.8 km) s. Facility: 105 units, some kitchens and condominiums. 2 stories, interior corridors. Parking: on-site (fee) and street. Terms: check-in 4 pm. Activities: whirlpool, putting green, exercise room.

/SOME UNITS FEE

WHERE TO EAT

BEAMER'S COFFEE BAR 403/678-3988

Coffee/Tea. Quick Serve. $3-$10 AAA Inspector Notes: In a convenient spot, the contemporary coffeehouse draws both locals and those en route to the ski hills. Among healthy offerings are magnificent muffins, soups, breakfast bagels and, of course, Beamer's coffee. Big boy sandwiches are built on the premises with fresh, multigrain bread and a choice of toppings. For those with a sweet tooth, the display case features some tempting choices. Address: 1702A Bow Valley Tr T1W 1N5 Location: Trans-Canada Hwy 1 exit 86, 0.5 mi (0.8 km) s. B L

CHEF'S STUDIO JAPAN 403/609-8383

Japanese. Casual Dining. $10-$30 AAA Inspector Notes: If you're craving sushi, this restaurant is a treat. Its location, between two art galleries, appears to have inspired the chef, who utilizes fresh, high-quality ingredients to create Japanese works of art. Bar: full bar. Reservations: suggested. Address: 709 8th St T1W 2B2 Location: Between 6th and 7th aves; down a small laneway; downtown; behind Bank of Montreal. Parking: on-site and street. L D

CHEZ FRANCOIS 403/678-6111

French. Casual Dining. $8-$32 AAA Inspector Notes: Always popular with the locals, this establishment features classic French cuisine including house pâté, coquilles St. Jacques, duck à l'orange and a variety of beef, seafood and pasta dishes. Lunch is much more casual with a good variety of salads, sandwiches, pasta and lighter French fare including crêpes and sole amandine. Bar: full bar. Reservations: suggested. Address: 1602 2nd Ave T1W 1P7 Location: Trans-Canada Hwy 1 exit 89, 1.3 mi (2.1 km) e; in Econo Lodge Canmore. B L D CALL

COMMUNITEA CAFE 403/678-6818

Vegetarian. Quick Serve. $8-$12 AAA Inspector Notes: This bright and cheery café has great healthy and organic choices. Apple cinnamon breakfast crumble or a free-range egg panini are a good start to the day. Lunch includes daily soup and couscous salad as well as enticing sandwiches and rice or noodle bowls. Carnivores will find a few prawn and free-range chicken options. The sweet tooth is satisfied with squares and cookies with some gluten-free items. More than 80 teas are on offer as well as some delicious coffee. Address: 1001 6th Ave, #117 T1W 3L8 Location: Corner of 10th St; center. Parking: street only. B L CALL

CRAIG'S WAY STATION
403/678-2656

◆◆ American. Family Dining. $7-$18 **AAA Inspector Notes:** Well suited for family dining, this casual diner offers great mountain views through large windows and cozy seating in front of a stone fireplace. Popular comfort foods include fresh beef burgers, clam chowder, club or Western Denver sandwiches, Salisbury steak with onions and mushrooms, the 10-ounce "rustler" Alberta steak, veal cutlets, chicken fettuccine and stir-fries. Steak and eggs, blueberry pancakes and other breakfast items are served all day, and kids can order from the children's menu. **Bar:** beer & wine. **Address:** 1727 Mountain Ave T1W 2W1 **Location:** 3.6 mi (5.8 km) e of Banff National Park east gate on Hwy 1A (Bow Valley Tr). [B] [L] [D]

CRAZYWEED KITCHEN
403/609-2530

◆◆◆ New American. Casual Dining. $10-$32 **AAA Inspector Notes:** This contemporary kitchen offers creative and innovative dishes with influences from around the world. Skillfully created with choice ingredients, menu choices could run the gamut from salt and pepper calamari with nham jim dip; frites with choice of homemade ketchup, St. Agur cheese dip or Parmesan and tequila aioli; steamed black Alaskan cod; and chili-crusted Alberta rib-eye in red wine sauce. Wood-fired gourmet pizza and yummy desserts also are offered. Service is friendly and proficient. **Bar:** full bar. **Address:** 1600 Railway Ave T1W 1P6 **Location:** Trans-Canada Hwy 1 exit 86, 1.2 mi (1.9 km) se, then just s. [L] [D] [LATE] CALL [&M]

FRENCH QUARTER CAFE
403/678-3612

◆◆ Cajun. Casual Dining. $9-$27 **AAA Inspector Notes:** Inspired by a vacation years ago, the chef/owner has been serving up a taste of New Orleans ever since. Diners often will find him working the open kitchen in this new trendy bistro. Delicious gumbo and enticing appetizers and salads are great starters, followed by Louisiana shrimp Creole, jambalaya, crawfish etoufée, red snapper, catfish, beef Napoleon and sweet potato chicken breast. Finish with one of the homemade desserts, including Southern bread pudding with whiskey sauce. **Bar:** full bar. **Reservations:** suggested. **Address:** 1005 Cougar Creek Dr, Unit 100 T1W 1E1 **Location:** Trans-Canada Hwy 1 exit 89, 1.4 mi (2.3 km) se. **Parking:** on-site and street.

[B] [L] [D]

THE GRIZZLY PAW BREWING COMPANY
403/678-9983

◆◆ American. Gastropub. $10-$20 **AAA Inspector Notes:** A taste of local ales awaits at this popular brew pub, where beer is made on site. The menu features a variety of hearty pub food, ranging from hamburgers to fish and chips, jalapeno poppers, soups and salads. For a casual meal, this is a popular spot. **Bar:** full bar. **Address:** 622 Main St T1W 2B5 **Location:** Downtown. [L] [D]

HABITAT RESTAURANT & BAR
403/679-5228

◆◆◆ American. Casual Dining. $12-$42 **AAA Inspector Notes:** A delightful, bright and contemporary décor set the background for this restaurant featuring a menu with locally sourced and excellent-quality ingredients. Wonderful service contributes to a great evening out. Delicious house desserts are definitely worth leaving room for. **Bar:** full bar. **Reservations:** suggested. **Address:** 901 Mountain St T1W 0C9 **Location:** Trans-Canada Hwy 1 exit 89, 1 mi (1.6 km) sw; in The Grande Rockies Resort.

[B] [L] [D] CALL [&M]

INDOCHINE
403/675-3888

◆◆ Vietnamese. Casual Dining. $12-$20 **AAA Inspector Notes:** Entrées are well-prepared with fresh ingredients and presented in an appealing fashion at this casual restaurant. The decor is simple and smart while friendly servers dish up traditional favorites ranging from spring rolls and noodle soups to lemon grass chicken, beef and prawn noodles or rice dishes. **Bar:** full bar. **Address:** 190 Kananaskis Way T1W 3K5 **Location:** Trans-Canada Hwy 1 exit 89, 1.2 mi (2 km) s; in Falcon Crest Lodge. **Parking:** street only.

[L] [D] CALL [&M]

THE IRON GOAT PUB & GRILL
403/609-0222

◆ Canadian. Casual Dining. $10-$26 **AAA Inspector Notes:** This striking pub, with a soaring wood ceiling and huge stone fireplace, is only outmatched by the stunning views of the Three Sisters Mountains. Almost every item on the upscale and intriguing pub menu includes some high-grade local or regional ingredient. The lunch menu is less extensive, but just as delicious. Servers are attentive and friendly. An outdoor patio is popular in the summer. **Bar:** full bar. **Reservations:** suggested. **Address:** 703 Benchlands Tr T1W 3G9 **Location:** Trans-Canada Hwy 1 exit 89, 1.6 mi (2.6 km) se.

[L] [D] CALL [&M]

LA BELLE PATATE
403/678-0077

◆ Canadian Specialty. Quick Serve. $5-$13 **AAA Inspector Notes:** This simple and friendly little spot is all about the poutine, a Quebec tradition made with double cooked fries, cheese curds and gravy. They make about 15 different kinds like Mexican, meat lovers, or breakfast style complete with hand cut fries and fresh squeaky curds. And what would poutine be without a great Montreal smoked meat sandwich. Also on the menu are other sandwiches, hot dogs and burgers. **Bar:** beer only. **Address:** 102 Boulder Cres, Bay 4 T1W 1L2 **Location:** From Elk Run Blvd, just e on Glacier Dr; south end of town; in an industrial area. [L] [D] CALL [&M]

LUNA BLUE RESTAURANT
403/609-3221

◆ Italian. Casual Dining. $12-$22 **AAA Inspector Notes:** Charming accents of blue and moons are incorporated into the décor and artwork at this pasta and pizza eatery on the main street. Daily soups are made from scratch and there are some enticing salad or appetizer options. The fresh pasta is made locally and guests can find some delicious creations available in small or large sizes as well as thin, wood-fired pizza. **Bar:** full bar. **Reservations:** suggested. **Address:** 721 Main St, #107 T1W 2B2 **Location:** Jct 7th Ave; downtown. **Parking:** street only. [D] CALL [&M]

MOUNTAIN MERCATO SPECIALTY FOOD MARKET
403/609-6631

◆ Sandwiches. Quick Serve. $9-$12 **AAA Inspector Notes:** This attractive little shop with a range of specialty Italian foods also has a small menu of soup, salads and panini which you order at the counter and can enjoy in the small sitting area along with a nice cup of cappuccino or glass of wine. Both the Bundnerfleisch (air dried meat) and arugula salad with shaved Italian cheese and the tacchino (turkey) panini with cave aged Gruyère, pickled fennel and pesto were extremely flavorful. **Bar:** beer & wine. **Address:** 817 Main St, #102 T1W 2B3 **Location:** Between 7th and 8th aves; center. **Parking:** street only. [L] CALL [&M]

MURRIETA'S BAR & GRILL
403/609-9500

◆◆◆ Western Pacific Rim. Casual Dining. $11-$39 **AAA Inspector Notes:** Upstairs from street level, this classy, upbeat restaurant boasts West Coast cuisine, including a variety of sandwiches and salads at lunch and heartier dishes at dinner. Reservations are recommended at the popular spot in this mountain town, especially for the dinner hour. Lending to the restaurant's atmosphere are cozy mountain decor, wooden accents, a lounge and a fireplace. **Bar:** full bar. **Reservations:** suggested. **Address:** 200-737 Main St T1W 2B2 **Location:** Corner of 7th and Main sts; on 2nd Level; downtown. **Parking:** street only. [L] [D]

O BISTRO
403/678-3313

◆◆◆ French. Casual Dining. $13-$32 **AAA Inspector Notes:** There are just nine tables at this intimate little spot. They have a nicely put together, reasonably-priced menu for the area, with some great appetizers, salads and such entrées as a simple steak and frites. More complex items include beef Wellington with duck pate, cassoulet with duck confit and spicy sausage and seafood bouillabaisse. Lunch is a more casual affair but with plenty of options including crepes, pasta and a variety of deluxe sandwiches. **Bar:** full bar. **Reservations:** suggested. **Address:** 626 Main St, #2 T1W 2B5 **Location:** Downtown. **Parking:** street only. [L] [D] CALL [&M]

PATRINOS STEAKHOUSE & PUB
403/678-4060

◆◆ International Casual Dining $10-$32 **AAA Inspector Notes:** This simple, family-run, roadside restaurant features a good selection of comfort foods, ranging from pizza and pasta to steaks. Guests can eat in the casual dining room or grab something in the lounge next door. Expect friendly, attentive service. **Bar:** full bar. **Reservations:** suggested. **Address:** 1602 Bow Valley Tr T1W 1N5 **Location:** Trans-Canada Hwy 1 exit 86, 0.6 mi (1 km) s. [L] [D] CALL [&M]

RAILWAY DELI
403/678-3637

▼ Deli. Quick Serve. $7-$14 **AAA Inspector Notes:** The delicious breakfast offerings at this cafeteria-style deli will get you going on weekend mornings. The cafeteria section closes at 3 pm so guests can enjoy the numerous lunch offerings such as fresh soup, assorted meat and veggie pies, quiche, rotisserie chicken, sandwiches, burgers and schnitzel until then. Afterward, the outstanding deli remains open until 7 pm so locals and tourists alike can pick up anything from cheese, bread, sausage, pastries and pies to frozen soups and stews. **Bar:** beer & wine. **Address:** 702 Bow Valley Tr, Unit 101 T1W 2H4 **Location:** Trans-Canada Hwy 1 exit 89, 0.7 mi (1.1 km) s. [B] [L] CALL [&M]

ROCKY MOUNTAIN FLATBREAD COMPANY
403/609-5508

▼ ▼ Pizza. Family Dining. $12-$27 **AAA Inspector Notes:** The comfortable, casual restaurant offers diners a wide selection of thin-crust pizzas, fresh soup and home-baked desserts, many of which are cooked in the hand-built masonry oven. The menu features many organic and oceanwise ingredients and has initiatives in place to help support the environment. **Bar:** full bar. **Address:** 838 10th St, Unit 101 T1W 2A8 **Location:** Corner of 8th Ave and 10th St; downtown. **Parking:** on-site and street. [L] [D]

RUSTICA STEAKHOUSE
403/678-1600

▼▼▼ Steak. Fine Dining. $40-$60 **AAA Inspector Notes:** Enjoy your meal from an oversize high back arm chair as you appreciate the views from the picture windows or the crackling fire in the huge stone fireplace. A prix fixe menu is offered here with a fine selection of appetizers like tempura shrimp with house teriyaki sauce, entrées of Canadian Prime beef with Madeira reduction or almond crusted rack of lamb and desserts like white chocolate crème brûlée. The off season menu shrinks a bit but is still worth a visit. **Bar:** full bar. **Address:** 2000 Silvertip Tr T1W 3J4 **Location:** Trans-Canada Hwy 1 exit 89, just s on Palliser Tr, then 1.1 mi (1.8 km) n; at Silvertip Golf Course. [D] CALL [&M]

SAGE BISTRO
403/678-4878

▼▼▼ New Canadian. Casual Dining. $16-$29 **AAA Inspector Notes:** On its own by the gas station, this log cabin would be easy to drive by. Inside this rustic space, the kitchen elevates Canadian comfort food to new levels by using local products, including produce and game. **Bar:** full bar. **Reservations:** suggested. **Address:** 1712 Bow Valley Tr T1W 1P2 **Location:** 3.1 mi (5.2 km) e of Banff National Park east gate on Hwy 1A (Bow Valley Tr); jct 17th St.

[L] [D] [K]

SANTA LUCIA TRATTORIA
403/678-3414

▼ ▼ Italian. Casual Dining. $13-$21 **AAA Inspector Notes:** The attractive and fresh décor is not what you typically find in an Italian trattoria, but the classic dishes are. The menu is simple but well prepared and nicely presented, and the chef/owner uses fresh, high-quality ingredients to craft delicious appetizers, pastas, veal, chicken and pizza. It is well worth a visit to this long established little spot. **Bar:** full bar. **Reservations:** suggested. **Address:** 714 Main St T1W 2B6 **Location:** Trans-Canada Hwy 1 exit 89, 1.1 mi (1.9 km) se. **Parking:** street only. [D]

TAPAS RESTAURANT
403/609-0583

▼▼▼ Mediterranean. Casual Dining. $8-$32 **AAA Inspector Notes:** Diners should come in groups to sample and savor the widest variety of memorable tapas preparations. Drawing on influences from both Spain and Portugal, selections are mouthwatering. Delicious favorites include fiery sweet potato tapas, eggplant and paella for two. The casual spot is popular with locals and visitors alike for its comfortable surroundings and superb food. **Bar:** full bar. **Reservations:** suggested. **Address:** 633 10th St T1W 2A2 **Location:** Downtown; next to Paintbox Lodge. **Parking:** street only. [D] CALL [&M]

THE TROUGH DINING CO.
403/678-2820

▼▼▼ New American. Fine Dining. $29-$39 **AAA Inspector Notes:** This small restaurant emits a warm, inviting ambience that beckons patrons to relax and savor imaginative cuisine. The kitchen staff incorporates fresh local and regional ingredients, creating outstanding dishes. Do not be surprised to find some extra goodies served with menu choices. The highly competent service staff helps make the dining experience memorable. Closed for lunch November through April. **Bar:** full bar. **Reservations:** suggested. **Address:** 725 9th St T1W 2V7 **Location:** Downtown; on Walk of Champions. **Parking:** street only. [D]

CARDSTON (K-6) pop. 3,580,
elev. 1,185m/3,888'
• Restaurants p. 102

A son-in-law of Brigham Young, Charles Ora Card, led 10 Mormon families from Utah into Canada in 1887, hoping to find freedom from American anti-polygamy laws. Settling in Cardston, the immigrants founded the country's first Mormon settlement and named the town after their leader, who became its first mayor.

Today, a considerable percentage of Cardston residents are Mormon. Completed and dedicated in 1923, Cardston Alberta Temple of the Church of Jesus Christ of Latter-day Saints, 348 3rd St. W., serves a large area of western Canada and Montana. Non-Mormons are not permitted to enter the structure but can tour the grounds, where a visitor center offers information; phone (403) 653-1696.

Cardston & District Chamber of Commerce: 490 Main St., P.O. Box 1212, Cardston, AB, Canada T0K 0K0. **Phone:** (403) 795-1032.

CARD PIONEER HOME is at 337 Main St. The log cabin of Mormon leader Charles Ora Card is restored and refurnished with hand-carved furniture. **Time:** Allow 30 minutes minimum. **Hours:** Mon.-Sat. 11-7, July-Aug. **Cost:** Donations. **Phone:** (403) 653-3366.

COURTHOUSE MUSEUM is at 89 3rd Ave. W. Local pioneer memorabilia is displayed in a stone courthouse dating from 1907. **Time:** Allow 1 hour minimum. **Hours:** Mon.-Sat. 10-7, July-Aug. **Cost:** Donations. **Phone:** (403) 653-3366.

▼GEM [SAVE] **REMINGTON CARRIAGE MUSEUM** is at 623 Main St. More than 250 19th- and early 20th-century horse-drawn vehicles are showcased. Interactive displays and exhibit galleries provide the feeling of riding in the horse-drawn transportation of that era, and an introductory multimedia presentation provides an overview of that time.

The exhibit galleries, which include a blacksmith shop and livery stable, carriage factory, carriage dealership, working restoration shop, frontier settlement and racetrack, depict 19th-century society and its dependence on this mode of transportation. Sound effects, lighting and audiovisual presentations enhance many of the presentations. Horses may be seen being groomed and harnessed in a working stable. In summer visitors may schedule 15-minute rides on vintage and reproduction carriages.

Tours: Guided tours are available. **Time:** Allow 1 hour, 30 minutes minimum. **Hours:** Daily 9-5, June-Aug.; 9-4, rest of year. Carriage rides are offered daily 11-noon and 1-5. Closed Jan. 1, Easter, Christmas Eve and Christmas. **Cost:** $10; $8 (ages 65+); $5 (ages 7-17); $22 (family, two adults and two children). Carriage ride $4; $2.50 (ages 4-17); $12 (family, two adults and two children). **Phone:** (403) 653-5139. [¶] [⚐]

RECREATIONAL ACTIVITIES
White-water Rafting
- **Kimball River Sports** is 9 km (5.5 mi.) s.e. on Hwy. 501. **Hours:** Trips are offered June-Aug. Schedule varies; phone ahead. **Phone:** (403) 653-1099.

THE COBBLESTONE MANOR RESTAURANT & B&B
403/653-2701
▼▼▼ American. Casual Dining. $11-$38 **AAA Inspector Notes:** Classic Historic. This little restaurant is located in a historic house listed as one of National Geographic's Crowns of the Continent. Completed in 1926, the restaurant has three rooms with distinct decor featuring hardwoods from around the world, accented by Tiffany glass. A simple menu lists such dinner entrees as maple chicken breast, wild Canadian salmon and Alberta beef, all at very reasonable prices. **Reservations:** suggested. **Address:** 173 7th Ave W T0K 0K0 **Location:** Hwy 5 (1st Ave), 0.7 mi (1.1 km) s on Main St, just w. [L] [D]

PIZZAS & CREAM
403/653-4143
▼ Pizza. Quick Serve. $6-$9 **AAA Inspector Notes:** A play on words, this retro diner's name aptly describes its food: pizza and ice cream. Upon entering this spot, diners can appreciate its whimsical, nostalgic memorabilia, which ranges from Trivial Pursuit and Lite Brite to roller skates and pop bottles. Guests seat themselves in one of the sparkly, red and silver booths. Piping-hot pizza is delivered atop an old-fashioned pizza stand, and it tastes great with a frothy milkshake. **Address:** 325 Main St T0K 0K0 **Location:** Downtown. **Parking:** street only. [L] [D]

CLARESHOLM (J-6) pop. 3,758

CLARESHOLM MUSEUM is on Hwy. 2 at 5126 1st St. W. Displays are housed in a former Canadian Pacific Railway station. The sandstone building features early 20th-century items that represent pioneer life. Town history is highlighted in railway, medical and educational displays. On the grounds are a visitor center, a one-room schoolhouse, a historic log cabin, a caboose, a playground and the Louise McKinney Memorial Gardens. **Hours:** Daily 9:30-5:30, mid-May through second Mon. in Oct.; by appointment rest of year. **Cost:** Donations. **Phone:** (403) 625-1742.

BLUEBIRD MOTEL
403/625-3395
▼▼▼ Motel. Rates not provided. **Address:** 5505 1st St W T0L 0T0 **Location:** 0.3 mi (0.5 km) n on Hwy 2. **Facility:** 23 units, some two bedrooms, efficiencies and kitchens. 1 story, exterior corridors. **Parking:** winter plug-ins. **Amenities:** high-speed Internet. **Guest Services:** valet laundry.

MOTEL 6 CLARESHOLM
(403)625-4646
▼▼ Hotel $86-$96 **Address:** 11 Alberta Rd (Hwy 2) T0L 0T0 **Location:** North end of town. **Facility:** 69 units. 3 stories, interior corridors. **Parking:** winter plug-ins. **Amenities:** high-speed Internet. **Guest Services:** coin laundry.

COALDALE (J-7) pop. 7,493

THE ALBERTA BIRDS OF PREY CENTRE is at 2124 16th Ave. The facility, a working conservation center, rehabilitates injured and orphaned birds of prey and prepares them for release back into the wild. A captive breeding program returns threatened and endangered species to their native habitats. A self-guiding nature walk provides a close-up view of captive hawks, falcons, owls, eagles and vultures. Birds fly freely during daily demonstrations at this 28-hectare (70-acre) prairie wetland site.

Tours: Guided tours are available. **Time:** Allow 1 hour, 30 minutes minimum. **Hours:** Daily 9:30-5, early May-early Sept. **Cost:** $9.50; $8.50 (ages 60+); $6.50 (ages 6-17); $5.50 (ages 3-5). **Phone:** (403) 345-4262.

COCHRANE (H-5) pop. 17,580
- Part of Calgary area — see map p. 54

Cochrane—named for Sen. Matthew Henry Cochrane, who began the first large-scale cattle ranch in the area in the 1880s—is known locally for its homemade ice cream, made by the same family since 1948; hang gliding; horseback riding; and canoe trips down the Bow River. Stoney Indian Reserve, 16 kilometres (10 mi.) west on Hwy. 1A, was the filming site of several movies, including Arthur Penn's "Legends of the Fall" and "Little Big Man," and of the television series "Lonesome Dove."

Downtown Cochrane's Western-style architecture provides a backdrop for local arts and crafts and specialty shops. Of particular interest is Studio West, a foundry and art gallery where visitors can view the 3,000-year-old sculpting technique known as the "lost wax" process.

Also noteworthy is the town's "Trust" mural, on display at The Cochrane RancheHouse at 101 RancheHouse Rd. A montage of small paintings, the collective work of nearly 200 artists, forms a large Western image of a cowboy and his horse. The mural is accessible Mon.-Fri. 8:30-4:30. Closed holidays.

Cochrane & District Chamber of Commerce: 205 First St. E., P.O. Box 986, Cochrane, AB, Canada T4C 1X6. **Phone:** (403) 932-0320.

COCHRANE RANCHE HISTORIC SITE is near jct. hwys. 1A and 22. This 60-hectare (150-acre) site is where Sen. Matthew Henry Cochrane began his large-scale cattle operation in 1881. A visitor center, interpretive programs and walking trails are available. The "Men of Vision" bronze statue overlooks the grounds. **Time:** Allow 30 minutes minimum. **Hours:** Daily 9-5, mid-May through Labour Day. **Cost:** Free. **Phone:** (403) 932-4705.

DAYS INN & SUITES COCHRANE
(403)932-5588
▼▼▼ Hotel $99-$180 **Address:** 5 West Side Dr T4C 1M1 **Location:** Jct Hwy 1A, 0.3 mi (0.5 km) s on Hwy 22, just e on Quigley Dr, then just s. **Facility:** 61 units, some efficiencies and kitchens. 4 stories, interior corridors. **Terms:** check-in 4 pm, cancellation fee imposed. **Amenities:** high-speed Internet. Some: safes. **Pool(s):** heated indoor. **Activities:** exercise room. **Guest Services:** valet and coin laundry.

RAMADA COCHRANE
(403)932-6355

▼▼▼▼ **Hotel** $115-$165 **Address:** 10 West Side Dr T4C 1M1 **Location:** Jct Hwy 1A, 0.3 mi (0.5 km) s on Hwy 22, just e on Quigley Dr, then just s. **Facility:** 72 units, some efficiencies. 4 stories, interior corridors. **Parking:** winter plug-ins. **Amenities:** high-speed Internet. *Some:* video games. **Pool(s):** heated indoor. **Activities:** whirlpool, waterslide, exercise room. **Guest Services:** valet and coin laundry.

ECO 〔¶▸〕 ⊇ 〔BIZ〕 🛜 ✕ 🖥 🖨 🖵
/ SOME UNITS FEE 🐾

SUPER 8 COCHRANE
(403)932-1410

▼▼ ▼ **Hotel** $120-$150 **Address:** 11 West Side Dr T4C 1M1 **Location:** Jct Hwy 1A, 0.3 mi (0.5 km) s on Hwy 22, just e on Quigley Dr, then just s. **Facility:** 48 units. 3 stories (no elevator), interior/exterior corridors. **Parking:** winter plug-ins. **Amenities:** high-speed Internet. **Activities:** whirlpool, steamroom, exercise room. **Guest Services:** valet and coin laundry.

〔¶▸〕 〔BIZ〕 🛜 ✕ 🖥 🖨 🖵 / SOME UNITS FEE 🐾

WHERE TO EAT

BLUE DOG CAFE
403/932-4282

▼▼▼ Cajun. Casual Dining. $10-$26 **AAA Inspector Notes:** With a touch of jazz and a taste of funk, this eclectic café offers an intimate, memorable dining experience in this small town. The dining room has a mere 15 tables. On the menu are Cajun specialty dishes, including jambalaya and catfish. **Bar:** full bar. **Reservations:** suggested. **Address:** 110 Third Ave W T0L 0W0 **Location:** Hwy 1A, 2 blks w. 〔L〕〔D〕

PORTOFINO ITALIAN RISTORANTE
403/932-1777

▼▼▼ Italian. Casual Dining. $15-$38 **AAA Inspector Notes:** A little taste of finer dining takes place here with both the casually elegant décor and service style which is not overly stuffy. A well-prepared menu is served with such items as minestrone, artichoke hearts salad and a nice array of pasta and risotto. Find meat dishes including veal scaloppini al Parmigiana, chicken cacciatore and such seafood as baked scampi or cioppino seafood stew. If you are lucky they will have the warm and frothy zabaglione on the dessert menu. **Bar:** full bar. **Reservations:** suggested. **Address:** 205 1st St E, Bay 18 T4C 1X6 **Location:** Corner of River Ave; in a small complex.

〔L〕〔D〕 CALL 🖥M

PRAIRIE SMOKE RESTAURANT
403/932-9001

▼▼ ▼ American. Casual Dining. $8-$24 **AAA Inspector Notes:** Within walking distance to all of the hotels, who would have guessed that this slightly Spanish feeling restaurant does not have a wide selection of Tex-Mex favorites. Instead, the casual eatery offers a menu of such contemporary favorites as burgers, pasta and steak. **Bar:** full bar. **Reservations:** suggested. **Address:** 19 West Side Dr T4C 1M1 **Location:** Hwy 1A, 0.6 mi (1 km) sw on Hwy 22. 〔L〕〔D〕

COLD LAKE (D-9) pop. 13,839, elev. 555m/1,820'

COLD LAKE MUSEUMS is 5.1 km (3.12 mi.) s.w. on Hwy. 28 (8th Ave.)/Hwy. 55 (51st St.) at 6503 51st St. Four separate buildings connected by an enclosed passageway are situated on the site of a former radar facility. Showcased is the original 13-metre (42-ft.) radar height finder antenna, part of the Distant Early Warning Line during the Cold War.

The Aboriginal Museum displays Dene Suline and Cree artifacts and crafts. Interactive exhibits focusing on the area's oil sands industry are featured in The Oil & Gas Gallery, while the Heritage Museum highlights some of Cold Lake's other industries in addition to local history. Several aircraft and military vehicles are parked just outside the Cold Lake Air Force Museum, which relates the story of the Canadian Forces in the region.

Tours: Guided tours are available. **Time:** Allow 1 hour minimum. **Hours:** Tues.-Sat. 10-4, Victoria Day weekend-Labour Day. **Cost:** Donations. **Phone:** (780) 593-8047 for general information, (780) 594-3546 for the Cold Lake Air Force Museum, or (800) 840-6140 in the off-season. 🎫

BEST WESTERN COLD LAKE INN
780/594-4888

▼▼ ▼
Hotel
Rates not provided

AAA Benefit: Members save up to 20%, plus 10% bonus points with Best Western Rewards®.

Address: 4815 52nd St T9M 1P1 **Location:** Corner of 55th Ave (Hwy 26 and 55) and 52nd St; south end of city. **Facility:** 137 units, some efficiencies. 2-4 stories, interior/exterior corridors. **Parking:** winter plug-ins. **Amenities:** high-speed Internet. *Some:* safes. **Dining:** Sawmill Prime Rib & Steak House, see separate listing. **Pool(s):** heated indoor. **Activities:** whirlpool, waterslide, exercise room. **Guest Services:** valet laundry. **Free Special Amenities:** continental breakfast and high-speed Internet.

SAVE 〔¶▸〕 〔 〕 CALL 🖥M ⊇ 〔BIZ〕 🛜 ✕ 🖥 🖨 🖵 / SOME UNITS FEE 🐾

WHERE TO EAT

CLARKS GENERAL STORE & EATERY
780/639-4782

▼▼ ▼ American. Casual Dining. $9-$21 **AAA Inspector Notes:** This very popular restaurant is located in the old Clark's General Store, complete with a 1940s lunch counter and original copper bearing panel ceilings. You sure won't be bored because there are tons of antiques, collectibles and photos to look at. A mannequin, "Lucy" as she is affectionately known, gets a regular change of clothes with the season. A variety of good comfort food is on hand, including fish and chips, liver and onions, burgers, haddock, curry, Nathan's hot dogs and homemade pies. **Bar:** full bar. **Reservations:** suggested. **Address:** 701 Lakeshore Dr T9M 1N1 **Location:** Jct Hwy 55/28 and 16th Ave, 1.4 mi (2.4 km) ne, then just n; in North Cold Lake across from marina. **Parking:** street only. 〔L〕〔D〕

SAWMILL PRIME RIB & STEAK HOUSE
780/594-5985

▼▼▼ Steak. Casual Dining. $10-$39 **AAA Inspector Notes:** One of the finer spots in town, the contemporary decor accents the sawmill business. They feature a great Alberta AAA steak and prime rib menu with tasty starters like a shrimp martini with mint citrus salad or chicken pot stickers (dumplings) along with a variety of soups. If you don't fancy steak, you can choose other entrées of lobster, chicken, salmon and lamb. **Bar:** full bar. **Reservations:** suggested. **Address:** 4815 52nd St T9M 1P1 **Location:** Corner of 55th Ave (Hwy 26 and 55) and 52nd St; south end of city; in BEST WESTERN Cold Lake Inn. 〔B〕〔L〕〔D〕 CALL 🖥M

COLUMBIA ICEFIELD—See Jasper National Park p. 151.

CROWSNEST PASS (J-5) pop. 5,565

An area of wild beauty and haunting legends, the municipality of Crowsnest Pass is an amalgamation of the former coal-mining towns of Bellevue, Blairmore, Coleman, Frank and Hillcrest. Scenic Hwy. 3 through Crowsnest Pass connects Burmis to Fernie, British Columbia, via the Rocky Mountain Range and the Continental Divide.

The area provides visitors with recreational opportunities and stimulates the imagination with such stories as the curse of the Lost Lemon Gold Mine, rum-running and the shoot-out at Bellevue Cafe.

The town of Frank made national headlines April 29, 1903, when close to 70 residents were killed in the dramatic slide of Turtle Mountain on the east side of the pass. Ninety million tons of limestone swept over 1.5 kilometres (.9 mi.) of the valley before dawn, destroying part of the town and burying a mine plant and railway. The old town was at the western edge of the slide; many cellars still are visible.

BELLEVUE UNDERGROUND MINE TOUR is n. off Hwy. 3 Bellevue exit, following signs to the Bellevue Underground Mine access road at 21814 28th Ave. Participants don a miner's helmet and lamp, strap on a battery pack and follow guides along the same path taken by coal miners 1903-61, when this was an active coal mine. The 1-hour tour provides insights into the process of coal mining and the events that led to the mine's closing.

Note: The temperature in the mine can reach 7 C (45 F); dress in warm clothing and wear sturdy footwear. **Time:** Allow 1 hour minimum. **Hours:** Tours depart daily every 30 minutes 10-6:30, mid-May through Labour Day. **Cost:** $12; $11 (ages 65+); $8 (ages 6-17); $35 (family). **Phone:** (403) 564-4700.

FRANK SLIDE INTERPRETIVE CENTRE is 1.5 km (.9 mi.) n. off Hwy. 3 at w. edge of Frank Slide. The center overlooks the site of the 1903 rockslide. Visitors experience the impact of Canada's deadliest rockslide through interactive exhibits and multimedia presentations. Walkways outside the center provide spectacular views of the surrounding Canadian Rockies. A 1.5-kilometre (.9-mi.) self-guiding trail over the slide allows visitors to view the debris. Interpretive programs are offered in summer.

Time: Allow 1 hour, 30 minutes minimum. **Hours:** Daily 9-6, July-Aug.; 10-5, rest of year. Closed Jan. 1, Easter, Christmas Eve and Christmas. **Cost:** $10; $8 (ages 65+); $5 (ages 7-17); $22 (family, two adults and children). **Phone:** (403) 562-7388.

LEITCH COLLIERIES PROVINCIAL HISTORIC SITE is 3 km (1.9 mi.) e. of Bellevue on Hwy. 3. Founded in 1907, this was the first wholly Canadian-owned mine. The area was the site of a sophisticated early colliery—a coal mine and the buildings and equipment connected with it. The remains of the power house, washery, mine manager's residence and coke ovens still stand.

Interpretive signs explain the mining and processing methods. **Hours:** Self-guiding tours are available year-round. Interpreters are on-site daily 10-5 and offer guided tours at 11 and 2, mid-May through Labour Day. **Cost:** Donations. **Phone:** (403) 562-7388.

DEAD MAN'S FLATS pop. 121
• Part of Banff National Park area — see map p. 37

COPPERSTONE RESORT HOTEL	(403)678-0303

Condominium $129-$299

Address: 250 2nd Ave T1W 2W4 **Location:** Trans-Canada Hwy 1 exit 98, just n on 2nd St, then just e. **Facility:** Spacious and upscale suites feature granite kitchen countertops, an electric fireplace, a flat-screen television, stereo system and private balcony. 62 condominiums. 2-3 stories, interior corridors. **Terms:** check-in 4 pm, cancellation fee imposed. **Activities:** whirlpool, exercise room. **Guest Services:** complimentary laundry. **Free Special Amenities:** local telephone calls and early check-in/late check-out.

Resort located just out of Canmore, in beautiful natural surroundings, close to area attractions

DEVON (E-6) pop. 6,510, elev. 680m/2,230'
• Part of Edmonton area — see map p. 109

Canada's first planned community, Devon was created by Imperial Oil Resources Ltd. in 1948 to provide accommodations for the workers employed in the company's oilfields. Imperial Leduc No. 1, the area's first well, had just put the town of Devon on the map. The town's name was derived from the Devonian formation, the oil's source, a stratum 1,524 metres (5,000 ft.) underground.

Devon is on the banks of the North Saskatchewan River, where fishing often yields northern pike, walleye and goldeye. Year-round recreational activities include canoeing, cross-country skiing, golf, hiking, ice-skating and swimming.

Town of Devon: 1 Columbia Ave. W., Devon, AB, Canada T9G 1A1. **Phone:** (780) 987-8300.

LEDUC #1 ENERGY DISCOVERY CENTRE is 2 km (1.2 mi.) s. on Hwy. 60. The center not only provides insight into the workings of the oil industry but also looks at area history, the story behind Leduc No. 1 and how Canada became self-sufficient in oil production. A 15-minute video presentation, interactive energy displays, geological exhibits, equipment, artifacts, photographs, scale models, murals and an outdoor interpretive trail help explain how oil is produced and refined.

A 53-metre (174-ft.) replica of the original derrick has been erected on the discovery site. **Time:** Allow 1 hour minimum. **Hours:** Mon.-Sat. 9-5, Sun. noon-5, mid-May to early Sept.; Mon.-Fri. 9-5, rest of year. **Cost:** $9; $8 (ages 65+); $6 (ages 6-18); $21 (family). **Phone:** (780) 987-4323 or (866) 987-4323.

DICKSON (G-5) pop. 60

DICKSON STORE MUSEUM is at 1928 2nd Ave. Renovated to a style typical of the 1930s, this general store once served as the town post office and a local gathering place. Now operating as a museum, it features exhibits of dry goods, hardware and groceries common to that time. Costumed interpreters also lead visitors through the restored second-floor living quarters.

Time: Allow 30 minutes minimum. **Hours:** Mon.-Sat. 10-5:30, Sun. 12:30-5:30, mid-May through Labour Day; Sat. 10-5:30, Sun. 12:30-5:30, day after Labour Day-last Sun. in Sept. **Cost:** Donations. **Phone:** (403) 728-3355.

DONALDA (F-7) pop. 259

Situated in the heart of Alberta, Donalda was established in 1911 and named after the niece of Donald A. Mann, an official with the Canadian National Railway. It overlooks the scenic Meeting Creek Coulee. The region's unusual Paskapoo sandstone rock formations attract sportsman, hikers, artists and photographers. Donalda also claims an unusual man-made distinction. A 12.8-metre (42-ft.) lamp, said to be the world's largest, was built in the town center by local residents. It glows at the east end of Main Street each evening.

DONALDA & DISTRICT MUSEUM is at Main St. and Railway Ave. More than 900 lamps ranging from the antique bicycle variety to colorful living room types are displayed. Some 40 tiny courting lamps, which hold only an hour's worth of fuel and were used in the 1800s to signal the end of a suitor's visit, also can be seen. In addition more than 4,000 artifacts depicting the area's history are exhibited. An art gallery housed in a 1928 bank building, a 1909 railway station and a creamery also are on-site.

Time: Allow 30 minutes minimum. **Hours:** Mon.-Fri. 9-5, Sat.-Sun. 11-5, early May-second Mon. in Oct.; Mon.-Fri. 9-5, rest of year. **Cost:** Donations. **Phone:** (403) 883-2100.

DRAYTON VALLEY pop. 7,049

HOLIDAY INN EXPRESS HOTEL & SUITES
(780)515-9888

Hotel
$139-$169

Address: 5001 Brougham Dr T7A 0A1 **Location:** Hwy 22 exit Drayton Valley, 1.5 mi (2.4 km) n. **Facility:** 96 units. 3 stories, interior corridors. **Parking:** winter plug-ins. **Terms:** cancellation fee imposed. **Amenities:** high-speed Internet. **Activities:** whirlpool, exercise room. **Guest Services:** valet and coin laundry.

LAKEVIEW INNS & SUITES
780/542-3200

Hotel
Rates not provided

Address: 4302 50th St T7A 1M4 **Location:** Hwy 22 exit Drayton Valley, 1.5 mi (2.4 km) n. **Facility:** 90 units. 3 stories (no elevator), interior corridors. **Parking:** winter plug-ins. **Amenities:** high-speed Internet. **Activities:** sauna, exercise room. **Guest Services:** valet and coin laundry. **Free Special Amenities: expanded continental breakfast and high-speed Internet.**

SAVE | | | BIZ | | | | / SOME UNITS FEE

RAMADA INN DRAYTON VALLEY
(780)514-7861

Hotel **$140-$220 Address:** 2051 50th St T7A 1S5 **Location:** Just n on Hwy 39; south end of town. **Facility:** 82 units, some efficiencies. 4 stories, interior/exterior corridors. **Parking:** winter plug-ins. **Amenities:** high-speed Internet. **Pool(s):** heated indoor. **Activities:** whirlpool, waterslide, exercise room. **Guest Services:** valet and coin laundry.

ECO CALL | BIZ | | | | / SOME UNITS FEE

WHERE TO EAT

FLUIDS BAR & GRILL
780/621-3341

American. Casual Dining. $9-$28 **AAA Inspector Notes:** The establishment might look like an Irish pub but the food is anything but typical, except for the Guinness battered halibut and classic burger. For starters, try the smoked chicken and asparagus risotto followed by spicy chorizo pasta, bouillabaisse or lamb tenderloin. Service is casual and efficient. **Bar:** full bar. **Address:** 5-5505 50th St T7A 1W2 **Location:** Hwy 22 north access, just se; in strip mall.
L D CALL

MITCH'S FAMILY RESTAURANT
780/542-7525

American. Family Dining. $8-$25 **AAA Inspector Notes:** Comfortable and casual describes the décor at this establishment, and the menu follows suit with pub-style appetizers, burgers, po' boy and sub sandwiches, a good variety of pizzas, barbecue chicken, steaks and tender bison, pork or beef ribs. Service is quick and friendly. **Address:** 4341 50th St, Unit 102 T7A 1M4 **Location:** Hwy 22 exit Drayton Valley, 1.6 mi (2.7 km) n; east end of town. B L D CALL

THREE KNIGHTS STEAK HOUSE & PIZZA
780/542-5222

American. Casual Dining. $8-$28 **AAA Inspector Notes:** Not much has changed at this local favorite and folks will feel as though they have walked back in time-not quite to the Middle Ages but at least to the 1970s. A small suit of armor greets guests at the door, while a few shields adorn the walls at this second-generation, family-owned eatery. Expect a well-prepared traditional AAA Alberta Angus steak, seafood, pasta and pizza menu along with classic burgers and sandwiches as well as friendly and efficient service. **Bar:** full bar. **Address:** 5211 50 St T7A 1R5 **Location:** Hwy 22 north access, 0.6 mi (1 km) se; in strip mall. L D CALL

DRUMHELLER (H-7) pop. 8,029
• Hotels p. 107 • Restaurants p. 107

About 65 million years before Sam Drumheller began promoting the 1910 townsite later named for him, the surrounding Red Deer Valley was the home of immense dinosaurs. Plant-eating hadrosaurs, flesh-eating tyrannosaurs and their formidable cousins stomped through the swampy lowlands and forests bordering the Mowry Sea, which once covered the North American plains. Fossils of prehistoric creatures often are discovered in the multi-layered sedimentary walls of the valley; several life-size dinosaur replicas can be seen in town.

A larger-than-life version of one of these prehistoric beings, a 25-metre-tall (84-ft.) facsimile of a tyrannosaurus rex, has been built over the top of the

Drumheller & District Chamber of Commerce at 60 1st Ave. W. Visitors can climb up to a viewing platform in the dinosaur's mouth.

Although the local coal industry founded in 1911 by American Jesse Gouge has declined, remnants of old mines still exist. Six kilometres (3.7 mi.) w. on N. Dinosaur Trail (Hwy. 838), Midland Provincial Park features a self-guiding walking trail that leads to the former site of Midland Mine. Gas and oil wells sporadically dot the nearby rolling prairies, but the shortgrass country is occupied mostly by geese and antelope.

Hoodoos—mushroom-shaped pillars of rock that have been carved into unusual formations by centuries of wind and rain—can be seen 18 kilometres (11 mi.) southeast on Hwy. 10. Because of their fragile nature, climbing these formations is not permitted.

Another nearby remarkable natural site is Horseshoe Canyon, 17 kilometres (11 mi.) southwest on Hwy. 9. Deriving its name from its horseshoe shape, the canyon is in an area of badlands amidst the Alberta prairies. Viewpoints provide opportunities to survey multicolored canyon walls and unusual rock formations.

A natural amphitheater is the site in early July for six performances of The Canadian Badlands Passion Play. In a setting closely resembling the Holy Land, a cast of 150 and a 100-voice choir relate the life of Christ; phone (403) 823-2001 or (888) 823-2001.

Stretching over the Red Deer River, the Rosedale Suspension Bridge on Hwy. 10 originally was used to carry miners across the river to the now-abandoned Star Mine. In 1931 the swinging bridge replaced the original cable car system and was used until the mine closed in 1957. A park with picnic facilities is available.

Drumheller & District Chamber of Commerce: 60 1st Ave. W., P.O. Box 999, Drumheller, AB, Canada T0J 0Y0. **Phone:** (866) 823-8100.

ATLAS COAL MINE NATIONAL HISTORIC SITE is 18 km (11 mi.) s.e. on Hwy. 10. This site explores the coal mining history of the Drumheller Valley. Visitors can take a guided tour of what is said to be the last remaining wooden tipple (coal screening plant) in Canada; take a ride on a 1936 Mancha locomotive; see restored mine offices, a lamp house and a miner's shack; hike on interpretive trails; and climb on antique mining machines. A 75-minute underground tunnel tour and a 1-hour ghost walk tour also are offered.

Time: Allow 1 hour, 30 minutes minimum. **Hours:** Daily 9:30-8:30, July-Aug.; 9:30-6 in June and Sept. Tour schedules vary; phone ahead. **Cost:** Historic site $7; free (ages 0-6); $21 (family, two adults and two children). Tunnel tour (includes historic site) $15; free (ages 4-6); $45 (family, two adults and two children). Tipple, mine train or ghost walk tour (includes historic site) $10; free (ages 0-6); $30 (family, two adults and two children). Under 4 are not permitted on the tunnel tour. **Phone:** (403) 822-2220.

DINOSAUR TRAIL (HWYS. 838 AND 837) is a 48-km (30-mi.) looping drive trip that connects Drumheller with the Red Deer River Valley, part of Alberta's Canadian Badlands. The trail is marked, and several museums, parks and observation points are along the route. The arid terrain is distinguished by hoodoos—mushroom-shaped rock pillars carved by thousands of years of wind and rain.

On the north side of the trail is The Little Church, a meditation chapel that holds six visitors. The cable-run Bleriot Ferry crosses the Red Deer River. **Hours:** Highway open daily. The ferry departs daily as needed dawn-dusk, early May to mid-Oct. **Cost:** Highway and ferry free. **Phone:** (866) 823-8100.

HOMESTEAD MUSEUM is .7 km (.5 mi.) n.w. via Hwy. 9 to 901 N. Dinosaur Tr. (Hwy. 838). Pioneer and First Nations items as well as clocks, gramophones, radios, early cars, fine china, jewelry, tractors and farm implements are displayed. There also are collections of military badges, medals and early 20th-century clothing. **Time:** Allow 1 hour, 30 minutes minimum. **Hours:** Daily 10-5, May 1 to mid-Oct. (also Thurs.-Sun. 5-8, July 1-Labour Day). **Cost:** $7; $5 (ages 6-17 and 65+); $15 (family). **Phone:** (403) 823-2600.

REPTILE WORLD, 95 3rd Ave. E., is home to more than 150 species of reptiles and amphibians, including snakes, frogs and turtles. Still, the facility's most well-known resident is Fred, a 272-kilogram (600-lb.) alligator. **Time:** Allow 30 minutes minimum. **Hours:** Daily 10-6, July-Aug.; Thurs.-Fri. and Mon. noon-5, Sat.-Sun. 10-5, rest of year. Public feedings are Sat. at 5:30 p.m., in summer. Closed major holidays. Phone ahead to confirm schedule. **Cost:** $8.50; $5.50 (ages 5-17 and 65+); $25 (family, two adults and children). **Phone:** (403) 823-8623.

ROYAL TYRRELL MUSEUM is 6 km (4 mi.) n.w. on N. Dinosaur Tr. (Hwy. 838) in Midland Provincial Park. The museum is in the badlands of the Red Deer River Valley, surrounded by one of the richest fossil deposits in the world. Dinosaurs that once roamed Alberta are now showcased in the museum's Dinosaur Hall, where more than 35 skeletons and lifelike models are displayed.

Fossils, models, computers, DVD centers, a preparation laboratory, hands-on exhibits and an indoor garden illustrate millions of years of geological and biological development. Educational programs are offered Victoria Day weekend through Labour Day. The Cretaceous Garden contains plants that are virtually the same today as they were more than 65 million years ago. The museum also houses a research center and operates a field station near Patricia (see attraction listing p. 174).

Time: Allow 3 hours minimum. **Hours:** Daily 9-9, Victoria Day weekend-Labour Day; Tues.-Sat. 10-5, rest of year. Closed Jan. 1 and Christmas. Phone ahead to confirm schedule. **Cost:** $11; $8 (ages 65+); $6 (ages 7-17); $30 (family, two adults and children). **Phone:** (403) 823-7707, or (888) 440-4240 out of Alberta.

VALLEY DOLL MUSEUM is at 60-249 3rd Ave. W. More than 700 dolls are displayed in themed settings. Celebrity dolls include Marilyn Monroe, Elvis Presley and John Wayne. Unusual figures fashioned from such materials as coal, wax and felt also are exhibited. **Note:** The facility is not wheelchair accessible. **Time:** Allow 30 minutes minimum. **Hours:** Mon.-Sat. 10-7, Sun. noon-5, in summer; Tues.-Sat. 10-5, rest of year. Closed Jan. 1, third Mon. in Feb., Thanksgiving, Christmas and day after Christmas. **Cost:** $5.50; $4.50 (ages 12-17); $3.50 (ages 5-11). **Phone:** (403) 823-3655.

CANALTA JURASSIC HOTEL
403/823-7700

Hotel. Rates not provided. **Address:** 1103 Hwy 9 S T0J 0Y0 **Location:** Hwy 9, southeast access to town. **Facility:** 48 units, some efficiencies. 2 stories (no elevator), interior/exterior corridors. **Parking:** winter plug-ins. **Activities:** whirlpool, steamroom, exercise room. **Guest Services:** coin laundry.

INN AND SPA AT HEARTWOOD
403/823-6495

Boutique Hotel $105-$315 **Address:** 320 N Railway Ave E T0J 0Y4 **Location:** Jct Hwy 9 and 575 (S Railway Ave SE), just n, then just e. **Facility:** Classic, old-fashioned touches distinguish this inn, a heritage home which has been skillfully renovated. 10 units, some houses and cottages. 2 stories (no elevator), interior/exterior corridors. **Parking:** winter plug-ins. **Terms:** check-in 4 pm, 2 night minimum stay - weekends, age restrictions may apply, 3 day cancellation notice-fee imposed. **Activities:** spa. **Guest Services:** coin laundry.

RAMADA INN & SUITES
(403)823-2028

Hotel $150-$220 **Address:** 680 2nd St SE T0J 0Y0 **Location:** Jct Hwy 9 and 575 (S Railway Ave SE), just ne. **Facility:** 74 units. 4 stories, interior/exterior corridors. **Parking:** winter plug-ins. **Amenities:** high-speed Internet. **Pool(s):** heated indoor. **Activities:** whirlpool, waterslide, exercise room. **Guest Services:** coin laundry.

SUPER 8
(403)823-8887

Hotel $140-$180 **Address:** 600-680 2nd St SE T0J 0Y0 **Location:** Jct Hwy 9 and 575 (S Railway Ave SE), just ne. **Facility:** 72 units, some two bedrooms, efficiencies and kitchens. 2-3 stories, interior/exterior corridors. **Terms:** cancellation fee imposed. **Amenities:** high-speed Internet. **Pool(s):** heated indoor. **Activities:** whirlpool, waterslide, exercise room. **Guest Services:** valet and coin laundry.

TASTE THE PAST BED & BREAKFAST
403/823-5889

Historic Bed & Breakfast $115-$125 **Address:** 281 2nd St W T0J 0Y0 **Location:** Hwy 9 exit 2nd St W; center. **Facility:** Built by a coal baron in 1910, the large home features a working 1930s billiards table in the lounge area. 3 units. 3 stories (no elevator), interior corridors. **Parking:** winter plug-ins. **Terms:** check-in 4 pm, cancellation fee imposed.

WHERE TO EAT

CAFE ITALIANO
403/823-4443

Coffee/Tea. Casual Dining. $6-$12 **AAA Inspector:** The small downtown cafe is best known for its panini and dessert offerings, not to mention a good cup of coffee and lively bantering between the owner and locals. **Address:** 35 3rd Ave W T0J 0Y0 **Location:** Downtown. **Parking:** street only. B L

FLAVOURZ
403/823-4447

Indian. Casual Dining. $7-$20 **AAA Inspector Notes:** There's a simple decor here and the menu is not extensive but it is cooked from scratch, quite tasty and served by friendly helpful servers. You can find items like samosas and fish pakoras to start followed by lamb, chicken or beef curries, butter chicken and other chicken dishes as well as a good variety of vegetarian items. They also have wings and a few wraps and sandwiches. The same menu is offered in the lounge where you can catch a game or shoot some pool. **Bar:** full bar. **Reservations:** suggested. **Address:** 1102C Hwy 9 S T0J 0Y0 **Location:** Hwy 9, southeast access to town; in small strip mall. L D CALL M

O'SHEA'S EATERY & ALE HOUSE
403/823-2460

American. Casual Dining. $7-$24 **AAA Inspector Notes:** This attractive Irish theme restaurant showcases beautiful stained-glass work and offers up an extended pub menu as well as a good selection of salads, pasta, fish, ribs and steak. And they do not forget to include such Irish classics as fish and chips, Guinness beef stew, shepherd's pie and cheese steak boxty. **Bar:** full bar. **Address:** 680 2nd St SE, 600B T0J 0Y0 **Location:** Jct Hwy 9 and 575 (S Railway Ave SE), just ne; next to Ramada Inn & Suites. L D CALL M

VINTAGE PUB & GRILL
403/823-5123

American. Casual Dining. $6-$22 **AAA Inspector Notes:** This casual pub has a wide-open space with a contemporary feel where diners can relax and visit while enjoying the wall-mounted TVs and pool table. A very good selection of pub grub includes delicious burgers, sandwiches, pasta, steaks, ribs, grilled salmon, jambalaya and fish and chips. Guests must be of legal drinking age to enter the premises. **Bar:** full bar. **Address:** 30 Railway Ave E T0J 0Y0 **Location:** Jct Hwy 9 and 575 (S Railway Ave SE), just n, then just e. **Parking:** street only. L D CALL M

DUNVEGAN (B-2)

SAVE **DUNVEGAN PROVINCIAL PARK** is off Queen Elizabeth II Hwy. on the n. side of the Peace River beside Dunvegan Suspension Bridge. The park was a fur-trading post and the site of one of the first Roman Catholic missions in Alberta. Three original buildings remain: the 1877-78 Factor's House, part of the Hudson's Bay Co.'s fort, along with the 1885 church of St. Charles Mission and its 1889 rectory.

Guided walks and educational programs explain the site's history. A visitor center offers a video about the history of Dunvegan. *See Recreation Areas Chart.* **Time:** Allow 1 hour minimum. **Hours:** Daily 10-5, May 15-Labour Day. **Cost:** $3; $2 (ages 65+); $1.50 (ages 7-17); $8 (family). **Phone:** (780) 835-7150.

Edmonton

Then & Now

From trading post to metropolis within some 200 years, Edmonton continues to surprise visitors by its size, quality of life, sophistication and beautiful river valley location.

In 1795 the Hudson's Bay Co. founded Fort Edmonton on the banks of the North Saskatchewan River. Traders bartered with Cree and Blackfoot Indians for luxuriant and sought-after pelts of otters, beavers, muskrats, minks and foxes. A trading settlement developed and became the main stopping point on routes to the north and to the Pacific.

This stopping point became a starting point for gold seekers rushing to the Klondike; they gathered supplies in Edmonton for the harsh trip north. When gold failed to materialize and many prospectors realized they weren't going to get rich, let alone get rich quick, they returned to Edmonton to settle for a slower but surer way of life.

A bust for prospectors was a boom for Edmonton. The city grew to six times its previous size, making it a prime choice for the provincial capital when Alberta was formed in 1905.

In the years that followed, the capital city earned its nickname, "Gateway to the North," because of its status as a transportation hub and gateway to the regions beyond. In 1915 Edmonton became a major link in the Canadian Pacific Transcontinental Railroad, emerging as an important crossroads stop between east and west as well as north and south.

The city's reputation as a transportation center was reinforced during the 1930s as bush pilots transported vital medical supplies, food and mail to northern communities. And when construction began on the Alaska Highway in 1942, Edmonton found itself again in the role of a major distribution and supply center.

In February 1947, the Leduc No. 1 Well gushed crude oil 40 kilometres (25 mi.) southwest of Edmonton. Since then more than 2,250 wells within a 40-kilometre (25-mi.) radius of Edmonton have coaxed the precious natural resource to the surface. Enormous industrial growth resulted; the city's population quadrupled in the 25 years following the Leduc gusher. Today more than 450,000 barrels of crude oil are refined daily in Greater Edmonton.

With about 938,000 residents in the greater metropolitan area, Edmonton has been careful not to sacrifice the natural resource that makes it livable—its green space. Edmonton's river valley parkland is reputed to be the largest stretch of urban parkland in North America, encompassing 7,340 hectares (18,348 acres). The city contains more than 11,000 hectares (27,181 acres) of parkland, playgrounds and open areas. Stretches of parks along the

Alberta Legislature Building

(Continued on p. 110.)

Destination Edmonton

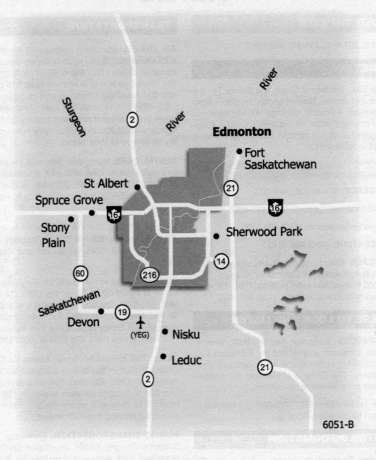

Edmonton

Sturgeon River

St Albert

Spruce Grove

Stony Plain

Fort Saskatchewan

Sherwood Park

Saskatchewan

Devon

(YEG)

Nisku

Leduc

6051-B

This map shows cities in the Edmonton vicinity where you will find attractions, hotels and restaurants. Cities are listed alphabetically in this book on the following pages.

Fast Facts

ABOUT THE CITY

POP: 812,201 ■ **ELEV:** 670 m/2,198 ft.

MONEY

SALES TAX: The federal Goods and Service Tax is 5 percent and applies to most goods, food/beverages and services, including lodgings. Alberta does not have a provincial sales tax but does impose a 4 percent hotel tax. A 1-2 percent tourism levy also is charged in some areas.

WHOM TO CALL

EMERGENCY: 911 or (780) 426-3232

POLICE (non-emergency): (780) 423-4567

FIRE (non-emergency): (780) 496-3900

TEMPERATURE: (780) 468-4940

HOSPITALS: Grey Nuns Community Hospital, (780) 735-7000 ■ Misericordia Community Hospital, (780) 735-2000 ■ Royal Alexandra Hospital, (780) 735-4111 ■ University of Alberta Hospital, (780) 407-8822.

WHERE TO LOOK AND LISTEN

NEWSPAPERS: Edmonton has two daily newspapers, the *Edmonton Journal* and the *Edmonton Sun,* both distributed in the morning. Canada's national newspapers, *The Globe and Mail* and the *National Post,* also are available at newsstands.

RADIO: Radio station CBC (740 AM) is a member of Canadian Broadcasting Corp.

VISITOR INFORMATION

Edmonton Tourism: 9990 Jasper Ave. N.W., Edmonton, AB, Canada T5J 1P7. **Phone:** (780) 496-8400 or (800) 463-4667.

Gateway Park Information Center: 2404 Gateway Blvd. S.W./Queen Elizabeth II Hwy., Edmonton, AB, Canada T6W 1A1. **Phone:** (780) 496-8400 or (800) 463-4667.

Visitor information also is available at the Edmonton International Airport.

TRANSPORTATION

AIR TRAVEL: Edmonton International Airport (YEG) is 29 kilometres (18 mi.) south of the city center; for information phone (780) 890-8382 or (800) 268-7134. Sky Shuttle service to downtown costs $18 one way and $30 round-trip (phone to confirm fares); phone (780) 465-8515 or (888) 438-2342. Taxi service between the airport and downtown typically costs $49; a limousine costs $60. In addition many hotels offer free shuttle service for their guests.

RENTAL CARS: Hertz, downtown or at the airport, offers discounts to CAA and AAA members; phone (780) 423-3431 downtown, (780) 890-4435 at the airport, (800) 263-0600 in Canada or (800) 654-3080 out of Canada.

RAIL SERVICE: The VIA Rail station is at 12360 121st St.; phone (780) 448-2575 for baggage information, (888) 842-7245 for arrival and departure information.

BUSES: The downtown depot for Greyhound Lines Inc. is at 10324 103rd St.; phone (780) 413-8747 or (800) 661-8747. The south side depot is at 5723 104th St. Red Arrow Express offers luxury motor coach service between Edmonton, Calgary, Fort McMurray and Red Deer; phone (780) 424-3339 or (800) 232-1958.

TAXIS: Taxi companies include Alberta Co-Op Taxi, (780) 425-2525 ■ Barrel Taxi (780) 489-7777 ■ and Yellow Cab, (780) 462-3456. Taxi rates start at $3.60, plus 20c is charged for each additional 135 metres (about 1/12 mile) or a portion thereof. Taxis can be hailed, but phoning is recommended.

PUBLIC TRANSPORTATION: Edmonton Transit System's Churchill Station Information Centre, 99th Street and 102A Avenue, is open Mon.-Fri. 8:30-5:30; phone (780) 496-1611. Buses operate 6 a.m.-1 a.m., Mon.-Sat., 6:30 a.m.-12:30 a.m., Sun. and holidays; hours may be extended for special events. The Light-Rail Transit (LRT) operates 5:30 a.m. to 1 a.m. Fare is $3. A 1-day pass is $8.55. Disabled Adult Transit System (DATS) serves those who can't use other transit facilities. Visitors may request a temporary registration number by phoning (780) 496-4570. DATS reservations are accepted up to 3 days in advance.

(Continued from p. 108.)
North Saskatchewan River Valley let residents and visitors spend long summer days enjoying such warm-weather activities as golf, hiking and water sports. When the cold weather arrives, the park system provides a playground for cross-country skiing, ice-skating, dog sledding and snowshoeing.

An extensive system of underground and overhead "pedways" in the downtown area makes it possible to travel in climate-controlled comfort regardless of the weather. Those who'd rather play indoors head to West Edmonton Mall, which combines 800-plus retail stores with restaurants and such attractions as an amusement park, a water park, an aquarium and an ice-skating rink. The largest of its kind in North America, this shopping and entertainment center has undergone three major expansions since its 1981 opening and draws an estimated 28.4 million people each year.

Must Do: AAA Editor's Picks

- Travel back in time at ⟱ **Fort Edmonton Park,** dubbed Canada's largest living-history park. Staffed by costumed interpreters, the site features both original and re-created historical structures—everything from a replicated Hudson's Bay Co. fort to a 1920s-style midway.

- Spend a few loonies at the ⟱ **West Edmonton Mall,** the largest shopping and entertainment center in North America. The gargantuan complex boasts an amusement park, a water park, an aquarium, a shooting range and an ice rink. Despite such impressive amenities, Clara, Kelpie and Pablo, the three California sea lions working the mall crowd daily, usually garner the most accolades. (And by "accolades," we mean fish, natch.)

- Attend a show at the **Francis Winspear Centre for Music.** Built in 1997, the main performance space is a modern interpretation of such shoebox-style concert halls as the Tonhalle in Zurich and the Musikverein in Vienna. The downtown Edmonton facility is renowned for its acoustics as well as a stunning 6,551-pipe concert organ fashioned by Orgues Létourneau Limitée of Québec.

- Wrap your head around architect Randall Stout's **Art Gallery of Alberta,** a curvy blend of steel and glass inspired by such undulating natural treasures as the aurora borealis and the North Saskatchewan River. When you're done ogling the ultra-modern exterior, head inside and admire the handiwork of such Canadian painters as Maxwell Bates, Emily Carr and David Milne.

- Scan the ⟱ **Muttart Conservatory.** Readable by smartphones, matrix barcodes posted in four futuristic pyramid-shaped greenhouses put descriptions of walking tours and changing exhibitions in the palm of your hand. Low-tech printed tour brochures also are available, as are weekend guided tours.

- Cheer on the National Hockey League's Edmonton Oilers at **Rexall Place,** once the stomping ground of Wayne Gretzky. "The Great One" led his team to four Stanley Cup victories, an achievement commemorated when a bronze statue of the frequent MVP was erected outside the arena in 1989, just 1 year after Gretzky was traded to the Los Angeles Kings.

- Eat, drink and be merry in **Old Strathcona,** a five-block historic district now dominated by bohemian java joints, funky stores, live performance venues, restaurants and bars. Whether the agenda calls for a bit of window-shopping or some late-night carousing, your best bet is to stick to the section of Whyte Avenue between 99th and 109th streets.

- Explore Edmonton's "Ribbon of Green," a 48-kilometre (30-mi.) stretch of the **North Saskatchewan River Valley** with bragging rights to more than 20 major parks and public facilities. In winter, strap on your cross-country skis and traverse 130-hectare (1.3-sq.-mi.) William Hawrelak Park. Or, if the weather's warm, play a round at Victoria Golf Course, said to be the oldest municipal golf course in Canada.

- Party like an Edmontonian. An overbooked calendar filled with more than 30 annual events—including July's **Edmonton International Street Performers Festival,** August's **Edmonton Folk Music Festival** and November's **Canadian Finals Rodeo**—earned the provincial capital the nickname "The Festival City."

- Tour the 1912 Beaux Arts **Alberta Legislature Building** for sure. But spend the bulk of your time strolling the handsome grounds—monuments dedicated to military veterans, immigrant groups and prominent Albertans dot the 23-hectare (57-acre) park. Wading pools and shooting water fountains are huge kid magnets in summer, and the holiday light and ice sculpture displays that arrive come winter dazzle visitors of all ages.

Art Gallery of Alberta

Edmonton 1-day Itinerary

AAA editors suggest these activities for a great short vacation experience.

Morning

- Operating from late May through early October, the **High Level Streetcar** is a fun way to travel between downtown Edmonton (where you can browse Jasper Avenue boutiques or hit the slots at the **Baccarat Casino**) and Old Strathcona (a historic district now sheltering a bastion of independent businesses). As your vintage vehicle crosses the 1913 High Level Bridge, you'll catch a glimpse—and likely a shaky snapshot or two—of the idyllic North Saskatchewan River Valley.

- For eats, the **Blue Plate Diner** is a few blocks east of the streetcar's northern terminus (which is downtown, south of Jasper Avenue and west of 109th Street). Your typical brunch dishes are doled out on weekends, as are more unconventional mid-morning morsels, like lemon ricotta pancakes and tofu-topped crostini.

- Along the streetcar line are three intermediary stops, including one in the Garneau neighborhood. If you disembark here, try a specialty brew from Transcend, 8708 109th St. N.W., a local coffee chain that's been hawking gourmet blends and ethically sourced beans since 2006. Hankering for something special to dunk in your cup of joe? Look no further than the **Highlevel Diner,** an eclectic space known far and wide for its cakey, supersize cinnamon buns.

- At the High Level Streetcar's southern terminus (at 103rd Street and 84th Avenue) is the Strathcona Streetcar Barn Museum, where rail buffs can peruse antique model trains and ticket punches. The museum is at the north end of the Old Strathcona Farmers' Market, open every Saturday from 8 a.m. to 3 p.m.

- On rainy days or during the streetcar's off-season, spend the morning at the ▽ **Royal Alberta Museum.** Housing the Natural History Gallery, the Syncrude Gallery of Aboriginal Culture and the Wild Alberta Gallery, the impressive facility was known as the Provincial Museum of Alberta until Elizabeth II rechristened it in 2005 during the province's 100th anniversary celebrations.

Afternoon

- First-time visitors to Edmonton will no doubt want to check the home of more than 800 stores and services (as well as a myriad of fashion-forward mannequins) off their to-do lists. After raiding the sales racks at the ▽ **West Edmonton Mall,** strike a few cover model poses in the shopping center's three "theme streets": Bourbon Street, Chinatown and Europa Boulevard.

- Naturally, there are plenty of places to grab a bite inside WEM. However, we suggest you skip the mall food court and head about 5 kilometres (3 mi.) north to family-owned **Fife N' Dekel** for delectable deli meats sandwiched between slices of freshly baked sunflower

Old Strathcona historic district

bread. More importantly, for dessert, there's pie! Drool-worthy flavors run the gamut from banana cream to strawberry rhubarb.

- If The Mall is on your been-there, done-that list (*and* you're a sucker for geraniums and cacti), enjoy an afternoon at the ▽ **Muttart Conservatory.** Changing displays of ornamental flowering plants as well as flora from tropical, temperate and arid regions keep so-called "floraphiles" content inside four glass pyramids. Hungry tree huggers will appreciate the health-conscious soups, salads and sandwiches of the on-site café, **Culina Muttart.**

Evening

- If the menus at downtown darlings like the **Hardware Grill** (innovative Canadian cuisine) and **Khazana** (upscale Indian) don't excite you, the views from **The Harvest Room** and **La Ronde Revolving Restaurant** surely will. After dinner, see a show at the Citadel Theatre complex. In a city with a surplus of stages, this renowned Arts District facility is acknowledged as Edmonton's premier performing arts venue.

- Before turning in, cab it back to Old Strathcona. During your morning visit you probably noticed the prevalence of watering holes, tattoo shops and independent theaters that make this a popular late-night destination. Although the nightlife here revolves around people watching (mostly along Whyte Avenue) and live music (for jazz, Yardbird Suite is without equal), the district's allure with college-age revelers also opens the door to a wide range of drunken shenanigans.

Arriving
By Car

Two major highways run through Edmonton. The Trans-Canada Yellowhead Hwy. (Hwy. 16) provides access from the east and west; Queen Elizabeth II Hwy. runs north and south between Edmonton and Calgary.

Getting Around
Street System

Edmonton's street system is a grid with streets running north and south and avenues running east and west. Most streets and avenues are numbered starting from the southeast corner of the city; a few are named.

Edmonton's street plan includes several traffic circles. When approaching a traffic circle, make sure you are in the correct lane. Use the right lane if you plan to exit, the left lane if you are traveling around the circle. When in the circle, the vehicle on the outside must yield to the vehicle on the inside.

The city speed limit is 50 kilometres per hour (30 mph) or as posted. A right turn on red after stopping is permitted; U-turns are not. A sign that reads "Bus and Taxi Lane Only" means it is illegal to drive, park or stop any vehicle other than the above in that lane.

Parking

Street parking restrictions vary throughout the city; watch for and heed the signs. Parking is not permitted in the residential areas surrounding Northlands Park, TELUS Field and Commonwealth Stadium during major events; cars parked there will be towed.

Rates for city-operated parking meters are $2-$4 per hour. Most meters are free after 6 p.m. and on Sundays and holidays; however, there are some 24-hour meters. Rates for downtown parking lots range $2-$4 per half-hour during the day.

Shopping

For the intrepid shopper, there is nothing like **West Edmonton Mall** *(see attraction listing p. 119)*, which occupies a 44-hectare (110-acre) site at 87th Avenue and 170th Street. Inside are more than 800 stores and services.

South Edmonton Common offers about 130 hectares (320 acres) of retail space. The massive outdoor shopping complex at 23rd Avenue and Calgary Trail is home to more than 155 businesses, including IKEA, Liz Claiborne, Nike and Sears Home.

For those who want shopping on a less imposing scale, other popular malls include **Kingsway Garden Mall,** 109th Street and Princess Elizabeth Avenue; **Londonderry Mall,** 137th Avenue and 66th Street; and **Southgate Centre,** 111th Street and 51st Avenue.

Downtown offers boutiques and restaurants as well as covered shopping areas joined by enclosed walkways or pedways. The **Edmonton City Centre** complex between 100th and 103rd streets on 102nd Avenue contains Hudson's Bay Co., 140 other shops and a nine-screen theater among its four glittering floors.

ManuLife Place, 102nd Avenue and 101st Street, contains designer boutiques and Holt Renfrew, an elegant retail store with a quaint in-store café. Connected to ManuLife Place is **Commerce Place,** which features several shops with signature fashions. **Rice Howard Way,** an attractive outdoor pedestrian area lined with sidewalk seating and eateries, is downtown at 100th Street and 101A Avenue. It is particularly popular in summer.

At 102nd Avenue and 97th Street, the Chinatown Gate symbolizes friendship and welcomes visitors to **Chinatown,** which features several ethnic restaurants, shops and outdoor vendors selling fresh produce.

The **124th Street & Area** commercial district, which extends from Jasper Avenue north to 111th Avenue, is home to a wide variety of businesses, including the handful of art galleries comprising the 12-block **Gallery Walk** area.

Old Strathcona at Whyte Avenue (82nd Avenue from 99th to 109th streets), the main outdoor shopping street on the south side of the city, has the look of historic Edmonton and offers boutiques, specialty shops, restaurants, bistros and coffee bars.

Don't forget that the major museums have interesting shops with items sometimes impossible to find elsewhere. Of particular interest are the six period shops in **Fort Edmonton Park** and the shop in the interpretive center at the **Alberta Legislature Building.**

Browse over 800 stores at the West Edmonton Mall

Edmonton Heritage Festival

Big Events

Edmonton offers a smorgasbord of events. Concerts, workshops, club dates and outdoor events characterize the **Edmonton International Jazz Festival,** held mid- to late June. Also in June, **The Works Art and Design Festival** brings together artists and artisans.

Edmonton Celebrate Canada is a 12-day celebration, beginning late June with National Aboriginal Day. On June 24 are Francophone festivities honoring St. Jean Baptiste. The celebration concludes on Canada Day (July 1), with a full day of events and the Fireworks Finale.

During late June to mid-July the **Freewill Shakespeare Festival** presents two shows on alternating nights in **William Hawrelak Park.** Edmonton International Street Performers Festival in early July offers 10 days of free performances by street acts including magicians, clowns, jugglers, mime artists, musicians and comics.

The city's biggest event is ⌁ **Edmonton's K-Days,** a 10-day celebration held in July. Parades, casinos, gold panning, a chuck wagon derby and various other forms of entertainment keep the city alive with activities such as **Sunday in the City** and **A Taste of Edmonton.** Another major draw in July is the **Edmonton Indy,** offering racing excitement, concerts, exhibits and live demonstrations.

The 3-day ⌁ **Edmonton Heritage Festival** in early August offers more than 60 outdoor ethnic pavilions showcasing international music, dance, art and cuisine. Also in August are the ⌁ **Edmonton Folk Music Festival;** the **Cariwest Caribbean Arts Festival;** the **Labatt Blues Festival;** the

Dragon Boat Festival; and the ⌁ **Edmonton International Fringe Theatre Festival,** an 11-day extravaganza of plays, dance, music, mime and street performances.

In September is the Edmonton Symphony Orchestra's 5-day **Symphony Under the Sky Festival** at **Hawrelak Park.** Post-summer events include the **Edmonton International Film Festival,** featuring independent short and feature-length movies in October, the ⌁ **Canadian Finals Rodeo** in early November, and New Year's Eve special events.

Sports & Rec

Whatever the season, there are opportunities for both indoor and outdoor recreation. The **North Saskatchewan River Valley** is an oasis of parkland, with 122 kilometres (76 mi.) of trails, four lake systems and 22 parks. Depending on the time of year, you can **golf, hike, jog, cycle, ride horseback, fish, ski (cross-country** and **downhill), skate** or even pan for gold in a park.

The largest park is **Capital City Recreation Park,** composed of many smaller areas in the center and on the east side of the city. Within the park are 30 kilometres (19 mi.) of paths for **bicycling** and **jogging.** For information about activities and facilities phone Community Services at (780) 496-7275 Monday through Friday.

Playing host to three major sporting events—the Commonwealth Games in 1978, the World University Games in 1983 and the World Championships in Athletics in 2001—has provided Edmonton with a legacy of world-class sporting facilities. Several multiple-purpose centers—including **Kinsmen Sports Centre,** 9100 Walterdale Hill, (780) 944-7400, and **Mill Woods Recreation Centre,** 7207 28th Ave., (780) 496-2900—offer such activities as **swimming, diving, racquetball, squash** and **track** events.

Bring your set of clubs and try out one of more than 70 **golf** courses scattered about the Edmonton area. Three courses in the city's river valley are **Riverside,** on Rowland Road (106th Avenue) on the south side of the Dawson Bridge; **Rundle Park,** in the east end of Edmonton off 118th Avenue and Victoria Trail; and **Victoria,** said to be the oldest municipal golf course in Canada, on River Valley Road, accessible from Groat Road or from either 109th Street via the Walterdale Bridge from the south, or from 101st Street from the north.

Spectator sports can be enjoyed throughout the year. **Castrol Motorsports Park,** 2 kilometres (1.2 mi.) west of Queen Elizabeth II Hwy. on Hwy. 19, offers **motorsport racing** May through September; phone (780) 461-5801 or (780) 955-5540. **Northlands Park,** 7300 116th Ave., offers a chance to watch **harness racing** from early March to mid-June and from October to mid-December; phone (780) 471-7379 to confirm the dates for the racing schedule. **Thoroughbred racing** takes place from June to October; phone (780) 471-7379.

Note: Policies concerning admittance of children to pari-mutuel betting facilities vary. Phone for information.

Home to four professional sports teams, Edmonton is referred to fondly as the City of Champions. The **Edmonton Oilers,** several-time Stanley Cup champions of the National **Hockey** League, play from September to April in **Rexall Place** at 118th Avenue and 74th Street; phone (780) 414-4625. The **Edmonton Eskimos football** team, many times the Grey Cup champions of the Canadian Football League, play at **Commonwealth Stadium,** 111th Avenue and Stadium Road, from June to November; phone (780) 448-3757.

Golden League **Baseball** is played by the **Edmonton Capitals** from April to September at **TELUS Field,** south of downtown at 96th Avenue and 102nd Street; phone (780) 414-4625. National League **Lacrosse** is played by the **Edmonton Rush** from January through April in Rexall Place at 118th Avenue and 74th Street; phone (780) 732-7874.

Performing Arts

Theater season runs from September through May. For live theater visit the **Citadel Theatre** complex, 99th Street and 101A Avenue, which consists of four theaters, an amphitheater and a beautiful atrium; phone (780) 425-1820. Family-themed theater, produced by **Fringe Theatre Adventures,** can be enjoyed by all ages in October, December and February at the Arts Barns in Old Strathcona at 103rd Street and 84th Avenue; phone (780) 448-9000.

Prominent Canadian and American performers take to the stage at **Mayfield Dinner Theatre** at Mayfield Inn & Suites, 166th Street and 109th Avenue; phone (780) 483-4051 or (877) 529-7829. **Jubilations Dinner Theatre,** in the West Edmonton Mall at the intersection of 87th Avenue and 170th Street, features musical comedy; phone (780) 484-2424.

The **Alberta Ballet,** (780) 428-6839, and the **Edmonton Opera,** (780) 429-1000, perform in **Northern Alberta Jubilee Auditorium** on the University of Alberta campus at 87th Avenue and 114th Street; phone (780) 427-2760 for auditorium information. The **Edmonton Symphony Orchestra,** (780) 428-1414, performs at the **Francis Winspear Centre for Music,** 4 Sir Winston Churchill Sq.; phone (780) 428-1414 for concert information. The Winspear Centre also plays host to a variety of concerts ranging from classical music to rock, as do the **Shaw Conference Centre,** the Northern Alberta Jubilee Auditorium and **Rexall Place.**

The free publications *See Magazine, Vue Magazine* and *Where Edmonton* give detailed, up-to-date information about arts and entertainment in Edmonton, and local newspapers provide current performance information. Ticketmaster outlets handle ticket sales for most sports, recreation, theater and concert events; phone (780) 451-8000.

⚑ ATTRACTIONS

ALBERTA AVIATION MUSEUM is at 11410 Kingsway Ave. This hangar was part of a training facility for air crews during World War II. The museum displays more than 30 historic aircraft including a carefully restored Fairchild 71, a fighter-bomber version of the de Havilland Mosquito, a fully operational Boeing 737 airliner, as well as 1920s biplanes and jet fighters from the Cold War era. Other displays detail the history of aviation in Edmonton and Alberta.

Guided tours are available by appointment. **Time:** Allow 1 hour minimum. **Hours:** Mon.-Fri. 10-6, Sat.-Sun. and holidays 10-4. Closed Jan. 1, Christmas, day after Christmas and Dec. 31. **Cost:** $10; $8 (ages 60+); $7 (ages 13-17); $6 (ages 6-12); $25 (family, two adults and four children). **Phone:** (780) 451-1175.

ALBERTA LEGISLATURE BUILDING is at 10800 97th Ave. Public-use parkland, monuments, reflecting pools and fountains surround the building, which was built with sandstone and marble and completed in 1912. Displays outline Alberta's history and parliamentary traditions. Guided 45-minute tours begin in the Legislature Interpretive Centre.

Time: Allow 1 hour minimum. **Hours:** Guided tours are offered daily on the hour 9-3, May 1-Oct. 15; on the hour Mon.-Fri. 9-3, Sat.-Sun. and holidays noon-4, rest of year. Closed Jan. 1, Good Friday and Christmas. **Cost:** Free. **Phone:** (780) 427-7362.

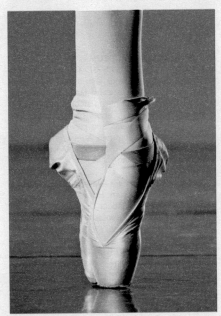
Watch a performance by the Alberta Ballet

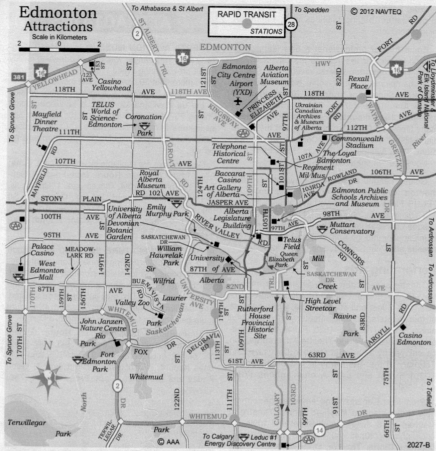

Edmonton
Attractions
Scale in Kilometers

ALBERTA RAILWAY MUSEUM is 2 km (1.2 mi.) s. of Hwy. 37 at 24215 34th St. The museum resembles a railway terminal, with a train yard, locomotive and car shops, a water tank and a station. More than 60 pieces of rolling stock are displayed. There are many exhibits about railway history, including telegraph systems and railway technology. Some weekends in July and August a 20-minute ride aboard a steam or diesel-powered train is offered (weather permitting).

Tours: Guided tours are available. **Time:** Allow 1 hour, 30 minutes minimum. **Hours:** Sat.-Sun. 10-5, Victoria Day weekend-Labour Day. **Cost:** $5; $3.50 (students with ID and senior citizens); $2 (ages 3-12). Train ride $4. **Phone:** (780) 472-6229.

ART GALLERY OF ALBERTA, 2 Sir Winston Churchill Sq., is dedicated to the exhibition and preservation of Canadian art and visual culture. Fine and applied arts are exhibited in a stunning three-level building—a work of art in and of itself—designed by Los Angeles architect Randall Stout. Focusing primarily on Albertan and Canadian artists, revolving

displays include paintings, sculptures and other visual art pieces. The permanent exhibit space features items from the museum's collection of more than 6,000 pieces.

Tours: Guided tours are available. **Time:** Allow 2 hours minimum. **Hours:** Tues.-Fri. 11-7, Sat.-Sun. and holidays 11-5. Closed major holidays. **Cost:** $12.50; $8.50 (ages 65+ and students with ID); free (ages 0-6); $26.50 (family, two adults and four children). **Phone:** (780) 422-6223.

EDMONTON PUBLIC SCHOOLS ARCHIVES AND MUSEUM is at 10425 99th Ave. The archives and museum is in the historic 1905 McKay Avenue School, site of the first two sessions of the Alberta Legislature. The building has been carefully restored and features the 1906 legislative chamber, period classrooms and displays tracing the history of Edmonton public schools.

Also on the grounds is the restored Edmonton 1881 Schoolhouse, the first free public school in Alberta. **Time:** Allow 1 hour minimum. **Hours:** Tues.-Fri. 12:30-4, Sun. 1-4, May-Sept.; Tues.-Fri.

12:30-4, rest of year. Closed major holidays. **Cost:** Free. **Phone:** (780) 422-1970.

FORT EDMONTON PARK is at jct. Fox and Whitemud drs. at 7000 143rd. St. Reputed to be Canada's largest living-history park, it depicts Edmonton in four eras: as an 1846 Hudson's Bay Co. fur-trading fort and Cree encampment, as an 1885 settlement, as a developing capital in 1905 and as a 1920 business community.

Costumed interpreters give demonstrations. Visitors may play horseshoes and old-time children's games, ride in antique cars, fire a round in the shooting gallery, learn to bead and sample pioneer foods such as bannock. Steam train and streetcar rides as well as a 1920s-style midway are included.

Pets are not permitted. **Time:** Allow 3 hours minimum. **Hours:** Daily 10-6, late June-Labour Day; Mon.-Fri. 10-4, Sat.-Sun. 10-6, late May-late June; Sat.-Sun. 10-4, day after Labour Day-Sept. 30. Guided tours are available at 11, noon, 1, 2 and 3. **Cost:** $15.75; $11.75 (ages 2-17 and 65+); $55 (family, two adults and children). Prices may vary; phone ahead. **Phone:** (780) 496-8787 or (780) 496-8776.

JOHN JANZEN NATURE CENTRE is at jct. Fox and Whitemud drs., adjacent to Fort Edmonton Park. The center has exhibits, self-guiding nature trails through the river valley, small animals, hands-on exhibits for children, and interpretive programs and events designed to promote awareness and appreciation of wildlife and the environment.

Time: Allow 1 hour minimum. **Hours:** Daily 10-5, late Aug.-late Dec.; Mon.-Fri. 10-5, Sat.-Sun. and holidays 11-6, early Apr.-late Aug. Closed Jan. 1 and Christmas. **Cost:** $5; free (ages 0-1); $10 (family). Prices may vary. **Phone:** (780) 496-8787.

THE LOYAL EDMONTON REGIMENT MILITARY MUSEUM is at 10440 108th Ave. in the Prince of Wales Armouries Heritage Centre. The museum's two galleries examine the history of The Loyal Edmonton Regiment, Alberta's oldest infantry unit, and explore military life. Displays include weapons, military equipment, uniforms, medals and badges, photographs and documents. **Time:** Allow 1 hour minimum. **Hours:** Mon.-Fri. 10-4. Phone ahead to confirm schedule. **Cost:** Donations. **Phone:** (780) 421-9943.

MUTTART CONSERVATORY is at 9626 96A St., at the e. end of the James MacDonald Bridge. Four pyramid-shaped glass greenhouses showcase a variety of flora. Palm trees, orchids and hibiscus, typical of warm, moist climates, thrive in the rain forest atmosphere of the Tropical Pyramid, while the Arid Pyramid displays vegetation indigenous to parts of North America and Africa. The Temperate Pyramid shows seasonal changes, and the Show Pyramid features changing floral displays. The conservatory's outdoor grounds can be enjoyed on a stroll.

Guided and self-guiding tours are available. **Time:** Allow 1 hour minimum. **Hours:** Mon.-Fri. 10-5 (also Thurs. 5-9), Sat.-Sun. and holidays 11-5. Guided tours are given Sat.-Sun. at noon, 1:30 and 3. Closed Christmas. Phone ahead to confirm schedule. **Cost:** $11.75; $10.60 (ages 13-17 and 65+); $6.25 (ages 2-12); $34.50 (family). Prices may vary. **Phone:** (780) 496-8787.

ROYAL ALBERTA MUSEUM is at 12845 102nd Ave. Alberta's natural and human history museum houses a permanent collection in three main galleries, with changing displays and events scheduled throughout the year.

The Natural History Gallery offers specimens of plants, animals, birds, live insects, fossils and minerals depicting the 1 billion-year odyssey from dinosaurs to rare minerals and gems. A fossil gallery displays extinct beasts from ancient Alberta, while The Bug Room contains live specimens from around the world.

The Syncrude Gallery of Aboriginal Culture tells the story of 11,000 years of aboriginal history. The Wild Alberta gallery encourages visitors to look at Alberta's environment from a different perspective.

Time: Allow 2 hours minimum. **Hours:** Daily 9-5. Hours may vary during special exhibits. Closed Christmas Eve and Christmas. **Cost:** $11; $8 (ages 65+); $7 (students with ID); $5 (ages 7-17); $28 (family, two adults and children); half-price (Sat.-Sun. 9-11 a.m.). An additional fee may be charged during special exhibitions. **Phone:** (780) 453-9100.

RUTHERFORD HOUSE PROVINCIAL HISTORIC SITE is at 11153 Saskatchewan Dr. on the University of Alberta campus. The structure was home to A.C. Rutherford, Alberta's first premier and a founder of the University of Alberta. Completed in 1911, the elegant Jacobethan (a blend of Jacobean and Elizabethan styles) Revival house established a new standard in domestic architecture and marked the end of the pioneer style in Alberta. Historical interpreters in period dress conduct house tours upon request. Events are scheduled throughout the year.

Time: Allow 1 hour minimum. **Hours:** Daily 10-5, May 15-Labour Day; Tues.-Sun. noon-5, rest of year. Closed Jan. 1, Good Friday and Christmas. **Cost:** $4; $3 (ages 7-17 and 65+); $12 (family, two adults and two children). **Phone:** (780) 427-3995 or (780) 422-2697.

TELEPHONE HISTORICAL CENTRE is in the Prince of Wales Armouries Heritage Centre at 10440 108th Ave. The center presents the history of telecommunications in Edmonton dating from the introduction of telephone service in 1885. The facility features numerous interactive exhibits and a 30-minute theater presentation with Xeldon the Robot. **Time:** Allow 1 hour minimum. **Hours:** Tues.-Fri. 10-3 (also Mon. 10-12:30, Victoria Day-Labour Day). Phone ahead to confirm schedule. **Cost:** Donations. **Phone:** (780) 433-1010.

Ukrainian Cultural Heritage Village

GEM **SAVE** **TELUS WORLD OF SCIENCE—EDMONTON** is at 142nd St. and 111th Ave. Five galleries house exhibits that explain and explore unusual phenomena: Space Gallery, which focuses on space exploration; The Health Gallery, which includes large-scale models of body parts; Forensics Gallery, where visitors must collect and analyze clues to solve a crime; The Environment Gallery, a living backyard that teaches visitors about nature and conservation; and Discoveryland, an interactive area designed for children ages 2 through 8.

In addition you'll enjoy live science demonstrations, an observatory, films offered in an IMAX theater and digital shows presented in the Margaret Zeidler Star Theatre. On weekends, you can program your own robot in the Robotics Lab.

Hours: Center daily 10-7, Victoria Day weekend-Labour Day; 10-5, rest of year. Observatory Fri. 7-10, Sat. 1-4 and 7-10, Sun. and holidays 1-4 (weather permitting). Robotics Lab Sat.-Sun. noon-4. Science demonstrations are given daily on the hour noon-4, July 1-Labour Day; Sat.-Sun. and holidays on the hour noon-4, rest of year. IMAX shows are offered daily on the hour beginning at 11. Closed Christmas.

Cost: Exhibit galleries (includes Margaret Zeidler Star Theatre) $16.95; $13.95 (ages 13-17 and 65+); $10.95 (ages 3-12); $63.95 (family, two adults and four children). IMAX film $13.95; $11.95 (ages 13-17 and 65+); $9.50 (ages 3-12); $54.95 (family, two adults and four children). Combination ticket $24.95; $20.95 (ages 13-17 and 65+); $16.95 (ages 3-12); $109.95 (family, two adults and four children). Prices may vary; phone ahead. **Phone:** (780) 451-3344. 🍴

UKRAINIAN CANADIAN ARCHIVES & MUSEUM OF ALBERTA is at 9543 110th Ave. Exhibits trace the history of Alberta's Ukrainian pioneers. Displays include traditional apparel and musical instruments, costumes, Ukrainian currency, photographs, church artifacts and folk art. **Time:** Allow 1 hour minimum. **Hours:** Tues.-Fri. 10-5, Sat. noon-5. Closed major holidays. Phone ahead to confirm schedule. **Cost:** $5. **Phone:** (780) 424-7580.

GEM **SAVE** **UKRAINIAN CULTURAL HERITAGE VILLAGE** is 50 km (31 mi.) e. on Hwy. 16, 3 km e. of the entrance to Elk Island National Park. The lifestyle of the region's Ukrainian immigrant population is portrayed in a village re-created to resemble a typical east central Alberta settlement 1892-1930.

Living-history demonstrations center around more than 30 restored historical buildings, including houses, farm buildings, churches and stores. Costumed interpreters depicting a wide variety of characters from the turn of the 20th century re-create the lives of those who lived in each of the buildings, demonstrating the settlers' daily routines. Special events are held throughout the summer.

Time: Allow 2 hours minimum. **Hours:** Daily 10-5, Victoria Day weekend-Labour Day. **Cost:** $9; $7 (ages 65+); $4 (ages 7-17); $20 (family, two adults and children). Rates may be increased during special events. **Phone:** (780) 662-3640. 🎡

SAVE **UNIVERSITY OF ALBERTA DEVONIAN BOTANIC GARDEN** is 14 km (9 mi.) s. on Hwy. 60 from jct. Hwy. 16W and the Devon Hwy. overpass. Comprising 32 hectares (80 acres) of cultivated gardens and 44.5 hectares (110 acres) of natural area, the garden includes a Japanese garden, a butterfly house, ecological reserves and collections of native and alpine plants. Nature trails and guided tram tours also are offered.

Time: Allow 2 hours minimum. **Hours:** Daily 10-6 (also Thurs. 6-8 p.m.), late May-Labour Day; 10-5, May 1-late May and day after Labour Day to mid-Oct. Tram tours are given daily on the hour 11-3, July 1-Labour Day (also daily at 4, July-Aug.); Thurs.-Sun. on the hour 11-3, in June; Sat.-Sun. on the hour 11-3, in May. Tram tour schedule may vary; phone ahead. **Cost:** $13; $8.50 (ages 65+); $5 (ages 13-17); $3 (ages 7-12); $26 (family, two adults and four children). Tram tour $5.25; $2.10 (ages 0-17). Prices may vary. **Phone:** (780) 987-3054 or (780) 987-3055. 🍴🎡

VALLEY ZOO is at Buena Vista Rd. (87th Ave.) and 134th St. More than 300 domestic, endangered and exotic animals from around the world call the zoo home. Animal interpretive programs are featured year-round. A merry-go-round, paddleboats, a miniature train and a children's discovery zoo are available in summer.

Time: Allow 1 hour, 30 minutes minimum. **Hours:** Daily 9:30-6, early May-late Aug.; Mon.-Fri. 9:30-4, Sat.-Sun. and holidays 9:30-6, late Aug. to mid-Oct.; daily 9:30-4, rest of year. Closed Christmas. Phone ahead to confirm schedule. **Cost:** Early May to mid-Oct. $11.75; $10.60 (ages 13-17 and 65+); $6 (ages 2-12); $34.50 (family). Rest of year $8; $6 (ages 13-17 and 65+); $6.50 (ages 2-12); $36.50 (family). Prices may vary. **Phone:** (780) 496-8787, ext. 2.

WEST EDMONTON MALL is at jct. 87th Ave. and 170th St. The huge, two-level complex is North America's largest shopping and entertainment center. It contains more than 800 stores and services, more than 100 eateries and 10 theme attractions.

Galaxyland features 25 rides and attractions. Sea Life Caverns contains approximately 200 species of marine life. World Waterpark offers more than 2 hectares (5 acres) of indoor fun, including a giant wave pool. The mall also is home to three sea lions (a program allowing patrons to swim with the creatures is offered); the Ice Palace, an NHL-size ice rink; two miniature golf courses; and a recreation center offering bowling, billiards and arcade games.

Time: Allow a full day. **Hours:** Shops open Mon.-Sat. 10-9, Sun. 11-5, most holidays 10-6. Hours for attractions, theaters and restaurants vary; phone ahead. **Cost:** Prices for individual attractions vary. **Phone:** (780) 444-5321 for general mall information, (780) 444-5300, or (800) 661-8890 for more information about attractions, including hours of operation and prices. *(See ad this page.)*

GAMBLING ESTABLISHMENTS
- **Baccarat Casino** is at 10128 104th Ave. N.W. **Hours:** Slot machines daily 10 a.m.-3 a.m. Table games daily noon-2 a.m. Poker daily 24 hours. Closed Christmas. **Phone:** (780) 413-3178.
- **Casino Edmonton** is at 7055 Argyll Rd. **Hours:** Slot machines daily 10 a.m.-3 a.m. Table games daily noon-2 a.m. Poker daily 24 hours. Closed Christmas. **Phone:** (780) 463-9467.
- **Casino Yellowhead** is at 12464 153rd St. N.W. **Hours:** Slot machines daily 10 a.m.-3 a.m. Table games daily noon-2 a.m. Poker daily 24 hours. Closed Christmas. **Phone:** (780) 424-9467.
- **Palace Casino** is at 2710 West Edmonton Mall, 8882 170th St. N.W., Upper Level Entrance #9. **Hours:** Slot machines daily 10 a.m.-3 a.m. Table games daily noon-2 a.m. Poker daily 24 hours. **Phone:** (780) 444-2112.

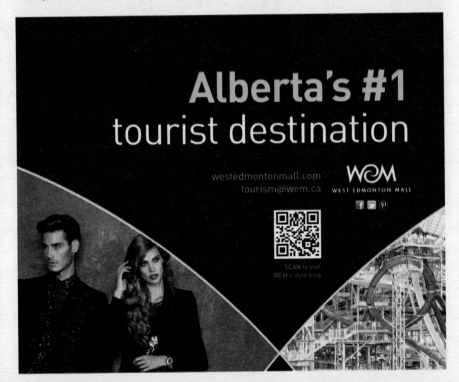

Sightseeing

Driving Tours

The most scenic areas in Edmonton are along the North Saskatchewan River Valley. On the south side, the drive north along Saskatchewan Drive from 76th Avenue and 120th Street to 99th Street offers a picturesque trip around the University of Alberta campus. The views from the Royal Alberta Museum, 102nd Avenue and 128th Street, and the residential district of Glenora are impressive.

Streetcar Tours

HIGH LEVEL STREETCAR departs from the Old Strathcona stop at 103rd St. and 84th Ave. and from downtown s. of Jasper Ave. and w. of 109th St. A vintage streetcar takes passengers along the old Canadian Pacific Railway (CPR) line across the High Level Bridge, built 1911-13 to link Old Strathcona and downtown Edmonton. The narrated, 6-kilometre (3.7-mi.) trip offers excellent views of the city and the North Saskatchewan River Valley.

The Strathcona Streetcar Barn Museum features exhibits relating the history of the Edmonton Streetcar System; included are conductor uniforms, photographs and antique ticket punches. **Time:** Allow 45 minutes minimum. **Hours:** Streetcars operate Sun.-Fri. 11-3:40, Sat. 9-3:40, late May-Labour Day; Fri.-Sun. 11-3:40, day after Labour Day-early Oct. Hours extended to 10 p.m. during the Fringe Festival in Aug. Museum open Sat. 10-2, late May-early Oct. Phone ahead to confirm schedule. **Cost:** Round-trip streetcar fare $5; free (ages 0-5); $15 (family, two adults and children). Museum free. **Phone:** (780) 442-5311 or (780) 437-7721.

Walking Tours

Heritage Trail leads from the Shaw Conference Centre to the Alberta Legislature Building, a route that links government and industry by way of Edmonton's past. Old Strathcona, south of the North Saskatchewan River, offers a view of many original buildings and street scenes characteristic of an early 20th-century prairie town. Edmonton Gallery Walk joins nine private art galleries around Jasper Avenue and 124th Street.

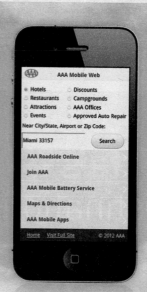

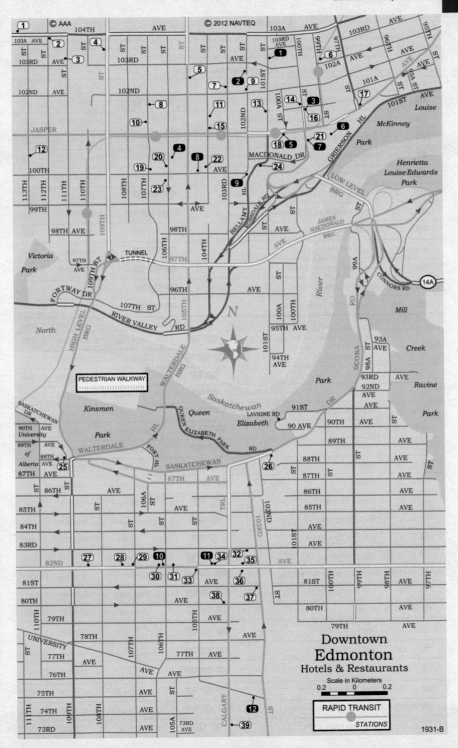

Downtown
Edmonton
Hotels & Restaurants

Scale in Kilometers
0.2   0   0.2

RAPID TRANSIT
STATIONS

1931-B

Downtown Edmonton

This index helps you "spot" where approved hotels and restaurants are located on the corresponding detailed maps. Hotel daily rate range is for comparison only. Restaurant price range is a combination of lunch and/or dinner. Turn to the listing page for more detailed rate and price information and consult display ads for special promotions.

DOWNTOWN EDMONTON

Map Page	Hotels	Diamond Rated	Rate Range	Page
1 p. 121	The Sutton Place Hotel Edmonton	◈◈◈	$259-$450	128
2 p. 121	**Delta Edmonton Centre Suite Hotel**	◈◈◈	$109-$339 SAVE	128
3 p. 121	**The Westin Edmonton**	◈◈◈◈	$119-$489 SAVE	129
4 p. 121	**Days Inn Downtown Edmonton**	◈◈◈	$105-$160 SAVE	128
5 p. 121	**Union Bank Inn**	◈◈◈	$209-$409 SAVE	128
6 p. 121	Courtyard by Marriott Edmonton Downtown	◈◈◈	$155-$171	128
7 p. 121	**The Fairmont Hotel Macdonald**	◈◈◈◈	$189-$399 SAVE	128
8 p. 121	**Holiday Inn Express Edmonton Downtown**	◈◈◈	$149-$199 SAVE	128
9 p. 121	Coast Edmonton House	◈◈◈	$129-$300	128
10 p. 121	Varscona Hotel on Whyte	◈◈◈	$125-$400	128
11 p. 121	Metterra Hotel on Whyte	◈◈◈	$130-$200	128
12 p. 121	Days Inn Edmonton South	◈◈◈	$115-$130	128

Map Page	Restaurants	Diamond Rated	Cuisine	Price Range	Page
1 p. 121	4th & Vine Wine Bar & Bistro	◈◈	American	$15-$28	129
2 p. 121	Wild Tangerine	◈◈◈	Asian	$13-$30	132
3 p. 121	Louisiana Purchase	◈◈	Cajun	$10-$28	130
4 p. 121	Mikado	◈◈	Japanese	$12-$29	131
5 p. 121	Characters Fine Dining	◈◈◈	New American	$13-$42	129
6 p. 121	Zinc Restaurant	◈◈◈	New American	$12-$44	132
7 p. 121	The Creperie	◈◈	French	$10-$29	129
8 p. 121	Khazana	◈◈	Indian	$10-$20	130
9 p. 121	L'azia	◈◈◈	International	$10-$40	130
10 p. 121	Doan's Restaurant	◈◈	Vietnamese	$8-$17	130
11 p. 121	Blue Plate Diner	◈◈	International	$10-$28	129
12 p. 121	Bua Thai Restaurant	◈◈	Thai	$15-$22	129
13 p. 121	Lux steakhouse & bar	◈◈◈	Steak	$14-$46	130
14 p. 121	Moriarty's Bistro & Wine Bar	◈◈◈	New World	$12-$28	131
15 p. 121	Tzin Wine and Tapas	◈◈◈	New World	$20-$30	132
16 p. 121	Share	◈◈◈	American	$15-$35	132
17 p. 121	Hardware Grill	◈◈◈	Regional Canadian	$30-$50	130
18 p. 121	Madison's Grill	◈◈◈	New Canadian	$12-$42	130
19 p. 121	Wildflower Grill	◈◈◈	Northern Canadian	$15-$46	132
20 p. 121	Cafe Select	◈◈◈	Continental	$15-$35	129
21 p. 121	**The Harvest Room**	◈◈◈	New Canadian	$17-$49	130
22 p. 121	The Free Press Bistro	◈◈	American	$10-$26	130

Map Page	Restaurants (cont'd)	Diamond Rated	Cuisine	Price Range	Page
㉓ p. 121	The Marc Restaurant	▼▼▼	French	$11-$29	131
㉔ p. 121	La Ronde Revolving Restaurant	▼▼▼	New Canadian	$32-$42	130
㉕ p. 121	Highlevel Diner	▼▼	American	$10-$22	130
㉖ p. 121	New Asian Village	▼▼	Eastern Indian	$15-$27	131
㉗ p. 121	Cafe Mosaics	▼	Vegetarian	$10-$15	129
㉘ p. 121	Tokyo Noodle Shop	▼▼	Japanese	$10-$20	132
㉙ p. 121	The King & I	▼▼	Thai	$10-$25	130
㉚ p. 121	O'Byrne's Irish Pub	▼	Irish	$11-$20	131
㉛ p. 121	Continental Treat Fine Bistro	▼▼	European	$17-$40	129
㉜ p. 121	Packrat Louie's Kitchen & Bar	▼▼▼	New American	$12-$42	131
㉝ p. 121	Chianti Cafe & Restaurant	▼▼	Italian	$9-$23	129
㉞ p. 121	Yiannis Taverna	▼▼	Greek	$8-$22	132
㉟ p. 121	The Pourhouse Bier Bistro	▼▼	American	$12-$19	131
㊱ p. 121	Block 1912	▼	Coffee/Tea	$7-$13	129
㊲ p. 121	Von's Steak House & Oyster Bar	▼▼▼	Steak	$25-$55	132
㊳ p. 121	Bee-Bell Health Bakery	▼	Breads/Pastries	$2-$9	129
㊴ p. 121	Billingsgate Seafood Market Lighthouse Cafe	▼▼	Seafood	$8-$40	129

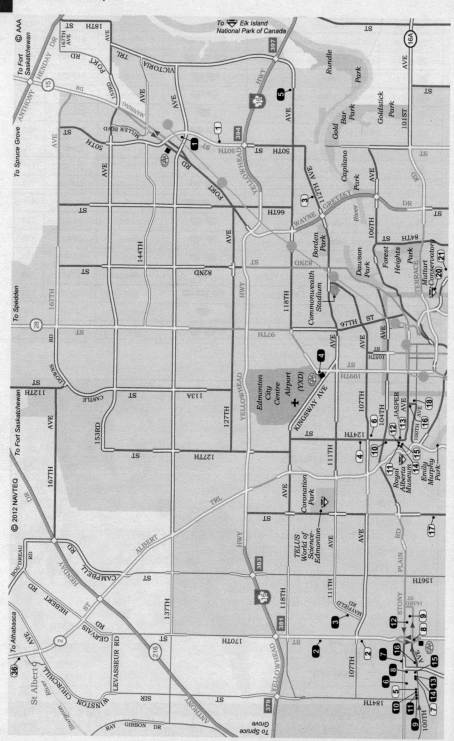

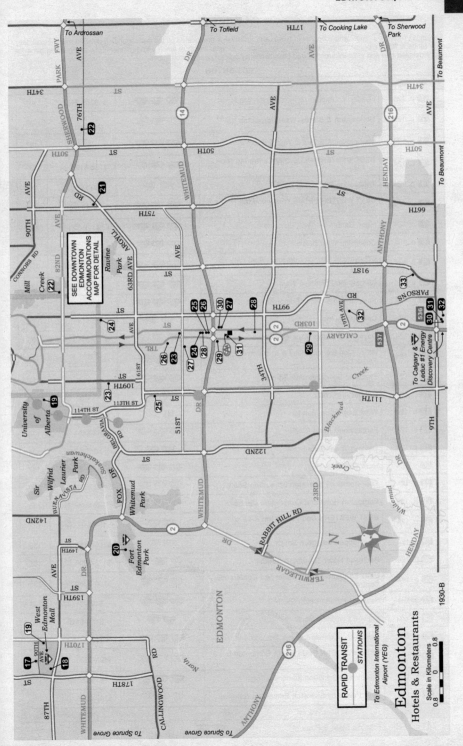

Edmonton
Hotels & Restaurants

1930-B

Edmonton

This index helps you "spot" where approved hotels and restaurants are located on the corresponding detailed maps. Hotel daily rate range is for comparison only. Restaurant price range is a combination of lunch and/or dinner. Turn to the listing page for more detailed rate and price information and consult display ads for special promotions.

EDMONTON

Map Page	Hotels	Diamond Rated	Rate Range	Page
1 p. 124	Holiday Inn Express & Suites Edmonton North	◆◆◆	$139-$159	137
2 p. 124	**Holiday Inn & Suites, West Edmonton**	◆◆◆	Rates not provided (SAVE)	137
3 p. 124	Mayfield Inn & Suites at West Edmonton	◆◆◆	Rates not provided	137
4 p. 124	**BEST WESTERN PLUS City Centre Inn** *(See ad p. 133.)*	◆◆◆	$135-$199 (SAVE)	132
5 p. 124	**Travelodge Edmonton East**	◆	$89-$99 (SAVE)	138
6 p. 124	**BEST WESTERN PLUS Westwood Inn** *(See ad p. 134.)*	◆◆◆	$140 (SAVE)	134
7 p. 124	Hilton Garden Inn-West Edmonton	◆◆◆	$129-$219	137
8 p. 124	Quality Inn West Harvest	◆◆◆	$115-$135	137
9 p. 124	Courtyard by Marriott Edmonton West *(See ad p. 135.)*	◆◆◆	$139-$169	135
10 p. 124	Wingate Inn Edmonton West	◆◆◆	$125-$225	138
11 p. 124	Hampton Inn & Suites Edmonton West	◆◆◆	$149-$189	137
12 p. 124	**Continental Inn**	◆◆	$110-$145 (SAVE)	134
13 p. 124	**Days Inn & Suites West Edmonton**	◆◆	$109-$159 (SAVE)	135
14 p. 124	Holiday Inn Express Hotel & Suites, West Edmonton	◆◆◆	Rates not provided	137
15 p. 124	Executive Royal Inn West Edmonton	◆◆◆	$120	136
16 p. 124	**Comfort Inn West**	◆◆	$99-$139 (SAVE)	134
17 p. 124	**West Edmonton Mall Inn**	◆◆	$119-$194 (SAVE)	138
18 p. 124	**Fantasyland Hotel** *(See ad p. 119.)*	◆◆◆	$168-$498 (SAVE)	136
19 p. 124	Campus Tower Suite Hotel	◆◆	$143-$211	134
20 p. 124	Hotel Selkirk	◆◆◆	$110-$150	137
21 p. 124	**Four Points by Sheraton Edmonton South**	◆◆◆	$125 (SAVE)	136
22 p. 124	**Edmonton Hotel and Convention Centre**	◆◆◆	$139-$299	135
23 p. 124	**BEST WESTERN Cedar Park Inn** *(See ad p. 133.)*	◆◆	$130-$160 (SAVE)	132
24 p. 124	**Travelodge Edmonton South**	◆◆	$105-$135 (SAVE)	138
25 p. 124	**Radisson Hotel Edmonton South**	◆◆◆	$175-$300 (SAVE)	137
26 p. 124	**Delta Edmonton South Hotel and Conference Centre**	◆◆◆	$100-$350 (SAVE)	135
27 p. 124	Sawridge Inn Edmonton South	◆◆◆	$109-$189	137
28 p. 124	Super 8 Edmonton South	◆◆	$120-$140	138
29 p. 124	Holiday Inn Express & Suites Edmonton South	◆◆◆	$129-$159	137
30 p. 124	**BEST WESTERN PLUS South Edmonton Inn & Suites**	◆◆◆	$120-$230 (SAVE)	132
31 p. 124	Hampton Inn by Hilton Edmonton South	◆◆◆	$149-$239	137
32 p. 124	**Four Points by Sheraton Edmonton Gateway**	◆◆◆	$149-$249 (SAVE)	136

Map Page	Restaurants	Diamond Rated	Cuisine	Price Range	Page
1 p. 124	Franco's Steak & Pizza	◆◆	Italian	$8-$27	139

Map Page	Restaurants (cont'd)	Diamond Rated	Cuisine	Price Range	Page
② p. 124	Fife N' Dekel	▽	Deli	$6-$10	139
③ p. 124	Highlands Kitchen	▽▽▽	New European	$8-$26	139
④ p. 124	Col. Mustard's Canteen	▽▽	American	$10-$26	138
⑤ p. 124	Homefire Bar & Grill	▽▽	International	$11-$30	139
⑥ p. 124	The Blue Pear	▽▽	French	$35-$89	138
⑦ p. 124	ConYac's Bar & Grill	▽▽	American	$11-$26	138
⑧ p. 124	Guru Fine Indian Cuisine	▽▽	Indian	$14-$24	139
⑨ p. 124	Bucas & Pastas	▽	Italian	$7-$13	138
⑩ p. 124	The Dish Bistro	▽▽	American	$13-$19	139
⑪ p. 124	Urban Diner	▽▽	American	$9-$17	141
⑫ p. 124	La Favorite Pastry Shop	▽	Breads/Pastries	$3-$8	140
⑭ p. 124	Violino Gastronomia Italiana	▽▽▽	Italian	$11-$35	141
⑮ p. 124	Manor Casual Bistro	▽▽	International	$12-$34	140
⑯ p. 124	Normand's Fine Regional Cuisine	▽▽▽	French	$14-$39	140
⑰ p. 124	Delux Burger Bar	▽▽	American	$10-$20	139
⑱ p. 124	Il Pasticcio Trattoria	▽▽	Italian	$12-$35	139
⑲ p. 124	Famoso Neapolitan Pizzeria	▽▽	Pizza	$7-$15	139
⑳ p. 124	Culina Muttart	▽▽	American	$11-$16	139
㉑ p. 124	Red Ox Inn	▽▽▽	New American	$28-$34	140
㉒ p. 124	Unheardof Restaurant	▽▽▽	American	$35-$45	140
㉓ p. 124	Parkallen Restaurant	▽▽▽	Lebanese	$8-$45	140
㉔ p. 124	Barb & Ernie's	▽	German	$8-$25	138
㉕ p. 124	Jack's Grill	▽▽▽	Regional Canadian	$28-$43	139
㉖ p. 124	The Bothy Wine & Whisky Bar	▽▽▽	New American	$12-$25	138
㉗ p. 124	Lemongrass Cafe	▽▽	Vietnamese	$10-$19	140
㉘ p. 124	Koutouki	▽▽	Greek	$15-$35	140
㉙ p. 124	Tom Goodchilds Moose Factory	▽▽	Steak	$12-$50	140
㉚ p. 124	Creations Dining Room & Lounge	▽▽▽	New American	$11-$39	139
㉛ p. 124	Century Grill	▽▽▽	New Pacific Rim	$17-$41	138
㉜ p. 124	Local Public Eatery	▽▽	American	$13-$19	140
㉝ p. 124	Zaika Indian Bistro Bar	▽▽	Indian	$14-$19	141

ST. ALBERT

Map Page	Restaurant	Diamond Rated	Cuisine	Price Range	Page
㊱ p. 124	River House Grill	▽▽▽	Regional Canadian	$24-$38	179

DOWNTOWN EDMONTON
• Hotels & Restaurants map & index p. 121

COAST EDMONTON HOUSE
(780)420-4000 **9**

▼▼▼ **Condominium** $129-$300 **Address:** 10205 100th Ave T5J 4B5 **Location:** Just se of jct 102nd St and 100th Ave. **Facility:** These apartment-style accommodations offers good views of the city and river valley. 297 condominiums. 35 stories, interior corridors. **Parking:** winter plug-ins. **Terms:** cancellation fee imposed. **Amenities:** safes. *Some:* microwaves. **Pool(s):** heated indoor. **Activities:** exercise room. **Guest Services:** valet and coin laundry, area transportation-downtown.

ECO ▨ ▥ ✈ ▤ BIZ 🖥 ▤ ▤ ▤
/ SOME UNITS FEE ▤

COURTYARD BY MARRIOTT EDMONTON DOWNTOWN
(780)423-9999 **6**

▼▼▼ **Hotel** $155-$171 **Address:** 1 Thornton Ct T5J 2E7 **Location:** Just off Jasper Ave; between 99th and 97th sts. **Facility:** 177 units. 11 stories, interior corridors. **Parking:** on-site (fee) and valet. **Amenities:** high-speed Internet. **Activities:** exercise room. **Guest Services:** valet and coin laundry.

AAA Benefit: AAA hotel discounts of 5% or more.

FEE ▤ ▥ ▥ CALL ▤ BIZ 🖥 ✕ ▤ ▤
▤ / SOME UNITS FEE ▤ ▤

DAYS INN DOWNTOWN EDMONTON
(780)423-1925 **4**

▼▼▼ **Hotel** $105-$160 **Address:** 10041 106th St T5J 1G3 **Location:** Just s of Jasper Ave. **Facility:** 76 units. 4 stories, interior corridors. **Parking:** winter plug-ins. **Activities:** exercise room. **Guest Services:** valet and coin laundry. **Free Special Amenities:** early check-in/late check-out and high-speed Internet.

SAVE ECO FEE ▤ ▥ BIZ 🖥 ✕ ▤
/ SOME UNITS ▤ ▤

DAYS INN EDMONTON SOUTH
(780)430-0011 **12**

▼▼▼ **Hotel** $115-$130 **Address:** 10333 University Ave T6E 6N3 **Location:** Just s of Whyte Ave; between 103rd and 104th sts. **Facility:** 85 units. 4 stories, interior corridors. **Parking:** winter plug-ins. **Amenities:** high-speed Internet. **Activities:** whirlpool, exercise room. **Guest Services:** valet and coin laundry.

▥ BIZ 🖥 ✕ ▤ ▤ ▤

DELTA EDMONTON CENTRE SUITE HOTEL
(780)429-3900 **2**

▼▼▼ **Hotel** $109-$339 **Address:** 10222 102nd St NW T5J 4C5 **Location:** At 102nd St NW and 103rd Ave NW. Attached to a shopping center. **Facility:** 169 units. 7 stories, interior corridors. **Parking:** on-site (fee) and valet, winter plug-ins. **Terms:** cancellation fee imposed. **Amenities:** video games (fee), high-speed Internet. **Activities:** whirlpool, steamroom, exercise room. **Guest Services:** complimentary and valet laundry.

SAVE ECO ▥ ▥ CALL ▤ BIZ 🖥 ✕ ▨ ▤
▤ / SOME UNITS FEE ▤

Share a New View on Travel at AAATravelViews.com

THE FAIRMONT HOTEL MACDONALD
(780)424-5181 **7**

▼▼▼▼ **Historic Hotel** $189-$399 **Address:** 10065 100th St T5J 0N6 **Location:** Just s of Jasper Ave. **Facility:** This landmark hotel with its majestic ambiance is perched above the river valley, and the elegant lobby lounge has a beautiful view. Guest rooms, available in a variety of sizes and styles, have upscale décor. 199 units. 9 stories, interior corridors. **Parking:** on-site (fee) and valet, winter plug-ins. **Terms:** 3 day cancellation notice. **Amenities:** high-speed Internet (fee). *Some:* safes. **Dining:** The Harvest Room, see separate listing. **Pool(s):** heated indoor. **Activities:** sauna, whirlpool, steamroom. *Fee:* massage. **Guest Services:** valet laundry.

SAVE ECO ▥ ▥ ▤ ▤ CALL ▤ ✈ ▤ BIZ
🖥 ▨ ▤ / SOME UNITS FEE ▤ ▤

HOLIDAY INN EXPRESS EDMONTON DOWNTOWN
(780)423-2450 **8**

▼▼▼ **Hotel** $149-$199 **Address:** 10010 104th St T5J 0Z1 **Location:** Corner of 100th Ave; center. **Facility:** 140 units. 7 stories, interior corridors. **Parking:** on-site (fee). **Terms:** check-in 4 pm. **Amenities:** video games (fee), high-speed Internet. **Pool(s):** heated indoor. **Activities:** whirlpool, steamrooms, exercise room. **Guest Services:** valet and coin laundry. **Free Special Amenities:** expanded continental breakfast and high-speed Internet.

SAVE ECO FEE ▤ ▥ CALL ▤ ✈ BIZ 🖥 ✕
▨ ▤ / SOME UNITS FEE ▤ ▤

METTERRA HOTEL ON WHYTE
(780)465-8150 **11**

▼▼▼ **Boutique Hotel** $130-$200 **Address:** 10454 82nd Ave (Whyte Ave) T6E 4Z7 **Location:** Just e of 105th St. **Facility:** Trendy, chic and upscale surroundings await you at this hotel centered on Whyte Avenue. Wine and cheese is offered most evenings. 98 units. 8 stories, interior corridors. **Parking:** valet and street only, winter plug-ins. **Amenities:** high-speed Internet. *Some:* safes. **Activities:** exercise room. **Guest Services:** valet laundry.

▥ ▤ CALL ▤ BIZ 🖥 ✕ ▤ ▤
/ SOME UNITS FEE ▤ ▤

THE SUTTON PLACE HOTEL EDMONTON
(780)428-7111 **1**

▼▼▼ **Hotel** $259-$450 **Address:** 10235 101st St T5J 3E9 **Location:** 102nd Ave at 101st St. **Facility:** 313 units. 26 stories, interior corridors. **Parking:** on-site (fee) and valet. **Terms:** cancellation fee imposed. **Amenities:** *Some:* high-speed Internet, safes. **Pool(s):** heated indoor. **Activities:** saunas, whirlpool. **Guest Services:** valet laundry.

ECO FEE ▤ ▥ ▤ ▥ ✈ FEE ▤ BIZ 🖥
✕ ▨ ▤ ▤ / SOME UNITS FEE ▤ FEE ▤

UNION BANK INN
(780)423-3600 **5**

▼▼▼ **Boutique Hotel** $209-$409 **Address:** 10053 Jasper Ave T5J 1S5 **Location:** Corner of 101st St. **Facility:** This upscale inn partly housed in a 1911 building has modern or heritage units with goose-down bedding, gas fireplaces and nightly wine and cheese service. Warm and hospitable service is the norm. 34 units. 3-5 stories, interior corridors. **Parking:** on-site (fee). **Terms:** cancellation fee imposed. **Amenities:** high-speed Internet, safes. **Dining:** Madison's Grill, see separate listing. **Activities:** limited exercise equipment. **Guest Services:** valet laundry.

SAVE FEE ▤ ▥ ▥ BIZ 🖥 ✕ ▤ / SOME UNITS ▤

VARSCONA HOTEL ON WHYTE
(780)434-6111 **10**

▼▼▼ **Hotel** $125-$400 **Address:** 8208 106th St T6E 6R9 **Location:** Corner of 82nd Ave (Whyte Ave) and 106th St. **Facility:** 89 units. 6 stories, interior corridors. **Parking:** on-site and valet, winter plug-ins. **Terms:** cancellation fee imposed. **Amenities:** high-speed Internet. **Activities:** exercise room. **Guest Services:** valet laundry.

ECO ▥ ▤ ▥ BIZ 🖥 ✕ ▤ ▤
/ SOME UNITS FEE ▤ ▤

(See map & index p. 121.)

THE WESTIN EDMONTON (780)426-3636 ③

WESTIN HOTELS & RESORTS

Hotel
$119-$489

AAA Benefit: Enjoy up to 20% off your next stay, plus Starwood Preferred Guest® bonuses.

Address: 10135 100th St T5J 0N7 **Location:** 101st Ave at 100th St. **Facility:** Expect professional service at this elegant downtown hotel offering a mix of well-appointed guest rooms in two separate towers. 416 units, some two bedrooms. 20 stories, interior corridors. **Parking:** on-site (fee) and valet. **Terms:** cancellation fee imposed. **Amenities:** safes. *Some:* high-speed Internet (fee). **Dining:** Share, see separate listing. **Pool(s):** heated indoor. **Activities:** saunas, exercise room, spa. **Guest Services:** valet laundry.

[SAVE] [ECO] [FEE] [icons] [BIZ] [icons] [SOME UNITS] [icons]

WHERE TO EAT

4TH & VINE WINE BAR & BISTRO 780/497-7858 ①
American. Casual Dining. $15-$28 **AAA Inspector Notes:** The contemporary setting of this bistro features subdued lighting and friendly, laid back service which complements the wonderfully distinct and creative menu. A host of tapas include charcuterie and cheese plates. Beef, chicken, lamb and fish entrées are innovatively prepared with a variety of delicious sauces. Delectable homemade desserts and wine from an eclectic list are available. Patrons must be 18 years of age or older. **Bar:** full bar. **Address:** 11358 104th Ave T5H 3G7 **Location:** Jct Hwy 16 (Yellowhead Tr) and 127th St, 3.2 mi (5.2 km) s. **Parking:** street only. [D]

BEE-BELL HEALTH BAKERY 780/439-3247 ㊳
Breads/Pastries. Quick Serve. $2-$9 **AAA Inspector Notes:** Although there are no places to sit and eat, the bakery is a favorite for those planning a picnic in the park or a festival outing. Patrons step up to the counter to order a variety of breads, quiches and delectable desserts. **Address:** 10416 80th Ave T6E 5T7 **Location:** E at 80th Ave to 104th St. **Parking:** street only. [B] [L]

BILLINGSGATE SEAFOOD MARKET LIGHTHOUSE CAFE
780/433-0091 ㊴
Seafood. Casual Dining. $8-$40 **AAA Inspector Notes:** Patrons walk past displays of fresh seafood to the lively, bright restaurant, where seafood lovers indulge in jewels from the ocean. Fresh halibut, salmon, trout and a catch of the day are sure to delight, as does traditional fish and chips. Desserts made on the premises are well worth saving room for. The cafe-style restaurant bustles at lunchtime, and a distinctive East Coast flair characterizes the decor. **Bar:** full bar. **Address:** 7331 104th St T6E 4B9 **Location:** Corner of 73rd Ave and 104th St. [L] [D]

BLOCK 1912 780/433-6575 ㊱
Coffee/Tea. Quick Serve. $7-$13 **AAA Inspector Notes:** There's a bit of an interesting mix to the decor of this European feeling room, and it could be the decidedly Indian artwork that hangs on the walls. Primarily a coffee shop, the large space is perfectly placed as a pit stop among the shops of Whyte Avenue. Offerings include a decent selection of sandwiches, house-made gelato and freshly baked sweet and savory baked goods. **Bar:** full bar. **Address:** 10361 82nd Ave NW T6E 1Z9 **Location:** Jct Calgary Tr NW; on historic Whyte Ave. **Parking:** street only. [B] [L] [D]

BLUE PLATE DINER 780/429-0740 ⑪
International. Casual Dining. $10-$28 **AAA Inspector Notes:** In the heart of downtown, the diner displays comfortable yet eclectic decor, which includes exposed brick walls and bright paint, and is as far from a classic diner as it gets. Offering an ever-changing menu, the kitchen produces a good selection of vegetarian dishes, as well as a variety of creative takes on down-home comfort food. **Bar:** full bar. **Reservations:** suggested. **Address:** 10145 104th St T5J 0Z9 **Location:** Just s of Jasper Ave. **Parking:** street only. [L] [D]

BUA THAI RESTAURANT 780/482-2277 ⑫
Thai. Casual Dining. $15-$22 **AAA Inspector Notes:** For fantastic Thai food, diners need look no further than this family-run restaurant just south of Jasper Avenue. Because locals frequent this place, it's a good idea to make a reservation. Dishes range from pad thai to various curries, and are sure to please. **Bar:** full bar. **Reservations:** suggested. **Address:** 10049 113th St NW T5K 1N9 **Location:** Just s of Jasper Ave at 113th St. [L] [D]

CAFE MOSAICS 780/433-9702 ㉗
Vegetarian. Casual Dining. $10-$15 **AAA Inspector Notes:** An eclectic and funky respite for vegetarians, this small cafe is along trendy Whyte Avenue. Home-cooked meals, including a large selection of vegetarian entrees, are served in a cozy setting. Whether a hearty bowl of soup, a distinctive pizza or an entree-sized spinach salad, the servings are large and a good value for the dollar. This place is nice for spending hours catching up with a friend over a cup of tea. **Bar:** full bar. **Address:** 10844 82nd Ave T6E 2B3 **Location:** On Whyte Ave (82nd Ave), just e of 109th St. **Parking:** street only. [B] [L] [D]

CAFE SELECT 780/428-1629 ⑳
Continental. Casual Dining. $15-$35 **AAA Inspector Notes:** Patrons unwind in a comfortable, intimate atmosphere while contemplating a menu of traditional favorites, such as rack of lamb and beef tenderloin as well as lighter fare ranging from salads to fondue. Patio dining is available in season. Whether in a hurry or prepared for a long, lingering meal, expect appropriate service. The waitstaff is fast, friendly, cordial and unobtrusive. Closed for lunch Saturday and Sunday. **Bar:** full bar. **Reservations:** suggested. **Address:** 10018 106th St T5J 1G1 **Location:** Just s of Jasper Ave. **Parking:** street only. [L] [D]

CHARACTERS FINE DINING 780/421-4100 ⑤
New American. Fine Dining. $13-$42 **AAA Inspector Notes:** Polished hardwood floors, brick walls and a glimmering open-concept kitchen set the tone for this fresh contemporary restaurant. The seasonally inspired menu changes, but can include a variety of offerings including duck, lamb, Alberta pork and beef. An impressive wine list will ensure a memorable experience. Closed for dinner on Monday and lunch on Saturday. **Bar:** full bar. **Reservations:** suggested. **Address:** 10257 105th St T5J 1E3 **Location:** Just n of jct 102nd Ave and 105th St. [L] [D] CALL [icons]

CHIANTI CAFE & RESTAURANT 780/439-9829 ㉝
Italian. Casual Dining. $9-$23 **AAA Inspector Notes:** In a former post office building on trendy Whyte Avenue, the lively, long-established restaurant serves entrees of pasta, veal, seafood and chicken, and most menu items can be served in half portions. This place is ideal for large gatherings or an evening out in a festive atmosphere. When busy, service might suffer a bit, but expect friendly, knowledgeable assistance in general. **Bar:** full bar. **Address:** 10501 82nd Ave NW T6E 2A3 **Location:** Corner of 105th St. **Parking:** street only. [L] [D]

CONTINENTAL TREAT FINE BISTRO 780/433-7432 ㉛
European. Fine Dining. $17-$40 **AAA Inspector Notes:** Nothing much has changed in the all the years since this spot was established in 1982. They still serve traditional fine food from Eastern and Central Europe. Escargot, smoked salmon, pierogi, dill pickle soup, French onion soup, stroganoff, schnitzel, filet mignon with various sauces and rainbow trout are just some of the many offerings. A pleasing décor with an Old World flair and polite service add to overall enjoyment as does the size of the beer menu which is quite astonishing. **Bar:** full bar. **Reservations:** suggested. **Address:** 10560 82nd Ave NW T6E 2A4 **Location:** Corner of 106th St NW. **Parking:** street only. [L] [D]

THE CREPERIE 780/420-6656 ⑦
French. Casual Dining. $10-$29 **AAA Inspector Notes:** Patrons can prepare themselves for delectable French cuisine-including outstanding stuffed crepes-in the cozy restaurant, just below street level. Menu options, such as seafood and vegetarian dishes, are varied enough to tempt any palate. **Bar:** full bar. **Reservations:** suggested. **Address:** 10220 103rd St T5J 0Y8 **Location:** Just n of 102nd Ave. **Parking:** street only. [L] [D]

(See map & index p. 121.)

DOAN'S RESTAURANT 780/424-3034 10
▼▼ Vietnamese. Casual Dining. $8-$17 **AAA Inspector Notes:** Visitors to the simple, neatly furnished and spacious dining room can enjoy classic Vietnamese dishes, such as hearty rice and noodle soup. Several meat dishes are expertly spiced by the restaurant's signature sauces. **Bar:** full bar. **Reservations:** suggested. **Address:** 10130 107th St NW T5J 1J4 **Location:** Just n of Jasper Ave at 107th St. L D

THE FREE PRESS BISTRO 780/497-7784 22
▼▼ American. Casual Dining. $10-$26 **AAA Inspector Notes:** This quiet and casual restaurant seems miles away from the hustle and bustle of nearby Jasper Avenue. Offerings include a good selection of panini (more than 20) and homemade soups as well as such substantial entrées as pasta and maple-honey pork chops. **Bar:** full bar. **Reservations:** suggested, for lunch. **Address:** 10014 104th St, #80 T5J 0Z1 **Location:** Center; attached to Holiday Inn Express Edmonton Downtown. **Parking:** street only. L D

HARDWARE GRILL 780/423-0969 17
▼▼▼ Regional Canadian. Fine Dining. $30-$50 **AAA Inspector Notes:** Superb service, fine surroundings and a wonderful menu combine to create a truly memorable dining experience in the former hardware store. The warehouse-like dining room is open and airy, and there are hints of history throughout. Representative of seasonally-inspired Canadian cuisine are such choices as mocha-crusted bacon-wrapped elk, applewood smoked Kurobuta pork loin and cedar-planked salmon. The grand finale is exceptional desserts, including warm gingerbread cake. Dinner only on Saturdays. **Bar:** full bar. **Reservations:** suggested. **Address:** 9698 Jasper Ave T5H 3V5 **Location:** Corner of 97th St. **Parking:** street only. L D

THE HARVEST ROOM 780/424-5181 21
▼▼▼▼

New Canadian Fine Dining $17-$49

AAA Inspector Notes: The atmosphere is warm and vibrant in the elegant surroundings of this restaurant. Views of the North Saskatchewan River are beautiful. Creative Canadian prairie cuisine is prepared in the open-concept kitchen. Among tempting entrees are preparations of Alberta beef and venison. Professional, upscale service complements the delicious, upscale food presentations. **Bar:** full bar. **Reservations:** suggested. **Address:** 10065 100th St T5J 0N6 **Location:** Just s of Jasper Ave; in The Fairmont Hotel Macdonald. **Parking:** on-site (fee) and valet. B L D CALL &M

HIGHLEVEL DINER 780/433-0993 25
▼▼ American. Casual Dining. $10-$22 **AAA Inspector Notes:** Diners can find this great diner at the top of the hill just off the High Level Bridge. There is no bland comfort food here—just fabulously flavored dishes made from local and organic produce. Daily soups and quiche, salads, chicken tostada, Guinness shepherd's pie, black bean chili and turkey burgers are just some of the items available. An enticing breakfast menu also is offered as well as the famous and humongous cinnamon buns. Gluten-free options are offered. **Bar:** full bar. **Address:** 10912 88th Ave NW T6G 0Z1 **Location:** Jct 109th St and Saskatchewan Dr. **Parking:** street only. B L D

JOEY RESTAURANTS 780/420-1996
▼▼ American. Casual Dining. $13-$33 **AAA Inspector Notes:** The cuisine blends Mediterranean and Asian cooking styles and emphasizes finger foods for sharing. Those who aren't big fans of tapas can consider full meal offerings centered on steaks and chops. **Bar:** full bar. **Address:** 11228 Jasper Ave T5K 2V2 **Location:** At 112th NW. L D LATE

KHAZANA 780/702-0330 8
▼▼ Indian. Casual Dining. $10-$20 **AAA Inspector Notes:** This eatery features an authentic, tasty tandoori cuisine of papadams, fresh naan bread, peshawari kebab (lamb), boti kebab (prime beef) and murgh tandoori (chicken). The inviting, upscale decor includes original artwork from New Delhi. Buffets are offered at lunch and also Wednesday and Sunday evenings. **Bar:** full bar. **Reservations:** suggested. **Address:** 10177 107 St T5J 1J5 **Location:** Corner of 102nd Ave. **Parking:** street only. L D CALL &M

THE KING & I 780/433-2222 29
▼▼ Thai. Casual Dining. $10-$25 **AAA Inspector Notes:** Zesty vegetarian, meat, seafood and poultry dishes provide sensational, savory variety at this pleasant southside curry house, just off Whyte Avenue. Steaming regional Thai curries are an aromatic, tasty choice to enjoy with friends. Thai art and comfy, padded booths and chairs create a comfortable atmosphere in which to enjoy zesty vegetarian, meat, seafood and poultry dishes with sensational, savory variety. Friendly and unobtrusive, servers are helpful to the first-timer. Closed for lunch on Sunday. **Bar:** full bar. **Reservations:** suggested. **Address:** 8208 107th St T6E 6P4 **Location:** Corner of 107th St, just n of 82nd Ave (Whyte Ave). **Parking:** street only. L D CALL &M

LA RONDE REVOLVING RESTAURANT 780/420-8366 24
▼▼▼ New Canadian. Fine Dining. $32-$42 **AAA Inspector Notes:** Located on the top of the Crowne Plaza Hotel, this revolving rooftop restaurant offers a short, yet high elevator ride to the top as well as a panoramic view of the city. The atmosphere is elegant, yet casual, and the menu focuses heavily on local and Canadian products. Prix fixe selections cater to couples and include aperitifs and champagnes. Seafood, beef, rabbit, pork and other delectable dishes are just a few of the offerings available from the mouthwatering menu. **Bar:** full bar. **Reservations:** suggested. **Address:** 10111 Bellamy Hill T5J 1N7 **Location:** Jct 101st St, MacDonald Dr and Bellamy Hill; in Crowne Plaza Edmonton-Chateau Lacombe. D CALL &M

L'AZIA 780/990-0188 9
▼▼▼ International. Casual Dining. $10-$40 **AAA Inspector Notes:** Inside a downtown shopping center, the restaurant entices hordes of office workers on their lunch hours. Upscale global cuisine is featured with dishes that exhibit creative and unusual twists on foods from around the world including Italy, Spain and Asia. **Bar:** full bar. **Reservations:** suggested. **Address:** 10200 102nd Ave, A113 T5J 4B7 **Location:** Center; in Edmonton City Centre; beside the bay. **Parking:** on-site (fee). L D LATE CALL &M

LOUISIANA PURCHASE 780/420-6779 3
▼▼ Cajun. Casual Dining. $10-$28 **AAA Inspector Notes:** For more than 20 years this warm and inviting restaurant with its brick walls and New Orleans décor has been serving up delicious, well-priced meals. Gumbos, fresh oysters on the half shell or grilled with vegetable cream and Parmesan, alligator kebobs, jambalayas, blackened catfish and pecan pork medallions are just some of the tasty dishes that you will find. Everything is prepared from scratch. Good music, attentive service and good-size portions add to your overall enjoyment. **Bar:** full bar. **Reservations:** suggested. **Address:** 10320 111th St T5K 1L2 **Location:** Jct 109th St NW and 104th Ave NW, just w, then just s. L D CALL &M

LUX STEAKHOUSE & BAR 780/424-0400 13
▼▼▼ Steak. Fine Dining. $14-$46 **AAA Inspector Notes:** In the heart of downtown, this contemporary restaurant features Alberta prime-aged, AAA beef along with salmon, chicken and lamb. A good range of appetizers, decadent side dishes like truffle lobster mac and cheese, and house-made desserts complete the menu. Popular for after work revelry, the restaurant features a lounge with a long, New York-style bar. **Bar:** full bar. **Reservations:** suggested. **Address:** 10150 101st St, Commerce Pl T5J 4G8 **Location:** Just n of Jasper Ave at 101st St. **Parking:** on-site (fee). L D

MADISON'S GRILL 780/401-2222 18
▼▼▼ New Canadian. Fine Dining. $12-$42 **AAA Inspector Notes:** Peep into this restaurant and see a striking decor with very comfortable seating where the chef creates a gorgeous menu utilizing some of the freshest local ingredients possible. Pacific halibut, wild boar, Four Whistle Farm duck and Spring Creek Ranch natural beef are just some of the staples the meals might be based upon. House desserts are definitely worth saving room for and diners can expect professional service. Closed for lunch on weekends. **Bar:** full bar. **Reservations:** suggested. **Address:** 10053 Jasper Ave T5J 1S5 **Location:** Corner of 101st St; in Union Bank Inn. **Parking:** on-site (fee) and street. B L D

(See map & index p. 121.)

THE MARC RESTAURANT 780/429-2828 23

♦♦♦ French. Casual Dining. $11-$29 **AAA Inspector Notes:** Expect wonderful preparations that are simple, yet sophisticated, on the seasonally-changing menu. Try the poached prawn and scallop salad with lavender butter vinaigrette, veal medallions with lobster cream and dense chocolate cake with Cointreau-soaked cherries. The modern open space is surrounded by a bank of windows and mirrors along the back wall. Servers are knowledgeable and able to assist with menu choices. Lunch becomes a much lighter affair. **Bar:** full bar. **Reservations:** suggested. **Address:** 9940 106th St, 100 Sterling Pl T5K 2N2 **Location:** Just s of Jasper Ave. **Parking:** street only. L D

MIKADO 780/425-8096 4

♦♦ Japanese. Casual Dining. $12-$29 **AAA Inspector Notes:** This eatery is a hot spot for sushi. As they enter, patrons are greeted with a warm towel and a friendly smile. The bright, contemporary spot offers a variety of seating options-private dining rooms, main restaurant or the sushi bar. The chef creates a wide variety of sushi and sashimi. Highlights include dragon eyes (a deep-fried salmon roll with a heavenly sauce) or mango tango (eel, cucumber and red pepper wrapped in mango and avocado). Open for dinner only on Sundays and holidays. **Bar:** full bar. **Reservations:** suggested. **Address:** 10350 109th St T5J 4X9 **Location:** Jct 103rd Ave and 109th St; in shopping plaza. L D CALL 🚹M

MORIARTY'S BISTRO & WINE BAR 780/757-2005 14

♦♦♦ New World. Gastropub. $12-$28 **AAA Inspector Notes:** This delightful French-inspired bistro menu is supported by local and organic products as well as quality imported items. Featured are such distinctive appetizers as a tasting of tomatoes with frozen balsamic grape tomatoes, heirloom tomatoes and tomato sushi; French pastry flatbreads; a porcini mushroom sirloin burger; or more substantial items like a flank steak pinwheel with duck and black trumpet mushroom pierogies. A fine selection of wine features an ecosystem wine preservation unit. **Bar:** full bar. **Reservations:** suggested, weekends. **Address:** 10154 100th St T5J 0P6 **Location:** Between 102nd and 102A aves. **Parking:** street only. L D CALL 🚹M

NEW ASIAN VILLAGE 780/433-3804 26

♦♦ Eastern Indian. Casual Dining. $15-$27 **AAA Inspector Notes:** East Indian cuisine is served in a cozy maharajah room or in the main dining room, which affords views of the city. Sounds of Indian music and scents of curry pique the senses, arousing an appetite for dishes such as tasty tandoori chicken, goat and lamb. A buffet is served during peak meal times and an a la carte menu is otherwise offered. **Bar:** full bar. **Reservations:** suggested. **Address:** 10143 Saskatchewan Dr T6E 4R5 **Location:** From 109th St, just e. L D CALL 🚹M

O'BYRNE'S IRISH PUB 780/414-6766 30

♦ Irish. Casual Dining. $11-$20 **AAA Inspector Notes:** In a trendy area, the Irish pub welcomes travelers from around the globe. The restaurant offers a lively atmosphere, friendly service and live entertainment, as well as an all-day Irish breakfast and an excellent selection of Irish beers on tap. **Bar:** full bar. **Address:** 10616 82nd Ave (Whyte Ave) NW T6E 2A7 **Location:** Corner of 106th St. **Parking:** on-site (fee) and street. L D LATE

PACKRAT LOUIE'S KITCHEN & BAR 780/433-0123 32

♦♦♦ New American. Casual Dining. $12-$42 **AAA Inspector Notes:** Guests will find a warm and inviting dining room of exposed brick and cork-filled walls at this restaurant where the chefs cook in a semi-open kitchen preparing creative and fresh-market cuisine. The menu includes the likes of pan-seared squid with curry butter or lime coconut crème fraîche or wood-fired pizza. Entrées could include chili-rubbed venison, prosciutto wrapped ahi tuna or free-range chicken and house gnocchi. Knowledgeable friendly staff will assist with menu and wine choices. **Bar:** full bar. **Reservations:** suggested. **Address:** 10335 83rd Ave T6E 2C6 **Location:** Jct 103rd St and 83rd Ave, 1 blk n of Jasper Ave. L D

THE POURHOUSE BIER BISTRO 780/757-7687 35

♦♦ American. Gastropub. $12-$19 **AAA Inspector Notes:** With a warm and funky décor featuring exposed brick and chandeliers, this bistro is not just about the more than 70 beers on hand or the special selection that changes every month or so. It is about the pride they have in offering a great food menu which includes gourmet hamburgers, sandwiches and such entrées as AAA striploin with red wine demi-glacé or albacore tuna with ginger wasabi. Be sure to save room for the delicious house desserts. **Bar:** full bar. **Reservations:** suggested. **Address:** 10354 82nd Ave NW T6E 1Z8 **Location:** Jct Calgary Tr NW; on historic Whyte Ave. **Parking:** street only. L D LATE

RIC'S GRILL 780/429-4333

♦♦♦ Steak. Casual Dining. $16-$42 **AAA Inspector Notes:** *Historic.* "Funky and modern" describes the decor and the food at the upscale steakhouse, which bustles with activity. Steaks are well worth it, but then again, so are the salmon, chicken and pasta dishes. A wide variety of distinctive appetizers rounds out the menu. Servers are friendly and attentive. **Bar:** full bar. **Reservations:** suggested. **Address:** 10190 104th St T5J 1A7 **Location:** Corner of 104th St and 102nd Ave; in historic Metals Building. **Parking:** street only. L D CALL 🚹M

(See map & index p. 121.)

SHARE
780/493-8994   16

American. Fine Dining. $15-$35 **AAA Inspector Notes:** This elegant dining room invites diners to peruse an excellent menu utilizing regional ingredients. Guests are sure to enjoy the interesting fare blending health-conscious choices with Alberta beef, seafood, chicken and pork dishes. The signature zesty bread dip is a favorite, as are the delicious house desserts-the sweet potato pecan pie with cinnamon ice cream is a delight. Expect professional, friendly service. **Bar:** full bar. **Reservations:** suggested. **Address:** 10135 100th St T5J 0N7 **Location:** 101st Ave at 100th St; in The Westin Edmonton. **Parking:** on-site (fee) and valet. [B] [L] [D]

TOKYO NOODLE SHOP
780/430-0838   28

Japanese. Casual Dining. $10-$20 **AAA Inspector Notes:** The popular restaurant gives diners a choice of good, affordable sushi selections. **Bar:** full bar. **Address:** 10736 82nd Ave T6E 6P4 **Location:** On Whyte Ave (82nd Ave) at 107th St. **Parking:** street only. [L] [D]

TZIN WINE AND TAPAS
780/428-8946   15

New World Small Plates. Casual Dining. $20-$30 **AAA Inspector Notes:** This tiny spot has an open kitchen and a dining room with a Bohemian feel—guests enter the draped room through a curtain and dine on banquettes lined with cushions. Sourced mainly from local farmers, the chef prepares a delicious range of tapas including crab-stuffed prawns with lemon chili aioli, wild mushroom and Gruyère tart or house chorizo with bean salad. The wines are carefully selected to provide some beautiful matches. Under age 18 are not permitted. **Bar:** full bar. **Reservations:** required. **Address:** 10115 104th St T5J 0Z9 **Location:** Just s of Jasper Ave. [D]

VON'S STEAK HOUSE & OYSTER BAR
780/439-0041   37

Steak. Casual Dining. $25-$55 **AAA Inspector Notes:** In Strathcona, an old part of town south of the river, the restaurant offers casual dining in a subdued, intimate atmosphere. The dining room sports wood beams and a large river stone fireplace. Beef and seafood are mainstays on a menu of choices that display Louisiana and Mediterranean influences. **Bar:** full bar. **Reservations:** suggested. **Address:** 10309 81st Ave T6E 1X3 **Location:** Just s of 82nd Ave (Whyte Ave) at 103rd St. **Parking:** street only. [D]

WILDFLOWER GRILL
780/990-1938   19

Northern Canadian. Fine Dining. $15-$46 **AAA Inspector Notes:** Diners should be prepared to be wowed by fabulous food at this stylish and classy grill where the decor is accented by exposed stone, wine walls and lovely wild flower art. The award-winning chef utilizes high-quality Canadian products in the design of the distinctive menu ranging from Alberta beef Carpaccio with shallot chipotle jam and lobster-braised spot prawns, to Thai green curry garganelli pasta and Saskatoon berry-infused venison with saffron-wild cherry couscous with venison ragout. **Bar:** full bar. **Reservations:** suggested. **Address:** 10009 107th St NW T5J 1J1 **Location:** Just s of Jasper Ave. **Parking:** street only. [L] [D] CALL &M

WILD TANGERINE
780/429-3131   2

Asian. Casual Dining. $13-$30 **AAA Inspector Notes:** Across from Grant McEwan College and a bevy of condominium developments, the hip and colorful restaurant nurtures a cozy atmosphere amid its limited number of tables. Traditional Asian cuisine is overhauled in a decidedly playful and contemporary manner in reasonably priced creations such as shrimp lollipops with wasabi yogurt and five-spice octopus salad with peppers, taro, lotus root and citrus dressing. Service is lively. **Bar:** full bar. **Reservations:** suggested. **Address:** 10383 112th St T5K 1M9 **Location:** Jct 104th Ave; at Coinfield Shopping Center. [L] [D] CALL &M

YIANNIS TAVERNA
780/433-6768   34

Greek. Casual Dining. $8-$22 **AAA Inspector Notes:** This lively, traditional restaurant is reminiscent of a cozy tavern in Greece, complete with a quaint sidewalk patio. Music, art and atmosphere combine to provide an enjoyable experience. Weekend entertainment features the hasapiko dance, belly dancing at 8:30 pm and later in the evening, the Zorba dance, in which patrons are encouraged to participate. Service is friendly, efficient and, at times, laced with Greek phrases. **Bar:** full bar. **Reservations:** suggested. **Address:** 10444 82nd Ave NW (Whyte Ave) T6E 2A2 **Location:** Corner of 104th St. **Parking:** street only. [L] [D] CALL &M

ZINC RESTAURANT
780/392-2501   6

New American. Casual Dining. $12-$44 **AAA Inspector Notes:** Like the building they are located in, Art Gallery of Alberta, the food here is attractive to look at along with the great views of downtown Edmonton through huge windows overlooking city hall. The chef makes wonderful concoctions with locally-sourced products where components of each dish add something to the overall complexity of flavors. This takes time to create so plan for a leisurely lunch or dinner. **Bar:** full bar. **Reservations:** suggested. **Address:** 2 Sir Winston Churchill Sq T5J 2C1 **Location:** Corner of 102A Ave and Rue Hull; in Art Gallery of Alberta. **Parking:** street only. [L] [D] CALL &M

EDMONTON (E-6)
- **Restaurants p. 138**
- **Hotels & Restaurants map & index p. 124**

BEST WESTERN CEDAR PARK INN
(780)434-7411   23

Hotel $130-$160

AAA Benefit: Members save up to 20%, plus 10% bonus points with Best Western Rewards®.

Address: 5116 Gateway Blvd T6H 2H4 **Location:** Hwy 2 (Gateway Blvd) at 51st Ave. **Facility:** 195 units. 4-5 stories, interior corridors. **Parking:** winter plug-ins. **Terms:** 7 day cancellation notice-fee imposed, resort fee. **Amenities:** *Some:* safes. Pool(s): heated indoor. **Activities:** exercise room. **Guest Services:** valet laundry. **Free Special Amenities:** local telephone calls and high-speed Internet. (See ad p. 133.)

SAVE [icons] CALL &M [icons] BIZ [icons] / SOME UNITS FEE [icons]

BEST WESTERN PLUS CITY CENTRE INN
(780)479-2042   4

Hotel $135-$199 PLUS

AAA Benefit: Members save up to 20%, plus 10% bonus points with Best Western Rewards®.

Address: 11310 109th St T5G 2T7 **Location:** From Kingsway Ave NW, just n. **Facility:** 109 units. 2 stories, interior/exterior corridors. **Parking:** winter plug-ins. **Terms:** cancellation fee imposed. **Amenities:** high-speed Internet. **Pool(s):** heated indoor. **Activities:** whirlpool, waterslide, exercise room. **Guest Services:** valet and coin laundry. **Free Special Amenities:** local telephone calls and high-speed Internet. (See ad p. 133.)

SAVE ECO FEE [icons] / SOME UNITS [icons]

BEST WESTERN PLUS SOUTH EDMONTON INN & SUITES
(780)801-3580   30

Hotel $120-$230 PLUS

AAA Benefit: Members save up to 20%, plus 10% bonus points with Best Western Rewards®.

Address: 1204 101st St T6X 0P1 **Location:** Hwy 2 exit Ellerslie Rd. **Facility:** 105 units. 4 stories, interior corridors. **Parking:** winter plug-ins. **Terms:** check-in 4 pm, 7 day cancellation notice-fee imposed. **Amenities:** high-speed Internet. **Pool(s):** heated indoor. **Activities:** whirlpool, waterslide, exercise room. **Guest Services:** valet and coin laundry. **Free Special Amenities:** full breakfast and local telephone calls.

SAVE ECO [icons] CALL &M [icons] BIZ [icons] [icons]

▼ See AAA listing p. 132 ▼

- Complimentary Wireless High-Speed Internet
- Business Centre
- Fitness Room & Pool
- Restaurant & Lounge
- 20 Minutes to West Edmonton Mall

Scan this tag on your smartphone and start saving today!

BEST WESTERN Cedar Park Inn

5116 Gateway Blvd. Edmonton, AB T6H 2H4 CAN

780.434.7411

1.800.661.9461 | bestwestern.com/aaa

Get the free mobile app at http://gettag.mobi

▼ See AAA listing p. 132 ▼

For business or Leisure, there's always a little something extra at our BEST WESTERN PLUS.

BEST WESTERN PLUS City Centre Inn
11310 109th Street
Edmonton, AB T5G 2T7
780-479-2042 800-666-5026

bestwestern.com/aaa

- AAA/CAA Preferred hotel
- Minimum 10% discount off published rates
- FREE Best Western Rewards® program
- Indoor Pool with waterslide & Jacuzzi
- Dataports and HSIA available in all rooms
- Refrigerators in all rooms

GREEN KEY
Eco-Rating Program

Hertz offers AAA/CAA members exclusive discounts and benefits including:

THE ONLY CAR RENTAL COMPANY ENDORSED BY AAA/CAA

- Free use of a child seat • Additional qualified AAA/CAA driver at no charge • 50% off SIRIUS XM Radio® rental • 10% Off Hertz Fuel Purchase Option • 10% Off U.S. prepaid rates • FREE Hertz Gold Plus Rewards + Free day after 1st Gold rental

SHOW YOUR AAA/CAA CARD AND SAVE

hertz.com/hertz.ca
For restrictions, visit your AAA/CAA office.

Click AAA.com/Hertz or CAA.ca/Hertz Call 800-654-3080 or 888-333-3120

(See map & index p. 124.)

BEST WESTERN PLUS WESTWOOD INN
(780)483-7770

Hotel
$140

AAA Benefit: Members save up to 20%, plus 10% bonus points with Best Western Rewards®.

Address: 18035 Stony Plain Rd T5S 1B2 **Location:** Hwy 16A (Stony Plain Rd) at 180th St. **Facility:** 172 units. 3-6 stories, interior corridors. **Parking:** winter plug-ins. **Terms:** check-in 4 pm, 7 day cancellation notice. **Amenities:** *Some:* safes. **Pool(s):** heated indoor. **Activities:** exercise room. *Fee:* game room. **Guest Services:** valet laundry. Free **Special Amenities:** local telephone calls and high-speed Internet. *(See ad this page.)*

Visit your AAA/CAA Travel office

to book a AAA Vacations®

Disney package

CAMPUS TOWER SUITE HOTEL
(780)439-6060 **19**

Extended Stay Hotel $143-$211 **Address:** 11145 87th Ave T6G 0Y1 **Location:** At 111th St and 87th Ave. Located near university and hospital campuses. **Facility:** 90 units, some two bedrooms and efficiencies. 16 stories, interior corridors. **Parking:** winter plug-ins. **Terms:** check-in 4 pm, cancellation fee imposed, resort fee. **Amenities:** safes. *Some:* high-speed Internet. **Dining:** 2 restaurants. **Activities:** exercise room. **Guest Services:** valet and coin laundry.

COMFORT INN WEST
(780)484-4415 **16**

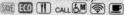
Hotel
$99-$139

Address: 17610 100th Ave T5S 1S9 **Location:** At 176th St. **Facility:** 100 units. 2 stories (no elevator), interior corridors. **Parking:** winter plug-ins. **Terms:** cancellation fee imposed. **Guest Services:** valet and coin laundry.

CONTINENTAL INN
(780)484-7751 **12**

Hotel
$110-$145

Address: 16625 Stony Plain Rd T5P 4A8 **Location:** On Hwy 16A (Stony Plain Rd) at 166th St. **Facility:** 100 units. 6 stories, interior corridors. **Parking:** winter plug-ins. **Terms:** 6 day cancellation notice-fee imposed. **Amenities:** high-speed Internet. **Activities:** exercise room. **Guest Services:** valet and coin laundry. Free **Special Amenities:** early check-in/late check-out and airport transportation.

(See map & index p. 124.)

COURTYARD BY MARRIOTT EDMONTON WEST
(780)638-6070

AAA Benefit:
AAA hotel discounts of 5% or more.

 Hotel $139-$169 **Address:** 10011 184th St T5S 0C7 **Location:** From Anthony Henday Dr, 0.8 mi (1.3 km) e. **Facility:** 136 units. 5 stories, interior corridors. **Parking:** winter plug-ins. **Amenities:** high-speed Internet. **Pool(s):** heated indoor. **Activities:** whirlpool, exercise room. **Guest Services:** valet and coin laundry. *(See ad this page.)*

DAYS INN & SUITES WEST EDMONTON
(780)444-4440 **13**

Hotel
$109-$159

Address: 10010 179A St T5S 2T1 **Location:** From Anthony Henday Dr, 1.2 mi (2 km) e. **Facility:** 108 units, some efficiencies. 4 stories, interior corridors. **Parking:** winter plug-ins. **Terms:** check-in 4 pm, cancellation fee imposed. **Amenities:** video games (fee), high-speed Internet. **Dining:** ConYac's Bar & Grill, see separate listing. **Pool(s):** heated indoor. **Activities:** whirlpool, exercise room. **Guest Services:** valet and coin laundry. **Free Special Amenities:** local telephone calls and high-speed Internet.

DELTA EDMONTON SOUTH HOTEL AND CONFERENCE CENTRE
(780)434-6415 **26**

 Hotel
$100-$350

Address: 4404 Gateway Blvd T6H 5C2 **Location:** Jct Calgary Tr (Hwy 2) and Whitemud Dr. **Facility:** 237 units. 11 stories, interior corridors. **Parking:** on-site and valet, winter plug-ins. **Terms:** cancellation fee imposed. **Amenities:** high-speed Internet. **Pool(s):** heated indoor. **Activities:** whirlpool, exercise room. **Guest Services:** valet laundry.

EDMONTON HOTEL AND CONVENTION CENTRE
(780)468-5400 **22**

Hotel
$139-$299

Address: 4520 76th Ave T6B 0A5 **Location:** Hwy 14, just s via 50th St exit, then just e. **Facility:** 168 units. 6 stories, interior corridors. **Parking:** winter plug-ins. **Amenities:** video games (fee), high-speed Internet. **Pool(s):** heated indoor. **Activities:** whirlpool, steamroom, exercise room. **Guest Services:** valet and coin laundry. **Free Special Amenities:** full breakfast and high-speed Internet.

Download eTourBook guides
for top destinations at
AAA.com/ebooks

(See map & index p. 124.)

EDMONTON MARRIOTT AT RIVER CREE RESORT
(780)484-2121

Hotel
$139-$329

AAA Benefit: AAA hotel discounts of 5% or more.

Address: 300 E Lapotac Blvd T7X 3Y3 **Location:** 1 mi (1.6 km) w of jct Hwy 216 (Anthony Henday Dr) and Whitemud Dr W. **Facility:** Located on the western outskirts of Edmonton and ten minutes from West Edmonton Mall, this hotel offers spacious guest rooms with contemporary décor. 249 units. 9 stories, interior corridors. **Parking:** winter plug-ins. **Terms:** check-in 4 pm. **Amenities:** high-speed Internet (fee). **Dining:** Sage Restaurant, see separate listing. **Pool(s):** heated indoor. **Activities:** whirlpool, exercise room. **Guest Services:** valet and coin laundry, area transportation-West Edmonton Mall. (See ad this page.)

SAVE ECO FEE CALL BIZ

EXECUTIVE ROYAL INN WEST EDMONTON
(780)484-6000 **15**

Hotel $120 **Address:** 10010 178th St T5S 1T3 **Location:** Corner of 178th St and 100th Ave. **Facility:** 235 units. 4 stories, interior corridors. **Parking:** winter plug-ins. **Amenities:** video games (fee). Some: high-speed Internet. **Activities:** whirlpools, exercise room. **Guest Services:** valet laundry.

ECO /SOME UNITS FEE

Plan.
Map.
Go.
TripTik® Travel Planner
AAA.com and CAA.ca

FANTASYLAND HOTEL
(780)444-3000 **18**

Hotel
$168-$498

Address: 17700 87th Ave T5T 4V4 **Location:** At 178th St. Located in West Edmonton Mall at southwest end; adjacent to amusement park. **Facility:** 355 units. 12 stories, interior corridors. **Parking:** on-site and valet, winter plug-ins. **Terms:** check-in 4 pm, cancellation fee imposed. **Amenities:** safes. **Activities:** spa. Fee: waterslide, miniature golf, ice skating. **Guest Services:** valet laundry. (See ad p. 119.)

SAVE ECO FEE CALL FEE BIZ /SOME UNITS

FOUR POINTS BY SHERATON EDMONTON GATEWAY
(780)801-4000 **32**

Hotel
$149-$249

FOUR POINTS BY SHERATON

AAA Benefit: Members get up to 20% off, plus Starwood Preferred Guest® bonuses.

Address: 10010 12th Ave SW T6X 1C8 **Location:** Hwy 2 exit Ellerslie Rd. **Facility:** 154 units. 8 stories, interior corridors. **Parking:** winter plug-ins. **Amenities:** safes. **Pool(s):** heated indoor. **Activities:** whirlpool, exercise room. **Guest Services:** valet and coin laundry. **Free Special Amenities:** local telephone calls and high-speed Internet.

SAVE CALL BIZ

FOUR POINTS BY SHERATON EDMONTON SOUTH
(780)465-7931 **21**

Hotel
$125

FOUR POINTS BY SHERATON

AAA Benefit: Members get up to 20% off, plus Starwood Preferred Guest® bonuses.

Address: 7230 Argyll Rd T6C 4A6 **Location:** Hwy 2 (Gateway Blvd), 2.3 mi (3.7 km) e at 63rd Ave (which becomes Argyll Rd); at 75th St. **Facility:** 139 units. 7 stories, interior corridors. **Parking:** winter plug-ins. **Terms:** 7 day cancellation notice-fee imposed. **Amenities:** high-speed Internet. **Pool(s):** heated indoor. **Activities:** sauna, steamroom, exercise room. **Guest Services:** valet laundry. **Free Special Amenities:** local telephone calls and high-speed Internet.

SAVE CALL BIZ /SOME UNITS FEE

▼ See AAA listing this page ▼

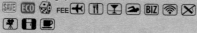

(See map & index p. 124.)

HAMPTON INN & SUITES EDMONTON WEST

(780)484-7280 **11**

▼▼▼▼ **Hotel** $149-$189 **Address:** 18304 100th Ave T5S 2V2 **Location:** From Anthony Henday Dr, 0.8 mi (1.3 km) e. **Facility:** 103 units. 5 stories, interior corridors. **Parking:** winter plug-ins. **Terms:** check-in 4 pm, 1-7 night minimum stay, cancellation fee imposed. **Amenities:** high-speed Internet, safes. **Pool(s):** heated indoor. **Activities:** whirlpool, exercise room. **Guest Services:** valet and coin laundry.

AAA Benefit: Members save up to 10%!

HAMPTON INN BY HILTON EDMONTON SOUTH

(780)801-2600 **31**

▼▼▼ **Hotel** $149-$239 **Address:** 10020 12th Ave T6X 0P6 **Location:** Hwy 2 exit Ellerslie Rd. **Facility:** 100 units. 4 stories, interior corridors. **Parking:** winter plug-ins. **Terms:** 1-7 night minimum stay, cancellation fee imposed. **Amenities:** high-speed Internet. **Pool(s):** heated indoor. **Activities:** whirlpool, exercise room. **Guest Services:** valet and coin laundry.

AAA Benefit: Members save up to 10%!

HILTON GARDEN INN-WEST EDMONTON

(780)443-2233 **7**

▼▼▼ **Hotel** $129-$219 **Address:** 17610 Stony Plain Rd T5S 1A2 **Location:** From 176th St, just w. **Facility:** 160 units. 6 stories, interior corridors. **Parking:** winter plug-ins. **Terms:** 1-7 night minimum stay, cancellation fee imposed. **Amenities:** video games (fee), high-speed Internet, safes. **Pool(s):** heated indoor. **Activities:** whirlpool, exercise room. **Guest Services:** valet and coin laundry.

AAA Benefit: Unparalleled hospitality at a special Member rate.

HOLIDAY INN & SUITES, WEST EDMONTON

(780)444-3110 **2**

Hotel **Rates not provided** **Address:** 11330 170th St T5S 2X1 **Location:** Between 113th and 114th aves. **Facility:** 112 units. 4 stories, interior corridors. **Parking:** winter plug-ins. **Terms:** check-in 4 pm. **Amenities:** high-speed Internet. **Pool(s):** heated indoor. **Activities:** whirlpool, exercise room. **Guest Services:** valet and coin laundry. **Free Special Amenities:** local telephone calls and high-speed Internet.

HOLIDAY INN EXPRESS & SUITES EDMONTON NORTH

(780)476-9898 **1**

▼▼▼ **Hotel** $139-$159 **Address:** 13742 50th St NW T5A 4Y3 **Location:** Hwy 16 (Yellowhead Tr); 1 mi (1.6 km) n on 50th St (Hwy 15). **Facility:** 95 units. 6 stories, interior corridors. **Parking:** winter plug-ins. **Amenities:** high-speed Internet. **Pool(s):** heated indoor. **Activities:** whirlpool. **Guest Services:** valet laundry.

Learn about inspections and Diamond Ratings at AAA.com/Diamonds

HOLIDAY INN EXPRESS & SUITES EDMONTON SOUTH

(780)440-5000 **29**

▼▼▼ **Hotel** $129-$159 **Address:** 2440 Calgary Tr T6J 5J6 **Location:** Hwy 2, just w at 31st Ave, then 0.5 mi (0.8 km) s on 104th St; Hwy 2 northbound, just w at 23 Ave, then just n. **Facility:** 191 units. 6 stories, interior corridors. **Pool(s):** heated indoor. **Activities:** whirlpool, exercise room. **Guest Services:** valet and coin laundry.

HOLIDAY INN EXPRESS HOTEL & SUITES, WEST EDMONTON

780)483-4000 **14**

▼▼▼ **Hotel** **Rates not provided** **Address:** 10017 179A St T5S 2L4 **Location:** On 100th Ave, just w of 178th St. **Facility:** 102 units. 4 stories, interior corridors. **Parking:** winter plug-ins. **Terms:** check-in 4 pm. **Amenities:** video games (fee). **Pool(s):** heated indoor. **Activities:** whirlpool, exercise room. **Fee:** game room. **Guest Services:** valet and coin laundry.

HOTEL SELKIRK

(780)496-7227 **20**

▼▼▼ **Hotel** $110-$150 **Address:** 7000 143rd St T5J 2R7 **Location:** From Whitemud Dr exit Fox Dr, follow signs for Fort Edmonton. **Facility:** 29 units. 2 stories, interior corridors. **Terms:** closed 9/3-5/24, check-in 4 pm, 3 day cancellation notice-fee imposed. **Activities:** hiking trails.

MAYFIELD INN & SUITES AT WEST EDMONTON

(780)484-0821 **3**

▼▼▼ **Hotel** **Rates not provided** **Address:** 16615 109th Ave T5P 4K8 **Location:** 1 mi (1.6 km) n of jct Hwy 2 (170th St) and 16A (Stony Plain Rd). **Facility:** 327 units, some kitchens. 10 stories, interior corridors. **Parking:** winter plug-ins. **Amenities:** high-speed Internet. **Dining:** 2 restaurants, nightclub. **Pool(s):** heated indoor. **Activities:** saunas, whirlpool, steamroom, racquetball courts, spa. **Guest Services:** valet and coin laundry.

QUALITY INN WEST HARVEST

(780)484-8000 **8**

▼▼▼ **Hotel** $115-$135 **Address:** 17803 Stony Plain Rd NW T5S 1B4 **Location:** Jct Hwy 16A (Stony Plain Rd) and 178th St. **Facility:** 159 units. 3 stories, interior corridors. **Parking:** winter plug-ins. **Terms:** check-in 4 pm, cancellation fee imposed. **Amenities:** video games (fee). **Activities:** exercise room. **Guest Services:** valet and coin laundry.

RADISSON HOTEL EDMONTON SOUTH

(780)437-6010 **25**

Hotel **$175-$300** **Address:** 4440 Gateway Blvd NW T6H 5C2 **Location:** Between Whitemud Dr and 45th Ave. **Facility:** 235 units. 4 stories, interior corridors. **Parking:** winter plug-ins. **Terms:** cancellation fee imposed. **Amenities:** high-speed Internet. **Pool(s):** heated indoor. **Activities:** sauna, whirlpool, steamroom, sports court. **Fee:** massage. **Guest Services:** valet and coin laundry. **Free Special Amenities:** local telephone calls and high-speed Internet.

SAWRIDGE INN EDMONTON SOUTH

(780)438-1222 **27**

▼▼▼ **Hotel** $109-$189 **Address:** 4235 Gateway Blvd T6J 5H2 **Location:** Just s of Whitemud Dr. **Facility:** 136 units. 5 stories, interior corridors. **Parking:** winter plug-ins. **Amenities:** video games (fee). **Dining:** Creations Dining Room & Lounge, see separate listing. **Guest Services:** valet laundry, area transportation-West Edmonton Mall.

(See map & index p. 124.)

SUPER 8 EDMONTON SOUTH (780)433-8688 [28]
▽▽ **Hotel** $120-$140 **Address:** 3610 Gateway Blvd T6J 7H8 **Location:** Jct 36th Ave. **Facility:** 104 units. 4 stories, interior corridors. **Parking:** winter plug-ins. **Amenities:** high-speed Internet. **Pool(s):** heated indoor. **Activities:** whirlpool, waterslide. **Guest Services:** coin laundry.

FEE 🔌 🍴 CALL 🅼 🚗 FEE 🐾 BIZ 📶 ✕
🛗 💻 /SOME UNITS FEE 🐕 🖼

TRAVELODGE EDMONTON EAST (780)474-0456 [5]
▽▽ ▽▽
Hotel
$89-$99
Address: 3414 118th Ave T5W 0Z4 **Location:** 5 mi (8 km) e of Capilano Dr, 0.6 mi (1 km) s from W Hwy 16 (Yellowhead Tr) exit Victoria Tr. **Facility:** 86 units. 2 stories (no elevator), interior corridors.
Parking: winter plug-ins. **Amenities:** Some: high-speed Internet. **Guest Services:** coin laundry. **Free Special Amenities:** continental breakfast and local telephone calls.

SAVE ECO 🍴 🍸 BIZ 📶 🛗 💻 /SOME UNITS FEE 🐕

TRAVELODGE EDMONTON SOUTH (780)436-9770 [24]

Hotel
$105-$135
Address: 10320 45th Ave S T6H 5K3 **Location:** Jct Calgary Tr (Hwy 2) and 45th Ave, just n of Whitemud Dr. **Facility:** 219 units. 3 stories, interior corridors. **Parking:** winter plug-ins.
Amenities: video games (fee). Some: high-speed Internet. **Pool(s):** heated indoor. **Activities:** whirlpool, limited exercise equipment. **Guest Services:** valet and coin laundry.

SAVE ECO 🍴 🚗 BIZ 📶 📹 💻
/SOME UNITS FEE 🐕 🛗 🖼

WEST EDMONTON MALL INN (780)444-9378 [17]
▽▽
Hotel
$119-$194
Address: 17504 90th Ave T5T 6L6 **Location:** From Whitemud Dr exit 170th St N, just w. Next to a mall. **Facility:** 88 units. 3 stories, interior corridors. **Parking:** winter plug-ins. **Terms:** check-in 4 pm, cancellation fee imposed, resort fee. **Amenities:** high-speed Internet (fee). **Guest Services:** valet laundry.

SAVE 🍴 CALL 🅼 📶 ✕ 🛗 💻 /SOME UNITS FEE 🐕

WINGATE INN EDMONTON WEST (780)443-1000 [10]
▽▽▽ **Hotel** $125-$225 **Address:** 18220 100th Ave T5S 2V2 **Location:** From Anthony Henday Dr, 0.9 mi (1.5 km) e at 182nd St. **Facility:** 105 units. 4 stories, interior corridors. **Parking:** winter plug-ins. **Terms:** cancellation fee imposed. **Amenities:** video games (fee), high-speed Internet, safes. **Dining:** Homefire Bar & Grill, see separate listing. **Pool(s):** heated indoor. **Activities:** whirlpool, waterslide, exercise room. **Guest Services:** valet and coin laundry.

🍴 🚗 BIZ 📶 ✕ 📹 🛗 💻 🖼
/SOME UNITS FEE 🐕

WHERE TO EAT

BARB & ERNIE'S 780/433-3242 [24]
▽ German. Casual Dining. $8-$25 **AAA Inspector Notes:** Ask any local for a favorite breakfast place, and this well-established family-run eatery often is mentioned. Lunch and dinner are popular as well. Among the homey restaurant's pleasing array of Bavarian dishes are sauerkraut and sausages. **Bar:** full bar. **Address:** 9906 72nd Ave NW T6E 0Z3 **Location:** 99th St S, just w.
B L D

Visit AAA.com/Travel or CAA.ca/Travel for complete trip planning and reservations

THE BLUE PEAR 780/482-7178 [6]
▽▽▽ French. Fine Dining. $35-$89 **AAA Inspector Notes:** The name of the upscale restaurant is derived from its previous name, D'Anjou. After ringing the doorbell, guests enter a small dining room with a lovely serene décor. Featuring French cooking techniques and regional ingredients, there is a five-course prix fixe menu as well as a la carte choices. Representative of typical menu fare are veal osso buco with saffron risotto and butter-poached Australian Bay lobster layered in herb lasagna. Servers are well-versed in food and wine pairings. **Bar:** full bar. **Reservations:** suggested. **Address:** 10643 123rd St T5N 1P3 **Location:** Southeast corner of 123rd St and 7th Ave. D CALL 🅼

THE BOTHY WINE & WHISKY BAR 780/761-1761 [26]
▽▽▽ New American. Gastropub. $12-$25 **AAA Inspector Notes:** This intimate bar creates delicious seasonal food using local products with a contemporary mix of American-style food and Scottish pub favorites of meat pies, fish and chips and even haggis, along with more complex entrées and fabulous desserts. Make sure to start with the mix and match charcuterie plate teamed with tasty condiments. Guests must be 18 years old and older. **Bar:** full bar. **Address:** 5482 Calgary Tr T6H 4J8 **Location:** Just s of 55th Ave; in a small strip mall. L D LATE CALL 🅼

BUCAS & PASTAS 780/496-2461 [9]
▽ Italian. Quick Serve. $7-$13 **AAA Inspector Notes:** Green-and-white check tablecloths cheer up this simple little café. At the counter, choose a fresh homemade pasta such as Cajun linguine or whole wheat, then add one of the sauces and they will dish it up right there for you to take to the table. Opt for a small, large or all-you-can-eat portion. They also have a few house salads and simple desserts to add to the meal and at dinner they add some meat specials. **Bar:** full bar. **Address:** 16516 100th Ave T5P 4Y2 **Location:** Just e of 166th St; in small industrial plaza. L D

CENTURY GRILL 780/431-0303 [31]
▽▽▽ New Pacific Rim. Casual Dining. $17-$41 **AAA Inspector Notes:** Chic and contemporary, this upscale restaurant features a lovely open-concept dining room with black and gray decor. Patrons can dine in the restaurant or the more casual lounge. Creative cuisine boldly pairs varied tastes and sensations. The menu focuses heavily on regional ingredients and also exhibits a Californian flair. Open only for dinner on Saturday and Sunday. **Bar:** full bar. **Reservations:** suggested. **Address:** 3975 Calgary Tr T6J 6S6 **Location:** Calgary Tr S at 39th Ave. L D CALL 🅼

THE CHEESECAKE CAFE 780/486-0440
▽▽ International. Casual Dining. $10-$25 **AAA Inspector Notes:** As might be expected, cheesecake is the signature item, and it is worth saving room for one of the lip-smacking varieties made on the premises. A huge dessert display case greets guests upon arrival. Offerings on the extensive lunch and dinner menu range from sandwiches and entree salads to pasta, pizza and seafood selections. It takes a while to get through the menu. **Bar:** full bar. **Address:** 17011 100th Ave NW T5S 1T9 **Location:** Jct 100th Ave NW and 170th St NW. L D CALL 🅼

COL. MUSTARD'S CANTEEN 780/448-1590 [4]
▽▽ American. Casual Dining. $10-$26 **AAA Inspector Notes:** There are sandwiches galore at this popular lunch spot with more than 30 kinds and that is not counting the design-your-own styles. It may seem more pricey than the average sandwich shop since it is extra for salad, soup and sides, but they only use the best ingredients and the sandwiches are filling. They also make personal-size pizza and simpler items like lasagna. Dinner morphs into a bistro-style menu with such items as pan-seared salmon or roasted rib-eye. **Bar:** beer & wine. **Address:** 10802 124th St NW T5M 0H3 **Location:** Just n of 107th Ave NW. **Parking:** street only. L D

CONYAC'S BAR & GRILL 780/483-2255 [7]
▽▽ American. Casual Dining. $11-$26 **AAA Inspector Notes:** As far as hotel restaurants go, this place does not fit into the conventional mold. Seats and booths in the comfortably decorated dining room are designed to be cozy for longer visits. While the menu does not take any risks, diners can find all of the classic dishes solidly executed and tasty. **Bar:** full bar. **Address:** 10010 179A St T5S 2T1 **Location:** From Anthony Henday Dr, 1.2 mi (2 km) e; in Days Inn & Suites West Edmonton. B L D CALL 🅼

(See map & index p. 124.)

CREATIONS DINING ROOM & LOUNGE 780/989-4439 30

WWW New American. Casual Dining. $11-$39 **AAA Inspector Notes:** This beautifully designed restaurant offers lots of stone and wood, distinctive lighting and a gas fireplace. Native and Western whimsy accents the room along with a giant dream catcher over a hoodoo sculpture. With a name like it has one has to expect a creative menu and diners will not be disappointed since the chef really uses his imagination with quality local ingredients to produce some amazing and tantalizing food choices. **Bar:** full bar. **Reservations:** suggested. **Address:** 4235 Gateway Blvd T6J 5H2 **Location:** Just s of Whitemud Dr; in Sawridge Inn Edmonton South.

B L D CALL &M

CULINA MUTTART 780/935-7094 20

WW American. Casual Dining. $11-$16 **AAA Inspector Notes:** This bright and casual café at the Muttart Conservatory has wonderful gourmet sandwiches made with local products. Examples might be chicken and Brie with cranberry chutney and greens or Spring Creek Ranch steak with horseradish mushroom jus on sweet potato bread. They are served with the daily soup or the delicious Culina salad with mixed greens, quinoa, dried fruit, cheese and almonds. They also serve dinner on Thursday night and brunch on the weekends. **Bar:** full bar. **Address:** 9626 96A St T6C 4L8 **Location:** Just s of 98th Ave NW; in Muttart Conservatory. L CALL &M

DELUX BURGER BAR 780/420-0101 17

WW American. Casual Dining. $10-$20 **AAA Inspector Notes:** Burgers almost seem out of place at this upbeat and stylish space, but the menu lists several gourmet varieties, such as the Black Angus-infused burger, in addition to lobster nachos, sweet potato fries and the signature deluxe donuts. **Bar:** full bar. **Address:** 9682 142th St T5N 4B2 **Location:** Jct 97th Ave NW; in shopping plaza.

L D

THE DISH BISTRO 780/488-6641 10

WW American. Casual Dining. $13-$19 **AAA Inspector Notes:** While in the art district, stop by this little bistro, a great place for a healthy, quick bite or a quaint, leisurely meal. Among interesting creations are tomato basil cream soup, pear and cambozola flatbread, mango curry chicken wraps, crab cakes and sweet potato shepherd's pie. Original artwork, hardwood floors and large, street-view windows create a cozy atmosphere in the dining room. **Bar:** full bar. **Reservations:** suggested. **Address:** 12417 Stony Plain Rd T5N 3N3 **Location:** Just w of jct Hwy 16A (Stony Plain Rd) and 124th St. **Parking:** street only. L D

EARLS RESTAURANT 780/473-9008

WWW American. Casual Dining. $13-$33 **AAA Inspector Notes:** Offering an experience that falls between fast food and fine dining, the fun, relaxed restaurant prepares great food at a great price. Choices range from juicy burgers, hearty sandwiches, fresh salads, wings and pizza to full entrees of steak, chops and seafood. Made-from-scratch soups and assorted breads, as well as a nice choice of wines and beers, round out the offerings. This is a fitting spot for impromptu get-togethers and festive occasions. **Bar:** full bar. **Address:** 13330 50th St T5A 4Z8 **Location:** Hwy 16 (Yellowhead Tr); 0.9 mi (1.5 km) n on 50th St (Hwy 15). L D LATE CALL &M

FAMOSO NEAPOLITAN PIZZERIA 780/487-0046 19

WW Pizza. Casual Dining. $7-$15 **AAA Inspector Notes:** This rustic, yet modern, pizzeria is proud of the thin-crust pizza made with Campania tomatoes, fior-di-latte cheese and fresh basil that are fire-roasted in ovens imported from Italy. Both Neapolitan classics and modern styles are offered as well as tomato bisque, salads, appetizers and Italian desserts. This is atypical service where diners seat themselves, look over the menu and then head to the counter to order. Friendly servers deliver the food and look after guests' needs. **Bar:** full bar. **Address:** 8882 170th St, Unit 1951 T5T 4M2 **Location:** Just e on 90th Ave NW; northeast corner of West Edmonton Mall parking lot. L D CALL &M

FIFE N' DEKEL 780/489-6436 2

W Deli. Quick Serve. $6-$10 **AAA Inspector Notes:** Quick, healthy lunch options are plentiful at the cafeteria-style eatery. Guests order at the counter and watch their sandwich being made. In addition to such sandwiches as roasted turkey, beef, ham and vegetarian, the menu lists soups, salads and tempting selections from a dessert case full of sumptuous options. Because this place draws a good crowd at lunch, patrons should arrive early to avoid lines. **Address:** 10646 170th St T5S 1P3 **Location:** At 106th Ave; in industrial shopping plaza; on west side of road. B L

FRANCO'S STEAK & PIZZA 780/476-4333 1

WW Italian. Casual Dining. $8-$27 **AAA Inspector Notes:** After more than 30 years, this family-run eatery must be doing something right. Cheerful Italian country décor with a wall mural along with a warm welcome await along with straightforward, but tasty, fare. Choose from a few typical appetizers and salads, followed by staples of hearty familiar pasta, including a variety of oven-baked styles as well as steaks, lobster, a smattering of other Italian dishes and pizza which as highly rated in Edmonton. **Bar:** full bar. **Address:** 12981 50th St NE T5A 3P3 **Location:** Hwy 16 (Yellowhead Tr), 0.6 mi (1 km) n on 50th St (Hwy 15). L D

GURU FINE INDIAN CUISINE 780/484-4300 8

WWW Indian. Casual Dining. $14-$24 **AAA Inspector Notes:** This contemporary spot has a lovely décor with some stand-out light fixtures and back-lit art designs as well as a well-prepared menu crafted using the best ingredients and spices. Samosas with butter chicken filling are a great way to start off and there is a good range of tandoori kebabs like their own Guru secret recipe chicken or adraki seekh beef. Curries, vindaloo and goat cooked in tomato onion gravy with ginger are some of the other choices along with a selection of naan and roti. **Bar:** full bar. **Reservations:** suggested. **Address:** 17021 100th Ave T5S 1T9 **Location:** Corner of 170th St. L D CALL &M

HIGHLANDS KITCHEN 780/477-2422 3

WWW New European. Casual Dining. $8-$26 **AAA Inspector Notes:** This bistro with a simple, cute décor offers dishes utilizing local farms and producers. An East Asian influence provides an intriguing meal experience. I loved every bit starting with fluffy goat cheese custard followed by lamb koftas (a spicy meatball) and finishing off with a decadent dense chocolate pate and crème fraîche. The Kalyna platter of pyrohy, grilled kubassa and lazy cabbage rolls is popular. Other entrées include wild salmon and free-range chicken. Closed for dinner on Sundays. **Bar:** full bar. **Reservations:** suggested. **Address:** 6509 112th Ave T5W 0P1 **Location:** Just e of Wayne Gretzky Dr NW. **Parking:** street only.

L D AC

HOMEFIRE BAR & GRILL 780/489-8086 5

WW International. Casual Dining. $11-$30 **AAA Inspector Notes:** This upscale yet comfortable restaurant features a large central fireplace that serves to remind guests that this place specializes in forno dishes. In addition to oven-baked pasta, pizza and rotisserie chicken, the menu also offers some distinctively Canadian items such as buffalo meatloaf with Saskatoon berry sauce and the locally-farmed Katahdin lamb burger with pancetta, Gouda and Saskatoon berry relish. **Bar:** full bar. **Reservations:** suggested. **Address:** 18210 100th Ave T5S 2V2 **Location:** From Anthony Henday Dr, 0.9 mi (1.5 km) e at 182nd St; in Wingate Inn Edmonton West.

L D CALL &M

IL PASTICCIO TRATTORIA 780/488-9543 18

WW Italian. Casual Dining. $12-$35 **AAA Inspector Notes:** Just a block south of Jasper Avenue, this funky little trattoria nurtures a cozy atmosphere, complete with an open kitchen where diners can watch the chefs toss homemade pasta and put together traditional Italian meat dishes. Boldly painted walls and black tablecloths set the scene. Servers are prompt and friendly. Also open for lunch on Thursday and Friday. **Bar:** full bar. **Address:** 11520 100th Ave T5K 0J7 **Location:** Corner of 116th St and 100th Ave. **Parking:** on-site (fee). D

JACK'S GRILL 780/434-1113 25

WWW Regional Canadian. Casual Dining. $28-$43 **AAA Inspector Notes:** Be impressed with both the personal attention guests receive from the owner of this relaxed, casual grill, and the unusual cuisine created by the talented chef. Fresh ingredients, bold flavors and French and West Coast influences are staples in the inventive fare. Regardless of whether sitting in the upscale, elegant dining room or on the seasonal patio, diners can expect flawless, professional service. **Bar:** full bar. **Reservations:** suggested. **Address:** 5842 111th St T6H 3G1 **Location:** Whitemud Dr exit 111th St, 0.5 mi (0.8 km) n, then just w on 57th Ave; in strip mall. D CALL &M

JOEY RESTAURANTS 780/465-1880

WWW American. Casual Dining. $13-$33 **AAA Inspector Notes:** The cuisine blends Mediterranean and Asian cooking styles and emphasizes finger foods for sharing. Those who aren't big fans of tapas can consider full meal offerings centered on steaks and chops. **Bar:** full bar. **Address:** 9911 19th Ave NW T6N 1M4 **Location:** South Edmonton Commons. L D LATE

(See map & index p. 124.)

KOUTOUKI
780/432-3660 (28)

▼▼▼ Greek. Casual Dining. $15-$35 **AAA Inspector Notes:** This restaurant served as a set in the Food Network Canada TV series "The Family Restaurant," a behind-the-scenes drama about the ongoing antics of a local restaurateur and his Greek family. Cool, comfortable décor is reflective of Greece, with many white and blue accents, terra cotta tiles and fake grape-covered arbors hanging from the ceiling. Not surprisingly, the menu is typical Greek, listing such favorites as souvlaki, moussaka and roasted lamb. Belly dancers occasionally perform. **Bar:** full bar. **Reservations:** suggested, for dinner. **Address:** 10310 45th Ave T6H 5K3 **Location:** Jct Gateway Blvd NW; just n of Whitemud Dr. L D CALL M

LA FAVORITE PASTRY SHOP
780/482-7024 (12)

▼ Breads/Pastries. Quick Serve. $3-$8 **AAA Inspector Notes:** Opening into a bookstore, this pastry shop generates the smells of chocolate and sugar that tend to waft through both. Guests can take a seat at one of several small tables or at a stool along the window as they sip fresh coffee in between bites of luscious cake. For those a little more hungry, a limited selection of panini-style sandwiches and soup is available. **Address:** 12431 102nd Ave NW T5N 0M2 **Location:** Just w of jct 124th St W. L

LEMONGRASS CAFE
780/413-0088 (27)

▼▼ Vietnamese. Casual Dining. $10-$19 **AAA Inspector Notes:** This restaurant has a deceptively unassuming exterior. Just behind the doors is a bright, cheerful, airy cafe offering exciting, fresh, healthy entrees. Traditional Vietnamese fare includes salad rolls, curries and the house specialty: spiced salmon wrapped in banana leaf with vermicelli. Guests can finish off the meal with a single malt scotch or an innovative dessert. **Bar:** full bar. **Address:** 10417 51st Ave T6H 0K4 **Location:** Just w of 104th St on Allard Way; in small strip mall. L D

LOCAL PUBLIC EATERY
780/989-5898 (32)

▼▼ American. Gastropub. $13-$19 **AAA Inspector Notes:** The first thing guests notice at this contemporary eatery is the loud music and the many TVs blaring sporting events. A typical, jazzed up, pub menu is offered, including gourmet burgers and sandwiches, seasonal fish and chips and tacos with braised beans. Stolen from the owner's previous incarnation, OPM Asian Bistro, is the tender Szechuan wok-fired squid and the drunken chicken in ginger sesame sauce. Also available is a decent wine list, some house cocktails and more than twelve tap pours. **Bar:** full bar. **Address:** 1820 99th St T6N 1M5 **Location:** On east side of South Edmonton Commons. L D LATE CALL M

MANOR CASUAL BISTRO
780/482-7577 (15)

▼▼ International. Casual Dining. $12-$34 **AAA Inspector Notes:** The cafe occupies the beautifully restored home of one of Alberta's former attorney generals. Decor is charming, warm and intimate, with a casual feel. The bistro-style menu includes progressive and innovative international dishes. **Bar:** full bar. **Reservations:** suggested. **Address:** 10109 125th St T5N 1S7 **Location:** Just s of 102nd Ave NW. L D CALL M

MOXIE'S CLASSIC GRILL

▼▼ American. Casual Dining. $10-$30 **AAA Inspector Notes:** This sleek, funky and popular restaurant presents an extensive menu of creatively prepared dishes, including pizza, pasta, rice, noodles, signature salads and burgers. Other menus include one for children and one for Sunday brunch. Lending to the upbeat, stylish decor are dark wood appointments and river rock fireplaces. **Bar:** full bar.

L D LATE

For additional information, visit AAA.com

LOCATIONS:
Address: 1670 8882-170th St T5T 4M2 **Location:** In West Edmonton Mall; in Bourbon Street District. **Phone:** 780/484-6669
Address: 17109 100th Ave NW T5S 2GS **Location:** Jct 170th St NW and 100th Ave NW. **Phone:** 780/484-2040

NORMAND'S FINE REGIONAL CUISINE
780/482-2600 (16)

▼▼▼ French. Casual Dining. $14-$39 **AAA Inspector Notes:** Guests are made to feel welcome, usually by Normand himself, at this warm and inviting room. Superb selections of classics ranging from escargot, frog legs and thyme-onion soup to bouillabaisse and pork tenderloin Dijonnaise are offered. What really sets them apart are the locally-sourced meats including bison, wild boar, elk, venison and pheasant in addition to a good selection of seafood. Such desserts as the chocolate three-nut pie are worth saving room for. **Bar:** full bar. **Reservations:** suggested. **Address:** 11639A Jasper Ave NW T5K 0M9 **Location:** Between 116th and 117th sts NW. **Parking:** on-site and street. L D

PARKALLEN RESTAURANT
780/436-8080 (23)

▼▼ Lebanese. Casual Dining. $8-$45 **AAA Inspector Notes:** A popular spot with the locals, this family-run restaurant is considered to be one of the city's best ethnic restaurants. The menu centers on selections of traditional Lebanese fare, including fatouche salad, baba ghanoush and marinated kebabs. Those not in the mood for Lebanese cuisine can also try award-winning pizza. The wine list is extensive. The casually elegant dining room displays traditional art. Servers are friendly and knowledgeable. Closed for lunch on Sunday. **Bar:** full bar. **Reservations:** suggested. **Address:** 7018 109th St NW T6H 3C1 **Location:** Corner of 70th Ave and 109th St. L D

RED OX INN
780/465-5727 (21)

▼▼▼ New American. Casual Dining. $28-$34 **AAA Inspector Notes:** This tiny pearl, hidden away in a residential area, offers an inspired menu influenced by local producers. The menu always is evolving but examples to start might include smoked salmon with cornbread and buttermilk or pork belly with sweet and sour marmalade, followed by such enticing entrées as pheasant with ancho romesco sauce and wild mushroom truffle lasagna. Finish with a cheese plate or a homemade dessert. A nice wine list along with hospitable and fine service can be expected. **Bar:** full bar. **Reservations:** suggested. **Address:** 9429 91st St T6C 3P4 **Location:** Jct Connors Rd NW, just n; in a residential area. **Parking:** street only. D K

RICKY'S ALL DAY GRILL
780/486-7109

▼▼ American. Family Dining. $12-$27 **AAA Inspector Notes:** The comfortable eatery, which employs friendly servers, presents a varied menu that includes pasta dishes, wraps, omelets, stir-fry preparations and burgers. Portions are generous. Children's and senior selections are offered. Guests can request seating in a booth or at a table. **Bar:** full bar. **Address:** 9917 170th St T5P 4S2 **Location:** Just s of jct 100th Ave NW. B L D CALL M

SAGE RESTAURANT
780/930-2626

▼▼▼ Steak. Fine Dining. $25-$45 **AAA Inspector Notes:** Just off the casino floor, this cool, trendy restaurant offers a lovely oasis from all the gambling action with an upscale décor of stone and wood work, glass wine walls and a large curved oyster bar just inside the entrance. Designed for the high roller, the expensive menu includes freshly baked bread warm from the oven, tantalizing appetizers, seafood, organic chicken and excellent cuts of meat from local farms with superb preparations. Friendly servers are attentive without being overbearing. **Bar:** full bar. **Reservations:** suggested. **Address:** 300 E Lapotac Blvd T7X 3Y3 **Location:** 1 mi (1.6 km) w of jct Hwy 216 (Anthony Henday Dr) and Whitemud Dr W; in Edmonton Marriott at River Cree Resort. D

TOM GOODCHILDS MOOSE FACTORY
780/437-5616 (29)

▼▼ Steak. Casual Dining. $12-$50 **AAA Inspector Notes:** The restaurant does not look big from the outside, but inside the formal yet comfortable dining area, guests have the choice of being seated in one of several differently decorated rooms. Tuxedoed servers have a casual edge that makes everyone feel at home. Known for its steaks, the menu is a carnivore's dream come true. **Bar:** full bar. **Reservations:** suggested. **Address:** 4810 Calgary Tr S T6H 5H5 **Location:** Just n of Whitemud Dr NW. L D CALL M

UNHEARDOF RESTAURANT
780/432-0480 (22)

▼▼ American. Fine Dining. $35-$45 **AAA Inspector Notes:** In an old house along the east end of Whyte Avenue, this cozy eatery draws patrons for its fine food and splendid service. Food made from regional ingredients is offered from a prix fixe menu or a la carte. The wine list is fantastic. This place is a favorite for special occasions. **Bar:** full bar. **Reservations:** suggested. **Address:** 9602 82nd Ave T6C 1A1 **Location:** Corner of 82nd Ave (Whyte Ave) and 96th St. **Parking:** street only. D

(See map & index p. 124.)

URBAN DINER   780/488-7274   ⓫

WWW American. Casual Dining. $9-$17 **AAA Inspector Notes:** While there is a definite upscale diner feel to this place, the kitchen presents a tight little menu of comfort food and regularly, sometimes daily, changing specials. Using top-notch ingredients, much of them sourced locally, the chefs displays their talents in the partially open kitchen and evoke clean and distinct flavors from even the simplest of dishes. Open for breakfast on the weekends but closed for dinner on Sunday. **Bar:** full bar. **Address:** 12427 102nd Ave T5N 0M2 **Location:** Just w of jct 124th St W. L D CALL M

VIOLINO GASTRONOMIA ITALIANA   780/757-8701   ⓮

WWWW Italian. Fine Dining. $11-$35 **AAA Inspector Notes:** Old World meets new at this 1913 mansion where well-prepared Italian dishes are offered with a modern touch. Some of the menu items include bruschetta with seasonal mushrooms and truffle oil, fresh fusilli with authentic Genova pesto cream sauce, rainbow trout in roasted shallots and a Quebec veal chop with basil-infused tomato sauce. Professional servers provide attentive service and some tableside presentations. Lunch is simplified with the addition of wood-fired gourmet pizza and sandwiches. **Bar:** full bar. **Reservations:** suggested. **Address:** 10133 125th St T5N 1S7 **Location:** Just s of 102nd Ave NW. L D CALL M

ZAIKA INDIAN BISTRO BAR   780/462-8722   ㉝

WW Indian. Casual Dining. $14-$19 **AAA Inspector Notes:** The spiffy blend of contemporary and East Indian décor with sparkly light fixtures and large illuminated photographs differentiate this restaurant. A menu is available but most people partake in the buffet which offers appetizers, a salad section including some Indian versions, chutneys and pickles as well as a good range of changing entrées and some desserts. Servers are friendly and accommodating. **Bar:** full bar. **Reservations:** suggested. **Address:** 2303 Ellwood Dr SW T6X 0A9 **Location:** Just e of 91st St SW; in industrial complex. L D CALL M

THE SHERLOCK HOLMES PUB   780/426-7784

fyi Not evaluated. Great spot for pub food with an English flair and a casual ambiance. **Address:** 10012-101 A Ave T5J 3Z1

EDSON   pop. 8,475

BEST WESTERN HIGH ROAD INN   (780)712-2378

WWWW
Hotel
$139-$149

AAA Benefit: Members save up to 20%, plus 10% bonus points with Best Western Rewards®.

Address: 300 52nd St T7E 1V8 **Location:** On 2nd Ave; center. **Facility:** 114 units. 4 stories, interior corridors. **Parking:** winter plug-ins. **Amenities:** high-speed Internet. **Pool(s):** heated indoor. **Activities:** whirlpool, waterslide, exercise room. **Guest Services:** valet laundry. **Free Special Amenities:** full breakfast and local telephone calls.

SAVE ❎ ❎ CALL M ❎ BIZ ❎ ❎ ❎ ❎ ❎ / SOME UNITS FEE ❎

EDSON COMFORT INN & SUITES   (780)723-7303

WWWW
Hotel
$100-$110

Address: 5517 4th Ave T7E 1L6 **Location:** Hwy 16; west end of town. **Facility:** 40 units, some kitchens. 4 stories, interior corridors. **Parking:** winter plug-ins. **Terms:** cancellation fee imposed. **Amenities:** high-speed Internet. **Activities:** exercise room. **Guest Services:** valet and coin laundry. **Free Special Amenities:** continental breakfast and early check-in/late check-out.

SAVE ❎ CALL M BIZ ❎ ❎ ❎ ❎

Get an insider view from AAA/CAA travel experts at AAATravelViews.com

GUEST HOUSE INN & SUITES   780-723-4486

WW WW Motel. Rates not provided. **Address:** 4411 4th Ave T7E 1B8 **Location:** 0.6 mi (1 km) e on Hwy 16. **Facility:** 108 units, some two bedrooms and kitchens. 1-3 stories (no elevator), interior/exterior corridors. **Parking:** winter plug-ins. **Amenities:** high-speed Internet. **Activities:** sauna, steamroom, exercise room. **Guest Services:** coin laundry.

❎ ❎ BIZ ❎ ❎ ❎ ❎ / SOME UNITS ❎

HOLIDAY INN EXPRESS HOTEL & SUITES EDSON   (780)723-4011

WWWW Hotel $129-$179 **Address:** 4520 2nd Ave T7E 1C3 **Location:** 0.6 mi (1 km) e on Hwy 16. **Facility:** 79 units. 4 stories, interior corridors. **Parking:** winter plug-ins. **Amenities:** high-speed Internet. **Pool(s):** heated indoor. **Activities:** whirlpool, waterslide, exercise room. **Guest Services:** valet and coin laundry.

ECO ❎ CALL M ❎ BIZ ❎ ❎ ❎ ❎ ❎

LAKEVIEW INN & SUITES EDSON AIRPORT WEST   780/723-7508

◆◆ Hotel Rates not provided   **Address:** 528 63rd St T7E 1M1 **Location:** Hwy 16, west end of town. **Facility:** 69 units. 2 stories (no elevator), interior corridors. **Parking:** winter plug-ins. **Terms:** check-in 4 pm. **Amenities:** high-speed Internet. **Activities:** exercise room. **Guest Services:** valet and coin laundry. **Free Special Amenities:** continental breakfast and high-speed Internet.

SAVE ECO CALL M ❎ ❎ ❎ ❎ / SOME UNITS FEE ❎

LAKEVIEW INNS & SUITES EAST   (780)723-2500

◆◆ Hotel $94-$114   **Address:** 4300 2nd Ave T7E 1B8 **Location:** 0.6 mi (1 km) e on Hwy 16. **Facility:** 45 units. 2 stories (no elevator), interior corridors. **Parking:** winter plug-ins. **Terms:** cancellation fee imposed. **Amenities:** Some: high-speed Internet. **Guest Services:** coin laundry. **Free Special Amenities:** continental breakfast and high-speed Internet.

SAVE ECO ❎ ❎ ❎ ❎ ❎ / SOME UNITS FEE ❎

WHERE TO EAT

MOJO'S JAVA   780/517-5619

W Coffee/Tea. Quick Serve. $5-$9 **AAA Inspector Notes:** There is an inviting décor at this pleasant coffee spot with a variety of seating including some cushy armchairs. Simple and fresh daily soup and sandwiches, salad and some tasty muffins and squares are on the menu along with great coffee. Ice cream treats also are available. **Address:** 5202 2nd Ave T7E 1X5 **Location:** Between 52nd and 53rd sts. B L D CALL M

MOUNTAIN PIZZA & STEAK HOUSE   780/723-3900

WW Steak. Casual Dining. $9-$28 **AAA Inspector Notes:** This casual, busy restaurant has been a popular spot for more than 30 years. Inside the pyramid-shaped building is a stained wooden roof with a skylight and a large fig tree as the focal point. Tourists from around the world return to sample the top-secret, spiced steaks. Also featured is shish kebabs, Italian veal and chicken dishes and, of course, pizza. Leave room for a slice of homemade carrot cake or cheesecake. **Bar:** full bar. **Reservations:** suggested. **Address:** 5102 4th Ave T7E 1T8 **Location:** Hwy 16 westbound at 51st St. L D CALL M

THE OLIVE TREE   780/723-4433

WW Mediterranean. Casual Dining. $13-$35 **AAA Inspector Notes:** This friendly and hospitable restaurant is one of the finer spots to dine in Edson with a low lighting ambience. They offer a range of appetizers such as mussels or pita baked with spinach, herbs and feta. A good mix of entrées includes flavorful souvlaki, kebabs, Moroccan lamb and pasta. They also serve up a few other European dishes like schnitzel along with steak and seafood. **Bar:** full bar. **Reservations:** suggested, weekends. **Address:** 221 50th St T7E 1T8 **Location:** Between 2nd and 4th (Yellowhead Hwy 16) aves; center. **Parking:** street only. D CALL M

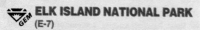

ELK ISLAND NATIONAL PARK
(E-7)

Elevations in the park range from 709 metres (2,326 ft.) at Goose Lake to 754 metres (2,475 ft.) at Tawayik Lake. Refer to CAA/AAA maps for additional elevation information.

About 35 kilometres (22 mi.) east of Edmonton, Elk Island National Park is reached by Hwy. 15 from the north and Hwy. 16 from the south. The lakes, ponds, forests and meadows of this 194-square-kilometre (75-sq.-mi.) park provide a haven for many species of animals and plants.

The park occupies the Beaver Hills region, which first was settled by Sarcee and Plains Cree Indians. They trapped beavers and hunted bison and elk, as did the European fur traders who arrived between the late 18th and the mid-19th centuries. Soon the animals became nearly extinct, and the natives were forced to seek sustenance elsewhere.

In 1906 five local men asked that the government establish a wildlife refuge to preserve the remaining elk. A year later 400 plains bison were added, while another preserve near Wainwright was being established. Most of these animals later were transferred, but about 50 stayed and produced the plains bison herd of more than 300 that remains today north of Hwy. 16. A herd of several hundred wood bison, a threatened subspecies, is kept separate from this herd south of Hwy. 16.

As the wildlife populations grew, so did the park's area; more land was added to the refuge in 1922, 1947, 1956 and 1978. Many small lakes dot the landscape, but the major bodies are Tawayik and Astotin, the latter being the larger. The lakes and marshes support the more than 250 bird species, including ducks, grebes, gulls, loons, pelicans, rare trumpeter swans and terns.

Marsh marigolds and several types of lilies are among several plants rarely seen outside the park. Song birds occupy the many aspen, spruce and birch forests, but few fish inhabit the waters due to low oxygen levels. The herd of elk for which the park was established flourish among the meadows and forests, as do reintroduced colonies of beavers. Deer, moose and coyotes also roam the park.

General Information and Activities

The park is open daily all year. Most recreation facilities center on Astotin Lake, which offers non-motorized boating, wildlife observations, picnic facilities, a nine-hole golf course, camping, hiking and walking trails. A campground is on the east side of the lake. Interpretive talks, events and displays explain the park's history and features.

A visitor information center is .8 kilometres (.5 mi.) north of Hwy. 16 before the park's south gate entrance. Staff members and displays describe Elk Island and other national parks. The center is open Thursday through Monday, mid-May through Labour Day; phone (780) 922-5790 to confirm schedule.

Camping and picnicking are popular in summer. The park's approximately 100 kilometres (60 mi.) of trails are popular with hikers and cross-country skiers. Hunting and fishing are prohibited. *See Recreation Areas Chart.*

ADMISSION to the park is $19.60 per private vehicle (three to seven persons). Otherwise admission per person is $7.80; $6.80 (ages 65+); $3.90 (ages 6-16). An annual pass, valid at all Canadian national parks, is available.

PETS must be kept on a leash at all times.

ADDRESS inquiries for additional information to Elk Island National Park, Site 4, R.R. 1, Fort Saskatchewan, AB, Canada T8L 2N7; phone (780) 992-2950.

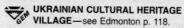 **UKRAINIAN CULTURAL HERITAGE VILLAGE**—see Edmonton p. 118.

ELK POINT (D-8) pop. 1,412, elev. 594m/1,948'

[SAVE] **FORT GEORGE AND BUCKINGHAM HOUSE PROVINCIAL HISTORIC SITE**, 13 km (8 mi.) s.e. on Hwy. 646, encompasses the archeological remains of two fur trade forts. A scenic interpretive trail complemented by wild flowers—including the rare yellow lady's slipper orchid—allows for closer inspection of the site and its various structural remains. Staff members are available at the visitor center, which offers displays about the area's heritage and fur trading industry.

Educational programs are offered. **Tours:** Guided tours are available. **Time:** Allow 2 hours minimum. **Hours:** Daily 10-5, May 15-Labour Day. **Cost:** $3; $2 (senior citizens); $1.50 (ages 7-17); $8 (family, two adults and two children). **Phone:** (780) 724-2611, or (780) 645-6256 in the off-season. 🎟

ELKWATER (J-9) pop. 50

Before Europeans came to the Elkwater region, Assiniboine, Blackfoot, Cree and Sioux shared the land with grizzly bears, wolves, bison and a large number of elk. After settlers and trappers arrived, the wolves and elk were hunted to extinction; the elk population since has been reintroduced. An 1873 massacre of Assiniboine Indians by wolf hunters and whiskey traders prompted the formation of the North West Mounted Police and the establishment of Fort Walsh.

The Cypress Hills area, shared by Alberta and Saskatchewan, is noted for its lodgepole pine forests, water resources and wildlife. The hills, which rise to more than 1,466 metres (4,810 ft.), offer visitors a cool climate, scenic views and diverse flora and fauna. Elkwater serves as the area's hub.

CYPRESS HILLS INTERPROVINCIAL PARK is 1.5 km (.9 mi.) s. on Hwy. 41. Fossils of early mammals dating back 40 million years have been found in the hills. An aboriginal culture flourished in the area for more than 7,000 years. Ruminants, beavers, coyotes and varied birds and plants now live in the park.

Park interpreters schedule programs May through September. The visitor center offers information, displays and audiovisual presentations. *See Recreation Areas Chart.*

Hours: Grounds daily 24 hours. Visitor center daily 9:30-7, early July-Labour Day; daily 9:30-5 (also Fri.-Sat. 5-7), Victoria Day weekend-early July; Wed.-Sun. 9-4, May 1-day before Victoria Day weekend. Special events are offered year-round. **Cost:** Free. **Phone:** (403) 893-3833, (403) 893-3782 for camping reservations, or (403) 893-3777 for the visitor center. 🅰 🍴 ⊗ 🐕 ⛺

FORT MACLEOD (J-6) pop. 3,117, elev. 955m/3,133'

In 1874 at the end of their 1,126-kilometre (700-mi.) march through the prairie wilderness to rid western Canada of whiskey traders, the North West Mounted Police, now the Royal Canadian Mounted Police, chose the site of what is now Fort Macleod as their first headquarters.

A commanding view of the countryside and the natural protection afforded by the Oldman River made Fort Macleod an important outpost; a cairn at 2nd Avenue and 25th Street commemorates the fort's founding. Guided walking tours of the historic district, ranging from 30 minutes to 1 hour, can be arranged in advance during the summer by contacting the Main Street Office, (403) 553-2500, or The Fort Museum of the North West Mounted Police (*see attraction listing*).

The highland physical geography that made the Fort Macleod outpost successful also helped the Plains Indians survive long before the first traders appeared in the area. In order to kill the buffalo for food, the Plains hunters stampeded them over the high cliffs.

SAVE **THE FORT MUSEUM OF THE NORTH WEST MOUNTED POLICE**, 219 25th St., creates the atmosphere of the original Fort Macleod. Exhibits set among historical structures focus on the history of the North West Mounted Police, southern Alberta natives and pioneer settlers. Of particular interest are the summer Mounted Patrol Musical Rides in which horseback riders in replicas of 1878 RCMP uniforms perform precision movements to music.

Time: Allow 1 hour minimum. **Hours:** Daily 9-6, July 1-Labour Day; 9-5, early May-June 30; Wed.-Sun. 10-4, day after Labour Day-early Oct. Musical rides are presented daily (weather permitting) at 10, 11:30, 2 and 3:30, July 1-Labour Day. **Cost:** July 1-Labour Day $12; $10 (ages 65+); $8 (ages 12-17); $6 (ages 6-11); $27 (family). Early May-June 30 and day after Labour Day-early Oct. $10; $8 (ages 65+); $6 (ages 12-17); $5 (ages 6-11); $25 (family). **Phone:** (403) 553-4703 or (866) 273-6841.

GEM SAVE **HEAD-SMASHED-IN BUFFALO JUMP INTERPRETIVE CENTRE** is 3 km (1.9 mi.) n. on Queen Elizabeth II Hwy., then 16 km (10 mi.) w. on Hwy. 785. For at least 6,000 years the Plains Indians stampeded herds of buffalo over sandstone cliffs to their deaths. The hunters then butchered the kill at their campsite below the cliffs. This is one of the oldest, best-preserved buffalo jump sites. A 12-minute film re-creates the hunts.

The site's name is derived from a young brave who stood under a ledge of the cliff to watch the buffalo as they fell past him. As the number of carcasses multiplied, his skull was crushed as he became trapped between the animals and the cliff.

Built into that cliff today is a seven-story interpretive center with displays. Exhibits focus on the geographical and climatic factors affecting these tribes as well as their lifestyle and history. The hunting site is preserved; short trails lead to the main areas.

Time: Allow 2 hours minimum. **Hours:** Daily 10-6, July 1-Labour Day; 10-5, rest of year. Closed Jan. 1, Easter, Christmas Eve and Christmas. **Cost:** $10; $8 (ages 66+); $5 (ages 7-17); $22 (family). **Phone:** (403) 553-2731. 🍴

SUNSET MOTEL   403/553-4448

Motel
$80-$88

Address: 104 Hwy 3 W T0L 0Z0 **Location:** 0.6 mi (1 km) w on Hwy 2 and 3. **Facility:** 22 units, some two bedrooms and kitchens. 1 story, exterior corridors. **Parking:** winter plug-ins. **Amenities:** high-speed Internet. **Free Special Amenities: continental breakfast and high-speed Internet.**

SAVE 📶 🛏 🖼 🖵 / SOME UNITS 🐾

WHERE TO EAT

JOHNNY'S RESTAURANT   403/553-3939

♦♦ Chinese. Family Dining. $7-$24 **AAA Inspector Notes:** The highly trained chef/owner prepares an extensive selection of Western and Chinese dishes. Fresh ingredients, generous portions and good value make this a gem of a place. All members of the family take part in serving and exhibit unsurpassed friendliness. Entrees include selections of salmon, veal, prawns, ribs and steak as well as fresh pasta and lighter sandwiches. An old-fashioned sign serves as a beacon to this downtown restaurant, which is quite popular with the locals. **Bar:** full bar. **Reservations:** suggested. **Address:** 225 24th St (Main St) T0L 0Z0 **Location:** Center; next to Empress Theatre. **Parking:** street only. L D

FORT McMURRAY (A-8) pop. 61,374
• Hotels p. 144 • Restaurants p. 144

At the confluence of the Clearwater and Athabasca rivers in the fur country of northern Alberta, Fort McMurray began as the home of the Woodland Cree and Chipewyan Indians. In 1778 explorers and fur traders led by Peter Pond opened the vast fur trade region of the Mackenzie River basin. In 1870 Henry John Moberly built a post and named it Fort McMurray after his chief factor, William McMurray of Hudson's Bay Co.

Soon after a steamboat terminus was established near Fort McMurray in 1884, the region's vast resources began to attract attention. Oil sands containing some 1.7 trillion barrels of oil were found around Lake Athabasca. The first commercially successful extractions, however, did not take place until the late 1960s. Since then Fort McMurray has boomed, serving oil recovery plants that now extract from the sands more than 600,000 barrels of synthetic crude oil per day.

The city is the southern terminus of the vast water transportation system that navigates Great Slave Lake and the Mackenzie River en route to the Arctic. Logging and tourism further bolster the economy. Fort McMurray is a service center for surrounding areas and the oil sands plants.

Re-creating the city's past is Heritage Park, on the banks of the Hangingstone River just off King Street on Tolen Drive. A museum highlights the history of boat building, aviation, river travel, lumbering, fishing, salt production and fur trading; phone (780) 791-7575.

Fort McMurray Tourism: 400 Sakitawaw Tr., Fort McMurray, AB, Canada T9H 4Z3. **Phone:** (780) 791-4336 or (800) 565-3947.

OIL SANDS DISCOVERY CENTRE is at 515 MacKenzie Blvd. Exhibits relate the geology, history and technology of the Athabasca Oil Sands, said to be the world's single largest oil deposit. Oil sands mining, technology and new methods of exploration are explained through interpretive displays, demonstrations and the video presentation "Quest for Energy." Outside in the Industrial Garden are a seven-story bucket-wheel excavator and other pieces of massive mining equipment.

Seasonal bus tours to view the production facilities of Suncor Energy depart from the discovery center; reservations for the 3.5-hour tours can be arranged through Fort McMurray Tourism.

Note: Photo ID is required for the bus tour. **Time:** Allow 1 hour, 30 minutes minimum. **Hours:** Daily 9-5, mid-May through Labour Day; Tues.-Sun. 10-4, rest of year. Closed Jan. 1, Good Friday, Christmas Eve, Christmas and day after Christmas. Bus tours to Suncor, generally one per day, are given Fri.-Sat., Victoria Day weekend-Labour Day. Phone ahead to confirm schedule.

Cost: Discovery center $7; $5 (ages 65+); $4 (ages 7-17); $20 (family, two adults and children). Bus tour (includes admission to Heritage Park and Oil Sands Discovery Centre) $45; $40 (ages 12-17 and 65+). Tour prices may vary. Under 12 are not permitted on the bus tour. Because tours are generally given only once a day and are in high demand, make reservations well in advance of your visit. In any event, reservations for the bus tour are required and must be made at least 24 hours in advance. **Phone:** (780) 743-7167 for the Oil Sands Discovery Centre, (780) 791-4336 for Fort McMurray Tourism, or (800) 565-3947 for tour reservations.

CLEARWATER SUITE HOTEL   780/799-7676
Extended Stay Hotel. Rates not provided. **Address:** 4 Haineault St T9H 1L6 **Location:** Hwy 63 (Sakitawaw Tr), just n on Hardin St, just e on Franklin Ave, then just s. **Facility:** 150 efficiencies. 4 stories, interior corridors. **Parking:** winter plug-ins. **Amenities:** high-speed Internet. **Activities:** sauna, whirlpool, steamroom, exercise room, spa. **Guest Services:** complimentary laundry.

FRANKLIN SUITE HOTEL   780/788-2199
Hotel. Rates not provided. **Address:** 10030 Franklin Ave T9H 0A5 **Location:** Hwy 63 (Sakitawaw Tr), just n on Morrison St, just w. **Facility:** 75 units. 5 stories, interior corridors. **Parking:** winter plug-ins. **Amenities:** high-speed Internet. **Activities:** exercise room. **Guest Services:** coin laundry.

MERIT HOTEL & SUITES   (780)714-9444
Hotel $189-$289 **Address:** 8200 Franklin Ave T9H 2H9 **Location:** Hwy 63 (Sakitawaw Tr) exit King St, 0.6 mi (1 km) n. **Facility:** 160 units, some two bedrooms. 3 stories, interior corridors. **Parking:** winter plug-ins. **Terms:** cancellation fee imposed. **Amenities:** high-speed Internet. **Pool(s):** heated indoor. **Activities:** whirlpool, exercise room. **Guest Services:** valet laundry.

SUPER 8   (780)799-8450
Hotel $165-$210 **Address:** 321 Sakitawaw Tr T9H 5E7 **Location:** Just w of Hwy 63 (Sakitawaw Tr), 3.1 mi (5 km) s. **Facility:** 140 units. 2-4 stories (no elevator), interior corridors. **Parking:** winter plug-ins. **Terms:** cancellation fee imposed. **Amenities:** Some: high-speed Internet. **Activities:** whirlpool, exercise room. **Guest Services:** coin laundry.

VANTAGE INN & SUITES   780/713-4111
Hotel. Rates not provided. **Address:** 200 Parent Way T9H 5E6 **Location:** 3.1 mi (5 km) s on Hwy 63 (Sakitawaw Tr). **Facility:** 83 units. 4 stories, interior corridors. **Parking:** winter plug-ins. **Amenities:** high-speed Internet. **Activities:** exercise room. **Guest Services:** coin laundry.

WHERE TO EAT

EARLS RESTAURANT   780/791-3275
American. Casual Dining. $11-$29 **AAA Inspector Notes:** Offering an experience that falls between fast food and fine dining, the fun, relaxed restaurant prepares great food at a great price. Choices range from juicy burgers, hearty sandwiches, fresh salads, wings and pizza to full entrees of steak, chops and seafood. Made-from-scratch soups and assorted breads, as well as a nice choice of wines and beers, round out the offerings. This is a fitting spot for impromptu get-togethers and festive occasions. **Bar:** full bar. **Address:** 9802 Morrison St T9H 5B8 **Location:** Hwy 63 N (Sakitawaw Tr), just n on Hardin St, just w on MacDonald Ave, then just s.

THE FISH PLACE   780/791-4040
Seafood. Casual Dining. $12-$33 **AAA Inspector Notes:** A well-known fact about Fort McMurray is that the largest population of Newfoundlanders outside of Newfoundland is found here. As a result, the superb fish restaurant was established to accommodate that population. Seven days a week, the nautical, cozy restaurant is busy serving seafood and evening specials. Seafood lovers looking for a hearty meal with speedy service should look no further. **Bar:** full bar. **Reservations:** suggested. **Address:** 412 Thickwood Blvd T9K 1P1 **Location:** Hwy 63 (Sakitawaw Tr) exit Thickwood Blvd, 1 mi (1.6 km) w; in small shopping plaza.

GARDENIA CAFE   780/714-9266
International. Casual Dining. $7-$30 **AAA Inspector Notes:** One of the more decent spots in town to dine, this café has an appealing and cozy décor. The dinner menu draws from cuisine of the world and diners might find Syrian kebabs, shawarma, Cajun chicken, seafood or chicken paella, and Tuscan or Bombay vegetable pasta. Some interesting international dishes at breakfast and lunch are offered. Not licensed for alcohol, guests can bring a bottle of wine in for a corkage fee. **Reservations:** suggested. **Address:** 300 Thickwood Blvd, #400 T9K 1Y1 **Location:** Hwy 63 (Sakitawaw Tr) exit Thickwood Blvd, 1 mi (1.6 km) w; in small shopping plaza. **Parking:** street only.

MOXIE'S CLASSIC GRILL
780/791-1996

◆◆◆ ◆◆ American. Casual Dining. $10-$29 **AAA Inspector Notes:** This sleek, funky and popular restaurant presents an extensive menu of creatively prepared dishes, including pizza, pasta, rice, noodles, signature salads and burgers. Other menus include one for children and one for Sunday brunch. Lending to the upbeat, stylish decor are dark wood appointments and river rock fireplaces. **Bar:** full bar. **Address:** 9521 Franklin Ave, #100 T9H 3Z7 **Location:** Hwy 63 (Saki-tawaw Tr) exit Hospital St, just ne, then 0.5 mi (0.8 km) nw; in shopping plaza. Ⓛ Ⓓ ⃝LATE CALL Ⓜ

FORT SASKATCHEWAN pop. 19,051
• **Part of Edmonton area — see map p. 109**

HAMPTON INN BY HILTON FORT SASKATCHEWAN
(780)997-1001

◆◆◆◆ Hotel $120-$151 **Address:** 8709 101st St T8L 0H9 **Location:** Just s of Hwy 15/21. **Facility:** 124 units, 4 stories, interior corridors. **Parking:** winter plug-ins. **Terms:** 1-7 night minimum stay, cancellation fee imposed. **Amenities:** high-speed Internet. **Pool(s):** heated indoor. **Activities:** exercise room. **Guest Services:** valet and coin laundry.

| **AAA Benefit:** Members save up to 10%! |

⃝ CALL Ⓜ ⃝ BIZ ⃝ ⃝ ⃝ ⃝ ⃝

LAKEVIEW INNS & SUITES
780/998-7888

◆◆◆ Hotel Rates not provided **Address:** 10115 88th Ave T8L 2T1 **Location:** Just w of Hwy 15/21 and 101st St. **Facility:** 69 units. 4 stories, interior corridors. **Parking:** winter plug-ins. **Amenities:** Some: high-speed Internet. **Activities:** exercise room. **Guest Services:** valet and coin laundry. **Free Special Amenities:** continental breakfast and high-speed Internet.

⃝SAVE ⃝ECO ⃝ ⃝ BIZ ⃝ ⃝ ⃝

/ SOME UNITS FEE ⃝ ⃝

MUSGRAVE'S HOSPITALITY INNS & SUITES
(780)998-2770

◆◆◆ Hotel $139-$199 **Address:** 9820 86th Ave T8L 4P4 **Location:** Just sw of Hwy 15/21 and 101st St. **Facility:** 99 units. 4 stories, interior corridors. **Parking:** winter plug-ins. **Terms:** check-in 4 pm. **Amenities:** high-speed Internet. **Activities:** whirlpool, exercise room. **Guest Services:** valet and coin laundry, area transportation. **Free Special Amenities:** full breakfast and high-speed Internet.

⃝SAVE ⃝ ⃝ CALL Ⓜ BIZ ⃝ ⃝ ⃝ ⃝ ⃝

/ SOME UNITS FEE ⃝

SUPER 8 HOTEL-FORT SASKATCHEWAN
(780)998-2898

◆◆ ◆◆ Hotel $128-$148 **Address:** 8750 84th St T8L 4P5 **Location:** Just e of jct Hwy 15/21. **Facility:** 87 units, some kitchens. 3 stories, interior corridors. **Parking:** winter plug-ins. **Amenities:** high-speed Internet. **Pool(s):** heated indoor. **Activities:** whirlpool, exercise room. **Guest Services:** coin laundry.

⃝ ⃝ ⃝ BIZ ⃝ ⃝ ⃝ ⃝ ⃝

WHERE TO EAT

ORIGINAL JOE'S RESTAURANT & BAR
780/998-0520

◆◆ ◆◆ American. Gastropub. $11-$25 **AAA Inspector Notes:** Good eats, good drinks, good tunes and a casual atmosphere are found here along with delicious, seemingly familiar, pub food except it is notched up with good quality ingredients and little twists. Great appetizers, soups, salads, pizza and a few other yummy entrées (butter chicken, halibut and chips and Long Beach fish tacos) are on the bill of fare. Sides for burgers and sandwiches are creative and as a bonus you get two. The restaurant is restricted to legal adult diners only. **Bar:** full bar. **Address:** 9372 Southfort Dr, #103 T8L 0C5 **Location:** Jct Hwy 15/21, just s; in a small retail complex.

Ⓛ Ⓓ ⃝LATE CALL Ⓜ

GIROUXVILLE (B-3) pop. 266

GIROUXVILLE MUSEUM is on Main St. (Hwy. 49). More than 6,000 artifacts tell the story of the indigenous people, devout missionaries and rugged pioneers who lived here. The museum also displays mounted birds and fur-bearing animals (the most famous being a five-legged squirrel) and the works of local artists Leon Tremblay and Alfred Gaboury.

Transportation Means of Yesterday includes sleighs, an antique snowmobile, a birch bark canoe and a 1927 Chevrolet truck. **Time:** Allow 1 hour minimum. **Hours:** Mon.-Fri. 9:30-4:30, May-Sept.; by appointment rest of year. **Cost:** $3; $1.50 (ages 6-17). **Phone:** (780) 323-4252.

GLEICHEN (I-7) pop. 336, elev. 899m/2,952'

BLACKFOOT CROSSING HISTORICAL PARK is 11 km (7 mi.) e. on Hwy. 1, then 9.7 km (6 mi.) s. on Hwy. 842. Used by the Siksika (Blackfoot) Indians as a wintering grounds, Blackfoot Crossing was the site of the signing of Treaty No. 7 by representatives of the Blackfoot Confederacy and the Canadian and British governments in 1877. An on-site cultural center offers several galleries that describe the culture and history of the Siksika people.

Housed in a striking, eco-friendly edifice are exhibits about hunting, early life, societies, storytelling and warriors. The collection features such artifacts as tools, weapons, clothing and utensils as well as multimedia displays. The building's architectural features also document First Nations heritage, with tepee-shaped skylights and stained glass eagle feather fans incorporated into the structure's design.

Self-guiding tours of the Blackfoot Crossing area are offered; guided tours of the cultural center and of the surroundings also are available by appointment. **Time:** Allow 1 hour, 30 minutes minimum. **Hours:** Tues.-Sat. 9-5, mid-May through Sept. 30; Tues.-Fri. 9-5, Sat. 10-4, rest of year. **Cost:** $10; $8 (ages 8-17 and 65+). **Phone:** (403) 734-5171 or (888) 654-6274. ⃝ ⃝

GRANDE CACHE (D-2) pop. 4,319
• **Hotels p. 146**

Grande Cache was named after a large shipment of furs cached nearby in 1821 by Ignace Giasson, an Iroquois working for Hudson's Bay Co. The Grande Cache area historically served as a major trading area for marten, lynx and beaver pelts.

Grande Cache is known for the many recreational activities available nearby. The town is surrounded on three sides by Willmore Wilderness Park, which has the Continental Divide and Jasper National Park as its western and southern borders, respectively; the park can be accessed only by horseback, mountain bike or by hiking.

Lakes, rivers and mountains are favorites with outdoor enthusiasts, who come for white-water rafting, horseback riding, hiking, kayaking, fishing, canoeing and mountain biking. Pacific Western Helicopter Tours offers various sightseeing trips; phone (780) 827-3911.

Local events accommodate those with an adventurous streak. During the Canadian Death Race, held the first weekend in August, runners must travel 125 kilometres (78 mi.) over rough mountain trails—with part of the race occurring after dusk—and then cross a major river by raft. An accompanying festival offers food, concerts and carnival rides and games.

Interpretive displays in the tourism center, on the south side of Grande Cache, feature dinosaur tracks, artifacts from the ice age and memorabilia from the fur trade era.

Grande Cache Tourism and Interpretive Centre: 9701 100th St., P.O. Box 300, Grande Cache, AB, Canada T0E 0Y0. **Phone:** (780) 827-3300 or (888) 827-3790.

RECREATIONAL ACTIVITIES
White-water Rafting
- **Wild Blue Yonder White Water Rafting** is w. off Hwy. 40. **Hours:** Trips are offered daily, May-Sept. Departure times vary. **Phone:** (780) 827-5450 or (877) 945-3786.

BEST WESTERN GRANDE MOUNTAIN GETAWAYS & HOTEL   780/827-3303

Hotel
Rates not provided

AAA Benefit: Members save up to 20%, plus 10% bonus points with Best Western Rewards®.

Address: 9901 100th St T0E 0Y0 **Location:** Hwy 40 (100th St); south end of town. **Facility:** 145 units, some efficiencies. 3 stories, interior corridors. **Parking:** winter plug-ins. **Amenities:** *Some:* high-speed Internet. **Activities:** sauna, whirlpool, exercise room. **Guest Services:** coin laundry. **Free Special Amenities:** early check-in/late check-out and high-speed Internet.

🅢🅐🅥🅔 🍴 🍸 CALL &M BIZ 📶 ✕ 🛗 🖨 🖵

GRANDE PRAIRIE (C-2) pop. 55,032

Surrounded by a colorful checkerboard of rich farmland along the gateway to the Alaska Hwy., Grande Prairie serves as the business and transportation center of Alberta's Peace River country.

Glimpses into the Peace River region's past are evident in the Kleskun Hills, just east via Hwy. 43. Erosion of the glacial drift of clay, sand, gravel and boulders has uncovered dinosaur tracks and aquatic fossils embedded in a prehistoric river delta formed more than 70 million years ago.

The Art Gallery of Grande Prairie, in the Montrose Cultural Centre at 9839 103rd Ave., houses a permanent artwork collection and also offers temporary exhibitions; phone (780) 532-8111. Muskoseepi Park has hiking and bicycling trails, picnicking areas and recreation facilities. Other area recreational pursuits include swimming, boating, bird-watching and fishing. A pioneer-oriented event is the Grande Prairie Stompede the first weekend in June. Other festivals celebrated throughout the summer highlight the region's diversity.

Grande Prairie Regional Tourism Association: 11330 106th St., Suite 217, Grande Prairie, AB, Canada T8V 7X9. **Phone:** (780) 539-7688 or (866) 202-2202.

Shopping areas: Prairie Mall, 11801 100th St., features Shopper's and Zellers.

GRANDE PRAIRIE MUSEUM is at 102nd St. and 102nd Ave. in Muskoseepi Park. The 10-building village features a one-room schoolhouse, a country store, a church and a log homesteader's cabin. The main exhibit building houses artifacts depicting the life of Peace River area pioneers 1908-16. The gallery also features natural history items and aboriginal artifacts. **Hours:** Mon.-Fri. 8:30-4:30, Sat. 10-4:30, Sun. noon-4:30. **Cost:** $5; $4 (ages 66+); $3 (ages 6-17); $12 (family, two adults and children); $10 (family, one adult and children). **Phone:** (780) 532-5482.

HERITAGE DISCOVERY CENTRE is at 11330 106th St. on the lower level of Centre 2000, Grand Prairie's visitor information center. Operated by the Grand Prairie Museum *(see attraction listing)*, the hands-on interpretive center depicts regional history through pioneer artifacts, a geology timeline, an animatronic dinosaur named Piper, a tepee, photographs, films, a caboose and computer games. Changing exhibits also are featured.

Tours: Guided tours are available. **Hours:** Mon.-Fri. 8:30-4:30, Sat.-Sun. 10-4:30. Closed Jan. 1, third Mon. in Feb., Good Friday, Christmas and day after Christmas. **Cost:** $5; $4 (senior citizens); $3 (students with ID); free (ages 0-6). **Phone:** (780) 532-5790.

GAMBLING ESTABLISHMENTS
- **Great Northern Casino** is at 10910-107 A Ave. **Hours:** Mon.-Sat. 10 a.m.-2 a.m., Sun. 10 a.m.-1 a.m. **Phone:** (780) 539-4454.

BEST WESTERN GRANDE PRAIRIE HOTEL & SUITES   (780)402-2378

Hotel
$169-$174

AAA Benefit: Members save up to 20%, plus 10% bonus points with Best Western Rewards®.

Address: 10745 117th Ave T8V 7N6 **Location:** Corner of Hwy 43 (100th Ave) and 117th Ave. **Facility:** 100 units. 4 stories, interior corridors. **Parking:** winter plug-ins. **Terms:** resort fee. **Amenities:** video games (fee). *Some:* high-speed Internet. **Pool(s):** heated indoor. **Activities:** whirlpool, exercise room. **Guest Services:** valet laundry. **Free Special Amenities:** full breakfast and high-speed Internet.

🅢🅐🅥🅔 🄴🄲🄾 ✈ 🍴 🍸 🐾 BIZ 📶 🐾 🛗 🖵
/ SOME UNITS FEE 🐕 🖨

DAYS INN GRANDE PRAIRIE   (780)532-2773

▽▽▽ **Hotel** $110-$145 **Address:** 10218 162nd Ave T8V 0P2 **Location:** Jct Hwy 2 and 43 (100th Ave), just s. **Facility:** 90 units, some kitchens. 4 stories, interior corridors. **Parking:** winter plug-ins. **Amenities:** high-speed Internet. **Activities:** exercise room. **Guest Services:** valet and coin laundry.

BIZ 📶 🛗 🖨 🖵 / SOME UNITS FEE 🐕

HOLIDAY INN HOTEL & SUITES (780)402-6886

Hotel
$150-$180

Address: 9816 107th St T8V 8E7 **Location:** Jct Hwy 43 (100th Ave) and 40 (108th St). **Facility:** 145 units. 4 stories, interior corridors. **Amenities:** video games (fee); high-speed Internet. **Pool(s):** heated indoor. **Activities:** whirlpool, exercise room, spa. **Guest Services:** complimentary and valet laundry. **Free Special Amenities: high-speed Internet and airport transportation.**

SAVE ECO ⊁ ❙❙ 🍴 Y CALL &M 🏊 BIZ 🛜 🎥
🔲 📷 💻 /SOME UNITS FEE 🐕

MOTEL 6 GRANDE PRAIRIE #5709 (780)830-7744

Hotel $76-$81 **Address:** 15402 101st St T8V 0P7 **Location:** Jct Hwy 2 and 43 (100th Ave), just s. **Facility:** 132 units. 4 stories, interior corridors. **Parking:** winter plug-ins. **Amenities:** high-speed Internet. **Guest Services:** valet and coin laundry.

ECO CALL &M 🔲 📷 /SOME UNITS 🐕 🐕

PODOLLAN INN & SPA (780)830-2000

Hotel $149-$169 **Address:** 10612 99th Ave T8V 8E8 **Location:** Jct Hwy 43 (100th Ave) and 40 (108th St), just e. **Facility:** 108 units. 4 stories, interior corridors. **Terms:** 3 day cancellation notice-fee imposed, resort fee. **Amenities:** high-speed Internet. **Dining:** Jax Grill & Lounge, see separate listing. **Activities:** spa. **Guest Services:** valet laundry.

❙❙ 🛜 🎥 🔲 📷 💻 /SOME UNITS FEE 🐕

POMEROY HOTEL (780)532-5221

Hotel $119-$299 **Address:** 11633 100th St T8V 3Y4 **Location:** Jct Hwy 43 (100th Ave) and 116th Ave. **Facility:** 203 units. 5-6 stories, interior corridors. **Parking:** winter plug-ins. *Some:* safes. **Pool(s):** heated indoor. **Activities:** whirlpool, steamroom, exercise room. *Fee:* massage. **Guest Services:** valet laundry.

ECO ❙❙ Y 🏊 BIZ 🛜 🎥 💻
/SOME UNITS FEE 🐕 🔲 📷

POMEROY INN & SUITES, GRANDE PRAIRIE (780)831-2999

Extended Stay
Hotel
$150-$160

Address: 11710 102nd St T8V 7S7 **Location:** 102nd St at 117th Ave. **Facility:** 152 units, some kitchens. 3-4 stories, interior corridors. **Parking:** winter plug-ins. **Terms:** cancellation fee imposed. **Amenities:** high-speed Internet. **Pool(s):** heated indoor. **Activities:** whirlpool, waterslide, exercise room. **Guest Services:** valet and coin laundry. **Free Special Amenities: full breakfast and high-speed Internet.**

SAVE ECO ⊁ ❙❙ 🏊 BIZ 🛜 🎥 🔲 📷 💻
/SOME UNITS FEE 🐕

QUALITY HOTEL & CONFERENCE CENTRE GRANDE PRAIRIE (780)539-6000

Hotel
$129-$169

Address: 11201 100th Ave T8V 5M6 **Location:** 1.8 mi (2.9 km) w on Hwy 2. **Facility:** 102 units, some efficiencies. 10 stories, interior corridors. **Parking:** winter plug-ins. **Terms:** cancellation fee imposed. **Amenities:** high-speed Internet. **Activities:** exercise room. **Guest Services:** valet laundry. **Free Special Amenities: full breakfast and local telephone calls.**

SAVE ECO ⊁ ❙❙ Y BIZ 🛜 🎥 🔲 📷 💻
/SOME UNITS FEE 🐕

SERVICE PLUS INNS AND SUITES 780/538-3900

Hotel. **Rates not provided. Address:** 10810 107A Ave T8V 7A9 **Location:** 1.4 mi (2.2 km) w on Hwy 2, just n. Adjacent to a casino. **Facility:** 123 units. 4 stories, interior corridors. **Parking:** winter plug-ins. **Pool(s):** heated indoor. **Activities:** whirlpool, waterslide, exercise room. **Guest Services:** valet laundry.

⊁ ❙❙ 🏊 🛜 🔲 📷 💻 /SOME UNITS FEE 🐕

STANFORD INN (780)539-5678

Hotel $99-$120 **Address:** 11401 100th Ave T8V 5M6 **Location:** Hwy 2 and 43 (100th Ave), just e of 116 St. **Facility:** 204 units, some two bedrooms, efficiencies and kitchens. 2 stories (no elevator), interior/exterior corridors. **Parking:** winter plug-ins. **Terms:** cancellation fee imposed. **Amenities:** *Some:* high-speed Internet. **Activities:** exercise room. **Guest Services:** valet and coin laundry.

ECO ❙❙ Y 🛜 🔲 📷 💻 /SOME UNITS FEE 🐕

STONEBRIDGE HOTEL (780)539-5561

Hotel $129-$189 **Address:** 12102 100th St T8V 5P1 **Location:** 100th St at 121st Ave. **Facility:** 124 units. 3 stories, interior corridors. **Parking:** winter plug-ins. **Terms:** cancellation fee imposed, resort fee. **Amenities:** *Some:* high-speed Internet. **Dining:** 3 restaurants. **Activities:** exercise room. **Guest Services:** valet and coin laundry.

⊁ ❙❙ Y BIZ 🛜 🔲 📷 💻 /SOME UNITS FEE 🐕

SUPER 8 (780)532-8288

Hotel $110-$170 **Address:** 10050 116th Ave T8V 4K5 **Location:** 102nd St at 117th Ave. **Facility:** 148 units, some two bedrooms and kitchens. 4 stories, interior corridors. **Parking:** winter plug-ins. **Amenities:** video games (fee). **Pool(s):** heated indoor. **Activities:** whirlpool, waterslide, exercise room. **Guest Services:** valet and coin laundry.

ECO ⊁ ❙❙ 🏊 🛜 🎥 🔲 📷 💻
/SOME UNITS FEE 🐕 📷

WHERE TO EAT

ACROPOLIS 780/538-4424

Greek. Casual Dining. $22-$39 **AAA Inspector Notes:** A taste of Greece is found at this downtown eatery, where diners find fare ranging from spanakopita and souvlaki to moussaka and baklava. Portions are not skimpy and are served by friendly, attentive staff members. **Bar:** full bar. **Reservations:** suggested. **Address:** 10011 101st Ave T8V 0X9 **Location:** Corner of 100th St and 101st Ave; downtown. **Parking:** street only. D

BURGER HEAVEN 780/814-7015

Burgers. Casual Dining. $10-$19 **AAA Inspector Notes:** If your idea of paradise is a menu packed with burgers then this is the place. From chicken, fish, beef and bison to a plethora of themes—Greek, Hawaiian, Baja, marinara, cordon blue, Neptune and Ernie's mile high with eight patties. Diners also can build their own version from a large selection of toppings. Burgers come with fresh-cut potato wedges or fries. Start with classic appetizers, salad or soup and finish with assorted pies and cakes. Service is casual, friendly and quick. **Bar:** beer & wine. **Address:** 10016 110th Ave T8V 2N1 **Location:** Jct Hwy 43 (100th Ave) and 116th Ave, 0.5 mi (0.8 km) s, then just e. L D

CATMINT TEAHOUSE & MARTINI BAR 780/538-3798

Chinese. Casual Dining. $6-$22 **AAA Inspector Notes:** A quirky mix of contemporary accents along with classic Chinese bits and pieces and a red, back-lit bar highlight the décor of this restaurant, which dishes up cuisine with in-house sauces and no monosodium glutamate. Dim sum-style appetizers such as crabmeat spring roll and shrimp dumplings and such entrées as gong bao chicken and prawns with mustard sauce are found on the menu. Eighty martini choices and a good variety of loose-leaf tea also are featured. **Bar:** full bar. **Reservations:** suggested. **Address:** 10833 100th St T8V 2M7 **Location:** Jct Hwy 43 (100th Ave) and 116th Ave, 0.6 mi (1 km) s. L D CALL &M

THE CHOPPED LEAF 780/897-2562

Specialty. Quick Serve. $6-$10 **AAA Inspector Notes:** A fresh alternative to traditional fast food, this spot crafts designer salads and wraps or guests can build their own from a variety of ingredients. Fresh daily soup, chicken quesadillas and sandwiches, cookies, bars and granola, along with some healthy breakfast options round out the menu. Tightly spaced tables and counters are available for dining in. **Address:** 10902 105th Ave, #108 T8V 7Y5 **Location:** Just e of 108th St; in Gateway Power Centre Shopping Complex. B L D

GUERINO'S ITALIAN KITCHEN
780/513-3630

Italian. Quick Serve. $11-$12 **AAA Inspector Notes:** Check tablecloths and bright art cheer up this simple little café. There is nothing complicated here, just simple pasta combinations dished up right at the counter for diners to take to their table. Pick a soup or salad, choose meatballs, chicken or veal, then the pasta and top it with Alfredo, meat sauce or tomato sauce. And there it is—a tasty and quick meal with friendly service. **Bar:** beer & wine. **Address:** 10635 West Side Dr, #103 T8V 8E6 **Location:** Jct Hwy 43 (100th Ave) and 40 (108th St), just s, then just e. L D CALL 🛒M

HONG FAH THAI RESTAURANT
780/357-9988

Thai. Casual Dining. $14-$15 **AAA Inspector Notes:** This is the only Thai restaurant in town but diners do not need to look any farther. The fresh and simple décor is complemented by exceedingly well-prepared dishes with all the classics, including fresh spring rolls, Thai satay, Tom yum kung soup, pad thai noodles and a variety of yellow, green and red curries. Do not worry about the spice level, it can be adjusted from mild to hottest of hot. A friendly waitstaff is more than happy to help patrons choose their dishes. **Bar:** full bar. **Reservations:** suggested. **Address:** 11735 105th St T8V 8L1 **Location:** Hwy 43 (100th Ave), just n; in strip mall. L D CALL 🛒M

JAX GRILL & LOUNGE
780/830-2000

International. Casual Dining. $12-$34 **AAA Inspector Notes:** This intimate and stylish lounge, with cushy banquettes and high-top tables, features an enticing menu from around the world with such items as tangy Indian butter chicken, Mexican dishes and Asian ginger beef. More traditional fare includes steaks, burgers, cedar-planked salmon and pasta dishes. The yummy sweet potato fries are a must try. **Bar:** full bar. **Reservations:** suggested. **Address:** 10612 99th Ave T8V 8E8 **Location:** Jct Hwy 43 (100th Ave) and 40 (108th St), just e; in Podollan Inn & Spa. L D CALL 🛒M

JEFFERY'S CAFE COMPANY
780/830-0140

American. Casual Dining. $8-$15 **AAA Inspector Notes:** Prepared using fresh-made breads, this little café's gourmet sandwiches will definitely lighten up the day, as do the surrounding windows. Select from such toppings as pesto, teriyaki or curry chicken; smoked turkey; or Italian meatballs. Patrons will also find intriguing salads, hearty soups and pasta or rich dishes on the menu. The sinfully delicious desserts are a must-have. **Reservations:** suggested, for lunch. **Address:** 106-10605 West Side Dr T8V 8E6 **Location:** Jct Hwy 43 (100th Ave) and 40 (108th St), just s, then just e. L D CALL 🛒M

MOXIE'S CLASSIC GRILL
780/532-4401

American. Casual Dining. $15-$35 **AAA Inspector Notes:** This sleek, funky and popular restaurant presents an extensive menu of creatively prepared dishes, including pizza, pasta, rice, noodles, signature salads and burgers. Other menus include one for children and one for Sunday brunch. Lending to the upbeat, stylish decor are dark wood appointments and river rock fireplaces. **Bar:** full bar. **Address:** 11801 100th St, #212 T8V 3Y2 **Location:** Jct Hwy 43 (100th Ave) and 116th Ave, just n; in Prairie Mall. L D CALL 🛒M

TITO'S BISTRO & CAFE
780/539-4881

Lebanese. Quick Serve. $8-$15 **AAA Inspector Notes:** Homemade and healthy choices line the menu at this cafeteria-style restaurant. Select from such choices as sandwich-style beef and chicken shawarma, the full-meal deal with rice and a salad, donairs, souvlaki, Greek salad and an array of pastries and desserts. The less adventurous diner might opt for a sandwich, burger or classic breakfast offering. Tuesday is open-mike night so don't forget the guitar. **Address:** 10006 101st Ave T8V 0Y1 **Location:** Corner of 100th St and 101st Ave; downtown. B L D

GRIMSHAW pop. 2,515

POMEROY INN & SUITES
780/332-2000

Extended Stay Hotel. Rates not provided. **Address:** 4311 51st St T0H 1W0 **Location:** On Hwy 2; south end of town. **Facility:** 62 units, some kitchens. 3 stories, interior corridors. **Parking:** winter plug-ins. **Amenities:** high-speed Internet. **Pool(s):** heated indoor. **Activities:** whirlpool, waterslide, exercise room. *Fee:* game room. **Guest Services:** coin laundry.

ECO 🏊 BIZ 🛜 🛏 🖥 🖨 / SOME UNITS FEE 🐾

HANNA (H-7) pop. 2,673

HANNA PIONEER VILLAGE & MUSEUM is at Pioneer Tr. and 4th Ave. E. Restored and partially furnished 19th-century buildings, arranged in a pioneer village setting, include a general store, a school, a four-room hospital, a church, a power windmill, a Canadian National Railway station, a telephone office, a ranch house and smithy, and the Hanna archives. Among the displays are antique automobiles and farm machinery.

Tours: Guided tours are available. **Time:** Allow 1 hour, 30 minutes minimum. **Hours:** Daily 10-6, July-Aug.; by appointment May-June and in Sept. Last tour begins 1 hour, 30 minutes before closing. **Cost:** $7; $2 (ages 0-12). **Phone:** (403) 854-4244.

SUPER 8 HANNA
(403)854-2400

Hotel $130-$140 **Address:** 113 Palliser Tr T0J 1P0 **Location:** Hwy 9, just n. **Facility:** 63 units, some efficiencies. 2 stories (no elevator), interior/exterior corridors. **Parking:** winter plug-ins. **Amenities:** *Some:* high-speed Internet. **Activities:** exercise room. **Guest Services:** coin laundry.

ECO 🛗 BIZ 🛜 🛏 🖥 🖨 / SOME UNITS FEE 🐾

HIGH LEVEL pop. 3,641

BEST WESTERN PLUS MIRAGE HOTEL & RESORT
(780)821-1000

Hotel $177-$197

AAA Benefit: Members save up to 20%, plus 10% bonus points with Best Western Rewards®.

Address: 9616 Hwy 58 T0H 1Z0 **Location:** Jct Hwy 35 and 58; north end of town. **Facility:** 92 units, some two bedrooms and kitchens. 2 stories, interior/exterior corridors. **Parking:** winter plug-ins. **Terms:** check-in 4 pm, 2-4 night minimum stay - seasonal, cancellation fee imposed. **Amenities:** video games (fee), high-speed Internet. **Dining:** Mirage Restaurant, see separate listing. **Pool(s):** heated indoor. **Activities:** whirlpool, waterslide, exercise room. **Guest Services:** valet and coin laundry, area transportation-local businesses. **Free Special Amenities:** local telephone calls and high-speed Internet.

SAVE ✈ 🛗 🍴 BIZ 🛜 🎥 🛏 🖥 / SOME UNITS FEE 🐾 🖨

SUPER 8 HIGH LEVEL
780/841-3448

Hotel $135

Address: 9502 114th Ave T0H 1Z0 **Location:** Hwy 35, just se; south end of town. **Facility:** 81 units. 4 stories, interior/exterior corridors. **Parking:** winter plug-ins. **Amenities:** video games (fee), high-speed Internet. **Pool(s):** heated indoor. **Activities:** whirlpool, waterslide, exercise room. **Guest Services:** valet and coin laundry. **Free Special Amenities:** expanded continental breakfast and high-speed Internet.

SAVE ECO ✈ 🍴 CALL 🛒M 🏊 BIZ 🛜 🎥 🛏 🖥 🖨 / SOME UNITS FEE 🐾

WHERE TO EAT

MIRAGE RESTAURANT
780/821-8300

Canadian. Casual Dining. $10-$32 **AAA Inspector Notes:** It is nice to find an eatery this far north dedicated to providing fresh and high-quality, Canadian-sourced ingredients with highlights of free-range chicken, wild seafood and fresh vegetables. Sample menu items include tasty lobster corn dogs with mango ketchup and sweet chili mustard and tender Carmen Creek flat-iron bison steak with port demi-glacé. The dining room proper is an open space off the lobby with skylight roofing and tropical plants or there is a more casual lounge tucked in back. **Bar:** full bar. **Address:** 9616 Hwy 58 T0H 1Z0 **Location:** Jct Hwy 35 and 58; north end of town; in BEST WESTERN PLUS Mirage Hotel & Resort. B L D CALL 🛒M

HIGH PRAIRIE pop. 2,600

PEAVINE INN & SUITES (780)523-2398

 Hotel $129-$169 **Address:** 3905 51st Ave T0G 1E0 **Location:** Hwy 2, just n; east end of town. **Facility:** 91 units, some kitchens. 4 stories, interior/exterior corridors. **Parking:** winter plug-ins. **Amenities:** high-speed Internet. **Pool(s):** heated indoor. **Activities:** whirlpool, waterslide, exercise room. **Guest Services:** valet and coin laundry.

 / SOME UNITS FEE

HIGH RIVER (I-6) pop. 12,920

A ranching and farming town, High River counts among its events Little Britches Rodeo and Parade, held Victoria Day weekend in late May, as well as the North American Chuckwagon Championship and the Guy Weadick Memorial Rodeo, both held in June. The winter holiday season is ushered in the first weekend in December with the evening Santa Claus Parade.

High River Tourism and Economic Development: 309B Macleod Tr. S.W., High River, AB, Canada T1V 1Z5. **Phone:** (403) 652-8622.

HIGH RIVER HISTORICAL MURALS are at various locations throughout town. Many colorful paintings illustrate area history. The murals present a variety of subjects, ranging from cattle ranching and polo to well-known residents, including author W.O. Mitchell and former Prime Minister Joe Clark.

Hours: Murals visible daily 24 hours. Brochures are available at the High River Tourism and Economic Development office and from the Museum of the Highwood Mon.-Fri. 10-6, Sat.-Sun. 12:30-5, May-Oct.; otherwise varies. Closed Jan. 1 and Christmas. **Cost:** Free. **Phone:** (403) 603-3101.

MUSEUM OF THE HIGHWOOD is at 406 1st St. S.W. The museum takes its name from the nearby Highwood River. Changing exhibits are housed in a 1911 sandstone building once used as a Canadian Pacific Railway station. Displays detail local history, primarily from the mid-19th century to the present. A family discovery room has interactive exhibits.

Time: Allow 30 minutes minimum. **Hours:** Mon.-Fri. 9-4:30, Sun. noon-4. Closed statutory holidays in the off-season. **Cost:** Donations. **Phone:** (403) 652-7156.

HERITAGE INN HOTEL & CONVENTION CENTRE (403)652-3834

 Hotel $129-$185 **Address:** 1104 11th Ave SE T1V 1M4 **Location:** Trans-Canada Hwy 2 exit 23, 0.5 mi (0.8 km) w. **Facility:** 73 units. 2 stories (no elevator), interior corridors. **Parking:** winter plug-ins. **Terms:** check-in 4 pm, cancellation fee imposed. **Amenities:** Some: high-speed Internet. **Pool(s):** heated indoor. **Activities:** whirlpool.

/ SOME UNITS FEE

SUPER 8 (403)652-4448

 Hotel $120-$140 **Address:** 1601 13th Ave SE T1V 2B1 **Location:** Trans-Canada Hwy 2 exit High River, just w. **Facility:** 60 units, some efficiencies. 3 stories, interior corridors. **Parking:** winter plug-ins. **Amenities:** high-speed Internet. **Pool(s):** heated indoor. **Activities:** whirlpool, waterslide, exercise room. **Guest Services:** coin laundry.

/ SOME UNITS FEE

WHERE TO EAT

WHISTLESTOP CAFE 403/652-7026

 American. Casual Dining. $9-$10 **AAA Inspector Notes:** Simple, well-prepared food is one of the reasons to come to this distinctive eatery. Its location in a 1947 Canadian Pacific rail coach car, complete with CP memorabilia, is a winner. On the menu is a wide variety of comfort foods, including sandwiches, quiche, quesadillas and fried green tomatoes. The dessert selection is extensive. Guests can enjoy lunch or afternoon tea and imagine the car swaying gently along the tracks as it did long ago. **Reservations:** suggested. **Address:** 406 1st St SW T1V 1S2 **Location:** 0.6 mi (1 km) n at 3rd Ave; next to museum. L

HINTON (E-3) pop. 9,640, elev. 1,049m/3,444'
• Restaurants p. 150
• Part of Jasper National Park area — see map p. 151

RECREATIONAL ACTIVITIES

Horseback Riding
• **Larry's Riding Stables** is 8 km (5 mi.) w. off Hwy. 16. Other activities are offered. **Hours:** Daily 10-6. **Phone:** (780) 865-9223.

BEST WESTERN WHITE WOLF INN (780)865-7777

 Hotel $150-$160 **AAA Benefit:** Members save up to 20%, plus 10% bonus points with Best Western Rewards®.

Address: 828 Carmichael Ln T7V 1T1 **Location:** At west end of town; just off Hwy 16. **Facility:** 42 units, some efficiencies and kitchens. 2 stories (no elevator), exterior corridors. **Parking:** winter plug-ins. **Terms:** check-in 4 pm. **Amenities:** Some: high-speed Internet. **Activities:** whirlpool, limited exercise equipment. **Guest Services:** valet laundry. **Free Special Amenities:** continental breakfast and high-speed Internet.

SAVE / SOME UNITS FEE

HOLIDAY INN EXPRESS (780)865-2048

 Hotel $139-$173 **Address:** 462 Smith St T7V 2A1 **Location:** 1.2 mi (2 km) e on Hwy 16. **Facility:** 99 units. 4 stories, interior corridors. **Parking:** winter plug-ins. **Terms:** check-in 4 pm, cancellation fee imposed. **Amenities:** high-speed Internet. **Pool(s):** heated indoor. **Activities:** sauna, whirlpool, waterslide, exercise room. **Guest Services:** valet and coin laundry.

ECO CALL

HOLIDAY INN HINTON (780)865-3321

 Hotel $139-$159 **Address:** 393 Gregg Ave T7V 1N1 **Location:** 0.3 mi (0.5 km) w on Hwy 16. **Facility:** 104 units, some two bedrooms. 2 stories (no elevator), interior corridors. **Parking:** winter plug-ins. **Amenities:** video games (fee). Some: high-speed Internet. **Pool(s):** heated indoor. **Activities:** sauna, whirlpool, waterslide, exercise room. **Guest Services:** valet and coin laundry.

ECO CALL / SOME UNITS FEE

LAKEVIEW INNS & SUITES 780/865-2575

 Hotel Rates not provided **Address:** 500 Smith St T7V 2A1 **Location:** 1.1 mi (1.7 km) e on Hwy 16. **Facility:** 55 units, some kitchens. 2 stories (no elevator), interior/exterior corridors. **Parking:** winter plug-ins. **Terms:** check-in 4 pm. **Activities:** limited exercise equipment. **Guest Services:** complimentary and valet laundry. **Free Special Amenities:** expanded continental breakfast and high-speed Internet.

SAVE ECO / SOME UNITS FEE

OVERLANDER MOUNTAIN LODGE (780)866-2330

WW WW Country Inn $139-$249 **Address:** Hwy 16 T7V 1X5 **Location:** Hwy 16, 15 mi (24 km) w; just outside Jasper National Park gates. **Facility:** 41 units, some efficiencies, cabins and cottages. 1-2 stories (no elevator), interior/exterior corridors. **Parking:** winter plug-ins. **Terms:** check-in 4 pm, 3 day cancellation notice-fee imposed. **Dining:** Stone Peak Restaurant & Lounge, see separate listing. **Activities:** hiking trails.

SUPER 8 (780)817-2228

WW WW Hotel $100-$200 **Address:** 284 Smith St T7V 2A1 **Location:** 1 mi (1.6 km) e on Hwy 16. **Facility:** 48 units, some efficiencies and kitchens. 2 stories (no elevator), interior corridors. **Parking:** winter plug-ins. **Pool(s):** heated indoor. **Activities:** whirlpool. **Guest Services:** valet and coin laundry.

WHERE TO EAT

GUS'S PIZZA 780/865-4232

WW WW Pizza. Casual Dining. $13-$25 **AAA Inspector Notes:** This place is unassuming and overall pretty basic and while they serve other items like simple pasta and steak, it really is all about the pizza here. Classic pizza choices come steaming hot with lots of cheese, tangy sauce and crunchy crust. **Bar:** full bar. **Address:** 346 Hardisty Ave T7V 1E8 **Location:** Corner of Switzer Dr; east end of town. D

L & W FAMILY RESTAURANT 780/865-4892

WW American. Family Dining. $7-$17 **AAA Inspector Notes:** Ask any local in town for a good place to eat, and this diner is mentioned time and time again. Order at the counter from the huge menu board, then take a seat at one of the cozy booths or tables in the modern dining room with a fireplace at one end and stone trim throughout. Diners can pick up their food when their number is called. Nosh on ample portions of Greek specialties, such as donairs, souvlaki and spanakopita, as well as hamburgers, pizza, simple pasta and grilled steaks. **Bar:** full bar. **Address:** 414 Carmichael Ln T7V 1X7 **Location:** West end of city on Hwy 16; across from Holiday Inn Hinton.

RANCHER'S SPORTS BAR & GRILL 780/865-9785

WW American. Family Dining. $10-$28 **AAA Inspector Notes:** Situated in a gas station travel complex, this dining room has a simple, but pleasing, contemporary décor. The menu offers a fairly broad choice including burgers, sandwiches, tacos and enchiladas, simple pasta, pizza, steaks and other entrées including veal cutlets, pork chops and liver and onions. A buffet also is offered weekdays for lunch. There is a lounge attached. **Bar:** full bar. **Reservations:** suggested, weekends. **Address:** 438 Smith St T7V 2A1 **Location:** 1.2 mi (2 km) e on Hwy 16; in Esso Travel Centre.

SMITTY'S 780/865-6151

WW WW International. Family Dining. $7-$20 **AAA Inspector Notes:** The family-oriented restaurant satisfies patrons with its ever-popular all-day breakfast items, as well as tasty and wholesome soups and salads at lunchtime. A relaxed mood characterizes the dining space. **Address:** 445 Gregg Ave T7V 1X8 **Location:** 0.4 mi (0.7 km) w on Hwy 16. B L D CALL &M

STONE PEAK RESTAURANT & LOUNGE 780/866-2330

WW WW WW International. Casual Dining. $10-$41 **AAA Inspector Notes:** Just outside of town, the restaurant is worth the drive. Diners can enjoy seasonally inspired cuisine in the log interior, which features a cozy décor. Chocolate pecan pie, created from a recipe so secret that the chef won't allow his staff to see him make it, is a great way to finish a fine meal. The cozy surroundings afford views of the mountains in the distance. **Bar:** full bar. **Reservations:** suggested. **Address:** Hwy 16 T7V 1X5 **Location:** Hwy 16, 15 mi (24 km) w; just outside Jasper National Park gates; in Overlander Mountain Lodge. B L D

INNISFAIL (G-6) pop. 7,876, elev. 945m/3,100'

DISCOVERY WILDLIFE PARK is off Queen Elizabeth II Hwy. N. Innisfail exit; take Hwy. 2A 2 blks. n.e., then just n.w. on 42nd Ave., following signs. The 36-hectare (90-acre) park is home to a variety of rescued exotic and native animals, including jaguars, lions, bears, monkeys, tigers and wolves. Some of the creatures are trained to work in show business and have been featured in major film and television productions. Educational shows and interactive programs are offered daily. A children's train also is on-site.

Time: Allow 1 hour, 30 minutes minimum. **Hours:** Daily 10-7, May 1 to mid-Oct. **Cost:** $14; $12 (ages 13-17 and senior citizens); $8 (ages 3-12); $1 (ages 0-2). **Phone:** (403) 227-3211.

INNISFAIL & DISTRICT HISTORICAL VILLAGE, 5140 42nd St., is home to 17 buildings, including a blacksmith shop, barn and pioneer church. The 2-acre site features several furnished structures as well as The Bowden Train Station, which displays various relics. Originally located about 6 kilometres (4 mi.) north of Innisfail, the 19th-century "Spruces" building once served as a depot on the stagecoach trail between Calgary and Edmonton and is purportedly the last surviving stopping house from the route. Historical gardens also grace the village grounds.

Time: Allow 30 minutes minimum. **Hours:** Mon.-Sat. 10-6, Sun. and holidays noon-5, Victoria Day weekend-Labour Day. **Cost:** Donations. **Phone:** (403) 227-2906.

BEST WESTERN INNISFAIL INN (403)227-4405

WWW
Hotel
$100-$200

 AAA Benefit: Members save up to 20%, plus 10% bonus points with Best Western Rewards®.

Address: 5010 40th Ave T4G 1Z1 **Location:** Hwy 2 exit Hwy 54 (Innisfail/Caroline), just w. **Facility:** 66 units. 3 stories, interior corridors. **Parking:** winter plug-ins. **Terms:** cancellation fee imposed. **Amenities:** high-speed Internet. **Pool(s):** heated indoor. **Activities:** whirlpool, exercise room. **Guest Services:** coin laundry. **Free Special Amenities:** expanded continental breakfast and high-speed Internet.

IRRICANA (H-6) pop. 1,162

PIONEER ACRES OF ALBERTA MUSEUM is off Hwy. 9, 1 km n., then 1 km w. The museum features one of the largest collections of antique farm equipment in western Canada. It also displays furniture, tools, memorabilia, clothing and vehicles. A collection of early buildings includes a school, a steam-engine shop and a blacksmith shop. **Tours:** Guided tours are available. **Time:** Allow 1 hour, 30 minutes minimum. **Hours:** Daily 9-5, May 15-Sept. 30. **Cost:** $8; $5 (ages 6-12). **Phone:** (403) 935-4357.

Keep seasonal vehicles travel-ready with a AAA/CAA Battery Tender®

JASPER NATIONAL PARK (E-2)
• Attractions map p. 153

Elevations in the park range from 1,067 metres (3,500 ft.) in the town of Jasper to 3,747 metres (12,293 ft.) at Mount Columbia. Refer to CAA/AAA maps for additional elevation information.

The largest of Canada's seven national parks in the Rocky Mountains, Jasper preserves a spectacular wilderness of forested glacial valleys, dazzling snow-capped peaks, roaring waterfalls and sparkling blue-green lakes. Jasper is less developed and less crowded than Banff National Park to the south, so it tends to attract those seeking the solitude and tranquility that are among the park's greatest assets. More than a thousand kilometres (600 mi.) of trails help visitors escape into the virtually pristine countryside.

The park's wildlife is as diverse as its peaks and valleys. Mountain goats and bighorn sheep inhabit the crags and highlands, although the sheep frequently wander down from the heights and into the camera viewfinders of tourists. The lower slopes and meadows are home to deer, elk and moose. Bears, coyotes, wolves, lynx and other predators usually avoid humans.

The Whistlers, whose peak looms above the town of Jasper *(see place listing p. 154)*, is named for the whistling call of the hoary marmot, which looks like something between a squirrel and a beaver. You might encounter marmots along Jasper National Park's trails, along with Columbian ground squirrels and tiny pikas, which look like mice but are actually related to rabbits, as you might guess from their other name: rock rabbits.

The park was named for Jasper Hawes who operated Jasper's House, an early 19th-century fur-trading post in the area. The town, originally called Fitzhugh, adopted the name of the surrounding park in 1913. It's a laid-back place with a surprisingly

This map shows cities in Jasper National Park where you will find attractions, hotels and restaurants. Cities are listed alphabetically in this book on the following pages.

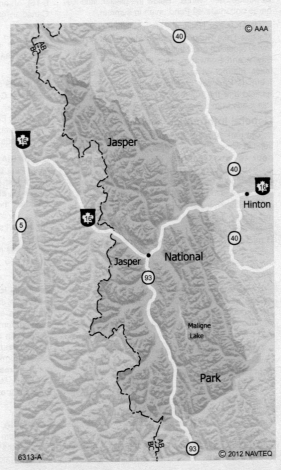

6313-A

© 2012 NAVTEQ

small-town feel despite catering to the millions who visit the park annually. You will find one of the park's two information centers in a rustic cobblestone building on the town's main street. Completed in 1914, it once housed the park's headquarters; its design established the style now common for national park buildings.

Looked at from above, the town's curved layout appropriately enough resembles the letter J. Take a look for yourself by making the 7-minute journey via the Jasper Tramway (see attraction listing p. 154) to the upper station on The Whistlers, 2,277 metres (7,472 ft.) above sea level. The view of the town, the Athabasca River Valley and surrounding mountains is unforgettable.

Strolling the streets of Jasper, you can't help but notice the distinctive profile of Mount Edith Cavell with its contrasting parallel bands of rock and snow. A half-hour drive will take you to the mountain, called the White Ghost by the Stoney Indians. Trails there lead to the wildflower-strewn Cavell Meadows and offer fantastic views of Angel Glacier, named for its outstretched "wings." Below the glacier, little icebergs bob in Cavell Pond, even in summer.

Other Jasper National Park highlights: the scenic Maligne Lake Road connecting Malign Canyon and lovely Medicine and Maligne lakes; thundering Athabasca and Sunwapta falls; Pyramid and Patricia lakes; Marmot Basin ski resort; and the breathtaking Icefields Parkway running south to the Columbia Icefield and the Athabasca Glacier, where a short trail leads from the parkway right up to the glacier.

General Information and Activities

The park is open all year, though weather conditions in winter make some portions inaccessible except to cross-country skiers and those on snowshoes. Some facilities are open only from May to September or October. A Parks Canada information center is in the townsite of Jasper.

Many hiking trails, including the 11.2-kilometre (7-mi.) trip to Valley of Five Lakes and the loop to Lac Beauvert, depart from Old Fort Point, 1.6 kilometres (1 mi.) east of Jasper on Hwy. 93. The Valley of Five Lakes also can be accessed from the trailhead on the Icefields Parkway, 9 km (6 mi.) south of the townsite.

Hikers and skiers staying overnight in the backcountry must have a valid backcountry use permit. These permits are available at the Parks Canada information center in Jasper and at the Columbia Icefield Centre from early June to mid-October.

Campgrounds are open varying durations, and limited camping facilities are available in winter. For more information, phone (780) 852-6176.

There are many ways to explore the park's features, either alone or with a guide. One- or multiple-day bus tours to attractions within the park depart from Jasper. Several stables in the Jasper area offer 1-hour and half- and full-day trail rides from mid-May to mid-September and sleigh rides in winter.

Winter sports include curling, skating, tobogganing, ice climbing, snowshoeing and hockey. Cross-country skiing tours operate out of Jasper. Downhill skiing is available at Marmot Basin; cross-country trails also traverse the Maligne and Pyramid lake areas. Interpretive guides share their insights in theatrical productions. Wildlife tours also are available. Audio tours by CCInc. Auto Tape Tours are available at the Friends of Jasper store in the Parks Canada information center, 415 Connaught Dr.; phone (780) 852-4767.

Note: Since hunting is illegal, some animals may have lost their fear of human activity; be alert for animals on the highways both day and night, and never feed them. Fishing permits can be obtained at information centers, campgrounds and local sport fishing shops. Boats with electric motors are allowed on lakes unless signs indicate otherwise. See Recreation Areas Chart.

ADMISSION to the park is $19.60 per private vehicle (two to seven persons). Otherwise admission per person is $9.80; $8.30 (ages 65+); $4.90 (ages 6-16). An annual pass, valid at Jasper and 26 other Canadian national parks, is available. **Cards:** MC, VI.

PETS are allowed in some areas of the park but must be leashed, crated or physically restrained at all times.

ADDRESS inquiries to the Jasper National Park Information Centre, Jasper National Park, P.O. Box 10, Jasper, AB, Canada T0E 1E0; phone (780) 852-6176. For other area information contact Jasper Park Chamber of Commerce, P.O. Box 98, Jasper, AB, Canada T0E 1E0; phone (780) 852-3858.

COLUMBIA ICEFIELD, just inside the Jasper National Park boundary next to Banff National Park, is the largest ice mass in the Rocky Mountains. Its main bulk, about 16 by 24 kilometres (10 by 15 mi.), straddles the Great Divide, part of the British Columbia border and portions of Banff and Jasper national parks. The ice covers about 325 square kilometres (130 sq. mi.) to an estimated depth of 300 metres (984 ft.). Three glaciers—Stutfield, Athabasca and Dome—can be seen from Icefields Parkway.

Columbia Icefield Centre is 105 km (64 mi.) s. of the town of Jasper on Hwy. 93. The center overlooks Athabasca and Dome glaciers and offers views of major mountain peaks surrounding the Columbia Icefield. An interpretive center contains models of the ice field and an ice cave. The center offers maps, information and details about interpretive programs. **Time:** Allow 30 minutes minimum. **Hours:** Daily 9-6, May-Sept.; 10-4 in Apr. and Oct. **Cost:** Free. **Phone:** (780) 852-5288 or (877) 423-7433. 🍴

COLUMBIA ICEFIELD GLACIER EXPERIENCE departs from Columbia Icefield Centre, 105 km (64 mi.) s. of the town of Jasper on Hwy. 93. Tours provide an opportunity to see and walk on a field of

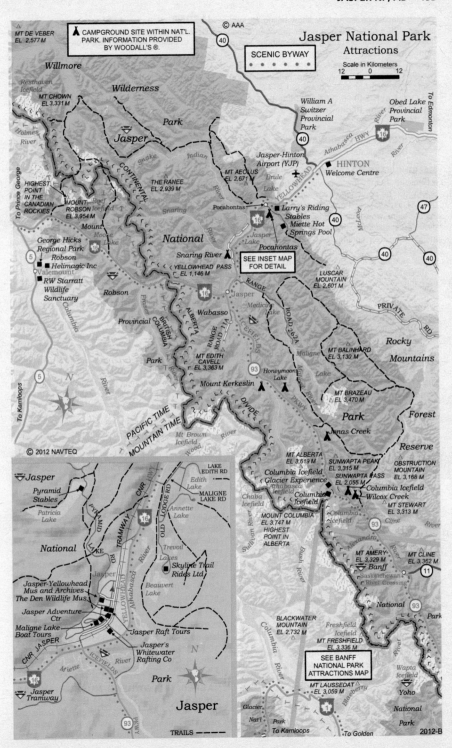

Jasper National Park
Attractions

CAMPGROUND SITE WITHIN NAT'L. PARK. INFORMATION PROVIDED BY WOODALL'S ®.

SCENIC BYWAY

Scale in Kilometers
12   0   12

© AAA

MT DE VEBER EL 2,577 M

Willmore

Wilderness

Park

Jasper

Resthaven Icefield

MT CHOWN EL 3,331 M

Holmes River

HIGHEST POINT IN THE CANADIAN ROCKIES

MOUNT ROBSON EL 3,954 M

Reef Icefield

Moose Lake

George Hicks Regional Park

Robson

Helimagic Inc

RW Starratt Wildlife Sanctuary

Valemount

CONTINENTAL

Snake River

Indian River

THE RANEE EL 2,939 M

MT AEOLUS EL 2,671 M

Snaring River

National

Snaring River

YELLOWHEAD PASS EL 1,146 M

Mount

BRITISH COLUMBIA / ALBERTA

Robson

Provincial

Park

Fraser River

Columbia River

Wabasso

RANGE ROAD 1A

MT EDITH CAVELL EL 3,363 M

Mount Kerkeslin

PACIFIC TIME

MOUNTAIN TIME

Mt Brown Icefield

Wood River

William A Switzer Provincial Park

Jasper-Hinton Airport (YJP)

Brule Lake

Pocahontas

Larry's Riding Stables

Miette Hot Springs Pool

Jasper Lake

Pocahontas

SEE INSET MAP FOR DETAIL

LUSCAR MOUNTAIN EL 2,601 M

RANGE ROAD 262A

Medicine Lake

ICEFIELDS

Maligne River

Maligne Lake

MT BALINHARD EL 3,130 M

MT BRAZEAU EL 3,470 M

Honeymoon Lake

DIVIDE

Jonas Creek

MT ALBERTA EL 3,619 M

Columbia Icefield Glacier Experience

Columbia Icefield

MOUNT COLUMBIA EL 3,747 M HIGHEST POINT IN ALBERTA

SUNWAPTA PEAK EL 3,315 M

SUNWAPTA PASS EL 2,055 M

Columbia Icefield Wilcox Creek

MT STEWART EL 3,313 M

Columbia Icefield

Cline River

Alexandra River

MT AMERY EL 3,329 M

Banff

Saskatchewan River Crossing

Bush River

MT CLINE EL 3,362 M

Rocky

Mountains

Park

Forest

Reserve

PRIVATE RD

HINTON

Welcome Centre

Athabasca HWY

YELLOWHEAD

Athabasca River

McLeod River

To Edmonton

To Prince George

To Kamloops

Obed Lake Provincial Park

National

BLACKWATER MOUNTAIN EL 2,732 M

MT FRESHFIELD EL 3,336 M

Freshfield Icefield

Park

Saskatchewan River

Columbia River

Blackberry River

MT LAUSSEDAT EL 3,059 M

SEE BANFF NATIONAL PARK ATTRACTIONS MAP

Glacier Nat'l Park

To Kamloops

To Golden

Wapta Icefield

Yoho

National

Park

© 2012 NAVTEQ

© 2012 NAVTEQ

Jasper

Pyramid Stables

Patricia Lake

Jasper-Yellowhead Mus and Archives

The Den Wildlife Mus

Jasper Adventure Ctr

Maligne Lake Boat Tours

Jasper's Whitewater Rafting Co

Jasper Tramway

National

PYRAMID LAKE RD

TRAMWAY RD

YELLOWHEAD

CNR HWY

OLD LODGE RD

LAKE EDITH RD

Edith Lake

MALIGNE LAKE RD

Annette Lake

Trevoil Lakes

Beauvert Lake

Skyline Trail Rides Ltd

Jasper Raft Tours

Athabasca River

Miette River

ICEFIELDS

CNR JASPER

Park

Jasper

TRAILS - - - - -

2012-B

moving glacier ice formed by snow falling as long
ago as 400 years. The bus driver provides anec-
dotes and information during this 80-minute excursion. **Time:** Allow 1 hour, 30 minutes minimum.
Hours: Tours depart daily every 15-30 minutes
(weather permitting) 9-6, June-Aug.; 9-5 in May and
Sept.; 10-4, mid-Apr. through Apr. 30 and Oct. 1 to
mid-Oct. **Cost:** $49.95; $24.95 (ages 6-15); free
(ages 0-5 in lap). **Phone:** (403) 762-6700 or (877)
423-7433.

ICEFIELDS PARKWAY (HWY. 93)—see
Banff National Park p. 39.

MALIGNE LAKE BOAT TOURS is 48 km (30 mi.)
s.e. of the Jasper townsite via Maligne Lake Rd.;
tickets can be purchased from the office at 616 Patricia St. in Jasper and at some area hotels. The 90-
minute tours, which offer a brief stop at Spirit Island,
provide exceptional views of Maligne Narrows and
insight into area geology and wildlife. Hiking and
trout-fishing trips as well as boat, canoe and sea
kayak rentals are available June to September.
Shuttles to the cruise departure point are available
from the town of Jasper.

Time: Allow 1 hour, 30 minutes minimum. **Hours:**
Boat tours depart daily on the hour (weather permit-
ting) 10-5, July-Aug.; 10-4 in June and Sept. **Cost:**
Boat fare $55; $27.50 (ages 5-14). Shuttle fare $40.
Phone: (780) 852-3370 for general information and
shuttle schedule. *(See ad p. 155.)*

MIETTE HOT SPRINGS POOL is e. on Hwy. 16
from the town of Jasper for 44 km (27.3 mi.) to the
Pocahontas Bungalows and jct. Miette Rd., then s.
17 km (11 mi.) on Miette Rd. Man-made pools are
fed by sulfur hot springs, with the water temperature
ranging between 38 C (100 F) and 42 C (108 F).
One pool is about 1.5 metres (5 ft.) deep; another
pool averages one-half metre (18 in.) deep. Visitors
also can cool off in two swimming pools.

Wildlife viewing opportunities often are available
in the area, and hiking trails are nearby. Changing
rooms and bathing suit and towel rentals are available. **Time:** Allow 30 minutes minimum. **Hours:**
Daily 8:30 a.m.-10:30 p.m., mid-June through Labour Day; 10:30-9, early May to mid-June and day
after Labour Day to mid-Oct. **Cost:** $6.05; $5.15
(ages 3-17 and 65+); $18.35 (family, two adults and
two children). Prices may vary; phone ahead.
Phone: (780) 866-3939 or (800) 767-1611.

RECREATIONAL ACTIVITIES
White-water Rafting
- **Jasper's Whitewater Rafting Co.** departs from
  the parking lot .3 km (.19 mi.) s. of Sunwapta Falls
  Rocky Mountain Lodge off Hwy. 93 (Sunwapta
  River trip) or from the RV parking lot off Hazel
  Ave. in the Jasper townsite (Athabasca River
  trips). **Hours:** Trips are offered May 1-early Oct.
  Schedule varies; phone ahead. **Phone:** (780)
  852-7238.

JASPER (F-2) pop. 4,051
- Restaurants p. 159
- Part of Jasper National Park area — see map
  p. 151

THE DEN WILDLIFE MUSEUM is in the lower level
of Whistler's Inn at 105 Miette Ave. Displayed are
more than 150 mounted animals in simulated habitats. Nearly all of the animals shown were native to
the area. **Time:** Allow 30 minutes minimum. **Hours:**
Daily 8 a.m.-10 p.m. **Cost:** $3; free (ages 0-6); $6
(family). **Phone:** (780) 852-3361.

JASPER ADVENTURE CENTRE is on Connaught
Dr. The company offers guided interpretive van
tours, wildlife tours and walking tours. Summer adventures include exploration of the Columbia Icefield, Maligne Valley and Morro Peak. Some winter
treks encompass such activities as snowshoeing,
dog sledding and cross-country skiing. Horseback
riding trips, rafting tours and icewalks also are offered seasonally. **Hours:** Daily 8-6. Closed
Christmas. **Cost:** Fares $55-$350. **Phone:** (780)
852-5595 or (800) 565-7547.

JASPER TRAMWAY is 3 km (1.8 mi.) s. on
Hwy. 93, then 4 km (2.5 mi.) w. at Whistlers
Mountain Rd. Take a short, narrated tram ride in an
enclosed gondola 973 metres (3,243 ft.) up into the
alpine zone on Whistlers Mountain, where stunning
scenic views await. From the aerial tramway's upper
station at 2,277 metres (7,472 ft.) you can see six
surrounding mountain ranges, several glacial-fed
lakes, the Athabasca River and the town of Jasper.
On a clear day you may even see Mount Robson in
British Columbia, the highest mountain in the Canadian Rockies.

Once at the upper station, you can stroll along the
wooden boardwalk and read the interpretive panels
posted along the way, or if you're feeling energetic,
climb the remaining 189 metres (620 ft.) up to the
summit where you'll have a breathtaking 360-degree
view.

Step carefully here; the plants that cling to life in
this harsh alpine climate are delicate, small and
easily damaged. Several have tiny but beautiful
flowers. Ptarmigans are the most common birds in
this rugged environment, and other frequently seen
inhabitants include the diminutive pika and the hoary
marmot, although you may hear these creatures before you ever see them. Pikas make a recognizable
"eep" sound while the hoary marmot's call resembles a whistle, which is how Whistlers Mountain
got its name.

Time: Allow 1 hour minimum. **Hours:** Daily 9-8,
late June-late Aug.; 9:30-6:30, late May-late June;
10-5, mid-Apr. to late May and late Aug.-second
Mon. in Oct. **Cost:** $30.95; $15.48 (ages 5-14).
Phone: (780) 852-3093. *(See ad p. 155.)*

**JASPER-YELLOWHEAD MUSEUM AND AR-
CHIVES** is at 400 Bonhomme St. Exhibits depict
Jasper history, highlighting the area's fur trade, pioneers and railways. Early tourism within Jasper National Park also is documented. An art gallery

features the works of local artists, while the archives contain photographs, maps and documents.

Time: Allow 30 minutes minimum. **Hours:** Daily 10-5, Victoria Day-second Mon. in Oct.; Thurs.-Sun. 10-5, rest of year. Closed Jan. 1, Christmas and day after Christmas. **Cost:** $6; $5 (ages 65+ and students with ID); free (ages 0-5); $13 (family). **Phone:** (780) 852-3013.

RECREATIONAL ACTIVITIES

Horseback Riding

- **Pyramid Stables** is 4 km (2.5 mi.) n. on Pyramid Lake Rd. **Hours:** Daily 8:30-4:30, mid-May to late Sept. **Phone:** (780) 852-7433.
- **Skyline Trail Rides Ltd.** departs The Fairmont Jasper Park Lodge on Old Lodge Rd. **Hours:** Daily 9:30-6:30, late Apr.-late Oct. **Phone:** (780) 852-4215 or (888) 852-7787.

White-water Rafting

- **Jasper Raft Tours** is at 604 Connaught Dr. **Hours:** Trips are offered daily, May 15-Sept. 30. Departure times vary. **Phone:** (780) 852-2665 or (888) 553-5628.
- **Raven Adventures Ltd.** is at 610 Patricia St. Other activities are offered. **Hours:** Trips are offered daily, May-Sept. Departure times vary. **Phone:** (780) 852-4292.
- **Rocky Mountain River Guides** is at 626 Connaught Dr. **Hours:** Trips are offered daily, mid-May through Sept. 30. Departure times vary. **Phone:** (780) 852-3777 or (866) 952-3777.

Get more from your
membership with an
upgrade to Plus or Premier

ALPINE VILLAGE 780/852-3285

Cabin
$120-$320

Address: Hwy 93A T0E 1E0 **Location:** Jct Hwy 16 and 93, 0.9 mi (1.4 km) s on Hwy 93, then just e. **Facility:** These upscale cabins, which range in size and decor, are in a wooded, riverfront setting outside of town; a 16-foot outdoor hot tub is on site. 50 cabins, some kitchens. 1 story, exterior corridors. **Terms:** closed 10/15-5/2, check-in 4 pm, 2-3 night minimum stay - seasonal and/or weekends, 14 day cancellation notice-fee imposed. **Activities:** hiking trails, playground. **Guest Services:** valet laundry. **Free Special Amenities:** local telephone calls and high-speed Internet. *(See ad p. 156.)*

 /SOME UNITS

AMETHYST LODGE (780)852-3394

Hotel
$85-$285

Address: 200 Connaught Dr T0E 1E0 **Location:** 0.3 mi (0.5 km) e. **Facility:** 97 units. 3 stories, interior/exterior corridors. **Parking:** winter plug-ins. **Terms:** check-in 4 pm, cancellation fee imposed. **Activities:** whirlpools. **Guest Services:** valet laundry, area transportation-bus & train stations. **Free Special Amenities:** local telephone calls and high-speed Internet.

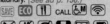
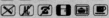
/SOME UNITS FEE

BECKER'S CHALETS 780/852-3779

Cabin
$145-$200

Address: Hwy 93 S T0E 1E0 **Location:** 4.3 mi (6.8 km) s. Located in a quiet rustic area. **Facility:** 118 units, some two bedrooms, three bedrooms, efficiencies, kitchens and cabins. 2 stories (no elevator), exterior corridors. **Terms:** closed 10/14-5/1, check-in 4 pm, 7 day cancellation notice. **Activities:** fishing, hiking trails, playground. **Guest Services:** coin laundry. *(See ad p. 156.)*

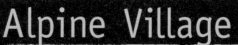

BEST WESTERN JASPER INN & SUITES

(780)852-4461

Hotel
$150-$240

AAA Benefit: Members save up to 20%, plus 10% bonus points with Best Western Rewards®.

Address: 98 Geikie St T0E 1E0 **Location:** Corner of Geikie and Bonhomme sts. Located in a residential area. **Facility:** 143 units, some two bedrooms and kitchens. 2-3 stories (no elevator), interior/exterior corridors. **Parking:** winter plug-ins. **Terms:** check-in 4 pm, 2 night minimum stay - seasonal and/or weekends, 3 day cancellation notice-fee imposed, resort fee. **Amenities:** safes. **Pool(s):** heated indoor, whirlpool, steamroom. **Guest Services:** coin laundry. **Free Special Amenities:** early check-in/late check-out and high-speed Internet. *(See ad this page.)*

CHATEAU JASPER

(780)852-5644

Hotel
$109-$295

Address: 96 Geikie St T0E 1E0 **Location:** Corner of Juniper and Geikie sts. Located in a residential area. **Facility:** 119 units. 3 stories, interior corridors. **Parking:** winter plug-ins. **Terms:** check-in 4 pm, cancellation fee imposed. **Amenities:** safes. **Pool(s):** heated indoor. **Activities:** whirlpool, exercise room. **Guest Services:** valet laundry, area transportation-bus & train stations. **Free Special Amenities:** local telephone calls and high-speed Internet.

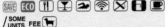

THE FAIRMONT JASPER PARK LODGE

780/852-3301

Resort Hotel
Rates not provided

Address: 1 Old Lodge Rd T0E 1E0 **Location:** 3 mi (4.8 km) ne via Hwy 16, 2 mi (3.2 km) se off highway via Maligne Rd, follow signs. **Facility:** It's said that at one time Marilyn Monroe frequented this resort set along two lakes just outside of town in a spectacular mountain setting. Activities and scenic grounds await along with superlative services. 446 units. 1-2 stories (no elevator), exterior corridors. **Parking:** on-site and valet, winter plug-ins. **Terms:** check-in 4 pm. **Amenities:** safes. *Some:* high-speed Internet (fee). **Dining:** 4 restaurants, also, Cavell's Restaurant & Terrace, The Moose's Nook Northern Grill, see separate listings, entertainment. **Pool(s):** heated outdoor. **Activities:** saunas, steamrooms, rental boats, rental canoes, rental paddleboats, boat dock, 2 tennis courts, cross country skiing, ice skating, tobogganing, recreation programs, rental bicycles, hiking trails, playground, basketball, horseshoes, shuffleboard, volleyball, exercise room, spa. *Fee:* fishing, golf-18 holes, horseback riding, game room. **Guest Services:** valet laundry, area transportation (fee)-ski hill.

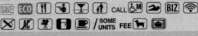

The ***Fairmont***
JASPER PARK LODGE

Surrounded by captivating mountains and sparkling lakes, The Fairmont Jasper Park Lodge welcomes you

▼ *See AAA listing this page* ▼

Experience our year round playground in Jasper National Park!

- 10 minutes walking distance to the heart of Jasper
- Indoor pool, jacuzzi, sauna & steam room

- Inn Restaurant & Terrace; a local favorite
- Choose from a variety of family suites

To Edmonton
Jasper National Park
GEIKIE ST
BW Jasper Inn & Suites
CONNAUGHT DR
Athabasca R.
16
Jasper National Park
To Hwy 93 & Banff

BEST WESTERN Jasper Inn & Suites

98 Geikie St. • Jasper, AB T0E 1E0
780.852.4461 | 1.800.661.1933
bestwesternjasperinn.com

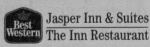
Show Your Card & Save

Best Western
Jasper Inn & Suites
The Inn Restaurant

JASPER HOUSE BUNGALOWS   780/852-4535

 Cabin. Rates not provided. **Address:** Hwy 93 S T0E 1E0 **Location:** 2.5 mi (4 km) s on Hwy 93. Located in a quiet rustic area. **Facility:** 56 cabins, some kitchens. 1 story, exterior corridors. **Activities:** hiking trails, horseshoes. **Guest Services:** coin laundry.

LOBSTICK LODGE   (780)852-4431

Hotel
$99-$255

Address: 94 Geikie St T0E 1E0 **Location:** Corner of Geikie and Juniper sts. **Facility:** 139 units, some kitchens. 3 stories, interior corridors. **Parking:** winter plug-ins. **Terms:** check-in 4 pm, cancellation fee imposed. **Pool(s):** heated indoor. **Activities:** sauna, whirlpools, exercise room. **Guest Services:** valet and coin laundry, area transportation-bus & train stations. **Free Special Amenities: local telephone calls and high-speed Internet.**

MARMOT LODGE   (780)852-4471

Motel
$89-$255

Address: 86 Connaught Dr T0E 1E0 **Location:** 1 mi (1.6 km) ne. **Facility:** 107 units, some two bedrooms and kitchens. 2 stories (no elevator), exterior corridors. **Parking:** winter plug-ins. **Terms:** check-in 4 pm, cancellation fee imposed. **Pool(s):** heated indoor. **Activities:** sauna, whirlpools. **Guest Services:** valet and coin laundry, area transportation-bus & train stations. **Free Special Amenities: local telephone calls and high-speed Internet.**

MOUNT ROBSON INN   (780)852-3327

Motel
$114-$339

Address: 902 Connaught Dr T0E 1E0 **Location:** 0.6 mi (1 km) sw. **Facility:** 80 units. 2 stories (no elevator), exterior corridors. **Parking:** winter plug-ins. **Terms:** check-in 4 pm. **Amenities:** *Some:* video games. **Activities:** whirlpools. **Guest Services:** coin laundry, area transportation-train station. **Free Special Amenities: continental breakfast and high-speed Internet.**

Now featuring complimentary continental breakfast! Family owned with family style hospitality.

PARK PLACE INN   780/852-9770

Boutique Hotel
$129-$269

Address: 623 Patricia St T0E 1E0 **Location:** Downtown. **Facility:** Looking to go shopping or explore the national park? This upscale and intimate property, one floor up from the hustle of downtown, is the perfect spot from which to do so. 14 units. 2 stories, interior corridors. **Terms:** check-in 4 pm, 5 day cancellation notice. **Free Special Amenities: local telephone calls.**

PATRICIA LAKE BUNGALOWS   780/852-3560

 Cabin $87-$325 **Address:** Pyramid Lake Rd T0E 1E0 **Location:** 3 mi (4.8 km) nw via Pyramid Lake Rd. **Facility:** 49 cabins. 1 story, exterior corridors. **Terms:** closed 10/16-5/3, check-in 4 pm, 3 night minimum stay - seasonal, 7 day cancellation notice. **Activities:** whirlpool, rental boats, rental canoes, rental paddleboats, boat dock, fishing, rental bicycles, playground. **Guest Services:** coin laundry.

PYRAMID LAKE RESORT   (780)852-4900

Hotel
$161-$368

Address: Pyramid Lake Rd T0E 1E0 **Location:** Jct Connaught Dr and Cedar St, 3.8 mi (6 km) nw via Pyramid Lake Rd. Located in a quiet area. **Facility:** 62 units, some efficiencies. 2 stories (no elevator), exterior corridors. **Parking:** winter plug-ins. **Terms:** closed 10/13-4/18, cancellation fee imposed. **Amenities:** safes. **Activities:** whirlpool, steamroom, rental boats, rental canoes, rental paddleboats, boat dock, cross country skiing, rental bicycles, hiking trails, exercise room. *Fee:* fishing, ice skating. **Guest Services:** coin laundry.

SAWRIDGE INN & CONFERENCE CENTRE JASPER   (780)852-5111

Hotel
$92-$284

Address: 76 Connaught Dr T0E 1E0 **Location:** 1.1 mi (1.7 km) e. **Facility:** 153 units. 3 stories, interior corridors. **Parking:** winter plug-ins. **Terms:** check-in 4 pm, 2 night minimum stay - weekends, 3 day cancellation notice-fee imposed. **Amenities:** video games (fee). *Some:* high-speed Internet. **Dining:** 2 restaurants, nightclub. **Pool(s):** heated indoor. **Activities:** sauna, whirlpools, recreation programs in summer, exercise room, spa. **Guest Services:** valet and coin laundry, area transportation-downtown. **Free Special Amenities: local telephone calls and high-speed Internet.**

SUNWAPTA FALLS ROCKY MOUNTAIN LODGE   (780)852-4852

Cabin
$99-$409

Address: Hwy 93 T0E 1E0 **Location:** 34.7 mi (55 km) s on Icefields Pkwy (Hwy 93). Located in a quiet secluded setting. **Facility:** 53 cabins. 1-2 stories (no elevator), exterior corridors. **Terms:** closed 10/10-5/17, check-in 4 pm, cancellation fee imposed. **Activities:** rental bicycles, hiking trails. *Fee:* fishing. **Free Special Amenities: local telephone calls and room upgrade (subject to availability with advance reservations).**

TONQUIN INN   (780)852-4987

 Motel $135-$400 **Address:** 100 Juniper St T0E 1E0 **Location:** Corner of Juniper and Geikie sts. **Facility:** 137 units, some two bedrooms and kitchens. 2-3 stories, exterior corridors. **Parking:** winter plug-ins. **Terms:** check-in 4 pm, cancellation fee imposed. **Pool(s):** heated indoor. **Activities:** saunas, whirlpools, exercise room. **Guest Services:** coin laundry.

WHERE TO EAT

BEAR'S PAW BAKERY 780/852-3233

Breads/Pastries. Quick Serve. $4-$10 **AAA Inspector Notes:** Guests can savor the aroma of freshly baked goods at this cozy hide-away bakery. Representative of the many temptations are the signature Bear's Paw cinnamon buns, a selection of muffins, cinnamon rolls and chocolate croissants. The bakery does make a limited number of excellent sandwiches to-go but they tend to sell out very quickly. Grab a sweet and a cup of coffee and head out into the mountain air. **Address:** 4 Cedar Ave T0E 1E0 **Location:** Just w off Connaught Dr at Cedar Ave. **Parking:** street only. [B] [L] [AC]

BECKER'S GOURMET RESTAURANT 780/852-3535

Continental
Fine Dining
$22-$42

AAA Inspector Notes: About a 10 minute drive from Jasper along the Ice-field Highway, this restaurant was a secret, only known to a few locals who made it a favorite. However, a few years ago they let the cat out of the bag and people now ask for a table overlooking mounts Kerkeslin and Hardisty. It is not just the decidedly Canadian décor of warm oak and firs and the large stone fireplace that keep customers coming back—the chefs change the menu on a daily basis to create innovative dishes. **Bar:** full bar. **Reservations:** suggested. **Address:** Hwy 93 T0E 1E0 **Location:** On Hwy 93, 4.3 mi (6.8 km) s. [B] [D] [AC]

CAFE MONDO 780/852-9676

Canadian. Quick Serve. $6-$15 **AAA Inspector Notes:** This popular casual eatery has a fresh and bright décor, perfect for sitting and relaxing with one of the magazines or papers while you wait for one of the enticing pita melts or wraps. Fresh and tasty soups, salads, pizza or ready-made sandwiches and a great variety of baked goods, all prepared in house, can be enjoyed with a cold beverage or freshly made cup of coffee from the espresso bar. **Bar:** full bar. **Address:** 616 Patricia St T0E 1E0 **Location:** Center. **Parking:** street only. [B] [L] [D]

CASSIO'S ITALIAN RESTAURANT 780/852-4070

Italian. Casual Dining. $15-$32 **AAA Inspector Notes:** This bright and cheery spot offers a great menu. Appetizers include smoked salmon, mussels and clams, bruschetta, flatbreads and the house salad with prosciutto and mozzarella. A good selection of pasta and hearty entrées of wild salmon, veal picatta and Alberta Gold Label AAA steak are each accompanied by a pasta, polenta or gnocchi. More casual dishes feature a buffalo burger and a thin-crust gourmet pizza. Service is efficient and friendly. Open for breakfast on weekends during the season. **Bar:** full bar. **Reservations:** suggested. **Address:** 602 Connaught Dr T0E 1E0 **Location:** Between Miette and Hazel aves. **Parking:** street only. [D] CALL [&M]

CAVELL'S RESTAURANT & TERRACE 780/852-6052

American
Casual Dining
$17-$42

AAA Inspector Notes: Good views of nearby Mount Edith Cavell and Lac Beauvert can be had from the dining room of the mountain's namesake restaurant. Fresh, quality ingredients focus on Fairmont Lifestyle Cuisine which utilizes local, organic and sustainable items. Start with tasty salads, soups and appetizers. Entrees run the gamut from a bison burger and butter chicken to more complex dishes such as pan-seared halibut and a spring creek rib-eye. For breakfast enjoy a full buffet or a la carte dining. **Bar:** full bar. **Reservations:** suggested. **Address:** 1 Old Lodge Rd T0E 1E0 **Location:** 3 mi (4.8 km) ne via Hwy 16, 2 mi (3.2 km) se off highway via Maligne Rd, follow signs; in The Fairmont Jasper Park Lodge. **Parking:** on-site and valet. [B] [L] [D] CALL [&M]

EARLS RESTAURANT 780/852-2393

American. Casual Dining. $13-$31 **AAA Inspector Notes:** Offering an experience that falls between fast food and fine dining, the fun, relaxed restaurant prepares great food at a great price. Choices range from juicy burgers, hearty sandwiches, fresh salads, wings and pizza to full entrees of steak, chops and seafood. Made-from-scratch soups and assorted breads, as well as a nice choice of wines and beers, round out the offerings. This is a fitting spot for impromptu get-togethers and festive occasions. **Bar:** full bar. **Address:** 600 Patricia St T0E 1E0 **Location:** Corner of Miette Ave, 2nd Level. **Parking:** street only. [L] [D] [LATE]

EVIL DAVE'S GRILL 780/852-3323

New American. Casual Dining. $20-$37 **AAA Inspector Notes:** Guests need not be frightened to dine at this casual spot as the only thing out of world here is the delicious food. Crazy names are attached to the contemporary menu items like the malevolent meatloaf made with Alberta bison; malicious sockeye salmon; and porco loco, a ginger-rubbed pork chop. The great food, a warm and intimate decor (with a slight Asian and African feel) and a blazing fire displayed on a flat-screen TV, as well as proficient and friendly servers, makes for a great night out. **Bar:** full bar. **Reservations:** suggested. **Address:** 622 Patricia St T0E 1E0 **Location:** Corner of Hazel Ave. **Parking:** street only. [D] CALL [&M]

FIDDLE RIVER RESTAURANT 780/852-3032

Canadian. Casual Dining. $20-$38 **AAA Inspector Notes:** Located on the second floor, this cozy restaurant is often missed by tourists as they walk on by. Upstairs, the candlelit windows offer a view of the nearby Colin Range Mountains. The owner drives daily to the local farms in the Robson Valley to pick the freshest produce to use in the restaurant's recipes. Innovative specialties include Alberta beef, bison and such seasonal fish as Arctic char, salmon and pickerel. **Bar:** full bar. **Reservations:** suggested. **Address:** 620 Connaught Dr T0E 1E0 **Location:** At Hazel Ave; upstairs. **Parking:** street only. [D]

JASPER BREWING CO 780/852-4111

American. Gastropub. $11-$30 **AAA Inspector Notes:** More than average pub grub, this spot serves up quality ingredients with innovative twists. Appetizers include double-dip calamari with sweet onion peanut sauce and chili aioli, and monkey fingers (banana-panko crusted chicken with mango curry and sweet chili sauce). Homemade burgers and other items include spaghetti with cheddar-filled meatballs, buckets of cream ale-battered fish and chips, and AAA Alberta beef with roast garlic butter. As expected, there are some hand-crafted beers. **Bar:** full bar. **Address:** 624 Connaught Dr T0E 1E0 **Location:** Between Miette and Hazel aves. **Parking:** street only. [L] [D] [LATE]

JASPER PIZZA PLACE 780/852-3225

Pizza. Family Dining. $10-$22 **AAA Inspector Notes:** Those looking for pizza need search no further. Thick crusted pies are available with unusual toppings, such as spinach, barbecue chicken and artichokes. At night, the wood-fired oven gets going and the menu lists even more exotic combinations. In additional to pizza, the menu lists casual noodle and pasta dishes, burgers, wraps, salads and steak and chicken entrées. The rooftop patio is popular during the summer. Closed for lunch on weekdays from October through May. **Bar:** full bar. **Address:** 402 Connaught Dr T0E 1E0 **Location:** Center. **Parking:** street only. [L] [D] CALL [&M] [AC]

KAROUZO'S STEAKHOUSE 780/852-4640

Steak. Casual Dining. $9-$58 **AAA Inspector Notes:** On the main street leading into town, this family-run steak and seafood restaurant features a wide variety of entrees, including some pasta dishes. **Bar:** full bar. **Address:** 628 Connaught Dr T0E 1E0 **Location:** Between Spruce and Hazel aves. **Parking:** street only. [L] [D]

KIMCHI HOUSE 780/852-5022

Korean. Casual Dining. $13-$25 **AAA Inspector Notes:** Guests will often be greeted by the truly hospitable owner of this simple, little eatery. Classic dishes include the delicious bin dae duk, an appetizer of mung bean pancake batter with pork and kimchi (spicy pickled cabbage). A host of hot pots, noodles and other soups, along with a good variety of chicken, beef, seafood and vegetable dishes, all are presented in a variety of distinctive bowls and plates. As a small side dish, try their namesake kimchi. **Bar:** full bar. **Reservations:** suggested. **Address:** 407 Patricia St T0E 1E0 **Location:** Between Cedar and Elm aves. **Parking:** street only. [L] [D] CALL [&M]

LA FIESTA 780/852-0404

Mexican. Casual Dining. $15-$30 **AAA Inspector Notes:** A fusion of Mexican and Spanish cuisines awaits in the cozy restaurant boasting friendly, casual service. Daily-made soups complement the more-Mexican-than-Spanish menu, but a definite modern twist is evident in all the dishes. Adobe-spiced mahi mahi or ancho chili burritos are enticing items you might find. Since the chef creates everything from scratch, diners enjoy each bite. **Bar:** full bar. **Reservations:** suggested. **Address:** 504 Patricia St T0E 1E0 **Location:** Between Elm and Miette aves; across from Information Centre. **Parking:** street only. [D] [AC]

L & W FAMILY RESTAURANT   780/852-4114

◆◆ International. Family Dining. $8-$23 **AAA Inspector Notes:** Those looking for good value for the dollar will find this family-run restaurant a good choice. Overflowing with an abundance of huge, rubber plants and other greenery, the eatery's menu has something for everyone. Guests have their choice of Greek dishes, burgers, pizza and sandwiches. **Bar:** full bar. **Address:** 101 Pine Ave T0E 1E0 **Location:** Corner of Hazel Ave and Patricia St. **Parking:** street only. [L] [D]

THE MOOSE'S NOOK NORTHERN GRILL   780/852-6052

◆◆◆
Regional
Canadian
Fine Dining
$22-$42

AAA Inspector Notes: This nook of a restaurant is casual, but the food is anything but. Representative of creative, inventive regional cuisine are Alberta beef and pork entrées, seasonal greens and tempting desserts. The service and ambience are upscale without being pretentious and laid-back yet classy. This spot should not be missed for those looking for a taste of Canada. Check for seasonal closures. **Bar:** full bar. **Reservations:** suggested. **Address:** 1 Old Lodge Rd T0E 1E0 **Location:** 3 mi (4.8 km) ne via Hwy 16, 2 mi (3.2 km) se off highway via Maligne Rd, follow signs; in The Fairmont Jasper Park Lodge. **Parking:** on-site and valet. [D] CALL [⌖M]

PAPA GEORGE'S RESTAURANT   780/852-2260

◆◆◆ Canadian. Family Dining. $9-$39 **AAA Inspector Notes:** Named after Papa George Andrews, one of Jasper's business pioneers, this 1925 eatery continues to produce hearty, yet innovative food using free-range Alberta game and beef, local wild mushrooms, organic grains and beans and seasonal vegetables. Try the caramelized vegetable fries or Brome Lake duck wings to start, followed by elk tenderloin or wild salmon. Finish with one of the delicious house desserts. A small, take-out espresso café with freshly baked pastries is on site. **Bar:** full bar. **Reservations:** suggested. **Address:** 404 Connaught Dr T0E 1E0 **Location:** Center; in Astoria Hotel. [B] [L] [D]

PATRICIA STREET DELI   780/852-4814

◆ Deli. Quick Serve. $8-$16 **AAA Inspector Notes:** It would be easy to walk past the small, unassuming entrance to this simple delicatessen. However, it is worth seeking out for delicious and freshly-made, build-your-own sandwiches which can be eaten at one of the limited tables or one of the many picnic areas with scenic vistas surrounding Jasper. Also on the menu is rotisserie chicken, wings, deli meats and cheeses and some simple baked goods. **Address:** 606 Patricia St T0E 1E0 **Location:** Center. **Parking:** street only. [B] [L] [Ⓚ]

SOFT ROCK CAFÉ   780/852-5850

◆ Breakfast Sandwiches. Quick Serve. $4-$12 **AAA Inspector Notes:** While the café may look a little rough at times-what with the scuffed hardwood floors, scratched tables and understated decor-few patrons come for the decor. The food is what brings skiers and families out for oversize portions of fabulously rustic grub: fluffy omelets, pancakes and sinful, home-baked goods. The place is more or less self-service; diners place an order at the counter and wait for their name to be called. Open for dinner during summer. **Bar:** full bar. **Address:** 632 Connaught Dr T0E 1E0 **Location:** Just n of Hazel Ave. **Parking:** street only. [B] [L]

SYRAHS OF JASPER   780/852-4559

◆◆ International. Casual Dining. $23-$31 **AAA Inspector Notes:** Sharing an entranceway with one of the best wine stores in town, this bistro boasts a great wine list. Swiss-born-and-trained chef Andy is respected for his robust fare with clean, distinct flavors. The classic menu changes often to feature local, in-season ingredients such as wild game, organic fruits, vegetables and herbs that are procured locally. As expected some Swiss influence can be found on the menu. Everything is cooked a la minute so guests should be prepared for a leisurely meal. **Bar:** full bar. **Reservations:** suggested. **Address:** 606 Patricia St T0E 1E0 **Location:** Center. **Parking:** street only. [D]

TREELINE RESTAURANT   780/852-3093

◆ American. Quick Serve. $6-$22 **AAA Inspector Notes:** A spectacular view awaits above the trees in the tundra just south of town. For an additional fee, a tram whisks you up past the tree line for views of five mountain ranges, lakes and the town. You can work up an appetite climbing to the summit of Whistlers Mountain and then enter the cafeteria-style restaurant for soups, sandwiches, spaghetti, burgers and hotdogs. In the high season the evening menu expands to include entrées such as crab-stuffed salmon, steak sandwiches and fish and chips. **Bar:** beer & wine. **Address:** Top of Whistler Mountain Rd T0E 1E0 **Location:** 1.8 mi (3 km) s on Hwy 93, 2.5 mi (4 km) w at Whistlers Campground; tram ride to restaurant for an additional charge. [B] [L] [D] [Ⓚ]

VILLA CARUSO   780/852-3920

◆◆◆ Steak. Casual Dining. $11-$37 **AAA Inspector Notes:** Established in 1977, this longstanding steakhouse sits above street level but is accessible via elevator. The spacious lodgelike setting has wood beams and hardwood floors, and guests seated near the windows are treated to a great view of the mountains. Alberta beef is the house specialty, but other Canadian specialties, including salmon, also find their way onto the menu. **Bar:** full bar. **Reservations:** suggested. **Address:** 640 Connaught Dr T0E 1E0 **Location:** Connaught Dr and Hazel Ave; 2nd Level. **Parking:** street only. [D] CALL [⌖M]

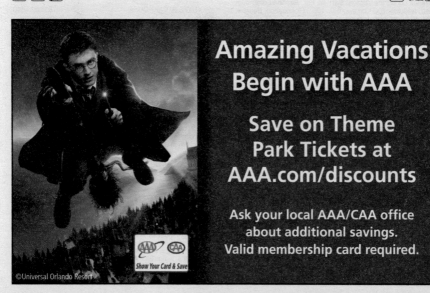

KANANASKIS pop. 249

- Part of Banff National Park area — see map p. 37

PASSING OF THE LEGENDS MUSEUM is at

Rafter Six Ranch Resort, 2 km (1.2 mi.) s. of Hwy. 1 overpass after the Seebe exit. Guided tours of the museum highlight the movies and television commercials that have been filmed on the property, First Nations and North West Mounted Police exhibits, pioneer memorabilia, antique carriages and artwork. Adventure programs, including trail riding, ziplining, rock climbing, and white-water rafting and hiking tours, can be organized at the ranch.

Hours: Museum daily 10-4, May-Sept. **Cost:** $10; $8 (senior citizens); $6 (ages 5-12). **Phone:** (403) 673-3622, (403) 264-1251, or (888) 267-2624 (Rafter Six Ranch Resort).

RECREATIONAL ACTIVITIES

Skiing

- **Nakiska Ski Resort** is just n. of Kananaskis Village on Hwy. 40. **Hours:** Daily 9-4, early Dec. to mid-Apr. **Phone:** (403) 591-7777, (403) 256-8473 or (800) 258-7669.

Give the gift of security, value and peace of mind: Gift Membership

---

DELTA LODGE AT KANANASKIS (403)591-7711

WWWW Resort Hotel $159-$309 **Address:** Kananaskis Village T0L 2H0 **Location:** Trans-Canada Hwy 1, 14.7 mi (23.5 km) s on Hwy 40 (Kananaskis Tr), then 1.8 mi (3 km) on Kananaskis Village access road, follow signs. Located in a quiet area. **Facility:** This beautiful resort, nestled in a tranquil mountain village, consists of three separate buildings within easy reach of multiple recreational activities. 412 units, some two bedrooms. 3 stories, interior corridors. **Parking:** on-site (fee) and valet, winter plug-ins. **Terms:** check-in 4 pm, 3 day cancellation notice-fee imposed. **Amenities:** video games (fee), high-speed Internet. *Some:* safes. **Dining:** 3 restaurants, also, The Fireweed Grill, see separate listing. **Pool(s):** heated indoor. **Activities:** sauna, whirlpool, steamroom, 6 lighted tennis courts, cross country skiing, ice skating, tobogganing, recreation programs, rental bicycles, hiking trails, jogging, playground, sports court, spa. *Fee:* horseback riding, game room. **Guest Services:** valet and coin laundry, area transportation-golf course & Nakiska Ski Resort. *(See ad this page.)*

ECO FEE ⊞ ⊞ ⊞ ⊞ ⊞ ⊞ ⊞ ⊞ BIZ ⊞
⊠ ⊞ ⊞ ⊞ / SOME UNITS FEE ⊞ ⊞

WHERE TO EAT

THE FIREWEED GRILL 403/591-7711

WW American. Casual Dining. $14-$40 **AAA Inspector Notes:** Located in the main lodge at the village, this comfortable, casual restaurant is a popular pick for both hotel guests and day trippers alike. Dinner entrées run the gamut from smoked Queen Charlotte sablefish to Alberta lamb cassoulet or Alberta beef. A trimmed down lunch menu offers soup, salads, pizza, pasta and sandwiches. **Bar:** full bar. **Reservations:** suggested, for dinner. **Address:** Kananaskis Village T0L 2H0 **Location:** Trans-Canada Hwy 1, 14.7 mi (23.5 km) s on Hwy 40 (Kananaskis Tr), then 1.8 mi (3 km) on Kananaskis Village access road, follow signs; in Delta Lodge at Kananaskis. **Parking:** on-site (fee) and valet. *(See ad this page.)* B L D CALL ⊞M

KANANASKIS COUNTRY (I-5)

Kananaskis Country is a four-season, multiuse recreation area encompassing more than 4,200 square kilometres (1,622 sq. mi.) of mountains and foothills. West of Calgary, the area contains Bow Valley, Bragg Creek, Canmore Nordic Centre, Peter Lougheed, Sheep River and Spray Valley provincial parks. In addition there are Blue Rock, Bow Valley, Don Getty and Elbow-Sheep wildland parks. There are also numerous provincial recreation areas with campgrounds, day use areas and trails (see Recreation Areas Chart).

Year-round recreational activities are offered, including hiking, horseback riding, snowmobiling, kayaking, mountain biking, fishing, snowshoeing and downhill and cross-country skiing. The area begins just south of Hwy. 1 and extends south to the intersection of hwys. 940 and 532. Animals, including elk, deer, bighorn sheep, lynx, moose, mountain goats, bears and porcupines, can be observed in the area.

Three major visitor information centers within Kananaskis Country provide brochures, maps, displays and other travel information. The Barrier Lake Visitor Information Centre is 6.5 kilometres (4 mi.) south of Hwy. 1 on Hwy. 40, and Peter Lougheed Provincial Park Visitor Information Centre is 50 kilometres (31 mi.) south off Hwy. 40 on Kananaskis Lakes Trail. Elbow Valley Visitor Information Centre is 5 kilometres (3 mi.) west of Hwy. 22 on Hwy. 66. Campground amphitheaters offer interpretive programs Wednesday through Sunday evenings in July and August. The area is open daily; however, Hwy. 40 is closed December 1 to June 15 between the Kananaskis Lakes Trail and the junction of hwys. 541 and 940.

Kananaskis Country General Inquiries: Provincial Building, 800 Railway Ave., Suite 201, Canmore, AB, Canada T1W 1P1. **Phone:** (403) 678-5508 or (403) 673-3985.

LAC LA BICHE (C-7) pop. 2,544

South of town, Portage La Biche was discovered in 1798 by renowned geographer and explorer David Thompson of the North West Co. This area encompasses the land between the Churchill and

Athabasca-Mackenzie basins. Soon after its discovery the portage became a key link in Canada's main fur trade routes and a passageway to the Pacific Ocean.

The 1853 founding of Lac La Biche Mission played a vital role in the settlement of the area, which quickly developed into a major transportation center of the north.

Lakeland Provincial Park *(see Recreation Areas Chart)*, 13 kilometres (8 mi.) east off Hwy. 663, provides such recreational opportunities as bicycling, bird-watching, camping, cross-country skiing, fishing, hiking and swimming. The park also offers Alberta's only backcountry canoe circuit. Sir Winston Churchill Provincial Park *(see Recreation Areas Chart)*, 11 kilometres (6.8 mi.) northeast off Hwy. 881, is the largest of the 12 islands on Lac La Biche and offers opportunities for camping, hiking and bird-watching.

Lac La Biche Regional Community Development Corp.: 10106 102nd Ave., P.O. Box 2188, Lac La Biche, AB, Canada T0A 2C0. **Phone:** (780) 623-2662 or (877) 623-9696.

LACOMBE (F-6) pop. 11,707, elev. 846m/2,775'

Lacombe is the site of the Canadian Agriculture Department's experimental farm; visitors can tour the facility. At Gull Lake 17 kilometres (11 mi.) west on Hwy. 12, Aspen Beach Provincial Park is a noteworthy area resort affording such recreational activities as cross-country skiing, ice fishing and water skiing *(see Recreation Areas Chart)*.

ELLIS BIRD FARM, 8 km (5 mi.) e. on Hwy. 12, then 8 km (5 mi.) s. on Prentiss Rd., is a working bird-conservation facility encouraging the propagation of mountain bluebirds and tree swallows. Such species as house wrens, owls and warblers also are attracted to the vibrant grounds. A network of trails afford access to butterfly, native wildflower, hummingbird and water gardens. A visitor center displaying mounted bird specimens is on-site as is a pond where children can try to net beetles and damselflies.

Time: Allow 1 hour minimum. **Hours:** Daily 11-5, Victoria Day weekend-Labour Day. Guided tours are offered Sun. at 2, June-July. **Cost:** Admission by donation. Guided tour $2. **Phone:** (403) 885-4477, or (403) 346-2211 in the off-season. 🍴 🎡

KRAAY FAMILY FARM AND LACOMBE CORN MAZE is off Hwy. 2 (Queen Elizabeth II) exit 422; take Hwy. 12 3 km (1.9 mi.) w., then 1 km (.6 mi.) s., following signs. Geared toward families with young children, the site is home to such farm animals as chickens, goats and pigs and offers visitors more than 20 activities, including miniature golf, a giant air-filled jumping pillow and a pedal cart track. The three sections of the 15-acre corn maze range from easy to hard. A barrel train ride through the maze, the Corn Cannon and Pumpkin Blaster, and a gem mining area are offered for an additional fee.

Note: Sturdy walking shoes are recommended. **Time:** Allow 2 hours minimum. **Hours:** Mon.-Sat. 10:30-8, late July-Labour Day; Tues.-Thurs. 4-8 p.m., Fri.-Sat. 10:30-9, day after Labour Day to mid-Oct. (weather permitting). Pig races are held Mon.-Fri. at 2, Sat.-Sun. at 1:30 and 4. Phone ahead to confirm schedule. **Cost:** $12; $10 (ages 4-12 and 65+). **Phone:** (403) 302-1709. 🍴 🎡 🌳

LAKE LOUISE (H-4)
• **Hotels p. 164** • **Restaurants p. 164**
• **Part of Banff National Park area — see map p. 37**

LAKE LOUISE is 4 km (2.4 mi.) w. of Hwy. 1/93 behind The Fairmont Chateau Lake Louise hotel. Incredibly aqua in summer and glistening with snow and ice in winter, the lake has been the subject of countless photographs. Viewed from the hotel side of the lake, the milky blue water creates a striking foreground framed by steep, densely forested mountains on either side and at the far end, the rocky bulk of Mount Victoria blanketed by a sparkling layer of glacial ice. It's the grinding of this ice against the mountain that creates the fine rock particles that wash down into the lake, giving it the unusual hue.

Benches along the shore near the hotel offer a place to relax and take in the magnificent view, but if you're here in summer, especially in the late morning or early afternoon, you'll have plenty of competition for those seats. It's at this time when RVs and automobiles cruise the parking lots endlessly, searching for a coveted spot, while one bus after another disgorges throngs of tourists.

It's an amazingly beautiful place, but during the high season, not a very peaceful one. To escape the crowds, choose one of the several trails that begin near the hotel and make your escape. The easy Lakeshore Trail follows the northern edge of Lake Louise for about 2 kilometres one way (1.2 mi.). If you continue another 3.3 kilometres (2 mi.), the trail becomes much more challenging, but eventually you'll reach the Plain of Six Glaciers, a rocky area created by advancing and retreating glaciers. A quaint teahouse sells refreshments here, and the view extends all the way to the other side of the valley. Another way to explore the lake is by canoe, which you can rent at the boathouse on the lake's west shore.

The Lake Louise Visitor Information Centre in nearby Samson Mall has maps and information. Nearby Moraine Lake *(see attraction listing p. 40)* is another spectacular Banff National Park location worth visiting. **Phone:** (403) 522-3833 for the visitor center.

LAKE LOUISE SIGHTSEEING GONDOLA AND INTERPRETIVE CENTRE is just n. of Hwy. 1 interchange at 1 Whitehorn Rd. A lift offers an impressive aerial view of Lake Louise and the mountains of the Continental Divide. At the interpretive center staff members present a brief visitor orientation session; interpretive programs, including guided walks, are offered daily for an additional fee. Ride and dine packages also are offered. **Hours:** Daily 9-4:30, May 15-Sept. 30. **Cost:** Gondola $27.75; $13.75 (ages 6-15). Interpretive center free. **Phone:** (403) 522-3555. ▯

RECREATIONAL ACTIVITIES
Skiing
- **Lake Louise Ski Area** is 6.5 km (4 mi.) e. at 1 Whitehorn Rd. Other activities are offered. **Hours:** Daily, early Nov.-May 31. Hours vary; phone ahead. **Phone:** (403) 522-3555 or (877) 956-8473.

THE FAIRMONT CHATEAU LAKE LOUISE
403/522-3511

Historic Resort Hotel
Rates not provided

Address: 111 Lake Louise Dr T0L 1E0 **Location:** 1.8 mi (3 km) up the hill from the village. **Facility:** Surrounded by mountains and set alongside Lake Louise, the historic château-style property features a grand lobby and a lounge overlooking the lake. A variety of tastefully appointed rooms are offered. 554 units, some two bedrooms. 8 stories, interior corridors. **Parking:** on-site (fee) and valet, winter plug-ins. **Terms:** check-in 4 pm. **Amenities:** high-speed Internet (fee), safes. **Dining:** Chateau Deli, also, Chateau Deli, Fairview Dining Room, see separate listings. **Pool(s):** heated indoor. **Activities:** whirlpool, steamroom, rental canoes, recreation programs, hiking trails, exercise room, spa. **Fee:** cross country skiing, ice skating, horseback riding. **Guest Services:** valet laundry, area transportation-ski area.

The Fairmont
CHATEAU LAKE LOUISE
Enveloped by soaring mountain peaks is the magnificent The Fairmont Chateau Lake Louise.

LAKE LOUISE INN
403/522-3791

▼▼ **Hotel.** Rates not provided. **Address:** 210 Village Rd T0L 1E0 **Location:** Just w of 4-way stop. **Facility:** 247 units, some two bedrooms, efficiencies and kitchens. 2-3 stories, interior/exterior corridors. **Parking:** winter plug-ins. **Terms:** check-in 4 pm. **Dining:** 2 restaurants. **Pool(s):** heated indoor. **Activities:** whirlpools, steamroom, ice skating, hiking trails, exercise room. **Guest Services:** coin laundry, area transportation-ski area.

MOUNTAINEER LODGE
(403)522-3844

Hotel
$179-$339

Address: 101 Village Rd T0L 1E0 **Location:** Just e of 4-way stop. **Facility:** 78 units, some two bedrooms. 2 stories (no elevator), interior/exterior corridors. **Terms:** check-in 4 pm, cancellation fee imposed. **Activities:** whirlpool, steamroom. **Free Special Amenities:** continental breakfast and high-speed Internet.

MOUNTAINEER LODGE
Family owned and operating in both Jasper and Lake Louise.

POST HOTEL & SPA
(403)522-3989

▼▼▼ ▼▼▼ **Hotel** $275-$715 **Address:** 200 Pipestone Rd T0L 1E0 **Location:** Just w of main intersection; in Lake Louise village. **Facility:** Mountain decor, luxurious bathrooms, upscale rooms and fine service await at this cozy hotel. 96 units, some cabins. 3 stories, interior corridors. **Parking:** on-site and valet, winter plug-ins. **Terms:** closed 10/9-11/30, 14 day cancellation notice-fee imposed. **Amenities:** safes. **Dining:** Post Hotel Dining Room, see separate listing. **Pool(s):** heated indoor. **Activities:** whirlpool, steamroom, exercise room, spa. **Guest Services:** valet laundry.

WHERE TO EAT

CHATEAU DELI
403/522-3511

▼ Deli. Quick Serve. $9-$16 **AAA Inspector Notes:** Long lines are not uncommon at this delicatessen, which features custom-made sandwiches and hot entrées. Choose a selection from the limited wine list to complement your meal and give in to the tempting desserts. **Bar:** beer & wine. **Address:** 111 Lake Louise Dr T0L 1E0 **Location:** 1.8 mi (3 km) up the hill from the village; in The Fairmont Chateau Lake Louise. **Parking:** on-site (fee) and valet.

B L D 24 CALL ☏M

FAIRVIEW DINING ROOM
403/522-1818

New American Fine Dining
$59-$75

AAA Inspector Notes: *Historic.* Ask for a seat by the oversized windows and be rewarded with commanding views of Lake Louise and the Victoria Glacier. From start to finish, diners can expect professional and knowledgeable service amid exquisite surroundings. The tantalizing table d'hôte menu explores a diverse seasonal selection of cuisine utilizing top-notch ingredients, ranging from Quebec foie gras and Alberta bison tartare to organic king salmon and AAA Alberta beef, not to mention delectable desserts. It is a good idea to check for off-season closures. **Bar:** full bar. **Reservations:** required. **Address:** 111 Lake Louise Dr T0L 1E0 **Location:** 1.8 mi (3 km) up the hill from the village; in The Fairmont Chateau Lake Louise. **Parking:** on-site (fee) and valet.

D CALL ☏M

LAGGAN'S MOUNTAIN BAKERY & DELI
403/522-2017

Deli Quick Serve
$6-$7

AAA Inspector Notes: One of the few village restaurants not located in a hotel, the very popular bakery serves an extensive range of baked goods and freshly made sandwiches, as well as several soups of the day. **Address:** 101 Lake Louise Dr T0L 1E0 **Location:** Center; in Samson Mall.

B L D

LAKE LOUISE STATION
403/522-2600

▼▼ American. Casual Dining. $16-$34 **AAA Inspector Notes:** This restaurant is located in a beautifully restored heritage railway station that includes a 1925 dining car. Offerings from the fine menu include entrées ranging from pasta, chicken, pork, lamb and AAA aged Alberta beef. **Bar:** full bar. **Reservations:** suggested. **Address:** 200 Sentinel Rd T0L 1E0 **Location:** From 4-way stop, just s on underpass, 0.6 mi (1 km) w.

L D

MOUNT FAIRVIEW DINING ROOM
403/522-4202

Regional Canadian Fine Dining
$29-$40

AAA Inspector Notes: This restaurant is tucked behind the lounge of a historic hotel deep in the heart of the Rockies. With windows on three sides, every seat affords commanding views of the mountains and the nearby château hotel. An extraordinary wine list includes selections perfectly matched to the creative and artistic food, which blends the best seasonal and local ingredients. This place is well known for its preparations of game, most of which is raised in a ranch outside of Calgary. **Bar:** full bar. **Reservations:** suggested. **Address:** 80 Lake Louise Dr T0L 1E0 **Location:** 1.8 mi (3 km) up the hill from village; in Deer Lodge Hotel.

B L D

POST HOTEL DINING ROOM
403/522-3989

▼▼▼ ▼▼▼
Continental
Fine Dining
$14-$52

AAA Inspector Notes: Delicious food lends to this restaurant's exceptional reputation. European classics are wonderfully flavored and colorfully presented. A less extensive menu is offered at lunch. **Bar:** full bar. **Reservations:** suggested, for dinner. **Address:** 200 Pipestone Rd T0L 1E0 **Location:** Just w of main intersection; in Lake Louise village; in Post Hotel & Spa.

[B] [L] [D] [AC]

LEDUC   pop. 24,279
• Restaurants p. 166
• Part of Edmonton area — see map p. 109

BEST WESTERN PLUS DENHAM INN & SUITES
(780)986-2241

▼▼▼
Hotel
$140-$155

AAA Benefit: Members save up to 20%, plus 10% bonus points with Best Western Rewards®.

Address: 5207 50th Ave T9E 6V3 **Location:** Hwy 2 exit Leduc/City Centre, just e. **Facility:** 95 units. 2-5 stories, interior corridors. **Parking:** winter plug-ins. **Terms:** check-in 4 pm. **Amenities:** high-speed Internet. **Activities:** whirlpool, exercise room. **Guest Services:** valet and coin laundry. **Free Special Amenities: local telephone calls and high-speed Internet.** *(See ad this page.)*

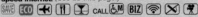

EDMONTON INTERNATIONAL AIRPORT-SUPER 8
(780)986-8898

▼▼ ▼▼ **Hotel** $119-$139 **Address:** 8004 Sparrow Cres T9E 7G1 **Location:** Hwy 2 exit N Sector Leduc. **Facility:** 64 units. 4 stories, interior corridors. **Parking:** winter plug-ins. **Amenities:** high-speed Internet. **Guest Services:** coin laundry.

HAMPTON INN & SUITES EDMONTON INTERNATIONAL AIRPORT
(780)980-9775

▼▼▼
Hotel
$149-$199

(Hampton logo) **AAA Benefit:** Members save up to 10%!

Address: 3916 84th Ave T9E 7G1 **Location:** Hwy 2 exit Edmonton International Airport, just e. **Facility:** 110 units. 4 stories, interior corridors. **Parking:** winter plug-ins. **Terms:** 1-7 night minimum stay, cancellation fee imposed. **Amenities:** high-speed Internet. **Pool(s):** heated indoor. **Activities:** whirlpool, exercise room. **Guest Services:** valet and coin laundry. **Free Special Amenities: expanded continental breakfast and airport transportation.**

HILTON GARDEN INN EDMONTON INTERNATIONAL AIRPORT
(780)612-2350

▼▼▼ **Hotel** $139-$159 **Address:** 8208 36th St T9E 0H7 **Location:** Hwy 2 exit 519, 1.1 mi (1.9 km) e. **Facility:** 165 units. 6 stories, interior corridors. **Parking:** winter plug-ins. **Terms:** check-in 4 pm, 1-7 night minimum stay, cancellation fee imposed. **Amenities:** high-speed Internet. **Pool(s):** heated indoor. **Activities:** whirlpool, exercise room. **Guest Services:** valet and coin laundry.

AAA Benefit: Unparalleled hospitality at a special Member rate.

Safety tip: Keep a current AAA/CAA Road Atlas in every vehicle

WHERE TO EAT

ZAMBELLIS RESTAURANT   780/980-9669
♥♥ ♥♥ International. Casual Dining. $11-$33 **AAA Inspector Notes:** Although it is described as a steak and pizza place, this restaurant presents a much more diverse menu. Greek food is a highlight, as are child- and senior-size portions. The large, bustling dining room features an open-concept kitchen and small sports lounge. Expect generous portions and friendly service. **Bar:** full bar. **Address:** 6210 50th St T9E 7G9 **Location:** Hwy 2 exit Leduc Business Centre (50th St). ⓛ ⓓ

LEGAL (D-6) pop. 1,225

Best known for its collection of building-sized historical murals, the small town of Legal is 50 kilometres (31 mi.) north of Edmonton. The Francophone community is named after Father Emile Legal, a French bishop, missionary and architect.

The town takes pride in its Francophone pioneer history, as is depicted by its huge outdoor murals. Subject matter ranges from the Grey Nuns—who built the first educational center for rural children—to Alexandre Lavoie, whose court battle helped French-Canadians throughout the country obtain federal services in French.

ACFA and Centralta Community Centre: 5109-46 St., P.O. Box 328, Legal, AB, Canada T0G 1L0. **Phone:** (780) 961-3665.

LETHBRIDGE (J-7) pop. 83,517,
elev. 930m/3,051'
• **Restaurants p. 168**

Founded in the 1870s, abundant agricultural resources helped Lethbridge to become one of Alberta's major feedlot and grain distribution centers. The region reportedly receives more hours of sunshine annually than any other spot in Canada and therefore requires irrigation to counterbalance the semiarid climate; more than 400,000 hectares (988,000 acres) produce crops of grain and sugar beets. Livestock, oil and gas also support the economic base.

Numerous parks and green spaces complement the city's commercial enterprises. Two popular areas are Lethbridge Nature Preserve in Indian Battle Park at 3rd Avenue S. and Scenic Drive, and Henderson Park at S. Parkside Drive and Mayor Magrath. The park has a golf course, a 60-acre lake with tennis courts, a picnic area and a campground. Rose and Japanese gardens, a stadium and an ice-skating center are included. Lethbridge holds Whoop-Up Days in summer.

Chinook Country Tourist Association: 2805 Scenic Dr. S., Lethbridge, AB, Canada T1K 5B7. **Phone:** (403) 320-1222 or (800) 661-1222.

Shopping areas: Hudson's Bay Co. anchors Lethbridge Centre, off Hwy. 3 at 200 4th Ave. S. Park Place Mall, 1st Avenue S. on Scenic Drive, has more than 100 stores and features Sears.

BREWERY GARDENS is just w. off 1st Ave. S. at Brewery Hill on Scenic Dr. Developed by a former brewery, the gardens present eight floral displays May through the first frost, as well as displays for Easter, Halloween, Remembrance Day and Christmas. The gardens are not walk-through gardens, but are a 1 hectare (2.5 acre) plot on the side of a coulee. Visitors view them across the coulee. **Hours:** Daily dawn-dusk. **Cost:** Free. **Phone:** (403) 320-1223.

GALT MUSEUM & ARCHIVES is at 502 1st St. S. at the w. end of 5th Ave. S. Housed in a 1910 building that once served as a hospital, the museum is named for the founder of North Western Coal and Navigation Co. The Discovery Hall exhibit gallery highlights the history of the Kainai people and southern Alberta. The High Level Bridge can be seen from the Viewing Gallery, which overlooks the Oldman River Valley.

Time: Allow 30 minutes minimum. **Hours:** Museum Mon.-Sat. 10-5 (also Thurs. 5-9), Sun. and holidays 1-5; closed Jan. 1, Easter, Christmas and day after Christmas. Archives Mon.-Fri. 10-4:30 (also Thurs. 4:30-9); closed statutory holidays. **Cost:** $6; $4 (students with ID and senior citizens); $3 (ages 7-17); $12 (family, two adults and two children). **Phone:** (403) 320-3898, (403) 320-4258 for recorded information, or (866) 320-3898 in Canada.

INDIAN BATTLE PARK is 1 km (.6 mi.) w. of jct. Scenic Dr. and 3rd Ave. S. under the High Level Bridge. This was the 1870 site of the last intertribal battle in North America, between the Cree and Blackfoot Indians. Within the park are attractions, self-guiding trails and playground facilities. **Hours:** Daily 7 a.m.-10:30 p.m., May-Sept.; 7 a.m.-8:30 p.m., rest of year. **Cost:** Free. 🅰

Coal Banks Interpretive Sites are scattered throughout the city. Five informational signs explain the origin of coal mining in the area. Three of the signs are in or near the park at Helen Schuler Nature Centre *(see attraction listing)*, by the Elks Recreation Centre, and between the Lodge and the Galt Museum & Archives *(see attraction listing)*. The others are at Brewery Gardens *(see attraction listing)* and on Queen Elizabeth II Hwy. near Kipp. **Hours:** Daily 24 hours. **Phone:** (403) 320-3898 (Galt Museum & Archives).

Fort Whoop-Up is on the river in Indian Battle Park, 1 km (.6 mi.) w. of jct. Scenic Dr. and 3rd Ave. S. This is a replica of a fort built in 1869 by American traders in Canadian territory. Trade in guns and illegal alcohol, in addition to reports of an American flag flying in Canada, led to the formation of the North West Mounted Police and to their march west in 1874. Wagon rides through the park are available in summer; they must be booked in advance during winter months.

Time: Allow 30 minutes minimum. **Hours:** Wed.-Mon. 10-5, June-Sept.; Wed.-Sun. noon-4, Apr.-May; Sat.-Sun. noon-4, rest of year. Guided tours are available Tues.-Sun. at 10:30, 1:30 and 2:30, July-Aug. **Cost:** June-Sept. $7; $6 (ages 65+); $5 (ages 5-18); $18.69 (family). Rest of year $5; $4 (ages 65+); $3 (ages 13-18); $2 (ages 5-12); $14 (family). **Phone:** (403) 329-0444.

Helen Schuler Nature Centre is at the n. of Indian Battle Park, 1 km (.6 mi.) w. of jct. Scenic Dr. and 3rd Ave. S. Desertlike flora and fauna are found on the coulee slopes and in cottonwood forests along the Oldman River. The center is surrounded by the 79-hectare (196-acre) Lethbridge Nature Reserve, home to the great horned owl, porcupines and white-tailed deer. Most of the park is accessible via three self-guiding trails. The center offers seasonal exhibits.

Note: The nature center is closed for renovations through spring 2014; in the interim, a temporary facility (in Indian Battle Park, south of the High Level Bridge) is available. Phone ahead for more information. Pets, bicycles, inline skates and skateboards are not permitted. **Time:** Allow 30 minutes minimum. **Hours:** Daily 10-6, June-Aug.; Tues.-Sun. 1-4, rest of year. Closed Jan. 1 and Christmas. Phone ahead to confirm schedule. **Cost:** Free. **Phone:** (403) 320-3064.

High Level Bridge spans the Oldman River in Indian Battle Park, 1 km (.6 mi.) w. of jct. Scenic Dr. and 3rd Ave. S. Reputedly this is the longest and highest bridge of its type and construction in North America. The 1909 trestle bridge extends 1.6 kilometres (1 mi.) across the coulees and is 97 metres high (300 ft.). The best place to view the bridge is from the information center/rest area on the west end of 1st Avenue, south of Hwy. 3 on Brewery Hill. **Hours:** Daily 24 hours. **Cost:** Free.

NIKKA YUKO JAPANESE GARDEN is on Mayor Magrath Dr. at 9th Ave. Five basic types of traditional Japanese gardens are incorporated into the overall design, which is one of the most authentic of its kind in North America. A pavilion, bridges, a bell tower imported from Japan and cypress wood from Taiwan are featured; paths punctuated by footbridges over ponds and streams weave through the gardens.

A variety of ongoing activities are offered. Visitors can take in art exhibitions or learn pruning and gardening techniques. Guides in traditional kimonos also conduct half-hour tours as needed. Special events, which take place on select Saturdays at 2, include traditional Japanese art demonstrations of bonsai, flower arranging, origami, sand art and calligraphy. A tea ceremony is offered Sundays at 2.

Time: Allow 1 hour minimum. **Hours:** Daily 9-5, May-Oct. Phone ahead to confirm schedule. **Cost:** $8; $5.50 (ages 65+); $4 (ages 6-17). **Phone:** (403) 328-3511.

ST. MARY'S RIVER DAM is 78 km (47 mi.) s. off Hwy. 5. This earth-filled dam is one of the largest in Canada. Water sports and a campground are available. **Phone:** (403) 382-4097 (Park Lake Provincial Park).

SOUTHERN ALBERTA ART GALLERY is at 601 3rd Ave. S. Exhibits showcase works of Canadian and international artists with an emphasis on contemporary art. **Time:** Allow 30 minutes minimum. **Hours:** Tues.-Sat. 10-5, Sun. 1-5. **Cost:** $5; $4 (students with ID and senior citizens); free (ages 0-11 and to all Sun.). **Phone:** (403) 327-8770.

GAMBLING ESTABLISHMENTS

• **Casino Lethbridge** is at 3756 2nd Ave. S. **Hours:** Daily 9:30 a.m.-3 a.m. Closed Christmas. **Phone:** (403) 381-9467.

CANADAS BEST VALUE INN   403/328-4436

▼▼ **Motel.** Rates not provided. **Address:** 1142 Mayor Magrath Dr S T1K 2P8 **Location:** Hwy 3 (Crowsnest Tr) exit Mayor Magrath Dr S, 1 mi (1.6 km) s. **Facility:** 56 units, some efficiencies. 2 stories (no elevator), exterior corridors. **Parking:** winter plug-ins. **Pool(s):** outdoor. **Guest Services:** coin laundry.

COMFORT INN   (403)320-8874

▼▼ ▼▼ **Hotel** $107-$179 **Address:** 3226 Fairway Plaza Rd S T1K 7T5 **Location:** Hwy 3 (Crowsnest Tr) exit Mayor Magrath Dr S, 1.8 mi (3 km) s, then just e on 24th Ave. **Facility:** 58 units. 4 stories, interior corridors. **Parking:** winter plug-ins. **Terms:** cancellation fee imposed. **Amenities:** high-speed Internet. **Pool(s):** heated indoor. **Activities:** whirlpool, exercise room. **Guest Services:** valet and coin laundry.

DAYS INN LETHBRIDGE   (403)327-6000

▼▼ ▼▼ **Hotel** $99-$120 **Address:** 100 3rd Ave S T1J 4L2 **Location:** Corner of 3rd Ave and Scenic Dr; center. **Facility:** 87 units. 2 stories (no elevator), interior/exterior corridors. **Parking:** winter plug-ins. **Terms:** cancellation fee imposed. **Pool(s):** heated indoor. **Activities:** whirlpool, waterslide. **Guest Services:** valet and coin laundry.

HAMPTON INN & SUITES BY HILTON LETHBRIDGE
                                         (403)942-2142

◆▼◆▼ **Hotel** $139-$189 **Address:** 4073 2nd Ave S T1J 1Z2 **Location:** Hwy 3 (Crowsnest Tr), just s on WT Hill Blvd, then just e. **Facility:** 87 units. 4 stories, interior corridors. **Parking:** winter plug-ins. **Terms:** 1-7 night minimum stay, cancellation fee imposed. **Amenities:** high-speed Internet. **Pool(s):** heated indoor. **Activities:** whirlpool, waterslide, exercise room. **Guest Services:** valet and coin laundry.

> **AAA Benefit:**
> Members save up to 10%!

HOLIDAY INN EXPRESS HOTEL & SUITES LETHBRIDGE
                                         403/394-9292

▼▼▼ **Hotel.** Rates not provided. **Address:** 120 Stafford Dr S T1J 4W4 **Location:** Hwy 3 (Crowsnest Tr) exit Stafford Dr, just s; downtown. **Facility:** 102 units. 4 stories, interior corridors. **Parking:** winter plug-ins. **Amenities:** high-speed Internet. **Pool(s):** heated indoor. **Activities:** whirlpool, waterslide, exercise room. **Guest Services:** valet and coin laundry.

HOLIDAY INN HOTEL LETHBRIDGE (403)380-5050

▼▼▼▼ **Hotel** $139-$199 **Address:** 2375 Mayor Magrath Dr S T1K 7M1 **Location:** Hwy 3 (Crowsnest Tr) exit Mayor Magrath Dr S, 1.8 mi (3 km) s, then just e on 22nd St. **Facility:** 119 units, some two bedrooms. 4 stories, interior corridors. **Parking:** winter plug-ins. **Terms:** cancellation fee imposed. **Amenities:** video games (fee). **Pool(s):** heated indoor. **Activities:** whirlpool, waterslide, exercise room. *Fee:* game room. **Guest Services:** valet and coin laundry.

LETHBRIDGE LODGE HOTEL AND CONFERENCE CENTRE (403)328-1123

▼▼▼ Hotel $109-$199 **Address:** 320 Scenic Dr T1J 4B4 **Location:** Scenic Dr at 4th Ave S; center. **Facility:** 190 units. 4 stories, interior corridors. **Parking:** winter plug-ins. **Terms:** check-in 4 pm, cancellation fee imposed. **Dining:** nightclub. **Pool(s):** heated indoor. **Activities:** whirlpool, exercise room. **Guest Services:** valet laundry. **Free Special Amenities: local telephone calls and high-speed Internet.**

PREMIER INN & SUITES (403)380-6677

▼▼ ▼▼ Hotel $100-$140 **Address:** 2225 Mayor Magrath Dr S T1K 7M1 **Location:** Hwy 3 (Crowsnest Tr) exit Mayor Magrath Dr S, 1.8 mi (3 km) s, then just e on 22nd St. **Facility:** 50 units. 4 stories, interior corridors. **Parking:** winter plug-ins. **Terms:** cancellation fee imposed. **Amenities:** high-speed Internet. **Activities:** whirlpool, exercise room. **Guest Services:** coin laundry. **Free Special Amenities: expanded continental breakfast and high-speed Internet.**

QUALITY INN & SUITES (403)331-6440

▼▼ ▼▼ Hotel $105-$195 **Address:** 4070 2nd Ave S T1J 3Z2 **Location:** Hwy 3 (Crowsnest Tr), just s on WT Hill Blvd, then just e. **Facility:** 60 units. 4 stories, interior corridors. **Parking:** winter plug-ins. **Terms:** cancellation fee imposed. **Amenities:** high-speed Internet. **Pool(s):** heated indoor. **Activities:** whirlpool, waterslide, exercise room. **Guest Services:** valet and coin laundry. **Free Special Amenities: local telephone calls and newspaper.**

RAMADA LETHBRIDGE (403)329-0555

▼▼ ▼▼ Hotel $120-$150 **Address:** 1303 Mayor Magrath Dr S T1K 2R1 **Location:** Hwy 3 (Crowsnest Tr) exit Mayor Magrath Dr S, 1.8 mi (3 km) s. **Facility:** 66 units. 9 stories, interior corridors. **Parking:** winter plug-ins. **Amenities:** safes. *Some:* high-speed Internet. **Dining:** Namu Korean & Western Grill, see separate listing. **Activities:** sauna, exercise room. **Guest Services:** valet laundry. **Free Special Amenities: expanded continental breakfast and high-speed Internet.**

SANDMAN HOTEL LETHBRIDGE (403)328-1111

▼▼ ▼▼ **Hotel** $114-$179 **Address:** 421 Mayor Magrath Dr S T1J 3L8 **Location:** Hwy 3 (Crowsnest Tr) exit Mayor Magrath Dr S, just s. **Facility:** 139 units. 8 stories, interior corridors. **Parking:** winter plug-ins. **Terms:** check-in 4 pm, cancellation fee imposed. **Amenities:** high-speed Internet. **Pool(s):** heated indoor. **Activities:** exercise room. **Guest Services:** valet laundry.

WHERE TO EAT

BAADSHAH ROYAL EAST INDIAN CUISINE 403/381-1353

▼▼▼ Indian. Casual Dining. $10-$16 **AAA Inspector Notes:** Great food can be found at this bright and cheery restaurant. A huge variety of vegetarian dishes is offered along with plenty of chicken, beef and seafood courses as well as biryani and other rice dishes. Sample the yummy tandoori chicken and the lovely Indian breads all baked in the tandoori oven (my favorite was the onion kulcha). The fish pakora appetizer is beautifully spiced so it is worth a try. Be sure to save room for one of the interesting, traditional desserts. **Bar:** beer & wine. **Reservations:** suggested, weekends. **Address:** 310 5th St S T1J 2B2 **Location:** Between 3rd and 4th aves S. **Parking:** street only.

THE CHEESECAKE CAFE 403/394-2253

▼▼▼ American. Casual Dining. $10-$26 **AAA Inspector Notes:** As might be expected, cheesecake is the signature item, and it's worth saving room for one of the lip-smacking varieties made on the premises. A huge dessert display case greets guests upon arrival. Offerings on the extensive lunch and dinner menu range from sandwiches and entree salads to pasta, pizza and seafood selections. It takes a while to get through the menu. **Bar:** full bar. **Address:** 904 2nd Ave S T1J 0C6 **Location:** At Stafford Dr and 2nd Ave S; downtown.

COCO PAZZO ITALIAN CAFE 403/329-8979

▼▼▼ Italian. Casual Dining. $8-$25 **AAA Inspector Notes:** The cozy Italian cafe has a fun, casual atmosphere. Finely tuned, guest-oriented service enhances the meals, which range from wood-fired-oven pizzas and fresh pasta to seafood and other nicely prepared meat and poultry dishes. **Bar:** full bar. **Address:** 1264 3rd Ave S T1J 0J9 **Location:** Corner of 12th St.

LIGHTHOUSE AKARI SUSHI JAPANESE RESTAURANT 403/328-4828

▼▼▼ Japanese. Casual Dining. $10-$20 **AAA Inspector Notes:** Considered one of the best in the city, this restaurant sports a simple décor with plenty of semi-private bench seating and produces a good selection of classic sushi and sashimi dishes. Chicken, beef, freshwater eel (unagi), Donburi rice bowls, sunomono octopus, shrimp salad and assorted appetizers and tempura also are offered. Service is polite and friendly. **Bar:** beer & wine. **Reservations:** suggested. **Address:** 708 3rd Ave S T1J 0H6 **Location:** Hwy 3 (Crowsnest Tr) exit Hwy 4 (Mayor Magrath Dr), 1.3 mi (2.2 km) e. **Parking:** street only.

MIRO BISTRO 403/394-1961

▼▼ Continental. Casual Dining. $12-$29 **AAA Inspector Notes:** This relaxed and comfortable bistro features a diverse menu with French, Italian and German influences that is well prepared and flavorsome. Highlights include fresh daily soup or bouillabaisse, a good selection of fine salads and appetizers of seared scallops with yam vichyssoise or steamed asparagus with shaved Parmesan. Gourmet pizza, pasta and such entrées as lamb ragout, seared wild sockeye salmon or sautéed beef tenderloin often are delivered by the chef himself. **Bar:** full bar. **Reservations:** suggested, weekends. **Address:** 212 5th St S T1J 2B3 **Location:** Hwy 3 (Crowsnest Tr) exit Stafford Dr S, just s to 1st Ave, then just w. **Parking:** street only.

NAMU KOREAN & WESTERN GRILL 403/328-5077

▼▼ Korean. Casual Dining. $9-$18 **AAA Inspector Notes:** The focus here is on Korean food with such items as madoo (fried pork dumpling) and kimbab rolls to start, and entrées of Korean-style barbecue or bibimbap (seasoned beef and vegetables on rice topped with egg). There are a few other Asian-style dishes. For the less adventurous there are such Western-style items as burgers. Servers are pleasant and the décor is pleasing with some privacy offered by the design and layout. **Bar:** beer & wine. **Address:** 1303 Mayor Magrath Dr S T1K 2R1 **Location:** Hwy 3 (Crowsnest Tr) exit Mayor Magrath Dr S, 1.8 mi (3 km) s; in Ramada Lethbridge.

PENNY COFFEE HOUSE 403/320-5282

▼ Coffee/Tea. Quick Serve. $7-$12 **AAA Inspector Notes:** Postage stamp art adorns the walls of this local coffee shop, which features a wide range of soups, salads and sandwiches. Many of the pastries are made on the premises. **Address:** 331 5th St S T1J 2B4 **Location:** Jct 3rd Ave; center. **Parking:** street only.

PLUM   403/394-1200

▼▼ Canadian. Casual Dining. $20-$39 **AAA Inspector Notes:**
Distinctive decor at this spot features warm tones, exposed brick and
huge pieces of original artwork providing a chic spot to relax. The tiny
but tempting menu features exquisite Canadian cuisine presented
with a simple artfulness. Favorites include such appetizers as shrimp
and ginger wontons or pork croquettes with chipotle cream sauce. A
fresh daily soup, pasta, fish, game hen, lamb and AAA Alberta Angus
beef tenderloin are offered. This eatery serves patrons 18 years and
older. **Bar:** full bar. **Reservations:** suggested. **Address:** 330 6th St
S T1J 2G2 **Location:** Hwy 3 (Crowsnest Tr) exit Stafford Dr S, just s
to 3rd Ave, just w, then just s; downtown. **Parking:** street only.

D CALL 🅼

RIC'S GRILL   403/317-7427

▼▼▼ Steak. Casual Dining. $14-$45 **AAA Inspector Notes:**
"Funky and modern" describes the decor and the food at the upscale
steakhouse, which bustles with activity. Steaks are well worth it, but
then again, so are the salmon, chicken and pasta dishes. A wide variety of distinctive appetizers rounds out the menu. Servers are
friendly and attentive. **Bar:** full bar. **Reservations:** suggested. **Address:** 103 Mayor Magrath Dr S T1J 4Y8 **Location:** Hwy 3
(Crowsnest Tr) exit Mayor Magrath Dr S, just s; in water tower.

L D CALL 🅼

STREATSIDE EATERY   403/328-8085

▼▼ American. Casual Dining. $10-$29 **AAA Inspector Notes:**
A local favorite for more than 20 years, this casual downtown eatery
prepares homemade comfort food from fresh ingredients. Known for
its vegetable fritters, Caesar salad, tender garlic boneless ribs, quiche
and delicious cheesecakes, guests also can try a host of tasty salads,
sandwiches, burgers, pasta and such entrees as maple pork tenderloin, Greek chicken, souvlaki and Cajun blackened salmon. The red
brick interior with street lamps and outdoor patio contribute to a
pleasant atmosphere. **Bar:** full bar. **Address:** 317 8th St S T1J 2J5
Location: At 3rd Ave and 8th St; downtown. **Parking:** street only.

L D

TREATS EATERY   403/380-4880

▼▼ American. Casual Dining. $12-$25 **AAA Inspector Notes:**
This fun, casual restaurant features unique original metal wall sculptures and artwork. On the menu are deli-style burgers, sandwiches
and quiche, as well as health-conscious dishes and more elaborate
dinner items. Fresh homemade pies and cakes await your sweet
tooth. **Bar:** full bar. **Address:** 1104 Mayor Magrath Dr T1K 2P9 **Location:** 2 mi (3.2 km) se on Hwy 4 and 5 exit Mayor Magrath Dr; at
10th Ave S. L D CALL 🅼

LLOYDMINSTER (E-9) pop. 18,032
• **Restaurants p. 170**

Lloydminster is the province's only city with one
foot planted in Saskatchewan and the other in Alberta. Four 31-metre-tall (100-ft.) border markers—
shaped like the survey stakes used during the
original survey of the border between the two
provinces—represent four themes: oil and gas, agriculture, the Barr Colonists and native North Americans. The downtown monument, erected in 1994,
denotes the city's bi-provincial status.

Many nearby lakes, regional parks and campgrounds offer opportunities for fishing, bird-watching
and other pursuits. Other recreational opportunities
include an 18-hole golf course and an aquatic leisure center with a wave pool and a waterslide.

Summer events include Canada Day celebrations, which are held July 1 in Weaver Park; Colonial
Days, a 4-day fair with a parade, agricultural exhibits
and grandstand entertainment held in mid-July; and
racing action at the Canadian Professional Chuckwagon Finals in mid-August.

Lloydminster Tourism: 5420 50th Ave., Lloydminster, AB, Canada T9V 0X1. **Phone:** (780) 875-8881
or (800) 825-6180.

BARR COLONY HERITAGE CULTURAL CENTRE
is on Hwy. 16E at 45th Ave. in Saskatchewan. This
complex of museums, galleries and changing exhibits chronicles the history of one of North America's largest organized colonizations. The center is
next to Weaver Park, where English colonists led by
Rev. Isaac Barr built their first settlement in 1903.
The facilities and exhibits include The Richard
Larsen Museum, The Fuchs Wildlife Exhibit, The Imhoff Art Collection and The Oilfield Technical Society
Heavy Oil Science Centre.

Hours: Cultural center Mon.-Sat. 9-5, Sun.
noon-8, Victoria Day weekend-Labour Day; Tues.-
Sat. 9-5, rest of year. **Cost:** $3.38; $2.88 (ages 60+
and students with ID); $2 (ages 6-12); $1.50 (ages
2-5); $10 (family). **Phone:** (306) 825-5655.

BORDER CITY PETTING ZOO is 8 km (5 mi.) e. on
Hwy. 16 in Saskatchewan. The zoo shelters bears,
exotic cattle, chickens, deer, ducks, lions, pigs,
sheep and wolves as well as a large collection of
reptiles, including crocodiles, tortoises and the zoo's
mascot, Peanut, a royal ball python. Visitors can
take a ride in a covered wagon pulled by two Percheron draft horses. **Time:** Allow 1 hour minimum.
Hours: Daily 10:30-8, May-Sept. **Cost:** $6; $5 (ages
3-16). Wagon ride $2. **Phone:** (306) 825-4472.

🍴 🏕

BUD MILLER ALL SEASONS PARK is at 2902
59th Ave. in Alberta. The park consists of 81 hectares (200 acres) of walking and bicycling trails, gardens, picnic areas, playgrounds, sports facilities and
a skateboard park. Fishing, tennis, beach volleyball,
lawn bowling and miniature golf are among the activities offered. An aquatic complex offers a wave
pool, waterslide, whirlpool, steam room and sauna.
Self-guiding interpretive trails are available. *See
Recreation Areas Chart.*

Hours: Park open daily 7 a.m.-11 p.m. Aquatic
complex hours vary with seasons and events; phone
ahead. **Cost:** Park admission free. Aquatic complex
$6.75; $5.75 (ages 13-17 and 60+); $4 (ages 6-12);
$3 (ages 2-5); $15 (family). **Phone:** (780) 875-4497,
(780) 875-4499 or (800) 825-6180. 🚫 🏕

DAYS HOTEL & SUITES LLOYDMINSTER   (780)875-4404

▼▼▼ Hotel $150-$225 **Address:** 5411 44th St T9V 0A9 **Location:** 0.5 mi (0.8 km) w on Hwy 16 from jct Hwy 17. **Facility:** 128
units. 6 stories, interior corridors. **Parking:** winter plug-ins. **Amenities:** *Some:* high-speed Internet. **Pool(s):** heated indoor. **Activities:**
exercise room. **Guest Services:** valet laundry.

🍴 🍸 🏊 BIZ 🛜 🎥 🛗 🖥 🖵

EXECUTIVE ROYAL HOTEL LLOYDMINSTER SOUTH
                                        (780)875-8884

▼▼▼ Hotel $139-$159 **Address:** 1402 50th Ave T9V 2K5 **Location:** Hwy 16, 1.9 mi (3.1 km) s. **Facility:** 80 units, some two bedrooms and efficiencies. 4 stories, interior corridors. **Parking:** winter
plug-ins. **Terms:** check-in 4 p.m. **Amenities:** high-speed Internet.
Guest Services: valet and coin laundry.

ECO 🍴 ⊕ BIZ 🛜 ✕ 🛗 🖥 🖵

HOLIDAY INN HOTEL & SUITES (780)870-5050

Hotel
$149-$190

Address: 5612 44th St T9V 0B6 **Location:** Jct Hwy 16 and 17, 0.6 mi (1 km) w. **Facility:** 100 units. 4 stories, interior corridors. **Parking:** winter plug-ins. **Terms:** check-in 4 pm. **Amenities:** high-speed Internet. **Pool(s):** heated indoor. **Activities:** whirlpool, exercise room. **Guest Services:** valet and coin laundry.

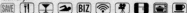

WEST HARVEST INN (780)875-6113

   Hotel $129-$169 **Address:** 5620 44th St T9V 0B6 **Location:** Jct Hwy 16 and 17, 0.6 mi (1 km) w. **Facility:** 96 units. 2 stories (no elevator), interior/exterior corridors. **Parking:** winter plug-ins. **Terms:** check-in 4 pm, cancellation fee imposed. **Amenities:** Some: high-speed Internet. **Activities:** steamrooms, exercise room. **Guest Services:** valet and coin laundry.

WHERE TO EAT

MR BILL'S FAMILY RESTAURANT 780/875-3388

Continental. Family Dining. $9-$45 **AAA Inspector Notes:** In a border town that features predominantly chain eateries, this excellent family restaurant serves burgers, sandwiches, pasta and everything from liver to lobster along with a few Greek dishes. Popular with locals, the spot offers fast, friendly service amid comfortable, trendy decor. Settle into a booth or choose a table. Diners can expect fast, friendly service. **Bar:** full bar. **Reservations:** suggested. **Address:** 5405 44th St, Suite 10 T9V 0A9 **Location:** Corner of Hwy 16 and 54th Ave; in strip mall. L D

MR MIKE'S STEAKHOUSE & BAR 780/875-6663

American. Casual Dining. $11-$28 **AAA Inspector Notes:** This bustling, casual restaurant offers such familiar choices as great burgers, steaks, ribs, chicken, salmon, noodle bowls and stir-fries. Local prairie photographs provide some visual stimulation while guests dine. **Bar:** full bar. **Address:** 2606 50th Ave T9V 2S3 **Location:** Hwy 16, 1.3 mi (2.2 km) s. L D CALL M

SPIRO'S 780/875-4241

Mediterranean. Family Dining. $9-$25 **AAA Inspector Notes:** A great place to take a family for a meal, the steak and pizza house has something for everyone on its menu. In addition to the requisites, this place serves sandwiches and some Greek dishes. **Bar:** full bar. **Reservations:** suggested. **Address:** 1408 50th Ave T9V 0Y1 **Location:** Hwy 16, 1.9 mi (3.1 km) s. L D

LONGVIEW (I-6) pop. 307

BAR U RANCH NATIONAL HISTORIC SITE is 15 km (9 mi.) s. on Hwy. 22. The site focuses on the history of ranching in Canada and the role that occupation played in the country's development. Visitors learn the history of the Bar U Ranch, from the days of open range ranching through its prominence as a breeding center for cattle and Percheron horses to its position as part of a multiple-ranch cattle operation.

The visitor center has exhibits and a presentation about the site, one of Canada's largest ranching operations 1882-1950. Guests can tour the 158-hectare (390-acre) site on foot or via a hay wagon. Historic structures include the 1882-83 saddle horse barn, blacksmith shop, stud horse barn, wintering pens, 1910 cook house, storage sheds and ranch office/post office. Ranch chores also are demonstrated.

Hours: Daily 9-5, Victoria Day-Sept. 30. **Cost:** $7.80; $6.55 (ages 65+); $3.90 (ages 6-16); $19.60 (family). **Phone:** (403) 395-2212, (403) 395-3044 or (888) 773-8888.

MARKERVILLE (G-6) pop. 42

On June 27, 1888, 50 Icelanders from the drought-plagued Dakota Territory crossed the Red Deer River to settle in Markerville, where they hoped to maintain their language and customs. For a time they produced woolen outerwear, pastries, sweets and smoked mutton in the traditional Icelandic manner.

During the 1920s, however, an increase in intermarriage with other ethnic groups and improved transportation diluted their cultural isolation. Less than 10 percent of the population is now of purely Icelandic descent, but many traditional customs are celebrated during heritage days.

HISTORIC MARKERVILLE CREAMERY MUSEUM is off hwys. 781 and 592 on Creamery Way. Begun by 34 Icelandic farmers as a cooperative in 1899 and in operation until 1972, the creamery has been restored to depict the operation as it was in the 1930s. Costumed guides offer tours. **Time:** Allow 30 minutes minimum. **Hours:** Mon.-Sat. 10-5:30, Sun. noon-5:30, May 15-Labour Day; by appointment rest of year. **Cost:** $3; $2 (ages 7-17 and 65+); $10 (family, two adults and two children). **Phone:** (403) 728-3006.

STEPHANSSON HOUSE PROVINCIAL HISTORIC SITE is 7 km (4 mi.) n., following signs. Historical displays highlight the Icelanders who founded Markerville, including Stephan G. Stephansson, a prominent poet and farmer. His home, restored to its 1927 appearance, contains original furnishings. Costumed guides give 15- to 30-minute tours and demonstrations of 1920s homemaking chores such as spinning.

Self-guiding tours are available. **Time:** Allow 30 minutes minimum. **Hours:** Daily 10-5, May 15-Labour Day. **Cost:** $3; $2 (ages 7-17 and 65+); $8 (family, two adults and children). **Phone:** (403) 728-3929 May 15-Labour Day, or (780) 427-1787 rest of year.

MEDICINE HAT (J-9) pop. 60,005,
elev. 715m/2,346'
• Restaurants p. 172

According to popular legend the name Medicine Hat originated because of a battle between Cree and Blackfoot Indians on the banks of a southern Alberta river. The Cree fought bravely until their medicine man deserted them, losing his headdress in midstream. Believing this to be a bad omen, the Cree put down their weapons and were killed by the Blackfoot. This site became known as "Saamis," which translates as "medicine man's hat."

A buried prehistoric river, or aquifer, serves as a source of unlimited cool water. More than 20 billion cubic metres (26 billion cu. yd.) of natural gas reserves inspired Rudyard Kipling in 1907 to describe Medicine Hat as possessing "all hell for a basement."

Outdoor opportunities include swimming and fishing at Echo Dale Regional Park. Circuit cowboys and spectators gather for 4 days in late July for the Medicine Hat Exhibition & Stampede.

Tourism Medicine Hat: 8 Gehring Rd. S.W., Medicine Hat, AB, Canada T1B 4W1. **Phone:** (403) 527-6422 or (800) 481-2822.

Shopping areas: Medicine Hat Mall, 3292 Dunmore Rd. S.E., features The Bay, Sears and Zellers among its more than 100 stores.

ESPLANADE ARTS & HERITAGE CENTRE, 401 First St. S.E., houses a state-of-the-art theater, art galleries featuring works by both local and national artists, a museum and archives. The museum presents audiovisual displays detailing the region's cultural heritage as well as a collection encompassing more than 25,000 artifacts. Included are pioneer items and pieces related to the area's petroleum industry.

Time: Allow 1 hour minimum. **Hours:** Exhibit galleries and box office Mon.-Fri. 10-5, Sat.-Sun. and holidays noon-5. Closed Jan. 1, Good Friday, Christmas and day after Christmas. **Cost:** Exhibit galleries $4.15; $3.10 (ages 7-17 and students with ID); free (ages 0-6 and to all Thurs.); $12.45 (family). Prices for shows vary; phone ahead. **Phone:** (403) 502-8580. 〔¶〕

MEDICINE HAT CLAY INDUSTRIES NATIONAL HISTORIC DISTRICT is at 713 Medalta Ave. S.E. Brick, tile and pottery manufacturing were prominent industries in Medicine Hat starting in the late 19th century due to a supply of clay deposits, natural gas and the availability of railroad transportation. The city once boasted several potteries, such as Medalta Potteries and Medicine Hat Potteries (later Hycroft China Ltd.). Today only the brick industry remains.

At the Medalta Potteries site, visitors can see beehive kilns constructed in the early 1920s. Artifacts and production machines also are displayed. Semiguided tours are offered in summer. **Time:** Allow 1 hour minimum. **Hours:** Daily 9:30-5, mid-May through Labour Day; Tues.-Sat. 10-4, rest of year. **Cost:** $10; $8 (ages 7-16 and 60+); $25 (family, two adults and two children). **Phone:** (403) 529-1070.

SAAMIS TEEPEE is at jct. Hwy. 1 and South Ridge Dr. Made of steel, the tepee stands approximately 20 stories high. Storyboards incorporated in the tepee stand 3.6 metres (12 ft.) high and depict Indian history. Used during the 1988 Olympics in Calgary, the tepee was moved to Medicine Hat where it now stands on Saamis Archaeological Site—the location of a 16th-century buffalo camp. **Time:** Allow 1

hour minimum. **Hours:** Daily 24 hours. **Cost:** Free. **Phone:** (403) 527-6422.

GAMBLING ESTABLISHMENTS

• **Casino by Van Shaw** is at 1051 Ross Glen Dr. S.E. **Hours:** Daily 10 a.m.-3 a.m. Closed Christmas. **Phone:** (403) 504-4584.

BEST WESTERN PLUS SUN COUNTRY   (403)527-3700

Hotel
$116-$150

AAA Benefit: Members save up to 20%, plus 10% bonus points with Best Western Rewards®.

Address: 722 Redcliff Dr T1A 5E3 **Location:** On Trans-Canada Hwy 1, 0.3 mi (0.4 km) w of jct Hwy 3, access 7th St SW. **Facility:** 122 units, some efficiencies. 2 stories (no elevator), interior/exterior corridors. **Parking:** winter plug-ins. **Terms:** 30 day cancellation notice. **Amenities:** video games (fee). *Some:* high-speed Internet. **Pool(s):** 2 heated indoor. **Activities:** sauna, whirlpools, exercise room. **Guest Services:** valet and coin laundry. **Free Special Amenities:** full breakfast.

〔SAVE〕〔ECO〕〔⟨⟩〕〔¶¶〕〔CALL〕〔&M〕〔⟳〕〔BIZ〕〔ⓦ〕〔✕〕〔▦〕
〔🛏〕〔💻〕/SOME UNITS FEE〔🐾〕〔▣〕

COMFORT INN & SUITES   (403)504-1700

Hotel
$93-$210

Address: 2317 Trans-Canada Way SE T1B 4E9 **Location:** Trans-Canada Hwy 1, just n on Dunmore Rd, then just w. Opposite Medicine Hat Mall. **Facility:** 100 units. 3 stories, interior corridors. **Parking:** winter plug-ins. **Terms:** check-in 4 pm, cancellation fee imposed. **Amenities:** high-speed Internet. **Pool(s):** heated indoor. **Activities:** whirlpool, exercise room. **Guest Services:** valet and coin laundry. **Free Special Amenities:** full breakfast and high-speed Internet.

〔SAVE〕〔ECO〕〔¶¶〕〔⟳〕〔BIZ〕〔ⓦ〕
〔🛏〕〔▣〕〔💻〕/SOME UNITS FEE〔🐾〕

Complimentary Hot Breakfast & High-Speed Internet. Pet Friendly. Close to Shopping and Restaurants.
Comfort INN & SUITES

DAYS INN-MEDICINE HAT   (403)580-3297

〔▽▽▽〕 Hotel $130-$140 **Address:** 24 Strachan Ct SE T1B 4R7 **Location:** Trans-Canada Hwy 1 exit Dunmore Rd, just sw. **Facility:** 97 units. 4 stories, interior corridors. **Parking:** winter plug-ins. **Terms:** check-in 4 pm. **Amenities:** *Some:* video games, high-speed Internet. **Pool(s):** heated indoor. **Activities:** whirlpool, waterslide, playground, limited exercise equipment. **Guest Services:** valet and coin laundry.

〔ECO〕〔¶¶〕〔⟳〕〔BIZ〕〔ⓦ〕〔🛏〕〔▣〕〔💻〕

HOLIDAY INN EXPRESS HOTEL & SUITES   (403)504-5151

〔▽▽▽〕 Hotel $159-$189 **Address:** 9 Strachan Bay SE T1B 4Y2 **Location:** Trans-Canada Hwy 1, just s on Dunmore Rd, then just e; east end of city. **Facility:** 93 units, some efficiencies. 4 stories, interior corridors. **Parking:** winter plug-ins. **Amenities:** high-speed Internet. **Pool(s):** heated indoor. **Activities:** whirlpool, waterslide, exercise room. **Guest Services:** valet and coin laundry.

〔ECO〕〔¶¶〕〔CALL〕〔&M〕〔⟳〕〔BIZ〕〔ⓦ〕〔✕〕〔🛏〕〔▣〕〔💻〕
/SOME UNITS 〔🐾〕

MEDICINE HAT LODGE RESORT, CASINO & SPA
(403)529-2222

♦♦♦ **Hotel** $114-$194 **Address:** 1051 Ross Glen Dr SE T1B 3T8 **Location:** Trans-Canada Hwy 1, just n on Dunmore Rd. **Facility:** A variety of rooms are offered at this casino hotel, including some poolside units. Children will enjoy the indoor waterslides. 222 units. 4 stories, interior corridors. **Parking:** winter plug-ins. **Terms:** check-in 4 pm. **Amenities:** video games (fee). *Some:* high-speed Internet, safes. **Dining:** M Grill, see separate listing. **Pool(s):** heated indoor. **Activities:** whirlpool, waterslide, exercise room, spa. *Fee:* game room. **Guest Services:** valet and coin laundry.

[icons] / SOME UNITS FEE [icons]

MOTEL 6 MEDICINE HAT
(403)527-1749

♦ **Hotel** $85-$95 **Address:** 20 Strachan Ct SE T1B 4R7 **Location:** Trans-Canada Hwy 1, just s on Dunmore Rd, then just w; southeast end of city. **Facility:** 79 units. 3 stories, interior corridors. **Parking:** winter plug-ins. **Terms:** check-in 4 pm. **Guest Services:** coin laundry.

[icons] / SOME UNITS [icons]

SUPER 8
(403)528-8888

♦♦ **Hotel** $96-$110 **Address:** 1280 Trans-Canada Way SE T1B 1J5 **Location:** Trans-Canada Hwy 1 at 13th Ave SE; just n off Trans-Canada Hwy 1. **Facility:** 70 units, some kitchens. 2-3 stories (no elevator), interior/exterior corridors. **Parking:** winter plug-ins. **Terms:** check-in 4 pm, cancellation fee imposed. **Pool(s):** heated indoor. **Activities:** whirlpool, exercise room. **Guest Services:** valet laundry.

[icons] / SOME UNITS FEE [icons]

WHERE TO EAT

THE GARAGE PUB AND EATERY
403/580-2588

♦♦ American. Casual Dining. $6-$12 **AAA Inspector Notes:** Located in an old gas station, the funky diner has a great collection of vintage gas and air pumps, auto and gas memorabilia and, of course, a jukebox. All the classic pub food is featured, including burgers, but fresh-made wraps and sandwiches are the way to go. Make sure you try some hubcaps (hot, seasoned potato chips), but diners won't be able to tempt a sweet tooth, as there are no desserts. In the summer there is a great patio on which to unwind. This spot caters to those 18 and older. **Bar:** full bar. **Address:** 710 Gershaw Dr SW T1A 5C8 **Location:** On Trans-Canada Hwy 1, just e of jct Hwy 3 (Crowsnest Tr). [L] [D]

HAT'S RESTAURANT
403/529-9739

♦ Chinese. Casual Dining. $10-$15 **AAA Inspector Notes:** Locals claim the wonderful Chinese restaurant as a favorite for its flavorful, reasonably priced food. Traditional foods line the all-you-can-eat buffet, as well as the a la carte menu. Also offered is a smattering of Western cuisine. Friendly servers keep drinks full and tables cleared. **Bar:** full bar. **Address:** 1701 Dunmore Rd SE T1A 1Z8 **Location:** In Crestwood Shopping Centre. [L] [D]

MADHATTER COFFEE ROASTERY
403/529-2344

♦ Coffee/Tea. Quick Serve. $3-$5 **AAA Inspector Notes:** This downtown spot takes its coffee seriously, as evidenced by the coffee roaster set in the middle of the space. A limited variety of baked goods are available at the front counter. Local musicians are sometimes on hand to serenade you while you sip your brew or loose leaf tea. **Address:** 513 3rd St SE T1A 0H2 **Location:** Jct 5th Ave; downtown. **Parking:** street only. [B] [L]

M GRILL
403/529-2222

♦♦♦ American. Casual Dining. $18-$40 **AAA Inspector Notes:** This restaurant's elegant garden setting lends to a refined and relaxed atmosphere. The menu is quite interesting with a great selection starting with such items as truffled mushroom chowder or cowboy sashimi—seared blue tenderloin with ponzu dipping sauce. Great cuts of AAA Alberta beef, along with succulent fish, like sable fish, are perfectly prepared in a variety of ways. **Bar:** full bar. **Reservations:** suggested. **Address:** 1051 Ross Glen Dr SE T1B 3T8 **Location:** Trans-Canada Hwy 1, just n on Dunmore Rd; in Medicine Hat Lodge, Casino & Spa. [D]

THAI ORCHID ROOM
403/580-8210

♦♦ Thai. Casual Dining. $14-$26 **AAA Inspector Notes:** The restaurant, which boasts a contemporary decor, prides itself on the use of the finest and freshest ingredients available. While not an extensive menu, the dishes are well made and seasoned to taste along with vibrantly colored vegetables and housemade sauces. Servers are smartly clad and friendly. **Bar:** full bar. **Address:** 3-36 Strachan Ct SE T1B 4R7 **Location:** Trans-Canada Hwy 1, just s on Dunmore Rd, then just w. [L] [D] CALL [icons]

TWIST WINE BISTRO & RESTAURANT
403/528-2188

♦♦ International. Casual Dining. $12-$24 **AAA Inspector Notes:** Guests can grab a seat at a high-top table or a comfy banquette at this delightful little bistro. With a diverse menu encompassing flavors from around the globe, appetizers include Moroccan chicken kebabs, deep-fried Manchego cheese and shrimp and crab cocktail. Entrées range from mesquite steak and pork Marsala to red Thai curry and butter chicken. Homemade desserts are scrumptious and the staff is friendly and knowledgeable. Lunch is a simpler version with the addition of gourmet panini. **Bar:** full bar. **Reservations:** suggested, weekends. **Address:** 531-3rd St SE T1A 0H2 **Location:** Between 5th and 6th aves; downtown. **Parking:** street only. [L] [D]

THE ZUCCHINI BLOSSOM MARKET AND CAFE   403/526-1630

♦ Deli. Quick Serve. $6-$12 **AAA Inspector Notes:** This attractive little café has tables set among the colorful art and shelves of enticing oils, vinegars and other gourmet groceries. The menu is focused on fresh, creative and delicious soups, salads, grilled panini and some appealing cakes, squares and cookies. Daily muffins, scones, pizza and quiche also are offered as well as great coffee and tea. Vegetarian, lactose-free and gluten-free items are available. **Address:** 62 3rd St NE T1A 5L8 **Location:** Just nw on 2nd Ave NE, then just w; just n of center. **Parking:** street only. [B] [L] CALL [icons]

MILK RIVER (K-7) pop. 811

Milk River is on the east side of Milk River Ridge, an area more than 1,200 metres (3,900 ft.) high, 39 kilometres (24 mi.) long and 29 kilometres (18 mi.) wide. Quartzite, granite and gneiss rock formations indicate prehistoric glacial action; meltwater carved the Milk River Valley 10,000 years ago. The river, formed from small streams and springs in southwest Alberta and northern Montana, joins the Missouri and Mississippi rivers to flow to the Gulf of Mexico.

Throughout the area and predominantly in Writing-on-Stone Provincial Park *(see attraction listing)* are mushroom-shaped sandstone hoodoos, odd rock formations that once led Indians to believe spirits inhabited the valley.

The Alberta Tourism Information and Interpretive Centre: General Delivery, Milk River, AB, Canada T0K 1M0. **Phone:** (800) 252-3782.

WRITING-ON-STONE PROVINCIAL PARK is 35 km (21.9 mi.) e. on Hwy. 501, 7 km (4.5 mi.) s. on Hwy. 130, then 6 km (3.9 mi.) e. on Hwy. 500, following signs. The archeological preserve overlooks the Milk River. Massive sandstone outcrops display pictographs and petroglyphs created by nomadic Shoshone and Blackfoot Indians. Fire-burned stones, broken bones, horn tools and other implements have been found at former campsites. Interpretive programs are presented mid-May to early September. *See Recreation Areas Chart.*

Note: Temperatures in excess of 40 C (104 F) are often recorded along the trail. **Hours:** Grounds daily

24 hours. Guided 90-minute tours depart Sat.-Sun. at 2, mid-May to early Sept. Tour departure times vary; phone ahead. **Cost:** Grounds free. Guided tour $12; $8 (ages 7-17); $2 (ages 0-6); $34 (family). **Phone:** (403) 647-2364. 🅰 🗙 🕾 🏛

MORLEY (H-5)

GAMBLING ESTABLISHMENTS

• **Stoney Nakoda Casino** is at Hwy. 1 & Hwy. 40. **Hours:** Slot machines Sun.-Wed. 10 a.m.-midnight, Thurs.-Sat. 10 a.m.-2 a.m. Table games Mon.-Wed. 4 p.m.-midnight, Thurs.-Fri. 4 p.m.-2 a.m., Sat. 2 p.m.-2 a.m., Sun. noon-midnight. **Phone:** (403) 881-2830 or (888) 862-5632.

STONEY NAKODA RESORT   403/881-2830
▼▼▼ Hotel $99-$169 **Address:** Jct Trans-Canada Hwy 1 and Hwy 40 T0L 1N0 **Location:** Jct Hwy 40, just s. Located in a rural area. **Facility:** The hotel features a lovely contemporary lobby with stone walls, water features and native theme art. Comfortable, well-appointed guest rooms provide a respite from the casino. 111 units. 4 stories, interior corridors. **Parking:** winter plug-ins. **Terms:** check-in 4 pm, cancellation fee imposed. **Amenities:** high-speed Internet, safes. **Dining:** 2 restaurants. **Pool(s):** heated indoor. **Activities:** whirlpool, waterslide, exercise room. **Guest Services:** area transportation-Canmore & Banff.
🐾 🍴 🍷 🚲 BIZ 📶 🔌 💲 / SOME UNITS FEE 🕾 🖴

MOUNTAIN VIEW pop. 80

ROCKY RIDGE COUNTRY LODGE   403/653-2350
▼▼ Bed & Breakfast $65-$265 **Address:** 523 2nd St N T0K 1N0 **Location:** Just n of Village Church, follow signs. **Facility:** 7 units, some cabins. 2 stories (no elevator), interior corridors. *Bath:* some shared. **Parking:** winter plug-ins. **Terms:** 7 day cancellation notice. **Activities:** whirlpool, game room.
📶 🗙 📺 🚲 / SOME UNITS 🎿 🔌 🖴 🖴

MUNDARE (E-7) pop. 855

BASILIAN FATHERS MUSEUM is 2 km (1.2 mi.) n. of Hwy. 16 on Hwy. 855. Operated by the Basilian Fathers, the museum houses exhibits about Ukrainian immigration and the religious order's work in east central Alberta and throughout Canada. **Tours:** Guided tours are available. **Hours:** Mon.-Fri. 10-4 (also Sat.-Sun. 1-5, July-Aug.). Closed major holidays. **Cost:** Donations. **Phone:** (780) 764-3887.

NANTON (I-6) pop. 2,132

BOMBER COMMAND MUSEUM OF CANADA is s. on Queen Elizabeth II Hwy. following signs. Exhibits honor Royal Canadian Air Force and Royal Air Force members who waged bombing operations during World War II. The highlight of the museum's collection is a Canadian-built Lancaster bomber.

Other bombers also are displayed, along with training planes, simulators, gun turrets and instrumentation and photographs of training aircraft in action. **Time:** Allow 1 hour minimum. **Hours:** Daily 9-5, mid-Apr. to mid-Oct.; Sat.-Sun. 10-4, rest of year. Closed Jan. 1, Christmas and day after Christmas. **Cost:** Donations. **Phone:** (403) 646-2270.

NISKU
• **Part of Edmonton area — see map p. 109**

HOLIDAY INN EXPRESS & SUITES EDMONTON INT'L AIRPORT   (780)955-1000
▼▼▼ Hotel $159-$199 **Address:** 1102 4th St T9E 8E2 **Location:** Hwy 2 exit Edmonton International Airport/Nisku Business Park (10th Ave), 0.5 mi (0.9 km) e. **Facility:** 120 units. 4 stories, interior corridors. **Parking:** winter plug-ins. **Amenities:** high-speed Internet. **Pool(s):** heated indoor. **Activities:** whirlpool, waterslide, exercise room. **Guest Services:** valet and coin laundry. **Free Special Amenities:** full breakfast and airport transportation.
SAVE 🔌 🍴 CALL 🔑 🚲 BIZ 📶 🗙 🎿 🔌 🖴 🖴

QUALITY INN & SUITES-AIRPORT   (780)955-3001
▼▼ Hotel $119-$160 **Address:** 501 11th Ave T9E 7N5 **Location:** Hwy 2 exit Edmonton International Airport/Nisku Business Park (10th Ave), 0.8 mi (1.3 km) e. **Facility:** 73 units. 2-4 stories (no elevator), interior corridors. **Parking:** winter plug-ins. **Terms:** cancellation fee imposed. **Amenities:** *Some:* high-speed Internet. **Activities:** exercise room. **Guest Services:** valet laundry.
🔌 🍴 🍷 BIZ 📶 🖴 / SOME UNITS 🔌 🖴

NORDEGG (F-4) elev. 1,453m/4,470'

NORDEGG HERITAGE CENTRE AND THE BRAZEAU COLLIERIES is .5 km s. of Hwy. 11. The center offers a small museum that documents Nordegg's heritage and coal mining industry history through a collection of photos and artifacts. In addition guided tours of the Brazeau Collieries, once Canada's largest producer of coal briquettes, depart from the museum.

The mine site and processing plant operated until 1955. Brazeau's technical aspects are explored during the 2.5-hour Technical Tour, which takes visitors to the mine portals (but not underground) and through the briquette processing plant buildings; a 1-hour overview tour also is offered some months.

Note: Guided tours of the Brazeau Collieries involve a lot of walking and climbing; in addition it is necessary to maneuver through remnants of the operation and ascend steep ladders in tight spaces. The tours are organized at the museum, but visitors must drive their own private vehicles to the mine site.

Hours: Museum daily 9-5, Victoria Day weekend to mid-Sept. Technical tours are given daily at 1, Victoria Day weekend-Aug. 31; Sat.-Sun. at 1, Sept. 1 to mid-Sept. Overview tours are given daily at 10, July-Aug. **Cost:** Museum admission by donation. Technical tour $8; $2 (ages 7-12). Overview tour $5. **Phone:** (403) 845-4444. 🍴 🏛

OKOTOKS (I-6) pop. 24,511, elev. 1,036m/3,400'
• **Hotels p. 174**
• **Part of Calgary area — see map p. 54**

Incorporated in 1904, Okotoks thrived on brick making, lumber and oil distribution in its early days. Today Okotoks is a commuter community of Calgary. The town gets its name from the Blackfoot name *okatoks,* meaning "rocks." Big Rock, 7 kilometres (4 mi.) west, is the continent's largest known glacial boulder, having been carried here during an ice age.

A popular recreational retreat, Okotoks offers such leisure pursuits as fishing and hiking. Events include a parade and Youth Festival in mid-June and the Coors Pro Rodeo and Western Art Show on Labour Day.

Okotoks & District Chamber of Commerce: 14 McRae St., P.O. Box 1053, Okotoks, AB, Canada T1S 1B1. **Phone:** (403) 938-2848.

Self-guiding tours: Heritage Walking Tour brochures are available from the information desk at The Station Cultural Centre, 53 N. Railway St.

LAKEVIEW INNS & SUITES (403)938-7400

Hotel
$125-$130

Address: 22 Southridge Dr T1S 1N1 **Location:** Hwy 2 exit 2A, 2.4 mi (4 km) s to Southridge Dr. **Facility:** 64 units. 2 stories, interior corridors. **Parking:** winter plug-ins. **Terms:** 14 day cancellation notice-fee imposed. **Amenities:** *Some:* high-speed Internet. **Activities:** exercise room. **Guest Services:** coin laundry. **Free Special Amenities:** continental breakfast and high-speed Internet.

  / SOME UNITS FEE

OLDS pop. 8,235

BEST WESTERN OF OLDS (403)556-5900

Hotel
$125

Best Western

AAA Benefit: Members save up to 20%, plus 10% bonus points with Best Western Rewards®.

Address: 4520 46th St T4H 1P7 **Location:** Hwy 2 exit 340B (Olds/Rt 27), 3 mi (5 km) w. **Facility:** 41 units. 2 stories (no elevator), interior corridors. **Parking:** winter plug-ins. **Amenities:** *Some:* high-speed Internet. **Pool(s):** heated indoor/outdoor. **Activities:** whirlpool, exercise room. **Guest Services:** complimentary laundry. **Free Special Amenities:** local telephone calls and high-speed Internet.

/ SOME UNITS

PATRICIA (I-8) pop. 108

DINOSAUR PROVINCIAL PARK is 13 km (8 mi.) n.e. via Hwy. 210, following signs. The park, declared a UNESCO World Heritage Site in 1979, covers 81 square kilometres (31 sq. mi.) of badlands and prairie along the Red Deer River. One of the richest fossil beds in the world, it contains the remains of 39 species of dinosaurs from 75 million years ago as well as crocodile, fish, flying reptile, small mammal and turtle fossils.

Five self-guiding trails explore three habitats: prairie grassland, badlands and riverside. Each offers opportunities for bird-watching. Interpretive programs are offered seasonally. *See Recreation Areas Chart.* **Time:** Allow a full day. **Hours:** Grounds daily 24 hours. **Cost:** Grounds free. Prices for interpretive programs vary; reservations are recommended. **Phone:** (403) 378-4344, or (403) 378-3700 for camping reservations.

Dinosaur Provincial Park Visitor Centre and Field Station is 13 km (8 mi.) n.e. via Hwy. 210. The interpretive center and research facility contains dinosaur skeletons, a theater, interpretive displays depicting the park's geological and paleontological

resources, and the park administration office. **Hours:** Daily 8:30-5 (also Fri.-Sat. 5-7), Victoria Day weekend-day before Labour Day; 9-4, rest of year. Phone ahead to confirm schedule. **Cost:** $3; $2.50 (ages 65+); $2 (ages 7-17); $8 (family). **Phone:** (403) 378-4342.

PEACE RIVER (A-3) pop. 6,744

Formed by the confluence of the Smoky and Heart rivers, the Peace River flows north and east of the town of the same name to Lake Athabasca and to the west into British Columbia. The area was known as "The Forks" by trappers and traders in the 1700s and "Sagitawa" (meeting of the waters) by the Cree Indians. On his historic trek across the northern continent, Alexander Mackenzie explored the region and built a fort and wintered here 1792-93.

A wooden statue honors prospector and local legend Henry Fuller "Twelve-Foot" Davis. The Vermont native, known for his generosity and hospitality, achieved great social stature when he mined $15,000 worth of gold from a 3.5-metre (12-ft.) plot between two gold claims. Davis said on his deathbed that he was not afraid to die because "I never kilt nobody, I never stole from nobody and I kept open house for travelers all my life." His grave overlooks the confluence of the Peace, Heart and Smoky rivers.

Nearby forests, rivers and streams make Peace River a popular center for year-round recreation in northern Alberta. Golfing, swimming, canoeing, downhill skiing and dog sledding are all options.

Peace River and District Chamber of Commerce: 9309 100th St., P.O. Box 6599, Peace River, AB, Canada T8S 1S4. **Phone:** (780) 624-4166.

PINCHER CREEK (K-6) pop. 3,685

Pincher Creek was established in 1878 by the North West Mounted Police as a horse farm to provide remounts for Fort Macleod *(see place listing p. 143).* The town was named for a pair of pincers that presumably were left behind by prospectors. After hearing that the area had ample grassland, other settlers soon arrived.

Pincher Creek & District Chamber of Economic Development and Information Centre: 1300 Hewetson Ave. Bay 4, P.O. Box 2287, Pincher Creek, AB, Canada T0K 1W0. **Phone:** (403) 627-5855.

KOOTENAI BROWN PIONEER VILLAGE is at 1037 Bev McLachlin Dr. Displays include more than 16,000 local relics—including military uniforms, agricultural equipment, jewelry, clothing and books about local history—in 12 historical buildings. On the grounds is the restored log cabin of George "Kootenai" Brown, an Irish adventurer and one of the region's first settlers who helped establish Waterton Lakes National Park. Other period buildings are on the grounds.

Time: Allow 2 hours minimum. **Hours:** Daily 10-8, Victoria Day weekend-Labour Day; Mon.-Fri. 10-4:30, rest of year. Closed Christmas Eve-Jan. 2. **Cost:** $10; $7 (ages 7-17 and 65+); free (ages 0-6 with adult); $25 (family). **Phone:** (403) 627-3684.

RECREATIONAL ACTIVITIES
Skiing
• **Castle Mountain Resort** is off CR 507, just w. on CR 774. **Hours:** Daily 9-4, mid-Dec. to early Apr. **Phone:** (403) 627-5101.

HERITAGE INN & HOTEL CONVENTION CENTRE PINCHER
CREEK   (403)627-5000
▼▼ ▼▼ **Hotel** $125-$269 **Address:** 919 Waterton Ave (Hwy 6) T0K
1W0 **Location:** Jct Hwy 785, just s. **Facility:** 78 units, some two bedrooms and efficiencies. 2 stories, interior corridors. **Parking:** winter plug-ins. **Terms:** cancellation fee imposed. **Amenities:** Some: high-speed Internet. **Pool(s):** heated indoor. **Activities:** whirlpool, exercise room. **Guest Services:** valet and coin laundry.

⊣⊢ 𝗬 🏊 🛜 🔋 💻 / SOME UNITS FEE 🐕 📷

RAMADA INN & SUITES   (403)627-3777
▼▼▼▼ **Hotel** $140-$219 **Address:** 1132 Table Mountain St T0K
1W0 **Location:** Hwy 3 (Crowsnest Trl), 1.3 mi (2.1 km) s on Hwy 6. **Facility:** 78 units, some efficiencies. 3 stories, interior/exterior corridors. **Parking:** winter plug-ins. **Terms:** cancellation fee imposed. **Amenities:** high-speed Internet. **Pool(s):** heated indoor. **Activities:** whirlpool, waterslide, exercise room. **Guest Services:** valet and coin laundry.

ECO ⊣⊢ 🏊 BIZ 🛜 ✕ 🔋 📷 💻
/ SOME UNITS FEE 🐕

RAVEN (G-5)

MEDICINE RIVER WILDLIFE CENTRE is 4 km (2.5 mi.) s. of Hwy. 54, then 2 km (1.2 mi.) e. The organization provides rehabilitation for injured and orphaned wildlife. It also serves as an environmental education center, offering a video presentation and displays about wildlife. A trail leads to an observation tower that affords excellent bird-watching around a 30-hectare (75-acre) marsh. **Time:** Allow 1 hour minimum. **Hours:** Daily 10-5, May 1-Labour Day; by appointment rest of year. **Cost:** Donations. **Phone:** (403) 728-3467.

RED DEER (G-6) pop. 90,564, elev. 905m/2,969'
• Hotels p. 176 • Restaurants p. 177

Red Deer's name comes from the Cree Indian word *waskasoo*, meaning "elk." Early Scottish settlers mistook the native elk for the red deer of their homeland and the name stuck. A creek and park running through Red Deer still bear the name Waskasoo.

The original settlement was several kilometres upstream on the Red Deer River where the water was shallow and easy to cross. Dr. Leonard Gaetz, a Methodist minister who arrived in 1884, persuaded the Calgary and Edmonton Railway to cross the river on his property by donating half of his land for use as a townsite. The trains came through, and the town took root at its current site. Agriculture and petroleum products are the major local industries.

City Hall Park, 48th Avenue and Ross Street, is a landscaped oasis known for its Christmas light and flower displays. West of town is Sylvan Lake, which accommodates Jarvis Bay and Sylvan Lake provincial parks *(see Recreation Areas Chart)*.

Tourism Red Deer: 101-4200 Queen Elizabeth II Hwy. (Hwy. 2), Red Deer, AB, Canada T4N 1E3. **Phone:** (403) 346-0180 or (800) 215-8946.

Self-guiding tours: A brochure outlining a walking tour of the historic downtown is available from the Red Deer Museum + Art Gallery and from the visitor information center west of Heritage Ranch in Waskasoo Park *(see attraction listings)*.

Shopping areas: Bower Place, Gaetz Avenue and 28th Street, is anchored by The Bay and Zellers. Parkland Mall, 67th Street and Gaetz Avenue, has Sears and 120 smaller shops.

ALBERTA SPORTS HALL OF FAME & MUSEUM is n. of 32nd St. by Heritage Ranch at 102-42 Queen Elizabeth II Hwy. (Hwy. 2). Alberta's sports history and heroes are celebrated through the display of 7,000 artifacts, archival material and interactive exhibits. Visitors can play an Alpine ski racer game in the Ice and Snow—the Spirit of Winter gallery or try out five different sports via a virtual computer system. Also onsite are a climbing wall and a putting green.

Time: Allow 1 hour, 30 minutes minimum. **Hours:** Daily 9-5. Closed Jan. 1, Good Friday, Easter, Christmas and day after Christmas. **Cost:** $5; $3 (ages 4-17); $12 (family, two adults and children). **Phone:** (403) 341-8614. ⊣⊢ 🏛

RED DEER MUSEUM + ART GALLERY is at 4525 47A Ave. Its collections tell the story of diverse cultures who lived in the Red Deer River Valley from the days of the First Nations to the start of modern civilization. Changing art exhibits are featured. **Hours:** Mon.-Sat. 9-4:30, Sun. noon-4:30. Closed major holidays. **Cost:** $5; $2 (ages 6-17, ages 65+ and students with ID); $10 (family). **Phone:** (403) 309-8405.

ST. MARY'S CHURCH is at 6 McMillan Ave. This ultramodern 1968 structure of unusual design is the work of architect Douglas Cardinal. Local architect Graham Leadbeater designed the parish center addition. Alois Peter Marx of Germany created the sculpture displays. **Hours:** Mon.-Fri. 8:30-4. Closed major holidays. **Cost:** Free. **Phone:** (403) 347-3114.

SUNNYBROOK FARM MUSEUM AND INTERPRETIVE CENTRE, 4701 30th St., features several structures, including a windmill, a sawmill and a replica log house. Various types of farm equipment and tools are on display throughout the 10-acre site. The highlight of the museum and interpretive center's exhibits is its large collection of vintage tractors. Chickens, goats, pigs, sheep and other barnyard animals can be seen.

Tours: Guided tours are available. **Time:** Allow 30 minutes minimum. **Hours:** Daily 10-4, Victoria Day-Labour Day; Mon.-Fri. 1-4 or by appointment, rest of year. Closed Jan. 1 and Christmas. **Cost:** Donations. **Phone:** (403) 340-3511.

WASKASOO PARK borders the Red Deer River and runs throughout the city. The park has about 100 kilometres (62 mi.) of both paved and unpaved walking trails. Also within the park are Bower Ponds; the 1911 Victorian Cronquist House Multicultural Centre; Fort Normandeau, with an interpretive center; Heritage Ranch; Kerry Wood Nature Centre, which houses nature displays; and Gaetz Lake Sanctuary, a wildlife preserve. **Hours:** Grounds daily dawn-11 p.m. **Cost:** Grounds free. **Phone:** (403) 342-8159.

GAMBLING ESTABLISHMENTS

- **Cash Casino** is at 6350 67th St. **Hours:** Daily 10 a.m.-2 a.m. (also Fri.-Sat. 2-3 a.m.). Closed Christmas. **Phone:** (403) 346-3339.
- **Jackpot Casino Ltd.** is at 4950 47th Ave. **Hours:** Daily 10 a.m.-3 a.m. **Phone:** (403) 342-5825.

RECREATIONAL ACTIVITIES

Recreational Complex

- **Collicutt Centre** is at 3031 30th Ave. **Hours:** Mon.-Fri. 5:30 a.m.-10:30 p.m., Sat. 6:30 a.m.-10:30 p.m., Sun. 6:30 a.m.-9 p.m., holidays 10-8. Closed Christmas. **Phone:** (403) 358-7529.

BEST WESTERN PLUS RED DEER INN & SUITES
(403)346-3555

Hotel
$135-$145

AAA Benefit: Members save up to 20%, plus 10% bonus points with Best Western Rewards®.

Address: 6839 66th St T4P 3T5 **Location:** Hwy 2 exit 67th St, just e. **Facility:** 92 units. 4 stories, interior corridors. **Parking:** winter plug-ins. **Amenities:** high-speed Internet. *Some:* safes. **Pool(s):** heated indoor. **Activities:** whirlpool, exercise room. **Guest Services:** valet and coin laundry. **Free Special Amenities: full breakfast and high-speed Internet.**

COMFORT INN & SUITES
(403)348-0025

Hotel $130-$170 **Address:** 6846 66th St T4P 3T5 **Location:** Hwy 2 exit 67th St, just e. Located in a commercial area. **Facility:** 88 units. 4 stories, interior corridors. **Parking:** winter plug-ins. **Terms:** cancellation fee imposed. **Pool(s):** heated indoor. **Activities:** whirlpool, waterslide, exercise room. **Guest Services:** valet and coin laundry.

DAYS INN RED DEER
(403)340-3297

Hotel $115-$140 **Address:** 1000 5001 19th St T4R 3R1 **Location:** Hwy 2 exit 394 (Gaetz Ave), just w. **Facility:** 76 units. 4 stories, interior corridors. **Parking:** winter plug-ins. **Terms:** check-in 4 pm, cancellation fee imposed. **Amenities:** high-speed Internet. *Some:* video games. **Pool(s):** heated indoor. **Activities:** whirlpool, waterslide, exercise room. **Guest Services:** valet and coin laundry.

HAMPTON INN & SUITES BY HILTON RED DEER
(403)346-6688

Hotel $129-$139 **Address:** 37400 Hwy 2, #130 T4N 5E2 **Location:** Hwy 2 exit 391 (Gasoline Alley), just w. **Facility:** 110 units. 4 stories, interior corridors. **Terms:** 1-7 night minimum stay, cancellation fee imposed. **Amenities:** high-speed Internet. **Pool(s):** heated indoor. **Activities:** whirlpool, exercise room. **Guest Services:** valet and coin laundry.

AAA Benefit: Members save up to 10%!

HOLIDAY INN EXPRESS RED DEER
403/343-2112

Hotel. Rates not provided. **Address:** 2803 50th Ave T4R 1H1 **Location:** Hwy 2 exit 394 (Gaetz Ave), 1.8 mi (2.9 km) n. **Facility:** 91 units. 2 stories, interior corridors. **Parking:** winter plug-ins. **Pool(s):** heated indoor. **Activities:** sauna, whirlpool, exercise room. **Guest Services:** valet and coin laundry.

HOLIDAY INN HOTEL AND SUITES RED DEER SOUTH
(403)348-8485

Hotel $150-$180 **Address:** 37471 Hwy 2, Gasoline Alley T4E 1B3 **Location:** Hwy 2, Gasoline Alley; on east side. **Facility:** 114 units, some two bedrooms. 5 stories, interior corridors. **Parking:** winter plug-ins. **Terms:** cancellation fee imposed. **Amenities:** high-speed Internet. **Pool(s):** heated indoor. **Activities:** whirlpool, waterslide, exercise room. **Guest Services:** valet and coin laundry.

IHOTEL 67 STREET
(403)342-6567

Hotel $129-$149 **Address:** 6500 67th St T4P 1A2 **Location:** Hwy 2 exit 67th St, 0.5 mi (0.8 km) e. **Facility:** 142 units. 4 stories, interior corridors. **Parking:** winter plug-ins. **Terms:** cancellation fee imposed, resort fee. **Amenities:** video games (fee), high-speed Internet, safes. **Pool(s):** heated indoor. **Activities:** sauna, whirlpool, spa. **Guest Services:** valet and coin laundry. **Free Special Amenities: expanded continental breakfast and high-speed Internet.**

MOTEL 6-RED DEER
(403)340-1749

Hotel $75-$109 **Address:** 900-5001 19th St T4R 3R1 **Location:** Hwy 2 exit 394 (Gaetz Ave), just w; in Southpointe Common Shopping District. Located in a commercial area. **Facility:** 79 units. 3 stories, interior corridors. **Parking:** winter plug-ins. **Terms:** cancellation fee imposed. **Amenities:** high-speed Internet. **Guest Services:** coin laundry.

QUALITY INN NORTH HILL
(403)343-8800

Hotel $129-$199 **Address:** 7150 50th Ave T4N 6A5 **Location:** Hwy 2 exit 401 (67th St), 1.7 mi (2.9 km) e, then 0.5 mi (0.8 km) n. **Facility:** 114 units. 3 stories, interior corridors. **Parking:** winter plug-ins. **Dining:** nightclub. **Pool(s):** indoor. **Activities:** whirlpool. **Guest Services:** valet and coin laundry. **Free Special Amenities: continental breakfast and high-speed Internet.**

Plan complete trip routings with the TripTik®

Travel Planner on AAA.com/CAA.ca

RED DEER LODGE HOTEL AND CONFERENCE CENTRE
403/346-8841

▽▽▽▽
Hotel
Rates not provided

Address: 4311 49th Ave T4N 5Y7 **Location:** Hwy 2 exit 394 (Gaetz Ave), 2.6 mi (4.2 km) n. **Facility:** 233 units. 3-7 stories, interior corridors. **Parking:** winter plug-ins. **Amenities:** high-speed Internet. **Pool(s):** heated indoor. **Activities:** whirlpool, exercise room, spa. **Guest Services:** valet laundry. **Free Special Amenities:** local telephone calls and high-speed Internet.

[SAVE] [ECO] [⏏] [Y] [≋] [BIZ] [🛜] [🖥] [☕]
/ SOME UNITS [🐾] [🖨]

SANDMAN HOTEL RED DEER
(403)343-7400

▽▽▽ **Hotel** $129-$149 **Address:** 2818 Gaetz Ave T4R 1M4 **Location:** 1 mi (1.6 km) n on Hwy 2A (Gaetz Ave). **Facility:** 143 units. 4 stories, interior corridors. **Parking:** winter plug-ins. **Terms:** cancellation fee imposed. **Amenities:** high-speed Internet. **Dining:** 2 restaurants, also, Moxie's Classic Grill, see separate listing. **Pool(s):** heated indoor. **Activities:** whirlpool, exercise room. **Guest Services:** valet laundry.

[ECO] [⏏] [Y] [≋] [BIZ] [🛜] [🐾] [☕]
/ SOME UNITS [FEE] [🐾] [🖥] [🖨]

SHERATON RED DEER HOTEL
(403)346-2091

▽▽▽▽
Hotel
$119-$299

(S) Sheraton HOTELS & RESORTS

AAA Benefit: Members get up to 20% off, plus Starwood Preferred Guest® bonuses.

Address: 3310 50th Ave T4N 3X9 **Location:** 1.3 mi (2 km) n on Hwy 2A (Gaetz Ave). **Facility:** 241 units, some two bedrooms. 2-14 stories, interior corridors. **Parking:** winter plug-ins. **Terms:** cancellation fee imposed, resort fee. **Amenities:** video games (fee). *Some:* high-speed Internet. **Dining:** 2 restaurants. **Pool(s):** heated outdoor. **Activities:** sauna, exercise room. **Guest Services:** valet laundry. **Free Special Amenities:** newspaper and high-speed Internet.

[SAVE] [⏏] [Y] [≋] [BIZ] [🛜] [✕] [🐾] [☕]
/ SOME UNITS [FEE] [🐾] [🖥] [🖨]

SUPER 8 CITY CENTRE
(403)358-7722

▽▽ **Hotel** $108 **Address:** 4217 50th Ave T4N 3Z4 **Location:** At 42nd St; center. **Facility:** 86 units. 4 stories, interior corridors. **Parking:** winter plug-ins. **Activities:** limited exercise equipment. **Guest Services:** valet and coin laundry.

[CALL] [🖥M] [🛜] [✕] [🐾] [🖥] [☕]

WHERE TO EAT

BISTRO ON GAETZ
403/309-0905

▽ Coffee/Tea. Quick Serve. $7-$10 **AAA Inspector Notes:** This is a cheery little spot downtown where guests can get simple and fresh sandwiches, soup, salads, cookies and squares along with a tasty cup of specialty coffee or Italian soda. **Address:** 4810 50th Ave, #1 T4N 4A3 **Location:** Between 48th and 49th sts; center. **Parking:** street only. [B] [L] CALL [🖥M]

CITIES GASTRO PUB
403/309-9989

▽▽ American. Gastropub. $9-$24 **AAA Inspector Notes:** Taking pub food to a whole new level, local organic ingredients are sourced as much as possible for the creative menu. Poutine is a specialty with build-your-own or custom choices and there is a great selection of appealing appetizers and delightful salads. Burgers are named for cities around the world with matching themes. Other entrées include butter chicken, fish tacos, jerk halibut or braised lamb shank. Over 60 beers are showcased for the aficionado. Minors are allowed until 5 pm. **Bar:** full bar. **Address:** 3301 50th Ave T4N 3T2 **Location:** 1.3 mi (2 km) n on Hwy 2A (Gaetz Ave). [L] [D] [LATE] CALL [🖥M]

EARLS RESTAURANT
403/342-4055

▽▽ American. Casual Dining. $10-$28 **AAA Inspector Notes:** Offering an experience that falls between fast food and fine dining, the fun, relaxed restaurant prepares great food at a great price. Choices range from juicy burgers, hearty sandwiches, fresh salads, wings and pizza to full entrees of steak, chops and seafood. Made-from-scratch soups and assorted breads, as well as a nice choice of wines and beers, round out the offerings. This is a fitting spot for impromptu get-togethers and festive occasions. **Bar:** full bar. **Address:** 2111 Gaetz Ave T4R 1Z4 **Location:** Hwy 2 exit 394 (Gaetz Ave), 0.9 mi (1.4 km) n. [L] [D] [LATE]

FUSION CAFE
403/348-5268

▽▽ Asian. Casual Dining. $9-$24 **AAA Inspector Notes:** This hugely popular spot, with its simple and cheery décor, has a wide variety of Vietnamese and Chinese selections as well as Japanese and Thai. Food is freshly prepared and there are some interesting presentations such as fresh pineapple rice dishes which come in a carved and decorated pineapple. Western fare features on the menu with a variety of such appetizers as chicken quesadillas or stuffed mushroom caps and some pretty impressive chicken, rib and seafood entrées. **Bar:** full bar. **Address:** 6842 50th Ave, Unit 6 T4N 4E3 **Location:** Jct Hwy 2A (Gaetz Ave) and 11 (67th St), just n; in strip mall. [L] [D] CALL [🖥M]

LA CASA PERGOLA
403/342-2404

▽▽▽ Italian. Casual Dining. $12-$38 **AAA Inspector Notes:** Warm and cozy vine-draped nooks are the setting for this popular establishment. Enjoy classic Italian soups, salads and pasta. Creative entrées include the artichoke and Asiago dip that comes with the calamari or the beef tenderloin with cremini mushroom and black truffle cream sauce. Lunch fare is a little scaled down. **Bar:** full bar. **Reservations:** suggested. **Address:** 4909 48th St T4N 1S8 **Location:** Hwy 2A N (Gaetz Ave), just e; center. **Parking:** street only.

[L] [D] CALL [🖥M]

MOHAVE GRILL
403/340-3463

▽▽ Southwestern. Casual Dining. $10-$28 **AAA Inspector Notes:** Diners will find mainly Mexican food at the funky, festive restaurant, just off the highway. However, the eclectic menu takes some chances by delving into Cajun, Southwestern and Jamaican influences. Each dish is sure to please, and the servings are plentiful. **Bar:** full bar. **Address:** 6608 Orr Dr T4P 3T5 **Location:** Hwy 2 exit 67th St, 0.3 mi (0.5 km) e; next to Service Plus Inns & Suites. [L] [D] CALL [🖥M]

MOXIE'S CLASSIC GRILL
403/340-0111

▽▽ American. Casual Dining. $10-$29 **AAA Inspector Notes:** This sleek, funky and popular restaurant presents an extensive menu of creatively prepared dishes, including pizza, pasta, rice, noodles, signature salads and burgers. Other menus include one for children and one for Sunday brunch. Lending to the upbeat, stylish decor are dark wood appointments and river rock fireplaces. **Bar:** full bar. **Address:** 2828 Gaetz Ave T4R 1M4 **Location:** 1 mi (1.6 km) n on Hwy 2A (Gaetz Ave); in Sandman Hotel Red Deer.

[B] [L] [D] [LATE] CALL [🖥M]

REDSTONE GRILL
403/342-4980

▽▽▽ New American. Fine Dining. $10-$38 **AAA Inspector Notes:** Contemporary and comfortable, the restaurant features a sleek design and a menu to match. Service is friendly, and servers like to take care of you. Food is tasty, and menu highlights include rack of lamb, sea bass, salmon and AAA beef. Live music is featured some evenings. **Bar:** full bar. **Reservations:** suggested. **Address:** 5018 45th St, #101 T4N 1K9 **Location:** Hwy 2 exit 394 (Gaetz Ave), 2.5 mi (4 km) n, then just w. [L] [D] [Ⓚ]

RUSTY PELICAN
403/347-1414

▽▽ American. Casual Dining. $10-$29 **AAA Inspector Notes:** Ask any local for a great place to eat, and this place is mentioned often. The large, loft-like dining room creates a casual atmosphere, and most tables feature a large umbrella. Many entrees amid the menu's eclectic array exhibit Asian influences. Among selections are lettuce wraps, sumptuous salmon, pasta and assorted sandwiches. **Bar:** full bar. **Address:** 2079 50th Ave T4R 1Z4 **Location:** Hwy 2 exit 394 (Gaetz Ave), just n. [L] [D] CALL [🖥M]

RIMBEY (F-5) pop. 2,378

PAS-KA-POO HISTORICAL PARK is at 5620 51st St. The park's Smithson International Truck Museum features 19 half-ton trucks, a collection of license plates, farm machinery and photographs. A restored village features 10 historic structures and two museums. A 1902 schoolhouse, a 1915 town office, a train station, a replica trapper's cabin, a 1932 homesteader's cottage, a 1908 church, a barbershop and a blacksmith shop are on-site. Each building contains artifacts and memorabilia.

Tours: Guided tours are available. **Hours:** Truck museum daily 9-4. Village daily 9-4, mid-May to early Sept. Closed Jan. 1 and Christmas. **Cost:** $5; free (ages 0-10 with adult). **Phone:** (403) 843-2004.

BEST WESTERN RIMSTONE RIDGE HOTEL
(403)843-2999

Hotel
$135-$160

AAA Benefit: Members save up to 20%, plus 10% bonus points with Best Western Rewards®.

Address: 5501 50th Ave T0C 2J0 **Location:** Hwy 20, 1.2 mi (2 km) w. **Facility:** 60 units, some efficiencies. 3 stories, interior corridors. **Parking:** winter plug-ins. **Terms:** cancellation fee imposed. **Amenities:** high-speed Internet. **Pool(s):** heated indoor. **Activities:** whirlpool, waterslide, exercise room. **Guest Services:** coin laundry. **Free Special Amenities:** full breakfast and high-speed Internet.

New Hotel near Hospital, Arena, TownCentre. Free Full Breakfast, Licensed Dining, Pet/Rider Friendly

---

ROCKY MOUNTAIN HOUSE pop. 6,933

BEST WESTERN ROCKY MOUNTAIN HOUSE INN & SUITES
403/844-3100

Hotel
Rates not provided

AAA Benefit: Members save up to 20%, plus 10% bonus points with Best Western Rewards®.

Address: 4407 41st Ave T4T 1A5 **Location:** Hwy 11 and 22, just w on 42nd Ave, then just s; east end of town. **Facility:** 81 units. 4 stories, interior corridors. **Parking:** winter plug-ins. **Amenities:** high-speed Internet. **Pool(s):** heated indoor. **Activities:** whirlpool, waterslide, exercise room. **Guest Services:** valet and coin laundry. **Free Special Amenities:** continental breakfast and high-speed Internet.

ROCKY INN EXPRESS
403/845-2871

Hotel. Rates not provided. **Address:** 4715 45th St T4T 1B1 **Location:** Hwy 11 and 22, just e on 47th Ave, then just n. **Facility:** 40 units, some kitchens. 2 stories (no elevator), interior corridors. **Parking:** winter plug-ins. **Guest Services:** valet laundry.

SUPER 8
(403)846-0088

Hotel $135-$155 **Address:** 4406 41st Ave T4T 1J6 **Location:** Hwy 11 and 22, just w on 42nd Ave, then just s; east end of town. **Facility:** 97 units, some efficiencies. 3 stories, interior/exterior corridors. **Parking:** winter plug-ins. **Amenities:** high-speed Internet. *Some:* video games. **Pool(s):** heated indoor, waterslide, exercise room. **Guest Services:** valet and coin laundry.

ROCKY MOUNTAIN HOUSE NATIONAL HISTORIC SITE (G-5)

In west central Alberta about 80 kilometres (50 mi.) west of Red Deer on Hwy. 11 and 6 kilometres (4 mi.) west from the town of Rocky Mountain House via Hwy. 11A, following signs, Rocky Mountain House National Historic Site tells the story of the fur trade era that existed 1799-1875. The site, on the banks of the North Saskatchewan River, protects the remains of four fur-trading posts.

Both the North West Co. and Hudson's Bay Co. were expanding in an attempt to reach the area's native peoples. The two rivals arrived here within a week of each other in 1799, their goal being to stimulate trade with the Kootenai, who were on the western side of the Rocky Mountains. The Blackfoot people blocked the planned trade. Rocky Mountain House traded with eight different aboriginal groups in its 76 years of operation.

Well-known cartographer and fur trader David Thompson used Rocky Mountain House for a time as a base for exploring routes over the mountains. Thompson was the first person of European descent to cross Howse Pass, accomplishing this feat in 1807.

Trade competition remained intense between the two companies until their merger in 1821. The influx of illegal whiskey traders into southern Alberta in 1869 disrupted trade with the aboriginal people, and in 1875 the last of the four posts was abandoned.

Two walking trails along the North Saskatchewan River and through a scenic wooded area connect the remains of the four forts. Eight listening stations and illustrated interpretive panels are spaced along the trail system. A 30-minute walk leads past the two later forts, the reconstructed chimneys at the last fort site, a replica flat-bottom York boat, a Red River cart and a fur press. A longer 90-minute walk travels to the first two forts built at Rocky Mountain House, passing tepees, the 1967 Centennial Canoe Race exhibit and a buffalo viewing area. Visitors often can see deer, coyotes, bluebirds and hawks along the trails.

The visitor center contains exhibits of trade items and aboriginal objects and a theater presenting films. Interpretive programs and special events are offered daily during July and August. Bicycle rentals are available.

The visitor center is open daily 10-5, Victoria Day weekend-Sept. 30. Admission is $3.90; $3.40 (ages

65+); $1.90 (ages 6-16); $9.80 (family, two adults and four children). **Cards:** AX, MC, VI. **Phone** (403) 845-2412.

ROSEBUD (H-7) pop. 88

A pioneer ranching settlement founded in the 1880s, Rosebud has become a thriving cultural center. The community participates in the activities of Rosebud School of the Arts. Rosebud Theatre offers dinner and theater entertainment at matinees and evening performances Wednesday through Saturday from March through December. Matinees also are offered on Sundays from July through August; phone (403) 677-2350 or (800) 267-7553.

Among Rosebud's historical buildings is an early 20th-century Chinese laundry, which now is home to Centennial Museum. The museum displays local memorabilia and an array of western Canadiana. Works by Alberta artists are exhibited in Akokiniskway Art Gallery and other shops along the town's self-guiding historical walking tour.

ST. ALBERT (E-6) pop. 61,466
• **Hotels & Restaurants map & index p. 124**
• **Part of Edmonton area — see map p. 109**

Alberta's oldest non-fortified community, St. Albert was established in 1861. The city is the site of the first cathedral west of Winnipeg. Its founder—Father Albert Lacombe—devoted 62 years to acting as a peacemaker between the Cree and the Blackfoot and as a negotiator between the Blood Indians and the Canadian Pacific Railway.

St. Albert lays claim to western Canada's largest outdoor farmers market, which operates every Saturday July through September, as well as an interactive water play park and a vibrant arts community. Grain Elevator Park, 4 Meadowview Dr., features two grain elevators from the early 20th century and a replica of a 1920s-era train station. The site is open Wed.-Sun. 10-5, late May-Labour Day; phone (780) 419-7354 for more information.

The Rainmaker Rodeo & Exhibition takes place the fourth weekend in May. The International Children's Festival—a showcase for performers in theater, music, dance, storytelling and puppetry—is traditionally held the weekend after the rodeo.

St. Albert Business and Tourism Development: 71 St. Albert Tr., St. Albert, AB, Canada T8N 6L5. **Phone:** (780) 459-1631.

FATHER LACOMBE CHAPEL is just w. of Queen Elizabeth II Hwy. on St. Vital Ave. The log chapel, built by Father Albert Lacombe and his Métis helpers in 1861, is said to be Alberta's oldest building. Guided tours explain the importance of Lacombe and the St. Albert Roman Catholic Mission to the French/Métis community as well as the priest's role as spiritual leader, peacemaker and negotiator in the 1860s. Conducted in English and French, tours include the chapel, crypt, cemetery and grotto. **Time:** Allow 30 minutes minimum. **Hours:** Tours are

given daily by request 10-6, May 15-Labour Day. **Cost:** Donations. **Phone:** (780) 459-7663, or (780) 431-2300 in the off-season.

MUSÉE HERITAGE MUSEUM is w. of Queen Elizabeth II Hwy. at 5 St. Anne St. in St. Albert Place. Exhibits are dedicated to the heritage of St. Albert. Changing displays are featured. **Time:** Allow 1 hour minimum. **Hours:** Tues.-Sat. 10-5 (also Sun. 1-5, Sept.-June). Closed major holidays. **Cost:** Donations. **Phone:** (780) 459-1528.

BEST WESTERN PLUS THE INN AT ST. ALBERT
(780)470-3800

Hotel
$145-$160

AAA Benefit: Members save up to 20%, plus 10% bonus points with Best Western Rewards®.

Address: 460 St. Albert Tr T8N 5J9 **Location:** Hwy 2 (St. Albert Tr), just w at Lennox Dr. **Facility:** 90 units. 4 stories, interior corridors. **Parking:** winter plug-ins. **Terms:** check-in 4 pm. **Amenities:** high-speed Internet. **Pool(s):** heated indoor. **Activities:** whirlpool, exercise room. **Guest Services:** valet and coin laundry. **Free Special Amenities: local telephone calls and high-speed Internet.**

/ SOME UNITS FEE

WHERE TO EAT

RIC'S GRILL 780/460-6602

 Steak. Casual Dining. $14-$38 **AAA Inspector Notes:** "Funky and modern" describes the decor and the food at the upscale steakhouse, which bustles with activity. Steaks are well worth it, but then again, so are the salmon, chicken and pasta dishes. A wide variety of distinctive appetizers rounds out the menu. Servers are friendly and attentive. **Bar:** full bar. **Reservations:** suggested, weekends. **Address:** 24 Perron St T8N 1E7 **Location:** Hwy 2 N (St. Albert Tr), just e at St. Anne St; corner of St. Anne and Perron sts.

RIVER HOUSE GRILL 780/458-2232 **(36)**

 Regional Canadian. Casual Dining. $24-$38 **AAA Inspector Notes:** Located in a picturesque, converted Victorian red house on the banks of the Sturgeon River, there is a real effort to use local, fresh ingredients and the mix of flavors does not overpower. Food preparation is as close to flawless as one can get. The atmosphere is friendly but intimate with hardwood floors, a cozy dining room with art decorated walls and scenic outdoor patio. **Bar:** full bar. **Reservations:** suggested. **Address:** 8 Mission Ave T8N 1H4 **Location:** Jct Hwy 2 (St. Albert Rd); downtown.

SHERWOOD PARK pop. 65,475
• **Restaurants p. 180**
• **Part of Edmonton area — see map p. 109**

BEST WESTERN PLUS SHERWOOD PARK INN & SUITES
(780)416-7800

Hotel
$135-$150

AAA Benefit: Members save up to 20%, plus 10% bonus points with Best Western Rewards®.

Address: 300 Lakeland Dr T8H 0N6 **Location:** Hwy 16 exit 400B westbound or 400C eastbound (Broadmoor Blvd), 0.9 mi (1.5 km) s, then just e. **Facility:** 90 units. 4 stories, interior corridors. **Parking:** winter plug-ins. **Terms:** check-in 4 pm, cancellation fee imposed. **Amenities:** high-speed Internet. **Pool(s):** heated indoor. **Activities:** whirlpool, exercise room. **Guest Services:** coin laundry. **Free Special Amenities: expanded continental breakfast and high-speed Internet.**

    CALL

COAST EDMONTON EAST HOTEL   (780)464-4900

WWWW **Hotel** $139-$159 **Address:** 2100 Premier Way T8H 2G4 **Location:** Hwy 16 exit Broadmoor Blvd, 0.6 mi (1 km) sw. Next to Millennium Place Recreation Centre. **Facility:** 258 units, some two bedrooms. 5 stories, interior corridors. **Parking:** winter plug-ins. **Terms:** check-in 4 pm, cancellation fee imposed. **Amenities:** high-speed Internet. **Activities:** exercise room. **Guest Services:** valet and coin laundry.

FRANKLIN'S INN   (780)467-1234

WW WW
Hotel
$129-$169

Address: 2016 Sherwood Dr T8A 3X3 **Location:** At Granada Blvd. Next to shopping complex. **Facility:** 40 units. 3 stories, interior corridors. **Parking:** winter plug-ins. **Terms:** 3 day cancellation notice. **Dining:** Sawmill Prime Rib & Steak House, see separate listing. **Guest Services:** valet laundry. **Free Special Amenities:** full breakfast and high-speed Internet.

HOLIDAY INN EXPRESS & SUITES   (780)417-3388

WWW WW
Hotel
$143-$169

Address: 11 Portage Ln T8H 2R7 **Location:** Hwy 16 exit Broadmoor Blvd, 0.6 mi (1 km) sw. **Facility:** 90 units. 4 stories, interior corridors. **Parking:** winter plug-ins. **Terms:** check-in 4 pm. **Amenities:** high-speed Internet. **Activities:** whirlpool, exercise room. **Guest Services:** valet laundry. **Free Special Amenities:** expanded continental breakfast and high-speed Internet.

MAINSTAY SUITES EAST EDMONTON/SHERWOOD PARK   (780)570-8080

WWW WW
Extended Stay
Hotel
$149-$169

Address: 201 Palisades Way T8H 0N3 **Location:** Hwy 16 exit 403 (Sherwood Dr), 0.9 mi (1.5 km) s. **Facility:** 118 efficiencies. 4 stories, interior corridors. **Parking:** winter plug-ins. **Amenities:** high-speed Internet. **Activities:** exercise room. **Guest Services:** valet and coin laundry. **Free Special Amenities:** expanded continental breakfast and airport transportation.

RAMADA LIMITED-EDMONTON EAST/SHERWOOD PARK   (780)467-6727

WWW WWW **Hotel** $120-$150 **Address:** 30 Broadway Blvd T8H 2A2 **Location:** Hwy 16 exit Broadmoor Blvd, 1.2 mi (2 km) s. **Facility:** 63 units. 4 stories, interior corridors. **Parking:** winter plug-ins. **Amenities:** safes. **Activities:** exercise room. **Guest Services:** valet and coin laundry.

SUPER 8 SHERWOOD PARK/EDMONTON AREA   (780)464-1000

WW WW **Hotel** $129-$144 **Address:** 26 Strathmoor Dr T8H 2B6 **Location:** Hwy 16 exit Broadmoor Blvd, just sw. Next to truck stop. **Facility:** 120 units. 2 stories, interior corridors. **Parking:** winter plug-ins. **Amenities:** video games (fee). **Dining:** 2 restaurants. **Activities:** exercise room. **Fee:** game room. **Guest Services:** coin laundry.

WHERE TO EAT

CAFE DE VILLE   780/449-4765

WWWW International. Casual Dining. $12-$35 **AAA Inspector Notes:** Expertly prepared cuisine inspired by global influence is found at this charming little spot. Menu examples could be a lovely spinach salad with goat feta, mission figs, macadamia nuts and strawberry rhubarb peppercorn dressing or Thai dumplings with a tangy dressing to start. Follow that with herb-crusted pizza, gourmet pasta and such specialties as beef filet with roast garlic demi, sun-dried cherries and a pepper-herb crust. This is a must save room for dessert spot. **Bar:** full bar. **Reservations:** suggested. **Address:** 25 Sioux Rd T8A 4C7 **Location:** From Baseline Rd, just s on Broadmoor Blvd; in small strip mall.

CAFE HAVEN   780/417-5523

W Coffee/Tea. Quick Serve. $8-$11 **AAA Inspector Notes:** This bright and cheery spot is really popular with locals. Super sandwiches and salads with fresh and local ingredients are found as well as a delicious daily soup. A breakfast bagel, sandwich and wraps are served until 11 a.m. but guests might just want to settle for one of the delightfully sinful cinnamon buns. There also is a very good weekend brunch menu. **Bar:** beer & wine. **Address:** 9 Sioux Rd T8A 4C7 **Location:** From Baseline Rd, just s on Broadmoor Blvd; in small strip mall.

FULTON MARKET BURGER COMPANY   780/467-8388

W Burgers. Quick Serve. $7-$14 **AAA Inspector Notes:** The AAA prime rib burgers here are thick and juicy. Just grab an order form at the entry and choose from signature burgers including the smoky barbecue and ultimate mushroom and onion. Or build your own choosing from a wide variety of toppings and add such sides as crispy sea salt fries, onion rings or coleslaw. Alternatives are the bison, chicken, vegetarian and turkey burgers or a simple Caesar salad. Thick delicious milkshakes made with Chapman's premium ice cream also are great. **Address:** 160 Broadway Blvd, #144 T8H 2A3 **Location:** From Baseline Rd, just n.

JOEY RESTAURANTS   780/449-1161

WWW American. Casual Dining. $13-$35 **AAA Inspector Notes:** The cuisine blends Mediterranean and Asian cooking styles and emphasizes finger foods for sharing. Those who aren't big fans of tapas can consider full meal offerings centered on steaks and chops. **Bar:** full bar. **Address:** 360-222 Baseline Rd T8H 1S8 **Location:** Between 17th St NE and Sherwood Dr.

SAWMILL PRIME RIB & STEAK HOUSE   780/467-1144

WWW WW
Steak
Casual Dining
$12-$29

AAA Inspector Notes: This large steakhouse features smart-looking rooms showcasing a fireplace, water wall and a wall of neat looking wood cutouts. The newest addition to a long-established local group, this spot offers a great Alberta AAA steak and prime rib menu. If you don't fancy steak, there are lobster, king crab, chicken, salmon and veal dishes. They also have one of the best salad bars I have seen in a long while with more than twenty salads, fresh oysters, peel and eat shrimp and cheeses. **Bar:** full bar. **Reservations:** suggested, weekends. **Address:** 2016 Sherwood Dr T8A 3X3 **Location:** At Granada Blvd; in Franklin's Inn.

THE SOUP & SANDWICH CO.   780/467-8530

W Soup Sandwiches. Quick Serve. $5-$8 **AAA Inspector Notes:** Crowds often line out the front door in this cozy little restaurant, which seems lost in the generic-looking commercial plaza near the Holiday Inn Express. Patrons get good value for the dollar in the varied homemade soups, made-to-order sandwiches and salads. **Address:** 2833 Broadmoor Blvd, Unit 144 T8H 2H3 **Location:** Hwy 16 exit Broadmoor Blvd, 0.6 mi (1 km) s.

SUMO SUMO SUSHI BAR & GRILL   780/416-7866

WW WW Sushi. Casual Dining. $9-$24 **AAA Inspector Notes:** This gem of a restaurant appeals to those with sumo appetites but who do not want to pay sumo prices. A wonderful selection of traditional and nouveau sushi is available, as is a teppanyaki bar. Locals frequent this place. **Bar:** full bar. **Reservations:** suggested, weekends. **Address:** 220 Lakeland Dr, #300 T8H 1S8 **Location:** Jct Hwy 16 and 21, just s, then just e.

VICKY'S BISTRO WINE BAR   780/417-1750

▼▼▼ International. Family Dining. $8-$34 **AAA Inspector Notes:** Having moved to trendy new digs, this well-known family-run restaurant still serves excellent homemade food. Patrons can choose from such Greek specialties as saganaki and souvlaki or try Atlantic salmon with lemon-dill Hollandaise, chicken penne Alfredo or AAA steaks. They also have an Enomatic wine preservation system with a selection of premium wines available from one ounce and up. **Bar:** full bar. **Reservations:** suggested. **Address:** 100 501 Festival Ave T8A 4X3 **Location:** From Sherwood Dr, just e; next to Strathcona Public Library. [L] [D] CALL [♿M]

SLAVE LAKE (C-5) pop. 6,782

Slave Lake is on the southeast shore of Lesser Slave Lake, the second-largest lake in Alberta. Popular with bird-watchers and recreationalists, the expansive body of water is easily accessible by automobile. Six kilometres (4 mi.) north on Hwy. 88, Lesser Slave Lake Provincial Park *(see Recreation Areas Chart)* hugs the lake's east shore and provides snowshoeing and cross-country skiing opportunities in winter as well as camping and hiking during the summer. The park also is home to the Lesser Slave Lake Bird Observatory and the Boreal Centre for Bird Conservation. Riverboat Daze takes place the second week in July, and the Alberta Open Sand Sculpture Championship is held the third weekend in July.

In May 2011 a devastating fire that originated in a nearby forest ravaged the Slave Lake community, necessitating the complete evacuation of the town. At the time, the displacement of nearly 7,000 residents was reported to be the largest in Alberta's history. Although about a third of Slave Lake was destroyed in the fire—which gutted the town hall, library and radio station—the community is steadfastly rebuilding, encouraged by an outpouring of material and financial support from across Canada.

HOLIDAY INN EXPRESS HOTEL & SUITES
                                    (780)849-4819

Hotel
$147-$167

Address: 1551 Main St SE T0G 2A0 **Location:** Hwy 2, just s. **Facility:** 96 units. 4 stories, interior corridors. **Parking:** winter plug-ins. **Terms:** resort fee. **Amenities:** high-speed Internet.
Activities: whirlpool, exercise room. **Guest Services:** valet and coin laundry. **Free Special Amenities: full breakfast and high-speed Internet.**

[SAVE] [†+] CALL [♿M] [BIZ] [📶] [▨] [🛏] [🖥] [💻]

LAKEVIEW INNS & SUITES   (780)849-9500

Hotel
$121-$190

Address: 1550 Holmes Tr SE T0G 2A3 **Location:** Hwy 2, just n; east end of town. **Facility:** 68 units. 3 stories, interior corridors. **Parking:** winter plug-ins. **Terms:** cancellation fee imposed. **Amenities:** high-speed Internet. **Activities:** whirlpool, exercise room. **Guest Services:** valet and coin laundry. **Free Special Amenities: expanded continental breakfast and high-speed Internet.**

[SAVE] [ECO] [BIZ] [📶] [🛏] [🖥] [💻] / SOME UNITS FEE [🐾]

WHERE TO EAT

TAO RESTAURANT & LOUNGE   780/849-6658

▼▼▼ Asian. Casual Dining. $10-$32 **AAA Inspector Notes:** Upon entry, guests will be greeted by the warmth of a fireplace at this trendy spot. The menu tempts with a huge variety of Asian favorites as well as some steaks and burgers. Later in the evening, the restaurant opens up to the nightclub. **Bar:** full bar. **Address:** 109 2nd Ave NW T0G 2A1 **Location:** Just e of Main St; downtown. **Parking:** street only. [L] [D] CALL [♿M]

SMOKY LAKE (D-7) pop. 1,022

[SAVE] **VICTORIA SETTLEMENT PROVINCIAL HISTORIC SITE** is 10 km (6 mi.) s. on Hwy. 855 and 6 km (3.6 mi.) e. on Victoria Tr. Settlement began in 1862 as a Methodist mission. A Hudson's Bay Co. fur-trading post soon followed, and by the beginning of the 20th century the village was known as Pakan. Guided tours are offered of the 1906 Methodist Church and the 1864 Clerk's Quarters, which is furnished with pioneer articles. A video presentation describes local history.

Time: Allow 1 hour minimum. **Hours:** Daily 10-5, May 15-Labour Day. **Cost:** $3; $2 (ages 65+); $1.50 (ages 7-17); $8 (family, two adults and children). **Phone:** (780) 656-2333.

SPRUCE GROVE (E-6) pop. 26,171
• Part of Edmonton area — see map p. 109

Olympic gold medalist Jennifer Heil, a freestyle skier, hails from Spruce Grove, as does Carla MacLeod, a retired member of Canada's national women's hockey team. Located just 35 kilometres (22 mi.) west of downtown Edmonton, the city also attracts athletic day-trippers from the provincial capital with such impressive recreational features as the state-of-the-art TransAlta Tri Leisure Centre, the adjacent Bruce and Jeannette Fuhr Sports Park, and Heritage Grove Park, a network of bicycle paths that connects several neighborhoods.

Other local draws include the Horizon Stage Performing Arts Centre, 1001 Calahoo Rd., (780) 962-8995, and the Spruce Grove Grain Elevator Museum, 100 Railway Ave., home to one of the last wood grain elevators in the province. Guided tours of the historical grain elevator are offered May through September. The museum also comprises the Spruce Grove Archives; phone (780) 960-4600.

SPRUCE VIEW (G-5) pop. 163

Founded at the turn of the 20th century, Spruce View was named for its omnipresent spruce trees. Such recreational opportunities as boating, camping, fishing and picnicking are available at Dickson Dam-North Valley Provincial Recreation Area.

Trust your vehicle to AAA/CAA Approved Auto Repair facilities

DICKSON DAM VISITOR CENTRE is 6 km (4 mi.) e. on Hwy. 54, following signs. Perched on a hillside, the center offers a bird's-eye view of Dickson Dam. Exhibits and a short video focus on the dam's history and topography. **Hours:** Tues. and Fri. 8:15-3:30, June-Oct. **Cost:** Free. **Phone:** (403) 227-1106.

STETTLER (G-7) pop. 5,748

Stettler is named after Carl Stettler, a Swiss immigrant who arrived in Alberta in 1903. He helped establish a Swiss community known as Blumenau not far from present-day Stettler. With the arrival of the railroad, the Stettler settlement was established and the residents of Blumenau relocated there.

ALBERTA PRAIRIE RAILWAY EXCURSIONS depart the train station at 47th Ave. and 46th St. Steam- and diesel-powered rail excursions are offered through the Alberta countryside in vintage passenger coaches. Trips last 5 to 6 hours; all include a buffet-style meal at the destination in the summer or on-board dining during the winter. Theme trips also are scheduled.

Hours: Trains operate Sat.-Sun. and selected weekdays, May-Oct. Departure times vary. **Cost:** Fares $90-$155; $65-$130 (ages 11-17); $40-$130 (ages 4-10). Prices may vary. Reservations are required. **Phone:** (403) 742-2811, or (800) 282-3994 in Canada.

STONY PLAIN (E-6) pop. 15,051
• Part of Edmonton area — see map p. 109

Plentiful water and abundant fish and game attracted the first settlers to the region in 1881. By 1892 the name of the community itself was changed from Dog Creek to Stony Plain. The Stony Plain of today is an agricultural community.

Murals depicting historical remembrances, events and pioneers prominent in the early settlement of Stony Plain have been painted by local artists on 26 buildings in town. Memories of an early 1900s Christmas from a child's point of view are the basis for one mural, while another shows the multiculturalism of the area's early residents. The Heritage Walk Murals can be seen on a walking tour.

Town of Stony Plain: 4905 51st Ave., Stony Plain, AB, Canada T7Z 1Y1. **Phone:** (780) 963-2151.

MULTICULTURAL HERITAGE CENTRE AND OPPERTSHAUSER HOUSE is at 5411 51st St. Restored buildings feature local history and art exhibits, programs and events. The center, built as the area's first high school in 1925, offers regional archives as well as a living-history museum, a demonstration farm, an art gallery and the 1910 Oppertshauser House. **Time:** Allow 30 minutes minimum. **Hours:** Daily 9-4. Closed Christmas Eve-Jan. 2. A country market takes place Sat. 9-1, May-Oct. **Cost:** Donations. **Phone:** (780) 963-2777. ⑪

BEST WESTERN SUNRISE INN & SUITES

(780)968-1716

Hotel
$151-$221

AAA Benefit: Members save up to 20%, plus 10% bonus points with Best Western Rewards®.

Address: 3101 43rd Ave T7Z 1L1 **Location:** Hwy 16A (Township Rd 530), just s at S Park Dr, then just e. **Facility:** 110 units. 4 stories, interior corridors. **Parking:** winter plug-ins. **Terms:** check-in 4 pm, cancellation fee imposed. **Amenities:** safes. *Some:* high-speed Internet. **Pool(s):** heated indoor. **Activities:** whirlpool, steamroom, waterslide, exercise room. **Guest Services:** valet and coin laundry. **Free Special Amenities:** expanded continental breakfast and local telephone calls.

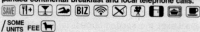

MOTEL 6 STONY PLAIN

780/968-5123

Hotel. Rates not provided. **Address:** 66 Boulder Blvd T7Z 1V7 **Location:** Just off Hwy 16A (Township Rd 530). **Facility:** 78 units, some kitchens. 2 stories, interior corridors. **Parking:** winter plug-ins. **Amenities:** high-speed Internet. **Guest Services:** coin laundry.

RAMADA INN & SUITES

(780)963-0222

Hotel $111-$139 **Address:** 3301 43rd Ave T7Z 1L1 **Location:** Hwy 16A (Township Rd 530), just s on S Park Dr, then just e. **Facility:** 88 units, some two bedrooms, efficiencies and kitchens. 2 stories (no elevator), interior/exterior corridors. **Parking:** winter plug-ins. **Terms:** check-in 4 pm, cancellation fee imposed. **Amenities:** safes. **Pool(s):** heated indoor. **Activities:** sauna, whirlpool. **Guest Services:** valet and coin laundry.

STRATHMORE pop. 12,305
• Part of Calgary area — see map p. 54

BEST WESTERN STRATHMORE INN

403/934-5777

Hotel
Rates not provided

AAA Benefit: Members save up to 20%, plus 10% bonus points with Best Western Rewards®.

Address: 550 Hwy 1 T1P 1M6 **Location:** Trans-Canada Hwy 1, jct Hwy 817; center. **Facility:** 81 units, some two bedrooms. 3 stories (no elevator), interior corridors. **Parking:** winter plug-ins. **Terms:** check-in 4 pm. **Pool(s):** heated indoor. **Activities:** whirlpool, exercise room. **Guest Services:** coin laundry. **Free Special Amenities:** local telephone calls and high-speed Internet.

DAYS INN & SUITES

(403)934-1134

Hotel
$130-$150

Address: 400 Ranch Market T1P 0B2 **Location:** Trans-Canada Hwy 1, just n at Lakeside Blvd (Centre St). **Facility:** 102 units. 4 stories, interior corridors. **Parking:** winter plug-ins. **Amenities:** high-speed Internet. **Pool(s):** heated indoor. **Activities:** whirlpool, waterslide, exercise room. **Guest Services:** coin laundry. **Free Special Amenities:** full breakfast and high-speed Internet.

TRAVELODGE STRATHMORE

(403)901-0000

Hotel $129-$144 **Address:** 350 Ridge Rd T1P 1B5 **Location:** Just n of Trans-Canada Hwy 1; at Ridge Rd. **Facility:** 121 units, some two bedrooms and kitchens. 3 stories, interior corridors. **Parking:** winter plug-ins. **Terms:** check-in 4 pm, cancellation fee imposed. **Amenities:** high-speed Internet. **Pool(s):** heated indoor. **Activities:** whirlpool, waterslide, exercise room. **Guest Services:** valet and coin laundry.

STRATHMORE STATION RESTAURANT & PUB   403/934-0000

WWW ◆ American. Family Dining. $12-$33 **AAA Inspector Notes:** Families and groups alike will enjoy the nostalgia of the Strathmore Station, which has a medley of comfort foods, including pizza, steak, pasta and oversize salads. Railway enthusiasts will enjoy the train decor, complete with black-and-white photos from the railway days, large colorful murals and a special caboose dining car. **Bar:** full bar. **Address:** 380 Ridge Rd T1P 1B5 **Location:** Trans-Canada Hwy 1, just w of jct Hwy 817. [B] [L] [D]

SYLVAN LAKE pop. 12,327

BEST WESTERN PLUS CHATEAU INN   (403)887-7788

Hotel
$150-$190

AAA Benefit: Members save up to 20%, plus 10% bonus points with Best Western Rewards®.

Address: 5027 Lakeshore Dr T4S 1R3 **Location:** Jct Hwy 11 and 781 (50th St), 1.9 mi (3.1 km) n, just e. **Facility:** 72 units. 4 stories, interior corridors. **Parking:** winter plug-ins. **Amenities:** high-speed Internet. **Pool(s):** heated indoor. **Activities:** whirlpool, exercise room. **Guest Services:** valet and coin laundry. **Free Special Amenities: continental breakfast and high-speed Internet.**

[SAVE] [🛏️] [🛥️] [BIZ] [🛜] [✕] [🚪] [📷] [💻] / SOME UNITS FEE [🐾]

CHATEAU SUITES AT SYLVAN BAY   (403)887-6699

WWW ◆ Condominium $169-$310 **Address:** 5100 Lakeshore Dr, #1 T4S 2L7 **Location:** Waterfront. Jct Hwy 11 and 781 (50th St), 1.9 mi (3.1 km) n. **Facility:** Next to a large water park, these fully equipped suites have a modest but pleasing décor. Most impressive is the view of the lake from your balcony, which is furnished with a gas grill, table and chairs. 61 condominiums. 5 stories, exterior corridors. **Terms:** check-in 4 pm, 2 night minimum stay - seasonal and/or weekends, cancellation fee imposed. **Amenities:** high-speed Internet. **Activities:** exercise room. *Fee:* massage. **Guest Services:** complimentary laundry. [🛏️] [🚪] [📷] [💻] / SOME UNITS [🐾]

BAY VIEW CAFE   403/887-8524

WWW American. Quick Serve. $8-$12 **AAA Inspector Notes:** Simple and tasty soups, salads, sandwiches, quiche and in-house baked goods along with smoothies and specialty coffees are found at this cute little spot featuring counter service. Prime seating is along the ledge top at the windows where you have good views of the lake. **Address:** 5100 Lakeshore Dr, #9 T4S 2L7 **Location:** Jct Hwy 11 and 781 (50th St), 1.9 mi (3.1 km) n. [B] [L] CALL [📱M]

SMUGGLER'S INN   403/887-0213

WWW ◆ Steak. Casual Dining. $20-$38 **AAA Inspector Notes:** Life-size pirate figures greet you as you reach the top of the stairs where you find a dark, cozy space with oversize captain's chairs. Sample the all-you-can-eat soup and salad bar with any entrée. The menu centers on steak, prime rib and chicken. **Bar:** full bar. **Reservations:** suggested. **Address:** 5000 Lakeshore Dr T4S 2L7 **Location:** Jct Hwy 11 and 781 (50th St), 1.9 mi (3.1 km) n. [D]

TABER pop. 8,104

HERITAGE INN HOTEL & CONVENTION CENTRE TABER   (403)223-4424

WWW WWW Hotel $100-$160 **Address:** 4830 46th Ave T1G 2A4 **Location:** Jct Hwy 3 and 36 S, 1.5 mi (2.5 km) se. **Facility:** 74 units. 2 stories (no elevator), interior corridors. **Terms:** check-in 4 pm, cancellation fee imposed. **Amenities:** *Some:* high-speed Internet. **Activities:** sauna, whirlpool. *Fee:* game room.

[🍴] [🍷] [🛜] [💻] / UNITS FEE [🐾] [🚪] [📷]

SUPER 8 TABER   (403)223-8181

WWW WWW Hotel $96-$107 **Address:** 5700 46th Ave T1G 2B1 **Location:** Jct Hwy 3 and 36 S, 0.5 mi (0.9 km) se. **Facility:** 48 units. 2 stories (no elevator), interior/exterior corridors. **Parking:** winter plug-ins. **Guest Services:** coin laundry.

[🛜] [🚪] [💻] / SOME UNITS FEE [🐾]

THREE HILLS pop. 3,198

BEST WESTERN DIAMOND INN   (403)443-7889

Hotel
$120-$125

AAA Benefit: Members save up to 20%, plus 10% bonus points with Best Western Rewards®.

Address: 351 7th Ave N T0M 2A0 **Location:** Hwy 21 and 27, 1.1 mi (1.9 km) w. **Facility:** 52 units. 3 stories, interior corridors. **Parking:** winter plug-ins. **Amenities:** high-speed Internet. **Activities:** whirlpool, exercise room. **Guest Services:** valet and coin laundry. **Free Special Amenities: expanded continental breakfast and high-speed Internet.**

[SAVE] [BIZ] [🛜] [🚪] [📷] [💻] / SOME UNITS FEE [🐾]

TROCHU (G-6) pop. 1,072

ST. ANN RANCH TRADING CO. PROVINCIAL HISTORIC SITE is .5 km (.3 mi.) s. on King George Ave. This reconstructed 1905 French settlement contains restored historic houses and reproductions of period buildings. The site includes a small school, post office, hospital and chapel.

An interpretive center contains displays recounting the history of the settlement, which was founded by aristocratic officers from the French cavalry. **Time:** Allow 30 minutes minimum. **Hours:** Museum and interpretive center open daily 9-9. **Cost:** $2. **Phone:** (888) 442-3924 in Canada.

TWIN BUTTE pop. 10

TWIN BUTTE COUNTRY GENERAL STORE   403/627-4035

WWW Mexican. Casual Dining. $10-$15 **AAA Inspector Notes:** Find this small but cheerful Mexican-themed diner halfway between Pincher Creek and Waterton on the Cowboy Trail. Head to the back of the country store to order from a menu of simple, yet tasty, Western and Mexican dishes. **Bar:** full bar. **Reservations:** suggested. **Address:** Box 461 T0K 2J0 **Location:** 16.9 mi (27 km) s of Dinchis Creek, on Hwy 6 (Cowboy Tr). [B] [L] [D]

VALLEYVIEW pop. 1,761

WESTERN VALLEY INN   780/524-4000

WWW WWW Motel $79-$139 **Address:** 5402 Highway St T0H 3N0 **Location:** Just w of jct Hwy 43 and 49. **Facility:** 50 units, some efficiencies. 2 stories (no elevator), interior corridors. **Parking:** winter plug-ins. **Amenities:** high-speed Internet. **Activities:** limited exercise equipment. **Guest Services:** coin laundry. **Free Special Amenities: full breakfast and high-speed Internet.**

[SAVE] [🏊] [🍴] [🍷] [BIZ] [🛜] [🚪] [📷] [💻] / SOME UNITS FEE [🐾]

VEGREVILLE (E-7) pop. 5,717

The center of eastern Alberta's Ukrainian culture, Vegreville has the distinction of possessing the largest known *pysanka*, or Easter egg, in the world. The 9.4-metre-high (31-ft.) egg, decorated to reflect Ukrainian folk art, was erected in 1975 for the centennial of the formation of the Royal Canadian Mounted Police in Alberta.

The egg's bronze, gold and silver design, made from more than 3,500 pieces of aluminum, illustrates the local settlers' struggles and the protection the mounted police provided them. Queen Elizabeth and Prince Phillip unveiled the plaque next to the giant egg in Elks/Kinsmen Park during their visit in 1978. The Ukrainian Pysanka Festival is held in early July.

Town of Vegreville Parks, Recreation & Tourism: 4509 48th St., P.O. Box 640, Vegreville, AB, Canada T9C 1K8. **Phone:** (780) 632-3100.

WAINWRIGHT (F-8) pop. 5,925

WAINWRIGHT & DISTRICT MUSEUM is at 1001 1st Ave. Displays include items and memorabilia relating to family life in the town since its founding in 1908. The histories of a local prisoner of war camp and the now defunct Buffalo National Park also are presented. The museum is housed in an original Canadian National Railway station built in 1929. **Time:** Allow 30 minutes minimum. **Hours:** Daily 9-5, May-Aug.; 1-5, rest of year. Closed Jan. 1, Good Friday and Christmas. **Cost:** $5; $3 (ages 6-17). **Phone:** (780) 842-3115.

BEST WESTERN WAINWRIGHT INN & SUITES
(780)845-9934

Hotel
$140

AAA Benefit: Members save up to 20%, plus 10% bonus points with Best Western Rewards®.

Address: 1209 27th St T9W 0A2 **Location:** Jct Hwy 14 and 41, just e. **Facility:** 85 units. 4 stories, interior corridors. **Parking:** winter plug-ins. **Terms:** check-in 4 pm. **Amenities:** high-speed Internet. **Pool(s):** heated indoor. **Activities:** whirlpool, exercise room. **Guest Services:** valet and coin laundry. **Free Special Amenities: continental breakfast and local telephone calls.**

SAVE CALL &M ⊇ BIZ 🛜 💺 🖪 🖻 🖵
/SOME UNITS FEE 🐾

WHERE TO EAT

THE HONEY POT EATERY & PUB   780/842-4094

▼▼ American. Casual Dining. $11-$28 **AAA Inspector Notes:** There is something for everyone at this pub where a good meal with an excellent value go hand-in-hand with tasty sauces and spicing. Choose from fresh bread, classic appetizers, great salads, bison or beef burgers, an assortment of chicken dishes, wild salmon, Pacific cod, Certified Angus beef and bison steaks. Be sure to save room for one of the creative desserts. Choose a seat inside the attractive dining room, in the livelier pub or on the seasonal patio. **Bar:** full bar. **Reservations:** suggested. **Address:** 823 2nd Ave T9W 1C5 **Location:** Hwy 14, 0.8 mi (1.3 km) sw on Main St, just nw at clock tower. **Parking:** street only. L D CALL &M

WARNER (K-7) pop. 331, elev. 1,017m/3,336'

DEVIL'S COULEE DINOSAUR HERITAGE MUSEUM is in the County of Warner Administration Building w. off Hwy. 4, following signs. Embryonic fossils in their nests were found on the Milk River Ridge in 1987. The specimens were from a hadrosaur (a duck-billed dinosaur); the location was the first nesting site found in Canada. A 2-hour walking tour allows for first-hand inspection of the dinosaur egg site, where ongoing excavations often yield new scientific discoveries. Museum displays feature a hadrosaur nest, embryo, fossils and models of dinosaurs. Also included is an exhibit about early area settlement.

Note: The guided hikes are organized at the museum, but visitors must drive their own private vehicles to the dig site. The nesting site is in a primitive area not suitable for small children or those with mobility or medical problems. Allow 30 minutes minimum for the museum, 3 hours minimum for tour and museum.

Hours: Museum daily 9-5, July 1-Labour Day; Wed.-Mon. 9-5, Victoria Day-June 30; by appointment rest of year. Tours of the nesting site are given daily at 10 and 1, July 1-Labour Day; Sat.-Sun. at 10 and 1, Victoria Day-June 30 (weather permitting). Phone ahead to confirm schedule. **Cost:** Museum $4; free (ages 0-5); $12 (family). Tour of dig site $12; $30 (family). Combination ticket $14; $38 (family). Reservations are recommended for the tour. **Phone:** (403) 642-2118.

◤GEM WATERTON LAKES NATIONAL PARK (K-5)

Elevations in the park range from 1,279 metres (4,200 ft.) in the town of Waterton Park to 2,920 metres (9,580 ft.) at Mount Blakiston. Refer to CAA/AAA maps for additional elevation information.

The most direct approach into the national park from the south is over Chief Mountain International Hwy. (SR 17/Hwy. 6) from Glacier National Park in Montana; the park also is accessible via Hwy. 5 from Cardston or Hwy. 6 from Pincher Creek. Covering 505 square kilometres (195 sq. mi.), Waterton Lakes National Park adjoins Glacier National Park. Together the two parks form Waterton-Glacier International Peace Park. The customs office is open daily 7 a.m.-10 p.m., June 1-Sept. 1; 9-6, Victoria Day weekend-May 31 and Sept. 2-30.

For thousands of years this was aboriginal territory, where the Kootenai and Blackfoot were the primary aboriginal tribes. In 1858 Lt. Thomas Blakiston became the first European on record to explore the area; he named the lakes for Charles Waterton, an 18th-century English naturalist.

Local rancher Fred Godsal, American journalist and naturalist George Bird Grinnell and others lobbied their respective governments in the late 19th century to set aside parts of this wilderness area for future generations. They succeeded, and Waterton Lakes and Glacier national parks were established in 1895 and 1910, respectively.

Waterton Lake is divided into three parts: Upper, Middle and Lower Waterton lakes. The townsite, the location of park headquarters, is on the north shore of Upper Waterton Lake, which juts 4.7 kilometres (3 mi.) into Glacier National Park. The mountains on either side tower 900 to 1,200 metres (3,000 to 4,000 ft.) above the lake. Mount Crandell rises to the north; Sofa Mountain and Vimy Peak are east across the lake.

Wildlife ranging from squirrels and marmots to deer and bears inhabits the park. A small herd of plains bison is in the buffalo paddocks on the northern boundary, 1.6 kilometres (1 mi.) north of the Waterton River Bridge on Hwy. 6. Thousands of waterfowl visit the lakes during spring and fall migrations. Hunting is prohibited.

Among the many rare wildflowers that grace prairie and mountain landscapes are bear grass, pygmy poppy and mountain lady-slipper. Evergreens blanket the slopes and peaks below mountain goat country at an altitude of about 2,286 metres (7,500 ft.).

General Information and Activities

The park is open all year, though most concessions operate only from Victoria Day weekend through the second Monday in October. Red Rock Canyon, 15 kilometres (11 mi.) northwest of Waterton, offers a .7-kilometre (.4-mi.) loop trail along the canyon and a 1-kilometre (.6-mi.) trail to Blakiston Falls. Riding stables are 2.5 kilometres (1.5 mi.) north of town near the main entrance road; horses can be rented.

Just north of the townsite is an 18-hole public golf course that is open daily, Victoria Day weekend through the second Monday in October. A free four-court tennis facility is on Cameron Falls Drive.

The park visitor center, at the junction of the entrance road and Prince of Wales Road, is open daily 8-7, mid-June through Labour Day; 9-5, mid-May to mid-June; 9-4:30, day after Labour Day-second Mon. in Oct. Interpretive display centers at Cameron Lake and the Waterton townsite describe the park's subalpine forest and the history of the International Peace Park. All are open daily 24 hours.

Illustrated talks are given every evening at 8 at the park's indoor theaters. There also are guided walks and other interpretive programs; phone (403) 859-5133.

Those wishing to camp in Waterton's backcountry campsites must obtain a park use permit ($9.80) at the visitor center. You also can register your outing with the Park Warden Service.

Hunting is prohibited. Anglers need a fishing license, which can be obtained along with fishing regulations at the park offices, information center, campgrounds, from park wardens and at service stations in the townsite. Motorboats are permitted on both Upper and Middle Waterton lakes; water skiing, however, is permitted only on Middle Waterton Lake. *See Recreation Areas Chart.*

ADMISSION to the park is $19.60 per private vehicle (up to seven persons). Otherwise admission per person is $7.80; $6.80 (ages 65+); $3.90 (ages 6-16). An annual pass, valid at all Canadian national parks, is available.

PETS must be leashed at all times while in the park.

ADDRESS inquiries to the Superintendent, Waterton Lakes National Park, P.O. Box 200, Waterton Park, AB, Canada T0K 2M0; phone (403) 859-2224.

WATERTON INTER-NATION SHORELINE CRUISE CO. departs from the Waterton Marina. Narrated sightseeing trips lasting 2.25 hours cross Waterton Lake, which is surrounded by the majestic scenery of the Rocky Mountains. From early June through late September the cruise includes a 30-minute stop at Goat Haunt in Montana; passengers also may stay at Goat Haunt for daylong hiking trips and return on a later boat. Hikes to Crypt Lake also may be enjoyed, with a shuttle picking up and dropping off patrons at Crypt Landing mid-May to early October.

Note: A passport must be presented by any passenger choosing to disembark at Goat Haunt for the day-long hiking trips. **Hours:** Sightseeing trips landing at Goat Haunt depart daily at 10, 1 and 4, early June-late Sept. (also at 7 p.m., July-Aug.). Non-landing sightseeing trips depart daily at 10 and 2:30, early May-early June and late Sept.-second Mon. in Oct. Crypt Landing shuttle trips depart daily at 9 and 10, mid-May to early Oct. **Cost:** Sightseeing trip $40; $18 (ages 13-17); $12 (ages 4-12). Crypt Landing shuttle $20; $10 (ages 4-12). **Phone:** (403) 859-2362.

RECREATIONAL ACTIVITIES
Horseback Riding
- **Alpine Stables** is in Waterton Lakes National Park, following signs. **Hours:** Daily 9-5, July-Aug.; 10-5, May-Sept. Phone ahead to confirm schedule. **Phone:** (403) 859-2462, or (403) 653-2449 in the off-season.

WATERTON PARK pop. 88

ASPEN VILLAGE INN (403)859-2255

Motel
$89-$259

Address: 111 Windflower Ave T0K 2M0 **Location:** Center. **Facility:** 51 units, some two bedrooms, efficiencies, kitchens and cottages. 1-2 stories (no elevator), exterior corridors. **Terms:** closed 10/8-4/30, check-in 4 pm, cancellation fee imposed. **Activities:** playground. **Free Special Amenities: high-speed Internet.**

BAYSHORE INN RESORT & SPA (403)859-2211

Motel
$122-$282

Address: 111 Waterton Ave T0K 2M0 **Location:** Center. **Facility:** 70 units, some two bedrooms. 2 stories (no elevator), interior/exterior corridors. **Terms:** closed 10/10-5/3, check-in 4 pm, 3 day cancellation notice-fee imposed. **Amenities:** safes. **Dining:** Bayshore Lakeside Chophouse, see separate listing, nightclub. **Activities:** hiking trails, spa. **Guest Services:** coin laundry. **Free Special Amenities: local telephone calls and early check-in/late check-out.**

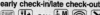

CRANDELL MOUNTAIN LODGE (403)859-2288

Hotel
$99-$245

Address: 102 Mt. View Rd T0K 2M0 **Location:** Center. **Facility:** 17 units, some two bedrooms, efficiencies and kitchens. 2 stories (no elevator), interior corridors. **Terms:** closed 10/8-3/31, check-in 4 pm, cancellation fee imposed. **Activities:** hiking trails. **Free Special Amenities: high-speed Internet.**

WATERTON GLACIER SUITES (403)859-2004

Hotel
$99-$292

Address: 107 Windflower Ave T0K 2M0 **Location:** Center. **Facility:** 26 units. 2 stories (no elevator), exterior corridors. **Terms:** check-in 4 pm, 3 day cancellation notice-fee imposed. **Amenities:** safes. **Free Special Amenities: local telephone calls and early check-in/late check-out.**

WATERTON LAKES RESORT (403)859-2150

Hotel
$149-$289

Address: 101 Clematis Ave T0K 2M0 **Location:** Center. **Facility:** 80 units, some efficiencies and kitchens. 2 stories (no elevator), interior/exterior corridors. **Terms:** check-in 4 pm, cancellation fee imposed. **Dining:** Vimy's Lounge & Grill, see separate listing. **Pool(s):** heated indoor. **Activities:** sauna, whirlpool, steamroom, hiking trails, game room. **Free Special Amenities: high-speed Internet.**

PRINCE OF WALES HOTEL 403/859-2231

fyi Not evaluated. **Address:** Waterton Lakes National Park T0K 2M0 **Location:** Through park gates, 4 mi (6.4 km) sw, then just se. Facilities, services, and décor characterize a mid-scale property. **(See ad this page.)**

WHERE TO EAT

BAYSHORE LAKESIDE CHOPHOUSE 403/859-2211

American. Casual Dining. $10-$40 **AAA Inspector Notes:** Diners can often view deer grazing outside the windows of the dining room, which boasts a wonderful view of Waterton Lake. The menu lists a variety of Alberta beef, salmon, trout and chicken dishes. **Bar:** full bar. **Reservations:** suggested. **Address:** 111 Waterton Ave T0K 2M0 **Location:** Center; in Bayshore Inn Resort & Spa.

B L D

BEL LAGO RISTORANTE 403/859-2213

Italian. Casual Dining. $9-$30 **AAA Inspector Notes:** Contemporary Italian cuisine featuring local and organic ingredients is offered at this smart and casual bistro. Starters include calamari with scallion aioli or Bel Lago salad with robiola cheese and an orange-honey vinaigrette. Follow with homemade pasta or such entrees as lamb osso buco or game hen with fig and hazelnut stuffing. A simpler version of the menu is offered at lunch. The sheltered side patio is popular in seasonal weather. **Bar:** full bar. **Reservations:** suggested. **Address:** 110 Waterton Ave T0K 2M0 **Location:** Center. **Parking:** street only. L D

▼ See AAA listing this page ▼

PIZZA OF WATERTON   403/859-2660

▽ Pizza. Casual Dining. $8-$17 **AAA Inspector Notes:** This little spot has just a few tables inside and some picnic table seating on the patio. They dish up some tasty pizza and calzone made with their own flavorful tomato sauce as well as soup, salad, simple appetizers and a build-your-own rotini. Check the daily homemade dessert to see if you need to leave some room for that sweet delight. **Bar:** full bar. **Address:** 302 Windflower Ave T0K 2M0 **Location:** Center. **Parking:** street only. [D]

VIMY'S LOUNGE & GRILL   403/859-2150

▽▽▽ American. Casual Dining. $11-$35 **AAA Inspector Notes:** This restaurant sits on the second level above the lounge and there are great views of the mountains from the big picture windows. A number of familiar dishes are found on the menu but they have some distinctive elements and ingredients sourced from as little as 20 minutes away. One of the most interesting items on the menu is the yak-crossed beef which can be prepared in different ways. If the meatballs are on the menu, they are quite delicious. **Bar:** full bar. **Reservations:** suggested. **Address:** 101 Clematis Ave T0K 2M0 **Location:** Center; in Waterton Lakes Resort. [B] [L] [D]

WIENERS OF WATERTON   403/859-0007

▽ Hot Dogs. Quick Serve. $6-$9 **AAA Inspector Notes:** Started by two enterprising and engaging young men, hot dogs are taken to a new level with superior quality wieners from local and afar, as well as their own homemade falafel version. Buns are baked daily on premise, dogs are grilled to order and they have a good variety of toppings. The best crispy yam fries I have ever tried are served with a choice of their homemade gourmet dips. And they now offer breakfast dogs and coffee. In the height of season, line-ups go out the door all day. **Address:** 301 Windflower Ave T0K 2M0 **Location:** Center. **Parking:** street only. [B] [L] [D]

ZUM'S EATERY & MERCANTILE   403/859-2388

▽▽ American. Casual Dining. $8-$22 **AAA Inspector Notes:** Attached to a gift shop, this restaurant has a bright and cheerful decor with checkered tablecloths and an extensive collection of license plates from around the world. The menu consists of simple and ample portions of soups, salads, burgers, sandwiches and their famous country-fried chicken. Dinner sees the addition of a few more entrées such as Salisbury steak and schnitzel. A full hot breakfast features omelets, corned beef hash and eggs, waffles and French toast. **Bar:** full bar. **Address:** 116 Waterton Ave T0K 2M0 **Location:** Center. **Parking:** on-site (fee). [B] [L] [D]

WESTEROSE

VILLAGE CREEK COUNTRY INN   780/586-0006

▽▽ Hotel $129-$199 **Address:** 15 Village Dr, RR 2 T0C 2V0 **Location:** Hwy 2 exit 482, 17.5 mi (28 km) w on Hwy 13; in Village at Pigeon Lake. **Facility:** 35 units, some two bedrooms, kitchens and condominiums. 2 stories, interior/exterior corridors. **Parking:** winter plug-ins. **Terms:** 3 day cancellation notice. **Activities:** whirlpool, spa.

[icons] / SOME UNITS FEE

WHERE TO EAT

DAISY MCBEANS ICE CREAM & COFFEE   780/586-0771

▽ American. Quick Serve. $6-$10 **AAA Inspector Notes:** This is a cute little place to stop for a quick breakfast or lunch. Soup, salads and fresh sandwiches made with in-house roasted meats are offered as well as hot dogs, smokies and their own creation of a taco in a bag. Fabulous homemade fruit and cream pies and other treats will satisfy the sweet tooth along with a big selection of ice cream. Guests also can shop for cool candy and other nifty gift items. **Address:** 22 Village Dr, RR 2 T0C 2V0 **Location:** Hwy 2 exit 482, 17.5 mi (28 km) w on Hwy 13; in Village at Pigeon Lake. [B] [L] CALL [M]

ECO CAFE   780/586-2627

▽▽ International. Casual Dining. $9-$15 **AAA Inspector Notes:** In the Village of Pigeon Lake development, near the beaches, this intimate café is easy to miss among other coffee shops and gift stores. However, it is worth finding for its cheerfully decorated dining area and standard mix of coffee and treats, in addition to flavorful regional cuisine made from organically grown and raised foods, ranging from elk to bison. Owners raise their own lamb, pork and chicken, while other ingredients are raised down the road. **Bar:** wine only. **Address:** 10 Village Dr T0C 2V0 **Location:** Hwy 2 exit 482, 17.5 mi (28 km) w on Hwy 13. [B] [L] [D]

WESTLOCK   pop. 4,823

BEST WESTERN WESTLOCK   780/349-4102

Hotel
Rates not provided

AAA Benefit: Members save up to 20%, plus 10% bonus points with Best Western Rewards®.

Address: 10520 100th St T7P 2C6 **Location:** Jct Hwy 18 and 44, just e. **Facility:** 59 units. 2 stories (no elevator), interior/exterior corridors. **Parking:** winter plug-ins. **Activities:** whirlpool, exercise room. **Guest Services:** valet laundry. **Free Special Amenities:** full breakfast and high-speed Internet.

[SAVE] [icons] / SOME UNITS FEE

WETASKIWIN (F-6) pop. 12,525

• Hotels p. 188 • Restaurants p. 188

Wetaskiwin got its name from a Cree phrase meaning "the hills where peace was made." It is believed that a peace agreement between the warring Cree and Blackfoot tribes was made in the area. A stop between the growing outposts of Calgary and Edmonton, Wetaskiwin flourished due to its proximity to the Canadian Pacific Railway; the city was incorporated in 1906. Today Wetaskiwin boasts progressive commercial, agricultural and industrial ties, while a restored downtown area highlights the community's historic roots.

Wetaskiwin City Hall: 4705 50th Ave., P.O. Box 6210, Wetaskiwin, AB, Canada T9A 2E9. **Phone:** (780) 361-4417.

 [GEM] [SAVE] **REYNOLDS-ALBERTA MUSEUM** is 2 km (1.2 mi.) w. on Hwy. 13 to 6426 40th Ave. Displays interpret the history of ground and air transportation, agriculture and industry in Alberta. Audiovisual presentations, displays and demonstrations supplement the actual operation of vintage automobiles, bicycles, and farm and industrial machinery. One area features a reproduction of a small drive-in theater, complete with old films, metal speakers and seats shaped like the back end of 1950-era automobiles.

The museum also is home to Canada's Aviation Hall of Fame, situated in a separate exhibit building. Vintage aircraft are displayed. Canadians who have contributed significantly to aviation history are recognized. **Time:** Allow 2 hours minimum. **Hours:** Daily 10-5, Victoria Day-Labour Day; Tues.-Sun. and Mon. holidays 10-5, rest of year. Closed Jan. 1, Christmas

Eve and Christmas. **Cost:** $10; $7 (ages 65+); $5 (ages 7-17); $25 (family, two adults and children). **Phone:** (780) 361-1351 or (800) 661-4726. ⟨Ⅱ⟩

WETASKIWIN & DISTRICT HERITAGE MUSEUM is at 5007 50th Ave. Housed in a historic building, the museum depicts local history and includes displays about the military, hospitals, early businesses, and Swedish and Chinese immigrants. The Origins Exhibit offers interactive games as well as such archeological finds as dinosaur fossils and Cree Indian artifacts. Women of Aspenland profiles notable women from the community.

A hands-on gallery for children features a blacksmith's shop, a one-room schoolhouse and a pioneer kitchen. **Time:** Allow 30 minutes minimum. **Hours:** Tues.-Sat. 10-5, Victoria Day weekend-Labour Day; Tues.-Fri. 10-5, rest of year. Closed Jan. 1, Good Friday and Christmas. **Cost:** Donations. **Phone:** (780) 352-0227.

BEST WESTERN WAYSIDE INN   (780)312-7300

 Hotel $125-$140

 AAA Benefit: Members save up to 20%, plus 10% bonus points with Best Western Rewards®.

Address: 4103 56th St T9A 1V2 **Location:** On Hwy 2A, just n of jct Hwy 13 W. **Facility:** 28 units. 2 stories (no elevator), interior corridors. **Parking:** winter plug-ins. **Terms:** check-in 4 pm. **Amenities:** Some: high-speed Internet. **Activities:** exercise room. **Free Special Amenities:** newspaper and high-speed Internet.

⬛ 🍴 🐾 🍸 BIZ 🛜 ✕ 🛢 🖥 💻 / SOME UNITS FEE 🐕

SUPER 8   (780)361-3808

Hotel $120-$130 **Address:** 3820 56th St T9A 2B2 **Location:** On Hwy 2A, just s of jct Hwy 13 W. **Facility:** 89 units. 2 stories (no elevator), interior/exterior corridors. **Parking:** winter plug-ins. **Terms:** check-in 4 pm. **Guest Services:** coin laundry.

🍴 BIZ 🛜 🛢 🖥 💻 / SOME UNITS

WHERE TO EAT

HUCKLEBERRY'S CAFE   780/352-3111

🍷🍷 American. Casual Dining. $8-$30 **AAA Inspector Notes:** This popular restaurant features a homelike country and Western decor and offers up quick, efficient service. On the menu is a wide variety of burgers, pasta dishes and sandwiches that emphasize local ingredients. Find Alberta turkey and beef as well as the famous huckleberry, a berry from the mountains. Not surprisingly, the berry, which is plumper and juicier than the blueberry, found its way into the cafe's name and desserts, including the homemade pie. **Bar:** full bar. **Reservations:** suggested. **Address:** 103-3840 56th St T9A 2B2 **Location:** Just e of Hwy 2A; s of jct Hwy 13 W; behind Super 8.

Ⓛ Ⓓ

PIPESTONE FOOD COMPANY STEAK HOUSE   780/352-9596

🍷 Canadian. Casual Dining. $11-$40 **AAA Inspector Notes:** A sophisticated menu contrasts the rustic interior at this inviting spot. The menu features local naturally-raised meats and fresh wild-caught fish as well as king crab and lobster. Steaks can be enhanced with such decadent toppings as blue cheese au poivre or bacon and brie. Rounding out the menu is lamb, chicken and pasta entrées as well as gourmet burgers. Open for dinner only on Saturday. **Bar:** full bar. **Reservations:** suggested. **Address:** 4911 51st St T9A 2A4 **Location:** Between 49th and 50th aves; downtown. **Parking:** street only.

Ⓛ Ⓓ CALL 📶M

WHITECOURT (D-4) pop. 9,605, elev. 732m/2,404'

THE WHITECOURT AND DISTRICT FOREST INTERPRETIVE CENTRE is 1 km (.6 mi.) e. on Hwy. 43. The center includes multimedia exhibits detailing the role of the forest in the evolution of Whitecourt. Visitors can view a storyboard describing the manufacturing process of wood products, a tepee, and a variety of wood artifacts and tools.

Next to the building, Heritage Park re-creates an early 20th-century logging town through a collection of restored buildings and vehicles. Tools and other artifacts from this period also are on display. Guided tours are available by appointment. **Time:** Allow 30 minutes minimum. **Hours:** Mon.-Fri. 8:30-6, Sat.-Sun. and holidays 11-6, June 1-early Sept.; Mon.-Fri. 8:30-4:30, rest of year. Closed statutory holidays in winter. **Cost:** $1.50; 50c (ages 6-10). **Phone:** (780) 778-3433. ⟨🏛⟩

HOLIDAY INN EXPRESS & SUITES WHITECOURT   (780)778-2512

🍷🍷🍷 Hotel $149-$159 **Address:** 4721 49th St T7S 1N5 **Location:** Hwy 43, just n on 51st St, just e. **Facility:** 96 units. 4 stories, interior corridors. **Parking:** winter plug-ins. **Amenities:** high-speed Internet. **Activities:** whirlpool, exercise room. **Guest Services:** valet and coin laundry.

🍴 CALL 📶M BIZ 🛜 🎥 🛢 🖥 💻 / SOME UNITS FEE 🐕

LAKEVIEW INNS & SUITES   (780)706-3349

🍷🍷 Hotel $109-$130 **Address:** 3325 Caxton St T7S 1P2 **Location:** Hwy 43, just n of Park Dr. **Facility:** 50 units. 2 stories (no elevator), interior corridors. **Parking:** winter plug-ins. **Terms:** check-in 4 pm, cancellation fee imposed. **Amenities:** high-speed Internet. **Activities:** whirlpool, exercise room. **Guest Services:** valet and coin laundry. **Free Special Amenities:** continental breakfast and high-speed Internet.

⬛ ECO BIZ 🛜 🛢 🖥 💻

SUPER 8   (780)778-8908

🍷🍷 Hotel $135-$145 **Address:** 4121 Kepler St T7S 0A3 **Location:** On Hwy 43, just e of Hwy 32. **Facility:** 59 units. 3 stories, interior corridors. **Parking:** winter plug-ins. **Terms:** cancellation fee imposed. **Amenities:** video games (fee). Some: high-speed Internet. **Activities:** exercise room. **Guest Services:** valet and coin laundry. **Free Special Amenities:** continental breakfast and local telephone calls.

⬛ ECO 🍴 BIZ 🛜 🎥 🛢 🖥 💻 / SOME UNITS FEE 🐕

WHERE TO EAT

MOUNTAIN PIZZA & STEAK HOUSE   780/778-3600

🍷🍷 Steak. Casual Dining. $10-$28 **AAA Inspector Notes:** This casually elegant restaurant features steaks, shish kebabs, Italian veal and chicken dishes as well as pizza, all served by a friendly and efficient staff. The highly-secret steak spice is apparently world famous, customers from around the world come back to sample it. **Bar:** full bar. **Reservations:** suggested. **Address:** 3827 Caxton St T7S 1P3 **Location:** Hwy 43, just s on Pine Rd.

Ⓛ Ⓓ CALL 📶M

WOOD BUFFALO NATIONAL PARK—

See Northwest Territories and Nunavut p. 511.

Get Your Car Vacation Ready!

Before setting out on vacation, have your car checked out by a dependable AAA/CAA Approved Auto Repair **facility.**

Queen Elizabeth Park, Vancouver

British Columbia

Sailing along Vancouver Island's untamed coast in 1842, James Douglas visited the site of present-day Victoria and reported: "The place itself appears a perfect Eden...one might be pardoned for supposing it had been dropped from the clouds..."

Today, Edenic gardens are the province's forte: From Victoria's renowned, blossom-loaded Butchart Gardens to lush Queen Elizabeth Park atop Vancouver's tallest hill, horticultural delights are everywhere.

And if a single apple was enough to tempt Adam and Eve, they would no doubt have found BC's fertile Okanagan Valley irresistible. Its orchards produce more than a third of Canada's apples, and the valley also lures vacationers with sunny weather, sandy lakefront beaches and picturesque rolling hills striped by orderly rows of grapevines.

If you were searching for the Garden of Eden on Earth, British Columbia wouldn't be a bad place to start.

Pacific Rim National Park Reserve

Into the Woods

Indeed, a trip here just might recapture a lost youthful expectation of adventure. BC's snowcapped mountains and mist-filled rain forests seem to have sprung from the pages of a novel full of exciting new experiences.

Take a walk among centuries-old Douglas firs in MacMillan Provincial Park's Cathedral Grove; you'll feel child-size by comparison. Look up at the high, dim ceiling of needle-heavy boughs arching overhead and you'll understand how this grove got its name. Stands of old-growth forests continue to thrive in Pacific Rim National Park Reserve and Strathcona Provincial Park.

Another of these sylvan sanctuaries is Vancouver's Stanley Park, an evergreen woodland so extensive that while wandering its paths you might forget you're in the heart of Canada's third largest city.

Especially intriguing are the stylized figures carved into totem poles. A thicket of these cedar columns is at the park's eastern edge, each one communicating its own story—possibly a family history, notable event or age-old myth. More examples carved by the Bella Coola, Haida, Kwakwaka'wakw, Nootka, Salish, Tlingit and Tsimshian peoples rise along the province's mainland coast or offshore islands.

In the Canadian Rockies, Kootenay National Park preserves land that seems equally imbued with magic. At the park's southern end are the Radium Hot Springs, which bubble forth hot, mineral water no matter what time of year.

On the other hand, changing seasons at Victoria's Butchart Gardens make a huge difference. As some plants bloom, others fade, producing a dramatic shift in hues. Meandering paths among blossoming trees and shrubs pass softly splashing fountains and countless flower beds in this floral heaven.

Vancouver's VanDusen Botanical Garden is also endowed. This former golf course is now a showplace of lakes, streams, hedge mazes and whimsical topiaries.

Recreation

The Rocky Mountain and Cascade ranges, a lush valley and rivers, lakes and protected ocean waterways are the hallmarks of British Columbia's natural beauty and the sources of unlimited recreational possibilities.

Extended canoeing trips await you on the Outside Trail, a chain of lakes in the Kootenay region's Champion Lakes Provincial Park, and the coast's Powell Forest Canoe Route, eight lakes connected by portage routes.

The 116-kilometre (72-mi.) canoeing and kayaking circuit (plus portage routes) in Bowron Lake Provincial Park is so popular that reservations are required and daily access is limited to 25 boats. Paddling through this unspoiled wildlife sanctuary could take up to 7 days, depending on the weather or how much time you spend gawking at wildlife or the beautiful Cariboo Mountains.

In addition to spectacular mountain scenery, canoeists will find calm, turquoise glacial lakes nestled in the snowcapped Rockies; two of these, O'Hara and Emerald, are in Yoho National Park.

If rushing water is more your speed, try negotiating the Thompson and Fraser rivers. They converge near Lytton, said to be Canada's white-water rafting capital; outfitters and guides are plentiful.

Hiking trails throughout BC bring you up close with its natural wonders. One of the best coastal hikes is in Pacific Rim National Park Reserve. The Long Beach Unit near Ucluelet offers eight moderately challenging hiking venues ranging from beaches to rain forests. The park's pride and joy, the rugged West Coast Trail, follows the shoreline from Port Renfrew to Bamfield.

But that's just the tip of the iceberg. A National Marine Conservation Area as well as seven national and nearly 650 provincial parks and recreation areas await your discovery.

You can swim, water ski or windsurf at one of Okanagan Lake's seven provincial beach parks or at Osoyoos Lake, the province's warmest; both are in the desertlike Okanagan Valley. The valley's climate and terrain also invite other activities. The Kettle Valley Railway bed, west of Penticton, provides easy mountain biking; tougher trails cross nearby Campbell Mountain and Ellis Ridge.

The skiing amenities at Whistler and Blackcomb mountains north of Vancouver—39 high-speed lifts, 200 trails and 12 alpine bowls—are world renowned and make up one of North America's largest ski resorts. Off the slopes, unlimited après ski options exist in Whistler Village's eclectic mix of pubs, dance clubs and culinary nightspots, shops, spas and art galleries.

The Okanagan Valley's gentle slopes and rolling hills draw snowboarders and cross-country skiers. Resorts and ski areas near Osoyoos, Oliver, Penticton, West Kelowna (Westbank) and Kelowna have quite a following; most offer night skiing, too. Some of western Canada's best cross-country skiing is farther north, from 100 Mile House to Quesnel west of the Cariboo Mountains.

Enjoy windsurfing on Okanagan Lake

Historic Timeline

1750	The Queen Charlotte Islands are occupied by Haida First Nation.
1774	Spanish explorers first sight the coast of Vancouver Island.
1792	George Vancouver, an English explorer, surveys the British Columbian coast.
1820	The powerful Hudson's Bay Co. controls fur trading in the Pacific Northwest.
1849	Vancouver Island becomes a crown colony.
1858	Gold is discovered in the Fraser River Valley.
1871	British Columbia becomes the sixth province of the Dominion of Canada.
1885	A transcontinental railroad links British Columbia with eastern Canada.
1986	Vancouver celebrates its centennial with a world's fair, Expo '86.
1998	The Nisga'a Treaty ends 20 years of negotiations with the Nisga'a nation over land, resources and self-government.
2010	Vancouver and Whistler host the 2010 Olympic Winter Games.

What To Pack

Temperature Averages Maximum/Minimum (Celsius)	JANUARY	FEBRUARY	MARCH	APRIL	MAY	JUNE	JULY	AUGUST	SEPTEMBER	OCTOBER	NOVEMBER	DECEMBER
Fort St. John	-11 / -19	-7 / -16	-1 / -11	8 / -2	15 / 3	19 / 8	21 / 10	20 / 9	14 / 4	8 / -1	-3 / -11	-9 / -18
Kamloops	-2 / -9	3 / -5	10 / -2	16 / 2	21 / 7	25 / 11	28 / 13	28 / 13	22 / 8	14 / 3	5 / -2	0 / -7
Prince George	-6 / -14	-1 / -11	4 / -6	11 / -2	16 / 3	19 / 6	22 / 8	21 / 7	16 / 3	9 / -1	1 / -7	-5 / -13
Prince Rupert	4 / -3	6 / -1	7 / 0	9 / 1	12 / 4	14 / 7	16 / 9	16 / 10	15 / 7	11 / 4	7 / 1	4 / -2
Vancouver	6 / 0	8 / 1	9 / 2	12 / 4	16 / 8	19 / 11	22 / 12	22 / 13	18 / 10	13 / 6	9 / 3	6 / 1
Victoria	6 / 0	8 / 1	10 / 2	13 / 3	16 / 6	19 / 9	22 / 11	22 / 11	19 / 8	14 / 5	9 / 2	7 / 1

From the records of The Weather Channel Interactive, Inc.

Good Facts To Know

ABOUT THE PROVINCE

AREA: 944,735 sq km (364,762 sq mi.); ranks 5th.

CAPITAL: Victoria.

HIGHEST POINT: 4,663 m (15,295 ft.), Mount Fairweather.

LOWEST POINT: Sea level, Pacific Ocean.

TIME ZONE(S): Mountain/Pacific. DST in portions of the province.

GAMBLING

MINIMUM AGE FOR GAMBLING: 19.

REGULATIONS

TEEN DRIVING LAWS: The minimum age for an unrestricted driver's license is 19 (18 years, 3 months with approved driver's ed). No more than one unrelated passenger is permitted unless accompanied by a driver age 25 or older. For more information about British Columbia driver's license regulations phone (800) 663-3051.

SEAT BELT/CHILD RESTRAINT LAWS: Seat belts are required for driver and all passengers ages 16 and over. Children ages 9-15 or 145 centimetres (57 in.) tall and over are required to use a booster seat or seat belt; booster seats are required for children under age 9 or under 145 centimetres (57 in.) tall. Infants under 40 pounds must be in a rear-facing seat until they are either 12 months old or big enough for booster seats, which must not be placed in front of an air bag.

CELLPHONE RESTRICTIONS: The use of handheld phones and text messaging while driving are prohibited.

HELMETS FOR MOTORCYCLISTS: Required for all riders.

RADAR DETECTORS: Permitted.

MOVE OVER LAW: Drivers approaching a stopped emergency vehicle displaying flashing lights must slow down and, if traffic permits, move over into the adjacent lane in order to pass by.

FIREARMS LAWS: By federal law, all nonresidents entering Canada with a firearm must declare their weapon in writing and pay a fee of $25 (Canadian). Contact the Canadian Firearms Centre at (800) 731-4000 to receive a declaration form or for additional information.

ALCOHOL CONSUMPTION: Legal age 19.

HOLIDAYS

HOLIDAYS: Jan. 1 ▪ Family Day, Feb. 11 ▪ Good Friday ▪ Easter Monday ▪ Victoria Day, May 24 (if a Mon.) or closest prior Mon. ▪ Canada Day, July 1 ▪ British Columbia Day, Aug. (1st Mon.) ▪ Labour Day, Sept. (1st Mon.) ▪ Thanksgiving, Oct. (2nd Mon.) ▪ Remembrance Day, Nov. 11 ▪ Christmas, Dec. 25 ▪ Boxing Day, Dec. 26.

MONEY

TAXES: British Columbia has a single tax known as a harmonized sales tax (HST); the rate is 12 percent. Hotel accommodations are subject to the harmonized tax.

VISITOR INFORMATION

INFORMATION CENTERS: British Columbia has more than 136 visitor information centers throughout the province. Of these more than 80 are open all year and can be found in all major cities including Victoria and Vancouver. The smaller community travel information centers are open June through August. For further information phone Hello BC at (800) 435-5622.

ROAD CONDITIONS: DriveBC provides current information about road conditions; phone (800) 550-4997 in British Columbia or anywhere in North America.

FURTHER INFORMATION FOR VISITORS:
1-800-HELLO BC
1166 Alberni St., Unit 600
Vancouver, BC V6C 3L6
Canada
(800) 435-5622

FISHING AND HUNTING REGULATIONS:
British Columbia Ministry of Environment
Fish and Wildlife Branch
P.O. Box 9391, Stn. Prov. Gov't.
Victoria, BC V8W 9M8
Canada
(250) 387-9771

RECREATION INFORMATION:
BC Parks
P.O. Box 9398, Stn. Prov. Gov't.
Victoria, BC V8W 9M9
Canada
(800) 689-9025 (camping reservations)

British Columbia Annual Events
Please call ahead to confirm event details.

JANUARY

- Polar Bear Swim
  Vancouver
  604-665-3424
- Brackendale Winter Eagle
  Festival and Count
  Brackendale
  604-898-3333
- Winter Carnival / Rossland
  250-362-5666

FEBRUARY

- Vernon Winter Carnival
  Vernon
  250-545-2236
- BC Home and Garden
  Show / Vancouver
  905-951-4051
- Cariboo Gold Rush
  Marathon / 100 Mile House
  250-395-3487

MARCH

- CelticFest Vancouver
  Vancouver
  604-727-3984
- Cowboy Festival
  Kamloops
  888-763-2224
- Pacific Rim Whale Festival
  Ucluelet
  250-726-4641

APRIL

- Victoria Harbour Boat Show
  Victoria
  604-683-2628
- TELUS World Ski &
  Snowboard Festival
  Whistler
  604-664-5614
- Goodbye Chums
  Maple Ridge
  604-462-8643

MAY

- Fire and Ice Street Festival
  Qualicum Beach
  250-752-2300
- Cloverdale Rodeo and
  Country Fair / Surrey
  604-576-9461
- Victoria Highland Games
  and Celtic Festival / Victoria
  250-598-8961

JUNE

- Sam Steele Days
  Cranbrook
  250-426-4161
- Seafest / Prince Rupert
  250-624-9118
- Vancouver International
  Children's Festival
  Vancouver
  604-708-5655

JULY

- Kimberley Old Time
  Accordion Championships
  Kimberley
  250-427-3666
- Billy Barker Days / Quesnel
  250-992-1234
- Discovery Coast Music
  Festival / Bella Coola
  800-663-5885

AUGUST

- Abbotsford International Air
  Show / Abbotsford
  604-852-8511
- Victoria Dragon Boat
  Festival / Victoria
  250-472-2628
- MusicFest Vancouver
  Vancouver
  604-688-8441

SEPTEMBER

- Gibsons Landing Salmon
  Festival / Gibsons
  604-886-2325
- Vancouver International
  Fringe Festival / Vancouver
  604-257-0350
- Coho Festival
  West Vancouver
  604-926-6956

OCTOBER

- The Mane Event--Equine
  Education and Trade Fair
  Chilliwack
  250-578-7518
- Ghosts of Victoria Festival
  Victoria
  800-953-2022
- Okanagan Fall Wine
  Festival / Kelowna
  250-861-6654

NOVEMBER

- Kris Kringle Craft Market
  Parksville
  250-758-9750
- Cornucopia--Whistler's
  Celebration of Wine and
  Food / Whistler
  604-932-2394
- Heritage Christmas at
  Burnaby Village / Burnaby
  604-294-7201

DECEMBER

- WinterFest / Prince Rupert
  250-624-9118
- Magic of Christmas
  Brentwood Bay
  250-652-4422
- Festival of Lights
  Vancouver
  604-257-8665

Victoria Butterfly Gardens,
Brentwood Bay

VanDusen Botanical
Garden, Vancouver

Royal BC Museum, Victoria

Little Qualicum Falls, Qualicum Beach

A busy marina, Prince Rupert

Index: Great Experience for Members

AAA editor's picks of exceptional note

Barkerville Historic Town

Kootenay National Park

McLean Mill National Historic Site

Britannia Mine Museum

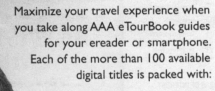

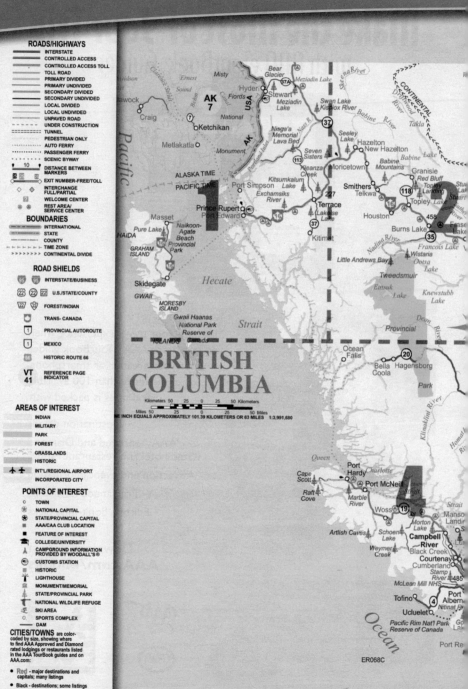

British Columbia
Atlas Section

ROADS/HIGHWAYS

	INTERSTATE
	CONTROLLED ACCESS
	CONTROLLED ACCESS TOLL
	TOLL ROAD
	PRIMARY DIVIDED
	PRIMARY UNDIVIDED
	SECONDARY DIVIDED
	SECONDARY UNDIVIDED
	LOCAL DIVIDED
	LOCAL UNDIVIDED
	UNPAVED ROAD
	UNDER CONSTRUCTION
	TUNNEL
	PEDESTRIAN ONLY
	AUTO FERRY
	PASSENGER FERRY
	SCENIC BYWAY
10	DISTANCE BETWEEN MARKERS
	EXIT NUMBER-FREE/TOLL
	INTERCHANGE FULL/PARTIAL
	WELCOME CENTER
	REST AREA/ SERVICE CENTER

BOUNDARIES

	INTERNATIONAL
	STATE
	COUNTY
	TIME ZONE
>>>>>>>>	CONTINENTAL DIVIDE

ROAD SHIELDS

85 85	INTERSTATE/BUSINESS
22 22	U.S./STATE/COUNTY
27 27	FOREST/INDIAN
	TRANS- CANADA
1	PROVINCIAL AUTOROUTE
1	MEXICO
66	HISTORIC ROUTE 66
VT 41	REFERENCE PAGE INDICATOR

AREAS OF INTEREST

	INDIAN
	MILITARY
	PARK
	FOREST
	GRASSLANDS
	HISTORIC
✈ ✈	INT'L/REGIONAL AIRPORT
	INCORPORATED CITY

POINTS OF INTEREST

○	TOWN
✳	NATIONAL CAPITAL
✹	STATE/PROVINCIAL CAPITAL
■	AAA/CAA CLUB LOCATION
◆	FEATURE OF INTEREST
▲	COLLEGE/UNIVERSITY
▲	CAMPGROUND INFORMATION PROVIDED BY WOODALL'S®
⊛	CUSTOMS STATION
	HISTORIC
⊺	LIGHTHOUSE
▲	MONUMENT/MEMORIAL
▲	STATE/PROVINCIAL PARK
	NATIONAL WILDLIFE REFUGE
⅀	SKI AREA
○	SPORTS COMPLEX
	DAM

CITIES/TOWNS are color-coded by size, showing where to find AAA Approved and Diamond rated lodgings or restaurants listed in the AAA TourBook guides and on AAA.com:

- Red - major destinations and capitals; many listings
- Black - destinations; some listings
- Grey - no listings

BRITISH COLUMBIA

Kilometers 50 25 0 25 50 Kilometers

Miles 50 25 0 25 50 Miles

ONE INCH EQUALS APPROXIMATELY 101.39 KILOMETERS OR 63 MILES 1:3,991,680

ER068C

Use driving maps from the AAA Road Atlas to plan your itinerary and route. Purchase the complete 2013 AAA Road Atlas at participating AAA/CAA offices, retail stores and online booksellers.

Atlas
ROAD
AAA
2013

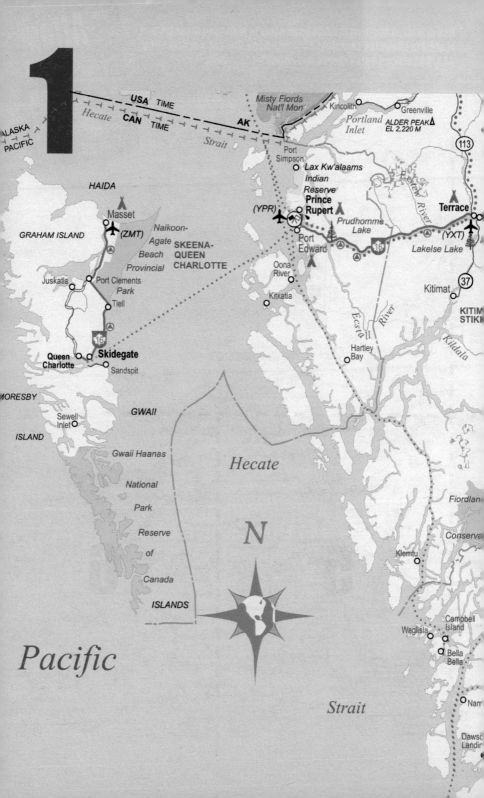

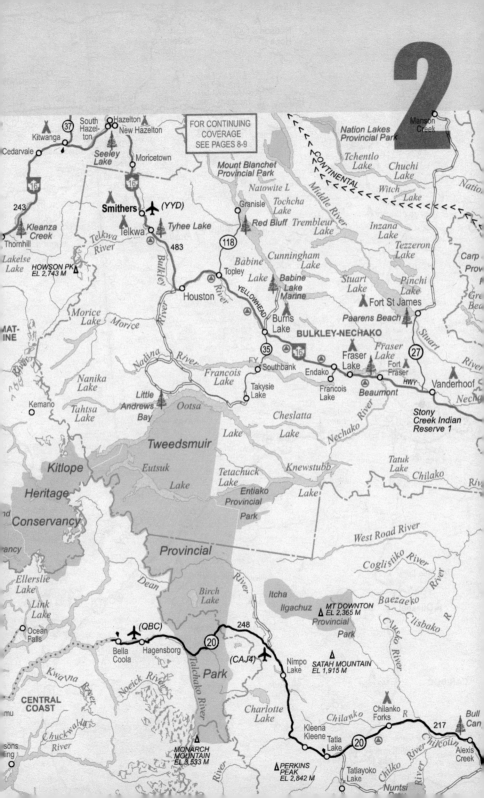

2

FOR CONTINUING
COVERAGE
SEE PAGES 8-9

Kitwanga
37
South
Hazel-
ton
Hazelton
New Hazelton
Cedarvale
Seeley
Lake
Moricetown

16

243

Thornhill
Kleanza
Creek
HOWSON PK
EL 2,743 M

Lakelse
Lake

Smithers (YYD)
Telkwa
Telkwa
River
Tyhee Lake
483

16

Bulkley River

Houston

Morice
Lake
Morice

Nanika
Lake

Kemano

Tahtsa
Lake

Little
Andrews
Bay

Nadina River

Francois
Lake

Takysie
Lake

Ootsa

Lake

Kitlope

Heritage

Conservancy

Eutsuk

Lake

Tetachuck
Lake

Entiako
Provincial
Park

Cheslatta

Lake

Tweedsmuir

Knewstubb

Lake

Granisle
Red Bluff
118

Natowite L

Babine
Topley
Lake

Tochcha
Lake

Cunningham
Lake

Babine
Lake
Marine

YELLOWHEAD

Burns
Lake

35

16

FY
Southbank

Endako

Francois
Lake

BULKLEY-NECHAKO

Fraser
Lake

Beaumont

Nation Lakes
Provincial Park

Manson
Creek

CONTINENTAL

Tchentlo
Lake

Middle River

Chuchi
Lake

Witch
Lake

Natio

Trembleur
Lake

Inzana
Lake

Tezzeron
Lake

Carp
Lake

Gre
Bea

Stuart
Lake

Pinchi
Lake

Fort St James

Paarens Beach

Fraser
Lake
Fort
Fraser

HWY

27

Stuart
River

Vanderhoof

Nech

Stony
Creek Indian
Reserve 1

MAT-
INE

Tatuk
Lake

Chilako

Rive

West Road River

Coglistiko River

Ellerslie
Lake

Link
Lake

Ocean
Falls

Dean

Birch
Lake

River

Provincial

Park

Itcha
Ilgachuz

MT DOWNTON
EL 2,365 M

Provincial

Park

Baezaeko
River

Clisbako R

Clusko River

(QBC)

Bella
Coola
Hagensborg

Kwatna River

248
20

Talchako River

CENTRAL
COAST

Noeick River

(CAJ4)

Nimpo
Lake

SATAH MOUNTAIN
EL 1,915 M

Charlotte
Lake

Chilanko

Chilanko
Forks

Bull
Can

217

mu

sons
ing

Chuckwalla River

MONARCH
MOUNTAIN
EL 3,533 M

PERKINS
PEAK
EL 2,842 M

Kleena
Kleene
Tatla
Lake

Tatlayoko
Lake

20

Chilko River

Chilcotin River

Alexis
Creek

Nuntsi

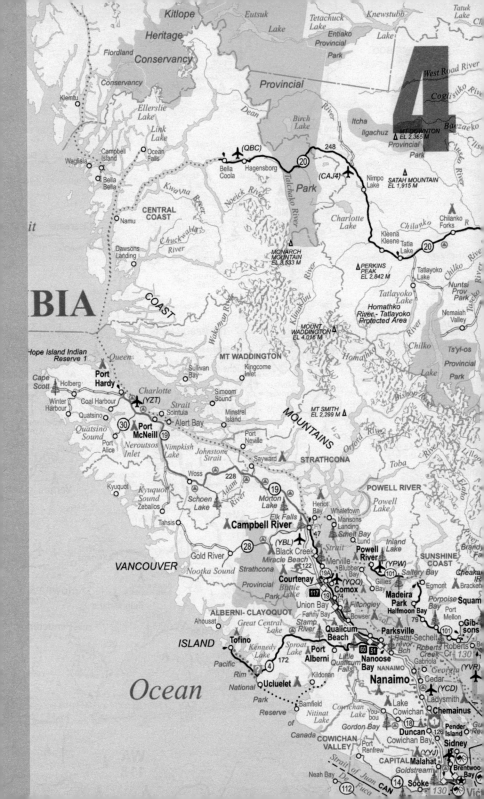

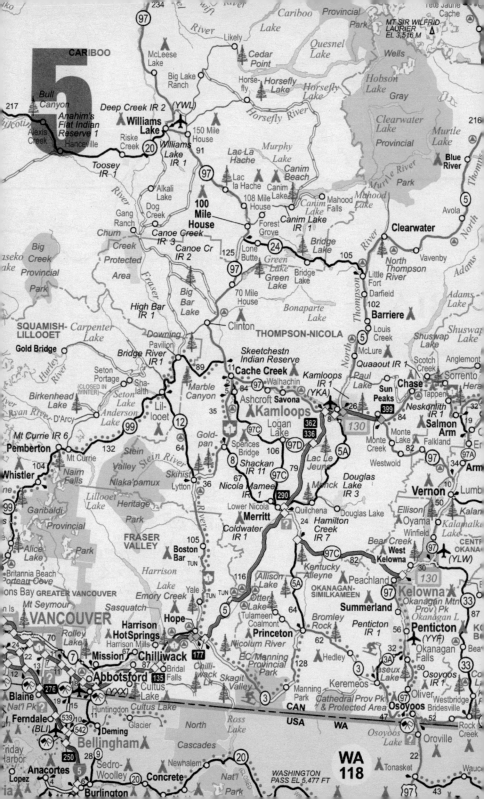

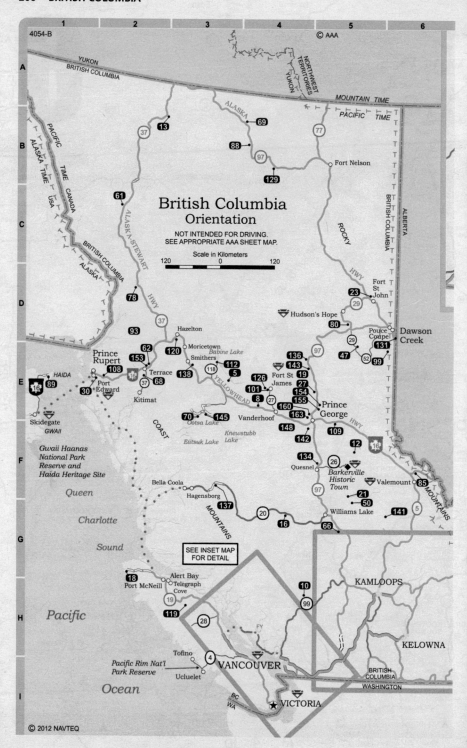

4054-B

© AAA

British Columbia
Orientation

NOT INTENDED FOR DRIVING.
SEE APPROPRIATE AAA SHEET MAP.

Scale in Kilometers
120   0   120

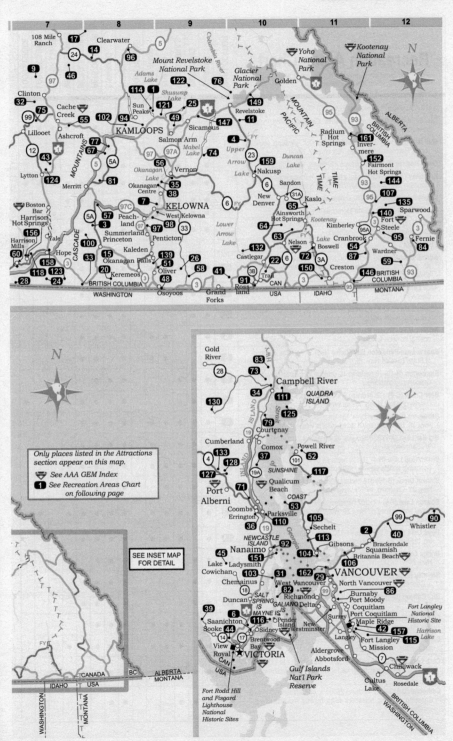

Recreation Areas Chart

The map location numerals in column 2 show an area's location on the preceding map.

	MAP LOCATION	CAMPING	PICNICKING	HIKING TRAILS	BOATING	BOAT RAMP	BOAT RENTAL	FISHING	SWIMMING	PETS ON LEASH	BICYCLE TRAILS	WINTER SPORTS	VISITOR CENTER	LODGE/CABINS	FOOD SERVICE
NATIONAL PARKS (See place listings.)															
Glacier (A-10) 1,350 square kilometres. Camping, caving, mountaineering, wildlife viewing.		•	•	•				•		•			•	•	•
Gulf Islands (H-10) 33 square kilometres. Golf, kayaking, scuba diving. Recreational activities vary on each island.		•	•	•	•		•		•	•					
Gwaii Haanas (F-1) 1,495 square kilometres. Kayaking.		•			•	•			•						
Kootenay (A-11) 1,406 square kilometres. Horseback riding, mountain biking, wildlife viewing. Power boats prohibited.		•	•	•				•	•	•	•	•	•	•	
Mount Revelstoke (A-9) 260 square kilometres.		•	•					•				•	•	•	
Pacific Rim (I-3) 510 square kilometres.		•	•	•	•	•		•	•					•	
Yoho (A-11) 1,310 square kilometres. Cross-country skiing; horseback riding. Power boats prohibited.		•	•	•	•		•	•	•		•	•	•		•
PROVINCIAL															
Adams Lake (A-8) 56 hectares 30 km n. of Chase off Hwy. 1. Archeological sites. Canoeing, scuba diving, water skiing, windsurfing.	❶	•	•	•	•	•		•	•	•	•		•		
Alice Lake (G-11) 396 hectares 13 km n. of Squamish on Hwy. 99. Canoeing.	❷	•	•	•				•	•	•	•				
Allison Lake (C-8) 23 hectares 28 km s. of Princeton on Hwy. 5A. Canoeing, water skiing	❸	•	•					•	•	•	•				
Arrow Lakes (Shelter Bay) (B-10) 93 hectares on Hwy. 23. Canoeing, horseback riding	❹	•	•		•	•		•	•	•					
Babine Lake-Pendleton Bay Marine (E-3) 37 hectares 45 km n. of Burns Lake off Hwy. 16.	❺	•			•	•		•	•	•					
Bamberton (H-10) 28 hectares 45 km n. of Victoria off Hwy. 1. Canoeing, windsurfing	❻	•	•	•				•	•	•					
Bear Creek (C-8) 178 hectares 9 km n. off Hwy. 97 w. of Kelowna. Canoeing, water skiing, wildlife viewing	❼	•	•	•				•	•	•	•				•
Beaumont (E-4) 192 hectares 134 km w. of Prince George on Hwy. 16. Canoeing, water skiing, wildlife viewing, windsurfing	❽	•	•	•				•	•	•					
Big Bar Lake (A-7) 332 hectares 42 km n.w. of Clinton off Hwy. 97. Canoeing	❾	•	•		•	•		•	•	•					
Birkenhead Lake (H-4) 10,439 hectares 54 km n.e. of Pemberton. Canoeing, wildlife viewing, windsurfing	❿	•	•	•	•	•		•	•	•	•		•		
Blanket Creek (B-10) 318 hectares 25 km s. of Revelstoke on Hwy. 23. Canoeing, wildlife viewing	⓫	•	•	•				•	•	•					
Bowron Lake (F-5) 149,207 hectares 120 km e. of Quesnel via a gravel access road off Hwy. 26. Water circuit of connecting lakes. Canoeing	⓬	•	•	•	•	•		•	•	•	•		•	•	
Boya Lake (B-2) 4,597 hectares 150 km n. of Dease Lake. Canoeing, hunting, kayaking, wildlife viewing	⓭	•		•	•	•		•	•	•					
Bridge Lake (A-8) 11 hectares 51 km e. of 100 Mile House off Hwy. 24.	⓮	•			•	•		•	•	•					
Bromley Rock (C-8) 149 hectares 21 km e. of Princeton on Hwy. 3. Canoeing	⓯	•	•					•	•	•	•				
Bull Canyon (G-4) 369 hectares 6 km w. of Alexis Creek off Hwy. 20.	⓰	•	•	•				•		•	•				
Canim Beach (A-7) 6 hectares on Canim Lake, 43 km n.e. of 100 Mile House off Hwy. 97. Canoeing, kayaking.	⓱		•	•	•	•		•	•	•					
Cape Scott (G-2) 22,294 hectares 64 km w. of Port Hardy. Canoeing, hunting, kayaking, wildlife viewing	⓲	•						•	•	•			•		
Carp Lake (E-4) 38,149 hectares 32 km s.w. of McLeod Lake off Hwy. 97. Canoeing, hunting, ice fishing, kayaking, wildlife viewing	⓳	•	•	•	•	•		•	•	•	•		•		
Cathedral (D-8) 33,272 hectares 24 km w. of Keremeos off Hwy. 3. Canoeing, climbing, horseback riding, hunting, mountaineering, wildlife viewing	⓴	•	•	•				•	•					•	

Recreation Areas Chart

The map location numerals in column 2 show an area's location on the preceding map.

Area	MAP LOCATION	CAMPING	PICNICKING	HIKING TRAILS	BOATING	BOAT RAMP	BOAT RENTAL	FISHING	SWIMMING	PETS ON LEASH	BICYCLE TRAILS	WINTER SPORTS	VISITOR CENTER	LODGE/CABINS	FOOD SERVICE
Cedar Point (F-5) 8 hectares 118 km n.e. of Williams Lake off Hwy. 97 on Quesnel Lake. Canoeing, water skiing; mining displays.	21	•	•	•	•	•	•	•	•	•	•				
Champion Lakes (C-10) 1,426 hectares 10 km s. of Castlegar off Hwy. 3B. Canoeing, cross-country skiing, ice fishing, wildlife viewing, windsurfing. Power boats prohibited.	22	•	•	•	•	•	•	•	•	•	•	•			
Charlie Lake (D-5) 176 hectares 11 km n. of Fort St. John off Hwy. 97.	23	•	•	•	•	•	•	•	•	•	•				
Chilliwack Lake (D-7) 9,528 hectares 64 km s.e. of Chilliwack via an access road off Hwy. 1. Canoeing, hunting, water skiing. ATVs or unlicensed motorbikes prohibited.	24	•	•	•	•	•	•	•	•	•	•				
Cinnemousun Narrows (A-9) 176 hectares 22.5 km n. of Sicamous via boat. Canoeing, houseboating, scuba diving, water skiing, windsurfing.	25	•	•	•	•	•	•	•	•	•				•	
Conkle Lake (C-9) 587 hectares 28 km n.e. of Osoyoos via Hwy. 3, then 26 km to entrance. Canoeing, windsurfing.	26	•	•	•	•	•	•	•	•	•	•				
Crooked River (E-4) 970 hectares 70 km n. of Prince George on Hwy. 97. Canoeing, cross-country skiing, ice fishing, wildlife viewing, windsurfing.	27	•	•	•				•	•	•	•	•			
Cultus Lake (D-7) 2,561 hectares 11 km s.w. of Chilliwack off Hwy. 1. Canoeing, horseback riding, water skiing, wildlife viewing, windsurfing. *(See Cultus Lake p. 234.)*	28	•	•	•	•	•	•	•	•	•	•	•			
Cypress (G-11) 3,012 hectares off Hwy. 1 exit 8 in West Vancouver, then w. following signs. Cross-country and downhill skiing, snowmobiling, wilderness camping, wildlife viewing. *(See West Vancouver p. 421.)*	29		•	•						•	•	•			
Diana Lake (E-1) 233 hectares 16 km e. of Prince Rupert on Hwy. 16. Canoeing, kayaking and paddling.	30		•	•				•	•	•					
Dionisio Point (G-10) 142 hectares on Galiano Island via car ferry. Scuba diving, wildlife viewing, winter camping.	31	•	•	•				•	•	•	•				
Downing (A-7) 100 hectares 18 km s.w. of Clinton off Hwy. 97. Canoeing	32	•	•		•	•		•	•	•					
E.C. Manning (C-8) 70,844 hectares on Hwy. 3 between Hope and Princeton. Scenic. Canoeing, horseback riding, hunting, wildlife viewing; Cross-country and downhill skiing, mountain biking, snowshoeing. Horse and kayak rentals. No motorized or electric motorized boats. *(See Hope p. 249.)*	33	•	•	•	•			•	•	•	•	•	•	•	•
Elk Falls (E-10) 1,087 hectares 3 km n.w. of Campbell River off Hwy. 28. Mountain biking (on designated trails), winter camping, wildlife viewing; waterfall.	34	•	•	•				•	•	•	•				
Ellison (B-9) 200 hectares on Okanagan Lake, 16 km s.w. of Vernon off Hwy. 97. Canoeing, scuba diving, rock climbing.	35	•	•	•				•	•	•	•			•	
Englishman River Falls (G-10) 97 hectares 13 km s.w. of Parksville off Hwy. 4. Wildlife viewing.	36	•	•	•				•	•	•	•				
Fillongley (F-10) 23 hectares on Denman Island via ferry from Buckley Bay. Canoeing, kayaking, wildlife viewing, winter camping.	37	•	•	•				•	•	•					
Fintry (C-9) 361 hectares 34 km n. of Kelowna off Hwy. 97. Canoeing, hunting, scuba diving, water skiing, wildlife viewing, windsurfing.	38	•	•	•	•	•	•	•	•	•				•	
French Beach (H-9) 59 hectares 22 km w. of Sooke off Hwy. 14. Wildlife viewing, windsurfing.	39	•	•					•	•	•	•				
Garibaldi (G-12) 194,650 hectares accessible by five trails from Hwy. 99 in Squamish. Canoeing, climbing; cross-country skiing, winter camping. Snowmobiling prohibited. *(See Squamish p. 329.)*	40	•	•	•				•	•			•	•		
Gladstone (D-9) 39,387 hectares 5 km e. of Christina Lake on Hwy. 3. Canoeing, cross-country skiing, horseback riding, hunting, scuba diving, snowshoeing, water skiing.	41	•	•	•	•	•	•	•	•	•	•	•			
Golden Ears (H-12) 62,540 hectares 11 km n. of Maple Ridge off Hwy. 7. Water skiing, windsurfing. Canoeing, horse rental, rock climbing.	42	•	•	•	•	•	•	•	•	•	•	•			

Recreation Areas Chart

The map location numerals in column 2 show an area's location on the preceding map.

Area	MAP LOCATION	CAMPING	PICNICKING	HIKING TRAILS	BOATING	BOAT RAMP	BOAT RENTAL	FISHING	SWIMMING	PETS ON LEASH	BICYCLE TRAILS	WINTER SPORTS	VISITOR CENTER	LODGE/CABINS	FOOD SERVICE
Goldpan (B-7) 5 hectares 10 km s. of Spences Bridge adjacent to Hwy. 1 on the e. bank of the Thompson River. Canoeing, kayaking, wildlife viewing	43	•	•					•	•	•					
Goldstream (H-9) 477 hectares 16 km n.w. of Victoria via Hwy. 1. Wildlife viewing, winter camping. Salmon spawning in fall.	44	•	•	•				•	•	•					
Gordon Bay (G-9) 51 hectares 14 km w. of Lake Cowichan off Hwy. 18. Canoeing, freshwater diving, waterskiing, windsurfing, winter camping.	45	•	•	•	•	•	•	•	•	•	•				
Green Lake (A-7) 347 hectares 16 km n.e. of Hwy. 97 at 70 Mile House. Canoeing, horseback riding, water skiing.	46	•	•	•	•	•	•	•	•	•	•				
Gwillim Lake (E-5) 32,326 hectares 56 km. s.e. of Chetwynd on Hwy. 29. Canoeing, horseback riding, hunting, kayaking, rock climbing, scuba diving, water skiing, wildlife viewing, windsurfing.	47	•	•	•	•	•	•	•	•	•	•	•			
Haynes Point (D-9) 38 hectares 2 km s. of Osoyoos on Hwy. 97. Canoeing, water skiing, wildlife viewing.	48	•	•	•	•	•	•	•	•	•					
Herald (B-9) 79 hectares 14 km e. of Tappen off Hwy. 1. Canoeing, scuba diving, water skiing, windsurfing.	49	•	•	•	•	•	•	•	•	•					
Horsefly Lake (G-5) 148 hectares 65 km e. of 150 Mile House off Hwy. 97. Canoeing, scuba diving, water skiing, wildlife viewing, windsurfing.	50	•	•	•	•	•	•	•	•	•					
Inkaneep (C-9) 21 hectares 6 km n. of Oliver on Hwy. 97. Canoeing, kayaking, wildlife viewing	51	•		•				•		•	•				
Inland Lake (F-11) 2,763 hectares 12 km n. of Powell River on Inland Lake Rd. Canoeing, hunting, kayaking, wildlife viewing; wheelchair accessible trail. *(See Powell River p. 306.)*	52	•	•	•	•	•	•	•	•	•					
Jedediah Island Marine (G-10) 243 hectares between Lasqueti and Texada islands in the Sabine Channel of the Strait of Georgia. Accessible only via boat from Lasqueti Island. Canoeing, kayaking, wilderness camping, winter camping; sandy bays.	53	•		•				•	•	•					
Jimsmith Lake (C-11) 14 hectares 5 km e. of Cranbrook off Hwy. 3. Canoeing. Power boats prohibited.	54	•	•	•				•	•	•					
Juniper Beach (B-8) 260 hectares 19 km e. of Cache Creek on Hwy. 1. Canoeing	55	•	•						•	•					
Kalamalka Lake (B-9) 4,209 hectares 8 km s. of Vernon off Hwy. 6. Canoeing, cross-country skiing, horseback riding, kayaking, snowshoeing, water skiing, wildlife viewing. *(See Vernon p. 393.)*	56		•	•	•			•	•	•	•	•			
Kentucky Alleyne (C-8) 144 hectares 38 km s. of Merritt on Hwy. 5A. Horsepower restriction for boats.	57	•						•	•	•					
Kettle River (D-9) 179 hectares 5 km n. of Rock Creek on Hwy. 33. Cross-country skiing, snowshoeing.	58	•	•	•				•	•	•		•			
Kikomun Creek (C-12) 682 hectares 64 km s.e. of Cranbrook via Hwy. 3, then 11 km s. to entrance. Canoeing, hunting; playground.	59	•	•	•	•	•	•	•	•	•				•	•
Kilby (C-7) 3 hectares 2 km e. of Harrison Mills on Hwy. 7. Historic. Water skiing, wildlife viewing.	60	•	•	•		•		•	•						
Kinaskan Lake (C-2) 1,800 hectares on Hwy. 37 100 km s. of Dease Lake. Canoeing.	61	•	•	•	•	•		•	•	•					
Kleanza Creek (E-2) 269 hectares 15 km e. of Terrace on Hwy. 16. Canoeing, snowshoeing, wildlife viewing.	62	•	•	•						•	•	•			
Kokanee Creek (C-10) 260 hectares 19 km e. of Nelson on Hwy. 3A. Cross-country skiing, snowshoeing, water skiing, canoeing, wildlife viewing, windsurfing; adventure playground.	63	•	•	•	•	•		•	•	•			•	•	
Kokanee Glacier (C-10) 32,035 hectares 19 km n.e. of Nelson on Hwy. 3A. Back- and cross-country skiing, snowshoeing. Non-motorized boats allowed. No pets allowed.	64	•		•				•				•		•	
Kootenay Lake (Davis Creek/Lost Ledge) (C-10) 343 hectares n. of Kaslo on Hwy. 31. Canoeing, water skiing, windsurfing.	65	•	•		•	•		•	•	•					
Lac La Hache (G-5) 24 hectares 13 km n. of Lac la Hache on Hwy. 97. Canoeing, water skiing; adventure playground	66	•	•	•	•	•		•	•	•					

Recreation Areas Chart

The map location numerals in column 2 show an area's location on the preceding map.

Name	MAP LOCATION	CAMPING	PICNICKING	HIKING TRAILS	BOATING	BOAT RAMP	BOAT RENTAL	FISHING	SWIMMING	PETS ON LEASH	BICYCLE TRAILS	WINTER SPORTS	VISITOR CENTER	LODGE/CABINS	FOOD SERVICE
Lac Le Jeune (B-8) 213 hectares 37 km s. of Kamloops off Hwy. 5. Nature programs. Canoeing, cross-country skiing, ice skating, snowshoeing, wildlife viewing; playground.	67	•	•	•	•	•		•	•	•	•	•			
Lakelse Lake (E-2) 354 hectares 20 km s. of Terrace on Hwy. 37. Canoeing, water skiing, windsurfing.	68	•	•	•	•	•	•	•	•	•	•	•			
Liard River Hot Springs (B-4) 1,082 hectares at Liard River at Km-post 765 on Hwy. 97 (Alaska Hwy.). Winter camping, wildlife viewing; playground.	69	•	•	•				•	•	•		•	•		
Little Andrews Bay (E-3) 45 hectares 95 km s. of Houston on Oosta Lake. Canoeing.	70	•	•		•	•		•	•	•					
Little Qualicum Falls (F-10) 440 hectares 19 km w. of Parksville off Hwy. 4. Canoeing, kayaking, scuba diving, water skiing, windsurfing; adventure playground.	71	•	•	•				•	•	•	•				
Lockhart Beach (C-11) 3 hectares 40 km n. of Creston on Hwy. 3A. Canoeing.	72	•	•	•	•			•	•	•	•				
Loveland Bay (E-10) 30 hectares 16 km w. of Campbell River off Hwy. 28. Canoeing, waterskiing, windsurfing.	73	•						•	•	•	•				
Mabel Lake (B-9) 187 hectares 60 km n.e. of Vernon via an access road off Hwy. 6. Canoeing, water skiing, wildlife viewing	74	•	•	•	•	•	•	•	•	•					
Marble Canyon (B-7) 355 hectares 40 km n.w. of Cache Creek off Hwy. 99. Canoeing, rock climbing, scuba diving, wildlife viewing.	75	•	•	•	•			•	•	•					
Martha Creek (A-9) 71 hectares 20 km n. of Revelstoke on Hwy. 23. Canoeing, kayaking.	76	•	•	•				•	•	•					
McConnell Lake (B-8) 102 hectares 35 km s. of Kamloops off Hwy. 5. Canoeing, cross-country skiing, ice fishing, kayaking, snowshoeing.	77		•	•	•	•		•	•	•		•			
Meziadin Lake (D-2) 335 hectares 50 km e. of Stewart off Hwy. 37. Canoeing, wildlife viewing	78	•	•		•	•		•	•	•					
Miracle Beach (F-10) 137 hectares 22 km n. of Courtenay off Hwy. 19. Canoeing, wildlife viewing, winter camping.	79	•	•	•				•	•	•	•				•
Moberly Lake (D-5) 98 hectares 25 km n.w. of Chetwynd on Hwy. 29. Canoeing, water skiing, windsurfing; playground.	80	•	•	•	•	•		•	•	•					
Monck (B-8) 92 hectares 22 km n. of Merritt off Hwy. 5A. Canoeing, water skiing, wildlife viewing, windsurfing; playground.	81	•	•	•	•	•		•	•	•					
Montague Harbour Marine (H-10) 97 hectares on Galiano Island via car ferry. Middens. Canoeing.	82	•	•	•	•	•		•	•	•					
Morton Lake (E-10) 74 hectares 27 km n.w. of Campbell River on Hwy. 19. Canoeing. Winter camping.	83	•	•	•	•	•		•	•	•					
Mount Fernie (C-12) 259 hectares 3 km s. of Fernie on Hwy. 3.	84	•	•	•				•		•		•			
Mount Robson (F-6) 224,866 hectares bordering Jasper National Park on Hwy. 16. Canoeing, rock climbing, spelunking, winter camping; horse rental, playground. *(See Valemount p. 340.)*	85	•	•	•				•	•	•	•	•	•		
Mount Seymour (H-12) 3,508 hectares 24 km n.e. of North Vancouver off Hwy. 1. Cross-country skiing, horseback riding, winter camping. *(See North Vancouver p. 283.)*	86	•	•	•				•	•	•	•	•		•	•
Moyie Lake (C-11) 91 hectares 20 km s. of Cranbrook on Hwy. 3. Canoeing, ice fishing, kayaking, windsurfing; playground.	87	•	•	•	•	•		•	•	•	•	•			
Muncho Lake (B-3) 86,079 hectares on Hwy. 97 at Muncho Lake at Km-post 681 of the Alaska Hwy. Canoeing, hunting, kayaking, scuba diving, water skiing, hunting, wildlife viewing.	88	•	•	•	•	•	•	•	•	•				•	
Naikoon (E-1) 69,166 hectares on n. tip of Graham Island in Haida Gwaii. Canoeing, hunting.	89	•	•					•						•	
Nairn Falls (G-12) 170 hectares 32 km n. of Whistler on Hwy. 99. Wildlife viewing.	90	•	•	•				•		•	•				
Nancy Greene (D-10) 203 hectares 29 km n.w. of Rossland via Hwy. 3B. Canoeing, cross-country skiing, windsurfing.	91	•	•	•				•	•	•	•	•			
Newcastle Island Marine (G-10) 336 hectares e. of Nanaimo via foot passenger ferry. *(See Nanaimo p. 276.)*	92	•	•	•				•	•	•					•

Recreation Areas Chart

The map location numerals in column 2 show an area's location on the preceding map.

Area	MAP LOCATION	CAMPING	PICNICKING	HIKING TRAILS	BOATING	BOAT RAMP	BOAT RENTAL	FISHING	SWIMMING	PETS ON LEASH	BICYCLE TRAILS	WINTER SPORTS	VISITOR CENTER	LODGE/CABINS	FOOD SERVICE
Nisga'a Memorial Lava Bed (D-2) 17,683 hectares 100 km n. of Terrace on Nisga'a Hwy. (first 70 km is paved). Canoeing, hunting, wildlife viewing. *(See Terrace p. 337.)*	93	•	•	•	•	•		•	•	•	•	•	•	•	•
Niskonlith Lake (B-8) 238 hectares 8 km n.w. of Chase off Hwy. 1. Cross-country skiing, ice fishing, scuba diving, snowshoeing, windsurfing, wildlife viewing.	94	•			•	•		•	•	•		•			
Norbury Lake (C-12) 97 hectares 16 km s. of jct. hwys. 93 and 95 at Fort Steele. Canoeing.	95	•	•	•	•	•		•	•	•	•				
North Thompson River (A-8) 126 hectares 5 km s. of Clearwater off Hwy. 5. Playground.	96	•	•	•											
Okanagan Lake (C-9) 98 hectares 11 km n. of Summerland off Hwy. 97. Canoeing, water skiing, windsurfing, wildlife viewing; playground.	97	•	•	•	•	•		•	•	•					•
Okanagan Mountain (C-9) 11,038 hectares 25 km n. of Penticton off Hwy. 97. Canoeing, horseback riding, hunting, wildlife viewing, kayaking, water skiing.	98	•	•	•				•	•	•				•	
One Island Lake (E-5) 59 hectares 30 km s. of Tupper off Hwy. 2. Canoeing, kayaking, scuba diving, water skiing, windsurfing; playground.	99	•	•		•	•		•	•	•					
Otter Lake (C-8) 51 hectares on Otter Lake, 33 km w. of Princeton off Hwy. 5A. Canoeing, ice fishing, water skiing.	100	•	•	•	•	•		•	•	•					
Paarens Beach (E-4) 43 hectares 11 km s.w. of Fort St. James off Hwy. 27. Canoeing, water skiing, windsurfing; playground.	101	•	•		•	•		•	•	•					
Paul Lake (B-8) 670 hectares 5 km n. of Kamloops off Hwy. 5. Canoeing, cross-country skiing, snowshoeing, wildlife viewing.	102	•	•	•	•	•		•	•	•		•	•		
Pirates Cove Marine (G-10) 31 hectares 16 km s.e. of Nanaimo on DeCourcy Island via boat. Canoeing, wildlife viewing	103	•	•	•				•	•	•					
Plumper Cove Marine (G-11) 66 hectares on Keats Island. Boat and ferry access only. Canoeing, winter camping.	104	•	•	•				•	•	•	•				
Porpoise Bay (G-11) 61 hectares 4 km n. of Sechelt on East Porpoise Bay Rd. Canoeing. Playground.	105	•	•	•				•	•	•	•				
Porteau Cove (G-11) 50 hectares 38 km n. of Vancouver on Hwy. 99. Canoeing, scuba diving, windsurfing, wildlife viewing, winter camping.	106	•	•	•	•	•		•	•	•		•		•	
Premier Lake (C-12) 662 hectares 12 km s. of Skookumchuck via Hwy. 95. Canoeing, hunting, wildlife viewing, winter camping; playground.	107	•	•	•	•			•	•	•		•			
Prudhomme Lake (E-2) 7 hectares 16 km e. of Prince Rupert on Hwy. 16. Canoeing.	108	•		•				•	•	•					
Purden Lake (F-5) 2,521 hectares 64 km e. of Prince George off Hwy. 16. Canoeing, hunting, water skiing, wildlife viewing, windsurfing; playground.	109	•	•	•	•	•		•	•	•					
Rathtrevor Beach (G-10) 347 hectares 3 km s. of Parksville on Hwy. 19. Nature programs. Canoeing, wildlife viewing, windsurfing, winter camping; playground.	110	•	•	•				•	•	•	•				
Rebecca Spit Marine (E-10) 177 hectares on Quadra Island via ferry from Campbell River, then 5 km e. on Heriot Bay Rd. Canoeing, scuba diving, windsurfing.	111		•	•	•	•		•	•	•	•				
Red Bluff (E-3) 148 hectares 45 km n. of Topley via Hwy. 118. Canoeing, wildlife viewing.	112	•	•	•				•	•	•	•				
Roberts Creek (G-11) 40 hectares 9 km s. of Sechelt on Hwy. 101.	113	•	•	•				•	•	•					
Roderick Haig-Brown (A-8) 1,076 hectares 5 km n. of Squilax off Hwy. 1 on both sides of the Adams River. Salmon spawning beds. Non-motorized boats only. Canoeing, wildlife viewing.	114		•	•	•			•			•	•	•		
Rolley Lake (H-12) 115 hectares 23 km n.w. of Mission off Hwy. 7. Canoeing, wildlife viewing.	115	•	•	•				•	•	•	•				
Ruckle (H-10) 486 hectares at Beaver Point on Salt Spring Island via ferry from Swartz Bay. Canoeing, scuba diving, wildlife viewing, windsurfing, winter camping. *(See Salt Spring Island p. 324.)*	116	•	•	•				•	•	•	•				

Recreation Areas Chart

The map location numerals in column 2 show an area's location on the preceding map.

	MAP LOCATION	CAMPING	PICNICKING	HIKING TRAILS	BOATING	BOAT RAMP	BOAT RENTAL	FISHING	SWIMMING	PETS ON LEASH	BICYCLE TRAILS	WINTER SPORTS	VISITOR CENTER	LODGE/CABINS	FOOD SERVICE
Saltery Bay (F-11) 69 hectares 1 km n. of Saltery Bay ferry landing on Hwy. 101. Canoeing, kayaking, scuba diving, wildlife viewing.	117	•	•	•				•	•	•	•				
Sasquatch (D-7) 1,217 hectares 6.4 km n. of Harrison Hot Springs via an access road off Hwy. 7. Canoeing, water skiing, windsurfing, wildlife viewing; playground.	118	•	•	•	•	•		•	•	•	•				
Schoen Lake (H-3) 8,430 hectares 45 km s. of Sayward, 38 km s. of Hwy. 19. Backcountry skiing, canoeing, hunting, snowshoeing.	119	•	•	•		•		•		•	•	•	•		
Seeley Lake (E-3) 24 hectares 10 km w. of Hazelton on Hwy. 16. Electric motors only.	120	•	•	•		•		•		•					
Shuswap Lake (A-9) 149 hectares 19 km n. of Squilax. Nature programs. Canoeing, cross-country skiing, kayaking, snorkeling, snowshoeing, water skiing, windsurfing; playground.	121	•	•	•	•	•	•	•	•	•	•				
Silver Beach (A-9) 130 hectares at n. end of Shuswap Lake at Seymour Arm. Canoeing, scuba diving, water skiing, windsurfing.	122	•		•	•	•		•	•						
Skagit Valley (D-7) 27,948 hectares 3 km w. of Hope via Hwy. 1, then 37 km s. on entrance portal via Silver Skagit Rd. Interpretive programs. Canoeing, hunting; horse trails, playground.	123	•	•	•	•	•		•		•		•	•		
Skihist (B-7) 33 hectares 6 km e. of Lytton on Hwy. 1. Canoeing, wildlife viewing.	124	•	•	•				•		•		•			
Smelt Bay (E-10) 16 hectares on s.w. side of Cortes Island via ferry from Campbell River. Canoeing, kayaking.	125	•	•		•	•		•	•	•	•				
Sowchea Bay (E-4) 13 hectares on Stuart Lake, 20 km w. of Fort St. James off Hwy. 27. Canoeing, water skiing, windsurfing.	126	•			•	•		•	•						
Sproat Lake (F-9) 43 hectares 13 km n.w. of Port Alberni on Sproat Lake Rd. Canoeing, scuba diving, water skiing, windsurfing. Prehistoric petroglyphs (K'ak'awin).	127	•	•	•	•	•		•	•	•	•				
Stamp River (F-10) 327 hectares 14 km w. of Port Alberni on Stamp River Rd. Winter camping.	128	•		•				•		•		•			
Stone Mountain (B-4) 25,690 hectares 140 km w. of Fort Nelson on Hwy. 97. Canoeing, horseback riding, hunting, kayaking, wildlife viewing.	129	•	•	•	•	•		•		•		•	•		
Strathcona (E-9) 245,807 hectares 48 km w. of Campbell River via Hwy. 28. Cross-country skiing, horseback riding, mountain biking, rock climbing, snowshoeing, water skiing, wildlife viewing, windsurfing. Snowmobiles prohibited.	130	•	•	•	•	•		•	•	•		•		•	
Swan Lake (E-5) 82 hectares at Tupper, 35 km s.e. of Dawson Creek via Hwy. 2. Canoeing, kayaking, scuba diving, water skiing, windsurfing; playground.	131	•	•	•	•	•		•	•	•	•				
Syringa (C-10) 4,417 hectares 19 km n.w. of Castlegar off Hwy. 3. Canoeing, hunting, kayaking, water skiing, windsurfing; playground.	132	•	•	•	•	•		•	•	•	•				
Taylor Arm (F-9) 71 hectares 23 km n.w. of Port Alberni on Hwy. 4. Hunting, winter camping.	133	•		•				•	•	•					
Ten Mile Lake (F-4) 260 hectares 12 km n. of Quesnel on Hwy. 97. Canoeing; cross-country and water skiing.	134	•	•	•	•	•		•	•	•	•		•		
Top of the World (C-12) 8,790 hectares 48 km n.e. of Kimberley off Hwy. 93. Cross-country skiing, hunting, mountain biking, snowshoeing, winter camping; horse trails.	135	•		•				•		•	•	•		•	
Tudyah Lake (E-4) 56 hectares 9 km n. of McLeod Lake on Hwy. 97. Canoeing, ice fishing, water skiing.	136	•	•		•	•		•	•	•	•				
Tweedsmuir South (G-3) 506,000 hectares 365 km n.w. of Williams Lake on Hwy. 20. Canoeing circuit, cross-country and downhill skiing, horseback riding, hunting.	137	•	•	•	•	•		•		•		•		•	
Tyhee Lake (E-3) 33 hectares 10 km e. of Smithers off Hwy. 16. Canoeing, cross-country skiing, ice skating, kayaking, water skiing, wildlife viewing.	138	•	•	•				•	•	•		•	•		
Vaseux Lake (C-9) 12 hectares 25 km s. of Penticton on Hwy. 97. Canoeing, ice skating, kayaking, wildlife viewing.	139	•	•	•				•	•	•	•				

Recreation Areas Chart

The map location numerals in column 2 show an area's location on the preceding map.

	MAP LOCATION	CAMPING	PICNICKING	HIKING TRAILS	BOATING	BOAT RAMP	BOAT RENTAL	FISHING	SWIMMING	PETS ON LEASH	BICYCLE TRAILS	WINTER SPORTS	VISITOR CENTER	LODGE/CABINS	FOOD SERVICE
Wasa Lake (C-12) 144 hectares 21 km n. of Fort Steele off Hwy. 93/95. Canoeing, water skiing, windsurfing; playground.	140	•	•	•	•	•	•	•	•	•	•				
Wells Gray (G-6) 540,000 hectares 67 km n. of Clearwater via an access road off Hwy. 5. Interpretive programs. Canoeing, cross-country skiing, horseback riding, hunting, kayaking, snowshoeing, wildlife viewing; horse rental. *(See Clearwater p. 229.)*	141	•	•	•	•	•	•	•	•	•	•	•	•	•	•
West Lake (F-4) 256 hectares 22 km s.w. of Prince George off Hwy. 16. Canoeing, cross-country skiing, water skiing, wildlife viewing, windsurfing.	142		•	•	•	•		•	•	•	•				
Whiskers Point (E-4) 116 hectares 130 km n. of Prince George off Hwy. 97. Canoeing, hunting, kayaking, water skiing, windsurfing; nature trail, playground.	143	•	•	•	•	•		•	•	•					
Whiteswan Lake (B-12) 1,994 hectares 22 km e. of Canal Flats off Hwy. 93/95. Canoeing, hunting, kayaking.	144	•	•	•	•	•		•	•	•	•				
Wistaria (E-3) 40 hectares 60 km w. of Hwy. 35, s.w. of Burns Lake on Ootsa Lake.	145		•		•	•		•	•		•				
Yahk (D-11) 9 hectares on Hwy. 3/93 at Yahk. Canoeing.	146	•	•					•			•	•			
Yard Creek (B-9) 175 hectares 15 km e. of Sicamous on Hwy. 1.	147	•	•	•				•	•	•					
OTHER															
Berman Lake (F-4) 38 hectares 45 km w. of Prince George. Canoeing.	148		•	•					•	•					
Canyon Hot Springs (A-10) Hot mineral springs 35 km e. of Revelstoke on Hwy. 1. *(See Revelstoke p. 312.)*	149	•	•	•				•	•	•				•	•
Creston Valley Wildlife Management Area (D-11) 7,000 hectares 13 km w. of Creston on Hwy. 3. Bird-watching, hunting. *(See Creston p. 234.)*	150		•	•				•		•	•	•	•		
Descanso Bay Regional Park (G-10) 16 hectares 1 km e. of Nanaimo on Gabriola Island via ferry. Kayaking.	151	•	•	•	•			•	•	•	•				
Fairmont Hot Springs (B-12) Hot mineral springs on Hwy. 95 in Fairmont Hot Springs. Downhill skiing, fly fishing, ice fishing, rock climbing, snowshoeing, wildlife viewing, winter camping; horse rental. *(See place listing p. 237.)*	152	•	•					•	•	•	•	•		•	•
Ferry Island (E-2) 61 hectares 1 km e. of Terrace off Hwy. 16. Cross-country skiing.	153	•	•	•	•	•	•	•				•		•	
Giscome Portage (E-4) 160 hectares 40 km n. of Prince George. Historic. Cross-country skiing, snowshoeing.	154		•									•			
Harold Mann (E-4) 13 hectares 50 km n.e. of Prince George. Canoeing; nature trail.	155		•	•				•	•	•			•		
Harrison Hot Springs (C-7) Hot mineral springs on Harrison Lake, 5 km n. of Hwy. 7 on Hwy. 9. Canoeing, golf, hunting, rock hunting; horse rental. *(See place listing p. 248.)*	156	•	•	•	•	•	•	•	•	•				•	•
Kanaka Creek (H-12) 400 hectares 2 km e. of Haney. Canoeing, kayaking; fish hatchery, horse trails. *(See Maple Ridge p. 272.)*	157		•	•				•	•			•	•		
Kawkawa Lake (C-7) 7 hectares 2.5 km e. of Hope off Hwy. 5. Canoeing, jet skiing, kayaking, tubing. Buggy rentals.	158	•	•	•	•			•	•						
Nakusp Hot Springs (B-10) Hot mineral springs 14 km n. of Nakusp on Nakusp Hot Springs Rd. Cross-country skiing, kayaking, mountain biking, snowmobiling. *(See Nakusp p. 275.)*	159	•	•					•	•		•	•	•	•	
Ness Lake (E-4) 14 hectares 35 km n.w. of Prince George. Canoeing, cross-country skiing, ice fishing.	160		•	•				•	•	•					
Radium Hot Springs (B-11) Hot mineral springs near the w. entrance of Kootenay National Park. Hunting, skiing; horse rental. *(See Kootenay National Park p. 267.)*	161	•	•	•				•	•			•	•	•	•
Whytecliff Park (G-11) 16 hectares near Horseshoe Bay in West Vancouver. Scuba diving; playground.	162		•	•				•	•	•					•
Wilkins Park (E-4) 57 hectares 15 km w. of Prince George. Cross-country skiing; nature trail.	163		•	•	•	•				•		•			

100 MILE HOUSE pop. 1,886

100 MILE HOUSE SUPER 8
(250)395-8888

 Motel $79-$149 **Address:** 989 Alder Ave V0K 2E0 **Location:** 0.6 mi (1 km) s on Hwy 97. **Facility:** 28 units, some efficiencies. 2 stories (no elevator), exterior corridors. **Parking:** winter plug-ins. **Terms:** cancellation fee imposed.

CALL  / SOME UNITS FEE

WHERE TO EAT

HAPPY LANDING RESTAURANT
250/395-5359

 Swiss. Casual Dining. $10-$20 **AAA Inspector Notes:** Behind the village restaurant's charming blue shutters, diners are welcomed to savor the flavors of traditional Swiss cuisine. Among choices are steaks, wonderful schnitzels, roestis and other European favorites. **Bar:** full bar. **Reservations:** suggested. **Address:** 725 Alder Ave V0K 2E0 **Location:** Hwy 97, 0.6 mi (1 km) s on Service Rd. [L] [D]

SMITTY'S
250/395-4655

 American. Casual Dining. $7-$20 **AAA Inspector Notes:** The family-oriented restaurant satisfies patrons with its ever-popular all-day breakfast items, as well as tasty and wholesome soups and salads at lunchtime. A relaxed mood characterizes the dining space. **Bar:** full bar. **Address:** 451 Caribou Hwy V0K 2E0 **Location:** On Hwy 97; by tourist information booth. [B] [L] [D]

Theme Park Savings

AAA.com/discounts

Download eTourBook guides for
top destinations at AAA.com/ebooks

108 MILE RANCH (A-7) pop. 2,559

South Cariboo Visitor Info Centre: 155 Airport Rd., Box 340, 100 Mile House, BC, Canada V0K 2E0. **Phone:** (250) 395-5353 or (877) 511-5353.

108 HERITAGE SITE is at 4690 Cariboo Tr. The site comprises eight historical buildings depicting the famous mile houses, which were established as a stopover for weary travelers. With the discovery of gold in 1858 and the influx of miners increasing, the houses served a need by providing meals or a place to sleep. A 1908 log barn and 1890 church also are on-site. **Time:** Allow 30 minutes minimum. **Hours:** Daily 10-5, Victoria Day-Labour Day weekend. **Cost:** Donations. **Phone:** (250) 791-5288 or (250) 791-1971.

ABBOTSFORD (H-11) pop. 133,497, elev. 58m/190'

Abbotsford is the regional shopping center as well as the center of trade and industry for the fruit, livestock, poultry and dairy farms of the surrounding Fraser Valley. Several area industries and farms offer tours, including Clayburn Industries Ltd., at Railway and Pine streets, which produces refractory products. Castle Park Golf and Games Amusement Park, 36165 N. Parallel Rd., provides a range of family entertainment.

The city is also the site of the Abbotsford International Air Show, held in early August. In addition to more than 2 dozen planes on display, more than 30 planes, both military and civilian, take to the air.

Tourism Abbotsford Visitor Centre: 34561 Delair Rd., Abbotsford, BC, Canada V2S 2E1. **Phone:** (604) 859-1721 or (888) 332-2229.

TRETHEWEY HOUSE HERITAGE SITE ON MILL LAKE is at 2313 Ware St., next to John Mahoney Park. Restored and furnished to its 1925 appearance, this Arts and Crafts-style house features reconstructions of a playhouse and a carriage house as well as period gardens.

Tours: Guided tours are available. **Time:** Allow 30 minutes minimum. **Hours:** House open daily 9-5, Victoria Day-Labour Day; Mon.-Fri. 1-5, rest of year. Closed statutory holidays. **Cost:** Donations. **Phone:** (604) 853-0313.

BEST WESTERN BAKERVIEW INN   (604)859-1341

 Motel $110-$140

 AAA Benefit: Members save up to 20%, plus 10% bonus points with Best Western Rewards®.

Address: 1821 Sumas Way V2S 4L5 **Location:** Trans-Canada Hwy 1 exit 92 (Town Centre), just n on Hwy 11. **Facility:** 61 units, some efficiencies. 2 stories (no elevator), exterior corridors. **Terms:** 3 day cancellation notice-fee imposed. **Pool(s):** heated indoor. **Activities:** whirlpool. **Guest Services:** coin laundry. **Free Special Amenities:** local telephone calls and use of on-premises laundry facilities.

▼ See AAA listing p. 218 ▼

BEST WESTERN PLUS REGENCY INN & CONFERENCE CENTRE
(604)853-3111

Hotel
$106-$160

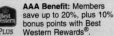

AAA Benefit: Members save up to 20%, plus 10% bonus points with Best Western Rewards®.

Address: 32110 Marshall Rd V2T 1A1 **Location:** Trans-Canada Hwy 1 exit 87 (Clearbrook Rd). Located behind an elementary school. **Facility:** 128 units, some efficiencies. 2-3 stories, interior corridors. **Amenities:** video games (fee). *Some:* high-speed Internet. **Pool(s):** 2 heated indoor. **Activities:** whirlpools, exercise room. **Guest Services:** valet and coin laundry. **Free Special Amenities:** full breakfast and high-speed Internet. *(See ad this page.)*

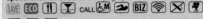

SWEET DREAMS LUXURY INN
(604)851-5101

Bed & Breakfast $195-$300 **Address:** 32288 King Rd V2T 5Z5 **Location:** Trans-Canada Hwy 1 exit 87 (Clearbrook Rd), 1 mi (1.6 km) s to King Rd, then just e. **Facility:** Amazingly spacious guest rooms feature deep soaker tubs for two, rain showers in separate stalls and luxurious Egyptian cotton linens. A gourmet breakfast is served. 4 units. 2 stories (no elevator), interior corridors. **Terms:** check-in 4 pm, age restrictions may apply, 7 day cancellation notice.

MILESTONES GRILL AND BAR
604/850-3826

American. Casual Dining. $8-$28 **AAA Inspector Notes:** Popular with locals, the bustling eatery is a great gathering place. The menu features such items as wild Pacific coho salmon, Angus beef, gluten-free burgers, Kobe style beef sliders, "share plate" appetizers, soups, salads, "pasta & bowls," Angus top sirloin, Mediterranean chicken, portobello mushroom chicken, sandwiches, burgers, prime rib, roll-ups, taster or full desserts. There is a great selection of wines by the glass and creative specialty cocktails. **Bar:** full bar. **Address:** 200-2070 Sumas Way V2S 2C7 **Location:** Corner of S Fraser Way and Sumas Way (Hwy 11); in Abbotsford Village Mall.

SWISS CHALET
604/864-4002

Chicken. Casual Dining. $10-$21 **AAA Inspector Notes:** The popular restaurant is known for its rotisserie chicken and ribs and the tangy Chalet sauce that gives food its special zip. Diners munch on a half or quarter chicken with sides such as steamed vegetables, fries, baked potatoes and salads. Lunch guests often go for the great soup and sandwich combination. Take-out and delivery service are popular options. **Bar:** full bar. **Address:** 32470 S Fraser Way V2T 1X3 **Location:** S Fraser Way at Trethewey.

Learn about inspections and Diamond Ratings at AAA.com/Diamonds

▼ See AAA listing this page ▼

Share a New View on Travel at AAATravelViews.com

Read stories, tips and trends from AAA insiders. Post comments and get your questions answered by our travel experts.

AINSWORTH HOT SPRINGS (C-11)
elev. 538m/1,766'

AINSWORTH HOT SPRINGS RESORT is on Hwy. 31. Overlooking Kootenay Lake, the springs feature a natural, odorless mineral cave pool with an average temperature of 40-44 C (104-111 F), and a main pool averaging 35 C (97 F). The cold plunge pool, fed by a natural spring, has an average temperature of 4 C (40 F). Towels can be rented. **Hours:** Daily 10-9:30. Last admission 30 minutes before closing. **Cost:** $11; $10 (ages 13-17 and 60+); $9 (ages 3-12). **Phone:** (250) 229-4212 or (800) 668-1171. ⓣ

AINSWORTH HOT SPRINGS RESORT   (250)229-4212

Hotel
$139-$249

Address: 3609 Hwy 31 V0G 1A0 **Location:** On Hwy 31. **Facility:** 43 units, some efficiencies. 4 stories, interior/exterior corridors. **Terms:** check-in 4 pm, cancellation fee imposed. **Dining:** The Springs, see separate listing. **Activities:** Fee: massage. **Guest Services:** complimentary laundry.

[SAVE] ⓣ ⓨ CALL ⓈM 🛜 ✕ 🖥 /SOME UNITS 🅱

WHERE TO EAT

THE SPRINGS   250/229-4212

▼▼▼ American. Casual Dining. $10-$27 **AAA Inspector Notes:** The gorgeous view of Kootenay Lake is the focal point in the simply designed dining room where you will find professional and friendly service. A good variety of tasty appetizers along with Asian dishes, steak, chicken, salmon and halibut entrées and house-made desserts are featured. The chef puts out well-prepared dishes and likes to source local ingredients when possible. Lunch is toned down a bit to burgers, sandwiches, fish and chips and more simple entrées, but it's just as worthwhile. **Bar:** full bar. **Reservations:** suggested. **Address:** 3609 Hwy 31 V0G 1A0 **Location:** On Hwy 31; in Ainsworth Hot Springs Resort. Ⓑ Ⓛ Ⓓ CALL ⓈM

ALDERGROVE (H-11) elev. 61m/200'
• Part of Vancouver area — see map p. 343

A small town on the Lower Fraser Valley's southern side, Aldergrove is near the Fraser River and the Canada-United States border. Dairy, chicken, strawberry and raspberry farms dot the surrounding area. Just northeast of Aldergrove, Bradner grows about 400 varieties of daffodils.

GREATER VANCOUVER ZOO is at 5048 264th St. The 49-hectare (120-acre) zoo is devoted to the preservation of endangered species. More than 600 animals represent 121 species from around the world, including hippopotami, monkeys, giraffes and tigers. A narrated train ride takes passengers around the zoo's perimeter; a bus tour travels through the North American Wilds exhibit.

Time: Allow 2 hours minimum. **Hours:** Daily 9-7, Apr.-Sept.; 9-4, rest of year. **Cost:** $22.25; $20.25 (ages 16+ with student ID); $16.25 (ages 3-15 and 65+); $70.25 (family, two adults and two children). Train ride $5. **Parking:** Parking $6. Rates may vary; phone ahead. **Phone:** (604) 856-6825. ⓣ 🅰

BEST WESTERN PLUS COUNTRY MEADOWS INN
(604)856-9880

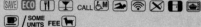

▼▼▼
Hotel
S89-$149

Best Western PLUS

AAA Benefit: Members save up to 20%, plus 10% bonus points with Best Western Rewards®.

Address: 3070 264th St V4W 3E1 **Location:** Trans-Canada Hwy 1 exit 73 (264th St/Aldergrove), 3.1 mi (5 km) s on 264th St (Hwy 13). **Facility:** 77 units, some efficiencies. 2 stories, interior corridors. **Parking:** on-site (fee). **Terms:** check-in 4 pm. **Amenities:** Some: high-speed Internet. **Pool(s):** heated indoor. **Activities:** whirlpool, exercise room. **Guest Services:** valet and coin laundry. **Free Special Amenities:** full breakfast and local telephone calls. (See ad p. 216.)

[SAVE] [ECO] ⓣ ⓨ CALL ⓈM 🛝 🛜 ✕ 🅱 🖥 /SOME UNITS FEE 🐾

ALERT BAY (H-2) pop. 445, elev. 15m/49'

On crescent-shaped Cormorant Island off Vancouver Island's northeast coast, Alert Bay is a fishing village reached by ferry from Port McNeill (see place listing p. 305). The influence of indigenous cultures is evident in the many totem poles, including a memorial pole for totem carver Chief Mungo Martin.

Christ Church on Front Street is an 1881 cedar church with stained-glass windows that reflect the blending of native and European cultures; phone the Travel InfoCentre for information.

Alert Bay Travel InfoCentre: 116 Fir St., Bag Service 2800, Alert Bay, BC, Canada V0N 1A0. **Phone:** (250) 974-5024.

ALERT BAY PUBLIC LIBRARY AND MUSEUM is at 118 Fir St. This small museum houses Kwakwaka'wakw artifacts and items depicting local history. Its archives include Alert Bay newspapers and more than 6,000 photographs. **Time:** Allow 30 minutes minimum. **Hours:** Mon.-Sat. 1-4, July-Aug.; Mon. and Fri.-Sat. 1-4, Wed. 1-5, rest of year. Closed major holidays. **Cost:** Donations. **Phone:** (250) 974-5721.

TOTEM POLE is near the corner of Park and Front sts. Erected in 1973, the 53-metre (173-ft.) pole is considered to be the world's tallest. It features 22 figures, including a sun at the top. Binoculars are recommended for viewing. The totem pole stands near the 'Namgis Big House, a Kwakwaka'wakw ceremonial center not open to the public. **Time:** Allow 30 minutes minimum. **Hours:** Daily dawn-dusk. **Cost:** Free.

U'MISTA CULTURAL CENTRE & MUSEUM is 2 km (1.2 mi.) w. of the ferry on Front St. The collection includes elaborately carved masks, traditional and historical carvings, woven cedar pieces, ceremonial regalia, paintings and other artifacts from Indian potlatches—the gift-giving ceremonies that mark such important occasions as birth, marriage and death. The exhibits tell the stories of the people who speak Kwak'wala, the Kwakwaka'wakw First Nation of British Columbia; for generations they have been hosting potlatches, which continue to play a central and unifying role in community life. The potlatch was banned 1885-1951.

The potlatch masks and other regalia in the Big House Gallery were surrendered to the police after an illegal potlatch in 1921. After the ban ended, the Kwakwaka'wakw negotiated for decades for the return of their sacred regalia that had ended up in museums and private collections, and most came back. The word *u'mista* is Kwak'wala and means, "the return of something important."

There are also films and small galleries with short-term exhibits. **Tours:** Guided tours are available. **Hours:** Daily 9-5, Victoria Day-Sept. 30; Tues.-Sat. 9-5, rest of year. **Cost:** $10; $9 (ages 8-18 and 65+); 7 (students); $1 (ages 0-11). **Phone:** (250) 974-5403 or (800) 690-8222.

ARMSTRONG pop. 4,815
• Part of Okanagan Valley area — see map p. 286

VILLAGE CHEESE COMPANY   250/546-8651

Sandwiches Soup. Quick Serve. $5-$7 **AAA Inspector Notes:** Inside a working cheese factory, the bistro has a small seating area. As they nosh on pre-made sandwiches and desserts, guests can watch cheese being made and browse the vast choice of retail cheeses and cheese-related knick-knacks. **Address:** 3475 Smith Dr V0E 1B0 **Location:** Just w of Hwy 97. L

ASHCROFT (B-7) pop. 1,628, elev. 305m/1,000'

Ashcroft Manor, a roadside house on Cariboo Waggon Road, was named for the English home of its settlers, Clement and Henry Cornwall. The Cornwalls established themselves as cattlemen in 1862 and lived the pioneer life in the style of gentlemen, practicing such rituals as afternoon tea and riding to hounds through sagebrush and scrub in pursuit of coyotes. The manor is south of town on Hwy. 1.

ASHCROFT MUSEUM is at 404 Brink St. Exhibits recount the history of the southern Cariboo, the Indian tribes that first settled Ashcroft. Artifacts and photographs are displayed in the windows of old shops, churches and houses along a board sidewalk, depicting life as it was in Ashcroft's glory days between the first settlement in 1884 and the great fire in 1916. A re-creation of the Hat Creek Mine also is displayed.

Hours: Mon.-Fri. 9-5, Sat.-Sun. noon-8, July-Aug.; Mon.-Fri. 9-5, mid-Apr. through June 30 and Sept. 1-late Oct. Closed major holidays. Phone ahead to confirm schedule. **Cost:** Donations. **Phone:** (250) 453-9232.

BARKERVILLE HISTORIC TOWN
(F-5)

Barkerville is approximately 80 kilometres (50 mi.) east of Quesnel via Hwy. 26. The restored 1870s gold rush town once had the largest population north of San Francisco and west of Chicago. In those days when more than $50 million of gold—at $16 per ounce—had been mined from the area, soap cost $1 a bar and a dance with a hurdy-gurdy girl cost $1 a whirl.

The town was named for Billy Barker, a Cornish miner who first found gold in large quantities in the early 1860s. Barkerville became a virtual ghost town a few years later when the gold ran out.

The Barkerville Hotel, St. Saviours Church, the Mason and Daly General Store and the Wake Up Jake Cafe are just a few of the 125 original or reconstructed buildings in the town; many are manned by attendants in period dress. Board sidewalks and dirt streets help preserve the essence of the original site.

Theatre Royale presents period melodrama, dance and music Victoria Day through September 30. Treasure seekers can pan for gold at Eldorado Mine. A visitor center presents videos and exhibits about the history of Barkerville. Guided town, Chinatown and cemetery tours as well as living-history programs are offered.

Pets are not permitted. The townsite is open daily 8-8. Full visitor services operate daily, mid-May through Sept. 30. Admission mid-May through Sept. 30, $14; $13 (ages 65+); $8.50 (ages 13-18); $4.50 (ages 6-12); $2 (second-day admission with first-day receipt); $33.50 (family, two adults and four children). Free rest of year. Phone (250) 994-3332 or (888) 994-3332.

BARRIERE pop. 1,326

MOUNTAIN SPRINGS MOTEL & RV PARK   250/672-0090

Motel $70-$80 **Address:** 4253 Yellowhead Hwy V0E 1E0 **Location:** 0.6 mi (1 km) s on Hwy 5 (Yellowhead Hwy). **Facility:** 12 units, some efficiencies. 1 story, exterior corridors. **Parking:** winter plug-ins. **Terms:** cancellation fee imposed. **Guest Services:** coin laundry.

CALL / SOME UNITS

BELLA COOLA (F-3) pop. 95, elev. 590'

BELLA COOLA VALLEY MUSEUM is just e. of jct. MacKenzie Hwy. and Bentinck Ave. at 269 Hwy. 20. The museum, in an 1892 heritage building, contains artifacts and interpretive exhibits about the Bella Coola Valley from the late 18th century, when Europeans first discovered the area's aboriginal people, to the mid-20th century. **Tours:** Guided tours are available. **Time:** Allow 30 minutes minimum. **Hours:** Daily 9-noon and 1-5, early June-early Sept. **Cost:** $2.50; $2 (students with ID); $1 (ages 0-9). **Phone:** (250) 799-5767, or (250) 982-2130 for Archives.

BLUE RIVER

GLACIER MOUNTAIN LODGE   250/673-2393

Hotel $99-$209 **Address:** 869 Shell Rd V0E 1J0 **Location:** On Hwy 5 (Yellowhead Hwy); at Shell Rd, follow signs. **Facility:** 35 units. 2 stories (no elevator), interior corridors. **Parking:** winter plug-ins. **Activities:** whirlpool. **Guest Services:** complimentary and valet laundry. / SOME UNITS FEE

BOSTON BAR (C-7) pop. 206, elev. 309m/1,013'

Boston Bar, which began as a gold mining town, was named for a Dutchman who came from Boston to prospect in the 1860s. Because Boston was the home port to many of the ships bringing prospectors, local Indians called the newcomers Boston men. Boston Bar is a logging and trade center, with the Canadian National Railway passing through town. The Canadian Pacific Railway parallels the National on the other side of Fraser River Canyon and passes through the village of North Bend.

Boston Bar is the access point for the Nahatlach Valley, which features the Nahatlach River and a chain of lakes. Recreation includes camping, fishing and white-water rafting.

HELL'S GATE AIRTRAM is 11 km (7 mi.) s. on Hwy. 1 to 43111 Trans-Canada Hwy. in Fraser River Canyon. The 25-passenger gondola descends 153 metres (502 ft.) across the river to the narrowest part of Fraser Canyon and across Hell's Gate Fishways, where millions of salmon annually swim upstream to their spawning grounds. Visitors can see eight fishways from observation decks or a suspension bridge.

A film about the life cycle of the salmon is shown at the education center. Simon's Wall is an interactive photo exhibit that pays tribute to the 200th anniversary of explorer Simon Fraser's journey. Panning for gold is available. An exhibit displays how Chinese labourers lived during the construction of the Canadian Pacific Railway in the 1880s.

Time: Allow 1 hour minimum. **Hours:** Daily 10-5, May 18-Sept. 3; daily 10-4, Apr. 26-May 17 and Sept. 4-Oct. 14. Phone ahead to confirm schedule. **Cost:** $21; $19 (ages 65+ and students with ID); $15 (ages 6-18); $57 (family). **Phone:** (604) 867-9277. 🍴

RECREATIONAL ACTIVITIES
White-water Rafting

- **REO Rafting Adventure Resort** is 18 km (11 mi.) n.w. on Hwy. 1 in Fraser Canyon. **Hours:** One-day Nahatlatch River trips operate May-Sept. Other trips are available. **Phone:** (604) 461-7238 or (800) 736-7238.

SIMON'S CAFE   604/867-9277

🍷 Burgers. Cafeteria. $9-$15 **AAA Inspector Notes:** You travel to this restaurant on a thrilling Hell's Gate Airtram ride over the mighty Fraser River. Regular Airtram admission applies with a $2 discount for CAA/AAA members. The menu features homemade salmon chowder and salmon burgers. It's well worth the stop. **Bar:** beer & wine. **Address:** 43111 Trans-Canada Hwy V0K 1C0 **Location:** 6.6 mi (11 km) s on Trans-Canada Hwy 1; at Hell's Gate Airtram.
Ⓛ CALL ⒼⓂ

BOSWELL (C-11) elev. 533m/1,748'

THE GLASS HOUSE is s. on Hwy. 3A (Southern Trans-Canada Hwy.). This six-room, castlelike house is made of empty 16-ounce embalming fluid bottles. A funeral director built the house, archway and several terraces on the landscaped lakefront

grounds. **Time:** Allow 30 minutes minimum. **Hours:** Daily 8-8, July-Aug.; 9-5, May-June and Sept. 1 to mid-Oct. **Cost:** $10; $8 (ages 13-19); $5 (ages 6-12). **Phone:** (250) 223-8372.

BRACKENDALE (G-11)

GLACIER AIR TOURS is at 46001 Government Rd. at Squamish Municipal Airport. Helicopter and airplane sightseeing flights and glacier-landing flights are offered. The latter may include dining on a glacier. Weight restrictions apply; phone ahead for details. **Hours:** Daily 8-8, in summer; otherwise varies (weather permitting). Departure times vary. Closed Jan. 1 and Christmas. **Cost:** Sightseeing flights start at $79; $74 (ages 2-12). All fares are per person based on a two person minimum. Reservations are recommended. **Phone:** (604) 898-9016, or (800) 265-0088 within Canada.

RECREATIONAL ACTIVITIES
White-water Rafting

- **Sunwolf Rafting** is at 70002 Squamish Valley Rd. Other activities are available. **Hours:** Daily 8-8, mid-May to mid-Sept. (weather permitting). **Phone:** (604) 898-1537 or (877) 806-8046.

BRENTWOOD BAY (H-10)
• Part of Victoria area — see map p. 397

BUTCHART GARDENS is 2 km (1.2 mi.) s. on W. Saanich Rd., then w. to 800 Benvenuto Ave. The magnificent floral displays of Butchart Gardens owe their existence to Jennie Butchart, wife of Robert Pim Butchart, a successful Portland cement pioneer.

When the limestone quarry near their home became depleted in the early 1900s, Jennie lined the empty pit with topsoil and the gardens began to take shape. The Sunken Garden, the site of the former quarry, was soon joined on the 22-hectare (55-acre) site with the Rose Garden, Japanese Garden and Italian Garden as well as the Star Pond and Ross Fountain. The Butcharts named their estate *Benvenuto*, Italian for "welcome."

The spring season brings azaleas, tulips, daffodils and other delicate blossoms. Breathtaking roses, annuals and perennials bloom in summer, while bursts of colorful foliage appear in autumn; subtle colored lighting illuminates the gardens June 15 through Sept. 15.

Two electrically operated boats offer 45-minute tours of the local coastline, including the location of the now-gone factory that produced cement from the limestone quarried in what is now the Sunken Garden. The cruise along Tod Inlet and Brentwood Bay often provides sightings of seals, herons, eagles and otters. The Rose Carousel in the Children's Pavilion offers old-fashioned rides on 30 hand-carved animals and two chariots.

July through August, nightly entertainment is offered with fireworks displays Saturday nights. The sparkle of holiday lights and decorations complement the colorful berries on shrubs and trees from Dec. 1 to Jan. 6 during Christmas at Butcharts. An outdoor skating rink, with skate rental, also is available in Waterwheel Square.

Time: Allow 2 hours minimum. **Hours:** Gardens open daily at 9 (at 1 on Dec. 25). Closing times vary depending on the season; phone ahead. Boat tours depart the dock daily every half-hour 11-5, mid-June to mid-Sept.; 11-4, late May to mid-June.

Cost: June 15-Sept. 30, $30.20; $15.10 (ages 13-17); $3 (ages 5-12). Admission in Oct., $25.25; $12.56 (ages 13-17); $2 (ages 5-12). Admission in Nov. $19.55; $9.80 (ages 13-17); $2 (ages 5-12). Admission in Dec., $25; $12.50 (ages 13-17); $3 (ages 5-12). Admission Jan. 7-Jan. 14, $16.70; $8.35 (ages 13-17); $2 (ages 5-12). Admission Jan. 15-Mar. 20, $22.40; $11.20 (ages 13-17); $2 (ages 5-12). Admission Mar. 21-June 14, $28.10; $14.05 (ages 13-17); $2 (ages 5-12). Boat tours $17.25; $13.25 (ages 13-17); $10.50 (ages 5-12). Carousel rides $2. Rates may vary; phone ahead. **Phone:** (250) 652-5256 or (866) 652-4422. 🍴

VICTORIA BUTTERFLY GARDENS is 2 km (1.2 mi.) s. at jct. Benvenuto Ave. and Keating Cross Rd. at 1461 Benvenuto Ave. This 1,110-square-metre (12,000-sq.-ft.) indoor tropical garden was designed specifically for the housing and breeding of more than 75 exotic butterfly and moth species. Guided tours and a videotape presentation explain the transformations the butterflies undergo during their life cycle. Between 600 and 1,200 pupae are imported each week and displayed in the Emerging Room.

Up to 6,000 butterflies—from the 2.5-centimetre-long (1-in.) helicon to the 30.5-centimetre-long (1-ft.) atlas moth—fly free among tropical plants and flowers, including an orchid exhibit and a carnivorous bog. Water falls into a stream that is home to koi fish and tropical ducks. Parrots, flamingos, songbirds and rare species such as the South African turacos also call the gardens home. Other garden residents include poison dart frogs, geckos, chameleons and sulcata tortoises.

Time: Allow 1 hour minimum. **Hours:** Daily 10-5, May 1-day after Labour Day; 10-7, in Dec.; 10-5, rest of year. Last admission 1 hour before closing. Closed Jan. 1 and Christmas. Phone ahead to confirm schedule. **Cost:** All-day admission $15; $10 (ages 13-17, ages 65+ and students with ID); $5 (ages 5-12). **Phone:** (250) 652-3822 or (877) 722-0272.

BRENTWOOD BAY RESORT & SPA   (250)544-2079

▼▼ ▼▼ ▼▼   **Address:** 849 Verdier Ave V8M 1C5 **Location:** Hwy 17 exit 18 (Brentwood
Contemporary Hotel   Bay), 1.8 mi (3 km) w on Keating Rd, 0.9 mi (1.5 km) n on W Saanich Rd, then 0.6 mi (1 km) w to Mill Bay Ferry. **Facility:**
$199-$599   Rooms in this standout luxury hotel offer ocean and marina views, private sun decks, deep soaker tubs, gas fireplaces and soft, fine linens on every bed. Expect the finest couples treatments at the spa. 33 units. 3 stories, exterior corridors. **Terms:** 7 day cancellation notice-fee imposed. **Amenities:** high-speed Internet, safes. **Dining:** Seagrille, see separate listing. **Pool(s):** heated outdoor. **Activities:** whirlpool, exercise room, spa. **Fee:** marina. **Guest Services:** valet and coin laundry. **Free Special Amenities:** local telephone calls and high-speed Internet.

🅂🅰🆅🅴 🄴🄲🄾 🍴 🍸 CALL 🛗 🛏 🛜 ✕ 🐾 🖥

WHERE TO EAT

SEAGRILLE   250/544-2079

▼▼ ▼▼ Pacific Northwest. Fine Dining. $19-$36 **AAA Inspector Notes:** In one of the city's finest luxury oceanfront resorts, the restaurant is just minutes from famous Butchart Gardens. Fresh fish, Alberta beef and local produce factor in exquisite, creatively prepared dishes. An extensive wine list features many award-winning British Columbia wines. **Bar:** full bar. **Reservations:** suggested. **Address:** 849 Verdier Ave V8M 1C5 **Location:** Hwy 17 exit 18 (Brentwood Bay), 1.8 mi (3 km) w on Keating Rd, 0.9 mi (1.5 km) n on W Saanich Rd, then 0.6 mi (1 km) w to Mill Bay Ferry; in Brentwood Bay Resort & Spa. B D CALL 🛗

SMITTY'S   250/652-1764

▼▼ ▼▼ American. Casual Dining. $8-$20 **AAA Inspector Notes:** The family-oriented restaurant satisfies patrons with its ever-popular all-day breakfast items, as well as tasty and wholesome soups and salads at lunchtime. A relaxed mood characterizes the dining space. **Bar:** full bar. **Address:** 6719 W Saanich Rd V8M 1R4 **Location:** Corner of W Saanich and Keating Cross rds. B L D

ZANZIBAR CAFE   250/652-1228

▼▼ ▼▼ Breakfast Sandwiches. Casual Dining. $11-$27 **AAA Inspector Notes:** Wildly popular with locals, this charming café is open early for breakfast, and until 4 pm for lunch. Thursday through Saturday they're open for dinner; reservations are recommended. All the favorite breakfast items are served, including eggs Benedict and made-to-order oatmeal. The lunch menu features delicious chicken and avocado melts, grilled turkey paninis, and gourmet burgers made with the likes of lamb and albacore tuna. **Bar:** full bar. **Address:** 1164 Stelly's Cross Rd V8M 1H3 **Location:** Hwy 17 exit 18 (Brentwood Bay), 1.8 mi (3 km) w on Keating Rd, then 1.2 mi (2 km) n on N Saanich Rd. B L 🅰

BRITANNIA BEACH (G-11) pop. 254, elev. 6m/20'

From 1930 to 1935 the Britannia Mine at Britannia Beach was the largest producer of copper in the British Empire. No longer in operation, the mine is now part of the Britannia Mine Museum.

Shopping areas: At the CRS Trading Post on Hwy. 99 the wood and soapstone carvings, silver jewelry, spirit masks, jade pieces, handcrafted walking sticks, moccasins and other items are created by Coast Salish artists in British Columbia. Look for the rocks displaying hand-painted scenes by well-known local artist Ken Skoda.

Visit AAA.com/Travel or CAA.ca/Travel for complete trip planning and reservations

BRITANNIA MINE MUSEUM is off Hwy. 99, following signs. The Britannia Mine was an important 20th-century copper mining site during its 70-year existence. The company town included libraries, swimming pools and a gym, and social events were held throughout the year.

The towering 20-story 1923 mill building, through which the ore would move as it was crushed and the valuable minerals separated from the rest of the rock, is now a museum. Fourteen other historic buildings also can be seen. Mining artifacts document the history of the site, and other items depict the social history of mining communities. The Canadian Mining Hall of Fame and a theater are on-site.

An underground mine tunnel ride is a highlight of the museum, which chronicles mining history through hands-on demonstrations and exhibits. On site is a 235-ton super mine truck. Gold panning is included with admission.

Note: The tunnel temperature is a constant 12 C (54 F); warm clothing and comfortable walking shoes are recommended. Hard hats are provided. **Tours:** Guided tours are available. **Time:** Allow 1 hour, 30 minutes minimum. **Hours:** Daily 9-5. Phone ahead for tour times. Closed major holidays. **Cost:** $21.50; $16 (ages 13-18 and 65+ and students with ID); $13.50 (ages 6-12); $72 (family, two adults and up to three children). **Phone:** (604) 896-2233 or (800) 896-4044.

BURNABY (H-11) pop. 223,218, elev. 40m/130'
- **Attractions map p. 355**
- **Hotels & Restaurants map & index p. 368**
- **Part of Vancouver area — see map p. 343**

Burnaby is more than just a suburban, bedroom community of hills, ridges, valleys, plain, and stunning views; it is an urban center which is home to Simon Fraser University and the British Columbia Institute of Technology.

DEER LAKE PARK is 14.5 km (9 mi.) s.e. at 6450 Deer Lake Ave. at Canada Way. The park contains the Century Gardens, with its distinctive rhododendron display and rose gardens. The Shadbolt Centre for the Arts offers community arts programs as well as theater and dance performances in its James Cowan Theatre. Several walking trails provide scenic views throughout the park. **Hours:** Daily 24 hours. **Cost:** Free. **Phone:** (604) 294-7450 or (604) 291-6864.

Burnaby Village Museum & Carousel is off Hwy. 1 Kensington Ave. S. exit to 6501 Deer Lake Ave. The 4-hectare (10-acre) village re-creates the sights and sounds of an 1890-1925 settlement in lower mainland British Columbia. Costumed townspeople welcome visitors to more than 30 shops and homes, including a printshop and schoolhouse. A restored 1912 Parker carousel is on the site. The Heritage Christmas celebration from late November to early January features carolers, entertainment, crafts and a chat with Father Christmas.

Time: Allow 1 hour minimum. **Hours:** Tues.-Sun. 11-4:30, May 4-Sept. 2; otherwise varies. Heritage Christmas daily noon-4:30 p.m., Nov. 24-Jan. 4 (also 4:30-8, Dec. 15-Jan. 4). Spring Break Scavenger Hunt daily noon-4, Mar. 16-24. Closed Christmas Eve and Christmas. **Cost:** Free. Carousel rides $2.30. **Phone:** (604) 297-4565. 🍴

RECREATIONAL ACTIVITIES
Boating
- **Deer Lake Boat Rentals** is at 5435 Sperling Ave. **Hours:** Daily 10-8, mid-June through Labour Day; Mon.-Fri. by appointment, Sat.-Sun. 10-8, Apr. 1 to mid-June; Mon.-Fri. by appointment, Sat.-Sun. 10-7, day after Labour Day-second Mon. in Oct. **Phone:** (604) 839-3949.

ACCENT INNS   (604)473-5000 **18**

Hotel
$109-$179

Address: 3777 Henning Dr V5C 6N5 **Location:** Trans-Canada Hwy 1 exit 28 (Grandview Hwy), just n on Boundary Rd. **Facility:** 128 units, some efficiencies. 3 stories, exterior corridors. **Terms:** cancellation fee imposed. **Activities:** sauna, whirlpool, limited exercise equipment. **Guest Services:** valet and coin laundry, area transportation-within 3 mi (5 km). **Free Special Amenities:** newspaper and high-speed Internet.

(See map & index p. 368.)

BEST WESTERN PLUS KINGS INN & CONFERENCE CENTER (604)438-1383 **22**

 Hotel $99-$139

AAA Benefit: Members save up to 20%, plus 10% bonus points with Best Western Rewards®.

Address: 5411 Kingsway V5H 2G1 **Location:** Trans-Canada Hwy 1 exit 29 (Willingdon Ave), 1.9 mi (3 km) s to Kingsway, then 1.2 mi (2 km) e. **Facility:** 137 units, some efficiencies and kitchens. 2 stories (no elevator), exterior corridors. **Amenities:** *Some:* high-speed Internet. **Pool(s):** heated outdoor. **Guest Services:** valet and coin laundry. **Free Special Amenities: expanded continental breakfast and high-speed Internet.** *(See ad this page.)*

DELTA BURNABY HOTEL AND CONFERENCE CENTRE (604)453-0750 **19**

 Hotel $129-$1300

Address: 4331 Dominion St V5G 1B2 **Location:** Trans-Canada Hwy 1 exit 29 (Willingdon Ave), just w on Canada Way, then n on Sumner St. **Facility:** Among the city's newest hotels, this luxurious spot is geared for both business and pleasure with its spacious meeting areas as well as an on-site casino featuring two floors of 24-hour entertainment. 200 units. 21 stories, interior corridors. **Parking:** on-site (fee) and valet. **Amenities:** high-speed Internet, safes. **Dining:** Ebo Restaurant and Lounge, see separate listing. **Activities:** whirlpool, steamroom, exercise room. **Guest Services:** valet laundry, area transportation-within 7 mi (11.2 km).

Enjoy exclusive member discounts and benefits from Hertz

HILTON VANCOUVER METROTOWN (604)438-1200 **20**

 Hotel $116-$197 **Address:** 6083 McKay Ave V5H 2W7 **Location:** Trans-Canada Hwy 1 exit 29 (Willingdon Ave), 1.8 mi (3 km) s to Kingsway, then just e. Next to Metrotown Shopping Mall.

AAA Benefit: Members save 5% or more!

Facility: 283 units. 18 stories, interior corridors. **Parking:** on-site (fee) and valet. **Terms:** 1-7 night minimum stay, cancellation fee imposed. **Amenities:** high-speed Internet. *Some:* safes. **Dining:** Reflect Social Dining + Lounge, see separate listing. **Pool(s):** heated outdoor. **Activities:** whirlpool, exercise room. **Guest Services:** valet laundry.

HOLIDAY INN EXPRESS METROTOWN (604)438-1881 **21**

 Hotel $139-$194 **Address:** 4405 Central Blvd V5H 4M3 **Location:** Trans-Canada Hwy 1 exit 29 (Willingdon Ave), 3.1 mi (5 km) s to Central Blvd, then just e. Adjacent to a large shopping center. **Facility:** 100 units. 6 stories, interior corridors. **Terms:** check-in 4 pm, cancellation fee imposed. **Pool(s):** heated outdoor. **Activities:** limited exercise equipment. **Guest Services:** valet and coin laundry.

HOWARD JOHNSON NORTH BURNABY BOUTIQUE HOTEL (604)298-7232 **17**

 Boutique Hotel $99-$410 **Address:** 4125 E Hastings St V5C 2J3 **Location:** Trans-Canada Hwy 1 exit 26 (E Hastings St), 1 mi (1.6 km) e to Gilmore Ave. **Facility:** Although guest rooms are small you'll find them sporting modern décor at this property located a short drive of the PNE and Hastings Park. 42 units. 2 stories (no elevator), interior corridors. **Amenities:** safes. **Guest Services:** valet and coin laundry.

WHERE TO EAT

CACTUS CLUB CAFE 604/291-6606

Canadian. Casual Dining. $11-$37 **AAA Inspector Notes:** This bustling, casual restaurant serves huge burgers, sandwiches, pasta, salads, soups, quesadillas, fajitas, vegetarian dishes, steak, ribs, chicken and fish. Featured are certified Angus beef and fresh wild British Columbia salmon. **Bar:** full bar. **Address:** 4219B Lougheed Hwy V5C 3Y6 **Location:** Between Gilmore and Madison aves.

▼ See AAA listing this page ▼

For business or leisure, we're thoughtfully designed for every type of trip.

Scan this tag on your smartphone for more information

Get the free mobile app at
http://gettag.mobi

BEST WESTERN PLUS Kings Inn & Conference Center
5411 Kingsway, Burnaby BC V5H 2G1
604- 438-1383
bestwestern.com/aaa

(See map & index p. 368.)

EARLS RESTAURANT   604/205-5025

▼▼ ▼▼ American. Casual Dining. $10-$28 **AAA Inspector Notes:** Offering an experience that falls between fast food and fine dining, the fun, relaxed restaurant prepares great food at a great price. Choices range from juicy burgers, hearty salads, wings and pizza to full entrees of steak, chops and seafood. Made-from-scratch soups and assorted breads, as well as a nice choice of wines and beers, round out the offerings. This is a fitting spot for impromptu get-togethers and festive occasions. **Bar:** full bar. **Address:** 3850 Lougheed Hwy V5C 6N4 **Location:** Just e of Boundary Rd.

[L] [D] [LATE] CALL [&M]

EBO RESTAURANT AND LOUNGE   604/453-0750 ③④

▼▼▼▼ Pacific Northwest. Casual Dining. $12-$36 **AAA Inspector Notes:** Patrons enjoy panoramic views of Burnaby and the North Shore Mountains from this second-floor dining room. Vancouver Aquarium recommends this place, which participates in sustainable food practices, as a choice for ocean-friendly seafood, specifically the freshest bounty of the Pacific Northwest. Breakfast comes in the form of a full buffet, while lunch and dinner are a la carte. **Bar:** full bar. **Reservations:** suggested. **Address:** 4331 Dominion St V5G 1B2 **Location:** Trans-Canada Hwy 1 exit 29 (Willingdon Ave), just w on Canada Way, then n on Sumner St; in Delta Burnaby Hotel and Conference Centre. **Parking:** on-site and valet. [B] [L] [D] CALL [&M]

HART HOUSE RESTAURANT   604/298-4278 ③⑤

▼▼▼▼ Pacific Northwest. Fine Dining. $14-$34 **AAA Inspector Notes:** The turn-of-the-20th-century Tudor-style country home has been turned into a lovely restaurant overlooking Deer Lake and 2 acres of lush lawn. The menu features rack of lamb, fish and pasta, along with lighter fare for lunch. **Bar:** full bar. **Reservations:** suggested. **Address:** 6664 Deer Lake Ave V5E 4H3 **Location:** Trans-Canada Hwy 1 exit 33 (Kensington S), 0.6 mi (1 km) e on Canada Way to Sperling Ave, follow signs to Burnaby Village Museum.

[L] [D] CALL [&M]

HORIZONS   604/299-1155 ③③

▼▼▼▼ Pacific Rim. Fine Dining. $14-$36 **AAA Inspector Notes:** The restaurant's hilltop location in Burnaby Mountain Park gives you a spectacular view of the city and mountains. Its menu specializes in alder wood-fired fresh seafood and steak as well as rack of lamb and roasted duck. This is a casual, fine dining experience. **Bar:** full bar. **Reservations:** suggested. **Address:** 100 Centennial Way V5A 2X9 **Location:** Lougheed Hwy, 3.1 mi (5 km) n on Gaglardi Way, 0.6 mi (1 km) w on Burnaby Mountain Pkwy, then just n, follow signs. [L] [D] CALL [&M]

REFLECT SOCIAL DINING + LOUNGE   604/438-1200 ③⑥

▼▼ ▼▼ Pacific Northwest. Casual Dining. $12-$35 **AAA Inspector Notes:** On the third floor of the Hilton Vancouver Metrotown, the renovated restaurant and lounge cater to those who like to linger before and after a meal. Fusion cooking at its best blends the flavors of Canada's West Coast with those of Europe and Asia. Dishes are meant to be shared. **Bar:** full bar. **Reservations:** suggested. **Address:** 6083 McKay Ave V5H 2W7 **Location:** Trans-Canada Hwy 1 exit 29 (Willingdon Ave), 1.8 mi (3 km) s to Kingsway, then just e; in Hilton Vancouver Metrotown. **Parking:** on-site and valet.

[B] [L] [D] CALL [&M]

SWISS CHALET   604/299-1761

▼▼ ▼▼ Chicken. Casual Dining. $9-$22 **AAA Inspector Notes:** The popular restaurant is known for its rotisserie chicken and ribs and the tangy Chalet sauce that gives food its special zip. Diners munch on a half or quarter chicken with sides such as steamed vegetables, fries, baked potatoes and salads. Lunch guests often go for the great soup and sandwich combination. Take-out and delivery service are popular options. **Bar:** full bar. **Address:** 3860 Lougheed Hwy V5C 6N4 **Location:** Jct Boundary Rd. [L] [D]

CACHE CREEK (B-7) pop. 1,040, elev. 450m/1,500'

 HISTORIC HAT CREEK RANCH is 11 km (7 mi.) n. on Hwy. 97 at jct. hwys. 97 and 99. The 130-hectare (320-acre) ranch, on one of the few sections of the Cariboo Waggon Road still accessible to the public, consists of more than 20 historic buildings constructed 1863-1915 when the ranch served as a roadhouse for the horse-drawn stagecoaches and freight wagons of the B.C. Express line (known as the B.X.).

Docents in period costumes conduct guided tours of the 1860s roadhouse, and visitors can explore a heritage apple orchard, a Shuswap village, a blacksmith shop and a collection of pioneer agricultural machinery. Visitors also can enjoy stagecoach rides and try their hand at gold panning.

Hours: Daily 9-6, July-Aug.; 9-5, May-June and in Sept. **Cost:** $12; $11 (ages 55+); $8 (ages 6-12); $25 (family, two adults and three children). **Phone:** (250) 457-9722 or (800) 782-0922. [A] [TI]

BONAPARTE MOTEL   250/457-9693

▼▼ ▼▼
Motel
$59-$129

Address: 1395 Hwy 97 N V0K 1H0 **Location:** Just n of jct Trans-Canada Hwy 1. **Facility:** 24 units, some two bedrooms, efficiencies and kitchens. 1 story, exterior corridors. **Parking:** winter plugins. **Pool(s):** heated outdoor. **Activities:** sauna, whirlpool. **Free Special Amenities:** early check-in/late check-out and high-speed Internet.

[SAVE] [icons] / SOME UNITS FEE [icon]

CAMPBELL RIVER (E-10) pop. 31,186, elev. 18m/59'

An important lumber, mining and commercial fishing center, Campbell River is near a noted Vancouver Island timber stand. The Elk Falls Pulp and Paper Mill offers tours in the summer. Campbell River is headquarters of the Tyee Club, whose members must catch a salmon of 14 kilograms (30 lbs.) or more while fishing from a rowboat in the raging waters of Discovery Passage.

Provincial parks preserve the area's natural beauty, typified by waterfalls and mountainous wilderness. At Elk Falls Provincial Park the Campbell River drops 27 metres (90 ft.) into a deep canyon. Strathcona Provincial Park contains Mount Golden Hinde, at 2,200 metres (7,218 ft.) the highest mountain on Vancouver Island, and 440-metre (1,445-ft.) Della Falls, the highest waterfall in Canada. Scuba diving is popular during the winter when the waters are particularly clear. *See Recreation Areas Chart.*

The 183-metre-long (600-ft.) Campbell River Fishing Pier, 655 Island Hwy., is available for fishing, strolling or watching the cruise ships pass through the Strait of Georgia.

Campbell River Visitor Centre: 1235 Shoppers Row, Campbell River, BC, Canada V9W 2C7. **Phone:** (250) 830-0411 or (877) 286-5705.

MUSEUM AT CAMPBELL RIVER is at 470 Island Hwy. with an entrance off 5th Ave. The museum displays artifacts crafted by the native inhabitants of northern Vancouver Island. Exhibits also follow the island's pioneer and industrial history, including vintage logging and fishing equipment and replicas of a pioneer cabin and a float house. The outdoor historical interpretation park includes indigenous plant gardens, a cod fishing boat and a logging steam donkey.

Time: Allow 1 hour minimum. **Hours:** Daily 10-5, mid-May through Sept. 30; Tues.-Sun. noon-5, rest of year. Closed Jan 1, Good Friday and Dec. 25. **Cost:** $6; $4 (students with ID); free (ages 0-5); $15 (family). **Phone:** (250) 287-3103.

QUINSAM RIVER SALMON HATCHERY is .5 km (.3 mi.) w. on Hwy. 28, then 2.4 km (1.5 mi.) s. on Quinsam Rd. to 4217 Argonaut Rd. The salmon enhancement project produces pink, coho and chinook salmon and steelhead trout. A display room chronicles the life cycle of a salmon. Facilities include various hatchery sensing containers. Adult salmon viewing is best from mid-September to mid-November. Also available are picnic sites and a network of hiking trails along the river. **Hours:** Daily 8-4. **Cost:** Free. **Phone:** (250) 287-9564. 🚻

ANCHOR INN & SUITES   (250)286-1131
▼▼ Hotel $99-$149 **Address:** 261 Island Hwy V9W 2B3 **Location:** On Island Hwy 19A, 1.3 mi (2 km) s. **Facility:** 77 units. 7 stories, interior corridors. **Terms:** cancellation fee imposed. **Amenities:** Some: high-speed Internet. **Pool(s):** heated indoor. **Activities:** whirlpool, exercise room. **Guest Services:** valet and coin laundry.

🍴 🍸 CALL 🛦 🛥 📶 💆 🎧 📺 🖥 / SOME UNITS FEE 🐾

Be a better driver.
Keep your mind on the road.

OCEAN RESORT   250/923-4281
▼▼ Motel $125-$145 **Address:** 4834 S Island Hwy V9H 1E8 **Location:** 11 mi (18 km) s on Island Hwy 19A. **Facility:** 28 units, some kitchens. 2 stories (no elevator), interior corridors. **Activities:** saunas, steamroom, exercise room. **Fee:** massage. **Guest Services:** coin laundry. 📶 ❌ 🎧 🖥 / SOME UNITS FEE 🐾

TOWN CENTRE INN   250/287-8866
▼▼ Motel $79-$94 **Address:** 1500 Dogwood St V9W 3A6 **Location:** Follow Island Hwy 19A through town, follow signs, just e; corner of 16th Ave. **Facility:** 34 units, some efficiencies. 2 stories (no elevator), exterior corridors. **Activities:** sauna. **Guest Services:** coin laundry. 🍴 📶 🎧 🖥 💻 / SOME UNITS FEE 🐾

TRAVELODGE CAMPBELL RIVER   (250)286-6622
▼▼ Motel $72-$140 **Address:** 340 S Island Hwy V9W 1A5 **Location:** 1.9 mi (3 km) s on Island Hwy 19A. **Facility:** 40 units. 2 stories (no elevator), interior corridors. **Terms:** cancellation fee imposed. **Pool(s):** heated indoor. **Activities:** whirlpool. **Guest Services:** coin laundry. ECO CALL 🛦 🛥 📶 ❌ 📵 🖥 💻 / SOME UNITS FEE 🐾

WHERE TO EAT

BAAN THAI RESTAURANT   250/286-4850
▼▼ Thai. Casual Dining. $8-$15 **AAA Inspector Notes:** The traditional flavors and aromas of Thailand's distinctive cuisine are honored at this contemporary downtown restaurant. The second-floor spot also features a small rooftop patio. **Bar:** full bar. **Reservations:** suggested, for dinner. **Address:** 1090B Shoppers Row V9W 2C6 **Location:** At 11th Ave; downtown. **Parking:** street only.
L D 🎧

BEST WOK   250/287-2831
▼▼ Chinese. Casual Dining. $5-$16 **AAA Inspector Notes:** Contemporary Chinese and Western food is on the menu at the downtown restaurant. Combination meals serve two, four, six or eight to 10 diners. Plenty of on-site parking is available, but for those who can't dine in, take-out and delivery also are offered. **Bar:** full bar. **Address:** 968 Alder St V9W 2P9 **Location:** From Shoppers Row, just e on 10th Ave, then just s. L D CALL 🛦

THE DRIFTWOOD RESTAURANT   250/923-5505
▼▼ Chinese. Casual Dining. $8-$18 **AAA Inspector Notes:** A 15-minute drive south along scenic Island Highway and across from the Oyster Bay rest area, this Chinese restaurant sets up a nightly dinner buffet, as well as a lunch buffet on Friday, Saturday and Sunday. Guests also have the option of ordering from the extensive menu. Dishes are prepared with 100 percent vegetable oil and no monosodium glutamate. **Bar:** full bar. **Address:** 4329 S Island Hwy V9H 1B7 **Location:** 10 mi (16 km) s on Island Hwy 19A. L D CALL 🛦

FUSILLI GRILL   250/830-0090
▼▼ Pacific Northwest. Casual Dining. $9-$26 **AAA Inspector Notes:** Away from the busy downtown area, you'll find this cute eatery located in a small strip mall. Ask any local for directions; everyone knows about this place. The menu features Italian dishes as well as tasty comfort foods and daily specials. Sample some wonderful British Columbia wines or enjoy a hearty cocktail. **Bar:** full bar. **Reservations:** suggested, for dinner Fri & Sat. **Address:** 4-220 Dogwood St V9W 2X9 **Location:** Island Hwy 19A, 1.5 mi (2.4 km) se; in Dogwood Plaza. L D CALL 🛦

MOXIE'S CLASSIC GRILL   250/830-1500
▼▼ American. Casual Dining. $11-$18 **AAA Inspector Notes:** This sleek, funky and popular restaurant presents an extensive menu of creatively prepared dishes, including pizza, pasta, rice, noodles, signature salads and burgers. Other menus include one for children and one for Sunday brunch. Lending to the upbeat, stylish decor are dark wood appointments and river rock fireplaces. **Bar:** full bar. **Address:** 1360 Island Hwy V9W 8C9 **Location:** From Island Hwy 19A, just n on Discovery Cres; in Discovery Harbour Mall. L D LATE CALL 🛦

QUAY WEST KITCHEN & CATERING   250/286-9988
▼▼ ▼▼ Pacific Northwest. Casual Dining. $10-$27 **AAA Inspector Notes:** On the waterfront, every table offers stunning views of Quadra Island, located just across the waters of Johnson Strait. This casual restaurant focuses on local, seasonal seafood, which you'll find featured on the "daily fresh sheet." Only the best AAA-graded Canadian beef is used for their specialty burgers and sirloin steaks. The owner is also the chef, so you know the food is going to be great. **Bar:** full bar. **Reservations:** suggested. **Address:** 921 Island Hwy V9W 2C2 **Location:** Just s on Island Hwy 19A from downtown. L D CALL &M

RICKY'S ALL DAY GRILL   250/286-3448
▼▼ ▼▼ American. Casual Dining. $8-$15 **AAA Inspector Notes:** The comfortable eatery, which employs friendly servers, presents a varied menu that includes pasta dishes, wraps, omelets, stir-fry preparations and burgers. Portions are generous. Children's and senior selections are offered. Guests can request seating in a booth or at a table. **Bar:** full bar. **Address:** 811 13th Ave V9W 4G9 **Location:** Island Hwy 19A, just s on Dogwood St, then just e. B L D CALL &M

CASTLEGAR (C-10) pop. 7,816, elev. 494m/1,620'

At the junction of hwys. 3 and 3A, Castlegar is considered the crossroads of the Kootenays. Just north is the 51-metre-high (167-ft.) Hugh Keenleyside Dam. The upper and lower Arrow Lakes, created by the dam, offer popular summer recreation areas including Arrow Lakes Provincial Park (Shelter Bay) and Syringa Provincial Park *(see Recreation Areas Chart)*.

Castlegar Chamber of Commerce: 1995 Sixth Ave., Castlegar, BC, Canada V1N 4B7. **Phone:** (250) 365-6313.

CANADIAN PACIFIC RAILWAY (CPR) MUSEUM is at 400 13th Ave. at jct. 3rd St. The train station was originally built in 1902 and reconstructed following a fire in 1906. Exhibits include a collection of antique tools, machines, a 1929 Harley Davidson, a newspaper collection dating 1947-2005 and a Doukhobor display.

Theme rooms depict music, sewing and agriculture. A bedroom has clothing from the 1930s to the 1960s, including cosmetics, gloves, shoes and corsets. A restored yellow caboose is a highlight for children. **Time:** Allow 1 hour minimum. **Hours:** Tues.-Sat. 10-5. Phone ahead to confirm schedule. **Cost:** $2. **Phone:** (250) 365-6440. 🐕 🏕

DOUKHOBOR DISCOVERY CENTRE is opposite the airport just off Hwy. 3A to 112 Heritage Way. The site replicates the communal settlement of the Doukhobors, a pacifist group of Russian immigrants who settled near the Columbia River 1908-13. Highlights include an Audio Visual Gallery, showing documentaries and temporary exhibits; traditional music; thousands of artifacts reflecting the settlement; and the Art Gallery/Craft Center, depicting Doukhobor-related handiwork.

Spinning and weaving demonstrations occur July through September. **Time:** Allow 30 minutes minimum. **Hours:** Daily 10-5, May-Sept. **Cost:** $10; $8 (senior citizens); $5 (students with ID); free (ages 0-5). Cash only. **Phone:** (250) 365-5327.

KOOTENAY GALLERY OF ART is opposite the airport just off Hwy. 3A at 120 Heritage Way, next to Doukhobor Discovery Centre. Two galleries feature rotating exhibitions of local, national and international origin. Workshops and musical events are held throughout the year.

Time: Allow 30 minutes minimum. **Hours:** Daily 10-5, in Dec.; Tues.-Sat. 10-5, Mar.-Nov. Closed Dec. 25-31 and statutory holidays. Phone ahead to confirm schedule. **Cost:** Donations. **Phone:** (250) 365-3337.

ZUCKERBERG ISLAND HERITAGE PARK is at 7th Ave. and 9th St. A suspension bridge leads to the island at the confluence of the Columbia and Kootenay rivers. Walking tours offers such sights as an Indian Kekuli or pit house, a cemetery, a log house, a sculpture of a seated woman carved from a tree stump and the Chapel House with its Russian Orthodox onion dome. The Castlegar Station Museum is in a restored 19th-century Canadian Pacific Railway (CPR) station.

Time: Allow 30 minutes minimum. **Hours:** Zuckerberg Island Wed.-Sun. 10-5, May-Sept. Station museum Mon.-Sat. 10-5. Island tours are available year-round. Phone ahead to confirm schedule. **Cost:** $2. **Phone:** (250) 365-6440. 🏕

QUALITY INN CASTLEGAR   (250)365-2177
▼▼ ▼▼ Hotel $90-$130 **Address:** 1935 Columbia Ave V1N 2W8 **Location:** Jct Hwy 3A and 3B, just s. Some two bedrooms and kitchens. 2 stories (no elevator), interior/exterior corridors. **Terms:** cancellation fee imposed. **Activities:** limited exercise equipment.
🍴 📶 ✖ 🛏 🖥 🖨 / SOME UNITS FEE 🐕

SUPER 8-CASTLEGAR   (250)365-2700
▼▼ ▼▼ Hotel $125-$150 **Address:** 651 18th St V1N 2N1 **Location:** Jct Hwy 3, just n on Hwy 22. **Facility:** 56 units, some efficiencies. 3 stories, interior corridors. **Terms:** check-in 4 pm, cancellation fee imposed. **Amenities:** *Some:* high-speed Internet. **Pool(s):** heated indoor. **Activities:** whirlpool, waterslide. **Guest Services:** valet and coin laundry.
ECO 🍴 🍽 🚲 📶 ✖ 🛏 🖥 🖨 / SOME UNITS FEE 🐕

WHERE TO EAT

BLACK ROOSTER CLASSIC BAR & GRILL   250/365-7779
▼▼ ▼▼ American. Casual Dining. $10-$30 **AAA Inspector Notes:** A giant black rooster dominates the entrance to this casual establishment, where the varied menu ranges from sandwiches, burgers and pizza to more serious fare such as rack of lamb or seared wild salmon. **Bar:** full bar. **Reservations:** suggested. **Address:** 651 18th St V1N 2N1 **Location:** Hwy 3 exit City Centre; next to Super 8-Castlegar. L D CALL &M

CAFE MICHAEL   250/365-8308
▼▼ International. Casual Dining. $9-$25 **AAA Inspector Notes:** The attractive décor at this restaurant is accentuated with stained-glass and wood accents. Popular with the locals, the well-prepared menu features classic Italian dishes such as pizza, pasta, chicken and veal Parmesan, as well as seafood, steaks and ribs. Service is fast and friendly. **Bar:** full bar. **Reservations:** suggested. **Address:** 143 Columbia Ave V1N 3K3 **Location:** Jct Hwy 3 and 22, 2.2 mi (3.7 km) n. L D

CHASE pop. 2,495

CHASE COUNTRY INN MOTEL (250)679-3333

 Motel $69-$99 **Address:** 576 Coburn St V0E 1M0 **Location:** Trans-Canada Hwy 1 and Coburn St. **Facility:** 21 units, some efficiencies and kitchens. 2 stories (no elevator), exterior corridors. **Parking:** winter plug-ins. **Terms:** cancellation fee imposed. **Guest Services:** coin laundry.

QUAAOUT LODGE & SPA, TALKING ROCK GOLF
(250)679-3090

Resort Hotel $100-$350

Address: 1663 Little Shuswap Lake Rd W V0E 1M0 **Location:** Trans-Canada Hwy 1 exit Squilax Bridge, 1.5 mi (2.5 km) w on Little Shuswap Rd. Located in a quiet secluded area. **Facility:** Native interpretive trails criss-cross the grounds of this lakefront lodge, which offers brightly decorated guest rooms. 70 units. 3 stories, interior corridors. **Terms:** 3 day cancellation notice-fee imposed. **Amenities:** high-speed Internet. **Pool(s):** indoor. **Activities:** whirlpool, steamroom, boat dock, putting green, hiking trails, volleyball, exercise room, spa. *Fee:* golf-18 holes. **Guest Services:** coin laundry. **Free Special Amenities:** local telephone calls and high-speed Internet.

CHEMAINUS (H-10) pop. 3,035, elev. 6m/20'

A lumber and manufacturing town, Chemainus added tourism to its economy with the creation of murals. More than 40 professional paintings on the walls of buildings portray the history of the Chemainus Valley. Subjects range from North American Indians to dramatic depictions of the logging industry.

Begun by local artists, the series of murals has attracted artists from around the world. Recent additions include interpretations of images created by noted Canadian artist Emily Carr, including a trompe l'oeil mural on the wall of the Chemainus Theatre. Walking tour maps can be bought at the kiosk in the central parking area. Prearranged guided tours and horse-drawn carriage tours also are available for a fee; phone (250) 246-5055 or (250) 246-0063.

The Chemainus Theatre offers dramas, comedies and musical productions; phone (250) 246-9820 or (800) 565-7738.

Chemainus Chamber of Commerce: 9796 Willow St., P.O. Box 575, Chemainus, BC, Canada V0R 1K0. **Phone:** (250) 246-3944.

Tell Us How We're Doing

If your visit to a TourBook-listed property doesn't meet your expectations, tell us about it.

AAA.com/TourBookComments

BEST WESTERN PLUS CHEMAINUS INN
(250)246-4181

Hotel $137-$199

AAA Benefit: Members save up to 20%, plus 10% bonus points with Best Western Rewards®.

Address: 9573 Chemainus Rd V0R 1K5 **Location:** Trans-Canada Hwy 1 exit Henry Rd, 0.9 mi (1.4 km) e. **Facility:** 75 units, some efficiencies. 4 stories, interior corridors. **Terms:** check-in 4 pm. **Amenities:** high-speed Internet, safes. **Pool(s):** heated indoor. **Activities:** whirlpool, exercise room. *Fee:* massage. **Guest Services:** valet and coin laundry. **Free Special Amenities:** full breakfast and high-speed Internet.

 All Suite Style Hotel with Indoor Pool Free Full Breakfast Across golf course In Arts Cultural Town

WHERE TO EAT

ODIKA CAFE 250/324-3303

International. Casual Dining. $11-$25 **AAA Inspector Notes:** The name of this café comes from the seed of the African wild mango as the husband and wife owner come from Africa. The menu includes dishes inspired by many countries, especially recipes passed down from a loving mother. Highlights include classic Indian curry, African lamb shanks and Jamaican jerk chicken. The town's live stage theater is just around the corner so make it a dinner and show evening out. **Bar:** full bar. **Address:** 2976 Mill St V0R 1K0 **Location:** Between Chemainus Rd and Willow St; downtown. **Parking:** street only. L D

CHETWYND pop. 2,635

LAKEVIEW INNS & SUITES (250)788-3000

Hotel $129

Address: 4820 N Access Rd V0C 1J0 **Location:** Hwy 29 and 97, just n on 48th St, then just e. **Facility:** 57 units, some efficiencies and kitchens. 4 stories, interior corridors. **Parking:** winter plug-ins. **Terms:** cancellation fee imposed. **Amenities:** high-speed Internet. **Activities:** exercise room. **Guest Services:** valet and coin laundry. **Free Special Amenities:** expanded continental breakfast and high-speed Internet.

POMEROY INN & SUITES (250)788-4800

Extended Stay Hotel $161 **Address:** 5200 N Access Rd V0C 1J0 **Location:** Hwy 29 and 97, just n on 52nd St. **Facility:** 87 units, some kitchens. 4 stories, interior corridors. **Parking:** winter plug-ins. **Amenities:** *Some:* high-speed Internet. **Pool(s):** heated indoor. **Activities:** whirlpool, waterslide, exercise room. **Guest Services:** valet and coin laundry.

CHILLIWACK (H-12) pop. 77,936, elev. 10m/33'
• Hotels p. 228 • Restaurants p. 228

In the heart of the upper Fraser River Valley, Chilliwack is the center of a prosperous farming and dairy region. The surrounding lakes, rivers, mountains and nearby provincial parks offer such varied recreation as skiing, hiking, fishing, rock hunting and white-water rafting. Scenic views and picnic facilities are available at Chilliwack Lake Provincial Park, 84 kilometres (54 mi.) southeast off Hwy. 1 *(see Recreation Areas Chart)*, and Cultus Lake Provincial Park, 11 kilometres (7 mi.) southwest off Hwy. 1 *(see Recreation Areas Chart)*.

Tourism Chilliwack Visitor Information Centre: 44150 Luckakuck Way, Chilliwack, BC, Canada V2R 4A7. **Phone:** (604) 858-8121 or (800) 567-9535.

BRIDAL VEIL FALLS PROVINCIAL PARK is 16 km (10 mi.) e. off Hwy. 1 exit 135, following signs. An easy 15-minute hike leads visitors to a lovely view of the area, characterized by valleys and emerald-colored rounded mountains. The main attraction is the falls, Canada's sixth highest, which cascade 60 metres (197 ft.) over slick rock and create the appearance of a glassy bridal veil. The park is the former site of Popkum, a 1700s village.

Note: In winter, the falls may freeze and cause the base to be slippery as well as allow rock and ice to fall. **Time:** Allow 30 minutes minimum. **Hours:** Daily dawn-dusk. **Cost:** Free.

CHILLIWACK MUSEUM is at 45820 Spadina Ave. between Main St. and Yale Rd. Books, pictures, clothing and farming supplies are among the approximately 7,500 objects that tell the story of Chilliwack's history. Housed in the old city hall building, the exhibits focus on life in the area from the late 1800s, when it was settled, to World War II. **Time:** Allow 30 minutes minimum. **Hours:** Mon.-Fri. 9-4:30, Sat. 11-3:30. Closed Jan. 1 and Christmas. **Cost:** $3; $2 (students with ID and senior citizens). **Phone:** (604) 795-5210.

GREAT BLUE HERON NATURE RESERVE is at 5200 Sumas Prairie Rd. This 130-hectare (321-acre) site includes an interpretive center, an observation tower, fish-spawning channels and a self-guiding interpretive walking trail. More than 90 herons build nests here; painted turtles, tailed frogs, beavers, bald eagles and a variety of other birds also dwell at the reserve.

Time: Allow 1 hour minimum. **Hours:** Nature reserve open daily 8-8. Interpretive center open daily 10-4; phone ahead in winter. **Cost:** Donations. **Phone:** (604) 823-6603.

MINTER GARDENS is 19 km (12 mi.) e. on Hwy. 1 to exit 135 (Hwy. 9) at 52892 Bunker Rd. Covering about 13 hectares (32 acres), 12 thematic gardens display seasonal colors and plants from around the world. Highlights include an ever-green living maze, topiary sculptures and, in the spring, 100,000 tulips.

Tours: Guided tours are available. **Time:** Allow 1 hour minimum. **Hours:** Daily 9-7, July-Aug.; 9-6, June and Sept. 2-5; 9-5:30, May and in Sept.; 10-5, Apr. and Oct. 1-14 (weather permitting). Phone ahead to confirm schedule. **Cost:** $17; $15 (ages 65+); $9.50 (ages 13-18); $6.50 (ages 6-12); $38 (family). **Phone:** (604) 794-7191 or (888) 646-8377.

BEST WESTERN RAINBOW COUNTRY INN

(604)795-3828

 Hotel $105-$140

 AAA Benefit: Members save up to 20%, plus 10% bonus points with Best Western Rewards®.

Address: 43971 Industrial Way V2R 3A4 **Location:** Trans-Canada Hwy 1 exit 116 (Lickman Rd). **Facility:** 74 units. 2 stories (no elevator), interior corridors. **Terms:** 7 day cancellation notice, resort fee. **Amenities:** *Some:* high-speed Internet. **Dining:** 2 restaurants. **Pool(s):** heated indoor. **Activities:** sauna, whirlpool. **Guest Services:** valet and coin laundry. **Free Special Amenities:** local telephone calls and high-speed Internet.

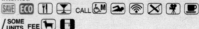

THE COAST CHILLIWACK HOTEL (604)792-5552

Hotel $109-$164 **Address:** 45920 First Ave V2P 7K1 **Location:** Trans-Canada Hwy 1 exit 119, 1.8 mi (2.9 km) n on Vedder Rd, then just e. **Facility:** 110 units. 9 stories, interior corridors. **Terms:** cancellation fee imposed. **Amenities:** safes. **Pool(s):** heated indoor. **Activities:** whirlpool, steamroom, exercise room. **Guest Services:** valet laundry, area transportation.

COMFORT INN (604)858-0636

Motel $97-$135 **Address:** 45405 Luckakuck Way V2R 3C7 **Location:** Trans-Canada Hwy 1 exit 119, s on Vedder Rd, then 0.6 mi (1 km) w. **Facility:** 83 units. 2 stories (no elevator), interior corridors. **Terms:** cancellation fee imposed. **Guest Services:** valet laundry.

TRAVELODGE HOTEL, CHILLIWACK (604)792-4240

 Hotel $96-$130

Address: 45466 Yale Rd W V2R 3Z8 **Location:** Trans-Canada Hwy 1 exit 119, just n. **Facility:** 82 units, some two bedrooms and efficiencies. 2 stories (no elevator), interior corridors. **Terms:** 3 day cancellation notice. **Pool(s):** heated indoor. **Activities:** whirlpool. **Guest Services:** coin laundry. **Free Special Amenities:** local telephone calls and high-speed Internet.

WHERE TO EAT

EARLS RESTAURANT 604/858-3360

American. Casual Dining. $10-$28 **AAA Inspector Notes:** Offering an experience that falls between fast food and fine dining, the fun, relaxed restaurant prepares great food at a great price. Choices range from juicy burgers, hearty sandwiches, fresh salads, wings and pizza to full entrees of steak, chops and seafood. Made-from-scratch soups and assorted breads, as well as a nice choice of wines and beers, round out the offerings. This is a fitting spot for impromptu get-togethers and festive occasions. **Bar:** full bar. **Address:** 45585 Luckakuck Way V2R 1A1 **Location:** Trans-Canada Hwy 1 exit 119, just s on Vedder Rd, then just w; in Cottonwood Shopping Centre. L D CALL

RICKY'S ALL DAY GRILL 604/858-5663

American. Casual Dining. $11-$27 **AAA Inspector Notes:** The comfortable eatery, which employs friendly servers, presents a varied menu that includes pasta dishes, wraps, omelets, stir-fry preparations and burgers. Portions are generous. Children's and senior selections are offered. Guests can request seating in a booth or at a table. **Bar:** full bar. **Address:** 45389 Luckakuck Way V2R 3C7 **Location:** Trans-Canada Hwy 1 exit 119, just s on Vedder Rd, then 0.6 mi (1 km) w. B L D CALL

CHRISTINA LAKE pop. 1,168

NEW HORIZON MOTEL   (250)447-9312

ⓦⓦ **Motel** $85-$175 **Address:** 2037 Hunter Frontage Rd (Hwy 3) V0H 1E2 **Location:** Just e on Hwy 3. **Facility:** 25 units, some kitchens. 1-2 stories (no elevator), exterior corridors. **Terms:** 2 night minimum stay - seasonal and/or weekends, 14 day cancellation notice-fee imposed. **Amenities:** *Some:* high-speed Internet. **Activities:** basketball, volleyball.

ECO CALL 🚹Ⓜ 🛜 ✕ 🛢 💻 /SOME UNITS FEE 🐾 📷

CLEARWATER (A-8) pop. 2,331

Clearwater gets its name from the clear waters of the nearby Clearwater River. Opportunities for riding, hiking, canoeing, skiing and fishing abound in the surrounding North Thompson Valley.

Wells Gray Provincial Park, north off Hwy. 5, offers a variety of scenery, particularly with regard to water. Scattered throughout its boundaries are five large lakes, two river systems, many streams and waterways and a multitude of waterfalls. Helmcken Falls, which drops 141 metres (465 ft.), is said to be the fourth highest in Canada. At Bailey's Chute Loop in late summer, visitors can view salmon jumping upstream to spawn. Extinct volcanoes and lava beds recall the region's fiery past. *See Recreation Areas Chart.*

Clearwater & District Chamber of Commerce: 201 - 416 Eden Rd., Clearwater, BC, Canada V0E 1N1. **Phone:** (250) 674-2646.

RECREATIONAL ACTIVITIES
White-water Rafting

- **Interior Whitewater Expeditions** is at 73 W. Old N. Thompson Hwy. **Hours:** Daily 8-8, May-Sept. (depending on water level). **Phone:** (250) 674-3727 in Can. or (800) 661-7238.

CLEARWATER VALLEY RESORT & KOA KAMPGROUND
                                      (250)674-3909

ⓦⓦ **Address:** 373 Clearwater Valley Rd
Cottage V0E 1N1 **Location:** Jct Hwy 5 (Yellow-head Hwy) and Clearwater Valley Rd.
$110-$170 **Facility:** 18 units. 1-2 stories (no elevator), exterior corridors. **Terms:** closed 10/13-4/30, 3 night minimum stay - weekends, cancellation fee imposed. **Pool(s):** heated outdoor. **Activities:** miniature golf, playground, horseshoes, volleyball. *Fee:* game room. **Guest Services:** coin laundry.

SAVE 🍴 🍸 🛶 🛜 ✕ 🛢 💻
/SOME UNITS FEE 🐾 🚭 📷

WHERE TO EAT

THE PAINTED TURTLE RESTAURANT   250/674-3560

ⓦⓦ Canadian. Casual Dining. $10-$33 **AAA Inspector Notes:** On the edge of Dutch Lake, the restaurant treats patrons to lovely views of the lake and water lilies from seating inside or outside on the covered veranda. Dinner choices run from salmon, halibut and trout to AAA steaks, mushroom dill chicken, pasta or the specialty of pork stuffed with cream cheese and dried cranberries. Lunch fare — such as prime rib burgers, the bison steak sandwich and salads — is a little simpler. Scrumptious desserts are prepared in house. **Bar:** full bar. **Reservations:** suggested. **Address:** 361 Ridge Dr V0E 1N0 **Location:** Hwy 5 (Yellowhead Hwy), 0.9 mi (1.5 km) w on Old Hwy 5A; in Dutch Lake Resort & RV Park. B L D CALL 🚹Ⓜ 🜔

CLINTON (A-7) pop. 636, elev. 274m/898'

During the gold rush of the late 1850s and early 1860s Clinton was the junction of several wagon roads leading to northern goldfields. In 1863 Queen Victoria changed the town's name from Junction to Clinton. Retaining much of its frontier look, Clinton is a supply center for surrounding resorts, fishing camps and ranches. Summer activities include boating, fishing and camping at area lakes, which also attract various wildlife.

The Village of Clinton: 1423 Cariboo Hwy., P.O. Box 309, Clinton, BC, Canada V0K 1K0. **Phone:** (250) 459-2261.

CLINTON MUSEUM is at 1419 Cariboo Hwy. (Hwy. 97). Built in 1892, this building has served as the town's schoolhouse and courthouse. Displays include photographs and pioneer artifacts. **Time:** Allow 30 minutes minimum. **Hours:** Daily 9-5, June-Sept. Phone ahead to confirm schedule and availability in Sept. **Cost:** Donations. **Phone:** (250) 459-2442.

COMOX (F-10) pop. 13,627
- **Hotels p. 230** • **Restaurants p. 230**

Comox was founded in the mid-1800s, taking its name from the Salish word *Koumuckthay,* meaning "land of plenty." Once an important port for ships of the Royal Navy, the east coast village became the home of a Royal Air Force base in 1942. CFB Comox maintains search-and-rescue operations, maritime patrols and support of naval and air force defense.

COMOX AIR FORCE MUSEUM is e. on Ryan Rd. following signs to CFB Comox main entrance. Museum displays outline the history of the base and West Coast aviation. Two squadrons continue to fly Cormorant helicopters and Buffalo and Aurora aircraft. Nearby, a heritage aircraft park displays vintage aircraft. Canada's flight pioneers are recognized in a videotape presentation.

On weekends visitors may view a Spitfire that is being restored. A comprehensive aviation library also is on site. **Time:** Allow 30 minutes minimum. **Hours:** Museum Tues.-Sun. 10-4. Heritage aircraft park daily 10-4, May-Sept. Closed Jan. 1 and Dec. 25-26 and 31. **Cost:** Donations. **Phone:** (250) 339-8162.

FILBERG HERITAGE LODGE AND PARK is at 61 Filberg Rd. The 1929 heritage lodge and outbuildings stand on 4 hectares (9 acres) of landscaped grounds on Comox Bay. The timber lodge is restored and furnished in period. Rare and exotic trees, rhododendrons and herb gardens adorn the park, which offers 1-hour concerts most Sundays at 2 in July and August. A petting farm is available from mid-June to mid-August.

Pets are not permitted. **Time:** Allow 1 hour minimum. **Hours:** Lodge tours offered Thurs.-Sun. 11-4, May-early Sept.; Sat.-Sun. 11-3, Mar.-Apr. and mid-Sept. to Dec. (based on volunteer staff availability). Park open daily 8-dusk. Closed Jan. 1, two weeks around British Columbia Day for Filberg Festival, second Mon. in Oct., Christmas Eve, Christmas and day after Christmas. Phone ahead to confirm schedule. **Cost:** Lodge by donations. Park free; admission is charged during special events. **Phone:** (250) 339-2715.

PORT AUGUSTA INN & SUITES   (250)339-2277

Motel
$65-$150

Address: 2082 Comox Ave V9M 1P8 **Location:** Hwy 19A (Cliffe Ave), follow signs to Comox Ave, then 2.5 mi (4 km) e. **Facility:** 67 units, some efficiencies and kitchens. 2 stories (no elevator), interior/exterior corridors. **Pool(s):** heated outdoor. **Free Special Amenities: expanded continental breakfast and high-speed Internet.**

SAVE CALL ⊠M ➥ 📶 🅱 💻 /SOME UNITS FEE 🛍 🎱

WHERE TO EAT

BLACKFIN PUB AT THE MARINA   250/339-5030

▼▼ American. Gastropub. $11-$25 **AAA Inspector Notes:** Right near the entrance to the marina, this pub has satisfied with great brews and incredible scenery for more than 20 years. Among signature dishes are grilled beef tenderloin, oven-baked halibut and Jack Daniel's baby back ribs. No one younger than 19 is admitted to this pub, where beverages include 30 varieties of Scotch and 10 draft beers and ales. **Bar:** full bar. **Address:** 132 Port Augusta St V9M 3N7 **Location:** Between Comox and Beaufort aves; next to Marina Park. [L] [D] CALL ⊠M

SMITTY'S   250/339-3911

▼▼ American. Casual Dining. $7-$20 **AAA Inspector Notes:** The family-oriented restaurant satisfies patrons with its ever-popular all-day breakfast items, as well as tasty and wholesome soups and salads at lunchtime. A relaxed mood characterizes the dining space. **Bar:** full bar. **Address:** 1747 Comox Ave V9M 3M2 **Location:** Between Port Augusta and Nordin sts. [B] [L] [D] CALL ⊠M

COOMBS (G-10) pop. 1,547

Coombs retains the atmosphere of a quaint village settled around 1910. The Coombs General Store, which has operated continuously since the settlement days, and the Old Country Market, which is unusual for the goats that are kept on the roof in summer, are two landmarks.

The town is on Vancouver Island, midway between Little Qualicum Falls Provincial Park *(see Recreation Areas Chart)* and Englishman River Falls Provincial Park *(see Recreation Areas Chart)*, where there are many recreational opportunities.

VANCOUVER ISLAND BUTTERFLY WORLD & ORCHID GARDENS is 1 km (.6 mi.) w. on Hwy. 4A at 1080 Winchester Rd. A walk-through tropical garden contains more than 30 species of free-flying butterflies; the insect's life cycle is portrayed through displays.

Other exhibits include birds in an outdoor aviary, a Japanese water garden with exotic fish, an orchid garden with some 800 orchids, a turtle pond, a petting zoo in the summer and Big Bug Jungle—an insectary housing large live jungle insects. An indoor water garden displays hundreds of orchids from around the world set amidst waterfalls and ponds.

Time: Allow 30 minutes minimum. **Hours:** Daily 10-5. Phone ahead to confirm schedule. **Cost:** $11; $10 (ages 65+); $6 (ages 12-18); $5 (ages 3-12). Phone ahead to confirm prices. **Phone:** (250) 248-7026.

COQUITLAM (H-11) pop. 126,456, elev. 137m/449'

• **Attractions map p. 355**
• **Hotels & Restaurants map & index p. 368**
• **Part of Vancouver area — see map p. 343**

Named for a type of landlocked salmon, Coquitlam borders Pitt Lake and encompasses Burke Mountain. Recreational opportunities, including swimming, canoeing, hiking and fishing, are available throughout the area.

Nearby parks and lakes include Mundy Park, 4 kilometres (2.5 mi.) south off Mariner Way; Belcarra Park, 15 kilometres (9 mi.) northwest off loco and Bedwell Bay roads; Buntzen Lake, 12 kilometres (7 mi.) northwest off East and Sunnyside roads; Minnekhada Regional Park, 13 kilometres (8 mi.) northeast off Victoria Drive and Quarry Road; Town Centre Park and Lafarge Lake, on Pinetree Way just north of Lougheed Highway; and Burke Mountain, 11 kilometres (7 mi.) northeast off Coast Meridian and Harper roads.

Coquitlam Tourist/Visitor Info Booth: 1209 Pinetree Way, Coquitlam, BC, Canada V3B 7Y3. **Phone:** (604) 464-2716.

BEST WESTERN PLUS CHELSEA INN

(604)525-7777 **27**

▼▼▼
Hotel
$119-$139
Best Western
PLUS

AAA Benefit: Members save up to 20%, plus 10% bonus points with Best Western Rewards®.

Address: 725 Brunette Ave V3K 6A6 **Location:** Trans-Canada Hwy 1 exit 40B (Brunette Ave N). **Facility:** 61 units, some efficiencies. 3 stories, interior corridors. **Pool(s):** heated outdoor. **Activities:** sauna, limited exercise equipment. **Guest Services:** coin laundry. **Free Special Amenities: expanded continental breakfast and high-speed Internet.**

SAVE CALL ⊠M ➥ 📶 ❌ 🐾 🅱 📺 💻

BEST WESTERN PLUS COQUITLAM INN CONVENTION CENTRE

(604)931-9011 **25**

▼▼▼
Hotel
$140-$180
Best Western
PLUS

AAA Benefit: Members save up to 20%, plus 10% bonus points with Best Western Rewards®.

Address: 319 North Rd V3K 3V8 **Location:** Trans-Canada Hwy 1 exit 37 (Cariboo Rd/Gaglardi Way), 1.2 mi (2 km) e on Lougheed Hwy (Hwy 7), then just s. **Facility:** 106 units, some two bedrooms and kitchens. 2 stories (no elevator), interior/exterior corridors. **Terms:** cancellation fee imposed. **Amenities:** safes. **Dining:** 2 restaurants. **Pool(s):** heated indoor. **Activities:** sauna, whirlpool, exercise room. **Guest Services:** valet laundry. **Free Special Amenities: local telephone calls and high-speed Internet.**

SAVE ECO 🍽 🍸 CALL ⊠M ➥ 📶 ❌ 🐾 🅱 💻 /SOME UNITS 🖥

Keep seasonal vehicles travel-ready with a AAA/CAA Battery Tender®

(See map & index p. 368.)

RAMADA COQUITLAM   (604)931-4433 **26**
🎖🎖 **Hotel** $99-$139 **Address:** 631 Lougheed Hwy V3K 3S5 **Location:** Trans-Canada Hwy 1 exit 44 (Coquitlam), 1.9 mi (3 km) w on Lougheed Hwy (Hwy 7). **Facility:** 84 units. 2 stories (no elevator), interior/exterior corridors. **Pool(s):** heated indoor. **Activities:** whirl-pool, exercise room. **Guest Services:** valet and coin laundry.

🍴 🍸 🚲 🛰 🚫 💻 / SOME UNITS FEE 🐾 📞 🖨

WHERE TO EAT

CACTUS CLUB CAFE   604/777-0440
🎖🎖 American. Casual Dining. $11-$37 **AAA Inspector Notes:** This bustling, casual restaurant serves huge burgers, sandwiches, pasta, salads, soups, quesadillas, fajitas, vegetarian dishes, steak, ribs, chicken and fish. Featured are certified Angus beef and fresh wild British Columbia salmon. **Bar:** full bar. **Address:** 110-101 Schoolhouse St V3K 4X8 **Location:** From Lougheed Hwy (Hwy 7), just n. 🅛 🅓 LATE CALL 🖹M

JOEY RESTAURANTS   604/939-3077
🎖🎖 American. Casual Dining. $13-$35 **AAA Inspector Notes:** The cuisine blends Mediterranean and Asian cooking styles and em-phasizes finger foods for sharing. Those who aren't big fans of tapas can consider full meal offerings centered on steaks and chops. **Bar:** full bar. **Address:** 550 Lougheed Hwy V3K 353 **Location:** Trans-Canada Hwy 1 exit 37 (Gaglardi Way) eastbound, 2.3 mi (3.8 km) e on Hwy 7 (Lougheed Hwy); exit 44 (Coquitlam) westbound, 1.9 mi (3.2 km) w. 🅛 🅓 LATE CALL 🖹M

RICKY'S ALL DAY GRILL   604/468-8000
🎖🎖 American. Casual Dining. $11-$27 **AAA Inspector Notes:** The comfortable eatery, which employs friendly servers, presents a varied menu that includes pasta dishes, wraps, omelets, stir-fry preparations and burgers. Portions are generous. Children's and senior selections are offered. Guests can request seating in a booth or at a table. **Bar:** full bar. **Address:** 2929 Barnet Hwy, Unit 2660 V3B 5R5 **Location:** Just off Barnet Hwy; in Coquitlam Centre Mall.

🅑 🅛 🅓

COURTENAY (F-10) pop. 24,099, elev. 25m/82'
• Restaurants p. 232

Courtenay was established in the late 1860s when settlers began a major farming community near the Comox Valley. Known for a garden called the Mile of Flowers, the town is now a year-round recreation area with good skiing and sailing nearby.

The 1989 Puntledge River discovery of the fossil-ized intact skull of a 14-metre-long (46-ft.) elasmo-saur, a long-necked Cretaceous marine reptile 80 million years old, brought Courtenay to the attention of the world of paleontology.

Courtenay is the terminus of the Powell River Ferry, which makes round-trip excursions to the mainland.

Comox Valley Visitor Centre: 2040 Cliffe Ave., Courtenay, BC, Canada V9N 2L3. **Phone:** (250) 334-3234 or (888) 357-4471.

COURTENAY MUSEUM is at 207 Fourth St., down-town at jct. Fourth St. and Cliffe Ave. Permanent ex-hibits, enhanced by audiovisuals, focus on native history, exploration, agriculture, logging and pioneer life. A reconstruction of an elasmosaur is displayed along with locally excavated fossil evidence from the age of dinosaurs. The museum has archival material pertaining to the nearby Comox Valley. Guided fossil discovery tours are available.

Time: Allow 1 hour minimum. **Hours:** Mon.-Sat. 10-5, Sun. noon-4, Victoria Day-Labour Day; Tues.-Sat. 10-5, rest of year. Closed Jan. 1, Good Friday, Victoria Day, Labour Day and Christmas. **Cost:** Do-nations. **Phone:** (250) 334-0686.

PUNTLEDGE HATCHERY is 3 km (1.9 mi.) w. on Lake Trail Rd., then 2 km (1.2 mi.) n. on Power-house Rd. following signs. The hatchery nurtures and releases several varieties of salmon into the Puntledge River. Photographic displays outline the species' various stages of development. **Hours:** Daily 8-4; closed statutory holidays. **Cost:** Free. **Phone:** (250) 703-0907.

RECREATIONAL ACTIVITIES
Skiing
• **Mt. Washington Alpine Resort** is 31 km (19 mi.) n.w. on the Strathcona Pkwy. Other activities are available. **Hours:** Daily 9-3:30, Dec. 1 to mid-Apr. Phone ahead to confirm schedule. **Phone:** (250) 338-1386 or (888) 231-1499.

THE ANCO MOTEL   250/334-2451
🎖🎖 **Motel** $70-$100 **Address:** 1885 Cliffe Ave V9N 2K9 **Loca-tion:** Just s of Hwy 19A Connector. **Facility:** 67 units, some efficien-cies. 2 stories (no elevator), exterior corridors. **Terms:** cancellation fee imposed. **Amenities:** Some: high-speed Internet. **Pool(s):** heated outdoor. **Guest Services:** coin laundry.

CALL 🖹M 🚲 🛰 📞 💻 / SOME UNITS 🅚 🖨

BEST WESTERN PLUS THE WESTERLY HOTEL &
CONVENTION CENTRE   (250)338-7741
🎖🎖🎖 **Hotel** $110-$200 **Best Western PLUS** **AAA Benefit:** Members save up to 20%, plus 10% bonus points with Best Western Rewards®.
Address: 1590 Cliffe Ave V9N 2K4 **Location:** Corner of Cliffe Ave and Island Hwy. **Facility:** 142 units. 3 stories, inte-rior corridors. **Terms:** cancellation fee imposed. **Pool(s):** heated indoor. **Activities:** saunas, whirlpool, game room, exercise room. **Guest Services:** valet and coin laundry. **Free Special Amenities:** full breakfast and high-speed Internet.

SAVE ECO 🍴 🍸 CALL 🖹M 🚲 BIZ 🛰 🚫 🐾
💻 / SOME UNITS FEE 🐾 📞 🖨

CROWN ISLE RESORT & GOLF COMMUNITY   (250)703-5050
🎖🎖 **Resort Hotel** $139-$279 **Address:** 399 Clubhouse Dr V9N 9G3 **Location:** Island Hwy 19A N, 0.9 mi (1.5 km) n on Comox Ave, then 1.6 mi (2.5 km) ne on Ryan Rd, follow signs. **Facility:** A spectacular golf course and wonderful condo-like rooms (all with a view of the course) await at this unique resort, which is just a short drive from the downtown district. 88 units, some two bedrooms, effi-ciencies and kitchens. 2-3 stories (no elevator), exterior corridors. **Amenities:** Some: high-speed Internet. **Dining:** 2 restaurants. **Ac-tivities:** steamrooms, exercise room. **Fee:** golf-18 holes. **Guest Ser-vices:** complimentary laundry.

🍴 🍸 CALL 🖹M 🛰 🚫 💻
/ SOME UNITS FEE 🐾 📞 🖨

HOLIDAY INN EXPRESS & SUITES COMOX VALLEY
                                    (778)225-0010
🎖🎖🎖 **Hotel** $130-$150 **Address:** 2200 Cliffe Ave V9N 2L4 **Lo-cation:** 0.6 mi (1.1 km) s on Island Hwy 19A S. **Facility:** 91 units, some two bedrooms. 4 stories, interior corridors. **Terms:** cancellation fee imposed. **Amenities:** high-speed Internet. **Pool(s):** heated in-door. **Activities:** whirlpool, waterslide, exercise room. **Guest Ser-vices:** coin laundry.

CALL 🖹M 🚲 BIZ 🛰 🚫 📞 🖨 💻
/ SOME UNITS FEE 🐾

KINGFISHER OCEANSIDE RESORT & SPA

(250)338-1323

Hotel
$115-$415

Address: 4330 S Island Hwy V9N 9R9 **Location:** 3.8 mi (6 km) s on Island Hwy 19A S, follow signs. **Facility:** 64 units, some efficiencies. 2 stories, exterior corridors. **Terms:** 2 night minimum stay - weekends, cancellation fee imposed. **Dining:** The Breakwater Restaurant, see separate listing. **Pool(s):** heated outdoor. **Activities:** sauna, whirlpool, steamroom, tennis court, rental bicycles, exercise room, spa. **Guest Services:** valet laundry. **Free Special Amenities:** early check-in/late check-out and high-speed Internet.

TRAVELODGE COURTENAY

(250)334-4491

Motel $85-$102 **Address:** 2605 Cliffe Ave V9N 2L8 **Location:** 0.8 mi (1.2 km) s on Island Hwy 19A S. Adjacent to Driftwood Mall. **Facility:** 91 units, some efficiencies. 2 stories (no elevator), exterior corridors. **Amenities:** Some: high-speed Internet. **Pool(s):** heated outdoor. **Guest Services:** coin laundry.

WHERE TO EAT

ATLAS CAFE

250/338-9838

International. Casual Dining. $11-$23 **AAA Inspector Notes:** This funky downtown cafe presents an eclectic menu with a mix of Italian dishes, Mexican entrees and global cuisine such as curry-glazed wild salmon, vegetable lasagna and Asian soba noodles. This place opens early for breakfast. **Bar:** full bar. **Address:** 250 6th St V9N 1M1 **Location:** Jct Island Hwy 19A N, 0.5 mi (0.8 km) n on Cliffe Ave. **Parking:** street only. [B] [L] [D]

THE BREAKWATER RESTAURANT

250/338-1323

Pacific Northwest. Casual Dining. $12-$35 **AAA Inspector Notes:** Amazing water views from every table and a warm and inviting atmosphere await both guests staying at the resort and those simply stopping in for a delightful meal. The restaurant uses fresh local ingredients, including seafood and meats, not to mention vegetables grown locally on area farms and in its own gardens. The very popular Sunday brunch starts at 9 a.m. **Bar:** full bar. **Reservations:** suggested. **Address:** 4330 S Island Hwy V9N 9R9 **Location:** 3.8 mi (6 km) s on Island Hwy 19A S, follow signs; in Kingfisher Oceanside Resort & Spa. [B] [L] [D] CALL

MONTE CHRISTO ON THE RIVER

250/338-1468

American. Casual Dining. $9-$21 **AAA Inspector Notes:** This long-established restaurant sits on a peaceful river bank that's popular with birds; grab a window seat if possible. The lunch menu features daily specials and wonderfully tasty homemade soups. At the heart of the dinner menu are steak, seafood, pasta and barbecue dishes. Also offered are many choices aimed to please seniors and kids. **Bar:** full bar. **Address:** 975 Comox Rd V9N 3P7 **Location:** Island Hwy 19A N. [L] [D]

THE OLD HOUSE RESTAURANT

250/338-5406

Canadian. Casual Dining. $12-$26 **AAA Inspector Notes:** This locally popular dining spot is housed in a Comox Valley Heritage site, a unique rustic 1938 home that has been renovated inside with a very modern décor, yet the exterior still features its old farmhouse-like charm and it sits right along the river. Reopened after a fire in late 2009, the restaurant offers their 'casual format' menu featuring burgers, sandwiches and more hearty dinner entrées like slow roasted prime rib, wild sockeye salmon, seared halibut filet and New York steak. **Bar:** full bar. **Reservations:** suggested. **Address:** 1760 Riverside Ln V9N 8C7 **Location:** Island Hwy 19A, just n on 19th St; in Old House Village Hotel & Spa. [B] [L] [D] CALL

RICKY'S ALL DAY GRILL

250/334-9638

American. Casual Dining. $11-$16 **AAA Inspector Notes:** The comfortable eatery, which employs friendly servers, presents a varied menu that includes pasta dishes, wraps, omelets, stir-fry preparations and burgers. Portions are generous. Children's and senior selections are offered. Guests can request seating in a booth or at a table. **Bar:** full bar. **Address:** 795 Ryan Rd V9N 3R6 **Location:** Island Hwy 19A N, just ne; in Washington Park Centre Mall. [B] [L] [D] CALL

CRANBROOK (C-11) pop. 19,319, elev. 940m/3,083'

Cranbrook is the key city of the eastern Kootenays (see Kootenay National Park p. 267) and the center of many circle tours. Nearby lakes, rivers and mountains provide such recreational opportunities as swimming, fishing, hiking, hunting and skiing. A scenic portion of Hwy. 93 runs north from Cranbrook through Kootenay National Park into Alberta to the junction with Hwy. 16 in Jasper National Park. (A valid park pass is required to travel on the Icefields Parkway section of Hwy. 93.)

Cranbrook Chamber of Commerce: 2279 Cranbrook St. N. (Hwy. 3/95), P.O. Box 84, Cranbrook, BC, Canada V1C 4H6. **Phone:** (250) 426-5914 or (800) 222-6174.

Self-guiding tours: Information about driving and walking tours is available from the chamber of commerce.

CANADIAN MUSEUM OF RAIL TRAVEL is at 57 Van Horne St. (Hwy. 3/95). The museum restores and preserves vintage Canadian Pacific Railway passenger train sets, including cars from the luxury Trans-Canada Limited. The lifestyle of rail travel is reflected in trains from 1880 to 1955, including cars of state, business and royalty. On the grounds is the original three-story café from the Canadian Pacific Railway's Royal Alexandra Hotel of Winnipeg. Several guided tours are available and can be taken in various combinations. The Grand Tour includes 17 railcars and three historic rooms.

Time: Allow 1 hour, 30 minutes minimum. **Hours:** Museum open daily 9:45-6, Victoria Day-second Mon. in Oct.; Tues.-Sat. 11:45-5, rest of year. Guided tours are given daily every 45 minutes. Last tour begins 45 minutes before closing. Closed Jan. 1, Christmas and day after Christmas. **Cost:** Grand Tour $21.30; $18 (ages 65+); $10.85 (students with ID); free (ages 0-5); $61.30 (family). Exhibits inside museum free. **Phone:** (250) 489-3918 to verify tour schedule and rates.

GAMBLING ESTABLISHMENTS

• **St. Eugene Golf Resort Casino** is at 7777 Mission Rd. **Hours:** Sun.-Thurs. 10 a.m.-midnight, Fri.-Sat. and holidays 10 a.m.-2 a.m. Closed Christmas. **Phone:** (250) 420-2000 or (877) 417-3133.

BEST WESTERN CRANBROOK HOTEL

250/417-4002

Hotel
Rates not provided

AAA Benefit: Members save up to 20%, plus 10% bonus points with Best Western Rewards®.

Address: 1019 Cranbrook St N V1C 3S4 **Location:** Hwy 3 and 95; center. **Facility:** 94 units, some two bedrooms and efficiencies. 4 stories, interior corridors. **Amenities:** high-speed Internet. **Pool(s):** indoor. **Activities:** waterslide, exercise room. **Fee:** game room. **Guest Services:** valet and coin laundry. **Free Special Amenities:** high-speed Internet and children's activities.

DAYS INN CRANBROOK (250)426-6683

▼▼ ▼▼ **Hotel** $95-$124 **Address:** 600 Cranbrook St N V1C 3R7 **Location:** Corner of 6th St and Cranbrook St N. **Facility:** 87 units, some kitchens. 4 stories, interior corridors. **Parking:** winter plug-ins. **Terms:** check-in 4 pm. **Dining:** Bavarian Chalet, see separate listing, nightclub. **Pool(s):** heated outdoor. **Activities:** sauna, whirlpool. **Guest Services:** valet laundry.

⬛ 🍴 🍸 🏊 🛜 🖥 🖨 💻 / SOME UNITS FEE 🐾

HERITAGE INN HOTEL & CONVENTION CENTRE CRANBROOK (250)489-4301

▼▼ ▼▼ **Hotel** $112-$220 **Address:** 803 Cranbrook St N V1C 3S2 **Location:** Hwy 3 and 95; center. **Facility:** 100 units, some two bedrooms. 3 stories (no elevator); interior corridors. **Parking:** winter plug-ins. **Terms:** check-in 4 pm, cancellation fee imposed. **Amenities:** Some: high-speed Internet, safes. **Pool(s):** heated indoor. **Activities:** whirlpool, limited exercise equipment.

FEE ✚ 🍴 🍸 CALL 🅼 🏊 🛜 💻 / SOME UNITS FEE 🐾 🖥 🖨

ST. EUGENE GOLF RESORT & CASINO (250)420-2000

▼▼▼ ▼▼

Hotel
$129-$189

Address: 7731 Mission Rd V1C 7E5 **Location:** Hwy 3 exit Kimberley/Airport (Hwy 95A) to Mission Rd, 2.8 mi (4.5 km) n. **Facility:** This vine-covered upscale hotel, in a scenic setting, has extremely comfortable and lovely rooms. There's many options for entertaining yourself, including a year-round outdoor pool and hot tub area. 125 units. 3 stories, interior corridors. **Terms:** check-in 4 pm, cancellation fee imposed. **Amenities:** video games (fee), high-speed Internet, safes. **Dining:** Purcell Grill, see separate listing. **Pool(s):** heated outdoor. **Activities:** sauna, whirlpools, steamroom, hiking trails, exercise room. *Fee:* golf-18 holes. **Guest Services:** valet laundry. **Free Special Amenities:** high-speed Internet and airport transportation.

🅢 ⬛ ✱ ✚ 🍴 🍸 🏊 BIZ 🛜 ✕ 🎥
🖥 💻 / SOME UNITS FEE 🐾 🖨

WHERE TO EAT

ALLEGRA MEDITERRANEAN CUISINE 250/426-8812

▼▼ ▼▼ Mediterranean. Casual Dining. $14-$28 **AAA Inspector Notes:** This bright, bistro-style restaurant has an interesting take on French, Italian and Spanish Mediterranean cuisines thanks to its Swiss chef/owner. The menu lists a variety of pastas, chicken, veal, pork tenderloin and lamb dishes, all offering good value. Service is simple, yet friendly. **Bar:** full bar. **Reservations:** suggested. **Address:** 1225B Cranbrook St N V1C 3S6 **Location:** Hwy 3 and 95, just s of Theatre Rd; in strip mall. D

BAVARIAN CHALET 250/489-3305

▼▼ ▼▼ Continental. Casual Dining. $8-$25 **AAA Inspector Notes:** The restaurant is a favorite for simple, hearty food, a relaxing atmosphere and European touches. Among menu choices are ribs, chicken cordon bleu, schnitzels and German spaetzle, as well as excellent prime rib specials Thursday through Saturday nights. Delicious apple strudel merits a sweet splurge. **Bar:** full bar. **Reservations:** suggested. **Address:** 600 Cranbrook St N V1C 3R7 **Location:** Corner of 6th St and Cranbrook St N; in Days Inn Cranbrook. L D

HEIDI'S EUROPEAN & INTERNATIONAL CUISINE
250/426-7922

▼▼ ▼▼

International
Casual Dining
$8-$34

AAA Inspector Notes: Located in the heart of Cranbrook, the cozy, comfortable, European-style restaurant serves an extensive menu of international fare, including rotisserie chicken, schnitzel, bratwurst and steak. Prime rib is offered Fridays and Saturdays. Dim lights add to an intimate ambience, and charming, friendly servers will recommend their favorite dishes. **Bar:** full bar. **Reservations:** suggested. **Address:** 821 C Baker St V1C 1A3 **Location:** On 9th Ave S; center. **Parking:** street only. *Menu on AAA.com*

L D CALL 🅼

MR MIKE'S STEAKHOUSE & BAR 250/417-2542

▼▼ ▼▼ Steak. Casual Dining. $10-$26 **AAA Inspector Notes:** "It's a West Coast Thing" is the theme at this casual restaurant so you find kayaks and bike gear as part of the décor. Steaks, burgers, ribs, noodle bowls and stir-fry's are some of the features on the menu. **Bar:** full bar. **Address:** 1028 Cranbrook St N V1C 3S3 **Location:** Between 6th St NW and Theatre Rd. L D

PURCELL GRILL 250/420-2025

▼▼▼ ▼▼ American. Casual Dining. $30-$45 **AAA Inspector Notes:** Creative, artistic dishes are created with many regional ingredients. The setting, in the old St. Eugene Mission School, lends to a sense of history with exposed brick walls, heavy overhead beams and views of the golf course. Service is friendly and attentive. **Bar:** full bar. **Reservations:** suggested. **Address:** 7731 Mission Rd V1C 7E5 **Location:** Hwy 3 exit Kimberley/Airport (Hwy 95A) to Mission Rd, 2.8 mi (4.5 km) n; in St. Eugene Golf Resort & Casino.

B D CALL 🅼

CRESTON (D-11) pop. 5,306, elev. 636m/2,086'
• Hotels p. 234 • Restaurants p. 234

The unusual Kutenai canoe, which has a bow and stern that both meet the waterline, was used by Indians in the area around Creston in pre-pioneer days. The only other place such a canoe has been found is the Amur River region in southeastern Russia. The canoe's use in this area supports the theory that Asians migrated to North America over a frozen Bering Strait.

In the 1930s about 8,100 hectares (20,000 acres) of land were reclaimed from the Kootenay Delta for agriculture. The Creston Valley floor is now quilted with a variety of seed and root crops, grains and fruit orchards. Other Creston industries include forestry, dairying and brewing.

The Columbia Brewing Co., 1220 Erickson St., offers narrated tours of its facilities mid-May to mid-October; closed toe shoes are mandatory. Complimentary beer is available at the end of the tour; phone (250) 428-1238. Free guided tours of a candlemaking factory are offered year-round at Kootenay Candles, 1511 Northwest Blvd.; phone (250) 428-9785 or (866) 572-9785

Hikers can trek along the old Dewdney Trail, which carried gold seekers from Hope to the Wild Horse goldfields in the 1860s.

Creston Visitor Centre: 121 Northwest Blvd., Creston, BC, Canada V0B 1G0. **Phone:** (250) 428-4342 or (866) 528-4342.

CRESTON MUSEUM is at 219 Devon St. via Hwy. 3A N. The 1957 Stone House, which has four stone fireplaces and walls more than one-third metre (1 ft.) thick, contains in excess of 10,000 pioneer and Indian artifacts, including a replica of a Kutenai Indian canoe and early agricultural tools. A schoolroom exhibit can be seen in the restored Kingsgate Schoolhouse on the museum grounds.

Time: Allow 1 hour minimum. **Hours:** Daily 10-5, mid-June to late Aug.; Mon.-Sat. 10-3:30, mid-May to mid-June and late Aug. to mid-Sept.; Tues.-Sat. 9-noon and 1-4, early Jan. to mid-May and mid-Sept. to mid-Dec. Closed major holidays. Phone ahead to confirm schedule. **Cost:** $4; $3 (ages 6-16). **Phone:** (250) 428-9262.

CRESTON VALLEY WILDLIFE MANAGEMENT AREA is 13 km (6 mi.) w. on Hwy. 3. The 7,000-hectare (17,297-acre) area permits hiking, seasonal camping, bicycling, hunting, canoeing and picnicking in a managed waterfowl habitat. A variety of programs and canoe trips originate at the Interpretation Centre, which houses natural history displays and a theater. *See Recreation Areas Chart.*

Hours: Daily 9-4, July-Aug.; Tues.-Sat. 9-4, May-June and Sept.-Oct. **Cost:** $4; $3 (ages 0-11); $12 (family, two adults and two children). **Phone:** (250) 402-6908.

SKIMMERHORN INN   (250)428-4009

Motel
$65-$155

Address: 2711 Hwy 3 V0B 1G0 **Location:** Hwy 3, 0.8 mi (1.3 km) e. **Facility:** 25 units, some two bedrooms, efficiencies and kitchens. 2 stories (no elevator), exterior corridors. **Parking:** winter plug-ins. **Terms:** cancellation fee imposed. **Pool(s):** heated outdoor. **Activities:** playground, horseshoes. **Free Special Amenities: high-speed Internet and children's activities.**

 / SOME UNITS FEE

SUNSET MOTEL   250/428-2229

Motel
$79-$109

Address: 2705 Canyon St (Hwy 3 E) V0B 1G0 **Location:** Hwy 3, 0.8 mi (1.3 km) e. **Facility:** 24 units, some efficiencies and kitchens. 1-2 stories (no elevator), exterior corridors. **Parking:** winter plug-ins. **Terms:** cancellation fee imposed. **Pool(s):** heated outdoor.

 / SOME UNITS FEE

WHERE TO EAT

A BREAK IN TIME CAFFE   250/428-5619

International. Casual Dining. $8-$14 **AAA Inspector Notes:** This cheerful cafe produces delicious gourmet sandwiches. The Midnight Cuban sandwich with smoked ham and shredded pork is stupendous, but you also can try a naan melt, quesadilla, burrito, wrap or burger. Also available are salads, homemade soups, samosas and desserts. Entrées include Cajun prime rib, smoked pork chops, grilled salmon and shrimp Alfredo pasta. Local cheese, meat and coffee producers are supported, and organic foods are promoted. Order at the counter or grab a menu and sit down. **Bar:** beer & wine. **Address:** 1417 Canyon St V0B 1G0 **Location:** On Hwy 3/3A; center. **Parking:** street only. [B] [L] [D]

CULTUS LAKE (I-12) pop. 15, elev. 45m/150'

Cultus Lake Provincial Park, 11 kilometres (7 mi.) southwest of Chilliwack off Hwy. 1, is a popular recreational area and offers camping, boating, fishing, horseback riding and hiking *(see Recreation Areas Chart)*. Cultus Lake Waterpark, Hwy. 1 exit 119A, has giant waterslides, twisting tunnels, pools and inner tube rides; phone (604) 858-7241 for more information.

CUMBERLAND (F-10) pop. 3,398

Cumberland's origins are rooted in the rigors of coal mining. From 1888 until the last of its nine mines closed in 1966, the village produced some 25 million tons of high-grade coal. The lucrative enterprise solidified Cumberland's economy and contributed to its multi-ethnic mix, drawing miners from locations as diverse as England, Scotland, Italy, China and Japan. The village and many of its streets were named for the mining region in England known as Cumbria.

Nestled in the foothills of the Beaufort Mountains and a stone's throw from Comox Lake, Cumberland offers ample snow skiing, hiking, fishing and boating opportunities.

Cumberland Visitor Centre: 2680 Dunsmuir, P.O. Box 250, Cumberland, BC, Canada V0R 1S0. **Phone:** (250) 336-8313 or (866) 301-4636.

CUMBERLAND MUSEUM & ARCHIVES is off Hwy. 19 Cumberland exit, 2 km (1.2 mi.) w. on Cumberland Rd./4th St., then just w. to jct. 1st St. and Dunsmuir Ave. Visitors can walk through a replica of a coal mine and view exhibits about Cumberland's mining history. Outdoor heritage tours are offered.

Time: Allow 30 minutes minimum. **Hours:** Daily 9-5, July-Aug.; Mon.-Sat. 9-5, rest of year. Phone ahead to confirm schedule. **Cost:** $4; $3 (ages 60+); $2 (ages 13-18). Tours $2. **Phone:** (250) 336-2445.

DAWSON CREEK (D-6) pop. 11,583, elev. 655m/2,148'

Named for George Mercer Dawson of the Geological Survey of Canada, Dawson Creek was settled in 1912. Growth accelerated during World War II, as this was the southern terminus of the Alaska Highway. The highway was then called the Alcan Military Highway, and it served as a supply road to bases in Alaska. The Mile Zero Cairn, which marks the start of the Alaska Highway, and the Zero Milepost are in the center of town. Alpine skiing, camping, hiking and fishing are popular recreational activities.

Dawson Creek Visitor's Centre: 900 Alaska Ave., Dawson Creek, BC, Canada V1G 1M5. **Phone:** (250) 782-9595 or (866) 645-3022.

DAWSON CREEK STATION MUSEUM is at 900 Alaska Ave. Artifacts, fossils and mounted animals and birds from the Peace River region are displayed. Highlights include an early 1900s railway caboose and a 1930s grain elevator as well as an art gallery and a video presentation about construction of the Alaska Highway.

Hours: Daily 8-7, May 3-Sept. 6; Mon.-Sat. 9-5, Sept. 7-Oct. 3; Tues.-Sat. 10-5, Oct. 4-Apr. 4; Mon.-Sat. 9-6, Apr. 5-May 2. Closed Jan. 1 and Good Friday. Phone ahead to confirm schedule. **Cost:** Donations. **Phone:** (250) 782-9595 or (866) 645-3022.

WALTER WRIGHT PIONEER VILLAGE is just w. of jct. Hwy. 97N (Alaska Hwy.) and Hwy. 97S (Hart Hwy.). The complex of pioneer buildings includes a log schoolhouse, log cabin, general store, smithy and two churches. All contain period furnishings.

An extensive collection of farm machinery and implements also is featured as well as nine flower gardens, a memorial rose garden and a lake for swimming. **Time:** Allow 1 hour minimum. **Hours:** Daily 10-5, Victoria Day-Labour Day. **Cost:** $2; $5 (family). **Phone:** (250) 782-7144. 🚽

BEST WESTERN DAWSON CREEK INN   250/782-6226

Hotel
Rates not provided

AAA Benefit: Members save up to 20%, plus 10% bonus points with Best Western Rewards®.

Address: 500 Hwy 2 V1G 0A4 **Location:** Jct Hwy 49, 1.6 mi (2.6 km) s on 8th St (Hwy 2), then just e; south end of town. **Facility:** 100 units, some efficiencies. 3 stories, interior corridors. **Parking:** winter plug-ins. **Amenities:** high-speed Internet. **Pool(s):** heated indoor. **Activities:** whirlpool, waterslide, exercise room. **Guest Services:** valet laundry. **Free Special Amenities: expanded continental breakfast and local telephone calls.**

🆚 🌿 🍴 📶 🍸 CALL 📶 🏊 BIZ 🛜 🐾 🖥️ 📠 💻 / SOME UNITS FEE 🐕

DAWSON CREEK SUPER 8   (250)782-8899

Hotel
$146-$337

Address: 1440 Alaska Ave V1G 1Z5 **Location:** Jct Hwy 2 and 49, 0.5 mi (0.8 km) ne. **Facility:** 66 units, some efficiencies. 2 stories (no elevator), interior corridors. **Parking:** winter plug-ins. **Amenities:** *Some:* high-speed Internet. **Dining:** Sola's Bar & Grill, see separate listing. **Activities:** exercise room. **Guest Services:** coin laundry. **Free Special Amenities: expanded continental breakfast and high-speed Internet.**

🆚 🍴 🍸 BIZ 🛜 ✂️ 📷 🖥️ 📠 💻 / SOME UNITS FEE 🐕

DAYS INN DAWSON CREEK   (250)782-8887

Hotel
$140

Address: 640 122nd Ave V1G 0A4 **Location:** Hwy 2, just n on 7th St; southeast end of town. Next to Walmart. **Facility:** 85 units. 4 stories, interior corridors. **Parking:** winter plug-ins. **Amenities:** high-speed Internet. **Activities:** exercise room. **Guest Services:** valet and coin laundry.

🆚 🌿 🍴 BIZ 🛜 🖥️ 📠 💻

POMEROY INN & SUITES   (250)782-3700

Extended Stay Hotel $170-$329 **Address:** 540 Hwy 2 V1G 0A4 **Location:** Jct Hwy 49, 1.6 mi (2.6 km) s on 8th St (Hwy 2), then just e; south end of town. **Facility:** 94 units, some two bedrooms and kitchens. 4 stories, interior corridors. **Parking:** winter plug-ins. **Terms:** cancellation fee imposed, resort fee. **Amenities:** high-speed Internet. **Pool(s):** heated indoor. **Activities:** whirlpool, waterslide, exercise room. **Guest Services:** valet laundry.

🍴 🏊 BIZ 🛜 🐾 🖥️ 📠 💻 / SOME UNITS FEE 🐕

WHERE TO EAT

BROWNS SOCIAL HOUSE   250/782-2400

International. Gastropub. $12-$25 **AAA Inspector Notes:** This spot is boisterous and hip with tables packed around the bar, low lighting and a décor that focuses on an assortment of nifty light fixtures. The menu has a global influence with a good range of made-for-sharing appetizers like edamame, spicy tempura tuna roll or calamari. Other menu items include interesting salads, hand-pressed burgers, gourmet pizza, blackened chicken, Tahitian tuna rice bowls, cashew curry, and beer-battered halibut and chips. **Bar:** full bar. **Address:** 1100 Alaska Ave, #104 V1G 4V8 **Location:** Jct Hwy 2 and 49, just ne. 🅛 🅓 LATE CALL 📶

HUG A MUG COFFEE SHOP   250/782-6659

Coffee/Tea. Quick Serve. $5-$12 **AAA Inspector Notes:** This is a homey spot with a simple design focusing around a bright blue mural along the entrance wall. Though known for delicious soups and quiche, the place also has a fresh-made sandwich bar. Home-style treats include cookies, squares and pies. Fresh cinnamon buns are available Monday, Wednesday and Friday. You'll also find specialty coffees, teas, smoothies and frozen yogurt on the menu. **Address:** 1012 102nd Ave V1G 2B8 **Location:** Just s of Hwy 2; center. **Parking:** street only. 🅑 🅛

MR MIKES STEAKHOUSE & BAR   250/782-1577

American. Casual Dining. $11-$33 **AAA Inspector Notes:** This bustling, casual restaurant offers such familiar choices as great burgers, steaks, ribs, chicken, salmon, noodle bowls and stir-fry dishes. Be prepared for friendly and fast service. **Bar:** full bar. **Address:** 1501 Alaska Ave V1G 1Z8 **Location:** Jct Hwy 2 and 97, 0.5 mi (0.8 km) ne. 🅛 🅓 CALL 📶

SOLA'S BAR & GRILL   250/782-8890

American. Casual Dining. $10-$30 **AAA Inspector Notes:** A large stone fireplace dominates the popular and bustling restaurant's contemporary dining room. On the menu is a little something for everyone, including a variety of burgers and sandwiches as well as classic entrées of prime rib, lemon pepper chicken or grilled salmon. You'll also find international dishes such as tandoori chicken. The friendly staff provides swift service. **Bar:** full bar. **Address:** 1440 Alaska Ave V1G 1Z5 **Location:** Jct Hwy 2 and 49, 0.5 mi (0.8 km) ne; in Dawson Creek Super 8. 🅛 🅓 CALL 📶

DELTA (H-11) pop. 99,863, elev. 10m/33'

• Hotels p. 236 • Restaurants p. 236
• Hotels & Restaurants map & index p. 368
• Part of Vancouver area — see map p. 343

Delta, composed of the three distinct communities of Ladner, Tsawwassen and North Delta, is an amalgam of commerce, fisheries, industry, farmland, beaches and suburban residences. The warm-water beaches on Boundary Bay and Tsawwassen are popular spots for swimming and sunbathing. Other recreational opportunities in the area include fishing for salmon and boating on the Fraser River and the Strait of Georgia.

Delta Visitor Centre: 6201 60th Ave., Delta, BC, Canada V4K 4E2. **Phone:** (604) 946-4232.

DELTA MUSEUM AND ARCHIVES is at 4858 Delta St. The museum houses marine, fishing and farming exhibits, pioneer and native peoples displays, reconstructed rooms of a late Victorian household and an early 1900s Delta street scene. **Time:** Allow 1 hour minimum. **Hours:** Museum open Tues.-Fri. 10-4:30. Archives open Tues.-Fri. 10-4:30. Closed major holidays. **Cost:** Donations. **Phone:** (604) 946-9322.

REIFEL MIGRATORY BIRD SANCTUARY is at 5191 Robertson Rd. on Westham Island. More than 286 species of birds have been observed at the refuge, which comprises 344 hectares (850 acres). This major bird-watching area offers superb observation from 7 kilometres (4 mi.) of trails bordering sloughs and ponds. Bird sightings reach their peak in November and nesting activity is in April and May. **Time:** Allow 1 hour minimum. **Hours:** Daily 9-4. **Cost:** $5; $3 (ages 2-14 and 60+). Bird seed 50c per bag. **Phone:** (604) 946-6980.

(See map & index p. 368.)

THE COAST TSAWWASSEN INN   (604)943-8221 **58**

WWWW
Hotel
$111-$233

Address: 1665 56th St V4L 2B2 **Location:** Hwy 99 exit 28 (Tsawwassen Ferries), 5 mi (8 km) w on Hwy 17; 3.1 mi (5 km) from Tsawwassen Ferry Terminal. **Facility:** 90 units, some kitchens. 3 stories, interior corridors. **Terms:** cancellation fee imposed. **Amenities:** video games (fee). **Pool(s):** heated indoor. **Activities:** sauna, whirlpool, exercise room. **Guest Services:** valet and coin laundry, area transportation-ferry terminal. **Free Special Amenities: expanded continental breakfast and high-speed Internet.**

[SAVE] [ECO] [↑↓] [Y] CALL [&M] [⊃] [⌂] [✕] [✦] [⊟]
[▭] [▱] / SOME UNITS FEE [⊢]

DELTA TOWN & COUNTRY INN   (604)946-4404 **57**

WWWW
Hotel
$102-$112

Address: 6005 Hwy 17 V4K 5B8 **Location:** Hwy 17 at Hwy 99 exit 28 (River Rd). Located in a quiet rural area. **Facility:** 49 units. 2 stories (no elevator), interior corridors. **Pool(s):** heated outdoor. **Activities:** exercise room. **Fee:** 5 tennis courts (4 indoor, 5 lighted). **Guest Services:** valet and coin laundry. **Free Special Amenities: local telephone calls and high-speed Internet.**

[SAVE] [ECO] [↑↓] [Y] [⊃] [BIZ] [⌂] [✕] [▱]
/ SOME UNITS [⊟] [▭]

WHERE TO EAT

CACTUS CLUB CAFE   604/591-1707

WW American. Casual Dining. $9-$29 **AAA Inspector Notes:** This bustling, casual restaurant serves huge burgers, sandwiches, pasta, salads, soups, quesadillas, fajitas, vegetarian dishes, steak, ribs, chicken and fish. Featured are certified Angus beef and fresh wild British Columbia salmon. **Bar:** full bar. **Address:** 7907 120th St V4C 6P6 **Location:** Just s from 80th Ave.

[L] [D] [LATE] CALL [&M]

RICKY'S ALL DAY GRILL   604/599-1784

WW American. Casual Dining. $6-$15 **AAA Inspector Notes:** The comfortable eatery, which employs friendly servers, presents a varied menu that includes pasta dishes, wraps, omelets, stir-fry preparations and burgers. Portions are generous. Children's and senior selections are offered. Guests can request seating in a booth or at a table. **Bar:** full bar. **Address:** 7135 120th St V4E 2A9 **Location:** Just s of 72nd Ave. [B] [L] [D] CALL [&M]

DUNCAN (H-10) pop. 4,932, elev. 15m/49'

Founded in 1887 as Alderlea, Duncan was renamed in 1912 in honor of farmer William Duncan, who gave his land for the original townsite. Settlers were attracted by the promise of copper and coal on nearby Mount Sicker, where abandoned mines and original homesteads still can be seen. The growth of the logging and farming industries brought increasing numbers to Duncan and the Cowichan Valley.

The area around Duncan is known for the handspun woolen sweaters produced by the Cowichan Indians. West on Hwy. 18 is the Cowichan Valley Demonstration Forest with scenic viewpoints and signs describing forest management practices and ecology. More than 80 totem poles dot the town of Duncan.

Duncan-Cowichan Chamber of Commerce: 381 Trans-Canada Hwy., Duncan, BC, Canada V9L 3R5. **Phone:** (250) 746-1111 or (888) 303-3337.

Shopping areas: Whippletree Junction, a group of shops and boutiques with late 1800s storefronts, is 5 kilometres (3 mi.) south on the Trans-Canada Highway.

BC FOREST DISCOVERY CENTRE is 1.5 km (1 mi.) n. off Hwy. 1 to 2892 Drinkwater Rd. The site has more than 40 hectares (99 acres) of forest and interactive displays and videotapes depicting British Columbia's forestry heritage, management practices and renewal efforts. In addition to a logging museum there are Douglas fir trees, forestry equipment and an old-time logging camp. A nature trail and a ride on a logging train are available July through August; a Christmas train ride and related events take place in late November and December.

Hours: Daily 10-4:30, June 1-Labour Day; Thurs.-Mon. 10-4, late Apr.-May 31 and day after Labour Day-early Oct. Phone ahead for Dec. schedule. Closed second Mon. in Oct. **Cost:** June 1-Labour Day $15; $13 (ages 13-18 and 65+); $10 (ages 5-12); $55 (family). Admission rest of year $11; $9 (ages 13-18 and 65+); $7 (ages 5-12). Christmas train $7; $5 (ages 2-12). Prices and schedule may vary; phone ahead. **Phone:** (250) 715-1113 or (866) 715-1113.

QUW'UTSUN' CULTURAL AND CONFERENCE CENTRE is 1 blk. w. of Hwy. 1 at 200 Cowichan Way. The 2.4-hectare (6-acre) site consists of a living-history museum and a gallery dedicated to the preservation and dissemination of the culture of the Northwest Coast Indians. Exhibits include numerous totem poles and historical artifacts as well as the Comeakin longhouse and Khenipsen Carving House. Interpretive tours, craft demonstrations and a film presentation also are featured.

Time: Allow 1 hour minimum. **Hours:** Mon.-Sat. 10-4, June 1-Sept. 24. Guided tours are offered on the hour; multimedia presentations begin on the half-hour. Closed statutory holidays. **Cost:** $13; $10 (ages 12-18 and 55+); $6 (ages 5-11). Rates may vary; phone ahead. **Phone:** (250) 746-8119 or (877) 746-8119. [↑↓]

BEST WESTERN COWICHAN VALLEY INN
                                           (250)748-2722

WW
Hotel
$119-$169

AAA Benefit: Members save up to 20%, plus 10% bonus points with Best Western Rewards®.

Address: 6474 Trans-Canada Hwy 1 V9L 6C6 **Location:** 1.8 mi (3 km) n. **Facility:** 42 units. 2 stories (no elevator), interior corridors. **Pool(s):** heated outdoor. **Activities:** limited exercise equipment. **Guest Services:** valet laundry. **Free Special Amenities: local telephone calls and high-speed Internet.**

[SAVE] [↑↓] [Y] [⊃] [⌂] [✕] [⊟] [▱] / SOME UNITS FEE [⊢]

SUPER 8 HOTEL   (250)748-0661

WW Hotel $89-$139 **Address:** 5325 Trans-Canada Hwy V9L 5J2 **Location:** 1 mi (1.6 km) s at Chaster Rd. **Facility:** 35 units, some kitchens. 3 stories (no elevator), interior corridors. **Dining:** Smitty's, see separate listing. **Guest Services:** coin laundry.

[↑↓] [Y] [↔] [⌂] [✕] [⊟] [▱] / SOME UNITS [⊢] [▭]

TRAVELODGE DUNCAN   (250)748-4311
 **Hotel** $109-$200 **Address:** 140 Trans-Canada Hwy V9L 3P7 **Location:** Just n of Silver Bridge. Located by Duncan Village Mall. **Facility:** 34 units, some kitchens. 2 stories (no elevator), exterior corridors. **Terms:** cancellation fee imposed. **Amenities:** high-speed Internet.

WHERE TO EAT

DOGHOUSE A FAMILY RESTAURANT   250/746-4614
American. Family Dining. $5-$17 AAA Inspector Notes: Patrons have been coming to the Doghouse since 1955, and it's easy to see why. Quality home-style cooking, generous family servings and reasonable prices might make a regular out of you, too. Fish and chips is a specialty not to be missed, and the veal cutlets and homemade desserts are worth mentioning. **Bar:** full bar. **Address:** 271 Trans-Canada Hwy V9L 3R1 **Location:** Corner of Trans-Canada Hwy and Trunk Rd. B L D CALL

SMITTY'S   250/597-1818
American. Casual Dining. $12-$16 AAA Inspector Notes: The family-oriented restaurant satisfies patrons with its ever-popular all-day breakfast items, as well as tasty and wholesome soups and salads at lunchtime. A relaxed mood characterizes the dining space. **Bar:** full bar. **Address:** 5325 Trans-Canada Hwy V9L 5J2 **Location:** 1 mi (1.6 km) s at Chaster Rd; in Super 8 Hotel. B L D CALL

ERRINGTON (G-10) pop. 2,678

NORTH ISLAND WILDLIFE RECOVERY ASSOCIATION is .7 km (.4 mi.) e. on Grafton Ave., then .4 km (.25 mi.) n. to 1240 Leffler Rd. Bald eagles, owls, hawks, swans and black bears are among the animals that can be viewed at this 3-hectare (8-acre) rehabilitation facility. An eagle flight cage houses eagles waiting to be released into the wild.

A nature museum, wildlife learning center, nature trails and a release pond are on the grounds. **Time:** Allow 30 minutes minimum. **Hours:** Daily 9-5, mid-Mar. through Dec. 19. Raptor presentation Wed.-Fri. at 1:30, July-Aug. **Cost:** $8; $5 (ages 3-11). **Phone:** (250) 248-8534.

FAIRMONT HOT SPRINGS (B-11) pop. 476, elev. 810m/2,657'

At the north end of Columbia Lake, Fairmont Hot Springs were discovered about 1840. This popular resort area offers four hot mineral springs with temperatures averaging 35 to 45 C (95 to 113 F). Water sports and alpine and cross-country skiing also are available. *See Recreation Areas Chart.*

RECREATIONAL ACTIVITIES
Skiing
• **Fairmont Hot Springs Resort** is at 5225 Fairmont Resort Rd. Other activities are available. **Hours:** Skiing daily 9:30-4, mid-Dec. to early Apr. **Phone:** (250) 345-6000 or (800) 663-4979.

AAA/CAA travel information: Available in print, online and on the go!

FAIRMONT HOT SPRINGS RESORT   250/345-6070
 Resort Hotel $105-$355 **Address:** 5225 Fairmont Resort Rd V0B 1L1 **Location:** 1 mi (1.6 km) e off Hwy 93 and 95. **Facility:** The resort's outstanding feature is its landscaped grounds, which includes an area with natural hot springs pools. 143 units, some two bedrooms, efficiencies, cabins and cottages. 3 stories, interior/exterior corridors. **Parking:** winter plug-ins. **Terms:** check-in 4 pm, 7 day cancellation notice-fee imposed. **Amenities:** *Some:* high-speed Internet. **Dining:** 2 restaurants. **Pool(s):** heated outdoor. **Activities:** sauna, whirlpool, steamroom, fishing, 2 tennis courts, cross country skiing, ice skating, recreation programs in summer, rental bicycles, hiking trails, jogging, playground, volleyball, exercise room, spa. *Fee:* golf-45 holes, miniature golf, downhill skiing, horseback riding. **Guest Services:** coin laundry. **Free Special Amenities:** high-speed Internet.

FAIRMONT HOT SPRINGS RESORT

Experience Canada's largest natural mineral hot springs! Located in the BC Rocky Mountains.

FERNIE (C-12) pop. 4,448
• Restaurants p. 238

At the foot of Trinity Mountain in the British Columbia Rockies, Fernie is a year-round recreation center. The many surrounding lakes and mountains provide opportunities for boating, fishing, hiking, camping and skiing. Mount Fernie Provincial Park is 4.8 kilometres (3 mi.) east *(see Recreation Areas Chart)*. Prentice and Rotary parks are downtown.

Fernie Chamber of Commerce: 102 Hwy. 3, Fernie, BC, Canada V0B 1M5. **Phone:** (250) 423-6868.

RECREATIONAL ACTIVITIES
Skiing
• **Fernie Alpine Resort** is 5 km (3 mi.) s.w. off Hwy. 3 at 5339 Fernie Ski Hill Rd. Other activities are offered. **Hours:** Daily 9-4, early Dec.-Apr. 30. **Phone:** (250) 423-4655 or (800) 258-7669.

White-water Rafting
• **Mountain High River Adventures Inc.** collects passengers at Riverside Mountain Lodge at 100 Riverside Way. Other activities are offered. **Hours:** Daily 8-8, Victoria Day-Sept. 30. **Phone:** (250) 423-5008 or (877) 423-4555.

BEST WESTERN PLUS FERNIE MOUNTAIN LODGE
                                  (250)423-5500
 Hotel $150-$210

AAA Benefit: Members save up to 20%, plus 10% bonus points with Best Western Rewards®.

Address: 1622 7th Ave V0B 1M0 **Location:** Jct Hwy 3 and 7th Ave; east end of town. **Facility:** 95 units, some efficiencies. 3 stories, interior corridors. **Parking:** winter plug-ins. **Amenities:** high-speed Internet. **Pool(s):** heated indoor. **Activities:** whirlpools, exercise room. *Fee:* massage. **Guest Services:** valet and coin laundry. **Free Special Amenities:** full breakfast and high-speed Internet.

CORNERSTONE LODGE   (250)423-6855

 **Condominium** $154-$392 **Address:** 5339 Ski Hill Rd V0B 1M6 **Location:** 4 mi (6.5 km) w on Hwy 3, 0.8 mi (1.4 km) n. **Facility:** Right on the ski hill, these comfortable condominiums are equipped as a home away from home. 26 condominiums. 3 stories, interior corridors. **Parking:** winter plug-ins. **Terms:** off-site registration, check-in 4 pm, 2 night minimum stay, 30 day cancellation notice-fee imposed. **Amenities:** high-speed Internet. **Dining:** 2 restaurants. **Activities:** whirlpool, cross country skiing, limited exercise equipment. *Fee:* downhill skiing, snowmobiling. **Guest Services:** complimentary laundry.

LIZARD CREEK LODGE AND CONDOMINIUMS AT FERNIE ALPINE RESORT   (250)423-2057

Condominium
$145-$570
Address: 5346 Highline Dr V0B 1M6 **Location:** 4 mi (6.5 km) w on Hwy 3, 0.8 mi (1.4 km) on Ski Area Rd, follow signs. **Facility:** Featuring ski-in/ski-out access and heated underground parking, the luxurious property offers a mix of fully-equipped studios in the main lodge, as well as one to three bedroom units in separate buildings. 99 condominiums. 3 stories, interior corridors. **Parking:** on-site and valet. **Terms:** check-in 4 pm, 30 day cancellation notice. **Amenities:** *Some:* high-speed Internet. **Dining:** Lizard Creek Lodge Dining Room, see separate listing. **Pool(s):** heated outdoor. **Activities:** whirlpools, steamroom, cross country skiing, hiking trails, exercise room. *Fee:* downhill skiing, snowmobiling, horseback riding, massage. **Guest Services:** coin laundry. **Free Special Amenities: local telephone calls and high-speed Internet.**

PARK PLACE LODGE   (250)423-6871

Hotel
$132-$272
Address: 742 Hwy 3 V0B 1M0 **Location:** At 7th St. **Facility:** 64 units, some efficiencies and kitchens. 3 stories, interior corridors. **Parking:** winter plug-ins. **Terms:** check-in 4 pm, cancellation fee imposed, resort fee. **Amenities:** video games, high-speed Internet. **Dining:** Max Restaurant, see separate listing. **Pool(s):** heated indoor. **Activities:** sauna, whirlpool, hiking trails, exercise room. **Guest Services:** valet laundry. **Free Special Amenities:** local telephone calls and high-speed Internet.

WHERE TO EAT

THE BLUE TOQUE DINER   250/423-4637

Breakfast. Casual Dining. $11-$15 AAA Inspector Notes: This tiny spot serves up all-day, one-of-a-kind breakfasts that are delicious and beautifully presented. Fresh house-made soups, salads, sandwiches and desserts at lunchtime complete the menu. Located in The Art Station, a historic Canadian Pacific Railway station, it's popular with locals and tourists alike, so be prepared to wait. Full bar. **Address:** 601 1 Ave V0B 1M0 **Location:** Corner of 6 St and 1 Ave. **Parking:** street only. [B] [L]

KELSEY'S   250/423-2444

American. Casual Dining. $10-$26 AAA Inspector Notes: A fun, relaxed atmosphere and tasty menu of casual fare make the restaurant a popular favorite with locals. Diners might start a meal with some tempting appetizers, such as wings, loaded potato skins or nachos, and follow them with an old-time favorite, such as a burger, wrap, pizza or pasta dish. For a heartier meal, it's hard to beat pork back ribs or a steak. The diverse menu has broad appeal. Bar: full bar. **Address:** 5339 Ski Hill, Fernie Alpine Resort Rd V0B 1M0 **Location:** At base of ski hill. [L] [D]

LIZARD CREEK LODGE DINING ROOM   250/423-2057

American. Casual Dining. $11-$39 AAA Inspector Notes: Considered to be one of the best places in Fernie, this upscale dining room is a superb place for a fine meal. After a day on the ski hill, guests can explore a regional menu of creative dishes or more casual lunch offerings. During the winter, Sunday brunch is offered. **Bar:** full bar. **Reservations:** suggested. **Address:** 5346 Highline Dr V0B 1M1 **Location:** 4 mi (6.5 km) w on Hwy 3, 0.8 mi (1.4 km) on Ski Area Rd, follow signs; in Lizard Creek Lodge and Condominiums at Fernie Alpine Resort. [B] [L] [D] CALL [&M]

MAX RESTAURANT   250/423-6871

American. Casual Dining. $8-$29 AAA Inspector Notes: The open room has an elegant décor with huge brass chandeliers and lovely large pieces of art. The menu features a really good range of casual fare as well as more complex entrées like chicken cordon bleu with mountain mushroom demi-glace, wild salmon with mango salsa and AAA Alberta beef with a choice of sauces and delicious house desserts. Lunch is simpler with a good choice of salads, sandwiches, wraps and burgers. **Bar:** full bar. **Address:** 742 Hwy 3 V0B 1M0 **Location:** At 7th St; in Park Place Lodge. [B] [L] [D] CALL [&M]

MUGSHOTS CAFE   250/423-8018

Coffee/Tea. Quick Serve. $7-$10 AAA Inspector Notes: Quirky and eclectic best describes the funky coffeehouse, which prepares a wide selection of soups, sandwiches, ground coffees and sumptuous desserts. The downtown spot is popular with locals and visitors alike, not only for the hearty, healthy food but also for its Internet café. **Address:** 592 3 Ave V0B 1M0 **Location:** Corner of 5th St and 3rd Ave; downtown. **Parking:** street only. [B] [L] CALL [&M]

YAMAGOYA JAPANESE RESTAURANT   250/430-0090

Japanese. Casual Dining. $10-$20 AAA Inspector Notes: The classic mountain log cabin exterior hides the fresh and stylish décor found inside this exceedingly popular spot. Lineups start before the doors even open; be prepared to wait, especially if you want one of the coveted private booths. You won't be disappointed by the well-crafted sushi, including some challenging fusion rolls. Tasty appetizers, including tender edamame and great tempura dishes, and teriyaki stir-fries round out the menu. **Bar:** full bar. **Address:** 711 7th Ave V0B 1M6 **Location:** Hwy 3/3B, just e. **Parking:** street only. [D] [C]

FORT LANGLEY (H-11) elev. 12m/39'

BRITISH COLUMBIA FARM MACHINERY AND AGRICULTURAL MUSEUM is at 9131 King St. This complex of buildings features artifacts and exhibits devoted to the development of farm machinery in British Columbia. Included are a handwrought plow, a threshing machine, carriages and buckboards, and a Tiger-Moth airplane used for crop dusting. A research library also is available.

Time: Allow 30 minutes minimum. **Hours:** Daily 10-4:30, Apr. 1-second Mon. in Oct. **Cost:** $6; $4 (ages 13-19 and 60+); $3 (ages 6-12). **Phone:** (604) 888-2273.

LANGLEY CENTENNIAL MUSEUM is at 9135 King St. Regional artifacts reflect the lifestyle of early explorers, fur traders and native peoples. Re-created period rooms include a parlor, a kitchen and a general store. Displays also feature wood carvings, stone artifacts and baskets from the Coast Salish culture. Permanent and changing exhibits focus on art, science and Canadian and world history.

Hours: Mon.-Sat. 10-4:45, Sun. 1-4:45. Closed Jan. 1, Good Friday, Easter Monday, second Mon. in Oct., Nov. 11 and Dec. 25-31. **Cost:** Donations. **Phone:** (604) 888-3922.

FORT LANGLEY NATIONAL HISTORIC SITE (I-10)

Fort Langley National Historic Site is 6.5 kilometres (4 mi.) north of Langley off Hwy. 1 at 23433 Mavis Ave. On the bank of the Fraser River, the 19th-century Hudson's Bay Company trading post was an important supply link in the company's network of fur trading forts west of the Rockies. British Columbia was proclaimed a colony at the site in 1858.

The site preserves an original 1840 storehouse and reconstructed wooden buildings, including a cooperage and blacksmith's shop and a log palisade. Interpreters in period costumes demonstrate fur-trading activities daily. A visitor center displays contemporary exhibits. Special events are presented throughout the year.

Picnicking is permitted. Allow 1 hour minimum. Daily 9-5, July 1-Labour Day; 10-5, rest of year. Closed Jan. 1, Christmas and day after Christmas. Admission $7.80; $6.55 (ages 65+); $3.90 (ages 6-16); $19.60 (family). Phone (604) 513-4777.

FORT NELSON (B-5) pop. 3,902, elev. 405m/1,350'

Originally a fur-trading post, Fort Nelson thrived with the building of the Alaska Highway during World War II. Nearby mountains, lakes, parks, forests and diverse wildlife populations make Fort Nelson a destination for adventurous tourists, anglers and hunters.

Fort Nelson Visitor Centre: 5500 Alaska Hwy., Fort Nelson, BC, Canada V0C 1R0. **Phone:** (250) 774-6400.

FORT NELSON HERITAGE MUSEUM is w. on Hwy. 97 at Mile 300 on the Alaska Hwy. An albino moose is among the stuffed animals displayed at the museum, which chronicles the history of Fort Nelson. Exhibits include vintage cars, photographs of the construction of the Alaska Highway and a trapper's log cabin.

Time: Allow 30 minutes minimum. **Hours:** Daily 8:30-7:30, mid-May to mid-Sept. Closed July 1 for morning parade. **Cost:** $5; $3 (ages 5-16 and senior citizens); $10 (family). **Phone:** (250) 774-3536.

LAKEVIEW INN & SUITES (250)233-5001

Hotel
$130-$140

Address: 4507 50th Ave S V0C 1R0 **Location:** Just off Hwy 97 (Alaska Hwy); at 44th St. **Facility:** 82 units, some two bedrooms and efficiencies. 4 stories, interior corridors. **Parking:** winter plug-ins. **Terms:** cancellation fee imposed. **Amenities:** high-speed Internet. **Activities:** whirlpool, steamroom, limited exercise equipment. **Guest Services:** coin laundry. **Free Special Amenities:** expanded continental breakfast and high-speed Internet.

  / SOME UNITS FEE

WOODLANDS INN & SUITES (250)774-6669

Hotel
$154-$164

Address: 3995 50th Ave S V0C 1R0 **Location:** On Hwy 97 (Alaska Hwy). **Facility:** 202 units, some efficiencies and kitchens. 4 stories, interior corridors. **Parking:** winter plug-ins. **Terms:** 7 day cancellation notice-fee imposed. **Amenities:** high-speed Internet. **Dining:** The One, see separate listing. **Activities:** whirlpool, steamroom, exercise room. **Guest Services:** coin laundry.

THE ONE 250/774-6669

American
Casual Dining
$12-$39

AAA Inspector Notes: You'll find friendly service and a contemporary flair in this newly designed dining room. The comfortable banquettes feature blue lights along the baseboards to guide your way. The great lighting enhances the dark wood accents. The menu highlights Alberta beef, salmon, halibut, burgers, pasta and pizza. **Bar:** full bar. **Address:** 3995 50th Ave S V0C 1R0 **Location:** On Hwy 97 (Alaska Hwy); in Woodlands Inn & Suites.

B D CALL ☾M

FORT RODD HILL AND FISGARD LIGHTHOUSE NATIONAL HISTORIC SITES (I-9)
• Part of Victoria area — see map p. 397

Fourteen kilometres (9 mi.) west of Victoria via Hwy. 1A, Fort Rodd Hill was a coastal artillery fort 1895-1956. Of interest are the loophole walls, underground magazines, artillery stores, command posts, barracks and gun and searchlight emplacements. Audiotape and videotape presentations, along with period rooms, depict life at the fort. The 1860 Fisgard Lighthouse, restored to its 1873 appearance, was the first built on this part of the coast. Still operational, the lighthouse has two floors of historical exhibits. A nature trail follows the paths formerly used by soldiers. Historical exhibits also are featured. Picnic facilities are available. Pets are not allowed on the grounds.

Allow 1 hour, 30 minutes minimum. Park open daily 10-5:30, Feb. 15-Oct. 31; 9-4:30, rest of year. Exhibits daily 10-5, Mar.-Oct.; 9-4, rest of year. Buildings and exhibits close 30 minutes prior to park closing. Closed Christmas. Admission (includes fort and lighthouse) $3.90; $3.40 (ages 65+); $1.90 (ages 6-16). **Cards:** MC, VI. Phone (250) 478-5849.

FORT ST. JAMES (E-4) pop. 1,691, elev. 680m/2,230'

Established in 1806 by Simon Fraser and John Stuart, the fur-trading post of Fort St. James became the capital of New Caledonia in 1821. Furs from outlying New Caledonia posts were brought overland to Fort St. James by dog sled and then shipped south during the spring thaw to the coast by canoe and horse.

During this time George Simpson, governor of the Hudson's Bay Co.'s vast empire, visited the fort. Determined to impress the Carrier Indians, Simpson organized a flamboyant procession complete with flute, bugle and bagpipe players in Highland dress, accompanied by a dog with a music box around its neck. Thereafter, the awe-struck Indians reverently referred to Simpson as the "great chief whose dog sings."

A Roman Catholic mission was founded at the fort in 1843. Services continue to be held in Our Lady of Good Hope Church, which was built in 1873 and is one of the oldest churches in British Columbia.

Mining activity supplemented the capital's trapping enterprises after the discovery of gold in the Omineca region in 1869. Interest in mining rekindled during World War II when the Pinchi Mine a few kilometres north yielded more mercury than any other mine in the British Commonwealth.

A lack of highways and railways prompted Fort St. James to pioneer bush flying as a means of transportation; it has served as an air base since the earliest days of charter flight.

The north shore of Stuart Lake, 16 kilometres (10 mi.) west, features some of the earliest signs of habitation in the form of prehistoric rock paintings just above the high-water mark. Although Fort St. James has emerged from relative wilderness, its surrounding evergreen forests continue to be among the best big-game hunting areas in the province. Alpine skiing is available nearby.

Fort St. James Visitor Centre: 115 Douglas Ave., P.O. Box 1164, Fort St. James, BC, Canada V0J 1P0. **Phone:** (250) 996-7023.

FORT ST. JAMES NATIONAL HISTORIC SITE is 2 blks. w. of Hwy. 27. Established on the southern shore of Stuart Lake by the North West Co. in 1806, Fort St. James contains one of the largest groups of original wooden buildings from Canada's fur trade. A massive fur warehouse is a noted example of Red River framing. The fully restored Hudson's Bay Co. post on the site served as a hub of commerce between fur traders and the indigenous peoples—and as the capital of New Caledonia, now central British Columbia.

The visitor center provides pictorial displays, artifacts and an audiovisual presentation. Changing exhibits also are offered seasonally. Interpreters in period costume provide living-history demonstrations throughout the day. **Time:** Allow 2 hours minimum. **Hours:** Daily 9-5, June 1 through mid-Sept.; by appointment rest of year. **Cost:** $7.80; $6.55 (ages 66+); $3.90 (ages 6-16); $19.60 (family). Prices may vary; phone to confirm. **Phone:** (250) 996-7191.

FORT ST. JOHN (D-5) pop. 18,609, elev. 695m/2,280'

One of the oldest European settlements in the province, Fort St. John was established in 1793 as a fur-trading outpost called Rocky Mountain Fort. Residents engage in gas and oil exploration as well as the lumber industry and cattle ranching. There are coalfields to the south and west.

Recreational activities include fishing for Arctic grayling and gray trout in nearby Charlie Lake *(see Recreation Areas Chart)*, canoeing the rapids of the Peace River, skiing, and hunting for mountain caribou, mountain goats and black bears in the Rocky Mountain foothills. Floatplanes operating out of Charlie Lake provide access to the wilderness surrounding Fort St. John, and Hwy. 29 provides scenic driving to Chetwynd.

Fort St. John Visitor Centre: 9523-100 St., Fort St. John, BC, Canada V1J 4N4. **Phone:** (250) 785-3033 or (877) 785-6037.

LAKEVIEW INNS & SUITES   (250)787-0779

Hotel
$116-$143

Address: 10103 98th Ave V1J 1P8 **Location:** Corner of 100th Ave; center of downtown. **Facility:** 71 units, some efficiencies. 3 stories (no elevator), interior corridors. **Parking:** winter plug-ins. **Terms:** cancellation fee imposed. **Amenities:** high-speed Internet. **Activities:** exercise room. **Guest Services:** valet and coin laundry. **Free Special Amenities:** expanded continental breakfast and high-speed Internet.

POMEROY HOTEL   (250)262-3233

Hotel
$179-$249

Address: 11308 Alaska Rd V1J 5T5 **Location:** Just w on Hwy 97 (Alaska Hwy). **Facility:** Get a good night's sleep here thanks to the signature Opulence Sleep System, which, along with the wet bar area and large desk, enhances the comfort in the inviting rooms. 125 units, some kitchens. 3 stories, interior corridors. **Parking:** winter plug-ins. **Terms:** 14 day cancellation notice. **Amenities:** high-speed Internet. **Pool(s):** heated indoor. **Activities:** whirlpool, waterslide, exercise room. **Guest Services:** valet and coin laundry. **Free Special Amenities:** continental breakfast and manager's reception.

POMEROY INN & SUITES   (250)262-3030

Extended Stay
Hotel
$129-$159

Address: 9320 Alaska Rd V1J 6L5 **Location:** Just s on Hwy 97 (Alaska Hwy). **Facility:** 92 units, some kitchens. 4 stories, interior corridors. **Parking:** winter plug-ins. **Terms:** cancellation fee imposed, resort fee. **Amenities:** video games (fee), high-speed Internet. **Activities:** exercise room. **Guest Services:** valet laundry. **Free Special Amenities:** continental breakfast and high-speed Internet.

QUALITY INN NORTHERN GRAND   (250)787-0521

Hotel $179-$189 **Address:** 9830 100th Ave V1J 1Y5 **Location:** Center. **Facility:** 125 units. 6 stories, interior corridors. **Parking:** winter plug-ins. **Terms:** cancellation fee imposed. **Dining:** J. D. Fitzgeralds, see separate listing, nightclub. **Pool(s):** heated indoor. **Activities:** sauna, whirlpool, exercise room. **Guest Services:** valet laundry.

SUPER 8-FORT ST. JOHN   (250)785-7588

Hotel
$150

Address: 9500 W Alaska Rd V1J 6L5 **Location:** Just s on Hwy 97 (Alaska Hwy). **Facility:** 93 units. 4 stories, interior corridors. **Parking:** winter plug-ins. **Terms:** cancellation fee imposed. **Amenities:** high-speed Internet. **Pool(s):** heated indoor. **Activities:** whirlpool, waterslide, exercise room. **Guest Services:** valet and coin laundry. **Free Special Amenities:** expanded continental breakfast and high-speed Internet.

WHERE TO EAT

J. D. FITZGERALDS
250/261-6961
▼▼▼ Irish. Casual Dining. $12-$26 **AAA Inspector Notes:**
Jazzy Irish décor awaits at this attractive eatery and pub where you
will find lovingly prepared traditional favorites such as Irish potato and
seafood chowder, halibut and fresh-cut chips, beef and Guinness
stew, bangers and mash, and meat pasties made with fresh and flaky
pastry. Other menu items include classic pub fare as well as a
double-cut pork chop, steak and West Coast salmon. Friendly, efficient service and live music on the weekends cap off your experience. **Bar:** full bar. **Address:** 9830 100th Ave V1J 1Y5 **Location:**
Center; in Quality Inn Northern Grand. **Parking:** on-site and street.

[B] [L] [D] [LATE] CALL [M]

MASTARO SUSHI
250/261-6595
▼▼ Japanese. Casual Dining. $10-$29 **AAA Inspector Notes:**
Almost a thousand kilometres from the nearest coast, the restaurant
nevertheless prepares an expansive selection of sushi and sashimi,
in addition to classic appetizers such as edamame (salted soy beans)
and gyoza (dumplings). The menu also lists many noodle dishes,
pan-fried yakisoba and udon soups, rice items and teriyaki. **Bar:** full
bar. **Address:** 9823 100th St V1J 3Y2 **Location:** Downtown.

[L] [D] CALL [M]

MONDO RESTAURANT
250/787-1454
▼▼ International. Casual Dining. $9-$37 **AAA Inspector
Notes:** The menu here is quite eclectic. To suit many palates, it offers
a little bit of everything: coquille St. Jacques scallops, sushi appetizers, burgers, seafood crepes, chicken with thyme cream sauce,
pastas, lamb rack and steaks. The room is pleasingly divided with
raised sections and plants. Décor is marked by earthy tones, wood
floors and stone work. A good breakfast selection also is offered. **Bar:**
full bar. **Address:** 10403 100th Ave V1J 1Z1 **Location:** Just e of
100th St; center. [B] [L] [D] CALL [M]

MR MIKES STEAKHOUSE & BAR
250/262-4151
▼▼ American. Casual Dining. $10-$29 **AAA Inspector Notes:**
Be prepared for fast, friendly service at this bustling restaurant where
you can dig in to familiar burgers, steaks, ribs, chicken, salmon,
noodle bowls and stir-fries. **Bar:** full bar. **Address:** 9324 Alaska Rd
V1J 6L5 **Location:** Just s on Hwy 97 (Alaska Hwy).

[L] [D] [LATE] CALL [M]

WHOLE WHEAT 'N' HONEY CAFE & COFFEEHOUSE
250/787-9866
▼ American. Quick Serve. $6-$10 **AAA Inspector Notes:** Since
this bright spot is so popular, it has an obviously successful philosophy: provide wholesome and appetizing nourishment. Fresh ingredients make up the tasty soup, sandwiches, wraps and salads.
Classic breakfast items include egg burritos and pancakes. Among
the baked treats you'll find cinnamon buns and huge cookies. **Bar:**
beer & wine. **Address:** 10003 100th St V1J 1Y5 **Location:** Corner of
100th Ave; center. **Parking:** street only. [B] [L] CALL [M]

FORT STEELE (C-12) elev. 771m/2,529'

Founded during the 1864 Kootenay gold rush,
Fort Steele, then known as Galbraith's Ferry, became the site of the first North West Mounted Police
west of the Rockies. In 1888 the settlement's name
was changed to honor police superintendent
Samuel Steele, who peacefully settled tensions between European settlers and the Ktunaxa people.

As a result of the mining boom of the 1890s the
town became a thriving center of trade, transportation, communication and social activity, with a population of more than 2,000. In 1898 the British
Columbia Southern Railroad bypassed Fort Steele
in favor of Cranbrook, 16 kilometres (10 mi.) southwest, and the town began its decline. At the end of
World War II Fort Steele had fewer than 50
residents.

FORT STEELE HERITAGE TOWN is 3 km
(1.9 mi.) s.w. at 9851 Hwy. 93/95. The 11-
hectare (27-acre) site preserves an 1890s boomtown. More than 60 restored, reconstructed or
original buildings include an operating bakery, restaurant, tinsmith shop, blacksmith shop and newspaper office. Street dramas and demonstrations
such as quilting, horse farming and ice cream
making help re-create life in the era.

Fort Steele's Clydesdales give wagon rides daily
mid-June through Labour Day and perform a six-
horse hitch show on July 1. Live entertainment is
presented in the Wild Horse Theatre late June
through Labour Day. Steam train rides are available
during this time. A visitor reception center contains
exhibits about the town's history.

Hours: Grounds open daily 9:30-7, July 1-Labour
Day; 9:30-5, May-June and day after Labour Day-
Oct. 9; 10-4, rest of year. Last admission 1 hour before closing. Programs, including street skits
depicting daily life of the late 1890s, are presented
daily 9:30-5:30, late June-Labour Day. Closed
Christmas and day after Christmas. **Cost:** May
1-second Sun. in Oct. $5; free (ages 0-5). By dona-
tions rest of year. **Phone:** (250) 417-6000 or (250)
426-7352.

BULL RIVER GUEST RANCH
250/429-3760
▼▼▼ Resort Ranch. Rates not provided. **Address:** 2975 Bull
River Rd V1C 4H7 **Location:** Hwy 95, 12.9 mi (21.4 km) se of town
on Ft Steele-Wardner Rd, 7.2 mi (12 km) ne on gravel road; Hwy 3
W, 24.6 mi (41 km) e of Cranbrook, 5 mi (8.2 km) n on Ft Steele-
Wardner Rd, 7.2 mi (12 km) ne on gravel road. Located in a quiet
rustic area. **Facility:** Lovely landscaping features enhance the natural
mountain setting at this secluded ranch with comfortable one-
bedroom log cabins and bunkhouse units. The owners can organize
fly fishing and river rafting trips. 12 units, some cabins. 1 story, exterior corridors. *Bath:* shower only. **Activities:** sauna, whirlpools, canoeing, fishing, bicycles, hiking trails, jogging, playground,
horseshoes, volleyball. *Fee:* horseback riding. **Guest Services:** complimentary laundry.

[BIZ] [🛜] [✕] [K] [W] [🅿] [🛏] [▣]
/ SOME UNITS FEE [🐾] [▣]

GALIANO ISLAND (H-10) pop. 1,138
• Hotels p. 242 • Restaurants p. 242

Named after Spanish explorer Dionisio Alcala Galiano, Galiano Island, part of the Gulf Islands chain,
is a long narrow island that is a haven for bird
watchers and naturalists. Bicycling, horseback
riding, kayaking, fishing, sailing, diving, swimming
and hiking are popular recreational activities. The efforts of hikers and cyclists are rewarded with grand
vistas and viewpoints. Mount Galiano provides
climbers with eye-catching views of the southern
Gulf Islands and the Olympic Mountains.

Montague Harbour Marine Provincial Park has
3,000-year-old middens; camping facilities are available at the park as well as at Dionisio Point Provincial Park. The Descanso Bay Regional Park offers
30 camping sites. *See Recreation Areas Chart.*

Galiano Island Chamber of Commerce: P.O. Box
73, Galiano Island, BC, Canada V0N 1P0. **Phone:**
(250) 539-2233.

GALIANO INN & SPA   (250)539-3388
▼▼▼▼ Hotel $199-$425 Address: 134 Madrona Dr V0N 1P0
Location: From Sturdies Bay Ferry Terminal, just ne on Sturdies Bay
Rd. Facility: 20 units, some kitchens. 2 stories (no elevator),
interior/exterior corridors. Terms: 2 night minimum stay - weekends,
7 day cancellation notice-fee imposed. Dining: eat@ Galiano Inn
Restaurant, see separate listing. Activities: whirlpool, spa. Guest
Services: coin laundry.

🍴 🍸 CALL 📶 🛰 ✕ 𝄞 🔒 💻
/ SOME UNITS FEE 🐾

WHERE TO EAT

EAT@ GALIANO INN RESTAURANT   250/539-3388
▼▼▼▼ Pacific Northwest. Fine Dining. $20-$30 AAA Inspector
Notes: Galiano Island's only oceanfront restaurant serves delightful
West Coast cuisine that reflects an array of such fresh local ingredients as Salt Spring Island organic goat cheese, West Coast seafood
like Pacific salmon and the finest selection of British Columbia wines
selected by the restaurant's very own sommelier. It's open for lunch
mid-May to mid September. Hours vary during the off season, so call
ahead. Bar: full bar. Reservations: suggested, for dinner. Address:
134 Madrona Dr V0N 1P0 Location: From Sturdies Bay Ferry Terminal, just ne on Sturdies Bay Rd; in Galiano Oceanfront Inn & Spa.

📀 𝄞

GALIANO GRAND CENTRAL EMPORIUM   250/539-9885
▼▼ American. Casual Dining. $7-$18 AAA Inspector Notes: Not
far from the Sturdies Bay Ferry Terminal, this simple restaurant is one
of the few open all year long. The building isn't much to look at, but
the food is really good. Order from the wall-mounted blackboard-style
menu, grab a seat and enjoy. Daily homemade soups, lunchtime
sandwiches and morning breakfasts make this a unique stop while
waiting for the ferry. It's open for breakfast and lunch all year and for
weekend dinners only during the off season. Bar: full bar. Address:
2740 Sturdies Bay Rd V0N 1P0 Location: Just nw of Sturdies Bay
Ferry Terminal. 🅱 🅛 𝄞

HUMMINGBIRD INN PUB   250/539-5472
▼▼ American. Casual Dining. $10-$19 AAA Inspector Notes:
Dining choices on the island are limited, but those who visit can expect pub-style food. Flat screen TVs are on all the time, showing the
latest hockey game or golf tournament. The pub is now licensed to
accept children in the dining section. Bar: full bar. Address: 47 Sturdies Bay Rd V0N 1P0 Location: From Sturdies Bay Ferry Terminal,
1.8 mi (3 km) nw. 🅛 📀 𝄞

GIBSONS (G-11) pop. 4,437

SUNSHINE COAST MUSEUM & ARCHIVES is at
716 Winn Rd. Two floors of exhibits explain the history of the Sunshine Coast and its inhabitants. The
main floor features displays about the area's maritime past; the upper floor recounts information about
the native peoples and pioneers as well as natural
history and industries. **Time:** Allow 1 hour minimum.
Hours: Tues.-Sat. 10:30-4:30; closed statutory holidays. **Cost:** Donations. **Phone:** (604) 886-8232.

BONNIEBROOK LODGE OCEANFRONT INN   (604)886-2887
▼▼▼ Country Inn $159-$328 Address: 1532 Ocean Beach
Esplanade V0N 1V5 Location: Hwy 101, 3.8 mi (6 km) s on Veterans
Rd to Fichett Rd, just sw to King Rd, 0.6 mi (1 km) sw to Chaster Rd,
then 5 mi (8 km) sw to Gower Pt Rd, follow signs. Facility: Built in
1922, this lodge features four adult-only suites that overlook the
ocean and duplex-style cottages located just behind the lodge. Pets
and children are allowed only in the cottage units. 7 units. 1-3 stories
(no elevator), interior/exterior corridors. Terms: closed 1/1-2/15,
check-in 4 pm, 2-3 night minimum stay - weekends, 7 day cancellation notice-fee imposed. Amenities: high-speed Internet. Activities:
beach access.

🍴 🍸 🛰 ✕ 𝄞 🔒 💻 / SOME UNITS FEE 🐾

WHERE TO EAT

MOLLY'S REACH RESTAURANT   604/886-9710
▼▼ American. Casual Dining. $6-$17 AAA Inspector Notes:
The famous landmark originally was built as a set for "The Beach-
combers," a popular CBC TV series of the late 1970s and early '80s.
Today, it's a family restaurant, well worth the stop for the memories
alone. Bar: full bar. Address: 647 School Rd V0N 1V0 Location: Jct
School Rd and Gibsons Way; on waterfront.

🅱 🅛 📀 CALL 📶 𝄞

GLACIER NATIONAL PARK (A-10)

Elevations in the park range from 800 metres
(2,625 ft.) at the lower portion of the Beaver
River to 3,380 metres (11,089 ft.) at Hasler
Peak on Mount Dawson. Refer to CAA/AAA
maps for additional elevation information.

West of the Rockies in the southeast interior of
British Columbia, Glacier National Park and its
smaller counterpart Mount Revelstoke National Park
(see place listing p. 275) encompass portions of the
rugged Columbia Mountains. The park's 1,350
square kilometres (521 sq. mi.) of hard rock terrain
present a jagged profile of angular mountains with
narrow steep-walled valleys. The steep mountain
slopes and enormous snowfall make this region sus-
ceptible to avalanches.

Rogers Pass National Historic Site, located in the
heart of the park became the scene of a pitched
19th-century battle between the railroad engineers
and the surrounding mountains. Sheer walls, numerous slide areas and severe weather proved almost insurmountable obstacles to the completion of
Canada's first transcontinental railroad. Some of the
largest railroad trestles then known were built to
carry the line across raging streams to the summit of
this pass.

The tracks crossed to the southern wall of the
valley on several loops to avoid the numerous avalanche slopes and reduce the steep downgrade. Despite the ingenuity of its engineers, the new railroad
eventually had to be abandoned to the area's devastating winter forces. Avalanches attaining speeds
of up to 325 kilometres (202 mi.) per hour tore up
sections of the new track and left other sections
buried under tons of snow.

Thirty-one snowsheds were built to shield the
track, but even this was not enough. In 1910, 58
men were killed by an avalanche as they were
clearing snow from an earlier slide. This incident,
mounting costs and the dangerous grades of this
section convinced the railroad to tunnel under Mount
MacDonald.

The Trans-Canada Highway met similar obstacles
as it crossed the pass, but the use of mobile howit-
zers to dislodge potential slides and other methods
of controlling avalanches have held the road's position. Evidence of the struggle to build the railroad is
visible from the road and the park's various
campgrounds.

Several short trails follow the railroad's progress,
winding past the ruins of Glacier House, a 19th-
century resort hotel, remains of former snow sheds

and the stone pillars that once supported the railroad trestles.

History is only part of the park's attractions. Twelve percent of the park is covered perpetually by snow and ice; more than 400 glaciers are scattered throughout the park. The contrast of the deep green forests and meadows with the glacial whites of these crags makes the park especially scenic.

Towering above the richly wooded valleys, the 3,284-metre (10,774-ft.) Mount Sir Donald rises to the east of the campgrounds, with Eagle and Uto peaks to the north. Day-hiking trails lead toward the Illecillewaet and Asulkan glaciers.

General Information and Activities

The park is open all year. In the winter, ski touring enthusiasts take advantage of the park's world-class ski touring opportunities. During the summer months, some of the popular activities include camping, hiking and mountaineering.

Parks Canada staff lead a variety of interpretive programs from Illecillewaet campground in July and August.

In addition, an extensive network of challenging day-hiking trails leads to such attractions as the Illecillewaet and Asulkan glaciers; Abbott Ridge; and the Hermit. Grizzly and black bears are common in Glacier National Park; be cautious and make noise frequently as you hike. Climbers and overnight hikers may voluntarily register at the Rogers Pass Discovery Centre before and after every trip. Guides are available through the Friends of Mount Revelstoke and Glacier store in the Rogers Pass Discovery Centre. Park use permits also can be purchased at the Rogers Pass Discovery Centre. *See Recreation Areas Chart.*

ADMISSION to the park is $7.80; $6.80 (ages 65+); $3.90 (ages 6-16); $19.60 (all occupants of a private vehicle with up to seven people). **Cards:** AX, MC, VI.

PETS are permitted in the park provided they are on a leash at all times.

ADDRESS inquiries to the Superintendent, Glacier and Mount Revelstoke National Parks, P.O. Box 350, Revelstoke, BC, Canada V0E 2S0; phone (250) 837-7500.

ROGERS PASS DISCOVERY CENTRE is 1.3 km (.8 mi.) e. of the Rogers Pass summit. Modeled after the snowsheds that once protected the railroad from avalanches, the discovery center includes a theatre, an exhibit hall with railway models and displays about natural history. **Time:** Allow 30 minutes minimum. **Hours:** Daily 7-5, Dec.-Mar. and April 1-25; daily 8-6, June 11-Sept. 3; daily 9-5, Apr. 26-June 10 and Sept. 4-Oct. 10; Thur.-Mon. 7-3, Nov. 8-30. Phone ahead to confirm schedule. **Cost:** Free with park entry; park admission $7.80; $6.80 (ages 65+); $3.90 (ages 6-16); $19.60 (all occupants of a private vehicle with up to seven people). **Phone:** (250) 837-7550.

GOLD BRIDGE pop. 10

TYAX WILDERNESS RESORT & SPA   (250)238-2221

▼▼▼▼ **Resort Hotel** $199-$289 **Address:** 1 Tyaughton Lake Rd V0K 1P0 **Location:** 5 mi (8 km) n from the Tyaughton Lake turnoff, follow signs. **Facility:** Choose from rooms in the large log lodge or the one log cottage that sleeps up to six people at this summertime resort offering family-oriented wilderness activities. 28 units, some cottages. 2-3 stories (no elevator), interior corridors. **Terms:** closed 10/16-5/14, check-in 4 pm, 30 day cancellation notice-fee imposed. **Activities:** saunas, whirlpool, steamroom, canoeing, paddleboats, fishing, hiking trails, playground, limited exercise equipment, spa. *Fee:* bicycles, horseback riding. **Guest Services:** coin laundry.

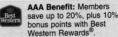

GOLDEN (A-11) pop. 3,701, elev. 785m/2,575'
• Restaurants p. 244

On the Trans-Canada Highway at the confluence of the Columbia and Kicking Horse rivers, Golden is between Glacier *(see place listing)* and Yoho national parks *(see place listing p. 434)* and located west of Banff National Park *(see place listing in Alberta p. 37)*. The community also is an outfitting point for sports enthusiasts.

The Golden and District Museum is at 11th Avenue and 13th Street. The museum is housed in a restored one-room schoolhouse and contains local historical items.

Kicking Horse Country Chamber of Commerce: 500 10th Ave. N., P.O. Box 1320, Golden, BC, Canada V0A 1H0. **Phone:** (250) 344-7125 or (800) 622-4653.

RECREATIONAL ACTIVITIES
White-water Rafting
• **Alpine Rafting Co.** is at 101 Golden Donald Upper Rd. **Hours:** Trips depart daily 8 a.m.-9 p.m., mid-May to early Sept. **Phone:** (250) 344-6778 or (888) 599-5299.

• **Glacier Raft Company** is at 612 N. 7th St. **Hours:** Trips depart daily 8-6, mid-May through Labour Day. **Phone:** (250) 344-6521 or (877) 344-7238.

• **Wild Water Adventures** is 25 km (15 mi.) s.e. on Hwy. 1. **Hours:** Trips are offered twice daily (weather permitting), mid-May to mid-Sept. **Phone:** (403) 522-2211 or (888) 647-6444.

BEST WESTERN MOUNTAINVIEW INN   (250)344-2333

▼▼▼ Hotel $120-$200 | **AAA Benefit:** Members save up to 20%, plus 10% bonus points with Best Western Rewards®.

Address: 1024 11th St N V0A 1H2 **Location:** Just w of jct Hwy 95 and Trans-Canada Hwy 1; on S Service Rd. **Facility:** 72 units. 3 stories, interior corridors. **Parking:** winter plug-ins. **Amenities:** *Some:* high-speed Internet. **Pool(s):** heated indoor. **Guest Services:** valet and coin laundry. **Free Special Amenities:** local telephone calls and high-speed Internet.

Safety tip: Keep a current AAA/CAA
Road Atlas in every vehicle

COLUMBIA VALLEY B&B
250-348-2508

▼▼ **Bed & Breakfast** $145 **Address:** 2304 Hwy 95 S V0A 1H4 **Location:** 14.4 mi (24 km) s of jct Trans-Canada Hwy 1. **Facility:** 4 units. 2 stories (no elevator), interior/exterior corridors. **Parking:** winter plug-ins. **Terms:** closed 10/1-5/1, check-in 4 pm, 3 day cancellation notice-fee imposed. **Activities:** rental canoes.

[BIZ] 🛜 ⊠ [𝄃] [⊘] / SOME UNITS [▥] [📷] [▭]

DAYS INN GOLDEN
(250)344-2216

▼▼ ▼▼ **Motel** $150-$205 **Address:** 1416 Golden View Rd V0A 1H1 **Location:** On Trans-Canada Hwy 1, 1 mi (1.6 km) e of jct Hwy 95. **Facility:** 81 units, some two bedrooms and kitchens. 2-3 stories (no elevator), exterior corridors. **Parking:** winter plug-ins. **Terms:** cancellation fee imposed. **Pool(s):** heated indoor. **Activities:** sauna, whirlpool, waterslide. **Guest Services:** coin laundry.

[𝄃] [Y] [🛏] [BIZ] 🛜 [▥] [▭] / SOME UNITS FEE [🐾] [📷]

WHERE TO EAT

CEDAR HOUSE RESTAURANT & CHALETS
250/344-4679

Canadian
Casual Dining
$23-$34

AAA Inspector Notes: Rocky Mountain dining is what's to be expected at the small bistro-style restaurant. The cozy, comfortable dining room has many rustic features yet a surprising elegance. Menu selections ranging from salmon to lamb to other Canadian specialties often incorporate produce grown in the chef's own garden. Service is laid back and friendly, and even the owner has been known to come out and greet guests. **Bar:** full bar. **Reservations:** suggested. **Address:** 735 Hefti Rd V0A 1H2 **Location:** 4.6 mi (7.4 km) s of town, just e at Almberg Rd, follow signs. [D] CALL [♿M] [🎦]

ELEVEN 22 GRILL & LIQUIDS
250/344-2443

▼▼ ▼▼ International. Casual Dining. $11-$26 **AAA Inspector Notes:** Head to this restored centennial home for some tasty international fare. The charming eatery nurtures a warm, casual ambiance, just the spot to enjoy a well-prepared menu that runs the gamut from appetizers like Jamaican chicken and Mediterranean dips to entrées such as Indian butter chicken, Italian cannelloni and French-style duck. In the wintertime, a weekly fondue is a nice treat. **Bar:** full bar. **Reservations:** suggested. **Address:** 1122 10th Ave S V0A 1H0 **Location:** Just e at 12th St; center. [D] CALL [♿M] [🎦]

GOLDEN GRIZZLY COOKHOUSE
250/439-1833

▼▼ ▼▼ American. Casual Dining. $13-$30 **AAA Inspector Notes:** This cookhouse with a cabin-like interior sports a collection of archive newspaper photos of local events and townsfolk and a chandelier over one large table in the corner. Tables are covered in brown paper with bear paws, and crayons are provided for those with an artistic bent to while the time (which isn't long, as service is speedy and friendly). Simple but tasty and filling fare includes salads, pastas, pizza, ribs, burgers and hot sandwiches. **Bar:** full bar. **Address:** 1001 Trans-Canada Hwy 1 E V0A 1H1 **Location:** Jct Trans-Canada Hwy 1 and 95, just n. [L] [D] CALL [♿M]

THE ISLAND RESTAURANT
250/344-2400

▼▼ ▼▼ New Canadian. Casual Dining. $11-$33 **AAA Inspector Notes:** In a renovated cabin, the décor features an eclectic yet tasteful mix of accent pieces. The chef has dubbed his cuisine "Canadian mountain fusion," as most dishes take on an international twist. Try the curry calamari, Jamaican jerk sandwich or braised Asian short ribs. But be sure to save room for the warm bumbleberry shortbread ravioli or crabapple crème brûlée. In nice weather, the veranda is a popular dining spot. **Bar:** full bar. **Reservations:** suggested. **Address:** 101 Gould's Island, 10th Ave V0A 1H0 **Location:** Just between the bridges; downtown. [B] [L] [D] CALL [♿M]

THE KICKING HORSE GRILL
250/344-2330

▼▼ ▼▼ International. Casual Dining. $15-$38 **AAA Inspector Notes:** The restaurant's small lodge-like interior is perfect for a casual meal with friends. Dark wood beams criss-cross the ceiling and line the walls, creating a true Rocky Mountain feel. Interesting and eclectic menu choices draw on many influences, ranging from Asian to Swedish and even some Canadian elements. **Bar:** full bar. **Reservations:** suggested. **Address:** 1105 9th St S V0A 1H0 **Location:** Hwy 95, just e; downtown. [D] [🎦]

LEGENDZ DINER
250/344-5059

▼▼ American. Family Dining. $8-$18 **AAA Inspector Notes:** Appointed in a 1950s theme, the diner is a popular stopover for residents and those just passing through. In addition to an extensive list of diner classics, this place prepares burgers, steaks and some hot entrees. The homemade pies are legendary. **Bar:** beer & wine. **Address:** 1405 N Trans-Canada Hwy V0A 1H0 **Location:** Jct Trans-Canada Hwy 1 and 95, 0.6 mi (1 km) n. [B] [L] [D] CALL [♿M]

WHITETOOTH MOUNTAIN BISTRO
250/344-5120

▼▼ ▼▼ New Canadian. Casual Dining. $10-$28 **AAA Inspector Notes:** Delicious twists happen when bistro meets Canadian-inspired comfort food. At this smart-looking casual spot you might want to start with daily mussels, duck confit poutine, an artisan cheese plate or an inspired salad, followed by a classic bistro entrée like bouillabaisse or coq au vin, or buffalo meatloaf, mac 'n' cheese with chorizo sausage, fresh fish or Certified Angus beefsteak. Tantalizing desserts test your willpower, and Pacific Northwest wines are a specialty of the house. **Bar:** full bar. **Address:** 427 9th Ave N V0A 1H0 **Location:** Just e of Hwy 97 (10th Ave N); center. **Parking:** on-site and street. [B] [L] [D]

GOLD RIVER (E-9) pop. 1,267, elev. 122m/400'

At the joining of the Gold and Heber rivers, the town of Gold River was built in 6 months in 1965 for employees of a pulp mill. The town, with its beautiful untamed countryside, has become popular with fishermen, photographers, hikers and campers.

The MV *Uchuck III* departs from the dock on Hwy. 28. The full-day and overnight cruises explore Tahsis, Nootka Sound and Friendly Cove, where Capt. James Cook met Chief Maquinna and the Nootka Indians when he landed on Vancouver Island in 1778; phone (250) 283-2418 for the tourist information center or (250) 283-2207 for the municipal office during off-season.

GRAND FORKS (D-9) pop. 3,985

Settlement at the confluence of the Kettle and Granby rivers began in the late 1800s when copper, gold and silver were discovered in the area. After 20 years of prosperity Grand Forks suffered reverses when the local copper smelter, said to be the largest in the British Empire, closed due to faltering copper prices. The logging industry and seed growing operations later restored stability to the community.

The downtown Boundary District contains preserved historic homes, stores and civic buildings from the settlement period. It is flanked on the south and east by rivers, on the west by 5th Avenue and on the north by 75th Avenue. A walking tour map is available at the Boundary Museum *(see attraction listing).*

Chamber of Commerce of the City of Grand Forks: 524 Central Ave., P.O. Box 2140, Grand Forks, BC, Canada V0H 1H0. **Phone:** (250) 442-5835.

BOUNDARY MUSEUM is 2 km (1.2 mi.) w. on Hwy. 3, then 1 km (.6 mi.) n. on Reservoir Rd., following signs. The museum depicts the area's history from the late 1800s. Artifacts, maps and photographs show the lifestyles of the native peoples as well as the Doukhobor. Other exhibits include a scale model and display of Grand Forks' Chinatown in the 1900s, a wildlife exhibit and a 1929 fire truck.

Hours: Tues.-Thurs. 10-4. Guided tours are available by appointment outside of regular hours. Phone ahead to confirm schedule. **Cost:** Donations. **Phone:** (250) 442-8266.

WESTERN TRAVELLER MOTEL   (250)442-5566

Motel
$69-$139

Address: 1591 Central Ave V0H 1H0
Location: West end of town on Hwy 3.
Facility: 34 units, some efficiencies. 2 stories (no elevator), exterior corridors.
Terms: cancellation fee imposed.

GULF ISLANDS

Separated from the San Juan Islands in Washington only by an international boundary, the almost 200 islands of various shapes and sizes that make up the Gulf Islands nestle against the southeast coast of Vancouver Island. Formed by a series of moving land masses beginning about 100 million years ago, today's Gulf Islands are the result of a mass collision of land that produced the long ridges of sandstone, conglomerate and shale that constitute the islands' geology.

The area was discovered by Capt. George Vancouver while on a quest to find a northwest passage to the Orient in 1792. Erroneously named Gulf of Georgia by Vancouver, the water separating Vancouver Island from the southwestern portion of British Columbia was later correctly termed the Strait of Georgia. The islands, however, retained the designation Gulf Islands.

The area features a climate that is sunnier and milder than that found on the nearby mainland. The quiet waters promote a much quieter lifestyle as well, and the islands are a haven from the frantic pace of nearby cities. Each island, though similar in many respects, has its own distinct identity. Easily reached from the mainland, they have become popular weekend retreats offering varying degrees of amenities and activities. Artists and professionals have joined the population of local fishermen who relish the peaceful lifestyle created by the sparkling waters, cliffs, winding roads and parks.

The main components of the southern Gulf Islands are Galiano, Mayne, North and South Pender, Salt Spring and Saturna islands. Although they can be explored by automobile, the best way to experience the islands is by bicycle or foot. The Islands Trust, a governmental agency, is charged with preserving and protecting the islands and waters in the Strait of Georgia.

BC Ferries provides year-round service to the main islands from Tsawwassen, south of Vancouver, and Swartz Bay, near Victoria. Vehicle reservations are recommended for travel between the mainland and the islands, but are not available for travel between Vancouver Island and the Gulf Islands or for inter-island travel. It is advisable to make reservations as far in advance as possible for summer and holiday travel. For schedule information and reservations phone (250) 386-3431 from the Victoria area and outside British Columbia or (888) 223-3779 from elsewhere in the province. Air service also is available.

GULF ISLANDS NATIONAL PARK
RESERVE (H-10)

Elevations in the park range from sea level to
401 metres (1,316 ft.) at Mt. Warburton Pike
on Saturna Island. Refer to CAA/AAA maps
for additional elevation information.

Gulf Islands National Park Reserve protects an
island landscape of rocky headlands, forested hills
and shorelines studded with colourful tide pools.
The park encompasses areas of lands scattered
over fifteen larger islands and includes many
smaller islets and reefs. Waters adjacent to park
lands, extending 200 metres (650 ft.) seaward, also
are under Parks Canada management.

The park shares the larger populated islands of
Mayne, Saturna and the Penders with communities
that offer a range of tourist amenities. Facilities and
services inside the national park reserve are currently limited. The populated larger islands are accessible by vehicle, bicycle and BC Ferries from
Vancouver and Victoria. The smaller islands are accessible by only boat or kayak. Water taxis also operate in several areas. Many local tour operators
offer such recreational opportunities as cycling,
kayaking, scuba diving, whale-watching or hiking.
Comfortable, sturdy shoes and water are recommended for all hiking excursions.

The islands are a haven for various wildlife, including such endangered species as the anatum
peregrine falcon, the sharp-tailed snake,
Townsend's big-eared bat, the western meadowlark
and the orca whale. The southern Gulf Islands are
home to the endangered Garry Oak ecosystem.
Various shorebirds, waterfowl, great blue herons,
seals and sea lions also inhabit the area.

For more information contact the Gulf Islands National Park Reserve InfoCentre, 2220 Harbour Rd.,
Sidney, BC, Canada V8L 2P6; phone (250)
654-4000 or toll free (866) 944-1744. *See Recreation Areas Chart.*

GWAII HAANAS NATIONAL PARK
RESERVE AND HAIDA HERITAGE SITE
(F-1)

Elevations in the park range from sea level
along Kunghit and Moresby islands to 1,123
metres (696 ft.) at Mount de la Touche. Refer
to CAA/AAA maps for additional elevation
information.

Off the British Columbia coast west of Prince Rupert, Gwaii Haanas National Park Reserve, National
Marine Conservation Area Reserve, and Haida Heritage Site is in the southern part of Haida Gwaii, a
remote island chain formerly known as the Queen
Charlotte Islands *(see place listing p. 246)*. Haida
Gwaii translates to "islands of the people." This protected area is jointly managed by the Government of
Canada and the Council of the Haida Nation. In
2010, Gwaii Haanas became the only area in the
world protected from mountain top to ocean floor.

The 1,470 square kilometres (912 sq. mi.) of
Gwaii Haanas offer a rich and fascinating diversity of
flora, sea creatures and wildlife. Whales, bald
eagles, nesting seabirds, black bears, sea lions and
river otters are commonly seen.

Remnants of Haida village sites on the 138 islands capture the history of the Haida. Haida Gwaii
Watchmen basecamps have been established at
major sites of cultural significance. Watchmen act as
hosts and also provide site security and protection
of the cultural features.

Access is challenging: The only way to and
around Gwaii Haanas is by air or sea. Solo travel is
recommended only for the experienced outdoor
traveler. Licensed tour operators provide a variety of
excursions. Sea kayaking, sailboat and powerboat
charters are the most popular ways to tour Gwaii
Haanas. There are no maintained trails or designated campsites, and only limited visitor facilities are
provided within the protected area.

Haida Gwaii can be reached by air from Vancouver and Prince Rupert. BC Ferries also provides
year-round service between the islands and Prince
Rupert. Arrangements for ferry transportation should
be made well in advance and reservations are
highly recommended; phone (250) 386-3431 from
the Victoria area and outside British Columbia or
(888) 223-3779 from elsewhere in the province.

Single-day admission $19.60; $16.60 (ages 65+);
$9.80 (ages 6-16); $49 (family, up to two adults and
seven people total). Reservations are required to
visit the reserve May through September. Regulations allow for no more than 12 people on shore in
one place at one time.

Note: If traveling independently (without a guide),
visitors must participate in one 60-minute orientation
session offered daily at visitor centers in Sandspit
and Queen Charlotte; phone (250) 559-8818 to
guarantee a place. For more information write to
Gwaii Haanas National Park Reserve, National Marine Conservation Area Reserve, and Haida Heritage Site, P.O. Box 37, Queen Charlotte, BC,
Canada V0T 1S0 or phone (250) 559-8818 or (877)
559-8818. *See Recreation Areas Chart.*

HAGENSBORG (F-3) pop. 219, elev. 495'

SNOOTLI HATCHERY is 4 km (2.5 mi.) w. on Hwy.
20, following signs. The hatchery raises chinook,
chum, coho and sockeye salmon as well as steelhead trout for release into local rivers. **Time:** Allow
30 minutes minimum. **Hours:** Mon.-Fri. 8-4. Guided
tours are available 8:30-3:30, June-Sept. **Cost:**
Free. **Phone:** (250) 982-2214.

HAIDA GWAII (E-1)

Haida Gwaii ("islands of the people"), formerly
the Queen Charlotte Islands, were occupied by
Haida Indians when Spanish sea captain Juan
Pérez sighted the archipelago in 1774. A seafaring
and artistic people, the Haida traded sea otter pelts
with European traders during the early 1800s. By

the late 19th century, however, the Haida had to vacate many of their ancestral villages to escape a devastating smallpox epidemic.

Only a fraction of their original number still inhabit the islands—at Haida, near Masset, and Skidegate, near Queen Charlotte City. Continuing their cultural traditions, they carve elaborate works of art from argillite, a black slatelike stone found only in mountain deposits off the coast.

A group of about 150 islands forming an elongated triangle, Haida Gwaii stretches 250 kilometres (157 mi.) from north to south, 90 kilometres (56 mi.) off the coast of British Columbia. Characterized by fog and low clouds, these islands also are known as the Misty Islands. The towns are small and decidedly rural; the entire population of Haida Gwaii is about 5,000.

The two main islands are Graham and Moresby. The largest and most populated is Graham. In the north on its broad and flat eastern side are most of the archipelago's communities—Masset, Old Masset, Port Clements, Queen Charlotte City, Skidegate, and Tlell—which are linked by a paved road. An airport is at Masset as well as at Sandspit, on the northeastern tip of Moresby Island. A 20-minute ferry ride connects the two islands.

A temperate marine climate supports dense coniferous forests, which, as the basis of the islands' economy, have been logged extensively. The fish and shellfish in the coastal waters supply the islands' important commercial fishing industry.

Visitors are attracted by the pristine wilderness, the hunting and fishing prospects, kayaking and hiking opportunities, and the handicrafts and art of the Haida. In fact the main destination of many travelers to Haida Gwaii is Gwaii Haanas National Park Reserve, National Marine Conservation Area Reserve and Haida Heritage Site *(see place listing p. 246)*, in the southern part of the island chain on Moresby Island.

Wildlife is abundant here; tiny Sitka deer and bald eagles frequent the shores, and seals, sea lions, porpoises and migrating whales often appear in the inlets. Bird-watching, wildlife viewing, hiking, kayaking and freshwater and saltwater fishing are popular activities.

Points of interest include Naikoon Provincial Park *(see Recreation Areas Chart)* on Graham Island, the remote Haida village sites, the Delkatla Wildlife Sanctuary in Masset, the Haida Heritage Centre at Kaay Llnagaay *(see attraction listing p. 328)* in Skidegate and the various carving sheds in Skidegate and Old Masset.

Permission to visit Haida unoccupied village sites must be obtained from Band Council offices; phone (250) 559-8225.

The islands' main visitor center in Queen Charlotte City has videos and interactive displays that provide information about life on the islands and in the waters that surround them. The center is open year-round.

Haida Gwaii can be reached by air from Prince Rupert and Vancouver and by ferry from Prince Rupert. Phone BC Ferries at (888) 223-3779 for ferry reservations. Kayak rentals, fishing charters and various guided boat and land tours are available.

Queen Charlotte Visitor Centre: 3220 Wharf St., P.O. Box 819, Queen Charlotte City, BC, Canada V0T 1S0. **Phone:** (250) 559-8316.

GRACIE'S PLACE   250/559-4262

[fyi] **Motel** Did not meet all AAA rating requirements for locking devices in some guest rooms at time of last evaluation on 05/07/2008. **Address:** 3113 Ocean View Dr V0T 1S0 **Location:** On Graham Island; in Queen Charlotte; from BC Ferries and Skidegate Landing, 1.8 mi (3 km) s. Facilities, services, and décor characterize an economy property.

HECATE INN   250/559-4543

[fyi] **Motel** Did not meet all AAA rating requirements for locking devices in some guest rooms at time of last evaluation on 05/07/2008. **Address:** 321 Ocean View Dr V0T 1S0 **Location:** On Graham Island; in Queen Charlotte; from BC Ferries and Skidegate Landing, 2.4 mi (4 km) s. Facilities, services, and décor characterize an economy property.

PREMIER CREEK LODGING   250/559-8415

[fyi] **Motel** Did not meet all AAA rating requirements for locking devices in some guest rooms at time of last evaluation on 05/07/2008. **Address:** 3101 Ocean View Dr V0T 1S0 **Location:** On Graham Island; in Queen Charlotte; from BC Ferries and Skidegate Landing, 1.8 mi (3 km) s. Facilities, services, and décor characterize an economy property.

WHERE TO EAT

JAGS BEANSTALK   250/559-8826

Coffee/Tea Breads/Pastries. Quick Serve. $5-$15 **AAA Inspector Notes:** Fresh coffee, pastries and wrapped sandwiches can be purchased at this coffee shop housed inside a garden store. A few tables and chairs are set up inside as well as on the deck, which offers views of the ocean strait. **Address:** 100 Hwy 16 V0T 1S1 **Location:** On Graham Island; in Skidegate; 1 mi (1.6 km) n of Skidegate Ferry Terminal, on Hwy 16. [L] [AC]

OCEANA   250/559-8886

Chinese. Casual Dining. $8-$18 **AAA Inspector Notes:** This place is popular with locals looking for good Chinese food in a restaurant that's always open. **Bar:** beer & wine. **Address:** 3119 Ocean View Dr V0T 1S0 **Location:** On Graham Island; in Queen Charlotte; from BC Ferries and Skidegate Landing, 1.8 mi (3 km) s. [L] [D] [AC]

HALFMOON BAY pop. 396

ROCKWATER SECRET COVE RESORT   604/885-7038

[fyi] **Hotel** Did not meet all AAA rating requirements for locking devices in some guest rooms at time of last evaluation on 04/09/2012. **Address:** 5356 Ole Rd V0N 1Y2 **Location:** 4.4 mi (7 km) n on Hwy 101, follow signs. Facilities, services, and décor characterize a mid-scale property.

WHERE TO EAT

ROCKWATER SECRET COVE RESORT DINING ROOM
                                                   604/885-7038

Pacific Northwest. Fine Dining. $12-$32 **AAA Inspector Notes:** Diners are treated to stunning water views from every table. Among offerings of wonderful West Coast cuisine are a fish of the day, as well as rack of lamb and hearty steaks. The homemade chuck steak burger is a good lunch choice. **Bar:** full bar. **Reservations:** suggested, for dinner. **Address:** 5356 Ole's Cove Rd V0N 1Y2 **Location:** 4.4 mi (7 km) n on Hwy 101, follow signs; in Rockwater Secret Cove Resort. [B] [L] [D] [AC]

HARRISON HOT SPRINGS (C-7)
pop. 1,468, elev. 11m/36'

At the foot of Harrison Lake, Harrison Hot Springs *(see Recreation Areas Chart)* is a well-known health and vacation resort with two mineral springs and a sandy beach on the lakeshore. Strong area winds make this a favorite spot for windsurfing. The surrounding mountains are known as Sasquatch country, where sightings of the legendary apelike creature twice the size of a man have been reported dozens of times.

More likely to be found in the mountains are mutton-fat jades, garnets, agates, fossils and gold; the area is renowned among rock hounds.

Harrison Hot Springs Visitor InfoCentre: 499 Hot Springs Rd., P.O. Box 255, Harrison Hot Springs, BC, Canada V0M 1K0. **Phone:** (604) 796-5581.

HARRISON BEACH HOTEL   (604)796-1111

Hotel
$99-$269

Address: 160 Esplanade Ave V0M 1K0 **Location:** Just w; on lakefront. **Facility:** 42 efficiencies. 4 stories, interior corridors. **Parking:** on-site (fee). **Terms:** 3 day cancellation notice-fee imposed. **Amenities:** high-speed Internet. **Pool(s):** heated indoor. **Activities:** whirlpool, limited exercise equipment. **Guest Services:** coin laundry. **Free Special Amenities:** local telephone calls and high-speed Internet.

HARRISON HOT SPRINGS RESORT & SPA
(604)796-2244

Resort Hotel
$119-$289

Address: 100 Esplanade Ave V0M 1K0 **Location:** Just w; on lakefront. **Facility:** When you think of "hot springs" the first thing that comes to mind is soaking in warm therapeutic mineral water. At this full-service hotel, the hot springs water is kept at a constant 102 degrees. 337 units, some cottages. 8 stories, interior corridors. **Parking:** on-site (fee) and valet. **Terms:** check-in 4 pm, 1-2 night minimum stay - seasonal and/or weekends, 3 day cancellation notice-fee imposed. **Amenities:** video games (fee). **Dining:** The Copper Room, see separate listing, entertainment. **Pool(s):** 3 heated outdoor, 2 heated indoor. **Activities:** steamrooms, rental boats, 2 tennis courts, hiking trails, jogging, game room, exercise room, spa. *Fee:* golf-9 holes. **Guest Services:** valet laundry. **Free Special Amenities:** newspaper and high-speed Internet. *(See ad this page.)*

WHERE TO EAT

BLACK FOREST RESTAURANT   604/796-9343
German. Casual Dining. $10-$26 **AAA Inspector Notes:** Stepping inside this place, you're transported to a little restaurant in Germany. You must try their wonderful schnitzel and a side of spätzle; ask your server to describe the latter. **Bar:** full bar. **Reservations:** suggested, in summer. **Address:** 180 Esplanade Ave V0M 1K0 **Location:** Just w; on lakefront. **Parking:** street only. D

▼ *See AAA listing this page* ▼

THE COPPER ROOM   604/796-2244

▼▼▼ Pacific Rim. Fine Dining. $25-$36 **AAA Inspector Notes:** In the mood for dinner and dancing? The room hosts a live, soft jazz band to go along with their delicious, slow-roasted prime rib, hearty steaks and Fraser Valley roast chicken. Doors open nightly at 6 pm; dressy-casual attire is requested. **Bar:** full bar. **Reservations:** suggested. **Address:** 100 Esplanade Ave V0M 1K0 **Location:** Just w; on lakefront; in Harrison Hot Springs Resort & Spa. **Parking:** on-site (fee) and valet. D CALL ⑤M

KITAMI JAPANESE RESTAURANT   604/796-2728

▼▼ Japanese. Casual Dining. $5-$26 **AAA Inspector Notes:** Operated by Japanese owners since 1991, this restaurant prepares favorites such as sushi rolls, in addition to varied combination plates that incorporate teriyaki, tempura and sushi preparations. The selection of sakes is extensive. **Bar:** beer & wine. **Address:** 318 Hot Springs Rd V0M 1K0 **Location:** Just s of Cedar Ave. D

HARRISON MILLS (C-7) pop. 405, elev. 11m/36'

KILBY HISTORIC SITE is 1.6 km (.9 mi.) s. of Hwy. 7 at 215 Kilby Rd. Costumed interpreters conduct tours of this 2-hectare (5-acre) living-history site, once the heart of a thriving community of lumber mills. The 1906 General Store contains forgotten foodstuffs, a wood stove and the traditional checkerboard. Other highlights include the Heritage Post Office, the Manchester House Hotel and animals of the Waterloo Farm.

Hours: Daily 11-5, May 17-Sept. 3; Thurs.-Mon. 11-4, Apr. 5-May 16, Sept. 3-Oct. 15 and Dec. 6-17. **Cost:** $9; $8 (ages 60+); $7 (ages 6-18); $24 (family). **Phone:** (604) 796-9576. ▲ ⑪

HAZELTON (D-3) pop. 270, elev. 306m/1,004'

A showplace of indigenous culture, Hazelton originally was called Git-an-maks, meaning "where people fish by torchlight." European settlers arriving in 1872 renamed the area Hazelton, after the profusion of hazelnut trees covering the fertile farmland.

Considered holy by the Gitxsan Indian community, the forest land within a 64.4-kilometre (40-mi.) radius of Hazelton has the province's greatest concentration of standing totem poles, many portrayed in paintings by British Columbia artist Emily Carr.

'KSAN HISTORICAL VILLAGE & MUSEUM is 5 km (3 mi.) s. on Hwy. 62. The Gitxsan Indian village consists of seven tribal houses. The 'Ksan Museum, the Frog House of the Stone Age, the Wolf House or Feast House, the Eagle House, the Fireweed House, the studio, the 'Ksan Shop, and the carving shed and workshop are decorated with paintings, carved interior poles and painted scenes in classic West Coast Indian style.

Tours: Guided tours are available. **Hours:** Daily 9-5, May-Sept. **Cost:** $10; $8.50 (ages 65+ and students with ID); $6.50 (ages 6-17); $33.30 (family). **Phone:** (250) 842-5544 or (877) 842-5518.

HOPE (C-7) pop. 5,969, elev. 39m/127'
• Hotels p. 250 • Restaurants p. 250

At the entrance to the Fraser River Valley, Hope dates from 1848 when the Hudson's Bay Co. established a fort. The town developed rapidly, especially during the gold rush of 1858. The 1859 Anglican Christ Church is one of the province's oldest churches.

From Hope the Trans-Canada Highway leads north to Fraser Canyon. Kawkawa Lake (see Recreation Areas Chart), Lake of the Woods, Mount Hope, Mount Ogilvie and Skagit Valley (see Recreation Areas Chart) are just some of the nearby places that offer year-round recreational opportunities.

The result of the 1965 Hope Slide is evident about 16 kilometres (10 mi.) east beside Hwy. 3. A plaque at the edge of the present roadway explains the collapse of the side of Johnson Peak, which buried the highway under 45 metres (148 ft.) of rubble.

The Hope Museum, inside the Hope Visitor InfoCentre, portrays the town's history through native artifacts and historical settings; phone (604) 869-2021. Hope was the location of several films, including "Rambo: First Blood," "Shoot to Kill" with Sidney Poitier, and Disney's "Far From Home: The Adventures of Yellow Dog."

The Hope Arts Gallery, 349 Fort St., features the work of more than 20 artists; phone (604) 869-2408. More art can be found scattered throughout downtown Hope. Wood carvings in such shapes as a gold prospector with his horse to a bald eagle holding a salmon in his talons were created from dying trees with a chainsaw; most are on the grounds of Memorial Park. Brochures about the more than two dozen carvings can be picked up at the Hope Visitor InfoCentre.

Hope Visitor InfoCentre: 919 Water Ave., P.O. Box 370, Hope, BC, Canada V0X 1L0. **Phone:** (604) 869-2021 or (866) 467-3842.

E.C. MANNING PROVINCIAL PARK is e. on Hwy. 3. The mountain park includes the Hope-Princeton Hwy. (Hwy. 3), a 134-kilometre (83-mi.) ride that climbs from near sea level at Hope to the 1,346-metre (4,416-ft.) summit of Allison Pass. Blackwall Road off Hwy. 3 leads to Cascade Lookout and offers access to a subalpine meadow.

Recreational activities include hiking, camping, canoeing, bird-watching, cross-country skiing, mountain biking and horseback riding. See Recreation Areas Chart. **Hours:** The park is open daily 24 hours. Campgrounds are open May-Oct. **Cost:** Park free. Camping $14-$22 per night. **Phone:** (250) 840-8822 or (800) 330-3321. ▲ ⑪ 𝖷 🐕 ⊞

▼ GEM **HELL'S GATE AIRTRAM**—see Boston Bar p. 220.

OTHELLO-QUINTETTE TUNNELS are off Hwy. 3 exit 170 in Coquihalla Canyon Provincial Park; take 6th St. 1 blk. n. to Kawkawa Lake Rd., then 5 km (3 mi.) e. to Tunnels Rd. Five tunnels were built 1911-16 to complete a railroad through Coquihalla Canyon. The Coquihalla River zigzags through the canyon, presenting a challenge to engineer Andrew

McCulloch, who used dynamite to blast through the canyon walls to create the narrow tunnels.

The railway ceased operations in 1959; wooden walkways now bridge the river's serpentine course between the tunnels and allow close-up views of the rushing waters.

Note: Wear shoes with good traction, as the gravel path through the tunnels may be wet and slippery. A flashlight is recommended for visibility. **Time:** Allow 1 hour, 30 minutes minimum. **Hours:** Daily dawn-dusk, Apr.-Oct. **Cost:** Free. **Parking:** $1 per hour, $3 per day. **Phone:** (604) 476-9069.

ALPINE MOTEL
(604)869-9931

Motel
$72-$115

Address: 505 Old Hope-Princeton Way V0X 1L0 **Location:** Trans-Canada Hwy 1 exit 173 westbound; exit 170 eastbound, just n from lights. **Facility:** 14 units, some efficiencies. 1 story, exterior corridors. **Free Special Amenities: local telephone calls and high-speed Internet.**

BEST CONTINENTAL MOTEL
604/869-9726

Motel
$69-$115

Address: 860 Fraser Ave V0X 1L0 **Location:** Trans-Canada Hwy 1 exit 170 to downtown; at Fort St. **Facility:** 14 units. 2 stories (no elevator), exterior corridors. **Terms:** cancellation fee imposed. **Free Special Amenities: local telephone calls and high-speed Internet.**

COLONIAL '900' MOTEL
(604)869-5223

Motel
$89-$125

Address: 900 Old Hope-Princeton Way V0X 1L0 **Location:** Trans-Canada Hwy 1 exit 173 westbound; exit 170 eastbound, 0.6 mi (1 km) n from lights. **Facility:** 17 units, some efficiencies and kitchens. 1 story, exterior corridors. **Terms:** cancellation fee imposed. **Free Special Amenities: local telephone calls and high-speed Internet.**

HERITAGE INN
(604)869-7166

Motel
$78-$116

Address: 570 Old Hope-Princeton Way V0X 1L0 **Location:** Trans-Canada Hwy 1 exit 173 westbound; exit 170 eastbound, just n from lights. **Facility:** 27 units, some efficiencies. 1-2 stories (no elevator), exterior corridors. **Terms:** cancellation fee imposed. **Guest Services:** coin laundry. **Free Special Amenities: local telephone calls and high-speed Internet.**

SKAGIT MOTOR INN
604/869-5220

Motel
$83-$190

Address: 655 3rd Ave V0X 1L0 **Location:** Trans-Canada Hwy 1 exit 170 to downtown, just e of Water Ave. **Facility:** 31 units, some efficiencies. 1 story, exterior corridors. **Terms:** 3 day cancellation notice-fee imposed. **Activities:** whirlpool. **Guest Services:** coin laundry. **Free Special Amenities: local telephone calls and high-speed Internet.**

Get pet travel tips and enter the photo contest at AAA.com/PetBook

TRAVELODGE
(604)869-9951

Motel
$90-$115

Address: 350 Old Hope-Princeton Way V0X 1L0 **Location:** Trans-Canada Hwy 1 exit 173 westbound; exit 170 eastbound, just n from lights. **Facility:** 25 units, some efficiencies. 2 stories (no elevator), interior corridors. **Pool(s):** heated indoor. **Activities:** whirlpool. **Free Special Amenities: continental breakfast and high-speed Internet.**

WHERE TO EAT

HOME RESTAURANT
604/869-5558

American. Casual Dining. $8-$15 **AAA Inspector Notes:** Burgers, meat loaf, club sandwiches, mountain-man breakfasts and homemade soups are menu mainstays at this popular family-style eatery. One look at the dessert case will make you want to skip the meal and go right for the sweets instead. Food is king here, and you'll want to come back again and again. **Bar:** beer & wine. **Address:** 665 Old Hope-Princeton Way V0X 1L4 **Location:** Trans-Canada Hwy 1 exit 173 westbound; exit 170 eastbound, just n from lights.

B L D CALL

HOPE DRIVE-IN & RESTAURANT
604/869-5380

American. Casual Dining. $7-$16 **AAA Inspector Notes:** Remember when going to the drive-in meant juicy hamburgers, crispy hot fries and some of the best pies on the planet? This popular diner carries on that same tradition. The prices are very reasonable, so feeding the whole family won't break the budget. **Bar:** full bar. **Address:** 590 Old Hope-Princeton Way V0X 1L0 **Location:** Trans-Canada Hwy 1 exit 173 westbound; exit 170 eastbound, just n from lights.

B L D CALL

PAPANDREAS GREEK TAVERNA
604/869-7218

Greek. Casual Dining. $11-$21 **AAA Inspector Notes:** On the north end of town next door to Colonial 900 Motel, this restaurant features fine Greek dishes along with steaks and some really good pizza. Guests can dine in or take out. **Bar:** full bar. **Address:** 904 Old Hope-Princeton Way V0X 1L0 **Location:** Trans-Canada Hwy 1 exit 173 westbound; exit 170 eastbound, 0.6 mi (1 km) n from lights.

D CALL

ROLLY'S RESTAURANT
604/869-7448

American. Casual Dining. $6-$15 **AAA Inspector Notes:** This casual family-dining restaurant serves breakfast all day. The home-style menu fare includes an ever-changing daily special and a fresh-made soup of the day. You won't be able to look away from the tempting dessert display case, so you may as well try one of their pies. A guilty pleasure, to be sure. **Bar:** full bar. **Address:** 888 Fraser Ave V0X 1L0 **Location:** Trans-Canada Hwy 1 exit 170 to downtown; jct Hudson Bay St. B L D CALL

HUDSON'S HOPE (D-5) pop. 970, elev. 520m/1,706'

Hudson's Hope is one of the oldest settlements in the province: Only two communities on Vancouver Island have been continuously occupied from earlier dates. First discovered in 1793 by Alexander Mackenzie, the area was the site of a small fur-trading post built in 1805. In 1900 the post was moved to the present site of Hudson's Hope on the north side of the Peace River, where it flourished as a center of trade for the Hudson's Bay Co.

Hudson's Hope is an important supplier of hydroelectricity; its two dams generate about 38 percent of the hydropower used in British Columbia. The dams also are major recreation centers for the area.

Hudson's Hope Visitor Centre: 9555 Beattie Dr., P.O. Box 330, Hudson's Hope, BC, Canada V0C 1V0. **Phone:** (250) 783-9154 May-Oct., or (250) 783-9901 rest of year.

HUDSON'S HOPE MUSEUM is at 9510 Beattie Dr. Housed in a 1942 Hudson's Bay Co. store, the museum contains local artifacts and a collection of prehistoric items including ichthyosaur fossils and tracks. Outbuildings include an active log church built in 1938, a trapper's cabin, a fur cache and a pioneer house. A steam boiler and other antique machines are displayed on the grounds. Children can have fun at the Dino Dig and Walking in the Footsteps of the Dinos exhibits.

Hours: Daily 9-5, late May to mid-Sept.; Mon.-Fri. 9-5, rest of year. Phone ahead to confirm schedule and for hours during the holiday season. **Cost:** Donations. **Phone:** (250) 783-5735.

GEM **PEACE CANYON DAM** is 4 km (2.5 mi.) s. on Hwy. 29. Completed in 1980, the dam is 50 metres (165 ft.) high and 533 metres (1,750 ft.) long. It reuses water that has generated electricity at the W.A.C. Bennett Dam, 23 kilometres (14 mi.) upstream on the Peace River. Nearby recreational facilities include a campground, picnic facilities and a boat launch to Dinosaur Lake, the dam's reservoir. **Hours:** Daily 8-4, mid-May through Labour Day.

Peace Canyon Dam Visitor Centre is next to the powerhouse. Exhibits reflect the area's natural history, its pioneer past and the Peace Canyon Project. Highlights include a replica of the stern-wheeler SS *Peace River,* a large-scale model of a generating unit, displays about the damming of the Peace River, and mammoth tusks found during excavation. Visitors can view the project's central control system, walk across the dam or visit the observation area on the main floor.

Guided tours of the visitor center are available. **Hours:** Daily 8-4, May 1-Labour Day; Mon.-Fri. 8-4, rest of year. Closed Jan. 1, Easter, second Mon. in Oct., Nov. 11 and Dec. 25-26. **Cost:** Free. **Phone:** (250) 783-7418.

GEM **W.A.C. BENNETT DAM** is 21 km (13 mi.) w. on Canyon Dr. following signs. A major hydroelectric project on the Peace River, the dam was completed in 1967 to produce electrical power for British Columbia. It is 183 metres (600 ft.) high, 2 kilometres (1.2 mi.) long and .8 kilometre (.5 mi.) thick at the base. Backup water from the dam forms 164,600-hectare (406,727-acre) Williston Lake, British Columbia's largest lake. Its shoreline stretches for 1,770 kilometres (1,100 mi.).

W.A.C. Bennett Dam Visitor Centre is about 1 km (.6 mi.) s.e. of the dam. Photographs and artifacts chronicle the history and geology of the region and the construction of the dam and powerhouse. A participatory exhibit demonstrates the generation of electricity and magnetism. Underground bus tours into the powerhouse and manifold chambers are available. A 40-minute multimedia presentation also is offered in the theater.

Note: Cameras, purses and bags are not permitted on the tour. **Hours:** Visitor center daily 10-6, Victoria Day-Labour Day; by appointment rest of year. Underground powerhouse tours are available 10:30-4:30. Last tour begins at 4:30. Phone ahead to confirm times for tours. **Cost:** Visitor center free. Tour $6; $5 (ages 6-17 and 55+); $15 (family). Reservations are required for the tour. **Phone:** (250) 783-5048 or (888) 333-6667.

BEST WESTERN HUDSON'S HOPE INN & SUITES
250/783-2300

Extended Stay Hotel
Rates not provided

AAA Benefit: Members save up to 20%, plus 10% bonus points with Best Western Rewards®.

Address: 9006 Clark Ave V0C 1V0 **Location:** Hwy 29, north end of town. **Facility:** 86 units, some efficiencies and kitchens. 3 stories, interior corridors. **Parking:** winter plug-ins. **Amenities:** high-speed Internet. **Activities:** whirlpool, exercise room. **Guest Services:** valet and coin laundry. **Free Special Amenities: local telephone calls and high-speed Internet.**

SAVE CALL BIZ / SOME UNITS FEE

INVERMERE (B-11) pop. 2,955

• Hotels p. 252 • Restaurants p. 252

Nestled in the "Valley of a Thousand Peaks" between the Rocky and Purcell mountain ranges, Invermere's bucolic location on Lake Windermere's north shore makes it the ideal spot for summer recreation, including hiking, camping, fishing, boating and sailboarding. Hang gliders frequently take flight off nearby Mount Swansea.

Birds of a different feather fly freely at Wilmer National Wildlife Area, about 5 kilometres (3 mi.) north of town; bring your binoculars to peep at songbirds, woodpeckers, waterfowl and birds of prey as well as four-legged creatures including deer, elk, muskrats and beavers.

Roam down Main Street in Invermere's downtown, where flowers bloom in abundance and small-town charm pervades the boutiques, antique shops and cafés. Take in a first-run flick at the 1952 Toby Theatre; it also hosts a film festival from September through June.

Invermere Visitor Centre: 651 Hwy. 93/95, P.O. Box 1019, Invermere, BC, Canada V0A 1K0. **Phone:** (250) 342-2844.

WINDERMERE VALLEY MUSEUM is at 222 6th Ave. Pioneer artifacts and local archives are displayed in a complex in a small park. The six log outbuildings have thematic displays. **Time:** Allow 1 hour minimum. **Hours:** Daily 10-4, June-Aug.; daily noon-4, in early Sept.; Tues. noon-4 and 7-9 or by appointment, rest of year. Phone ahead to confirm schedule. **Cost:** Donations. **Phone:** (250) 342-9769.

RECREATIONAL ACTIVITIES

Skiing

- **Panorama Mountain Village** is 18 km (11.2 mi.) w. on Panorama Dr. Other activities are offered.

Hours: Daily 9-4, Dec.-Apr. **Phone:** (250) 342-6941 or (800) 663-2929.

BEST WESTERN INVERMERE INN (250)342-9246

Hotel
$119-$199

AAA Benefit: Members save up to 20%, plus 10% bonus points with Best Western Rewards®.

Address: 1310 7th Ave V0A 1K0 **Location:** Hwy 93 and 95 exit Invermere, 1.8 mi (3 km) w; center. **Facility:** 46 units. 3 stories, interior corridors. **Parking:** winter plug-ins. **Terms:** check-in 4 pm. **Activities:** whirlpool, exercise room. **Guest Services:** coin laundry. **Free Special Amenities: full breakfast and high-speed Internet.**

[SAVE] [icons] / SOME UNITS FEE [icon]

COPPERPOINT RESORT 250/341-4000

Hotel. Rates not provided. Address: 760 Cooper Rd V0A 1K2 **Location:** Hwy 93 and 95, just w. **Facility:** 173 units, some two bedrooms, three bedrooms and kitchens. 4 stories, interior corridors. **Amenities:** high-speed Internet, safes. **Dining:** Elements Grill, see separate listing. **Pool(s):** heated outdoor, heated indoor. **Activities:** whirlpools, lighted tennis court, hiking trails, playground, basketball, exercise room, spa. *Fee:* golf-36 holes. **Guest Services:** valet laundry.

[icons] / SOME UNITS FEE [icon]

SUPER 8 INVERMERE (250)342-8888

Hotel $109-$159 **Address:** 8888 Arrow Rd V0A 1K0 **Location:** On Hwy 95. **Facility:** 49 units. 3 stories, interior corridors. **Parking:** winter plug-ins. **Dining:** Rocky River Grill, see separate listing. **Activities:** whirlpool. [icons]

WHERE TO EAT

BLACK FOREST STEAK & SCHNITZEL HOUSE 250/342-9417

Continental
Casual Dining
$17-$39

AAA Inspector Notes: On the menu is a good selection of schnitzels, bratwurst, steak and seafood finely prepared with a respect for tradition. Table d'hotes are offered daily, and the decor and relaxed ambience are inspired by Europe. The restaurant is a favorite with birders, who can enjoy watching the owner's pets while dining. **Bar:** full bar. **Reservations:** suggested. **Address:** 540 Hwy 93 & 95 V0A 1K0 **Location:** Center. [D]

BLUE DOG CAFE 250/342-3814

American. Casual Dining. $9-$11 AAA Inspector Notes: A favorite of the locals, this small cafe prepares fresh and wholesome soups, salads, wraps and sandwiches, staying as far away from monosodium glutamate and preservatives as it can. Baked goods, chutneys, dressings and vinaigrettes all are prepared from scratch. Breakfast is served with a variety of Kicking Horse coffees. **Bar:** beer & wine. **Address:** 1213 7th Ave V0A 1K0 **Location:** On Main St; downtown. **Parking:** street only. [B] [L]

ELEMENTS GRILL 250/341-4000

American. Casual Dining. $12-$25 AAA Inspector Notes: Enjoy the smart modern décor with slate walls and high windows providing lovely views of the mountains from most tables. After perusing the well-prepared contemporary menu you might decide to start with tender salt-and-pepper squid with lemon aioli or bison carpaccio with pickled mushrooms and white cheddar. Entrées like fresh wild salmon with crab risotto or AAA Alberta beef with roasted mushrooms and jus are among the choices. In season there is a lovely patio with a separate menu. **Bar:** full bar. **Reservations:** suggested. **Address:** 760 Cooper Rd V0A 1K2 **Location:** Hwy 93 and 95, just w; in Copperpoint Resort. [B] [L] [D] CALL [M]

ROCKY RIVER GRILL 250/342-8885

American. Casual Dining. $11-$25 AAA Inspector Notes: Popular with the locals, the restaurant has a contemporary décor and is dominated by a huge fish tank. The menu offers a good range of appetizers and salads, as well as all your favorites, including burgers, sandwiches, pastas, salmon, ribs and steak. A nice touch is the house-cut chips and fries. Seating also is available in the sports lounge or on the outside patio in good weather. **Bar:** full bar. **Address:** 8888 Arrow Rd V0A 1K0 **Location:** On Hwy 95; in Invermere Super 8. [B] [L] [D] CALL [M]

STRAND'S OLD HOUSE RESTAURANT 250/342-6344

Continental. Casual Dining. $18-$39 AAA Inspector Notes: *Historic.* The restaurant offers intimate dining in a restored historic house. The varied menu includes such offerings as lamb, game, seafood, a selection of pastas and dinner-size salads. A good number of daily specials complements the menu. A covered porch provides a bright, airy alternative to the more secluded corners of the main dining room. Servers are friendly and courteous. **Bar:** full bar. **Reservations:** suggested. **Address:** 818 12th St V0A 1K0 **Location:** Center. [D] CALL [M]

KALEDEN (C-8) pop. 1,224
• Part of Okanagan Valley area — see map p. 286

DOMINION RADIO ASTROPHYSICAL OBSERVATORY is at 717 White Lake Rd. The site features radio telescopes used to study the universe. A self-guiding tour includes a 26-metre (85-ft.) parabolic antenna and an array of more sophisticated, computer-linked, 9-metre (30-ft.) antennae.

Note: Since automobile ignitions cause radio interference, visitors are asked to leave their vehicles at the road and walk the 600 metres (.4 mi.) to the facility. **Time:** Allow 30 minutes minimum. **Hours:** Visitor center daily 10-5, Easter weekend-second Mon. in Oct.; Mon.-Fri. 10-5, rest of year. Guided 1-hour tours led by astronomers are given Sat.-Sun. 2-5, July-Aug. Closed major holidays. **Cost:** Free. **Phone:** (250) 497-2300.

KAMLOOPS (H-5) pop. 85,678,
elev. 345m/1,131'
• Hotels p. 254 • Restaurants p. 260

Founded in 1812 as a North West Co. depot, Kamloops later was a Hudson's Bay Co. post. Developed where the north and south branches of the Thompson River converge to form Kamloops Lake, Kamloops was named after a Secwepemc (Shuswap) word, *Tk'emlúps,* or "the meeting of the waters" or, alternatively, a similar French phrase, *camp des loups,* or "camp of wolves." During the gold rush of the 1860s the Overlanders reached the city by rafting down the North Thompson. A bronze statue at city hall commemorates their arrival and their contributions to the city.

Since the Cariboo's gold supply disappeared in the 1860s, Kamloops has developed as a center of cattle and sheep ranching, forestry and lumber and, in more recent years, tourism.

Kamloops Heritage Railway, at #6-510 Lorne St., operates *The Spirit of Kamloops* in the summer months. The restored 1912 steam locomotive, with its restored hayrack cars, heritage coaches and caboose, departs the Canadian National Railway station and carries passengers on a sightseeing tour, passing St. Joseph's Church along the way, surviving a train robbery on the return trip; phone (250) 374-2141.

With an abundance of lakes in the area, Kamloops offers good fishing. In fact, local trout are known to jump a few feet in the air after being hooked. Outdoor enthusiasts also enjoy golfing, nature trails, wildlife viewing, boating, kayaking, canoeing, hiking and mountain biking. Many urban parks also offer recreational activities, including hiking, biking, picnicking and strolling, and skiing can be enjoyed on nearby slopes.

Culturally speaking, Western Canada Theatre and Project X Theatre Productions stage plays virtually year-round; phone (250) 372-3216 and (250) 682-9055 respectively. And the Kamloops Symphony, (250) 374-5483, presents orchestral and chamber music performances September to May.

Kamloops Visitor Centre: 1290 W. Trans-Canada Hwy., Kamloops, BC, Canada V2C 6R3. **Phone:** (250) 374-3377 or (800) 662-1994.

Self-guiding tours: Kamloops is the site of several historical attractions, including the provincial courthouse and several old houses and churches. Self-guiding tour brochures are available from Kamloops Museum and Archives.

BRITISH COLUMBIA WILDLIFE PARK is 17 km (10 mi.) e. on Hwy. 1 to 9077 Dallas Dr. Sixty-five species of local and endangered wildlife, including grizzly bears, timber wolves, cougars, moose, snakes and birds of prey live in natural habitats at this 50-hectare (120-acre) park. Highlights include interpretive talks, animal encounters, a children's play area and splash park, and a seasonal miniature train. The Discovery Centre features interactive displays. Wildlights, a holiday light display, is offered in December and January.

Hours: Park open daily 9:30-4, May-Sept.; 9:30-9, Oct. 19-21 and 26-28 with Boo at the Zoo. Train departs daily 9-5, June-Sept.; 9:30-4, Mar. 15-May 31 and in Oct. Last admission 30 minutes before closing. Closed Christmas. Phone ahead to confirm schedule. **Cost:** May-Sept. $13.95; $11.95 (ages 65+); $9.95 (ages 3-17). Admission rest of year $11; $9 (ages 65+); $7 (ages 3-17). Admission may vary; phone ahead. **Phone:** (250) 573-3242.

KAMLOOPS ART GALLERY is at 101-465 Victoria St. Works by diverse regional, national and international artists are featured. Changing exhibits include paintings, sculptures, prints, drawings, photographs, videos and indigenous art. The gallery supports contemporary and historical visual arts and practices on a local, national and international level.

Time: Allow 30 minutes minimum. **Hours:** Mon.-Sat. 10-5 (also Thurs. 5-9). Closed statutory holidays. **Cost:** $5; $3 (ages 62+ and students with ID); $10 (family); free (Thurs.). Admission may vary for certain exhibits; phone ahead. **Phone:** (250) 377-2400.

KAMLOOPS MUSEUM AND ARCHIVES is at 207 Seymour St. Permanent history galleries portray the area's past through displays of indigenous culture, fly-fishing, a reconstructed Hudson's Bay Co. fur-trading cabin, pioneer and Victorian artifacts and tableaux, transportation items, natural history specimens and changing temporary exhibits. A children's museum and rocks and minerals geology gallery are available. The archives has collections of photographs and manuscripts.

Tours: Guided tours are available. **Time:** Allow 1 hour minimum. **Hours:** Tues.-Sat. 9:30-4:30 (also Thurs. 4:30-7:30, late May-Oct. 31). Closed major holidays. **Cost:** Donations. **Phone:** (250) 828-3576.

ST. JOSEPH'S CHURCH is n. on Mount Paul Way, then w. to end of Chilcotin St. Constructed by Roman Catholic missionaries and the Kamloops Indian Band in the late 19th century, the church has been meticulously renovated. The building's elaborate gilded altar and its many period religious artifacts also have been restored. **Time:** Allow 30 minutes minimum. **Hours:** Wed.-Sat. 12:30-7:30, July 1-Labour Day. Phone ahead to confirm schedule. **Cost:** Donations. **Phone:** (250) 374-7323.

SECWEPEMC MUSEUM AND HERITAGE PARK is at 101-355 Yellowhead Hwy. The 5-hectare (12-acre) park interprets the history and culture of the Secwepemc, or Shuswap, Nation. A walking trail leads through the archeological remains of a 2,000-year-old Shuswap winter village, pit house reconstructions and a summer village. The park also features a museum and ethnobotanical gardens.

Time: Allow 1 hour minimum. **Hours:** Daily 8:30-4:30, May 1-Oct. 15; Mon.-Fri. 8:30-4:30, rest of

year. Closed first week in Jan. and the last week in Dec. **Cost:** $10; $7 (ages 60+ and students with ID); $6 (ages 7-17); $20 (family, two adults and two children). **Phone:** (250) 828-9749.

GAMBLING ESTABLISHMENTS

• **Lake City Casino** is at 540 Victoria St. **Hours:** Daily 10 a.m.-2 a.m. **Phone:** (250) 372-2281.

ACCENT INNS
(250)374-8877

Motel
$99-$179

Address: 1325 Columbia St W V2C 6P4 **Location:** Trans-Canada Hwy 1 exit 369 (Columbia St) eastbound, at Notre Dame Dr; exit 370 (Summit Dr) westbound. **Facility:** 84 units, some efficiencies. 3 stories, exterior corridors. **Parking:** winter plug-ins. **Terms:** cancellation fee imposed. **Amenities:** high-speed Internet. **Pool(s):** heated outdoor. **Activities:** sauna, whirlpool, limited exercise equipment. **Guest Services:** valet and coin laundry. **Free Special Amenities:** newspaper and high-speed Internet.

BEST WESTERN PLUS KAMLOOPS HOTEL
(250)374-7878

Hotel
$125-$225

AAA Benefit: Members save up to 20%, plus 10% bonus points with Best Western Rewards®.

Address: 660 Columbia St W V2C 1L1 **Location:** Trans-Canada Hwy 1 exit 369 (Columbia St) eastbound, 1.3 mi (2 km) n; exit 370 (Summit Dr) westbound to Columbia St via City Centre, then just n. **Facility:** 81 units. 4 stories, interior corridors. **Parking:** winter plug-ins. **Pool(s):** heated indoor. **Activities:** whirlpool, exercise room. **Guest Services:** valet and coin laundry. **Free Special Amenities:** local telephone calls and high-speed Internet. *(See ad this page.)*

CANADAS BEST VALUE INN AND SUITES
(250)374-8100

Motel
$69-$199

Address: 1200 Rogers Way V1S 1N5 **Location:** Trans-Canada Hwy 1 exit 368 (Hillside Ave), just s. **Facility:** 38 units, some efficiencies. 2 stories (no elevator), exterior corridors. **Parking:** winter plug-ins. **Terms:** cancellation fee imposed. **Pool(s):** outdoor. **Guest Services:** coin laundry. **Free Special Amenities:** continental breakfast and high-speed Internet.

THE COAST KAMLOOPS HOTEL & CONFERENCE CENTRE
(250)828-6660

 Hotel $130-$185 **Address:** 1250 Rogers Way V1S 1N5 **Location:** Trans-Canada Hwy 1 exit 368 (Hillside Ave), just s. **Facility:** 203 units, some two bedrooms. 3 stories, interior corridors. **Parking:** winter plug-ins. **Amenities:** high-speed Internet. *Some:* safes. **Pool(s):** heated indoor. **Activities:** sauna, whirlpool, exercise room. **Guest Services:** valet laundry. *(See ad p. 255.)*

COMFORT INN & SUITES
250/372-0987

 Hotel. Rates not provided. **Address:** 1810 Rogers Pl V1S 1T7 **Location:** Trans-Canada Hwy 1 exit 368 (Hillside Ave), just w. **Facility:** 87 units. 3 stories, interior corridors. **Parking:** winter plug-ins. **Pool(s):** heated indoor. **Activities:** whirlpool, waterslide, exercise room. **Guest Services:** valet and coin laundry. *(See ad p. 255.)*

─────────── ▼ *See AAA listing this page* ▼ ───────────

▼ See AAA listing p. 254 ▼

Kamloops' premier business & leisure hotel!

The Coast
Kamloops Hotel
& Conference Centre

Reservations: 1-800-663-1144
www.coastkamloopshotel.com

Freshly renovated
Indoor pools, sauna & hot tub
Complimentary wireless internet
Aberdeen Private Liquor Store on-site
In-house restaurant & lounge
Complimentary parking

1250 Rogers Way
Kamloops, B.C. V1S 1N5
(250) 828-6660

▼ See AAA listing p. 254 ▼

KAMLOOPS, BC

Comfort Inn & Suites®. Truly Yours.

- Walk to Kamloops Convention Center, Aberdeen Mall
- Complimentary hot breakfast
- Free Internet access
- Free newspaper
- Indoor pool with waterslide, hot tub, and fitness center

choicehotels.com
1810 Rogers Pl
Kamloops, BC V1S 1T7
800.228.1222
250.372.0987

Get the free mobile app at
http://gettag.mobi

FOUR POINTS BY SHERATON KAMLOOPS

(250)374-4144

Hotel
$105-$225

AAA Benefit: Members get up to 20% off, plus Starwood Preferred Guest® bonuses.

Address: 1175 Rogers Way V1S 1R5 **Location:** Trans-Canada Hwy 1 exit 368 (Hillside Ave), just s. **Facility:** 78 units, some two bedrooms, efficiencies and kitchens. 4 stories, interior corridors. **Parking:** winter plug-ins. **Terms:** cancellation fee imposed. **Amenities:** safes. **Dining:** Ric's Grill, see separate listing. **Pool(s):** heated indoor. **Activities:** sauna, whirlpool, waterslide, exercise room. **Guest Services:** valet and coin laundry. *(See ad this page.)*

HAMPTON INN BY HILTON

(250)571-7897

Hotel
$129-$209

AAA Benefit: Members save up to 10%!

Address: 1245 Rogers Way V1S 1R9 **Location:** Trans-Canada Hwy 1 exit 368 (Hillside Ave), just s via Hillside Way. **Facility:** 81 units. 3 stories, interior corridors. **Parking:** winter plug-ins. **Terms:** 1-7 night minimum stay, cancellation fee imposed. **Amenities:** video games (fee), high-speed Internet. **Pool(s):** heated indoor. **Activities:** whirlpool, waterslide, exercise room. **Guest Services:** valet and coin laundry. **Free Special Amenities:** expanded continental breakfast and high-speed Internet. *(See ad p. 257.)*

HOLIDAY INN & SUITES

(250)376-8288

Hotel
$129-$199

Address: 675 Tranquille Rd V2B 3H7 **Location:** Trans-Canada Hwy 1 exit 374 (Jasper Ave), 2.5 mi (4 km) w on Halston Connector Rd, 1.8 mi (3 km) s on 8th St to Fortune Dr, then just s. **Facility:** 89 units. 4 stories, interior corridors. **Parking:** winter plug-ins. **Terms:** cancellation fee imposed. **Amenities:** high-speed Internet. **Pool(s):** heated indoor. **Activities:** whirlpool, exercise room. **Guest Services:** valet and coin laundry, area transportation-downtown. **Free Special Amenities:** high-speed Internet and local transportation. *(See ad p. 257.)*

HOLIDAY INN EXPRESS KAMLOOPS

(250)372-3474

Hotel $130-$165 **Address:** 1550 Versatile Dr V1S 1X4 **Location:** Trans-Canada Hwy 1 exit 367 (Pacific Way), just w. **Facility:** 80 units. 4 stories, interior corridors. **Parking:** winter plug-ins. **Terms:** cancellation fee imposed. **Amenities:** high-speed Internet. **Pool(s):** heated indoor. **Activities:** whirlpool, exercise room. **Guest Services:** valet laundry.

KAMLOOPS SUPER 8

(250)374-8688

Motel $70-$120 **Address:** 1521 Hugh Allan Dr V1S 1P4 **Location:** Trans-Canada Hwy 1 exit 367 (Pacific Way). **Facility:** 48 units. 2 stories (no elevator), interior corridors.

Plan complete trip routings with the TripTik® Travel Planner on AAA.com/CAA.ca

KAMLOOPS TRAVELODGE MOUNTVIEW
(250)374-4788

Motel
$89-$115

Address: 1225 Rogers Way V1S 1R9 **Location:** Trans-Canada Hwy 1 exit 368 (Hillside Ave), just s. **Facility:** 53 units, some two bedrooms and efficiencies. 3 stories, exterior corridors. **Terms:** cancellation fee imposed. **Amenities:** *Some:* high-speed Internet. **Pool(s):** heated outdoor. **Activities:** whirlpool. **Guest Services:** coin laundry.

SAVE 🍽️ CALL 🅜 🛥️ 🛜
📺 🖼️ 🖨️

Spectacular mountain views. Spacious renovated rooms. Free Wi-Fi and Breakfast.

QUALITY INN
(250)851-0111

Motel
$79-$129

Address: 1860 Rogers Pl V1S 1T7 **Location:** Trans-Canada Hwy 1 exit 368 (Hillside Ave). **Facility:** 63 units, some efficiencies. 2 stories (no elevator), interior corridors. **Parking:** winter plug-ins. **Terms:** cancellation fee imposed. **Pool(s):** heated outdoor. **Activities:** sauna, whirlpool. **Guest Services:** coin laundry. **Free Special Amenities: expanded continental breakfast and high-speed Internet.**

SAVE 🍽️ CALL 🅜 🛥️ 🛜
📺 /SOME UNITS FEE 🐾 🖨️ 🖼️

Located near shopping mall & restaurants. Continental breakfast Lovely outdoor pool & indoor hot tub.

MAVERICK MOTOR INN & WATERSLIDE   (250)374-9666

Motel $70-$200 **Address:** 1250 W Trans-Canada Hwy 1 V2C 6R3 **Location:** Trans-Canada Hwy 1 exit 368 (Hillside Ave), just w. **Facility:** 42 units, some efficiencies. 2 stories (no elevator), interior corridors. **Parking:** winter plug-ins. **Dining:** Beijing Restaurant, see separate listing. **Pool(s):** heated indoor. **Activities:** whirlpool, waterslide. **Guest Services:** coin laundry.

🍽️ 🛥️ 🛜 ✖️ 🖨️ 📺 /SOME UNITS 🖼️

PACIFIC HOST INN & SUITES   (250)372-0952

Hotel $120-$170 **Address:** 1820 Rogers Pl V1S 1T7 **Location:** Trans-Canada Hwy 1 exit 368 (Hillside Ave), just w. **Facility:** 39 units, some efficiencies. 3 stories, interior corridors. **Parking:** winter plug-ins. **Terms:** cancellation fee imposed. **Dining:** Vittorio's Italian Restaurant, see separate listing. **Pool(s):** heated outdoor. **Activities:** whirlpool, exercise room. **Guest Services:** valet and coin laundry.

🍽️ CALL 🅜 🛥️ 🛜 ✖️ 🎥 📺 /SOME UNITS FEE 🐾 🖨️ 🖼️

RAMADA KAMLOOPS   (250)374-0358

Hotel $115-$155 **Address:** 555 W Columbia St V2C 1K7 **Location:** Trans-Canada Hwy 1 exit 369 (Columbia St) eastbound, 1.3 mi (2 km) n; exit 370 (Summit Dr) westbound to Columbia St via City Centre. **Facility:** 88 units. 2-3 stories, interior corridors. **Parking:** winter plug-ins. **Activities:** whirlpool, exercise room. **Guest Services:** valet and coin laundry. *(See ad this page.)*

ECO 🍽️ 🍸 CALL 🅜 BIZ 🛜 ✖️ 📺 /SOME UNITS 🖨️ 🖼️

RANCHLAND MOTEL   (250)828-8787

Motel $79-$125 **Address:** 2357 Trans-Canada Hwy 1 E V2C 4A8 **Location:** 2.8 mi (4.5 km) e on Trans-Canada Hwy 1 exit River Rd, then just w along service access road. **Facility:** 36 units, some efficiencies. 2 stories (no elevator), exterior corridors. **Parking:** winter plug-ins. **Activities:** sauna, whirlpool. **Guest Services:** coin laundry.

CALL 🅜 🛜 🖨️ 📺 /SOME UNITS FEE 🐾

Contact us about AAA/CAA Approved properties at AAA.com/TourBookComments

SCOTT'S INN & RESTAURANT (250)372-8221

Motel
$80-$130

Address: 551 11th Ave V2C 3Y1 **Location:** Trans-Canada Hwy 1 exit 369 (Columbia St) eastbound, 3.1 mi (5 km) n; exit City Centre westbound, 1 mi (1.6 km) s on Columbia St. Located in residential area across from a playground. **Facility:** 51 units, some two bedrooms, efficiencies and kitchens. 2 stories (no elevator), exterior corridors. **Parking:** winter plug-ins. **Terms:** cancellation fee imposed. **Pool(s):** heated indoor. **Activities:** whirlpool. **Guest Services:** coin laundry. **Free Special Amenities: expanded continental breakfast and high-speed Internet.** *(See ad this page.)*

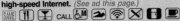

THE THOMPSON HOTEL & CONFERENCE CENTRE
(250)374-1999

   Hotel $139-$209 **Address:** 650 Victoria St V2C 2B4 **Location:** Trans-Canada Hwy 1 exit 369 (Columbia St) eastbound to City Centre; exit 370 (Summit Dr) westbound, just n on 6th Ave; downtown. **Facility:** 98 units. 3 stories, interior corridors. **Parking:** on-site (fee), winter plug-ins. **Terms:** cancellation fee imposed, resort fee. **Dining:** 2 restaurants. **Pool(s):** heated indoor. **Activities:** whirlpool, game room, exercise room. **Guest Services:** valet laundry.

Save on theme park tickets
at AAA.com/discounts

▼ See AAA listing this page ▼

WHERE TO EAT

BEIJING RESTAURANT   250-372-3355

♦♦ Chinese. Casual Dining. $11-$28 **AAA Inspector Notes:**
Wonderful views of the Kamloops Valley can be taken in from this
hilltop restaurant offering authentic Szechuan- and Cantonese-style
cuisine. There are plenty of a la cart dishes of chicken, pork, beef and
seafood, vegetables and rice, but you also can try their combination
dinners for groups of two all the way up to eight people. **Bar:** full bar.
Address: 1250 W Trans-Canada Hwy 1 V2C 6R3 **Location:** Trans-
Canada Hwy 1 exit 368 (Hillside Ave); in Maverick Motor Inn &
Waterslide. [L] [D]

CHAPTERS VIEWPOINT RESTAURANT & CATERING
                                        250-374-3224

♦♦ American. Casual Dining. $8-$40 **AAA Inspector Notes:**
This restaurant's great location offers a spectacular view of the city
and surrounding hills. The well-prepared menu features New
Mexican cuisine, beef and prime rib, chicken and seafood. The décor
is Pacific Northwest and makes use of the Douglas fir beams. **Bar:**
full bar. **Reservations:** suggested. **Address:** 550 W Columbia St
V2C 1L1 **Location:** Trans-Canada Hwy 1 exit 369 (Columbia St)
eastbound, 1.2 mi (2 km) n; exit 370 (Summit Dr) westbound to Columbia St via City Centre; in Panorama Howard Johnson Inn.
[B] [L] [D]

FLAVOURS OF INDIA   250-374-0340

♦♦ Indian. Casual Dining. $8-$20 **AAA Inspector Notes:** This
hilltop location along Columbia Street offers wonderful city views, but
the highlight is the excellent Indian food. The staff gladly accommodate any taste from mild to spicy. A buffet is served at lunch and on
weekends. **Bar:** full bar. **Address:** 550 W Columbia St V2C 1K6 **Location:** Trans-Canada Hwy 1 exit 369 (Columbia St) eastbound, 1.3
mi (2 km) n; exit 370 (Summit Dr) westbound to Columbia St via City
Centre; in Hospitality Inn. [L] [D]

ORIENTAL GARDENS RESTAURANT   250-372-2344

♦♦ Chinese. Casual Dining. $10-$20 **AAA Inspector Notes:**
Delicious Japanese and Chinese entrees are featured at this restaurant, where a full sushi bar and Japanese-style, private dining booths
are also offered. The restaurant will validate parking for those guests
who park in the lot to the side. **Bar:** full bar. **Address:** 545 Victoria St
V2C 2B1 **Location:** Victoria St at 5th Ave; downtown. **Parking:** on-
site (fee) and street. [D]

RIC'S GRILL

♦♦ Steak. Casual Dining. $11-$30 **AAA Inspector Notes:**
"Funky and modern" describes the decor and the food at the up-
scale steakhouse, which bustles with activity. Steaks are well
worth it, but then again, so are the salmon, chicken and pasta
dishes. A wide variety of distinctive appetizers rounds out the
menu. Servers are friendly and attentive. **Bar:** full bar.
[L] [D] CALL [⚙M]
For additional information, visit AAA.com
LOCATIONS:
Address: 227 Victoria St V2C 2A1 **Location:** Between 2nd and
3rd aves. **Phone:** 250/372-7771
Address: 1175 Rogers Way V1S 1R5 **Location:** Trans-Canada
Hwy 1 exit 368 (Hillside Ave), just s; in Four Points by Sheraton
Kamloops. **Phone:** 250/377-3113

VITTORIO'S ITALIAN RESTAURANT   250/851-2112

♦♦
Italian
Casual Dining
$13-$25

AAA Inspector Notes: "Come hungry,
leave full" is the motto for this family-
friendly Italian restaurant. The portions
are huge, and the staff will prepare and
send you on your way with a doggie
bag. The pizza dough is made from
scratch and the entrée choices include
all the Italian favorites. **Bar:** full bar. **Reservations:** suggested.
Address: 1820 Rogers Pl V1S 1T7 **Location:** Trans-Canada
Hwy 1 exit 368 (Hillside Ave), just w; in Pacific Host Inn & Suites.
[D] CALL[⚙M]

KASLO (C-11) pop. 1,026, elev. 588m/1,929'

Kaslo began as a mill site in 1888. Following
large silver strikes in 1893 the town quickly expanded to city proportions. A village once again,
Kaslo is a distribution center for the Lardeau Valley.

Duncan Dam, 42 kilometres (26 mi.) north, was
the first of the three dams constructed by B.C. Hydro
in accordance with the Columbia River Treaty, rati-
fied by British Columbia and the United States in
1964. Southwest of the dam is the Kokanee
Spawning Channel, built to compensate for the loss
of natural spawning areas resulting from the dam's
construction. The 3.2-kilometre (2-mi.) channel, one
of the longest in the world, is said to be the first constructed for freshwater fish.

SS *MOYIE* NATIONAL HISTORIC SITE is 1 blk. n.
off Hwy. 31 at 324 Front St., following signs. Considered the world's oldest intact passenger stern-
wheeler, the *Moyie* operated on Kootenay Lake
1898-1957, hauling travelers and freight from
Nelson to northern destinations along the shore. It is
the last active commercial stern-wheeler in the province and contains artifacts, antiques, a model of
Kaslo Harbor, a railway display and a photograph
exhibit relating to the history of the vessel and its
crew.

Time: Allow 30 minutes minimum. **Hours:** Daily
9-5, mid-May to mid-Oct. **Cost:** $7.50; $5.30 (ages
13-18 and 65+); $3.30 (ages 6-12); $18 (family, two
adults and two or more children ages 6-12). **Phone:**
(250) 353-2525.

KELOWNA (H-6) pop. 117,312,
elev. 420m/1,387'
• Hotels p. 262 • Restaurants p. 264
• Hotels & Restaurants map & index p. 290
• Part of Okanagan Valley area — see map p. 286

Kelowna is the center of a fruit and vineyard region around Lake Okanagan, from which one-third
of all apples harvested in Canada are shipped. The
lake also is known for its legendary monster, the
Ogopogo, a Loch Ness type beast reportedly 9 to 21
metres (30-69 ft.) long with a head resembling that
of a horse, goat or sheep.

The Kelowna Community Theatre stages productions during fall and winter; phone (250) 763-9018.
The Okanagan Symphony Orchestra is another
prominent cultural feature; phone (250) 763-7544.

Recreation in the area includes water sports,
fishing and golf. City Park on Lake Okanagan is the
city's largest park, with a beach, tennis courts and a
children's water park. The Kelowna Princess II sets
sail from the park's lakefront (end of Bernard
Street). Departures are subject to weather conditions; for information and sailing times phone (250)
869-6696.

The fall grape harvest is celebrated for 10 days in
early October at the ♦ Okanagan Fall Wine Festival. Wine and food lovers congregate to take in
more than 165 events that take place throughout the
Okanagan Valley.

(See map & index p. 290.)

Kelowna Visitor Centre: 544 Harvey Ave., Kelowna, BC, Canada V1Y 6C9. **Phone:** (250) 861-1515 or (800) 663-4345.

B.C. ORCHARD INDUSTRY MUSEUM is at 1304 Ellis St. Housed in the historic Laurel Packing House, the museum explores the Okanagan's roots in the orchard industry. A 15-metre (50-ft.) model train layout is displayed. Other displays explain fruit production from planting to processing and preserving. The Apple Tree Activities Centre is available for children. **Time:** Allow 30 minutes minimum. **Hours:** Tues.-Fri. 10-5, Sat. 10-4. Phone for holiday hours. Closed Jan. 1, Christmas and day after Christmas. **Cost:** Donations. **Phone:** (778) 478-0347.

The BC Wine Museum & VQA Wine Shop is at 1304 Ellis St. Housed in a converted 1917 packing house, the museum displays machines used for pressing and bottling as well as exhibits featuring the history of wine production in the area. Wine tastings are offered. Guided tours are available by appointment. **Hours:** Open Mon.-Fri. 10-6, Sat. 10-5, Sun. and holidays 11-5. Closed Jan. 1, Christmas and day after Christmas. **Cost:** Donations. **Phone:** (250) 868-0441.

ELYSIUM GARDENS is at 2834 Belgo Rd. The site covers 1.2 hectares (3 acres) and includes organically grown perennial gardens and a Japanese garden. Featured are herb gardens, cut flower and kitchen gardens, xeriscape gardens, ornamental grasses and rock and scree beds.

Dependent on the season, visitors will discover peonies, roses, primroses, tulips, day lilies and hydrangeas in full, fragrant bloom. Mountains and countryside views provide a backdrop for the gardens. **Time:** Allow 1 hour minimum. **Hours:** Tues.-Sun. and holidays 10-5, May-Sept. **Cost:** $10; $6.25 (ages 12-18). **Phone:** (250) 491-1368.

GEERT MAAS SCULPTURE GARDENS AND GALLERY is 10 km (6.2 mi.) n. on Hwy. 97N, then 2 km (1.2 mi.) w. on Sexsmith Rd. to 250 Reynolds Rd. Maas' semi-abstract sculptures of bronze, aluminum, stainless steel, stoneware and mixed media are exhibited in the gallery and in the .4-hectare (1-acre) sculpture garden. The complex contains one of the largest collections of bronze sculptures in Canada.

Medallions, paintings, etchings and reliefs can be seen in the permanent collection; changing exhibits also are offered. **Time:** Allow 1 hour minimum. **Hours:** Mon.-Sat. 10-5, May 1 to mid-Sept.; by appointment rest of year. Phone ahead to confirm schedule. **Cost:** Donations. **Phone:** (250) 860-7012.

KELOWNA ART GALLERY is at 1315 Water St. This architecturally striking museum offers permanent and changing exhibits as well as art classes and lectures. Its permanent collection contains paintings, drawings and photographs created mainly by contemporary Okanagan and British Columbian artists. There are works by other Canadian artists as well. Metered street parking and pay lot are nearby. **Time:** Allow 1 hour minimum. **Hours:** Tues.-Sat. 10-5 (also Thurs. 5-9), Sun. 1-4. Closed Jan. 1 and Dec. 24-28 and 31. **Cost:** $5; $4 (students with ID and senior citizens); $10 (family). **Phone:** (250) 762-2226.

OKANAGAN HERITAGE MUSEUM is at 470 Queensway Ave. Natural history displays offer a glimpse back into the history and settlement of the Okanagan Valley. The museum features a natural history gallery as well as rotating special exhibitions that explore regional and contemporary themes. **Hours:** Mon.-Fri. 10-5, Sat. 10-4. Closed Jan. 1, Christmas and day after Christmas. **Cost:** Donations. **Phone:** (250) 763-2417.

OKANAGAN MILITARY MUSEUM is at 1424 Ellis St. between Queensway and Doyle Ave. Permanent exhibits focus on the contributions of Okanagan Valley residents in the military. Items from the Boer War, World War I, World War II and others are on display. A reference library holds books on military history, and volunteer veterans are on-site to answer questions. **Time:** Allow 30 minutes minimum. **Hours:** Tues.-Sat. 10-4, June-Sept.; Tues., Thurs. and Sat. 10-4, rest of year. **Cost:** Donations. **Phone:** (250) 763-9292.

GAMBLING ESTABLISHMENTS

- **Lake City Casino** is at 1300 Water St. **Hours:** Sun.-Thurs. 9 a.m.-2 a.m., Fri.-Sat. 9 a.m.-3 a.m. **Phone:** (250) 860-9467.

RECREATIONAL ACTIVITIES

Skiing

- **Big White Ski Resort** is 54 km (34 mi.) e. on Hwy. 33 at 5315 Big White Rd. **Hours:** Daily 8-4:30, mid-Nov. to mid-Apr. (weather permitting). **Phone:** (250) 765-3101 or (800) 663-2772.

WINERIES

- **CedarCreek Estate Winery** is 12 km (7 mi.) s. at 5445 Lakeshore Rd., following signs. **Hours:** Tastings daily 10-6, May-Oct.; 11-5, rest of year. Tours are given daily at 11, 1 and 3, May-Oct. Closed Jan. 1, Christmas and day after Christmas. **Phone:** (250) 764-8866, ext. 107, or (800) 730-9463 in Canada.

- **Quails' Gate Estate Winery** is at 3303 Boucherie Rd. at jct. Sunnyside Rd. **Hours:** Tastings daily 9:30-7, June 22-Sept. 1; 10-7, May 3-June 21 and Sept. 2-Oct. 14; 10-6, rest of year. Tours on the hour 11-4, June 22-Sept.1; at 11, 1 and 3, May 3-June 21 and Sept. 2-Oct. 14; at 11, rest of year. Phone ahead to confirm schedule. **Phone:** (250) 769-4451 or (800) 420-9463.

- **Summerhill Pyramid Organic Winery** is at 4870 Chute Lake Rd. **Hours:** Tastings daily 9-7, May 19-Oct. 9; 10-6, rest of year. **Phone:** (250) 764-8000 or (800) 667-3538.

(See map & index p. 290.)

ACCENT INNS (250)862-8888 **17**

Hotel
$89-$189

Address: 1140 Harvey Ave V1Y 6E7 **Location:** Corner of Hwy 97 N (Harvey Ave) and Gordon Dr. Across from shopping mall. **Facility:** 102 units, some efficiencies. 3 stories, exterior corridors. **Parking:** winter plug-ins. **Terms:** cancellation fee imposed. **Pool(s):** heated outdoor. **Activities:** sauna, whirlpool, limited exercise equipment. **Guest Services:** valet and coin laundry. **Free Special Amenities:** newspaper and high-speed Internet.

A VISTA VILLA STAY, DINE & TOUR (250)762-7837 **12**

Bed & Breakfast $259-$419 **Address:** 962 Ryder Dr V1Y 7T5 **Location:** Hwy 97 N (Harvey Ave), 1.6 mi (2 km) n on Spall St to Summit Rd, just e to Valley Rd, follow Valley Rd (which becomes Ryder Dr). Located in a residential area. **Facility:** Though classified as a B&B, this romantic adults-only retreat features lovely guest rooms, all with private jetted tub. Inquire about the on-site day spa treatments, geared to honeymooners and couples. 4 units. 2 stories (no elevator), interior/exterior corridors. **Terms:** closed 11/15-4/1, check-in 4 pm, 3 night minimum stay - seasonal, age restrictions may apply, 30 day cancellation notice-fee imposed. **Amenities:** safes. **Pool(s):** heated outdoor. **Activities:** sauna. **Guest Services:** complimentary laundry.

BEST WESTERN PLUS KELOWNA HOTEL & SUITES (250)860-1212 **23**

Hotel
$139-$219

AAA Benefit: Members save up to 20%, plus 10% bonus points with Best Western Rewards®.

Address: 2402 Hwy 97 N V1X 4J1 **Location:** 0.6 mi (1 km) s of jct Hwy 33 and 97 N (Harvey Ave); corner of Leckie Rd. **Facility:** 176 units, some two bedrooms, efficiencies and kitchens. 2-8 stories, interior corridors. **Terms:** check-in 4 pm. **Amenities:** video games (fee), high-speed Internet. **Pool(s):** heated indoor/outdoor. **Activities:** whirlpools, steamroom, exercise room, spa. **Guest Services:** valet and coin laundry. **Free Special Amenities:** full breakfast and high-speed Internet. *(See ad this page.)*

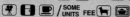

Plan.
Map.
Go.

TripTik® Travel Planner

Where premier mapping technology meets complete travel information. Only on AAA.com and CAA.ca.

▼ *See AAA listing this page* ▼

(See map & index p. 290.)

COMFORT SUITES
(250)861-1110 **16**

Hotel
$115-$289

Address: 2656 Hwy 97 N V1X 4J4 **Location:** Jct Hwy 97 N and 33, 0.5 mi (0.9 km) n. **Facility:** 83 units, some two bedrooms. 4 stories, interior corridors. **Parking:** winter plug-ins. **Terms:** cancellation fee imposed. **Amenities:** high-speed Internet, safes. **Pool(s):** heated indoor. **Activities:** whirlpool, waterslide, exercise room. **Guest Services:** valet and coin laundry. **Free Special Amenities: full breakfast and high-speed Internet.**

SAVE ECO [+] CALL &M 🔊🔊 BIZ 🛰 ✕ 🖥 🖼 💻 / SOME UNITS FEE 🐾

Kelowna's Newest Hotel. Choice Gold Award. FREE Hot Breakfast. Waterslide. Some Pet Rooms.

COMFORT SUITES

DELTA GRAND OKANAGAN RESORT & CONFERENCE CENTRE
(250)763-4500 **11**

Resort Hotel $119-$399 **Address:** 1310 Water St V1Y 9P3 **Location:** Hwy 97 (Harvey Ave), 0.6 mi (1 km) w along Water St. **Facility:** The hotel is undergoing guest room renovations. Property highlights include a full-service spa, a casino and fabulous waterfront views. Large condos with full kitchens available. 395 units, some kitchens and condominiums. 3-10 stories, interior corridors. **Parking:** on-site (fee) and valet. **Terms:** check-in 4 pm, 3 day cancellation notice, 5/1-9/30-fee imposed. **Amenities:** Some: high-speed Internet (fee), safes. **Dining:** Grand Bay Cafe, Hanna's Lounge & Grill, see separate listings. **Pool(s):** heated outdoor, heated indoor/outdoor. **Activities:** sauna, whirlpools, rental boats, rental canoes, rental paddleboats, recreation programs in summer, rental bicycles, spa. Fee: waterskiing. **Guest Services:** valet and coin laundry.

ECO 🌀 ⑪ 🐕 ⅄ CALL &M 🔊🔊 🐾 BIZ 🛰 ✕ 🎥 💻 / SOME UNITS FEE 🐾 🖥 🖼

DILWORTH INN
(250)762-9666 **24**

Motel
$79-$149

Address: 1755 Dilworth Dr V1Y 8R1 **Location:** Hwy 97 N (Harvey Ave), just w. Located behind White Spot Restaurant. **Facility:** 50 units, some efficiencies and kitchens. 3 stories (no elevator), interior corridors. **Terms:** cancellation fee imposed. **Pool(s):** heated indoor. **Activities:** sauna, whirlpool, limited exercise equipment. **Guest Services:** coin laundry. **Free Special Amenities: continental breakfast and high-speed Internet.**

SAVE [+] CALL &M 🔊🔊 🛰 ✕ 🖥 🖼 💻

ECONO LODGE
(250)762-3221 **19**

Motel
$89-$134

Address: 1780 Gordon Dr V1Y 3H2 **Location:** Hwy 97 N (Harvey Ave), just s. Across from mall. **Facility:** 43 units, some two bedrooms and kitchens. 2 stories (no elevator), exterior corridors. **Terms:** check-in 4 pm, cancellation fee imposed. **Pool(s):** heated indoor. **Activities:** whirlpool. **Guest Services:** coin laundry. **Free Special Amenities: continental breakfast and high-speed Internet.**

SAVE [+] 🔊🔊 🛰 ✕ 🖥 🖼 💻 / SOME UNITS FEE 🐾 🖼

Trust your vehicle to AAA/CAA
Approved Auto Repair facilities

FAIRFIELD INN & SUITES BY MARRIOTT KELOWNA
(250)763-2800 **20**

Hotel $125-$195 **Address:** 1655 Powick Rd V1X 4L1 **Location:** Just s of jct Hwy 97 N (Harvey Ave) and 33. **Facility:** 160 units. 4 stories, interior corridors. **Terms:** check-in 4 pm. **Amenities:** high-speed Internet. **Pool(s):** heated outdoor. **Activities:** whirlpool, waterslide, exercise room. **Guest Services:** valet and coin laundry.

AAA Benefit:
AAA hotel discounts
of 5% or more.

ECO [+] CALL &M 🔊🔊 BIZ 🛰 ✕ 🖥 🖼 💻 / SOME UNITS FEE 🐾 🖼

HOLIDAY INN EXPRESS KELOWNA CONFERENCE CENTRE
(250)763-0500 **22**

Hotel $129-$199 **Address:** 2429 Hwy 97 N V1X 4J2 **Location:** 0.6 mi (1 km) s of jct Hwy 97 N (Harvey Ave) and 33. **Facility:** 190 units. Interior corridors. **Terms:** check-in 4 pm. **Amenities:** Some: high-speed Internet. **Dining:** Ricky's All Day Grill, see separate listing. **Pool(s):** heated indoor. **Activities:** whirlpool, waterslide, exercise room. **Guest Services:** valet and coin laundry.

ECO ⑪ CALL &M 🔊🔊 BIZ 🛰 ✕ 🖥 🖼 💻

HOTEL ELDORADO
(250)763-7500 **28**

Hotel $109-$449 **Address:** 500 Cook Rd V1W 3G9 **Location:** Hwy 97 (Harvey Ave), 2.5 mi (4 km) s on Pandosy St (which becomes Lakeshore Rd). **Facility:** 53 units. 3-4 stories, interior corridors. **Terms:** 7 day cancellation notice-fee imposed, resort fee. **Amenities:** Some: high-speed Internet. **Dining:** Eldorado Dining Room & Bar, see separate listing. **Pool(s):** heated indoor. **Activities:** whirlpool, steamroom, rental boats, marina, exercise room. Fee: waterskiing. **Guest Services:** valet laundry.

ECO ⑪ ⅄ 🔊🔊 🛰 ✕ / SOME UNITS 🖥 🖼 💻

KELOWNA INN & SUITES
(250)762-2533 **14**

Motel $95-$195 **Address:** 1070 Harvey Ave V1Y 8S4 **Location:** Corner of Hwy 97 N (Harvey Ave) and Gordon Dr. Across from mall. **Facility:** 112 units, some two bedrooms, efficiencies and kitchens. 2 stories (no elevator), interior/exterior corridors. **Dining:** Mekong Restaurant, see separate listing. **Pool(s):** heated indoor. **Activities:** whirlpool, steamroom. **Guest Services:** coin laundry.

ECO ⑪ CALL &M 🔊🔊 🛰 🖥 🖼 💻 / SOME UNITS FEE 🐾 🖼

LAKE OKANAGAN RESORT
(250)769-3511 **10**

Resort Hotel $119-$299 **Address:** 2751 Westside Rd V1Z 3T1 **Location:** From Floating Bridge, 1.5 mi (2.5 km) sw on Hwy 97 (Harvey Ave), 10.6 mi (17 km) nw on Westside Rd (narrow winding road), follow signs. **Facility:** Located 20 to 25 minutes from town, this spread out, older property features a mix of accommodations—from standard hotel rooms to upscale condo units with full kitchens. 125 units, some condominiums. 3-6 stories, exterior corridors. **Terms:** check-in 4 pm, 2 night minimum stay - seasonal, 14 day cancellation notice, in summer-fee imposed. **Amenities:** Some: high-speed Internet. **Dining:** 3 restaurants. **Pool(s):** 3 heated outdoor. **Activities:** saunas, whirlpools, rental boats, rental canoes, rental paddleboats, 2 lighted tennis courts, recreation programs, hiking trails, jogging, playground, horseshoes, volleyball, limited exercise equipment, spa. Fee: marina, waterskiing, golf-9 holes. **Guest Services:** coin laundry.

ECO ⑪ ⅄ CALL &M 🔊🔊 🛰 ✕ 🖥 🖼 💻

MANTEO RESORT-WATERFRONT HOTEL & VILLAS
(250)860-1031 **27**

Resort Hotel $145-$740 **Address:** 3762 Lakeshore Rd V1W 3L4 **Location:** Hwy 97 (Harvey Ave), 2.5 mi (4 km) s on Pandosy St (which becomes Lakeshore Rd). **Facility:** Set along the lake, this resort offers extensive recreational facilities as well as large, upscale rooms ranging from studios to condo-style accommodations with cooking facilities. 101 units, some two bedrooms, three bedrooms and kitchens. 4 stories, interior/exterior corridors. **Terms:** check-in 4 pm, cancellation fee imposed. **Amenities:** safes. Some: high-speed Internet. **Dining:** Wild Apple Restaurant, see separate listing. **Pool(s):** 2 heated outdoor, heated indoor. **Activities:** whirlpools, waterslide, rental boats, rental canoes, rental paddleboats, boat dock, putting green, lighted tennis court, recreation programs in summer, playground, exercise room. Fee: massage. **Guest Services:** valet and coin laundry.

ECO ⑪ ⅄ CALL &M 🔊🔊 BIZ 🛰 ✕ 🖥 🖼 💻 / SOME UNITS 🖼

(See map & index p. 290.)

RAMADA HOTEL & CONFERENCE CENTRE
(250)860-9711 **25**

WWW **Hotel** $129-$239 **Address:** 2170 Harvey Ave V1Y 6G8 **Location:** Hwy 97 N (Harvey Ave) at Dilworth Dr. **Facility:** 135 units. 2-3 stories, interior/exterior corridors. **Terms:** check-in 4 pm. **Amenities:** video games (fee). **Pool(s):** heated indoor. **Activities:** whirlpool, exercise room. **Guest Services:** valet laundry.

[icons] / SOME UNITS FEE

RECREATION INN & SUITES
(250)860-3982 **21**

WWW
Motel
$69-$129

Address: 1891 Parkinson Way V1Y 7V6 **Location:** Hwy 97 (Harvey Ave), just n on Spall Rd. **Facility:** 49 units, some two bedrooms, efficiencies and kitchens. 2 stories (no elevator), exterior corridors. **Terms:** cancellation fee imposed. **Pool(s):** heated outdoor. **Activities:** sauna, whirlpool. **Guest Services:** coin laundry. **Free Special Amenities:** high-speed Internet.

[icons] / SOME UNITS FEE

THE ROYAL ANNE HOTEL
(250)763-2277 **13**

WWW
Hotel
$89-$199

Address: 348 Bernard Ave V1Y 6N5 **Location:** Corner of Pandosy St (which becomes Lakeshore Rd) and Bernard Ave; downtown. **Facility:** 64 units. 5 stories, interior corridors. **Activities:** saunas, limited exercise equipment. **Guest Services:** valet laundry. **Free Special Amenities:** expanded continental breakfast and high-speed Internet.

[icons] / SOME UNITS FEE

In the heart of downtown Kelowna. Free deluxe continental breakfast and high-speed internet.

SIESTA SUITES
(250)763-5013 **26**

WWW **Motel** $87-$279 **Address:** 3152 Lakeshore Rd V1W 3T1 **Location:** Hwy 97 (Harvey Ave), 1.8 mi (2.8 km) s on Pandosy St (which becomes Lakeshore Rd). **Facility:** 96 units, some two bedrooms, efficiencies and kitchens. 2 stories (no elevator), exterior corridors. **Terms:** 3 night minimum stay - seasonal and/or weekends. **Pool(s):** heated outdoor, heated indoor. **Activities:** sauna, whirlpools, exercise room. **Guest Services:** coin laundry.

[icons] / SOME UNITS

SUPER 8 KELOWNA
(250)762-8222 **18**

WWW **Motel** $81-$140 **Address:** 2592 Hwy 97 N V1X 4J4 **Location:** Jct Hwy 33, just n on Hwy 97 N (Harvey Ave). **Facility:** 61 units. 2 stories (no elevator), exterior corridors. **Terms:** cancellation fee imposed. **Pool(s):** heated outdoor. **Activities:** whirlpool.

[icons]

WHERE TO EAT

BOUCHONS BISTRO
250/763-6595 **10**

WWW **French. Fine Dining.** $20-$39 **AAA Inspector Notes:** Located a few blocks from the waterfront and downtown, the restaurant could have been lifted directly off the streets of Nice or Rennes. Offering classic bistro fare, meals are prepared using fresh, local ingredients. Cassoulet, the house specialty, is superb. The wine list consists of healthy doses of both French and local Okanagan wines. Decor features cork flooring, ochre walls, stained-glass panels and handwritten menus. Service is decidedly professional and many staff speak French. **Bar:** full bar. **Reservations:** suggested. **Address:** 105-1180 Sunset Dr V1Y 9W6 **Location:** Jct Water St. **Parking:** street only. [D] CALL

CABANA BAR AND GRILLE
250/763-1955 **25**

WWW **American. Casual Dining.** $15-$32 **AAA Inspector Notes:** This ultra-cool space has a menu that is extremely well prepared and flavorful with high-quality local products. The twists on the appetizers, burgers, pizzas and pastas as well as the meat and seafood entrées will tantalize your taste buds. Sauce choices include peppercorn and truffle butter and local apple barbecue. A trendy lounge for more casual dining is available, as is a huge patio with flaming grills. Cabana is open for lunch between the May and September long weekends. **Bar:** full bar. **Address:** 3799 Lakeshore Rd V1W 3K5 **Location:** Hwy 97 (Harvey Ave), 2.5 mi (4 km) s on Pandosy St (which becomes Lakeshore Rd). **Parking:** onsite and street. [D] CALL

CHRISTOPHER'S
250/861-3464 **15**

WW **Steak Seafood. Casual Dining.** $14-$46 **AAA Inspector Notes:** Patrons appreciate the charming restaurant's quaint dining room, personalized attention and fresh seafood. Selections also include steak, salad bar offerings and desserts. Large groups are accommodated at this local favorite. The atmosphere can be boisterous. **Bar:** full bar. **Reservations:** suggested. **Address:** 242 Lawrence Ave V1Y 6L3 **Location:** Downtown. **Parking:** street only. [D]

DAWETT FINE INDIAN CUISINE
250/717-1668 **13**

WW **Indian. Casual Dining.** $11-$16 **AAA Inspector Notes:** Considered one of the best Indian restaurants in the Okanagan Valley, this place doesn't disappoint with its traditional ethnic cuisine. Guests can tantalize their taste buds with tandoori chicken, chicken masala, pakoras and samosas, all made with top-quality ingredients. Vegetarians will find many choices of fine food to enjoy in a simple, comfortable dining room. **Bar:** full bar. **Reservations:** suggested. **Address:** 1435 Ellis St V1Y 2A3 **Location:** Between Bernard and Doyle aves; downtown. **Parking:** street only. [L] [D]

ELDORADO DINING ROOM & BAR
250/763-7500 **26**

WWW **Regional Canadian. Fine Dining.** $12-$46 **AAA Inspector Notes:** The casual yet elegant restaurant is right along the water and offers views of Lake Okanagan and the valley. Preparations of regionally diverse cuisine exceed expectations. In addition to seafood and pasta options, diners can select from several meat dishes. Known for its brunch, this place is a must stop for those visiting Kelowna. **Bar:** full bar. **Reservations:** suggested. **Address:** 500 Cook Rd V1W 3G9 **Location:** Hwy 97 (Harvey Ave), 2.5 mi (4 km) s on Pandosy St (which becomes Lakeshore Rd); in Hotel Eldorado. [B] [L] [D] CALL

GRAND BAY CAFE
250/869-3508 **11**

WWW **Pacific Northwest. Casual Dining.** $14-$34 **AAA Inspector Notes:** Offering some of the best warm-weather waterfront patio dining in the city, the restaurant's menu lines up a wide variety of local produce and the largest selection of B.C. wines. **Bar:** full bar. **Reservations:** suggested. **Address:** 1310 Water St V1Y 9P3 **Location:** Hwy 97 (Harvey Ave), 0.6 mi (1 km) w along Water St; in Delta Grand Okanagan Resort & Conference Centre. **Parking:** on-site (fee) and valet. [B] [L] [D] CALL

(See map & index p. 290.)

HANNA'S LOUNGE & GRILL   250/860-1266 12

▼▼▼ Pacific Northwest. Casual Dining. $11-$35 **AAA Inspector Notes:** Patrons can access the restaurant from the waterfront entrance or walk through the hotel. Inside is a modern, upbeat atmosphere and a menu that features a West Coast flair along with many local Okanagan wines. The 2nd floor location offers wonderful views of the lake and distant hills. You'll find parking at street meters or at the nearby yacht club pay lot. **Bar:** full bar. **Address:** 1352 Water St V1Y 9P3 **Location:** Hwy 97 (Harvey Ave), 0.6 mi (1 km) w along Water St; in Delta Grand Okanagan Resort & Conference Centre. **Parking:** street only.

L D CALL &M

THE JAMMERY   250/766-1139 9

▼▼ American. Casual Dining. $8-$14 **AAA Inspector Notes:** A play on the winery concept, the restaurant uses locally grown fruits in its creations and teaches guests about the jam that's being made on site. The menu lays out an excellent and fresh selection of breakfast choices, daily soups, salads, paninis, sandwiches and wraps and desserts. Afternoon tea also is served. The great choice of loose-leaf teas can be purchased in the gift shop along with a multitude of jams and jellies. **Address:** 8038 Hwy 97 N V1X 6A6 **Location:** Hwy 97 N (Harvey Ave), 7.4 mi (12 km) n.

B L CALL &M

JOEY RESTAURANTS   250/860-8999

▼▼ American. Casual Dining. $11-$32 **AAA Inspector Notes:** The cuisine blends Mediterranean and Asian cooking styles and emphasizes finger foods for sharing. Those who aren't big fans of tapas can consider full meal offerings centered on steaks and chops. **Bar:** full bar. **Address:** 300-2475 Hwy 97 N V1X 4J2 **Location:** Hwy 97 N (Harvey Ave); between Banks and Powick rds.

L D LATE CALL &M

MAMMA ROSA RESTAURANT   250/763-4114 17

▼▼ Italian. Casual Dining. $13-$34 **AAA Inspector Notes:** As the name suggests, the restaurant is known for Italian food prepared just as Mama might have made it. The extensive menu lists homemade dishes in various forms ranging from cannelloni and lasagna to manicotti and penne. Also tempting is a fine selection of pizzas. Red-and white-checked tablecloths and Italian décor lend to a cozy atmosphere. The service is super. **Bar:** full bar. **Reservations:** suggested. **Address:** 561 Lawrence Ave V1Y 6L8 **Location:** Between Bertram and Ellis sts; downtown. **Parking:** street only.

D CALL &M

THE MARMALADE CAT CAFE   250/861-4158 22

◆ Sandwiches Desserts. Quick Serve. $6-$9 **AAA Inspector Notes:** Many people accidentally discover this cute and tiny restaurant as they wander through the aisles of the gift shop that seems to surround it. Guests line up to order choices from a good selection of hearty and creative sandwiches, hot daily specials that seem to sell out quickly, and assorted small tasty desserts. **Address:** 2903 Pandosy St V1Y 1W1 **Location:** Hwy 97 (Harvey Ave), 1.8 mi (2.5 km) s; corner of West Ave. **Parking:** street only.

B L

MEKONG RESTAURANT   250/763-8000 19

▼▼ Chinese. Casual Dining. $8-$17 **AAA Inspector Notes:** The restaurant prepares fresh, mouthwatering Szechuan cuisine. Patrons are encouraged to ask about the signature deluxe meals, which involve ginger chicken or steak strips with black pepper sauce for two to 10 people. The decor is bright, fresh and contemporary. Peak meal times can be busy. **Bar:** full bar. **Address:** 1030 Harvey Ave V1Y 8S4 **Location:** Corner of Hwy 97 N (Harvey Ave) and Gordon Dr; in Kelowna Inn & Suites.

L D CALL &M

MINSTREL CAFE & BAR   250/764-2301 27

▼▼▼ Pacific Northwest. Casual Dining. $8-$30 **AAA Inspector Notes:** A little off the beaten path, the distinctive café is considered one of Kelowna's best-kept secrets, especially for lunch. Upon entry, guests notice a large tree decorated in lights on the large outdoor patio, while the inside dining room is set against soft olive walls adorned with original local art. The menu lists a wide range of tapas, soups, salads, pasta and pizza. Live entertainment is featured every weekend and some weekday evenings. **Bar:** full bar. **Reservations:** suggested. **Address:** 4638 Lakeshore Rd V1W 1X5 **Location:** Hwy 97 (Harvey Ave), 5.6 mi (9 km) s at Pandosy St (which becomes Lakeshore Rd).

L D CALL &M

MIZU JAPANESE RESTAURANT   250/862-8022 21

▼▼ Sushi. Casual Dining. $8-$14 **AAA Inspector Notes:** This eat-in/take-out eatery has just seven small tables for those who want to dine-in. Otherwise, you'll be joining the swarm of locals at the take-out counter. This is one seriously popular hole-in-the-wall sushi restaurant. **Address:** 2684 Pandosy St V1Y 1V6 **Location:** Hwy 97 (Harvey Ave), 1.8 mi (3 km) s on Pandosy St (which becomes Lakeshore Rd); in Southgate Plaza.

L D

MOXIE'S CLASSIC GRILL   250/861-6110

▼▼ American. Casual Dining. $10-$29 **AAA Inspector Notes:** This sleek, funky and popular restaurant presents an extensive menu of creatively prepared dishes, including pizza, pasta, rice, noodles, signature salads and burgers. Other menus include one for children and one for Sunday brunch. Lending to the upbeat, stylish decor are dark wood appointments and river rock fireplaces. **Bar:** full bar. **Address:** 1730 Cooper Rd V1Y 8V5 **Location:** Hwy 97 (Harvey Ave), just e; corner of Enterprise Way.

L D LATE CALL &M

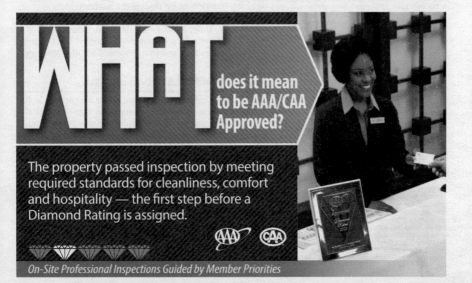

(See map & index p. 290.)

PEARSON'S EUROPEAN DELI   250/762-0800   (20)
▼ Deli. Quick Serve. $7-$12 **AAA Inspector Notes:** When diners enter the small delicatessen they are hit with the smell of fresh bread. Before them is a case of salads ranging from pasta to curried chicken. Behind the counter is a chalkboard with several sandwich options, as well as such listings as cabbage rolls and pierogies. Made on thick slabs of fresh bread, sandwiches are incredible. This spot fits the bill for a healthy, quick meal. **Address:** 2070 Harvey Ave, Unit 30 V1Y 8P8 **Location:** On Hwy 97 S; jct Cooper Rd; in strip mall. [L]

PHEASANT & QUAIL PUB   250/860-6606   (23)
▼▼ American. Casual Dining. $10-$26 **AAA Inspector Notes:** Modeled after an English ale house, the cozy restaurant invites patrons to drop in for a pint and some good pub food. The lounge area features some plush armchairs and banquettes for relaxing in. Fish and chips, sandwiches, burgers, pizza, pastas and salads make up the menu, and the friendly servers share information about the local brews. **Bar:** full bar. **Address:** 3110 Lakeshore Rd V1W 3T1 **Location:** 1.8 mi (3 km) s on Pandosy St (which becomes Lakeshore Rd). [L] [D] CALL [&M]

POPPADOMS   778/753-5563   (14)
▼▼ Indian. Casual Dining. $10-$27 **AAA Inspector Notes:** Fresh, contemporary Indian décor and an authentic menu that includes a few modern twists describes this bustling place. Food is fresh and tasty with an extensive choice of items to leave you wanting more. Appetizers include a special chaat with prawns, avocado, chicken and fish; mulligatawny vegetable soup; and Indian salad. You will find all the classic Indian entrées as well as such signature items as masala fish and chips with poppadom fries, and lamb popsicles in creamy fenugreek curry. **Bar:** full bar. **Reservations:** suggested. **Address:** 948 McCurdy Rd, Unit 118 V1X 2P7 **Location:** Jct Trans-Canada Hwy 1 and 33, 1 mi (1.6 km) ne, then just e; in McCurdy Corner shopping center. [L] [D] CALL [&M]

RICKY'S ALL DAY GRILL   250/763-4141
▼▼ American. Family Dining. $9-$26 **AAA Inspector Notes:** The comfortable eatery, which employs friendly servers, presents a varied menu that includes pasta dishes, wraps, omelets, stir-fry preparations and burgers. Portions are generous. Children's and senior selections are offered. Guests can request seating in a booth or at a table. **Bar:** full bar. **Address:** 2435 Hwy 97 N V1X 4J2 **Location:** 0.6 mi (1 km) s of jct Hwy 97 N (Harvey Ave) and 33; in Holiday Inn Express Kelowna Conference Centre. [B] [L] [D] CALL [&M]

RIC'S GRILL   250/869-1586
▼▼ Steak Seafood. Casual Dining. $14-$37 **AAA Inspector Notes:** "Funky and modern" describes the decor and the food at this upscale steakhouse, which bustles with activity. Steaks are well worth it, but then again, so are the salmon, chicken and pasta dishes. A wide variety of distinctive appetizers rounds out the menu. Servers are friendly and attentive. **Bar:** full bar. **Reservations:** suggested. **Address:** 210 Lawrence Ave V1Y 6L3 **Location:** Corner of Lawrence Ave and Abbott St; downtown. **Parking:** street only. [L] [D] CALL [&M]

SUMMERHILL SUNSET BISTRO   250/764-8000   (28)
▼▼ Pacific Northwest. Casual Dining. $10-$38 **AAA Inspector Notes:** Overlooking the Okanagan Valley, the winery restaurant affords spectacular views. Guests can make their way to the eatery after a tour and tasting, or come directly for a special meal. Several menu items incorporate regional ingredients and a Bavarian smokehouse cooking technique. Starters are large enough to share. **Bar:** wine only. **Reservations:** suggested. **Address:** 4870 Chute Lake Rd V1W 4M3 **Location:** 9 mi (15 km) e at Pandosy St (which becomes Lakeshore Rd), just s at Chute Lake Rd, follow signs. [L] [D] CALL [&M]

WILD APPLE RESTAURANT   250/860-4488   (24)
▼▼▼ Pacific Northwest. Casual Dining. $12-$35 **AAA Inspector Notes:** A fresh, bright, contemporary dining room awaits guests of the restaurant along the waterfront. Featuring an open-concept kitchen and light, bright colors, the dining room transforms in the evening to become a bit more intimate. Upbeat, creative meals include pasta and sandwiches at lunch, and creative seafood and meat preparations at dinner. **Bar:** full bar. **Reservations:** suggested. **Address:** 3762 Lakeshore Rd V1W 3L4 **Location:** Hwy 97 (Harvey Ave), 2.5 mi (4 km) s on Pandosy St (which becomes Lakeshore Rd); in Manteo Resort-Waterfront Hotel & Villas. [B] [L] [D] CALL [&M]

YAMAS TAVERNA GREEK RESTAURANT   250/763-5823   (18)
▼▼ Greek. Casual Dining. $11-$35 **AAA Inspector Notes:** A typical and traditional Greek feel envelops the downtown restaurant, which is popular with the business crowd at lunch. Guests can choose from the all-you-can-eat lunch buffet or from delicious entrees on the menu. **Bar:** full bar. **Reservations:** suggested. **Address:** 1630 Ellis St V1Y 8L1 **Location:** Hwy 97 (Harvey Ave), just w. **Parking:** street only. [L] [D] CALL [&M]

THE YELLOWHOUSE RESTAURANT   250/763-5136   (16)
▼▼▼ Pacific Northwest. Fine Dining. $12-$45 **AAA Inspector Notes:** Located in a Victorian heritage house downtown, guests will experience a warm welcome and be able to enjoy a delicious menu where the freshest ingredients are used and everything is made from scratch in house. Taste buds will be tantalized with entrées such as duck with pecan, spinach and thyme stuffing or the signature seafood orechiette with lemon pepper dill cream. Service is attentive and professional. **Bar:** full bar. **Reservations:** suggested. **Address:** 526 Lawrence Ave V1Y 6L7 **Location:** Hwy 97 (Harvey Ave), just n on Bertram St, then just w; downtown. **Parking:** street only. [L] [D] CALL [&M]

KEREMEOS (D-8) pop. 1,330, elev. 430m/1,414'

The rich soil and desert climate of the Similkameen Valley drew early settlers, who planted the first fruit trees there in 1880. Today Keremeos is considered one of the best fruit-growing regions in British Columbia. Cherries, apples, grapes, peaches and apricots are among the area's bounties.

Keremeos Visitor Centre: 417 7th Ave., Keremeos, BC, Canada V0X 1N0. **Phone:** (250) 499-5225.

THE GRIST MILL AND GARDENS AT KEREMEOS is 1.5 km (.9 mi.) n.e. on Hwy. 3A, then .8 km (.5 mi.) e. on Upper Bench Rd. Demonstrations of the principles of milling and restoration are offered at this 1877 flour mill, which features a working waterwheel and flume. A visitor center provides a schedule of living-history presentations for the Apple House Theatre and the summer kitchen. On the grounds are Victorian-era gardens, an heirloom apple orchard, heritage wheat fields and a tearoom.

Time: Allow 1 hour minimum. **Hours:** Daily 9-4, Victoria Day-Thanksgiving Sunday. **Cost:** $6; $5 (ages 5-19 and 65+). **Phone:** (250) 499-2888. [▲]

KIMBERLEY (C-11) pop. 6,652

Kimberley is a winter sports center with a Bavarian theme and a pedestrian mall—the Platzl—complete with wandering minstrels and a huge cuckoo clock. The Kimberley Community Gardens present colorful views June through October.

Built on the slopes of Sullivan and North Star hills, Kimberley is one of Canada's highest cities. It is perhaps best known as the site of the Sullivan Mine, one of the world's largest underground silver, lead and zinc mines. The mine closed in 2001 after 92 years of production, yielding more than $20 billion in ore.

In keeping with the Bavarian theme, the city presents the 🚲 Kimberley Old Time Accordion Championships for a week each year in early July.

Kimberley Visitor Centre: 270 Kimberley Ave., Kimberley, BC, Canada V1A 0A3. **Phone:** (250) 427-3666 or (866) 913-3666.

KIMBERLEY HERITAGE MUSEUM is in the Platzl at 105 Spokane St. Permanent and changing exhibits depict local history and the legacy of mining in the area. Archives are available for research by request. **Hours:** Tues.-Sat. 9-4:30, July-Aug.; Mon.-Fri. 1-4, rest of year. Closed last two weeks of Dec. and holidays except July 1. **Cost:** Donations. Walking guide $6. **Phone:** (250) 427-7510.

KIMBERLEY'S UNDERGROUND MINING RAILWAY departs the lower train station, 2 blks. n.w.

of the Platzl. The railway offers narrated 1-hour train rides, transporting passengers through the Mark Creek Valley on a narrow-gauge mine track. Interactive mining displays are offered in an underground tunnel.

Hours: Departures daily at 11, 1 and 3, July 1-Labour Day weekend; Sat.-Sun. at 11, 1 and 3, Victoria Day-June 30. Phone ahead to confirm schedule. **Cost:** $20; $15 (ages 13-18); $8 (ages 4-12). **Phone:** (250) 427-0022.

RECREATIONAL ACTIVITIES
Skiing

- **Kimberley Alpine Resort** is above town via Gerry Sorenson Way to 301 North Star Blvd. Other activities are offered. **Hours:** Daily 9-4, mid-Dec. to mid-Apr. **Phone:** (250) 427-4881 or (800) 258-7669.

TRICKLE CREEK LODGE   (250)427-5175

Extended Stay Hotel
$163-$272

Address: 500 Stemwinder Dr V1A 2Y6 **Location:** From Gerry Sorenson Way, follow signs. **Facility:** 80 kitchen units, some two bedrooms. 3 stories, interior corridors. **Terms:** check-in 4 pm, 7 day cancellation notice-fee imposed. **Pool(s):** heated outdoor. **Activities:** whirlpools, hiking trails, exercise room. *Fee:* golf-18 holes, downhill skiing. **Guest Services:** coin laundry.

THE BEAN TREE   250/427-7889

Sandwiches. Quick Serve. $6-$7 **AAA Inspector Notes:** This casual spot offers counter service for a quick lunch or just cup of coffee or tea. Homemade fresh soups, salads, interesting grilled sandwiches (like the grilled Marrakesh on rye), wraps and baked goodies are the mainstay here. Beverages range from 15 types of tea to Italian sodas, wine, beer and, of course, coffee. Entertainment is on tap some evenings. **Bar:** beer & wine. **Address:** 295 Spokane St V1A 2E6 **Location:** Hwy 95A, just n on Wallinger Ave. **Parking:** street only.

KITIMAT (E-2) pop. 8,335, elev. 130m/426'

Kitimat is a planned city built in the early 1950s by Alcan Smelters and Chemicals Ltd. The company chose the wilderness site for a new plant because of the area's deepwater harbor, flat land and hydroelectric plant.

Kitimat Chamber of Commerce: 2109 Forest Ave., P.O. Box 214, Kitimat, BC, Canada V8C 2G7. **Phone:** (250) 632-6294 or (800) 664-6554.

KOOTENAY NATIONAL PARK (A-11)

Elevations in the park range from 901 metres (2,956 ft.) at the park's west gate to 3,424 metres (11,235 ft.) at Deltaform Mountain. Refer to CAA/AAA maps for additional elevation information.

Straddling the Banff-Windermere Highway (Hwy. 93) from the Continental Divide to the Rocky Mountain Trench, Kootenay National Park encompasses 1,406 square kilometres (543 sq. mi.) of Rocky Mountain landscape. Following the Vermilion and Kootenay river valleys, this slender 94-kilometre-long (63-mi.) park embraces several significant geologic features and is part of the Canadian Rocky Mountain Parks UNESCO World Heritage Site.

Kootenay's western entrance provides one of the most dramatic gateways to any of the national parks in Canada. The highway clings to a sheer cliff before snaking through a narrow gorge and running along an iron-red rock face where bighorn sheep are a frequent sight. Visitors driving this scenic highway will see dramatic landscapes as they travel the Golden Triangle or Hot Springs routes.

Wildfires and prescribed burns in the northern part of the park have left charred trees visible from the road, but nature's renewal is visible through stunning wildflower displays in the burn areas during the summer.

Extensive faults created two of the park's most significant features: the Radium Hot Springs and the Paint Pots. Located in the southern end of the park, Radium Hot Springs is a result of rainwater and runoff being vaporized deep underground. The steam returns to the surface and is condensed in these clear, odourless springs. First used by the indigenous peoples in the area, the hot springs were later popularized by health buffs at the turn of the 20th century.

At the opposite end of the park are the Paint Pots, cold springs with a spiritual significance to the region's inhabitants. These iron-rich mineral springs bubble up into small, emerald green pools before staining the surrounding earth red. The Siksika, Nakoda and Ktunaxa First Nations once used the bright bronze mud called ochre to decorate their homes and draw the rock paintings once visible near Sinclair Canyon.

Good grazing conditions bring herds of bighorn sheep. Bears, deer, mountain goats, mountain goats, elk and countless species of birds are commonly seen throughout the park.

General Information and Activities

The park is open year-round, and its three main campgrounds—Redstreak, Marble Canyon and McLeod Meadows—are open during the summer months, with Redstreak staying open the longest. In the winter season, camping is available at the Dolly Varden campground. Phone ahead to confirm schedule.

Kootenay provides a variety of trails ranging from easy hikes to multiday backcountry treks. All backcountry campers must obtain a wilderness pass. Information about trails, park features and facilities can be obtained from the visitor centre in the village of Radium Hot Springs from the Victoria Day weekend through Labour Day and at the park's west gate during the remainder of the year.

Nonmotorized watercraft are permitted on all lakes and rivers in the park. *See Recreation Areas Chart.*

ADMISSION to the park is $9.80; $8.30 (ages 65+); $4.90 (ages 6-16); $19.60 (all occupants of a private vehicle with up to seven people). **Cards:** AX, MC, VI.

PETS must be leashed at all times. Pets are permitted in the backcountry overnight.

ADDRESS inquiries to the Superintendent, Kootenay National Park, Box 220, Radium Hot Springs, BC, Canada V0A 1M0; phone (250) 347-9505.

MARBLE CANYON is on Hwy. 93 at the northern end of Kootenay National Park and close to the Alberta border. The walls of marblelike gray limestone make this one of the most beautiful canyons in the Rockies. Tokumm Creek has cut a sheer, narrow cleft to the depth of about 40 metres (130 ft.). A self-guiding trail follows the top edge of the canyon and leads to a waterfall. Interpretive signs describe the power of water in shaping the canyon's features. **Time:** Allow 30 minutes minimum.

RADIUM HOT SPRINGS is just n. of the w. entrance to Kootenay National Park. Water temperatures range from 37 to 40 C (98 to 104 F). There is a hot pool, a cool pool and a 372-square-metre (4,000-sq.-ft.) day spa. Iron oxide also colors the towering sandstone cliffs, giving a perpetual sunset quality. *See Recreation Areas Chart.*

Hours: Pools open daily 9 a.m.-11 p.m., mid-May to mid-Oct.; Sun.-Thurs. noon-9, Fri.-Sat. noon-10, rest of year. **Cost:** $6.30; $5.40 (ages 3-17 and 65+); $19.10 (family, two adults and two children; each additional child $3.40). **Phone:** (250) 347-9331, (250) 343-6783 in southeastern British Columbia or (888) 347-9331.

▲ 🍴 ⊗ 🏕 🏕

LADYSMITH (G-10) pop. 7,921, elev. 40m/131'

On the 49th parallel, Ladysmith is noted for its scenic position between mountain and sea. Founded during the Boer War, Ladysmith was named for a sister city in South Africa. Transfer Beach Park offers a playground, picnic tables and a swimming area watched by lifeguards.

Ladysmith Visitor Centre: 411 B 1st Ave., Ladysmith, BC, Canada V9G 1A4. **Phone:** (250) 245-2112.

LAKE COWICHAN (G-10) pop. 2,974

KAATZA STATION MUSEUM AND ARCHIVES is at 125 S. Shore Rd. Housed in the renovated Esquimalt and Nanaimo railway station, the museum features murals, exhibits, photographs and archives pertaining to various industries as well as pioneer life in the area. **Time:** Allow 30 minutes minimum. **Hours:** Daily 10-4, Jan. 16-Dec. 14. Closed winter statutory holidays. Phone ahead to confirm schedule. **Cost:** Donations. **Phone:** (250) 749-6142.

LANGLEY (H-11) pop. 25,081, elev. 10m/33'
• Restaurants p. 271
• Hotels & Restaurants map & index p. 368
• Part of Vancouver area — see map p. 343

Langley, the site of a Hudson's Bay Co. fort built in 1840 *(see Fort Langley National Historic Site p. 238)*, is also an important farming and wine-growing region. Orchards, berry farms, horse ranches, vineyards and lavender and heirloom vegetable farms make a patchwork of the countryside.

The city's position on the banks of the Fraser River makes it an easy proposition to enjoy water-based activities. Kayaks and voyageur canoes can be rented and launched at the Fort Langley Marina.

(See map & index p. 368.)

Langley Visitor Centre: 7888 200th St., Unit 2, Langley, BC, Canada V2Y 3J4. **Phone:** (604) 888-1477 or (888) 788-1477.

CANADIAN MUSEUM OF FLIGHT is at Hangar 3, 5333 216th St., at the Langley airport. The museum, which is devoted to restoring, preserving and showcasing the history of Canadian aviation, features a collection of more than 25 aircraft, both static and flying.

Aircraft include a World War II Handley Page Hampden bomber (said to be the only one on display in the world), a Lockheed T-33 Silver Star trainer, helicopters and jets. The aircraft and artifacts displayed represent Canada's aviation heritage 1909 to the present day. A collection of other aviation memorabilia as well as a children's activity center is available. Exhibits are inside and outside; dress according to weather.

Time: Allow 30 minutes minimum. **Hours:** Daily 10-4. Closed Jan. 1, Christmas Eve, Christmas and day after Christmas. **Cost:** $10; $7 (ages 6-15 and 60+); $25 (family, two adults and up to five children). **Phone:** (604) 532-0035.

GAMBLING ESTABLISHMENTS

- **Cascades Casino** is at 20393 Fraser Hwy. **Hours:** Daily 24 hours. **Phone:** (604) 530-2211.

WINERIES

- **Domaine de Chaberton Estate Winery** is at 1064 216th St. **Hours:** Tastings are given Mon.-Sat. 10-6, Sun. 11-6. Closed Jan. 1, Christmas and day after Christmas. **Phone:** (604) 530-1736 or (888) 332-9463.

BEST WESTERN PLUS LANGLEY INN
(604)530-9311

Hotel
S117-S142

 AAA Benefit: Members save up to 20%, plus 10% bonus points with Best Western Rewards®.

Address: 5978 Glover Rd V3A 4H9 **Location:** Trans-Canada Hwy 1 exit 66 (232nd St), 3.6 mi (6 km) s, follow signs. **Facility:** 78 units, some two bedrooms, efficiencies and kitchens. 2 stories, interior corridors. **Terms:** 2 night minimum stay - seasonal. **Pool(s):** heated indoor. **Activities:** whirlpool, limited exercise equipment. **Guest Services:** valet and coin laundry. **Free Special Amenities: expanded continental breakfast and high-speed Internet.** (See ad this page.)

CANADAS BEST VALUE INN LANGLEY   (604)534-9238

Motel $69-$99 **Address:** 19682 Fraser Hwy V3A 4C7 **Location:** Trans-Canada Hwy 1 exit 58 (200th St/Langley City), 3.1 mi (5 km) s on 200th St, 0.6 mi (1 km) w on Hwy 10, then just w. **Facility:** 55 units, some kitchens. 1 story, exterior corridors. **Guest Services:** coin laundry.

▼ See AAA listing this page ▼

Visit your AAA/CAA Travel office to book
a AAA Vacations® Disney package

(See map & index p. 368.)

COAST HOTEL & CONVENTION CENTRE
(604)530-1500

Hotel
$112-$149

Address: 20393 Fraser Hwy V3A 7N2 **Location:** Trans-Canada Hwy 1 exit 58 (200th St/Langley City), 3.9 mi (6.3 km) s on 200th St, then just e. **Facility:** The hotel is attached to a large casino where the excitement never ends. There's a 420-seat theater featuring various shows plus huge convention space. 77 units. 6 stories, interior corridors. **Amenities:** high-speed Internet. **Dining:** 2 restaurants. **Activities:** spa. **Guest Services:** valet laundry. **Free Special Amenities:** continental breakfast and room upgrade (subject to availability with advance reservations).

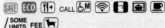

DAYS INN & SUITES LANGLEY
(604)539-0100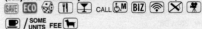

Hotel
$75-$119

Address: 20250 Logan Ave V3A 4L6 **Location:** Trans-Canada Hwy 1 exit 58 (200th St/Langley City), 3.9 mi (6.3 km) s on 200th St, then just e. **Facility:** 62 units. 4 stories, interior corridors. **Terms:** cancellation fee imposed. **Activities:** limited exercise equipment. **Guest Services:** coin laundry. **Free Special Amenities:** expanded continental breakfast and early check-in/late check-out.

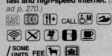

HOLIDAY INN EXPRESS HOTEL & SUITES LANGLEY
(604)882-2000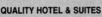

Hotel
$109-$169

Address: 8750 204th St V1M 2Y5 **Location:** Trans-Canada Hwy 1 exit 58 (200th St/Langley City), just e on 88th Ave. **Facility:** 85 units. 4 stories, interior corridors. **Amenities:** high-speed Internet. **Pool(s):** heated indoor. **Activities:** sauna, whirlpool, steamroom, exercise room. **Guest Services:** valet and coin laundry. **Free Special Amenities:** full breakfast and high-speed Internet. (See ad p. 270.)

QUALITY HOTEL & SUITES
(604)534-5110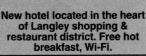

Hotel
$79-$109

Address: 6465 201st St V2Y 0G8 **Location:** From Trans Canada Hwy 1 exit 58, 1.8 mi (3 km) s on 200th St, just e on 64 Ave, then just s. **Facility:** 50 units. 4 stories, interior corridors. **Amenities:** Some: high-speed Internet. **Activities:** limited exercise equipment. **Guest Services:** coin laundry. **Free Special Amenities:** full breakfast and high-speed Internet.

New hotel located in the heart of Langley shopping & restaurant district. Free hot breakfast, Wi-Fi.

SANDMAN HOTEL LANGLEY
(604)888-7263

Hotel $109-$139 **Address:** 8855 202nd St V1M 2N9 **Location:** Trans-Canada Hwy 1 exit 58 (200th St/Langley City), just e on 88th Ave. **Facility:** 144 units, some efficiencies. 4 stories, interior corridors. **Activities:** limited exercise equipment. **Guest Services:** valet laundry.

WHERE TO EAT

RICKY'S ALL DAY GRILL
American. Casual Dining. $11-$27 **AAA Inspector Notes:** The comfortable eatery, which employs friendly servers, presents a varied menu that includes pasta dishes, wraps, omelets, stir-fry preparations and burgers. Portions are generous. Children's and senior selections are offered. Guests can request seating in a booth or at a table. **Bar:** full bar. B L D CALL

For additional information, visit AAA.com

LOCATIONS:
Address: 8720 204th St V3A 8G5 **Location:** Trans-Canada Hwy 1 exit 58 (200th St/Langley City), just e on 88th Ave. **Phone:** 604/888-4211
Address: 22314 Fraser Hwy V3A 8M6 **Location:** Between 222nd and 223A sts. **Phone:** 604/530-4317

SONOMA GRILL
604/534-2104 56
Continental. Casual Dining. $10-$30 **AAA Inspector Notes:** Named after the famous wine valley in Northern California, the Sonoma Grill features seafood, pasta, chicken, steak, pork and their popular schnitzels. The theme of this restaurant is "Try, Taste, Indulge". **Bar:** full bar. **Reservations:** suggested. **Address:** 20598 Fraser Hwy V3A 4G2 **Location:** Corner of Fraser Hwy and 206th St; downtown. L D CALL

LILLOOET (B-7) pop. 2,322, elev. 290m/951'

Lillooet, on the Fraser River, marked the first leg of the Cariboo Waggon Road and was therefore sometimes referred to as "Mile 0." The trail reached north to such destinations as 100 Mile House and 150 Mile House, named for their distances from the start of the trail. In 1859, during the Cariboo Gold Rush, the 15,000 inhabitants of Lillooet made it the most populous city north of San Francisco and west of Chicago. The surrounding area now is of particular interest to rockhounds.

LILLOOET MUSEUM AND VISITOR CENTRE is at 790 Main St. Displays in the former Anglican church include local pioneer relics, farm equipment, Indian artifacts, Chinese utensils and late 19th-century rooms. Gold rush, early pioneer and First Nations displays also are available. The museum houses the newspaper equipment collection of Margaret "Ma" Murray, Lillooet's beloved publisher. **Hours:** Daily 9-5, July-Aug.; Tues.-Sat. 10-4, Apr.-June and Sept.-Oct. **Cost:** Donations. **Phone:** (250) 256-4308.

MIYAZAKI HOUSE is at 643 Russell Ln., near jct. Main St. and 6th Ave., following signs. Originally owned by Caspar and Cerise Phair, the late 19th-century house was built in the same architectural style as Mrs. Phair's family home in Ireland. In the 1940s Dr. Masajiro Miyazaki and his family purchased the house. Visitors will learn about this family's history, including a period when the doctor treated residents of a local Japanese internment camp.

Tours: Guided tours are available. **Time:** Allow 30 minutes minimum. **Hours:** Tues.-Sat. 10-4:30, June-Aug.; Mon.-Fri. 11-3, rest of year. **Cost:** Donations. **Phone:** (250) 256-6808, or (250) 256-4289 for tour appointments.

LYTTON (B-7) pop. 228, elev. 199m/650'

At the junction of the Thompson and Fraser rivers, Lytton derives its livelihood from its location. Native peoples harvested salmon from this river junction. Their trail along the Fraser became a major route to the gold fields, with Lytton as a base of supplies. This community calls itself the Rafting Capital of Canada and claims some of the warmest weather in the country.

Lytton & District Chamber of Commerce: 400 Fraser St., P.O. Box 460, Lytton, BC, Canada V0K 1Z0. **Phone:** (250) 455-2523.

RECREATIONAL ACTIVITIES
White-water Rafting

• **Kumsheen Rafting Resort** is 6 km (4 mi.) n.e. on Trans-Canada Hwy. Other activities are offered. **Hours:** Trips operate daily 8-8, May-Sept. **Phone:** (250) 455-2296 or (800) 663-6667.

MADEIRA PARK

PAINTED BOAT RESORT SPA & MARINA   604/883-2456

▼▼▼ **Vacation Rental Condominium** $175-$390 **Address:** 12849 Lagoon Rd V0N 2H0 **Location:** Hwy 101, just w on Gonzales Rd, then just s, follow signs. **Facility:** This new condominium complex overlooks a spectacular private marina. All of the units are two bedrooms, but some feature an extra loft or den. The rates are based on four adults. 30 condominiums. 2-3 stories (no elevator), exterior corridors. **Terms:** check-in 4 pm, 3 day cancellation notice. **Amenities:** high-speed Internet. **Dining:** The Restaurant at Painted Boat, see separate listing. **Pool(s):** heated outdoor. **Activities:** whirlpool, exercise room, spa. **Guest Services:** complimentary laundry.

▢▢▢▢▢▢▢ / SOME UNITS FEE ▢

SUNSHINE COAST RESORT & MARINA   (604)883-9177

▼▼▼ **Vacation Rental Condominium** $99-$215 **Address:** 12695 Sunshine Coast Hwy V0N 2H0 **Location:** Just n of Madeira Park Rd, follow signs. **Facility:** On the beautiful Sunshine Coast, this accommodation offers spacious suites with either a soaker tub or a whirlpool bath. All the rooms sit high on a hillside offering stunning views of the harbor and marina. 17 units, some cottages and condominiums. 3 stories, interior/exterior corridors. **Terms:** 2 night minimum stay - seasonal and/or weekends, 21 day cancellation notice-fee imposed. **Amenities:** high-speed Internet. **Activities:** sauna, whirlpool, rental boats, rental canoes, fishing. *Fee:* marina, charter fishing. **Guest Services:** coin laundry.

CALL ▢▢▢▢▢▢ / SOME UNITS FEE ▢ ▢

■■■ **WHERE TO EAT** ■■■

THE RESTAURANT AT PAINTED BOAT   604/883-3000

▼▼▼ Pacific Northwest. Fine Dining. $12-$35 **AAA Inspector Notes:** This contemporary, casually elegant bistro is open for lunch during the spring and summer months and dinner nightly. The menu focuses on fresh ingredients from the Sunshine Coast, sustainable seafood and free-range chicken and beef. The management company that owns the restaurant also owns a bison ranch in Alberta; look for bison on the menu. The views of the private marina from the waterfront deck, which opens up on warm sunny evenings, are stunning. **Bar:** full bar. **Reservations:** suggested. **Address:** 12849 Lagoon Rd V0N 2H0 **Location:** Hwy 101, just w on Gonzales Rd, just s, follow signs; in Painted Boat Resort Spa & Marina. ▢

MALAHAT
• **Part of Victoria area — see map p. 397**

MALAHAT MOUNTAIN INN   250/478-1979

▼▼ ◆ Regional Canadian. Casual Dining. $10-$30 **AAA Inspector Notes:** Gourmet cuisine with a Regional Canadian influence is served in a relaxed setting. Perched 600 feet above Saanich Inlet, the dining room and patio deck afford stunning mountain and ocean views. **Bar:** full bar. **Reservations:** suggested. **Address:** 265 Trans-Canada Hwy 1 V0R 2L0 **Location:** Trans-Canada Hwy 1, 16 mi (26 km) n of Victoria, watch for signs. ▢ ▢ ▢

MAPLE RIDGE (H-11) pop. 76,052, elev. 30m/98'
• **Part of Vancouver area — see map p. 343**

Maple Ridge lies on the north shore of the Fraser River, with the Coast Mountains to the north and the Stave and Pitt Rivers forming its east and west boundaries. Snow-capped peaks overlook this Fraser Valley community.

The Fraser River Heritage Walk, which starts at Port Haney Wharf, passes many of the town's notable spots. The Haney House at 11612 224th St. was built in 1876 and contains many furnishings and artifacts owned by three generations of the Haney family; phone (604) 463-1377. Displays at Maple Ridge Museum, 22520 116th Ave., reflect the history and geography of the area; phone (604) 463-5311.

Kanaka Creek Regional Park *(see Recreation Areas Chart)* offers hiking and horseback riding trails as well as canoeing, kayaking, fishing and picnic facilities. A fish hatchery is on the grounds. Phone (604) 530-4983. Maple Ridge also has a large per capita horse population and an extensive riding trail system.

Tourism Maple Ridge and Pitt Meadows: 12492 Harris Rd., Pitt Meadows, BC, Canada V3Y 2J4. **Phone:** (604) 460-8300, or (877) 465-8300 in Canada.

UBC MALCOLM KNAPP RESEARCH FOREST is n. at 14500 Silver Valley Rd. Trails of various lengths lead visitors on tours through the forest, a research facility of the University of British Columbia. Bicycles, motorbikes, pets and horses are not permitted. **Hours:** Forest daily dawn-dusk. Office open Mon.-Fri. 8-4. Closed major holidays. Phone ahead to confirm schedule. **Cost:** Free. **Phone:** (604) 463-8148.

BEST WESTERN MAPLE RIDGE   (604)467-1511

Motel $90-$130   **AAA Benefit:** Members save up to 20%, plus 10% bonus points with Best Western Rewards®.

Address: 21650 Lougheed Hwy V2X 2S1 **Location:** 1.2 mi (2 km) w on Lougheed Hwy (Hwy 7). **Facility:** 56 units, some efficiencies. 2 stories, interior corridors. **Terms:** cancellation fee imposed. **Pool(s):** heated indoor. **Activities:** sauna, whirlpool, exercise room. **Guest Services:** coin laundry. **Free Special Amenities:** continental breakfast and high-speed Internet.

▢▢ CALL ▢▢▢▢▢▢ / SOME UNITS ▢

QUALITY INN

(604)463-5111

Hotel
$89-$209

Address: 21735 Lougheed Hwy V2X 2S2 **Location:** 1.2 mi (2 km) w on Lougheed Hwy (Hwy 7). **Facility:** 61 units. 2 stories (no elevator), exterior corridors. **Terms:** cancellation fee imposed. **Amenities:** high-speed Internet. **Activities:** limited exercise equipment. **Guest Services:** valet and coin laundry. **Free Special Amenities: continental breakfast and early check-in/late check-out.**

WHERE TO EAT

SWISS CHALET   604/460-8033

Chicken. Casual Dining. $9-$22 **AAA Inspector Notes:** The popular restaurant is known for its rotisserie chicken and ribs and the tangy Chalet sauce that gives food its special zip. Diners munch on a half or quarter chicken with sides such as steamed vegetables, fries, baked potatoes and salads. Lunch guests often go for the great soup and sandwich combination. Take-out and delivery service are popular options. **Bar:** full bar. **Address:** 20395 Lougheed Hwy, Unit 680 V2X 2P9 **Location:** Jct 203rd St.

MAYNE ISLAND (H-10) pop. 1,074

Although visited by the Spanish in the 1790s, it was not until the 1850s that British Capt. George Richards surveyed and mapped the area. Capt. Richards named Mayne Island after his lieutenant, Richard Charles Mayne. During the gold rush of the mid-1800s the island, in the Gulf Islands group halfway between Victoria and the mouth of the Fraser River, was a stopping point for miners heading for the riches to be found at the gold fields along the river.

The island is known as a haven for artists and artisans. Small and sparsely settled, Mayne offers quiet beaches and hiking trails; wildflowers; a landscape heavy with trees; seals, sea lions, salmon and sole offshore; and a large variety of birds, from tiny hummingbirds to soaring bald eagles.

Mayne Island Community Chamber of Commerce: P.O. Box 2, Mayne Island, BC, Canada V0N 2J0.

McBRIDE pop. 586

NORTH COUNTRY LODGE

250/569-0001

Motel
$85-$90

Address: 868 N Frontage Rd V0J 2E0 **Location:** Just w of village main exit, on Hwy 16 north service road. **Facility:** 48 units, some two bedrooms and efficiencies. 2 stories (no elevator), exterior corridors. **Parking:** winter plug-ins. **Terms:** cancellation fee imposed. **Activities:** whirlpool. **Free Special Amenities: local telephone calls and early check-in/late check-out.**

MERRITT (C-8) pop. 7,113, elev. 858m/2,814'
• Restaurants p. 274

Merritt is known for its many lakes. Of particular interest is Nicola Lake, a large warm-water lake 10 kilometres (6 mi.) north of town. For a view of the landmarks, including a giant Canadian flag, hike to the Merritt Lookout from Juniper Drive. Recreational activities in the area include swimming, fishing, sailing, water skiing and windsurfing. Monck Provincial Park, on the west side of the lake, offers camping and picnic facilities.

Merritt Visitor Centre: 2202 Voght St., P.O. Box 1105, Merritt, BC, Canada V1K 1B8. **Phone:** (250) 378-0349.

NICOLA VALLEY MUSEUM & ARCHIVES is off Coldwater Ave. at 1675 Tutill Ct. The history of the region is chronicled in exhibits about mining, logging and ranching. Indian and pioneer artifacts are displayed, along with photographs depicting the lives of early settlers.

Time: Allow 30 minutes minimum. **Hours:** Tues.-Sat. 9-5, Mon. 10-3, July-Aug.; Mon.-Fri. 10-3 (also Wed.-Thurs. 3-4), rest of year. Closed Jan. 1-3 and Dec. 17-31. Phone ahead to confirm schedule. **Cost:** Donations. **Phone:** (250) 378-4145.

QUALITY INN   (250)378-4253

Hotel
$90-$135

Address: 4025 Walters St V1K 1K1 **Location:** Hwy 5 exit 290, 0.6 mi (1 km) w. **Facility:** 56 units. 2 stories (no elevator), exterior corridors. **Parking:** winter plug-ins. **Amenities:** *Some:* high-speed Internet. **Pool(s):** heated indoor. **Activities:** whirlpool, limited exercise equipment. **Guest Services:** coin laundry. **Free Special Amenities: expanded continental breakfast and local telephone calls.**

Indoor pool & hot tub. Free Internet. A minute from Exit 290, Hwy #5. Fully renovated in 2013.

RAMADA   (250)378-3567

Motel
$80-$135

Address: 3571 Voght St V1K 1C5 **Location:** Hwy 5 exit 290, just w. **Facility:** 52 units, some two bedrooms, efficiencies and kitchens. 3 stories (no elevator), exterior corridors. **Parking:** winter plug-ins. **Pool(s):** heated indoor. **Activities:** sauna, whirlpool, waterslide, limited exercise equipment. **Guest Services:** coin laundry. **Free Special Amenities: expanded continental breakfast and local telephone calls.**

Huge indoor-outdoor waterslide, spacious pool, free breakfast, wireless internet, free newspaper.

Learn about inspections and Diamond Ratings at AAA.com/Diamonds

SUPER 8 MERRITT (250)378-9422

▼▼ ▼▼ **Motel** $75-$185 **Address:** 3561 Voght St V1K 1C5 **Location:** Hwy 5 exit 290, just w. **Facility:** 35 units, some efficiencies and kitchens. 2 stories (no elevator), exterior corridors. **Dining:** Home Restaurant, see separate listing. **Pool(s):** heated indoor. **Activities:** whirlpool.

[symbols row]

WHERE TO EAT

HOME RESTAURANT 250/378-9112

▼▼ ▼▼ American. Casual Dining. $9-$18 **AAA Inspector Notes:** This popular and very busy restaurant serves good old-fashioned comfort food for the weary traveler. You'll find great sandwiches, thick juicy burgers and great dinner entrées; there's even a kid's menu. Many of the desserts are made in house and displayed in a glass case near the front door. **Bar:** beer & wine. **Address:** 3561 Voght St V1K 1C5 **Location:** Hwy 5 exit 290, just w; in Super 8 Merritt.

[B] [L] [D] CALL 📶

MISSION (H-11) pop. 36,426, elev. 55m/180'
• Part of Vancouver area — see map p. 343

Mission developed from a Roman Catholic mission built in 1861 to serve First Nations tribes. The site became a popular stopping place for trappers, settlers and other river travelers.

The Fraser River provides opportunities for swimming, fishing, boating and water sports; its sandbars are good for rockhounds in search of agates, jades and garnets. Motocross and boat races are held at Mission Raceway from March through October.

Mission Regional Chamber of Commerce: 34033 Lougheed Hwy., Mission, BC, Canada V2V 5X8. **Phone:** (604) 826-6914.

FRASER RIVER SAFARI departs from the harborfront at 33428 Harbour Ave. A 3-hour narrated cruise along the Fraser River in a fully covered jet boat comes complete with scenic mountain views; possible sightings of bears, seals, deer and birds; and entertaining folklore about native legends, fur traders, gold miners and Sasquatch. A stop is made at Kilby Historic Site in Harrison Mills *(see attraction listing p. 249)*.

Time: Allow 3 hours, 30 minutes minimum. **Hours:** Trips depart daily at 9:30 and 2, July-Sept.; at 10, rest of year. Closed Christmas. **Cost:** $99; $90 (ages 60+); $70 (ages 5-16); $300 (family, two adults and two children). Reservations are required. **Phone:** (604) 826-7361 or (866) 348-6877.

MISSION MUSEUM is downtown at 33201 Second Ave. at jct. Welton St. The museum, in a 1907 prefabricated building shipped to Mission to serve as the Canadian Bank of Commerce, was also the town's library before becoming a museum. The building now houses a parlor and a kitchen reminiscent of the 1920s and permanent exhibits about the indigenous people and the history of the city. A themed exhibit changes each year. **Time:** Allow 30 minutes minimum. **Hours:** Thurs.-Fri. 10-4, Sat. 1-4. **Cost:** Donations. **Phone:** (604) 826-1011.

POWER HOUSE AT STAVE FALLS is 1.3 km (.8 mi.) w. on Ferndale Ave. from jct. Stave Lake St. and Ferndale Ave., then 12.9 km (8 mi.) n.w. on Dewdney Trunk Rd. to 31338 Dewdney Trunk Rd. Through interactive science games and historic displays, the facility tells the story of how power helped build British Columbia. Within a 50-seat theater, visitors may start their self-guiding tour with a 9-minute video that introduces life in the early 1900s. On display are generators and turbines within a 1912 generating station.

Time: Allow 1 hour minimum. **Hours:** Daily 10-5, Apr. 5-Sept. 2; otherwise varies. Closed Jan. 1-2, Christmas Eve, Christmas, day after Christmas and Dec. 31. Phone ahead to confirm schedule. **Cost:** $6; $5 (ages 6-18, 55+ and students with ID); $15 (family, two adults and two children). **Phone:** (604) 462-1222.

WESTMINSTER ABBEY is 1.5 km (.9 mi.) e., .7 km (.5 mi.) n. of Hwy. 7 to 34224 Dewdney Trunk Rd. The Seminary of Christ the King is managed by Benedictine monks. Of interest are the view and architecture. Modest dress is required. **Time:** Allow 30 minutes minimum. **Hours:** Mon.-Sat. 1:30-4:30, Sun. 2-4:30. Grounds open daily 8-8. **Cost:** Free. **Phone:** (604) 826-8975.

XÁ:YTEM LONGHOUSE INTERPRETIVE CENTRE is at 35087 Lougheed Hwy. (Hwy. 7). Xá:ytem (pronounced HAY-tum) is said to be British Columbia's oldest known dwelling site. It is evidence of one of many large villages that were once inhabited by the ancestors of today's Stó:lō people. Of note is a replica of a *skumel*, or underground pithouse, and the "Rock"—a physical manifestation of Stó:lō spirituality. Among the items housed at the cedar longhouse are artifacts found at the site.

Tours: Guided tours are available. **Time:** Allow 1 hour minimum. **Hours:** Mon.-Sat. 9-4:30. Closed major holidays. Phone ahead to confirm schedule. **Cost:** $12; $10 (ages 55+ and students with ID); $9 (ages 6-12). **Phone:** (604) 820-9725. 🅿️

BEST WESTERN PLUS MISSION CITY LODGE
(604)820-5500

▼▼ ▼▼
Hotel
$97-$107

AAA Benefit: Members save up to 20%, plus 10% bonus points with Best Western Rewards®.

Address: 32281 Lougheed Hwy V2V 1A3 **Location:** Just w of Hwy 11; corner of Lougheed Hwy (Hwy 7) and Hurd St. **Facility:** 80 units, some efficiencies. 4 stories, interior corridors. **Amenities:** high-speed Internet. **Pool(s):** heated indoor. **Activities:** sauna, whirlpool, exercise room. **Guest Services:** valet and coin laundry. **Free Special Amenities:** expanded continental breakfast and high-speed Internet.

[symbols row]

MORICETOWN (E-3) elev. 411m/1,348'

Moricetown is a Wet'suwet'en community that still practices the traditional hereditary system of governance. Originally known as Kyah Wiget, it was once the largest village of the Bulkley River Carrier tribe, a settlement built some 4,000 years ago. The town later took the name of Father A.G. Morice, a missionary who lived among the Carrier Indians in the late 19th century.

MORICETOWN CANYON is off Hwy. 16 and Telkawa High Rd. The Bulkley River plunges through this narrow gorge in a series of waterfalls. The canyon was vital to native tribes, whose diet depended on salmon. Visitors can view fish ladders that help five species of salmon reach their annual spawning grounds. During the summer Wet'suwet'en Indians still can be seen gaffing salmon as the fish fight their way upstream. **Time:** Allow 1 hour minimum.

MOUNT REVELSTOKE NATIONAL PARK (A-9)

Elevations in the park range from 480 metres (1,575 ft.) at the bottom of Mount Revelstoke to 2,639 metres (8,658 ft.) at the Mount Revelstoke summit at the Inverness Peaks. Refer to CAA/AAA maps for additional elevation information.

On the west edge of the Selkirk Range in southeastern British Columbia, Mount Revelstoke National Park is 260 square kilometres (100 sq. mi.) of sharp peaks, heavily timbered slopes and flowering meadows. The Selkirk Range, flanked on the east by the Purcell Range and on the west by the Monashee Range, are distinguished by their height and geologic complexity.

Erosion by glaciers and the heavy rainfall of the region have carved the rock of the Selkirks into jagged forms. Complementing the park's dense green forests and lush wildflower meadows are glacier-fed streams and lakes as well as the deep snows that blanket the slopes until late June.

Deer inhabit the lower slopes; black and grizzly bears and mountain caribou also may be seen in the park. Most mountain species of birds are represented, including Fox Sparrows, Hermit Thrushes and Northern Hawk Owls.

The Trans-Canada Highway (Hwy. 1) passes through the southeastern portion of the park for 13 kilometres (8 mi.) and parallels its southern boundary for 18 kilometres (11 mi.).

General Information and Activities

Visitor facilities and accommodations are available in the city of Revelstoke at the western entrance. A park pass must be purchased at the park kiosk at Rogers Pass Discovery Centre or at the park kiosk at the base of the Meadows in the Sky Parkway. Phone ahead for schedule.

From Hwy. 1, the Meadows in the Sky Parkway, a 26-kilometre (16-mi.) hard surface road that is open only in summer leads to the summit of Mount Revelstoke and provides an excellent panoramic view. Along its length are 16 switchbacks and several viewpoints. Picnic areas are available at Monashee, the 8-kilometre (5-mi.) viewpoint on this road, and at Balsam Lake, 1 kilometre (.6 mi.) from the summit.

Other picnic areas and nature trails are along the Trans-Canada Highway.

Recreation includes subalpine hiking, mountain climbing and fishing. August is the best time to view wildflowers. More than 60 kilometres (37 mi.) of hiking trails lead to such sites as Miller and Jade lakes. Voluntary registration for backcountry travellers is available. Fishing is by permit, available at the park administrative office in Revelstoke. *See Recreation Areas Chart.*

ADMISSION to the park is $7.80; $6.80 (ages 65+); $3.90 (ages 6-16); $19.60 (all occupants of a private vehicle with up to seven people). Buses, trailers and Class A motor homes are not permitted on the Meadows in the Sky Parkway. **Cards:** AX, MC, VI.

PETS are permitted in the park provided they are on leashes at all times.

ADDRESS inquiries to the Superintendent, Mount Revelstoke and Glacier National Parks, P.O. Box 350, Revelstoke, BC, Canada V0E 2S0; phone (250) 837-7500.

NAKUSP (B-10) pop. 1,569, elev. 914m/2,998'
• Restaurants p. 276

Nakusp, on the shore of Upper Arrow Lake between the Selkirk and Monashee mountain ranges, is named for an Indian word meaning "bay of quiet waters." Arrow Lake, part of the Columbia River system, is a popular destination for trout and dolly fishing. A waterfront walkway with gardens and a beach as well as a campground are nearby.

Heli-skiing, snowmobiling, cross-country skiing, winter fishing and a small ski hill are among the many cold-weather attractions offered.

Nakusp Chamber of Commerce: 92 6th Ave. N.W., P.O. Box 387, Nakusp, BC, Canada V0G 1R0. **Phone:** (250) 265-4234, or (800) 909-8819 within British Columbia.

NAKUSP HOT SPRINGS is 14 km (9 mi.) n. on Nakusp Hot Springs Rd. The quiet, natural mineral spring pools are nestled in the woods and surrounded by mountains. Indoor change rooms and showers are available. Pool temperatures range from 36 to 41 C (97-107 F). *See Recreation Areas Chart.*

Hours: Daily 9:30-9:30, Victoria Day to mid-Oct.; 1-9, rest of year. Phone ahead to confirm schedule. **Cost:** One swim $9.50; $8.50 (ages 6-17 and 60+); $29 (family, two adults and up to four children). Day pass $14; $11.50 (ages 6-17 and 60+); $38 (family, two adults and up to four children). **Phone:** (250) 265-4528 or (866) 999-4528.

THE SELKIRK INN	250/265-3666

▼▼▼ ◆◆
Motel
$65-$105

Address: 210 W 6th Ave NW V0G 1R0 **Location:** Center. **Facility:** 39 units, some efficiencies. 2 stories (no elevator), interior corridors. **Terms:** cancellation fee imposed.

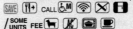

WHERE TO EAT

WOOD FIRE PIZZA N' MORE   250/265-0060
♥♥ International. Casual Dining. $9-$19 **AAA Inspector
Notes:** This casual little spot has a bit of a Mediterranean flair to the
decor. When first opened, the restaurant started out with tasty
gourmet pizzas crafted with good quality fresh ingredients. The N'
More came along when the German owners decided to expand and
added some schnitzel and spaetzle dishes along with salads, pasta
and barbecue chicken or ribs. You can be sure everything is made
from scratch in-house. **Bar:** full bar. **Address:** 312 Broadway St V0G
1R0 **Location:** Between 3rd and 4th aves SW; center. **Parking:**
street only. [L] [D] CALL [&M] [X]

NANAIMO (G-10) pop. 83,810, elev. 30m/98'
• Restaurants p. 278

Some 120 kilometres (75 mi.) north of Victoria,
Nanaimo began as a Hudson's Bay Co. outpost
called Colvilletown, established for miners brought
from England and Scotland to mine coal. A thriving
forest and marine products industry replaced coal's
influence, and the economy of contemporary
Nanaimo is centered on technology, service, manufacturing, tourism and recreation.

Offshore islands and nearby mountains and lakes
provide a variety of recreational opportunities including hiking, swimming, camping and picnicking.
Charter companies offer wildlife tours year-round to
view animals such as the area's bald eagles and
sea lions.

For a touch of wilderness in the middle of the city,
check out Bowen Park, on the Millstone River just
north of downtown. This 36-hectare (89-acre) expanse provides an outlet for a variety of activities.
Trails wind through forests of fir, hemlock, cedar and
maple, and kids enjoy the 4-H barnyard open July
through August. A rhododendron grove, a nature
center, duck pond, picnic shelters, swimming pool
and sports fields complete the complex. In winter,
tobogganers take to the park's big hills.

Exotic trees provide a setting for picnicking at
Harmac Arboretum, 11 kilometres (7 mi.) south at
Harmac Pulp Mill and Duke Point roads. Newcastle
Island *(see Recreation Areas Chart)* is a marine provincial park accessible by a 10-minute ferry ride
from Maffeo-Sutton Park on the harborfront. Automobiles are not permitted; the ferry operates daily
every 20 minutes in spring and summer.

In addition to the ferry, salmon sport fishing,
scuba diving, windsurfing and sailing are also available from Nanaimo's natural harbor. An intertidal
park with three lighted water curtains and a
4-kilometre (2.5-mi.) walkway along the seawall
graces Nanaimo's waterfront. St. Jean's Custom
Cannery is one of three factories where fishing enthusiasts can have their catch canned or smoked.

On a landscaped hillside, Vancouver Island University offers views of the city and harbor below and
also is the site of Nanaimo Art Gallery *(see attraction
listing).* Visitors interested in prehistoric art can see
sandstone carvings at Petroglyph Park, 3.25 kilometres (2 mi.) south on scenic Hwy. 1. Other cultural
endeavors can be enjoyed at The Port Theatre, an
800-seat performing arts center at 125 Front St. that
hosts local, national and international events; phone
(250) 754-8550 for ticket information.

Nanaimo is accessible from the mainland by BC
Ferries, which sails from Horseshoe Bay to Departure Bay and from Tsawwassen to Duke Point, 8
kilometres (5 mi.) south of Nanaimo. For more information phone (888) 223-3779.

Tourism Nanaimo: 2290 Bowen Rd., Nanaimo, BC,
Canada V9T 3K7. **Phone:** (250) 756-0106 or (800)
663-7337.

NANAIMO ART GALLERY is on the Vancouver Island University campus at 330-900 Fifth St. Two galleries display local, regional and national exhibits;
the second gallery is downtown at 150 Commercial
St. New exhibits are installed frequently.

Time: Allow 1 hour minimum. **Hours:** Campus
gallery Mon.-Fri. 10-5, Sat. noon-4. Downtown gal-
lery Tues.-Sat. 10-5. Closed major holidays. **Cost:**
Donations. **Phone:** (250) 740-6350 for the Fifth
Street gallery, or (250) 754-1750 for the Commercial
Street gallery.

NANAIMO MUSEUM is at 100 Museum Way on the
second floor of the Vancouver Island Conference
Centre. Nanaimo's history is explored through exhibits depicting life for the city's earliest settlers, its
days as a 19th-century mining center and its transi-
tion into the 21st century. Visitors can discover stories about the Snunéymuxw First Nation and check
out a replica coal mine to feel what it was like to be
an underground miner.

Time: Allow 1 hour minimum. **Hours:** Daily 10-5,
May-Sept.; Mon.-Sat. 10-5, rest of year. Closed Jan.
1, Nov. 11, Christmas and day after Christmas.
Phone ahead to confirm schedule. **Cost:** $2; $1.75
(ages 55+ and students with ID); 75c (ages 7-18).
Phone: (250) 753-1821.

The Bastion is on Front St. across from the Coast
Bastion Inn. The small fort was built in 1853 to pro-
tect early settlers. A display shows how the bastion
was used in the 1860s. A noon ceremonial cannon
firing is conducted by staff dressed in period cos-
tumes. **Hours:** Daily 10-5, Victoria Day weekend-
Labour Day; Mon.-Sat. 10-5, rest of year. Closed
Jan. 1, Good Friday, second Mon. in Oct., Nov. 11,
Christmas, day after Christmas and Dec. 31. **Cost:**
Donations. **Phone:** (250) 753-1821.

GAMBLING ESTABLISHMENTS
• **Great Canadian Casinos Nanaimo** is at 620 Ter-
  minal Ave. **Hours:** Sun.-Thurs. 10 a.m.-midnight,
  Fri.-Sat. 10 a.m.-2 a.m. **Phone:** (250) 753-3033.

RECREATIONAL ACTIVITIES
Bungee Jumping
• **Wildplay Element Park** is at 35 Nanaimo River
  Rd. Other activities are offered. **Hours:** Daily
  10-6, Victoria Day-Labour Day; Fri.-Mon. 10-6,
  rest of year. Phone ahead to confirm schedule.
  Phone: (250) 716-7874 or (888) 716-7374.

Hiking

- **Tracks Outdoor Adventures** meets participants at pre-arranged pickup points. Other activities are available. **Hours:** Daily 9-5, May-Oct. **Phone:** (250) 754-8732 or (877) 898-8732.

BEST WESTERN NORTHGATE INN (250)390-2222

 Hotel $130-$200

 AAA Benefit: Members save up to 20%, plus 10% bonus points with Best Western Rewards®.

Address: 6450 Metral Dr V9T 2L8 **Location:** Hwy 19A (Island Hwy), just w on Aulds Rd, then just s. **Facility:** 72 units, some efficiencies. 3 stories, interior corridors. **Amenities:** safes. **Activities:** sauna, whirlpool, limited exercise equipment. **Guest Services:** valet and coin laundry. **Free Special Amenities:** continental breakfast and local telephone calls.

 / SOME UNITS FEE

BEST WESTERN PLUS DORCHESTER HOTEL (250)754-6835

 Hotel $99-$189

AAA Benefit: Members save up to 20%, plus 10% bonus points with Best Western Rewards®.

Address: 70 Church St V9R 5H4 **Location:** Hwy 19A (Island Hwy) to Comox Rd; downtown. **Facility:** 70 units. 4 stories, interior corridors. **Amenities:** safes. *Some:* high-speed Internet. **Activities:** bicycles, exercise room. **Guest Services:** valet and coin laundry. **Free Special Amenities:** high-speed Internet and use of on-premises laundry facilities.

 / SOME UNITS FEE

BUCCANEER INN 250/753-1246

Motel $70-$179

Address: 1577 Stewart Ave V9S 4E3 **Location:** 1 mi (1.6 km) e; just before Departure Bay Ferry Terminal. **Facility:** 14 units, some kitchens. 2 stories (no elevator), exterior corridors. **Terms:** 3 day cancellation notice-fee imposed. **Guest Services:** coin laundry.

DAYS INN NANAIMO HARBOURVIEW (250)754-8171

Hotel $90-$120 **Address:** 809 Island Hwy S V9R 5K1 **Location:** On Island Hwy 1, 1.3 mi (2 km) s. **Facility:** 79 units, some efficiencies. 2 stories (no elevator), interior corridors. **Pool(s):** heated indoor. **Activities:** whirlpool. **Guest Services:** valet and coin laundry.

/ SOME UNITS FEE

THE GRAND HOTEL NANAIMO (250)758-3000

Hotel $119-$320 **Address:** 4898 Rutherford Rd V9T 4Z4 **Location:** 3.8 mi (6 km) n on Hwy 19A (Island Hwy) from Departure Bay Ferry Terminal, then just e. **Facility:** 72 units. 4 stories, interior corridors. **Terms:** cancellation fee imposed. **Amenities:** high-speed Internet. **Pool(s):** heated indoor. **Activities:** exercise room. **Guest Services:** valet laundry.

/ SOME UNITS FEE

INN ON LONG LAKE (250)758-1144

Hotel $109-$299

Address: 4700 Island Hwy N Hwy N V9T 1W6 **Location:** 3.1 mi (5 km) n on Hwy 19A (Island Hwy) from Departure Bay Ferry Terminal. **Facility:** 62 units, some efficiencies and kitchens. 3 stories, exterior corridors. **Activities:** sauna, whirlpool, rental canoes, rental paddleboats, boat dock, limited exercise equipment. **Guest Services:** valet and coin laundry. **Free Special Amenities:** expanded continental breakfast and high-speed Internet. *(See ad this page.)*

/ SOME UNITS FEE

RAMADA INN NANAIMO (250)716-2009

Hotel $115-$169 **Address:** 315 Rosehill St V9S 1E3 **Location:** 1 mi (1.6 km) n on Hwy 19A (Island Hwy). **Facility:** 65 units. 4 stories, interior corridors. **Terms:** cancellation fee imposed. **Amenities:** high-speed Internet, safes. **Activities:** exercise room. **Guest Services:** valet and coin laundry.

▼ See AAA listing this page ▼

WHERE TO EAT

BLUE GINGER SUSHI BAR & SATAY GRILL 250/751-8238

▼▼ Asian. Casual Dining. $6-$20 **AAA Inspector Notes:** The restaurant represents an interesting idea: combining three Asian tastes, Japanese, Chinese and Thai, on a single menu. Dishes reflect a melange of flavors and are a fun twist on the typical Asian dining experience. **Bar:** full bar. **Address:** 5769 Turner Rd, Unit 1 V9T 6L8 **Location:** Hwy 19A (Island Hwy), at Turner Rd; in Longwood Station. L D CALL 📶

CACTUS CLUB CAFE 250/729-0011

▼▼ American. Casual Dining. $11-$37 **AAA Inspector Notes:** This bustling, casual restaurant serves huge burgers, sandwiches, pasta, salads, soups, quesadillas, fajitas, vegetarian dishes, steak, ribs, chicken and fish. Featured are certified Angus beef and fresh wild British Columbia salmon. **Bar:** full bar. **Address:** 801-5800 Turner Rd V9T 6J4 **Location:** Hwy 19A (Island Hwy), just e before Uplands Dr. L D LATE CALL 📶

EARLS RESTAURANT 250/756-4100

▼▼ American. Casual Dining. $9-$29 **AAA Inspector Notes:** Offering an experience that falls between fast food and fine dining, the fun, relaxed restaurant prepares great food at a great price. Choices range from juicy burgers, hearty sandwiches, fresh salads, wings and pizza to full entrees of steak, chops and seafood. Made-from-scratch soups and assorted breads, as well as a nice choice of wines and beers, round out the offerings. This is a fitting spot for impromptu get-togethers and festive occasions. **Bar:** full bar. **Address:** 100-2980 Island Hwy N V9T 5V4 **Location:** 2.5 mi (4 km) n on Hwy 19A (Island Hwy). B L D 24 CALL 📶

GINA'S MEXICAN CAFE 250/753-5411

▼▼ Mexican. Casual Dining. $8-$16 **AAA Inspector Notes:** One of the busiest restaurants in downtown, Gina's has been serving Mexican food to hungry diners for more than 20 years in one of the gaudiest houses imaginable! Lines out the door are not uncommon, and the cramped interior and tacky Mexican decor add to its popularity. Nothing on the menu is more than $16, and portions are large. Parking is at street meters or in a nearby pay lot. **Bar:** full bar. **Address:** 47 Skinner St V9R 5K4 **Location:** Hwy 19A (Island Hwy), just e on Comox Rd, then just s on Chapel St. **Parking:** street only. L D ❌

KELSEY'S 250/729-8882

▼▼ American. Casual Dining. $10-$24 **AAA Inspector Notes:** A fun, relaxed atmosphere and tasty menu of casual fare make the restaurant a popular favorite with locals. Diners might start a meal with some tempting appetizers, such as wings, loaded potato skins or nachos, and follow them with an old-time favorite, such as a burger, wrap, pizza or pasta dish. For a heartier meal, it's hard to beat pork back ribs or a steak. The diverse menu has broad appeal. **Bar:** full bar. **Address:** 4711 Rutherford Rd V9T 4K6 **Location:** In Rutherford Mall. L D CALL 📶

LONGWOOD BREWPUB 250/729-8225

▼▼ American. Gastropub. $12-$28 **AAA Inspector Notes:** Families are welcomed in the restaurant section, but the pub, which offers all the amenities of the restaurant, is strictly for adults. Patrons can sample hand-crafted lagers and ales, as well as hearty pub food, such as sandwiches, burgers, pastas and varied dinner entrees. **Bar:** full bar. **Address:** 5775 Turner Rd V9T 6L8 **Location:** Hwy 19A (Island Hwy) at Turner Rd; in Longwood Station. L D LATE CALL 📶

MOXIE'S CLASSIC GRILL 250/390-1079

▼▼ American. Casual Dining. $10-$29 **AAA Inspector Notes:** This sleek, funky and popular restaurant presents an extensive menu of creatively prepared dishes, including pizza, pasta, rice, noodles, signature salads and burgers. Other menus include one for children and one for Sunday brunch. Lending to the upbeat, stylish decor are dark wood appointments and river rock fireplaces. **Bar:** full bar. **Address:** 6750 Island Hwy N, #102 V9V 1S3 **Location:** Hwy 19A (Island Hwy); in Nored Plaza. L D

RICKY'S ALL DAY GRILL 250/390-1227

▼▼ American. Casual Dining. $11-$27 **AAA Inspector Notes:** The comfortable eatery, which employs friendly servers, presents a varied menu that includes pasta dishes, wraps, omelets, stir-fry preparations and burgers. Portions are generous. Children's and senior selections are offered. Guests can request seating in a booth or at a table. **Bar:** full bar. **Address:** 6550 Island Hwy N V9V 1K8 **Location:** Corner of Hwy 19A (Island Hwy) and Hammond Bay Rd. B L D

SMITTY'S 250/716-8887

▼▼ Canadian. Casual Dining. $8-$17 **AAA Inspector Notes:** The family-oriented restaurant satisfies patrons with its ever-popular all-day breakfast items, as well as tasty and wholesome soups and salads at lunchtime. A relaxed mood characterizes the dining space. **Bar:** full bar. **Address:** 50 10th St V9R 6L1 **Location:** Hwy 19A (Island Hwy S), just w. B L D

SWISS CHALET 250/729-7120

▼▼ Chicken. Casual Dining. $9-$19 **AAA Inspector Notes:** The popular restaurant is known for its rotisserie chicken and ribs and the tangy Chalet sauce that gives food its special zip. Diners munch on a half or quarter chicken with sides such as steamed vegetables, fries, baked potatoes and salads. Lunch guests often go for the great soup and sandwich combination. Take-out and delivery service are popular options. **Bar:** full bar. **Address:** 3290 N Island Hwy V9T 1W1 **Location:** Hwy 19A (Island Hwy) at Bowen Rd. L D

ZOUGLA 250/716-3233

▼▼ Mediterranean. Casual Dining. $12-$30 **AAA Inspector Notes:** Diners will enjoy this restaurant's steak and seafood as well as such Mediterranean specialties as moussaka, spanakopita and souvlaki. Floor-to-ceiling windows offer a great view of the ocean and mountains. Couples and travelers like the relaxing ambience. **Bar:** full bar. **Address:** 2021 Estevan Rd V9S 3Y9 **Location:** Hwy 19A (Island Hwy) and Brechin Rd; on road to Departure Bay Ferry Terminal. L D CALL 📶

NANOOSE BAY pop. 5,471

THE LANDING WEST COAST GRILL 250/468-2400

▼▼ Pacific Rim. Casual Dining. $12-$35 **AAA Inspector Notes:** Two 6,000-gallon saltwater aquariums dominate this restaurant; each is stocked with such local area fish as salmon, crab, sea urchins, herring, perch and abalone. Enjoy a menu focused on local ingredients with West Coast and Mediterranean influences. **Bar:** full bar. **Reservations:** suggested. **Address:** 1-1600 Stroulger Rd V9P 9B7 **Location:** Hwy 19 exit 46 (Parksville), 0.5 mi (0.8 km) n on Old Island Hwy (19A), just e on Franklin's Gull Rd, 1.5 mi (2.4 km) s on Northwest Bay Rd, then just e on Beaver Creek Wharf Rd; in Pacific Shores Resort & Spa. L D CALL 📶

NARAMATA pop. 1,647
- Hotels & Restaurants map & index p. 290
- Part of Okanagan Valley area — see map p. 286

THE VILLAGE MOTEL   (250)496-5535 **39**

▼▼ **Motel** $95-$145 **Address:** 244 Robinson Ave V0H 1N0 **Location:** 8.8 mi (14 km) n on Naramata Rd from Penticton. **Facility:** 9 units, some efficiencies. 1 story, exterior corridors. **Terms:** closed 11/1-3/31, 2-3 night minimum stay - seasonal and/or weekends, 14 day cancellation notice-fee imposed.

[🛋️] [📶] [✕] [🍴] [🎱] [🚬] [💲] [🖥️] / SOME UNITS [📷]

WHERE TO EAT

COBBLESTONE WINE BAR & RESTAURANT
250/496-6808 **31**

▼▼▼ Canadian. Casual Dining. $10-$34 **AAA Inspector Notes:** There is an intimate, cozy feel among the brick floors and walls of this restaurant, set in the basement of the Naramata Heritage Inn & Spa. This is casual dining at its best, with a menu that features many artistic dishes with regional ingredients. Servers will impress you with their extensive wine knowledge, helping to create a lovely and enjoyable meal. **Bar:** full bar. **Reservations:** suggested. **Address:** 3625 1st St V0H 1N0 **Location:** 11.4 mi (19 km) ne of Penticton; from Naramata Rd, w along Robinson Ave to 1st St, just s; in Naramata Heritage Inn & Spa. [L] [D] CALL [♿M]

NELSON (C-10) pop. 10,230, elev. 535m/1,755'
- Restaurants p. 280

An old iron and silver mining town, Nelson was settled by prospectors in the late 1880s. With the depletion of its mines, the town turned to logging, sawmilling and area trade. However, the legacy of the bonanza days lives on in the more than 350 heritage sites. Most of Nelson's historic commercial buildings are open to the public, but homes are private and closed to visitors. If Fido comes along with you, be sure to follow Nelson's dog ordinance and keep him out of restricted zones.

Nearby parks, lakes, streams and mountains offer all types of summer and winter recreation. Kokanee Creek and Kokanee Glacier provincial parks *(see Recreation Areas Chart)* are 19 kilometres (12 mi.) northeast on Hwy. 3A.

Nelson Chamber of Commerce: 225 Hall St., Nelson, BC, Canada V1L 5X4. **Phone:** (250) 352-3433 or (877) 663-5706.

Self-guiding tours: Maps detailing walking and driving tours are available from the chamber of commerce.

◆GEM◆ **INTERNATIONAL SELKIRK LOOP** is a 405-kilometre (280-mi.) scenic byway through southeastern British Columbia and adjoining parts of Washington and Idaho. From Nelson the main route follows Hwy. 6 south to the U.S. border at Nelway. The other leg of the loop heads east on Hwy. 3A to Balfour, where what is said to be the world's longest free ferry service transports vehicles and passengers across Kootenay Lake. Hwy. 3A continues south along the lake's east shore to Creston, where Hwy. 21 connects with the U.S. border at Rykerts.

One 166-kilometre (103-mi.) side route follows Hwys. 3A, 6 and 22 from Nelson to Castlegar and Trail, then Hwy. 3B and 3 from Rossland to Salmo.

Another 217-kilometre (135-mi.) side route connects Nelson with Slocan Lake via Hwys. 3A and 6, then continues east from New Denver to Kaslo on Hwy. 31, completing the loop back to Nelson following Hwys. 31 and 3A.

Scenic highlights of the loop include Kootenay Lake, thick coniferous forests, snowcapped peaks and the lush Creston Valley. Museums, historic mining towns, heritage architecture, crafts villages and seasonal produce stands beckon travelers.

Recreational activities abound, including golf, fishing, boating, swimming, hunting, camping, hiking, mountain biking, horseback riding, skiing and snowmobiling. You also can tour a gold mine and soak in a hot spring.

Towns with attraction listings on the loop and its side routes include Ainsworth Hot Springs, Boswell, Castlegar, Creston, Kaslo, Nelson, New Denver, Rossland, Sandon and Trail.

Chambers of commerce and visitor centers on the loop provide maps and more information. Visitors also can write the International Selkirk Loop, P.O. Box 920, Bonners Ferry, ID 83805, United States; or in Canada, P.O. Box 2079, Creston, BC V0B 1G0. **Phone:** (208) 267-0822 or (888) 823-2626.

TOUCHSTONES NELSON: MUSEUM OF ART AND HISTORY is at s.e. corner of jct. Vernon and Ward sts. at 502 Vernon St. This renovated building features permanent visual and interactive exhibitions which examine the area's cultural, developmental and economic history. The Shawn Lamb Archives houses a thorough collection of materials relating to the region's diversified origins. Temporary exhibits and galleries also are available and change monthly.

Hours: Mon.-Sat. 10-5 (also Thurs. 5-8), Sun. 10-4, mid-May to mid-Sept.; Wed.-Sat. 10-5 (also Thurs. 5-8), Sun. 10-4, rest of year. Closed major holidays. **Cost:** $8; $6 (ages 60+ and college students with ID); $4 (ages 7-18); by donation (Thurs. 5-8); $22 (family). **Phone:** (250) 352-9813.

RECREATIONAL ACTIVITIES
Skiing
- **Whitewater Winter Resort** is 20 km (12 mi.) s. off Hwy. 6 at #1 Whitewater Ski Hill Rd. **Hours:** Daily 9-3:30, early Dec. to mid-Apr. **Phone:** (250) 354-4944 or (800) 666-9420.

BEST WESTERN PLUS BAKER STREET INN & CONVENTION CENTRE   (250)352-3525

▼▼▼ Hotel $130-$175 **Best Western PLUS**

AAA Benefit: Members save up to 20%, plus 10% bonus points with Best Western Rewards®.

Address: 153 Baker St V1L 4H1 **Location:** Jct Hwy 6 and 3A. **Facility:** 70 units. 4 stories, interior corridors. **Amenities:** high-speed Internet. **Activities:** whirlpool, exercise room. **Guest Services:** coin laundry. **Free Special Amenities:** local telephone calls and high-speed Internet.

[SAVE] [ECO] [🍴] [🍸] CALL [♿M] [BIZ] [📶] [✕] [🚬] [📷] [🖥️] / SOME UNITS FEE [🛒]

NORTH SHORE INN   (250)352-6606

▼ **Motel** $62-$85 **Address:** 687 Hwy 3A V1L 5P7 **Location:** 1.9 mi (3 km) n on Hwy 3A via Nelson Bridge. **Facility:** 30 units, some kitchens. 3 stories (no elevator), interior corridors.

[‖] [📶] [✕] [🖥] [📷] / SOME UNITS FEE [🐾]

WHERE TO EAT

ALL SEASONS CAFE   250/352-0101

▼▼▼ American. Casual Dining. $19-$32 **AAA Inspector Notes:** True to its name, this funky restaurant features a regional and seasonal menu, incorporating the best of the area and time of year in terms of ingredients. Everything is made from scratch, and dishes are beautiful. In a small house-like setting a block away from downtown, this is a true gem in the heart of Nelson. Guests can eat in the dimly lit, romantic dining room or in the glass-enclosed veranda, with a view of the rock garden. **Bar:** full bar. **Reservations:** suggested. **Address:** 620 Herridge Ln V1L 6A7 **Location:** Just e of Baker St; between Josephine and Hall sts, down alleyway. **Parking:** street only.

[D] [🅺]

FUSION BISTRO   250/352-3011

▼▼▼ Small Plates. Casual Dining. $15-$25 **AAA Inspector Notes:** This intimate and contemporary spot serves beautifully presented dishes utilizing fine ingredients. A variety of tapas such as tiger prawns stuffed with goat cheese, garlic wrapped in prosciutto and spicy crispy green beans with chili garlic sauce are showcased. Try one of the classic bistro dishes which include French onion soup and cassoulets. Truly decadent desserts are a great way to end the meal. All is prepared in the open-grill kitchen and served up by engaging and knowledgeable staff. **Bar:** full bar. **Reservations:** suggested. **Address:** 301 Baker St V1L 4H6 **Location:** Jct Hwy 3A/3B and 6, just nw, then just ne. **Parking:** street only. [D] CALL [♿M]

THE PRESERVED SEED   250/352-0325

▼ Natural/Organic. Quick Serve. $5-$9 **AAA Inspector Notes:** Climb up or down the stairs to reach this cafe, which has a small menu but boasts fresh, often organic, ingredients that frequently come from its own farm. Fresh salads, soups and hot sandwiches, as well as a rice medley made with an organic mix of rices and weekly sauces, are finished off with exceptional coconut cream pie, date squares or Mate energy bars. Organic coffee is on hand, but the signature beverage is Yerba Mate, a traditional drink not unlike tea. Outside dining is available. **Address:** 202 Vernon St V1L 4E2 **Location:** Jct Hwy 3A and 6, 0.4 mi (0.7 km) n; on covered stairway; access up from Vernon St or down from Falls St off Baker St. **Parking:** street only. [B] [L] [D] [🅺]

THOR'S PIZZA   250/352-1212

▼ Pizza. Quick Serve. $5-$15 **AAA Inspector Notes:** Named after the owner's dog, the eatery uses the freshest quality ingredients and Italian-style bread crust. Surely the pooch has impeccable taste in pizza, what with a certified chef de cuisine in front of the oven. Most ingredients in the fabulous pizzas are sourced locally or made in house, so there is no wonder why customers line up out the door on weekends. Ciabatta subs, grilled panini sandwiches, calzones and individual slices also are available. Guests can take advantage of the limited seating or grab their food to go. **Address:** 303 Victoria St V1L 4K3 **Location:** Between Kootenay and Stanley sts; downtown. **Parking:** street only. [L] [D]

NEW DENVER (C-10) pop. 504,
elev. 555m/1,850'

In 1891 prospectors poured into the area; New Denver sprang up as a supply point on the shores of Slocan Lake. Here goods and passengers switched from rail to lake stern-wheelers. The town also provided a more sedate environment to raise a family and conduct business than the rowdy mining camps of the so-called Silvery Slocan.

The Kohan Reflection Garden, at the foot of First Avenue, honors the Japanese-Canadians interned here during World War II. Shacks that formerly housed internees can still be seen around town. The Silvery Slocan Historical Society Museum, housed in the 1897 former Bank of Montreal Building on Sixth Avenue, contains artifacts and exhibits about the town's history; phone (250) 358-2316.

NIKKEI INTERNMENT MEMORIAL CENTRE is at 306 Josephine St. Dedicated to remembering the Japanese internment experience during World War II, the center commemorates the 22,000 Nikkei (people of Japanese descent) removed from their British Columbia homes and relocated to camps. Exhibits include a typical two-family shack, an outhouse and a peace garden. Tribute also is paid to the first generation of Japanese who arrived in Canada in 1877.

Tours: Guided tours are available. **Time:** Allow 30 minutes minimum. **Hours:** Daily 10-5, May-Sept.; by appointment rest of year. Phone ahead for guided tour information. **Cost:** $8.50; $6.50 (ages 60+ and students with ID); free (ages 0-5); $20 (family). **Phone:** (250) 358-7288.

SWEET DREAMS GUESTHOUSE   250/358-2415

▼▼ **Country Inn.** Rates not provided. **Address:** 702 Eldorado St V0G 1S0 **Location:** Just w of Hwy 6 on Slocan Ave. Across street from lake. **Facility:** 5 units. 2 stories (no elevator), interior corridors. **Bath:** some shared. **Terms:** check-in 5 pm.

[‖] [📶] [✕] [🅺] [Ⓦ] [✉] / SOME UNITS [🐾]

NEW WESTMINSTER (H-11) pop. 65,976,
elev. 75m/246'
- **Attractions map p. 355**
- **Hotels & Restaurants map & index p. 368**
- **Part of Vancouver area — see map p. 343**

The oldest incorporated city in Western Canada, New Westminster—also known as the Royal City—was named by Queen Victoria. Transformed into a boomtown by the lure of gold in 1857, it plunged into a depression when the gold rush subsided in the late 1860s. The city was the provincial capital until 1868.

New Westminster also is known for its architecture. Parts of the city were built by the Royal Engineers, sent in 1855 to keep order in the new crown colony. Former members of this organization later formed the New Westminster Regiment, whose history is recounted in the Museum of the Royal Westminster Regiment at Sixth Street and Queens Avenue; phone (604) 526-5116.

Other places of interest include old houses, many of which survived a devastating fire in 1898. The houses can be toured in May. Tickets must be purchased in advance; for information phone the New Westminster Hyack Festival Association at (604) 522-6894.

Westminster Quay Public Market, on the waterfront, maintains a tradition started in 1892 when farmers, hunters and settlers came to barter for goods. Fresh meat, baked goods, produce and local crafts can be purchased daily.

Antique Alley, on historic Front Street, is known for its heritage buildings housing stores featuring an array of antiques and collectibles.

(See map & index p. 368.)

Also of interest is *Sampson V* Maritime Museum aboard the stern-wheeler berthed on the Fraser River at the foot of Tenth Street. The stern-wheeler, the last steam-powered paddlewheeler to operate on the Fraser, can be toured; phone (604) 522-6894. The Canadian Lacrosse Hall of Fame, which celebrates Canada's national summer sport, is at 65 E. Sixth Ave. at junction McBride Boulevard; phone (604) 527-4640.

New Westminster Visitor Centre: 788 Quayside Dr., New Westminster, BC, Canada V3M 6Z6. **Phone:** (604) 526-1905 or (604) 551-4974.

JAPANESE FRIENDSHIP GARDEN is next to City Hall at 511 Royal Ave. Waterfalls, pathways and flowering trees and shrubs adorn the garden, which features 100 Yoshino cherry trees, a gift from the city of Moriguchi, Japan. **Time:** Allow 1 hour, 30 minutes minimum. **Hours:** Daily dawn-dusk. **Cost:** Free. **Phone:** (604) 527-4567.

NEW WESTMINSTER MUSEUM AND ARCHIVES is at 302 Royal Ave. This 1864 mansion was built in the San Francisco Gothic Revival style for Capt. William Irving, a pioneer of the riverboat trade on the Fraser River. Furnished in period, the 14-room residence is bedecked in Victorian Christmas decor during December. The adjacent museum features artifacts, local history displays and an 1876 coach built to carry the governor general of Canada to the Cariboo goldfields.

Time: Allow 1 hour minimum. **Hours:** Museum, house and archives Wed.-Sun. noon-5, in summer; noon-4, rest of year. Closed major holidays. Phone ahead to confirm schedule. **Cost:** Donations. **Phone:** (604) 527-4640.

PADDLEWHEELER RIVERBOAT TOURS departs from the boardwalk of the New Westminster Quay Public Market at 788 Quayside Dr. Narrated sightseeing tours of various lengths are offered aboard an authentic paddlewheeler. The MV *Native* is a replica of a late 19th-century riverboat that carried passengers on the historic Gold Rush Trail via the Fraser River. Evening entertainment cruises also are available.

Hours: Cruises depart daily year-round. Phone ahead to confirm schedule. **Cost:** Fare $49.95-$89.95; $44.95-$79.95 (ages 60+); $29.95-$59.95 (ages 6-12). Some fares may include meals. Reservations are required. **Phone:** (604) 525-4465 or (877) 825-1302.

QUEENS PARK is at 6th St. and McBride Blvd. in the center of town. The park includes a Salish totem pole, a picnic area, tennis courts, botanical gardens, nature trails, a stadium, an arena and a band shell in which concerts are presented in July and August. Splash pools, playgrounds and a petting zoo are open in summer. In Centennial Lodge, the Art Gallery in the Park features works by emerging and established artists.

Time: Allow 1 hour, 30 minutes minimum. **Hours:** Park open daily dawn-dusk. Art gallery daily 1-5, July-Aug.; Tues.-Sun. 1-5, rest of year. Splash pools daily 10-7, Victoria Day weekend-Labour Day weekend; Sat.-Sun. 10-7, day after Labour Day weekend-Sept. 30. Petting zoo daily 10-5:30, June-Aug. **Cost:** Donations. **Phone:** (604) 777-5111 for the park, or (604) 525-3244 for the gallery.

INN AT THE QUAY   (604)520-1776 **30**
▼▼▼▼ **Hotel** $140-$230 **Address:** 900 Quayside Dr V3M 6G1 **Location:** Along waterfront, follow signs to Westminster Quay. Adjacent to public market. **Facility:** 126 units. 9 stories, interior corridors. **Parking:** on-site (fee). **Terms:** cancellation fee imposed. **Dining:** The Boathouse Restaurant, see separate listing. **Activities:** sauna, whirlpool, exercise room. **Guest Services:** valet laundry.
ECO ▯▮ ▽ CALL ⟨ᴍ ⧉ ✕ ⧉ ▭

WHERE TO EAT

THE BOATHOUSE RESTAURANT   604/525-3474
▼▼ ▼▼ Steak Seafood. Casual Dining. $12-$40 **AAA Inspector Notes:** Along the water at Westminster Quay and next to the Inn at Westminster Quay, the relaxed restaurant lets diners look out over the Fraser River. An extensive selection of wines and cocktails complements the great seafood dishes. **Bar:** full bar. **Reservations:** suggested. **Address:** 900 Quayside Dr V3M 6G1 **Location:** Along waterfront, follow signs to Westminster Quay; in Inn at the Quay. **Parking:** on-site (fee). B L D CALL ⟨ᴍ

BURGER HEAVEN   604/522-8339 **39**
▼ Burgers Sandwiches. Casual Dining. $8-$20 **AAA Inspector Notes:** This locally popular dining spot features all kinds of burgers—chicken, veggie or beef—cooked to order and served with many different fresh toppings. The menu also lists a wide variety of sandwiches, beer, wine and coolers. Guests should watch their heads in the living room-style dining room, as the ceiling has several hanging plants. Both the walls and tabletops are adorned with hundreds of customer pictures. The friendly staff carries out casual service. **Bar:** beer & wine. **Address:** 77 10th St V3M 3X4 **Location:** From Royal Ave, just e. **Parking:** street only. L D

NORTH VANCOUVER (H-11) pop. 48,196, elev. 99m/325'
• Hotels p. 284 • Restaurants p. 284
• Attractions map p. 355
• Hotels & Restaurants map & index p. 368
• Part of Vancouver area — see map p. 343

North Vancouver is a city, and it's also a district. All visitors really need to know, however, is that this North Shore destination is definitely worth checking out.

Lumbering and shipbuilding were important early on, and by the early 20th century the town across Burrard Inlet from Vancouver had incorporated. Today there are no discernible distinctions among the various municipalities that make up the North Shore. The city of North Vancouver does have its own impressive skyline, easily visible from the downtown Vancouver waterfront, while the district of North Vancouver is a bit of a hodgepodge, with pockets of industry and commercial development mixed in with parks and green spaces. It's also the location of Grouse Mountain and the Capilano Suspension Bridge Park *(see attraction listings)*, two of the North Shore's most popular tourist attractions.

From Vancouver, take either the Lions Gate Bridge or the Ironworkers Memorial Second Narrows

(See map & index p. 368.)

Crossing (Hwy. 1) to North Vancouver. (The bridge's name honors 27 workers who were killed when several spans collapsed during construction.) But the most scenic approach is aboard TransLink's SeaBus, with terminals on Vancouver's downtown waterfront (near Canada Place) and in North Vancouver next to the Lonsdale Quay Market. These 400-passenger catamaran ferries make the one-way trip across Burrard Inlet in about 12 minutes. Ferries depart both terminals every 15 minutes Mon.-Fri. 6 a.m.-6:30 p.m., Sat. 10:15-6:45, Sun. 11:15-6:45. TransLink's fare system allows passengers to travel freely between buses, the SeaBus and the SkyTrain rapid transit system. For additional schedule and fare information phone (604) 953-3333.

If you arrive via the SeaBus, the first place you must explore is the Lonsdale Quay Market. It's a classic Vancouver fresh market with an abundance of vendors selling fruit, veggies, flowers, seafood and baked goods, plus yummy soups, sauces and other specialty items. You'll be hard pressed to decide on something to go from one of the international food bars—the choices are many and tempting, from noodle stir fries to seafood chowder—but once the decision is made, eat outside on the deck so you can watch the ferry boats come and go with downtown Vancouver as a backdrop. A farmers market sets up on the East Plaza at the Quay Saturdays from 10 to 3, May 10-Oct. 25. Organic farmers, bakers, jam and salsa makers and crafters all peddle their wares.

If peace and quiet are what you're seeking, head to Cates Park. From Vancouver, take the first exit off the Second Narrows bridge, following the signs for Deep Cove; then proceed east on Dollarton Highway about 8 kilometres (5 mi.) to the park entrance (on the right). There are grassy areas, a playground for kids and a pebble-sand beach. Watch the boats heading from Burrard Inlet into Indian Arm, check out the totem pole and indigenous canoe, hike a waterfront trail through stands of Douglas fir and big-leaf maple, or stretch out and take a nap under one of the huge cedar trees near the parking lot.

From Cates Park, get back on Dollarton Highway and continue north a couple of kilometres to the residential community of Deep Cove. The cove in question is a natural indentation of Indian Arm, a fiord-like extension of Burrard Inlet. In the 18th century Northwest tribes traveled up and down Indian Arm hunting and fishing, and lumbering was an important industry in this area in the first half of the 20th century.

What strikes you immediately about Deep Cove is how incredibly picturesque it is. Gallant Avenue is a quaint 2 blocks of eateries (fish and chips followed by a cone from Orca's Favourite Ice Cream makes a nice lunch combo), a shop or three and the Deep Cove Cultural Centre, which includes the Seymour Art Gallery and the Deep Cove Stage Society's community theater. The street ends at nicely landscaped Panorama Park, bright with flower beds in the

summer. Walk down the stairs to the beach and then out onto the pier.

Sheltered, serene Deep Cove harbor will take your breath away. Trees frame the cove on both sides. Rising beyond the water to the left are the thickly forested slopes of Mount Seymour Provincial Park *(see attraction listing and Recreation Areas Chart)*. The wooded hillsides to the right are speckled with houses that undoubtedly have views to die for. Across Indian Arm loom the Coast Mountains, dark masses in the distance. Sailboats bob on the cove's tranquil surface. Kayakers slice through the water. Canoeists paddle gracefully. It's quite an enchanting vista, one you'll likely end up gazing out on all afternoon.

CAPILANO SALMON HATCHERY is at 4500 Capilano Park Rd. Self-guiding tours allow visitors to view this architecturally acclaimed facility. Displays trace the development of coho, chinook and steelhead salmon. Live adult salmon may be seen in the fish ladder July through November. Scenic picnic areas are available. **Time:** Allow 30 minutes minimum. **Hours:** Daily 8-8, June-Aug.; 8-7 in May and Sept.; 8-4:45 in Apr. and Oct.; 8-4, rest of year. **Cost:** Free. **Phone:** (604) 666-1790. ⊞

GEM **CAPILANO SUSPENSION BRIDGE PARK** is off Hwy. 1 exit 14, then 2 km (1.2 mi.) n. to 3735 Capilano Rd.; a free shuttle is available from several locations in downtown Vancouver. The swinging 137-metre-long (450-ft.) footbridge spans a 70-metre-deep (230-ft.) densely wooded gorge above the Capilano River. George Grant Mackay, a Scottish civil engineer, built the original bridge in 1889 from hemp rope and cedar planks; the fourth structure on the site is reinforced with steel cables and concrete.

The site features gardens; a totem park; Treetops Adventure, a series of suspension bridges; Cliffwalk, a cliffside walkway with a rock-climber's view of the canyon; and a story center that displays artifacts of the bridge. The Living Forest includes interactive displays and naturalist exhibits which guide visitors through a West Coast rain forest. Artisans sculpt totem poles and masks in the Big House.

Wheelchairs are not permitted on the bridge. **Time:** Allow 1 hour minimum. **Hours:** Daily 8:30-8, May 29-Labour Day; 10-9 in Jan. and Dec.; 9-7, May 1-28; 9-6, Mar. 6- Apr. 30 and day after Labour Day-Oct. 2; 9-5, rest of year. Closed Christmas. Phone ahead to confirm schedule. **Cost:** $32.95; $30.95 (ages 65+); $26.95 (students with ID); $21.95 (ages 13-16); $12 (ages 6-12). **Phone:** (604) 985-7474 or (877) 985-7474. *(See ad p. 357, p. 315.)* ⊞

GEM **GROUSE MOUNTAIN** is at 6400 Nancy Greene Way. A skyride takes visitors to the top of the mountain where, from a height of 1,100 metres (4,100 ft.), the summit offers a panorama of the city. On clear nights floodlit buildings and twinkling lights are reflected in the still harbor.

(See map & index p. 368.)

Skiing, snowshoeing, snowboarding, ice skating and sleigh rides are possible in the winter. Helicopter tours; guided or self-guiding interpretive walks that provide information about area flora, fauna and geology; a 45-minute lumberjack show; and a Birds in Motion demonstration featuring free-flying birds of prey are popular in the summer. Sports events and shows take place year-round. An aerial tramway operates all year to the chalet.

Each hour year-round The Theatre in the Sky shows the film "Born to Fly," which provides an eagle's view of southwestern British Columbia, or "Tyto's Triumph," about a persevering barn owl and conservation efforts. The Grouse Mountain Refuge for Endangered Wildlife, a 2-hectare (5 acre) habitat also open year-round, is home to two orphaned grizzly bears and a pack of gray wolves. Grouse Grind, a grueling 2.9-kilometre (1.8-mi.) climb up the mountain, is popular with locals. Or, you can experience the beauty of the area from above on the Air Grouse zipline or tandem paragliding flights.

Daily bus service to the tramway is available. **Time:** Allow 1 hour minimum. **Hours:** Grouse Mountain open daily 9 a.m.-10 p.m. **Cost:** $39.95-$49.95; $35.95-$45.95 (ages 65+); $23.95-$33.95 (ages 13-18); $13.95 (ages 5-12). Fares may vary; phone ahead. **Phone:** (604) 980-9311. 🍴 🏕️

The Eye of the Wind is on top of Grouse Mountain. This 65-metre- (215 ft.) tall wind turbine erected on the mountaintop provides approximately 20 percent of Grouse Mountain's energy requirement. In addition, it offers the city's highest observation deck, the viewPOD.

One-hour guided tours provide information about sustainability and take visitors by elevator to the glassed-in observation deck (part of the floor is also glass) where they are rewarded with 360-degree views of Vancouver, the harbor, the Coastal Mountains and, on a clear day, mounts Baker, Rainier and Garibaldi. **Time:** Allow 1 hour minimum. **Hours:** Grouse Mountain open daily 9 a.m.-10 p.m. The Eye of the Wind tours depart daily on the hour 10-7 (weather permitting). Phone ahead to confirm schedule. **Cost:** Grouse Mountain $39.95; $35.95 (ages 65+); $23.95 (ages 13-18); $13.95 (ages 5-12). The Eye of the Wind Tour $19.95 additional; free (ages 0-4). Various combination tours are also available. Fares may vary; phone ahead. Reservations are recommended. **Phone:** (604) 980-9311. 🍴

LYNN CANYON ECOLOGY CENTRE is off Lynn Valley Rd. to the end of Peters Rd., following signs to 3663 Park Rd. The centre is in a municipal park that features paths, natural streams and rivers and a 50-metre-high (166-ft.) suspension bridge spanning a waterfall and the canyon. The ecology centre offers films, children's activities and nature displays. Interactive exhibits highlight the plants and animals of the coastal temperate rain forest.

Hours: Park open daily dawn-dusk. Center open daily 10-5, June-Sept.; Mon.-Fri. noon-4, Sat.-Sun. and holidays 10-5, rest of year. Closed Jan. 1, Christmas and day after Christmas. **Cost:** Donations. **Phone:** (604) 990-3755. 🍴

MAPLEWOOD FARM is at 405 Seymour River Pl. This park-farm specializes in the display of domestic farm animals and birds. Visitors may enjoy a pony ride, pet the inhabitants of Goathill and Rabbitat and view a cow-milking demonstration.

Time: Allow 1 hour minimum. **Hours:** Daily 10-4, Apr.-Oct.; Tues.-Sun. 10-4, rest of year. Closed Christmas. **Cost:** $7; $4 (ages 19 months-16 years and 55+). Prices may vary; phone ahead. **Phone:** (604) 929-5610.

MOUNT SEYMOUR PROVINCIAL PARK is 24 km (15 mi.) n.e. The scenic area of 3,508 hectares (8,668 acres) is on the slopes of 1,433-metre (4,701-ft.) Mount Seymour. A good highway goes to the 1,006-metre (3,330-ft.) level. Hiking trails and downhill skiing are available in season. *See Recreation Areas Chart.* **Hours:** Daily 7 a.m.-11 p.m. **Cost:** Free. **Parking:** $1 per hour or $3 per day. **Phone:** (604) 986-2261. 🔺 🍴 🎿 🥾 🏕️

NORTH VANCOUVER MUSEUM AND ARCHIVES is in Presentation House at 209 W. Fourth St. The museum's artifacts and photographs document the community's growth from pioneer days. Documentary and photographic collections are housed in the archives at 3203 Institute Rd. Temporary exhibits are available.

Time: Allow 1 hour minimum. **Hours:** Museum open Tues.-Sun. noon-5. Archives open Tues.-Sat. noon-5. Complex closed Jan. 1 and Dec. 25-31. **Cost:** Donations. **Phone:** (604) 990-3700.

PARK & TILFORD GARDENS is at jct. Cotton Rd. and Brooksbank Ave. at 333 Brooksbank Ave. The 2.8-acre botanical site consists of eight interconnected theme gardens. A variety of both native and exotic floral arrangements leads through arboreal displays and to aviaries, where visitors may see parrots and other tropical birds.

An aromatic blend of plant and flower enclosures composes the Rose Garden, home to 24 varieties of plant life and more than 250 rose plants. **Tours:** Guided tours are available. **Time:** Allow 1 hour minimum. **Hours:** Daily 9:30-dusk. **Cost:** Free. **Phone:** (604) 984-8200.

RECREATIONAL ACTIVITIES
Kayaking
- **Takaya Tours** depart from off Hwy. 1 exit 23A to Main St. (becomes Dollarton Hwy.), then 3.3 mi. e. to Cates Park docks, following signs. Shuttle transportation is available. **Hours:** Daily 9-7, May-Oct. **Phone:** (604) 904-7410 or (778) 835-5047.

(See map & index p. 368.)

BEST WESTERN CAPILANO INN & SUITES
(604)987-8185 **12**

Motel
$99-$149

AAA Benefit:
Members save up to 20%, plus 10% bonus points with Best Western Rewards®.

Address: 1634 Capilano Rd V7P 3B4 **Location:** Trans-Canada Hwy 1 exit 14 (Capilano Rd), 0.9 mi (1.5 km) s; from north end of Lions Gate Bridge, 0.6 mi (1 km) e on Marine Dr, then just n. **Facility:** 74 units, some two bedrooms, efficiencies and kitchens. 2 stories (no elevator), interior/exterior corridors. **Amenities:** Some: high-speed Internet. **Pool(s):** heated outdoor. **Guest Services:** coin laundry. **Free Special Amenities:** newspaper and high-speed Internet.

15 minutes to Downtown Vancouver. Near fine shopping centers, restaurants, attractions, ski slopes

---

COMFORT INN & SUITES
(604)988-3181 **10**

Motel
$99-$130

Address: 1748 Capilano Rd V7P 3B4 **Location:** Trans-Canada Hwy 1 exit 14 (Capilano Rd), 0.9 mi (1.5 km) s; from north end of Lions Gate Bridge, 0.6 mi (1 km) e on Marine Dr, then just n. **Facility:** 94 units, some two bedrooms, efficiencies and kitchens. 2 stories (no elevator), exterior corridors. **Terms:** check-in 4 pm, cancellation fee imposed. **Amenities:** Some: high-speed Internet. **Pool(s):** heated outdoor. **Activities:** whirlpool. **Guest Services:** valet and coin laundry. **Free Special Amenities:** full breakfast and local telephone calls.

HOLIDAY INN & SUITES NORTH VANCOUVER
(604)985-3111 **14**

Hotel
$139-$169

Address: 700 Old Lillooet Rd V7J 2H5 **Location:** Trans-Canada Hwy 1 exit 22 (Mt Seymour Pkwy), follow signs. **Facility:** 162 units, some efficiencies. 6 stories, interior corridors. **Amenities:** video games (fee), high-speed Internet, safes. **Pool(s):** heated indoor. **Activities:** sauna, whirlpool, exercise room, spa. **Guest Services:** valet and coin laundry. **Free Special Amenities:** local telephone calls and high-speed Internet.

Nestled at the foot of the majestic North Shore mountains, the perfect place to work, rest and play

---

Visit AAA.com/Travel or CAA.ca/Travel for complete trip planning and reservations

---

LIONSGATE TRAVELODGE
(604)985-5311 **11**

Motel $59-$169 **Address:** 2060 Marine Dr V7P 1V7 **Location:** Trans-Canada Hwy 1 exit 14 (Capilano Rd), 0.9 mi (1.5 km) s, then just w; from north end of Lions Gate Bridge, just e. **Facility:** 60 units. 2 stories (no elevator), exterior corridors.

NORTH VANCOUVER HOTEL
(604)987-4461 **9**

Motel
$79-$149

Address: 1800 Capilano Rd V7P 3B6 **Location:** Trans-Canada Hwy 1 exit 14 (Capilano Rd), 0.9 mi (1.5 km) s; from north end of Lions Gate Bridge, 0.6 mi (1 km) e on Marine Dr, then just n. **Facility:** 72 units, some kitchens. 2 stories (no elevator), exterior corridors. **Amenities:** high-speed Internet. **Pool(s):** heated outdoor. **Guest Services:** valet and coin laundry. **Free Special Amenities:** full breakfast and high-speed Internet.

PINNACLE HOTEL AT THE PIER
(604)986-7437 **13**

Contemporary Hotel $129-$259 **Address:** 138 Victory Ship Way V7L 0B1 **Location:** Corner of Esplanade St and Lonsdale Ave. **Facility:** 106 units. 8 stories, interior corridors. **Parking:** on-site (fee). **Terms:** cancellation fee imposed. **Amenities:** high-speed Internet, safes. **Dining:** The Lobby Restaurant, see separate listing. **Pool(s):** heated indoor. **Activities:** sauna, whirlpool, steamroom, exercise room. **Guest Services:** valet laundry.

WHERE TO EAT

CACTUS CLUB CAFE
604/986-5776

American. Casual Dining. $9-$29 **AAA Inspector Notes:** This bustling, casual restaurant serves huge burgers, sandwiches, pasta, salads, soups, quesadillas, fajitas, vegetarian dishes, steak, ribs, chicken and fish. Featured are certified Angus beef and fresh wild British Columbia salmon. **Bar:** full bar. **Address:** 1598 Pemberton Ave V7P 2S2 **Location:** From Marine Dr, just w at W 16th St.

THE EDGE BISTRO
604/985-9125 **27**

Italian. Fine Dining. $15-$30 **AAA Inspector Notes:** In the quaint Edgemont Shopping Village on the road to Grouse Mountain, this handsome bistro prepares a large selection of fresh, savory pastas in the most delightful sauces, or try their tasty poultry, meats and seafood. The wines are reasonably priced; servers will help you pick just the right bottle. You simply must try the amazing, fresh-made tiramisu. **Bar:** full bar. **Reservations:** suggested. **Address:** 3135 Edgemont Blvd V7R 2N7 **Location:** 1.1 mi (1.8 km) n on Capilano Rd, 0.6 mi (1 km) e on Ridgewood Dr, then just s; in Edgemont Village. **Parking:** street only.

GUSTO DI QUATTRO
604/924-4444 **30**

Italian. Fine Dining. $14-$35 **AAA Inspector Notes:** Translated, Gusto di Quattro means "a taste of Quattro." The North Shore favorite, which has a small dining space, is by Lonsdale Quay Market. Wonderful pastas and freshly made breads await. Patrons likely will have to wait for a table if they didn't make a reservation. A pay parking lot is right across the street. **Bar:** full bar. **Reservations:** suggested. **Address:** 1 Lonsdale Ave V7M 2E4 **Location:** Trans-Canada Hwy 1 exit 18 (Lonsdale Ave), 1.6 mi (2.5 km) s to Lonsdale Quay Market. **Parking:** street only.

JAGERHOF SCHNITZEL HOUSE
604/980-4316 **28**

German. Casual Dining. $10-$18 **AAA Inspector Notes:** Just north of the Sea Bus terminal and near the shops of Lonsdale Quay Market, the cozy little restaurant lures a loyal clientele for wonderful schnitzels. **Bar:** full bar. **Reservations:** suggested, for dinner. **Address:** 71 Lonsdale Ave V7M 2E5 **Location:** Between 1st and Esplanade sts. **Parking:** street only.

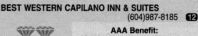

(See map & index p. 368.)

THE LOBBY RESTAURANT   604/986-7437   29
▼▼▼▼ Pacific Northwest. Fine Dining. $12-$28 **AAA Inspector Notes:** Inspired by a natural abundance of seafood and fresh regional ingredients, the dishes here reflect a wonderful West Coast flair. This cozy 85-seat restaurant offers breathtaking views of the harbor setting and distant downtown Vancouver skyline. **Bar:** full bar. **Reservations:** suggested. **Address:** 138 Victory Ship Way V7L 0B1 **Location:** Corner of Esplanade St and Lonsdale Ave; in Pinnacle Hotel at the Pier. [B] [L] [D] CALL ⟨&M⟩

RICKY'S ALL DAY GRILL   604/904-4430
▼▼▼ American. Casual Dining. $6-$15 **AAA Inspector Notes:** The comfortable eatery, which employs friendly servers, presents a varied menu that includes pasta dishes, wraps, omelets, stir-fry preparations and burgers. Portions are generous. Children's and senior selections are offered. Guests can request seating in a booth or at a table. **Bar:** full bar. **Address:** 1995 Lonsdale Ave V7M 2K3 **Location:** Between 20th and 19th sts. [B] [L] [D] CALL ⟨&M⟩

OAK BAY pop. 18,015
- **Hotels & Restaurants map & index p. 408**
- **Part of Victoria area — see map p. 397**

OAK BAY GUEST HOUSE BED & BREAKFAST
(250)598-3812   45
▼▼▼ **Historic Bed & Breakfast** $89-$179 **Address:** 1052 Newport Ave V8S 5E2 **Location:** 3 mi (4.8 km) e on Oak Bay Ave (which becomes Newport Ave). **Facility:** In keeping with the age of this historic building, the guest rooms are average size and some bathrooms are compact, as well. Overall, the B&B offers lush landscaped grounds and a very homey charm inside. 11 units. 2 stories (no elevator), interior corridors. **Terms:** check-in 4 pm, age restrictions may apply, 3 day cancellation notice-fee imposed.
[� icons]

WHERE TO EAT

THE MARINA RESTAURANT   250/598-8555   34
▼▼▼▼ Pacific Northwest. Fine Dining. $15-$36 **AAA Inspector Notes:** Located in the Oak Bay Marina, this restaurant provides beautiful, sweeping views of the ocean, harbor and mountains. Its menu features a Pacific Northwest cuisine, showcasing fresh, local and exotic seafood as well as items from a sushi bar and cafe deli. **Bar:** full bar. **Reservations:** suggested. **Address:** 1327 Beach Dr V8S 2N4 **Location:** 3.8 mi (6 km) e via Oak Bay Ave, just s. [L] [D] CALL ⟨&M⟩

OTTAVIO ITALIAN BAKERY & DELICATESSEN
250/592-4080   33
▼ Italian Deli Breads/Pastries. Quick Serve. $7-$14 **AAA Inspector Notes:** This pleasant café in the heart of Oak Bay offers a wide variety of fresh salads, grilled panini sandwiches and wonderful soups. The homemade gelato with fresh fruit is a hit. Choose dining inside or out on a lovely terrazzo overlooking a busy street scene. **Bar:** beer & wine. **Address:** 2272 Oak Bay Ave V8R 1G7 **Location:** At Monterey Ave. **Parking:** on-site and street. [B] [L] CALL ⟨&M⟩ [⟨]

PAPRIKA BISTRO   250/592-7424   31
▼▼▼ Pacific Northwest. Fine Dining. $16-$36 **AAA Inspector Notes:** In the small, neighborhood Estevan Shopping Centre, this bistro prepares some wonderful dishes that are always fresh and often include local ingredients. A fine selection of B.C. wines is available. It's a bit tricky to find, so ask your hotel or concierge for directions; it really is worth the drive. Lunch is served on Friday and Saturday. **Bar:** full bar. **Reservations:** suggested. **Address:** 2524 Estevan Ave V8R 2S7 **Location:** Between Dunlevy and Musgrave sts; in Estevan Shopping Centre. **Parking:** street only. [D] [⟨]

PENNY FARTHING ENGLISH PUB   250/370-9008   32
▼▼ Canadian. Gastropub. $11-$17 **AAA Inspector Notes:** The classic, relaxed British-style pub is decorated in rich dark wood with brass accents. Fine pub fare pairs with a wide selection of stouts, ales and lagers. Patrons younger than age 19 are not permitted. **Bar:** full bar. **Address:** 2228 Oak Bay Ave V8R 1G5 **Location:** Between Monterey Ave and Hampshire Rd. **Parking:** street only. [L] [D]

OKANAGAN VALLEY

It's one thing to read about a place; it's quite another to experience it in person. Evocatively written guides and glossy photo books can pique the curiosity and whet the appetite of almost any traveler, but when it comes down to it you really need to get out of the armchair and go. This is certainly true of the Okanagan (oh-ka-NOG-an) Valley; in a province almost embarrassingly gifted with scenic riches, it still manages to stand out.

British Columbia—like much of Canada—is notable for its sheer ruggedness: lofty mountains, expansive forests, rushing rivers. The valley, in contrast, is an anomaly; it could almost be Italy or some other sun-kissed land. The sun does indeed shine warmly, and the azure sky is huge. Tawny bluffs rise from the shores of steel-blue lakes. Scraggly pine trees and compact mounds of silvery gray sagebrush cloak hillsides. Parts of the Okanagan are arid enough to meet the meteorological criteria of a desert, but irrigation has transformed it into one of the most productive fruit- and vegetable-growing regions in North America.

A Land Created by Glaciers

This long, narrow valley was shaped over time by glacial movement. Layers of ice more than a mile thick began retreating some 10,000 years ago, scraping the surface of the land and leaving behind deposits of sediment. Flowing mountain rivers caused innumerable cycles of flooding and erosion. All this water action contributed to a slow but steady accumulation of nutrient-rich soils that over time formed fertile deltas, setting the stage for the valley's eventual blossoming as an agricultural powerhouse.

Impressive mountains, with some peaks topping 3,000 metres (9,800 ft.), flank both sides of the Okanagan Valley—the Monashee range to the east, the Cascades to the west. The mountain systems in this part of North America are oriented in a north-south direction paralleling the Pacific coast, and the intervening valleys follow suit. The entire area is part of

This map shows cities in Okanagan Valley where you will find attractions, hotels and restaurants. Cities are listed alphabetically in this book on the following pages.

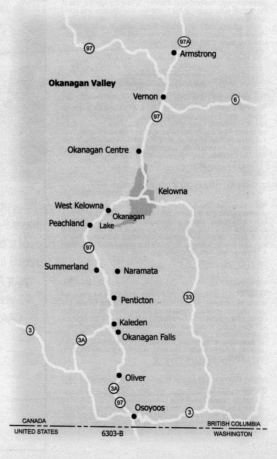

the vast Interior Plateau, an uplifted section of the Earth's crust that covers much of British Columbia's southern interior.

One of the Okanagan Valley's many virtues is its topographical variety—everything from desert to grassland to forest. The northern end is wetter and greener, with a panorama of snowcapped mountains rising off in the distance. As you head south into the heart of the valley the trees become more scattered; ponderosa pines speckling the hills are replaced by shrubs like antelope bush and hardy plants like bunch grass (so named because it grows in individual clumps or tufts rather than forming a uniform carpet), both of which are adapted to a drier climate.

Farther south the Okanagan verges on true desert. In and around Osoyoos the landscape is austere; towering cliffs and bare hillsides flaunt a palette of browns, beiges and grays, and the grasses and other low-growing plants are buffeted by persistent dry winds. The desert plants and animals that inhabit this arid environment are found nowhere else in Canada; the far southern end of the Okanagan Valley lies just above the northernmost reach of the Sonoran Desert, which extends south all the way into Mexico. This also is the country's warmest region, with relatively mild winters, hot summers and abundant sunshine, an ideal combination for irrigation-assisted agriculture.

Between Osoyoos to the east and Princeton to the west is the Similkameen Valley, nestled between steep rocky hills and threaded by the Similkameen River. Although a geographically separate region, it shares the southern Okanagan Valley's dramatic scenery and climatological characteristics. Similkameen country is known for its cattle ranches, horse farms and fruit orchards, and bills itself variously as the "Fruit Stand Capital of Canada" and "BC's Garden of Eden" in an attempt to step out of the better-known Okanagan's shadow.

Hwy. 3, also called the Crowsnest Highway, meanders along the province's southern border from Hope east to the Alberta border. Between Keremeos and Osoyoos the highway traverses an area that climatologists classify as a mid-altitude steppe, although it certainly looks like a desert. Away from the sweep of the ever-present irrigation sprinklers, this little portion of extreme southern British Columbia—known as Canada's "pocket desert"—is home to sagebrush, prickly pear cactus, Western rattlesnakes and even the odd scorpion, all of which thrive in these desert-like conditions.

The bracing beauty of the Similkameen countryside is particularly evident in the vicinity of Hedley, a small village about 76 kilometres (47 mi.) west of Osoyoos on Hwy. 3. Here the waters of Hedley Creek rush into the Similkameen River. Stemwinder Mountain looms to the west, Nickel Plate Mountain to the east. Marbled cliffs rise up on both sides of the highway (the Similkameen Indians named this area Sna-za-ist, meaning "the striped rock place"). Notes of color are supplied by a bright blue sky, the deep green of flourishing fruit trees and (in season) the gold and purple hues of ripening apricots, peaches, plums and grapes.

About 9 kilometres (5.5 mi.) west of Osoyoos is Spotted Lake, which gets its name from one of the world's highest concentrations of magnesium sulfate, calcium, sodium sulfates and other minerals. In summer much of the lake's water evaporates and the minerals crystallize into circles on the surface that can be white, pale yellow, green or blue, depending on the mineral composition. The lake is on private land, but you can view it from the highway.

The Okanagan Valley's distinguishing feature, in fact, is its chain of long, narrow lakes that stretch from north to south. Created by receding glaciers, they are kept fresh and full by snowmelt and runoff from the mountains that flank both sides of the valley. The largest is Okanagan Lake, which stretches north to south for some 111 kilometres (69 mi.) while averaging just 5 kilometres (3 mi.) wide. Skaha, Vaseux and Osoyoos lakes continue the chain to the south. To the east of Okanagan Lake are Kalamalka and Wood lakes; just north is little Swan Lake.

Cattle, Gold, Fruit and Wine

These valleys were first inhabited by the Okanagan Indians, an Interior Salish tribe. They hunted wild game, fished salmon runs, foraged for roots and berries and traded with other nations. The first European arrivals were fur traders searching for accessible routes to transport their goods to the Pacific. In the early 19th century they ventured north from Fort Okanogan, a Pacific Fur Co. trading post at the confluence of the Okanagan and Columbia rivers in present-day Washington state. Fur caravans were soon heading in and out of the valley region.

When the Oregon Treaty designated the 49th parallel as the border between the United States and the Canadian territory, Osoyoos became a port of entry, and vast herds of cattle were trailed through customs to supply food for miners who panned for placer gold along the Similkameen River. The bunch grass that grew along the river valley provided abundant forage, and ranches began to be established.

Father Charles Pandosy, an Oblate priest, founded a mission in 1859 on the eastern shore of Okanagan Lake. He and his followers endured a harsh first winter—they were forced to shoot their horses for food—but went on to build other missions in the Okanagan Valley, where Father Pandosy instructed the native people in European agricultural techniques in addition to performing baptisms, marriages and funerals.

The discovery of gold on the Fraser River in 1858 resulted in a full-fledged gold rush. British Columbia's southern interior was further opened up with the building of the Caribou Road (now Hwy. 97) and the Dewdney Trail (now Hwy. 3). By the late 19th century the Okanagan and Similkameen valleys were buzzing with gold camps and boom towns that began to spring up along the shores of the region's lakes.

The fruit industry that today is a hallmark of the Okanagan began with difficulty. Apple orchards were planted as early as 1892, but it wasn't until the 1920s that fruit crops proved economically successful. The valley's warm temperatures and long growing season—besides providing Canadians with approximately one-third of their apples—nurtures verdant orchards of apricots, cherries, peaches, pears and plums.

Commercial grape plantings near Kelowna supplied the Okanagan's first wineries. The local wine industry has grown exponentially since the introduction of large-scale irrigation, and almost all of British Columbia's wine comes from the Okanagan region. The diversity of growing conditions—from the hot, sandy desert soils of the south to the deep topsoil and clay of the cooler north, plus distinct microclimates created by the valley's lakes—help ensure a diversity of wines.

Vineyards at the southern end of the valley produce such vintages as Chardonnay, Merlot, Cabernet Sauvignon, Pinot Gris and Pinot Noir, while vineyards in the central and northern valley specialize in Pinot Blanc, Riesling and Gewürztraminer wines. Some grapes are left to freeze on the vine to produce icewine, a rich, sweet dessert wine. One of the Okanagan's most picturesque sights is orderly rows of grapevines, often covering a hillside that overlooks a deep blue lake.

Hwy. 97, which runs the length of British Columbia from the U.S. border just south of Osoyoos north to Watson Lake at the Yukon border, is the principal route through the Okanagan Valley. From Osoyoos it travels north to Penticton, then follows the western shore of Okanagan Lake before crossing the lake on a floating bridge (the largest in the country) that is scheduled to be replaced with an overhead bridge.

Okanagan Lake is said to be the home of Ogopogo, the best known of Canada's unexplained lake creatures. Sightings of the mythical beast—most often described as 5 to 6 metres (15 to 20 ft.) long, shaped like a log and with a head resembling that of a horse or goat—date back as far as 1872. Okanagan Indians believed that Ogopogo's home was small, barren Rattlesnake Island; they claimed that the island's rocky beaches were sometimes strewn with animal parts, presumably dinner remains, and when crossing the lake during bad weather always took along a small animal that would be thrown overboard in order to appease the monster. Interestingly, there are similarities between Okanagan Lake and Scotland's Loch Ness, home of the famed Loch Ness Monster; both bodies of water are long and narrow, and both lie at about the same latitude.

East of the lake Hwy. 97 winds north to Enderby, the unofficial northern end of the valley, before continuing on toward Sicamous. But whether you proceed from south to north or north to south, this 211-kilometre (131 mi.) journey through the heart of the Okanagan is utterly delightful. One minute the highway is running tantalizingly close to a sparkling lakeshore; the next it's in the shadow of a soaring, sagebrush-dotted bluff or looking down on checkerboard farmland. Each bend and turn reveals a new view, and each one is lovely. The scenery alone would be more than enough to recommend this drive, even if you didn't make a single stop.

Year-Round Fun

But of course you *will* want to stop, because this is Canada's No. 1 year-round recreation destination. Dozens of parks ring Okanagan Lake, offering myriad opportunities for hiking, backpacking, mountain biking and camping. Bear Creek Provincial Park, about 9 kilometres (6 mi.) west of Kelowna off Hwy. 97, has many hiking trails to explore, all beginning from a common trailhead at the park entrance. Bear Creek runs through the bottom of a tree-walled canyon, and the trails above wind past ponderosa pine, Douglas fir, juniper and prickly pear cactus that frame expansive lake views.

The lakes are, of course, ideal for water recreation, whether it's sailing, paddle boating, water skiing, jet skiing, kayaking, canoeing or freshwater fishing. Okanagan Lake is ringed with sandy beaches and sheltered coves, and numerous marina facilities provide equipment rentals.

For a northern Okanagan getaway head out to Kalamalka Lake Provincial Park, about 8 kilometres (5 mi.) southeast of Vernon off Hwy. 6. Kalamalka is known as a "marl lake," a process that begins when the water warms, forming calcium carbonate and limestone crystals that reflect sunlight. The water's distinctive blue-green color is often shot through with ribbons of deep blue, earning it the nickname "lake of a thousand colors." This largely undeveloped park encompasses rolling grasslands and forested ridges where Douglas fir and lodgepole pine grow; a paved trail leads to secluded beaches. Wildlife ranges from mule deer and minks to bobcats and western painted turtles. Bird-watching is rewarding, and the spring wildflower display is spectacular.

Nearly 40 golf courses are scattered from Vernon south to Osoyoos, with many of them concentrated around Kelowna. Due to the mild climate most courses open as early as March, and golfers frequently play into November. And this being the Okanagan, it's only natural that water and fruit trees figure into course layouts; the grounds of the Kelowna Springs Golf Club include seven spring-fed lakes, while fairways at the Harvest Golf Club are set in the midst of a huge hillside apple orchard and have prime views of Okanagan Lake.

Kelowna is the Okanagan Valley's largest city and a big summer vacation destination. Water sports—sailing, kayaking, windsurfing, fishing—rule the summer calendar, but downtown Kelowna also offers museums, art galleries, pretty lakeside parks, all kinds of restaurants and a lively nightlife. It makes a convenient base for touring the many small wineries in the vicinity.

Breezy Penticton has the best of both worlds; the north end of town fronts the southern tip of Okanagan Lake, while the south end brushes up against the north shore of Skaha Lake. Lakeside beaches give the city a summery feel, and families flock to Penticton's amusement centers, go-cart tracks, miniature golf course and waterslides. Stroll along Front Street, the original business corridor, which is lined with restaurants and funky little shops.

Situated between Swan, Kalamalka and Okanagan lakes, Vernon started out as a camp on the Okanagan Valley trail during the fur trade years; by the turn of the 20th century it was a bustling ranching center. Downtown Vernon truly earns the description "quaint": The tree-lined, flower-filled streets are packed with historic old buildings and specialty stores selling everything from Victorian crafts to homemade jams. Be sure to search out the 27 outdoor murals—some up to 91 metres (300 ft.) long—that depict Okanagan history, folklore and landscapes.

Just a stone's throw from the U.S. border, Osoyoos (oh-SOY-yoos) means, in the local Inkaneep native dialect, "where the water narrows"—a reference to its location spanning a narrow portion of Osoyoos Lake. Vineyards and orchards abound in the surrounding countryside, and the lake is one of Canada's warmest. Stroll along one of the lakeside parks in town while watching windsurfers and parasailing enthusiasts do their thing under sunny summer skies, and it's not that hard to believe you've happened onto some undiscovered Mediterranean resort.

The Okanagan Valley has something to offer regardless of the season. Downhill and cross-country skiers, snowboarders and other winter sports enthusiasts can choose from four ski resorts: Silver Star Mountain Resort, north of Vernon; Big White Ski Resort near Kelowna; Crystal Mountain resort near West Kelowna (Westbank); and Apex Mountain Resort, southwest of Penticton.

Spring and summer are seasons to experience the valley's agricultural bounty. In the spring fruit trees are in full glorious bloom. Spring into early summer also is the time when wildflowers make their appearance in the Okanagan's wilderness parks.

Harvest time for the region's famous fruits and vegetables begins in late June and lasts until mid-October. If you're here in the summer or fall stop at one of the ubiquitous roadside fruit stands, which seem almost as plentiful as the trees themselves. Cherries are first in the fruit parade, ripening from late June through mid-July. Peaches appear from mid-July through September; pears in August and September; plums in September; and apples from August through October.

Practically every town in the valley has a farmers market, and you'll want to check out every single one. In addition to all sorts of fruit, the markets offer tomatoes, pumpkins, squash, asparagus, organic preserves, homemade pies, artisanal cheeses, honey, herbs, flowers—just about everything. Most are open April or May through October.

Grapes are harvested September through mid-October, an ideal time to go winery hopping. Most of the Okanagan's roughly 100 wineries can be visited, many have an intriguing history to share, and practically all of them enjoy a picturesque rural setting. Before hitting the tasting bars, pick up information and maps at any local visitor center.

So when should you plan a trip? Come to think of it, just about *any* time is right.

Destinations in this region listed under their own names are Kaleden, Kelowna, Okanagan Centre, Okanagan Falls, Oliver, Osoyoos, Peachland, Penticton, Summerland, Vernon and West Kelowna (Westbank).

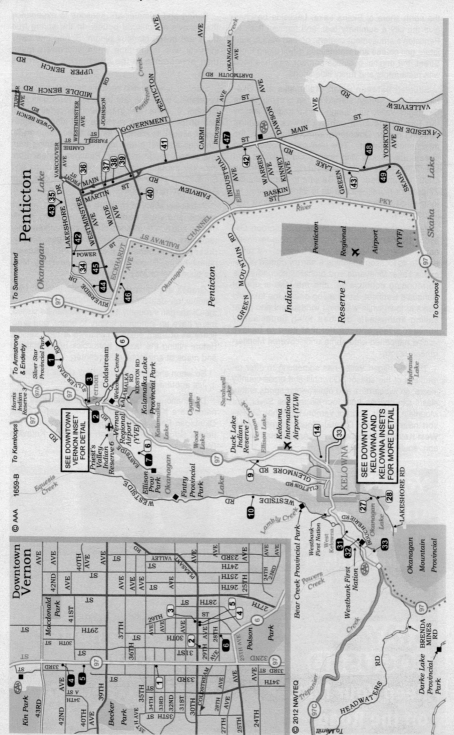

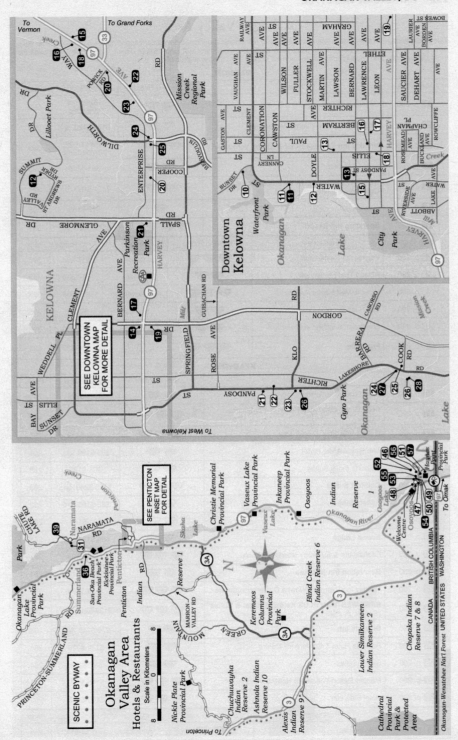

Okanagan Valley Area Hotels & Restaurants

SCENIC BYWAY

Scale in Kilometers

SEE PENTICTON INSET MAP FOR DETAIL

Downtown Kelowna

SEE DOWNTOWN KELOWNA MAP FOR MORE DETAIL

Okanagan Valley Area

This index helps you "spot" where approved hotels and restaurants are located on the corresponding detailed maps. Hotel daily rate range is for comparison only. Restaurant price range is a combination of lunch and/or dinner. Turn to the listing page for more detailed rate and price information and consult display ads for special promotions.

VERNON

Map Page	Hotels	Diamond Rated	Rate Range	Page
1 p. 290	Castle on the Mountain B & B	◆◆	Rates not provided	395
2 p. 290	**BEST WESTERN Villager Motor Inn**	◆◆	$100-$120 SAVE	395
3 p. 290	**Holiday Inn Express Hotel & Suites Vernon**	◆◆	Rates not provided SAVE	395
4 p. 290	Super 8 Vernon	◆◆	$85-$166	395
5 p. 290	**BEST WESTERN PLUS Vernon Lodge & Conference Centre** *(See ad p. 394.)*	◆◆	$114-$180 SAVE	394
6 p. 290	Journey Inn	◆	$79-$165	395
7 p. 290	**Sparkling Hill Resort**	◆◆◆◆	$340-$520 SAVE	395

Map Page	Restaurants	Diamond Rated	Cuisine	Price Range	Page
① p. 290	Intermezzo Restaurant	◆◆◆	Italian	$17-$34	395
② p. 290	Amarin Thai Restaurant	◆◆	Thai	$10-$16	395
③ p. 290	Eclectic Med Restaurant Inc	◆◆◆	Mediterranean	$16-$38	395
④ p. 290	Los Huesos	◆◆	Mexican	$9-$16	395
⑤ p. 290	The Italian Kitchen Company	◆◆	Italian	$12-$30	395
⑥ p. 290	**PeakFine**	◆◆◆	Pacific Northwest	$18-$39	395

KELOWNA

Map Page	Hotels	Diamond Rated	Rate Range	Page
10 p. 290	Lake Okanagan Resort	◆◆	$119-$299	263
11 p. 290	Delta Grand Okanagan Resort & Conference Centre	◆◆◆	$119-$399	263
12 p. 290	A Vista Villa Stay, Dine & Tour	◆◆◆	$259-$419	262
13 p. 290	**The Royal Anne Hotel**	◆◆	$89-$199 SAVE	264
14 p. 290	Kelowna Inn & Suites	◆◆	$95-$195	263
16 p. 290	**Comfort Suites**	◆◆◆	$115-$289 SAVE	263
17 p. 290	**Accent Inns**	◆◆	$89-$189 SAVE	262
18 p. 290	Super 8 Kelowna	◆◆	$81-$140	264
19 p. 290	**Econo Lodge**	◆◆	$89-$134 SAVE	263
20 p. 290	Fairfield Inn & Suites by Marriott Kelowna	◆◆◆	$125-$195	263
21 p. 290	**Recreation Inn & Suites**	◆◆	$69-$129 SAVE	264
22 p. 290	Holiday Inn Express Kelowna Conference Centre	◆◆◆	$129-$199	263
23 p. 290	**BEST WESTERN PLUS Kelowna Hotel & Suites** *(See ad p. 262.)*	◆◆◆	$139-$219 SAVE	262
24 p. 290	**Dilworth Inn**	◆◆	$79-$149 SAVE	263
25 p. 290	Ramada Hotel & Conference Centre	◆◆	$129-$239	264
26 p. 290	Siesta Suites	◆◆	$87-$279	264
27 p. 290	Manteo Resort-Waterfront Hotel & Villas	◆◆◆	$145-$740	263
28 p. 290	Hotel Eldorado	◆◆◆	$109-$449	263

Map Page	Restaurants	Diamond Rated	Cuisine	Price Range	Page
⑨ p. 290	The Jammery	◆◆	American	$8-$14	265

Map Page	Restaurants (cont'd)	Diamond Rated	Cuisine	Price Range	Page
⑩ p. 290	Bouchons Bistro	◈◈◈	French	$20-$39	264
⑪ p. 290	Grand Bay Cafe	◈◈◈	Pacific Northwest	$14-$34	264
⑫ p. 290	Hanna's Lounge & Grill	◈◈◈	Pacific Northwest	$11-$35	265
⑬ p. 290	Dawett Fine Indian Cuisine	◈◈	Indian	$11-$16	264
⑭ p. 290	Poppadoms	◈◈	Indian	$10-$27	266
⑮ p. 290	Christopher's	◈◈	Steak	$14-$46	264
⑯ p. 290	The Yellowhouse Restaurant	◈◈◈	Pacific Northwest	$12-$45	266
⑰ p. 290	Mamma Rosa Restaurant	◈◈	Italian	$13-$34	265
⑱ p. 290	Yamas Taverna Greek Restaurant	◈◈	Greek	$11-$35	266
⑲ p. 290	Mekong Restaurant	◈◈	Chinese	$8-$17	265
⑳ p. 290	Pearson's European Deli	◈	Deli	$7-$12	266
㉑ p. 290	Mizu Japanese Restaurant	◈◈	Sushi	$8-$14	265
㉒ p. 290	The Marmalade Cat Cafe	◈	Sandwiches	$6-$9	265
㉓ p. 290	Pheasant & Quail Pub	◈◈	American	$10-$26	266
㉔ p. 290	Wild Apple Restaurant	◈◈◈	Pacific Northwest	$12-$35	266
㉕ p. 290	Cabana Bar and Grille	◈◈◈	American	$15-$32	264
㉖ p. 290	Eldorado Dining Room & Bar	◈◈◈	Regional Canadian	$12-$46	264
㉗ p. 290	Minstrel Cafe & Bar	◈◈◈	Pacific Northwest	$8-$30	265
㉘ p. 290	Summerhill Sunset Bistro	◈◈◈	Pacific Northwest	$10-$38	266

WEST KELOWNA

Map Page	Hotels	Diamond Rated	Rate Range	Page
㉛ p. 290	**Super 8 West Kelowna Hotel**	◈◈	$90-$130 SAVE	419
㉜ p. 290	**BEST WESTERN PLUS Wine Country Hotel & Suites**	◈◈◈	$149-$249 SAVE	419
㉝ p. 290	The Cove Lakeside Resort	◈◈◈	$155-$889	419

SUMMERLAND

Map Page	Hotel	Diamond Rated	Rate Range	Page
㊱ p. 290	Summerland Motel	◈◈	$69-$159	332

NARAMATA

Map Page	Hotel	Diamond Rated	Rate Range	Page
㊴ p. 290	The Village Motel	◈◈	$95-$145	279

Map Page	Restaurant	Diamond Rated	Cuisine	Price Range	Page
㉛ p. 290	Cobblestone Wine Bar & Restaurant	◈◈◈	Canadian	$10-$34	279

PENTICTON

Map Page	Hotels	Diamond Rated	Rate Range	Page
㊷ p. 290	**Spanish Villa Resort**	◈	$68-$350 SAVE	302
㊸ p. 290	**Penticton Lakeside Resort, Convention Centre & Casino** (See ad p. 301.)	◈◈◈	$120-$246 SAVE	301
㊹ p. 290	Days Inn & Conference Centre Penticton	◈◈	$104-$194	301
㊺ p. 290	**Coast Penticton Hotel**	◈◈	$79-$269 SAVE	301
㊻ p. 290	**Ramada Inn & Suites**	◈◈◈	$99-$299 SAVE	301
㊼ p. 290	Super 8 Penticton	◈◈	$95-$320	302

PENTICTON (cont'd)

Map Page	Hotels (cont'd)	Diamond Rated	Rate Range	Page
48 p. 290	**BEST WESTERN PLUS Inn at Penticton**	◆◆◆	$89-$199 (SAVE)	300
49 p. 290	Empire Motel	◆◆	$69-$169	301

Map Page	Restaurants	Diamond Rated	Cuisine	Price Range	Page
34 p. 290	Salty's Beach House	◆◆	Caribbean	$12-$29	302
35 p. 290	Hooded Merganser Bar & Grill	◆◆◆	Pacific Northwest	$9-$29	302
36 p. 290	Fibonacci Roastery & Cafe	◆	Deli	$7-$10	302
37 p. 290	Navratan	◆◆	Indian	$10-$17	302
38 p. 290	Amante Bistro	◆◆◆	Pacific Northwest	$12-$35	302
39 p. 290	Theo's Restaurant	◆◆	Greek	$12-$23	302
40 p. 290	Bogner's of Penticton	◆◆◆	Continental	$27-$44	302
41 p. 290	La Casa Ouzeria	◆◆	Greek	$10-$45	302
42 p. 290	Shades on Main Family Restaurant	◆◆	American	$6-$12	302
43 p. 290	Iyara Thai Restaurant	◆◆	Thai	$8-$16	302

OSOYOOS

Map Page	Hotels	Diamond Rated	Rate Range	Page
52 p. 290	Spirit Ridge Vineyard Resort & Spa	◆◆◆	$129-$479	296
53 p. 290	Watermark Beach Resort	◆◆◆	$99-$699	296
54 p. 290	**Holiday Inn & Suites**	◆◆◆	$79-$219 (SAVE)	296
55 p. 290	The Coast Osoyoos Beach Hotel	◆◆	$79-$299	296
56 p. 290	**BEST WESTERN PLUS Sunrise Inn**	◆◆◆	$109-$179 (SAVE)	296
57 p. 290	Walnut Beach Resort	◆◆◆	$159-$650	296

Map Page	Restaurants	Diamond Rated	Cuisine	Price Range	Page
46 p. 290	Restaurant at Spirit Ridge	◆◆◆	Pacific Northwest	$11-$26	296
47 p. 290	Diamond Steak and Seafood House	◆◆	Steak	$10-$55	296
48 p. 290	Wildfire Grill	◆◆	Continental	$10-$24	297
49 p. 290	Sol Grill Room & Lounge	◆◆◆	Pacific Northwest	$12-$40	296
50 p. 290	Shores Lakeside Restaurant	◆◆	American	$8-$20	296
51 p. 290	Campo Marina	◆◆	Italian	$14-$23	296

OKANAGAN CENTRE (C-9) elev. 344m/1,129'
• Part of Okanagan Valley area — see map p. 286

WINERIES
• **Gray Monk Estate Winery** is at 1055 Camp Rd. Hours: Daily 9-9, July-Aug.; 10-7, May-June; 10-5, rest of year. Closed Jan. 1 and Christmas. Phone: (250) 766-3168 or (800) 663-4205.

OKANAGAN FALLS (C-8)
• Part of Okanagan Valley area — see map p. 286

WINERIES
• See **Ya Later Ranch** is 5 km (3 mi.) s.w. on Green Lake Rd. Hours: Daily 9:30-6, June 29-Sept. 3; daily 10-5, Apr. 1-June 28 and Sept. 4-Oct. 8; Wed.-Sun. 10-5, rest of year. Closed Jan. 1-18 and Dec. 23-31. Phone ahead to confirm schedule. Phone: (250) 497-8267.

OLIVER (D-8) pop. 4,824, elev. 307m/1,007'
• Part of Okanagan Valley area — see map p. 286

The northern tip of the American Great Basin Desert, which extends to Mexico, begins at Oliver. Irrigation begun in the 1920s converted the once desertlike valley floor and arid hillsides surrounding the town into productive orchards and vineyards. Abundant sunshine and little rain provide ideal conditions for growing wine grapes.

The area's climate also promotes numerous recreational activities. An 18-kilometre (11-mi.) paved bicycle trail travels through Oliver's rolling hills and along the Okanagan River. The valley lakes and streams offer boating and fishing. Vaseux Lake and Inkaneep provincial parks *(see Recreation Areas Chart)* are nearby, as are Bear and Madden lakes, known for excellent trout fishing.

The Fairview Townsite, 3 kilometres (1.9 mi.) west on Fairview Road, formerly was the site of an 1880s boomtown. The town disappeared along with the gold in 1906; plaques at the site provide historical information.

Oliver Visitor Centre: 36205 93rd St., P.O. Box 460, Oliver, BC, Canada V0H 1T0. **Phone:** (250) 498-6321 or (866) 498-6321.

WINERIES

• **Inniskillin Okanagan Vineyards** is 5 km (3 mi.) s. on Hwy. 97 to Rd. 11W. **Hours:** Tastings daily 10-5, July-Oct.; 9:30-6, rest of year. Tours are given daily, Nov.-Apr.; by appointment rest of year. Closed Jan. 1, Christmas Eve, Christmas and day after Christmas. **Phone:** (250) 498-6663, or (800) 498-6211 in Canada.

OSOYOOS (D-9) pop. 4,845, elev. 335m/1,099'

• **Hotels p. 296** • **Restaurants p. 296**
• **Hotels & Restaurants map & index p. 290**
• **Part of Okanagan Valley area — see map p. 286**

From Osoyoos on the east side of Osoyoos Lake, an area of desert sand extends 48 kilometres (30 mi.) north to Skaha Lake and 24 kilometres (15 mi.) west along the Similkameen River. The area's similarity to Spain in climate and terrain inspired the citizens to adopt an Iberian style in their buildings. Despite its arid surroundings, Osoyoos has 19 kilometres (12 mi.) of sandy beach lining one of Canada's warmest freshwater lakes.

Man-made recreational facilities include Wild Rapids on E. Lakeshore Drive, with three large waterslides, five giant hot tubs and two minislides. Skiing is available nearby.

A heavy concentration of minerals, including evaporated copper, silver, gold and sulfate and Epsom salts, can be found at Spotted Lake, west on Crowsnest Hwy. 3, which provides 446 kilometres (277 mi.) of scenic driving all the way to Hope.

Osoyoos & District Chamber of Commerce: 7610 Veterans Way, P.O. Box 227, Osoyoos, BC, Canada V0H 1V0. **Phone:** (250) 495-7142.

NK'MIP DESERT CULTURAL CENTRE is at 1000 Rancher Creek Rd. Visitors will experience a desert ecosystem and the traditions of the Okanagan people through interactive exhibits, artifacts, a re-created Okanagan village and self-guiding walking trails. The Village Trail is 1.4 kilometres (.9 mi.) long and has interpretive signs, benches and ramadas; the Loop Trail is 2 kilometres (1.2 mi.) and includes several uphill segments.

Tours: Guided tours are available. **Time:** Allow 1 hour minimum. **Hours:** Daily 9:30-6, Apr.-Oct. Phone ahead for guided tour information. **Cost:** $12; $11 (ages 5-18 and 65+); $36 (family, two adults and two or more children). **Phone:** (250) 495-7901 or (888) 495-8555.

OSOYOOS DESERT CENTRE is 2.9 km (1.9 mi.) n. of jct. hwys. 3 and 97, then 1.2 km (.7 mi.) w. to 14580 146th Ave. The 26.8-hectare (67-acre) ecological, interpretive and education center is within the northern outpost of the Great Basin Desert, part of the vast Sonoran Desert that extends from Washington south into Mexico.

In addition to hands-on exhibits and a native plant demonstration garden, the center offers narrated 60-minute guided tours on a 1.5-kilometre (1-mi.) boardwalk trail that allow visitors to learn about rare, threatened and endangered plant and animal species. Night tours offer a greater chance to catch a glimpse of the nocturnal animals that live in this harsh environment.

Pets are not permitted. **Time:** Allow 1 hour, 30 minutes minimum. **Hours:** Open daily 9:30-4:30, mid-May to mid-Sept.; 10-2, late Apr. to mid-May and mid-Sept. to early Oct. Guided tours depart at 10, noon and 2, mid-May to mid-Sept. Phone ahead to confirm schedule. **Cost:** $7; $6 (ages 13-17 and 65+); $5 (ages 6-12); $16 (family). **Phone:** (250) 495-2470, or (877) 899-0897 in British Columbia.

OSOYOOS AND DISTRICT MUSEUM & ARCHIVES is in Gyro Community Park at 19 Park Pl. The museum houses children's art from the Inkameep Day School Art Collection—art and photographs created 1931-43 under the guidance of Anthony Walsh, the teacher and principal who based his teaching on the importance of art in education.

The large range of exhibits also includes a butterfly collection, a Victorian parlor, native artifacts, pioneer and agricultural artifacts, military memorabilia, and an 1892 log building that served as a customs house, jail, school, residence and government office over the years.

Time: Allow 1 hour minimum. **Hours:** Museum open daily 10-4, July-Aug.; Tues.-Sat. 10-2, in June; Tues.-Fri. 10-3, rest of year. Archives open Tues.-Fri. 10-4, year-round. Last admission is 30 minutes before closing. Phone ahead to confirm schedule. **Cost:** $5; $2 (ages 6-14); $10 (family). **Phone:** (250) 495-2582.

WINERIES

• **Nk'Mip Cellars** is at 1400 Rancher Creek Rd. **Hours:** Tastings daily 9-9, June 29-Oct. 7; 9-8, Oct. 8-Jan. 2; 9-6, May 1-June 28; 9-5, rest of year. Phone ahead to confirm schedule. **Phone:** (250) 495-2985.

(See map & index p. 290.)

BEST WESTERN PLUS SUNRISE INN

(250)495-4000 **56**

Hotel
$109-$179

AAA Benefit: Members save up to 20%, plus 10% bonus points with Best Western Rewards®.

Address: 5506 Main St V0H 1V0 **Location:** Jct Hwy 97, 1.9 mi (3 km) on Hwy 3 (Main St). **Facility:** 66 units, some efficiencies and kitchens. 3 stories, interior corridors. **Terms:** check-in 4 pm, 2 night minimum stay - seasonal. **Pool(s):** heated indoor. **Activities:** whirlpool, exercise room. **Guest Services:** coin laundry. **Free Special Amenities:** full breakfast and high-speed Internet.

THE COAST OSOYOOS BEACH HOTEL (250)495-6525 **55**

Motel $79-$299 **Address:** 7702 Main St V0H 1V0 **Location:** Jct Hwy 97, 1.2 mi (2 km) e. **Facility:** 60 units, some two bedrooms and kitchens. 3 stories, interior/exterior corridors. **Terms:** check-in 4 pm, 14 day cancellation notice-fee imposed. **Amenities:** *Some:* high-speed Internet. **Pool(s):** heated indoor. **Activities:** whirlpool, waterslide, exercise room. **Guest Services:** coin laundry.

HOLIDAY INN & SUITES (250)495-7223 **54**

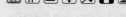
Hotel
$79-$219

Address: 7906 Main St V0H 1V0 **Location:** Jct Hwy 97, 1 mi (1.6 km) e on Hwy 3 (Main St). **Facility:** 118 units, some two bedrooms, efficiencies and kitchens. 4 stories, interior corridors. **Terms:** check-in 4 pm, 3 day cancellation notice-fee imposed. **Amenities:** video games (fee). **Dining:** Shores Lakeside Restaurant, Sol Grill Room & Lounge, see separate listings. **Pool(s):** heated indoor. **Activities:** whirlpool, exercise room. **Guest Services:** coin laundry. **Free Special Amenities:** local telephone calls and high-speed Internet.

SPIRIT RIDGE VINEYARD RESORT & SPA

(250)495-5445 **52**

Condominium $129-$479 **Address:** 1200 Rancher Creek Rd V0H 1V6 **Location:** Hwy 97 S, e on Hwy 3 (Main St), cross bridge, left on 45th St, then 0.9 mi (1.5 km) e. **Facility:** High on a hillside overlooking a vineyard, these wonderful Tuscan-style condos boast stunning views of the lake and township. Choose from ground-level units or units in a high-rise building. 226 condominiums. 2-4 stories, interior/exterior corridors. **Terms:** check-in 4 pm, 2 night minimum stay - seasonal and/or weekends, cancellation fee imposed, resort deposit. **Amenities:** high-speed Internet, safes. **Dining:** Restaurant at Spirit Ridge, see separate listing. **Pool(s):** 2 heated outdoor. **Activities:** whirlpools, steamroom, waterslide, beach access, rental boats, rental canoes, rental paddleboats, marina, rental bicycles, exercise room, spa. *Fee:* golf-9 holes. **Guest Services:** coin laundry, area transportation-marina.

WALNUT BEACH RESORT (250)495-5400 **57**

Hotel $159-$650 **Address:** 4200 Lakeshore Dr V0H 1V6 **Location:** 0.9 mi (1.5 km) s off Hwy 3 (Main St). **Facility:** 112 units, some two bedrooms, efficiencies and kitchens. 3 stories, interior corridors. **Terms:** check-in 4 pm, 7 day cancellation notice-fee imposed. **Amenities:** high-speed Internet. **Pool(s):** heated outdoor. **Activities:** sauna, whirlpools, steamroom, limited beach access, boat dock, exercise room. *Fee:* massage. **Guest Services:** valet and coin laundry.

WATERMARK BEACH RESORT (250)495-5500 **53**

Resort Condominium $99-$699 **Address:** 15 Park Pl V0H 1V0 **Location:** Corner of Park Pl and Main St; downtown. **Facility:** Right on the lake, this new condo hotel complex features spacious guest rooms with full kitchens. Perfect for those seeking a family vacation rental. Easy walk to shops. 153 condominiums. 4 stories, interior/exterior corridors. **Terms:** check-in 4 pm, 2-3 night minimum stay - seasonal and/or weekends, cancellation fee imposed. **Amenities:** high-speed Internet. *Some:* safes. **Pool(s):** heated outdoor. **Activities:** whirlpools, steamrooms, waterslide, limited beach access, exercise room, spa. **Guest Services:** complimentary laundry.

 **WHERE TO EAT**

CAMPO MARINA 250/495-7650 **51**

Italian. Casual Dining. $14-$23 **AAA Inspector Notes:** The established, family-run restaurant is sure to please with its hearty Italian dishes. The cozy, comfortable dining room welcomes guests to linger over linguine, tantalize their taste buds with tiramisu and savor pan-seared scallops. **Bar:** full bar. **Address:** 5907 Main St, (Hwy 3) V0H 1V3 **Location:** East end of town on Hwy 3 (Main St).

DIAMOND STEAK AND SEAFOOD HOUSE

250/495-6223 **47**

Steak Pizza. Casual Dining. $10-$55 **AAA Inspector Notes:** Tasty food and attentive service are hallmarks at the excellent family restaurant. The menu lists a nice selection of pasta, pizza and Greek specialties. Broiled chicken breast with peppercorn and brandy demi-glace sauce is simply delectable. **Bar:** full bar. **Reservations:** suggested, in summer. **Address:** 8903 Main St V0H 1V0 **Location:** Hwy 3 (Main St) at 89th St. **Parking:** street only.

RESTAURANT AT SPIRIT RIDGE 250/495-8007 **46**

Pacific Northwest. Casual Dining. $11-$26 **AAA Inspector Notes:** In addition to fantastic views of the lake and surrounding hillsides, among the individual tables you'll see a long, custom-built wood table which dominates the room. Here, you may find yourself seated communal-style with other diners, a fun way to introduce yourself to others at the resort. The menu highlights local produce (in season), BC seafood, good hearty beef from Alberta and a fantastic selection of wines from many local vineyards. **Bar:** full bar. **Reservations:** suggested. **Address:** 1200 Rancher Creek Rd V0H 1V6 **Location:** Hwy 97 S, e on Hwy 3 (Main St), cross bridge, left on 45th St, then 0.9 mi (1.5 km) e; in Spirit Ridge Vineyard Resort & Spa.

SHORES LAKESIDE RESTAURANT 250/495-4348 **50**

American. Family Dining. $8-$20 **AAA Inspector Notes:** This pleasant family-style restaurant is open all day long with breakfast served till 1:30 pm. Lunch and dinner consist of burgers, pasta, sandwiches and daily-made soup. **Address:** 7906 Main St V0H 1V0 **Location:** Jct Hwy 97, 1 mi (1.6 km) e on Hwy 3 (Main St); in Holiday Inn & Suites. **Parking:** on-site and street.

SOL GRILL ROOM & LOUNGE 250/495-6884 **49**

Pacific Northwest. Casual Dining. $12-$40 **AAA Inspector Notes:** The second-floor location offers stunning views of the lake and surrounding hillsides, making this one of the must-try spots in town. The menu features small plates as well as hearty entrée choices. Not only can you get a specialized ground chuck burger but also filet mignon, rib-eye steak and butter chicken tandoori masala. The highlight is the extensive local wine selection. The restaurant is adult-oriented and not suitable for children. **Bar:** full bar. **Reservations:** suggested. **Address:** 7906 Main St V0H 1V0 **Location:** Jct Hwy 97, 1 mi (1.6 km) e on Hwy 3 (Main St); in Holiday Inn & Suites. **Parking:** on-site and street.

(See map & index p. 290.)

WILDFIRE GRILL   250/495-2215 48

◆◆ ◆ Continental. Casual Dining. $10-$24 **AAA Inspector Notes:** As patrons enter the downtown restaurant's small dining room they are greeted by warm yellow walls and great background music. The chef/owner says his menu is "globally inspired," and that's the motto of this contemporary bistro, which serves B.C. salmon, chicken and pasta dishes, as well as hearty fresh salads. They open up their outdoor patio during the warm summer months. **Bar:** full bar. **Address:** 8526 Main St V0H 1V0 **Location:** Just e of jct Hwy 97 and 3 (Main St); downtown. **Parking:** street only. L D

PACIFIC RIM NATIONAL PARK RESERVE (I-3)

Elevations in the park range from sea level along the Long Beach area to 140 metres (459 ft.) at Radar Hill. Refer to CAA/AAA maps for additional elevation information.

On the west coast of Vancouver Island, Pacific Rim National Park Reserve consists of three geographically distinct sections with different entry points: the Long Beach unit between Ucluelet and Tofino; the Broken Group Island unit, a cluster of islands in Barkley Sound; and the 75-kilometre-long (47-mi.) West Coast Trail unit between Bamfield and Port Renfrew.

Numerous contrasts exist in the 510-square-kilometre (197-sq.-mi.) reserve, which has sandy beaches, tranquil estuaries and lakes, rugged headlands, dense rain forests and rocky islands. Wildflowers nurtured by the area's moist and temperate climate thrive in an immense old-growth rain forest.

A stopping place for geese and ducks during their yearly migrations, the shoreline zone also accommodates colonies of sea birds and wildlife. Each spring some 20,000 gray whales migrate through the reserve's waters.

General Information and Activities

The reserve is open all year, although many facilities are seasonal. The Long Beach Unit, about 16 kilometres (10 mi.) west of the junction of Hwy. 4 and the Ucluelet highway, has 19 kilometres (12 mi.) of sandy beach and shoreline which are popular year-round with surfers and beachwalkers; wheelchair-accessible trails are available. Long Beach Information Centre, open mid-March to mid-October, is on Hwy. 4 inside the park boundary. There are self-guiding nature trails in the surrounding rain forest and other interpretive programs. The Wickaninnish Interpretive Centre features displays and films chronicling marine life of the Pacific.

The Broken Group Islands, accessible only by boat, offer pristine wilderness spread over a 100-island cluster in the center of Barkley Sound. Eagles and sea lions are abundant, while varied sea life and sunken ships create a diver's paradise. Camping is available in designated areas on eight islands.

The West Coast Trail, which had its beginnings as a telegraph line and then an avenue of rescue for shipwrecked sailors, follows the national park's rugged coastline between Port Renfrew and Bamfield. The trail is recommended to experienced hikers only and offers spectacular coastal scenery along its challenging path. Remnants of former settlements and shipwrecks can be seen along the shoreline.

The West Coast Trail Information and Registration Centres at Pachena Bay near Bamfield and at Port Renfrew are open May through September. Reservations to hike the trail may be made for June 15 through September 15; phone (866) 727-5722. *See Recreation Areas Chart.*

ADMISSION to the Long Beach area is $7.80; $6.80 (senior citizens); $3.90 (ages 6-16); $19.60 (family, up to seven people). Camping fee at Long Beach is $16-$25 per person per night. Camping fee at other designated sites is $9 per person per night. West Coast Trail use permit $110; reservation fee $25 (non-refundable). Ferry fee $15.

PETS are permitted in the park provided they are on a leash at all times.

ADDRESS inquiries to the Superintendent, Pacific Rim National Park Reserve, P.O. Box 280, Ucluelet, BC, Canada V0R 3A0; phone (250) 726-7721, or (250) 726-4212 June 1 to mid-Sept.

PARKSVILLE (G-10) pop. 11,977, elev. 80m/262'
• Restaurants p. 298

With its 1.6-kilometre-long (1-mi.) sandy beach on the Strait of Georgia, Parksville is a popular summer resort. Nearby Englishman and Little Qualicum rivers and parks, with scenic waterfalls, provide many opportunities for recreation, as do other area lakes, streams, mountains and parks. Rathtrevor Beach Provincial Park offers a beach, camping and picnicking. *See Recreation Areas Chart.*

Artistic endeavors in sand are the main focus of the ◆ Parksville Beach Festival. Elaborate sand sculptures compete for prizes each August, and attendees can also enjoy fireworks, children's activities and a volleyball tournament.

Parksville & District Chamber of Commerce: 1275 E. Island Hwy., P.O. Box 99, Parksville, BC, Canada V9P 2G3. **Phone:** (250) 248-3613.

CRAIG HERITAGE PARK, MUSEUM & ARCHIVES is 4 km (2.5 mi.) s. at 1245 E. Island Hwy. The collection of historic buildings includes a church, a log house, a fire station, a turn-of-the-20th-century schoolhouse and two 19th-century post offices. Exhibits inside the buildings depict local history.

Time: Allow 30 minutes minimum. **Hours:** Daily 10-5, May-Sept. **Cost:** $5; $4 (ages 13-18, ages 60+ and students with ID); $3 (ages 6-12); $6 (family). **Phone:** (250) 248-6966.

ARBUTUS GROVE MOTEL   250/248-6422

◆◆ ◆◆ **Motel.** Rates not provided. **Address:** 1182 E Island Hwy V9P 1W3 **Location:** Island Hwy 19 exit 46 (Parksville), 1 mi (1.6 km) n on Hwy 19A. **Facility:** 10 units, some efficiencies. 1 story, exterior corridors. **Amenities:** high-speed Internet.

BEACH ACRES RESORT (250)248-3424

WWWW **Vacation Rental Cottage** $99-$414 **Address:** 1051 Resort Dr, Unit 25 V9P 2E4 **Location:** Island Hwy 19 exit 46 (Parksville), 1.6 mi (2.5 km) n on Hwy 19A. **Facility:** A mix of condos is dispersed over several acres; some are set back and secluded, some sit on a cliff overlooking the ocean and others are beachfront. 54 two-bedroom kitchen units, some cottages. 1-2 stories (no elevator), exterior corridors. **Terms:** check-in 4 pm, 3 night minimum stay - seasonal, 3 day cancellation notice, 30 day in season-fee imposed. **Pool(s):** heated indoor. **Activities:** sauna, whirlpool, 3 tennis courts, recreation programs, rental bicycles, playground, basketball, horseshoes, shuffleboard, volleyball. **Fee:** game room. **Guest Services:** coin laundry.

 / SOME UNITS FEE

THE BEACH CLUB RESORT (250)248-8999

WWWW
Contemporary
Resort Hotel
$169-$449

Address: 181 Beachside Dr V9P 2H5 **Location:** Island Hwy 19 exit 51 (Parksville/Coombs), 1.3 mi (2 km) e, then just n on Hwy 19A. **Facility:** This very impressive, newly constructed hotel sits near one of the most perfect sandy beaches. Choose from comfortable studio rooms and spacious one- or two-bedroom suites with full kitchens. 149 units, some kitchens. 4-9 stories, interior/exterior corridors. **Terms:** check-in 4 pm, 6 day cancellation notice-fee imposed. **Amenities:** safes. **Dining:** Pacific Prime Steak and Chop Restaurant, see separate listing. **Pool(s):** heated indoor. **Activities:** whirlpool, exercise room, spa. **Guest Services:** valet laundry.

SAVE ECO / SOME UNITS

OCEANSIDE VILLAGE RESORT 250/248-8961

WWWW **Vacation Rental Cottage** $115-$310 **Address:** 1080 Resort Dr V9P 2E3 **Location:** Island Hwy 19 exit 46 (Parksville), 1.8 mi (2.5 km) n on Hwy 19A. **Facility:** Situated on several acres these wonderfully modern, newly constructed cottages offer a home away from home. Whether it's just a couple or a group, the cottages can sleep up to six or eight persons. 67 kitchen cottage units, some two and three bedrooms. 1 story, exterior corridors. **Terms:** check-in 4 pm, 2 night minimum stay, 30 day cancellation notice-fee imposed. **Pool(s):** heated indoor. **Activities:** whirlpool, exercise room. **Guest Services:** complimentary laundry.

/ SOME UNITS FEE

Be a better driver.
Keep your mind on the road.

SANDCASTLE INN (250)248-2334

WWW
Hotel
$59-$149

Address: 374 W Island Hwy V9P 1K8 **Location:** Island Hwy 19 exit 51 (Parksville/Coombs), 1.3 mi (2 km) n, then just n on Hwy 19A. **Facility:** 36 units, some efficiencies. 3 stories, interior corridors. **Terms:** 3 day cancellation notice-fee imposed. **Guest Services:** coin laundry. **Free Special Amenities:** continental breakfast and high-speed Internet.

SAVE CALL / SOME UNITS

SUNRISE RIDGE WATERFRONT RESORT (250)248-4674

WWW
Contemporary
Hotel
$99-$429

Address: 1175 Resort Dr V9P 2E3 **Location:** Island Hwy 19 exit 46 (Parksville), 1.6 mi (2.5 km) n on Hwy 19A. **Facility:** 65 units, some two bedrooms, three bedrooms and kitchens. 2-3 stories, interior/exterior corridors. **Terms:** check-in 4 pm, 3 day cancellation notice-fee imposed. **Amenities:** Some: high-speed Internet. **Free Special Amenities:** local telephone calls and high-speed Internet.

SAVE

TIGH-NA-MARA SEASIDE SPA RESORT & CONFERENCE CENTRE (250)248-2072

WWW
Resort Hotel
$125-$237

Address: 1155 Resort Dr V9P 2E3 **Location:** Island Hwy 19 exit 46 (Parksville), 1.3 mi (2 km) n on Hwy 19A. **Facility:** This all-season, full-spa resort features a cluster of lovely log cottages and deluxe condo units set in a forest-like setting or along the spectacular sandy beach. Many feature a fireplace and whirlpool tub. 192 units, some two bedrooms, efficiencies, kitchens and cottages. 1-3 stories (no elevator), exterior corridors. **Terms:** check-in 4 pm, 2 night minimum stay - seasonal and/or weekends, 5 day cancellation notice-fee imposed. **Dining:** Cedar Room at Tigh-Na-Mara Seaside Spa Resort, see separate listing. **Pool(s):** heated indoor. **Activities:** sauna, whirlpool, tennis court, recreation programs, rental bicycles, playground, horseshoes, volleyball, exercise room, spa. **Guest Services:** valet and coin laundry, area transportation-ferry, bus & train stations. **Free Special Amenities:** local telephone calls and newspaper.

SAVE / SOME UNITS FEE

TRAVELODGE PARKSVILLE (250)248-2232

WW **Hotel** $89-$189 **Address:** 424 W Island Hwy V9P 1K8 **Location:** Island Hwy 19 exit 51 (Parksville/Coombs), 1.3 mi (2 km) e, then just n on Hwy 19A. **Facility:** 83 units. 3 stories. interior corridors. **Terms:** cancellation fee imposed. **Pool(s):** heated indoor. **Activities:** whirlpool, exercise room. **Guest Services:** coin laundry.

ECO CALL / SOME UNITS

V.I.P. MOTEL (250)248-3244

WW
Motel
$69-$169

Address: 414 W Island Hwy V9P 1K8 **Location:** Island Hwy 19 exit 51 (Parksville/Coombs), 1.3 mi (2 km) e, then just n on Hwy 19A. **Facility:** 21 units, some efficiencies. 1 story, exterior corridors. **Terms:** cancellation fee imposed. **Guest Services:** coin laundry. **Free Special Amenities:** continental breakfast and high-speed Internet.

SAVE / SOME UNITS FEE

 WHERE TO EAT

AMRIKKO'S FINE INDIAN CUISINE 250/951-0682

WW Indian. Casual Dining. $10-$15 **AAA Inspector Notes:** The goal of this Indian restaurant is simple: Offer a warm, casual atmosphere, polite service and superb food in generous portions. The menu offers tandoori barbecue, lamb, beef and vegetarian dishes and, of course, chicken specials such as butter chicken or chicken vindaloo. **Bar:** full bar. **Address:** 487 E Island Hwy V9P 2H6 **Location:** Island Hwy 19 exit 46 (Parksville), 2.2 mi (3.5 km) n on Hwy 19A. L D

BUGSYS BAR & GRILL
250/248-4545

▼▼▼ American. Casual Dining. $8-$23 **AAA Inspector Notes:** In gangster circles, the name Bugsy is a term of endearment or honor; here, Bugsy translates to pizza, calzones, ribs, chicken, pasta and burgers. A large bar features big screen TVs for all the sporting events you can handle, and the restaurant is open late. **Bar:** full bar. **Address:** 332 W Island Hwy V9P 1K8 **Location:** Island Hwy 19 exit 51 (Parksville/Coombs), 1.3 mi (2 km) e, then just n on Hwy 19A.

[L] [D] [LATE] CALL [&][M]

CEDAR ROOM AT TIGH-NA-MARA SEASIDE SPA RESORT
250/248-2333

▼▼▼▼

Pacific Northwest Casual Dining

$10-$36

AAA Inspector Notes: Although the menu focuses on West Coast seafood, it also lists pasta and steak dishes as well as more casual breakfast and lunch offerings, including daily soup and sandwich specials. Sunday brunch is popular. The authentic log cabin-style restaurant is nestled in a forest by the sea. **Bar:** full bar. **Reservations:** suggested, for dinner & Sunday brunch. **Address:** 1155 Resort Dr V9P 2E3 **Location:** Island Hwy 19 exit 46 (Parksville), 1.3 mi (2 km) n on Hwy 19A; in Tigh-Na-Mara Seaside Spa Resort & Conference Centre. [B] [L] [D] CALL [&][M]

KALVAS RESTAURANT
250/248-6933

▼▼ Steak Seafood. Casual Dining. $20-$40 **AAA Inspector Notes:** The restaurant has been built as an Alpine-style log cabin, making for a rather unique dining room. This is where hearty steaks and seafood are king. Live local crab, East Coast lobster and oysters are prepared to your liking by the chef/owner. Desserts are not to missed. **Bar:** full bar. **Reservations:** suggested. **Address:** 180 Moilliet St, Island Hwy N V9P 2H4 **Location:** Island Hwy 19 exit 51 (Parksville/Coombs), 1.3 mi (2 km) e, then just n on Hwy 19A.

[D] CALL [&][M]

LEFTY'S FRESH FOOD RESTAURANT
250/954-3886

▼▼ American. Casual Dining. $9-$20 **AAA Inspector Notes:** Three friends realized they all were left-handed and a new restaurant was born. The kitchen is committed to fresh ingredients in such dishes as the signature southpawtatoes, which are oven roasted in special seasoning, and the made-from-scratch desserts. The motto here: "Everyone is born right-handed; only the greatest overcome it.". **Bar:** full bar. **Address:** 101-280 E Island Hwy V9P 2G3 **Location:** Island Hwy 19 exit 46 (Parksville), 2.5 mi (4 km) n on Hwy 19A.

[B] [L] [D]

PACIFIC PRIME STEAK AND CHOP RESTAURANT
250/947-2109

▼▼▼▼

Pacific Northwest Fine Dining

$15-$35

AAA Inspector Notes: In the city's newest hotel, the restaurant offers the finest cuts of AAA Angus beef in juicy steaks and local seafood such as British Columbia clams and mussels and fresh seasonal salmon. There's even a great kids' menu. Floor-to-ceiling windows allow for some of the best ocean views in town. **Bar:** full bar. **Reservations:** suggested. **Address:** 181 Beachside Dr V9P 2H5 **Location:** Island Hwy 19 exit 51 (Parksville/Coombs), 1.2 mi (2 km) e, then just n on Hwy 19A; in The Beach Club Resort.

[B] [L] [D] CALL [&][M]

PARSON

ALEXA CHALETS-TIMBER INN & RESTAURANT   250/348-2228

▼▼ Country Inn. Rates not provided. **Address:** 3483 Hwy 95 V0A 1L0 **Location:** Just off Hwy 95; 21.3 mi (34 km) s of Golden. **Facility:** 14 units, some three bedrooms, efficiencies, cabins and condominiums. 2 stories (no elevator), interior/exterior corridors. **Terms:** check-in 4 pm. **Activities:** sauna, whirlpool, hiking trails, basketball, limited exercise equipment. *Fee:* massage. **Guest Services:** valet laundry.

/ SOME UNITS FEE [ ] [ ] [ ] [ ] [ ]

PEACHLAND (C-8) pop. 5,200,
elev. 366m/1,200'
• Part of Okanagan Valley area — see map p. 286

Peachland's rolling green countryside is a prosperous fruit growing, farming, lumber producing and mining area. The mining of molybdenum and copper from the Brenda Mines complex in the hills above Hwy. 97 spurred significant growth during the 1970s.

Nearby mountains, rivers and lakes, including Okanagan Lake *(see Recreation Areas Chart),* offer abundant opportunities for skiing, hiking, fishing and water sports.

HARDY FALLS REGIONAL PARK is off Hwy. 97 via Hardy Rd. This tucked-away little jewel of a park has a paved walking trail that runs along the wall of a steep-banked canyon. At the end of the trail a lovely little waterfall tumbles down a rocky hillside into the waters of Deep Creek. Bright red kokanee salmon provide a brilliant show of color in early September as they return to their spawning grounds to lay their eggs. **Time:** Allow 30 minutes minimum. **Hours:** Daily dawn-dusk. **Cost:** Free. **Phone:** (250) 763-4918.

PEMBERTON pop. 2,369

PEMBERTON VALLEY LODGE
(604)894-2000

▼▼▼ Hotel $129-$409 **Address:** 1490 Sea to Sky Hwy V0N 2L1 **Location:** Just e on Hwy 99 from Pioneer Junction. **Facility:** 85 units, some two bedrooms, efficiencies and kitchens. 3 stories, interior corridors. **Terms:** check-in 4 pm. **Amenities:** safes. **Pool(s):** heated outdoor. **Activities:** whirlpool, bicycles, limited exercise equipment. *Fee:* massage. **Guest Services:** complimentary laundry, area transportation-ski shuttle to Whistler Village.

[ECO] CALL [&][M] [ ] [ ] [ ] [ ] [ ] [ ] [ ]

/ SOME UNITS FEE [ ]

PENDER ISLANDS (H-10)
• Hotels p. 300 • Restaurants p. 300

Part of the Gulf Islands *(see place listing p. 246),* the Penders, consisting of North and South Pender islands, are connected by a one-lane wooden bridge that spans the canal linking Bedwell and Browning harbors. An archeological dig conducted at the time the bridge was built found evidence of island occupation dating back 4,000 years. The Pender Island Museum, set on national park lands at Roesland, offers an overview of area history from 10-4 on Saturdays and Sundays in July and August; otherwise varies. Phone (250) 629-6935.

The island's 20 public ocean access points and many coves allow ample opportunities for swimming and picnicking. Hiking, boating, fishing, golfing, bicycling, kayaking and scuba diving are other available recreational activities. Roadside stands offer locally grown produce. The view from the summit of Mount Norman, part of Gulf Islands National Park Reserve, is worth the climb.

POETS COVE RESORT & SPA   (250)629-2100
▼▼▼▼ Hotel $199-$309 **Address:** 9801 Spalding Rd V0N 2M3 **Location:** From Otter Bay Ferry Terminal, follow signs to South Pender Island, then 10 mi (16 km) s; Otter Bay Rd to Bidwell Harbour Rd to Canal Rd. **Facility:** 46 units, some cottages. 1-3 stories, interior/exterior corridors. **Parking:** on-site and valet. **Terms:** check-in 4 pm, 3 day cancellation notice-fee imposed. **Amenities:** high-speed Internet. **Dining:** Aurora Restaurant, see separate listing. **Pool(s):** 2 heated outdoor. **Activities:** whirlpools, exercise room, spa. *Fee:* marina. **Guest Services:** coin laundry.

🛎️ 🍽️ 🛍️ 📶 ⌧ 🅈 🎱 💻
/ SOME UNITS FEE 🐾 📷

WHERE TO EAT

AURORA RESTAURANT   250/629-2115
▼▼▼▼ Pacific Northwest. Fine Dining. $25-$45 AAA Inspector **Notes:** You will find this restaurant, where all of the tables overlook the marina, inside Pender Island's only upscale lodging. Enjoy West Coast cuisine with a modern interpretation on classic favorites. The chef uses only the highest quality ingredients, which are specially brought in just for this restaurant. A special herb, produce and flower garden grows on property. Dinner is very popular, so reservations are a must. **Bar:** full bar. **Reservations:** suggested, for dinner. **Address:** 9801 Spalding Rd V0N 2M3 **Location:** From Otter Bay Ferry Terminal, follow signs to South Pender Island, then 10 mi (16 km) s; Otter Bay Rd to Bidwell Harbour Rd to Canal Rd; in Poets Cove Resort & Spa. **Parking:** on-site and valet.

Ⓑ Ⓓ CALL 🄲🄼 🄺

PENTICTON (C-8) pop. 32,877,
elev. 345m/1,131'
• Restaurants p. 302
• Hotels & Restaurants map & index p. 290
• Part of Okanagan Valley area — see map p. 286

The first orchards in Okanagan Valley were planted by the Oblates at Okanagan Mission 1860-61, and the fruits, especially peaches, became a staple of the area. Tom Ellis established the first cattle ranch in 1865 and it was an empire when he sold it for a hefty sum in 1905; by 1909 orchards had replaced cattle in the agricultural economy. Today Penticton's fruit industry combines with tourism and lumber industries to keep the community strong.

Okanagan and Skaha lakes, at opposite ends of the city, offer ample expanses of shoreline for recreational pursuits. A popular summer activity is floating down the 8-kilometre (5-mi.) river channel from the mouth of Okanagan Lake *(see Recreation Areas Chart)* to Skaha Lake. The channel has rest and picnic areas and is paralleled by a bicycle path and a jogging trail. The *Casabella Princess*, a 48-passenger paddlewheeler departing from Penticton Marina, takes passengers on a 1-hour cruise of the south end of Okanagan Lake; phone (250) 492-4090.

Penticton Visitor Centre: 553 Railway St., Penticton, BC, Canada V2A 8S3. **Phone:** (250) 493-4055 or (800) 663-5052.

PENTICTON ART GALLERY is at 199 Marina Way. Four exhibition halls and an art loft comprise the facility on the shore of Okanagan Lake, where works by professional local, provincial and nationally known artists are displayed. **Time:** Allow 30 minutes minimum. **Hours:** Tues.-Fri. 10-5, Sat.-Sun. noon-5;

closed statutory holidays and Dec. 24-31. **Cost:** $2; free (Sat.-Sun.). **Phone:** (250) 493-2928.

PENTICTON MUSEUM & ARCHIVES is at 785 Main St. Displays describe the natural and social histories of the southern Okanagan Valley. A historic transportation exhibit about the Kettle Valley Railway is available along with an exhibit about the Canadian military. Summer programs include cemetery walks, heritage tours and children's activities. **Time:** Allow 1 hour minimum. **Hours:** Tues.-Sat. 10-5. Archives open Wed.-Fri. 10-4. Closed major holidays. **Cost:** Donations. **Phone:** (250) 490-2451.

SS *SICAMOUS* INLAND MARINE HERITAGE PARK is on Okanagan Lake Beach at 1099 Lakeshore Dr. Featured on-site is the *Sicamous*, the last steam-powered stern-wheeler to operate on Okanagan Lake. Visitors can experience what once was a major means of transportation in the area. Also on view is the 1914 tugboat SS *Naramata*; it is one of only two tugs from the steam era that has survived in the province.

    Time: Allow 30 minutes minimum. **Hours:** Daily 11-7, July-Aug.; 10-4, May-June and in Sept. **Cost:** $6.50; $4.50 (ages 13-19, ages 65+ and students with ID); $3.50 (ages 6-12). **Phone:** (250) 492-0403 or (866) 492-0403.

GAMBLING ESTABLISHMENTS
• **Lake City Casino** is at 21 Lakeshore Dr. W. **Hours:** Daily 10 a.m.-2 a.m. **Phone:** (250) 493-8221.

RECREATIONAL ACTIVITIES
Skiing
• **Apex Mountain Resort** is 32 km (20 mi.) w. off Green Mountain Rd. Other activities are available. **Hours:** Daily 9-3:30 (also Fri.-Sat. 3:30-9), Dec.-Mar. **Phone:** (250) 292-8222 or (877) 777-2739.

WINERIES
• **Hillside Estate Winery** is 3 km (2 mi.) n. of jct. McMillan Ave. and Naramata Rd. at 1350 Naramata Rd. **Hours:** Tastings and self-guiding tours daily 10-6, May 1 to mid-Oct.; 11-4, in Apr.; by appointment rest of year. **Phone:** (250) 493-6274 or (888) 923-9463.

BEST WESTERN PLUS INN AT PENTICTON
    (250)493-0311 **48**

▼▼▼▼
Hotel
$89-$199

AAA Benefit: Members save up to 20%, plus 10% bonus points with Best Western Rewards®.

Address: 3180 Skaha Lake Rd V2A 6G4 **Location:** From downtown, 2.5 mi (4 km) s. **Facility:** 67 units, some two bedrooms, efficiencies and kitchens. 2 stories (no elevator), exterior corridors. **Amenities:** *Some:* high-speed Internet. **Pool(s):** heated outdoor, heated indoor. **Activities:** whirlpool, playground, exercise room. **Guest Services:** valet and coin laundry. **Free Special Amenities:** local telephone calls and high-speed Internet.

SAVE ECO 🍽️ 🛍️ 📶 ⌧ 🎱 📷 💻
/ SOME UNITS FEE 🐾

(See map & index p. 290.)

COAST PENTICTON HOTEL   (250)492-0225 **45**

Hotel
$79-$269

Address: 950 Westminster Ave W V2A 1L2 **Location:** Hwy 97 (Eckhardt Ave W), just n to Westminster Ave W, then just e. **Facility:** 36 units. 3 stories, interior/exterior corridors. **Terms:** 7 day cancellation notice. **Amenities:** Some: high-speed Internet. **Pool(s):** heated outdoor, heated indoor. **Activities:** whirlpool. **Guest Services:** coin laundry. **Free Special Amenities:** newspaper and high-speed Internet.

DAYS INN & CONFERENCE CENTRE PENTICTON   (250)493-6616 **44**

 Hotel $104-$194 **Address:** 152 Riverside Dr V2A 5Y4 **Location:** Hwy 97, just n. **Facility:** 104 units, some kitchens. 2 stories (no elevator), interior corridors. **Terms:** cancellation fee imposed. **Amenities:** Some: high-speed Internet, safes. **Pool(s):** heated outdoor, heated indoor. **Activities:** whirlpool, limited exercise equipment, spa. **Guest Services:** coin laundry.

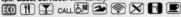

EMPIRE MOTEL   250/493-2323 **49**

 Motel $69-$169 **Address:** 3495 Skaha Lake Rd V2A 6G6 **Location:** From downtown, 2.8 mi (4.5 km) s. **Facility:** 32 units, some two bedrooms and kitchens. 2 stories (no elevator), exterior corridors. **Terms:** 2-5 night minimum stay - seasonal and/or weekends, 30 day cancellation notice-fee imposed. **Pool(s):** heated outdoor. **Activities:** playground.

PENTICTON LAKESIDE RESORT, CONVENTION CENTRE & CASINO   (250)493-8221 **43**

Hotel
$120-$246

Address: 21 Lakeshore Dr W V2A 7M5 **Location:** Main St at Lakeshore Dr W. **Facility:** This amazing lakefront hotel features an on-site casino as well as two lakefront restaurants. It's an easy walk to the downtown shops or you can follow the walking path that circles the shore. 203 units. 6 stories, interior corridors. **Parking:** on-site (fee) and valet. **Terms:** check-in 4 pm, cancellation fee imposed. **Dining:** Hooded Merganser Bar & Grill, see separate listing. **Pool(s):** heated indoor. **Activities:** whirlpool, limited beach access, rental boats, rental canoes, rental paddleboats, boat dock. **Guest Services:** valet laundry. (See ad this page.)

RAMADA INN & SUITES   (250)492-8926 **46**

Hotel
$99-$299

Address: 1050 Eckhardt Ave W V2A 2C3 **Location:** 0.8 mi (1.2 km) w on Hwy 97. **Facility:** 125 units, some kitchens. 1-3 stories, interior/exterior corridors. **Terms:** cancellation fee imposed. **Amenities:** Some: high-speed Internet. **Pool(s):** heated outdoor. **Activities:** whirlpool, playground, limited exercise equipment. **Guest Services:** valet and coin laundry. **Free Special Amenities:** newspaper and high-speed Internet.

▼ See AAA listing this page ▼

(See map & index p. 290.)

SPANISH VILLA RESORT
250/492-2922 (42)

Motel
S68-S350

Address: 890 Lakeshore Dr W V2A 1C1 **Location:** Corner of Power St and Lakeshore Dr W. **Facility:** 60 units, some two bedrooms, three bedrooms and two stories (no elevator), exterior corridors. **Terms:** 14 day cancellation notice-fee imposed. **Pool(s):** heated indoor. **Guest Services:** coin laundry. **Free Special Amenities:** newspaper and high-speed Internet.

SUPER 8 PENTICTON
(250)492-3829 (47)

Motel $95-$320 **Address:** 1706 Main St V2A 5G8 **Location:** Jct Main St and Industrial Ave. **Facility:** 53 units, some two bedrooms, efficiencies and kitchens. 2 stories (no elevator), interior/exterior corridors. **Pool(s):** heated indoor. **Activities:** whirlpool. **Guest Services:** coin laundry.

WHERE TO EAT

AMANTE BISTRO
250/493-1961 (38)

Pacific Northwest. Fine Dining. $12-$35 **AAA Inspector Notes:** "Urban chic" describes the décor at this cozy little bistro. The delightful menu features a variety of tapas-style appetizers made with fresh ingredients like Okanagan roasted garlic goat cheese, Black Angus steak tartare and BC Dungeness crab cakes. Entrées include BC sockeye salmon and jumbo pan-seared prawns and scallops. Prepare to enjoy a leisurely time in the warm and hospitable atmosphere. **Bar:** full bar. **Reservations:** suggested. **Address:** 101-483 Main St V2A 5C4 **Location:** Corner of Padmore Ave W and Main St; downtown. **Parking:** on-site and street. L D

BOGNER'S OF PENTICTON
250/493-2711 (40)

Continental. Fine Dining. $27-$44 **AAA Inspector Notes:** For somewhere special to eat, the 100-year-old heritage mansion fits the bill. On a quiet residential street, the rustic restaurant has an elegant dining room and attentive servers. Guests can sit back and enjoy flavorful creations from the kitchen. The chef draws largely on regional ingredients selected from the restaurant's own farm and chooses many local wines for the menu. **Bar:** full bar. **Reservations:** suggested. **Address:** 302 Eckhardt Ave W V2A 2A9 **Location:** 2 blks w of Main St; corner of Argyle St. D

FIBONACCI ROASTERY & CAFE
250/770-1913 (36)

Deli. Quick Serve. $7-$10 **AAA Inspector Notes:** A small Italian-style red coffee roaster is the centerpiece of this large, open-concept coffee shop. The aroma of freshly roasting coffee, brewed in small batches, wafts through the dining room. More than 40 types of loose-leaf teas come from organic and fair-trade roasted green beans. As for food, patrons find sandwiches and a limited selection of entrées, which are prepared to order. Staff call out customers' names when the order is ready. **Bar:** beer & wine. **Address:** 219 Main St V2A 5B1 **Location:** Between Front and Nanaimo sts; downtown. **Parking:** street only. B L D

HOODED MERGANSER BAR & GRILL
250/487-4663 (35)

Pacific Northwest. Casual Dining. $9-$29 **AAA Inspector Notes:** Practically sitting right on the lake, this beautifully designed restaurant offers gorgeous views from its huge picture windows. Food is well crafted with great quality ingredients. In addition to a great selection of appetizers such as Scotch-marinated beef carpaccio or chicken wings with a smoky pepper rub, the menu lists a good choice of salads, pasta, burgers, steaks and entrees such as smoked black cod or braised lamb shank. Service is friendly and warm. Parking is validated. **Bar:** full bar. **Reservations:** suggested. **Address:** 21 Lakeshore Dr W V2A 7M5 **Location:** Main St at Lakeshore Dr W; in Penticton Lakeside Resort, Convention Centre & Casino. **Parking:** on-site and valet. B L D CALL

IYARA THAI RESTAURANT
250/770-9791 (43)

Thai. Casual Dining. $8-$16 **AAA Inspector Notes:** In the south end of town toward Skaha Lake, the friendly restaurant serves authentic Thai cuisine from an extensive menu that includes dishes from mild to hot and spicy. Bangkok-trained chefs prepare fresh, delicious food, while eschewing the use of monosodium glutamate. **Bar:** full bar. **Address:** 2985 Skaha Lake Rd V2A 5J6 **Location:** From downtown, 2.2 mi (3.5 km) s. L D CALL

LA CASA OUZERIA
250/492-9144 (41)

Greek. Casual Dining. $10-$45 **AAA Inspector Notes:** This longtime family-run establishment features both Greek and Italian cuisine. The small taverna captures the essence of festive dining with soft, regional music playing overhead. Décor is warm and inviting. The food is excellent. Not to be missed. **Bar:** full bar. **Reservations:** suggested, weekends. **Address:** 1090 Main St V2A 5E5 **Location:** Corner of Main St and Nelson Ave. L D

NAVRATAN
250/490-4746 (37)

Indian. Casual Dining. $10-$17 **AAA Inspector Notes:** Diners step into another world at this small restaurant, where the Indian cuisine includes tandoori chicken and many other dishes cooked in the clay oven, in addition to well-prepared curries, vindaloos, korma, biryani and a choice of naan breads. **Bar:** full bar. **Address:** 413 Main St V2A 5C4 **Location:** Corner of Wade Ave W and Main St; downtown. **Parking:** street only. L D

RICKY'S ALL DAY GRILL
250/490-0375

American. Casual Dining. $9-$26 **AAA Inspector Notes:** The comfortable eatery, which employs friendly servers, presents a varied menu that includes pasta dishes, wraps, omelets, stir-fry preparations and burgers. Portions are generous. Children's and senior selections are offered. Guests can request seating in a booth or at a table. **Bar:** full bar. **Address:** 2111 Main St V2A 6W6 **Location:** Between Warren and McDougall aves; in Cherry Lane Shopping Centre. B L D CALL

SALTY'S BEACH HOUSE
250/493-5001 (34)

Caribbean. Casual Dining. $12-$29 **AAA Inspector Notes:** During his travels, the owner collected recipes for all kinds of fish and other seafood, including the daily fresh catch, in addition to ribs, Sterling Silver AAA beef and jerk chicken. The dishes reflect the flavors of the Caribbean, Hawaii, Thailand and other island destinations. An island theme punctuates the fun restaurant, which has an inviting summer patio overlooking the lake and the Black Pearl Lounge and Oyster Bar upstairs. **Bar:** full bar. **Reservations:** suggested. **Address:** 1000 Lakeshore Dr W V2A 1C1 **Location:** Hwy 97, 0.5 mi (0.8 km) n. **Parking:** street only. L D CALL

SHADES ON MAIN FAMILY RESTAURANT
250/493-0465 (42)

American. Family Dining. $6-$12 **AAA Inspector Notes:** For a quick, affordable meal that will please everyone in the family, the family-run restaurant hits the mark. On the menu is everything from grilled cheese sandwiches to burgers and fries. Guests shouldn't be surprised if the server addresses them as "honey" and knows almost all the regulars by name. **Bar:** full bar. **Address:** 1909 Main St V2A 5H5 **Location:** Corner of Main St and Okanagan Rd. B L D CALL

THEO'S RESTAURANT
250/492-4019 (39)

Greek. Casual Dining. $12-$23 **AAA Inspector Notes:** This established downtown restaurant is a favorite with the locals. This place adds its own little twists to classic dishes made from the freshest ingredients. On the menu you'll find Greek salads, dolmades, souvlaki, moussaka and roast lamb, as well as steak and seafood. The Mediterranean décor is warm and family oriented. Parking is available on the street or behind the restaurant. **Bar:** full bar. **Reservations:** suggested. **Address:** 687 Main St V2A 5C9 **Location:** On Main St at Eckhardt Ave. L D

Get more from your membership with an upgrade to Plus or Premier

PORT ALBERNI (F-9) pop. 17,743,
elev. 60m/197'
• Hotels p. 304 • Restaurants p. 304

A deepwater port and important fishing and lumber shipping center, Port Alberni was discovered in 1791 by Don Pedro Alberni, a Spanish sea captain. Industry began in 1860 when nine workmen arriving on the schooner *Meg Merrilees* built a sawmill on the harbor's edge.

Port Alberni's harbor remains the city's focal point, enhanced by the Alberni Harbour Quay at the foot of Argyle Street. The facility includes shops, an arts and crafts outlet and the Lady Rose Marine Services office *(see attraction listing)*. From the 1912 CPR Train Station, a logging locomotive takes visitors on a 35-minute journey along the waterfront to McLean Mill National Historic Site *(see attraction listing)*.

Surrounded by mountains, lakes and forests, the city is a good base for naturalists and outdoors enthusiasts. Alpine and cross-country skiing are available nearby. Sproat Lake Provincial Park *(see Recreation Areas Chart)* features Indian carvings of mythological beasts. There are hundreds of giant Douglas firs, many that date from the late 12th century, at Cathedral Grove in MacMillan Provincial Park, 16 kilometres (10 mi.) east.

The region's natural wonders are protected by the Martin Mars Water Bombers based at Sproat Lake. Designed to combat forest fires, these huge aircraft carry 6,000 imperial gallons (7,206 U.S. gallons) of water.

Port Alberni Visitor Centre: 2533 Port Alberni Hwy., Port Alberni, BC, Canada V9Y 8P2. **Phone:** (250) 724-6535.

ALBERNI VALLEY MUSEUM is at 4255 Wallace St. in the Echo Centre building. The community museum features collections relating to indigenous peoples as well as community and industrial history. Feature exhibits include basketry, folk art and textiles.

Visitors also can see displays about the area's industrial past in logging, fishing, mining and farming. An exhibit about the West Coast Trail tells of its early uses as a telegraph line and a rescue trail for shipwrecked sailors. Changing exhibitions also are offered. **Time:** Allow 30 minutes minimum. **Hours:** Tues.-Sat. 10-5 (also Thurs. 5-8). Closed statutory holidays. **Cost:** Donations. **Phone:** (250) 723-2181.

LADY ROSE MARINE SERVICES is at Argyle Pier in the Alberni Harbour Quay at the foot of Argyle St. The packet freighter MV *Frances Barkley* takes visitors on an all-day cruise, sailing down the Alberni Inlet to Bamfield, Ucluelet and the Broken Group Islands to deliver mail and cargo to isolated villages, fishing resorts and camps.

Note: Sensible shoes and a sweater or light jacket are advisable. **Hours:** Departures to Bamfield Tues., Thurs. and Sat. 8-5, Oct.-May. Sailings to Ucluelet and Broken Group Islands Mon., Wed. and Fri. at 8, early June to mid-Sept. Phone ahead to confirm schedule. **Cost:** Bamfield trip $68 round-trip; $34 (ages 8-15). Ucluelet trip $74 round-trip; $37 (ages 8-15). Fares may vary; phone ahead. All children must be accompanied by an adult. Reservations are recommended in summer. **Phone:** (250) 723-8313, or (800) 663-7192 Apr.-Sept. 🍴

MARITIME DISCOVERY CENTRE is on the waterfront at 2750 Harbour Rd. The area's maritime history is documented at this museum, which was built from a coastal lighthouse. Highlights include exhibits about the history of lighthouses, rescue stories, tsunamis and the 1964 tidal wave, and life as a lighthouse keeper. Traveling exhibits also are featured. **Time:** Allow 30 minutes minimum. **Hours:** Daily 10-5, July-Sept. **Cost:** Donations. **Phone:** (250) 723-6164.

McLEAN MILL NATIONAL HISTORIC SITE is 6 km (10 mi.) w. on Beaver Creek Rd., then 3 km (1.8 mi.) n. to 5633 Smith Rd., following signs. The 13-hectare (32-acre) site preserves a working 1926 steam sawmill that was operated by the R.B. McLean family until 1965. Thirty structures from the early days of British Columbia's forest industry include the camp where loggers and mill employees lived and worked. Interactive guided tours and stage shows and sawmill demonstrations are given Thursday through Monday.

Time: Allow 1 hour, 30 minutes minimum. **Hours:** Daily 10-4, mid-June through Labour Day. Phone ahead to confirm schedule. **Cost:** Mill and train tours $29.95; $22.50 (ages 13-18, ages 60+ and students with ID); $18.75 (ages 5-12); $79.95 (family). Rates may vary; phone ahead. Reservations are recommended. **Phone:** (250) 723-1376. 🍴

Alberni Pacific Railway departs from the CPR Station at Argyle and Kingsway sts. Passengers embark upon a 35-minute train ride to McLean Mill National Historic Site. **Hours:** Trips depart Thurs.-Mon. at 10 and 2, mid-June through Labour Day. Last train leaves the mill at 5. Phone ahead to confirm schedule. **Cost:** Round-trip fare (includes mill admission) $29.95; $22.50 (ages 13-18, ages 60+ and students with ID); $14.95 (ages 5-12); $79.95 (family). Rates may vary; phone ahead. **Phone:** (250) 723-1376.

ROBERTSON CREEK FISH HATCHERY is 5 km (3 mi.) w. on Hwy. 4, then 7 km (4 mi.) n.w. on Great Central Lake Rd. The hatchery has an annual output of 8 million chinook and 800,000 coho salmon and 150,000 steelhead trout. Displays explain the fish breeding process from incubation through release. Facilities include outdoor rearing ponds and raceways. **Hours:** Daily 8:30-3:30. Closed Christmas. **Cost:** Free. **Phone:** (250) 724-6521.

BEST WESTERN PLUS BARCLAY HOTEL

(250)724-7171

Hotel
$110-$170

AAA Benefit: Members save up to 20%, plus 10% bonus points with Best Western Rewards®.

Address: 4277 Stamp Ave V9Y 7X8 **Location:** Johnston Rd (Hwy 4), just s on Gertrude St. **Facility:** 86 units. 5 stories, interior corridors. **Amenities:** *Some:* high-speed Internet. **Pool(s):** heated outdoor. **Activities:** sauna, whirlpool, exercise room. **Guest Services:** valet laundry. **Free Special Amenities:** local telephone calls and high-speed Internet.

SAVE / SOME UNITS FEE [icons]

THE HOSPITALITY INN

(250)723-8111

Hotel
$85-$135

Address: 3835 Redford St V9Y 3S2 **Location:** 2 mi (3.2 km) sw of jct Hwy 4 via City Centre/Port Alberni South Route. **Facility:** 50 units. 2 stories (no elevator), interior corridors. **Terms:** cancellation fee imposed. **Amenities:** high-speed Internet. **Pool(s):** heated outdoor. **Activities:** whirlpool, exercise room. **Guest Services:** valet laundry. **Free Special Amenities:** local telephone calls and high-speed Internet.

SAVE ECO / SOME UNITS FEE [icons]

RIVERSIDE MOTEL

250/724-9916

Motel $99-$159 **Address:** 5065 Roger St V9Y 3Y9 **Location:** Johnston Rd (Hwy 4), just s on Gertrude St, then just w. **Facility:** 12 units, some efficiencies and kitchens. 1 story, exterior corridors. **Guest Services:** coin laundry.

[icons] / SOME UNITS FEE

SOMASS MOTEL

250/724-3236

Motel $65-$135 **Address:** 5279 River Rd V9Y 6Z3 **Location:** 2 mi (3.2 km) on River Rd (Hwy 4) from Johnston Rd. **Facility:** 14 units, some two bedrooms and kitchens. 1 story, exterior corridors. **Pool(s):** outdoor. **Guest Services:** coin laundry.

[icons] / SOME UNITS FEE

WHERE TO EAT

THE CLAM BUCKET RESTAURANT

250/723-1315

Seafood. Casual Dining. $12-$24 **AAA Inspector Notes:** As the name suggests, this place specializes in oysters, clams, shrimp and prawns. There's also Freddy's Fabulous fish and chips, plus halibut and salmon burgers. Whatever you order, be sure to begin with an appetizer of "chicken toes." No, not real chicken toes, which are much too crunchy, but strips of tender breaded chicken. The restaurant has a saying: "To get a better piece of chicken you'd have to be a rooster!" **Bar:** full bar. **Address:** 4479 Victoria Quay V9Y 5G1 **Location:** From Johnson Rd (Hwy 4), just e; downtown. **Parking:** street only. [L] [D]

LITTLE BAVARIA RESTAURANT

250/724-4242

German
Casual Dining
$8-$20

AAA Inspector Notes: This quaint restaurant features a pleasant Bavarian décor with an accent on good old-fashioned German food. Schnitzel, Hungarian goulash, cabbage rolls, steak, seafood and fondue for two are on the menu. Couples and business people like this place. **Bar:** full bar. **Reservations:** suggested. **Address:** 3035 4th Ave V9Y 2B8 **Location:** Between Argyle and Angus sts. **Parking:** street only. *Menu on AAA.com* [L] [D]

SMITTY'S

250/724-5022

Canadian. Casual Dining. $10-$17 **AAA Inspector Notes:** The family-oriented restaurant satisfies patrons with its ever-popular all-day breakfast items, as well as tasty and wholesome soups and salads at lunchtime. A relaxed mood characterizes the dining space. **Bar:** full bar. **Address:** 3426 3rd Ave V9Y 7M8 **Location:** Between Napier St and the Quadrant. [B] [L] [D]

PORT COQUITLAM (H-11) pop. 56,342, elev. 10m/33'
• Attractions map p. 355
• Part of Vancouver area — see map p. 343

Port Coquitlam is bordered by the Pitt and Fraser rivers to the east and south and mountains to the north. The rivers were coveted fishing grounds, and in fact, Coquitlam is derived from the Salish word *kwayhquitlum*, which means "red fish in the river," referring to the annual salmon spawning run. Before the 1800s, the area was occupied by the ancestors of the Kwayhquitlum First Nations tribe. With the arrival of the first European settlers, Port Coquitlam began its growth as a farming and logging community.

Opportunities for recreational activities abound. The 29-kilometre (18-mi.) PoCo Trail passes through wooded areas and runs alongside the Pitt River, providing plenty of opportunities to observe waterfowl and other wildlife; the Pitt Dikes can be seen from the trail. Activities such as hiking, jogging, bicycling and horseback riding also can be enjoyed.

EARLS RESTAURANT

604/941-1733

American. Casual Dining. $12-$28 **AAA Inspector Notes:** Offering an experience that falls between fast food and fine dining, the fun, relaxed restaurant prepares great food at a great price. Choices range from juicy burgers, hearty sandwiches, fresh salads, wings and pizza to full entrees of steak, chops and seafood. Made-from-scratch soups and assorted breads, as well as a nice choice of wines and beers, round out the offerings. This is a fitting spot for impromptu get-togethers and festive occasions. **Bar:** full bar. **Address:** 2850 Shaughnessy St V3C 6K5 **Location:** Corner of Shaughnessy St and Lougheed Hwy (Hwy 7); in Shaughnessy Station Shopping Complex. [L] [D] [LATE] CALL [M]

PORT EDWARD (E-1) pop. 544

Port Edward, on the Tsimpsean Peninsula, was named after King Edward VI. The town was founded in 1908 and incorporated in 1966.

The river of mists, as the Indians called the Skeena River, bursts through the Coast Range and empties into the Pacific Ocean near Port Edward. The river provides the community's major commodity, fish, which is processed by local canneries. Salmon and steelhead trout, besides being economic staples, also offer a recreational challenge to anglers. Because of the area's proximity to luxuriant rain forests, mountain ranges and the river, sporting types also will find ample opportunities for canoeing, kayaking, camping, hunting and hiking.

NORTH PACIFIC CANNERY HISTORIC SITE & MUSEUM is 10 km (6 mi.) s. of Hwy. 16 at 1889 Skeena Dr. For almost 100 years (1889-1980) this cannery, one of more than 200 such businesses operating along the West Coast at the industry's peak, processed and canned salmon from the Skeena River.

The site consists of 29 buildings and structures representing the factory operations and employee living quarters of a multiethnic workforce in one of the formative industries of British Columbia. The village includes the main cannery, reduction plant, staff housing and mess house. Artifacts of the fishing industry, such as boats, tools and machinery original to the shops as well as some of the workers' personal items are displayed throughout the complex. Guided tours feature a working canning line, and a live historical presentation is offered.

Tours: Guided tours are available. **Time:** Allow 1 hour minimum. **Hours:** Daily 9:30-5, May-June and in Sept.; Tues.-Sun. 9:30-5, July-Aug. Phone ahead to arrange tours. **Cost:** $12; $10 (ages 65+); $6 (ages 6-18). **Phone:** (250) 628-3538. 🍴

PORT HARDY pop. 4,008

AIRPORT INN   250/949-9434
⚜️ **Hotel.** Rates not provided. **Address:** 4030 Byng Rd V0N 2P0 **Location:** Hwy 19, 3.1 mi (5 km) ne, follow signs. **Facility:** 45 units, some efficiencies. 2 stories (no elevator), interior corridors. **Guest Services:** coin laundry. 📶 ✕ 🎞 💻 /SOME UNITS 📦

GLEN LYON INN   (250)949-7115
⚜️⚜️ **Hotel** $89-$185 **Address:** 6435 Hardy Bay Rd V0N 2P0 **Location:** Hwy 19, 0.9 mi (1.5 km) n, follow signs. **Facility:** 44 units, some efficiencies. 3 stories, exterior corridors. **Terms:** 3 day cancellation notice-fee imposed. **Guest Services:** coin laundry. 🍴 🍸 CALL 📶 ✕ 🎞 📦 💻 /SOME UNITS FEE 🐾 📦

QUARTERDECK INN & MARINA   250/902-0455
⚜️⚜️ **Hotel** $125-$145 **Address:** 6555 Hardy Bay Rd V0N 2P0 **Location:** Hwy 19, 0.9 mi (1.5 km) n. **Facility:** 40 units, some efficiencies. 4 stories, interior corridors. **Terms:** cancellation fee imposed. **Amenities:** high-speed Internet. **Guest Services:** coin laundry. 🍴 🍸 CALL 📶 ✕ 🎞 💻 /SOME UNITS FEE 🐾 📦

WHERE TO EAT

MARKET STREET CAFE   250/949-8110
⚜️ Breakfast Sandwiches. Quick Serve. $5-$12 **AAA Inspector Notes:** Serving homemade soup and sandwiches along with mouthwatering pastries, pie and muffins, the downtown cafe is in the heart of the business district. Booths line the walls. **Address:** 7030 Market St V0N 2P0 **Location:** Hwy 19, 0.6 mi (1 km) nw (towards water) on Granville St, then just ne. **Parking:** street only. B L 🎞

TOUDAI RESTAURANT   250/949-8755
⚜️⚜️ Japanese Sushi. Casual Dining. $5-$15 **AAA Inspector Notes:** The popular sushi restaurant featuring favorites such as maki, nigiri, sashimi, sushi combinations and bento box dinners. It's a good idea to come early, as this place fills up quickly. **Bar:** beer & wine. **Address:** 7370 Market St V0N 2P0 **Location:** Corner of Market and Douglas sts; downtown; in Northshore Inn. D 🎞

PORT McNEILL (H-2) pop. 2,505, elev. 15m/49'

In the scenic, untamed wilderness of northern Vancouver Island, Port McNeill occupies a rich lumber and fishing region popular with adventurous hikers, campers, spelunkers, fishermen and other sports enthusiasts.

Of interest to rock collectors and geologists are several nearby natural phenomena, including the Vanishing River, which plunges underground into a maze of caves and tunnels; the Devil's Bath, a huge rock bowl continuously filled by an underground spring; and the Eternal Fountain, which gushes from a rock crevice and then disappears underground again. All are reached by logging roads that are accessible only in summer.

An inter-island ferry operates a shuttle service between Port McNeill, Sointula and Alert Bay *(see place listing p. 218)*.

Port McNeill Visitor Centre: 1594 Beach Dr., P.O. Box 129, Port McNeill, BC, Canada V0N 2R0. **Phone:** (250) 956-3131 or (888) 956-3131.

BLACK BEAR RESORT   250/956-4900
⚜️⚜️ **Motel.** Rates not provided. **Address:** 1812 Campbell Way V0N 2R0 **Location:** Hwy 19, 1.3 mi (2 km) e. **Facility:** 40 units, some efficiencies. 2 stories (no elevator), exterior corridors. **Amenities:** high-speed Internet, safes. **Pool(s):** heated indoor. **Activities:** sauna, whirlpool, exercise room, spa. **Guest Services:** coin laundry. 🍴 CALL 📶 ✕ 🎞 📦 📦 💻

HAIDA-WAY MOTOR INN   250/956-3373
⚜️ **Motel** $109-$139 **Address:** 1817 Campbell Way V0N 2R0 **Location:** Hwy 19, 1.3 mi (2 km) e. **Facility:** 42 units. 3 stories (no elevator), interior corridors. **Terms:** check-in 4 pm, resort fee. **Dining:** Northern Lights Restaurant, see separate listing. **Guest Services:** coin laundry. 🍴 🍸 📶 🎞 📦 📦 💻

WHERE TO EAT

NORTHERN LIGHTS RESTAURANT   250/956-3263
⚜️⚜️ Canadian. Casual Dining. $10-$25 **AAA Inspector Notes:** Popular among the locals for tasty food, the restaurant offers summer choices that include fresh local seafood, steak, chicken or pasta dishes, not to mention the signature fish and chips. It's worth saving room for dessert, as there is always a nice selection. **Bar:** full bar. **Address:** 1817 Campbell Way V0N 2R0 **Location:** Hwy 19, 1.3 mi (2 km) e; in Haida-Way Motor Inn. L D CALL 📶

PORT MOODY (H-11) pop. 32,975, elev. 10m/33'
• Attractions map p. 355
• Part of Vancouver area — see map p. 343

Port Moody once was the terminus of the Canadian Pacific Railway—the first train from Montréal to the Pacific arrived July 4, 1886. A year later the line was extended 20 kilometres (12 mi.) west to Vancouver. Rocky Point Park on Burrard Inlet offers picnicking, swimming, boating and nature trails.

PORT MOODY STATION MUSEUM is at 2734 Murray St. The museum displays community and railway artifacts and historical information about Port Moody in a former Canadian Pacific Railway depot with working and living areas restored to their early 1900s appearance. A heritage garden, typical of Canadian Pacific Railway stations 1882-1912, is on the grounds. A restored 1921 sleeper car also is on site.

Hours: Daily 10-5, Victoria Day-Labour Day; Wed.-Sun. noon-4, rest of year. Closed Jan. 1 and Dec. 25-26. **Cost:** Donations. **Phone:** (604) 939-1648.

POUCE COUPE (D-6) pop. 738,
elev. 652m/2,139'

The village of Pouce Coupe is referred to as the gateway to Peace country because it is one of the first communities travelers will see when entering British Columbia from Alberta.

POUCE COUPE AND DISTRICT MUSEUM is at 5006 49th Ave. Pioneer artifacts are housed in the former Northern Alberta Railway station. **Hours:** Daily 8-5, May-Aug; by appointment rest of year. **Cost:** Donations. **Phone:** (250) 786-5555, or (250) 786-5794 for an appointment in the off-season.

POWELL RIVER (F-10) pop. 13,165,
elev. 55m/180'

Rich forests and abundant water brought the founders of the Powell River Company to the area in the early 1900s. The townsite is one of the oldest company-built communities in western Canada.

Separated from the mainland by Jervis Inlet, the area offers year-round recreation including freshwater and saltwater fishing, scuba diving, boating, kayaking, hiking and bicycling. The Powell Forest Canoe Route connects eight lakes around the Upper Sunshine Coast region with camping areas along the scenic circuit.

A panorama of the Strait of Malaspina unfolds from the Mount Valentine viewpoint, reached by a rock stairway in the heart of town. Bald eagles can be observed at any time of year, especially in late fall when they are attracted by salmon spawning in channels and small streams. Also of interest are Sliammon Fish Hatchery and Powell River Salmon Society Spawning Channel.

Guided 2-hour tours of the Catalyst Paper Mill are offered through the visitor center. Part of the tour is outdoors; appropriate dress and low-heeled, closed footwear are advised. For information and reservations phone (877) 817-8669.

Powell River Visitor Centre: 1760 Joyce Ave., Unit 111, Powell River, BC, Canada V8A 3B6. **Phone:** (604) 485-4701 or (877) 817-8669.

INLAND LAKE PROVINCIAL PARK is 12 km (7 mi.) n. on Inland Lake Rd. In a semi-remote area with abundant and varied wildlife, the park offers wheelchair-accessible facilities for camping, hiking and fishing.

A 13-kilometre-long (8-mi.) circuit of crushed limestone with minimal grades has eight picnic and rest areas and six fishing wharves. Amenities include cabins exclusively for use by the physically impaired, and wheelchair-accessible outhouses. *See Recreation Areas Chart.* **Hours:** Site open for day use daily 7 a.m.-10 p.m., Apr.-Oct. Phone ahead to confirm schedule. **Cost:** Free. **Phone:** (604) 888-3714.

POWELL RIVER HISTORICAL MUSEUM & ARCHIVES ASSOCIATION is on Marine Ave. across from Willingdon Beach. The museum houses artifacts, archival material and displays about the area's history. A children's treasure hunt is featured. **Time:** Allow 30 minutes minimum. **Hours:** Daily 9-4:30, June 15-Aug. 31; 9-4, rest of year. Closed major holidays. **Cost:** $2; $1 (ages 5-12 and students with ID). **Phone:** (604) 485-2222.

POWELL RIVER TOWN CENTRE HOTEL   (604)485-3000

▼▼ **Hotel** $109-$200 **Address:** 4660 Joyce Ave V8A 3B6 **Location:** 0.5 mi (0.8 km) e on Duncan St (Westview-Powell Ferry Terminal), then 0.6 mi (1 km) n. **Facility:** 71 units. 2 stories, interior corridors. **Terms:** cancellation fee imposed. **Amenities:** video games (fee). **Activities:** exercise room. **Guest Services:** valet laundry, area transportation-ferry terminal to Vancouver Island.

WHERE TO EAT

THE SHINGLEMILL PUB & BISTRO   604/483-2001

▼▼ Canadian. Casual Dining. $10-$24 **AAA Inspector Notes:** The popular, longstanding pub and bistro sits on the shores of Powell Lake, and large bay windows overlook the marina. The view is best from the second floor. Food is typical bistro fare: burgers, sandwiches and soups. Although it's a bit of a drive to get here, it's worth the trip. **Bar:** full bar. **Address:** 6233 Powell Pl V8A 4S6 **Location:** From Duncan St (Westview-Powell Ferry Terminal), 2.2 mi (3.5 km) n on Marine Ave, 0.9 mi (1.5 km) e on Arbutus Ave.

SNICKERS RESTAURANT   604/485-8441

▼▼ Pizza. Casual Dining. $10-$35 **AAA Inspector Notes:** Offering the "best pizza in town," this eatery also whips up various pasta dishes. A weekday lunch smorgasbord starts at 11:30 am. Afterward, diners can head out and walk Marine Avenue to explore its many unique gift shops and businesses. **Bar:** full bar. **Address:** 4591 Marine Ave V8A 2K7 **Location:** From Duncan St (Westview-Powell Ferry Terminal), just n. **Parking:** street only.

PRINCE GEORGE (E-4) pop. 71,974,
elev. 691m/2,267'

At the confluence of the Nechako and Fraser rivers, the area was visited in 1793 by Alexander Mackenzie in his trek down the Fraser to the Pacific. In 1807 it became the site for Simon Fraser's North West Co. fort. Fraser's canoe brigades soon gave way to paddlewheelers and then railroads, which converged on this important northern crossroads. Prince George remains a major transportation and trade center, a role enhanced by a thriving forest industry.

Despite its urban transformation, the city has retained much of its natural heritage in its 116 parks. Of interest are Fort George Park, which contains a replica of Fraser's trading post; Connaught Park's manicured gardens and scenic views; and Cottonwood Island Park, which includes the Prince George Railway & Forestry Museum and its collection of railroad artifacts and cars.

Prince George blends its pastoral features with such cultural centers as Studio 2880 and Vanier Hall. Studio 2880, home to six craft guilds, is the site of craft markets and special events throughout the year. Concerts by the Prince George Symphony and by visiting performers are held in Vanier Hall.

These cultural amenities coexist with the more rugged recreational opportunities available in the wilderness that surrounds the city. Nearby lakes, rivers and mountains present an array of activities ranging from rugged back-country hikes and fishing to skiing and ice skating.

Prince George Visitor Centre: 1300 First Ave., Suite 201, Prince George, BC, Canada V2L 2Y3. **Phone:** (250) 562-3700 or (800) 668-7646.

THE EXPLORATION PLACE MUSEUM & SCIENCE CENTRE is at the end of 20th Ave. at 333 Becott Pl. in Fort George Park. Fort George's history and development are explored through such topics as transportation, lumber and the indigenous culture. The Children's Gallery houses life-size dinosaur sculptures, skeletons and a dig pit. The Explorations Gallery features live animals and interactive computers. A SimEx virtual motion theater offers three rides daily. A steam locomotive ride is offered on weekends and holidays.

Time: Allow 1 hour minimum. **Hours:** Daily 9-5. Closed Jan. 1, Christmas and day after Christmas. **Cost:** Museum $9.95; $7.95 (ages 65+ and students with ID); $6.95 (ages 3-12); $22.95 (family, two adults and up to four children ages 0-18). Combination ticket with SimEx ride $10.95; $9.95 (ages 65+ and students with ID); $8.95 (ages 3-12); $29.95 (family, two adults and up to four children ages 0-18). **Phone:** (250) 562-1612 or (866) 562-1612.

HUBLE HOMESTEAD HISTORIC SITE is 38 km (24 mi.) n. on Hwy. 97, then 6 km (4 mi.) e. on Mitchell Rd. The site features several replicas of historic buildings as well as the original homestead of Al and Annie Huble. Along with his business partner Ed Seebach, Huble was instrumental in establishing a community within the Giscome Portage area. The homestead also offers weekend special events that feature demonstrations, live entertainment, games and contests.

Tours: Guided tours are available. **Time:** Allow 1 hour minimum. **Hours:** Daily 10-5, May 18-Sept. 2; Sat.-Sun. 10-5, Sept. 7-Oct. 7. Phone ahead to confirm schedule. **Cost:** $5; $3 (children and senior citizens); $10 (family). **Phone:** (250) 564-7033.

PRINCE GEORGE RAILWAY & FORESTRY MUSEUM is at 850 River Rd. The museum houses one of the largest collection of railway-related artifacts in British Columbia. Items, circa 1899-1960s, include a wooden snow plow, locomotives, box cars and cabooses.

Time: Allow 1 hour minimum. **Hours:** Tues.-Sat. 11-4, Victoria Day weekend-Labour Day weekend; 11-8, Dec. 18-23; 11-6 on Christmas Eve. Closed Nov. 11. Phone ahead to confirm schedule. **Cost:** $6; $5 (ages 12-17, students with ID and senior citizens); $3 (ages 3-11). **Phone:** (250) 563-7351.

CITY CENTRE INN   250/563-1267

◆◆ ◆◆ **Motel.** Rates not provided. **Address:** 910 Victoria St V2L 2K8 **Location:** Just n of Victoria St (Hwy 16) and Patricia Blvd; downtown. **Facility:** 53 units. 2 stories (no elevator), exterior corridors. **Pool(s):** heated indoor. **Activities:** exercise room. **Guest Services:** valet and coin laundry.

DAYS INN-PRINCE GEORGE   (250)562-7072

◆◆ ◆◆ **Hotel** $95 **Address:** 600 Quebec St V2L 1W7 **Location:** From Victoria St (Hwy 16), just n on 7th Ave. **Facility:** 76 units. 2 stories, interior corridors. **Terms:** 3 day cancellation notice-fee imposed. **Activities:** exercise room. **Guest Services:** valet and coin laundry.

FOUR POINTS BY SHERATON PRINCE GEORGE
(250)564-7100

◆◆◆ ◆◆◆ Hotel $109-$280
FOUR POINTS BY SHERATON

AAA Benefit: Members get up to 20% off, plus Starwood Preferred Guest® bonuses.

Address: 1790 Hwy 97 S V2L 5L3 **Location:** Hwy 97 exit Spruce northbound; exit City Center via Queensway southbound. **Facility:** 74 units. 3 stories, interior corridors. **Parking:** winter plug-ins. **Amenities:** high-speed Internet. **Pool(s):** heated indoor. **Activities:** whirlpool, exercise room. **Guest Services:** valet laundry. **Free Special Amenities:** newspaper and high-speed Internet.

TREASURE COVE CASINO HOTEL   (250)614-9111

◆◆◆ ◆◆◆ **Hotel** $144-$214 **Address:** 2005 Hwy 97 S V2N 7A3 **Location:** Corner of Hwy 97 and 16. **Facility:** The property features one of the area's largest casinos, a Vegas-style show lounge and a huge waterslide and pool. 82 units. 4 stories, interior corridors. **Terms:** check-in 4 pm, cancellation fee imposed. **Amenities:** high-speed Internet. **Pool(s):** heated indoor. **Activities:** whirlpool, waterslide, exercise room. **Guest Services:** valet laundry.

SANDMAN SIGNATURE HOTEL   250/645-7263

fyi Not evaluated. **Address:** 2990 Recreation Place Dr V2N 0B2 **Location:** Hwy 16, just w on Ferry Ave, then just s. Facilities, services, and décor characterize a mid-scale property.

WHERE TO EAT

CHINA SAIL RESTAURANT   250/564-2828

◆◆ ◆◆ Chinese. Casual Dining. $9-$15 **AAA Inspector Notes:** A local favorite for more than 20 years, this restaurant continues to serve delicious Chinese and Canadian dishes. Diners can select an individual meal, family dinner or combination plate; all are reasonably priced. **Bar:** full bar. **Address:** 4288 5th Ave V2M 7A2 **Location:** Hwy 97, 1 mi (1.7 km) w; corner of 5th Ave and Tabor Blvd.

EARLS RESTAURANT   250/562-1527

◆◆ ◆◆ American. Casual Dining. $13-$31 **AAA Inspector Notes:** Offering an experience that falls between fast food and fine dining, the fun, relaxed restaurant prepares great food at a great price. Choices range from juicy burgers, hearty sandwiches, fresh salads, wings and pizza to full entrees of steak, chops and seafood. Made-from-scratch soups and assorted breads, as well as a nice choice of wines and beers, round out the offerings. This is a fitting spot for impromptu get-togethers and festive occasions. **Bar:** full bar. **Address:** 1440 E Central St V2M 3C1 **Location:** Corner of Hwy 97 and 15th Ave.

AAA/CAA travel information:
Available in print, online and on the go!

MOXIE'S CLASSIC GRILL   250/564-4700

▼▼ ▼▼ American. Casual Dining. $11-$25 **AAA Inspector Notes:** This sleek, funky and popular restaurant presents an extensive menu of creatively prepared dishes, including pizza, pasta, rice, noodles, signature salads and burgers. Other menus include one for children and one for Sunday brunch. Lending to the upbeat, stylish decor are dark wood appointments and river rock fireplaces. **Bar:** full bar. **Address:** 1804 E Central St V2M 3C3 **Location:** Jct Hwy 97 and 18th Ave. [L] [D] [LATE] CALL [&M]

RIC'S GRILL   250/614-9096

▼▼ ▼▼ Steak Seafood. Casual Dining. $9-$45 **AAA Inspector Notes:** "Funky and modern" describes the decor and the food at the upscale steakhouse, which bustles with activity. Steaks are well worth it, but then again, so are the salmon, chicken and pasta dishes. A wide variety of distinctive appetizers rounds out the menu. Servers are friendly and attentive. **Bar:** full bar. **Reservations:** suggested. **Address:** 547 George St V2L 1R8 **Location:** Between 5th and 6th aves; downtown. **Parking:** street only. [L] [D] CALL [&M]

PRINCE RUPERT (E-1) pop. 12,508, elev. 50m/164'

At the turn of the 20th century Prince Rupert existed only in the imagination of Charles Hays, manager of the Grand Trunk Pacific Railway. Hays died with the sinking of the SS *Titanic,* but the Grand Trunk Pacific Railway carried out his intention to build a port to rival Vancouver on this rugged, uninhabited island bordered by a natural harbor. The new site was expected to be successful because it was closer to the Far East than Vancouver and would provide an outlet for the untapped resources of Canada's far north.

Prince Rupert has fulfilled that potential and is now one of Canada's major seaports. It is the southernmost port of the Alaska Ferry System, the northern terminus of the British Columbia Ferry Corp. and the western terminus of the Canadian National Railway. Cruise ships en route to coastal glaciers and fjords also stop at Prince Rupert's harbor, said to be the world's third largest natural ice-free deep-sea harbor.

Before the coming of the railroad the northern coast was home to the Tsimpsean and Haida, cultures whose ancestors inhabited the area for almost 5,000 years. Both are renowned for their stylized artworks, the most familiar of which are totem poles. Many of these graceful monuments are shown in such city parks as Service Park, the colorful terraced Sunken Gardens, and Roosevelt Park with its sweeping views of the Pacific.

On the waterfront, Kwinitsa Railway Station is a relic of the modern era. Restored and moved from its original location, Kwinitsa is one of the last of the Grand Trunk Pacific Railway stations; inside are exhibits about the railroad's history.

Just beyond the city, climate and soil have stunted and twisted lodgepole pines into a natural bonsai garden at Oliver Lake Provincial Park. Another interesting phenomenon is Butze Rapids, a series of reversing rapids between Wainwright and Morse basins that rival the reversing falls at Saint John, New Brunswick. A dramatic view of the rapids occurs during a falling tide and can be seen from a viewing point on Hwy. 16, which offers scenic driving east to Terrace *(see place listing p. 336).*

Guided tours are offered during the summer by Farwest Bus Lines Ltd., 225 Second Ave. W. Trans-Provincial Airlines and Northcoast Air Services offer flight tours of the region.

Prince Rupert Visitor Centre: 100 First Ave. W., Prince Rupert, BC, Canada V8J 1A8. **Phone:** (250) 624-5637 or (800) 667-1994.

Self-guiding tours: A walking tour that includes sunken gardens, the harbor, sections of the downtown area and various attractions is detailed on maps and brochures available from the visitor bureau at the Museum of Northern British Columbia *(see attraction listing).*

MUSEUM OF NORTHERN BRITISH COLUMBIA is at 100 First Ave. W. and McBride St. Models, maps, graphic displays and an ethnological collection explain pioneer history and the lifestyles of coastal groups from prehistoric times through their contacts with Europeans. Changing exhibits are displayed in the art gallery. Of interest are an early 20th-century steamroller and a modern carving shed with local artists on-site.

Hours: Daily 9-7, Victoria Day-Aug. 31; daily 9-5, in Sept.; Tues.-Sat. 9-5, rest of year. Closed Jan. 1, Christmas and day after Christmas. **Cost:** $6; $3 (ages 6-12 and students with ID); $10 (family). **Phone:** (250) 624-3207.

ALEEDA MOTEL   (250)627-1367

▼▼ Motel $60-$105 **Address:** 900 3rd Ave W V8J 1M8 **Location:** Corner of 3rd Ave W and 8th St. **Facility:** 31 units, some efficiencies. 2 stories (no elevator), interior corridors. **Terms:** cancellation fee imposed. [↑] [⬡] [✕] / SOME UNITS FEE [🐾] [🛏] [🖥]

INN ON THE HARBOUR   (250)624-9107

▼▼ ▼▼ Motel $99-$179 **Address:** 720 1st Ave W V8J 3V6 **Location:** Corner of 6th St. **Facility:** 49 units. 3 stories (no elevator), interior corridors. **Terms:** cancellation fee imposed. **Guest Services:** valet and coin laundry. [↑] CALL [&M] [⬡] [✕] [✕] [🛏] [🖥] / SOME UNITS FEE [🐾]

WHERE TO EAT

OPA SUSHI   250/627-4560

▼▼ ▼▼ Japanese Sushi. Casual Dining. $5-$30 **AAA Inspector Notes:** The sushi restaurant occupies an old loft originally used for taking the main conk lines off the nets and putting them into a pot filled with tar, which helped preserve the rope from rot and salt damage. The tar pot is still here, as is the tar on the floor. Seating is limited. Prices listed are for individual sushi rolls. **Bar:** beer & wine. **Reservations:** suggested. **Address:** 34 Cow Bay Rd V8J 1A5 **Location:** From 3rd Ave E, 0.6 mi (1 km) n; in Cow Bay. **Parking:** street only. [L] [D] [✕]

SMILES SEAFOOD CAFE   250/624-3072

▼▼ ▼▼ Seafood. Casual Dining. $8-$40 **AAA Inspector Notes:** In business since 1934, the distinctive diner-style restaurant serves locals and tourists alike with a variety of seafood, steaks, chops, sandwiches and salads. If you need directions, any local can point the way. **Bar:** full bar. **Address:** 113 Cow Bay Rd V8J 1A4 **Location:** From 3rd Ave E, 0.6 mi (1 km) n; in Cow Bay. **Parking:** street only. [L] [D] [✕]

PRINCETON (C-8) pop. 2,724

Named "Vermilion Forks" by fur traders in the early 1800s, Princeton developed as a ranching and mining outpost in the foothills of the Cascade Mountains. In 1860 the town was renamed to honor a visit by the Prince of Wales. Revitalized downtown storefronts boast murals and facades in keeping with Princeton's Western heritage.

Princeton & District Chamber of Commerce: 105 Hwy. 3E, P.O. Box 540, Princeton, BC, Canada V0X 1W0. **Phone:** (250) 295-3103.

Self-guiding tours: Maps detailing walking tours are available from the chamber of commerce.

PRINCETON & DISTRICT MUSEUM AND ARCHIVES is at 167 Vermilion Ave. The collection includes fossils and minerals, aboriginal baskets, lace and textiles, antique cooking utensils, mining tools and equipment, a large butterfly collection and a stagecoach. **Hours:** Daily 10-5, Easter-Aug. 31. **Cost:** Donations. **Phone:** (250) 293-7588.

CANADAS BEST VALUE PRINCETON INN & SUITES
(250)295-3537

Hotel
$110-$150

Address: 169 Hwy 3 V0X 1W0 **Location:** Hwy 3, just n on Vermilion Ave. **Facility:** 45 units, some kitchens. 2 stories (no elevator), exterior corridors. **Parking:** winter plug-ins. **Terms:** cancellation fee imposed. **Amenities:** Some: high-speed Internet. **Pool(s):** heated outdoor. **Activities:** sauna, whirlpool. **Free Special Amenities:** expanded continental breakfast and high-speed Internet.

WHERE TO EAT

BELAIRE RESTAURANT   250/295-7711
▼▼ American. Casual Dining. $9-$24 **AAA Inspector Notes:** This popular restaurant has been rebuilt after a fire. The menu features homemade burgers, sandwiches served with a choice of fries or homemade soup, and a selection of fresh salads sure to satisfy greens-loving vegetarians. Served after 5 pm, dinner entrees come with a garden salad or soup, along with a nightly dinner feature. **Bar:** full bar. **Address:** 157 Vermilion Ave V0X 1W0 **Location:** Hwy 3, just n. **Parking:** street only.

QUADRA ISLAND (E-11)

Totem poles are found within the Cape Mudge Reserve on Quadra Island, part of the Gulf Islands group, which is reached by a 15-minute ferry ride from Campbell River *(see place listing p. 224)*.

RECREATIONAL ACTIVITIES
Scuba Diving
• **Abyssal Dive Charters** departs from Quadra Island. Other activities are available. **Hours:** Daily 7:30 a.m.-10:30 p.m. **Phone:** (250) 204-3443 or (800) 499-2297.

Give the gift of security, value and peace of mind: Gift Membership

TAKU RESORT & MARINA   (250)285-3031
▼▼ ▼▼ Motel $99-$325 **Address:** 616 Taku Rd V0P 1H0 **Location:** From Campbell River Ferry Terminal, 4.1 mi (6.6 km) n on West Rd, then just e on Heriot Bay Rd, follow signs to Heriot Bay. **Facility:** 14 units, some two bedrooms, efficiencies, kitchens and cabins. 1 story, exterior corridors. **Terms:** 2 night minimum stay - seasonal, 30 day cancellation notice-fee imposed. **Activities:** whirlpool, fishing, tennis court, basketball, horseshoes, volleyball. *Fee:* boat dock. **Guest Services:** coin laundry.

TSA-KWA-LUTEN LODGE   (250)285-2042
▼▼ ▼▼ Hotel $105-$380 **Address:** 1 Lighthouse Rd V0P 1N0 **Location:** From Campbell River Ferry Terminal, just se on Green Rd, 0.6 mi (1 km) e on Noble Rd, 1.8 mi (2.9 km) se on Cape Mudge Rd to Joyce Rd, 0.6 mi (1 km) sw, then 1.4 mi (2.2 km) s. **Facility:** 36 units, some cottages. 1-2 stories (no elevator), interior/exterior corridors. **Terms:** closed 10/28-3/31, 3 day cancellation notice-fee imposed. **Dining:** Hama Elas Dining Room, see separate listing. **Activities:** sauna, whirlpool, bicycles, horseshoes, exercise room.

WHERE TO EAT

HAMA ELAS DINING ROOM   250/285-2042
▼▼▼ Pacific Northwest. Casual Dining. $12-$35 **AAA Inspector Notes:** The lodge's dining room features wonderful views of distant Campbell River and snow capped mountains across the water. The menu features a lovely mix of seafood, chicken, steak, pasta, rice and vegetarian dishes — something for everyone. **Bar:** full bar. **Reservations:** suggested. **Address:** 1 Lighthouse Rd V0P 1N0 **Location:** From Campbell River Ferry Terminal, just se on Green Rd, 0.6 mi (1 km) e on Noble Rd, 1.8 mi (2.9 km) se on Cape Mudge Rd to Joyce Rd, 0.6 mi (1 km) sw, then 1.4 mi (2.2 km) s; in Tsa-Kwa-Luten Lodge.

QUALICUM BAY pop. 334

SANDBAR CAFE   778/424-4478
▼ Canadian. Casual Dining. $7-$15 **AAA Inspector Notes:** The roadside-style diner offers a great view of the water. The traditional fare of good food includes a daily selection of tasty sandwiches and homemade soup. The coffee is always fresh, and service is friendly and prompt. **Bar:** full bar. **Address:** 6087 W Island Hwy V0R 1G0 **Location:** Hwy 19 exit 75 (Qualicum Bay/Bowser), 1.8 mi (3 km) e, follow Hwy 19A signs, then 1.5 mi (2.5 km) n on Hwy 19A.

QUALICUM BEACH (G-10) pop. 8,687, elev. 9m/30'
• Hotels p. 310 • Restaurants p. 310

A popular resort and arts community, Qualicum Beach is known for its white sand beaches. Nearby Little Qualicum Falls *(see Recreation Areas Chart)*, Englishman River Falls *(see Recreation Areas Chart)* and Horne Lake Caves provincial parks also present abundant recreational opportunities. Salmon and trout are raised at fish hatcheries on the Big and Little Qualicum rivers.

Qualicum Beach Visitor Information Centre: 2711 W. Island Hwy., Qualicum Beach, BC, Canada V9K 2C4. **Phone:** (250) 752-9532.

BIG QUALICUM HATCHERY is 2.5 km (1.5 mi.) s. on Hwy. 4W, 14.5 km (9 mi.) w. on Hwy. 19, then 2.4 km (1.5 mi.) s.w. on Horne Lake Rd. to Fisheries

Rd., following signs. Millions of chum, coho and chinook salmon are hatched here each year as part of the country's efforts to restore its salmon population. Steelhead and cutthroat trout also are raised. Visitors can see holding ponds, rearing channels and incubation units. Hiking trails are available. **Time:** Allow 30 minutes minimum. **Hours:** Daily 8-4. **Cost:** Donations. **Phone:** (250) 757-8412.

HORNE LAKE CAVES is 15 km (9 mi.) n. on Hwy. 19 to exit 75 (Horne Lake Rd.), then 14 km (9 mi.) w. on a gravel rd., following signs to the parking lot. A part of the Horne Lake Caves Provincial Park, the cave system is considered to be one of the best in Canada. Tours are guided and highlights include crystal formations, ancient fossils and a waterfall.

The 1.5-hour Family Cavern Tour teaches about the geology and history of the caves. The interpretive tour starts with a 25-minute walk to the entrance. Once inside the cave, visitors explore the easy passages; no crawling or maneuvering in tight spaces is necessary.

Other 3-, 4-, and 5-hour tours also are offered. Self-guiding exploration is available in Horne Lake Main and Lower caves year-round. A helmet and two sources of light are required. Helmets may be rented for $5 each during the summer only.

Note: The caves are mostly undeveloped and do not provide lighting. Floors are rocky and uneven; children ages 0-4 and visitors with mobility issues could encounter difficulty walking. Warm clothing and comfortable boots or shoes are highly recommended, as the caves remain cool even in hot weather. Cameras are permitted.

Time: Allow 1 hour, 30 minutes minimum. **Hours:** Tours require a minimum of three people. Family Cavern Tour is given on a first-come, first-served basis daily on the hour 10-5, late June-Labour Day; by appointment rest of year. Last tour leaves at closing. Closed Jan. 1 and Christmas. **Cost:** Family Cavern Tour $24; $20 (ages 0-11). Phone ahead to confirm rates. **Phone:** (250) 248-7829.

MILNER GARDENS AND WOODLAND, 2179 W. Island Hwy., comprises 4 hectares (60 acres) of Douglas fir woodland and 4 hectares (10 acres) of garden surrounding a gabled heritage house. Visitors may view the dining, sitting and drawing rooms as well as the library. Historical photos, artifacts and keepsakes of visits by members of the Royal family also are displayed.

Time: Allow 1 hour minimum. **Hours:** Daily 10-4:30, Apr. 25-Sept. 2; Thurs.-Sun. and Mon. holidays 10-4:30, Sept. 5-Oct. 14 and Mar. 28-Apr. 21; daily 11-2:30, Feb.-Mar. and Oct. 20-27. Phone ahead to confirm schedule. **Cost:** $11.20; $6.75 (students with ID); free (ages 0-12 when accompanied by an adult). **Phone:** (250) 752-6153.

QUALICUM BEACH HISTORICAL & MUSEUM SOCIETY is at 587 Beach Rd. Two floors of exhibits highlight the history of Qualicum Beach and

Canada. Included in the displays are murals, a diorama of a 1930s kitchen and a paleontology collection. The 1929 Powerhouse building also is on site and houses a variety of historical items. **Time:** Allow 30 minutes minimum. **Hours:** Tues.-Sat. 11-4, June-Sept.; Tues. and Thurs. 1-4, rest of year. **Cost:** Donations. **Phone:** (250) 752-5533.

OCEAN CREST MOTEL   250/752-5518

Motel $59-$119 **Address:** 3292 W Island Hwy V9K 2C6 **Location:** Hwy 19 exit 60 (Qualicum Beach/Port Alberni), 2.5 mi (4 km) e on Memorial Ave, then 1.9 mi (3 km) n on Hwy 19A. **Facility:** 19 units, some efficiencies. 2 stories (no elevator), exterior corridors. **Terms:** cancellation fee imposed.

OLD DUTCH INN (BY THE SEA)   250/752-6914

[fyi] Hotel. Rates not provided. Under major renovation, scheduled to be completed May 2013. **Last Rated:** Address: 2690 Island Hwy W V9K 1G8 **Location:** Hwy 19 exit 60 (Qualicum Beach/Port Alberni), 2.5 mi (4 km) on Memorial Ave; jct Hwy 19A. **Facility:** 35 units. 2 stories (no elevator), interior corridors. **Pool(s):** heated indoor. **Activities:** sauna, whirlpool.

GARY'S BISTRO   250/752-5800

American. Casual Dining. $9-$18 **AAA Inspector Notes:** Located downtown, this is a simple diner-style restaurant where burgers are king, frosty beers are on tap and there's a great selection of tasty appetizers. Open early for breakfast; try their famous "eggbennys" made with free-range eggs. **Bar:** full bar. **Address:** 115 W Second Ave V9K 1S7 **Location:** Between Primrose St and Memorial Ave. **Parking:** street only. [B] [L] [D]

THE SHADY REST WATERFRONT PUB RESTAURANT
                                               250/752-9111

American. Casual Dining. $11-$23 **AAA Inspector Notes:** The true highlight of this restaurant is its shore-front location, where every table has an amazing view of the water. At lunch, good pub food is served along with frosty beers on tap. You'll find heartier fare at dinner. Families are warmly welcomed. **Bar:** full bar. **Address:** 3109 Island Hwy W V9K 2C5 **Location:** Hwy 19 exit 60 (Qualicum Beach/Port Alberni), 2.4 mi (4 km) e on Memorial Ave, then 1.2 mi (2 km) n on Hwy 19A. [L] [D] CALL

QUESNEL (F-5) pop. 10,007, elev. 545m/1,788'

Discovery of gold in the surrounding area in the 1860s contributed to Quesnel's growth. The city is the center of a popular hunting and fishing region at the junction of the Fraser and Quesnel rivers. Lumber, pulp and plywood manufacturing, tourism, cattle ranching and mining are the city's primary sources of income.

East of the city on Hwy. 26 is a historic remnant of the gold rush days, Barkerville Historic Town (see place listing p. 219), a restored boomtown of that era. Just beyond Barkerville is Bowron Lake Provincial Park (see Recreation Areas Chart), which has a 116-kilometre (72-mi.) canoe circuit of interconnecting lakes. Alpine skiing is available nearby.

Quesnel Visitor Centre: 703 Carson Ave., Quesnel, BC, Canada V2J 2B6. **Phone:** (250) 992-8716 or (800) 992-4922.

COTTONWOOD HOUSE HISTORIC SITE is 28 km (17 mi.) e. on Hwy. 26. Cottonwood was built 1864-65 as a roadhouse for travelers on the Cariboo Wagon Road en route to the gold fields of Barkerville. The 11-hectare (26-acre) site includes a double barn, stable, animals, guesthouse, outbuildings and antique machinery. Costumed interpreters provide tours of Cottonwood House and wagon rides. A walking trail winds along the river.

Hours: Daily 10-5, mid-May through Labour Day. **Cost:** $4.50 (includes wagon ride); $3.50 (ages 60+); $2 (ages 13-18 and students with ID); $9 (family). **Phone:** (250) 992-2071 or (250) 983-6911.

QUESNEL & DISTRICT MUSEUM AND ARCHIVES is .7 km (.5 mi.) s. on Hwy. 97 at 705 Carson Ave. Marking the area's history from the days of Alexander Mackenzie's explorations and the 1862 gold rush, the museum includes exhibits about pioneer life, a hands-on area for children, items from the *Titanic,* Chinese artifacts from the gold rush, a doll that is said to be haunted and an archives.

Time: Allow 1 hour minimum. **Hours:** Daily 9-6, Victoria Day-Labour Day; Tues.-Sat. 9:30-4, day after Labour Day-Sept. 30; Wed.-Sat. 9:30-4, rest of year. Closed major holidays. **Cost:** $4; $2 (ages 13-18). **Phone:** (250) 992-9580.

BEST WESTERN PLUS TOWER INN   (250)992-2201

 Hotel $115-$125   **AAA Benefit:** Members save up to 20%, plus 10% bonus points with Best Western Rewards®.

Address: 500 Reid St V2J 2M9 **Location:** Hwy 97, just e on Shepherd Ave; downtown. **Facility:** 63 units. 4 stories, interior corridors. **Amenities:** high-speed Internet. **Activities:** exercise room. **Guest Services:** valet laundry. **Free Special Amenities: local telephone calls and high-speed Internet.**

QUALITY INN & SUITES   (250)992-7247

Motel $99-$179   **Address:** 753 Front St V2J 2L2 **Location:** Hwy 97, 0.6 mi (1 km) n of Carson Ave. **Facility:** 83 units, some efficiencies and kitchens. 2 stories (no elevator), interior corridors. **Parking:** winter plug-ins.
Amenities: Some: high-speed Internet. **Activities:** whirlpool, exercise room. **Guest Services:** coin laundry. **Free Special Amenities: expanded continental breakfast and high-speed Internet.**

 / SOME UNITS FEE

TRAVELODGE   (250)992-7071

Motel $77   **Address:** 524 Front St V2J 2K6 **Location:** Hwy 97, 0.5 mi (0.8 km) n of Carson Ave. **Facility:** 34 units, some two bedrooms, efficiencies and kitchens. 2 stories (no elevator), exterior corridors.
Parking: winter plug-ins. **Amenities:** Some: high-speed Internet. **Pool(s):** heated indoor. **Activities:** sauna. **Free Special Amenities: expanded continental breakfast and high-speed Internet.**

/ SOME UNITS FEE

WHERE TO EAT

GRANVILLE'S COFFEE   250/992-3667

Breads/Pastries Sandwiches. Quick Serve. $4-$9 **AAA Inspector Notes:** Patrons easily can become too busy viewing the eatery's eclectically decorated walls to finish their coffee. Good choices include jumbo muffins, deli sandwiches and homemade soups. Located downtown where fluent espresso is spoken. **Address:** 383 Reid St V2J 2M5 **Location:** Reid St at St. Laurent Ave; downtown. **Parking:** street only. B L D

TOKYO SUSHI   250/992-2822

Sushi. Casual Dining. $10-$20 **AAA Inspector Notes:** A nice spot for great sushi and sashimi, this place occupies a building easily recognized as a former Pizza Hut. Those who can't decide can opt for a combination or party tray. **Bar:** beer & wine. **Address:** 394 Front St V2J 2W4 **Location:** Corner of Hwy 97 and St. Laurent Ave. L D

RADIUM HOT SPRINGS (B-11) pop. 777,
elev. 805m/2,641'
• Restaurants p. 312

Renowned for its mineral hot springs *(see Kootenay National Park p. 267 and Recreation Areas Chart)*, Radium Hot Springs also is a popular departure point for scenic and white-water river excursions. More than 10 golf courses are in the vicinity.

RECREATIONAL ACTIVITIES
White-water Rafting

• **Kootenay River Runners** is at 4987 Hwy. 93. **Hours:** Daily 8 a.m.-10 p.m., June 1 to mid-Sept. **Phone:** (250) 347-9210 or (800) 599-4399.

BIGHORN MEADOWS RESORT   (250)347-2323

Condominium $139-$199   **Address:** 10 Bighorn Blvd V0A 1M0 **Location:** Hwy 93 and 95, 0.5 mi (0.9 km) sw on Stanley St; in Springs Golf Course. **Facility:** From smaller studio units to larger units, the resort includes varied rooms, including some lofts that let guests walk right onto the golf course. 189 condominiums. 3 stories, exterior corridors. **Parking:** winter plug-ins. **Terms:** check-in 4 pm, 3 day cancellation notice. **Amenities:** high-speed Internet. **Pool(s):** heated outdoor. **Activities:** whirlpool. **Fee:** golf-18 holes. **Free Special Amenities: local telephone calls and high-speed Internet.**

BIGHORN MOTEL   250/347-9111

Motel $70-$80   **Address:** 4881 St. Mary's St E V0A 1M0 **Location:** Jct Hwy 93 and 95, just s along Main St W, then just w. **Facility:** 20 units, some efficiencies. 1 story, exterior corridors. **Parking:** winter plug-ins.
Free Special Amenities: high-speed Internet and local transportation.

/ SOME UNITS FEE

CEDAR MOTEL   250/347-9463

Motel $75-$140 **Address:** 7593 Main St W V0A 1M0 **Location:** Hwy 93 and 95, just s of jct Hwy 93, on service road (Main St). **Facility:** 17 units, some efficiencies. 2 stories (no elevator), exterior corridors. **Parking:** winter plug-ins.

LIDO MOTEL   250/347-9533

Motel $65-$95 **Address:** 4876 McKay St V0A 1M0 **Location:** Jct Hwy 93 and 95, just s along Main St W, then just w. **Facility:** 10 units, some efficiencies. 1 story, exterior corridors. **Parking:** winter plug-ins. **Terms:** 7 day cancellation notice. **Activities:** miniature golf, horseshoes. / SOME UNITS FEE

PRESTIGE RADIUM HOT SPRINGS   (250)347-2300

Hotel
$130-$210

Address: 7493 Main St W V0A 1M0 **Location:** Jct Hwy 93 and 95. **Facility:** 87 units, some efficiencies and kitchens. 3 stories, interior corridors. **Parking:** winter plug-ins. **Terms:** cancellation fee imposed. **Pool(s):** heated indoor. **Activities:** whirlpool, exercise room, spa. **Guest Services:** valet and coin laundry. **Free Special Amenities:** high-speed Internet.

VILLAGE COUNTRY INN & FIRESIDE TEA SHOPPE
250/347-9392

Country Inn
$70-$175

Address: 7557 Canyon Ave V0A 1M0 **Location:** Jct Hwy 93 and 95, just w along Main St, then just s on St Joseph St. Located in a residential area across from playground. **Facility:** From the luxurious duvets to the serene setting, the Victorian property is suitable for short- or long-term stays and offers a retreat-like ambience. 14 units. 2 stories (no elevator), interior corridors. **Parking:** winter plug-ins. **Terms:** check-in 4 pm, 7 day cancellation notice-fee imposed. **Free Special Amenities:** high-speed Internet.

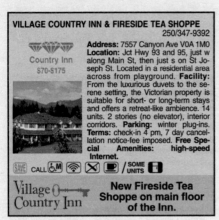

Village Country Inn

New Fireside Tea Shoppe on main floor of the Inn.

WHERE TO EAT

BACK COUNTRY JACKS   250/347-0097

American. Casual Dining. $10-$27 **AAA Inspector Notes:** Booming music keeps the mood lively at this Western-themed restaurant, a local hot spot for good eats. Canadian barbecue chicken, ribs, steaks, seafood, trout and salmon feature prominently on a menu that also lists soups, salads, hot sandwiches, meatloaf, chili and homemade pies. You might feel as if you're eating in a corral, thanks to Western-style murals and memorabilia lining the walls of the dining room. It's closed for lunch in winter months. **Bar:** full bar. **Address:** 7355 W Main St V0A 1M0 **Location:** Hwy 93 and 95, just s of jct Hwy 93, on service road (Main St). [D] CALL

THE OLD SALZBURG RESTAURANT   250/347-6553

Austrian
Casual Dining
$12-$27

AAA Inspector Notes: You'll get a friendly greeting when you enter this mountainside restaurant, which boasts a warm, mountain village ambience and lovely views. With traditional Austrian and Continental influences, the menu lists schnitzel, hearty spaetzle, pasta, chicken and steak. Patio seating is a nice option in the summer, but in the winter opt for a window seat to take in panoramic views of the surrounding valley and mountain ranges. Service is attentive. It's closed for lunch in the off season. **Bar:** full bar. **Reservations:** suggested, in summer. **Address:** 4943 Hwy 93 V0A 1M0 **Location:** Hwy 93 and 95, just w; center.

[D] CALL

REVELSTOKE (A-10) pop. 7,139,
elev. 440m/1,433'

Revelstoke is located on the Trans-Canada Highway between Rogers and Eagle passes—some of the world's most scenic mountain roads. Downhill skiing is available near the city.

Revelstoke Visitor Centre: 204 Campbell Ave., P.O. Box 490, Revelstoke, BC, Canada V0E 2S0. **Phone:** (250) 837-5345 or (800) 487-1493.

CANYON HOT SPRINGS is 35.5 km (22 mi.) e. on Hwy. 1. Bathers can dip in a pool of 40 C (104 F) mineral waters or swim in a pool that is 30 C (86 F). *See Recreation Areas Chart.*

Hours: Daily 9 a.m.-10 p.m., July-Aug.; 9-9, May-June and in Sept. Phone ahead to confirm schedule. **Cost:** Day passes $12.50; $10.50 (ages 5-14 and 60+); $32 (family pass, two adults and two children). Single swim $8.50; $7 (ages 5-14 and 60+); $23 (family, two adults and two children). Rates may vary; phone ahead. **Phone:** (250) 837-2420.

CRAZY CREEK HOT POOLS is 38 km (24 mi.) w. on Hwy. 1. Four pools—three geothermal heated pools (temperatures 99, 102 and 104 F) and a cold plunge pool—are part of Crazy Creek Resort. In addition to taking a dip, visitors can use the new pedestrian overpass to access the suspension bridge and boardwalks to view the two-stage waterfall and visit the high mountain patio.

Note: When entering from the resort side of property, the trail over the pedestrian overpass to the suspension bridge and high mountain patio is stair free. **Hours:** Pools open daily 9-9, year-round. Boardwalk, bridge and waterfalls open daily 9-4:30, mid-Apr. to mid-Oct. **Cost:** Pools *or* boardwalk, bridge and waterfalls $9.50; $5.70 (ages 3-16). All-day pool pass $16; $9.55 (ages 3-16). **Phone:** (250) 836-4097 or (855) 836-4097.

ENCHANTED FOREST is 32 km (20 mi.) w. on Hwy. 1 to 7060 Trans-Canada Hwy. More than 350 handmade figurines include Old World fairy folk, dragons and dungeons in a natural forest setting with giant cedars, a stump house, a fish pond and a towering tree house that is reputedly one of the province's tallest. Tree houses, swamp boat rides and a wetland boardwalk including lush vegetation, beaver dams and spawning salmon beds also are offered.

Hours: Daily 8-8, June 24-Aug. 25; 9-6, Aug. 26-Sept. 6; 9-5:30, May 1-June 23; 10-5:30, Sept. 8-Oct. 8. **Cost:** $11; $9 (ages 3-15). **Phone:** (250) 837-9477 or (866) 944-9744.

REVELSTOKE RAILWAY MUSEUM is at 719 Track St. W. off Victoria Rd. The building of the Canadian Pacific Railway is traced with artifacts, photographs and original equipment. One of the company's largest steam locomotives is displayed beside a restored 1929 solarium car inside the museum, while the yard features such rolling stock as a caboose, a snow plow and a flange car. A diesel cabin simulator allows visitors to experience the feeling of driving a train.

Time: Allow 30 minutes minimum. **Hours:** Daily 9-6, July-Aug.; daily 9-5, May-June and Sept.-Oct.; Thurs.-Sun. 11-4, rest of year. Closed Jan. 1,

Christmas Eve and Christmas. Phone ahead to confirm schedule. **Cost:** $10; $8 (ages 60+ and students with ID); $5 (ages 8-16); $2 (ages 4-7); $22 (family). **Phone:** (250) 837-6060 or (877) 837-6060.

THREE VALLEY GAP HERITAGE GHOST TOWN is 19 km (12 mi.) w. on Hwy. 1. Near the original site of the 19th-century lumber and mining town of Three Valley are more than 40 relocated buildings including a hotel, a general store, a church, two schoolhouses, a saloon and many examples of handcrafted log buildings. An exhibit chronicles the history of steam, transportation and communication. Live performances of a musical stage show take place most nights May through September.

Hours: Guided 1-hour tours depart daily dawn-dusk, mid-Apr. to early Oct. Phone ahead to confirm schedule. **Cost:** $12; $10 (ages 65+); $7 (ages 12-17); $5 (ages 6-11); $30 (family). An additional fee is charged for the stage show. Reservations are required. **Phone:** (250) 837-2109 or (888) 667-2109.

RECREATIONAL ACTIVITIES
Ziplines
• **SkyTrek Adventure Park Ltd.** is 32 km (20 mi.) w. on Hwy. 1 to 7060 Trans-Canada Hwy. **Hours:** Daily 9-7, July-Aug.; 10-6, rest of year. Phone ahead to confirm schedule. **Phone:** (250) 837-9477 or (866) 944-9744.

BEST WESTERN PLUS REVELSTOKE   (250)837-2043

Hotel
$180-$210

AAA Benefit: Members save up to 20%, plus 10% bonus points with Best Western Rewards®.

Address: 1925 Laforme Blvd V0E 2S0 **Location:** Trans-Canada Hwy 1, just n. **Facility:** 87 units. 4 stories, interior corridors. **Parking:** winter plug-ins. **Terms:** cancellation fee imposed. **Amenities:** high-speed Internet, safes. **Pool(s):** heated outdoor. **Activities:** whirlpools, exercise room. *Fee:* massage. **Guest Services:** complimentary and valet laundry. **Free Special Amenities:** expanded continental breakfast and high-speed Internet.

 / SOME UNITS FEE

THE HILLCREST HOTEL A COAST RESORT
(250)837-3322

Hotel
$131-$181

Address: 2100 Oak Dr V0E 2S0 **Location:** 2.7 mi (4.3 km) e on Trans-Canada Hwy 1, 0.6 mi (1 km) sw. **Facility:** 75 units. 3 stories, interior corridors. **Terms:** cancellation fee imposed. **Amenities:** safes. **Activities:** sauna, whirlpools, steamroom, exercise room, spa. **Free Special Amenities:** local telephone calls and high-speed Internet.

/ SOME UNITS FEE

The Hillcrest Hotel a Coast Resort
Revelstoke

Lodge style Lobby. Rock Fireplace. Patio dining with Mountain Views. Repose Day Spa. Free Wi-Fi.

SWISS CHALET MOTEL   250/837-4650

Motel
$89-$159

Address: 1101 W Victoria Rd V0E 2S0 **Location:** 0.6 mi (1 km) s from Trans-Canada Hwy 1; downtown. **Facility:** 22 units, some two bedrooms. 1-2 stories (no elevator), exterior corridors. **Parking:** winter plug-ins. **Free Special Amenities:** expanded continental breakfast and high-speed Internet.

WHERE TO EAT

MONASHEE FAMILY DINING ROOM   250/837-2109

Burgers Sandwiches. Family Dining. $7-$25 **AAA Inspector Notes:** A short 15-minute drive west of Revelstoke is the Three Valley Gap, featuring hotel rooms and restaurant, as well as a heritage ghost town, railway roundhouse and antique autos. Be sure to see everything it has to offer before you head on down the road. This easily accessible restaurant is a good place to stop for a rest and let the children browse. Fast, simple food is served in ample portions with a great view of Three Valley Lake and the mountains. **Bar:** full bar. **Address:** 8903 Trans-Canada Hwy 1 V0E 2S0 **Location:** 11.5 mi (19.2 km) w on Trans-canada Hwy 1, on Three Valley Lake; in Three Valley Gap Lake Chateau. B L D CALL M

THE NOMAD FOOD CO.   250/837-4211

Sandwiches Burgers. Quick Serve. $6-$13 **AAA Inspector Notes:** There's something for everyone at this little spot. The friendly staff here serves up great freshly made paninis, wraps, burgers, fried chicken, fish and chips and homemade soup. They boast that all of their food is made on premises with the freshest veggies, real meat, real cheese and no MSG. There's an ice cream bar for dessert. The restaurant is easily accessed from the Transcanada Highway. **Address:** 1601 Victoria Rd W V0E 3K0 **Location:** South side of Trans-Canada Hwy 1, just e of Columbia River Bridge at Victoria Rd. L D

THE ONE TWELVE STEAKHOUSE & LOUNGE
250/837-2107

Steak
Seafood
Casual Dining
$11-$36

AAA Inspector Notes: This restaurant maintains a cozy yet elegant atmosphere with the help of subdued lighting, soft music, an antique fireplace and friendly service. With the new ski resort nearby, the dining room gets packed in the evenings in winter. Your taste buds will be tempted with specialties like Alberta Sterling Silver steak, succulent veal, lamb and fresh B.C. seafood. The lounge is a great spot to have a drink after a long day of skiing. **Bar:** full bar. **Reservations:** suggested. **Address:** 112 1st St E V0E 2S0 **Location:** 1.2 mi (2 km) s from Trans-Canada Hwy 1, at Victoria Rd; downtown; in The Regent Inn. **Parking:** on-site and street. B D CALL M

ZALAS STEAK & PIZZA HOUSE   250/837-5555

Pizza Steak. Casual Dining. $14-$35 **AAA Inspector Notes:** A popular place to dine in town, this restaurant features a varied menu with some Greek twists and all your classic Canadian favorites. There's a large pizza menu with lots of various toppings to choose from, or you can try one of their specially grilled steaks. Entrées come with the salad bar. **Bar:** full bar. **Reservations:** suggested. **Address:** 1601 W Victoria Rd V0E 2S0 **Location:** South side of Trans-Canada Hwy 1, just e of Columbia River Bridge at Victoria Rd. D CALL M

RICHMOND (H-11) pop. 190,473, elev. 5m/16'

On an island at the mouth of the Fraser River, Richmond first was settled in 1879. The town grew and prospered with its farming, fishing and waterborne trade industries. Today, Richmond's major industries include aviation, berry farming, high technology and manufacturing.

(See map & index p. 368.)

Golden Village, in central Richmond, affords visitors the opportunity to experience the Asian culture through shopping, dining and festivals.

The Richmond Nature Park, 44 hectares (109 acres) at 11851 Westminster Hwy., has a bird pond, beehive displays, mounted birds, a quaking bog and plants identified by markers. A naturalist conducts hour-long tours of the park on Sunday.

Steveston, tucked away in Richmond's southwest corner, is a bit of a contradiction. It has a historic past, but it's also a residential neighborhood. Commercial fishing was once this area's lifeblood, but today you're just as likely to sample fish that's battered and sharing a plate with a pile of fries at a local restaurant as you are seeing one freshly caught. And while weather-beaten buildings hint at a hardscrabble past, there's also a Starbucks.

Sitting at the confluence of two major bodies of water—the Strait of Georgia and the Fraser River—Steveston's first flush of success was as a salmon canning center. The Fraser's south arm was a fertile fishing ground, and a settlement grew up around this favored coastal location in the 1880s. Salmon turned Steveston into a classic turn-of-the-20th-century boom town: It became one of the busiest fishing ports in the world, with windjammers loading up canned salmon bound for far-flung markets.

The town was boisterous with a capital "B." Saloons and gambling dens thrived, and on Saturday nights crowds of sailors, indigenous peoples and European, Chinese and Japanese immigrants—most of them fishermen and cannery workers—thronged the boardwalks. In the years leading up to World War I eager boosters dubbed Steveston "Salmonopolis," but the boom was not to last. The internment during World War II of Japanese-Canadian citizens, who made up a large part of the town's population, struck a serious blow. The canning industry slowly declined, finally coming to an end by the early 1990s. You can learn more about this aspect of town history at the Gulf of Georgia Cannery National Historic Site *(see attraction listing).*

Steveston, still an active fishing port that to a large degree has retained its salty character, makes a good day trip. From downtown Vancouver it's about a 30-minute drive. Take Granville Street south to Hwy. 99 (via 70th Avenue W.), then take Hwy. 99 south to exit 32 (Steveston Highway) and turn right (west). Summer, when the weather is usually sunny and a couple of annual festivals are on tap, is the time to go; during the chilly, rainy winter months many restaurants and attractions reduce their hours.

So what do you do? For starters, just explore where your feet take you. Follow the planked wooden boardwalk along the shore of Cannery Channel; interpretive panels provide background about Steveston's fishing and canning past. Have your picture taken sitting on a bench in the garden outside the Prickly Pear Garden Centre (on No. 1 Road, just off Bayview Street). In addition to lovely hanging flower baskets, the large, emerald-green leaves of a banana tree will have you scratching your head and reminding yourself that yes, you are in Canada.

Tramp around Garry Point Park (at the end of Moncton Street). Fronting the Strait of Georgia, it's basically undeveloped and has a wild and windswept look. Sunsets over the water can be showstoppers here, and the flat, open spaces bring out kite flyers. Stop at the Fisherman's Memorial, which takes the shape of a giant net-mending needle and is inscribed with a poem, "Spawning Cycle":

These spring days grow longer

Until the dark comes closing

What tides disclose they again conceal

We're out to fish until again

It's time to be ashore

Because the geese go by

I'll be here with you

'Till it's time to be alone: the way out,

The way back, and all ways this one.

Stroll the boardwalk along bustling Fisherman's Wharf, where seiners, trawlers and other vessels cruise in and out of the harbor. Depending on the season, some of the boats docked along the boardwalk sell fresh catches of salmon, cod, octopus or prawns.

The Steveston Museum, 3811 Moncton St., resembles a one-room country schoolhouse with its red-and-yellow clapboard exterior and steep gabled roof. This former Northern Bank building has a general store layout with displays of late 19th-century furniture and office equipment. It's also a working post office. Phone (604) 271-6868.

For lunch, it really has to be fish and chips. And there's a choice: Dave's Fish & Chips (3460 Moncton St.) or Pajo's (two locations—on the wharf at the corner of Bayview Street and 3rd Avenue, and a takeout stand in the large administrative building at Garry Point Park). Although the menus at both include such non-fishy items as burgers, do the right thing and order fish and chips (aficionados will go for the halibut over cod or salmon). Mushy peas are a veddy British accompaniment.

The big event of the year is the Steveston Salmon Festival, held on July 1 in conjunction with Canada Day. Floats, marching bands, vintage vehicles and local community groups are part of a big parade that begins at 10 a.m. There's a craft fair, an art show, a Japanese cultural show, carnival rides and a midway, martial arts demonstrations and a youth festival. The main attraction, though, is a salmon barbecue; hundreds of fillets are grilled to succulent perfection over open fire pits.

Summer in Steveston can get crowded, especially on nice sunny weekends. But there are several free parking lots in town, plenty of parking at Garry Point Park, and street parking if you're lucky enough to snag a space.

Tourism Richmond: 11980 Deas Thruway, Richmond, BC, Canada V6W 1L1. **Phone:** (604) 271-8280 or (877) 247-0777. *(See ad p. 315.)*

Stay in Richmond. play for FREE* in Metro Vancouver!

Get a FREE Vancouver Attractions Access Pass* and see the best of Vancouver by staying 25 minutes away in Richmond. Visit the Capilano Suspension Bridge Park, Science World at Telus World of Science, the Vancouver Art Gallery and much more! With a value of over $800 for a family of four it might just be the best summer getaway yet!

*Valid on new bookings for stays between June 15 and September 15, 2013 of three consecutive nights or more. No cash value. One Attraction Access Pass per person. For more details, visit:

richmondplayforfree.com/AAA
or call Tourism Richmond at 1.877.247.0777 to book your stay!

tourism Richmond
www.tourismrichmond.com

(See map & index p. 368.)

BRITANNIA HERITAGE SHIPYARD is at 5180 Westwater Dr. at the foot of Railway Ave. The site contains 10 buildings that were once part of a late 1880s fishing village which included canneries, boatyards and homes. Four buildings are open for touring; visitors can view displays about maritime history and watch as old wooden boats are restored. **Time:** Allow 30 minutes minimum. **Hours:** Tues.-Sun. 10-6, May-Sept.; Sat. 10-4, Sun. noon-4, rest of year. Phone ahead to confirm schedule. **Cost:** Free. **Phone:** (604) 718-8050.

 **GULF OF GEORGIA CANNERY NATIONAL HISTORIC SITE** is at 12138 Fourth Ave. in Steveston Village. The 1894 salmon cannery has been restored to serve as an interpretive center for Canada's West Coast fishing industry. Interactive video presentations, guided tours of the plant and replicated 1900-50 canning line, and equipment demonstrations are offered. Every 30 minutes the Boiler House Theatre presents a film about the West Coast fishing industry.

Hours: Daily 10-5. Closed Dec. 24-Jan. 3. **Cost:** $7.80; $6.55 (ages 65+); $3.90 (ages 6-16); $19.60 (family, up to seven people with a maximum of two adults). **Phone:** (604) 664-9009.

INTERNATIONAL BUDDHIST TEMPLE is at 9160 Steveston Hwy. This working temple offers visitors tranquility through its classical Chinese garden, ponds, small waterfalls and gazebos. A courtyard features bonsai plants and a striking ceramic mural. The temple houses Chinese artifacts that reveal the artisans' skill in sculpture, painting, carpentry and embroidery. Also on site is the Seven Buddha Mural; at 22 metres (73 ft.) long it is said to be the only Buddhist mural of this size in the world. **Time:** Allow 1 hour minimum. **Hours:** Daily 9:30-5:30. **Cost:** Donations. **Phone:** (604) 274-2822.

LONDON HERITAGE FARM is at 6511 Dyke Rd. The restored 1880s farmhouse, furnished in period, is the former residence of Charles and Henrietta London and their family. **Time:** Allow 1 hour minimum. **Hours:** Wed.-Sun. noon-5, July-Aug.; Sat.-Sun. noon-5, Feb.-June and Sept.-Dec. **Cost:** Donations. **Phone:** (604) 271-5220. 🛈

RICHMOND CULTURAL CENTRE is off Granville St. at 7700 Minoru Gate. Home to the Richmond Arts Centre, Archives, Museum and Art Gallery, the center presents programs and events in art, music, drama and dance. The gallery features works from local artists and traveling exhibits. The museum depicts Richmond's history through early household items, personal effects and articles relating to the area's agriculture, dairying, fishing and transportation. Archives preserve public and community records, which are available for research.

Time: Allow 1 hour minimum. **Hours:** Mon.-Fri. 9 a.m.-9:30 p.m.; Sat.-Sun. 10-5. Art gallery Mon.-Fri. 10-6, Sat.-Sun. 10-5. Archives Mon.-Thurs. 9-4:30. Closed major holidays. Phone ahead to confirm schedule. **Cost:** Donations. **Phone:** (604) 247-8300.

STEVESTON SEABREEZE ADVENTURES is at 12551 #1 Rd., Bldg. 43. A narrated whale-watching tour departs from historic Steveston village and transits the Fraser River Delta, Strait of Georgia and Gulf Islands. Hydrophones are used to listen to the whales vocalizing. The scenic trip affords passengers an opportunity to view other marine animals and wildlife.

Time: Allow 3 hours minimum. **Hours:** Departures daily at 9 and 2, mid-June to early Sept.; at 11, early Apr. to mid-June and early Sept.-late Oct. **Cost:** $120 (includes water/coffee and a snack); $100 (students with ID and senior citizens); $75 (ages 4-12). Reservations are recommended. **Phone:** (604) 272-7200 or (888) 272-7203.

VANCOUVER WHALE WATCH is at 210-12240 Second Ave. A 40-passenger, semi-covered vessel transports visitors through the Fraser River Delta, Strait of Georgia and Gulf Islands. Led by a naturalist, the narrated tour focuses on killer whales. Hydrophones are used to listen to the whales communicating. Other wildlife such as porpoises, sea lions, seals and eagles also may be seen. Binoculars are provided on loan.

Time: Allow 3 hours minimum. **Hours:** Departures daily 9-9, Apr. 1-Oct. 7. **Cost:** $120 (includes water and a snack); $100 (students with ID and senior citizens); $75 (ages 4-12). Reservations are recommended. **Phone:** (604) 274-9565.

GAMBLING ESTABLISHMENTS
- **River Rock Casino Resort** is at 8811 River Rd. **Hours:** Daily 24 hours. **Phone:** (604) 247-8900 or (866) 748-3718. *(See ad p. 320.)*

ACCENT INNS   (604)273-3311 **47**

Hotel
$89-$179

Address: 10551 St Edwards Dr V6X 3L8 **Location:** Hwy 99 exit 39 (Bridgeport Rd/Airport) northbound to St Edwards Dr; exit 39A (Richmond/Airport) southbound to St Edwards Dr. **Facility:** 206 units, some efficiencies. 3 stories, exterior corridors. **Terms:** cancellation fee imposed. **Amenities:** *Some:* high-speed Internet. **Activities:** whirlpool, limited exercise equipment. **Guest Services:** valet and coin laundry. **Free Special Amenities:** newspaper and airport transportation.

SAVE 🏧 🚭 📶 🍴 🍸 CALL 🅂🄼 🛜 ✕ 🐾 🎁
📺 / SOME UNITS FEE 🐾 🖨

(See map & index p. 368.)

BEST WESTERN PLUS ABERCORN INN
(604)270-7576 **43**

Hotel
$110-$150

AAA Benefit: Members save up to 20%, plus 10% bonus points with Best Western Rewards®.

Address: 9260 Bridgeport Rd V6X 1S1 **Location:** Hwy 99 exit 39 (Bridgeport Rd/Airport) northbound; exit 39A (Richmond/Airport) southbound. **Facility:** 98 units. 3 stories, interior corridors. **Amenities:** *Some:* safes. **Activities:** limited exercise equipment. **Guest Services:** valet laundry. **Free Special Amenities:** full breakfast and airport transportation. *(See ad this page.)*

COMFORT INN VANCOUVER AIRPORT   (604)278-5161 **41**

Hotel $75-$115 **Address:** 3031 No 3 Rd V6X 2B6 **Location:** Hwy 99 exit 39 (Bridgeport Rd/Airport) northbound; exit 39A (Richmond/Airport) southbound, just w. **Facility:** 122 units. 4 stories, interior corridors. **Parking:** on-site (fee). **Terms:** cancellation fee imposed. **Pool(s):** heated outdoor. **Activities:** limited exercise equipment. **Guest Services:** valet laundry.

DELTA VANCOUVER AIRPORT   (604)278-1241 **34**

Hotel
$149-$329

Address: 3500 Cessna Dr V7B 1C7 **Location:** Corner of Russ Baker Way and Cessna Dr; near Moray Bridge. **Facility:** 414 units. 10 stories, interior corridors. **Parking:** on-site (fee) and valet. **Amenities:** high-speed Internet (fee). **Dining:** 2 restaurants. **Pool(s):** heated outdoor. **Activities:** exercise room, spa. **Guest Services:** valet laundry, area transportation-casino, shopping mall & Steveston Village.

▼ See AAA listing this page ▼

(See map & index p. 368.)

THE FAIRMONT VANCOUVER AIRPORT
(604)207-5200 **33**

Hotel
$299-$399

Address: 3111 Grant McConachie Way V7B 0A6 **Location:** In Vancouver International Airport. **Facility:** Luxurious rooms feature sound-insulated windows and high-tech temperature and lighting controls; a full spa and jetted lap pool are on the premises. 392 units. 14 stories, interior corridors. **Parking:** on-site (fee) and valet. **Terms:** cancellation fee imposed. **Amenities:** safes. *Fee:* video games, high-speed Internet. **Dining:** Globe @ YVR, see separate listing. **Pool(s):** heated indoor. **Activities:** saunas, whirlpool, spa. **Guest Services:** valet laundry.

FOUR POINTS BY SHERATON VANCOUVER AIRPORT
(604)214-0888 **49**

Hotel
$155-$225

FOUR POINTS BY SHERATON

AAA Benefit: Members get up to 20% off, plus Starwood Preferred Guest® bonuses.

Address: 8368 Alexandra Rd V6X 4A6 **Location:** No 3 Rd, just e on Alderbridge Way, then just n on Hazelbridge Way. **Facility:** 139 units. 6 stories, interior corridors. **Parking:** on-site (fee). **Terms:** cancellation fee imposed. **Amenities:** video games (fee), high-speed Internet. **Activities:** exercise room. **Guest Services:** valet laundry. **Free Special Amenities:** high-speed Internet and airport transportation.

HAMPTON INN BY HILTON VANCOUVER AIRPORT
(604)232-5505 **39**

Hotel
$109-$175

AAA Benefit:
Members save up to 10%!

Address: 8811 Bridgeport Rd V6X 1R9 **Location:** Hwy 99 exit 39 (Bridgeport Rd/Airport) northbound; exit 39A (Richmond/Airport) southbound, just w. **Facility:** 109 units. 5 stories, interior corridors. **Terms:** 1-7 night minimum stay, cancellation fee imposed. **Amenities:** video games (fee). **Activities:** exercise room. **Guest Services:** valet laundry. **Free Special Amenities:** expanded continental breakfast and high-speed Internet.

2km from Vancouver airport, near Canada line Skytrain and just 15 minutes from downtown Vancouver.

HILTON VANCOUVER AIRPORT
(604)273-6336 **50**

Hotel
$169-$229

Hilton

AAA Benefit: Members save 5% or more!

Address: 5911 Minoru Blvd V6X 4C7 **Location:** Corner of Minoru Blvd and Westminster Hwy. **Facility:** 237 units, some two bedrooms. 15 stories, interior corridors. **Parking:** on-site (fee). **Terms:** 1-7 night minimum stay, cancellation fee imposed. **Amenities:** high-speed Internet (fee), safes. **Pool(s):** heated outdoor. **Activities:** whirlpool, tennis court, exercise room. **Guest Services:** valet laundry. **Free Special Amenities:** preferred room (subject to availability with advance reservations) and airport transportation.

HOLIDAY INN EXPRESS & SUITES RIVERPORT
(604)241-1830 **54**

Hotel $109-$199 **Address:** 10688 No. 6 Rd V6W 1E7 **Location:** Hwy 99 exit 32 (Steveston Hwy), just e. Next to Riverport Entertainment & Business Park. **Facility:** 105 units, some efficiencies and kitchens. 4 stories, interior corridors. **Amenities:** high-speed Internet. **Pool(s):** heated indoor. **Activities:** whirlpool, exercise room. **Guest Services:** valet and coin laundry.

HOLIDAY INN EXPRESS VANCOUVER-AIRPORT
(604)273-8080 **42**

Hotel $119-$179 **Address:** 9351 Bridgeport Rd V6X 1S3 **Location:** Hwy 99 exit 39 (Bridgeport Rd/Airport) northbound; exit 39A (Richmond/Airport) southbound. **Facility:** 107 units. 8 stories, interior corridors. **Parking:** on-site (fee). **Terms:** check-in 4 pm. **Activities:** exercise room. **Guest Services:** valet and coin laundry.

HOLIDAY INN VANCOUVER AIRPORT-RICHMOND
(604)821-1818 **48**

Hotel $115-$189 **Address:** 10720 Cambie Rd V6X 1K8 **Location:** Hwy 99 exit 39A (Bridgeport Rd/Airport) northbound to St. Edwards Dr, then 0.6 mi (1 km) n; exit 39B (No 4 Rd) southbound, just e. **Facility:** 163 units. 6 stories, interior corridors. **Parking:** on-site (fee). **Terms:** check-in 4 pm. **Amenities:** high-speed Internet. **Activities:** exercise room. **Guest Services:** valet and coin laundry.

HOTEL AT RIVER ROCK
604/247-8900 **37**

Hotel. Rates not provided. **Address:** 8888 River Rd V6X 3P8 **Location:** Hwy 99 exit 39 (Bridgeport Rd/Airport) northbound; exit 39A (Richmond/Airport) southbound, just w on Bridgeport Rd, then just n on Great Canadian Way. **Facility:** 193 units. 12 stories, interior corridors. **Parking:** on-site and valet. **Terms:** check-in 4 pm. **Amenities:** high-speed Internet, safes. **Guest Services:** valet laundry, area transportation-within 5 mi (8 km).

(See map & index p. 368.)

QUALITY HOTEL AIRPORT (SOUTH)

(604)244-3051 **51**

Hotel
$79-$129

Address: 7228 Westminster Hwy V6X 1A1 **Location:** Between Gilbert Rd and Alderbridge Way. **Facility:** 70 units. 4 stories, interior corridors. **Terms:** cancellation fee imposed. **Amenities:** high-speed Internet. **Guest Services:** valet laundry. **Free Special Amenities: expanded continental breakfast and high-speed Internet.**

Find thousands of places to show your card and save at AAA.com/discounts

RADISSON HOTEL VANCOUVER AIRPORT

(604)276-8181 **46**

Hotel
$139-$209

Address: 8181 Cambie Rd V6X 3X9 **Location:** Corner of No 3 and Cambie rds. **Facility:** 185 units. 12 stories, interior corridors. **Terms:** cancellation fee imposed. **Amenities:** safes. **Pool(s):** heated indoor. **Activities:** whirlpool, exercise room. **Guest Services:** valet laundry. **Free Special Amenities: full breakfast and high-speed Internet.** *(See ad this page.)*

▼ *See AAA listing this page* ▼

▼ See AAA listing p. 321 ▼

NOW
YOU'RE LIVING

thehotel
AT RIVER ROCK

8811 River Road
Richmond • BC • Canada
T/free 1.866.748.3718 • 604.273.1895
riverrock.com
Five minutes away from
Vancouver International Airport

HOTEL • CASINO • SHOW THEATRE
RESTAURANTS • LOUNGES • POOL • SPA
HEALTH CLUB • FREE PARKING

RiverRock
CASINO RESORT

(See map & index p. 368.)

RIVER ROCK CASINO RESORT   (604)247-8900 **38**

Hotel
$139-$189

Address: 8811 River Rd V6X 3P8 **Location:** Hwy 99 exit 39 (Bridgeport Rd/Airport) northbound; exit 39A (Richmond/Airport) southbound, just w on Bridgeport Rd, then just n on Great Canadian Way. **Facility:** From the airport to downtown, the Sky Train stops at this all-suite hotel, where there's always something happening—whether it's in the 950-seat theater, the 24-hour casino or full-service spa. 203 units, some two bedrooms. 9-11 stories, interior corridors. **Parking:** on-site and valet. **Terms:** check-in 4 pm, cancellation fee imposed. **Amenities:** high-speed Internet, safes. **Dining:** Tramonto, see separate listing. **Pool(s):** heated indoor. **Activities:** whirlpool, waterslide, exercise room, spa. *Fee:* marina. **Guest Services:** valet laundry, area transportation-within 5 mi (8 km). *(See ad p. 320.)*

SANDMAN HOTEL VANCOUVER AIRPORT
   (604)303-8888 **45**

Hotel $99-$169 **Address:** 3233 St Edwards Dr V6X 3K4 **Location:** Hwy 99 exit 39 (Bridgeport Rd/Airport) northbound to St Edwards Dr; exit 39A (Richmond/Airport) southbound. **Facility:** 172 units. 5 stories, interior corridors. **Terms:** check-in 4 pm, cancellation fee imposed. **Amenities:** high-speed Internet. **Dining:** Moxie's Classic Grill, see separate listing. **Pool(s):** heated indoor. **Activities:** whirlpool, exercise room. **Guest Services:** valet laundry.

SHERATON VANCOUVER AIRPORT HOTEL
   (604)273-7878 **52**

Hotel
$139-$359

AAA Benefit: Members get up to 20% off, plus Starwood Preferred Guest® bonuses.

Address: 7551 Westminster Hwy V6X 1A3 **Location:** Corner of Minoru Blvd and Westminster Hwy. **Facility:** 390 units. 6-7 stories, interior corridors. **Parking:** on-site (fee). **Terms:** cancellation fee imposed. **Amenities:** high-speed Internet (fee). **Pool(s):** heated outdoor. **Activities:** whirlpool, exercise room. **Guest Services:** valet laundry. **Free Special Amenities:** airport transportation.

TRAVELODGE HOTEL VANCOUVER AIRPORT
   (604)278-5155 **44**

Hotel
$79-$200

Address: 3071 St Edwards Dr V6X 3K4 **Location:** Hwy 99 exit 39 (Bridgeport Rd/Airport) northbound to St Edwards Dr; exit 39A (Richmond/Airport) southbound. **Facility:** 160 units. 10 stories, interior corridors. **Terms:** cancellation fee imposed. **Amenities:** video games (fee). **Pool(s):** heated indoor. **Activities:** whirlpool, limited exercise equipment. **Guest Services:** valet laundry.

Plan complete trip routings with
the TripTik® Travel Planner on
AAA.com/CAA.ca

VANCOUVER AIRPORT MARRIOTT
   (604)276-2112 **53**

Hotel $169-$259 **Address:** 7571 Westminster Hwy V6X 1A3 **Location:** Corner of Minoru Blvd and Westminster Hwy. **Facility:** 237 units, some two bedrooms. 18 stories, interior corridors. **Parking:** on-site (fee). **Amenities:** high-speed Internet (fee). **Pool(s):** heated outdoor. **Activities:** whirlpool, exercise room. **Guest Services:** valet and coin laundry.

AAA Benefit: AAA hotel discounts of 5% or more.

THE WESTIN WALL CENTRE VANCOUVER AIRPORT
   (604)303-6565 **40**

Hotel
$149-$409

WESTIN HOTELS & RESORTS

AAA Benefit: Enjoy up to 20% off your next stay, plus Starwood Preferred Guest® bonuses.

Address: 3099 Corvette Way V6X 4K3 **Location:** Hwy 99 exit 39 (Bridgeport Rd/Airport) northbound; exit 39A (Richmond/Airport) southbound, just w to No 3 Rd. **Facility:** This new high-rise hotel has extensive meeting spaces and an expanded health club. Guest rooms offer a modern décor. A casino and shopping malls are nearby; complimentary shuttles are available. 188 units. 15 stories, interior corridors. **Parking:** on-site (fee) and valet. **Amenities:** high-speed Internet (fee), safes. **Pool(s):** heated indoor. **Activities:** whirlpool, exercise room. *Fee:* massage. **Guest Services:** valet laundry, area transportation-casino. **Free Special Amenities:** newspaper and airport transportation. *(See ad p. 389.)*

WHERE TO EAT

CACTUS CLUB CAFE   604/244-9969

American. Casual Dining. $11-$37 **AAA Inspector Notes:** This bustling, casual restaurant serves huge burgers, sandwiches, pasta, salads, soups, quesadillas, fajitas, vegetarian dishes, steak, ribs, chicken and fish. Featured are certified Angus beef and fresh wild British Columbia salmon. **Bar:** full bar. **Address:** 5500 No 3 Rd V6X 2C8 **Location:** Corner of No 3 and Lansdowne rds.

FLYING BEAVER BAR & GRILL   604/273-0278 **43**

American. Casual Dining. $12-$18 **AAA Inspector Notes:** The pub is in the terminal of Harbour Air, a small float plane operation. While chowing down on a tasty burger or appetizers, you can gaze through large bay windows to watch planes land and take off. Signs to the South Terminal lead to this place, where there's plenty of free parking. Wednesday to Sunday, there's free shuttle service from Richmond area hotels; service begins at 6 pm. **Bar:** full bar. **Address:** 4760 Inglis Dr V7B 1W4 **Location:** Russ Baker Way, 0.6 mi (1 km) w on Inglis Dr towards south terminal.

GLOBE @ YVR   604/207-5200 **42**

Pacific Northwest. Fine Dining. $15-$42 **AAA Inspector Notes:** This restaurant treats diners to a memorable view of air traffic creeping in and out of the gates as service vehicles buzz around like bees. In addition to complete lunch and dinner service, the restaurant offers a wonderful Sunday-morning buffet breakfast, which is available until noon. The skilled culinary team keeps up the pace in the open kitchen. **Bar:** full bar. **Reservations:** suggested. **Address:** 3111 Grant McConachie Way V7B 1X9 **Location:** In Vancouver International Airport; in The Fairmont Vancouver Airport. **Parking:** on-site (fee) and valet.

(See map & index p. 368.)

MOXIE'S CLASSIC GRILL   604/303-1111

♦♦ ♦♦ Canadian. Casual Dining. $10-$29 **AAA Inspector Notes:** This sleek, funky and popular restaurant presents an extensive menu of creatively prepared dishes, including pizza, pasta, rice, noodles, signature salads and burgers. Other menus include one for children and one for Sunday brunch. Lending to the upbeat, stylish decor are dark wood appointments and river rock fireplaces. **Bar:** full bar. **Address:** 3233 St Edwards Dr V6X 3K4 **Location:** Hwy 99 exit 39 (Bridgeport Rd/Airport) northbound to St Edwards Dr; exit 39A (Richmond/Airport) southbound; in Sandman Hotel Vancouver Airport. [B] [L] [D] [LATE]

RICKY'S ALL DAY GRILL   604/233-7705

♦♦ ♦♦ American. Casual Dining. $11-$27 **AAA Inspector Notes:** The comfortable eatery, which employs friendly servers, presents a varied menu that includes pasta dishes, wraps, omelets, stir-fry preparations and burgers. Portions are generous. Children's and senior selections are offered. Guests can request seating in a booth or at a table. **Bar:** full bar. **Address:** 9100 Blundell Rd, #490 V6V 1K3 **Location:** Between Garden City Rd and Heather St.

[B] [L] [D]

STEVESTON SEAFOOD HOUSE   604/271-5252 [48]

♦♦♦♦ Seafood. Casual Dining. $20-$40 **AAA Inspector Notes:** Voted Best Seafood Restaurant in Richmond since 1999. This restaurant is located in the historic village of Steveston and offers a selection of ocean-fresh seafood based on availability. The prawns and scallops are delicious, and the warm and friendly decor is quite pleasant. Afterwards walk the village which is filled with quirky shops. **Bar:** full bar. **Reservations:** suggested. **Address:** 3951 Moncton St V7E 3A2 **Location:** Jct Moncton St and No 1 Rd; in Steveston Village. **Parking:** street only. [D]

TAPENADE BISTRO   604/275-5188 [47]

♦♦ ♦♦ Mediterranean. Casual Dining. $13-$28 **AAA Inspector Notes:** An urban bistro features a unique menu including seafood and chicken crepes, panini, daily pasta dishes, fresh fish, chicken, steak and pork. To complement your meal, a large selection of local wines are offered. **Bar:** full bar. **Reservations:** suggested, for dinner. **Address:** 3711 Bayview St V7E 3B6 **Location:** Between 2nd and 3rd aves; in Steveston Village. **Parking:** street only.

[L] [D] CALL [&M]

TRAMONTO   604/247-8900 [46]

♦♦♦♦ Italian. Fine Dining. $24-$43 **AAA Inspector Notes:** Spectacular views of the Fraser River await those who dine at this third-floor dining room, which is perfect for an intimate evening or entertaining an important client. The menu features a delicious selection of Italian items and an extensive wine cellar that boasts more than 500 red and white wines from a variety of countries. **Bar:** full bar. **Reservations:** suggested. **Address:** 8811 River Rock Rd V6X 3P8 **Location:** Hwy 99 exit 39 (Bridgeport Rd/Airport) northbound; exit 39A (Richmond/Airport) southbound, just w on Bridgeport Rd, then just n on Great Canadian Way; in River Rock Casino Resort. **Parking:** on-site and valet. [D] CALL [&M]

ROSEDALE (I-12)

BRIDAL FALLS WATER PARK is at jct. hwys. 1 and 9 at 53790 Popkum Rd. S. The park features 10 waterslides, a giant hot pool, miniature golf course, river ride, and picnic and barbecue facilities. **Time:** Allow 2 hours minimum. **Hours:** Daily 10-7, July 21-Aug. 19; 10-6, June 29-July 20 and Aug. 20-Sept. 3. Phone ahead to confirm schedule. **Cost:** $20; $14 (after 3 p.m.); free (ages 0-3). Admission may vary; phone ahead. **Phone:** (604) 794-7455, or (888) 883-8852 to verify schedule or rates. [‖]

ROSSLAND (D-10) pop. 3,556,
elev. 1,039m/3,408'

The 1890 gold rush on Red Mountain spurred the growth of Rossland from a prospectors' camp to a bustling town with 42 saloons, 17 law firms, four breweries and two distilleries. The area's vast mineral wealth, which supported a booming mining industry for 40 years, produced more than 6 million tons of ore valued at about $125 million.

Fishing, swimming and canoeing are available at Nancy Greene Provincial Park, 26 kilometres (16 mi.) northwest at hwys. 3 and 3B. *See Recreation Areas Chart.*

Rossland Visitor Centre: 1100 Hwy. 3B, Rossland, BC, Canada V0G 1Y0. **Phone:** (250) 362-7722 or (888) 448-7444.

ROSSLAND HISTORICAL MUSEUM AND ARCHIVES is at jct. hwys. 3B and 22. The museum has mining artifacts and rock and mineral samples. There also are outdoor exhibits. Gold panning is offered. Articles in the archives chronicle the history of Rossland and the nearby mining area.

Time: Allow 2 hours minimum. **Hours:** Daily 9-5, mid-May to mid-Sept. Phone ahead for winter hours and mine tour availability. **Cost:** Museum $10; $8 (ages 60+); $5 (students with ID); $3 (ages 6-13); $28 (family). **Phone:** (250) 362-7722 or (888) 448-7444.

RECREATIONAL ACTIVITIES
Skiing

• **Red Mountain Resort Ski Area** is 3 km (1.5 mi.) n. on Hwy. 3B at 4300 Red Mountain Rd. **Hours:** Daily 9-3:30, in winter; Mon.-Thurs. 8:30-4, Fri. 8:30-3:30, rest of year (weather permitting). Red Chair 10-3. Schedule may vary; phone ahead. **Phone:** (250) 362-7384 or (800) 663-0105.

CASA ALPINA   250/362-7364

♦♦ Motel. Rates not provided. **Address:** 1199 Nancy Greene Hwy V0G 1V0 **Location:** 0.6 mi (1 km) w on Royal Oak Dr, then just n. **Facility:** 42 units, some efficiencies and kitchens. 2 stories (no elevator), exterior corridors. **Activities:** whirlpool. **Guest Services:** coin laundry.

[icons] / SOME UNITS FEE [icons]

SAANICH pop. 109,752
• Hotels & Restaurants map & index p. 408
• Part of Victoria area — see map p. 397

HOWARD JOHNSON HOTEL & SUITES   (250)704-4656 [42]

♦♦ ♦♦ Hotel $99-$169 **Address:** 4670 Elk Lake Dr V8Z 5M2 **Location:** Blanshard St (Hwy 17), just w on Royal Oak Dr, then just n. **Facility:** 88 units, some kitchens. 3 stories, interior/exterior corridors. **Terms:** cancellation fee imposed. **Amenities:** high-speed Internet. **Pool(s):** heated outdoor. **Activities:** whirlpool, limited exercise equipment. **Guest Services:** coin laundry.

[icons] CALL [&M] [icons] / SOME UNITS FEE [icon]

QUALITY INN WADDLING DOG   (250)652-1146

♦♦ ♦♦

Hotel

$89-$139

Address: 2476 Mt Newton Crossroad V8M 2B8 **Location:** Corner of Blanshard St (Hwy 17) and Mt Newton Crossroad. **Facility:** 30 units. 3 stories, interior corridors. **Terms:** cancellation fee imposed. **Free Special Amenities:** local telephone calls and newspaper.

 [icons] / SOME UNITS FEE [icon]

SAANICHTON (H-10) elev. 58m/194'

• Part of Victoria area — see map p. 397

HERITAGE ACRES (SAANICH HISTORICAL ARTIFACTS SOCIETY) is off Hwy. 17, e. on Island View Dr., then n. to 7321 Lochside Dr. The society is dedicated to maintaining artifacts from the area's rural past on 12 hectares (29 acres) of parkland. A museum exhibits historic household items, furnishings and farm equipment. Also part of the complex are a blacksmith's shop, a sawmill, nature trails and a one-room log cabin. Rides are offered aboard model trains.

Time: Allow 30 minutes minimum. **Hours:** Daily 9:30-4, mid-June to mid-Sept.; 9:30-noon, rest of year. Closed Christmas. **Cost:** Donations. Admission is charged during events. **Phone:** (250) 652-5522. 🅰️

SALMON ARM (B-9) pop. 17,464, elev. 415m/1,364'

R.J. HANEY HERITAGE VILLAGE & MUSEUM is nearly 3 kilometres (2 mi.) e. on Hwy. 1, then just s. on Hwy. 97B. The village grew around the Haney House, built in 1910. Among the buildings in the community, all built in the early 20th century, are Salmon Arm's first gas station, a blacksmith shop, a Methodist church, a fire station and a schoolhouse.

In addition, the Beamish Building contains what is said to be Western Canada's largest collection of records and cylinders. A small museum, which changes displays every 2 years, focuses on local Shuswap history, and a 2-kilometre (1.2-mi.) nature walk, a tea house and a dinner theatre also are on the property. Guided tours of the Haney House are available.

Time: Allow 1 hour minimum. **Hours:** Village, museum and office open daily 10-5, July-Aug.; Mon.-Fri. 10-4, mid-May through June 30 and late Sept.-Oct. 29. Dinner theatre Wed., Fri. and Sun., July-Aug. Archives room Wed.-Thurs. 10-4, year-round. Phone ahead to confirm schedule. **Cost:** Donations. Reservations are required for the dinner theatre. **Phone:** (250) 832-5243. 🍴 🅰️

BEST WESTERN SALMON ARM INN (250)832-9793

Motel
$109-$249

AAA Benefit: Members save up to 20%, plus 10% bonus points with Best Western Rewards®.

Address: 61 10th St SW V1E 1E4 **Location:** 0.7 mi (1.1 km) w on Trans-Canada Hwy 1. **Facility:** 77 units, some efficiencies. 2 stories (no elevator), exterior corridors. **Terms:** cancellation fee imposed. **Pool(s):** heated indoor. **Activities:** whirlpool. **Free Special Amenities:** full breakfast and high-speed Internet.

SAVE ECO 🛗 CALL 🆓M 🍽️ 🛜 ✖️ 🔌 🖥️ 🖨️ / SOME UNITS FEE 🐾

COMFORT INN & SUITES (250)832-7711

▼▼▼▼ Hotel $123-$295 **Address:** 1090 22nd St NE V1E 2V5 **Location:** 0.5 mi (0.8 km) e on Trans-Canada Hwy 1. **Facility:** 114 units. 5 stories, interior corridors. **Terms:** check-in 4 pm, cancellation fee imposed. **Amenities:** video games (fee), high-speed Internet. **Pool(s):** heated indoor. **Activities:** whirlpool, waterslide, exercise room. **Guest Services:** valet and coin laundry.

ECO 🛗 CALL 🆓M 🍽️ BIZ 🛜 ✖️ 🔌 🖥️ / SOME UNITS FEE 🐾 🖨️

PODOLLAN INN (250)832-6025

▼▼ ▼▼ Hotel $109-$199 **Address:** 1460 Trans-Canada Hwy NE V1E 4N1 **Location:** Just e on Trans-Canada Hwy 1; at 14th St NE. **Facility:** 71 units, some efficiencies. 2-3 stories, interior/exterior corridors. **Terms:** 3 day cancellation notice-fee imposed, resort fee. **Dining:** Table 24 Restaurant, see separate listing. **Pool(s):** heated outdoor. **Activities:** whirlpools, spa.

🍴 🍽️ CALL 🆓M 🍽️ 🛗 🛜 ✖️ 🔌 🖨️ / SOME UNITS FEE 🐾 🖨️

SUPER 8 (250)832-8812

▼▼ ▼▼ Motel $80-$230 **Address:** 2901 10th Ave NE V1E 2S3 **Location:** 0.6 mi (1 km) e on Trans-Canada Hwy 1. **Facility:** 39 units. 2 stories (no elevator), interior corridors. **Guest Services:** coin laundry.

🛗 CALL 🆓M 🛜 ✖️ 🔌 🖥️ / SOME UNITS FEE 🐾

WHERE TO EAT

CHIANG MAI ORCHID THAI RESTAURANT 250/832-0699

▼▼ Northern Thai. Casual Dining. $9-$17 **AAA Inspector Notes:** Chefs trained in Thailand prepare both spicy and mild dishes in the classic northern style and from fresh ingredients. The entire family manages and staffs the simple dining room, and the chef often comes out to see how guests' meals are. Patrons need look no further for a taste of Thailand in the middle of British Columbia. **Bar:** full bar. **Address:** 131 Hudson Ave NE V1E 4N7 **Location:** Trans-Canada Hwy 1, just sw at Alexander St to Hudson Ave, then just e. **Parking:** street only. L D CALL 🆓M

PRIMAVERA RISTORANTE ITALIANO 250/833-0065

▼▼ ▼▼ Northern Italian. Casual Dining. $10-$25 **AAA Inspector Notes:** A small, authentic piece of Italy can be found just off the highway. Red-checkered tablecloths, vine-covered walls and Italian music create a cozy environment in which patrons can savor hearty dishes ranging from veal to seafood fettuccine. The owner makes all his own sauces. The restaurant is busy on weekends. Entertainers perform some nights of the week. **Bar:** full bar. **Reservations:** suggested, weekends. **Address:** 260 Ross St NE V0E 1H1 **Location:** Trans-Canada Hwy 1 exit Ross St, just n. **Parking:** street only.

L D

TABLE 24 RESTAURANT 250/832-5024

▼▼ ▼▼ Pacific Northwest Casual Dining $8-$29 **AAA Inspector Notes:** Offering a distant view of the lake, the restaurant proudly announces that they don't have a microwave or deep fryer in their kitchen, instead they make things from scratch with love and creativity. They shop locally wherever possible, using only the freshest ingredients. Entrées might include wild sockeye salmon with maple glaze, or duck breast with a cherry reduction and the freshest market vegetables. The menu changes frequently. **Bar:** full bar. **Reservations:** suggested, for dinner. **Address:** 1460 Trans-Canada Hwy NE V1E 4N1 **Location:** Just e on Trans-Canada Hwy 1; at 14th St NE; in Podollan Inn.

B L D CALL 🆓M

SALT SPRING ISLAND (H-10) pop. 10,322

Originally called Chuan Island, then Admiral Island, Salt Spring Island is the largest of the Gulf Island group and a popular spot for yachting, cycling, fishing and golfing. Bicycle and kayak rentals are available.

Although it is one of the most developed of the islands, it retains a rural feel. Mount Maxwell Park has a scenic drive leading to 610-metre (2,001-ft.) Baynes Peak. Ruckle Provincial Park (see Recreation Areas Chart) offers 7 kilometres (4.3 mi.) of shoreline and has walking trails; bicycling, fishing, kayaking and picnicking are permitted.

The island also features popular Saturday farmers markets and arts and crafts, and is home to many fine artists such as Robert Bateman and Carol Evans.

Ganges is the island's largest village and its commercial hub. Much of the seaside community's charm is the result of its status as an artist's colony. Visitors are welcome at many artists' studios, and locally made arts and crafts such as ceramics, jewelry, furniture, stained glass and woodcraft, are sold at many village shops.

A local Ganges landmark is a retired buoy that has been painted with a marine-themed mural. Marine life such as salmon, orcas, cod and octopus seals—all creatures that can be found near Salt Spring Island—join a Coast Guard cutter and kayaks as the mural's focal points.

Ferries operate daily from the island's three ferry terminals—between Swartz Bay and Fulford Harbour, between Crofton and Vesuvius Bay and between Long Harbour (the largest of the terminals) and Tsawwassen. For schedules and information phone BC Ferries, (250) 386-3431 from the Victoria area or outside British Columbia, or (888) 223-3779 from elsewhere in the province.

Salt Spring Island Visitor InfoCentre: 121 Lower Ganges Rd., Salt Spring Island, BC, Canada V8K 2T1. **Phone:** (250) 537-5252 or (866) 216-2936.

Self-guiding tours: Maps describing self-guiding tours to the studios of more than 30 resident artists are available at the island's visitor infocenter as well as at lodgings, the marina and on BC Ferries.

HARBOUR HOUSE HOTEL   250/537-5571
Hotel. Rates not provided. **Address:** 121 Upper Ganges Rd V8K 2S2 **Location:** 0.6 mi (1 km) n on Lower Ganges Rd, then just e, towards Long Harbour Ferry Terminal. **Facility:** 36 units. 2 stories (no elevator), interior/exterior corridors. **Dining:** Harbour House Restaurant, see separate listing.

SALT SPRINGS SPA RESORT   250/537-4111
Vacation Rental Cottage. Rates not provided. **Address:** 1460 N Beach Rd V8K 1J4 **Location:** From Ganges Township, 4.9 mi (8 km) n on North End Rd, 0.6 mi (1 km) ne on Fernwood Rd, then 6.8 mi (10.8 km) nw. **Facility:** Each self-contained cottage features a hydro-jetted tub filled with mineral water that is drawn from an underground spring. If you're looking for peace and quiet, you'll find it here. 13 cottages. 1 story, exterior corridors. **Terms:** check-in 4 pm. **Activities:** bicycles, spa. **Guest Services:** coin laundry.

HASTINGS HOUSE COUNTRY HOUSE HOTEL   250/537-2362
[fyi] Not evaluated. **Address:** 160 Upper Ganges Rd V8K 2S2 **Location:** 0.6 mi (1 km) n on Lower Ganges Rd, then just e; towards Long Harbour Ferry Terminal. Facilities, services, and décor characterize an upscale property.

WHERE TO EAT

BARB'S BAKERY & BISTRO   250/537-4491
Breads/Pastries. Quick Serve. $9-$20 **AAA Inspector Notes:** Delightfully Bohemian, the bright and bustling cafe/bakery tantalizes guests with the tempting aromas of fresh bread, pastries and coffee. Vegetarian and other health-conscious breakfast and lunch choices are all prepared with organic ingredients and served fresh. Take-home bakery items also are available. **Bar:** beer & wine. **Address:** 1-121 McPhillips Ave V8K 2T6 **Location:** In Ganges Township; from Lower Ganges Rd, just w; center. **Parking:** street only.

CALVIN'S SALTSPRING ISLAND BISTRO   250/538-5551
American. Casual Dining. $10-$28 **AAA Inspector Notes:** In the heart of the Ganges township right near the water, this simple bistro-style restaurant offers hearty meals like burgers, sandwiches and soups as well as a number of desserts. There's a choice of booth seating or tables set up near the large windows, which boast a great view of the water. **Bar:** full bar. **Reservations:** suggested, for dinner. **Address:** 133 Lower Ganges Rd V8K 2T2 **Location:** In Ganges Township; corner of Hereford Ave. **Parking:** street only.

HARBOUR HOUSE RESTAURANT   250/537-4700
American. Casual Dining. $10-$25 **AAA Inspector Notes:** The restaurant features an extensive menu with daily specials and a casual, pleasant décor. Tables set up against the window and a large outdoor garden patio ensure everyone has a nice view of the Ganges Harbour. Down-home comfort food is served with a smile. **Bar:** full bar. **Address:** 121 Upper Ganges Rd V8K 2S2 **Location:** 0.6 mi (1 km) n on Lower Ganges Rd, then just e, towards Long Harbour Ferry Terminal; in Harbour House Hotel.

HASTINGS HOUSE DINING ROOM   250/537-2362
Pacific Northwest Fine Dining $70-$85 **AAA Inspector Notes:** This restaurant holds a truly wonderful dining experience, dinner guests get their own personalized menu that features a three or four-course Chefs Tasting Menu with or without wine pairings. Guests are welcome to come earlier for drinks in the lounge. **Bar:** full bar. **Reservations:** required. **Address:** 160 Upper Ganges Rd V8K 2S2 **Location:** 0.6 mi (1 km) n on Lower Ganges Rd, then just e, towards Long Harbour Ferry Terminal; in Hastings House Country House Hotel.

RESTAURANT HOUSE PICCOLO   250/537-1844
Scandinavian. Fine Dining. $25-$29 **AAA Inspector Notes:** Reservations are a good idea at the cozy restaurant. Its location in a small house nestled away from the busy shops of Ganges offers limited seats amid its tightly spaced tables. An impressive selection of reasonably priced wines pair with delightful Scandinavian and European standards and seafood preparations. **Bar:** full bar. **Reservations:** suggested, required 8/1-9/30. **Address:** 108 Hereford Ave V8K 2V9 **Location:** In Ganges Township; cross street Lower Ganges Rd. **Parking:** street only.

SALT SPRING INN RESTAURANT   250/537-5339
American. Casual Dining. $11-$28 **AAA Inspector Notes:** Open all day long, this pleasant restaurant in the heart of Ganges Village serves good food at reasonable prices. The large veranda is open during warmer weather. There's no on-site parking, but a large lot is across the street. **Bar:** full bar. **Address:** 132 Lower Ganges Rd V8K 2S9 **Location:** In Ganges Township, corner of Hereford Ave; in Salt Spring Inn. **Parking:** street only.

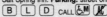

SANDON (C-10)

The remnants of one of western Canada's greatest mining towns nestle in the deep, wooded ravine of Carpenter Creek, high in the Selkirk Mountains. Pioneer prospectors Eli Carpenter and Jack Seaton discovered rich deposits of silver-lead ore here in 1891, triggering a rush. At its peak in the late 1890s, Sandon had over 5,000 residents, 29 hotels, 28 saloons, three breweries, theaters, an opera house, a school and a hospital.

Fire destroyed the central business district on May 3, 1900. The town was quickly rebuilt, channeling Carpenter Creek into a flume and converting its former course into the main street. The 1900s, however, ushered in a long decline. Rising metal prices during World War I briefly renewed prosperity, but the town disincorporated in 1920.

During World War II Sandon housed nearly 1,000 Japanese-Canadians, relocated from the Pacific coast, but by the early 1950s fewer than 200 residents remained. Much of the town remained intact until a major flood devastated the canyon in 1955.

Since the 1970s, volunteers have worked to preserve and restore the old mining town and to protect its heritage from souvenir hunters. Visitors are welcome to wander Sandon's scattered remnants. An old locomotive and other railroad rolling stock idle on a restored section of track. A steep gravel road (a high clearance vehicle is required) leads from the far end of town to Idaho Peak, where a short trail accesses a panoramic view. Galena Trail and K & S Railgrade Trail follow the former railroad routes. The Sandon Museum acts as a visitor center.

SANDON MUSEUM is in the former Slocan Mercantile Block in the center of town. Built in 1900, the museum was the only brick edifice ever erected in Sandon. It served as a general store and during World War II housed Japanese-Canadian internees.

The museum contains a large treasure trove of artifacts from the town's mining past, including historical archives, photos, maps and mining equipment. The basement contains grave markers from the local cemetery, moved to protect them from vandals. Videos portray the history of Sandon. **Time:** Allow 30 minutes minimum. **Hours:** Daily 10-5, Victoria Day weekend-Sept. 30. Phone ahead to confirm schedule. **Cost:** $4.50; $3.50 (ages 12-18 and 65+); $11.25 (family). **Phone:** (250) 358-7920.

SATURNA ISLAND (H-10) pop. 335

Saturna Island—remote, rugged and sparsely populated—is probably the least visited of the Gulf Islands as well as the southernmost isle. Mountain biking is one of the best ways to explore. Its bays, beaches and tidal pools offer glimpses of many varieties of marine life. Saturna offers hiking, bicycling and boating opportunities.

Camping is offered at Narvaez Bay as part of Gulf Islands National Park Reserve *(see place listing p. 246).* The seven-site camping area, is nestled by a tranquil bay. However, the best wildlife viewing is offered at East Point, also in the park reserve; it is the easternmost point of the islands surrounded by active currents where orcas and sea lions can often be spotted.

SECHELT (G-11) pop. 9,291

THE SUNSHINE COAST SALMONID ENHANCEMENT SOCIETY is at 4381 Parkway Dr. Visitors learn about the life-cycle of Pacific salmon. Throughout the facility, interpretive signs communicate the history of the Chapman Creek Hatchery and its function. **Time:** Allow 1 hour minimum. **Hours:** Mon.-Sat. 9-noon and 1-3:30 (also Sun. noon-3, June-Sept.). **Cost:** Donations. **Phone:** (604) 885-4136.

SICAMOUS (B-9) pop. 2,441, elev. 352m/1,155'

Flanked by Mara and Shuswap lakes, Sicamous has abundant recreational opportunities, including swimming, fishing, boating and other water sports. Full- and half-day cruises on Shuswap Lake *(see Recreation Areas Chart)* and 2- and 3-hour evening excursions on Mara Lake depart from the public wharf at the foot of Finlayson Street. Houseboats, which can be rented, are a popular way of touring the arms of Shuswap Lake.

At nearby Adams River almost 10 million scarlet sockeye salmon bury their eggs each October; it is one of the largest spawning grounds in the country. Several spawning grounds can be seen at Roderick Haig-Brown Provincial Park, 85 kilometres (53 mi.) northwest off Hwy. 1.

Sicamous Visitor Centre: 3-446 Main St., Sicamous, BC, Canada V0E 2V0. **Phone:** (250) 836-3313 or (866) 205-4055.

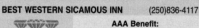

SIDNEY (H-10) pop. 11,178, elev. 9m/30'
• Part of Victoria area — see map p. 397

Salish Indians were the earliest known inhabitants of the area now called Sidney. Incorporated into a town in 1967, Sidney is known for its fishing and waterfront activity.

Booktown, the town's nickname, is the result of a dozen book shops concentrated in a five-block area around Beacon Avenue. Picnicking, beachcombing and camping are popular at Sidney Spit Marine Provincial Park.

Sidney Visitor Centre: 10382 Pat Bay Hwy., Sidney, BC, Canada V8L 5S8. **Phone:** (250) 656-0525.

BRITISH COLUMBIA AVIATION MUSEUM is at Victoria Airport at 1910 Norseman Rd. Displays of memorabilia and aircraft include World War II planes and bush planes, a model plane exhibit, photographs and aircraft engines. Additional displays are on view in the hangar. **Tours:** Guided tours are available. **Time:** Allow 1 hour minimum. **Hours:** Daily 10-4 May-Sept.; 11-3, rest of year. Closed Jan. 1 and Christmas. **Cost:** $8; $6 (ages 65+); $4 (ages 12-18). **Phone:** (250) 655-3300.

MINERAL WORLD AND THE SCRATCH PATCH is at 9808 Seaport Pl. An interpretive center offers hands-on exhibits that use minerals, crystals and fossils to demonstrate principles of earth science. Visitors may search and pan for semiprecious gemstones in the Scratch Patch.

Time: Allow 30 minutes minimum. **Hours:** Daily 10-5:30. Closed Christmas. **Cost:** Interpretive centre free. Searching for gemstones $6-$12. **Phone:** (250) 655-4367.

 SHAW OCEAN DISCOVERY CENTRE is at 9811 Seaport Pl. The main concentration of this waterfront aquarium and marine education center is the inland Salish Sea ecosystem. After experiencing the sensation of descending into the ocean in a simulated "elevator," visitors reach the Gallery of the Drifters to view plankton, algae and jellyfish.

The Ocean's Heartbeat, a classroomlike environment, has microscopes and live Internet links to undersea sites. The Gallery of the Salish Sea is where you'll find large aquarium habitats that are home to local marine life as well as works by native artists that depict the peoples' relationship with the ocean; an octopus den can be seen overhead.

Touch pools provide an opportunity to get up-close to some of the sea creatures such as sea urchins and sea stars, and docents, called "oceaneers," are available to answer questions. The diverse population of the center's 17 aquariums include wolf eels, rockfish, sea cucumbers and anemones.

Time: Allow 1 hour minimum. **Hours:** Daily 10-4. Closed Jan. 1, Christmas Eve and Christmas. Phone ahead to confirm schedule. **Cost:** $14; $8 (ages 7-17); $4 (ages 3-6). **Phone:** (250) 665-7511.

SIDNEY HISTORICAL MUSEUM & ARCHIVES is at 2423 Beacon Ave. The early lives of Sidney and North Saanich pioneers are portrayed through photographs and artifacts. **Time:** Allow 1 hour minimum. **Hours:** Daily 10-4; closed Jan 1 and Dec. 25-26. **Cost:** Donations. **Phone:** (250) 655-6355.

BEACON INN AT SIDNEY   (250)655-3288
▼▽▼ **Bed & Breakfast** $119-$259 **Address:** 9724 3rd St V8L 3A2 **Location:** Hwy 17 exit 28 (Sidney), 0.6 mi (1 km) e on Beacon Ave, then just s. **Facility:** The stately B&B features spacious guest rooms intricately appointed with have rich wood furnishings, plush velvet trim and regal feather beds. 9 units. 3 stories (no elevator), interior corridors. **Terms:** age restrictions may apply, cancellation fee imposed.

THE CEDARWOOD INN & SUITES   (250)656-5551

Hotel
$95-$255

Address: 9522 Lochside Dr V8L 1N8 **Location:** Hwy 17 exit 26, just e on McTavish Rd, then 0.8 mi (1.4 km) n. **Facility:** 46 units, some two bedrooms, efficiencies and kitchens. 2 stories (no elevator), exterior corridors. **Terms:** 3 day cancellation notice. **Amenities:** *Some:* high-speed Internet. **Guest Services:** coin laundry. **Free Special Amenities: newspaper and high-speed Internet.**

SAVE CALL 🛎 🛜 ✕ 🎿 🍴 ▯
/SOME UNITS FEE 🐾 📷

THE SIDNEY PIER HOTEL & SPA   (250)655-9445

Hotel
$139-$369

Address: 9805 Seaport Pl V8L 4X3 **Location:** Hwy 17 exit 28 (Beacon Ave), 0.6 mi (1 km) e. **Facility:** 55 units, some kitchens. 3 stories, interior corridors. **Parking:** on-site (fee). **Terms:** check-in 4 pm, cancellation fee imposed. **Amenities:** high-speed Internet, safes. **Dining:** Haro's Restaurant & Bar, see separate listing. **Activities:** steamrooms, exercise room, spa. **Guest Services:** valet and coin laundry. **Free Special Amenities: local telephone calls and high-speed Internet.**

SAVE ECO 🍴 🍸 CALL 🛎 🛜 ✕ 🍴 ▯
/SOME UNITS FEE 🐾 📷

VICTORIA AIRPORT TRAVELODGE SIDNEY
(250)656-1176

Hotel
$90-$160

Address: 2280 Beacon Ave V8L 1X1 **Location:** Hwy 17 exit 28 (Beacon Ave), just e. **Facility:** 90 units, some efficiencies. 2-4 stories, interior corridors. **Amenities:** *Some:* high-speed Internet. **Pool(s):** heated outdoor. **Guest Services:** valet and coin laundry. **Free Special Amenities: early check-in/late check-out and room upgrade (subject to availability with advance reservations).**

SAVE 🍸 CALL 🛎 🏊 🛜 🍴 📷 ▯
/SOME UNITS FEE 🐾

▼ See AAA listing p. 326 ▼

WHERE TO EAT

DEEP COVE CHALET   250/656-3541

French. Fine Dining. $18-$45 **AAA Inspector Notes:** Visitors and locals alike enjoy this delightful restaurant tucked away in a setting offering a lovely, manicured lawn and garden and spectacular views of the inlet. It may be a bit difficult to reach, but it's well worth the drive to sample the French cuisine. Fresh seafood, lamb, ostrich, caribou, wild boar and a nice variety of wines round out the menu. **Bar:** full bar. **Reservations:** suggested. **Address:** 11190 Chalet Rd V8L 4R4 **Location:** Hwy 17 exit 31 (Wain Rd/Deep Cove), 0.6 mi (1 km) w on Wain Rd, then 1.8 mi (3 km) nw on Tatlow Rd. L D CALL 🛎 🎿

HARO'S RESTAURANT & BAR   250/655-9700

Pacific Northwest. Casual Dining. $14-$32 **AAA Inspector Notes:** Affording sweeping views of Haro Strait, this relaxed waterfront restaurant has a heated outdoor terrace, comfortable lounge and bustling cafe-like atmosphere that appeals to almost anyone. The menu highlights ultra-fresh seafood, which is obtained only from sustainable fishery practices and combined with local and organic produce, homemade pasta and local meats to create wonderful seasonal specialties. **Bar:** full bar. **Reservations:** suggested. **Address:** 9805 Seaport Pl V8L 4X3 **Location:** Hwy 17 exit 28 (Beacon Ave), 0.6 mi (1 km) e; in The Sidney Pier Hotel & Spa. L D CALL 🛎

SMITTY'S   250/656-2423

Canadian
Casual Dining
$7-$20

AAA Inspector Notes: The family-oriented restaurant satisfies patrons with its ever-popular all-day breakfast items, as well as tasty and wholesome soups and salads at lunchtime. A relaxed mood characterizes the dining space. **Bar:** full bar. **Address:** 2306 Beacon Ave V8L 1X2 **Location:** Hwy 17 exit 28 (Sidney), just e; in BEST WESTERN PLUS Emerald Isle Motor Inn.
B L D CALL 🛎

Save on theme park tickets at AAA.com/discounts

SKIDEGATE (E-1)

HAIDA HERITAGE CENTRE AT KAAY LL-NAGAAY is just n. of the BC Ferries terminal on Second Beach Rd. The center, on the site of the old Haida seaside village of Kaay LInagaay, celebrates the relationship of the Haida people with the land and examines, through audiovisuals and interactive displays, Haida art, history and culture.

Traditional totem poles representing the 14 clans front the facility; three ancient poles are inside. A canoe house, a performing house and a carving shed also may be seen. The Haida Gwaii Museum includes exhibits about plants and wildlife as well as the Haida's belief in the natural and supernatural. A collection of argillite carvings and contemporary art is showcased.

Tours: Guided tours are available. **Time:** Allow 1 hour minimum. **Hours:** Daily 10-6, June-Aug.; Tues.-Sat. 10-5, rest of year. Closed holidays during the off-season. **Cost:** $15 (includes the heritage center and Haida Gwaii Museum); $10 (students with ID); $5 (ages 6-12). **Phone:** (250) 559-7885 or (877) 559-8818.

SMITHERS (E-3) pop. 5,404, elev. 520m/1,706'

Named for A.W. Smithers, one-time chairman of the Grand Trunk Pacific Railway, Smithers owes its location to railway construction crews who in 1913 selected the scenic spot at the base of Hudson Bay Mountain. It became a village in 1921 and officially a town in 1967. Today it is a distribution and supply center for local farms, mills and mines. Murals adorn many buildings within its alpine-style Main Street district.

Smithers is popular as a year-round skiing center thanks to 2,652-metre (8,700-ft.) Hudson Bay Mountain. The town also is a convenient starting point for fossil hunting, fishing, mountain climbing and trail riding.

Smithers Visitor Centre: 1411 Court St., P.O. Box 2379, Smithers, BC, Canada V0J 2N0. **Phone:** (250) 847-5072 or (800) 542-6673.

Self-guiding tours: Information about driving and walking tours is available at the chamber of commerce.

ADAMS IGLOO WILDLIFE MUSEUM is 10 km (6 mi.) w. on Hwy. 16. Mounted animals and birds native to British Columbia are displayed inside an igloo. **Time:** Allow 30 minutes minimum. **Hours:** Mon.-Sat. 9-6. **Cost:** $7.50; $5 (ages 65+); $3 (ages 5-12). **Phone:** (250) 847-3188.

Trust your vehicle to AAA/CAA
Approved Auto Repair facilities

ASPEN INN & SUITES　　　　　250/847-4551

Motel. Rates not provided. **Address:** 4628 Yellowhead Hwy V0J 2N0 **Location:** 0.9 mi (1.5 km) w on Hwy 16. **Facility:** 60 units, some efficiencies. 2 stories (no elevator), exterior corridors. **Parking:** winter plug-ins. **Pool(s):** heated indoor. **Activities:** saunas, whirlpool.

SUNSHINE INN & ESTATES　　　　250/847-6668

Hotel $109-$179 **Address:** 3880 Fourth Ave V0J 2N0 **Location:** Corner of Hwy 16 and Queen St. **Facility:** 58 units, some efficiencies and kitchens. 3 stories, interior corridors. **Parking:** winter plug-ins. **Amenities:** high-speed Internet. **Activities:** limited exercise equipment.

WHERE TO EAT

ALPENHORN BISTRO AND BAR　　　250/847-5366

American. Casual Dining. $12-$29 **AAA Inspector Notes:** Families are welcome in the casual, pub-like environment. Open late, you'll find many pub favorites like homemade soups, fresh salads, sandwiches, panini, burgers and pastas, plus a large selection of draft beers on tap. **Bar:** full bar. **Address:** 1261 Main St V0J 2N0 **Location:** Hwy 16, just s; between 3rd and 4th aves. **Parking:** street only.

SOOKE (H-9) pop. 11,435, elev. 38m/125'
• Part of Victoria area — see map p. 397

A natural harbor off the Juan de Fuca Strait, Sooke was discovered and claimed by the Spanish in 1790. The area, soon traded to the British by treaty, was named after a local Indian tribe, T'Soke. It is a popular fishing site and the center of a large forest industry. A scenic portion of Hwy. 14 runs 43 kilometres (27 mi.) east from Sooke to Victoria.

Sooke Visitor Centre: 2070 Phillips Rd., Box 774, Sooke, BC, Canada V9Z 0Y3. **Phone:** (250) 642-6351 or (866) 888-4748.

SOOKE REGION MUSEUM & VISITOR CENTRE is 1 km (.6 mi.) e. on Hwy. 14 at 2070 Phillips Rd. Exhibits about native peoples, early settlers and industrialization illustrate the history and economy of the west coast region. The 1870 Moss Cottage depicts late 19th-century family life, and visitors can see a 1910 lighthouse relocated from Cape Scott on Vancouver Island's northern tip. Documentary films are shown. In the summer salmon barbecues are scheduled; reservations are required.

Tours: Guided tours are available. **Time:** Allow 30 minutes minimum. **Hours:** Daily 9-5, May-Oct.; Tues.-Sun. 10-5, rest of year. **Cost:** Museum by donations. Moss Cottage tours $3. Lighthouse tours $3. Hours and rates may vary; phone ahead. **Phone:** (250) 642-6351 or (866) 888-4748.

RECREATIONAL ACTIVITIES
Ziplines

• **Adrena LINE Zipline Adventures Tours** departs from 5128C Sooke Rd. **Hours:** Two-hour trips depart daily 8:30-5:30, Mar.-Oct. **Phone:** (250) 642-1933 or (866) 947-9145.

BEST WESTERN PREMIER PRESTIGE OCEANFRONT RESORT
(250)642-0805

Contemporary Hotel
$130-$180

AAA Benefit: Members save up to 20%, plus 10% bonus points with Best Western Rewards®.

Address: 6929 W Coast Rd V9Z 0V1 **Location:** Oceanfront. 1 mi (1.6 km) w on Hwy 14. **Facility:** 122 units. 5 stories, interior corridors. **Amenities:** high-speed Internet. **Dining:** The Mix by Ric's, see separate listing. **Pool(s):** heated outdoor. **Activities:** whirlpool, exercise room, spa. **Guest Services:** coin laundry. **Free Special Amenities: local telephone calls and high-speed Internet.**

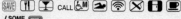

OCEAN WILDERNESS INN
(250)646-2116

Bed & Breakfast $130-$220 **Address:** 9171 W Coast Rd V9Z 1G3 **Location:** 8.6 mi (14 km) w on Hwy 14. Located in a secluded area. **Facility:** 7 units. 2 stories (no elevator), interior/exterior corridors. **Terms:** 2 night minimum stay - seasonal and/or weekends, 7 day cancellation notice-fee imposed. **Activities:** whirlpool.

SOOKE HARBOUR HOUSE
(250)642-3421

Country Inn
$230-$699

Address: 1528 Whiffen Spit Rd V9Z 0T4 **Location:** 1.2 mi (2 km) w on Hwy 14. **Facility:** Hear the name "Sooke" and you automatically think of this well-known, extensively written about lodging. Rooms are cozy with warm décor and water views; many also feature a wood-burning fireplace. 28 units. 4 stories, interior/exterior corridors. **Terms:** closed 1/4-1/24, 7 day cancellation notice-fee imposed. **Activities:** saunas. Fee: massage. **Free Special Amenities: high-speed Internet.**

SOOKE HARBOUR RESORT AND MARINA
250/642-3236

Condominium
Rates not provided

Address: 6971 W Coast Rd V9Z 0V1 **Location:** 1 mi (1.6 km) w on Hwy 14. **Facility:** Wonderfully large, modern condo units geared toward families and fishermen; the marina is located close by. 34 condominiums. 2-3 stories (no elevator), exterior corridors. **Terms:** check-in 4 pm. **Activities:** whirlpools. **Guest Services:** complimentary and valet laundry. **Free Special Amenities: high-speed Internet.**

WHERE TO EAT

THE EDGE RESTAURANT
778/425-3343

Pacific Northwest. Casual Dining. $10-$22 **AAA Inspector Notes:** This cozy bistro features house-cured meats and pork from the owner's personal farm, plus plenty of local seafood. The menu is quite affordable; all lunch items are under $15. Reservations aren't taken, so you may have to wait for a table. **Bar:** full bar. **Address:** 6686 Sooke Rd V9Z 1H5 **Location:** Jct Otter Point Rd and Hwy 14. L D

MARKUS' WHARFSIDE RESTAURANT
250/642-3596

Pacific Northwest. Fine Dining. $28-$31 **AAA Inspector Notes:** The chef/owner says it was his mother, an avid home cook, who inspired him to become a chef. Trained in Germany, he came to Canada in 1992 and began his long culinary career. Some 9 years ago the chef came to Sooke and opened this charming restaurant in an old fisherman's cottage. A fresh herb and vegetable garden dominates the front part of the restaurant, while the fresh seafood and organic meats are delivered each day. I recommend trying the three-course set menu. **Bar:** full bar. **Reservations:** suggested. **Address:** 1831 Maple Ave S V9Z 0N9 **Location:** 0.5 mi (0.9 km) w on Hwy 14. **Parking:** street only. D

THE MIX BY RIC'S
778/425-2529

American. Casual Dining. $12-$34 **AAA Inspector Notes:** You'll enjoy outstanding views of Sooke Harbour from the second-floor location, where as the restaurant likes to say, "Casual meets sophisticated." The reasonably priced tapas menu is good for those who want to sample and share. In the mood for something more hearty? Try the Sterling Silver AAA-grade beef. The steamed mussels and oysters come from Vancouver Island, while the small dessert selection is made in house. **Bar:** full bar. **Address:** 6929 W Coast Rd V9Z 0V1 **Location:** 1 mi (1.6 km) w on Hwy 14; in BEST WESTERN PREMIER Prestige Oceanfront Resort. L D CALL M

STONE PIPE GRILL
250/642-0566

American. Casual Dining. $7-$19 **AAA Inspector Notes:** The casual restaurant offers homestyle cooking with flair. The menu includes options from burgers and sandwiches to fine steaks and seafood, plus daily specials and homemade desserts. Portions are ample and incorporate the use of local ingredients in season. **Bar:** full bar. **Address:** 2038 Otter Point Rd V9Z 0S9 **Location:** Corner of Hwy 14. L D CALL M

SPARWOOD (C-12) pop. 3,667

Once known as a mining town, Sparwood offers guided tours of the Elkview Coal Mine during summer. Popular area recreational activities include fly fishing, white-water rafting, hiking and mountain biking.

Sparwood Visitor Centre: 141A Aspen Dr., P.O. Box 1448, Sparwood, BC, Canada V0B 2G0. **Phone:** (250) 425-2423 or (877) 485-8185.

SQUAMISH (G-11) pop. 17,158, elev. 5m/16'
• Hotels p. 330 • Restaurants p. 331

Overshadowed by Stawamus Chief Mountain and other snowcapped peaks, Squamish was named for the Indian word meaning "mother of the wind." It is a popular stopover for tourists and recreation seekers. Rock climbing and windsurfing are popular activities.

Picnic facilities are available 3 kilometres (1.9 mi.) south at Shannon Falls, and camping facilities are available at Alice Lake Provincial Park (see Recreation Areas Chart) 13 kilometres (8 mi.) to the north.

Squamish Visitor Centre: 38551 Loggers Ln., Squamish, BC, Canada V8B 0H2. **Phone:** (604) 815-4994 or (866) 333-2010.

GARIBALDI PROVINCIAL PARK is accessible by trail from Hwy. 99 or the British Columbia Railway. The 194,650-hectare (480,980-acre) park is a pristine wilderness of peaks, glaciers, meadows, lakes and streams.

Access to the Garibaldi Lake/Black Tusk Area is by a 7-kilometre (5-mi.) trail off Hwy. 99, about 37 kilometres (23 mi.) north of Squamish. A gravel road leads 16 kilometres (10 mi.) to the base camp parking lot, where a trail follows Paul Ridge 11 kilometres (7 mi.) to the Diamond Head Area. Glacier-fed Cheakamus Lake lies at an elevation of less than 914 metres (2,999 ft.). See Recreation Areas Chart. **Hours:** The park is open all year. **Cost:** Free. **Parking:** $3 per day. **Phone:** (604) 582-5200 for more information.

GLACIER AIR TOURS—see Brackendale p. 220.

WEST COAST RAILWAY HERITAGE PARK is 1 km (.6 mi.) w. off Hwy. 99 on Industrial Way, n. on Queensway Rd. to 39645 Government Rd. This outdoor museum is said to be home to western Canada's largest collection of heritage railway equipment. It features more than 60 railway heritage pieces dating to the early 1900s. Displays include steam and diesel locomotives, including a Royal Hudson locomotive; a sleeping car; caboose; bunk cars; a business car; and a new roundhouse.

A restoration exhibit demonstrates the process of restoring old railway cars. Visitors can ride a miniature train around the property on a 7.5-gauge track.

Time: Allow 30 minutes minimum. **Hours:** Daily 10-5, May-Sept.; 10-4, rest of year. Closed Jan. 1 and Christmas. **Cost:** $15; $12 (ages 60+); $10 (ages 6-18); $40 (family, two adults and three children). Miniature railway rides $3.50. **Phone:** (604) 898-9336.

BEST WESTERN MOUNTAIN RETREAT HOTEL
(604)815-0883

Hotel
$100

AAA Benefit: Members save up to 20%, plus 10% bonus points with Best Western Rewards®.

Address: 38922 Progress Way V8B 0K5 **Location:** 0.9 mi (1.5 km) n on Hwy 99; at Industrial Way. **Facility:** 87 units, some efficiencies. 4 stories, interior corridors. **Terms:** check-in 4 pm. **Amenities:** video games (fee). **Dining:** Timberwolf Restaurant & Lounge, see separate listing. **Pool(s):** heated indoor. **Activities:** whirlpool, waterslide, exercise room. **Guest Services:** coin laundry. **Free Special Amenities:** early check-in/late check-out and high-speed Internet.

EXECUTIVE SUITES HOTEL & RESORT SQUAMISH
(604)815-0048

Hotel
$119-$219

Address: 40900 Tantalus Rd V8B 0R3 **Location:** Hwy 99, just e on Garibaldi Way, then 0.6 mi (1 km) n. **Facility:** 111 units, some two bedrooms, efficiencies and kitchens. 4 stories, interior corridors. **Terms:** check-in 4 pm, cancellation fee imposed. **Dining:** Living Room Restaurant & Lounge, see separate listing. **Pool(s):** heated outdoor. **Activities:** whirlpool, exercise room. **Guest Services:** complimentary laundry. **Free Special Amenities:** local telephone calls and newspaper.

SEA TO SKY HOTEL
(604)898-4874

Hotel
$99-$189

Address: 40330 Tantalus Rd V0N 1T0 **Location:** 2.9 mi (4.5 km) n on Hwy 99 at Garibaldi Way. **Facility:** 52 units, some two bedrooms. 3 stories, interior corridors. **Terms:** cancellation fee imposed. **Activities:** sauna, whirlpool, limited exercise equipment. **Guest Services:** valet and coin laundry. **Free Special Amenities:** local telephone calls and high-speed Internet. *(See ad this page.)*

WHERE TO EAT

LIVING ROOM RESTAURANT & LOUNGE 604/815-0999

♦♦ ♦♦ American. Casual Dining. $12-$26 **AAA Inspector Notes:** In the city's newest lodging, the restaurant offers stunning views of the golf course and distant mountains. The menu features casual fare such as burgers, soups and various sandwiches at lunch and more complex offerings at dinner. **Bar:** full bar. **Address:** 40900 Tantalus Rd V8B 0R3 **Location:** Hwy 99, just e on Garibaldi Way, then 0.6 mi (1 km) n; in Executive Suites Hotel & Resort Squamish.

B L D CALL 🏃M

PARKSIDE RESTAURANT 604/892-2273

♦♦ ♦♦ Canadian. Casual Dining. $9-$38 **AAA Inspector Notes:** The cozy restaurant serves lunch and dinner, including salads, tapas, sandwiches, wraps, pasta and hearty dinner entrees such as chicken Marsala, prosciutto halibut and grilled salmon. The motto is: "Fresh ingredients made to order. Please be patient; the best things are worth waiting for!" **Bar:** full bar. **Reservations:** suggested, for dinner Fri & Sat. **Address:** 36996 Cleveland Ave V8B 0C2 **Location:** Hwy 99, 0.6 mi (1 km) w; corner of Victoria St. L D 🏃

TIMBERWOLF RESTAURANT & LOUNGE 604/815-4426

♦♦ ♦♦ American. Casual Dining. $6-$22 **AAA Inspector Notes:** Great food awaits the hungry traveler starting at 6 am, although breakfast can be ordered all day long. Lunch starts at 11 am. Daily specials include barbecue ribs on Mondays, prime rib on Wednesdays and seafood on Fridays. Seniors Night is Tuesday. **Bar:** full bar. **Address:** 38922 Progress Way V8B 0K5 **Location:** 0.9 mi (1.5 km) n on Hwy 99; at Industrial Way; in BEST WESTERN Mountain Retreat Hotel. B L D CALL 🏃M

SUMMERLAND (C-8) pop. 11,280, elev. 454m/1,489'

- Hotels p. 332
- Hotels & Restaurants map & index p. 290
- Part of Okanagan Valley area — see map p. 286

Surrounded by lush orchards and vineyards, Summerland depends on fruit cultivation as its main industry. Overlooking Okanagan Lake *(see Recreation Areas Chart)*, the first commercial orchard in the Okanagan Valley was planted in 1890. Fruit stands are still the best way to sample the region's bountiful produce.

Summerland also was the first town on the lake to employ electricity as an energy source; it was generated by a small hydroelectric plant built on the lakeshore in 1905. These and other historical landmarks are the focus of Summerland Museum at 9521 Wharton St.; phone (250) 494-9395.

Giants Head Park on 910-metre (2,986-ft.) Giants Head Mountain offers picnic facilities and views of Summerland, the valley below and Okanagan Lake.

Many beaches, including Sunoka, Peach Orchard, Powell and Rotary, line the shores of Okanagan Lake. Also of interest is the Summerland Trout Hatchery, 13405 Lakeshore Dr. S., where rainbow, brook and kokanee trout are raised; phone (250) 494-0491.

Summerland Visitor Centre: 15600 Hwy. 97, P.O. Box 130, Summerland, BC, Canada V0H 1Z0. **Phone:** (250) 494-2686.

KETTLE VALLEY STEAM RAILWAY is 5 km (3 mi.) w. on Prairie Valley Rd. to 18404 Bathville Rd. Passengers take a 1-hour, 45-minute narrated tour on the only preserved portion of the original Kettle Valley Railway Line, which ran from Midway to Hope.

Hours: The train departs from Prairie Valley Station Thurs.-Mon. at 10:30 and 1:30, late June-early Sept.; Sat.-Mon. at 10:30 and 1:30, mid-May to late June and early Sept.-second Mon. in Oct. **Cost:** $22; $20 (ages 65+); $17 (ages 13-18); $13 (ages 3-12). Fares may vary; phone ahead. **Phone:** (250) 494-8422, or (877) 494-8424 in Canada.

NIXDORF CLASSIC CARS, INC. is at 15809 Logie Rd. An inventory of more than 100 restored vehicles dating from 1936 to 1970 is rotated so that no fewer than half reside in the facility at one time. The cars, all of which are two-door hardtops or convertibles,

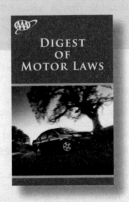

(See map & index p. 290.)

may also be rented for chauffeured wine tours. **Time:** Allow 1 hour minimum. **Hours:** Daily 9-5, May 1-Oct. 11; by appointment rest of year. **Cost:** $17; free (ages 0-11). **Phone:** (250) 494-4111.

SUMMERLAND ORNAMENTAL GARDENS is s. on Hwy. 97 to 4200 Hwy. 97 on the grounds of Pacific Agri-Foods Research Centre. Established in 1916, the 300-hectare (741-acre) site specializes in xeriscape landscaping, the use of drought-tolerant plants. English gardens, roses, meadow plants and wetland plants also are cultivated. A butterfly and hummingbird garden is featured. **Time:** Allow 1 hour minimum. **Hours:** Daily 8-8, in summer; 8-6 in fall and spring; 8-4, in winter (weather permitting). **Cost:** Donations. **Phone:** (250) 494-6385. 🎠

WINERIES

- **Dirty Laundry Vineyard** is at 7311 Fiske St. Other activities are available. **Hours:** Daily 10-5, Apr.-Oct.; Tues.-Sun. 11-4, Nov.-Dec. and in Apr. **Phone:** (250) 494-8815.
- **Sumac Ridge Estate Winery** is 1 km (.6 mi.) n. at 17403 Hwy. 97N. **Hours:** Tastings daily 9:30-6, late June-Labour Day; 10-5, May 4-June 30 and Sept. 1-early Oct.; 10-5, rest of year. Tours are given daily at 11 and 2 year-round. Closed Jan. 1-2, Christmas and day after Christmas. **Phone:** (250) 494-0451 or (877) 433-0451.

SUMMERLAND MOTEL · · · · · · · · · · 250/494-4444 **36**
💎 💎 **Motel** $69-$159 **Address:** 2107 Tait St V0H 1Z4 **Location:** 3.1 mi (5 km) s on Hwy 97 (32nd St). **Facility:** 58 units, some efficiencies and kitchens. 2 stories (no elevator), exterior corridors. **Terms:** closed 11/1-2/28, 2 night minimum stay - seasonal and/or weekends, 10 day cancellation notice-fee imposed. **Amenities:** Some: high-speed Internet. **Pool(s):** heated outdoor. **Activities:** exercise room. **Guest Services:** coin laundry.
CALL 🅑Ⓜ 🏊 🛜 ✕ 🅱 🖵 🖳 / SOME UNITS FEE 🐾 🖼

SUN PEAKS (B-8)

The resort community of Sun Peaks nestles amid firs and aspen at the base of Tod Mountain and Mount Morrisey in central British Columbia. The core of the village, 31 kilometres (19 mi.) east of Hwy. 5 at Heffley Creek, consists of three- to five-story alpine motif buildings clustered along pedestrian walkways.

With nearly 1,497 hectares (3,700 acres) of terrain, Sun Peaks is reportedly the third largest ski area in Canada, offering both alpine and Nordic skiing as well as a tube park, ice skating, sleigh rides, snowmobiling and dog sledding. Summer activities include golf, tennis, hiking, mountain biking, kayaking, canoeing, fishing and trail rides.

RECREATIONAL ACTIVITIES
Skiing

- **Sun Peaks Resort** is 54 km (32 mi.) n. on Hwy. 5 at 1280 Alpine Rd. Other activities are available. **Hours:** Daily 8:30-3:30, mid-Nov. to mid-Apr. Chairlifts open for summer activities daily 10-5, July 1-Sept. 3. Hours may vary; phone ahead to confirm schedule. **Phone:** (250) 578-5474 or (800) 807-3257.

COAST SUNDANCE LODGE · · · · · · · · · 250/578-0200
💎 💎 **Hotel. Rates not provided. Address:** 3160 Creekside Way V0E 5N0 **Location:** Hwy 5, 19.5 mi (31 km) ne on Todd Mountain Rd, follow signs to village. **Facility:** 84 units, some two bedrooms, efficiencies and kitchens. 4 stories, interior corridors. **Dining:** 3 restaurants. **Activities:** whirlpool, hiking trails, exercise room. **Fee:** downhill & cross country skiing. **Guest Services:** coin laundry.
🅔🅒🅞 🍴 ☕ CALL 🅑Ⓜ 🛜 ✕ 🅺 🅱 🖼 🖳
/ SOME UNITS FEE 🐾

DELTA SUN PEAKS RESORT · · · · · · · · (250)578-6000
💎💎💎 **Hotel** $89-$599 **Address:** 3240 Village Way V0E 5N0 **Location:** Hwy 5, 19.4 mi (31 km) ne on Todd Mountain Rd, follow signs to village. **Facility:** 261 units, some two bedrooms and kitchens. 4-5 stories, interior corridors. **Terms:** check-in 4 pm, cancellation fee imposed. **Amenities:** high-speed Internet. Some: video games (fee). **Dining:** Mantles Restaurant, see separate listing, nightclub. **Pool(s):** heated outdoor. **Activities:** sauna, whirlpools, steamroom, hiking trails, exercise room. **Fee:** game room, massage. **Guest Services:** coin laundry.
🅔🅒🅞 🍴 ☕ CALL 🅑Ⓜ 🏊 🄱🄸🅉 🛜 ✕ 🎦 🅱
🖳 / SOME UNITS FEE 🐾 🖼

HEARTHSTONE LODGE · · · · · · · · · · (250)578-8588
💎💎 **Hotel** $89-$499 **Address:** 3170 Creekside Way V0E 5N0 **Location:** Hwy 5, 19.4 mi (31 km) ne on Todd Mountain Rd, follow signs to village. **Facility:** 70 efficiencies. 4 stories, interior corridors. **Parking:** on-site (fee). **Terms:** check-in 4 pm, 3 day cancellation notice, 30 day in winter-fee imposed. **Amenities:** high-speed Internet. **Dining:** Bella Italia Ristorante, see separate listing. **Activities:** whirlpools, limited exercise equipment. **Guest Services:** coin laundry.
🅔🅒🅞 🍴 ☕ CALL 🅑Ⓜ 🛜 ✕ 🅺 🅱 🖼 🖳
/ SOME UNITS FEE 🐾

HEFFLEY BOUTIQUE INN · · · · · · · · · (250)578-8343
💎💎 **Extended Stay Hotel** $99-$425 **Address:** 3185 Creekside Way V0E 5N0 **Location:** Hwy 5, 19.4 mi (31 km) ne on Todd Mountain Rd, follow signs to village. **Facility:** 26 efficiencies. 3 stories, interior corridors. **Parking:** on-site (fee). **Terms:** check-in 4 pm, 30 day cancellation notice-fee imposed, resort fee. **Activities:** sauna, whirlpool.
🍴 ☕ CALL 🅑Ⓜ 🛜 ✕ 🅺 🅱 🖼 🖳

SUN PEAKS LODGE · · · · · · · · · · · (250)578-7878

💎💎💎
Hotel
$89-$299

Address: 3180 Creekside Way V0E 5N0 **Location:** Hwy 5, 19.4 mi (31 km) ne on Todd Mountain Rd, follow signs to village. **Facility:** 44 units. 3 stories, interior corridors. **Parking:** on-site (fee).
Terms: closed 4/1-4/30 & 10/1-12/5, 30 day cancellation notice-fee imposed. **Amenities:** safes. **Activities:** sauna, whirlpool, steamroom. **Free Special Amenities:** room upgrade (subject to availability with advance reservations) and high-speed Internet.
🆂🅰🆅🅴 🍴 ☕ CALL 🅑Ⓜ 🛜 ✕ 🅺 🅱 🖳
/ SOME UNITS 🖼

[WHERE TO EAT]

BELLA ITALIA RISTORANTE · · · · · · · · 250/578-7316
💎💎💎 **Italian. Casual Dining.** $17-$33 **AAA Inspector Notes:** This intimate restaurant is in a class of its own. While the menu is not as huge or typical as what's commonly found in Italian restaurants, it lists dishes made from the finest ingredients--and it shows in the quality of the finished product, which is prettily presented. Classic and not-so-classic dishes range from starters of bruschetta, minestrone and scallops with horseradish beet coulis to entrees of osso buco, wild Coho salmon with herb risotto and pancetta-wrapped beef tenderloin. **Bar:** full bar. **Reservations:** suggested. **Address:** 3170 Creekside Way V0E 5N0 **Location:** Hwy 5, 19.4 mi (31 km) ne on Todd Mountain Rd, follow signs to village; in Hearthstone Lodge. **Parking:** no self-parking. [D] CALL 🅑Ⓜ

MANTLES RESTAURANT 250/578-6060

▼▼▼ Pacific Northwest. Casual Dining. $11-$35 **AAA Inspector Notes:** Pacific Northwest fare is made in the vibrant family restaurant. The funky, upscale dining room, complete with an open-concept demonstration kitchen, sets the scene after a day on the ski hills. Among tempting starters are varied distinctive appetizers, ranging from scallops and portobello mushrooms to Caesar salad. The entrees are a piece of art. Good choices include salmon woven on a stalk of lemongrass, rack of lamb and oven-fired pizzas. **Bar:** full bar. **Reservations:** suggested. **Address:** 3240 Village Way V0E 5N0 **Location:** Hwy 5, 19.4 mi (31 km) n e on Todd Mountain Rd, follow signs to village; in Delta Sun Peaks Resort. **Parking:** on-site and valet. [B] [L] [D] CALL [&M]

POWDER HOUNDS RESTAURANT 250/578-0014

▼▼ International. Casual Dining. $15-$28 **AAA Inspector Notes:** You can always count on this restaurant being open, even during the slow periods here in Sun Peaks. Since 1997 they've been serving a mix of German specialties like schnitzels to hearty Canadian fare such as Angus beef steaks. For those looking for lighter fare there are pasta and seafood choices. **Bar:** full bar. **Reservations:** suggested. **Address:** 116-3190 Creekside Way V0E 5N0 **Location:** Hwy 5, 19.4 mi (31 km) n e on Todd Mountain Rd; in Fireside Lodge. [D] CALL [&M]

SUNSHINE COAST (F-10)

Lining the western edge of the British Columbia mainland, the Sunshine Coast offers a wide variety of marine and land habitats, from coastal rain forests and rocky beaches to an alpine wilderness with peaks reaching 2,500 metres (8,000 ft.).

Powell River *(see place listing p. 306)*, with more than 100 regional dive sites, exceptionally clear water and deep ocean currents, is called the "Dive Capital of Canada." Desolation Sound's warm, sheltered waters also contribute to the destination's popularity with scuba divers and kayakers. Sechelt *(see place listing p. 325)* is known for its rich artisan community, while Gibsons *(see place listing p. 242)* is home to up to 200 bird species throughout the year.

SURREY (H-11) pop. 468,251, elev. 80m/262'

Surrey's sights are popular with nature buffs. Bear Creek Park features a garden area that includes rhododendrons, azaleas, ornamental grasses and bulb displays. A shoreline walk extends from Crescent Beach to Peace Arch Park. Walkers can observe tide pools, dig for clams or watch the myriad native birds.

Surrey Visitor Centre: 730 176th St., Surrey, BC, Canada V3S 9S6. **Phone:** (604) 531-6646 or (888) 531-6646.

HISTORIC STEWART FARM is at 13723 Crescent Rd. Costumed guides offer tours of an 1890s farmhouse that has been restored to represent Victorian rural life. The site includes a pole barn, heritage gardens, an orchard and walking trails along the Nicomekl River. Demonstrations as well as seasonal special events and programs also are featured. **Time:** Allow 30 minutes minimum. **Hours:** Tues.-Fri. 10-4, Sat.-Sun. noon-4, early Feb.-late Dec. Closed major holidays. **Cost:** Donations. **Phone:** (604) 592-6956. 🪵

NEWTON WAVE POOL is at 13730 72nd Ave. The indoor aquatic center houses, in addition to the wave pool, two water slides, an interactive water fortress and a three-station water cannon platform. The complex also includes an exercise, a steam and 465-square-metre (5,000-sq.-ft.) weight room as well as a whirlpool.

Hours: Mon.-Sat. 8 a.m.-9 p.m., Sun. 8-8. Phone ahead for leisure swim times. **Cost:** Single drop-in swims $5.75; $4.50 (students with ID and ages 60+); $3 (ages 2-18). Prices may vary; phone ahead. **Phone:** (604) 501-5540.

SURREY MUSEUM is at 17710-56A Ave. Interactive exhibits and a 42-seat theater portray the history of Surrey. A textile library and weaving studio are featured on-site. Changing exhibits are offered. Also on the grounds is the Anderson cabin, the oldest remaining pioneer-era structure in Surrey. The cabin was built in 1872 by Eric Anderson, a Swedish immigrant and one of the first settlers in the area.

Time: Allow 1 hour minimum. **Hours:** Tues.-Fri. 9:30-5:30, Sat. 10-5, early Feb.-late Dec. Closed major holidays. **Cost:** Donations. **Phone:** (604) 592-6956.

(See map & index p. 368.)

COAST SURREY GUILDFORD HOTEL   604)930-4700 63
 Hotel. Rates not provided. Address: 10410 158th St V4N 5C2 **Location:** Trans-Canada Hwy 1 exit 50 (160th St), just w on 104th Ave. **Facility:** 77 units. 3 stories, interior corridors. **Amenities:** high-speed Internet. **Pool(s):** heated outdoor. **Activities:** whirlpool, limited exercise equipment. **Guest Services:** valet laundry.

COMFORT INN & SUITES SURREY   (604)576-8888 66
Hotel $99-$149 **Address:** 8255 166th St V4N 5R8 **Location:** Trans-Canada Hwy 1 exit 53 (176th St/Hwy 15), 2.9 mi (4.8 km) s to Fraser Hwy (Hwy 1A), then 1.6 mi (2.6 km) nw. Located near Roma Home Centre. **Facility:** 82 units. 4 stories, interior corridors. **Terms:** cancellation fee imposed. **Amenities:** high-speed Internet. **Activities:** limited exercise equipment. **Guest Services:** valet and coin laundry, area transportation-within 5 mi (8 km).

COMPASS POINT INN   (604)588-9511 62
Hotel $99-$129 **Address:** 9850 King George Blvd V3T 4Y3 **Location:** Jct Hwy 1A (Fraser Hwy) and 99A (King George Hwy). **Facility:** 81 units. 6 stories, interior corridors. **Terms:** 3 day cancellation notice-fee imposed. **Dining:** 2 restaurants. **Pool(s):** heated indoor. **Activities:** whirlpool, limited exercise equipment. **Guest Services:** valet and coin laundry.

HAMPTON INN & SUITES LANGLEY/SURREY
(604)530-6545 68

AAA Benefit: Members save up to 10%!

Hotel
$129-$159

Address: 19500 Langley Bypass V3S 7R2 **Location:** Trans-Canada Hwy 1 exit 58 (200th St/Langley City), 3.1 mi (5 km) s, then 0.7 mi (1.2 km) w on Hwy 10. **Facility:** 96 units, some efficiencies. 4 stories, interior corridors. **Terms:** 1-7 night minimum stay, cancellation fee imposed. **Amenities:** video games (fee), high-speed Internet. **Pool(s):** heated indoor. **Activities:** whirlpool, waterslide, exercise room. **Guest Services:** valet and coin laundry. **Free Special Amenities:** full breakfast and local telephone calls. (See ad p. 270.)

HOLIDAY INN EXPRESS & SUITES SURREY
(604)930-8510 64
Hotel $99-$149 **Address:** 15808 104th Ave V4N 5L2 **Location:** Trans-Canada Hwy 1 exit 50 (160th St), just w. **Facility:** 85 units. 4 stories, interior corridors. **Amenities:** high-speed Internet. **Pool(s):** heated indoor. **Activities:** sauna, whirlpool, limited exercise equipment. **Guest Services:** valet and coin laundry.

HOLIDAY INN HOTEL & SUITES   (604)576-8862 67

Hotel
$90-$150

Address: 17530 64th Ave V3S 1Y9 **Location:** Trans-Canada Hwy 1 exit 53 (176th St/Hwy 15), 4.2 mi (7 km) s, then just w. Located in the Cloverdale area. **Facility:** 76 units. 4 stories, interior corridors. **Amenities:** high-speed Internet. **Pool(s):** heated indoor. **Activities:** exercise room. **Guest Services:** valet and coin laundry. **Free Special Amenities:** local telephone calls and high-speed Internet.

▼ See AAA listing p. 333 ▼

(See map & index p. 368.)

RAMADA LANGLEY-SURREY   (604)576-8388 69

Hotel
$99-$149

Address: 19225 Hwy 10 (56 Ave) V3S 8V9 **Location:** Trans-Canada Hwy 1 exit 58 (200th St/Langley City), 3.1 mi (5 km) s on 200th St, then 1.2 mi (2 km) w on Rt 10 (56 Ave); corner of 192nd St and Rt 10. **Facility:** 85 units, some efficiencies. 3 stories, interior corridors. **Terms:** cancellation fee imposed. **Amenities:** safes. *Some:* high-speed Internet. **Pool(s):** heated indoor. **Activities:** whirlpool, exercise room. **Guest Services:** valet and coin laundry. **Free Special Amenities:** expanded continental breakfast and high-speed Internet.

Learn the local driving laws
at DrivingLaws.AAA.com

SHERATON VANCOUVER GUILDFORD HOTEL
(604)582-9288 61

Hotel
$105-$165

Sheraton
HOTELS & RESORTS

AAA Benefit: Members get up to 20% off, plus Starwood Preferred Guest® bonuses.

Address: 15269 104th Ave V3R 1N5 **Location:** Trans-Canada Hwy 1 exit 48 eastbound, 0.6 mi (1 km) s on 152nd St, then just e; exit 50 westbound, then just w. **Facility:** 279 units. 20 stories, interior corridors. **Parking:** on-site (fee) and valet. **Amenities:** video games (fee). **Pool(s):** heated outdoor. **Activities:** whirlpool, exercise room, spa. **Guest Services:** valet laundry. *(See ad this page.)*

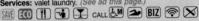

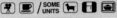

WHERE TO EAT

CRESCENT BEACH BISTRO   604/531-1882 52

Mediterranean. Casual Dining. $12-$28 **AAA Inspector Notes:** Diners enjoy a delightful setting either on the lovely outdoor terrace or in the quaint indoor dining room. Plants adorn both sections, and lively Mediterranean background music adds to the atmosphere. Menu highlights include Spanish paella, shrimp and scallops with tangy mango chutney, and a more traditional rack of lamb. It's best to phone ahead for reservations as it's very popular with the locals. **Bar:** full bar. **Reservations:** suggested. **Address:** 12251 Beecher St V4A 3A4 **Location:** 2 blks from Crescent Beach at McKenzie Ave. **Parking:** street only. L D 🐾

▼ See AAA listing this page ▼

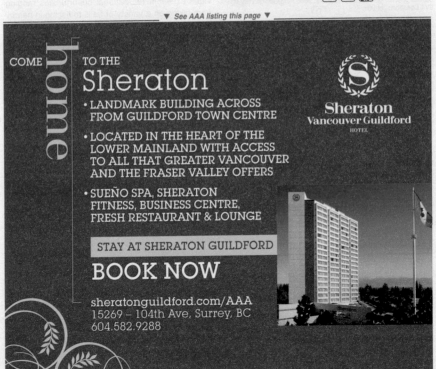

(See map & index p. 368.)

MOXIE'S CLASSIC GRILL   604/495-7020

▼▼ ▼▼ American. Casual Dining. $10-$29 **AAA Inspector Notes:** This sleek, funky and popular restaurant presents an extensive menu of creatively prepared dishes, including pizza, pasta, rice, noodles, signature salads and burgers. Other menus include one for children and one for Sunday brunch. Lending to the upbeat, stylish decor are dark wood appointments and river rock fireplaces. **Bar:** full bar. **Address:** 10608 151A St V3R 1J8 **Location:** Trans-Canada Hwy 1 exit 48 eastbound, 0.6 mi (1 km) s on 152nd St; exit 50 westbound, 0.6 mi (1 km) s on 104th Ave. ⓛ Ⓓ Ⓛⓐⓣⓔ

RICKY'S ALL DAY GRILL

▼▼ ▼▼ American. Casual Dining. $11-$27 **AAA Inspector Notes:** The comfortable eatery, which employs friendly servers, presents a varied menu that includes pasta dishes, wraps, omelets, stir-fry preparations and burgers. Portions are generous. Children's and senior selections are offered. Guests can request seating in a booth or at a table. **Bar:** full bar. Ⓑ ⓛ Ⓓ

For additional information, visit AAA.com

LOCATIONS:
Address: 3189 King George Hwy V4P 1B8 **Location:** Hwy 99 exit 10, 1.9 mi (3 km) s. **Phone:** 604/535-1789

Address: 8958 152nd St V3R 4L7 **Location:** Between Fraser Hwy and 88th Ave. **Phone:** 604/581-3212

Address: 1076 Central City V3T 2W1 **Location:** Between King George Hwy and 100th Ave. **Phone:** 604/582-2545

SWISS CHALET   604/583-0883

▼▼ ▼▼ Chicken. Casual Dining. $9-$22 **AAA Inspector Notes:** The popular restaurant is known for its rotisserie chicken and ribs and the tangy Chalet sauce that gives food its special zip. Diners munch on a half or quarter chicken with sides such as steamed vegetables, fries, baked potatoes and salads. Lunch guests often go for the great soup and sandwich combination. Take-out and delivery service are popular options. **Bar:** full bar. **Address:** 9666 King George Hwy V3T 2V4 **Location:** Jct 96th Ave. ⓛ Ⓓ

THE TURKEY HOUSE & DELI   604/531-6222 ⑤③

▼▼ Sandwiches Deli. Quick Serve. $7-$12 **AAA Inspector Notes:** Since 1973, the distinctive combination restaurant and delicatessen has been serving 100 percent turkey products and unforgettable home-cooked meals. On the menu are varied sandwiches and soups, as well as hot items that can be eaten here or taken out. Visitors can purchase turkey deli meats and pre-made dishes that can be warmed at home, including turkey pies, sausage rolls and lasagna. **Address:** 1433 King George Hwy V4A 4Z5 **Location:** Hwy 99 exit 2B southbound; from Canada/US border exit 2 northbound, then 0.6 mi (1 km) n. Ⓑ ⓛ CALL Ⓛ Ⓜ

VILLA VERDI RISTORANTE ITALIANO   604/591-2123 ⑤①

▼▼ ▼▼ ▼▼ Northern Italian. Casual Dining. $16-$32 **AAA Inspector Notes:** The Italian restaurant offers a choice among a wide selection of pasta dishes, including a pasta bar option that lets patrons customize a specialty dish from a list of pastas and sauces. Free parking is plentiful. **Bar:** full bar. **Reservations:** suggested. **Address:** 13620 80th Ave V3W 6M1 **Location:** Jct Fraser Hwy (Hwy 1A), 2.5 mi (4 km) s on 99A (King George Hwy). ⓛ Ⓓ CALL Ⓛ Ⓜ

TELEGRAPH COVE (H-3)

The bay community served as the northern terminus of the telegraph line along the coast of Vancouver Island and later became a logging and salmon fishing area. Whale watching, fishing and camping are popular during the summer.

STUBBS ISLAND WHALE WATCHING departs from the end of the #24 boardwalk. For excursions on the Johnstone Strait, vessels are equipped with underwater microphones for listening to whale vocalizations. Multiday tours also are available.

Warm clothing is recommended. **Time:** Allow 3 hours, 30 minutes minimum. **Hours:** Daily departures May 1-early Oct. Phone ahead to confirm schedule. **Cost:** Mid-day fare $94; $84 (ages 1-12 and 65+). Morning fare $84; $79 (ages 1-12 and 65+). Reservations are required. **Phone:** (250) 928-3185 or (800) 665-3066.

WHALE INTERPRETIVE CENTRE is at the end of the boardwalk. Interpreters provide hands-on presentations and share information about and promote awareness of the marine environment. Exhibits include whale skeletons and artifacts. An educational video about marine life also is featured. **Time:** Allow 45 minutes minimum. **Hours:** Daily 9-6, July-Aug.; 9-5, May-June and in Sept.; by appointment rest of year. Phone ahead to confirm schedule. **Cost:** $3; $1 (children). **Phone:** (250) 928-3129 or (250) 928-3117.

TELEGRAPH COVE MARINA & RV PARK   250/928-3163

▼▼ **Motel.** Rates not provided. **Address:** 1642 Telegraph Cove Rd V0N 3J0 **Location:** 9 mi (15 km) e on Beaver Cove Rd. **Facility:** 17 efficiencies. 2 stories (no elevator), exterior corridors. *Bath:* shower only. **Guest Services:** coin laundry.

⊞ ⊚ ⊠ Ⓧ ⊠ ⊟ ▦ ▣

TERRACE (E-2) pop. 11,486, elev. 215m/705'

On the banks of the Skeena River, Terrace is a major producer of forest products. The area provides excellent recreational opportunities ranging from hiking on a variety of trails to fishing in nearby rivers and creeks. Among the region's wildlife is a rare species of black bear, the white Kermodei. Native to the area, it is the city's symbol.

Among the most popular recreation areas are Lakelse Lake Provincial Park *(see Recreation Areas Chart)*; Lakelse River, a tributary of the Skeena River that harbors record-size salmon; and Williams Creek, which teems with spawning sockeye each August.

Several places of natural interest are nearby. At the eastern entrance to the city is Ferry Island, a park with hiking trails, swimming and camping *(see Recreation Areas Chart)*. About 20 kilometres (12 mi.) south of Terrace is Mount Layton Hot Springs Resort, which has waterslides and a pool filled with natural hot spring mineral water. Hwy. 16 offers a scenic drive west along the Skeena River to Prince Rupert.

Terrace Visitor Centre: 4511 Keith Ave., Terrace, BC, Canada V8G 1K1. **Phone:** (250) 635-4944 or (877) 635-4944.

HERITAGE PARK MUSEUM is at 4702 Kerby Ave. Historic buildings depict the history of pioneers in the region. The structures contain more than 4,000 artifacts pertaining to the life of settlers to the area 1890-1950. **Tours:** Guided tours are available. **Time:** Allow 1 hour minimum. **Hours:** Daily 10-6, June 1-Aug. 31; Mon.-Fri. 9:30-5:30, early Sept. to mid-May; Mon.-Fri. 10-6, May 15-31. Phone ahead to confirm schedule. **Cost:** Donations. **Phone:** (250) 635-4546.

NISGA'A MEMORIAL LAVA BED PROVINCIAL PARK is 100 km (62 mi.) n. on Kalum Lake Dr. (Nisga'a Hwy.); the first 70 km (44 mi.) is paved. Drivers should watch for logging trucks.

Miles of lava beds were formed by a volcanic eruption some 250 years ago that destroyed two Nisga'a tribal villages, causing 2,000 deaths. The valley floor resembles the moon's surface. Interpretive trails provide easy access through the park. The New Aiyansh Indian Village, 16 kilometres (10 mi.) north, features totem poles, a tribal council hall and a Nisga'a Lisims government building. Guided hiking tours to the volcanic cone are available. *See Recreation Areas Chart.*

Hours: Park daily dawn-dusk, May 1 to mid-Oct. Visitor center daily 10-6, mid-June to early Sept. Guided hiking tours of the volcanic cone are offered Thurs.-Mon., mid-June to early Sept. Phone ahead to confirm schedule. **Cost:** Park free. Visitor center $2; free (ages 0-12). Drop-in guided hiking tour $40; $30 (ages 16-18 and senior citizens); $25 (ages 8-15). Ages 0-5 are not permitted on the hiking tour. Prices may vary; phone ahead. **Phone:** (250) 633-2733.

BEST WESTERN PLUS TERRACE INN   250/635-0083

Hotel
Rates not provided

AAA Benefit: Members save up to 20%, plus 10% bonus points with Best Western Rewards®.

Address: 4553 Greig Ave V8G 1M7 **Location:** Hwy 16, just e on Greig Ave, follow City Centre signs. **Facility:** 68 units. 5 stories, interior corridors. **Amenities:** high-speed Internet. **Activities:** exercise room. **Guest Services:** valet laundry. **Free Special Amenities:** full breakfast and high-speed Internet.

COAST INN OF THE WEST   250/638-8141

Hotel. Rates not provided. **Address:** 4620 Lakelse Ave V8G 1R1 **Location:** Hwy 16 to City Centre; between Emerson and Kalum sts; downtown. **Facility:** 58 units. 2-4 stories, interior corridors. **Activities:** exercise room. **Guest Services:** valet laundry.

WHERE TO EAT

THE BAVARIAN INN STEAK & SEAFOOD GRILL   250/635-9161

German Steak Seafood. Casual Dining. $20-$35 **AAA Inspector Notes:** Downstairs is The Black Eddy Pub, while the more formal dining room, which offers great views, is upstairs. In addition to the expected German specialties, the menu lists steaks, seafood and pasta. This place is just east of the downtown mall. **Bar:** full bar. **Reservations:** suggested. **Address:** 4332 Lazelle Ave V8G 1N8 **Location:** Hwy 16 to City Centre, 0.6 mi (1 km) e. D

CASA MASALA HOT HOUSE RESTAURANT   250/615-5800

Indian. Casual Dining. $11-$20 **AAA Inspector Notes:** Located in a renovated house located right behind the McDonalds, this restaurant offers a unique take on the typical Indian restaurant. The flavors are the same, but in addition to items like their Indian Rice Bowls you can choose lighter fare such as wraps and sandwiches. Takeout is available. **Bar:** full bar. **Address:** 4728 Lazelle Ave V8G 1T2 **Location:** Between Eby and Sparks sts; behind McDonald's. **Parking:** on-site and street. L D CALL

TOFINO   (I-3) pop. 1,876
• Restaurants p. 338

A fishing and resort village with sandy beaches, Tofino is on the western side of Vancouver Island at the end of Hwy. 4. The area was the site of Fort Defiance, where Boston fur trader Robert Gray and his men spent the winter of 1791. The fort was stripped and abandoned the next spring, and all that remains are scattered bricks and ruins.

Near Clayoquot Sound and the northern end of Pacific Rim National Park Reserve, the town's shoreline and waters are popular with scuba divers and beachcombers. In the spring whales often can be seen migrating along the coast. The Whale Centre and Museum at 411 Campbell St. exhibits scientific and artistic displays, photographs and artifacts depicting past and present whale encounters.

Several companies, including Adventures Pacific, (250) 725-2811; Jamie's Whaling Station, (250) 725-3919; Remote Passages, (250) 725-3330; and Sea Trek Tours and Expeditions, (250) 725-4412, offer whale-watching excursions on Clayoquot Sound. Tours lasting up to 2.5 hours may afford sightings of sea lions, porpoises and eagles. Combination whale-watching and hot springs cruises that last approximately 6.5 hours also are available.

Tofino Visitor Centre: 455 Campbell St., Tofino, BC, Canada V0R 2Z0. **Phone:** (250) 725-3414 or (888) 720-3414.

TOFINO BOTANICAL GARDENS is at 1080 Pacific Rim Hwy. This site consists of 5 hectares (12 acres) of gardens that include a children's garden, a medicinal herb garden, 1,000-year-old cedar trees, an orchard and a berry patch, and a bird-watching area. An old homestead also is on the grounds. Pets and smoking are not permitted. **Time:** Allow 1 hour minimum. **Hours:** Daily 9-dusk. **Cost:** $10; $8 (senior citizens); $6 (students); free (ages 0-12). **Phone:** (250) 725-1220.

BEST WESTERN TIN WIS RESORT LODGE
   (250)725-4445

Hotel
$119-$319

AAA Benefit: Members save up to 20%, plus 10% bonus points with Best Western Rewards®.

Address: 1119 Pacific Rim Hwy V0R 2Z0 **Location:** 1.8 mi (3.5 km) s on Hwy 4. **Facility:** 85 units, some efficiencies. 2-3 stories, exterior corridors. **Amenities:** high-speed Internet. **Activities:** sauna, whirlpool, exercise room. **Guest Services:** coin laundry. **Free Special Amenities:** local telephone calls and high-speed Internet.

HIMWITSA LODGE   250/725-2017

Hotel. Rates not provided. **Address:** 300 Main St V0R 2Z0 **Location:** Just n via 1st St; downtown. **Facility:** 4 units. 2 stories (no elevator), interior corridors.

LONG BEACH LODGE RESORT
(250)725-2442

 Contemporary Hotel $169-$639 **Address:** 1441 Pacific Rim Hwy V0R 2Z0 **Location:** 4.7 mi (7.5 km) s on Hwy 4. **Facility:** 61 units, some cottages. 2-3 stories, interior/exterior corridors. **Terms:** check-in 4 pm, 2 night minimum stay - seasonal and/or weekends, 7 day cancellation notice-fee imposed. **Amenities:** high-speed Internet, safes. **Dining:** Restaurant at Long Beach Lodge Resort, see separate listing. **Activities:** whirlpool, steamroom, exercise room. **Guest Services:** coin laundry.

PACIFIC SANDS BEACH RESORT
(250)725-3322

 Hotel $195-$750 **Address:** 1421 Pacific Rim Hwy V0R 2Z0 **Location:** 4.7 mi (7.5 km) s on Hwy 4. **Facility:** 77 kitchen units, some two and three bedrooms. 1-3 stories (no elevator), exterior corridors. **Terms:** check-in 4 pm, 2-3 night minimum stay - seasonal and/or weekends, 7 day cancellation notice-fee imposed. **Activities:** recreation programs in summer, hiking trails. **Guest Services:** coin laundry. **Free Special Amenities:** local telephone calls and newspaper.

SCHOONER MOTEL
250/725-3478

Motel $85-$245 **Address:** 315-321 Campbell St V0R 2Z0 **Location:** Campbell and 2nd sts; downtown. **Facility:** 18 units, some efficiencies. 2 stories (no elevator), exterior corridors. **Terms:** 14 day cancellation notice-fee imposed. **Guest Services:** coin laundry.

TOFINO MOTEL
250/725-2055

Motel $75-$185 **Address:** 542 Campbell St V0R 2Z0 **Location:** Campbell and 4th sts; downtown. **Facility:** 13 units, some two bedrooms. 2 stories (no elevator), exterior corridors. **Terms:** cancellation fee imposed.

WICKANINNISH INN
(250)725-3100

 Contemporary Hotel $300-$580 **Address:** 500 Osprey Ln at Chesterman Beach V0R 2Z0 **Location:** 2.7 mi (4.3 km) e on Hwy 4. Located in a quiet area. **Facility:** One of the property's West Coast-style buildings has been built on the rocks overlooking the ocean. Be sure to ask for a room in the original section that overlooks the rocky shoreline; you'll get a real show when the waves come crashing in during one of Tofino's wild winter storms. 75 units, some kitchens. 3 stories, interior corridors. **Parking:** on-site and valet. **Terms:** check-in 4 pm, 2 night minimum stay - seasonal and/or weekends, 14 day cancellation notice-fee imposed. **Amenities:** high-speed Internet, safes. **Dining:** The Pointe Restaurant, see separate listing. **Activities:** steamroom, exercise room, spa. **Free Special Amenities:** local telephone calls and high-speed Internet.

BLUE HERON RESTAURANT
250/725-3277

American. Casual Dining. $11-$37 **AAA Inspector Notes:** On the shores of Porpoise Bay, the restaurant treats patrons to wonderful views. The specialty is wonderful fresh seafood, as well as chicken and steak, but mostly it's the seafood that keeps people coming back. **Bar:** full bar. **Reservations:** suggested, for dinner. **Address:** 634 Campbell St V0R 2Z0 **Location:** 0.6 mi (1 km) s of downtown; in Weigh West Marine Resort Tofino.

THE POINTE RESTAURANT
250/725-3106

Pacific Northwest Fine Dining $16-$42 **AAA Inspector Notes:** Built above the rocks and jutting out into the ocean, this restaurant offers breathtaking scenery. In winter wild waves crash on the rocks right outside the windows. Since opening in 1996, the restaurant has focused mainly on Canadian West Coast cuisine that reflects the bounty and tastes of Vancouver Island, especially its fresh seafood and amazing selection of B.C. wines. Walk-ins are welcome at breakfast and lunch. **Bar:** full bar. **Reservations:** required, for dinner. **Address:** 500 Osprey Ln at Chesterman Beach V0R 2Z0 **Location:** 2.7 mi (4.3 km) e on Hwy 4; in Wickaninnish Inn. **Parking:** on-site and valet.

RESTAURANT AT LONG BEACH LODGE RESORT
250/725-2442

Pacific Northwest. Fine Dining. $12-$42 **AAA Inspector Notes:** The restaurant is located on the second floor of a lodge that's situated right along a stunning beach cove. Most tables offer wonderful views of the waves, the sandy beach and surfers in their black wet suits out in the distant waves. The restaurant is proud of its fresh, local and sustainable products, which are bought daily and directly from the highest quality farmers, ranchers and fishermen from the province of B.C., giving guests a true West Coast experience. **Bar:** full bar. **Reservations:** suggested, for dinner. **Address:** 1441 Pacific Rim Hwy V0R 2Z0 **Location:** 4.7 mi (7.5 km) s on Hwy 4; in Long Beach Lodge Resort.

SCHOONER RESTAURANT
250/725-3444

Pacific Northwest. Casual Dining. $20-$36 **AAA Inspector Notes:** Great food has been a part of this building since 1949. Ask about Morris the Ghost, who lived here in the early '70s and always made the chowder. Now you can sample tasty seafood caught locally, as the restaurant supports sustainable fishing practices, 100-percent free-range beef and free-range organic chicken. During the tourist season from spring to fall the restaurant is open for breakfast. **Bar:** full bar. **Reservations:** suggested, for dinner. **Address:** 331 Campbell St V0R 2Z0 **Location:** Corner of 2nd St; downtown.

SHELTER RESTAURANT
250/725-3353

Pacific Northwest. Casual Dining. $11-$33 **AAA Inspector Notes:** On the edge of town, the tastefully renovated old village house welcomes diners with regional cuisine featuring market produce and local seafood. Seating is offered by the stone fireplace in the lounge or in the candlelit upstairs loft. **Bar:** full bar. **Reservations:** suggested. **Address:** 601 Campbell St V0R 2Z0 **Location:** Jct Campbell and Gibson sts; downtown.

SOBO RESTAURANT
250/725-2341

Pacific Rim. Casual Dining. $7-$26 **AAA Inspector Notes:** Locals are quick to rave about the food, which was once prepared from an old catering truck parked in the Tofino Botanical Gardens. The eatery has a new home in town, and the truck has been retired. Diners can still order seasonal specials, which are displayed on a colorful chalkboard, or such daily features as killer fish tacos, organic bean tostadas, crispy shrimp cakes, soba noodle salad and Caesar salad. **Bar:** full bar. **Address:** 311 Neill St V0R 2Z0 **Location:** Corner of Neill and 1st sts; downtown.

SPOTTED BEAR BISTRO
250/725-2215

Pacific Northwest. Fine Dining. $19-$30 **AAA Inspector Notes:** Located in a shopping complex, this small, intimate bistro features wonderfully distinctive Pacific Northwest cuisine featuring fresh ingredients, local seafood, pasta, vegetarian dishes and some red meats such as veal and lamb. Due to limited seating, reservations are recommended. **Bar:** full bar. **Reservations:** required. **Address:** 101-120 4th St V0R 2Z0 **Location:** 4th and Campbell sts; downtown. **Parking:** on-site and street.

TRAIL (D-10) pop. 7,681, elev. 430m/1,410'

At City Hall a sculptured screen titled "City of Lead and Zinc" illustrates how Trail's mineral and industrial strength steadily developed since the discovery of gold and copper in the area about 1890. Hydroelectric dams along the Kootenay River power extensive mining and smelting operations, dominated by Teck Cominco Ltd. Enjoy free concerts at Gyro Park, 1090 Charles Lakes Dr., on Thursday evenings in July and August.

Trail and District Chamber of Commerce and Visitor Centre: 1199 Bay Ave., Suite 200, Trail, BC, Canada V1R 4A4. **Phone:** (250) 368-3144, or (877) 636-9569 within British Columbia.

Self-guiding tours: Brochures for walking tours are available at the chamber of commerce.

TECK TRAIL OPERATIONS INTERPRETIVE CENTRE is downtown at 1199 Bay Ave., Suite 200. The center has hands-on science exhibits that explain the processes of smelting and refining and how metals affect our everyday life. Tours of one of the largest lead-zinc smelters in the world depart from the interpretive center.

Long pants, long-sleeved shirts and closed shoes are required for the tours; cameras and video equipment are prohibited. Individuals with pacemakers should not attend. Full mobility is required on the plant portion of the tour. All visitors must provide their own transportation to and from the interpretive center to the plant. **Time:** Allow 2 hours minimum. **Hours:** Center open daily 9-5, July-Aug.; Mon.-Fri. 9-5, rest of year. Tours depart Mon.-Fri. at 10, July-Aug.; by appointment rest of year. Closed major holidays. Phone ahead to confirm schedule. **Cost:** Free. Ages 0-11 are not permitted on tours. **Phone:** (250) 362-7722.

BEST WESTERN PLUS COLUMBIA RIVER HOTEL
(250)368-3355

WWW Hotel $130-$170

AAA Benefit: Members save up to 20%, plus 10% bonus points with Best Western Rewards®.

Address: 1001 Rossland Ave V1R 3N7 **Location:** On Hwy 3B; just n of center. **Facility:** 58 units. 4 stories, interior corridors. **Amenities:** high-speed Internet. **Activities:** whirlpool, exercise room. **Guest Services:** valet laundry. **Free Special Amenities:** local telephone calls and high-speed Internet.

SAVE 🍴 🍸 BIZ 🛜 ✕ 🛗 🖥

WHERE TO EAT

COLANDER RESTAURANT
250/364-1816

W Italian. Family Dining. $6-$21 **AAA Inspector Notes:** At lunch, Colander offers a small pasta buffet and items such as burgers, subs and sandwiches, while the dinner menu is more extensive. The menu also lists regional beers. While the atmosphere is pleasant, the eatery serves the masses, so guests may have to flag down the waitress for any special requests, like refills or dessert. To-go containers are available for a fee. **Bar:** full bar. **Reservations:** suggested, for dinner. **Address:** 1475 Cedar Ave V1R 4C5 **Location:** Center. **Parking:** street only. L D

TUMBLER RIDGE pop. 2,710

TREND MOUNTAIN HOTEL & CONFERENCE CENTER
250/242-2000

WWW **Extended Stay Hotel.** Rates not provided. **Address:** 375 Southgate V0C 2W0 **Location:** Hwy 29, just n on Monkman Way, then 0.5 mi (0.9 km) ne. **Facility:** 103 units, some efficiencies and kitchens. 4 stories, interior corridors. **Parking:** winter plug-ins. **Amenities:** high-speed Internet. **Activities:** exercise room. **Guest Services:** coin laundry.

🍴 🍸 CALL 🛗 BIZ 📺 🛗 🖥 🖥 / SOME UNITS FEE 🐾

UCLUELET (I-3) pop. 1,627
• Restaurants p. 340

On Barkley Sound, Ucluelet was named for an Indian word meaning "safe harbor." Charter boats for salmon fishing, whale watching, skin diving and nature excursions are available; phone the chamber of commerce. Lady Rose Marine Services makes round trips between Port Alberni and Ucluelet June through September *(see attraction listing in Port Alberni p. 303).*

He Tin Kis Park allows visitors to experience a Canadian rain forest and follow a boardwalk trail that leads to the ocean. The 5-kilometre (3-mi.) Wild Pacific Trail passes a lighthouse en route to cliffside ocean views.

Ucluelet Visitor Centre: 2791 Pacific Rim Hwy., Ucluelet, BC, Canada V0R 3A0. **Phone:** (250) 726-4600.

BLACK ROCK OCEANFRONT RESORT
(250)726-4800

WWW **Contemporary Hotel** $169-$559 **Address:** 596 Marine Dr V0R 3A0 **Location:** 1 mi (1.6 km) e on Peninsula Rd, just s on Matterson Rd, then just w. **Facility:** 133 units, some two bedrooms, efficiencies and kitchens. 2-4 stories, interior/exterior corridors. **Terms:** check-in 4 pm, 7 day cancellation notice-fee imposed, resort fee. **Amenities:** high-speed Internet, safes. **Dining:** Fetch Restaurant, see separate listing. **Pool(s):** heated outdoor. **Activities:** whirlpools, exercise room, spa.

ECO 🍴 🍸 CALL 🛗 🚣 🛜 ✕ 🎿 🛗 🖥 🖥 / SOME UNITS FEE 🐾

THORNTON MOTEL
250/726-7725

WW **Motel** $83-$190 **Address:** 1861 Peninsula Rd V0R 3A0 **Location:** E on Peninsula Rd; at Bay St. **Facility:** 16 units, some two bedrooms and efficiencies. 2 stories (no elevator), exterior corridors. **Terms:** cancellation fee imposed. **Guest Services:** coin laundry.

🛗 🛜 ✕ 🎿 🛗 🖥 / SOME UNITS 🖥

WHERE TO EAT

FETCH RESTAURANT 250/726-4800
▼▼▼▼ Pacific Northwest. Fine Dining. $10-$39 **AAA Inspector Notes:** Floor-to-ceiling windows overlook the stunning ocean, where crashing waves wash over the rocky shoreline. The West Coast-inspired menu features a wide selection of West Coast fish, along with hearty meat dishes of beef and chicken. The extensive wine cellar offer many bottle choices. **Bar:** full bar. **Reservations:** suggested, for dinner. **Address:** 596 Marine Dr V0R 3A0 **Location:** 1 mi (1.6 km) e on Peninsula Rd, just s on Matterson Rd, then just w; in Black Rock Oceanfront Resort. B L D CALL 🅼 🄰🄲

MATTERSON HOUSE RESTAURANT 250/726-2200
▼▼ American. Casual Dining. $6-$25 **AAA Inspector Notes:** The small restaurant is located in a converted older house situated along the main road through town. Open for breakfast on the weekends only, the restaurant offers a menu that features regular fare, such as wonderfully hearty soups, huge sandwiches for lunch, and more complex dinner entrées. **Bar:** full bar. **Reservations:** suggested, for dinner. **Address:** 1682 Peninsula Rd V0R 3A0 **Location:** Just e. L D 🄰🄲

OFFSHORE SEAFOOD RESTAURANT 250/726-2111
▼▼ Seafood. Casual Dining. $9-$25 **AAA Inspector Notes:** Just before entering the township you'll find this restaurant serving fresh seafood and sushi. The eclectic menu is sure to please everyone. **Bar:** full bar. **Address:** 2082 Peninsula Rd V0R 3A0 **Location:** At Forbes Rd; west end of town. L D CALL 🅼

VALEMOUNT (F-6) pop. 1,020, elev. 792m/2,600'

Valemount, the valley in the mountains, offers many activities for outdoor enthusiasts. The village, where the Rocky, Cariboo and Monashee mountain ranges meet, is popular for both summer and winter pursuits, including hiking, rafting, skiing and snowmobiling. The area is rich with birds and other wildlife. Off Hwy. 16 is Mount Terry Fox Provincial Park. A viewing area affords vistas of the peak named for the late athlete.

Valemount Visitor Centre: 825 Cranberry Lake Rd., P.O. Box 146, Valemount, BC, Canada V0E 2Z0. **Phone:** (250) 566-9893.

GEORGE HICKS REGIONAL PARK is off Hwy. 5 at 785 Cranberry Lake Rd. The site offers a bird's-eye view of Chinook salmon as they near the end of a 1,280-kilometre (768-mi.) upstream trip from mid-August to mid-September. **Hours:** Daily mid-May to mid-Sept. **Cost:** Donations. **Phone:** (250) 566-9893.

MOUNT ROBSON PROVINCIAL PARK is on Hwy. 16. Mount Robson, at 3,954 metres (12,972 ft.) is the highest peak in the Canadian Rockies. Other park highlights include glacier-fed lakes, valleys, canyons, waterfalls, rivers and streams. More than 180 species of birds reside here along with deer, moose, bears, elk and caribou. Fishing, camping, horseback riding and hiking are just a few of the outdoor activities to be enjoyed.

Scenic views abound on the many walking and hiking trails. A visitor center is at the Mount Robson viewpoint. *See Recreation Areas Chart.* **Hours:**

▼ *See AAA listing p. 341* ▼

Park open daily 24 hours. Visitor center open May-Sept. **Cost:** Donations. **Phone:** (250) 566-4325.

ROBSON HELIMAGIC INC. tours depart from the Yellowhead Helicopters hangar, 5 km (3 mi.) n. on Hwy. 5 to 3010 Selwyn Rd. Helicopters take passengers on 12-36 minute tours of the Valemount and Mount Robson areas, providing breathtaking views of glaciers, snow-covered mountains, alpine meadows, valleys, waterfalls, lakes and rivers.

Heli-skiing, heli-snowshoeing and heli-snowboarding also are offered in winter. Summer activities are available. **Hours:** Daily 8-7. Phone ahead to confirm schedule. **Cost:** $99-$219. **Phone:** (250) 566-4700 or (877) 454-7400.

R.W. STARRATT WILDLIFE SANCTUARY is 1 km (.6 mi.) s. on Hwy. 5. The refuge is home to more than 140 species of songbirds, waterfowl and other animals. Informational signs line a trail to two viewing platforms. There are 7 kilometres (4 mi.) of trails and walkways in the sanctuary, or if you prefer your sight-seeing from a boat, you can canoe through.

Time: Allow 30 minutes minimum. **Hours:** Daily 9-9, July-Aug.; 9-8, mid-June through June 30; 10-6, June 1 to mid-June; 9-5, Sept. 1-Labour Day; 10-5, late May-May 31 and day after Labour Day-Sept. 30; 10-4, early May to mid-May. Phone ahead to confirm schedule. **Cost:** Free. **Phone:** (250) 566-4846.

RECREATIONAL ACTIVITIES
White-water Rafting
- **Mount Robson Whitewater Rafting Co.** is 19 km (12 mi.) n. on Hwy. 5, then 3 km (1.8 mi.) e. on Hwy. 16. Other activities are offered. **Hours:** Departures daily, early June to mid-Sept. **Phone:** (250) 566-4879 or (888) 566-7238.
- **Stellar Descents White Water Rafting** is 19 km (12 mi.) n. on Hwy. 5, then 1 km (.6 mi.) w. on Hwy. 16 at the Tete Jaune Lodge. Other activities are offered. **Hours:** Departures daily 8:30-8:30, June-Sept. **Phone:** (250) 566-0040 or (866) 569-0188.

BEST WESTERN PLUS VALEMOUNT INN & SUITES
(250)566-0086

Hotel
$123-$176

AAA Benefit: Members save up to 20%, plus 10% bonus points with Best Western Rewards®.

Address: 1950 Hwy 5 S V0E 2Z0 **Location:** 0.9 mi (1.5 km) s on Hwy 5 (Yellowhead Hwy). Located near wildlife sanctuary. **Facility:** 77 units. 2 stories (no elevator), interior corridors. **Parking:** winter plug-ins. **Terms:** check-in 4 pm, cancellation fee imposed. **Amenities:** high-speed Internet. **Pool(s):** heated indoor. **Activities:** whirlpool, waterslide, hiking trails, limited exercise equipment. **Guest Services:** coin laundry. **Free Special Amenities:** high-speed Internet and use of on-premises laundry facilities. (See ad p. 340.)

RAMADA VALEMOUNT (250)566-8222

Hotel $105-$139 **Address:** 1501 Swift Creek Rd V0E 2Z0 **Location:** Just e of Hwy 5 (Yellowhead Hwy). **Facility:** 67 units, some efficiencies and kitchens. 2 stories, interior corridors. **Parking:** winter plug-ins. **Amenities:** safes. **Pool(s):** heated indoor. **Activities:** whirlpool, waterslide, exercise room. **Guest Services:** coin laundry.

WHERE TO EAT

CARIBOU GRILL 250/566-8244

American. Casual Dining. $10-$27 **AAA Inspector Notes:** The restaurant prepares casual fare about five blocks off Highway 97 in a beautiful log cabin toward the end of the main street. The menu, centered on Canadian cuisine, features traditional pasta, venison, Arctic caribou, vegetarian plates and fresh prime rib daily. Expect attentive, friendly service and original log house décor. **Bar:** full bar. **Address:** 1002 5th Ave V0C 2Z0 **Location:** Hwy 5 (Yellowhead Hwy), 0.6 mi (1 km) e at 5th Ave.

THE GATHERING TREE 250/566-0154

Sandwiches. Quick Serve. $6-$8 **AAA Inspector Notes:** With its charming, warm décor, this little spot offers some delicious made-to-order sandwiches, wraps and panini with a good choice of toppings. There's also tasty soup and lovely, homemade cakes and squares. After eating, make sure to browse through the attached gift shop. **Address:** 1150 5th Ave V0E 2Z0 **Location:** Center. **Parking:** street only.

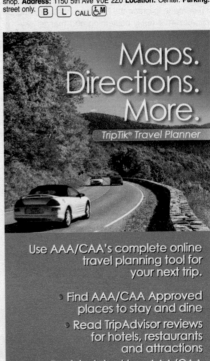

Vancouver

Then & Now

You're hiking along a wide, bark-mulched trail through an old-growth forest of towering Western red cedar, Douglas fir and Western hemlock. Salmonberry, huckleberry, bog buckbean and other native plants grow together in one luxurious tangle. A raccoon ambles by, giving you an inquisitive look. A goose honks in the distance. You stop and ask out loud, "Wait a minute—am I really in a city?" That question is answered a few minutes later when you emerge from Stanley Park to the hustle and bustle of Georgia Street.

There's no denying the beauty of Vancouver's natural setting. Vistas of green coastal mountains and the deep blue Strait of Georgia were tailor-made to grace the front of a postcard. And downtown is really something of a marvel: skyscrapers, human hubbub and quiet, tree-lined residential streets all coexisting harmoniously in one tightly packed urban cityscape. If that

pocket description sounds a bit like San Francisco, well, it's an apt comparison—but there really is no place like Vancouver.

No doubt the southwestern British Columbia wilderness impressed Capt. George Vancouver. An officer in the British Royal Navy, he sailed into Burrard Inlet on June 13, 1792, while searching for the Northwest Passage, the sea route that connects the Atlantic and Pacific oceans. Vancouver named the inlet after his friend Sir Harry Burrard, a member of Parliament, but lent his own moniker to the city and the large island that lies between the mainland and the Pacific.

Brockton Point Lighthouse, Stanley Park

Vancouver was incorporated in 1886, quite a young city given its present-day status. A Canadian Pacific Railway passenger train arrived the following year, showering exuberant spectators with soot and cinders. By the 1890s trans-Pacific shipping inaugurated the city as a major world port, and the future was looking rosy indeed.

That era produced colorful characters like John Deighton, aka "Gassy Jack," a saloon owner who set up shop in Gastown, the city's oldest section and a popular tourist hangout. The name is a reference not to excessive flatulence but to Deighton's vaunted reputation for tall-tale bluster. His likeness stands at the circle where Water, Alexander, Powell and Carrall streets converge, and having your picture snapped in front of the old salt is a prime Vancouver photo op.

Mandarin and Cantonese are the mother tongues in almost a third of Vancouver's homes, and only San Francisco's Chinatown is bigger. The Millennium Gate at Pender and Taylor

(Continued on p. 344.)

Destination Vancouver

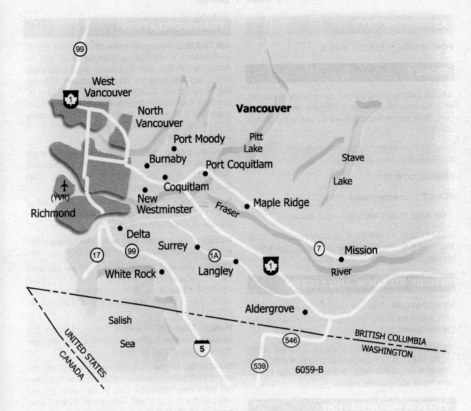

This map shows cities in the Vancouver vicinity where you will find attractions, hotels and restaurants. Cities are listed alphabetically in this book on the following pages.

Fast Facts

ABOUT THE CITY

POP: 603,502 ■ **ELEV:** 3 m/10 ft.

MONEY

SALES TAX: British Columbia has a single tax known as a harmonized sales tax (HST); the rate is 12 percent. Hotel accommodations are subject to the harmonized tax.

WHOM TO CALL

EMERGENCY: 911

POLICE (non-emergency): (604) 717-3321

TIME AND TEMPERATURE: (604) 664-9010

HOSPITALS: Mount Saint Joseph Hospital, (604) 874-1141 ■ St. Paul's Hospital, (604) 682-2344 ■ Vancouver General Hospital, (604) 875-4111.

WHERE TO LOOK AND LISTEN

NEWSPAPERS: The two major daily newspapers, both published in the morning, are the *Province* and the *Vancouver Sun*.

RADIO: Vancouver radio stations CBU-AM (690) ■ CBU-FM (105.7) ■ CHQM-FM (103.5) ■ CKCL-FM (104.9) ■ CKLG-FM (96.9) ■ and CKWX-AM (1130) have news and weather reports.

VISITOR INFORMATION

Vancouver Tourist InfoCentre: 200 Burrard St., Plaza Level, Vancouver, BC, Canada V6C 3L6. **Phone:** (604) 683-2000.

Maps, lodging reservations and literature about attractions as well as tickets for tours are available at the Vancouver Tourist InfoCentre which is open daily 8:30-6, Victoria Day weekend to mid-Sept.; Mon.-Sat. 8:30-5, rest of year.

TRANSPORTATION

AIR TRAVEL: Vancouver International Airport (YVR), in Richmond, is reached via Granville Street and the Arthur Lang Bridge, then Sea Island Way, which leads into Grant McConachie Way. Vancouver Airporter buses run every 20 minutes 8:55 a.m.-9:25 p.m. One-way bus service departs most major downtown hotels every 30 minutes. The fare is $13.50, round trip $21; phone (604) 946-8866 or (800) 668-3141. Taxis average $26 one-way.

RENTAL CARS: Hertz, at 1128 Seymour St., offers discounts to AAA and CAA members; phone (604) 606-4711, (800) 263-0600 in Canada, or (800) 654-3131 in North America.

RAIL SERVICE: The Via Rail passenger train terminal is at 1150 Station St.; phone (888) 842-7245 in Canada or in the United States.

BUSES: The bus terminal is at 1150 Station St.; phone (604) 482-8747 or (800) 661-8747.

TAXIS: Fares start at $2.75, plus $1.50 per kilometre (.6 mi.). Companies include Black Top, (604) 731-1111 ■ MacLure's, (604) 731-9211 ■ Yellow Cab, (604) 681-1111 ■ and Vancouver Taxi, (604) 255-5111.

PUBLIC TRANSPORTATION: TransLink offers bus service as well as SeaBus and SkyTrain service. *See Public Transportation for details.*

BOATS: BC Ferries links Vancouver Island with the rest of the province. Nanaimo and Sunshine Coast ferries leave from Horseshoe Bay, 21 kilometres (13 mi.) west of the city in West Vancouver. From Tsawwassen south of Vancouver automobile/passenger ferries make frequent trips to the southern Gulf Islands, Nanaimo and Swartz Bay, north of Victoria; Vancouver-Victoria bus service is available on most sailings.

For schedules phone the British Columbia Automobile Association, (604) 268-5555, British Columbia Ferries Information Centre, (250) 386-3431 outside British Columbia, (888) 223-3779 in British Columbia, or Tourism Vancouver, (604) 683-2000.

(Continued from p. 342.)
streets is a symbolic entryway that incorporates both eastern and western symbols. Between 1890 and 1920 Asian immigrants settled on back streets like Shanghai Alley off Pender Street; wall panels tell the story of their lives. Holding out your arms is almost enough to embrace the pencil-thin Sam Kee Building at 8 Pender St., which is a mere 6 feet wide.

Just as the city is a cosmopolitan blend of cultures, Vancouverites represent a melting pot of nationalities. The original inhabitants of coastal British Columbia were the Northwestern peoples, and their descendants live in urban areas as well as reserve communities located within ancestral territories. Diversity is the keynote, whether preserved in street names like Barclay and Granville or neighborhoods like Greektown and Little India.

It's only fitting, then, that Vancouver hosted the 2010 Winter Olympics. Besides being the Winter Olympic debut for such diverse nations as the Cayman Islands, Ghana, Montenegro, Pakistan and Peru, these games provided a storybook ending when the Canadian men's hockey team triumphed over rivals the United States to not only win the gold medal on home soil—but 7 minutes into overtime.

Not bad for a former lumber town, eh?

Must Do: AAA Editor's Picks

- One of the world's great outdoor food markets, **Granville Island Public Market** is the place to go for a slice of Vancouver life as well as the freshest fruits, vegetables, cheeses, meats, candy, baked goods and flowers.

- Enjoy fabulous waterside views while strolling, bicycling or in-line skating around the perimeter sea wall of **Stanley Park**. Or tour the park in a horse-powered trolley provided by **Stanley Park Horse-drawn Tours**. The park also has tennis courts, a pool, a golf course, woodland trails, playgrounds, totem poles and a miniature steam train. Beaches, gardens and woodland glades complete this 405-hectare (1,000-acre) urban sanctuary.

- Adorable white beluga whales steal the show at **Vancouver Aquarium Marine Science Centre** in Stanley Park; competing for attention are the center's thousands of marine animals including sea lions, sharks and walruses as well as rain forest creatures such as iguanas and crocodiles. Go behind the scenes in close encounters with dolphins, belugas, sea turtles, Steller sea lions and sea otters.

- Downtown's **Robson Street** beckons shoppers with its trendy designer boutiques, bookstores, jewelry shops and more. When you need a break, grab a seat and a cappuccino at a bistro or coffee shop and watch the world go by.

- On a clear day, you can see forever at **Grouse Mountain** in North Vancouver; the Skyride, an aerial cable car, presents a breathtaking view of Vancouver and the harbor. You can spend the day here and not run out of things to do: Ski down the mountain, zipline above an alpine rain forest, go paragliding or go on a sleigh ride, strap on snowshoes for a wintry hike, watch lumberjacks show off their axe and log-rolling skills, visit grizzly bears and grey wolves at a refuge and get a 360-degree view of Vancouver from the top of a 20-story-high wind turbine. Even those without skiing skills can enjoy traveling along trails and enjoying sensational views in a chauffeured Sno-Limo. After you've worked up an appetite, feast on fine cuisine at The Observatory or British Columbian dishes at Altitudes Bistro.

- Spot pods of orcas and other sea creatures on a scenic whale-watching cruise. Both **Steveston Seabreeze Adventures** and **Vancouver Whale Watch** in nearby Richmond also offer the opportunity to hear whales vocalize through the use of hydrophones; see marine animals like sea lions, porpoises and eagles; and travel through the Fraser River Delta, Strait of Georgia and the Gulf Islands.

- Dine in restaurants that rival New York's; an array of multicultural cuisines is available, but don't leave town without savoring mouth-watering Pacific Northwest and Asian cuisine featuring freshly caught seafood. Try such favorites as **CinCin**, **The Fish House in Stanley Park**, **Glowbal Grill Steaks & Satay**, **Joe Fortes Seafood & Chop House** and **Rain City Grill**.

- Discover one of Vancouver's trendiest neighborhoods; **Yaletown** has earned comparisons to New York's SoHo and rightfully so. Once a warehouse district, the area now attracts the young and hip with its of-the-moment shops, galleries, loft apartments, pubs and outdoor cafés.

- Confront your fear of heights with a walk through the tops of evergreens at **Capilano Suspension Bridge Park** in North Vancouver; the 137-metre (450-foot) bridge sways 70 metres (230 ft.) above the Capilano River Canyon. You can also take a guided tour on the forest floor, view the Totem Park and learn about its indigenous culture through storytelling and weaving and beadwork demonstrations.

Take a stroll on the Capilano Suspension Bridge

Vancouver 1-day Itinerary

AAA editors suggest these activities for a great short vacation experience. Those staying in the area for a longer visit can access a 3-day itinerary at AAA.com/TravelGuide.

Morning

- Kick off your tour at the **Vancouver Lookout at Harbour Centre Tower**. A glass elevator zips to the top of this 167-metre-tall (553-ft.) building, where 360-degree views of the skyline, the North Shore Mountains, English Bay, Coal Harbour and Stanley Park take your breath away.
- Head east on W. Georgia Street, then east on W. Pender Street to North America's second-largest **Chinatown**, between Carrall and Gore streets. Snap up some souvenirs at colorful emporiums; choose from Chinese curios, jewelry and fashions as well as bamboo, jade, brass and silk goods.
- Escape the bustling crowds at Chinatown's **Dr. Sun Yat-Sen Classical Chinese Garden**. Experience peace and harmony in this Ming Dynasty-style garden accented with pagodas, plum trees, bamboo and jade-hued ponds.

Afternoon

- Take your pick of three museums in Vanier Park, home to the **Museum of Vancouver**, **H.R. MacMillan Space Centre** and the **Vancouver Maritime Museum**, where you can tour a 1960s submarine and a 1940s schooner, the first vessel to circumnavigate North America.
- The Museum of Vancouver has a wealth of exhibits focusing on the region's art and history. Or stargaze at the H.R. MacMillan Space Centre's planetarium.
- Grab lunch at **Vera's Burger Shack**, half a kilometre (.3 mi.) south of Vanier Park on Cornwall Avenue. Expect a well-worth-it wait; the award-winning hamburgers are so popular they can't make them fast enough.
- Explore some of downtown's distinctive neighborhoods. You'll find funky boutiques, bookstores and coffee shops on Kitsilano's West Fourth Avenue, while antique shops, art galleries, pubs and street vendors line Gastown's cobblestone streets. Trendy Yaletown houses swank furniture and clothing shops, cafés and hip nightclubs. Robson Street, between Burrard and Jervis streets, has such mall chains as Banana Republic and Zara.

Evening

- For your evening repast, choose from an array of fine restaurants, many with picturesque waterfront views. Some of the best include **The Sandbar Seafood Restaurant** on Granville Island, or **C Restaurant** just across the Granville Street Bridge.
- After dinner, catch a hockey game when the Canucks take to the ice at **General Motors Place**, 800 Griffiths Way.
- Do you love the nightlife? Vancouver clubs run the gamut from frenetic discos, intimate lounges and swanky cabarets to beery pubs, sports bars and stadium concerts. Downtown's

Dr. Sun Yat-Sen Classical Chinese Garden

Granville Street is where the 24-hour party people go. Try **The Roxy** or **Caprice Nightclub** for starters.

- Gastown boasts **The Post Modern**, **Shine** and **Sonar**, all places to drink, dance and be merry. In Kitsilano, **The Cellar Restaurant and Jazz Club** hosts local and international talent. Watch flamenco dancers at **Kino Café** on Cambie Street; sip some sangria and clap along to the music.

- You'll find hipper-than-thou hangouts in Yaletown, home base for the city's young, stylish professionals. **Bar None** on Hamilton Street is a SoHo-style spot with a cigar lounge and martini bar, while homey **Yaletown Brewing Company**, with a fireplace and pool tables, is popular with the 9-to-5 crowd for microbrews and burgers. On Seymour Street is au courant **AuBAR**; Vancouver is known as Hollywood North and you may find celebs here. Go four blocks east to **The Shark Club**, a sports bar in the **Sandman Hotel Vancouver City Centre** on W. Georgia Street; masculine yet modern décor, pool tables, a shark tank, big-screen TVs and hockey fans fill the joint. After 10 p.m., live DJs and go-go dancers get the party started.

- Not a club-hopper? Wrap up your day with a dinner cruise provided by **Harbour Cruises**. Marvel at downtown's nighttime skyline ablaze with lights as you're treated to a West Coast-style buffet and live music. Watch an awe-inspiring sunset over the Pacific Ocean and check out the picture-postcard scenery, including the snow-sprinkled North Shore Mountains and West Vancouver's shoreline.

Arriving
By Car

Hwy. 1 and hwys. 1A and 7 are the major east-west routes to Vancouver. To reach downtown on the Trans-Canada Highway, use the First Avenue exit or continue to Hastings Street.

Hwy. 99 to S.W. Marine West becomes the major downtown artery, Granville Street. Before becoming a city street, Hwy. 99 begins its journey as I-5 at the Mexican border and crosses through California and the Pacific Northwest.

Getting Around
Street System

All streets and avenues in downtown Vancouver are named; many are one-way. Outside the business section, east-west avenues are numbered beginning with First Avenue, and north-south streets are named. Addresses begin at Ontario-Carrall streets for all east-west numbering and at Powell-Dundas streets for all north-south numbering.

The downtown peninsula is connected to western Vancouver by the Burrard, Granville and Cambie bridges and to North Vancouver and West Vancouver by the Lions Gate and the Iron Workers Memorial (Second Narrows) bridges.

Rush hours are 6-9:30 a.m. and 3-6:30 p.m. Right turns on red are permitted after a stop, unless otherwise posted; drivers must yield to pedestrians and vehicles in the intersection and to city buses pulling into traffic.

Parking

On-street parking, controlled by meter, is restricted on many thoroughfares during rush hours; violators' cars will be towed. Off-street parking is available in lots and garages at rates ranging from $1.25 per half-hour to $11 or more per day. Parking in a school zone between 8 and 5 on any school day is strictly prohibited unless otherwise posted.

Public Transportation

TransLink offers bus service to points throughout Vancouver and to all suburban areas; it also offers SeaBus and SkyTrain service as well as the West Coast Express commuter rail.

SeaBus service conveys commuters between North Vancouver and the city of Vancouver, connecting with the bus system at the foot of Granville Street.

SkyTrain, Vancouver's light rail rapid transit system, runs from Waterfront Station through downtown Vancouver to the suburbs of Burnaby and New Westminster and across the Fraser River to the suburb of Surrey.

SkyTrain's newest line, the Canada Line, connects downtown, Richmond and Sea Island (Vancouver International Airport). In addition to stations in those locations, it also includes an underground tunnel running south from downtown's Waterfront Station; park-and-ride facilities; bus exchanges; and elevated guideways. The 19-kilometre (12-mi.) line has 16 stations, including stops at Vancouver City Centre, Olympic Village, Broadway-City Hall, Marine Drive, Vancouver International Airport and four Richmond locations. The train ride from downtown to the airport takes 26 minutes.

Trains operate every 5 minutes Mon.-Fri. 5:30 a.m.-midnight, Sat. 6:50 a.m.-12:30 a.m., Sun. 7:50 a.m.-11:30 p.m. Fares are the same for any Translink service. A 1-zone fare Monday through Friday until 6:30 p.m. is $2.50, a 2-zone fare is $3.75 and a 3-zone fare is $5; for ages 5-13 and 65+ a 1-zone fare is $1.75, a 2-zone fare is $2.50 and a 3-zone fare is $3.50. The fare for weekdays after 6:30 p.m. and Saturday, Sunday and holidays for all zones is $2.50; for ages 5-13 and 65+ the fare for all zones is $1.75. A trip to or from the airport adds an additional $2.50.

Every SkyTrain station has information panels. A 1-day pass, available from SkyTrain and SeaBus ticket machines, Safeway food stores and 7-11 stores, costs $9; for ages 5-13 and 65+ the cost is $7. If you pay by cash on buses, exact change is required. Phone (604) 953-3333 Mon.-Sat. 6 a.m.-12:30 a.m., Sun. and holidays 8 a.m.-11 p.m. for more information.

Aquabus Ltd., (604) 689-5858, provides ferry service between Granville Island, Hornby Street, Yaletown, Stamps Landing and Science World at TELUS World of Science daily 7 a.m.-8 p.m. (10-6 in summer). Times vary according to destination. Fare ranges from $4-$6. The Aquabus from Granville Island to Hornby Street is equipped to carry bicycles for an extra 50c.

Daily bus service between Vancouver International Airport and Whistler is provided by Whistler

Lions Gate Bridge

Gastown shopping area

Skylynx. Passengers can be picked up and dropped off at major Vancouver and Whistler lodgings; reservations are required. Phone (604) 662-7575 or (800) 661-1725 for information.

Shopping

When you set out on a Vancouver shopping expedition be sure to bring along the AAA street map, because you're definitely going to want to hang out in every one of this town's cool and distinctively different urban neighborhoods.

The **West End** is as good a starting point as any. Denman Street anchors this area of leafy blocks and old apartment buildings backed up by downtown's office high-rises, with English Bay and Stanley Park at its doorstep. Sidewalk restaurants and cafes, specialty shops and the 30-odd stores of **Denman Place Mall** fill the six blocks of Denman between Davie and Robson streets.

Yaletown, reached via Davie Street, is the *de rigueur* downtown residential address for successful young professionals (just look at all those glass-walled condo towers). This former 19th-century rail yard district has morphed into an uber-stylish urban enclave; the industrial brick warehouses of yore are now hip clothing boutiques and designer furniture outlets.

Multilevel **Chintz & Company** (950 Homer St.) has a dazzling assemblage of interior design furnishings and accessories; browsing here is sensory overload. Art galleries are concentrated along Homer and Mainland streets; the **Coastal Peoples Fine Arts Gallery** (1024 Mainland St.) has an excellent collection of Northwest Coast Native artwork. Yaletown's many dog owners shop for trendy canine

accessories at **The Dog & Hydrant** (1146 Pacific Blvd.).

Robson Street, however, is downtown's shopping central. Stand at the intersection of Robson and Burrard on any given day and it's a sea of shopping bag-toting humanity. From Burrard up to Jervis Street Robson offers an uninterrupted stretch of window gazing: men's and women's fashions and accessories, shoes, jewelry, eyewear, gifts, chocolates, cosmetics and luggage, plus more restaurants than you can shake a stick at. For high-quality outdoor wear go to **Roots**, a popular Canadian chain. There are two locations, one for adults (1001 Robson St.) and one for kids (1153 Robson St.).

Very touristy but always enjoyable **Gastown**, the oldest section of the city, runs for several blocks along Water Street. The atmosphere is turn-of-the-20th-century renovated, with handsome brick buildings and white-globed lamp posts bedecked with flowery hanging baskets. There are lots of art galleries, antique shops and places to buy Canadian souvenirs. But Gastown isn't all about maple candy or a moose in a can; trendy home furnishings stores sell sleekly contemporary furniture by well-known Canadian and international designers.

There's a **Coastal Peoples Fine Arts Gallery** here as well (312 Water St.). Visit the **Jeffrey Boone Gallery** (140-1 E. Cordova St.) and the **Canvas Gallery** (99 Powell St.), which is associated with a popular Gastown nightspot, the **Canvas Lounge**. **Urbanity** (207 Abbott St.) sells beautiful knit sweaters, coats and blankets. There also are specialty shops like **Button Button** (318 Homer St.), with buttons in all shapes and sizes from around the world, and **Kites on Clouds** (131 Water St.), which stocks cool windsocks and mobiles as well as kites.

Walk a few blocks down Carrall Street into **Chinatown** *(see attraction listing)*, another neighborhood made for sidewalk exploration. You'll probably look rather than buy, since most of the businesses are where residents do their shopping. The produce and food markets lining Keefer and Main streets are fascinating, with unusual vegetables and bins full of dried fish, mushrooms and other foodstuffs. You'll also find a couple of jewelry shops selling bead necklaces and various trinkets.

Note: While the main thoroughfares in Gastown and Chinatown are fun to visit during the day, use big-city common sense regarding any encounters with panhandlers and street people, and avoid wandering around side streets after dark.

Downtown certainly isn't the only place to shop. In **Kitsilano**, along the south shore of English Bay, the blocks of West 4th Avenue between Fir and Larch streets are filled with grocers, wine shops and stores selling fashions, sportswear and sports gear from bikes to skis to snowboards.

Also within "Kits," the 10-block stretch of Granville Street between 6th and 16th avenues—dubbed **South Granville**—is where old-money families do their shopping; think expensive clothing boutiques, upscale furniture retailers and a plethora of home accessories stores like **18 Karat**, 3039 Granville St. (at 14th Avenue W.).

Much more down to earth is **Commercial Drive**, east of Kitsilano via Broadway E. From Venables Street south to Broadway is one of Vancouver's funkiest shopping experiences. Most of the shops and businesses are owner-operated; chains are few, which means that it's really fun to explore. Hit "the Drive" on a Saturday or Sunday afternoon. The heart of Commercial Drive is between Venables Street and 6th Avenue E. Books, CDs, vintage clothing and unusual gifts are all good bets.

Punjabi Market, in South Vancouver's Sunset neighborhood, is a small commercial district (along Main Street between 48th and 51st avenues) that serves the city's Indo-Canadian community and draws tourists as well. Restaurants and Indian businesses (grocers, sweet and spice shops, jewelry and fabric stores, Hindi video rentals) line Main Street. Several store windows feature mannequins outfitted in flowing, multicolored saris. Pick up some incense or a silk scarf.

You could easily spend an entire day doing **Granville Island**, but shoppers and foodies should focus on the **Granville Island Public Market**. The big building is crammed with vendors: produce, meat, seafood, baked goods, coffee and a head-spinning array of specialty foods. Take advantage of fresh B.C. salmon, artisanal cheeses and ripe, regionally grown fruit. Have lunch here, too; takeaway fast food counters offer Asian, Mexican, Indian, sushi, pizza and just about everything else.

There also are plenty of shops outside the market selling regionally produced art, food, jewelry, clothing, kids' toys and the like. And don't drive—it's much easier to take the False Creek Ferry. It's a 10-minute ride to Granville Island from the Aquatic Centre dock just off Beach Drive in the West End (ferries also depart from the dock at the foot of Davie Street in Yaletown).

Another popular destination is the **Lonsdale Quay Market**, at the foot of Lonsdale Avenue in North Vancouver. The lower level is a fresh market with vendors selling produce, seafood, baked goods and delicatessen items; specialty boutiques are on the upper level. Get a crab roll, fish and chips or a panini sandwich from one of the numerous stands at the international food bar and enjoy it outside on the dock, which has a great view of downtown and the harbor (don't feed the seagulls; they'll snitch a bite at any opportunity). There's a parkade for market customers (2 hours of free parking with proof of purchase, $1.50 per additional hour), but it often fills up; you also can take the Seabus, which shuttles between the downtown and North Vancouver terminals every 15 minutes.

Malls? Vancouver has several, if that's your shopping thing. Downtown, upscale **Pacific Centre** (corner of Georgia and Howe streets) is anchored by Sears and tony Holt Renfrew; other stores offer men's and ladies' wear, casual clothing, fashion accessories, shoes, electronics, sporting goods, handbags and cosmetics. On the North Shore, **Park Royal** (on either side of Marine Drive, just west of Taylor Way and the Lions Gate Bridge) consists of two enclosed malls with more than 280 stores and restaurants, plus **The Village**, specialty shops and cafés in an open-air setting.

For a true mega-mall experience, head to **Burnaby** and **Metropolis at Metrotown**, off Kingsway (Hwy. 1A/99A) between McKay and Nelson avenues. It's the province's largest shopping center, with The Bay (outfitters for the Canadian Olympic team), Sears and more than 450 other stores on three sprawling levels. Expect the usual chains and specialty outlets—everything from Absolute Dollar to Zellers—plus a food court and the latest box-office biggies at Famous Players SilverCity. Parking (plenty of it) is free.

CHINATOWN centers on E. Pender St. between Carrall and Gore sts. The second largest area of its kind in North America, Chinatown is lined with elaborately carved and gilded shops displaying jade, bamboo, rattan, brassware, silk and brocade. Sidewalk markets feature Oriental produce. Even the phone booths are topped with pagoda roofs. During Chinese New Year the streets resound with the din of drums and fireworks.

The Chinese Cultural Centre Museum & Archives, 555 Columbia St., has some displays and photographs on its second floor relating to the history of the Chinese in British Columbia. **Hours:** Chinese Cultural Centre Museum & Archives open Tues.-Sun. 11-5. Closed major holidays. **Phone:** (604)

Chinatown market

Granville Street nightlife

658-8850 for the Chinese Cultural Centre Museum & Archives.

Nightlife

Hip, cosmopolitan Vancouver has a buzzing nightlife, with plenty of spots where the young and beautiful congregate—and there are even a few options for the rest of us. Among the latter are several sophisticated hotel lounges where you can relax over drinks in a quiet, elegant atmosphere. The bar inside **Yew**, the restaurant at the Four Seasons Hotel Vancouver (downtown at 791 W. Georgia St.) is a lovely place to put a capper on a busy day. A 12-metre (40-ft.) ceiling makes this a breathtakingly lofty space, warmed by wood-paneled walls and a big sandstone fireplace. The bar is open until midnight Sun.-Wed., 1 a.m. Thurs.-Sat.

Bacchus Piano Lounge, in The Wedgewood Hotel & Spa (downtown at 845 Hornby St.), is an equally elegant spot to enjoy a glass of B.C. wine or a martini in surroundings that exude luxury—subdued lighting, antique furniture and vases of fresh flowers, with a softly tinkling piano in the background. There's dancing Thursday through Saturday evenings. Do dress up.

Opus Bar, in the Opus Hotel (322 Davie St.) is a cool, sleek lounge in hot-to-trot **Yaletown**. The decor is stylish with a capital "S": designer furniture, iridescent mood lighting, shimmer screens and live video feeds that allow you to keep an eye on the action at the bar and in the lounge. DJs spin dance music for a fashionably dressed, upwardly mobile crowd.

Baby boomers will feel right at home in **The Cascade Room**, 2616 Main St. (a block south of

Broadway). This restaurant and bar is a transplanted bit of British pub culture: Lampshades feature Queen Victoria's likeness, and a large glass panel advises patrons to "Keep calm and carry on"—a World War II slogan uttered by stiff-upper-lip Brits. Slide into one of the horseshoe-shaped booths for a cocktail, a beer or a pint of lager.

Granville Street is hopping with nightclubs, all with reasonable cover charges. Thirty-somethings hang out at **Republic**, (958 Granville St.). A bar runs almost the full length of the dance floor on the main level; a lounge with a glass-enclosed patio overlooking the Granville street scene is upstairs. DJs play music that varies from hip-hop, house and electro to dance mix mashups and reggae. **The Caprice** (967 Granville St.) has a lounge with an outdoor patio and TV screens showing sporting events. Special event nights augment DJ music (Wednesday through Saturday) that tends toward Top 40, R&B and dance hits.

The Roxy (932 Granville St.) draws a young, ready-to-party crowd with house bands pumping out rock and Top 40 and bartenders who put on their own show. If you don't feel like dancing, watch TV or play pool. It's open until 3 a.m. nightly. More sophisticated is **AuBAR** (674 Seymour St.), which has a New York feel—candlelit tables, intimate seating areas, two bars and a VIP lounge. There's usually a long line of very attractive people waiting to get in, and it's known to attract Hollywood types who are in town for on-location filming.

Touristy **Gastown** throngs with nightspots. The **Steamworks Pub & Brewery** (375 Water St.) is named for the Gastown steam line that runs through the premises. The hoist of choice here is beer (brewed on-site), from signature Lions Gate lager and Cascadia cream ale to such concoctions as Heroica oatmeal stout and sour cherry ale. Coffee drinkers will appreciate the Steamworks Grand, a combo of espresso and stout. The basement looks like a Bavarian-style drinking hall, while upstairs the atmosphere is clubbier, with leather chairs and windows overlooking the harbor.

In contrast, **The Post Modern** (7 Alexander St.) is an ultra-contemporary dance club replete with smoked glass and mirrors at every turn, the better to check out the scene as you sip a custom cocktail. The emphasis is on music, and the club books both Canadian and international DJ talent to provide hot dance mixes for cool kids. Cool kids also hang at **Celebrities** (1022 Davie St.) in **Davie Village**. Visiting DJs like Boy George take advantage of state-of-the-art sound and lighting, and the dance floor is invariably packed with chiseled, often shirtless young men. It's open every night but Monday.

The **Commodore Ballroom** (868 Granville St.) is an old-time dance hall that books everything from gospel choirs to death metal quadruple bills. This is the place to see up-and-coming bands as well as established acts that don't sell out arenas. The dance floor is in front of the stage and table seating is limited; arrive early unless you don't mind standing in the back of the room.

For a mellow evening, make it **O'Doul's Restaurant & Bar** (1300 Robson St. at Jervis, in the Listel Hotel). The West Coast cuisine is expertly prepared, the wine list is outstanding and live music is provided by the city's top jazz names. Solo artists perform Sunday through Wednesday, ensembles Thursday through Saturday. The music starts at 9 p.m.

If you want to hear blues in Vancouver, you go to the **Yale Hotel** (1300 Granville St., just south of Davie Street). This tavern has a lot of history—it was once a Canadian Pacific Railroad bunkhouse and then a hostelry with a reputation for wild nights—just the place, in other words, for musicians to get down and do their thing. Big names like Johnny Winter and Buckwheat Zydeco come through regularly, but there's plenty of local talent on tap, too. The Yale's weekend blues jams (Sat.-Sun. 3-7, no cover) are a tradition.

And here's a beautifully simple suggestion. On a balmy summer evening, head down to **English Bay Beach** (just off Beach Avenue at the south end of Denman Street). First, stop and get an ice cream cone or something from Starbucks (there's one at the corner of Davie and Denman). Then sit on a beach log or a bench, or stroll along the seawall promenade, and watch the sun set over the bay and the mountains rising beyond the North Shore, turning the water a pale luminescent blue or perhaps streaking the clouds fiery orange or crimson. It's just you and nature—plus the company of similar-minded souls.

Note: The *Georgia Straight,* a news and entertainment weekly that comes out on Thursday, has extensive arts and entertainment listings for greater Vancouver.

Big Events

Life in a city where your office is only 25 minutes from a ski slope is worth celebrating, and the residents of Vancouver celebrate their setting throughout the year. New Year's Day sees the **Polar Bear Swim** at **English Bay**; the event draws many swimmers and hundreds of spectators. February brings the Chinese New Year and with it the **Vancouver Chinese New Year Parade**, with colorful entries marching through Chinatown in a splendid celebration of the Chinese lunar year.

The **Vancouver International Children's Festival** in May ushers in summer, while cultural entertainment sails in with the **Rio Tinto Alcan Dragon Boat Festival** in mid-June. The **Vancouver Folk Music Festival** draws fans from as far away as Los Angeles for concerts during mid-July. **HSBC Celebration of Light** features 4 nights of fireworks displays and is held at English Bay the last week of July and the first week in August.

For 2 weeks in early August and staged in 10 venues throughout the city, **MusicFest Vancouver**

runs the gamut in musical offerings including classical, opera, jazz and chamber music. Virtually all facets of life and work in British Columbia are celebrated in the **Pacific National Exhibition**, held at the **Exhibition Grounds** from late August through Labour Day.

The Christmas season begins with the **Christmas Carol Ships**, which lead a flotilla of private watercraft decorated with Christmas lights around the harbor through mid-December. **Bright Nights in Stanley Park**, a holiday tradition of more than 30 years, turns the forest and the train into a wonderland with more than 2 million lights and animated displays. Additional information about events is available from your CAA or AAA club.

Sports & Rec

Vancouver offers such a diversity of recreational opportunities that anyone with a yen for variety can ski on Grouse Mountain in the morning, golf on the banks of the Fraser River in the afternoon, fish for salmon in Horseshoe Bay at dusk and top off the day with a dip in English Bay.

Vancouver's park system has tennis courts, swimming pools, putting greens, golf courses, lawn bowling greens, hiking paths and a comprehensive bike route. For park information phone the Vancouver Park Board at (604) 257-8400.

Swimming is available along English Bay, which is bordered by beaches from West Point Grey to Stanley Park. Beaches are easily accessible from Northwest Marine Drive in West Point Grey, Point Grey Road in Vancouver West and from Beach Avenue downtown.

Vancouver Chinese New Year Parade

Sea kayaking

White-water rafting is available April through September on the nearby Chilliwack River and a little farther afield on the Lillooet, Fraser and Thompson rivers. Vancouver rafting companies offering day trips as well as multiday trips include REO Rafting Adventure Resort, (604) 461-7238 or (800) 736-7238, and Kumsheen Rafting Resort, (250) 455-2296 or (800) 663-6667. Lotus Land Tours offers **sea kayaking** trips on Indian Arm and **whale-watching** tours from Steveston; phone (604) 684-4922 or (800) 528-3531.

Winter visitors with a penchant for **skiing** can tackle the challenging slopes of Grouse Mountain or Mount Seymour Park in North Vancouver. East of Vancouver are Hemlock Valley and Manning Park ski resorts, offering both downhill and cross-country treks. Cypress Provincial Park in West Vancouver also has cross-country and downhill skiing *(see attraction listing p. 421 and Recreation Areas Chart)*. Skiers can head north of Vancouver to Whistler and Blackcomb mountains.

When the waters sparkle from the summer sun, Vancouver becomes a **boating** paradise. For visitors without a boat, several companies have craft for hourly or daily rental. For charter yachts phone Harbour Cruises, (604) 688-7246, or Westin Bayshore Yacht Charters, (604) 250-8008. For **fishing** charters and boat rentals phone Sewell's Ltd., (604) 921-3474, at Horseshoe Bay.

Vancouver residents love spectator sports, especially **football, hockey** and **soccer.** The BC Lions of the Canadian Football League usually play before capacity crowds in BC Place Stadium. The Canucks of the National Hockey League compete in Rogers Arena. For football and hockey ticket information

phone TicketMaster, (855) 985-4357. **Baseball** is played by the Vancouver Canadians at Nat Bailey Stadium; phone (604) 872-5232 for schedule and ticket information. Indoor **lacrosse** can be enjoyed at Bill Copeland Sports Centre in Burnaby, (604) 291-1261; and at Queens Park Arena, (604) 777-5111, in New Westminster.

Thoroughbred racing with pari-mutuel betting is held at Hastings Park Race Course on the grounds of the Pacific National Exhibition; phone (604) 254-1631 *(see attraction listing p. 357).*

Note: Policies concerning admittance of children to pari-mutuel betting facilities vary. Phone for information.

Performing Arts

The Centre in Vancouver for Performing Arts, 777 Homer St., is a premier facility for theater, dance and music; phone (604) 602-0616 for event information. The **Queen Elizabeth Theatre** at the intersection of Hamilton and Georgia streets, (604) 665-3050, is home to **Ballet British Columbia,** (604) 732-5003, and the **Vancouver Opera Association,** (604) 683-0222. The adjacent **Vancouver Playhouse** presents professional theater, recitals and chamber music; phone (604) 873-3311. The **Vancouver Symphony Orchestra** performs at the **Orpheum Theatre,** Smithe and Granville streets; phone (604) 876-3434 for ticket information.

Other prominent metropolitan theaters presenting dramatic productions include the **Arts Club Theatre,** on Johnston Street on **Granville Island,** (604) 687-1644; the **Metro Theatre,** 1370 S.W. Marine Dr., (604) 266-7191; **Studio 58,** 100 W. 49th Ave., (604) 323-5227; and the **Vancouver East Cultural Centre,** 1895 Venables St., (604) 251-1363.

During the summer concerts and musicals are presented in Stanley Park's Malkin Bowl. **Kitsilano Showboat** at **Kitsilano Beach** presents an outdoor variety show Monday, Wednesday and Friday at 7:30 p.m. during July and August (weather permitting). For more information phone (604) 734-7332.

Concerts in such genres as classical, country, pop and rock are presented year-round at the **Pacific Coliseum,** 100 N. Renfrew St., (604) 253-2311, and **Rogers Arena,** 800 Griffiths Way, (604) 899-7000.

The daily papers carry listings of cultural events, as do weekly and monthly magazines. Ticket outlets include **Ticketmaster Head Office,** 1304 Hornby St.; and **Ticketmaster,** Pacific Centre Mall, 701 W. Georgia St.

INSIDER INFO:
A Stanley Park Jaunt

Stanley Park is the crown jewel in a city uncommonly blessed with scenic attributes. It is not only paradise for walkers, hikers and outdoor recreation enthusiasts but a truly delightful wooded retreat that's all the more special for being only a stone's throw away from downtown Vancouver's skyscrapers and urban congestion. And one of the best ways to experience the park is to walk the seawall promenade around its perimeter, a distance totaling a bit more than 9 kilometres (6 mi.) that you can take at a leisurely or vigorous pace.

A good starting point is English Bay Beach in the West End neighborhood; just follow the paved seawall path. (There are designated lanes for walkers and for cyclists and roller bladers.) One of the best things about this walk is that it offers an uninterrupted series of scenic water views. To your left, keep an eye out for the stone sculptures that people construct when the rocky beach is accessible during low tide; some of them are quite elaborate.

Once past the swimming pool and assorted recreational facilities at Second Beach you'll leave many of the casual strollers behind. Between Second Beach and Third Beach the waters of English Bay sparkle in the sun as the seawall runs along sandstone cliffs and conifer-covered hillsides. Third Beach is a good place to go beachcombing at low tide, when the receding waters reveal barnacle-encrusted rocks and pieces of driftwood.

Siwash Rock is a distinctive landmark you can't miss. This sea stack—a geologic feature formed when volcanic action caused a portion of rock to break free from the park foundation—is between 15 and 18 metres (50 and 60 ft.) tall. A small Douglas fir stands at its summit. Past Siwash Rock the seawall rounds the northern end of the park. At Prospect Point you'll be treated to outstanding views of the Lions Gate Bridge and mountains rising from the opposite North Shore.

On the other side of Prospect Point the seawall runs along Burrard Inlet. Stands of Douglas fir, western hemlock and western red cedar are in full view on this stretch of the walk. The fierce-looking green dragon arching toward the water is the Empress of Japan Figurehead, a replica of a prow ornament that once graced the RMS *Empress of Japan* ocean liner. Just beyond the dragon is "Girl in Wet Suit," a sculpture of a woman sitting on top of a rock about 9 metres (30 ft.) offshore. Although at first glance you might think she's a mermaid, this girl is wearing flippers and has a scuba mask atop her head.

Before reaching Brockton Point you'll see Stanley Park's totem poles standing in a clearing to your right. Interpretive plaques explain the significance of each pole's symbolic figures. Beyond the totems sits the squat Brockton Point Lighthouse. The 9 O'Clock Gun is an old cannon near the tip of Brockton Point; it used to be fired at 6 p.m. to signal the end of the fishing day. Although it goes off electronically these days, the sound is still loud enough to make you jump.

After curving around Brockton Point the seawall runs along the shore of Coal Harbour. There are superb views of the downtown skyline and the yachts and other pleasure craft docked at the harbor. Keep following the paved walkway until you reach the Georgia Avenue park entrance, which will take you back to the West End. Relaxing at one of the cafes

or casual restaurants along Denman Street is a perfect way to end this Stanley Park jaunt. You've earned it.

ATTRACTIONS

BC SPORTS HALL OF FAME AND MUSEUM is at jct. Beatty and Robson sts., Gate A of BC Place Stadium. British Columbia sports history is traced from native traditions to the modern Olympic games. Honorees include amateur and professional teams, athletes, journalists and sports pioneers. Interactive galleries provide opportunities for running, climbing, throwing, riding, rowing and even mini hockey.

Hours: Daily 10-5. Closed Jan. 1 and Christmas. **Cost:** $15; $12 (ages 6-17, ages 65+ and students with ID); $40 (family, two adults and two children). **Phone:** (604) 687-5520.

BILL REID GALLERY OF NORTHWEST COAST ART is downtown at 639 Hornby St. between W. Georgia and Dunsmuir sts. The museum is dedicated to Bill Reid, one of Canada's finest artists and a passionate proponent of Northwest Coast art. Reid was a master Haida goldsmith as well as a noted sculptor, carver, broadcaster, writer and spokesman for his native people.

His gold and silver jewelry forms the basis of the museum's permanent collection. Other highlights include his masterpiece, an 8.5-metre (28-ft.) bronze frieze titled "Mythic Messengers," and a massive 6.7-metre (22 ft.) totem pole carved in honor of the artist. Video displays alongside Reid's art allow visitors to watch him at work at different stages of his life.

Time: Allow 1 hour minimum. **Hours:** Wed.-Sun. 11-5. Closed major holidays. **Cost:** $10; $7 (students ages 18+ with ID and senior citizens); $5 (ages 5-17); $25 (family rate). Phone ahead to confirm hours and rates. **Phone:** (604) 682-3455.

BLOEDEL CONSERVATORY—see Queen Elizabeth Park p. 357.

CHINATOWN—see Shopping p. 349.

CHRIST CHURCH CATHEDRAL is at 690 Burrard St. One of Vancouver's oldest stone churches, the cathedral was completed in 1895. In addition to stone, it also is constructed of old-growth wood. Its 37 English and Canadian stained-glass windows are highlights. **Tours:** Guided tours are available. **Hours:** Mon.-Fri. 10-4. Phone ahead for tour information and schedule. **Cost:** Donations. **Phone:** (604) 682-3848.

DEELEY MOTORCYCLE EXHIBITION is s.e. off Hwy. 1 exit 27 (1st Ave.), between E. 2nd and 4th aves. at 1875 Boundary Rd. In the same complex that houses the Trev Deeley Harley-Davidson dealership, the museum features more than 250 vintage

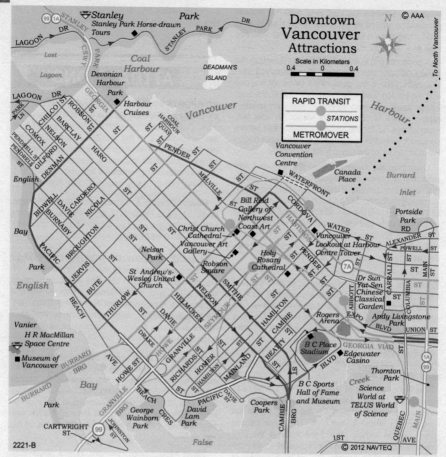

Downtown
Vancouver
Attractions

Scale in Kilometers

RAPID TRANSIT
STATIONS
METROMOVER

2221-B

© 2012 NAVTEQ

motorcycles representing 59 different manufacturers.

An interactive map has touch screens that let visitors choose highway rides across British Columbia and Washington state. **Time:** Allow 30 minutes minimum. **Hours:** Mon.-Fri. 10-5, Sat. 9:30-4:30, Sun. 11-4:30. Closed major holidays. **Cost:** $5. **Phone:** (604) 293-2221.

DR. SUN YAT-SEN CLASSICAL CHINESE GARDEN is at 578 Carrall St. What this walled garden lacks in size it more than makes up for in serene beauty. Located next to the Chinese Cultural Centre in the heart of Chinatown, it's a delightful respite from the surrounding hustle and bustle. Modeled after private gardens in the city of Suzhou, the garden embodies the Taoist philosophy of yin and yang, where every element—light, texture, vegetation—is balanced.

The architecture of the pavilions, covered walkways, terraces and viewing platforms evokes Ming Dynasty classical design. Rocks and water are integral elements, while trees and plants—from pine trees and bamboo to graceful weeping willows and

winter-flowering plum trees—all have symbolic connotations. The Jade Water Pavilion is graced with beautiful woodwork. Two of the garden's most intriguing elements are the 43 leak windows (each one has a different lattice pattern) and the groupings of Tai Hu rocks, interestingly shaped stones from China's Lake Tai that lend themselves to all sorts of artistic interpretations.

Visitors can walk through the garden on their own, but the guided tour offers historical perspective and encourages you to reflect on the design elements in different ways. Afterward, take a stroll through the adjacent public park, where pathways wind through clumps of bamboo and other plantings.

Art and horticultural exhibits and demonstrations also are offered. Festivals and concerts are featured throughout the year. **Time:** Allow 1 hour minimum. **Hours:** Daily 9:30-7, June 15-Aug. 31; daily 10-6, May 1-June 14 and in Sept.; Tues.-Sun. 10-4:30, rest of year. Closed Jan. 1 and Christmas. **Cost:** $14 (includes guided tour and tea); $11 (ages 6-17, ages 65+ and students with ID); $10 (students with

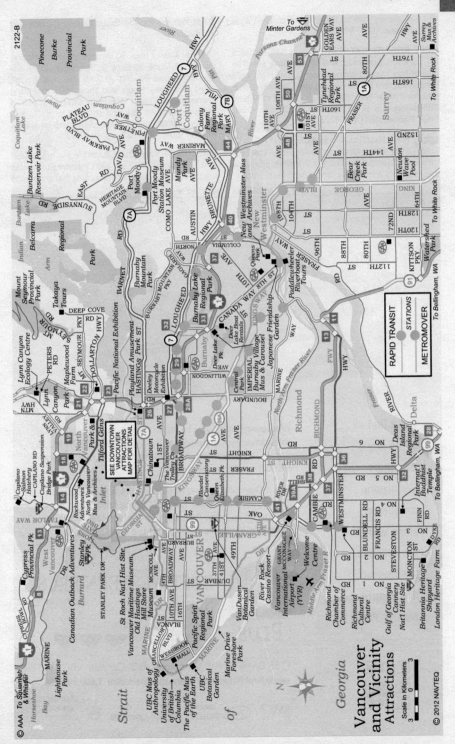

Vancouver and Vicinity Attractions

2122-B

© 2012 NAVTEQ

Scale in Kilometers
3 0 3

RAPID TRANSIT
STATIONS
METROMOVER

SEE DOWNTOWN VANCOUVER ATTRACTIONS MAP FOR DETAIL

To Minter Gardens

To Squamish & Whistler

To White Rock

To Bellingham, WA

To Bellingham, WA

ID); $28 (family, two adults and two children ages 0-17). **Phone:** (604) 662-3207.

HOLY ROSARY CATHEDRAL is at 646 Richards St. between Dunsmuir and W. Georgia sts. The church has stained-glass windows and eight bells hung in the rare English ringing style. **Hours:** Cathedral open Mon.-Sat. 6:30-6, Sun. 7:30 a.m.-9 p.m. Bell ringing Sun. at 10:30, Tues. at 7:30 p.m. **Cost:** Free. **Phone:** (604) 682-6774.

 H.R. MacMILLAN SPACE CENTRE is at 1100 Chestnut St. in Vanier Park. The centre's Planetarium Star Theatre presents programs dealing with astronomy and space exploration.

Other features include GroundStation Canada and an observatory.

Time: Allow 1 hour, 30 minutes minimum. **Hours:** Daily 10-5, June 30-Sept. 3; otherwise varies. Astronomy shows Fri.-Sat. at 7:30 p.m. and 9 p.m., July-Labour Day. Hours and show times may vary; phone ahead. Closed Christmas. **Cost:** $15; $10.75 (ages 5-18, ages 55+ and students with ID); $45 (family). Admission may vary depending on shows. **Phone:** (604) 738-7827.

MUSEUM OF VANCOUVER, on the s.w. end of Burrard St. in Vanier Park at 1100 Chestnut St., creates area-focused displays and programs that encourage

▼ *See AAA listing p. 375* ▼

dynamic conversations about what was, is, and can be Vancouver. Permanent exhibitions present the city's story 1900-1979, and are complemented by contemporary feature exhibits.

Hours: Daily 10-5 (also Thurs. 5-8), July 1-Labour Day weekend; Tues.-Sun. 10-5 (also Thurs. 5-8), rest of year. Closed Christmas. **Cost:** $12; $10 (ages 65+ and students with ID); $8 (ages 5-17); $35 (family, two adults and two children). **Phone:** (604) 736-4431.

OLD HASTINGS MILL STORE MUSEUM is at 1575 Alma St. in Hastings Mill Park. The mill was the first industrial facility on the south shore of what is now Vancouver. One of the few buildings to withstand the ravages of the 1886 fire, it contains relics of early Vancouver, including native basketry and a hansom cab. **Time:** Allow 30 minutes minimum. **Hours:** Tues.-Sun. 11-4, mid-June to mid-Sept.; Sat.-Sun. 1-4, mid-Sept. through Nov. 30 and Feb. 1 through mid-June. **Cost:** Donations. **Phone:** (604) 734-1212.

PACIFIC NATIONAL EXHIBITION is on E. Hastings St. between Renfrew and Cassiar sts. The site occupies 58 hectares (144 acres) and is home to Pacific Coliseum, a tradeshow and entertainment complex, and a skateboard park. The Pacific National Exhibition Fair is an end of summer highlight. Various trade and hobby shows, rock concerts and sporting events are scheduled throughout the year.

Hours: Fair daily 11 a.m.-midnight (weather permitting), mid- to late Aug. through Labour Day. Last admission 1 hour, 30 minutes before closing. **Cost:** Fair admission $20; $8 (ages 65+); free (up to five children ages 0-13 per paying adult age 21+). Rides are additional. Rates may vary; phone ahead. **Phone:** (604) 253-2311. 🍴

Playland Amusement Park is on E. Hastings St. between Renfrew and Cassiar sts. The 4-hectare (10-acre) park features games, miniature golf and rides, including a large wooden roller coaster and four "extreme" rides.

Hours: Mon.-Thurs. 10-7, Fri.-Sun. and holidays 10-8, July 1-late Aug.; Mon.-Fri. 10-3, in late June; Sat.-Sun. and holidays 10-6, late Apr.-late June and day after Labour Day-late Sept. Phone ahead to confirm schedule. **Cost:** $29.95; $19.95 (under 122 centimetres or 48 in. tall); $12.95 (parents when accompanied by a paying child ages 0-12); free (ages 0-3 and 65+). Rates may vary; phone ahead. **Phone:** (604) 253-2311.

QUEEN ELIZABETH PARK is off Cambie St. and W. 33rd Ave. On 167-metre (548-ft.) Little Mountain, the highest point in Vancouver, the park offers magnificent views of the city, harbor and North Shore Mountains. Other highlights include an arboretum; rose, sunken and quarry gardens; dancing fountains; tennis courts; and pitch and putt greens. **Hours:** Daily 24 hours. **Cost:** Free.

Bloedel Conservatory is at 33rd Ave. and Cambie St. Climatically varied species of plants grow in a climate-controlled, illuminated triodetic dome 43 metres (141 ft.) in diameter and 21 metres (70 ft.) high. Tropical birds and a fish pond are other highlights. **Time:** Allow 30 minutes minimum. **Hours:** Mon.-Fri. 9-8, Sat.-Sun. 10-9, May-Sept.; daily 10-5, rest of year. Closed Christmas. Phone ahead to confirm schedule. **Cost:** $5; $3.48 (ages 13-18 and 65+); $2.50 (ages 3-12). **Phone:** (604) 257-8584.

ST. ANDREW'S-WESLEY UNITED CHURCH is at 1022 Nelson St. at Burrard St. The Gothic structure includes a large collection of British, French and Canadian stained glass. **Hours:** Mon.-Fri. 10-4, Sun. 2-4. **Cost:** Donations. **Phone:** (604) 683-4574.

▼ *See AAA listing p. 282* ▼

SCIENCE WORLD AT TELUS WORLD OF SCIENCE, 1455 Quebec St., features hands-on exhibits and demonstrations that explain scientific phenomena. The Eureka! Mitchell Odyssey Foundation Gallery explores such themes as water, air, motion and invention. The Kidspace Gallery features activities for children ages 2 through 6. The Peter Brown Family Centre Stage presents live, zany science demonstrations daily. Human performance and nature are the subjects of additional galleries. Also of interest are the OMNIMAX Theatre, which presents nature and science films, and the new Ken Spencer Science Park, an outdoor sustainability gallery.

Time: Allow 2 hours minimum. **Hours:** Daily 10-6, late June-Labour Day and during spring and winter breaks; Tues.-Fri. 10-4, Sat.-Sun. 10-6, rest of year. Open 10-3, Dec. 31; noon-6, Jan. 1. Closed Sept. 4-7 and Christmas. Phone ahead to confirm schedule. **Cost:** Exhibits and Science Theatre $23.50; $19.75 (ages 13-18, ages 65+ and students with ID); $16.75 (ages 3-12). **Parking:** $5-$12. Rates may vary; phone ahead. **Phone:** (604) 443-7440. *(See ad p. 315.)*

STANLEY PARK shares the peninsula where the city's business district is located. Vancouver's first City Council made a momentous decision in 1886, when it petitioned the government to lease 400 hectares (1,000 acres) of largely logged-over land for public and recreation purposes. The result of this wise move was the creation of North America's third largest urban park—a cool, lush evergreen oasis right at downtown's doorstep.

Stanley Park

Named for Lord Stanley, Governor General of Canada when the park officially opened in 1888, Stanley Park was once land hunted and foraged by the Musqueam and Squamish First Nations peoples. And a large part of what makes it such a special place is the lush West Coast rain forest growth. One of the park's great pleasures, in fact, is exploring the network of bark-mulched trails that wind through Douglas fir, western hemlock and western red cedar trees. These giants create a hushed environment of subdued light and cool air that is all the more remarkable given such close proximity to downtown's hurly-burly.

Such a magnificent setting, of course, offers plenty of inspiring views. For example, follow Prospect Point Trail, an invigorating uphill trek, to Prospect Point at the northern tip of the peninsula; from this elevated perspective the vista of Burrard Inlet, the Lions Gate Bridge, the North Shore and the mountains beyond is a stunner. For a more relaxed jaunt, amble along Stanley Park Drive, the seawall that encircles the peninsula. The route totals about 10 kilometres (6 mi.), and you'll be gazing out over water essentially the entire time. There are separate lanes for walkers and cyclists/inline skaters.

There are other ways to enjoy nature. Walk to Beaver Lake, a body of water that is in the process of shrinking as it transitions from lake to bog (and may in time lose its watery aspects completely and become a meadow). Its surface is covered with yellow water lilies in summer. Or take a spin around Lost Lagoon, off the Georgia Street entrance to the park. This man-made body of water (created when the Stanley Park Causeway was built in 1916) provides a nesting ground for ducks, swans and Canada geese. The lagoon also is located on the Pacific Flyway, which makes it a favorite haunt of bird watchers as well as one of the park's most popular strolls.

Standing near the Brockton Oval (where you can watch a cricket match), just in from the seawall, are eight totem poles. They make a distinctive photo op, and you can learn about their history by reading the interpretive panels. You'll also want to take a ride in a horse-drawn carriage *(see sub-attraction listing);* breathing in the scent of the cedar trees while listening to the gentle clip-clop of a Clydesdale's hooves is an eminently relaxing way to tour the park.

There are free tennis courts near Lost Lagoon and the Beach Avenue entrance. The Second Beach Pool has English Bay as a backdrop. An 18-hole pitch-and-putt golf course also is located at Second Beach. At low tide, explore the rocky shoreline along Second and Third beaches. For kids there are three playgrounds—at Lumbermen's Arch, Second Beach and near the park's Rose Garden—as well as a miniature steam train *(see sub-attraction listing).*

Shows take place at the open-air Malkin Bowl/Theatre Under the Stars in July and August. A park information booth is just inside the Georgia Street entrance, next to the seawall. A free shuttle travels between the most popular destinations in summer; shuttles depart from the miniature railway parking lot.

Hours: Park open daily 24 hours. Information booth open 10-5, June 15-Sept. 15; 10-4, May 1-June 14 and Sept. 16-second Mon. in Oct. Booth hours may vary; phone ahead. Shuttle daily 10-6:30, July 1-Labour Day. **Cost:** Park free. **Phone:** (604) 681-6728. ⓘ ㋙

Miniature Train is near the Georgia St. entrance of Stanley Park off Pipeline Rd. Visitors can take a scenic ride through the park on this miniature train. The trip runs over trestles and through tunnels on its 2-kilometre (1.25-mi.) journey. Special excursions operate during Halloween and during the Christmas season.

Time: Allow 1 hour minimum. **Hours:** Daily 10:30-5, July 1-Labour Day; daily 11-4, Victoria Day weekend-June 30 (also Mar. spring break and Easter weekend); Sat.-Sun. 11-4, early Feb.-day before Victoria Day weekend and in mid-Sept. (weather permitting). Halloween ghost train operates early Oct.-Oct. 31; Christmas train operates late Nov.-Jan. 1. **Cost:** $10; $8 (ages 3-17 and 65+); a family rate is available. **Phone:** (604) 257-8531. ⓘ ㋙

Stanley Park Horse-drawn Tours depart from beside the information booth on Park Dr. off the Georgia St. entrance. The narrated, 1-hour tour highlights the park's points of interest. **Hours:** Tours depart daily every 20-30 minutes 9:30-5:30, July 1-Labour Day; 9:40-5, Apr.-June and day after Labour Day-Sept. 30; 9:40-4, Mar. 15-31 and in Oct. **Cost:** $30; $28 (ages 13-18, ages 65+ and students with ID); $16 (ages 3-12). **Phone:** (604) 681-5115 or (888) 681-5110.

Vancouver Aquarium Marine Science Centre is at 845 Avison Way. More than 70,000 marine animals are exhibited, with emphasis on such diverse habitats as the Canadian Arctic, the Amazon Rain Forest and the Pacific Northwest. Sharks, moray eels and colorful fish populate the Tropic Zone, while the Strait of Georgia exhibit features divers interacting with marine life.

Interactive multimedia displays in the Canada's Arctic exhibit allow visitors to meet the people of this region and explain the effects and impact of climate change on them and the area's marine life. Programs allowing animal encounters with sea lions, seals, otters and beluga whales are available for an additional fee.

Walk the BC Hydro Salmon Stream in Stanley Park to learn about a salmon's incredible life journey. Other highlights include daily whale and dolphin shows, shark dives and sea otter feedings as well as exhibits that feature sea lions and harbor seals.

Time: Allow 2 hours minimum. **Hours:** Daily 9:30-7, July 1-Labour Day; 9:30-5, rest of year. **Cost:** $27; $21 (ages 13-18, ages 65+ and students with ID); $17 (ages 4-12). Prices may vary during the peak of summer; phone ahead. **Parking:** $2-$2.50 per hour. **Phone:** (604) 659-3400 or (800) 931-1186. ⓘ

UNIVERSITY OF BRITISH COLUMBIA is on Point Grey. Encompassing 2,470 hectares (6,103 acres) overlooking the Strait of Georgia, the university is the largest in the province. **Hours:** Free campus tours are offered twice daily Mon.-Fri., mid-May through Aug. 31; phone ahead for information. **Phone:** (604) 822-2211.

Beaty Biodiversity Museum is at 2212 Main Mall on the University of British Columbia campus. This natural history museum exhibits more than 2 million specimens divided among five collections: the Cowan Tetrapod Collection, The Herbarium, the Spencer Entomological Collection, the Fish Collection, the Marine Invertebrate Collection and the Fossil Collection. A highlight is Canada's largest blue whale skeleton, which is suspended in the museum's two-story glass atrium.

Note: Pay parking is available at the Health Sciences Parkade and near the UBC Bookstore. **Time:** Allow 1 hour, 30 minutes minimum. **Hours:** Daily 10-5. Guided tours are given Mon.-Fri. at noon, 2 and 3:30. Closed Jan. 1 and Christmas. **Cost:** $12; $10 (ages 13-17, students with ID and senior citizens); $8 (ages 5-12); $35 (family). **Phone:** (604) 822-0862. ⓘ

The Pacific Museum of the Earth is just off the West Mall of the university on the main floor of the Earth and Ocean Science Building at 6339 Stores Rd. A highlight of the 30,000-piece mineral and fossil collection is an 80 million-year-old Lambeosaurus dinosaur. Also featured are a 2-metre-long (7-ft.) amethyst tube and a large sedimentary structure. **Time:** Allow 30 minutes minimum. **Hours:** Mon.-Fri. 9-5. Closed statutory holidays, Jan. 1-3 and Dec. 20-31. **Cost:** Donations. **Phone:** (604) 822-6992.

UBC Botanical Garden is at 6804 S.W. Marine Dr. More than 10,000 plants from around the world are cultivated on 28 hectares (69 acres). Themed gardens include Asian, alpine, perennial, food, medicinal and native plantings. Within the Asian garden is the Greenheart Canopy Walkway, a 308-metre (1,010-ft.) aerial trail through a West Coast forest canopy. Guided tours take participants across eight bridges more than 15 metres (49 ft.) above ground level to view plants and animals that live in this environment.

Nitobe Memorial Garden, one of the most accurately represented Japanese gardens in North America, features a tea garden and stroll garden with seasonal displays of irises, Japanese maples and flowering cherries.

Pets are not permitted. **Time:** Allow 1 hour minimum. **Hours:** Main garden and Nitobe Memorial Garden open daily 9:30-5. **Cost:** Main garden $8;

Vancouver Art Gallery

$6 (ages 13-17, senior citizens and non-UBC students with ID). Nitobe Memorial Garden $6; $4.50 (senior citizens); $3 (ages 6-12). There is an additional fee for the Greenheart Canopy Walkway. Various combination tickets are available. **Phone:** (604) 822-4208.

UBC Museum of Anthropology is at 6393 N.W. Marine Dr. on the Point Grey Cliffs. Traditional post and beam construction is utilized in this concrete and glass building designed by Canadian architect Arthur Erickson. The Great Hall, the main exhibition area, has soaring glass walls that let in natural light. It provides a striking setting for a major collection of Northwest Coast First Nations artwork, which includes totem poles, house posts, carved figures, feast dishes and other objects.

The Rotunda features one of the museum's highlights, "The Raven and the First Men" by Canadian artist Bill Reid. Reid, whose mother was a Haida, developed an interest in tribal folklore, and this carving—fashioned from a single block of laminated yellow cedar—powerfully depicts a Haida human creation myth. Four accompanying display cases contain more of Reid's works in gold, silver and argillite, a fine-grained sedimentary rock frequently used in Haida carvings.

In marked contrast to the often-monumental scale of the indigenous art is the 600-piece collection of 15th to 19th-century European ceramics—stoneware, lead-glazed earthenware and tin-glazed ware—on display in the Koerner Ceramics Gallery.

Time: Allow 1 hour minimum. **Hours:** Daily 10-5 (also Tues. 5-9), May 20-Oct. 14; Tues.-Sun. 10-5 (also Tues. 5-9), rest of year. Closed Christmas and day after Christmas. **Cost:** $16.75; $14.50 (ages 7-18, ages 65+ and students with ID); $44.75(family). **Phone:** (604) 822-5087.

 VANCOUVER AQUARIUM MARINE SCIENCE CENTRE—see Stanley Park p. 359.

VANCOUVER ART GALLERY is downtown at 750 Hornby St.; the museum encompasses a city block bounded by Georgia, Howe, Robson and Hornby sts. One of the largest art museums in Western Canada occupies a turn-of-the-20th-century building that originally was intended to serve as a provincial courthouse. Its stately exterior, however, is a contrast to much of the art inside, which tends to reflect the creative energy and hip, progressive style that the city itself embodies.

While historical masters are given their due, the focus of the gallery's changing thematic exhibitions is on contemporary artists and works from groundbreaking new visionaries that veer toward the cutting edge. The museum's four floors of mixed-media installations contain works by Emily Carr and other well-known Canadian artists.

Time: Allow 1 hour minimum. **Hours:** Daily 10-5 (also Tues. 5-9). Closed Jan. 1 and Christmas. **Cost:** $20; $15 (ages 65+ and students with ID); $6.25 (ages 5-12); $50 (family, two adults and two children); donations (Tues. 5-9). Rates may vary; phone ahead. **Phone:** (604) 662-4719. *(See ad p. 315.)*

VANCOUVER LOOKOUT AT HARBOUR CENTRE TOWER is at 555 W. Hastings St. Two glass elevators ascend the outside of this tower, which is crowned with an observation deck that offers a spectacular panoramic view of the city and outlying districts. Hourly guided tours point out the city's landmarks. The complex includes a revolving restaurant and a shopping mall.

Time: Allow 30 minutes minimum. **Hours:** Skylift elevators run daily 8:30 a.m.-10:30 p.m., early May-Sept. 30; 9-9, rest of year. **Cost:** $15; $12 (ages 60+); $10 (ages 13-18); $7 (ages 6-12). Rates may vary; phone ahead. **Phone:** (604) 689-0421.

VANCOUVER MARITIME MUSEUM is at 1905 Ogden Ave. at n. foot of Chestnut and Cypress sts. Discover the rich maritime traditions of the Pacific Northwest and the Canadian Arctic. Model ships, naval uniforms and other artifacts reveal explorers' interactions with the sea. Historic vessels are displayed outside in the harbor. Tour the circa 1944 *St. Roch*, Canada's celebrated RCMP schooner. The Alcan Children's Maritime Discovery Centre features hands-on activities to introduce youngsters to ships and pirates of the sea.

Time: Allow 1 hour minimum. **Hours:** Daily 10-5, Victoria Day-Labour Day; Tues.-Sat. 10-5, Sun. noon-5, rest of year. **Cost:** Museum (including the *St. Roch* National Historic Site) $11; $8.50 (ages 6-18 and 65+); $30 (family). **Phone:** (604) 257-8300.

St. *Roch* **National Historic Site** is next to the Vancouver Maritime Museum. The supply ship was built in 1928 for the Royal Canadian Mounted Police Arctic patrol. During World War II the St. *Roch* became the first vessel to travel from the Pacific to the Atlantic via the treacherous Northwest Passage in the Arctic; it completed the round trip in 1944. After the war, the schooner reached its destination via the Panama Canal, becoming the first ship to circumnavigate the North American continent. Preserved in dry dock, the vessel is displayed as it appeared in 1944.

Time: Allow 1 hour minimum. **Hours:** Daily 10-5, Victoria Day-Labour Day; Tues.-Sat. 10-5, Sun. noon-5, rest of year. **Cost:** Included in the admission for the Vancouver Maritime Museum. **Phone:** (604) 257-8300.

VANDUSEN BOTANICAL GARDEN is at 5251 Oak St. (between Oak and Granville sts.) at W. 37th Ave. One benefit of Vancouver's benevolent maritime climate is that it creates a favorable environment for gardening, and the plant collections at VanDusen Botanical Garden offer spectacular proof. The 22-hectare (55-acre) site, once owned by the Canadian Pacific Railway and logged at the turn of the 20th century, was nurtured into a garden in the early 1970s in order to prevent the land from being developed for housing.

This is a botanical garden, as much scientifically organized and carefully labeled as it is visually pleasing. Trees, shrubs and perennials dominate the plantings, and there's something beautiful to see regardless of the season. Camellias, cherry trees, azaleas, magnolias and rhododendrons bloom from March through May. The Rose Garden begins flowering in June. Late July and August find flowering summer annuals and perennials at their peak. Japanese maples flaunt crimson fall foliage from September into October. And during the winter months, 140 different kinds of hollies along the Holly Trail are bright with berries.

Special gardens include the Perennial Garden, the Canadian Heritage Garden (where there is a lovely Korean Pavilion built from red cedar posts), the peaceful retreat that is the Meditation Garden, and the dark-leaved plants in the intriguing Black Garden. Rocks and water are integral elements as well, and the lakes and ponds are lovely spots to stop and reflect. Kids can puzzle their way around the hedges that form the Elizabethan Maze.

Time: Allow 1 hour, 30 minutes minimum. **Hours:** Daily 10-8:30, June-Aug.; 10-8, in May; 10-7, in Sept.; 10-6, in Apr.; 10-5 in Mar. and Oct.; 10-4, rest of year. Closed Christmas. **Cost:** Admission Apr.-Sept. $10.25; $7.50 (ages 13-18 and 65+); $5.50 (ages 3-12); $24 (family, two adults and two children under 19). Admission rest of year $7.50; $5.50 (ages 13-18 and 65+); $4 (ages 3-12); $16 (family, two adults and two children under 19). **Phone:** (604) 257-8335. 🔲 🍽

GAMBLING ESTABLISHMENTS

- **Edgewater Casino** is at 311-750 Pacific Blvd. S. **Hours:** Daily 24 hours. **Phone:** (604) 687-3343 or (877) 688-3343.

Sightseeing

Opportunities to watch bustling harbor activities are available at several vantage points in Vancouver. Seaplanes, barges, tugboats, cargo ships, ferries and the SeaBus can be observed from Granville Square at the foot of Granville Street; from Canada Place at the foot of Howe St.; from Lonsdale Quay at the foot of Lonsdale Ave.; and from Stanley Park. Fine views of the city, sea and mountains are available at Cypress Bowl, Simon Fraser University atop Burnaby Mountain, Grouse Mountain and Queen Elizabeth Park.

Boat Tours

HARBOUR CRUISES departs from 501 Denman St., next to Stanley Park. Scenic 60-minute harbor tours are offered aboard an authentic paddle wheeler. Dinner and carol ship cruises also are available. Another option is a 4-hour lunch cruise that heads up Indian Arm, one of the continent's most southern fjords, passing forests, granite cliffs and a waterfall; herons, eagles, seals and salmon can frequently be spotted.

Hours: Harbor tours board daily at 11, 12:15, 1:30 and 2:45, Apr. 5-Sept. 30. Indian Arm cruise boards Fri.-Mon. at 10:30, July-Aug.; Sat.-Mon., May-June and in Sept. **Cost:** Harbor tours $29.95; $24.95 (ages 12-17 and 60+); $10 (ages 5-11). Tour of Indian Arm $64.95. Schedule and fares may vary; phone ahead. Reservations are required. **Phone:** (604) 688-7246 or (800) 663-1500. *(See ad p. 362.)*

Bus Tours

West Coast City and Nature Sightseeing Ltd. features sightseeing trips of the city and its surrounding natural areas in 12- to 30-passenger minibuses. Full-day trips to Victoria and the Whistler resort area also are available; phone (604) 451-1600 or (877) 451-1777.

Living Earth Eco Tours picks up at downtown area hotels. The company offers 4-hour Vancouver city tours with multilingual guides as well as tours of North Vancouver, a full-day tour to Victoria and Butchart Gardens, and an excursion to Whistler; phone (604) 999-8687.

SAVE Gray Line offers city tours as well as combination excursions that include Butchart Gardens and Victoria, Whistler, Capilano Suspension Bridge Park and Grouse Mountain; phone (604) 451-1600 or (877) 451-1777.

BIG BUS departs from 321 Water St.; the bus also can be boarded at any one of 22 other stops throughout the city. Ninety-minute tours on this large, red double-decker bus with covered and open seating offer hop-on, hop-off opportunities. Prerecorded commentary is available in seven languages.

Time: Allow 1 hour, 30 minutes minimum. **Hours:** Buses depart daily every 15-20 minutes 9-5, May-Sept.; every 45 minutes 9-3:45, rest of year. **Cost:** One-day pass $38; $35 (ages 13-17, ages 65+ and students with ID); $20 (ages 6-12); $90 (family, two adults and children ages 0-11). Two-day pass $45; $40 (ages 13-17, ages 65+ and students with ID); $25 (ages 6-12); $100 (family, two adults and children ages 0-11). **Phone:** (604) 299-0700, (604) 684-5605 or (877) 299-0701.

Industrial Tours

Tours are available of the Vancouver Post Office, (604) 662-5715, 349 W. Georgia St. Reservations are required.

Plane Tours

Another way to see Vancouver and its surroundings is by air. Harbour Air offers flights lasting from 35 minutes to 1.25 hours; departure is from downtown on Coal Harbour Road, one block west of Canada Place. Fares vary, and reservations are required; phone (604) 274-1277.

Train Tours

Rocky Mountaineer Vacations offers scenic, 2-day, all daylight, narrated rail tours between Vancouver or Whistler, British Columbia, and Banff, Calgary, or Jasper, Alberta. Westbound or eastbound departures are offered mid-April to mid-October, with winter rail trips available in December. Onboard meals and snacks as well as accommodations in Kamloops or Quesnel are included. A 3-hour trip on the Whistler Mountaineer also is available and runs between Vancouver and Whistler May through October. Phone (604) 606-7245 or (877) 460-3200, or (888) 687-7245 for information about Whistler trips.

Trolley Tours

Trolley tours provide a look at the city at a relaxed pace. The Downtown Historic Railway, comprised of two electric interurban railcars, skirts False Creek between Science World at TELUS World of Science and Granville Island and runs from mid-May to mid-October; phone (604) 665-3903.

THE VANCOUVER TROLLEY CO. departs from many downtown accommodations and attractions. Narrated tours highlight Vancouver's major attractions. Passengers may board, depart or re-board at any stop on the route. A Grouse Mountain sunset tour also is available.

Time: Allow 2 hours minimum. **Hours:** Narrated hop-on, hop-off tours daily 9-6:30. Sunset tours depart Victoria Day weekend-Labour Day. Closed Christmas. **Cost:** One-day hop-on, hop-off fare $38; $35 (ages 13-18 and 65+); $20 (ages 4-12). Two-day hop-on, hop-off trolley fare $40; $25 (ages 4-12). Combination tickets are available. Reservations are required for sunset tours. Hours and rates may vary; phone ahead. **Phone:** (604) 801-5515 or (888) 451-5581.

Walking Tours

ROCKWOOD ADVENTURES departs from downtown hotels. Half- and full-day guided nature walks are offered to area ecological destinations including Lynn Canyon, a rain forest in Capilano River Canyon, a coastal forest at Burrard Inlet and Mount Gardner on Bowen Island. All trips include a snack or lunch.

Hours: Half-day tours offered daily 9-4, Apr. 15-Oct. 15. **Cost:** $95; $85 (ages 12-25, ages 65+ and students with ID); $60 (ages 4-11). Rate may vary depending on tour. Reservations are required. **Phone:** (604) 913-1621 or (888) 236-6606.

▼ *See AAA listing p. 361* ▼

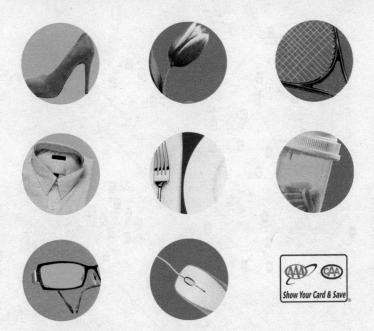

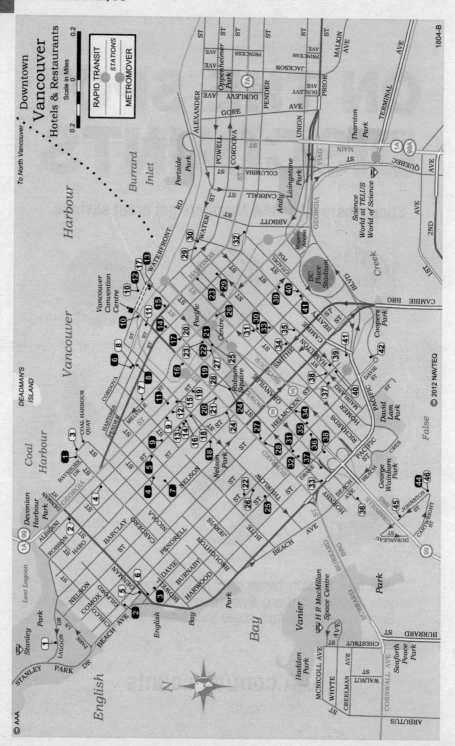

Vancouver
Downtown
Hotels & Restaurants

RAPID TRANSIT
STATIONS
METROMOVER

Scale in Miles
0.2   0.2

© AAA

1804-B

© 2012 NAVTEQ

Downtown Vancouver

This index helps you "spot" where approved hotels and restaurants are located on the corresponding detailed maps. Hotel daily rate range is for comparison only. Restaurant price range is a combination of lunch and/or dinner. Turn to the listing page for more detailed rate and price information and consult display ads for special promotions.

DOWNTOWN VANCOUVER

Map Page	Hotels	Diamond Rated	Rate Range	Page
1 p. 364	**The Westin Bayshore Vancouver** *(See ad p. 383.)*	◈◈◈	$189-$460 SAVE	383
2 p. 364	Sylvia Hotel	◈◈	$100-$400	382
3 p. 364	**BEST WESTERN PLUS Sands Hotel** *(See ad p. 356.)*	◈◈◈	$109-$260 SAVE	375
4 p. 364	West End Guest House	◈◈◈	$150-$325	382
5 p. 364	The Listel Hotel Vancouver	◈◈◈	$139-$299	377
6 p. 364	Renaissance Vancouver Harbourside Hotel	◈◈◈	$169-$329	379
7 p. 364	**Barclay House Bed and Breakfast**	◈◈◈	$90-$195 SAVE	374
8 p. 364	**Vancouver Marriott Pinnacle Downtown**	◈◈◈◈	$169-$329 SAVE	382
9 p. 364	**Blue Horizon Hotel**	◈◈◈	$109-$329 SAVE	375
10 p. 364	**Fairmont Pacific Rim**	◈◈◈◈	$269-$599 SAVE	376
11 p. 364	**Shangri-La Hotel Vancouver** *(See ad p. 380.)*	◈◈◈◈	Rates not provided SAVE	380
12 p. 364	**Pan Pacific Vancouver** *(See ad p. 378.)*	◈◈◈◈	$179-$439 SAVE	379
13 p. 364	**The Fairmont Waterfront**	◈◈◈◈	$199-$449 SAVE	376
14 p. 364	**Days Inn Vancouver Downtown**	◈◈◈	$113-$289 SAVE	375
15 p. 364	The Hotel at Terminal City Club	◈◈◈	Rates not provided	376
16 p. 364	**Hyatt Regency Vancouver**	◈◈◈◈	$125-$396 SAVE	377
17 p. 364	**Executive Hotel Le Soleil**	◈◈◈◈	$199-$399 SAVE	375
18 p. 364	'O Canada' House B&B	◈◈◈	Rates not provided	377
19 p. 364	**The Fairmont Hotel Vancouver**	◈◈◈◈	$179-$449 SAVE	375
20 p. 364	**The Sutton Place Hotel**	◈◈◈◈	Rates not provided SAVE	382
21 p. 364	**Four Seasons Hotel Vancouver**	◈◈◈◈	$225-$2950 SAVE	376
22 p. 364	**Rosewood Hotel Georgia**	◈◈◈◈	$215-$410 SAVE	379
23 p. 364	**Delta Vancouver Suites**	◈◈◈	$159-$299 SAVE	375
24 p. 364	**The Wedgewood Hotel & Spa**	◈◈◈	$238-$418 SAVE	382
25 p. 364	**Sunset Inn & Suites**	◈◈◈	$189-$500 SAVE	382
26 p. 364	St. Regis Hotel	◈◈◈	$134-$787	379
27 p. 364	**Sheraton Vancouver Wall Centre Hotel** *(See ad p. 381.)*	◈◈◈	$159-$509 SAVE	380
28 p. 364	The Burrard	◈◈	$129-$209	375
29 p. 364	Ramada Limited Downtown Vancouver	◈◈	$99-$224	379
30 p. 364	L'Hermitage Hotel	◈◈◈	$190-$595	377
31 p. 364	**Landis Hotel & Suites**	◈◈◈	$159-$299 SAVE	377
32 p. 364	**Residence Inn by Marriott Vancouver Downtown**	◈◈◈	Rates not provided SAVE	379
33 p. 364	**The Westin Grand, Vancouver**	◈◈◈	$169-$679 SAVE	383

DOWNTOWN VANCOUVER (cont'd)

Map Page	Hotels (cont'd)	Diamond Rated	Rate Range	Page
34 p. 364	**BEST WESTERN PLUS Chateau Granville** (See ad p. 374.)	◆◆◆	$79-$289 [SAVE]	374
35 p. 364	Howard Johnson Hotel Downtown Vancouver	◆◆	$79-$259	376
36 p. 364	**Ramada Inn & Suites Downtown Vancouver**	◆◆	$99-$299 [SAVE]	379
37 p. 364	Quality Hotel Downtown-The Inn at False Creek	◆◆	$79-$229	379
38 p. 364	**BEST WESTERN PLUS Downtown Vancouver**	◆◆◆	$99-$199 [SAVE]	375
39 p. 364	Sandman Hotel Vancouver City Centre	◆◆	$89-$179	379
40 p. 364	**Georgian Court Hotel**	◆◆◆	$159-$399 [SAVE]	376
41 p. 364	**Hampton Inn & Suites by Hilton, Downtown Vancouver**	◆◆◆	$163-$266 [SAVE]	376
44 p. 364	**Granville Island Hotel** (See ad p. 377.)	◆◆◆	$189-$550 [SAVE]	376

Map Page	Restaurants	Diamond Rated	Cuisine	Price Range	Page
1 p. 364	**The Fish House in Stanley Park**	◆◆◆	Seafood	$18-$35	384
2 p. 364	**Ciao Bella Ristorante**	◆◆	Italian	$16-$25	384
3 p. 364	Cardero's Restaurant	◆◆	Seafood	$9-$29	384
4 p. 364	Le Gavroche Restaurant Francais	◆◆◆	French	$16-$45	386
5 p. 364	Rain City Grill	◆◆◆	Pacific Northwest	$14-$32	387
6 p. 364	Won More Szechuan Cuisine	◆◆	Chinese	$7-$16	388
7 p. 364	Tableau Bar Bistro	◆◆◆	New French	$12-$24	387
8 p. 364	Show Case Restaurant	◆◆◆	Pacific Northwest	$15-$30	387
9 p. 364	Kirin Mandarin Restaurant	◆◆◆	Chinese	$4-$57	386
10 p. 364	**Five Sails Restaurant**	◆◆◆◆	New European	$30-$40	385
11 p. 364	Imperial Chinese Seafood Restaurant	◆◆◆	Chinese	$15-$58	385
12 p. 364	Oysi Oysi Japanese Restaurant	◆◆	Japanese	$7-$19	387
13 p. 364	CINCIN	◆◆◆	Mediterranean	$15-$38	384
14 p. 364	Zefferelli's Restaurant	◆◆	Italian	$11-$25	388
15 p. 364	**Market by Jean-Georges**	◆◆◆◆	Pacific Northwest	$16-$36	386
16 p. 364	**Tropika Malaysian & Thai Cuisine**	◆	Asian	$8-$20	387
17 p. 364	**Herons West Coast Kitchen + Bar**	◆◆◆	Pacific Northwest	$16-$35	385
18 p. 364	**Joe Fortes Seafood & Chop House**	◆◆◆	Seafood	$17-$40	386
19 p. 364	Kobe Japanese Steak House	◆◆	Japanese	$33-$58	386
20 p. 364	Copper Chimney	◆◆◆	Indian	$18-$34	384
21 p. 364	Fleuri Restaurant	◆◆◆◆	Pacific Northwest	$16-$39	385
22 p. 364	India Bistro	◆◆	Indian	$9-$14	385
23 p. 364	Diva at the Met	◆◆◆	Pacific Northwest	$16-$38	384
24 p. 364	**Le Crocodile**	◆◆◆◆	French	$15-$42	386
25 p. 364	Yew Restaurant & Bar	◆◆◆	Seafood	$18-$40	388
26 p. 364	Stepho's Souvlaki Greek Taverna	◆◆	Greek	$7-$12	387

Map Page	Restaurants (cont'd)	Diamond Rated	Cuisine	Price Range	Page
㉗ p. 364	Hawksworth Restaurant	▽▽▽▽	New Pacific Northwest	$18-$38	385
㉘ p. 364	**Bacchus Restaurant**	▽▽▽▽	French	$17-$46	383
㉙ p. 364	Al Porto Ristorante	▽▽▽	Northern Italian	$10-$29	383
㉚ p. 364	Water St. Cafe	▽▽	Italian	$11-$29	387
㉛ p. 364	Kingston Taphouse & Grille	▽▽	American	$11-$25	386
㉜ p. 364	Wild Rice	▽▽	Asian	$11-$21	388
㉝ p. 364	Il Giardino	▽▽▽	Italian	$19-$40	385
㉞ p. 364	Subeez Cafe	▽▽	Canadian	$11-$27	387
㉟ p. 364	Lupo Restaurant	▽▽▽	Italian	$15-$35	386
㊱ p. 364	C Restaurant	▽▽▽	Seafood	$18-$41	384
㊲ p. 364	Brix Restaurant & Wine Bar	▽▽▽	Pacific Northwest	$19-$29	384
㊳ p. 364	Blue Water Cafe + Raw Bar	▽▽▽▽	Seafood	$28-$46	383
㊴ p. 364	Glowbal Grill Steaks & Satay	▽▽▽	Steak	$13-$49	385
㊵ p. 364	Yaletown Brewing Company	▽▽	American	$12-$24	388
㊶ p. 364	La Terrazza	▽▽▽	Northern Italian	$24-$42	386
㊷ p. 364	Provence Marinaside	▽▽▽	Seafood	$14-$34	387
㊺ p. 364	The Sandbar Seafood Restaurant	▽▽	Seafood	$12-$35	387
㊻ p. 364	Dockside Restaurant (See ad p. 377.)	▽▽	Canadian	$14-$38	384

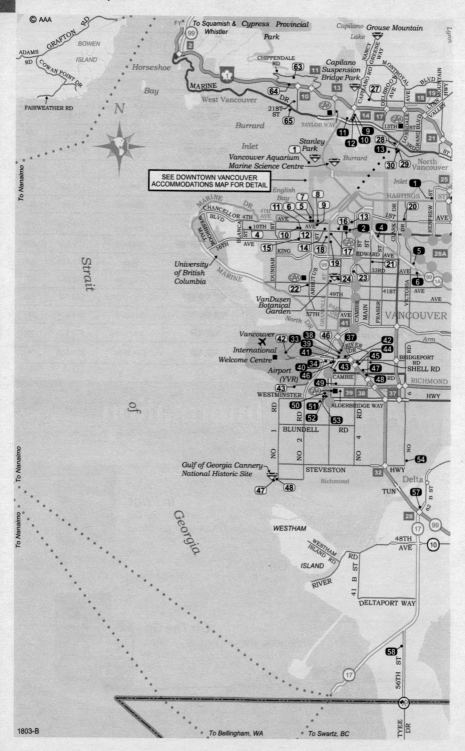

© AAA

SEE DOWNTOWN VANCOUVER
ACCOMMODATIONS MAP FOR DETAIL

1803-B

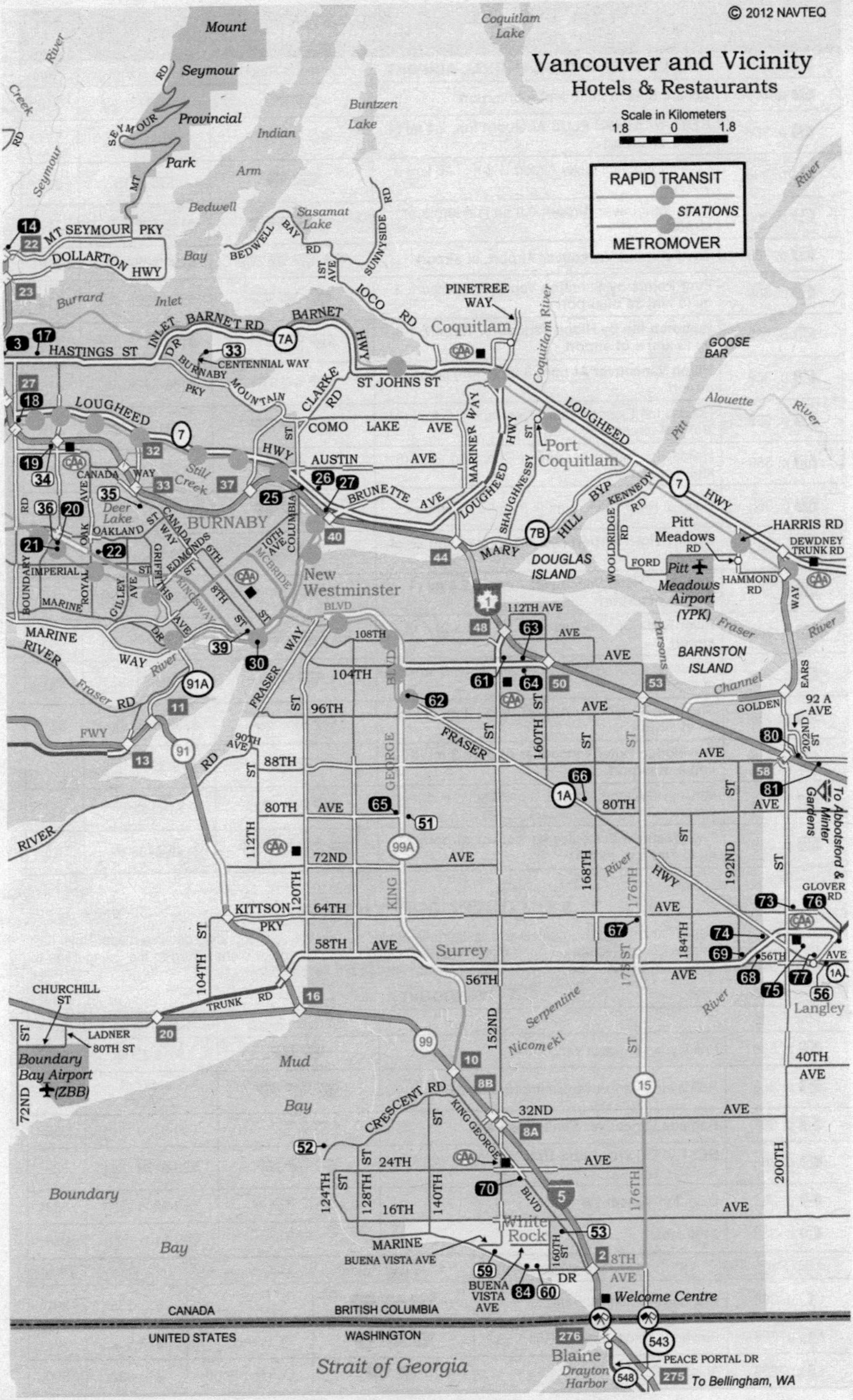

© 2012 NAVTEQ

Vancouver and Vicinity
Hotels & Restaurants

Scale in Kilometers
1.8   0   1.8

RAPID TRANSIT
STATIONS
METROMOVER

Mount
Seymour
Provincial
Park

Coquitlam
Lake

MT SEYMOUR PKY
DOLLARTON HWY

Burrard
Inlet

BARNET RD   BARNET
HASTINGS ST
CENTENNIAL WAY
BURNABY MOUNTAIN PKY

Coquitlam

PINETREE
WAY

IOCO RD

GOOSE
BAR

ST JOHNS ST

LOUGHEED

COMO LAKE AVE
AUSTIN AVE

Port
Coquitlam

LOUGHEED HWY

HARRIS RD
DEWDNEY
TRUNK RD

BURNABY

BRUNETTE AVE

MARY HILL BYP

DOUGLAS
ISLAND

Pitt
Meadows
RD

Pitt
Meadows
Airport
(YPK)

HAMMOND
RD

BARNSTON
ISLAND

New
Westminster

112TH AVE

108TH
104TH
96TH
88TH
80TH AVE
72ND

GOLDEN

92 A
AVE

Minter
Gardens

To Abbotsford &

GLOVER
RD

KITTSON

64TH
58TH AVE
56TH

Surrey

GEORGE
KING
FRASER

Serpentine
Nicomekl

River

Langley

CHURCHILL
ST
LADNER
80TH ST

TRUNK RD

Boundary
Bay Airport
(ZBB)

Mud
Bay

CRESCENT RD
KING GEORGE

24TH
16TH

32ND

40TH
AVE

Boundary
Bay

MARINE
BUENA VISTA AVE

White
Rock

BUENA
VISTA
AVE

Welcome Centre

CANADA
UNITED STATES

BRITISH COLUMBIA
WASHINGTON

Blaine
Drayton
Harbor

PEACE PORTAL DR

To Bellingham, WA

Strait of Georgia

✈ Airport Accommodations

Map Page	VANCOUVER INTERNATIONAL AIRPORT	Diamond Rated	Rate Range	Page
47 p. 368	Accent Inns, 3 mi (5 km) e of airport	◆◆	$89-$179 SAVE	316
43 p. 368	BEST WESTERN PLUS Abercorn Inn, 2.4 mi (4 km) e of airport	◆◆◆	$110-$150 SAVE	317
41 p. 368	Comfort Inn Vancouver Airport, 1.6 mi (2.6 km) e of airport	◆◆	$75-$115	317
34 p. 368	Delta Vancouver Airport, 0.9 mi (1.4 km) e of airport	◆◆◆	$149-$329 SAVE	317
33 p. 368	The Fairmont Vancouver Airport, at airport	◆◆◆◆	$299-$399 SAVE	318
49 p. 368	Four Points by Sheraton Vancouver Airport, 3 mi (5 km) se of airport	◆◆◆	$155-$225 SAVE	318
39 p. 368	Hampton Inn by Hilton Vancouver Airport, 1.8 mi (3 km) e of airport	◆◆◆	$109-$175 SAVE	318
50 p. 368	Hilton Vancouver Airport, 3 mi (5 km) se of airport	◆◆◆	$169-$229 SAVE	318
42 p. 368	Holiday Inn Express Vancouver-Airport, 2.4 mi (4 km) e of airport	◆◆◆	$119-$179	318
48 p. 368	Holiday Inn Vancouver Airport-Richmond, 3 mi (5 km) e of airport	◆◆◆	$115-$189	318
37 p. 368	Hotel at River Rock, 3 mi (4.8 km) e of airport	◆◆◆	Rates not provided	318
51 p. 368	Quality Hotel Airport (South), 3 mi (5 km) se of airport	◆◆	$79-$129 SAVE	319
46 p. 368	Radisson Hotel Vancouver Airport, 2.4 mi (4 km) se of airport	◆◆◆	$139-$209 SAVE	319
38 p. 368	River Rock Casino Resort, 3 mi (4.8 km) e of airport	◆◆◆◆	$139-$189 SAVE	321
45 p. 368	Sandman Hotel Vancouver Airport, 3 mi (5 km) e of airport	◆◆	$99-$169	321
52 p. 368	Sheraton Vancouver Airport Hotel, 3 mi (5 km) se of airport	◆◆◆	$139-$359 SAVE	321
44 p. 368	Travelodge Hotel Vancouver Airport, 3 mi (5 km) e of airport	◆◆	$79-$200 SAVE	321
53 p. 368	Vancouver Airport Marriott, 3 mi (5 km) se of airport	◆◆◆	$169-$259	321
40 p. 368	The Westin Wall Centre Vancouver Airport, 3 mi (5 km) e of airport	◆◆◆◆	$149-$409 SAVE	321

Vancouver and Vicinity

This index helps you "spot" where approved hotels and restaurants are located on the corresponding detailed maps. Hotel daily rate range is for comparison only. Restaurant price range is a combination of lunch and/or dinner. Turn to the listing page for more detailed rate and price information and consult display ads for special promotions.

VANCOUVER

Map Page	Hotels	Diamond Rated	Rate Range	Page
1 p. 368	Holiday Inn Express Vancouver	◆◆	$119-$309	388
2 p. 368	Holiday Inn Vancouver-Centre (Broadway)	◆◆◆	Rates not provided	388
3 p. 368	Ramada Vancouver Exhibition Park	◆◆	$90-$160 SAVE	388
4 p. 368	BEST WESTERN PLUS Uptown Hotel (See ad p. 389.)	◆◆◆	$89-$189 SAVE	388
5 p. 368	Days Inn-Vancouver Metro	◆◆	$59-$209 SAVE	388
6 p. 368	2400 Motel	◆	$89-$189 SAVE	388

Map Page	Restaurants	Diamond Rated	Cuisine	Price Range	Page
1 p. 368	Teahouse in Stanley Park	◆◆◆	Pacific Northwest	$17-$35	391
4 p. 368	Provence Mediterranean Grill	◆◆◆	French	$12-$32	391
5 p. 368	Abigail's Party	◆◆	Comfort Food	$14-$22	390

Map Page	Restaurants (cont'd)	Diamond Rated	Cuisine	Price Range	Page
6 p. 368	Bishop's	◆◆◆◆	Pacific Northwest	$30-$39	390
7 p. 368	Sophie's Cosmic Cafe	◆◆	American	$7-$19	391
8 p. 368	Las Margaritas Restaurante & Cantina	◆◆	Mexican	$12-$19	390
9 p. 368	REFUEL Restaurant & Bar	◆◆◆	Pacific Northwest	$15-$35	391
10 p. 368	Mistral French Bistro	◆◆◆	French	$16-$34	390
11 p. 368	Q4 Ristorante	◆◆	Italian	$17-$34	391
12 p. 368	Gramercy Grill	◆◆	Pacific Northwest	$10-$26	390
13 p. 368	Monk McQueen's Fresh Seafood & Oyster Bar	◆◆	Seafood	$14-$30	390
14 p. 368	Maurya Indian Cuisine	◆◆	Indian	$13-$25	390
15 p. 368	Trafalgars Bistro	◆◆	Regional Continental	$12-$27	391
16 p. 368	Tojo's Restaurant	◆◆◆	Japanese	$18-$45	391
17 p. 368	Vij's Restaurant	◆◆◆	New Indian	$24-$30	391
18 p. 368	West Restaurant	◆◆◆◆	Pacific Northwest	$15-$43	391
19 p. 368	The Ouisi Bistro	◆◆	Cajun	$10-$23	391
20 p. 368	Lombardo's Pizzeria & Ristorante	◆◆	Pizza	$12-$20	390
21 p. 368	Sawasdee Thai Restaurant	◆◆	Thai	$8-$13	391
22 p. 368	Avenue Grill	◆◆	Mediterranean	$11-$24	390
23 p. 368	Seasons in the Park Restaurant	◆◆◆	Pacific Northwest	$13-$36	391
24 p. 368	Shaughnessy Restaurant At VanDusen Garden	◆◆	Pacific Northwest	$14-$30	391

NORTH VANCOUVER

Map Page	Hotels	Diamond Rated	Rate Range	Page
9 p. 368	**North Vancouver Hotel**	◆◆	$79-$149 SAVE	284
10 p. 368	**Comfort Inn & Suites**	◆◆	$99-$130 SAVE	284
11 p. 368	Lionsgate Travelodge	◆	$59-$169	284
12 p. 368	**BEST WESTERN Capilano Inn & Suites**	◆◆	$99-$149 SAVE	284
13 p. 368	Pinnacle Hotel at the Pier	◆◆◆	$129-$259	284
14 p. 368	**Holiday Inn & Suites North Vancouver**	◆◆◆	$139-$169 SAVE	284

Map Page	Restaurants	Diamond Rated	Cuisine	Price Range	Page
27 p. 368	The Edge Bistro	◆◆◆	Italian	$15-$30	284
28 p. 368	Jagerhof Schnitzel House	◆◆	German	$10-$18	284
29 p. 368	The Lobby Restaurant	◆◆◆	Pacific Northwest	$12-$28	285
30 p. 368	Gusto di Quattro	◆◆◆	Italian	$14-$35	284

BURNABY

Map Page	Hotels	Diamond Rated	Rate Range	Page
17 p. 368	Howard Johnson North Burnaby Boutique Hotel	◆◆	$99-$410	223
18 p. 368	**Accent Inns**	◆◆	$109-$179 SAVE	222
19 p. 368	**Delta Burnaby Hotel and Conference Centre**	◆◆◆◆	$129-$1300 SAVE	223
20 p. 368	Hilton Vancouver Metrotown	◆◆◆	$116-$197	223
21 p. 368	Holiday Inn Express Metrotown	◆◆◆	$139-$194	223

BURNABY (cont'd)

Map Page	Hotels (cont'd)	Diamond Rated	Rate Range	Page
㉒ p. 368	**BEST WESTERN PLUS Kings Inn & Conference Center** *(See ad p. 223.)*	◇◇◇	$99-$139 SAVE	223

Map Page	Restaurants	Diamond Rated	Cuisine	Price Range	Page
㉝ p. 368	HORIZONS	◆◆◆	Pacific Rim	$14-$36	224
㉞ p. 368	Ebo Restaurant and Lounge	◆◆◆	Pacific Northwest	$12-$36	224
㉟ p. 368	Hart House Restaurant	◆◆◆	Pacific Northwest	$14-$32	224
㊱ p. 368	Reflect Social Dining + Lounge	◆◆	Pacific Northwest	$12-$35	224

COQUITLAM

Map Page	Hotels	Diamond Rated	Rate Range	Page
㉕ p. 368	**BEST WESTERN PLUS Coquitlam Inn Convention Centre**	◇◇◇	$140-$180 SAVE	230
㉖ p. 368	Ramada Coquitlam	◆◆	$99-$139	231
㉗ p. 368	**BEST WESTERN PLUS Chelsea Inn**	◇◇◇	$119-$139 SAVE	230

NEW WESTMINSTER

Map Page	Hotel	Diamond Rated	Rate Range	Page
㉚ p. 368	Inn at the Quay	◆◆◆	$140-$230	281

Map Page	Restaurant	Diamond Rated	Cuisine	Price Range	Page
㊴ p. 368	Burger Heaven	◆	Burgers	$8-$20	281

RICHMOND

Map Page	Hotels	Diamond Rated	Rate Range	Page
㉝ p. 368	**The Fairmont Vancouver Airport**	◇◇◇◇	$299-$399 SAVE	318
㉞ p. 368	**Delta Vancouver Airport**	◇◇◇	$149-$329 SAVE	317
㊲ p. 368	Hotel at River Rock	◆◆◆	Rates not provided	318
㊳ p. 368	**River Rock Casino Resort** *(See ad p. 320.)*	◇◇◇◇	$139-$189 SAVE	321
㊴ p. 368	**Hampton Inn by Hilton Vancouver Airport**	◇◇◇	$109-$175 SAVE	318
㊵ p. 368	**The Westin Wall Centre Vancouver Airport** *(See ad p. 389.)*	◇◇◇◇	$149-$409 SAVE	321
㊶ p. 368	Comfort Inn Vancouver Airport	◆◆	$75-$115	317
㊷ p. 368	Holiday Inn Express Vancouver-Airport	◆◆◆	$119-$179	318
㊸ p. 368	**BEST WESTERN PLUS Abercorn Inn** *(See ad p. 317.)*	◇◇◇	$110-$150 SAVE	317
㊹ p. 368	**Travelodge Hotel Vancouver Airport**	◇◇	$79-$200 SAVE	321
㊺ p. 368	Sandman Hotel Vancouver Airport	◆◆	$99-$169	321
㊻ p. 368	**Radisson Hotel Vancouver Airport** *(See ad p. 319.)*	◇◇◇	$139-$209 SAVE	319
㊼ p. 368	**Accent Inns**	◇◇	$89-$179 SAVE	316
㊽ p. 368	Holiday Inn Vancouver Airport-Richmond	◆◆◆	$115-$189	318
㊾ p. 368	**Four Points by Sheraton Vancouver Airport**	◇◇◇	$155-$225 SAVE	318
㊿ p. 368	**Hilton Vancouver Airport**	◇◇◇	$169-$229 SAVE	318
(51) p. 368	**Quality Hotel Airport (South)**	◇◇	$79-$129 SAVE	319
(52) p. 368	**Sheraton Vancouver Airport Hotel**	◇◇◇	$139-$359 SAVE	321
(53) p. 368	Vancouver Airport Marriott	◆◆◆	$169-$259	321
(54) p. 368	Holiday Inn Express & Suites Riverport	◆◆◆	$109-$199	318

Map Page	Restaurants	Diamond Rated	Cuisine	Price Range	Page
(42) p. 368	Globe @ YVR	◆◆◆	Pacific Northwest	$15-$42	321
(43) p. 368	Flying Beaver Bar & Grill	◆◆	American	$12-$18	321
(46) p. 368	Tramonto	◆◆◆	Italian	$24-$43	322
(47) p. 368	Tapenade Bistro	◆◆	Mediterranean	$13-$28	322
(48) p. 368	Steveston Seafood House	◆◆◆	Seafood	$20-$40	322

DELTA

Map Page	Hotels	Diamond Rated	Rate Range	Page
(57) p. 368	**Delta Town & Country Inn**	◆◆	$102-$112 SAVE	236
(58) p. 368	**The Coast Tsawwassen Inn**	◆◆◆	$111-$233 SAVE	236

SURREY

Map Page	Hotels	Diamond Rated	Rate Range	Page
(61) p. 368	**Sheraton Vancouver Guildford Hotel** *(See ad p. 335.)*	◆◆◆	$105-$165 SAVE	335
(62) p. 368	Compass Point Inn	◆◆	$99-$129	334
(63) p. 368	Coast Surrey Guildford Hotel	◆◆	Rates not provided	334
(64) p. 368	Holiday Inn Express & Suites Surrey	◆◆◆	$99-$149	334
(65) p. 368	**BEST WESTERN PLUS King George Inn & Suites** *(See ad p. 334.)*	◆◆◆	$79-$179 SAVE	333
(66) p. 368	Comfort Inn & Suites Surrey	◆◆◆	$99-$149	334
(67) p. 368	**Holiday Inn Hotel & Suites**	◆◆◆	$90-$150 SAVE	334
(68) p. 368	**Hampton Inn & Suites Langley/Surrey** *(See ad p. 270.)*	◆◆◆	$129-$159 SAVE	334
(69) p. 368	**Ramada Langley-Surrey**	◆◆◆	$99-$149 SAVE	335
(70) p. 368	**BEST WESTERN Peace Arch Inn**	◆◆	$99-$179 SAVE	333

Map Page	Restaurants	Diamond Rated	Cuisine	Price Range	Page
(51) p. 368	Villa Verdi Ristorante Italiano	◆◆◆	Northern Italian	$16-$32	336
(52) p. 368	Crescent Beach Bistro	◆◆	Mediterranean	$12-$28	335
(53) p. 368	The Turkey House & Deli	◆	Sandwiches	$7-$12	336

LANGLEY

Map Page	Hotels	Diamond Rated	Rate Range	Page
(73) p. 368	**Quality Hotel & Suites**	◆◆	$79-$109 SAVE	271
(74) p. 368	Canadas Best Value Inn Langley	◆	$69-$99	269
(75) p. 368	**Days Inn & Suites Langley**	◆◆	$75-$119 SAVE	271
(76) p. 368	**BEST WESTERN PLUS Langley Inn** *(See ad p. 269.)*	◆◆◆	$117-$142 SAVE	269
(77) p. 368	**Coast Hotel & Convention Centre**	◆◆◆	$112-$149 SAVE	271
(80) p. 368	Sandman Hotel Langley	◆◆	$109-$139	271
(81) p. 368	**Holiday Inn Express Hotel & Suites Langley** *(See ad p. 270.)*	◆◆◆	$109-$169 SAVE	271

Map Page	Restaurant	Diamond Rated	Cuisine	Price Range	Page
(56) p. 368	Sonoma Grill	◆◆	Continental	$10-$30	271

WHITE ROCK

Map Page	Hotel	Diamond Rated	Rate Range	Page
(84) p. 368	Ocean Promenade Hotel *(See ad p. 432.)*	◆◆◆	Rates not provided	432

Map Page	Restaurants	Diamond Rated	Cuisine	Price Range	Page
59 p. 368	Giraffe	▽▽▽	Pacific Rim	$12-$28	432
60 p. 368	La Baia Italian Restaurant	▽▽	Italian	$14-$27	432
WEST VANCOUVER					
Map Page	Restaurants	Diamond Rated	Cuisine	Price Range	Page
63 p. 368	Fraiche	▽▽▽	Pacific Northwest	$14-$38	421
64 p. 368	Salmon House on the Hill	▽▽▽	Seafood	$28-$39	421
65 p. 368	La Regalade French Bistro	▽▽	French	$18-$25	421

DOWNTOWN VANCOUVER
- Restaurants p. 383
- Hotels & Restaurants map & index p. 364

BARCLAY HOUSE BED AND BREAKFAST
604/605-1351 **7**

Historic Bed & Breakfast
$90-$195

Address: 1351 Barclay St V6E 1H6 **Location:** Between Broughton and Jervis sts. Located in a residential area. **Facility:** This classic Victorian adults-only B&B is located on a tree-lined street right in the heart of Vancouver's residential West End district. There's a lovely veranda that overlooks a quaint garden. 6 units. 3 stories (no elevator), interior/exterior corridors. **Terms:** check-in 4 pm, age restrictions may apply, 7 day cancellation notice-fee imposed. **Amenities:** safes. **Free Special Amenities:** full breakfast and high-speed Internet.

BEST WESTERN PLUS CHATEAU GRANVILLE
(604)669-7070 **34**

Hotel
$79-$289

AAA Benefit: Members save up to 20%, plus 10% bonus points with Best Western Rewards®.

Address: 1100 Granville St V6Z 2B6 **Location:** Between Davie and Helmcken sts. **Facility:** 150 units. 3-15 stories, interior corridors. **Parking:** on-site (fee). **Terms:** cancellation fee imposed. **Guest Services:** valet laundry. **Free Special Amenities:** local telephone calls and high-speed Internet. *(See ad this page.)*

(See map & index p. 364.)

BEST WESTERN PLUS DOWNTOWN VANCOUVER
(604)669-9888 **38**

Hotel
$99-$199

AAA Benefit: Members save up to 20%, plus 10% bonus points with Best Western Rewards®.

Address: 718 Drake St V6Z 2W6 **Location:** Between Howe and Granville sts. Located in Granville Street Entertainment District. **Facility:** 143 units, some efficiencies. 12 stories, interior corridors. **Parking:** on-site (fee). **Terms:** cancellation fee imposed. **Amenities:** high-speed Internet, safes. **Activities:** saunas, whirlpool, exercise room. **Guest Services:** valet and coin laundry, area transportation-downtown. **Free Special Amenities:** high-speed Internet and local transportation.

Full-service hotel, breakfast package available, complimentary drop-off shuttle, pet friendly & more

---

BEST WESTERN PLUS SANDS HOTEL
(604)682-1831 **3**

Hotel
$109-$260

AAA Benefit: Members save up to 20%, plus 10% bonus points with Best Western Rewards®.

Address: 1755 Davie St V6G 1W5 **Location:** Between Bidwell and Denman sts. **Facility:** 119 units, some efficiencies. 5 stories, interior corridors. **Parking:** on-site (fee). **Terms:** check-in 4 pm, cancellation fee imposed, resort fee. **Amenities:** video games (fee). **Activities:** sauna, exercise room. **Guest Services:** valet and coin laundry. **Free Special Amenities:** local telephone calls and high-speed Internet.
(See ad p. 356.)

BLUE HORIZON HOTEL
(604)688-1411 **9**

Hotel
$109-$329

Address: 1225 Robson St V6E 1C3 **Location:** Between Jervis and Bute sts. **Facility:** 214 units. 31 stories, interior corridors. **Parking:** on-site (fee). **Terms:** cancellation fee imposed. **Amenities:** high-speed Internet, safes. **Pool(s):** heated indoor. **Activities:** sauna, whirlpool, limited exercise equipment. **Guest Services:** valet laundry. **Free Special Amenities:** high-speed Internet.

Share a New View on Travel at AAATravelViews.com

THE BURRARD
(604)681-2331 **28**

Hotel $129-$209 **Address:** 1100 Burrard St V6Z 1Y7 **Location:** Between Helmcken and Davie sts. **Facility:** 72 units. 4 stories, exterior corridors. **Parking:** on-site (fee). **Terms:** check-in 4 pm, cancellation fee imposed. **Amenities:** safes. **Activities:** bicycles.

DAYS INN VANCOUVER DOWNTOWN
(604)681-4335 **14**

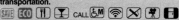

Hotel
$113-$289

Address: 921 W Pender St V6C 1M2 **Location:** Between Burrard and Hornby sts. Located in the financial district. **Facility:** 85 units. 9 stories, interior corridors. **Parking:** on-site (fee). **Terms:** cancellation fee imposed. **Amenities:** high-speed Internet, safes. **Guest Services:** valet and coin laundry. **Free Special Amenities:** newspaper and high-speed Internet.

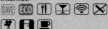

Located in the heart of downtown. Walking distance to Canada Place, Cruise Ships & Convention Center

---

DELTA VANCOUVER SUITES
(604)689-8188 **23**

Hotel
$159-$299

Address: 550 W Hastings St V6B 1L6 **Location:** Between Seymour and Richards sts; entrance in alley way. **Facility:** 225 units. 23 stories, interior corridors. **Parking:** on-site (fee) and valet. **Terms:** cancellation fee imposed. **Amenities:** high-speed Internet (fee), safes. **Activities:** exercise room. **Guest Services:** valet laundry.

EXECUTIVE HOTEL LE SOLEIL
(604)632-3000 **17**

Boutique Hotel
$199-$399

Address: 567 Hornby St V6C 2E8 **Location:** Between Dunsmuir and Pender sts. **Facility:** This charming boutique hotel features amazing attention to detail, from the cozy lobby to the guest suites, where every piece of art, furniture and fabric was hand-picked from European designers. 112 units. 16 stories, interior corridors. **Parking:** valet only. **Terms:** cancellation fee imposed. **Amenities:** high-speed Internet (fee), safes. **Dining:** Copper Chimney, see separate listing. **Guest Services:** valet laundry. **Free Special Amenities:** local telephone calls and high-speed Internet.

THE FAIRMONT HOTEL VANCOUVER
(604)684-3131 **19**

Classic Historic Hotel
$179-$449

Address: 900 W Georgia St V6C 2W6 **Location:** Corner of Burrard at W Georgia St; enter from Hornby St. Across from Vancouver Art Gallery. **Facility:** Built in 1939, this downtown historic landmark was officially opened by the Queen Mother and her husband, King George. 557 units. 15 stories, interior corridors. **Parking:** on-site (fee) and valet. **Terms:** cancellation fee imposed. **Amenities:** high-speed Internet (fee). **Dining:** entertainment. **Pool(s):** heated indoor. **Activities:** saunas, whirlpool, exercise room, spa. **Guest Services:** valet laundry.

(See map & index p. 364.)

FAIRMONT PACIFIC RIM   (604)695-5300

Hotel
$269-$599

Address: 1038 Canada Place V6C 0B9 **Location:** Between Burrard and Thurlow sts. **Facility:** Vancouver's newest luxury hotel treats you to breathtaking views of the north shore mountains, Stanley Park and the Inner Harbour. 377 units. 48 stories, interior corridors. **Parking:** on-site (fee) and valet. **Terms:** cancellation fee imposed, resort fee. **Amenities:** safes. *Fee:* video games, high-speed Internet. **Dining:** entertainment. **Pool(s):** heated outdoor. **Activities:** saunas, whirlpool, steamrooms, spa. **Guest Services:** valet laundry, area transportation-downtown.

THE FAIRMONT WATERFRONT   (604)691-1991 **13**

Hotel
$199-$449

Address: 900 Canada Place Way V6C 3L5 **Location:** Between Howe and Burrard sts. Opposite Canada Place. **Facility:** Near the cruise ship terminal and convention center, this guest-oriented property features pleasant, spacious rooms with either a harbor or city view. 489 units. 23 stories, interior corridors. **Parking:** on-site (fee) and valet. **Amenities:** high-speed Internet (fee), safes. **Dining:** Herons West Coast Kitchen + Bar, see separate listing. **Pool(s):** heated outdoor. **Activities:** whirlpool, steamrooms. *Fee:* massage. **Guest Services:** valet laundry. **Free Special Amenities: high-speed Internet and local transportation.**

FOUR SEASONS HOTEL VANCOUVER   (604)689-9333 **21**

Hotel
$225-$2950

Address: 791 W Georgia St V6C 2T4 **Location:** Between Howe and Granville sts. **Facility:** Known for providing lovely accommodations with impeccable service, this downtown hotel offers comfort and convenience. Standout features include the indoor/outdoor pool and huge outdoor deck on the third floor. 373 units. 28 stories, interior corridors. **Parking:** on-site (fee) and valet. **Terms:** cancellation fee imposed. **Amenities:** high-speed Internet (fee), safes. **Dining:** Yew Restaurant & Bar, see separate listing. **Pool(s):** heated indoor/outdoor. **Activities:** saunas, whirlpool. **Guest Services:** valet laundry.

GEORGIAN COURT HOTEL   (604)682-5555 **40**

Hotel
$159-$399

Address: 773 Beatty St V6B 2M4 **Location:** Between Georgia and Robson sts. Opposite BC Place Stadium. **Facility:** 180 units. 12 stories, interior corridors. **Parking:** on-site (fee). **Terms:** cancellation fee imposed. **Amenities:** high-speed Internet, safes. **Dining:** Frankie's Italian Kitchen & Bar, see separate listing. **Activities:** whirlpool, steamroom, exercise room. **Guest Services:** valet laundry, area transportation-downtown. **Free Special Amenities: high-speed Internet and local transportation.**

Downtown boutique hotel located near entertainment, shopping & sports venues. Luxury within reach!

GEORGIAN COURT
HOTEL

GRANVILLE ISLAND HOTEL   (604)683-7373 **44**

Hotel
$189-$550

Address: 1253 Johnston St V6H 3R9 **Location:** Granville Island; below the bridge, follow signs. **Facility:** 82 units. 3-4 stories, interior corridors. **Parking:** on-site (fee). **Terms:** cancellation fee imposed. **Amenities:** high-speed Internet, safes. **Dining:** Dockside Restaurant, see separate listing. **Activities:** sauna, whirlpool, rental bicycles, exercise room. **Guest Services:** valet laundry. **Free Special Amenities: local telephone calls and high-speed Internet.** *(See ad p. 377.)*

HAMPTON INN & SUITES BY HILTON, DOWNTOWN VANCOUVER   (604)602-1008 **41**

Hotel
$163-$266

Hampton

AAA Benefit: Members save up to 10%!

Address: 111 Robson St V6B 2A8 **Location:** Between Cambie and Beatty sts. Opposite BC Place Stadium. **Facility:** 132 units, some kitchens. 16 stories, interior corridors. **Parking:** on-site (fee). **Terms:** 1-7 night minimum stay, cancellation fee imposed. **Amenities:** video games (fee), high-speed Internet, safes. **Activities:** sauna, whirlpool, exercise room. **Guest Services:** valet and coin laundry, area transportation-downtown. **Free Special Amenities: full breakfast and local telephone calls.**

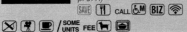

THE HOTEL AT TERMINAL CITY CLUB   604/681-4121 **15**

Hotel. Rates not provided. **Address:** 837 W Hastings St V6C 1B6 **Location:** Between Howe and Hornby sts. **Facility:** 60 units. 30 stories, interior corridors. **Parking:** on-site (fee). **Amenities:** high-speed Internet, safes. **Dining:** 3 restaurants. **Pool(s):** heated indoor. **Activities:** saunas, whirlpool, steamrooms, racquetball courts. **Guest Services:** valet laundry.

HOWARD JOHNSON HOTEL DOWNTOWN VANCOUVER   (604)688-8701 **35**

Hotel $79-$259 **Address:** 1176 Granville St V6Z 1L8 **Location:** Between Davie and Helmcken sts. Located in Granville Street Entertainment District. **Facility:** 110 units. 5 stories, interior corridors. **Parking:** on-site (fee). **Terms:** cancellation fee imposed. **Guest Services:** valet and coin laundry.

▼ See AAA listing p. 376 ▼

(See map & index p. 364.)

HYATT REGENCY VANCOUVER (604)683-1234 16

Hotel
$125-$396

AAA Benefit: Members save 10% or more everyday.

Address: 655 Burrard St V6C 2R7 **Location:** Between W Georgia and Melville sts. Connected to shopping center. **Facility:** In the heart of downtown, this convention-oriented hotel treats you to fantastic city views from many of its spacious, modern rooms. Request a room on the 20th floor or higher to enjoy an unusual rain shower system in which water falls from the ceiling rather than a wall-mounted shower head. 644 units. 34 stories, interior corridors. **Parking:** on-site (fee) and valet. **Terms:** check-in 4 pm, cancellation fee imposed. **Amenities:** high-speed Internet (fee), safes. **Pool(s):** heated outdoor. **Activities:** whirlpool, exercise room. **Guest Services:** valet laundry. **Free Special Amenities:** newspaper.

LANDIS HOTEL & SUITES (604)681-3555 31

Extended Stay Hotel
$159-$299

Address: 1200 Hornby St V6Z 1W2 **Location:** Between Drake and Davie sts. **Facility:** 51 two-bedroom kitchen units. 18 stories, interior corridors. **Parking:** on-site (fee). **Amenities:** safes. **Pool(s):** heated indoor. **Activities:** whirlpool, exercise room. **Guest Services:** valet and coin laundry, area transportation-downtown. **Free Special Amenities: continental breakfast and local telephone calls.**

Located in the heart of downtown, offering large 2 bedroom suites, ideal for short or extended stays.

THE LANDIS
HOTEL & SUITES

L'HERMITAGE HOTEL (778)327-4100 30

Boutique Hotel $190-$595 **Address:** 788 Richards St V6B 3A4 **Location:** Between Robson and W Georgia sts. **Facility:** The sophisticated boutique hotel is located blocks from BC Place Stadium and Robson Street's shopping district. Choose from large studio rooms to one-bedroom suites, each with stylish furnishings. 60 units, some two bedrooms and kitchens. 7 stories, interior corridors. **Parking:** on-site (fee) and valet. **Terms:** check-in 4 pm, cancellation fee imposed. **Amenities:** high-speed Internet, safes. **Pool(s):** heated outdoor. **Activities:** whirlpool, steamrooms, exercise room. **Guest Services:** valet laundry.

THE LISTEL HOTEL VANCOUVER (604)684-8461 5

Hotel $139-$299 **Address:** 1300 Robson St V6E 1C5 **Location:** Between Broughton and Jervis sts. **Facility:** 129 units. 6 stories, interior corridors. **Parking:** on-site (fee) and valet. **Terms:** cancellation fee imposed, resort fee. **Amenities:** high-speed Internet. **Activities:** exercise room. **Guest Services:** valet laundry.

'O CANADA' HOUSE B&B 604/688-0555 18

Historic Bed & Breakfast. Rates not provided. **Address:** 1114 Barclay St V6E 1H1 **Location:** Between Thurlow and Bute sts. Located in a residential area. **Facility:** This beautifully restored 1897 Victorian home is in the West End within easy walking distance of many restaurants and shops. The wonderfully decorated guest rooms are extra-large. 7 units, some cottages. 3 stories (no elevator), interior corridors. **Terms:** check-in 4 pm, age restrictions may apply.

▼ *See AAA listing p. 379* ▼

(See map & index p. 364.)

PAN PACIFIC VANCOUVER   (604)662-8111   12

▽▽▽▽
Hotel
$179-$439

Address: 300-999 Canada Pl V6C 3B5 **Location:** Between Howe and Burrard sts. Located at Canada Place. **Facility:** A Vancouver landmark, this harborside hotel, attached to the convention center and next door to the cruise ship terminal, is conveniently located near the famed Gastown area. 503 units, some two bedrooms and kitchens. 23 stories, interior corridors. **Parking:** on-site (fee) and valet. **Terms:** check-in 4 pm, cancellation fee imposed. **Amenities:** high-speed Internet (fee), safes. **Dining:** Five Sails Restaurant, see separate listing. **Pool(s):** heated outdoor. **Activities:** saunas, whirlpools, steamrooms, spa. **Guest Services:** valet laundry. **Free Special Amenities: newspaper and room upgrade (subject to availability with advance reservations).** *(See ad p. 378.)*

SAVE ECO 🍴 🍸 🏋 CALL &M ⛵ 👟 BIZ 🛜 ✕ 🎥 🖥 / SOME UNITS FEE 🐾 🖼

QUALITY HOTEL DOWNTOWN-THE INN AT FALSE CREEK
(604)682-0229   37

▽▽ Hotel $79-$229 **Address:** 1335 Howe St V6Z 1R7 **Location:** Between Drake and Pacific sts. **Facility:** 157 units, some kitchens. 7 stories, interior corridors. **Parking:** on-site (fee). **Terms:** cancellation fee imposed. **Pool(s):** heated outdoor. **Guest Services:** valet laundry.

ECO 🍸 CALL &M ⛵ 👟 BIZ 🛜 ✕ 🎥 🖥 / SOME UNITS FEE 🐾 🖼 🖼

RAMADA INN & SUITES DOWNTOWN VANCOUVER
(604)685-1111   36

▽▽▽
Hotel
$99-$299

Address: 1221 Granville St V6Z 1M6 **Location:** Between Davie and Drake sts. Located in Granville Street Entertainment District. **Facility:** 116 units, some efficiencies. 6 stories, interior corridors. **Parking:** on-site (fee) and valet. **Terms:** cancellation fee imposed. **Guest Services:** valet laundry. **Free Special Amenities: local telephone calls and high-speed Internet.**

SAVE ECO 🍴 🍸 👟 🛜 ✕ 🎥 🖥 / SOME UNITS FEE 🐾 🖼 🖼

🅰
RAMADA

Located in the heart of Downtown Vancouver's vibrant entertainment district. Newly Renovated.

RAMADA LIMITED DOWNTOWN VANCOUVER
(604)488-1088   29

▽▽ Hotel $99-$224 **Address:** 435 W Pender St V6B 1V2 **Location:** Between Homer and Richards sts. **Facility:** 80 units. 6 stories, interior corridors. **Parking:** valet only. **Terms:** cancellation fee imposed. **Guest Services:** valet and coin laundry.

ECO 🍴 CALL &M 🛜 ✕ 🖥 / SOME UNITS FEE 🖼

RENAISSANCE VANCOUVER HARBOURSIDE HOTEL
(604)689-9211   6

▽▽▽▽ Hotel $169-$329 **Address:** 1133 W Hastings St V6E 3T3 **Location:** Between Bute and Thurlow sts. **Facility:** 442 units. 19 stories, interior corridors. **Parking:** on-site (fee) and valet. **Amenities:** high-speed Internet (fee), safes. **Activities:** whirlpool, steamroom. **Guest Services:** valet laundry.

AAA Benefit: AAA hotel discounts of 5% or more.

ECO 🍴 🍸 CALL &M ⛵ 👟 🛜 ✕ 🎥 🖥 / SOME UNITS FEE 🐾

RESIDENCE INN BY MARRIOTT VANCOUVER DOWNTOWN
604)688-1234   32

▽▽▽
Extended Stay
Contemporary Hotel
Rates not provided

AAA Benefit: AAA hotel discounts of 5% or more.

Address: 1234 Hornby St V6Z 1W2 **Location:** Between Drake and Davie sts. **Facility:** 201 units, some efficiencies and kitchens. 22 stories, interior corridors. **Parking:** on-site (fee). **Terms:** check-in 4 pm. **Amenities:** high-speed Internet, safes. **Pool(s):** heated indoor. **Activities:** whirlpool, exercise room. *Fee:* bicycles. **Guest Services:** valet and coin laundry. **Free Special Amenities: full breakfast and high-speed Internet.**

SAVE ECO 🍴 🍸 CALL &M ⛵ 🛜 ✕ 🖥 / SOME UNITS FEE 🐾

ROSEWOOD HOTEL GEORGIA   (604)682-5566   22

▽▽▽▽▽
Boutique
Contemporary Hotel
$215-$410

Address: 801 W Georgia St V6C 1P7 **Location:** Between Hornby and Howe sts, entrance on Howe St. Across from Vancouver Art Gallery. **Facility:** Opened in 1927, the hotel has hosted such stars as Katherine Hepburn, Nat King Cole and British royalty. After an extensive renovation, it has reopened with a spa, chic lounge and fine restaurant. 156 units. 12 stories, interior corridors. **Parking:** valet only. **Terms:** cancellation fee imposed. **Amenities:** high-speed Internet, safes. **Dining:** Hawksworth Restaurant, see separate listing, nightclub, entertainment. **Pool(s):** heated indoor. **Activities:** exercise room, spa. **Guest Services:** valet laundry, area transportation-within 3 mi (4.8 km). **Free Special Amenities: newspaper and high-speed Internet.**

SAVE 🍴 👟 🍸 🏋 CALL &M ⛵ BIZ 🛜 ✕ 🎥 🖥 / SOME UNITS FEE 🐾

ST. REGIS HOTEL   (604)681-1135   26

▽▽▽ Boutique Contemporary Hotel $134-$787 **Address:** 602 Dunsmuir St V6B 1Y6 **Location:** Between Granville and Seymour sts. **Facility:** Set in a central and convenient location, the exceptional boutique-style hotel underwent extensive renovations that transformed the rooms into an elegant oasis. 65 units. 5 stories, interior corridors. **Parking:** on-site (fee) and valet. **Terms:** cancellation fee imposed. **Amenities:** high-speed Internet, safes. **Activities:** *Fee:* massage. **Guest Services:** valet laundry.

🍴 🍸 CALL &M 👟 BIZ 🛜 ✕ 🎥 🖥 / SOME UNITS 🖼

SANDMAN HOTEL VANCOUVER CITY CENTRE
(604)681-2211   39

▽▽ Hotel $89-$179 **Address:** 180 W Georgia St V6B 4P4 **Location:** Between Cambie and Beatty sts. Close to BC Place Stadium. **Facility:** 302 units. 11-14 stories, interior corridors. **Parking:** on-site (fee). **Terms:** check-in 4 pm, cancellation fee imposed. **Dining:** Moxie's Classic Grill, see separate listing. **Pool(s):** heated indoor. **Activities:** whirlpool. **Guest Services:** valet laundry.

ECO 🍴 🍸 CALL &M ⛵ FEE 👟 🛜 ✕ 🎥 🖥 / SOME UNITS FEE 🐾 🖼 🖼

(See map & index p. 364.)

SHANGRI-LA HOTEL VANCOUVER

604/689-1120

Boutique
Contemporary Hotel
Rates not provided

Address: 1128 W Georgia St V6E 0A8 **Location:** Between Thurlow and Bute sts. **Facility:** Luxurious guest rooms feature the latest and greatest amenities, from automatically closing drapes and sheers to centrally controlled lighting. 119 units. 15 stories, interior corridors. **Parking:** on-site (fee) and valet. **Amenities:** high-speed Internet, safes. **Dining:** Market by Jean-Georges, see separate listing, entertainment. **Pool(s):** heated outdoor. **Activities:** sauna, whirlpool, steamroom, spa. **Guest Services:** valet laundry, area transportation-downtown. **Free Special Amenities:** local telephone calls and high-speed Internet. (See ad this page.)

    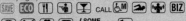

SHERATON VANCOUVER WALL CENTRE HOTEL

(604)331-1000

Hotel
$159-$509

AAA Benefit: Members get up to 20% off, plus Starwood Preferred Guest® bonuses.

Address: 1088 Burrard St V6Z 2R9 **Location:** Between Helmcken and Nelson sts. **Facility:** 733 units, some two bedrooms and kitchens. 27-35 stories, interior corridors. **Parking:** on-site (fee) and valet. **Amenities:** high-speed Internet, safes. **Pool(s):** heated indoor. **Activities:** saunas, whirlpools, spa. **Guest Services:** valet laundry, area transportation-downtown. **Free Special Amenities:** newspaper and high-speed Internet. (See ad p. 381.)

   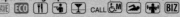 

Learn about inspections and Diamond Ratings at AAA.com/Diamonds

▼ See AAA listing this page ▼

▼ See AAA listing p. 380 ▼

Sheraton Vancouver
WALL CENTRE
HOTEL

Life is Better When Shared

Book today at www.sheratonvancouver.com or call 1-800-663-9255

Approved

(See map & index p. 364.)

SUNSET INN & SUITES (604)688-2474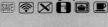

Hotel
$189-$500

Address: 1111 Burnaby St V6E 1P4 **Location:** Between Thurlow and Bute sts. **Facility:** 50 kitchen units. 11 stories, interior corridors. **Terms:** check-in 4 pm, cancellation fee imposed. **Amenities:** high-speed Internet, safes. **Activities:** exercise room. **Guest Services:** coin laundry. **Free Special Amenities:** continental breakfast and high-speed Internet.

 Get more for less. Enjoy lots of complimentary amenities & services. Walk to beach and Stanley Park.

THE SUTTON PLACE HOTEL 604/682-5511

Hotel
Rates not provided

Address: 845 Burrard St V6Z 2K6 **Location:** Between Smithe and Robson sts. **Facility:** Attractive yet understated rooms incorporate superior residential-style furnishings at this service-oriented hotel near Robson Street. 397 units. 21 stories, interior corridors. **Parking:** on-site (fee) and valet. **Amenities:** high-speed Internet (fee), safes. **Dining:** Fleuri Restaurant, see separate listing. **Pool(s):** heated indoor. **Activities:** whirlpool, steamroom, spa. **Guest Services:** valet laundry, area transportation-downtown.

SYLVIA HOTEL (604)681-9321

Historic Hotel $100-$400 **Address:** 1154 Gilford St V6G 2P6 **Location:** Between Pendrell St and Beach Ave. Across from English Bay. **Facility:** Vines have taken over most of the exterior of this historic older hotel, so in the spring and summer the building is covered in greenery. 120 units, some efficiencies and kitchens. 2-8 stories, interior corridors. **Parking:** on-site (fee). **Guest Services:** valet laundry.

VANCOUVER MARRIOTT PINNACLE DOWNTOWN (604)684-1128

Hotel
$169-$329

Marriott HOTELS & RESORTS **AAA Benefit:** AAA hotel discounts of 5% or more.

Address: 1128 W Hastings St V6E 4R5 **Location:** Between Thurlow and Bute sts. **Facility:** Located a few blocks from the Convention Centre in the heart of the downtown business district, guest rooms offer breathtaking views of the mountains, water and downtown Vancouver. 438 units. 25 stories, interior corridors. **Parking:** on-site (fee) and valet. **Terms:** check-in 4 pm. **Amenities:** high-speed Internet (fee). **Dining:** Show Case Restaurant, see separate listing. **Pool(s):** heated indoor. **Activities:** sauna, whirlpool, steamroom, exercise room. **Guest Services:** valet laundry.

THE WEDGEWOOD HOTEL & SPA (604)689-7777

Boutique Hotel
$238-$418

Address: 845 Hornby St V6Z 1V1 **Location:** Between Smithe and Robson sts. **Facility:** Wonderfully intimate, this stylish boutique property offers an alternative to downtown hotels with an institutional feel. Niceties include a newly expanded fitness room and a peaceful spa. 83 units. 13 stories, interior corridors. **Parking:** valet only. **Terms:** cancellation fee imposed, resort fee. **Amenities:** high-speed Internet, safes. **Dining:** Bacchus Restaurant, see separate listing, entertainment. **Activities:** steamroom, exercise room, spa. **Guest Services:** valet laundry. **Free Special Amenities:** newspaper and high-speed Internet.

WEST END GUEST HOUSE (604)681-2889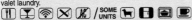

Historic Bed & Breakfast $150-$325 **Address:** 1362 Haro St V6E 1G2 **Location:** Between Broughton and Jervis sts. Located in a quiet residential area. **Facility:** This 1906 Victorian home is located in the heart of the West End. Inside the home is a mix of modern amenities with an ambiance of old heritage charm. A collection of early photos of the West End adorn a wall. 7 units. 2 stories (no elevator), interior corridors. **Terms:** 2-3 night minimum stay - weekends, age restrictions may apply, 7 day cancellation notice-fee imposed. **Activities:** bicycles.

(See map & index p. 364.)

THE WESTIN BAYSHORE VANCOUVER

(604)682-3377 **1**

WESTIN HOTELS & RESORTS

Hotel
$189-$460

AAA Benefit: Enjoy up to 20% off your next stay, plus Starwood Preferred Guest® bonuses.

Address: 1601 Bayshore Dr V6G 2V4 **Location:** Jct W Georgia and Cardero sts. **Facility:** Enjoy your own little oasis in the middle of downtown Vancouver. Wonderful grounds surround this marine hotel, whose every room offers spectacular harbour, city and mountain views. The large, heated outdoor pool is a standout feature with lush landscaping and a nearby pathway that leads to famous Stanley Park. 511 units. 9-16 stories, interior corridors. **Parking:** on-site (fee) and valet. **Terms:** check-in 4 pm, cancellation fee imposed. **Amenities:** safes. *Some:* high-speed Internet (fee). **Dining:** 2 restaurants. **Pool(s):** heated outdoor, heated indoor. **Activities:** whirlpool, jogging, exercise room, spa. **Guest Services:** valet laundry, area transportation-downtown. **Free Special Amenities: local telephone calls and high-speed Internet.** *(See ad this page.)*

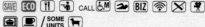

THE WESTIN GRAND, VANCOUVER

(604)602-1999 **33**

WESTIN HOTELS & RESORTS

Hotel
$169-$679

AAA Benefit: Enjoy up to 20% off your next stay, plus Starwood Preferred Guest® bonuses.

Address: 433 Robson St V6B 6L9 **Location:** Between Homer and Richards sts. **Facility:** 207 units. 26 stories, interior corridors. **Parking:** on-site (fee) and valet. **Terms:** cancellation fee imposed. **Amenities:** high-speed Internet (fee), safes. **Pool(s):** heated outdoor. **Activities:** sauna, whirlpool, steamrooms, exercise room. *Fee:* massage. **Guest Services:** valet laundry.

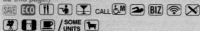

LODEN HOTEL

604/669-5060

fyi Not evaluated. **Address:** 1177 Melville St V6E 0A3 **Location:** Between Thurlow and Bute sts. Facilities, services, and décor characterize a mid-scale property.

WHERE TO EAT

AL PORTO RISTORANTE

604/683-8376 **29**

Northern Italian. Fine Dining. $10-$29 **AAA Inspector Notes:** In the heart of Old Gastown, this restaurant is housed in a century-old Hudson Bay Trading Co. warehouse. Tables upstairs offer a great harbor view; the downstairs area is like dining in a Tuscan villa. Prosciutto di parma is excellent. Parking can be found in a nearby lot or at street meters. **Bar:** full bar. **Reservations:** suggested. **Address:** 321 Water St V6B 1B8 **Location:** Between Richards and Cambie sts; in Gastown. **Parking:** street only.

BACCHUS RESTAURANT

604/608-5319 **28**

French
Fine Dining
$17-$46

AAA Inspector Notes: This elegant restaurant is on the lobby level of a wonderful, boutique-style downtown hotel. On warm summer evenings the windows of the lobby lounge, which shares space with the restaurant, are opened up so you can do some people-watching. The creative, French-influenced menu incorporates many B.C. ingredients, especially seafood from Vancouver Island, including succulent mussels, clams, halibut and wild B.C. salmon. **Bar:** full bar. **Reservations:** suggested. **Address:** 845 Hornby St V6Z 1V1 **Location:** Between Smithe and Robson sts; in The Wedgewood Hotel & Spa. **Parking:** valet only.

BLUE WATER CAFE + RAW BAR

604/688-8078 **38**

Seafood Sushi. Fine Dining. $28-$46 **AAA Inspector Notes:** This highly regarded Yaletown restaurant serves only the freshest, live-caught or sustainably farmed seafood. Oysters for the raw bar are flown in from all around B.C.'s west coast. Grab a seat at the sushi bar and watch the chefs prepare the freshest sushi you'll ever try. A fantastic dining experience, this Vancouver hot spot is busy every night of the week. **Bar:** full bar. **Reservations:** suggested. **Address:** 1095 Hamilton St V6B 5T4 **Location:** Between Nelson and Helmcken sts. **Parking:** valet and street only.

▼ *See AAA listing this page* ▼

(See map & index p. 364.)

THE BOATHOUSE RESTAURANT   604/669-2225

▼▼ ▼▼ Seafood. Casual Dining. $13-$45 **AAA Inspector Notes:** The restaurant's fantastic heated and covered patio, which is open all year and in all kinds of weather, affords spectacular views of English Bay. Casual bar food makes up the menu in the downstairs pub, while the more formal upstairs dining room serves fresh seafood. **Bar:** full bar. **Reservations:** suggested. **Address:** 1795 Beach Ave V6G 1Y9 **Location:** Between Bidwell and Denman sts. **Parking:** valet and street only. [L] [D] CALL [&M]

BRIX RESTAURANT & WINE BAR   604/915-9463   (37)

▼▼▼▼ Pacific Northwest. Fine Dining. $19-$29 **AAA Inspector Notes:** A nice place to drop in for a glass of wine and a bite, the restaurant is pure Yaletown—a funky old space with wood floors and high ceilings. A long list of wine-by-the-glass choices complements the small-plate selections, as well as B.C. seafood, duck, veal and Alberta beef dishes. **Bar:** full bar. **Reservations:** suggested. **Address:** 1138 Homer St V6B 2X6 **Location:** Between Helmcken and Davie sts. **Parking:** street only. [D] CALL [&M]

CACTUS CLUB CAFE

▼▼ ▼▼ American. Casual Dining. $14-$37 **AAA Inspector Notes:** This bustling, casual restaurant serves huge burgers, sandwiches, pasta, salads, soups, quesadillas, fajitas, vegetarian dishes, steak, ribs, chicken and fish. Featured are certified Angus beef and fresh wild British Columbia salmon. **Bar:** full bar.

[L] [D] [LATE] CALL [&M]

For additional information, visit AAA.com

LOCATIONS:

Address: 1136 Robson St V6E 1B2 **Location:** Between Bute and Thurlow sts. **Phone:** 604/687-3278

Address: 357 Davie St V6B 1R2 **Location:** Between Homer and Hamilton sts. **Phone:** 604/685-8070

Address: 1790 Beach Ave V6G 1Y9 **Location:** Between Bidwell and Denman sts. **Phone:** 604/681-2582

CARDERO'S RESTAURANT   604/669-7666   (3)

▼▼ ▼▼ Seafood. Casual Dining. $9-$29 **AAA Inspector Notes:** At the north end of Cardero and Nicola streets where the seawall weaves around the various condos sits this distinctive warehouse-like restaurant overlooking a marina and Vancouver's north shore. This place is known for its wonderfully prepared fish dishes and mouthwatering pizzas, which are baked in a wood oven. For oyster lovers, there's an open oyster bar. Comfy leather chairs in the cozy lounge are right next to a wood-burning fireplace. **Bar:** full bar. **Reservations:** suggested. **Address:** 1583 Coal Harbour Quay V6G 3E7 **Location:** Between Cardero and Nicola sts. **Parking:** valet and street only. [L] [D] [LATE] CALL [&M]

CIAO BELLA RISTORANTE   604/688-5771   (2)

▼▼▼ ▼▼▼

Italian
Casual Dining
$16-$25

AAA Inspector Notes: Good Italian food at very reasonable prices is the name of the game at this restaurant. The lunch special, which includes soup or salad and a pasta dish, is a great deal. For regular entrées, you'll find a long list of pasta sauces to choose from. There's live piano entertainment Wednesday through Sunday. A limited number of parking spaces are at the rear of the building, just off Alberni Street. Otherwise you'll need to feed the street parking meters. **Bar:** full bar. **Reservations:** suggested. **Address:** 703 Denman St V6G 2L6 **Location:** Between Robson and Alberni sts. **Parking:** on-site and street. [L] [D] CALL [&M]

CINCIN   604/688-7338   (13)

▼▼▼▼ Mediterranean. Fine Dining. $15-$38 **AAA Inspector Notes:** The menu at this restaurant blends Mediterranean and Italian dishes that have been delighting patrons for years. Choices include tasty pasta or thin-crust pizza cooked in a wood-fired oven. On the second floor overlooking Robson Street, the bustling spot has a trendy feel that sometimes lures film stars. Guests are encouraged to linger over cocktails. **Bar:** full bar. **Reservations:** suggested. **Address:** 1154 Robson St V6E 1B5 **Location:** Between Bute and Thurlow sts. **Parking:** street only. [L] [D]

COPPER CHIMNEY   604/689-8862   (20)

▼▼ ▼▼ Indian. Fine Dining. $18-$34 **AAA Inspector Notes:** West Coast and Indian influences are fused to create a wonderful blend of unique dishes like the melt-in-your-mouth butter chicken and lamb curry, which are always on the menu. The bustling bi-level dining room features a large open kitchen and a pleasant bar area as well as a loft-type dining area. **Bar:** full bar. **Reservations:** suggested. **Address:** 567 Hornby St V6C 2E8 **Location:** Between Dunsmuir and Pender sts; in Executive Hotel Le Soleil. **Parking:** valet and street only. [B] [L] [D] CALL [&M]

C RESTAURANT   604/681-1164   (36)

▼▼▼▼ Seafood. Fine Dining. $18-$41 **AAA Inspector Notes:** Located along the seawall just at the end of Howe Street, one of the biggest treats at this restaurant is the chance to dine on the outdoor patio during the summer. The restaurant features a wonderful array of fresh fish and seafood along with an extensive wine list that will complement each and every dish. **Bar:** full bar. **Reservations:** required, for dinner. **Address:** 2-1600 Howe St V6Z 2L9 **Location:** 1 blk below Beach Ave. **Parking:** street only. [L] [D] CALL [&M]

DIVA AT THE MET   604/602-7788   (23)

▼▼ ▼▼ Pacific Northwest. Fine Dining. $16-$38 **AAA Inspector Notes:** Dining here, you'll be supporting local suppliers from around Vancouver and Vancouver Island. The restaurant is proudly recognized as "ocean wise" by the Vancouver Aquarium for its sustainable fishing practices. Open all day long, the restaurant caters to the business crowd but really shines for those looking for a special occasion. A number of wonderful B.C. wines can be enjoyed. **Bar:** full bar. **Reservations:** suggested. **Address:** 645 Howe St V6C 2Y9 **Location:** Between Georgia and Dunsmuir sts; in Metropolitan Hotel Vancouver. **Parking:** valet only. [B] [L] [D] CALL [&M]

DOCKSIDE RESTAURANT   604/685-7070   (46)

▼▼ ▼▼ Canadian. Casual Dining. $14-$38 **AAA Inspector Notes:** Floor-to-ceiling windows offer views of the marina, and a 50-foot aquarium adds to the restaurant's charm. Breakfast, lunch and dinner are served. You can enjoy a selection of specialty beers from the restaurant's own microbrewery. During warmer weather the outdoor patio is open. **Bar:** full bar. **Reservations:** suggested, for dinner & weekends. **Address:** 1253 Johnston St V6H 3R9 **Location:** Granville Island; below the bridge, follow signs; in Granville Island Hotel. **Parking:** street only. *(See ad p. 377.)* [B] [L] [D] CALL [&M] [AC]

EARLS RESTAURANT

▼▼ ▼▼ American. Casual Dining. $12-$19 **AAA Inspector Notes:** Offering an experience that falls between fast food and fine dining, the fun, relaxed restaurant prepares great food at a great price. Choices range from juicy burgers, hearty sandwiches, fresh salads, wings and pizza to full entrees of steak, chops and seafood. Made-from-scratch soups and assorted breads, as well as a nice choice of wines and beers, round out the offerings. This is a fitting spot for impromptu get-togethers and festive occasions. **Bar:** full bar. [L] [D] [LATE] CALL [&M]

For additional information, visit AAA.com

LOCATIONS:

Address: 1185 Robson St V6E 1B5 **Location:** Between Bute and Thurlow sts. **Phone:** 604/669-0020

Address: 905 Hornby St V6Z 1V3 **Location:** Corner of Hornby and Smithe sts. **Phone:** 604/682-6700

THE FISH HOUSE IN STANLEY PARK
    604/681-7275   (1)

▼▼▼ ▼▼▼

Seafood
Fine Dining
$18-$35

AAA Inspector Notes: Located in the lush and quiet surroundings of Stanley Park, this restaurant features a wide variety of fresh seafood wonderfully prepared with a Canadian West Coast influence. Its casual atmosphere offers patio dining in season. The pay parking lot is in effect at all times. **Bar:** full bar. **Reservations:** suggested. **Address:** 8901 Stanley Park Dr V6G 3E2 **Location:** Beach Ave entrance to Stanley Park; next to tennis courts. **Parking:** on-site (fee). *Menu on AAA.com*
[L] [D] CALL [&M] [AC]

(See map & index p. 364.)

FIVE SAILS RESTAURANT 604/844-2855 [10]

New
European
Fine Dining
$30-$40

AAA Inspector Notes: Whether it's the sight of cruise ships docked at the adjoining piers or the beautiful harbor and mountain vistas, every table gets a view. The menu is driven by seasonal market availability, and the chef celebrates the bounty by staying true to his European roots. Depending on what the market bears, look for offerings to include a variety of seafood, domestic and game meats, sweetbreads and exotics like truffles and sturgeon roe, and artisanal cheeses stashed away in the kitchen. **Bar:** full bar. **Reservations:** suggested. **Address:** 999 Canada Pl, Suite 410 Pl V6C 3E1 **Location:** Between Howe and Burrard sts; in Pan Pacific Vancouver. **Parking:** on-site (fee) and valet.

D CALL &M

FLEURI RESTAURANT 604/682-5511 [21]

Pacific Northwest. Fine Dining. $16-$39 **AAA Inspector Notes:** In one of Vancouver's finest hotels, the restaurant offers a quiet respite from the hustle and bustle of the downtown streets. Open early, diners can come for breakfast, lunch or dinner. Everything is handled by a professional and personable staff. The menu is inspired by fresh, local B.C. produce and sustainable seafood practices, which means it changes seasonally to highlight ever-changing ingredients. A daily afternoon tea service starts at 2:30. **Bar:** full bar. **Reservations:** suggested. **Address:** 845 Burrard St V6Z 2K6 **Location:** Between Smithe and Robson sts; in The Sutton Place Hotel. **Parking:** on-site (fee) and valet.

B L D CALL &M

GLOWBAL GRILL STEAKS & SATAY 604/602-0835 [39]

Steak Fusion. Fine Dining. $13-$49 **AAA Inspector Notes:** The funky Yaletown district of downtown is full of restaurants, but this one is a real standout. Aged cuts of beef, rib-eye, strip and tenderloin are selected from a glass-walled meat cooler on display near the open kitchen. Once chosen, the meats are butchered to order. The satay bar offers a nice selection of individually priced items as well as a sampler dish meant to be shared. The restaurant is busy, fun and funky. After dinner, head to Afterglow, their sexy back lounge. **Bar:** full bar. **Reservations:** suggested. **Address:** 1079 Mainland St V6B 5P9 **Location:** Between Helmcken and Nelson sts. **Parking:** valet and street only. L D CALL &M

HAWKSWORTH RESTAURANT 604/673-7000 [27]

New Pacific Northwest. Fine Dining. $18-$38 **AAA Inspector Notes:** While the dining room is laid back and comfortable the food is anything but. Outstanding presentations can include a host of offerings such as the Hawksworth beef burger with applewood smoked bacon, an aged prosciutto or a Serrano ham, Quebec quail, Australian truffles, pan roasted halibut, grilled sturgeon, caramelized squid, or my personal favorite, rack of pork - all packed with rich, complex flavors and great visual impact. **Bar:** beer only. **Reservations:** suggested. **Address:** 801 W Georgia St V6C 1P7 **Location:** Between Hornby and Howe sts, entrance on Howe St; in Rosewood Hotel Georgia. **Parking:** valet and street only.

B L D CALL &M

HERONS WEST COAST KITCHEN + BAR
604/691-1818 [17]

Pacific Northwest
Fine Dining
$16-$35

AAA Inspector Notes: Located across from the Canada Place cruise ship terminal, the restaurant offers a menu showcasing the best of seasonal British Columbian cuisine. The open kitchen enables guests to view the staff as they prepare breakfast, lunch and dinner for hungry diners. Try the popular Sunday brunch. Validated parking for dinner starts at 6 pm. **Bar:** full bar. **Reservations:** suggested. **Address:** 900 Canada Place Way V6C 3L5 **Location:** Between Howe and Burrard sts; in The Fairmont Waterfront. **Parking:** on-site (fee) and valet.

B L D CALL &M

A culinary celebration of all things British Columbia

IL GIARDINO 604/669-2422 [33]

Italian. Fine Dining. $19-$40 **AAA Inspector Notes:** This very nice restaurant, which specializes in game, fowl and pasta, is designed to look like the Tuscan villa of the owner, Umberto Menghi, a well-known and longtime Vancouver restaurateur. The very charming décor has bright colors, open beams and exquisite furniture. During the warmer months they open their outdoor patio, which is surrounded by flowers. You can expect wonderful wine and good service. **Bar:** full bar. **Reservations:** suggested. **Address:** 1382 Hornby St V6Z 1W5 **Location:** Corner of Pacific and Hornby sts. **Parking:** valet and street only. L D JC

IMPERIAL CHINESE SEAFOOD RESTAURANT
604/688-8191 [11]

Chinese. Fine Dining. $15-$58 **AAA Inspector Notes:** In a restored heritage building, this long-established, chandeliered restaurant mixes traditional Chinese furnishings with modern décor. Floor-to-ceiling windows bring in plenty of light, but due to recent downtown developments the restaurant has lost its water view. Whether you come in for a light lunch, dim sum or a big dinner, you can enjoy fresh daily live seafood like lobster and crab and a wide assortment of Chinese dishes. Set menus for groups of 10 or more people also are available. **Bar:** full bar. **Reservations:** suggested. **Address:** 355 Burrard St V6C 2G8 **Location:** Between W Hastings and Cordova sts. **Parking:** valet and street only. L D CALL &M

INDIA BISTRO 604/684-6342 [22]

Indian. Casual Dining. $9-$14 **AAA Inspector Notes:** In the Davie Village, this wonderful Indian restaurant serves well-known and reasonably priced favorites, including naan bread, savory tandoori chicken and a good choice of vegetarian options. Friendly servers circulate through the bright, colorful dining area. Parking is at street meters or in nearby pay lots. **Bar:** full bar. **Reservations:** suggested, weekends for dinner. **Address:** 1157 Davie St V6E 1N2 **Location:** Between Bute and Thurlow sts. **Parking:** street only. L D

(See map & index p. 364.)

JOE FORTES SEAFOOD & CHOP HOUSE
604/669-1940 (18)

Seafood
Steak
Casual Dining
$17-$40

AAA Inspector Notes: A San Francisco-style seafood grill on trendy Robson Street, this restaurant features delightful rooftop garden dining in season. It also has a popular oyster bar and fireplace lounge. Be sure to ask about turn-of-the-century legend Joe Fortes. Valet parking is available weekdays and after 6 pm on Saturday and Sunday. **Bar:** full bar. **Reservations:** suggested. **Address:** 777 Thurlow St V6E 3V5 **Location:** Between Robson and Alberni sts. **Parking:** valet and street only. *Menu on AAA.com* L D CALL ♿M

KINGSTON TAPHOUSE & GRILLE
604/681-7011 (31)

American. Gastropub. $11-$25 **AAA Inspector Notes:** The restaurant has two large outdoor patios, one with a large fountain and concrete fireplace; the other, one of Vancouver's best-kept secrets, is on the roof. Because the restaurant is close to BC Place it welcomes sports fans both before the game and after. The food, like the made-for-sharing Kingston Appy Platter, wood-plank pizzas, burgers and, of course, steaks, is causal but done right. **Bar:** full bar. **Address:** 755 Richards St V6B 3A6 **Location:** Between Robson and W Georgia sts. **Parking:** street only. L D LATE CALL ♿M

KIRIN MANDARIN RESTAURANT
604/682-8833 (9)

Chinese. Fine Dining. $4-$57 **AAA Inspector Notes:** The specialty here is dim sum. The variety is outstanding, as it includes some rather exotic ingredients for the adventurous, while satisfying the tastes of those seeking more traditional fare. The menu encompasses many Chinese cooking styles and includes dumplings, soups, noodle and rice dishes, meats and seafood, and an assortment of desserts. The décor has an elegant feel, but the ambiance is casual. If you ever thought you'd like to try shark fin or bird nest soups, here's your chance. **Bar:** full bar. **Reservations:** suggested. **Address:** 1172 Alberni St V6E 3Z3 **Location:** Between Thurlow and Bute sts. **Parking:** street only. L D

KOBE JAPANESE STEAK HOUSE
604/684-2451 (19)

Japanese. Casual Dining. $33-$58 **AAA Inspector Notes:** Visitors and locals alike enjoy this restaurant's dinner style, which seats enjoyed guests together at a teppan table to watch the chef prepare steak, chicken, shrimp or lobster on the grill right in front of you. **Bar:** full bar. **Reservations:** required. **Address:** 1042 Alberni St V6E 1A3 **Location:** Between Burrard and Thurlow sts. **Parking:** street only. D

LA TERRAZZA
604/899-4449 (41)

Northern Italian. Fine Dining. $24-$42 **AAA Inspector Notes:** Near the Cambie Street bridge in Yaletown, the lovely restaurant features an impressive wine list with many bottles displayed in a huge rack against one wall. On the menu is an array of meat dishes--such as grilled venison, rack of lamb and Cornish game hen--along with some seafood and a choice of pasta. **Bar:** full bar. **Reservations:** suggested. **Address:** 1088 Cambie St & Pacific Blvd V6B 6J5 **Location:** By Cambie St Bridge. **Parking:** valet and street only.

D LATE CALL ♿M

LE CROCODILE
604/669-4298 (24)

French
Fine Dining
$15-$42

AAA Inspector Notes: The French restaurant's menu shows an emphasis on beef and seafood. Other offerings include grilled lamb chops and pan-fried Dover sole filleted tableside. The atmosphere is bustling when the place is full, which is nearly every night. The trained wine steward will help match your meal to a wonderful bottle of wine. Valet parking service begins at 5:30 pm. **Bar:** full bar. **Reservations:** suggested. **Address:** 100-909 Burrard St on Smithe St V6Z 2N2 **Location:** Jct Smithe and Burrard sts. **Parking:** on-site (fee) and valet. L D CALL ♿M

LE GAVROCHE RESTAURANT FRANCAIS
604/685-3924 (4)

French. Fine Dining. $16-$45 **AAA Inspector Notes:** In a small Victorian home, this charming French restaurant's second-floor dining room affords slight views of the North Shore. On the classical French menu, lamb, beef tenderloin, veal or veal sweetbread are prepared using recipes from the owner's childhood growing up in Portugal and France. The lunch special, which comes with soup or salad and a main entrée, is available for a very reasonable price of around $20. **Bar:** full bar. **Reservations:** suggested. **Address:** 1616 Alberni St V6G 1A6 **Location:** Between Cardero and Bidwell sts. **Parking:** street only. L D

LUPO RESTAURANT
604/569-2535 (35)

Italian. Fine Dining. $15-$35 **AAA Inspector Notes:** You'll enjoy modern Italian cooking in a relaxed atmosphere in this turn-of-the-century heritage house tucked away in the heart of downtown. Your favorite pastas and appetizers are just waiting to be explored. Gone are the white tablecloths and stuffy atmosphere; instead you will find great food at affordable prices. Parking is only at street meters or in nearby pay lots. **Bar:** full bar. **Reservations:** suggested. **Address:** 869 Hamilton St V6B 2R7 **Location:** Between Robson and Smithe sts. **Parking:** street only. D

MARKET BY JEAN-GEORGES
604/695-1115 (15)

Pacific Northwest
Fine Dining
$16-$36

AAA Inspector Notes: Internationally acclaimed chef Jean-Georges Vongerichten has put his name on this exciting restaurant on the third floor of the Shangri-La Hotel. Offering a truly West Coast experience, this place has three distinct dining areas: the heated terrace, the fine-dining room and the always busy bar. On weekdays, a must-try is the "50 minute Power Lunch," a choice of two plates plus dessert for $29. **Bar:** full bar. **Reservations:** suggested. **Address:** 1115 Alberni St V6E 4T9 **Location:** Between Thurlow and Bute sts; in Shangri-La Hotel Vancouver. **Parking:** on-site (fee) and valet. B L D CALL ♿M

MILESTONES GRILL AND BAR

American. Casual Dining. $13-$28 **AAA Inspector Notes:** Popular with locals, the bustling eatery is a great gathering place. The menu features such items as wild Pacific coho salmon, Angus beef, gluten-free burgers, Kobe style beef sliders, "share plate" appetizers, soups, salads, "pasta & bowls," Angus top sirloin, Mediterranean chicken, portobello mushroom chicken, sandwiches, burgers, prime rib, roll-ups, taster or full desserts. There is a great selection of wines by the glass and creative specialty cocktails. **Bar:** full bar.

L D LATE CALL ♿M

For additional information, visit AAA.com

LOCATIONS:
Address: 1145 Robson St V6E 1B5 **Location:** Between Bute and Thurlow sts. **Phone:** 604/682-4477

Address: 1109 Hamilton St V6B 5P6 **Location:** Between Helmcken and Davie sts. **Phone:** 604/684-9111

MOXIE'S CLASSIC GRILL

American. Casual Dining. $10-$29 **AAA Inspector Notes:** This sleek, funky and popular restaurant presents an extensive menu of creatively prepared dishes, including pizza, pasta, rice, noodles, signature salads and burgers. Other menus include one for children and one for Sunday brunch. Lending to the upbeat, stylish decor are dark wood appointments and river rock fireplaces. **Bar:** full bar.

L D CALL ♿M

For additional information, visit AAA.com

LOCATIONS:
Address: 808 Bute St V6E 1Y4 **Location:** Between Robson and Haro sts. **Phone:** 604/696-9986

Address: 180 W Georgia St V6B 4P4 **Location:** Between Cambie and Beatty sts; in Sandman Hotel Vancouver City Centre. **Phone:** 604/684-8434

Address: 1160 Davie St V6E 1N1 **Location:** Between Bute and Thurlow sts. **Phone:** 604/678-8043

(See map & index p. 364.)

OYSI OYSI JAPANESE RESTAURANT   604/682-0011   12

▼▼ Japanese. Casual Dining. $7-$19 **AAA Inspector Notes:** The downtown restaurant's menu lists fresh seafood, barbecue and sushi, as well as take-out combination trays. Guests can park in metered street spots or in a limited number of free spaces in underground parking lot stalls 200 through 300 available weekdays after 5 pm and all day Saturday and Sunday. **Bar:** beer & wine. **Address:** 1136 Alberni St V6E 1A5 **Location:** Between Bute and Thurlow sts. **Parking:** on-site and street.   L D

PROVENCE MARINASIDE   604/681-4144   42

▼▼▼ Seafood. Fine Dining. $14-$34 **AAA Inspector Notes:** The delightful restaurant faces the seawall and a small marina in an area known as Falsecreek. The menu spans breakfast, lunch and dinner, so guests can fit this place into any part of their day. In addition to choices from the antipasto display case, selections include wonderful pasta and panini, as well as beef, chicken and fish entrées. **Bar:** full bar. **Reservations:** suggested. **Address:** 1177 Marinaside Cres V6Z 2Y3 **Location:** End of Davie St, towards water. **Parking:** street only.   B L D CALL ⬥M

RAIN CITY GRILL   604/685-7337   5

▼▼▼ Pacific Northwest. Fine Dining. $14-$32 **AAA Inspector Notes:** Pacific Northwest cuisine makes up a menu that includes fresh ingredients and weekly changes. The atmosphere is simple yet stately, the service staff attentive and nicely attired, and the wine list extensive. Valet parking is available nightly in spring and summer and on Friday and Saturday nights from November through March. **Bar:** full bar. **Reservations:** suggested. **Address:** 1193 Denman St V6G 2N1 **Location:** Just n of jct Denman and Davie sts. **Parking:** valet and street only.   L D

RICKY'S ALL DAY GRILL

▼▼ American. Casual Dining. $11-$27 **AAA Inspector Notes:** The comfortable eatery, which employs friendly servers, presents a varied menu that includes pasta dishes, wraps, omelets, stir-fry preparations and burgers. Portions are generous. Children's and senior selections are offered. Guests can request seating in a booth or at a table. **Bar:** full bar.   B L D

For additional information, visit AAA.com

LOCATIONS:
Address: 23-200 Burrard St V6C 3L6 **Location:** Between W Hastings and Cordova sts. **Phone:** 604/669-2781
Address: 104-111 Dunsmuir St V6B 6A3 **Location:** Corner of Dunsmuir and Beatty sts. **Phone:** 604/602-9233

THE SANDBAR SEAFOOD RESTAURANT   604/669-9030   45

▼▼ Seafood. Casual Dining. $12-$35 **AAA Inspector Notes:** More than a century ago, Granville Island was known as "the great sandbar," where native tribes came to fish. Today, the 300-seat fresh seafood restaurant perches on the waterfront and offers great views from every seat. Complimentary parking is available for three hours during the day and all night after 7 pm. **Bar:** full bar. **Reservations:** suggested, for dinner. **Address:** 1535 Johnston St, Creekhouse #9 V6H 3R9 **Location:** Below the bridge, follow signs to Granville Island.   L D CALL ⬥M

SHOW CASE RESTAURANT   604/639-4040   8

▼▼▼ Pacific Northwest. Casual Dining. $15-$30 **AAA Inspector Notes:** Natural light shining through floor-to-ceiling windows illuminates the restaurant and adjoining bar. During the week the lunch crowd from nearby office buildings keeps this place hopping; a breakfast buffet is available on weekends. The ingredients are fresh. Some ingredients, like the smoked meats, are prepared right in the kitchen. **Bar:** full bar. **Reservations:** suggested. **Address:** 1128 W Hastings St V6E 4R5 **Location:** Between Thurlow and Bute sts; in Vancouver Marriott Pinnacle Downtown. **Parking:** on-site (fee) and valet.   B L D CALL ⬥M

Enjoy exclusive member discounts and benefits from Hertz

STEPHO'S SOUVLAKI GREEK TAVERNA   604/683-2555   26

▼▼ Greek. Casual Dining. $7-$12 **AAA Inspector Notes:** Amid the many shops, bars and coffee houses on bustling Davie Street, the longstanding restaurant is a favorite for its generous plates of reasonably priced rice, roasted potatoes, souvlaki, lamb and chicken. There's often a line, so diners are encouraged to arrive early. **Bar:** full bar. **Address:** 1124 Davie St V6E 1N1 **Location:** Between Bute and Thurlow sts. **Parking:** street only.   L D

SUBEEZ CAFE   604/687-6107   34

▼▼ Canadian. Casual Dining. $11-$27 **AAA Inspector Notes:** A downtown fixture for the past 18 years, the restaurant serves good comfort foods like sandwiches with West Coast greens, soups and meal-sized salads. Breakfast is served from 10 am to 3 pm. For those looking to satisfy the late night munchies, the café is open weekdays until midnight, and Friday and Saturday 'til 2 am. **Bar:** full bar. **Address:** 891 Homer St V6B 2W2 **Location:** Between Smithe and Robson sts. **Parking:** street only.
B L D LATE CALL ⬥M

TABLEAU BAR BISTRO   604/639-8692   7

▼▼▼ New French. Casual Dining. $12-$24 **AAA Inspector Notes:** This intimate restaurant and lounge is where funky meets upscale. That's the only way to describe this new restaurant located lobby level in one of Vancouver's newest boutique hotels. The French- and Asian-inspired cuisine features ingredients found locally or from organic growers from around the lower mainland of B.C. The lounge and background music tend to increase with the evening crowds. **Bar:** full bar. **Reservations:** suggested. **Address:** 1181 Melville St V6E 0A3 **Location:** Between Bute and Thurlow sts; in Loden Hotel. **Parking:** valet and street only.   L D CALL ⬥M

TROPIKA MALAYSIAN & THAI CUISINE
      604/737-6002   16

◆◆
Asian
Casual Dining
$8-$20

AAA Inspector Notes: A quick trip through the extensive menu, which combines Malaysian and Thai cuisine, turns up Thai curries that take 8 hours of preparation, pan-fried roti bread that disappears within seconds of reaching the table and Malaysian chili sauce dishes. A popular signature dish is the wonderfully aromatic K.L.Crab. The tom yum kung soup has lobster meat. The restaurant is on the second floor overlooking trendy Robson Street. **Bar:** full bar. **Reservations:** suggested. **Address:** 1128 Robson St V6E 1B2 **Location:** Between Bute and Thurlow sts. **Parking:** street only.   L D

VERA'S BURGER SHACK   604/228-8372

▼ Burgers Hot Dogs. Quick Serve. $6-$11 **AAA Inspector Notes:** Vera's, as it has come to be known, has received kudos for its burgers for the past few years. The secret to its success is simple, freshly ground beef that's cooked to perfection. In addition to burgers, guests might want to try the dogs, fries, onion rings or daily specials. Takeout available. **Bar:** beer only. **Address:** 1925 Cornwall Ave V6J 1C8 **Location:** Between Walnut and Cypress sts. **Parking:** street only.   L D

VERA'S BURGER SHACK   604/893-8372

▼ Burgers Hot Dogs. Quick Serve. $6-$11 **AAA Inspector Notes:** Vera's is known for fresh, never-frozen ground beef burgers, succulent hot dogs, huge onion rings and thick creamy milkshakes. They like to say they're a "full fat operation" so don't ask for a whole wheat bun and don't ask for skim milk in your milkshake! Eat in or take out. **Bar:** beer only. **Address:** 1030 Davie St V6E 1M3 **Location:** Between Thurlow and Burrard sts. **Parking:** street only.   L D CALL ⬥M

WATER ST. CAFE   604/689-2832   30

▼▼▼ Italian. Casual Dining. $11-$29 **AAA Inspector Notes:** In a Victorian building across from Old Gastown's steam clock landmark, the elegant yet casual restaurant prepares Continental and Italian cuisine with British Columbia and Canadian West Coast touches. A corner location makes this trendy spot perfect for people-watching. The wonderful selection of warmed breads makes mouths water. With its remnants of red brick walls and large bay windows, the interior evokes an old warehouse. **Bar:** full bar. **Reservations:** suggested. **Address:** 300 Water St V6B 1B6 **Location:** Corner of Cambie and Water sts; in Gastown. **Parking:** street only.   L D AC

(See map & index p. 364.)

WHITE SPOT

[diamond][diamond] American. Casual Dining. $10-$18 **AAA Inspector Notes:** Open for three meals a day, the popular casual restaurant prepares offerings such as sandwiches and burgers, fresh salads, pastas and stir-fries, fish and chips, chargrilled sirloin steaks and chicken, in addition to a selection of yummy desserts. **Bar:** full bar.

[B] [L] [D] CALL [&M]

For additional information, visit AAA.com

LOCATIONS:

Address: 718 Drake St V6Z 2W6 **Location:** Between Granville and Howe sts. **Phone:** 604/605-0045

Address: 1616 W Georgia St V6G 2V5 **Location:** Corner of W Georgia and Cardero sts. **Phone:** 604/681-8034

WILD RICE   604/642-2882   (32)

[diamond][diamond] Asian. Casual Dining. $11-$21 **AAA Inspector Notes:** This funky downtown east-side bar and Asian eatery caters to the nightclub crowd looking for appetizers to share along with a fancy and innovative drink menu. Located just up the street from the Tinseltown Cinema, this is a perfect spot to stop in before a movie or after. You'll want to park at a nearby lot as street spots are limited. **Bar:** full bar. **Reservations:** suggested. **Address:** 117 W Pender St V6B 1S4 **Location:** Between Beatty and Abbott sts. **Parking:** street only.

[D] CALL [&M]

WON MORE SZECHUAN CUISINE   604/688-8856   (6)

[diamond][diamond] Chinese. Casual Dining. $7-$16 **AAA Inspector Notes:** The second-floor restaurant overlooks English Bay. The wonderful eatery is known for its dry ginger beef and salt and pepper squid. Those who like it hot and spicy should look for the highlighted items on the menu. **Bar:** beer & wine. **Address:** 201-1184 Denman St V6G 2M9 **Location:** Between Davie and Pendrell sts. **Parking:** street only. [D]

YALETOWN BREWING COMPANY   604/681-2739   (40)

[diamond][diamond] American. Casual Dining. $12-$24 **AAA Inspector Notes:** In the trendy Yaletown area, the distinctive brewpub offers homemade beers to accompany its thin-crust pizzas and wonderful burgers. On warm days, patrons can unwind on the large outdoor patio. **Bar:** full bar. **Reservations:** suggested. **Address:** 1111 Mainland St V6B 2T9 **Location:** Between Helmcken and Davie sts. **Parking:** street only. [L] [D] [LATE] CALL [&M]

YEW RESTAURANT & BAR   604/692-4939   (25)

[diamond][diamond][diamond] Seafood. Fine Dining. $18-$40 **AAA Inspector Notes:** A unique dining room offers extra lofty ceilings, thick beams, wood-paneled walls and a floor-to-ceiling sandstone fireplace to enhance a West Coast feel. Capturing the essence of British Columbia, the chef relies on ingredients from the entire Pacific region. The menu features four meat choices, four fish choices and some pasta choices, and an extensive wine list highlights old world classics as well as favorites from British Columbia, the Pacific Northwest and California. **Bar:** full bar. **Reservations:** suggested. **Address:** 791 W Georgia St V6C 2T4 **Location:** Between Howe and Granville sts; in Four Seasons Hotel Vancouver. **Parking:** on-site (fee) and valet.

[B] [L] [D] CALL [&M]

ZEFFERELLI'S RESTAURANT   604/687-0655   (14)

[diamond][diamond] Italian. Casual Dining. $11-$25 **AAA Inspector Notes:** On the second floor above the Cactus Club, many tables offer spectacular views of bustling Robson Street. In operation since 1989, the restaurant boasts it is the best place for delicious pasta dishes, offering reasonably priced menu options with a fine selection of local wines. **Bar:** full bar. **Reservations:** suggested. **Address:** 1136 Robson St V6E 1B2 **Location:** Between Bute and Thurlow sts. **Parking:** street only. [L] [D]

FRANKIE'S ITALIAN KITCHEN & BAR   604/688-6368

[fyi] Not evaluated. Delightful fresh homemade Italian pasta. **Address:** 765 Beatty St V6B 2M4 **Location:** Between Georgia and Robson sts; in Georgian Court Hotel.

VANCOUVER (I-4)

- **Restaurants p. 390**
- **Hotels & Restaurants map & index p. 368**

2400 MOTEL   (604)434-2464   [6]

Motel [diamond] $89-$189

Address: 2400 Kingsway V5R 5G9 **Location:** 4.5 mi (7.2 km) se on Hwy 1A and 99A (Kingsway and 33rd Ave). **Facility:** 65 units, some two bedrooms and kitchens. 1 story, exterior corridors. **Free Special Amenities:** local telephone calls and early check-in/late check-out.

 [SAVE] [dining] [wifi] [X] [/SOME UNITS] FEE [pet] [gym] [fridge]

BEST WESTERN PLUS UPTOWN HOTEL   (604)267-2000   [4]

Hotel [diamond][diamond][diamond] $89-$189

AAA Benefit: Members save up to 20%, plus 10% bonus points with Best Western Rewards®.

Address: 205 Kingsway V5T 3J5 **Location:** Corner of E 10th St. **Facility:** 69 units. 4 stories, interior corridors. **Amenities:** high-speed Internet. **Activities:** exercise room. **Guest Services:** valet laundry. **Free Special Amenities:** expanded continental breakfast and high-speed Internet. *(See ad p. 389.)*

 [SAVE] [dining] [Y] CALL [&M] [wifi]
[X] [fridge] [/SOME UNITS] [gym] [icon]

DAYS INN-VANCOUVER METRO   (604)876-5531   [5]

Motel [diamond][diamond] $59-$209

Address: 2075 Kingsway V5N 2T2 **Location:** 3.8 mi (6 km) se on Hwy 1A and 99A (Kingsway/Victoria Dr). **Facility:** 66 units. 3 stories (no elevator), exterior corridors. **Terms:** cancellation fee imposed. **Free Special Amenities:** continental breakfast and high-speed Internet.

[SAVE] [ECO] [dining] [wifi] [X] [gym] [fridge] [/SOME UNITS] [icon]

HOLIDAY INN EXPRESS VANCOUVER   (604)254-1000   [1]

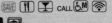 [diamond][diamond] Hotel $119-$309 **Address:** 2889 E Hastings St V5K 2A1 **Location:** Between Renfrew and Kaslo sts. **Facility:** 100 units. 4 stories, interior corridors. **Terms:** check-in 4 pm, cancellation fee imposed. **Activities:** sauna, exercise room. **Guest Services:** valet and coin laundry, area transportation-within 5 mi (8 km).

  [ECO] [dining] [Y] CALL [&M] [wifi] [X] [camera] [fridge]
[/SOME UNITS] FEE [pet] FEE [gym]

HOLIDAY INN VANCOUVER-CENTRE (BROADWAY)
                                 604/879-0511   [2]

[diamond][diamond][diamond] Hotel. Rates not provided. **Address:** 711 W Broadway V5Z 3Y2 **Location:** Between Heather and Willow sts. **Facility:** 200 units. 16 stories, interior corridors. **Parking:** on-site (fee). **Amenities:** high-speed Internet. **Pool(s):** heated indoor. **Activities:** exercise room. **Guest Services:** valet and coin laundry.

[ECO] [dining] [Y] CALL [&M] [pool] [BIZ] [wifi] [X] [camera] [fridge]
[/SOME UNITS] [gym]

RAMADA VANCOUVER EXHIBITION PARK
                                 (604)294-4751   [3]

Hotel [diamond][diamond] $90-$160

Address: 3475 E Hastings St V5K 2A5 **Location:** Trans-Canada Hwy 1 exit 26; jct Trans-Canada Hwy 1 and 7A. **Facility:** 57 units. 3 stories, interior corridors. **Activities:** limited exercise equipment. **Guest Services:** valet and coin laundry. **Free Special Amenities:** expanded continental breakfast and high-speed Internet.

 [SAVE] [dining] CALL [&M] [BIZ] [wifi] [gym] [icon] [fridge]

▼ See AAA listing p. 388 ▼

▼ See AAA listing p. 321 ▼

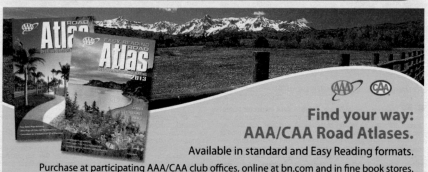

(See map & index p. 368.)

WHERE TO EAT

ABIGAIL'S PARTY   604/739-4677 5

▼▼ ▼▼ Comfort Food. Casual Dining. $14-$22 **AAA Inspector Notes:** The owners of this cheeky Kitsilano eatery chose this name because it's a fun and sexy place with a warm interior, low lighting and cool music. The menu changes seasonally and features locally harvested items whenever possible. The often-changing chalkboard wine list offers several vintages by the glass. Parking is at street meters, but you also can search the neighborhood for a 2-hour spot. **Bar:** full bar. **Reservations:** suggested. **Address:** 1685 Yew St V6K 3E6 **Location:** Between Cornwall and 1st aves; in Kitsilano District. **Parking:** street only. D LATE

AVENUE GRILL   604/266-8183 22

▼▼ ▼▼ Mediterranean. Casual Dining. $11-$24 **AAA Inspector Notes:** In the trendy Kerrisdale neighborhood, the long-established restaurant has limited space, making reservations a good idea, especially on weekends. Tables are tightly spaced, but seating is comfortable. The main draw is the food: standard breakfast selections, fresh sandwiches, daily soups and blue-plate specials for lunch; and many pasta dishes made from more than 40 toppings on the dinner menu. Most parking is along the street. **Bar:** full bar. **Reservations:** suggested, weekends. **Address:** 2114 W 41st Ave V6M 1Z1 **Location:** Between Yew St and W Boulevard. **Parking:** street only.

 B L D

BISHOP'S   604/738-2025 6

▼▼▼ ▼▼▼ Pacific Northwest. Fine Dining. $30-$39 **AAA Inspector Notes:** The restaurant has been serving wonderful, contemporary North American cuisine for more than 25 years. The weekly changing menu highlights the season's freshest ingredients such as British Columbia salmon, which has a short season. The chef/owner, John Bishop, has filled his restaurant with extraordinary Native artwork pieces and has produced several cookbooks that are available for sale in his restaurant. **Bar:** full bar. **Reservations:** required. **Address:** 2183 W 4th Ave V6K 1N7 **Location:** Between Arbutus and Yew sts. **Parking:** street only. D

CACTUS CLUB CAFE

▼▼ ▼▼ American. Casual Dining. $11-$37 **AAA Inspector Notes:** This bustling, casual restaurant serves huge burgers, sandwiches, pasta, salads, soups, quesadillas, fajitas, vegetarian dishes, steak, ribs, chicken and fish. Featured are certified Angus beef and fresh wild British Columbia salmon. **Bar:** full bar.

 L D LATE CALL 🖻M

For additional information, visit AAA.com

LOCATIONS:

Address: 575 W Broadway V5Z 1E6 **Location:** Corner of W Broadway and Ash St. **Phone:** 604/714-6000

Address: 1530 W Broadway V6J 5K9 **Location:** Between Fir and Granville sts. **Phone:** 604/733-0434

GRAMERCY GRILL   604/730-5666 12

▼▼ ▼▼ Pacific Northwest. Casual Dining. $10-$26 **AAA Inspector Notes:** Named for a New York district, the restaurant sports a dark-wood interior, comfortable booths and tables and a showpiece bar. During warm days and evenings, patrons gather on the pleasant patio. Prices for such dishes as osso buco, roast lamb sirloin, game hen and, of course, West Coast salmon are reasonable. Several wines by the glass are available. **Bar:** full bar. **Reservations:** suggested. **Address:** 2685 Arbutus St V6J 3Y4 **Location:** Between W 10th and W 11th aves. **Parking:** street only. L D CALL 🖻M

LAS MARGARITAS RESTAURANTE & CANTINA
604/734-7117 8

▼▼ ▼▼ Mexican. Casual Dining. $12-$19 **AAA Inspector Notes:** Las Margaritas features a bright, festive atmosphere accented with Mexican artifacts. The menu includes healthy choices and offers fajitas, grilled salmon burritos and chipotle chicken. Servers are prompt and attentive. There are six parking stalls behind the restaurant; metered street parking also is available. **Bar:** full bar. **Reservations:** suggested, except Fri-Sun. **Address:** 1999 W 4th Ave V6J 1M7 **Location:** Between Cypress and Maple sts. **Parking:** on-site and street. L D

LOMBARDO'S PIZZERIA & RISTORANTE   604/251-2240 20

▼▼ ▼▼ Pizza. Casual Dining. $12-$20 **AAA Inspector Notes:** Conveniently located near shopping, this place is known as one of the oldest brick-oven pizza houses in town, and it offers 20 types of pizza. The lasagna is very good also. Locals and visitors alike enjoy the family-style atmosphere, though seating is a bit limited. **Bar:** beer & wine. **Address:** 120 1641 Commercial Dr V5L 3A4 **Location:** Corner of 1st St and Commercial Dr; in Il Mercato Mall. **Parking:** on-site (fee) and street. L D

MAURYA INDIAN CUISINE   604/742-0622 14

▼▼ ▼▼ Indian. Casual Dining. $13-$25 **AAA Inspector Notes:** Representative of the cuisine are moist, flavorful tandoori chicken, vindaloo lamb and a number of vegetarian dishes. Don't forget to order naan bread with three dipping sauces. There's a daily lunch buffet starting around $14. Lending to the warm, inviting atmosphere are rich wood accents and professional decoration down to the last detail. Parking is at the back of the restaurant or at street meters. **Bar:** full bar. **Reservations:** suggested. **Address:** 1643 W Broadway V6J 1W9 **Location:** Between Fir and Pine sts. **Parking:** on-site and street. L D

MEMPHIS BLUES BARBEQUE HOUSE

▼▼ Barbecue. Casual Dining. $8-$26 **AAA Inspector Notes:** A sure sign that diners are likely to get messy fingers and faces is the roll of paper towels at each table. Savory favorites include slabs of ribs, pulled pork and, of course, heaps of barbecue wings. **Bar:** full bar. L D

For additional information, visit AAA.com

LOCATIONS:

Address: 1465 W Broadway V6H 1H6 **Location:** Between Granville and Hemlock sts. **Phone:** 604-738-6806

Address: 1342 Commercial Dr V5L 3X6 **Location:** Between Kitchener and Charles sts. **Phone:** 604/215-2599

MILESTONES GRILL AND BAR   604/678-8488

▼▼ ▼▼ Canadian. Casual Dining. $12-$28 **AAA Inspector Notes:** Popular with locals, the bustling eatery is a great gathering place. The menu features such items as wild Pacific coho salmon, Angus beef, gluten-free burgers, Kobe style beef sliders, "share plate" appetizers, soups, salads, "pasta & bowls," Angus top sirloin, Mediterranean chicken, portobello mushroom chicken, sandwiches, burgers, prime rib, roll-ups, taster or full desserts. There is a great selection of wines by the glass and creative specialty cocktails. **Bar:** full bar. **Address:** 2425 Cambie St V5Z 4M5 **Location:** Between W Broadway and W 8th Ave. **Parking:** on-site (fee) and street.

 L D LATE CALL 🖻M

MISTRAL FRENCH BISTRO   604/733-0046 10

▼▼▼ ▼▼▼ French. Casual Dining. $16-$34 **AAA Inspector Notes:** The quaint French bistro serves wonderful lunches and dinners with a heavy reliance on meats such as roast chicken, veal and New York grade A beef. Amazing desserts made on the premises are the highlight here. Parking is offered at metered spots along the street. **Bar:** full bar. **Reservations:** suggested. **Address:** 2585 W Broadway V6K 2E9 **Location:** Between Trafalgar and Larch sts. **Parking:** street only. L D CALL 🖻M

MONK MCQUEEN'S FRESH SEAFOOD & OYSTER BAR
604/877-1351 13

▼▼ ▼▼ Seafood. Casual Dining. $14-$30 **AAA Inspector Notes:** Known to locals simply as "Monks," this mostly seafood restaurant juts out onto the waters of False Creek. With the floor-to-ceiling windows diners have a magnificent view of the North Shore mountains. In spring and summer people flock to the outdoor patio. Sample fresh oysters or a pound of clams or mussels. Main Plate specials include wild salmon and pan-seared Arctic char. For the non-seafood person there's braised beef short ribs, AAA New York steak or oven-roasted chicken. **Bar:** full bar. **Reservations:** suggested. **Address:** 601 Stamps Landing V5Z 3Z1 **Location:** Just n of jct W 6th Ave and Moberly Rd; just w of Cambie St Bridge. **Parking:** valet and street only. D CALL 🖻M

MOXIE'S CLASSIC GRILL   604/678-9973

▼▼ ▼▼ American. Casual Dining. $10-$29 **AAA Inspector Notes:** This sleek, funky and popular restaurant presents an extensive menu of creatively prepared dishes, including pizza, pasta, rice, noodles, signature salads and burgers. Other menus include one for children and one for Sunday brunch. Lending to the upbeat, stylish decor are dark wood appointments and river rock fireplaces. **Bar:** full bar. **Address:** 1759 W Broadway V6J 4S5 **Location:** Between Burrard and Pine sts. **Parking:** on-site (fee). L D

(See map & index p. 368.)

THE OUISI BISTRO
604/732-7550 (19)

Cajun. Casual Dining. $10-$23 **AAA Inspector Notes:** In the mix of high-end shops and restaurants along trendy Granville Street, the low-key restaurant serves Louisiana Creole and Cajun dishes from its open kitchen. Certain times of the year usher in live jazz in the evenings. Parking is at street meters. **Bar:** full bar. **Reservations:** suggested. **Address:** 3014 Granville St V6H 3J8 **Location:** Between W 14th and W 15th sts. **Parking:** street only.

L D

PROVENCE MEDITERRANEAN GRILL
604/222-1980 (4)

French. Fine Dining. $12-$32 **AAA Inspector Notes:** The pleasant Point Grey restaurant serves casual southern French and Italian cuisine in a warm neighborhood atmosphere. At the end of the month, the owners have a culinary tasting or chef's three-course prix fixe menu. Guests can walk off their meal afterward by checking out the nearby shops. **Bar:** full bar. **Reservations:** suggested. **Address:** 100-4473 W 10th Ave V6R 2H2 **Location:** Between Sasamat and Trimble sts. **Parking:** street only.

L D CALL &M

Q4 RISTORANTE
604/734-4444 (11)

Italian. Casual Dining. $17-$34 **AAA Inspector Notes:** Located in the heart of Kitsilano, this place has a good local reputation of serving good pasta dishes along with a variety of antipasto items. During the warmer weather the restaurant opens its large outdoor patio. **Bar:** full bar. **Reservations:** suggested. **Address:** 2563 W Broadway V6K 2E9 **Location:** Between Trafalgar and Larch sts. **Parking:** street only. L D CALL &M

REFUEL RESTAURANT & BAR
604/288-7905 (9)

Pacific Northwest. Casual Dining. $15-$35 **AAA Inspector Notes:** Along trendy Fourth Avenue, the restaurant prepares weekly changing offerings of superb regional cuisine from ingredients purchased from local farmers and purveyors. The kitchen looks right out onto the street, providing a hook for captivated passers-by. **Bar:** full bar. **Reservations:** suggested. **Address:** 1944 W 4th Ave V6J 1M5 **Location:** Between Cypress and Maple sts. **Parking:** street only. L D CALL &M

SAWASDEE THAI RESTAURANT
604/876-4030 (21)

Thai. Casual Dining. $8-$13 **AAA Inspector Notes:** Sawasdee Thai likes to say this is where you'll find "the most authentic Thai food outside of Thailand." The flavorful food and pleasant service are hallmarks of this popular place located outside the downtown core. Main Street is known for its various other shops and restaurants, but this one is well worth the stop. The cozy dining room is comfortable and is adorned with framed posters of Thailand. It's almost like you're there. **Bar:** full bar. **Reservations:** suggested, weekends. **Address:** 4250 Main St V5V 3P9 **Location:** Main St and 27th Ave. **Parking:** street only. L D

SEASONS IN THE PARK RESTAURANT
604/874-8008 (23)

Pacific Northwest. Fine Dining. $13-$36 **AAA Inspector Notes:** Atop a small hill in gorgeous Queen Elizabeth Park, the restaurant offers absolutely stunning views of the park and its flowers and the distant downtown buildings. Market-fresh ingredients and great service are the hallmarks of this long-established restaurant. Take advantage of valet parking for a small charge. Access to the park and restaurant is available from either Cambie or Main streets. **Bar:** full bar. **Reservations:** suggested. **Address:** W 33rd Ave & Cambie St V6G 3E7 **Location:** Between Main and Cambie sts; at 33rd Ave; in Queen Elizabeth Park. **Parking:** on-site (fee) and valet. L D CALL &M

SHAUGHNESSY RESTAURANT AT VANDUSEN GARDEN
604/261-0011 (24)

Pacific Northwest. Casual Dining. $14-$30 **AAA Inspector Notes:** Overlooking the wonderful VanDusen Botanical Garden, the quiet haven uses fresh ingredients in beautiful lunch and dinner entrées. Among daily specials are homemade soups. Ask about the chicken pot pie, a longtime favorite. After the meal, enjoy a stroll through the gardens. **Bar:** full bar. **Reservations:** suggested. **Address:** 5251 Oak St V6M 4H1 **Location:** Between W 33rd and W 37th aves. ⊞ L D CALL &M ✗

SOPHIE'S COSMIC CAFE
604/732-6810 (7)

American. Casual Dining. $7-$19 **AAA Inspector Notes:** Be prepared to stand in line for this popular restaurant, where the walls are covered with decorations (many found at garage sales) that recall the '60s and '70s; think Bobby Vinton album covers, red Radio Flyer wagons and more fun reminders of the past. Parking is only at street meters. **Bar:** full bar. **Address:** 2095 W 4th Ave V6J 1N3 **Location:** Between Arbutus and Maple sts. **Parking:** street only.

B L D

SWISS CHALET
604/732-8100

Chicken. Casual Dining. $6-$19 **AAA Inspector Notes:** The popular restaurant is known for its rotisserie chicken and ribs and the tangy Chalet sauce that gives food its special zip. Diners munch on a half or quarter chicken with sides such as steamed vegetables, fries, baked potatoes and salads. Lunch guests often go for the great soup and sandwich combination. Take-out and delivery service are popular options. **Bar:** full bar. **Address:** 3204 W Broadway V6K 2H4 **Location:** Between Blenheim and Trutch sts. **Parking:** on-site and street. L D CALL &M

TEAHOUSE IN STANLEY PARK
604/669-3281 (1)

Pacific Northwest. Fine Dining. $17-$35 **AAA Inspector Notes:** In the charming country-garden setting of Stanley Park, the restaurant affords spectacular views of English Bay and the mountains. The menu standout is the fabulous roasted rack of lamb. Couples and visitors especially enjoy the atmosphere of casual elegance. Pay parking is in effect. **Bar:** full bar. **Reservations:** suggested. **Address:** 7501 Stanley Park Dr V6G 3E2 **Location:** Ferguson Point; in Stanley Park. **Parking:** on-site (fee). L D CALL &M

TOJO'S RESTAURANT
604/872-8050 (16)

Japanese. Fine Dining. $18-$45 **AAA Inspector Notes:** Each item on the MSG-free menu is prepared using traditional Japanese methods and only the freshest ingredients. Diners can try the Omakase dinners, similar to a chef's tasting menu, entrusting Tojo to arrange your meal for a cost of $70, $80 or $120, or simply go a la cart. There's no on-site parking, just street meters. The food gets raves from the locals and celebrities, whom you might even see dining there. **Bar:** full bar. **Reservations:** suggested. **Address:** 1133 W Broadway V6H 1G1 **Location:** Between Spruce and Alder sts. **Parking:** street only. D CALL &M

TRAFALGARS BISTRO
604/739-0555 (15)

Regional Continental. Casual Dining. $12-$27 **AAA Inspector Notes:** If you covet one of the limited seats at dinnertime, be sure to reserve ahead since table spacing is a little tight. Trafalgars Bistro occupies a small neighborhood shopping complex and serves brunch daily. The owners describe the food as being "French based with some Asian influences," but you'll likely describe it as being good and reasonably priced. The lamb and ground pork burger, fresh-made soups of the day and all-day egg dishes are popular choices. **Bar:** full bar. **Reservations:** suggested, for dinner. **Address:** 2603 W 16th Ave V6K 3C2 **Location:** Between Trafalgar and Stephens sts. **Parking:** street only. L D CALL &M

VIJ'S RESTAURANT
604/736-6664 (17)

New Indian. Casual Dining. $24-$30 **AAA Inspector Notes:** You'll find this restaurant in the South Granville district, just 5 minutes from downtown over the Granville Street Bridge. Because they don't take reservations patrons start lining up around 5 pm for the 5:30 opening. Once seated, your server will offer you a hot cup of sweet Chai tea. The all-female Punjabi kitchen staff works hard all day preparing the fresh spices to pair with locally grown meats, seafood and produce, making this restaurant a true standout. **Bar:** full bar. **Address:** 1480 W 11th Ave V6H 1L1 **Location:** Between Hemlock and Granville sts. **Parking:** street only. D CALL &M

WEST RESTAURANT
604/738-8938 (18)

Pacific Northwest. Fine Dining. $15-$43 **AAA Inspector Notes:** Located along the very trendy area known as South Granville Street, this restaurant has been recognized with a number of awards, especially for its innovative wine list and magnificent "wall of wine" that houses some 3,000 wines from 750 labels. The menu highlights B.C.'s finest seafood and game, and organic and local ingredients. The in-house pastry chef makes all the fresh breads, sorbets, ice creams, chocolates and desserts to please your sweet tooth. **Bar:** full bar. **Reservations:** suggested. **Address:** 2881 Granville St V6H 3J4 **Location:** Between 12th and 13th aves. **Parking:** street only. L D CALL &M

(See map & index p. 368.)

WHITE SPOT

♥♥ Canadian. Casual Dining. $11-$17 **AAA Inspector Notes:** Open for three meals a day, the popular casual restaurant prepares offerings such as sandwiches and burgers, fresh salads, pastas and stir-fries, fish and chips, chargrilled sirloin steaks and chicken, in addition to a selection of yummy desserts. **Bar:** full bar.

B L D CALL &M

For additional information, visit AAA.com

LOCATIONS:
Address: 2850 Cambie St V5Z 1V5 **Location:** Corner of Cambie and 13th sts. **Phone:** 604/873-1252
Address: 613A-650 41st Ave V5Z 2M9 **Location:** Jct 41st Ave and Cambie St; in Oakridge Mall. **Phone:** 604/261-2820

VANDERHOOF (E-4) pop. 4,480, elev. 915m/2,050'

When the last spike of the railroad was driven in 1914, the Grand Trunk Pacific Development Company offered land for sale. The decision of where to put the new settlement in the wilderness was decided by Herbert Vanderhoof, a railroad employee, and a town was built in just a few weeks. The site, unfortunately, was a poor choice, as the land flooded every spring. In 1919 the townspeople moved to higher ground on the opposite side of the tracks.

Mr. Vanderhoof's legacy to the town is its name, Dutch for "of the farm." The name is fitting, as farming has always been an economic mainstay in the area.

Vanderhoof District Chamber of Commerce: 2353 Burrard Ave., P.O. Box 126, Vanderhoof, BC, Canada V0J 3A0. **Phone:** (250) 567-2124 or (800) 752-4094.

VANDERHOOF COMMUNITY MUSEUM is w. on Hwy. 16 to 478 W. First St. The collection of reconstructed buildings depicts rural agriculture in the 1920s. Among the buildings restored and open are the 1914 Board of Trade Building, a café, a police office, a 1914 jail cell and a home typical of those built in the area by early Mennonite settlers. In the town square are examples of farm machines and equipment. **Time:** Allow 30 minutes minimum. **Hours:** Daily 9:30-5:30, Victoria Day weekend-Sept. 30. Phone ahead to confirm schedule. **Cost:** Donations. **Phone:** (250) 567-2991. [↑↑]

VERNON (B-9) pop. 38,150, elev. 383m/1,256'

• Hotels p. 394 • Restaurants p. 395
• Hotels & Restaurants map & index p. 290
• Part of Okanagan Valley area — see map p. 286

At the confluence of five valleys and bounded by three lakes, Vernon is an important shipping and trading center for the Okanagan region. The town's history is portrayed in 26 large murals painted on downtown buildings. On Hwy. 97 at 25th Avenue, Polson Park encompasses a Japanese garden, a Chinese tea house, a floral clock made of 3,500 plants and a children's water park.

Boating, fishing, hiking, mountain biking and golf are popular in summer; winter activities include skiing, dogsledding and snowshoeing. Several recreational opportunities are available at nearby Ellison Provincial Park *(see Recreation Areas Chart)* and Kalamalka Lake Provincial Park *(see attraction listing and Recreation Areas Chart).*

Silver Star Provincial Park offers mountain biking tours from late June to mid-September. A chairlift to the top of Silver Star Mountain operates daily, July 1 to mid-September.

For relaxation, the Kalamalka Lake viewpoint, 5 kilometres (3 mi.) south of 25th Avenue on Hwy. 97, provides an excellent view of the lake.

Tourism Greater Vernon: 701 Hwy. 97S, Vernon, BC, Canada V1B 3W4. **Phone:** (250) 542-1415 or (800) 665-0795.

ALLAN BROOKS NATURE CENTRE is on a ridgetop at 250 Allan Brooks Way in the old Vernon Upper Air Weather Station. The centre—named after naturalist and illustrator Allan Brooks—features a habitat exhibit about the Northern Okanagan region's ecosystems and describes local grasslands and forests. The Grassland Trail, Naturescape Gardens and scenic views can be enjoyed outdoors. To overlook the countryside and see wildlife, climb the hill for a quiet spot.

Comfortable walking shoes are recommended. **Tours:** Guided tours are available. **Time:** Allow 1 hour minimum. **Hours:** Mon.-Sat. 9-4, May-Oct. Closed Victoria Day, July 1, Labour Day and Thanksgiving. **Cost:** $4.50; $3.50 (ages 3-18 and 65+); $13 (family, parents and children ages 3-18). **Phone:** (250) 260-4227. [↑↑]

ATLANTIS WATERSLIDES LTD. is 8 km (5 mi.) n. on Hwy. 97A at Pleasant Valley Rd. The water park has a slide with 10 flumes of varying lengths and slopes, a giant hot tub, miniature golf and a picnic area. **Time:** Allow 2 hours, 30 minutes minimum. **Hours:** Daily 10-6, July 1-early Sept.; 10-5 in June (weather permitting). Closed Sept. 2. **Cost:** $21; $15 (ages 4-12); $10 (ages 65+); $60 (family, two adults and two children). **Phone:** (250) 549-4121. [↑↑]

DAVISON ORCHARDS COUNTRY VILLAGE is at 3111 Davison Rd. This family-run working farm, known mostly for its apples (including pies and cider), produces an assortment of fruits and vegetables. Twenty-minute tours, in wagons pulled by a tractor, are a fun way to see the operation.

The Crazy Cow Kid's Corral has a straw maze, a sand box, trikes to play on and a tree house; there's also a petting zoo. Older visitors enjoy the collection of vintage tractors and the country village with its market, pantry and produce barn. A corn maze and pumpkin picking are seasonal activities.

Time: Allow 1 hour, 30 minutes minimum. **Hours:** Daily 8:30-5:30. Phone ahead to confirm schedule. **Cost:** Village free. Train tours $6; $4 (children). Kid's corral $4 (ages 2-16); free (parents with paid children's admission). **Phone:** (250) 549-3266. [↑↑]

(See map & index p. 290.)

GREATER VERNON MUSEUM AND ARCHIVES is at 3009 32nd Ave. Exhibits include local and natural history items, Indian artifacts and period costumes and furniture. The Allan Brooks Gallery features works by the artist and naturalist. Archives and a research facility also are on the premises. **Time:** Allow 1 hour minimum. **Hours:** Museum Tues.-Sat. 10-5. Closed major holidays. **Cost:** Donations. **Phone:** (250) 542-3142.

HISTORIC O'KEEFE RANCH is at 9380 Hwy 97N. One of the earliest cattle empires in the Okanagan Valley, the 1867 O'Keefe homestead includes a dozen restored structures. Guided tours are offered of the family's Victorian mansion. Other buildings include a log house, a church, a general store, a blacksmith shop, a cowboy bunk house, barns and tool sheds. A museum depicts the family's history and the ranching way of life.

Time: Allow 1 hour, 30 minutes minimum. **Hours:** Daily 10-6, July-Aug.; 10-5, May-June and Sept. 1-second Mon. in Oct. **Cost:** $12; $11 (ages 60+); $9 (ages 13-18); $7 (ages 6-12); $30 (family, two adults and children ages 6-18). Prices may vary; phone ahead. **Phone:** (250) 542-7868.

KALAMALKA LAKE PROVINCIAL PARK is 8 km (5 mi.) s. off Hwy. 6. Largely undeveloped, the parkland protects an environment of north Okanagan grassland interspersed with stands of ponderosa pine and Douglas fir.

A paved trail winds down to the beaches at Jade and Juniper bays, popular swimming spots in summer. Other hiking trails crisscross the park, which provides refuge for a variety of mammals (white-tailed deer, coyotes and red foxes), birds, reptiles and other wildlife. Take in the panoramic vistas from the viewing platform atop Rattlesnake Point. *See Recreation Areas Chart.*

Hours: Daily dawn-dusk. **Cost:** Free. **Parking:** Day use $1 per hour; $3 per day. **Phone:** (250) 545-9943.

OKANAGAN SCIENCE CENTRE is at 2704 Hwy. 6 in Polson Park. Housed in one of the oldest brick schoolhouses in British Columbia, the center features hands-on exhibits focusing on such topics as rocks, fossils, illusions, recycling and the environment. **Time:** Allow 1 hour minimum. **Hours:** Mon.-Fri. 10-5, Sat. 11-5, July-Aug.; Tues.-Fri. 10-5, Sat. 11-5, rest of year. **Cost:** $7; $4 (ages 3-18 and 65+); $16 (family, up to six people). **Phone:** (250) 545-3644.

PLANET BEE HONEY FARM AND MEADERY, 1 km (.6 mi.) w. on 25th Ave. from jct. Hwy. 97, just n. on 41st St., then w. to 5011 Bella Vista Rd., provides a variety of tours at several apiaries. Visitors may witness the complex societal structure and diligent work habits of more than 10,000 bees in indoor and outdoor observatories. The Inside the Hive tour allows visitors to don gear and explore a working hive. Free taste samples of honey are available from a selection of global sources. Special educational presentations are offered daily in July and August and on weekends in May, June and September. A nominal fee is applicable and includes a personalized sample jar of honey.

Time: Allow 30 minutes minimum. **Hours:** Daily 8:30-5:30, with extended hours in summer. Guided tour hours vary; phone ahead. Closed Christmas and day after Christmas. **Cost:** Free. Guided tours $5-$12; $3-$4.50 (ages 4-10); $20 (family). **Phone:** (250) 542-8088 or (877) 233-9675.

VERNON PUBLIC ART GALLERY is at 3228 31st Ave. on the ground level of the Parkade Bldg. Three exhibition rooms feature works of regional and nationally known artists. Free gallery tours are available upon request. **Time:** Allow 30 minutes

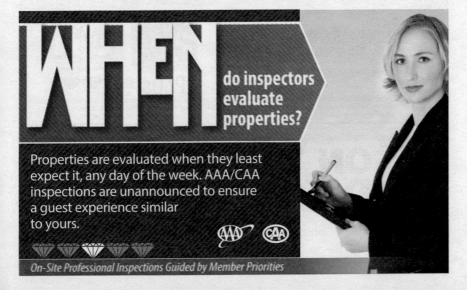

(See map & index p. 290.)

minimum. **Hours:** Mon.-Fri. 10-5, Sat. 11-4; closed statutory holidays. Phone ahead to confirm schedule. **Cost:** Donations. **Phone:** (250) 545-3173.

GAMBLING ESTABLISHMENTS

- **Lake City Casino** is at 4900 Anderson Way. **Hours:** Daily 9 a.m.-2 a.m. Phone ahead to confirm schedule. **Phone:** (250) 545-3505.

RECREATIONAL ACTIVITIES

Skiing

- **Silver Star Mountain Resort** is at 123 Shortt St. **Hours:** Daily 8:30-8:30, mid-Nov. to mid-Apr. Other activities are available. **Phone:** (250) 542-0224 for information, or (800) 663-4431 for reservations.

BEST WESTERN PLUS VERNON LODGE & CONFERENCE CENTRE   (250)545-3385 **5**

Hotel
$114-$180

AAA Benefit: Members save up to 20%, plus 10% bonus points with Best Western Rewards®.

Address: 3914 32nd St V1T 5P1 **Location:** 1 mi (1.6 km) n on Hwy 97 (32nd St). **Facility:** 127 units. 3 stories (no elevator), interior corridors. **Dining:** 2 restaurants. **Pool(s):** heated indoor. **Activities:** whirlpool, exercise room. **Guest Services:** valet laundry. **Free Special Amenities:** local telephone calls and high-speed Internet.

(See ad this page.)

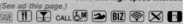

▼ See AAA listing this page ▼

(See map & index p. 290.)

(See map & index p. 290.)

WHERE TO EAT

BEST WESTERN VILLAGER MOTOR INN

(250)549-2224 **2**

Motel
$100-$120

AAA Benefit: Members save up to 20%, plus 10% bonus points with Best Western Rewards®.

Address: 5121 26th St V1T 8G4 **Location:** 1.5 mi (2.5 km) n on 27th St. Across from Village Green Mall. **Facility:** 53 units, some efficiencies. 2 stories (no elevator), exterior corridors. **Pool(s):** heated indoor. **Activities:** whirlpool. **Free Special Amenities:** local telephone calls and high-speed Internet.

SAVE [icons] CALL [icons] / SOME UNITS FEE [icon]

CASTLE ON THE MOUNTAIN B & B

250/542-4593 **1**

Bed & Breakfast. Rates not provided. **Address:** 8227 Silver Star Rd V1B 3M8 **Location:** Hwy 97A exit 48th Ave (which becomes Silver Star Rd), 6.3 mi (10 km) e. **Facility:** 7 units, some kitchens and cottages. 3 stories (no elevator), interior/exterior corridors. **Parking:** winter plug-ins. **Terms:** check-in 4 pm. **Activities:** whirlpool. [icons] / SOME UNITS [icons]

HOLIDAY INN EXPRESS HOTEL & SUITES VERNON

250/550-7777 **3**

Hotel
Rates not provided

Address: 4716 34th St V1T 5Y9 **Location:** Hwy 97 (32nd St) northbound at 48th Ave. **Facility:** 85 units. 3 stories, interior corridors. **Amenities:** high-speed Internet. **Pool(s):** heated indoor. **Activities:** whirlpool, exercise room. **Guest Services:** valet and coin laundry. **Free Special Amenities: continental breakfast and high-speed Internet.**

SAVE CALL [icons] BIZ [icons] / SOME UNITS FEE [icons]

JOURNEY INN

(250)545-2161 **6**

Motel $79-$165 **Address:** 3000 28th Ave V1T 1W1 **Location:** Hwy 97 (32nd St), just e on 28th Ave. Near Polson Park. **Facility:** 38 units. 2 stories (no elevator), exterior corridors. **Terms:** cancellation fee imposed. **Pool(s):** heated outdoor.

ECO [icons]

SPARKLING HILL RESORT

(250)275-1556 **7**

Boutique
Contemporary Hotel
$340-$520

Address: 888 Sparkling Pl V1H 2K7 **Location:** 6 mi (10 km) s on Hwy 97, 1.1 mi (1.9 km) n on Bailey Rd, 2.4 mi (4 km) nw on Commonage Rd, then 1.8 mi (3 km) w on Predator Ridge Dr, follow signs. **Facility:** Guest rooms and bathrooms at this spa retreat, offer floor to ceiling windows with panoramic lake and mountain views, and luxurious features such as over-sized soaking tubs and separate showers. 149 units. 3 stories, interior corridors. **Parking:** on-site and valet. **Terms:** check-in 4 pm, 3 day cancellation notice, resort fee. **Amenities:** safes. **Dining:** PeakFine, see separate listing. **Pool(s):** heated outdoor, heated indoor. **Activities:** saunas, whirlpool, steamrooms, exercise room, spa. **Free Special Amenities: full breakfast and high-speed Internet.**

SAVE FEE [icons] CALL [icons] / SOME UNITS FEE [icon]

SUPER 8 VERNON

(250)542-4434 **4**

Motel $85-$166 **Address:** 4204 32nd St V1T 5P4 **Location:** Hwy 97 (32nd St); jct 43rd Ave. **Facility:** 62 units, some two bedrooms. 3 stories, interior corridors. **Pool(s):** heated indoor. **Activities:** whirlpool.

[icons] CALL [icons] / SOME UNITS [icon]

AMARIN THAI RESTAURANT

250/542-9300 **2**

Thai. Casual Dining. $10-$16 **AAA Inspector Notes:** Located downtown, this enticing Thai restaurant features an extensive menu with spicy curries where you can choose from mild to hot. Vegetarian dishes are available for those who don't eat meat. The stylish décor, which includes Thai artifacts and art, is warm and appealing. Service is fine. Parking is limited to the street. **Bar:** full bar. **Reservations:** suggested. **Address:** 2903 31st St V1T 5H6 **Location:** Between 29th and 30th aves. **Parking:** street only. [L] [D]

ECLECTIC MED RESTAURANT INC

250/558-4646 **3**

Mediterranean. Casual Dining. $16-$38 **AAA Inspector Notes:** In a word, the restaurant can be summed up as "funky," with a varied and eclectic menu of Mediterranean food. The many tempting food choices are prepared with local ingredients wherever possible. Diners return time and again for appetizers such as calamari calabrese spiked with ground chorizo or roasted portobello mushrooms with pine nut and Parmesan pesto, in addition to entrees such as Alaskan black cod served two ways or cocoa-rubbed duck breast with red wine and orange-mocha reduction. **Bar:** full bar. **Reservations:** suggested. **Address:** 2915 30th Ave V1T 5Z1 **Location:** Jct Hwy 97 (32nd St) and 32nd Ave, just e. **Parking:** street only. [D]

INTERMEZZO RESTAURANT

250/542-3853 **1**

Italian. Fine Dining. $17-$34 **AAA Inspector Notes:** You'll enjoy the wide variety of pasta, chicken, seafood, barbecue ribs and the specialty veal, prepared in six classic ways, at Intermezzo, which is located downtown behind a small shopping complex. Meals are delicious and attractively presented. **Bar:** full bar. **Reservations:** suggested. **Address:** 3206 34th Ave V1T 7E2 **Location:** Hwy 97 (32nd St), just w. **Parking:** street only. [D]

THE ITALIAN KITCHEN COMPANY

250/558-7899 **5**

Italian. Casual Dining. $12-$30 **AAA Inspector Notes:** Hearty, delicious food awaits at the funky, upbeat restaurant along the main street downtown. Among offerings are traditional dishes, ranging from pastas to salads to savory soups. Hardwood floors and an exposed brick wall are accentuated by large works of local art in a bright and cheery décor. Service is friendly and attentive. **Bar:** full bar. **Reservations:** suggested. **Address:** 2916 30th Ave V1T 2B7 **Location:** Between 29th and 30th sts; downtown. **Parking:** street only. [L] [D]

LOS HUESOS

250/275-4820 **4**

Mexican. Casual Dining. $9-$16 **AAA Inspector Notes:** Mexican tunes greet patrons as they step off the street into the warm and inviting dining room. The straightforward menu lists classic burritos, chimichangas, tacos and fajitas, as well as daily specials. Margaritas are made with fresh fruit. Live music pumps up the atmosphere on weekends and every night during the summer. **Bar:** full bar. **Reservations:** suggested. **Address:** 2918 30th Ave V1T 2B7 **Location:** Between 29th and 30th sts; downtown. **Parking:** street only. [L] [D] CALL [icon]

PEAKFINE

250/275-1556 **6**

Pacific Northwest
Fine Dining
$18-$39

AAA Inspector Notes: Under a sparkling Swarovski crystal chandelier, every table in the dining room offers views of Okanagan Lake and the surrounding hillsides. The menu changes with the seasons, as well as the mood of the chef. Meat and produce comes from the many area farmers. The restaurant also serves flown-in, seasonal seafood favorites such as salmon and mussels. **Bar:** full bar. **Reservations:** required. **Address:** 888 Sparkling Pl V1H 2K7 **Location:** 6 mi (10 km) s on Hwy 97, 1.1 mi (1.9 km) n on Bailey Rd, 2.4 mi (4 km) nw on Commonage Rd, then 1.8 mi (3 km) w on Predator Ridge Dr, follow signs; in Sparkling Hill Resort. **Parking:** on-site and valet. [B] [L] [D] CALL [icon]

Victoria

Then & Now

"To realize Victoria," Rudyard Kipling wrote, "you must take all that the eye admires in Bournemouth, Torquay, the Isle of Wight, the Happy Valley at Hong Kong, the Doon, Sorrento, Camp's Bay, add reminiscences of the Thousand Islands and arrange the whole around the Bay of Naples with some Himalayas for the background."

Yet the capital of British Columbia remains quintessentially British. Along with its tearooms, double-decker buses, horse-drawn tallyho carriages and shops that sell china and woolens, Victoria proudly claims another, much older culture. Totem poles can be seen throughout local parks, reflecting the city's dual heritage.

Regarded as Canada's gentlest city, Victoria has uncluttered streets, gardens that bloom year-round and hotels that have been serving high tea for decades. Sharing a passion for gardening, Victoria residents tend their prim English gardens. The city's innumerable flower beds and hanging baskets, nurtured by its mild climate, bloom in bright displays while the rest of Canada shivers.

The heart of the city curves around the stone-walled Inner Harbour, alive with bobbing pleasure craft, fishing boats and coastal shipping vessels. Facing the harbor are the Parliament Buildings and the block-long, ivy-covered Empress Hotel.

Emily Carr, a native of Victoria, devoted her artistic career to capturing on canvas the brilliant totem poles carved by the vanishing Indian civilizations of the Pacific coast. Like those she found in deserted Indian villages, the fanciful totems in Thunderbird Park evoke the highly developed ancient culture that dominated the

Parliament Buildings

area long before Victoria was settled in the mid-19th century.

Fort Victoria was built by Hudson's Bay Co. in 1843. Six years later Vancouver Island became a crown colony, and as British Columbia's only port, it became a passage to the Cariboo goldfields on the mainland in 1858. Thousands of European and Asian miners descended on the city, forming the nucleus of today's diverse citizenry.

Violence around Bastion Square was so commonplace during this rowdy boomtown period that the *Victoria Gazette* reported no deaths "from natural causes in the city during the last 30 days." Local politicians supposedly settled their debates with fist fights.

After the gold fever broke, Victoria began to assume its characteristic cool reserve. Lured by modest land prices, English settlers developed their queen's namesake city into a thriving government and commercial center. In 1868 Victoria became the capital of the newly joined crown colonies of Vancouver Island and British Columbia and, a short

(Continued on p. 398.)

Destination Victoria

Strait of Georgia

BRITISH COLUMBIA
WASHINGTON

To Fort Rodd Hill and
Fisgard Lighthouse

(1)

(YYJ) Sidney
✈

Saanichton
Brentwood Bay   (17)

Malahat   •   Saanich

(14)

Oak
Bay

Sooke   •   View Royal

Victoria

Strait   CANADA
UNITED STATES
of
Juan de Fuca

6061-B

This map shows cities in the Victoria vicinity where you will find attractions, hotels and restaurants. Cities are listed alphabetically in this book on the following pages.

Fast Facts

ABOUT THE CITY

POP: 80,017 ▪ **ELEV:** 17m/56 ft.

MONEY

SALES TAX: British Columbia has a single tax known as a harmonized sales tax (HST); the rate is 12 percent. Hotel accommodations are subject to the harmonized tax.

WHOM TO CALL

EMERGENCY: 911

POLICE (non-emergency): (250) 475-4321

HOSPITALS: Gorge Road Hospital, (250) 519-3500 ▪ Royal Jubilee Hospital, (250) 370-8000 ▪ Victoria General Hospital, (250) 727-4212.

WHERE TO LOOK AND LISTEN

NEWSPAPERS: Victoria's daily paper is the *Times-Colonist,* which is distributed in the morning.

RADIO: Victoria radio stations CBC (90.5 FM) ▪ CIOC (98.5 FM) ▪ CFUV (102 FM) ▪ and C-FAX (1070 AM) have news and weather reports.

VISITOR INFORMATION

Tourism Victoria Visitor Information Centre: 812 Wharf St., Victoria, BC, Canada V8W 1T3. **Phone:** (250) 953-2033 or (800) 663-3883.

The center provides maps and brochures outlining various self-guiding walking and driving tours. The center is open daily 8:30-6:30, mid-May to mid-Sept.; 9-5, rest of year.

TRANSPORTATION

AIR TRAVEL: Victoria International Airport (YYJ) is 22 kilometres (12 mi.) north on Hwy. 17 (Patricia Bay Highway). Air Canada makes frequent flights to Victoria from Vancouver and Seattle. International air connections are made in Vancouver.

Airport Bus Service runs between the airport and downtown hotels; phone (250) 386-2525. Fare $15; free (ages 0-4).

RENTAL CARS: Auto rental agencies include Hertz, 1640 Electra Blvd. and 2634 Douglas St., which offers discounts to AAA and CAA members; phone (250) 656-2312 or (250) 952-3765 in Canada. Additional agencies are listed in the telephone directory.

RAIL SERVICE: From its depot at 450 Pandora Ave., Via Rail has weekday passenger service between Victoria and Courtenay; phone (888) 842-7245 in Canada or in the United States.

BUSES: Pacific Coach Lines, 700 Douglas St., provides daily bus service between Vancouver and Victoria via British Columbia Ferry. The vessels transport buses and personal vehicles; phone (604) 385-4411.

Island Coach Lines provides bus transportation between Victoria and Campbell River; Nanaimo; Port Alberni; Port Hardy; and Port McNeill. For information phone (250) 385-4411.

TAXIS: Taxis charge $2.85 minimum plus $1.45 per kilometre (.6 mi.). Companies include Blue Bird Cabs, (250) 382-4235 ▪ Empress Taxi, (250) 381-2222 ▪ and Victoria Taxi, (250) 383-7111.

PUBLIC TRANSPORTATION: BC Transit provides bus service for Greater Victoria. Buses serve the downtown area 6:30 a.m.-midnight. Fare $2.25; senior citizens, students and children $1.40. Buses run frequently between downtown and the ferry terminal. For route information phone (250) 382-6161.

BOATS: Several ferry systems make connections with mainland Canada and the United States. *See Arriving, By Boat.*

(Continued from p. 396.)

time later in 1871 when British Columbia joined the Canadian Confederation, it became the capital of the province.

Since commercial supremacy passed to Vancouver after the completion of the Canadian Pacific Railway, Victoria has adopted a slower pace with few heavy industries. The city is a center for commercial trade as well as the home of Canada's West Coast naval operations. The dry dock at the Canadian Forces Base-Pacific Command is one of the world's largest. Lumber and fishing also contribute to the bustle of this port.

The city's strong tourism industry is buoyed by the stream of travelers who come by ferry from Washington and throughout British Columbia. Those travelers come year round, thanks to Victoria's scenic setting and delightful climate, said to be the mildest in Canada. Flowers bloom all year, and the city only occasionally sees snow.

Victoria's climate and proximity to the Pacific Ocean also provide its citizens an opportunity for an active lifestyle. Marine-based activities such as fishing, sailing, kayaking, canoeing and whale-watching are popular, as are bicycling, hiking and exploring neighborhoods and parks.

Whether or not Victoria is more British than Britain remains an ongoing debate among Victoria's residents. Few would contest, however, that nature's blessings have endowed the city with ample charm in its own right. No one understood this better than its native Indians, whose awesome totems continue to speak the land's wonder.

Must Do: AAA Editor's Picks

- **Butchart Gardens,** in nearby Brentwood Bay, attracts gardeners and nature lovers from around the world. Thousands of spring bulbs and flowering trees offer an extravagant show of color from late March to mid-June—but October and November, when the Japanese Garden takes center stage, matches spring's glory with a stunning autumn parade of reds, russets and golds, plus dozens of varieties of chrysanthemums.

- There's more beauty at **Victoria Butterfly Gardens,** where more than 3,000 free-flying butterflies inhabit a 12,000-square-foot enclosure replete with tropical plants and koi-filled ponds. Swallowtails, brilliantly iridescent blue morphos and the impressively large Atlas moth are just a few of the species you'll see.

- Victoria's **Chinatown** isn't as large as Vancouver's, but it is no less authentic, founded by Chinese immigrants in 1858. Wander up and down Fisgard Street, where vibrant wall murals depict turn-of-the-20th century Chinese families and the opium dens, gambling houses and brothels of yore that are now restaurants and local businesses. Then hunt for souvenirs in the novelty shops along tiny Fan Tan Alley, reputedly Canada's narrowest street.

- **Miniature World** isn't always what you might think—two dollhouses, each furnished in exquisite detail, as well as a model of the Great Canadian Railway are among the largest examples of their kind in the world.

But there's also a miniscule, operational sawmill, an itty-bitty circus and scaled-down European castles. What makes this themed fantasyland particularly enthralling is that it's also hands-on; push a button and something, somewhere, will start moving.

- Minutes away from the Inner Harbour, **Government Street** is packed with stores and art galleries. Do some shopping before settling into a booth at Bard and Banker, a convivial pub housed in a grand old bank building where you can tuck into a plate of beer-battered fish and chips.

- Those who don't feel like walking can ride in elegant style on a horse-drawn carriage tour. **Victoria Carriage Tours** offers a 30-minute narrated excursion along the Inner Harbour that includes a peek at the architecturally grand homes in the historic James Bay neighborhood.

- **Craigdarroch Castle,** the former home of late 19th-century coal mining magnate Robert Dunsmuir, is a must see. The interior of this massive estate, capped with a distinctive red slate roof, is a feast of oak paneling, stained glass and period room furnishings.

- A sylvan retreat in the middle of downtown Victoria, beautifully landscaped **Beacon Hill Park** is named for a pair of masts strategically placed atop a hill that acted as navigational aids for mariners approaching Victoria's Inner Harbour. Quiet and tree shaded, it's a stroller's delight right down to the freely roaming peacocks.

- From Kwakwaka'wakw ceremonial masks to Northern sea lions, the **Royal BC Museum** explores every facet of British Columbia's natural and human history. Just how vast is this province? The Big Map, an animated audiovisual experience, provides a dramatic answer to that question.

- Indulge in afternoon tea on the lawn at **Point Ellice House,** which overlooks the scenic Gorge Waterway. The former home of Irish emigrant Peter O'Reilly is filled with family possessions that comprise one of Canada's largest collections of Victoriana.

- The **Swiftsure International Yacht Race** has been a springtime tradition for more than 80 years. Thousands of people gather along the Dallas Road waterfront to watch fleets of sporting craft navigate the tricky waters of the Strait of Juan de Fuca. The competition is known for exciting starts and nail-biting finishes.

Craigdarroch Castle

Victoria 1-day Itinerary

AAA editors suggest these activities for a great short vacation experience.

Morning

- Begin by visiting several of the gardens that serve as reminders of the city's British heritage (we'll get to the horse-drawn carriages and tearooms later in the day). Head to the Oak Bay neighborhood (where the ambiance is veddy English indeed) to **Abkhazi Garden**. Though petite in size, the garden is resplendent in its beauty. Set on a rocky slope, the dramatic landscape is planted in rhododendrons, Japanese maples, azaleas, evergreens and alpine plants.

- Nearby is Government House, home to the province's lieutenant governor. The formal themed **Government House and Gardens** include spaces devoted to heather, iris and roses and plantings typical of an English country garden.

- A turreted, 39-room, four-story estate is next up. **Craigdarroch Castle** was built in the 1880s by Robert Dunsmuir, a Scottish immigrant from a coal mining family who became one of the richest men in British Columbia. The impressive staircase, oak paneling, period furnishings and stained and leaded glass reflect 19th-century elegance.

- On your way back downtown, stop for lunch at **Haultain's Fish & Chips**. The restaurant has been frying up this traditional favorite since 1924. Choose between halibut and cod and fries or coleslaw. What could be more British?

Afternoon

- The rest of the day is in the lovely Inner Harbor area. Cultural and natural provincial history is the focus of the **Royal BC Museum**, a treasure trove of information about the province's development. Start at the First Peoples Gallery with its ceremonial masks and a full-size chief's house. A turn-of-the-20th-century street scene in the Modern History Gallery, complete with sounds and smells, encourages window peeping to learn about lifestyles of that time period. Hear what a mammoth might have sounded like as well as other sounds from the Ice Age in a gallery devoted to natural history. Then head outdoors to **Thunderbird Park**, which has a collection of Northwest Coast totem poles.

- Practically around the corner in **The Fairmont Empress** hotel is **Miniature World**, a favorite of all ages. Incredible attention to detail is obvious in more than 80 dioramas, all intricately created in miniature. The world of the circus is elaborately crafted in teensy elements, as are dollhouses, castles, battle scenes and a 17th-century London cityscape.

- The palatial Fairmont Empress itself is worth a visit. Resembling a castle, the hotel is a Victoria landmark. It's perhaps best-known, however, for its afternoon teas, a tradition since the hotel opened in 1908. Have a seat in the Tea Lobby and treat yourself to the English ritual (advance reservations are absolutely necessary). Served, in addition to tea, are raisin scones with heavy cream and

Spend the morning at Abkhazi Garden

strawberry preserves and an assortment of sandwiches and pastries (think mango and curried chicken sandwiches and lemon curd and berry tarts). Although worth a splurge, other options (the **White Heather Tea Room** is highly recommended) offer less expensive versions of the afternoon tea experience.

- After the formal tea ceremony, a stroll and shopping are in order. Take a walk up Government Street (the street the hotel's on). The Victorian lampposts and colorful hanging baskets add to the city's charming ambiance. Browse through some of the 19th-century shops selling English woolens, fine china and other British imports; chocolates; Northwestern Indian and Canadian art; clothing; and jewelry.

Evening

- For a very British way to begin the evening, what could be more relaxing than a ride in a horse-drawn carriage? Head over to the corner of Belleville and Menzies streets where the carriages queue up. Knowledgeable drivers provide a running commentary as the horse clip-clops past residential neighborhoods, parks and the downtown area.

- As evening approaches, take a romantic walk alongside the stone walls of the Inner Harbor. Enjoy the soothing breezes, the boats bobbing in the marinas and the lights illuminating the classic lines of the **Legislative Assembly of British Columbia**.

- If enticing aromas from waterside restaurants beckon, there are many options on or just off the harbor. Depending on your taste and pocketbook, you might want to consider **Restaurant Matisse**, **Il Terrazzo**, **Koto Japanese Restaurant**, **The Black Olive** or **Pagliacci's**.

Arriving
By Car

Victoria is the western terminus of the 7,760-kilometre (4,850-mi.) Trans-Canada Highway. The highway traverses the mainland to Horseshoe Bay in West Vancouver and resumes at the Departure Bay Ferry Terminal (Nanaimo). It then proceeds south along the island's eastern shore to Victoria. Hwy. 17, the other major artery into the city, connects Victoria with the ferry terminals at Swartz Bay and Sidney on the Saanich Peninsula.

By Boat

Several ferry systems connect Vancouver Island and Victoria with mainland Canada and the United States. The most direct route is the Tsawwassen-Swartz Bay automobile/passenger ferry service used by the intercity buses between Vancouver and Victoria. British Columbia Ferries also connects Nanaimo, 111 kilometres (69 mi.) north of Victoria, to Horseshoe Bay in West Vancouver. Phone (250) 386-3431 outside British Columbia or (888) 223-3779 within British Columbia for ferry information or reservations.

Ferries linking the southern end of the island and Victoria with the United States include Black Ball Transport Inc., (250) 386-2202, from Port Angeles, Wash.; and Washington State Ferries, (206) 464-6400, from Anacortes, Wash., to Sidney. Reservations are available for the Anacortes, Wash., to Sidney route; phone 1 day in advance to determine estimated waiting time. Victoria Express provides fast passenger ferry service from Port Angeles, Wash., and to Friday Harbor in Washington's San Juan Islands; phone (250) 361-9144. Victoria/San Juan Cruises has seasonal passenger boat service to Friday Harbor and Bellingham, Wash.; phone (800) 443-4552.

Connecting Seattle and Victoria is the high-speed passenger ferry, the Victoria Clipper; phone (250) 382-8100 or (800) 888-2535.

Departing from the north end of the island at Port Hardy, British Columbia Ferries' vessels voyage through the Inside Passage to Prince Rupert, where they connect with the Alaska State Ferry system. Information can be obtained from British Columbia Ferries, 1112 Fort St., Victoria, BC, Canada V8V 4V2; phone (250) 386-3431 outside British Columbia or (888) 223-3779 within British Columbia.

Getting Around
Street System

Most traffic activity is on Wharf, Government and Belleville streets, which embrace the Inner Harbour. Ferries arrive from Port Angeles, Wash., all year and from Seattle in summer. The main east-west streets are Yates, Fort and Johnson. Pandora Avenue, renamed Oak Bay Avenue in midtown, crosses the city from the Inner Harbour to Oak Bay.

Major north-south thoroughfares are Blanshard Street (Hwy. 17) and Douglas Street (Hwy. 1), which begins at Victoria's southern coast along the Juan de Fuca Strait. Dallas Road borders the shore and continues as Beach Drive along Victoria's eastern coast. Many Victoria streets are one-way.

Parking

On-street parking is controlled by meters and posted restrictions Mon.-Sat. 9-6. Vehicles parked on specially posted blocks are subject to towing during rush hours. Downtown off-street parking is available in civic parkades and shopping center lots.

Shopping

Lined with shops carrying English tweeds and fine china, **Government Street** maintains Victoria's heritage as a trading post of the British Empire. Such shops as **E.A. Morris Tobacconist** have distinguished Government Street since the 19th century. Established in 1833, **Rogers' Chocolate Shop** is a Victoria institution that counts British royalty in its clientele. The Rogers' factory, behind the store at 913 Government St., still produces its renowned bittersweet chocolate according to a guarded recipe.

Shoppers determined to bring home something other than a few extra pounds might want to explore the craft and specialty shops in the renovated squares and malls off Government Street. More than 30 quaint stores and restaurants in revitalized old buildings highlight **Market Square**, bounded by Johnson, Pandora and Store streets.

Trounce Alley, in the downtown core, is a hideaway of eclectic shops. Shops of mid-19th-century architecture display modern items in **Bastion Square**, once a hangout for prospectors and drifters. An attractive shopping arcade is in **Centennial Square** off Douglas Street. **Nootka Court** between Courtney and Humboldt streets contains small arts and crafts shops.

Ferries connect Victoria to the mainland

Old meets new in Bastion Square

Popular items available in Victoria include hand-woven woolens from Ireland and England, hand-knit Cowichan Indian sweaters, Eskimo jade sculpture and Northwest Indian masks and prints. **The Bay** department stores, 1150 and 3125 Douglas St., sell authentic Cowichan sweaters. Also in Victoria are **Hillside Shopping Centre**, 1644 Hillside Rd.; **Mayfair Shopping Centre**, 3147 Douglas St.; and **Sears**, 3190 Shelbourne St.

In keeping with its Victorian image, Victoria has more than 50 antique shops. Many are found along Government and Fort streets and Oak Bay Avenue.

Big Events

As a city of traditions, Victoria celebrates many events and festivals year after year. **Victoria Day**, a Canadian national holiday, launches a week of festivities highlighted by a parade. The weekend following Victoria Day features the classic **Swiftsure International Yacht Race**, which has drawn an armada of more than 185 sailboats from all over the world since 1930. The **Highland Games** take place in mid-May.

Boating enthusiasts will enjoy the **Classic Boat Festival** at **Inner Harbour** during Labour Day. There will be a steamboat cruise, rowing regatta, boat races and lots of nautical fun.

Autumn shows off its best colors along the rural **Saanich Peninsula**, where the **Saanich Fair** has been held in early September for more than a century. Fall's lower temperatures provide an energy boost for the **GoodLife Fitness Victoria Marathon**. In late October, however, guests can experience a chill that has nothing to do with the weather at the **Ghosts of Victoria Festival**.

Wrap up an incredible holiday journey with the "jolly old elf" himself at **Island Farms Santa's Light Parade** in the streets of Victoria.

Sports & Rec

The English spirit still is manifest in such games as **lawn bowling** at the corner of Belleville and Douglas streets and **cricket** at Beacon Hill Park. Any notion, however, that Victoria's sports are too staid is dispelled quickly by a **box lacrosse** game. This offspring of the Indian game of *baggataway* is a rough-and-tumble version of field lacrosse confined to a smaller, enclosed area. Canada's Parliament designated boxla, as it also is called, the national sport in 1867. The game is played from April to August at Memorial Arena, 1925 Blanshard.

All-star **wrestling** and **ice hockey**, two other spectator sports that hardly could be considered sedate, also are held at the arena.

Water sports have obvious appeal in this island city. The wide variety of game fish around southern Vancouver Island includes rockfish, lingcod, sole and flounder; fishing licenses are required. Surf **fishing** often yields rewarding catches of salmon and black sea bass. Clamming and oyster harvesting are popular activities on any of the Gulf Islands, which are accessible by ferry from Swartz Bay.

Oak Bay Marina, 1327 Beach Dr., offers fishing charters at an hourly rate. Fishing equipment, a tackle shop and marine store are available; phone (250) 598-3369. Other nearby marinas include Anglers Anchorage Marina, 933 Marchant, Brentwood Bay; North Saanich Marina, 1949 Marina Way, Sidney; and the West Bay Marina, 453 Head St.

Boating is enjoyed in the Strait of Georgia and the Saanich Inlet. Uplands Park on Oak Bay is equipped with boat ramps. Fine beaches border Dallas Road and Beach Drive.

With its scenic coastal location and balmy climate, Victoria offers excellent playing conditions for **golf**. On a peninsula jutting into the Juan de Fuca Strait, Victoria Golf Club is open to members of other clubs.

Other golf clubs include Ardmore (nine holes), 930 Ardmore Dr., North Saanich; Cedar Hill (18 holes), 1400 Derby Rd.; Cordova Bay (18 holes), 5333 Cordova Bay Rd.; Glen Meadows (18 holes), 1050 McTavish Rd.; Green Acres (nine holes), 3970 Metchosin Rd.; Henderson Park (nine holes), 2291 Cedar Hill Crossroad; Mount Douglas (nine holes), 4225 Blenkinsop Rd.; Olympic View Golf Course (18 holes), 643 Latoria Rd.; Prospect Lake (nine holes), 4633 Prospect Lake Rd.; and Royal Oak Golf Club (nine holes), 540 Marsett Pl.

Many parks are scattered throughout Victoria and its surrounding municipalities of Oak Bay, Saanich and Esquimalt. Some offer **swimming**, such as Elk/Beaver Lake Park, Island View Beach Park, Mount Work Park, Thetis Lake Park and Willows Beach Park. Swimmers also might wish to try the Crystal Pool in Central Park.

Hiking, nature and horse trails are found at several parks. For more information contact Victoria Downtown Park; phone (250) 361-0600. Bamberton Provincial Park *(see Recreation Areas Chart)* offers developed recreational facilities, including **camping.**

Swan Lake-Christmas Hill Nature Sanctuary, 6.5 kilometres (4 mi.) north via the Patricia Bay Highway, can be explored by hiking trails and floating walkways weaving through the area. Excellent views of Victoria and the sea are at Mount Douglas, Mount Tolmie and Beacon Hill Park.

Performing Arts

McPherson Playhouse in Centennial Square is the center of Vancouver Island's regional and professional theater. The restored old theater regularly presents noontime concerts and musical comedy productions in the evening; phone (250) 386-6121 or (888) 717-6121. The **Pacific Opera Victoria,** (250) 385-0222, performs at the **Royal Theatre.**

The Royal Theatre on Broughton Street is also the home of the **Victoria Symphony Orchestra,** (250) 385-6515, which offers a pop and masterworks series September through May. The **Victoria Conservatory of Music** sometimes offers performances; phone (250) 386-5311.

Comedy revues and music hall shows also are staged frequently at the **Belfry,** (250) 385-6815, 1291 Gladstone, and the Royal Theatre, (250) 386-6121, 805 Broughton. The **University of Victoria Auditorium** on Finnerty Road also presents various cultural events; phone (250) 721-8480. **Butchart Gardens** mounts musical stage shows during the summer. **Kaleidoscope Theatre,** an open-air theater at the Inner Harbour, also offers summer productions.

Top-name entertainers, rock groups and other performers draw large audiences to **Save-on-Foods Arena,** 1925 Blanshard. A carillon at the **Parliament Buildings** can be heard daily at 3 during the summer. The Royal BC Museum's **National Geographic IMAX Theatre** offers big-screen films complementing the museum's natural and human history themes; phone (250) 953-4629.

ATTRACTIONS

ABKHAZI GARDEN is e. at 1964 Fairfield Rd. at Shotbolt Rd. This small, residential garden was created and nurtured by an Englishwoman and an exiled Georgian prince. The two met in Paris in the

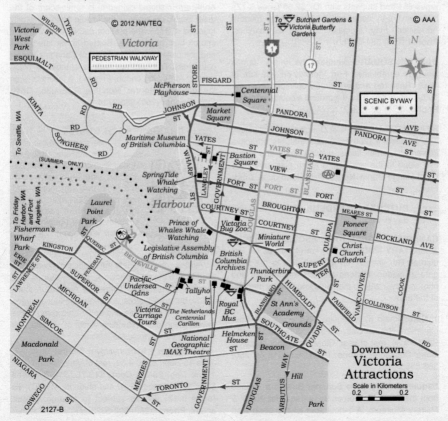

Downtown Victoria Attractions

1920s, spent time in separate World War II internment camps, reunited after the war, married and settled in Victoria.

Prince Nicholas and Princess Peggy Abkhazi built their home and developed this garden along rocky slopes meticulously planted with rhododendrons, Garry oaks and Japanese maples. The Abkhazis' home is now a tea room open for lunch and late afternoon tea.

Time: Allow 1 hour, 30 minutes minimum. **Hours:** Daily 11-5, Mar.-Oct.; 11:30-3:30, rest of year. Closed holidays Nov.-Feb. Last admission is 1 hour before closing. Phone ahead to confirm schedule. **Cost:** Admission Mar.-Oct. $12; $9 (ages 60+ and students with ID); free (ages 0-12); $30 (family). Admission by donation rest of year. **Phone:** (250) 598-8096.

ART GALLERY OF GREATER VICTORIA is at 1040 Moss St. The gallery presents contemporary, historical and Asian exhibitions, including a permanent Emily Carr exhibition. **Hours:** Mon.-Sat. 10-5 (also Thurs. 5-9), Victoria Day to mid-Sept.; Tues.-Sat. 10-5, rest of year. Closed major holidays. Phone ahead to confirm schedule. **Cost:** $13; $11 (ages 65+ and students with ID); $2.50 (ages 6-17); $28 (family); by donation (first Tues. of the month). Admission may increase for special exhibits. **Phone:** (250) 384-4171.

BASTION SQUARE overlooks the harbor. James Douglas established Fort Victoria on this site in 1843. Restored and preserved buildings from the 19th-century boom days surround a courtyard plaza. **Phone:** (250) 885-1387.

BEACON HILL PARK is at Douglas and Dallas sts. The 81-hectare (200-acre) park features attractive flowerbeds, small lakes, playing fields and lawns that slope to the sea, and a totem pole carved by Chief Mungo Martin. **Hours:** Daily dawn-dusk. **Cost:** Free.

 BUTCHART GARDENS—see Brentwood Bay p. 220.

CANADIAN FORCES BASE ESQUIMALT NAVAL & MILITARY MUSEUM is 6 km (4 mi.) w. on Esquimalt Rd., then n. on Admirals Rd. to the main gate at Naden. Historic artifacts, documents and photographs relate to the naval and military heritage of the area.

Note: Photo ID is required. **Time:** Allow 1 hour minimum. **Hours:** Daily 10-3:30, June-Aug.; Mon.-Fri. 10-3:30, rest of year. Closed statutory holidays. **Cost:** Donations. **Phone:** (250) 363-4312 or (250) 363-5655.

Esquimalt Navy Base Summer Bus Tour departs from the Canadian Forces Base Esquimalt Naval & Military Museum. A 1-hour tour of the base also passes the harbor, where navy warships can be seen. **Note:** Photo ID is required. **Hours:** Mon.-Fri. 8-3, July-Aug. **Cost:** Free. **Phone:** (250) 363-7060.

CENTRE OF THE UNIVERSE is at 5071 W. Saanich Rd. Housed within the Dominion Astrophysical Observatory, this interpretive center affords visitors a glimpse into the world of astronomy. The facility offers interactive exhibits, theater presentations and a look at the constellations in the Starlab Planetarium. Visitors may tour the 1.8-metre (5-ft.) Plaskett Telescope. Evening observing hours are available during summer star parties (weather permitting).

Tours: Guided tours are available. **Time:** Allow 1 hour, 30 minutes minimum. **Hours:** Tues.-Sat. 3:30-11:15, mid-July through day before Labour Day; Tues.-Fri. 1-4:30, Sat. 3:30-11, early May through June 30; Tues.-Fri. 1-4:30, Labour Day-Sept. 30. Phone ahead to confirm schedule. **Cost:** $13.50; $11.50 (students with ID and senior citizens); $8 (ages 4-12). Prices may vary; phone ahead. **Phone:** (250) 363-8262.

CHRIST CHURCH CATHEDRAL is at 911 Quadra St., between Burdett and Rockland sts. The Anglican-Episcopal cathedral is reminiscent of the great Gothic churches of the Middle Ages. Originally founded in 1856, the present cathedral is the third church built on this site. Started in the late 1920s and completed in 1986, it is one of Canada's largest cathedrals. The bells are replicas of those at Westminster Abbey in London, England. A labyrinth is on the grounds. **Hours:** Mon.-Fri. 8:30-4:30. **Cost:** Free. **Phone:** (250) 383-2714.

CRAIGDARROCH CASTLE is at 1050 Joan Crescent St. The sandstone mansion was built in the late 1880s for Robert Dunsmuir, a Scottish immigrant who attained wealth and fame through politics and coal mining. Dunsmuir died before the 39-room castle was completed. The building later served as a military hospital, a college and a music conservatory.

Visitors can appreciate the castle's stained-glass windows, intricate woodwork, ceiling murals and Victorian furnishings. There are numerous staircases, but no elevators. A self-guiding tour includes four floors of the castle and an 87-step climb to the tower, which offers stunning views of Victoria, the strait and the Olympic Mountains.

Time: Allow 1 hour minimum. **Hours:** Daily 9-7, June 15-Sept. 6; 10-4:30, rest of year. Closed Jan. 1 and Dec. 25-26. **Cost:** $13.75; $12.75 (ages 65+); $8.75 (ages 13-18 and students with ID); $5 (ages 6-12). Prices subject to change; phone ahead. **Phone:** (250) 592-5323.

EMILY CARR HOUSE is at 207 Government St. Built in 1864 a few blocks from the harbor, the house was the birthplace of artist and writer Emily Carr. The Victorian residence has been restored to the ambiance the Carr family experienced in the 1870s. Family possessions, including some of Carr's early pottery, are displayed. Special events are scheduled throughout the year; phone ahead to confirm schedule.

Hours: Tues.-Sat. 11-4, May-Sept. Last admission is at closing. **Cost:** $6.75; $5.75 (students with ID and senior citizens); $4.50 (ages 6-18); $17 (family). Rates may vary for special events. **Phone:** (250) 383-5843.

THE GARDENS AT HORTICULTURE CENTRE OF THE PACIFIC is off Hwy. 17 West Saanich/Quadra exit, then w. to Beaver Lake Rd., following signs to 505 Quayle Rd. More than 3 hectares (9 acres) of educational gardens feature more than 10,000 plant varieties and sculptures. Highlights of the developing site include the Winter Garden and the Takata Japanese Garden. The surrounding 36 hectares (90 acres) include forests, wetlands and a haven for migratory birds.

Time: Allow 1 hour minimum. **Hours:** Daily 8-6, May-Oct.; 9-4, rest of year. Closed Jan. 1, Christmas Eve, Christmas and day after Christmas. **Cost:** $11; $8.25 (ages 60+ and students with ID); free (ages 0-16). **Phone:** (250) 479-6162.

GOVERNMENT HOUSE AND GARDENS is at 1401 Rockland Ave. The grounds in front of the lieutenant governor's residence consist of 5.7 hectares (14 acres) of formal gardens, featuring perennials, herbs, roses, irises, azaleas, rhododendrons and other floral varieties. The property behind the house, a terraced rock garden, covers a 9-hectare (22-acre) rare Garry oak woodland that is native to southeast Vancouver Island. **Hours:** Formal gardens daily dawn-dusk. **Cost:** Gardens free. Fee for tours. **Phone:** (250) 387-2081.

HATLEY PARK NATIONAL HISTORIC SITE is at 2005 Sooke Rd. The 216.5-hectare (565-acre) Hatley Park estate offers a variety of hands-on, educational visitor experiences. With its preserved old-growth forests, heritage gardens and spectacular vistas that overlook the Esquimalt Lagoon and the Juan de Fuca Strait, the centerpiece of this magnificent site is a 40-room Edwardian home built in 1908 by former British Columbia premier and lieutenant governor James Dunsmuir.

The Hatley Park Museum, part of the historic site, has exhibits reflecting the estate's days as home to the Dunsmuir family, its days as Royal Roads Military College and its current use as the home of Royal Roads University. The site's formal gardens are organized into garden rooms (Japanese, Rose and Italian), recreational spaces (croquet lawn, terrace lawn), agricultural zones and surrounding forest.

Emily Carr House

Hours: Gardens and museum open daily 10-5, year-round. Guided tours are given daily 10:30-2:45, Apr. 15-Sept. 30. **Cost:** Guided tours $18; $15.50 (ages 60+); $10.50 (ages 6-17). Garden tours $9.50; $8.50 (ages 60+); $6.50 (ages 6-17). **Phone:** (250) 391-2666 or (866) 241-0674.

LEGISLATIVE ASSEMBLY OF BRITISH COLUMBIA overlooks the Inner Harbour and yacht basin. The seat of British Columbia's legislature, the buildings have elaborately carved facades and are surrounded by 5 hectares (12 acres) of lawns, gardens, fountains and statues of dignitaries. The rooms have mosaic tile floors, rotundas, stained-glass windows, woodcarvings and murals.

Guided 30- to 45-minute tours, conducted in several languages, are offered. Self-guiding tours also are available; a booklet can be picked up at the tour desk. **Hours:** Daily 9-5, mid-May through Labour Day; Mon.-Fri. 9-5, rest of year. Phone ahead to confirm schedule. **Cost:** Free. **Phone:** (250) 387-3046 for the tour office, or (800) 663-7867 in British Columbia.

MARITIME MUSEUM OF BRITISH COLUMBIA is at 28 Bastion Sq. The Pacific Northwest's maritime heritage is presented through ship models, figureheads, ships' tools and naval uniforms. Also featured is the 1860 *Tilikum*, an 11-metre (36-ft.) dugout canoe converted to a schooner, which sailed from Victoria to England 1901-04. The museum's 1889 building features one of the oldest operating birdcage elevators in North America.

Time: Allow 1 hour minimum. **Hours:** Daily 10-5. Closed Christmas. **Cost:** $12; $10 (ages 65+ and students with ID); $30 (family). **Phone:** (250) 385-4222.

MINIATURE WORLD is in The Fairmont Empress hotel at 649 Humboldt St. Animation, lighting, commentary and sound effects enhance more than 80 highly detailed miniature scenes. Displays include a circus, one of the world's largest dollhouses, a Swiss Family Robinson tree house, a classic car rally and a futuristic space diorama. Scenes illustrate historic battles, fairy tales, nursery rhymes, "Gulliver's Travels" and novels by Charles Dickens. The Great Canadian Railway exhibit re-creates rail transportation in late 19th-century Canada.

Time: Allow 1 hour minimum. **Hours:** Daily 9-9, mid-May through Labour Day; 9-5, rest of year. Closed Christmas. **Cost:** $12; $11 (senior citizens); $10 (ages 12-17 and students with ID); $8 (ages 5-11). **Phone:** (250) 385-9731.

PACIFIC UNDERSEA GARDENS is at 490 Belleville St. An observation room on the sea bottom allows visitors to view native marine life through large underwater windows. **Hours:** Daily 9-8, July-Sept.; Thurs.-Sun. 10-5, Mon.-Wed. 10-7, May-June; Mon.-Fri. 10-5, Sat.-Sun. 10-5, rest of year. Closed Jan. 1 and Christmas. **Cost:** $11.95; $10.50 (ages 65+); $8.75 (ages 12-17); $5.95 (ages 5-11). **Phone:** (250) 382-5717.

POINT ELLICE HOUSE is at 2616 Pleasant St. Built in 1861, the rambling Italianate residence contains many of its original furnishings. Lawns and a restored 19th-century garden surround the house.

Whale-watching tours are given year-round

Christmas teas are offered late November to mid-December. Self-guiding audiotapes are available.

Time: Allow 30 minutes minimum. **Hours:** Thurs.-Mon. 11-4, May 5-Labour Day. Schedule varies rest of year; phone ahead. **Cost:** $6; $4 (ages 12-18); $3 (ages 6-11). Tour and tea $23; $12 (ages 6-12). **Phone:** (250) 380-6506.

PRINCE OF WHALES WHALE WATCHING is at 812 Wharf St. Three-hour tours narrated by a marine biologist provide information about marine life. Passengers have a choice of sitting either outside on an open-air deck or inside in a heated cabin aboard the 19-metre (62-ft.) *Ocean Magic* cruiser. High-speed open-boat whale-watching tours in a Zodiac also are available. Hydrophones allow passengers to hear the whales vocalize. Sightseeing tours also are available.

Time: Allow 3 hours minimum. **Hours:** *Ocean Magic* departures daily at 9, 12:15 and 3:30, May-Oct.; schedule varies, rest of year. Passengers should arrive 30 minutes prior to departure. **Cost:** $100; $90 (ages 13-18 and senior citizens); $80 (ages 5-12). Phone ahead to confirm tour prices and schedule. Reservations are required. **Phone:** (250) 383-4884 or (888) 383-4884.

ROYAL BC MUSEUM is on the Inner Harbour at 675 Belleville St. at Government St. Two floors of displays reflect the human and natural history of British Columbia. An early 1900s frontier town has a theater with silent movies, a saloon, shops and a hotel. The Natural History Gallery showcases the Living Land, Living Sea exhibit with a coastal rain forest display highlighted by live plants and tidal-pool animals as well as a climate change exhibit which explores the province's future climate. The First Peoples Gallery includes an exhibit focusing on the historic Nisga'a agreement and the present-day Nisga'a community, and Haida argillite carvings.

The on-site IMAX Victoria Theatre offers films to complement the natural and human history theme of the museum as well as other exciting IMAX footage. Feature exhibits are presented annually.

Hours: Daily 10-5 (also Fri.-Sat. 5-10, early June-late Sept.). Closed Jan. 1 and Christmas. **Cost:** Museum $14.29; $9.06 (ages 6-18, ages 65+ and students ages 19+ with ID); $37.63 (family, two adults and two children). Admission may increase for feature exhibits. **Phone:** (250) 356-7226 or (888) 447-7977.

British Columbia Archives is at 655 Belleville St. Extensive public and private records are available to those conducting historical, genealogical or other research. Gardens containing native plants surround the building. **Hours:** The archives are open to the public Mon.-Fri. 10-8. Closed major holidays. **Cost:** Free. **Phone:** (250) 387-1952.

Helmcken House is on the grounds of the Royal BC Museum. One of the oldest houses in British Columbia still on its original site, the 1852 log structure was the home of John Sebastian Helmcken, a surgeon for Hudson's Bay Co. at Fort Victoria and a Father of Confederation. The restored house displays many original furnishings and an impressive collection of period medical instruments.

Time: Allow 30 minutes minimum. **Hours:** Daily noon-4, May 18-Labour Day; by appointment rest of year. Phone ahead to confirm schedule. **Cost:** Donations. **Phone:** (250) 356-7226.

The Netherlands Centennial Carillon is on the grounds of the Royal BC Museum at the corner of Government and Belleville sts. The largest carillon in Canada houses 62 bells donated by British Columbians of Dutch origin in celebration of the 1967 Canadian Confederation Centennial and in recognition of Canada's role in the liberation of the Netherlands during World War II. **Hours:** Carillon chimes ring hourly 10-5. **Cost:** Free. **Phone:** (250) 356-7226.

Thunderbird Park is at the corner of Douglas and Belleville sts. on the grounds of the Royal BC Museum. The park's collection of Northwest Coast totem poles was established in 1940 and re-carved via the Totem Restoration Program 1950-90, when the originals began to decay beyond repair. A new Kwakwaka'wakw pole was carved and raised in 2000.

Also showcased is Wawadit'la, the ceremonial bighouse built by noted carver and artist Mungo Martin in 1953 that bears the hereditary crests of his family. **Hours:** Park open daily dawn-dusk. **Cost:** Free. **Phone:** (250) 356-7226.

SPRINGTIDE WHALE WATCHING is at 1119 Wharf St. Depending on the season and in addition to killer whales, visitors also may encounter sea lions; seals; porpoises; humpback, grey and minke whales as well as a variety of birds. Tours are given on a 19-metre (61-ft.) motor yacht as well as on high-speed, open Zodiacs. A harbor tour is available year-round.

Time: Allow 3 hours minimum. **Hours:** Whale-watch tours are given daily at 10 and 2, Apr.-Oct. Other times are available; phone for schedule. **Cost:** Whale-watch tour $99; $95 (ages 65+); $79 (ages 13-18 and students with ID); $69 (ages 3-12). Reservations are recommended. **Phone:** (250) 384-4444, (250) 386-6016 or (800) 470-3474.

UNIVERSITY OF VICTORIA is on McKenzie Ave. at Gordon Head Rd. The 160-hectare (395-acre) campus includes the Mystic Vale Ecological Protection Area, several totems carved by local artists and Finnerty Gardens, known for its collection of more than 200 rhododendron species.

Guided tours of the campus are available; the meeting point is the University Centre. A self-guiding walking tour brochure is available from the MacPherson Library loans desk.

Hours: Guided tours are given Mon.-Sat. 1-2:30, May-Aug.; Mon.-Fri. at 1, rest of year. Closed Jan. 1,

Good Friday, Easter Monday, Victoria Day and Dec. 25-31. **Cost:** Free. Reservations are required for tours. **Parking:** $1.25 per hour. **Phone:** (250) 721-8949.

VICTORIA BUG ZOO is at 631 Courtney St. More than 50 species of tropical insects and arachnids from around the world are on display. Highlights include a leaf-cutter ant farm and the giant African millipede. For the more adventurous, the zoo also provides the opportunity for an environment conducive to a safe bug-handling experience.

Tours: Guided tours are available. **Time:** Allow 30 minutes minimum. **Hours:** Daily 11-5:30 (seasonal hours vary). Closed Jan. 1 and Christmas. Phone ahead to confirm schedule. **Cost:** $10; $9 (ages 65+); $8 (ages 11-18); $7 (ages 3-10). **Phone:** (250) 384-2847.

Sightseeing
Boat Tours

Sightseers using Victoria as a base for their travels can explore the Gulf Islands and Vancouver by ferry from Swartz Bay, north of Victoria via Hwy. 17; for schedule and toll phone the British Columbia Ferry Service at (250) 386-3431.

Opportunities for whale watching are offered by several boating companies, the oldest of which is Seacoast Expeditions, 146 Kingston St.; phone (250) 383-2254.

Bus and Carriage Tours

Guided tours of the city in red double-decker buses from London enhance Victoria's British atmosphere. Many of these tour operators are found along Belleville and Menzies streets by the harbor. SAVE Gray Line, 4196 Glanford Ave., (250) 388-6539 or (800) 663-8390, conducts bus tours.

Narrated horse-drawn carriage tours of the city are offered by several companies, including Black Beauty Line Ltd., phone (250) 507-0789; Tallyho, phone (250) 383-5067; and Victoria Carriage Tours, phone (250) 383-2207. All tours leave from the corner of Belleville and Menzies streets.

Driving Tours

The Greater Victoria Visitors Information Centre has information about such scenic routes as Marine Drive along the shoreline, a trip to Sooke Harbour on the west coast and the Malahat Drive, which runs along the east coast and reaches an elevation of 381 metres (1,250 ft.). The trip to Butchart Gardens is one of the most popular drives, following Hwy. 17 and Hwy. 17A through the rural communities and pastoral valleys of the Saanich Peninsula.

Walking Tours

Victoria is the perfect size for visitors keen on walking. A favorite thoroughfare of strollers and shoppers is Government Street, graced by banners and five-globe Victorian lampposts supporting baskets of geraniums and petunias.

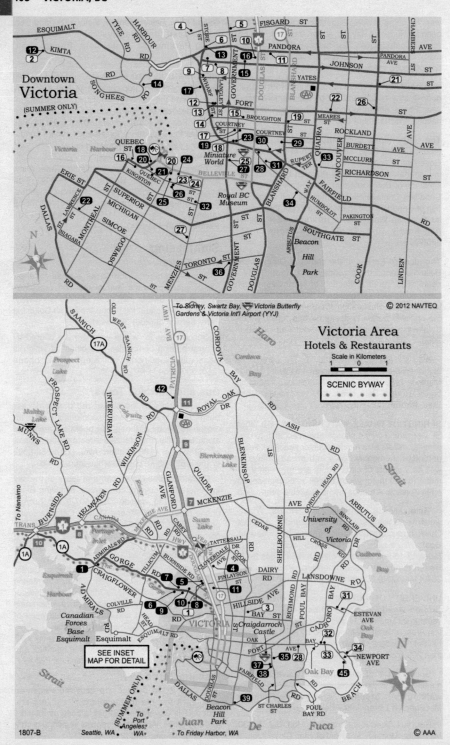

Downtown Victoria (SUMMER ONLY)

Victoria Harbour

Miniature World

Royal BC Museum

Beacon Hill Park

To Sidney, Swartz Bay, Victoria Butterfly Gardens & Victoria Int'l Airport (YYJ)

© 2012 NAVTEQ

Victoria Area
Hotels & Restaurants

Scale in Kilometers
1   0   1

SCENIC BYWAY

Prospect Lake

Maltby Lake

MUNNS

To Nanaimo

Swan Lake

University of Victoria

Cadboro Bay

Esquimalt Harbour

Canadian Forces Base Esquimalt

Craigdarroch Castle

VICTORIA

Oak Bay

SEE INSET MAP FOR DETAIL

Strait

of

Juan

De

Fuca

Beacon Hill Park

To Port Angeles, WA

Seattle, WA

To Friday Harbor, WA

1807-B

© AAA

Victoria

This index helps you "spot" where approved hotels and restaurants are located on the corresponding detailed maps. Hotel daily rate range is for comparison only. Restaurant price range is a combination of lunch and/or dinner. Turn to the listing page for more detailed rate and price information and consult display ads for special promotions.

VICTORIA

Map Page	Hotels	Diamond Rated	Rate Range	Page
1 p. 408	**Econo Lodge Inn & Suites**	◆◆	$109-$189 (SAVE)	413
4 p. 408	**Accent Inns**	◆◆	$79-$179 (SAVE)	411
5 p. 408	Mayfair Motel	◆◆	Rates not provided	414
6 p. 408	Ramada Victoria	◆◆	$65-$150	414
7 p. 408	**Robin Hood Motel**	◆◆	$54-$99 (SAVE)	415
8 p. 408	**Blue Ridge Inns**	◆◆	$59-$149 (SAVE)	412
9 p. 408	**Travelodge Victoria**	◆◆	$80-$130 (SAVE)	415
10 p. 408	**Howard Johnson Hotel-City of Victoria**	◆◆	$59-$124 (SAVE)	414
11 p. 408	**Comfort Hotel & Conference Centre**	◆◆◆	$99-$189 (SAVE)	413
12 p. 408	Spinnakers Gastro Brewpub and Guesthouses	◆◆	$149-$299	415
13 p. 408	Swans Suite Hotel	◆◆◆	$149-$359	415
14 p. 408	**Delta Victoria Ocean Pointe Resort and Spa**	◆◆◆◆	$129-$328 (SAVE)	413
15 p. 408	**BEST WESTERN PLUS Carlton Plaza Hotel**	◆◆◆	$89-$259 (SAVE)	411
16 p. 408	Hotel Rialto	◆◆◆	$109-$159	414
17 p. 408	**Victoria Regent Waterfront Hotel & Suites**	◆◆◆	$139-$369 (SAVE)	416
19 p. 408	**The Magnolia Hotel & Spa**	◆◆◆◆	$189-$369 (SAVE)	414
20 p. 408	**Huntingdon Hotel & Suites**	◆◆	$79-$389 (SAVE)	414
21 p. 408	**Harbour Towers Hotel & Suites**	◆◆	$94-$450 (SAVE)	414
22 p. 408	Heathergate House Bed & Breakfast	◆◆	$90-$155	414
23 p. 408	The Union Club of British Columbia	◆◆◆	$129-$259	415
24 p. 408	**Days Inn Victoria on the Harbour**	◆◆	$93-$173 (SAVE)	413
25 p. 408	**BEST WESTERN PLUS Inner Harbour** (See ad p. 412.)	◆◆◆	$109-$259 (SAVE)	412
26 p. 408	**Royal Scot Hotel & Suites** (See ad p. 415.)	◆◆◆	$120-$299 (SAVE)	415
27 p. 408	The Fairmont Empress	◆◆◆◆	$199-$499	414
28 p. 408	**Executive House Hotel**	◆◆	$99-$215 (SAVE)	413
29 p. 408	**Quality Inn Downtown Inner Harbour Victoria**	◆◆◆	$79-$159 (SAVE)	414
30 p. 408	**Chateau Victoria Hotel and Suites**	◆◆◆	$89-$249 (SAVE)	412
31 p. 408	**Victoria Marriott Inner Harbour**	◆◆◆◆	$209-$309 (SAVE)	416
32 p. 408	**Embassy Inn**	◆◆	$89-$370 (SAVE)	413
33 p. 408	Abigail's Hotel	◆◆◆	$159-$359	411
34 p. 408	Humboldt House Bed & Breakfast	◆◆	$147-$295	414
35 p. 408	Villa Marco Polo Inn	◆◆◆	$135-$305	416
36 p. 408	James Bay Inn Hotel & Suites	◆◆	$79-$199	414
37 p. 408	Abbeymoore Manor Bed & Breakfast Inn	◆◆◆	$139-$249	411
38 p. 408	Fairholme Manor	◆◆◆	$135-$325	413
39 p. 408	Dashwood Seaside Heritage Manor	◆◆	$139-$269	413

Map Page	Restaurants	Diamond Rated	Cuisine	Price Range	Page
1 p. 408	Glo Restaurant & Lounge	◆◆	Canadian	$13-$27	417
2 p. 408	Spinnakers Gastro Brewpub & Restaurant	◆◆	American	$10-$25	418
3 p. 408	Haultain's Fish & Chips	◆	Fish & Chips	$11-$20	417
4 p. 408	Canoe Brewpub Marina Restaurant	◆◆	American	$9-$28	417
5 p. 408	Brasserie L'Ecole	◆◆◆	French	$18-$31	416
6 p. 408	Wild Saffron Bistro & Wine Bar	◆◆◆	Pacific Rim	$18-$30	419
7 p. 408	Cafe Mexico	◆◆	Mexican	$11-$19	417
8 p. 408	Il Terrazzo	◆◆◆	Italian	$19-$36	417
9 p. 408	Restaurant Matisse	◆◆◆	French	$20-$33	418
10 p. 408	Veneto Tapa Lounge	◆◆◆	Pacific Northwest	$14-$20	418
11 p. 408	**The Black Olive**	◆◆◆	Mediterranean	$10-$30	416
12 p. 408	Koto Japanese Restaurant	◆◆	Japanese	$6-$20	417
13 p. 408	Siam Thai Restaurant	◆◆	Thai	$8-$18	418
14 p. 408	Nautical Nellie's Steak & Seafood Restaurant	◆◆	Steak	$13-$34	418
15 p. 408	Pagliacci's	◆◆	Italian	$6-$24	418
16 p. 408	Pablo's Dining Lounge	◆◆◆	New French	$17-$42	418
17 p. 408	Bon Rouge Bistro & Lounge	◆◆	French	$11-$25	416
18 p. 408	Pescatore's Seafood & Grill	◆◆◆	Seafood	$10-$33	418
19 p. 408	The Pink Bicycle	◆◆	Burgers	$10-$16	418
20 p. 408	Victoria Harbour House Restaurant	◆◆	Steak	$16-$37	418
21 p. 408	Passero's Mediterranean Cuisine	◆◆	Mediterranean	$12-$24	418
22 p. 408	Cafe Brio	◆◆	Pacific Northwest	$15-$28	417
23 p. 408	Jonathan's Restaurant	◆◆	Canadian	$10-$35	417
24 p. 408	**The Mark**	◆◆◆◆	Pacific Northwest	$32-$42	417
25 p. 408	The Empress Room	◆◆◆◆	Pacific Northwest	$30-$45	417
26 p. 408	Pluto's	◆◆	American	$7-$15	418
27 p. 408	James Bay Tea Room & Restaurant	◆◆	Canadian	$9-$16	417
28 p. 408	White Heather Tea Room	◆◆	Desserts	$10-$17	418

SAANICH

Map Page	Hotel	Diamond Rated	Rate Range	Page
42 p. 408	Howard Johnson Hotel & Suites	◆◆	$99-$169	322

OAK BAY

Map Page	Hotel	Diamond Rated	Rate Range	Page
45 p. 408	Oak Bay Guest House Bed & Breakfast	◆◆	$89-$179	285

Map Page	Restaurants	Diamond Rated	Cuisine	Price Range	Page
31 p. 408	Paprika Bistro	◆◆◆	Pacific Northwest	$16-$36	285
32 p. 408	Penny Farthing English Pub	◆◆	Canadian	$11-$17	285
33 p. 408	Ottavio Italian Bakery & Delicatessen	◆	Italian	$7-$14	285
34 p. 408	The Marina Restaurant	◆◆◆	Pacific Northwest	$15-$36	285

VICTORIA (I-4)
- **Restaurants p. 416**
- **Hotels & Restaurants map & index p. 408**

ABBEYMOORE MANOR BED & BREAKFAST INN
(250)370-1470 **37**

 Historic Bed & Breakfast $139-$249 **Address:** 1470 Rockland Ave V8S 1W2 **Location:** Blanshard St (Hwy 17), 1.2 mi (2 km) e on Fort St, just s on St Charles St, then just w. **Facility:** Once the residence of a lieutenant governor, the renovated B&B is in the Rockland neighborhood dotted with stately Victorian homes. Two modern suites with a kitchen can be rented for longer stays. 7 units, some efficiencies. 3 stories (no elevator), interior/exterior corridors. **Terms:** check-in 4 pm, age restrictions may apply, 14 day cancellation notice-fee imposed.

ABIGAIL'S HOTEL
(250)388-5363 **33**

 Boutique Hotel $159-$359 **Address:** 906 McClure St V8V 3E7 **Location:** Blanshard St (Hwy 17), just e on Fairfield Rd, then just n on Vancouver St. Located in a quiet residential area. **Facility:** Two large buildings house a wide variety of room choices. Rooms in the newest building include a TV, fridge and coffeemaker; rooms in the original building feature a fireplace and large claw-foot tub. 23 units. 2-3 stories (no elevator), interior corridors. **Terms:** 14 day cancellation notice-fee imposed. **Activities:** spa. **Guest Services:** valet laundry.

ACCENT INNS
(250)475-7500 **4**

Hotel
$79-$179

Address: 3233 Maple St V8X 4Y9 **Location:** 1.9 mi (3 km) n on Blanshard St (Hwy 17); corner of Blanshard St and Cloverdale Ave. **Facility:** 118 units, some efficiencies. 3 stories, exterior corridors. **Terms:** cancellation fee imposed. **Guest Services:** valet and coin laundry. **Free Special Amenities:** newspaper and high-speed Internet.

BEST WESTERN PLUS CARLTON PLAZA HOTEL
(250)388-5513 **15**

Hotel
$89-$259

AAA Benefit:
Members save up to 20%, plus 10% bonus points with Best Western Rewards®.

Address: 642 Johnson St V8W 1M6 **Location:** Between Douglas and Broad sts. **Facility:** 103 units, some efficiencies and kitchens. 7 stories, interior corridors. **Parking:** on-site (fee) and valet. **Amenities:** safes. **Activities:** exercise room. **Guest Services:** valet and coin laundry. **Free Special Amenities:** local telephone calls and high-speed Internet.

Award winning hotel is located in the centre of Victoria, featuring clean, well appointed rooms

Be a better driver.
Keep your mind on the road.

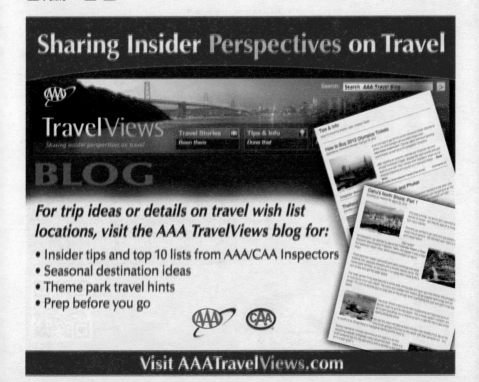

(See map & index p. 408.)

BEST WESTERN PLUS INNER HARBOUR
(250)384-5122

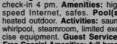
Extended Stay Hotel
$109-$259

AAA Benefit: Members save up to 20%, plus 10% bonus points with Best Western Rewards®.

Address: 412 Quebec St V8V 1W5 **Location:** Between Oswego and Menzies sts. **Facility:** 74 kitchen units. 8 stories, interior corridors. **Parking:** on-site (fee). **Terms:** check-in 4 pm. **Amenities:** high-speed Internet, safes. **Pool(s):** heated outdoor. **Activities:** sauna, whirlpool, steamroom, limited exercise equipment. **Guest Services:** valet and coin laundry. **Free Special Amenities:** full breakfast and high-speed Internet. *(See ad this page.)*

BLUE RIDGE INNS
(250)388-4345

Motel
$59-$149

Address: 3110 Douglas St V8Z 3K4 **Location:** Between Finlayson St and Speed Ave. **Facility:** 63 units, some two bedrooms, efficiencies, kitchens and cottages. 2 stories (no elevator), exterior corridors. **Terms:** cancellation fee imposed. **Pool(s):** heated indoor. **Activities:** sauna. **Guest Services:** coin laundry. **Free Special Amenities:** newspaper and high-speed Internet.

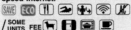

CHATEAU VICTORIA HOTEL AND SUITES
(250)382-4221

Hotel
$89-$249

Address: 740 Burdett Ave V8W 1B2 **Location:** Between Douglas and Blanshard (Hwy 17) sts. **Facility:** 177 units, some two bedrooms, efficiencies and kitchens. 19 stories, interior corridors. **Parking:** on-site (fee). **Terms:** cancellation fee imposed. **Amenities:** safes. *Some:* high-speed Internet. **Pool(s):** heated indoor. **Activities:** whirlpool, exercise room. **Guest Services:** valet laundry, area transportation-downtown. **Free Special Amenities:** local telephone calls and high-speed Internet.

▼ *See AAA listing this page* ▼

(See map & index p. 408.)

COMFORT HOTEL & CONFERENCE CENTRE
(250)382-4400 **11**

Hotel
$99-$189

Address: 3020 Blanshard St V8T 5C7 **Location:** 1.6 mi (2.6 km) n on Blanshard St (Hwy 17), just s of Finlayson St. **Facility:** 152 units, some efficiencies. 1-5 stories, interior/exterior corridors. **Terms:** check-in 4 pm, cancellation fee imposed. **Amenities:** video games (fee). Some: high-speed Internet. **Activities:** sauna, exercise room. **Guest Services:** valet and coin laundry.

[SAVE] [ECO] [icons] CALL [icons] / SOME UNITS [icon]

DASHWOOD SEASIDE HERITAGE MANOR
(250)385-5517 **39**

Historic Bed & Breakfast $139-$269 **Address:** 1 Cook St V8V 3W6 **Location:** 0.6 mi (1 km) e of Douglas St on Dallas Rd. Located in a residential area across from Beacon Hill Park. **Facility:** At the end of Cook Street sits this charming mansion. Built in 1912, it still retains the rich look of an English Tudor manor. This is the only B&B with a view of the ocean and Mt. Baker across the water. 10 units. 3 stories (no elevator), interior corridors. **Terms:** check-in 4 pm, 2 night minimum stay - seasonal and/or weekends, 14 day cancellation notice-fee imposed.

[icons] / SOME UNITS [icon]

DAYS INN VICTORIA ON THE HARBOUR
(250)386-3451 **24**

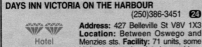

Hotel
$93-$173

Address: 427 Belleville St V8V 1X3 **Location:** Between Oswego and Menzies sts. **Facility:** 71 units, some kitchens. 4 stories, interior corridors. **Amenities:** safes. **Pool(s):** heated outdoor. **Activities:** whirlpool. **Guest Services:** valet laundry.

[SAVE] [ECO] [icons]

[icons] / SOME UNITS FEE [icons]

Perfectly located on Victoria's downtown Inner Harbour, walk to restaurants, shopping & attractions

DELTA VICTORIA OCEAN POINTE RESORT AND SPA
(250)360-2999 **14**

Hotel
$129-$328

Address: 45 Songhees Rd V9A 6T3 **Location:** Just w of Johnson St Bridge; Esquimalt at Tyee Rd. **Facility:** Located waterfront at the Inner Harbour, this resort lets you watch sea planes land and take off or the U.S. COHO ferry arrive, all from the comfort of your nicely decorated room. If you enjoy a good run, head out to the miles-long cement pathway that passes out front. 240 units. 8 stories, interior corridors. **Parking:** on-site (fee) and valet. **Terms:** check-in 4 pm, cancellation fee imposed. **Amenities:** high-speed Internet. **Pool(s):** heated indoor. **Activities:** sauna, whirlpool, 2 lighted tennis courts, racquetball court, spa. **Guest Services:** valet laundry, area transportation-downtown & Inner Harbour.

[SAVE] [ECO] [icons] CALL [icons] [BIZ] [icons]
[icons] / SOME UNITS FEE [icons]

ECONO LODGE INN & SUITES
(250)388-7861 **1**

Motel
$109-$189

Address: 101 Island Hwy V9B 1E8 **Location:** Douglas St, 3.1 mi (5 km) w on Gorge Rd, then just s on Admirals Rd. **Facility:** 101 units, some two bedrooms, efficiencies and kitchens. 2 stories (no elevator), interior/exterior corridors. **Terms:** check-in 4 pm, cancellation fee imposed. **Pool(s):** heated outdoor. **Activities:** rental bicycles. **Guest Services:** valet and coin laundry. **Free Special Amenities:** expanded continental breakfast and high-speed Internet.

[SAVE] [icons] / SOME UNITS FEE [icons]

Perfectly located on Victoria's quiet Gorge waterway; just minutes from downtown & major attractions.

EMBASSY INN
(250)382-8161 **32**

Hotel
$89-$370

Address: 520 Menzies St V8V 2H4 **Location:** Corner of Quebec St. Adjacent to Parliament buildings. **Facility:** 103 units, some efficiencies and kitchens. 3-4 stories, interior/exterior corridors. **Terms:** check-in 3:30 pm, cancellation fee imposed. **Pool(s):** heated outdoor. **Activities:** sauna. **Guest Services:** valet and coin laundry. **Free Special Amenities:** local telephone calls and high-speed Internet.

[SAVE] [icons] CALL [icons] / SOME UNITS [icons]

EXECUTIVE HOUSE HOTEL
(250)388-5111 **28**

Hotel
$99-$215

Address: 777 Douglas St V8W 2B5 **Location:** Between Blanshard (Hwy 17) and Douglas sts; downtown. **Facility:** 181 units, some two bedrooms, efficiencies and kitchens. 17 stories, interior corridors. **Parking:** on-site (fee) and valet. **Terms:** cancellation fee imposed. **Amenities:** high-speed Internet. **Dining:** 2 restaurants. **Activities:** whirlpool, steamroom, exercise room, spa. **Guest Services:** complimentary and valet laundry, area transportation-downtown & inner harbor. **Free Special Amenities:** high-speed Internet and use of on-premises laundry facilities.

[SAVE] [icons] [BIZ] [icons] / SOME UNITS FEE [icons]

FAIRHOLME MANOR
(250)598-3240 **38**

Historic Bed & Breakfast $135-$325 **Address:** 638 Rockland Pl V8S 3R2 **Location:** Blanshard St (Hwy 17), 1.2 mi (2 km) e on Fort St, just s on St. Charles St to Rockland Ave, follow Rockland Pl sign, then down alley. Located in historic Rockland District. **Facility:** Built in 1885, this carefully restored mansion has been converted into luxury suites and is surrounded by an acre of park-like gardens and lawn. All the bathrooms have been renovated with wonderful soaker tubs. 6 units, some two bedrooms. 2 stories (no elevator), interior/exterior corridors. **Terms:** check-in 4 pm, 2 night minimum stay - seasonal and/or weekends, age restrictions may apply, 14 day cancellation notice-fee imposed.

[icons]

(See map & index p. 408.)

THE FAIRMONT EMPRESS (250)384-8111 **27**

◈◈◈ ◈◈◈ **Classic Historic Hotel** $199-$499 **Address:** 721 Government St V8W 1W5 **Location:** Between Belleville and Humboldt sts. Located on Inner Harbour. **Facility:** Renowned for its tradition of afternoon tea, this landmark hotel built in 1908 impresses with creeping vines over the entrance and Victorian style. Guest rooms vary in aspects ranging from décor to whether there's a harbor view. However, all rooms are carefully decorated to fit the property's historic nature. 477 units. 8 stories, interior corridors. **Parking:** on-site (fee) and valet. **Terms:** check-in 4 pm, 3 day cancellation notice-fee imposed. **Amenities:** high-speed Internet (fee), safes. **Dining:** The Empress Room, see separate listing. **Pool(s):** heated indoor. **Activities:** saunas, whirlpool, exercise room, spa. **Guest Services:** valet laundry, area transportation-downtown.

ECO ❙❙ ▯ CALL ⬗M ⇨ 🛜 ✕ 🎥 🔒 🖵 / SOME UNITS FEE 🐾

HARBOUR TOWERS HOTEL & SUITES (250)385-2405 **21**

◈◈◈ ◈◈◈
Hotel
$94-$450
Address: 345 Quebec St V8V 1W4 **Location:** Between Oswego and Pendray sts. **Facility:** 196 units, some two bedrooms, efficiencies and kitchens. 12 stories, interior corridors. **Parking:** on-site (fee). **Terms:** cancellation fee imposed. **Amenities:** high-speed Internet. **Pool(s):** heated indoor. **Activities:** sauna, whirlpool. **Guest Services:** valet and coin laundry, area transportation-downtown. **Free Special Amenities: local telephone calls and high-speed Internet.**

SAVE ECO ❙❙ ▯ CALL ⬗M ⇨ 🛗 BIZ 🛜 ✕ 🎥 🖵 / SOME UNITS FEE 🐾 🔒 🖵

HEATHERGATE HOUSE BED & BREAKFAST (250)383-0068 **22**

◈◈ **Bed & Breakfast** $90-$155 **Address:** 122 Simcoe St V8V 1K4 **Location:** Between St. Lawrence and Montreal sts. **Facility:** 4 units, some two bedrooms, kitchens and cottages. 2 stories (no elevator), interior/exterior corridors. **Terms:** 2 night minimum stay - seasonal and/or weekends, 14 day cancellation notice-fee imposed.

🛜 ✕ 🎥 / SOME UNITS 🔒

HOTEL RIALTO 250/383-4157 **16**

◈◈◈ **Boutique Contemporary Hotel** $109-$159 **Address:** 653 Pandora Ave V8W 1N8 **Location:** Corner of Pandora Ave and Douglas St. **Facility:** This beautifully restored heritage building is located in the heart of downtown. The grand boutique-style hotel greets guests with sprawling Italian marble floors, exotic hardwood and fresco-style walls. 51 units. 4 stories, interior corridors. **Parking:** on-site (fee). **Terms:** 3 day cancellation notice-fee imposed. **Amenities:** high-speed Internet. **Dining:** Veneto Tapa Lounge, see separate listing. **Guest Services:** valet laundry.

❙❙ ▯ 🛜 ✕ 🎥 🔒 🖵 🖵

HOWARD JOHNSON HOTEL-CITY OF VICTORIA (250)382-2151 **10**

◈◈ ◈◈
Hotel
$59-$124
Address: 310 Gorge Rd E V8T 2W2 **Location:** From Douglas St, 0.6 mi (1.4 km) w; between Jutland St and Washington Ave. **Facility:** 80 units, some kitchens. 3 stories, interior corridors. **Terms:** cancellation fee imposed. **Amenities:** Some: high-speed Internet. **Pool(s):** heated indoor. **Activities:** saunas, limited exercise equipment. **Guest Services:** valet and coin laundry. **Free Special Amenities: newspaper and high-speed Internet.**

SAVE ECO ❙❙ ▯ 🐾 CALL ⬗M ⇨ 🛜 ✕ 🖵 / SOME UNITS FEE 🐾 🔒 🖵

HUMBOLDT HOUSE BED & BREAKFAST (250)383-0152 **34**

◈◈ ◈◈ **Historic Bed & Breakfast** $147-$295 **Address:** 867 Humboldt St V8V 2Z6 **Location:** Jct Humboldt and Quadra sts. Located in a quiet area. **Facility:** This romantic hideaway is within easy walking distance of downtown Victoria. Each morning, a full gourmet breakfast is delivered to your room. On arrival, enjoy handmade chocolate truffles. 6 units. 2 stories (no elevator), interior corridors. **Terms:** 7 day cancellation notice-fee imposed.

🛜 ✕ 🎥 🗘 🔒 / SOME UNITS 🕅

HUNTINGDON HOTEL & SUITES (250)381-3456 **20**

◈◈◈ ◈◈◈
Hotel
$79-$389
Address: 330 Quebec St V8V 1W3 **Location:** Between Oswego and Pendray sts. **Facility:** 115 units, some two bedrooms and kitchens. 3 stories, interior corridors. **Terms:** cancellation fee imposed. **Activities:** sauna, whirlpool. **Guest Services:** valet and coin laundry. **Free Special Amenities: local telephone calls and high-speed Internet.**

SAVE ❙❙ ▯ 🛜 ✕ 🔒 🖵 / SOME UNITS FEE 🐾 🎥 🖵

JAMES BAY INN HOTEL & SUITES (250)384-7151 **36**

◈◈ ◈◈ **Historic Hotel** $79-$199 **Address:** 270 Government St V8V 2L2 **Location:** Between Toronto and Marifield sts. **Facility:** In the heart of Victoria's heritage residential district, this historic hotel has a lovingly tended garden in the front. Due to the building's historic nature, rooms are compact in size. 45 units, some kitchens. 4 stories (no elevator), interior corridors. **Guest Services:** valet laundry.

ECO ❙❙ ▯ 🛜 ✕ 🎥 / SOME UNITS 🔒

THE MAGNOLIA HOTEL & SPA (250)381-0999 **19**

◈◈◈ ◈◈◈
Boutique Hotel
$189-$369
Address: 623 Courtney St V8W 1B8 **Location:** Corner of Courtney and Gordon sts. Located on Inner Harbour. **Facility:** This luxury hotel provides a convenient base for guests interested in visiting downtown Victoria and its popular attractions. Elegant guest rooms with floor-to-ceiling windows offer spectacular views. 64 units. 7 stories, interior corridors. **Parking:** valet only. **Terms:** check-in 4 pm, cancellation fee imposed. **Amenities:** high-speed Internet, safes. **Activities:** sauna, exercise room, spa. **Guest Services:** valet laundry. **Free Special Amenities: expanded continental breakfast and high-speed Internet.**

SAVE ECO ❙❙ ▯ 🛗 ▯ CALL ⬗M 🛜 ✕ 🖵 / SOME UNITS FEE 🐾

MAYFAIR MOTEL 250/388-7337 **5**

◈◈ **Extended Stay Motel.** Rates not provided. **Address:** 650 Speed Ave V8Z 1A4 **Location:** From downtown, 1.6 mi (2.5 km) n on Douglas St. **Facility:** 22 kitchen units. 4 stories, interior corridors. **Guest Services:** coin laundry. 🛜 ✕ 🎥 🔒

QUALITY INN DOWNTOWN INNER HARBOUR VICTORIA (250)385-6787 **29**

◈◈◈ ◈◈◈
Hotel
$79-$159
Address: 850 Blanshard St V8W 2H2 **Location:** Between Courtney St and Burnett Ave. **Facility:** 63 units, some efficiencies. 3 stories, interior corridors. **Parking:** on-site (fee). **Terms:** cancellation fee imposed. **Amenities:** Some: high-speed Internet. **Pool(s):** heated indoor. **Activities:** steamroom, limited exercise equipment. **Guest Services:** valet and coin laundry. **Free Special Amenities: newspaper and high-speed Internet.**

SAVE ECO ❙❙ ▯ 🐾 🛜 ✕ 🎥 🔒 🖵 / SOME UNITS FEE 🐾

RAMADA VICTORIA (250)386-1422 **6**

◈◈ ◈◈ **Hotel** $65-$150 **Address:** 123 Gorge Rd E V9A 1L1 **Location:** From Douglas St, 1.2 mi (2.4 km) w. **Facility:** 91 units, some efficiencies and kitchens. 4 stories, interior corridors. **Terms:** cancellation fee imposed. **Pool(s):** heated outdoor. **Activities:** limited exercise equipment. **Guest Services:** valet and coin laundry.

ECO ❙❙ ▯ 🐾 BIZ 🛜 ✕ 🔒 🖵 / SOME UNITS FEE 🐾 🖵

(See map & index p. 408.)

ROBIN HOOD MOTEL   (250)388-4302   7

Motel
$54-$99

Address: 136 Gorge Rd E Rd V9A 1L4 **Location:** From Douglas St, 1.2 mi (2.4 km) w. **Facility:** 54 units, some kitchens. 3 stories (no elevator), exterior corridors. **Guest Services:** coin laundry. **Free Special Amenities:** local telephone calls and high-speed Internet.

Family business, just 2 miles from the Inner Harbour. Free parking, wireless Internet & local calls.

ROYAL SCOT HOTEL & SUITES   (250)388-5463   26

Hotel
$120-$299

Address: 425 Quebec St V8V 1W7 **Location:** Between Menzies and Oswego sts. **Facility:** 176 units, some two bedrooms and kitchens. 4 stories, interior corridors. **Parking:** on-site (fee). **Terms:** cancellation fee imposed. **Amenities:** high-speed Internet, safes. **Dining:** Jonathan's Restaurant, see separate listing. **Pool(s):** heated indoor. **Activities:** saunas, whirlpool, game room, shuffleboard, exercise room. **Guest Services:** valet and coin laundry, area transportation-downtown. **Free Special Amenities:** high-speed Internet and local transportation. (See ad this page.)

SPINNAKERS GASTRO BREWPUB AND GUESTHOUSES
250/386-2739   12

Bed & Breakfast $149-$299 **Address:** 308 Catherine St V9A 3S8 **Location:** 1.3 mi (2 km) nw over Johnson St Bridge, then just s. **Facility:** 10 units, some efficiencies, kitchens and cottages. 2 stories (no elevator), interior/exterior corridors. **Terms:** 7 day cancellation notice-fee imposed. **Dining:** Spinnakers Gastro Brewpub & Restaurant, see separate listing.

SWANS SUITE HOTEL   (250)361-3310   13

Hotel $149-$359 **Address:** 506 Pandora Ave V8W 1N6 **Location:** Corner of Pandora Ave and Store St. **Facility:** 30 units, some two bedrooms, efficiencies and kitchens. 2 stories, interior corridors. **Parking:** street only. **Terms:** check-in 4 pm, cancellation fee imposed. **Amenities:** high-speed Internet. **Dining:** Wild Saffron Bistro & Wine Bar, see separate listing. **Guest Services:** valet and coin laundry.

TRAVELODGE VICTORIA   (250)388-6611   9

Hotel
$80-$130

Address: 229 Gorge Rd E V9A 1L1 **Location:** From Douglas St, 1.2 mi (2 km) w at Washington Ave. **Facility:** 73 units, some efficiencies and kitchens. 3 stories (no elevator), exterior corridors. **Terms:** cancellation fee imposed. **Amenities:** safes. **Pool(s):** heated indoor. **Activities:** saunas, exercise room. **Guest Services:** valet and coin laundry.

THE UNION CLUB OF BRITISH COLUMBIA
(250)384-1151   23

Classic Historic Hotel $129-$259 **Address:** 805 Gordon St V8W 1Z6 **Location:** Between Courtney and Humboldt sts. **Facility:** 22 units. 4 stories, interior corridors. **Parking:** on-site (fee). **Terms:** age restrictions may apply, cancellation fee imposed. **Amenities:** high-speed Internet. **Activities:** steamroom, exercise room. **Guest Services:** valet and coin laundry.

AAA/CAA travel information:
Available in print, online and on the go!

▼ See AAA listing this page ▼

(See map & index p. 408.)

VICTORIA MARRIOTT INNER HARBOUR
(250)480-3800   **31**

Hotel
$209-$309

AAA Benefit: AAA hotel discounts of 5% or more.

Address: 728 Humboldt St V8W 3Z5 **Location:** Between Blanshard (Hwy 17) and Douglas sts. **Facility:** Close to the Inner Harbour and downtown, the full-service hotel offers spacious rooms and lots of attractions within walking distance. For a view, ask for a room on a higher floor. 236 units. 16 stories, interior corridors. **Parking:** on-site (fee) and valet. **Terms:** check-in 4 pm. **Amenities:** high-speed Internet, safes. **Pool(s):** heated indoor. **Activities:** whirlpool, steamroom, exercise room. **Guest Services:** valet and coin laundry. **Free Special Amenities:** high-speed Internet.

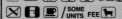

Marriott.
VICTORIA
INNER HARBOUR

**AAA members 10% off or more.
Short walk to harbor, dining, shopping.
Kids stay free. Pets welcome.**

VICTORIA REGENT WATERFRONT HOTEL & SUITES
(250)386-2211   **17**

Vacation Rental
Condominium
$139-$369

Address: 1234 Wharf St V8W 3H9 **Location:** Between Yates and Fort Sts. Located on the Inner Harbour. **Facility:** These amazing condo units sit right at the water's edge, where the harbor views are simply spectacular. Modern full kitchens and super large bedrooms are in the many condo units. 45 condominiums. 8 stories, interior corridors. **Terms:** cancellation fee imposed. **Amenities:** safes. **Guest Services:** valet and coin laundry. **Free Special Amenities:** expanded continental breakfast and high-speed Internet.

VR
VICTORIA REGENT
WATERFRONT HOTEL & SUITES

**Combine your 10% AAA Member
Discount with our free breakfast for
great value & exceptional comfort.**

VILLA MARCO POLO INN
(250)370-1524   **35**

Historic Bed & Breakfast $135-$305 **Address:** 1524 Shasta Pl V8S 1X9 **Location:** Blanshard St (Hwy 17), 1.3 mi (2 km) e on Fort St, then just s on St. Charles St. Located in a residential area. **Facility:** The renovated home is in one of Victoria's oldest neighborhoods; many of the spacious, nicely decorated bedrooms overlook the manicured grounds. 4 units. 2 stories (no elevator), interior corridors. **Terms:** 2 night minimum stay - seasonal and/or weekends, age restrictions may apply, 30 day cancellation notice-fee imposed.

WESTIN BEAR MOUNTAIN GOLF RESORT & SPA
(250)391-7160

WESTIN HOTELS & RESORTS

Hotel
$139-$599

AAA Benefit: Enjoy up to 20% off your next stay, plus Starwood Preferred Guest® bonuses.

Address: 1999 Country Club Way V9B 6R3 **Location:** Trans-Canada Hwy 1 exit 14 (Langford/Highlands), 1.1 mi (1.7 km) n on Millstream Rd, then 1.9 mi (3 km) ne on Bear Mountain Pkwy, follow signs. **Facility:** Victoria's hotel and golf resort is situated in an up-and-coming development called Bear Mountain. There's a choice of accommodations from standard hotel rooms to large one-bedroom suites with full kitchens. 156 units, some kitchens. 3-5 stories, interior corridors. **Parking:** on-site and valet. **Terms:** cancellation fee imposed, resort fee. **Amenities:** video games (fee), high-speed Internet, safes. **Dining:** 3 restaurants. **Pool(s):** heated outdoor. **Activities:** sauna, whirlpool, rental bicycles, hiking trails, jogging, spa. **Fee:** golf-36 holes, 2 tennis courts. **Guest Services:** valet and coin laundry. **Free Special Amenities:** newspaper and use of on-premises laundry facilities.

WHERE TO EAT

THE BLACK OLIVE
250/384-6060   **11**

Mediterranean
Casual Dining
$10-$30

AAA Inspector Notes: This charming downtown restaurant serves an interesting mix of Mediterranean dishes, some reflecting Italian influences. During the week, the restaurant features a daily lunch specials sheet for those pressed for time. The owner makes and sells his own olive oil. Parking is available on the street or in nearby pay lots. **Bar:** full bar. **Reservations:** suggested. **Address:** 739 Pandora Ave V8W 1N9 **Location:** Between Douglas and Blanshard sts. **Parking:** street only.

BON ROUGE BISTRO & LOUNGE
250/220-8008   **17**

French. Casual Dining. $11-$25 **AAA Inspector Notes:** At this charming bistro, located downtown, French-inspired classics are served amid décor marked by bright red walls, black upholstered seating and lots of black-and-white photos on the walls. In warmer weather, the sun-drenched patio hosts three gas fireplaces. Daily lunch and dinner specials are offered. Pay parking is along the street. **Bar:** full bar. **Address:** 611 Courtney St V8W 1B7 **Location:** Between Government and Gordon sts. **Parking:** street only.

BRASSERIE L'ECOLE
250/475-6260   **5**

French. Fine Dining. $18-$31 **AAA Inspector Notes:** This historic downtown building was once a Chinese schoolhouse. Today, it's home to a fantastic, unpretentious French bistro where the wines are from France, and the beers from Belgium. The owner/chef uses locally available produce and meats, and cooks in the classic French-country style. Many menu items change nightly. Reservations are not accepted. **Bar:** full bar. **Address:** 1715 Government St V8W 1Z4 **Location:** Between Herald and Fisgard sts; downtown. **Parking:** street only.

CACTUS CLUB CAFE
250/361-3233

American. Casual Dining. $11-$37 **AAA Inspector Notes:** This bustling, casual restaurant serves huge burgers, sandwiches, pasta, salads, soups, quesadillas, fajitas, vegetarian dishes, steak, ribs, chicken and fish. Featured are certified Angus beef and fresh wild British Columbia salmon. **Bar:** full bar. **Address:** 1125 Douglas St V8W 3L7 **Location:** Between Fort and View sts. **Parking:** street only.

Give the gift of security, value and peace of mind: Gift Membership

(See map & index p. 408.)

CAFE BRIO 250/383-0009 (22)

▼▼▼ Pacific Northwest. Casual Dining. $15-$28 **AAA Inspector Notes:** A delightfully warm and cozy bistro style atmosphere welcomes guests as soon as you walk through the door. Choose a booth and make the evening just about the two of you. Amazingly fresh seafood from around BC from up island muscles and oysters to wild BC Pacific salmon. Local farmers supply the restaurant year around — this why you'll find fresh lamb from Salt Spring Island and garden greens in season. A delightful selection of BC made cheeses make a perfect ending to any meal. **Bar:** full bar. **Reservations:** suggested. **Address:** 944 Fort St V8V 3K2 **Location:** Between Quadra and Vancouver sts. **Parking:** street only. D CALL 𝄢M

CAFE MEXICO 250/386-1425 (7)

▼ Mexican. Casual Dining. $11-$19 **AAA Inspector Notes:** If you haven't been to Mexico, this place is the next best thing. Located in downtown's Market Square, the restaurant offers an extensive menu of really good food. Décor is colorful and bright. **Bar:** full bar. **Address:** 1425 Store St V8W 3C6 **Location:** Between Pandora and Johnson sts; in Market Square. **Parking:** street only.

L D 𝄢

CANOE BREWPUB MARINA RESTAURANT

250/361-1940 (4)

▼ American. Gastropub. $9-$28 **AAA Inspector Notes:** Located along the waterfront in the historic City Light Building (just behind Chintz & Company). Food is served in both the brewpub as well as in a second-floor restaurant section. Enjoy an excellent selection of West Coast seafood choices along with regular pub food. Patio dining is available, weather permitting. **Bar:** full bar. **Reservations:** suggested. **Address:** 450 Swift St V8W 1S3 **Location:** Corner of Stone and Fisgard sts. **Parking:** on-site (fee) and street.

L D LATE 𝄢

THE EMPRESS ROOM 250/384-8111 (25)

▼▼▼ ▼▼▼ Pacific Northwest. Fine Dining. $30-$45 **AAA Inspector Notes:** *Historic.* Topping the list for fine dining in Victoria, this restaurant enables guests to dine surrounded by amazing tapestry walls and richly carved ceilings. The menu changes seasonally to showcase the best cuisine the province has to offer, including wild British Columbia salmon, fresh local mussels and clams and fine Alberta beef. **Bar:** full bar. **Reservations:** suggested. **Address:** 721 Government St V8W 1W5 **Location:** Between Belleville and Humboldt sts; in The Fairmont Empress. **Parking:** on-site and valet.

B D CALL 𝄢M

GLO RESTAURANT & LOUNGE 250/385-5643 (1)

▼▼ Canadian. Casual Dining. $13-$27 **AAA Inspector Notes:** This unique restaurant is a little tricky to find, but well worth the trouble. All of the tables overlook the Gorge Waterway, and there's a large outdoor patio. On the menu you'll find fun, tasty food along the lines of flat-bread pizzas, entrée salads, burgers, sandwiches and pasta. Street parking is available, but they will validate your ticket if you use a pay lot. **Bar:** full bar. **Reservations:** suggested. **Address:** 104-2940 Jutland Rd V8T 5K6 **Location:** Just sw of Gorge Rd. **Parking:** street only. L D LATE CALL 𝄢M

HAULTAIN'S FISH & CHIPS 250/383-8332 (3)

▼ Fish & Chips Burgers. Quick Serve. $11-$20 **AAA Inspector Notes:** Since 1975, patrons have been dining in and taking out orders from this small, neighborhood favorite in a quiet residential area. Fish and chips is the specialty, but burgers and specialty dinners also are served. Seating can be limited, but it's well worth the trip. **Bar:** beer & wine. **Address:** 1127 Haultain St V8T 1V4 **Location:** Blanshard St (Hwy 17), 0.6 mi (1 km) e on Bay St, then just n on Cook St. L D 𝄢

IL TERRAZZO 250/361-0028 (8)

▼▼▼ ▼▼▼ Italian. Casual Dining. $19-$36 **AAA Inspector Notes:** Situated in an old courtyard, Il Terrazzo offers excellent meals such as Australian lamb, ostrich, pasta and seafood, with emphasis on wood-burning oven specialties. Wine choices are extensive, with a nice by-the-glass selection. Fast, friendly service. **Bar:** full bar. **Reservations:** suggested. **Address:** 555 Johnson St V8W 1M2 **Location:** Jct Wharf St; near Market Square; main entrance off Waddington Alley. **Parking:** street only. L D CALL 𝄢M 𝄢

JAMES BAY TEA ROOM & RESTAURANT 250/382-8282 (27)

▼▼▼ Canadian. Casual Dining. $9-$16 **AAA Inspector Notes:** This popular place in a 1907 home has an intimate atmosphere featuring memorabilia and photos of Britain's Royal Family. The menu offers omelets, potpies, bangers and kidney pie. Afternoon tea is $18.50 and a light tea is $10.50. **Bar:** beer & wine. **Reservations:** suggested. **Address:** 332 Menzies St V8V 2G9 **Location:** Corner of Superior St; just s of the Parliament buildings. **Parking:** street only.

B L CALL 𝄢M

JONATHAN'S RESTAURANT 250/383-5103 (23)

▼▼ Canadian. Casual Dining. $10-$35 **AAA Inspector Notes:** This pleasant hotel restaurant is particularly popular with seniors, who appreciate the good Canadian fare, which changes on a regular basis. **Bar:** full bar. **Address:** 425 Quebec St V8V 1W7 **Location:** Between Menzies and Oswego sts; in Royal Scot Hotel & Suites.

B L D

KELSEY'S 250/978-5550

▼▼ American. Casual Dining. $10-$24 **AAA Inspector Notes:** A fun, relaxed atmosphere and tasty menu of casual fare make the restaurant a popular favorite with locals. Diners might start a meal with some tempting appetizers, such as wings, loaded potato skins or nachos, and follow them with an old-time favorite, such as a burger, wrap, pizza or pasta dish. For a heartier meal, it's hard to beat pork back ribs or a steak. The diverse menu has broad appeal. **Bar:** full bar. **Address:** 325 Burnside Rd W V8Z 7L6 **Location:** Burnside and Tillicum rds. L D

KOTO JAPANESE RESTAURANT 250/382-1514 (12)

▼▼ Japanese. Casual Dining. $6-$20 **AAA Inspector Notes:** Offerings include an extensive array of sushi and sashimi dishes, as well as teriyaki steak, sukiyaki, Japanese lunch boxes, ginger pork and a wide selection of tempura. The easy-to-follow, full-color, detailed descriptions of each dish help with decision making. The lovely space includes quiet booths in the tatami room and seats at the sushi bar where you can watch the chefs at work. Koto is located right downtown near the harbour. Metered street parking and pay lots are close by. **Bar:** full bar. **Reservations:** suggested. **Address:** 510 Fort St V8W 1E6 **Location:** Between Government and Wharf sts. **Parking:** street only. L D CALL 𝄢M

THE MARK 250/386-0450 (24)

▼▼▼ ▼▼▼
**Pacific Northwest
Fine Dining
$32-$42**

AAA Inspector Notes: With only 28 seats, the restaurant offers the discriminating guest a very intimate dining experience. The menu is constantly changing, but it always offers the finest in local ingredients. An excellent selection of wines will complement any meal. **Bar:** full bar. **Reservations:** suggested. **Address:** 463 Belleville St V8V 1X3 **Location:** Between Oswego and Menzies sts; in Hotel Grand Pacific. **Parking:** on-site (fee) and valet. D CALL 𝄢M

Innovative and playful
West Coast cuisine

MILESTONES GRILL AND BAR 250/381-2244

▼▼ Canadian. Casual Dining. $9-$27 **AAA Inspector Notes:** Popular with locals, the bustling eatery is a great gathering place. The menu features such items as wild Pacific coho salmon, Angus beef, gluten-free burgers, Kobe style beef sliders, "share plate" appetizers, soups, salads, "pasta & bowls," Angus top sirloin, Mediterranean chicken, portobello mushroom chicken, sandwiches, burgers, prime rib, roll-ups, taster or full desserts. There is a great selection of wines by the glass and creative specialty cocktails. **Bar:** full bar. **Address:** 812 Wharf St V8W 1T3 **Location:** Corner of Government and Humboldt sts. **Parking:** street only. L D CALL 𝄢M

MOXIE'S CLASSIC GRILL 250/360-1660

▼▼ American. Casual Dining. $11-$25 **AAA Inspector Notes:** This sleek, funky and popular restaurant presents an extensive menu of creatively prepared dishes, including pizza, pasta, rice, noodles, signature salads and burgers. Other menus include one for children and one for Sunday brunch. Lending to the upbeat, stylish decor are dark wood appointments and river rock fireplaces. **Bar:** full bar. **Address:** 1010 Yates St, #1 V8V 3M7 **Location:** Between Vancouver and Cook sts. L D CALL 𝄢M

(See map & index p. 408.)

NAUTICAL NELLIE'S STEAK & SEAFOOD RESTAURANT
250/380-2260 (14)
◆◆ Steak Seafood. Casual Dining. $13-$34 **AAA Inspector Notes:** A long established downtown restaurant with partial views of the Harbour. Nellie's serves wonderful seafood and certified Angus steaks that has been aged for 35 days. One of their signature dishes is their steak and mushroom pie featuring tender strip loin steak and big round mushrooms in a rich, creamy gravy capped with a flaky pastry topping. **Bar:** full bar. **Address:** 1001 Wharf St V8W 1T6 **Location:** Between Broughton and Fort sts. **Parking:** street only.
[L] [D] CALL [M]

PABLO'S DINING LOUNGE 250/388-4255 (16)
◆◆◆ New French. Fine Dining. $17-$42 **AAA Inspector Notes:** Located in a renovated heritage home close to Inner Harbour hotels, the restaurant has an exciting chef who prepares an interesting menu of French Continental cuisine. Plate presentations are exquisite, and all of the food products are purchased from local growers and farmers and prepared from scratch. The amazing wine list features two pages of wonderful wines by the glass. **Bar:** full bar. **Reservations:** suggested. **Address:** 225 Quebec St V8V 1W2 **Location:** Corner of Pendray and Quebec sts. [D] [K]

PAGLIACCI'S 250/386-1662 (15)
◆◆ Italian. Casual Dining. $6-$24 **AAA Inspector Notes:** A New York-style Italian eatery with a bustling Big Apple ambience, this place has the food to match. Flavorful pasta dishes include the exceptional ravioli or spaghetti Western, made with fresh tomatoes and topped with a couple of large meatballs. It's as Italian as it gets. **Bar:** full bar. **Address:** 1011 Broad St V8W 2A1 **Location:** Between Fort and Broughton sts. **Parking:** street only. [L] [D] [K]

PASSERO'S MEDITERRANEAN CUISINE 250/384-6474 (21)
◆◆ Mediterranean. Casual Dining. $12-$24 **AAA Inspector Notes:** The family-run restaurant serves a fine combination of Greek and Italian cuisine in large portions. Lending to the bistro there are lots of color and live plants. The patio opens seasonally. **Bar:** full bar. **Reservations:** suggested. **Address:** 1102 Yates St V8V 3M8 **Location:** Corner of Cook St. [L] [D]

PESCATORE'S SEAFOOD & GRILL 250/385-4512 (18)
◆◆◆ Seafood. Casual Dining. $10-$33 **AAA Inspector Notes:** Pescatore's is a chic bistro with excellent fresh seafood and such great beverage choices as espresso, cappuccino and martinis. This is a hip and funky fine dining spot with parking at street meters or pay lots. **Bar:** full bar. **Reservations:** suggested. **Address:** 614 Humboldt St V8W 1A4 **Location:** Between Gordon and Government sts. **Parking:** street only. [L] [D] CALL [M]

THE PINK BICYCLE 250/384-1008 (19)
◆ Burgers. Casual Dining. $10-$16 **AAA Inspector Notes:** This tiny but often packed spot is distinguished not only by its trademark pink bicycle parked outside the door but also by its menu packed with hand-made, mouthwatering gourmet burgers. The house specialty is the Pink Bike cheeseburger made from naturally raised Vancouver Island beef, but the adventurous are urged to try burger options such as the blue cheese lamb, mutton, bison, halibut or chicken with sauteed leeks. Among accompaniments are truffle fries, poutine and pink lemonade cheesecake. **Bar:** full bar. **Address:** 1008 Blanshard St V8W 2H5 **Location:** Between Fort and Broughton sts. **Parking:** street only. [L] [D] [K]

PLUTO'S 250/385-4747 (26)
◆◆ American. Casual Dining. $7-$15 **AAA Inspector Notes:** The funky-looking, turquoise-and-pink Art Deco structure used to be a gas station. In addition to the extensive breakfast menu, which is served until 2 pm, there also are varied wraps and burgers and a few Mexican items. **Bar:** full bar. **Address:** 1150 Cook St V8V 3Z9 **Location:** Corner of Cook and View sts. [B] [L] [D] [K]

RESTAURANT MATISSE 250/480-0883 (9)
◆◆◆ French. Fine Dining. $20-$33 **AAA Inspector Notes:** This eatery is a wonderful French restaurant located downtown. The first thing you'll notice is the bright sunlight-yellow decor that is warm and inviting. Daily specials along with what they do best include duck, beef and fish. **Bar:** full bar. **Reservations:** suggested. **Address:** 512 Yates St V8W 1K8 **Location:** Between Government and Wharf sts. **Parking:** street only. [D] CALL [M]

RICKY'S ALL DAY GRILL 250/383-9925
◆◆ American. Casual Dining. $11-$27 **AAA Inspector Notes:** The comfortable eatery, which employs friendly servers, presents a varied menu that includes pasta dishes, wraps, omelets, stir-fry preparations and burgers. Portions are generous. Children's and senior selections are offered. Guests can request seating in a booth or at a table. **Bar:** full bar. **Address:** 1501 Admirals Rd V9A 2P8 **Location:** Corner of Admirals and Glentana rds; on Admirals Walk Mall. [B] [L] [D] CALL [M]

SIAM THAI RESTAURANT 250/383-9911 (13)
◆◆ Thai. Casual Dining. $8-$18 **AAA Inspector Notes:** The secret of Thai cooking is to maintain a delicate balance between the spices and main ingredients. The restaurant accomplishes this in its soups, as well as dishes of fried rice, noodles, chicken, beef, pork, seafood and vegetarian items. Lunch specials are available. **Bar:** full bar. **Reservations:** suggested. **Address:** 512 Fort St V8W 1E6 **Location:** Between Government and Wharf sts. **Parking:** street only. [L] [D] [K]

SPINNAKERS GASTRO BREWPUB & RESTAURANT
250/386-2739 (2)
◆◆ American. Gastropub. $10-$25 **AAA Inspector Notes:** The fun and lively pub and restaurant features terrific breads and delicious homemade soups. Guests can tour the brew house, said to be Canada's first in-house brewery, or bring home treats from the on-site bakery. **Bar:** full bar. **Reservations:** suggested. **Address:** 308 Catherine St V9A 3S8 **Location:** 1.3 mi (2 km) nw over Johnson St Bridge, then just s; in Spinnakers Gastro Brewpub and Guesthouses. [L] [D] CALL [M]

SWISS CHALET 250/475-0334
◆◆ Chicken. Casual Dining. $9-$22 **AAA Inspector Notes:** The popular restaurant is known for its rotisserie chicken and ribs and the tangy Chalet sauce that gives food its special zip. Diners munch on a half or quarter chicken with sides such as steamed vegetables, fries, baked potatoes and salads. Lunch guests often go for the great soup and sandwich combination. Take-out and delivery service are popular options. **Bar:** full bar. **Address:** 3233 Douglas St V8Z 3K8 **Location:** Between Tolmie and Roderick sts. [L] [D] CALL [M]

VENETO TAPA LOUNGE 250/383-7310 (10)
◆◆◆ Pacific Northwest. Fine Dining. $14-$20 **AAA Inspector Notes:** Funky and cool are a couple of words that come to mind when stepping into this restaurant/bar. No one under 19 is allowed into this adults-only place where the cocktail menu and craft beer list is like nothing you've seen before. On weekends they'll sometimes have a DJ pumping out the tunes as you and friends enjoy a tapas-style menu where all of the dishes are meant to be shared. This is more than just dinner out, it's a real night out on the town. **Bar:** full bar. **Reservations:** suggested. **Address:** 1450 Douglas St V8W 2G1 **Location:** Corner of Pandora Ave and Douglas St; in Hotel Rialto. **Parking:** street only. [D] CALL [M]

VICTORIA HARBOUR HOUSE RESTAURANT
250/386-1244 (20)
◆◆ Steak Seafood. Fine Dining. $16-$37 **AAA Inspector Notes:** Just up from the U.S. ferry terminal in Victoria's Inner Harbour and surrounded by many hotels, sits this long-established restaurant that serves fresh seafood and fine steaks. If on-site parking is full, diners can park along the street. **Bar:** full bar. **Reservations:** suggested. **Address:** 607 Oswego St V8V 4W9 **Location:** Corner of Oswego and Quebec sts. [D] [K]

WHITE HEATHER TEA ROOM 250/595-8020 (28)
◆◆ Desserts Sandwiches. Casual Dining. $10-$17 **AAA Inspector Notes:** On Oak Bay, the wonderful tea room serves lunch and afternoon tea starting at 11:45 am. Among choices are the Wee Tea for $14.75, Not-So-Wee Tea for $18.95 and the Big Muckle, which is $43.95 for those with hearty appetites. The sconewiches, freshly baked scones with varied fillings, are popular. Everything is baked on site. **Bar:** beer & wine. **Reservations:** required. **Address:** 1885 Oak Bay Ave V8R 1C6 **Location:** Corner of Davie St. **Parking:** street only. [L]

(See map & index p. 408.)

WILD SAFFRON BISTRO & WINE BAR   250/361-3310 6
▽▽▽▽ Pacific Rim. Fine Dining. $18-$30 **AAA Inspector Notes:** The warm, contemporary bistro pairs its large selection of local and international wines--not to mention beers from the on-site brewery--with wonderful West Coast cuisine, including the seafood dishes for which this place is known, in addition to hearty lamb, game, poultry and vegetarian options. Artistic flair characterizes the plate presentations. **Bar:** full bar. **Reservations:** suggested. **Address:** 506 Pandora Ave V8W 1N6 **Location:** Corner of Pandora Ave and Store St; in Swans Suite Hotel. **Parking:** street only.

D CALL ⬛M Ⓧ

VIEW ROYAL (H-10) pop. 9,381, elev. 22m/72'
• Part of Victoria area — see map p. 397

CRAIGFLOWER NATIONAL HISTORIC SITE is at 1801 Admirals Rd. Built in 1856 by the Hudson's Bay Co. on an original homestead, the farmhouse is a fine example of early Georgian architecture.

The heavy oak door reinforced with iron studs is a reminder of the British class system. A kitchen garden complements the atmosphere. The schoolhouse, said to be the oldest in western Canada, was built by the Craigflower farmhouse workers for their children. **Time:** Allow 30 minutes minimum. **Hours:** Mon.-Fri. 10-4, May-Sept.; by appointment rest of year. **Cost:** Donations. **Phone:** (250) 386-1606.

WARDNER (C-12)

KOOTENAY TROUT HATCHERY is 8 km (5 mi.) n. on the e. side of the Kootenay River at 4522 Fenwick Rd. The facility raises 3 million trout annually. An aquarium contains fish species raised at the hatchery, including the rare white sturgeon. Displays explain fish raising. An outside moat holds large rainbow trout. **Time:** Allow 30 minutes minimum. **Hours:** Daily 8-3:30, May-Aug.; Mon.-Fri. 8-4, rest of year. Guided tours are available daily 9:30-3:30, in summer; otherwise varies. Phone ahead to confirm schedule. **Cost:** Donations. **Phone:** (250) 429-3214.

WEST KELOWNA (C-8) pop. 30,892, elev. 411m/1,348'
• Hotels & Restaurants map & index p. 290
• Part of Okanagan Valley area — see map p. 286

West Kelowna (Westbank) was a link on the fur-trading route from the north-central part of the province, called New Caledonia, to the Columbia River. In the early 1860s fortune seekers en route to the Cariboo gold mines followed the old trail through the Okanagan Valley.

Ideal climatic conditions in the Okanagan Valley nurture the city's many orchards and vineyards. Vacationers also are drawn by the favorable weather in the valley. Downhill and cross-country skiing in the surrounding countryside are popular in winter.

West Kelowna Visitor Centre: 2376 Dobbin Rd., Suite 4, West Kelowna, BC, Canada V4T 2H9. **Phone:** (250) 768-2712 or (866) 768-3378.

WINERIES
• **Mission Hill Family Estate** is 4.5 km (3 mi.) e. off Hwy. 97 via Boucherie Rd. to 1730 Mission Hill

Rd. **Hours:** Daily 9:30-7, late June-day before Labour Day; 10-6, Sept. 4-Oct. 8; 11-5, Oct. 9-Dec. 31. Tours are offered daily; phone for schedule. Closed Jan. 1, Christmas and day after Christmas. **Phone:** (250) 768-7611 or (250) 768-6448.

BEST WESTERN PLUS WINE COUNTRY HOTEL & SUITES   (250)707-1637 32
▽▽▽ ▽▽
Hotel
$149-$249

AAA Benefit: Members save up to 20%, plus 10% bonus points with Best Western Rewards®.

Address: 3460 Carrington Rd V4T 3C1 **Location:** Hwy 97 (Dobbin Rd), just e on Elk Rd, follow signs. **Facility:** 99 units. 4 stories, interior corridors. **Terms:** cancellation fee imposed. **Amenities:** high-speed Internet, safes. **Pool(s):** heated indoor. **Activities:** whirlpool, waterslide, exercise room. **Guest Services:** valet and coin laundry. **Free Special Amenities:** full breakfast and local telephone calls.

SAVE ECO 🍴 CALL ⬛M 🏊 BIZ 🛜 ✕ 🔌 🖨 💻

High speed Internet, pet friendly, full continental breakfast, in-room safes, meeting room.

THE COVE LAKESIDE RESORT   (250)707-1800 33
▽▽▽ ▽▽ Resort Hotel $155-$889 **Address:** 4205 Gellatly Rd V4T 2K2 **Location:** Hwy 97 (Dobbin Rd), 1 mi (1.6 km) s, follow signs. **Facility:** Along a private cove on the spectacular Okanagan Lake sits this premiere resort with tastefully appointed suites with gourmet kitchens, separate bedrooms, large living room areas and wonderful lake views. 105 kitchen units, some two and three bedrooms. 4 stories, interior corridors. **Terms:** check-in 4 pm, 3 day cancellation notice-fee imposed, resort fee. **Pool(s):** 2 heated outdoor. **Activities:** whirlpools, waterslide, limited beach access, putting green, tennis court, exercise room, spa. *Fee:* marina. **Guest Services:** complimentary and valet laundry.

ECO 🍴 🍷 CALL ⬛M 🏊 🛜 ✕ 🔌 🖨 💻
/ SOME UNITS FEE 🐾

SUPER 8 WEST KELOWNA HOTEL   (250)769-2355 31
▽▽▽ ▽▽
Hotel
$90-$130
Address: 1655 Westgate Rd V1Z 3P1 **Location:** Jct Hwy 97 (Harvey Ave) and Bartley Rd, s to Ross Rd. **Facility:** 81 units, some efficiencies. 2 stories (no elevator), interior corridors. **Terms:** cancellation fee imposed. **Pool(s):** heated indoor. **Activities:** whirlpool, limited exercise equipment. **Guest Services:** valet and coin laundry. **Free Special Amenities:** continental breakfast and high-speed Internet.

SAVE 🍴 🍷 CALL ⬛M 🏊 🛜 ✕ 💻
/ SOME UNITS FEE 🐾 🔌 🖨

WEST VANCOUVER (H-11) pop. 42,694

- **Attractions map p. 355**
- **Hotels & Restaurants map & index p. 368**
- **Part of Vancouver area — see map p. 343**

If you're not a Vancouverite—or you're unfamiliar with British Columbia's Lower Mainland—you might think that the North Shore is simply one more spectacularly scenic backdrop to a city already blessed with loads of scenic allure. And you would be wrong. The North Shore is not only uncommonly beautiful; it's also teeming with things to do.

The city and district of North Vancouver are east of the Lions Gate Bridge; the district of West Vancouver spreads along the northern shore of Burrard Inlet from the bridge west to Horseshoe Bay. There's no manufacturing or industry here; "West Van" is primarily residential. It's also affluent, and there are many gorgeous and expensive homes tucked away on winding little streets or perched high on hillsides. All of West Vancouver is situated on slopes of the Coast Mountains, which means that most of these homes enjoy enviable vistas of water, trees, mountains or all three.

The Lions Gate Bridge, which connects Stanley Park and the North Shore, is the gateway to West Vancouver. This suspension bridge crosses the first narrows of Burrard Inlet, which accounts for its official name, the First Narrows Bridge; "lions gate" is a reference to two mountains known as the Lions.

Construction of the 1,795-metre (5,890-ft.) span began in 1937, and the bridge opened to traffic in 1938. It's similar in appearance to San Francisco's Golden Gate Bridge (although bright green rather than bright orange). Another similarity it shares with Golden Gate is the view from the bridge—it's gorgeous whether you're coming or going. The Guinness family (of beer fame), who for a time owned land on the North Shore, purchased decorative white lights for the bridge in 1986 as a gift to Vancouver, turning it into a distinctive nighttime landmark.

Marine Drive is West Vancouver's main thoroughfare. It runs from the bridge west to Horseshoe Bay, usually within sight of water, passing lovely neighborhoods and commercial blocks packed with shops and restaurants. Ambleside, between 11th and 23rd streets, is one of West Vancouver's oldest neighborhoods. The Centennial Seawalk in Ambleside Park is a breezy waterfront promenade that's a favorite spot for walkers, joggers or anyone who loves to gaze out onto the water and contemplate the awesome views of the bridge and Stanley Park. There's a long, sandy beach and a concession stand where you can grab a cheeseburger or an ice cream cone.

Ambleside also has art galleries and antique shops. The Silk Purse Gallery, 1570 Argyle Ave. (on the waterfront near John Lawson Park), is a comfy old cottage that used to be a haven for honeymooners. It's now home to the West Vancouver Community Arts Council, which presents rotating art exhibits and a series of summer concerts; for ticket information phone (604) 925-7292. Local artists exhibit at the Ferry Building Gallery, a lovingly restored heritage building at 1414 Argyle Ave.

Dundarave is another exceedingly picturesque little seaside community. Stroll along the water once again at Dundarave Park, at the foot of 25th Street, with Cypress Mountain looming in the distance. Old-fashioned lamp posts are installed on Marine Drive between 23rd and 25th streets, flowers cascade from hanging baskets, and the 2 blocks are filled with eateries and specialty shops. It's a nice area to spend an hour or two. Have lunch at the Red Lion Bar & Grill (2427 Marine Dr.), a classic British-style pub—think dark wood walls, stained glass and several fireplaces when the weather's nippy—or stop for coffee and a muffin at Delaney's Coffee House.

Marine Drive presses on to Caulfeild (yes, that spelling is correct), an exclusive residential community of narrow, precipitously winding streets and expensive homes shielded by tall privacy hedges. Almost every bend and curve of the road offers a brief, tantalizing water view. Walking the trails in Lighthouse Park *(see attraction listing)*, a protected stand of old growth coastal forest, is well worth your time.

Past the Lighthouse Park turnoff Marine Drive winds north toward Horseshoe Bay. Side streets lead to tucked-away little green spaces like Kew Park (accessed via Kew Cliff Road and Seaside Place). The multimillion-dollar homes along Kew Cliff Road have stunning views of the Strait of Georgia. A bit farther north Marine Drive winds around Fisherman's Cove, bristling with the masts of pleasure craft moored at the West Vancouver Yacht Club.

Follow the signs to Horseshoe Bay, the North Shore's western bookend. This is where ferries depart for Vancouver Island and the Lower Mainland's "Sunshine Coast." The little community is another North Shore jewel. Take Nelson Avenue off Marine Drive, which leads to the ferry terminal and marina. BC Ferries chug in and out of port while sea gulls wheel overhead. Tree-covered slopes frame Horseshoe Bay, houses perch high above the water and the Coast Mountains loom in the distance. Charming really doesn't begin to describe it.

"Downtown" Horseshoe Bay has just a couple of streets, which makes it perfect for strolling. Browse a few art galleries. Lean against a dock piling and watch the waterfront activity. Get fish and chips or an oyster burger from one of the takeout restaurants on Bay Street and take your feast to Horseshoe Bay Park, where there's a little gravel beach, two totem poles and a massive cast-bronze propeller that came off a whaling ship. Listen to the gulls and breathe in the sea air. Now *this* is an afternoon outing.

Backtrack to Marine Drive and turn right instead of left (which will take you back to Hwy. 99). Stay on Marine Drive and you'll reach Whytecliff Marine Park *(see Recreation Areas Chart)*. Designated Canada's first salt water Marine Protected Area (MPA) in 1993, it's located at the entrance to Howe Sound and is known for

(See map & index p. 368.)

excellent scuba diving. Seals frolic along this rugged stretch of coastline, and there's a pebbly beach to explore. Or just relax at the park's observation pavilion and—you guessed it—admire the view.

CYPRESS PROVINCIAL PARK is off Trans-Canada Hwy. exit 8, then w. following signs. The park encompasses 3,012 hectares (7,443 acres) of mountains, lakes and forests. Winter offers skiing and other snow-related activates, while summer features bird-watching and a wide range of hiking and nature trails. *See Recreation Areas Chart.* **Hours:** Daily 24 hours. **Cost:** Free. **Phone:** (604) 924-2200.

🅰️ 🅰️ 🅰️

LIGHTHOUSE PARK is off Marine Dr. (watch for the park sign at the turnoff), then a short distance s. via Beacon Ln. to the parking area. Capt. George Vancouver sailed past the rocky peninsula at the entrance to Burrard Inlet in 1792 and named the site Point Atkinson. Today this lush remnant of old growth coastal forest is a peaceful haven and wonderful place to hike. The lofty Douglas firs and other conifers are up to 500 years old.

Several kilometres of trails crisscross the park; to get to the Point Atkinson Lighthouse take the Beacon Lane Trail south from the parking area. It's about a 15-minute walk to a viewpoint with an expansive vista (on clear days) of the lighthouse (a working one and therefore closed to the public), the inlet and downtown Vancouver on the opposite shore. From the lighthouse viewpoint, short East Beach Trail leads down to the rugged, rocky beach along Starboat Cove.

The group of buildings near the lighthouse were barracks during World War II, when a number of B.C. light stations were used for surveillance purposes. **Time:** Allow 30 minutes minimum. **Hours:** Daily dawn-dusk. **Cost:** Free. **Phone:** (604) 925-7000.

SEWELL'S MARINA is at the Horseshoe Bay Ferry Terminal at 6409 Bay St., following signs to the village. Points of interest on the 2-hour high-speed Sea Safari tour of coastal British Columbia may include Bowyer Island, Pam Rocks—birthing ground to seal pups in July—Ragged Island and The Strait of Georgia. **Hours:** Tours depart daily at 10, 1 and 4, Apr.-Oct. (weather permitting). Phone ahead to confirm schedule. **Cost:** $73; $65 (ages 65+ and students with ID); $43 (ages 5-12). **Phone:** (604) 921-3474.

Traveling With Your Pet?
AAA.com/PetBook

THE BOATHOUSE RESTAURANT   604/921-8188

♦♦ Seafood. Casual Dining. $13-$39 **AAA Inspector Notes:** In this picturesque area, the restaurant is just minutes from the Horseshoe Bay Ferry Terminal. Floor-to-ceiling windows take full advantage of the busy ferry terminal and marina. Diners can watch these massive ferries arrive and depart all day long from the comfort of their tables. The specialty is the hand-selected, fresh seafood, but you also can try premium cut, 35-day-aged Certified Angus beef. Lunch features reasonably priced seafood, burgers, soups and salads. **Bar:** full bar. **Reservations:** suggested. **Address:** 6695 Nelson Ave V7W 2B2 **Location:** Trans-Canada Hwy 1 to Horseshoe Bay Ferry Terminal, follow signs to "Village," just w on Bay St.

L D CALL 🅼

CACTUS CLUB CAFE   604/922-1707

♦♦ American. Casual Dining. $9-$29 **AAA Inspector Notes:** This bustling, casual restaurant serves huge burgers, sandwiches, pasta, salads, soups, quesadillas, fajitas, vegetarian dishes, steak, ribs, chicken and fish. Featured are certified Angus beef and fresh wild British Columbia salmon. **Bar:** full bar. **Address:** 855 Main St V7T 2Z3 **Location:** Just off Marine Dr; in Village at Park Royal.

L D LATE CALL 🅼

FRAICHE   604/925-7595   63

♦♦♦ Pacific Northwest. Fine Dining. $14-$38 **AAA Inspector Notes:** Nestled on a hillside in a newly constructed residential neighborhood sits this wonderful restaurant offering stunning views, warm, inviting décor and delicious food. The menu showcases fresh seasonal and regional cuisine like the organic beef burger and local sablefish. Because the chef uses as many local ingredients as possible, his menu changes seasonally. **Bar:** full bar. **Reservations:** suggested. **Address:** 2240 Chippendale Rd V7S 3J5 **Location:** Trans-Canada Hwy 1 exit 10 (21st St), just w to Folkestone Way, 0.9 mi (1.5 km) n, then just e. L D CALL 🅼

LA REGALADE FRENCH BISTRO   604/921-2228   65

♦♦ French. Casual Dining. $18-$25 **AAA Inspector Notes:** The tiny, family-run bistro blends fantastically fresh ingredients in heaping plates of great food. The chef/owner hails from France and has cooked at fine restaurants both in France and here in the city. Daily specials are listed on the wall chalkboard. Don't leave without trying one of the many homemade desserts on display. **Bar:** full bar. **Reservations:** suggested. **Address:** 2232 Marine Dr V7V 1K4 **Location:** Trans-Canada Hwy 1 exit 10 (22nd St), 0.9 mi (1.5 km) s, then just w. **Parking:** street only. L D CALL 🅼

SALMON HOUSE ON THE HILL   604/926-3212   64

♦♦♦ Seafood. Fine Dining. $28-$39 **AAA Inspector Notes:** Absolutely stunning views of downtown, Lions Gate Bridge and the water where many commercial ships anchor can be taken in from this hilltop restaurant. Fresh British Columbia salmon is a specialty, but the entire menu features ingredients from B.C.'s six growing regions. Each dish can be accompanied by a recommended B.C. wine. **Bar:** full bar. **Reservations:** suggested. **Address:** 2229 Folkestone Way V7S 2Y6 **Location:** Trans-Canada Hwy 1 exit 10 (21st St), follow signs. D CALL 🅼

WHISTLER (G-12) pop. 9,824,

elev. 640m/2,009'
• Hotels p. 426 • Restaurants p. 430
• Hotels & Restaurants map & index p. 425

Whistler would be a special place even without the whole enchilada it offers when it comes to winter sports. It would be special without the superb system of hiking and mountain biking trails that provide outdoor activity when the sun is warm and the snow isn't swirling. And it would be special without the amenities—all sorts of lodgings from basic to luxury, plenty of restaurants (and a few of culinary distinction), a nice selection of specialty shops, evening entertainment from mild to wild—that combine to create this covers-every-base active vacation destination.

(See map & index p. 425.)

The reason why has a lot to do with an old adage: location, location, location. About 2 hours north of Vancouver, Whistler snuggles in a Coast Mountains valley amid a cluster of shimmering small lakes, the reflection of forested slopes etched on their surfaces. Rivers rush through steep-walled canyons. Waterfalls plunge. The stark white of glacier ice contrasts with the black of mountain peaks, framed against a brilliantly blue sky. The wilderness is rugged and unspoiled, the air bracingly fresh. Given such a spectacular setting, it's easy to see why it has become one of Canada's best all-season resorts.

Although the 2010 Olympic Winter Games are now history, Whistler remains a pretty exciting place—and getting there is part of the fun. From Vancouver, the major road link is the Sea-to-Sky Highway (Hwy. 99). The primary road link between Vancouver and Whistler was widened and improved for the games. The approximately 2-hour drive offers a full plate of scenic views as the highway climbs from a coastal rain forest environment in the vicinity of Horseshoe Bay to the rugged mountain landscapes around Whistler. Even so, it's always a good idea to check road conditions before heading to Whistler; for information and traffic updates phone (877) 472-3399.

Between Horseshoe Bay and Squamish the road runs along the eastern edge of Howe Sound, punctuated by a series of fjords. From a distance, islands in the bay look like plump green mounds floating on water that is invitingly blue in sunny weather and a brooding gray on overcast days.

Just south of Squamish water is left behind as the highway veers inland. If you want to take a break or need to make a pit stop before reaching Whistler, there are gas stations and a scattering of fast-food outlets at the intersection of Hwy. 99 and Cleveland Road. Past Squamish, Hwy. 99 twists and turns around tree-covered granite crags and sheer rock faces that rise almost straight up from the side of the road. Be sure to pull off and stop at the designated viewpoints; great views are guaranteed.

Whistler has no grand entrance; there are just two primary access roads off Hwy. 99 (Village Gate Drive and Lorimer Road). Whistler Village may seem small, but it's compact. Sitting at the base of Whistler Mountain's ski runs, this is where lots of hotels, restaurants and shops are concentrated. Blackcomb Way divides Whistler Village from the Upper Village, which lies at the base of Blackcomb Mountain's ski runs. Distinctions are pretty much a moot point, although the Upper Village tends to have more upscale accommodations and Whistler Village a livelier scene after dark.

You can walk between the two villages in about 5 minutes along Fitzsimmons Trail, which crosses burbling Fitzsimmons Creek via a covered bridge. Branching off Fitzsimmons Trail is Bridge Meadows Trail, a pleasant walk through the woods that follows the creek and ends up near the new Squamish Lil'wat

Cultural Centre *(see attraction listing)*. Pick up a copy of the tear-off Whistler walking map at your hotel's front desk, fold it up and stash it in your pocket.

Whistler Mountain and Blackcomb Mountain are Whistler's twin peaks. Each mountain has more than 1,524 metres (5,000 ft.) of vertical rise and more than 100 marked runs that are serviced by multiple lifts; together they offer more than 3,238 hectares (8,000 acres) of ski-worthy terrain. Challenge your thighs on downhill runs, negotiate spectacular alpine bowls or embark on a cross-country trek through deep powder. You can even ski on a glacier. There are lessons and instruction for every skill level, all sorts of equipment rentals and a variety of ski packages to choose from. If skiing doesn't strike your fancy, go snowshoeing, snowboarding, ice skating or snowmobiling. And if you're not the active sort, sit back and relax under a comfy blanket with a mug of hot chocolate on a Blackcomb Mountain sleigh ride. Even active sorts would enjoy this.

Whistler boasts North America's first gondola connecting two mountain peaks, the Peak 2 Peak Gondola at Whistler-Blackcomb Resort. The gondola's passenger cabins travel the 4.4-kilometre (2.7-mi.) distance between the two towers at the summit of Whistler and Blackcomb mountains in 11 minutes, allowing skiers to take advantage of cruising both mountains in the same day. Each gondola cabin holds up to 28 people, and two of them feature glass floors for a dizzying bird's-eye view of Fitzsimmons Valley 435 metres (1,427 ft.) below. Purchase of a regular lift ticket includes gondola transportation.

But Whistler isn't just about winter sports. Summer is prime time for hiking, mountain biking, windsurfing and canoeing, among other activities. Ski lifts take hikers up the two mountains to explore trails free of snow, but if you'd rather go down a different path, walk to Lost Lake. It takes about 30 minutes to get there from Whistler Village (trail access is off Lorimer Road), a good jaunt if you want to leave the hustle and bustle behind for an afternoon.

This tranquil lake is surrounded by Lost Lake Park's evergreen forests, with lovely views of mountains in the distance. The shallow water makes for good swimming on warm days. Numerous hiking trails crisscross this wooded area. There's no parking at the lake, but free shuttle bus service departs from the Gondola Transit Exchange on Blackcomb Way in July and August.

Walkers, hikers, cyclists and inline skaters all take advantage of the paved Valley Trail, which wends its way for some 30.5 kilometres (19 mi.) around the greater Whistler area, connecting parks, residential neighborhoods and the villages. It's a popular commuter biking route.

Adrenaline junkies head to Whistler Mountain Bike Park, a lift-accessed mountain biking haven. The terrain here covers the bases from gently banked trails through a lush coastal forest environment to single-track trails twisting in a series of tight turns to death-defying descents down the side of steep rock faces (which sounds a bit like skiing on wheels). Access is by lift tickets or park passes;

(See map & index p. 425.)

bikes and accessories can be rented. The park is open from mid-May to mid-October.

With four championship courses, Whistler's got some very good golf. The Whistler Golf Club, (604) 932-3280 or (800) 376-1777, is the first course in Canada designed by Arnold Palmer. Robert Trent Jones Jr. was the course architect for the Fairmont Chateau Whistler Golf Club, (877) 938-2092, at The Fairmont Chateau Whistler. The Golden Bear designed the Nicklaus North Golf Course, (604) 938-9898 or (800) 386-9898. Big Sky Golf and Country Club, (604) 894-6106 or (800) 668-7900, is near Pemberton, about a 25-minute drive north of Whistler. With a Bob Cupp-designed layout along the Green River, you can be assured that water will come into play.

For pure sightseeing fun, take the Whistler Village Gondola up Whistler Mountain. The bird's-eye views of alpine lakes, meadows full of wildflowers (in summertime) and mountain slopes from the enclosed gondola are breathtaking. The ride up takes about 25 minutes. Once at the top, hike back-country trails or have a leisurely lunch at the Roundhouse Lodge, a cool 1,850 metres (6,069 ft.) above sea level, while taking in the scenery all around you. More intrepid souls can continue ascending on the Peak Chair to the 2,182-metre (7,160-ft.) level, where a 360-degree panorama of the Coast Mountains awaits.

And what do you do après skiing or otherwise testing your physical endurance? You stroll around Whistler Village. It's pedestrian-only, it's done in the style of a German mountain village, and it's *cute*. In winter the atmosphere is all woolen caps, puffy ski parkas and oversize mittens; summer brings out the hanging flower baskets and umbrella-shaded tables for outdoor cafe dining. Mogul's Coffee House, next to the drugstore at Village Square, is a funky little place to hang out for a spell.

Four large day-use lots between the two villages offer free parking. Whistler and Valley Express (WAVE) public buses operated by BC Transit provide service to the greater area. Various bus lines serve the resort; shuttle lines 5 and 6 are the most useful if you're staying in or near Whistler Village. The fare is $2; $1.50 (ages 65+ and students); free (ages 0-6). Exact change is required. WaveCards that are good for multiple rides can be purchased at the Whistler Visitor Centre, 4320 Gateway Dr. (in Whistler Village).

Tourism Whistler: 4230 Gateway Dr., Whistler, BC V0N 1B4. **Phone:** (604) 935-3357 or (877) 991-9988.

Shopping areas: With all kinds of specialty boutiques and eateries, Whistler Village is where it's at. Whistler's Marketplace (entrance off Lorimer Road) is the main shopping center. It has a ski lodge ambiance and retailers like the Escape Route, which carries a full lineup of outdoor recreation wear and accessories—body wear, head wear, hand wear, footwear, snowshoes, backpacks, you name it. Let kids loose in the

Great Glass Elevator Candy Shop and its head-turning display of sweets. It just may be enough to drive you to the more adult-oriented Upper Village Market, where you can stock up on gourmet groceries (they'll also deliver to your hotel room!)

Also in the Upper Village is Snowflake (in The Fairmont Chateau Whistler), with a selection of Canadian-designed fur and leather jackets, cashmere sweaters, scarves, shawls, boots and accessories for women. Bring lots of money. Back in Whistler Village, New Agers will want to waft into The Oracle (on Main Street) and check out the jewelry, candles, incense and gifts. Tarot card and palm readings are given, or you can give in to a relaxing reiki massage.

The Whistler Village Art Gallery exhibits contemporary paintings, sculpture and art and has two locations, in the Four Seasons Resort Whistler and at the Hilton Whistler Resort & Spa's Gallery Row. Also at the Hilton is the Black Tusk Gallery, which has a collection of masks, sculptures, totems and other objects created by Northwest Coast First Nations artists. Mountain Galleries at the Fairmont, in The Fairmont Chateau Whistler, exhibits museum-quality work—paintings, glass pieces, bronze sculptures, stone carvings—by respected Canadian artists.

Nightlife: Whistler's a family-oriented kind of place, but that doesn't mean it lacks hotspots for those itching to get down and *party*. Maxx Fish, below the Amsterdam Cafe in Village Square, has plush booths and plasma-screen TVs, plus a light show choreographed to the slammin' beats cooked up by resident and visiting DJs. A similar uninhibited mood and young, good-looking crowd prevails at Tommy Africa's, not far away on Gateway Drive next to the taxi loop.

Garfinkels, on Main Street in Whistler Village, throws club night bashes on different days of the week; locals and visitors alike flock to "Happy Thursdays," and Saturday is another big party night. The music is DJ dance mixes, augmented by occasional live hip-hop shows. "Garf's" also has VIP hosts and table service, so reservations are a good idea; phone (604) 932-2323. Also in the village is Buffalo Bills, a high-energy nightspot that packs 'em in with drink specials, a huge dance floor and a mix of mainstream and classic rock.

The Savage Beagle, in Whistler Village near Starbucks, has two levels: a relatively sedate upstairs lounge serving all sorts of cocktails, fresh-squeezed juice martinis and wines by the glass, and a downstairs dance floor where DJs pump up the volume. The après-ski crowd hangs out here.

On the other hand, if crowded clubs and earsplitting music isn't your cup of tea, you could catch a movie at the Village 8 Cinemas in Whistler Village. Or better yet, pick up a to-go pie at Avalanche Pizza (locals say it's the best in town) and chill out in your room, because you just might want to save your energy for the slopes.

BLACKCOMB SLEIGH RIDES depart from Base II on Blackcomb Mountain, at the end of Glacier Dr.

(See map & index p. 425.)

Fifty- to 60-minute scenic sleigh rides through Blackcomb's wooded countryside stop at a warming cabin for a cup of hot chocolate. Lunch, dinner and other sleigh ride options also are available. Carriage rides replace the sleigh rides in summer.

Hours: Tours depart every half-hour 4:30-7:30, early Nov.-Mar. 31 (weather permitting); by appointment rest of year. **Cost:** Fares $99; $49.50 (ages 3-12). Prices vary depending on tour. **Phone:** (604) 932-7631.

SQUAMISH LIL'WAT CULTURAL CENTRE is at 4584 Blackcomb Way, just s. of Whistler's Upper Village. Conceived as a joint venture between the Squamish and Lil'wat First Nations, this facility is a showcase meant to share and preserve the culture and heritage of these two peoples. The spectacular building, with its rounded contours, was constructed to resemble a traditional Squamish longhouse and a Lil'wat *istken* (an earthen dwelling with a fire pit). Whistler and Blackcomb mountains are on view from the outdoor deck.

Inside, the Great Hall has soaring 22-foot ceilings, cedar wood walls and beautiful polished stone floors inlaid with different patterns. Among the exhibits are two Squamish canoes, traditional clothing and regalia, wall weavings, textiles and baskets. Visitors can watch artists at work and learn how to make a craft. Make sure you see the 15-minute film "Where Rivers, Mountains and People Meet," which provides some fascinating historical and cultural context to what is on display.

Parking is available in Day Lot 4 adjacent to the center. **Time:** Allow 1 hour minimum. **Hours:** Daily 10-5; winter and holiday hours are subject to change. **Cost:** $18; $13.50 (senior citizens and students with ID); $8 (ages 6-12); $49 (family). **Phone:** (866) 441-7522. ⓣ

WHISTLER AIR SERVICES is 3 km (1.9 mi.) n. on Hwy. 99, following signs. The company offers 30-minute to 2-hour floatplane tours over glaciers, ice caps or alpine lakes. **Hours:** Trips depart daily Apr.-Nov. (weather permitting). **Cost:** $135-$265; half-price (ages 2-11 with two paying adults); free (ages

0-1 on parent's lap). Schedule and rates may vary; phone ahead. Reservations are required. **Phone:** (604) 932-6615 or (800) 806-0212.

WHISTLER MUSEUM is at 4333 Main St. behind the public library. Exhibits and videos about Whistler's natural and human history as well as the 2010 Winter Olympics document aspects of mountain life in the area. **Time:** Allow 1 hour minimum. **Hours:** Daily 11-5. Closed Jan. 1 and Christmas. **Cost:** $7; $5 (ages 65+ and students with ID); $4 (ages 7-18); $20 (family, up to six people). **Phone:** (604) 932-2019.

RECREATIONAL ACTIVITIES
Mountain Biking
- **Whistler Mountain Bike Park** is at the base of Whistler Mountain. Other activities are offered. **Hours:** Park opens daily at 10, mid-May to early Oct. Closing times vary; phone ahead. **Phone:** (604) 932-3434 or (866) 218-9690.

Skiing
- **Whistler/Blackcomb Mountain** is on Hwy. 99. Other activities are offered. **Hours:** Whistler daily mid-Nov. to mid-Apr. Blackcomb mid-Nov. to early June. **Phone:** (604) 932-3141 or (800) 766-0449.

White-water Rafting
- **Canadian Outback Adventures** departs from various locations in Whistler. Other activities are available. **Hours:** Tours daily 9-5, May-Sept. Shuttles depart at 7:30, 10:15 and 1. **Phone:** (604) 921-7250 or (800) 565-8735.
- **Wedge Rafting** departs from 4165 Springs Ln. at the base of the Whistler Mountain gondola in Whistler Village. Other activities are offered. **Hours:** Trips depart daily 8-8, mid-May through Labour Day. **Phone:** (604) 932-7171 or (888) 932-5899.

Ziplines
- **WildPlay Element Park Whistler** is at 4293 Mountain Square, Unit 218. Other activities are offered. **Hours:** Daily 9-5:30, June-Sept.; 10-4, rest of year. Phone ahead to confirm schedule. **Phone:** (604) 932-4086 or (888) 297-2222.
- **Ziptrek Ecotours** trips meet at the Carleton Lodge, 4340 Sundial Crescent, across from the gondola building. **Hours:** Departures several times daily, year-round. Reservations are recommended. **Phone:** (604) 935-0001 or (866) 935-0001.

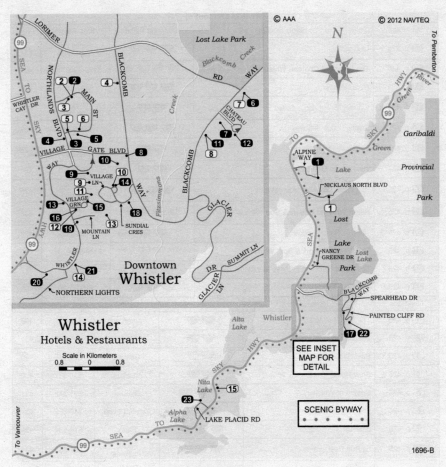

Whistler
Hotels & Restaurants

Scale in Kilometers

1696-B

Whistler

This index helps you "spot" where approved hotels and restaurants are located on the corresponding detailed maps. Hotel daily rate range is for comparison only. Restaurant price range is a combination of lunch and/or dinner. Turn to the listing page for more detailed rate and price information and consult display ads for special promotions.

WHISTLER

Map Page	Hotels	Diamond Rated	Rate Range	Page
1 this page	**Edgewater Lodge**	◈◈	$135-$339 SAVE	427
2 this page	Summit Lodge & Spa	◈◈◈	Rates not provided	428
3 this page	Whistler Pinnacle Hotel	◈◈	$129-$348	430
4 this page	Whistler Cascade Lodge	◈◈	$109-$533	430
5 this page	**Delta Whistler Village Suites**	◈◈◈	$109-$409 SAVE	427
6 this page	**Four Seasons Resort Whistler**	◈◈◈◈◈	$305-$920 SAVE	428
7 this page	Glacier Lodge	◈◈◈	$99-$1659	428
8 this page	Pan Pacific Whistler Village Centre	◈◈◈	Rates not provided	428
9 this page	**Blackcomb Lodge**	◈◈◈	$109-$503 SAVE	427
10 this page	Holiday Inn Whistler Village Centre	◈◈	$109-$469	428

WHISTLER (cont'd)

Map Page	Hotels (cont'd)	Diamond Rated	Rate Range	Page
11 p. 425	Le Chamois	▽▽▽	Rates not provided	428
12 p. 425	**The Fairmont Chateau Whistler** *(See ad p. 427.)*	▽▽▽▽	$179-$900 [SAVE]	427
13 p. 425	Aava Whistler	▽▽▽	$101-$450	426
14 p. 425	Whistler Village Inn + Suites	▽▽	Rates not provided	430
15 p. 425	Crystal Lodge & Suites	▽▽▽	$99-$339	427
16 p. 425	The Listel Hotel Whistler	▽▽	Rates not provided	428
17 p. 425	The Aspens On Blackcomb	▽▽	$109-$735	426
18 p. 425	Pan Pacific Whistler Mountainside	▽▽▽	Rates not provided	428
19 p. 425	**Hilton Whistler Resort & Spa** *(See ad p. 429.)*	▽▽▽▽	Rates not provided [SAVE]	428
20 p. 425	Tantalus Resort Lodge	▽▽	$139-$599	428
21 p. 425	**The Westin Resort & Spa, Whistler**	▽▽▽▽	$149-$949 [SAVE]	430
22 p. 425	The Coast Blackcomb Suites at Whistler	▽▽▽	$125-$799	427
23 p. 425	Nita Lake Lodge	▽▽▽	$150-$500	428

Map Page	Restaurants	Diamond Rated	Cuisine	Price Range	Page
1 p. 425	The Den Restaurant	▽▽	American	$12-$27	430
2 p. 425	Sachi Sushi	▽▽	Sushi	$6-$24	431
3 p. 425	**Bavaria Restaurant**	▽▽	German	$23-$45	430
4 p. 425	Brew House	▽▽	American	$16-$37	430
5 p. 425	Quattro at Whistler	▽▽▽	Italian	$21-$42	431
6 p. 425	The Flipside Restaurant	▽▽	Comfort Food	$12-$29	431
7 p. 425	Sidecut	▽▽▽	Steak	$14-$34	431
8 p. 425	La Rua Restaurante	▽▽▽	Pacific Northwest	$27-$35	431
9 p. 425	Araxi Restaurant & Bar	▽▽▽▽	Pacific Northwest	$29-$46	430
10 p. 425	21 Steps Kitchen & Bar	▽▽	Comfort Food	$9-$30	430
11 p. 425	LaBocca Restaurant & Bar	▽▽	American	$13-$38	431
12 p. 425	Bearfoot Bistro	▽▽▽	Pacific Northwest	$98-$148	430
13 p. 425	Sushi Village Japanese Cuisine	▽▽	Japanese	$6-$35	431
14 p. 425	The Aubergine Grille	▽▽▽	Pacific Northwest	$12-$32	430
15 p. 425	Rimrock Cafe	▽▽▽	Continental	$36-$53	431

AAVA WHISTLER   (604)932-2522 **13**
▽▽▽ **Hotel** $101-$450 **Address:** 4005 Whistler Way V0N 1B4
Location: Hwy 99, just e on Village Gate Blvd. **Facility:** 191 units,
some efficiencies. 4 stories, interior corridors. **Parking:** on-site (fee).
Terms: check-in 4 pm, 2-5 night minimum stay - seasonal and/or
weekends, 14 day cancellation notice, in winter-fee imposed. **Amenities:** high-speed internet, safes. **Pool(s):** heated outdoor. **Activities:**
sauna, whirlpool, exercise room. **Guest Services:** valet laundry, area
transportation-within Whistler Village.

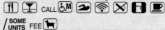

THE ASPENS ON BLACKCOMB   (604)932-7222 **17**
▽▽ **Vacation Rental Condominium** $109-$735 **Address:**
4800 Spearhead Dr V0N 1B4 **Location:** Hwy 99, 0.6 mi (1 km) e on
Lorimer Rd (Upper Village), just se on Blackcomb Way, then just w.
Facility: These self-contained condos geared for families or groups
of friends offer lots of space to move around. This is one of the rare
condo complexes to offers ski-in/ski-out access to Blackcomb Mountain. 77 condominiums. 4-5 stories, interior corridors. **Parking:** on-site
(fee). **Terms:** check-in 4 pm, 2-5 night minimum stay - seasonal, cancellation fee imposed, resort fee. **Amenities:** high-speed internet.
Pool(s): heated outdoor. **Activities:** sauna, whirlpools, exercise
room. **Guest Services:** coin laundry.

(See map & index p. 425.)

BLACKCOMB LODGE

(604)932-4155  **9**

Hotel
$109-$503

Address: 4220 Gateway Dr V0N 1B4 **Location:** Hwy 99, just e on Village Gate Blvd, then just s. **Facility:** 71 units, some efficiencies. 3 stories, interior corridors. **Parking:** on-site (fee). **Terms:** check-in 4 pm, 2-3 night minimum stay - seasonal, 30 day cancellation notice-fee imposed, resort fee. **Amenities:** safes. **Pool(s):** heated indoor. **Activities:** sauna, whirlpool. **Guest Services:** coin laundry. **Free Special Amenities:** early check-in/late check-out and high-speed Internet.

THE COAST BLACKCOMB SUITES AT WHISTLER

(604)905-3400 **22**

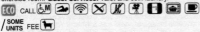 **Vacation Rental Condominium** $125-$799 **Address:** 4899 Painted Cliff Rd V0N 1B4 **Location:** Hwy 99, 0.6 mi (1 km) e on Lorimer Rd (Upper Village), just se on Blackcomb Way, then just w, follow road all the way to the end. **Facility:** Studio units and one- or two-bedroom units, each with a gas fireplace, occupy this facility on Blackcomb Mountain. 186 condominiums. 6 stories, interior corridors. **Parking:** on-site (fee). **Terms:** check-in 4 pm, 2-5 night minimum stay - seasonal and/or weekends, 60 day cancellation notice-fee imposed. **Pool(s):** heated outdoor. **Activities:** whirlpools, exercise room. **Guest Services:** valet and coin laundry.

CRYSTAL LODGE & SUITES

(604)932-2221 **15**

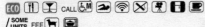 **Hotel** $99-$339 **Address:** 4154 Village Green V0N 1B4 **Location:** Hwy 99, just e on Village Gate Blvd, then follow road to Whistler Way. **Facility:** 158 units, some two bedrooms, three bedrooms, efficiencies and kitchens. 5 stories, interior corridors. **Parking:** on-site (fee). **Terms:** check-in 4 pm, 1-5 night minimum stay - seasonal and/or weekends, 30 day cancellation notice, in winter-fee imposed. **Amenities:** *Some:* high-speed Internet, safes. **Dining:** 2 restaurants, also, Ric's Grill, see separate listing. **Pool(s):** heated outdoor. **Activities:** sauna, whirlpool, exercise room. **Guest Services:** valet and coin laundry.

DELTA WHISTLER VILLAGE SUITES

(604)905-3987 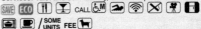 **5**

Extended Stay Hotel
$109-$409

Address: 4308 Main St V0N 1B4 **Location:** Hwy 99, just e on Village Gate Blvd, just n on Northlands Blvd, then just e. **Facility:** 205 units, some two bedrooms and kitchens. 6 stories, interior corridors. **Parking:** on-site (fee) and valet. **Terms:** check-in 4 pm, 30 day cancellation notice-fee imposed. **Amenities:** high-speed Internet. **Pool(s):** heated outdoor. **Activities:** sauna, whirlpools, exercise room, spa. **Guest Services:** valet and coin laundry, area transportation-ski area.

EDGEWATER LODGE

(604)932-0688 **1**

Hotel
$135-$339

Address: 8020 Alpine Way V0N 1B0 **Location:** 2.5 mi (4 km) n of Whistler Village via Hwy 99, then just e. **Facility:** 12 units. 1 story, exterior corridors. **Terms:** 14 day cancellation notice-fee imposed. **Activities:** whirlpool. **Free Special Amenities:** expanded continental breakfast and high-speed Internet.

THE FAIRMONT CHATEAU WHISTLER

(604)938-8000 **12**

Hotel
$179-$900

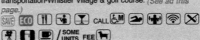

Address: 4599 Chateau Blvd V0N **Location:** Hwy 99, 0.6 mi (1 km) e on Lorimer Rd (Upper Village), just w on Blackcomb Way. **Facility:** Close to the Blackcomb chairlift, this inspiring château offers luxurious accommodations. The lobby lounge features a fireplace and plenty of seating. Downstairs are several high-end shops. 550 units, some two bedrooms. 12 stories, interior corridors. **Parking:** on-site (fee) and valet. **Terms:** check-in 4 pm, 3 day cancellation notice-fee imposed. **Amenities:** high-speed Internet (fee), safes. **Dining:** 4 restaurants. **Pool(s):** 2 heated outdoor. **Activities:** sauna, whirlpools, steamrooms, 3 tennis courts, spa. *Fee:* golf-18 holes. **Guest Services:** valet and coin laundry, area transportation-Whistler Village & golf course. *(See ad this page.)*

▼ See AAA listing this page ▼

(See map & index p. 425.)

FOUR SEASONS RESORT WHISTLER

(604)935-3400 **6**

Resort Hotel
$305-$920

Address: 4591 Blackcomb Way V0N 1B4 **Location:** Hwy 99, 0.6 mi (1 km) e on Lorimer Rd (Upper Village). **Facility:** This resort near Blackcomb Mountain offers warmly decorated guest rooms with wood accents, fireplaces and balconies with a view. 293 units, some two bedrooms, three bedrooms and kitchens. 6-9 stories, interior corridors. **Parking:** valet only. **Terms:** 30 day cancellation notice, in winter-fee imposed. **Amenities:** high-speed Internet, safes. **Dining:** Sidecut, see separate listing. **Pool(s):** heated outdoor. **Activities:** whirlpools, steamrooms, rental bicycles, jogging, spa. *Fee:* downhill skiing. **Guest Services:** valet laundry, area transportation-Whistler Village & golf course. **Free Special Amenities:** newspaper and high-speed Internet.

GLACIER LODGE

(604)905-0518 **7**

Boutique Hotel $99-$1659 **Address:** 4573 Chateau Blvd V0N 1B4 **Location:** Hwy 99, 0.6 mi (1 km) e on Lorimer Rd (Upper Village), then just w on Blackcomb Way. **Facility:** About half of the units are one bedrooms with kitchens, while the other half are standard hotel rooms with double beds and small kitchenettes. 77 units, some two bedrooms, three bedrooms, efficiencies and kitchens. 3 stories, interior corridors. **Parking:** on-site (fee). **Terms:** check-in 4 pm, 2-5 night minimum stay - seasonal and/or weekends, cancellation fee imposed, resort fee. **Pool(s):** heated outdoor. **Activities:** whirlpools, exercise room. **Guest Services:** coin laundry.

HILTON WHISTLER RESORT & SPA

604/932-1982 **19**

Hotel
Rates not provided

AAA Benefit: Members save 5% or more!

Address: 4050 Whistler Way V0N 1B4 **Location:** Hwy 99, just e on Village Gate Blvd, then follow Whistler Way. **Facility:** Boasting some of the largest hotel rooms in Whistler, Hilton Whistler's newly renovated facilities offer a pleasant, alpine-style ambiance. Each unit features a private balcony, an ideal spot to lounge. Skiers will appreciate the property's close proximity to the chair lifts at Whistler Mountain, which are within easy walking distance. 287 units, some two bedrooms, efficiencies and kitchens. 5-8 stories, interior corridors. **Parking:** on-site (fee) and valet. **Terms:** check-in 4 pm. **Amenities:** high-speed Internet, safes. **Pool(s):** heated outdoor. **Activities:** sauna, whirlpools, exercise room, spa. **Guest Services:** valet and coin laundry, area transportation-Whistler Village & golf courses. *(See ad p. 429.)*

HOLIDAY INN WHISTLER VILLAGE CENTRE

(604)938-0878 **10**

Hotel $109-$469 **Address:** 4295 Blackcomb Way V0N 1B4 **Location:** Hwy 99, just e on Village Gate Blvd. **Facility:** 115 units, some two bedrooms, efficiencies and kitchens. 6 stories, interior corridors. **Parking:** on-site (fee). **Terms:** check-in 4 pm, cancellation fee imposed. **Amenities:** high-speed Internet. **Activities:** whirlpool, exercise room. **Guest Services:** valet laundry.

LE CHAMOIS

604/932-4113 **11**

Hotel. Rates not provided. **Address:** 4557 Blackcomb Way V0N 1B4 **Location:** Hwy 99, 0.6 mi (1 km) e on Lorimer Rd (Upper Village), then just w. **Facility:** 41 units, some kitchens. 6 stories, interior corridors. **Terms:** check-in 4 pm. **Amenities:** high-speed Internet. **Dining:** 3 restaurants, also, La Rua Restaurante, see separate listing. **Pool(s):** heated outdoor. **Activities:** whirlpool, limited exercise equipment. **Guest Services:** coin laundry.

THE LISTEL HOTEL WHISTLER

604/932-1133 **16**

Hotel. Rates not provided. **Address:** 4121 Village Green V0N 1B4 **Location:** Hwy 99, just e on Village Gate Blvd, then follow Whistler Way. **Facility:** 98 units. 3 stories, interior corridors. **Parking:** on-site (fee). **Terms:** check-in 4 pm. **Amenities:** safes. **Dining:** Bearfoot Bistro, see separate listing. **Activities:** saunas, whirlpool. **Guest Services:** valet and coin laundry.

NITA LAKE LODGE

(604)966-5700 **23**

Hotel $150-$500 **Address:** 2131 Lake Placid Rd V0N 1B2 **Location:** 1.8 mi (3 km) s on Hwy 99, just w. **Facility:** 77 units, some two bedrooms. 4 stories, interior corridors. **Parking:** on-site (fee) and valet. **Terms:** check-in 4 pm, 2 night minimum stay - weekends, cancellation fee imposed. **Amenities:** high-speed Internet. **Dining:** 2 restaurants. **Pool(s):** heated outdoor. **Activities:** whirlpools, bicycles, exercise room, spa. **Guest Services:** valet and coin laundry, area transportation-ski area & Whistler Village.

PAN PACIFIC WHISTLER MOUNTAINSIDE

604/905-2999 **18**

Extended Stay Contemporary Hotel. Rates not provided. **Address:** 4320 Sundial Crescent V0N 1B4 **Location:** Hwy 99, just e on Village Gate Blvd, then just s on Blackcomb Way. **Facility:** 121 kitchen units, some two bedrooms. 8 stories, interior corridors. **Parking:** on-site (fee) and valet. **Amenities:** safes. **Pool(s):** heated outdoor. **Activities:** whirlpools, steamroom, exercise room. **Guest Services:** valet and coin laundry, area transportation-within Whistler Village.

PAN PACIFIC WHISTLER VILLAGE CENTRE

604/966-5500 **8**

Extended Stay Contemporary Hotel. Rates not provided. **Address:** 4299 Blackcomb Way V0N 1B4 **Location:** Hwy 99, just e on Village Gate Blvd. **Facility:** 83 units, some two bedrooms, three bedrooms, efficiencies and kitchens. 8 stories, interior corridors. **Parking:** on-site (fee) and valet. **Amenities:** safes. **Pool(s):** heated outdoor. **Activities:** sauna, whirlpools, exercise room, spa. **Guest Services:** valet and coin laundry, area transportation-within Whistler Village.

SUMMIT LODGE & SPA

604/932-2778 **2**

Hotel. Rates not provided. **Address:** 4359 Main St V0N 1B4 **Location:** Hwy 99, just n on Village Gate Blvd, then just w on Northlands Blvd. **Facility:** 81 efficiencies. 5 stories, interior corridors. **Parking:** on-site (fee). **Terms:** check-in 4 pm. **Amenities:** high-speed Internet. **Dining:** Sachi Sushi, see separate listing. **Pool(s):** heated outdoor. **Activities:** sauna, whirlpool, spa. **Guest Services:** valet and coin laundry.

TANTALUS RESORT LODGE

(604)932-4146 **20**

Condominium $139-$599 **Address:** 4200 Whistler Way V0N 1B4 **Location:** Hwy 99, just e on Village Gate Blvd, then follow Whistler Way to the end. **Facility:** 64 condominiums. 5 stories, interior corridors. **Parking:** on-site (fee). **Terms:** check-in 4 pm, cancellation fee imposed. **Amenities:** safes. **Pool(s):** heated outdoor. **Activities:** sauna, whirlpools, 2 tennis courts, playground, volleyball. **Guest Services:** coin laundry, area transportation-ski area.

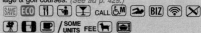

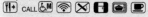

▼ See AAA listing p. 428 ▼

(See map & index p. 425.)

THE WESTIN RESORT & SPA, WHISTLER
(604)905-5000 **21**

WESTIN HOTELS & RESORTS
Hotel
$149-$949

AAA Benefit: Enjoy up to 20% off your next stay, plus Starwood Preferred Guest® bonuses.

Address: 4090 Whistler Way V0N 1B4 **Location:** Hwy 99, just e on Village Gate Blvd, then s. **Facility:** The upscale lodging comprises shops, conference facilities, a spa and health club as well as ski-in, ski-out convenience to Whistler Mountain. 400 units, some two bedrooms, efficiencies and kitchens. 11 stories, interior corridors. **Parking:** on-site (fee) and valet. **Terms:** check-in 4 pm, 21 day cancellation notice-fee imposed. **Amenities:** safes. *Fee:* video games, high-speed Internet. **Dining:** The Aubergine Grille, see separate listing. **Pool(s):** heated outdoor. **Activities:** sauna, whirlpools, steamrooms, spa. **Guest Services:** valet and coin laundry, area transportation-within Whistler Village.

[SAVE] [ECO] [icons] CALL [&M] [icons] [BIZ] [wifi] [X] [icons] / SOME UNITS [icons]

WHISTLER CASCADE LODGE
(604)905-4875 **4**

Vacation Rental Condominium $109-$533 **Address:** 4315 Northlands Blvd V0N 1B4 **Location:** Hwy 99, just e on Village Gate Blvd, then just n. **Facility:** Select from standard-style hotel rooms with a small kitchenette or a one-bedroom condo unit with a full kitchen and large living room area. 112 units, some two bedrooms, efficiencies, kitchens and condominiums. 6 stories, interior corridors. **Parking:** on-site (fee). **Terms:** check-in 4 pm, 2-5 night minimum stay - seasonal, cancellation fee imposed, resort fee. **Pool(s):** heated outdoor. **Activities:** saunas, whirlpools, limited exercise equipment. **Guest Services:** coin laundry.

[icons] [icons] [wifi] [X] [icons] [icons] [icons]

WHISTLER PINNACLE HOTEL
(604)938-3218 **3**

Extended Stay Hotel $129-$348 **Address:** 4319 Main St V0N 1B4 **Location:** Hwy 99, just e on Village Gate Blvd, just n on Northlands Blvd, then just s. **Facility:** 84 efficiencies. 4 stories, interior corridors. **Parking:** on-site (fee). **Terms:** check-in 4 pm, 2 night minimum stay - seasonal, 30 day cancellation notice, 11/1-4/30-fee imposed. **Amenities:** high-speed Internet. **Pool(s):** heated outdoor. **Activities:** whirlpool. **Guest Services:** coin laundry.

[icons] CALL [&M] [icons] [wifi] [X] [icons] [icons] [icons] / SOME UNITS FEE [icons]

WHISTLER VILLAGE INN + SUITES
604/932-4004 **14**

Hotel. Rates not provided. **Address:** 4429 Sundial Pl V0N 1B4 **Location:** Hwy 99, just e on Village Gate Blvd, then just s on Blackcomb Way to Sundial Pl. **Facility:** 87 units, some efficiencies. 3 stories, interior corridors. **Parking:** on-site (fee). **Terms:** check-in 4 pm. **Pool(s):** heated outdoor. **Activities:** saunas, whirlpools, exercise room. **Guest Services:** valet and coin laundry.

[icons] CALL [&M] [icons] [wifi] [X] [icons] / SOME UNITS [icons] [icons]

WHERE TO EAT

21 STEPS KITCHEN & BAR
604/966-2121 **10**

Comfort Food. Casual Dining. $9-$30 **AAA Inspector Notes:** Grab a table by the window and watch the people strolling around the village at this restaurant located 21 steps upstairs of St. Andrew's House in the heart of Whistler Village. The restaurant serves salads, soups, small plates, big plates that can be shared and course desserts. There is no on-site parking, so look for a space in one of Whistler's day lots. **Bar:** full bar. **Reservations:** suggested. **Address:** 4433 Sundial Pl, RR 4 V0N 1B4 **Location:** Hwy 99, just e on Village Gate Blvd, then just s on Blackcomb Way. **Parking:** no self-parking. [D] [LATE] CALL [&M]

ARAXI RESTAURANT & BAR
604/932-4540 **9**

Pacific Northwest. Fine Dining. $29-$46 **AAA Inspector Notes:** Outstanding! That's what comes to mind as Araxi features the freshest ingredients from B.C., Alberta, Quebec and the Maritimes using the best produce from each province and season. During the summer months enjoy their open air patio. Araxi was recognized for the winning chef on season 6 of Gordon Ramsay's Hell's Kitchen. The event was filmed during the Winter Olympic Games with the winner working alongside the executive chef. **Bar:** full bar. **Reservations:** suggested. **Address:** 4222 Village Square V0N 1B4 **Location:** In Whistler Village Square by the Blackcomb Lodge. **Parking:** on-site (fee). [D] CALL [&M]

THE AUBERGINE GRILLE
604/905-5000 **14**

Pacific Northwest. Fine Dining. $12-$32 **AAA Inspector Notes:** French for "eggplant," Aubergine features a show kitchen where guests can watch chefs assemble breakfast and dinner selections. The eclectic menu centers on West Coast seafood, including British Columbia salmon, but it also lists such comfort foods as steak, pizza and pasta. **Bar:** full bar. **Reservations:** suggested, for dinner & in winter. **Address:** 4090 Whistler Way V0N 1B4 **Location:** Hwy 99, just e on Village Gate Blvd, then s; in The Westin Resort & Spa, Whistler. **Parking:** on-site (fee) and valet. [B] [D] CALL [&M]

BAVARIA RESTAURANT
604/932-7518 **3**

German Casual Dining $23-$45

AAA Inspector Notes: Enjoy true German cuisine, like pork or veal schnitzel and fondue, with German beers and schnapps. Try their three-course dinner, which includes an appetizer, choice of schnitzel and dessert. Metered street parking in effect at all times. **Bar:** full bar. **Reservations:** suggested. **Address:** 101-4369 Main St V0N 1B4 **Location:** Hwy 99, just n on Village Gate Blvd, then just w on Northland Blvd; in Alpenglow Lodge. **Parking:** street only. [D] CALL [&M]

BEARFOOT BISTRO
604/932-3433 **12**

Pacific Northwest. Fine Dining. $98-$148 **AAA Inspector Notes:** The bistro features what is reputed to be the city's largest wine cellar, with more than 20,000 bottles. The dining room's strictly table d'hote menu lists a three-course meal at $39 (in summer) and $98 (in winter) and a five-course meal at $95 (in summer) and $148 (in winter). Those not inclined to eat in the dining room can visit the wine bar, where meals often are served with by-the-glass wines. **Bar:** full bar. **Reservations:** suggested. **Address:** 4121 Village Green V0N 1B4 **Location:** Hwy 99, just e on Village Gate Blvd, then follow Whistler Way; in The Listel Hotel Whistler. **Parking:** valet only. [D] CALL [&M]

BREW HOUSE
604/905-2739 **4**

American. Casual Dining. $16-$37 **AAA Inspector Notes:** This brewpub brews beer solely for consumption on the premises. Four flagship brews are always available to be enjoyed with a menu of pizza, pasta and rotisserie options. **Bar:** full bar. **Reservations:** suggested. **Address:** 4355 Blackcomb Way V0N 1B4 **Location:** Hwy 99, 0.6 mi (1 km) e on Lorimer Rd (Upper Village), then just w. **Parking:** on-site (fee). [L] [D] [LATE] CALL [&M]

THE DEN RESTAURANT
604/938-9898 **1**

American. Casual Dining. $12-$27 **AAA Inspector Notes:** This pub-like restaurant overlooks the golf course and nearby lake and is open for breakfast, lunch and dinner from early May through early October. It's dinner only in winter. There are tapas, burgers and sandwiches at lunch and more sophisticated fare for dinner, like Alberta beef and great seafood. Many microbrews are on tap. **Bar:** full bar. **Reservations:** suggested. **Address:** 8080 Nicklaus North Blvd V0N 1B8 **Location:** Hwy 99, 2 mi (3.5 km) n of Whistler Village, just e; in The Nicklaus North Golf Course Clubhouse. [D] CALL [&M]

EARLS RESTAURANT
604/935-3222

American. Casual Dining. $14-$38 **AAA Inspector Notes:** Offering an experience that falls between fast food and fine dining, the fun, relaxed restaurant prepares great food at a great price. Choices range from juicy burgers, hearty salads, fresh salads, wings and pizza to full entrees of steak, chops and seafood. Made-from-scratch soups and assorted breads, as well as a nice choice of wines and beers, round out the offerings. This is a fitting spot for impromptu get-togethers and festive occasions. **Bar:** full bar. **Address:** 4295 Blackcomb Way, Unit 220 V0N 1B4 **Location:** Hwy 99, just e on Village Gate Blvd, then just s. **Parking:** street only. [L] [D] [LATE] CALL [&M]

(See map & index p. 425.)

THE FLIPSIDE RESTAURANT   604/962-0030   **6**

▼▼ Comfort Food. Casual Dining. $12-$29 **AAA Inspector Notes:** Located along the village stroll, the restaurant is open late, which attracts locals who are just completing their evening night shifts. It's known for its chicken wings prepared four ways, hot, BBQ, Cajun or salt 'n' peppa, but you also can try the fresh calamari and B.C. mussels brought in from Salt Spring Island. Every main course comes with a Caesar or house salad plus a fresh baked baguette. Bring the kids because they're welcome, too. **Bar:** full bar. **Address:** 40 4314 Main St V0N 1B4 **Location:** Just n of Village Gate Blvd; in Whistler Village North. **Parking:** street only. D LATE CALL &M

LABOCCA RESTAURANT & BAR   604/932-2112   **11**

▼▼ American. Casual Dining. $13-$38 **AAA Inspector Notes:** This restaurant in the heart of Whistler Village is busy and popular with both the young and mature. The menu features fondue, rack of lamb, pizza, pasta and wok cooking, a real mix of items to suit almost every taste. The huge outdoor patio is open during the summer and great for people-watching. Simple fare with a range of sandwiches and burgers is served at lunch, while more formal fare is available at dinnertime. **Bar:** full bar. **Reservations:** suggested. **Address:** 4232 Village Stroll V0N 1B0 **Location:** In Whistler Village Square. **Parking:** no self-parking. B L D CALL &M ✗

LA RUA RESTAURANTE   604/932-5011   **8**

▼▼▼ Pacific Northwest. Fine Dining. $27-$35 **AAA Inspector Notes:** In the Upper Village, the long established restaurant affords wonderful views of Blackcomb Mountain and is known for its wild game and fish, warm and inviting atmosphere and great service. Complimentary parking is available in Le Chamois. **Bar:** full bar. **Reservations:** suggested. **Address:** 4557 Blackcomb Way V0N 1B0 **Location:** Hwy 99, 0.6 mi (1 km) e on Lorimer Rd (Upper Village), then just w; in Le Chamois. D CALL &M

QUATTRO AT WHISTLER   604/905-4844   **5**

▼▼▼ Italian. Fine Dining. $21-$42 **AAA Inspector Notes:** Next to Pinnacle International Resort, the restaurant offers a cozy atmosphere and an extensive wine list that represents several regions and includes some reasonably priced selections. Besides pasta, adventurous diners might try Cornish game hen, which is deboned and cooked on a panini grill; rack of lamb; pan-seared beef tenderloin; or baked salmon wrapped in phyllo pastry. The pazza a pezzi is a combination of five pastas. **Bar:** full bar. **Reservations:** suggested. **Address:** 4319 Main St V0N 1B4 **Location:** Hwy 99, just e on Village Gate Blvd, then just n on Northlands Blvd; in Whistler Pinnacle Hotel. **Parking:** street only. D CALL &M

Plan complete trip routings with
the TripTik® Travel Planner on
AAA.com/CAA.ca

RIC'S GRILL   604/932-7427

▼▼ Steak Seafood. Casual Dining. $16-$40 **AAA Inspector Notes:** "Funky and modern" describes the decor and the food at the upscale steakhouse, which bustles with activity. Steaks are well worth it, but then again, so are the salmon, chicken and pasta dishes. A wide variety of distinctive appetizers rounds out the menu. Servers are friendly and attentive. **Bar:** full bar. **Reservations:** suggested. **Address:** 4154 Village Green V0N 1B4 **Location:** Hwy 99, just e on Village Gate Blvd, then follow road to Whistler Way; in Crystal Lodge & Suites. **Parking:** street only. D CALL &M

RIMROCK CAFE   604/932-5565   **15**

▼▼▼ Continental. Fine Dining. $36-$53 **AAA Inspector Notes:** The hidden gem may be hard to find, but the locals know and love this place. Open for dinner with the last seating at 9:30 pm, the restaurant serves many seafood choices, including swordfish, salmon and halibut, in addition to an interesting selection of such wild game as buffalo and grilled caribou. Reservations are a must; it's that popular. **Bar:** full bar. **Reservations:** suggested. **Address:** 2117 Whistler Rd V0N 1B0 **Location:** From Whistler Village; Village Gate Blvd, 2.1 mi (3.5 km) s on Hwy 99, just e; in The Highland Lodge. D ✗

SACHI SUSHI   604/935-5649   **2**

▼▼ Sushi. Casual Dining. $6-$24 **AAA Inspector Notes:** Located at the Summit Lodge, this cozy Japanese restaurant aims to please sushi lovers with exceptionally fresh selections. Open for lunch Wednesday through Friday; dinner served nightly. You'll find metered parking along the street. **Bar:** full bar. **Address:** 106-4359 Main St V0N 1B4 **Location:** Hwy 99, just n on Village Gate Blvd, then just w on Northlands Blvd; in Summit Lodge & Spa. **Parking:** street only. D

SIDECUT   604/966-5280   **7**

▼▼▼ Steak Seafood. Fine Dining. $14-$34 **AAA Inspector Notes:** This steakhouse welcomes guests for breakfast, lunch and dinner. Excellent meats, poultry and fish are served a la carte with a selected rub and accompanied by six dipping sauces. The wine list includes some of the best selections that British Columbia has to offer. In keeping with Four Seasons tradition, guests are asked to consider stylish, casual resort wear for evening dining. **Bar:** full bar. **Reservations:** suggested. **Address:** 4591 Blackcomb Way V0N 1B4 **Location:** Hwy 99, 0.6 mi (1 km) e on Lorimer Rd (Upper Village); in Four Seasons Resort Whistler. **Parking:** valet only. B L D CALL &M

SUSHI VILLAGE JAPANESE CUISINE   604/932-3330   **13**

▼▼ Japanese. Casual Dining. $6-$35 **AAA Inspector Notes:** Opposite the Blackcomb gondola, this restaurant specializes in fresh, tasty sushi and sashimi. They also have tatami rooms for small or large groups. The relaxed and friendly place was among the original six restaurants in Whistler. Green salad, steamed rice, steamed vegetables and ice cream are offered. It's open for lunch on weekends. **Bar:** full bar. **Reservations:** suggested. **Address:** 4272 Mountain Square V0N 1B4 **Location:** Hwy 99, just e on Village Gate Blvd, then just s on Blackcomb Way; in Sundial Boutique Hotel. **Parking:** street only. D CALL &M

WHITE ROCK pop. 19,339
- Hotels & Restaurants map & index p. 368
- Part of Vancouver area — see map p. 343

OCEAN PROMENADE HOTEL   604/542-0102 **84**
▼▼▼▼ **Hotel.** Rates not provided. **Address:** 15611 Marine Dr V4B 1E1 **Location:** Hwy 99 exit 2B southbound; exit 2 (White Rock/8th Ave) northbound, 1.3 mi (2 km) w. **Facility:** 51 units, some kitchens. 3 stories, interior/exterior corridors. **Terms:** check-in 4 pm. **Amenities:** high-speed Internet, safes. **Activities:** limited exercise equipment. **Guest Services:** valet and coin laundry. *(See ad this page.)*

[!↕] CALL [&M] [📶] [✕] [▣] / SOME UNITS FEE [🐕] [🛏] [🖥]

▼ See AAA listing this page ▼

Contact us about AAA/CAA Approved properties at AAA.com/TourBookComments

GIRAFFE   604/538-6878 **59**
▼▼▼▼ Pacific Rim. Fine Dining. $12-$28 **AAA Inspector Notes:** All tables at the lovely, intimate restaurant face the water. Giraffe-centric decor, including the noteworthy napkin holders, suits this place's name. Daily specials, which are printed on a blackboard at the entrance, are can't-miss choices. The dining room's small size accounts for tight table spacing. Pay parking is in effect at all times. **Bar:** full bar. **Reservations:** suggested. **Address:** 15053 Marine Dr V4B 1C5 **Location:** Hwy 99 exit 2B southbound; exit 2 northbound, 1.8 mi (3 km) w. **Parking:** street only. [D]

LA BAIA ITALIAN RESTAURANT   604/531-6261 **60**
▼▼ Italian. Casual Dining. $14-$27 **AAA Inspector Notes:** Delicious rack of lamb and veal Marsala are among choices at the bright and airy restaurant, which displays antiques and offers a nice view of the park. The atmosphere is cozy, and service is friendly and attentive. Those who can't nab a free parking spot at the back can pay to park on the street. **Bar:** full bar. **Reservations:** suggested. **Address:** 15791 Marine Dr V4B 1E5 **Location:** Hwy 99 exit 2B southbound; exit 2 northbound, 0.9 mi (1.5 km) w. [D] [✕]

WILLIAMS LAKE (G-5) pop. 10,832

The rush for gold brought prospectors to the heart of the Cariboo in the 1860s, but it was the 1920s Canadian Railway push that put Williams Lake on the map. Cattle ranching and timber production now are the economic mainstays. Twenty kilometres (12 mi.) north of Williams Lake, Bull Mountain Trails offers 30 kilometres (19 mi.) of trails for cross-country skiing, hiking and mountain biking.

Williams Lake and District Chamber of Commerce: 1660 S. Broadway, Williams Lake, BC, Canada V2G 2W4. **Phone:** (250) 392-5025 or (877) 967-5253.

MUSEUM OF THE CARIBOO CHILCOTIN is at 113 N. Fourth Ave. Highlights include the BC Cowboys Hall of Fame and displays portraying the ranching and rodeo history of the Cariboo Chilcotin region. Artifacts and photographs depict the lifestyles of cowboys and ranchers as well as First Nations peoples. **Time:** Allow 30 minutes minimum. **Hours:** Mon.-Sat. 10-4, June-Sept.; Tues.-Sat. 11-4, rest of year. Closed Jan. 1, Good Friday and Dec. 25. **Cost:** $2; free (ages 0-12). **Phone:** (250) 392-7404.

SCOUT ISLAND NATURE CENTER is off Hwy. 97 just e. of jct. Hwy. 20, s. on McKenzie Ave., then e. on Borland Rd. Nature trails lead to views of Williams Lake. The island and marsh are prime nesting grounds for migratory birds. A nature house offers interactive displays, a marsh aquarium and a beehive. A viewing platform on the roof provides a vista of the marsh and valley. Walking trails, interpretive signs and an arboretum are on-site.

Hours: Grounds daily dawn-dusk. Nature house Sat.-Sun. 1-4, May-Oct. Phone ahead to confirm schedule; the center may close for school classes. **Cost:** Donations. **Phone:** (250) 398-8532.

DRUMMOND LODGE MOTEL   250/392-5334
▼ Motel $82-$145 **Address:** 1405 Cariboo Hwy V2G 2W3 **Location:** 0.6 mi (1 km) s on Hwy 97. **Facility:** 24 units, some efficiencies and kitchens. 1-2 stories (no elevator), exterior corridors. **Parking:** winter plug-ins. **Terms:** cancellation fee imposed. **Amenities:** *Some:* high-speed Internet. **Guest Services:** coin laundry.
[!↕] [📶] [🛏] [▣] / SOME UNITS FEE [🐕]

WILLIAMS LAKE SUPER 8 (250)398-8884

Motel
$100-$107

Address: 1712 Broadway Ave S V2G 2W4 **Location:** 1.2 mi (2 km) s on Hwy 97. **Facility:** 53 units. 3 stories (no elevator), interior corridors. **Parking:** winter plug-ins. **Amenities:** high-speed Internet. **Guest Services:** coin laundry. **Free Special Amenities: continental breakfast and high-speed Internet.**

WINDERMERE pop. 1,019

WINDERMERE CREEK BED AND BREAKFAST CABINS
(250)342-0356

Cabin $109-$159 **Address:** 1658 Windermere Loop Rd V0B 2L2 **Location:** Hwy 93/95 (south end of town), 0.6 mi (1 km) e on Kootenay 3 Rd, keep left at fork for 1.3 mi (2.2 km). Located in a quiet area. **Facility:** In a mountain valley, the property offers four modern cabins with kitchenettes as well as one rustic yet well-appointed 1887 cabin. 5 cabins, some efficiencies. 1 story, exterior corridors. **Parking:** winter plug-ins. **Terms:** 30 day cancellation notice-fee imposed. **Activities:** cross country skiing, hiking trails.

YALE (C-7) pop. 136

Settled at the southern entrance to Fraser Canyon, Yale was a major steamship port during the gold rush. The town was established in 1848 as a Hudson's Bay Co. fort, taking its name from the commander of Fort Langley. After gold was discovered on Hill's Bar in 1858, Yale's population swelled to 30,000. In later years the number dwindled to 200. Several buildings from the mid-1800s still stand, and a pioneer cemetery contains Victorian monuments to early settlers.

The Alexandra Suspension Bridge, 22 kilometres (14 mi.) north of town, was constructed in 1863 to ferry miners across the Fraser River. From the bridge, which was rebuilt in 1926 with the original foundations, the original wagon road to the Cariboo goldfields is visible. A hiking trail leading to the nearby Spirit Caves offers views of the canyon.

YALE HISTORIC SITE is at 31187 Douglas St. The museum displays artifacts about mining, paddlewheelers, the Canadian Pacific Railway, early settlers and native peoples. The Church of St. John the Divine has served the area since it was built in 1863. Guided walking tours of the old townsite are offered in the summer. Gold panning instructions and trips also are available.

Hours: Daily 10-5, July 1-Labour Day; Thurs.-Mon. 10-5, May-June and day after Labour Day to mid-Oct. Closed Labour Day. Phone ahead to confirm schedule. **Cost:** Museum $6; free (ages 0-5). **Phone:** (604) 863-2324.

RECREATIONAL ACTIVITIES
White-water Rafting
• **Fraser River Raft Expeditions** is 1 km (.6 mi.) w. on Hwy. 1. **Hours:** Daily mid-May to late Sept. Departure times vary with trip. **Phone:** (604) 863-2336 or (800) 363-7238.

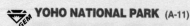

▽ YOHO NATIONAL PARK (A-11)

Elevations in the park range from 1,090 metres (3,576 ft.) at the west boundary to 3,562 metres (11,686 ft.) at the top of Mount Goodsir at the South Tower. Refer to CAA/AAA maps for additional elevation information.

Reached by hwys. 1 and 93, Yoho National Park covers 1,310 square kilometres (507 sq. mi.) and is west of the Great Divide and Banff National Park. In the Cree language, *yoho* is an exclamation of wonder appropriate to the park's spectacular rock walls and towering waterfalls.

At the centre of the park's history is Canada's first trans-continental railway. Following the route originally discovered by Sir James Hector, the Canadian Pacific Railway laid tracks through Kicking Horse Pass in 1884. The park was established two years later as a tourist destination for passengers on the newly completed rail line. In 1962, the Trans-Canada Highway opened along this same route.

Takakkaw Falls ("magnificent" in Cree) drops 380 metres (1,265 ft.) in all. Its highest sheer fall is 254 metres (833 ft.), making it one of the highest waterfalls in Canad and a visible landmark along the well-known Iceline trail.

Other highlights in the park include Natural Bridge, Emerald Lake, Wapta Falls and the Canadian Pacific Railway's Spiral Tunnels. Twisting their way under Mount Ogden and Cathedral Mountain, trains can be seen entering and exiting the Spiral Tunnels from the viewpoints on the Yoho Valley Road and the Trans-Canada Highway, 8 kilometres (5 mi.) east of Field.

Nestled high in the mountains are the famous Burgess Shale fossil beds. Discovered in 1909, these exquisitely preserved 505 million-year-old soft-bodied fossils draw visitors to Yoho National Park each year. The park's visitor centre, located in Field, hosts an interactive exhibit and display of some of the many fossils found in the park.

General Information and Activities

The park is open all year. In winter it is popular with ice climbers, and cross-country and back-country skiers as well as hikers and backpackers in other seasons. During the summer months, canoes and rowboats are available for rent at Emerald Lake.

The park's visitor centre, located on Hwy. 1 in Field, is open Apr. 1-Sept. 29; phone (250) 343-6783 for schedule. The adjoining washrooms are open year-round.

The Trans-Canada Highway traverses the park and provides access to most attractions. The 13-kilometre (7.8-mi.) Yoho Valley Road leading to Takakkaw Falls is open mid-June through September as weather permits.

Access to the Burgess Shale fossil beds is restricted to guided tours during July and August; fees range from $35-$70. Two hikes are available: Walcott Quarry, at 22 kilometres (14 mi.), and the Mount Stephen Fossil Beds, at 9 kilometres (6 mi.). Reservations are required; phone (800) 759-2429.

Yoho has five frontcountry campgrounds with site prices ranging from $15.70-$27.40 per night. Firewood and permits are an additional $8.80. Visitors venturing into the backcountry require a wilderness pass to stay overnight; passes are available from the visitor centre for $9.80 per person per night.

Fishing, particularly rewarding to those in search of char and many other varieties of trout, requires a $34.30 annual permit or a $9.80 1-day permit from the visitor centre. Anglers are allowed to fish in most lakes and rivers in the park. *See Recreation Areas Chart.*

ADMISSION to the park is $9.80; $8.30 (ages 65+); $4.90 (ages 6-16); $19.60 (all occupants of a private vehicle with up to seven people). **Cards:** AX, MC, VI.

PETS are permitted in the park provided they are on a leash at all times.

ADDRESS inquiries to the Superintendent, Yoho National Park, P.O. Box 99, Field, BC, Canada V0A 1G0; phone (250) 343-6783.

Winnipeg skyline

Manitoba

Waves pound a rock-strewn shore at the narrows of Lake Manitoba, producing a noise oddly like a beating drum. To the Cree Indians, this sound was the great spirit Manitou, whose name was given to the lake and, in 1870, the entire province.

From clear water lapping in giant lakes—Winnipeg, Winnipegosis and Manitoba—to the rustling sigh of wind across golden seas of wheat, the great spirit of this province speaks with many voices and conveys many moods.

It echoes in the plaintive cry of migrating geese winging south and the hoarse chuffing of a protective mother polar bear herding her cubs along Hudson Bay's icy shore.

The spirit sings within a chorus of steel wheels as trains carry freight across the prairies. It proclaims itself in the bustling streets of Winnipeg, where sundry languages—French, English, Ukrainian, Chinese and others—blend into a rich,

Wheat harvest

evocative murmur, and laughs amid the joyous din of the city's various celebrations.

Gem of the Prairies

Look north into the night sky. There. See it? A faint glow high above the horizon....

Watch as an arc of yellow light gradually forms. As it drifts upward, shimmering yellow-green streamers rise from it, rippling like a breeze-blown curtain. New arcs appear lined with bright amber streaks that curl like wisps of smoke. Eventually the swirls of color fade and darkness returns, ending your encounter with the aurora borealis.

In Manitoba you won't have to wait long for a repeat performance. This far north you can count on basking in the aurora's eerie luminescence nearly 90 nights a year. Even citizens of Winnipeg, the capital, are often treated to this celestial light show, despite living in the province's extreme south.

Sky-obscuring pollution may be the bane of many cities, but Winnipeg's clean air isn't likely to spoil your auroral view. And while multihued lights dance overhead, visitors to the "Gem of the Prairies" can enjoy an equally colorful cultural spectrum spread out before them. Home to more than half of all Manitobans, Winnipeg is a city of surprising diversity. It's not unusual to find a German butcher shop sandwiched between an Italian clothing store and a Vietnamese restaurant, all within a few steps of a Portuguese café.

In the 18th century, when conflicts escalated between French voyageurs and their

English rivals, Fort Rouge—site of modern Winnipeg—was established where the Red and Assiniboine rivers meet. Now known as The Forks, this riverfront park is where you can take a tree-shaded stroll past splashing fountains and vibrantly hued flower beds.

The Great White North

Follow your compass farther north and the chances of seeing Mother Nature's silent fireworks multiply. The northern lights not only occur more frequently in Manitoba's subarctic areas, but are brighter, too.

But the real stars in this small community are its big, furry neighbors: polar bears. Sightings of the great white animals are common in October, when they migrate onto freezing Hudson Bay to fish, and late June, when thawing ice forces a return to shore.

The best way to meet these deceptively cuddly looking carnivores is safely ensconced in a specially designed, balloon-tired tundra vehicle. Climb aboard one for an unforgettable in-the-wild encounter. And when you're ready to thaw out, visit Churchill's Eskimo Museum, which is filled with ancient Inuit tools and other artifacts.

Well-acquainted with the aurora's haunting glow, the Inuits crafted stories as elaborate as their carvings to explain what they saw. According to one tale, the lights are torches lit by spirits to guide those who will follow across the narrow bridge to heaven.

But you don't have to study Inuit mythology to appreciate the northern lights' otherworldly beauty; all you really need to know is that the skies are perfect for admiring them.

Recreation

The overwhelming bulk of Manitoba's populace resides in a thin strip just above the U.S. border, which leaves a vast region of unspoiled territory farther north that's prime for exploration.

Colorful sails glide across the surface of Lake Winnipeg as windsurfing enthusiasts take advantage of breezy days. Put in at Grand Beach Provincial Park, at the far southeast end of the lake. Canoeing down the Grass River, near the junction of hwys. 10 and 39, gives you the opportunity to see the beauty of the northern frontier.

Manitoba's lakes are home to dozens of species of fish, including walleye, northern pike, arctic grayling, sturgeon and channel catfish. Fly-in fishing—at such isolated spots as Aikens and Dogskin lakes, northeast of Bissett in Atikaki Provincial Park; Gods River, Knee Lake, and Island Lake, all in northeast Manitoba; and Big Sand, Egenolf,

and Nueltin lakes in the northwest region— attracts anglers of all skill levels.

When the lakes freeze over, ice fishing and ice-skating are favored pursuits. Smooth blankets of snow—at such places as Assiniboine Park in Winnipeg—are irresistible for snowshoeing and cross-country skiing.

Many adventurers, too, can't resist the snowmobiling trails that crisscross the province. Kick up some powder in Duck Mountain and Turtle Mountain provincial parks.

Although downhill skiing is hard to come by in a province that's known mostly for its lowlands, skiers can take on 25 runs at Asessippi Winter Park ski area.

For tobogganing fun, head for the hills and slides at Kildonan Park and more than a dozen park locations in Winnipeg.

Riding Mountain National Park rises from the flat prairie to provide a wealth of opportunity for activity. Self-guiding hiking trails range from the easy Beach Ridges Trail to the difficult Bald Hill Trail, named for the barren hill towering over scores of lush, green trees. Most memorable is the grueling but beautiful Ochre River Trail, which entices both trekkers and cross-country skiers.

Mountain bikers favor the exhilarating J.E.T. Trail, which rewards risk-takers with great views. The multiuse Central Trail, the longest at 73 kilometres (45 miles), is especially popular for horseback riding.

Sleepy polar bear, Churchill

Historic Timeline

1612	Capt. Thomas Button winters at Port Nelson on Hudson Bay and claims the land for England.
1690	Henry Kelsey of the Hudson's Bay Co. sets out on a 2-year exploration of the province.
1738	French fur-trader Pierre Gaultier de la Vérendrye arrives at the site now known as Winnipeg.
1812	The Red River Colony, one of Manitoba's earliest settlements, is established with a land grant from the Hudson's Bay Co.
1869	The Métis, native people of mixed ancestry, are led by Louis Riel in the Red River Rebellion.
1870	Manitoba becomes the fifth Canadian province.
1887	The Winnipeg Grain and Produce Exchange is established.
1912	Manitoba's boundary is extended north to Hudson Bay.
1986	The Supreme Court rules that all provincial laws passed since 1870 are invalid because they were written only in English.
1999	The Pan Am Games are held in Winnipeg.
2007	A tornado in Elie is Canada's first officially documented F5 tornado, the highest possible rating on the Fujita scale.

What To Pack

Temperature Averages Maximum/Minimum (Celsius)	JANUARY	FEBRUARY	MARCH	APRIL	MAY	JUNE	JULY	AUGUST	SEPTEMBER	OCTOBER	NOVEMBER	DECEMBER
Churchill	-23 / -32	-22 / -31	-16 / -26	-7 / -17	1 / -6	9 / 1	16 / 7	14 / 7	8 / 2	0 / -6	-10 / -19	-19 / -28
Hecla Island	-14 / -25	-9 / -21	-2 / -13	8 / -3	17 / 3	22 / 9	24 / 12	23 / 10	17 / 5	9 / -1	-2 / -10	-11 / -21
Swan River	-10 / -23	-6 / -19	1 / -12	9 / -5	17 / 2	22 / 7	24 / 10	24 / 8	17 / 3	9 / -2	-2 / -12	-9 / -20
The Pas	-17 / -26	-12 / -23	-4 / -17	6 / -6	15 / 2	21 / 9	23 / 12	22 / 11	14 / 5	7 / -1	-4 / -12	-14 / -22
Thompson	-19 / -31	-14 / -28	-6 / -21	4 / -10	13 / -1	19 / 5	22 / 8	21 / 7	12 / 2	4 / -4	-7 / -17	-17 / -27
Winnipeg	-13 / -23	-10 / -21	-2 / -13	9 / -3	18 / 4	23 / 10	26 / 13	24 / 12	18 / 6	11 / 0	-1 / -9	-10 / -19

From the records of The Weather Channel Interactive, Inc.

Good Facts To Know

ABOUT THE PROVINCE

POPULATION: 1,208,268.

AREA: 552,370 sq km (213,270 sq mi.); ranks 8th.

CAPITAL: Winnipeg.

HIGHEST POINT: 831 m (2,727 ft.), Baldy Mountain.

LOWEST POINT: Sea level, Churchill.

TIME ZONE(S): Central. DST.

GAMBLING

MINIMUM AGE FOR GAMBLING: 18.

REGULATIONS

TEEN DRIVING LAWS: Teens may not drive between midnight and 5 a.m. and no more than one passenger is permitted unless a supervising licensed driver is seated in the front passenger seat. When driving with a supervising driver, no more passengers than the number of backseat seat belts are permitted. The minimum age for an unrestricted driver's license is 17 years, 6 months.

SEAT BELT/CHILD RESTRAINT LAWS: Seat belts are required for driver and all passengers ages 18 and over. Children ages 5-18 and over 23 kilograms (50 lbs.) are required to be in a child restraint or seat belt; child restraints are required for children under age 5 and under 23 kilograms (50 lbs.).

CELL PHONE RESTRICTIONS: The use of handheld cell phones and text messaging while driving are prohibited.

HELMETS FOR MOTORCYCLISTS: Required for all riders.

MOVE OVER LAW: Driver is required to slow down and vacate the lane nearest stopped police, fire or rescue vehicles when those vehicles are using audible or flashing signals. The law also applies to tow trucks and other recovery vehicles.

RADAR DETECTORS: Not permitted.

FIREARMS LAWS: By federal law, all nonresidents entering Canada with a firearm must declare their weapon in writing and pay a fee of $25 (Canadian). Contact the Canadian Firearms Centre at (800) 731-4000 to receive a declaration form or for additional information.

ALCOHOL CONSUMPTION: Legal age 18.

SPECIAL REGULATIONS: Dogs and cats transported from the United States must have proof of rabies vaccination.

No person may smoke tobacco or have lighted tobacco in a motor vehicle while anyone under 16 is in the vehicle.

HOLIDAYS

HOLIDAYS: Jan. 1 ▪ Louis Riel Day (3rd Mon. in Feb.) ▪ Good Friday ▪ Easter ▪ Easter Monday ▪ Victoria Day, May 24 (if a Mon.) or the closest prior Mon. ▪ Canada Day, July 1 ▪ Civic Holiday, Aug. (1st Mon.) ▪ Labour Day, Sept. (1st Mon.) ▪ Thanksgiving, Oct. (2nd Mon.) ▪ Remembrance Day, Nov. 11 ▪ Christmas, Dec. 25 ▪ Boxing Day, Dec. 26.

MONEY

TAXES: In addition to Manitoba's provincial sales tax of 7 percent, there is a national 5 percent Goods and Services Tax (GST).

VISITOR INFORMATION

INFORMATION CENTERS: Free travel literature and information are available at the following locations: Canada/United States border, Hwy. 75 at Emerson ▪ Manitoba/Ontario boundary, Hwy. 1E just east of West Hawk Lake ▪ Manitoba/Saskatchewan boundary on Hwy. 1W west of Kirkella ▪ Manitoba/Saskatchewan boundary on Hwy. 16W near Russell ▪ and the Explore Manitoba Centre at The Forks National Historic Site in Winnipeg.

FURTHER INFORMATION FOR VISITORS:

Explore Manitoba Centre
21 Forks Market Rd.
Winnipeg, MB R3C 4T7
Canada
(204) 927-7838
(800) 665-0040

The Forks National Historic Site
401-25 Market Rd.
Winnipeg, MB R3C 4S8
Canada
(204) 983-6757
(888) 773-8888

Travel Manitoba
155 Carlton St., 7th Floor
Winnipeg, MB R3C 3H8
Canada
(204) 927-7800
(800) 665-0040

RECREATION INFORMATION:

Manitoba Conservation and Water Stewardship
Parks and Natural Areas
200 Saulteaux Crescent
Winnipeg, MB R3J 3W3
Canada
(204) 945-6784
(800) 214-6497

Manitoba Annual Events

Please call ahead to confirm event details.

JANUARY

- Master Playwright Festival
  Winnipeg
  204-956-1340
- Dakota Nation Winterfest
  Brandon
  204-726-3500
- Manitoba AgDays / Brandon
  204-534-2010

FEBRUARY

- Festival du Voyageur
  Winnipeg
  204-237-7692
- Optimist Clubs of Winnipeg
  Concert Band Festival
  Winnipeg
  204-663-1226
- Lieutenant Governor's
  Winter Festival / Brandon
  888-799-1111

MARCH

- Royal Manitoba Winter Fair
  Brandon
  204-727-4837
- Country Cottage Show
  Winnipeg
  250-554-1040
- Aurora Winterfest
  Churchill
  204-675-2022

APRIL

- Winnipeg Comedy Festival
  Winnipeg
  204-284-9477
- Scattered Seeds Spring
  Craft Show and Sale
  Winnipeg
  204-222-0111
- Brandon Home and Leisure
  Show / Brandon
  204-727-4837

MAY

- Manitoba Rocks! Provincial
  Mining Week / Winnipeg
  204-945-6569
- Winnipeg Wine Festival
  Winnipeg
  204-925-5633
- Victoria Day Weekend and
  Bioblitz / Selkirk
  204-785-6050

JUNE

- Manitoba Highland
  Gathering / Selkirk
  204-757-4007
- Red River Exhibition
  Winnipeg
  204-888-6990
- Manitoba Summer Fair
  Brandon
  204-726-3590

JULY

- Neepawa Lily Festival
  Neepawa
  204-476-8811
- Fringe Theatre Festival
  Winnipeg
  204-956-1340
- Manitoba Stampede and
  Exhibition / Morris
  204-746-2552

AUGUST

- Canada's National Ukrainian
  Festival / Dauphin
  204-622-4600
- Winkler Harvest Festival and
  Exhibition / Winkler
  204-325-5600
- Virden Indoor Rodeo and
  Wild West Daze / Virden
  204-748-2710

SEPTEMBER

- Fur Traders Rendezvous
  Dauphin
  204-638-6630
- Fall on the Farm
  Steinbach
  204-326-9661
- ManyFest: All Together
  Downtown / Winnipeg
  204-958-4640

OCTOBER

- Wheat City Stampede
  Brandon
  204-571-6618
- International Wine Festival
  of Manitoba / Winnipeg
  204-947-9084
- Marine Museum Halloween
  Haunt / Selkirk
  204-482-7761

NOVEMBER

- Manitoba Livestock Expo
  Brandon
  204-726-3590
- Festival of Trees and Lights
  Winnipeg
  204-895-4560
- Signatures Craft Show and
  Sale / Winnipeg
  613-241-5678

DECEMBER

- Winter Wonderland
  Winnipeg
  204-888-6990
- Christmas at the Fort
  Dauphin
  204-638-6630
- Island of Lights / Portage la
  Prairie
  204-239-8334

Inukshuk, Churchill

Northern lights, Birds Hill Provincial Park

Colorful architecture, Winnipeg

Winter in Manitoba

Limestone at Lake Manitoba

Index: Great Experience for Members

AAA editor's picks of exceptional note

Eskimo Museum

Lower Fort Garry
National Historic Site

International Peace
Garden

Royal Canadian Mint

Make the Most of Your Trip
with AAA eTourBook® Guides

Maximize your travel experience when you take along AAA eTourBook guides for your ereader or smartphone. Each of the more than 100 available digital titles is packed with:

- Destination details
- AAA Approved and Diamond Rated hotel and restaurant listings
- Attraction and event information
- Preplanned itineraries
- Editor's don't-miss picks

Download now at
AAA.com/ebooks

Manitoba
Atlas Section

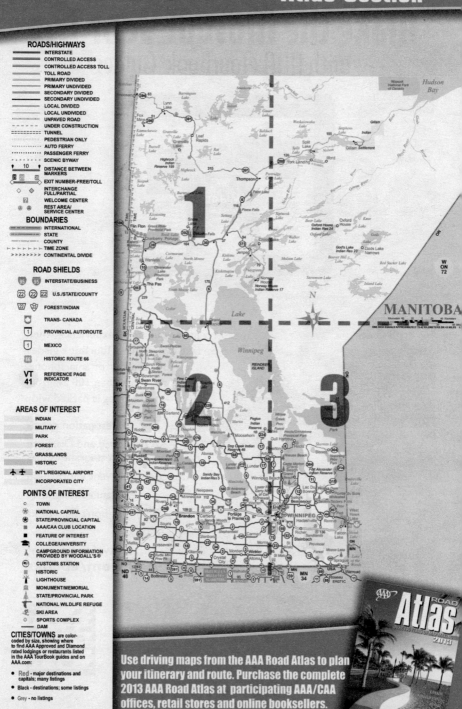

ROADS/HIGHWAYS
- INTERSTATE
- CONTROLLED ACCESS
- CONTROLLED ACCESS TOLL
- TOLL ROAD
- PRIMARY DIVIDED
- PRIMARY UNDIVIDED
- SECONDARY DIVIDED
- SECONDARY UNDIVIDED
- LOCAL DIVIDED
- LOCAL UNDIVIDED
- UNPAVED ROAD
- UNDER CONSTRUCTION
- TUNNEL
- PEDESTRIAN ONLY
- AUTO FERRY
- PASSENGER FERRY
- SCENIC BYWAY
- 10 DISTANCE BETWEEN MARKERS
- EXIT NUMBER-FREE/TOLL
- INTERCHANGE FULL/PARTIAL
- WELCOME CENTER
- REST AREA/ SERVICE CENTER

BOUNDARIES
- INTERNATIONAL
- STATE
- COUNTY
- TIME ZONE
- CONTINENTAL DIVIDE

ROAD SHIELDS
- 15 / 15 INTERSTATE/BUSINESS
- 22 / 22 / 22 U.S./STATE/COUNTY
- 27 / 27 FOREST/INDIAN
- TRANS- CANADA
- 1 PROVINCIAL AUTOROUTE
- 1 MEXICO
- 66 HISTORIC ROUTE 66
- VT 41 REFERENCE PAGE INDICATOR

AREAS OF INTEREST
- INDIAN
- MILITARY
- PARK
- FOREST
- GRASSLANDS
- HISTORIC
- ✈ INT'L/REGIONAL AIRPORT
- INCORPORATED CITY

POINTS OF INTEREST
- ○ TOWN
- ⊛ NATIONAL CAPITAL
- ⊛ STATE/PROVINCIAL CAPITAL
- AAA/CAA CLUB LOCATION
- ■ FEATURE OF INTEREST
- COLLEGE/UNIVERSITY
- CAMPGROUND INFORMATION PROVIDED BY WOODALL'S®
- CUSTOMS STATION
- HISTORIC
- LIGHTHOUSE
- MONUMENT/MEMORIAL
- STATE/PROVINCIAL PARK
- NATIONAL WILDLIFE REFUGE
- SKI AREA
- ○ SPORTS COMPLEX
- DAM

CITIES/TOWNS are color-coded by size, showing where to find AAA Approved and Diamond rated lodgings or restaurants listed in the AAA TourBook guides and on AAA.com:
- ● Red - major destinations and capitals; many listings
- ● Black - destinations; some listings
- ● Grey - no listings

Use driving maps from the AAA Road Atlas to plan your itinerary and route. Purchase the complete 2013 AAA Road Atlas at participating AAA/CAA offices, retail stores and online booksellers.

MANITOBA
SASKATCHEWAN

1:2,471,040
Scale in Kilometers

50   0   50

50   Scale in Miles   0

Berens River

Berens River
Indian Reserve 13

North Etomami R

Berens River

Pigeon River

Princess Harbour

Matheson Island

Bloodvein Indian
Reserve 12

Lake St George

Moose Creek Provincial

Fisher River
Indian Reserve 44

Forest

234

Hecla/Grindstone

Dallas

Indian ve 1B

224

Provincial Park

Hecla

Guli Harbour

8

Hodgson Fisher Branch

17

Riverton

Poplarfield

68

Arborg

Chatfield

419

17

7

Gimli

60

Fraserwood

229

Komarno

Oak Point

68

Winnipeg Bch

St Laurent

415

Teulon

14

Inwood

30

Scanterbury

West Shoal Lake

322

Gunton

9

Petersfield

59

Lake Francis

Argyle Stonewall

7

8

56

Libau

40

Selkirk

30

26

41

44

Garson

Marquette Warren

41

321

16

10

Beausejour

20

221

Birds Hill

12

Poplar Point

26

22

Headingley

Dugald

Anola

15

Oakville Elie

1

Beaudry

YWG

16

38

Ste Genevieve

248

Starbuck

100

Winnipeg

27

13

51

247

31

Ste Anne

Richer

1

Fannystelle

San-ford

Domain

St Adolphe

18

305

Brunkild

Niverville

Steinbach

Elm Creek

75

Aubigny

59

20

La Broquerie

18

Carman

3

332

Rosenort

200

St-Pierre Jolys

210

5 Roland

40

25

Morris

St Malo

Woodridge

79

32

428

306

18

Lowe Farm

St Malo

Rosa

Zhoda

203

5

18

44

Plum Coulee

Roseau River
Indian Reserve 46

302

Sundown

12

Winkler

14

Letellier

Stuartburn

Vita

201

201

Dominion City

Tolstoi

Piney

8

32

Gretna

421

Emerson

310

Warroad

18

Walhalla

75

59

Hallock

11

89

Roseau

Baudette

32

Cavalier

203

175

Lake Bronson

Greenbush

11

89

MN 60

Williams

39

Family Lake

Atikaki

Sasginnigak Lake

Provincial

Bloodvein River

Aikens Lake

Carroll Lake

Spoonbill Lake

Cairns Lake

McCusker Lake

Pikangiku

Park

Wallace Lake

Hollow Water 10
Indian Reserve

Wanipigow Lake

Wanipigow R

Manigotagan

Bissett

304

Nopiming

Larus Lake

Red Lake

Manigotagan River

Manigotagan Lake

Black River

Provincial

Eagle Lake

Werner Lake

Longlegged Lake

Sydney Lake

Park

ON 136

Fort Alexander
Indian Reserve 3

Powerview-Pine Falls

314

315

Umfreville Lake

Separat

11

Great Falls

Brightstone Sand
Hills Prov For

Belair Prov Forest

116

Stead

Pointe du Bois

313

Whitedog

525

Minaki

Brokenhead
Indian Res 4

317

Lac Du Bonnet

Pinawa

Crowduck Lake

Whiteshell

Tetu Lake

Swan Lake

Agassiz

214

Seven Sisters Falls

307

Provincial

596

44

Whitemouth

17

Park

34 17A

Elma

44

60

Rennie

42

17

Kenora

29

11

Falcon Lake

West Hawk Lake

Hadashville

54

Shoal Lake

308

East Braintree

Sandilands

Provincial

Whitemouth Lake Forest

Moose Lake

South Junction

Sprague

Middlebro

Buffalo Point
Indian Reserve 36

Woods

Lake

of the

40

9

600

MN CAN USA

22

Bloodvein

N ON

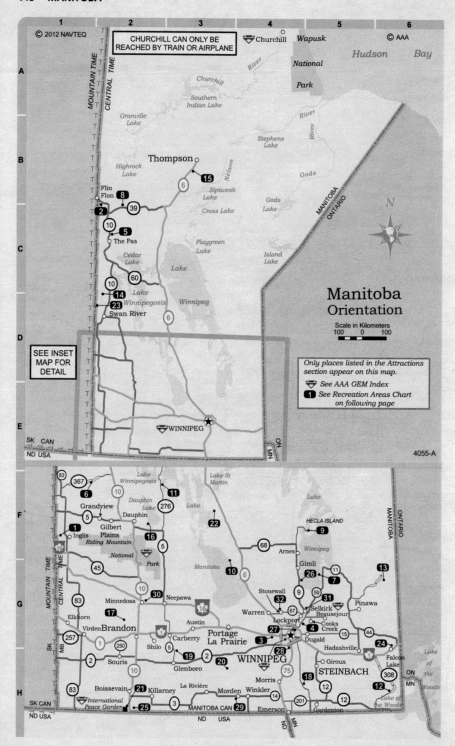

© 2012 NAVTEQ

CHURCHILL CAN ONLY BE
REACHED BY TRAIN OR AIRPLANE

Churchill

Wapusk

© AAA

Hudson Bay

Wapusk
National
Park

Churchill River

Southern
Indian Lake

Granville
Lake

Stephens
Lake

River

Thompson 15

Highrock
Lake

Nelson

Sipiwesk
Lake

Gods

Flin
Flon
2
8
39

Cross Lake

Gods
Lake

MANITOBA

ONTARIO

N

10
5
The Pas

Playgreen
Lake

Island
Lake

Manitoba
Orientation

Cedar
Lake

Lake
Winnipeg

Scale in Kilometers
100   0   100

10
60

14
23
Swan River

Lake
Winnipegosis

6

Only places listed in the Attractions
section appear on this map.

See AAA GEM Index

1 See Recreation Areas Chart
on following page

SEE INSET
MAP FOR
DETAIL

WINNIPEG

SK CAN
ND USA

ON

MN

4055-A

83
367
6
Grandview

Lake
Winnipegosis

Lake St
Martin

Lake

ONTARIO

MANITOBA

10
11
276
22

Dauphin
Lake

HECLA ISLAND
9

5
Gilbert
Plains
16
5

68
Arnes

Winnipeg

Gimli

1
Inglis
Riding Mountain

Dauphin

National

26
11
7
13

16

Park

Manitoba

10
6

50
31

Pinawa

45

MOUNTAIN TIME

CENTRAL TIME

Stonewall

9

Selkirk
Beausejour

83
Minnedosa
30
Neepawa

32
Warren

67
Lockport

4
Cooks
Creek

44
24

17
Elkhorn

16

Dugald

15

Falcon
Lake

Virden
Brandon

Austin

Portage
La Prairie

27
3
28
WINNIPEG

Hadashville
308

257
1
250
Carberry
Shilo
5

19
2
20

75

STEINBACH

ON
MN

2
Souris

Glenboro

18
Giroux

12

Lake
of
the
Woods

10

Morris

83
Boissevain
21
Killarney
La Rivière
Morden
Winkler
14

International
Peace Garden
25
3
MANITOBA CAN
29
Emerson
201
Gardenton

12

12
Lake of
the Woods

SK CAN
ND USA

ND   USA

ND

MN

Recreation Areas Chart

The map location numerals in column 2 show an area's location on the preceding map.

	MAP LOCATION	CAMPING	PICNICKING	HIKING TRAILS	BOATING	BOAT RAMP	BOAT RENTAL	FISHING	SWIMMING	PETS ON LEASH	BICYCLE TRAILS	WINTER SPORTS	VISITOR CENTER	LODGE/CABINS	FOOD SERVICE
NATIONAL PARKS *(See place listings.)*															
Riding Mountain (E-1) 2,978 square kilometres. Backpacking, cross-country skiing, golf, hiking, horseback riding, scuba diving, tennis, water skiing, wind surfing; boat cruises, paddleboats.		•	•	•	•	•	•	•	•	•	•	•	•	•	•
PROVINCIAL															
Asessippi (F-1) 2,330 hectares 13 km from Shellmouth Dam on Hwy. 83. Fishing, snowmobiling; nature trail.	1	•	•	•	•	•	•	•	•	•		•		•	
Bakers Narrows (C-2) 145 hectares 27 km s. of Flin Flon on Hwy. 10. Board sailing, canoeing, wildlife viewing; playground.	2	•	•	•	•	•	•	•	•	•		•		•	•
Beaudry (G-4) 939 hectares 10 km w. of Winnipeg on Roblin Blvd./Hwy. 241.	3		•	•				•				•			
Birds Hill (G-5) 3,550 hectares 24 km n.e. of Winnipeg on Hwy. 59. Cross-country skiing, horseback riding, snowmobiling, wildlife viewing; interpretive programs, playground.	4	•	•	•	•	•	•	•	•	•	•	•		•	
Clearwater Lake (C-2) 59,265 hectares 19 km n. of The Pas on Hwy. 10, then 2.5 km e. on Hwy. 287. Cross-country skiing, snowmobiling; interpretive trail.	5	•	•	•	•	•	•	•	•	•		•		•	
Duck Mountain (F-1) 142,430 hectares 56 km n. of Roblin off Hwy. 83. Canoeing, cross-country skiing, snowmobiling.	6	•	•	•	•	•	•	•	•	•		•		•	•
Grand Beach (G-5) 2,490 hectares 80 km n.e. of Winnipeg on Hwy. 59, then 6 km w. on Hwy 12. Cross-country skiing, sailing, snowmobiling, tennis, windsurfing; interpretive programs, sand beaches.	7	•	•	•	•	•	•	•	•	•	•	•	•	•	•
Grass River (B-2) 228,018 hectares at Cranberry Portage off Hwy. 10. Canoeing; interpretive trail.	8	•	•	•	•	•	•	•	•	•				•	•
Hecla/Grindstone (F-5) 108,440 hectares 165 km n. of Winnipeg via Hwy. 8. Cross-country skiing, golf, sailing, snowmobiling, tennis, windsurfing; interpretive programs. *(See Hecla Island p. 459.)*	9	•	•	•	•	•	•	•	•	•	•	•	•	•	•
Lundar Beach (G-3) 23 hectares 18 km w. of Lundar on Hwy. 419.	10							•	•	•			•		
Manipogo (F-3) 61 hectares 47 km n. of Dauphin on Hwy. 20. Board sailing, wildlife viewing; playground.	11	•	•					•	•	•					•
Moose Lake (H-6) 956 hectares 30 km n.e. of Sprague on Hwy. 308. Board sailing, canoeing, snowmobiling, wildlife viewing; playground.	12	•	•					•	•	•		•		•	•
Nopiming (G-6) 142,910 hectares 70 km n.e. of Lac du Bonnet. Canoeing; interpretive trail.	13	•	•	•	•	•	•	•	•	•				•	•
North Steeprock Lake (D-2) 13 hectares 3 km n. of Birch River on Hwy. 10, then 40 km w. on Hwy. 365.	14	•	•		•	•		•	•	•					
Paint Lake (B-3) 8,848 hectares 32 km s. of Thompson on Hwy. 6. Canoeing, cross-country skiing, ice skating, snowmobiling, tobogganing, windsurfing.	15	•	•	•	•	•	•	•	•	•		•		•	•
Rainbow Beach (F-2) 52 hectares 17 km e. of Dauphin on Hwy. 20. Board sailing, golf, wildlife viewing; playground.	16	•	•		•			•	•	•					
Rivers (G-2) 37 hectares 14 km n. of Brandon on Hwy. 10, then 26 km w. on Hwy. 25. Playground.	17	•	•		•			•	•	•					
St. Malo (H-5) 148 hectares 64 km s. of Winnipeg on Hwy. 59. Motorized boats not allowed.	18	•	•	•				•	•	•					
Spruce Woods (H-3) 26,950 hectares 25 km s.e. of Carberry on Hwy. 5. Canoeing, cross-country skiing, ice skating, snowmobiling, tobogganing; horse trails, interpretive programs. *(See Carberry p. 454.)*	19	•	•	•	•				•	•		•	•	•	
Stephenfield (H-3) 94 hectares 10 km w. of Carman on Hwy. 245. Board sailing, golf; playground.	20	•	•	•	•	•	•	•	•	•	•				•
Turtle Mountain (H-2) 18,570 hectares 23 km s. of Boissevain off Hwy. 10. Cross-country skiing, ice skating, snowmobiling, tobogganing; interpretive trail, horse trails. *(See Boissevain p. 451.)*	21	•	•	•	•	•	•		•	•		•		•	

Recreation Areas Chart

The map location numerals in column 2 show an area's location on the preceding map.

	MAP LOCATION	CAMPING	PICNICKING	HIKING TRAILS	BOATING	BOAT RAMP	BOAT RENTAL	FISHING	SWIMMING	PETS ON LEASH	BICYCLE TRAILS	WINTER SPORTS	VISITOR CENTER	LODGE/CABINS	FOOD SERVICE
Watchorn (F-3) 10 hectares 11 km w. of Moosehorn on Hwy. 237. Playground.	22	•	•		•	•		•	•	•					
Whitefish Lake (D-2) 24 hectares 13 km n. of Swan River, then 28 km w. on Hwy. 279. Playground.	23	•	•		•	•		•	•						
Whiteshell (G-6) 272,090 hectares off Hwy. 1 at Falcon Lake, near the Ontario border. Cross-country skiing, downhill skiing, golf, horseback riding, sailing, snowmobiling, tennis, tobogganing, windsurfing; interpretive programs, museum. *(See Falcon Lake p. 457.)*	24	•	•	•	•	•	•	•	•	•	•	•	•	•	•
William Lake (H-2) 199 hectares 7 km e. of Horton, then 8 km s. Amphitheater, playground.	25	•	•		•	•		•	•						
Winnipeg Beach (G-5) 41 hectares 45 km n. of Winnipeg on Hwy. 8, then 5 km e. on PR 229. Soccer, tennis, volleyball, wildlife viewing; playground.	26	•	•		•	•		•	•	•	•				
OTHER															
Kildonan (G-4) 39 hectares at 2021 Main St. in Winnipeg. Cross-country skiing, ice skating, tobogganing; pool. *(See Winnipeg p. 479.)*	27		•	•						•	•	•	•		
La Barriere (H-4) 21 hectares 6 km s. of jct. Waverley St. and Perimeter Hwy. in Winnipeg. Canoeing, cross-country skiing, naturalist-guided hikes, snowshoeing.	28		•	•				•		•	•	•			
Lake Minnewasta (H-4) 125 hectares 2 km w. of Morden on Hwy. 3, then 1 km s. on Hwy. 434.	29	•	•	•	•	•		•	•	•	•	•			
Minnedosa Lake and Beach (G-2) on Beach Dr. (PR 262). Cross-country skiing, ice fishing, ice hockey, snowmobiling; beach, playgrounds. Note: concessions are only offered in summer. *(See Minnedosa p. 461.)*	30										•	•	•		
Selkirk Park (G-5) 81 hectares on the banks of the Red River at Eveline St. in Selkirk. Cross-country skiing, ice fishing; bird sanctuary.	31	•	•	•	•	•		•		•	•	•			
Stonewall Quarry (G-4) 30 hectares 4 blks. n. on Main St. in Stonewall. Nature programs. Cross-country skiing, ice skating, tobogganing. *(See Stonewall p. 465.)*	32	•	•	•					•			•	•	•	

ARNES (F-4) elev. 225m/739'

An old fishing village, Arnes today offers sandy beaches, a marina and a nine-hole golf course. A monument to writer and explorer Vilhjalmur Stefansson is inscribed "I know what I have experienced, and I know what it has meant to me," a statement from his autobiography. Born in 1879, Stefansson traveled by boat and dog sled across the Arctic, mapping large areas of the archipelago and collecting ethnological data from the central Arctic coast. He proved through his explorations that it was possible to live off the land in this forbidding area.

AUSTIN (G-3) pop. 403, elev. 262m/860'

MANITOBA AGRICULTURAL MUSEUM, 2.5 km (1.6 mi.) s. of Hwy. 1 on Hwy. 34, includes a large collection of steam engines, gasoline tractors, farm equipment, artifacts of pioneer farmers and a pioneer village. The location also is home to the Manitoba Amateur Radio Museum. **Hours:** Daily 9-5, mid-May through Sept. 30; Mon.-Fri. 9-4:30, rest of year. **Cost:** $10; $8 (students with ID and senior citizens); $5 (ages 6-12); free (ages 0-5); $30 (family). **Phone:** (204) 637-2354.

Homesteaders' Village, at the Manitoba Agricultural Museum, 2.5 km (1.6 mi.) s. of Hwy. 1 on Hwy. 34, depicts pioneer life in the late 19th century through furnished buildings of the period. Included are log cabins, an 1883 schoolhouse, two churches, a printing office, blacksmith's shop, grain elevator, pioneer-style store and gristmill. **Hours:** Daily 9-5, mid-May through Sept. 30. **Cost:** included with Manitoba Agricultural Museum admission of $10; $8 (students with ID and senior citizens); $5 (ages 6-12); free (ages 0-5); $30 (family). **Phone:** (204) 637-2354.

BEAUSEJOUR (G-5) pop. 3,126, elev. 247m/810'

Just 46 kilometres (29 mi.) northeast of Winnipeg, Beausejour is on one of the main roads to Whiteshell Provincial Park (see attraction listing p. 457). Nature enthusiasts take advantage of the walking, hiking and cross-country ski trails available at Wally Chryplywy Nature Park on First Street.

Town of Beausejour: 639 Park Ave., Beausejour, MB, Canada R0E 0C0. **Phone:** (204) 268-7550.

BROKEN BEAU HISTORICAL SOCIETY PIONEER VILLAGE MUSEUM, 1 blk. n. of Park Ave. and Seventh St. N., features a reassembled pioneer village with a restored railroad station, a blacksmith shop, a school, an old church, a community hall, a general store, a tailor's shop, a harness shop and a house that was once the home of former premier and Governor General Edward Schreyer. **Time:** Allow 1 hour minimum. **Hours:** Mon.-Fri. 8:30-4:30, Sat.-Sun. and holidays 1-4:30, July-Aug.; by appointment rest of year. **Cost:** $5; free (ages 0-12). **Phone:** (204) 268-1318 or (204) 265-3204.

SUPERIOR INN   204/268-9050
◆◆ **Hotel.** Rates not provided. **Address:** 1055 Park Ave R0E 0C0 **Location:** On Hwy 215; jct Hwy 12/44/302. Located in a rural area. **Facility:** 36 units. 2 stories (no elevator), interior corridors. **Parking:** winter plug-ins. **Pool(s):** heated indoor. **Activities:** whirlpool. **Guest Services:** coin laundry.

BOISSEVAIN (H-2) pop. 1,572

Nearby Turtle Mountain Provincial Park (see Recreation Areas Chart) is named for the western painted turtle, which lives in the park's many shallow lakes. The park is the year-round home of a large number of waterfowl and of migratory birds in spring and fall. A wildlife center also is available.

As a connection to the park, the town has adopted as its symbol an 8.5-metre-tall (28-ft.) statue known as Tommy Turtle, which can be seen beside the visitor center on Hwy. 10.

An outdoor art gallery throughout the town depicts area history by way of more than 20 colorful wall-size murals, including a large scene painted on a grain elevator in downtown Boissevain. Scenic Hwy. 10 leads south to the North Dakota border and the International Peace Garden (see place listing p. 460).

Boissevain Visitors Centre: 298 Mountain St., P.O. Box 368, Boissevain, MB, Canada R0K 0E0. **Phone:** (204) 534-6303 or (800) 497-2393.

Self-guiding tours: Literature for a self-guiding walking tour of the city's historic buildings is available at the Boissevain Visitors Centre.

BECKONING HILLS MUSEUM is at 425 Mill Rd. S. The museum exhibits pioneer artifacts, mementos such as uniforms from World Wars I and II, farming equipment, early photographs and items relating to culture, education and literature. **Time:** Allow 1 hour minimum. **Hours:** Daily 1-5, June-Sept.; other times by appointment. **Cost:** Donations. **Phone:** (204) 534-6544.

BOISSEVAIN & DISTRICT MODEL RAILWAY, 200 Mountain St., displays three model railroads that feature miniature accessories such as a flour mill, school, water tower, oil well and historic houses as well as historical depictions of the Bunclody Bridge and the CPR passenger train on the Minto Hartney line. **Time:** Allow 30 minutes minimum. **Hours:** Daily 10-5, May 1-Sept. 15; by appointment rest of year. **Cost:** $2; $5 (family). Cash only. **Phone:** (204) 534-7172, (204) 534-6792 or (204) 534-3797.

IRVIN GOODON INTERNATIONAL WILDLIFE MUSEUM is at 298 Mountain St. (Hwy. 10). Visitors can gain a better understanding of wildlife through the mounted animals displayed in natural-like dioramas. Each setting provides information about the animals and their behavior. Examples of the wildlife displayed include a polar bear, grizzly bear, wolves, moose, elk, caribou, deer, geese and other fowl. A sod house and log cabin are on the grounds.

Tours: Guided tours are available. **Time:** Allow 1 hour minimum. **Hours:** Daily 10-7, Victoria Day weekend-Labour Day weekend; by appointment rest of year. **Cost:** $7; $3 (ages 6-16). **Phone:** (204) 534-6662, or (204) 534-2433 during the off-season.

MONCUR GALLERY & MUSEUM, in the Civic Centre/Library Complex at 420 S. Railway St., contains 10,000 years of archeological history of early southwestern Manitoba. Included in the collection are projectile points, scrapers, ceremonial items and food preparation utensils. **Time:** Allow 30 minutes minimum. **Hours:** Tues.-Sat. 10-5, July-Aug.; by appointment rest of year. **Cost:** $5; $2 (ages 12-17). **Phone:** (204) 534-6478.

BRANDON (G-2) pop. 46,061, elev. 409m/1,300'

An agricultural and industrial center, Brandon is the second largest city in the province after Winnipeg and is known for its small-town warmth and big-city amenities.

The Riverbank Discovery Centre, in addition to providing information about Brandon and the surrounding region, is the starting point for the Assiniboine Riverbank Trail System, 17 kilometres (10.5 mi.) of trails that wind throughout Brandon, linking the downtown area with parks, picnic spots and sports venues.

The Keystone Centre, with more than 4.8 hectares (12 acres) under one roof, plays host to some of Manitoba's larger events, concerts and sports competitions; phone (204) 726-3500. Brandon's Community Sportsplex offers both winter and summer recreational activities. Built for the 1979 Canada Winter Games, the structure houses racquetball courts, an ice arena, swimming pool, indoor water slide and an outdoor running track; phone (204) 729-2475.

The Brandon Hills Wildlife Management Area, just a short drive south of the city on Hwy. 10 and east along Beresford Road, provides a setting for a variety of recreational pursuits such as hiking, mountain bicycling, cross-country skiing and bird-watching.

Regional Tourism Centre/Riverbank Discovery Centre: #1-545 Conservation Dr., Brandon, MB, Canada R7A 7L8. **Phone:** (204) 729-2141 or (888) 799-1111.

Self-guiding tours: A historical walking tour of the residential area between 10th and 18th streets offers interesting architecture and turn-of-the-20th-century homes; a booklet describing the tour is available for $3.50 from the tourism center.

ART GALLERY OF SOUTHWESTERN MANITOBA, 710 Rosser Ave. (entrance via the Town Centre Mall parkade), features changing exhibits with an emphasis on community-based art and contemporary works. Displays change every 6-7 weeks. Workshops and art classes are offered for a fee. **Time:** Allow 1 hour minimum. **Hours:** Mon.-Fri. 10-5 (also Thurs. 6-9 p.m., Sept.-June), Sat. noon-5. Closed major holidays. **Cost:** Donations. **Phone:** (204) 727-1036.

COMMONWEALTH AIR TRAINING PLAN MUSEUM, in Hangar 1 at Brandon Airport, is dedicated to preserving the history of the British Commonwealth Air Training Plan of 1939-45. It has many of the aircraft used for training, photographs, artifacts and memorabilia. Three of the 11 aircraft displayed are in flying condition. A chapel has a book with names of more than 18,000 Canadian Air Force personnel who died during World War II.

Guided tours are available by appointment. **Hours:** Daily 10-4, May-Sept.; 1-4, rest of year. Closed Christmas. **Cost:** $6; $4 (ages 6-18). **Phone:** (204) 727-2444.

DALY HOUSE MUSEUM, 122 18th St., was built in 1882 as the home of Brandon's first mayor, Thomas Mayne Daly. It is furnished with late 19th-century upper middle-class pieces and houses photographs and artifacts that relate the city's history. Also featured are a general store and rotating exhibits. A research center on the third floor is available by appointment.

A Victorian Garden features benches, paved walkways, a bandstand, a gazebo, Victorian-era flowers and century-old elm trees. **Tours:** Guided tours are available. **Time:** Allow 1 hour minimum. **Hours:** Mon.-Sat. 10-noon and 1-5, Sun. 1-4, July-Aug.; Tues.-Sat. 10-noon and 1-5, rest of year. **Cost:** $6; $5 (ages 0-17 and 66+); $12 (family, two adults and two children). **Phone:** (204) 727-1722.

WESTMAN REPTILE GARDENS is 19 km (12 mi.) e. on PR 457 to the end of the road, 1.6 km (1 mi.) s. on Wagglesprings Rd. (gravel) to Thompson Rd., then just w. following signs. One of Canada's largest reptile exhibits, the zoo has more than 300 animals on display. Visitors can see rattlesnakes, crocodiles, cobras, monitors and turtles. **Hours:** Mon.-Sat. 10-8, Sun. and holidays noon-5, Apr.-Sept.; Tues.-Sat. noon-6, Sun. and holidays noon-5, rest of year. **Cost:** $6; $4 (ages 3-15). **Phone:** (204) 763-4030.

BEST WESTERN BRANDON INN   (204)727-7997

Hotel
$119-$150

AAA Benefit: Members save up to 20%, plus 10% bonus points with Best Western Rewards®.

Address: 205 Middleton Ave R7A 1A8 **Location:** Jct Trans-Canada Hwy 1 and 10; access via north service road. **Facility:** 79 units, some efficiencies. 3 stories, interior corridors. **Parking:** winter plug-ins. **Terms:** check-in 4 pm, 3 day cancellation notice. **Amenities:** high-speed Internet, safes. **Pool(s):** heated indoor. **Activities:** whirlpool, waterslide, exercise room. **Guest Services:** valet and coin laundry. **Free Special Amenities:** local telephone calls and high-speed Internet.

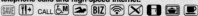

CANAD INNS-DESTINATION CENTRE BRANDON
(204)727-1422

Hotel
$120-$250

Address: 1125 18th St R7A 7C5 **Location:** On Hwy 10 (18th St); jct Brandon Ave. **Facility:** 159 units. 11 stories, interior corridors. **Parking:** winter plug-ins. **Amenities:** high-speed Internet. *Some:* video games. **Dining:** 2 restaurants, nightclub. **Pool(s):** heated indoor. **Activities:** whirlpools, waterslide, exercise room. **Guest Services:** valet laundry. **Free Special Amenities: newspaper and high-speed Internet.**

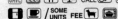

COMFORT INN BRANDON
(204)727-6232

Motel $101-$128 Address: 925 Middleton Ave R7C 1A8 **Location:** Trans-Canada Hwy 1; between Hwy 10 (18th St) N and 10 S; on northside of service road. Located in a commercial area. **Facility:** 81 units. 2 stories (no elevator), interior corridors. **Parking:** winter plug-ins. **Terms:** cancellation fee imposed. **Guest Services:** valet laundry.

DAYS INN BRANDON
(204)727-3600

Hotel $89-$170 Address: 2130 Currie Blvd R7B 4E7 **Location:** Jct Trans-Canada Hwy 1, 4.9 mi (7.9 km) s on Hwy 10 (18th St). Located in a commercial area. **Facility:** 61 units. 3 stories, interior corridors. **Parking:** winter plug-ins. **Terms:** check-in 4 pm. **Amenities:** high-speed Internet. **Pool(s):** heated indoor. **Activities:** whirlpool, exercise room. **Guest Services:** valet and coin laundry.

LAKEVIEW INNS & SUITES BRANDON
204/728-1880

Hotel
Rates not provided

Address: 1880 18th St N R7C 1A5 **Location:** On Hwy 10 (18th St), just s of jct Trans-Canada Hwy 1. Located in a commercial area. **Facility:** 66 units. 3 stories, interior corridors. **Parking:** winter plug-ins. **Pool(s):** heated indoor. **Activities:** exercise room. **Guest Services:** valet and coin laundry. **Free Special Amenities: continental breakfast and high-speed Internet.**

VICTORIA INN
(204)725-1532

Hotel $116-$199 Address: 3550 Victoria Ave R7B 2R4 **Location:** Jct Trans-Canada Hwy 1 and 10 (18 St), 3.1 mi (5 km) s, then 0.9 mi (1.4 km) w. Located in a residential/commercial area. **Facility:** 131 units. 2 stories (no elevator), interior corridors. **Parking:** winter plug-ins. **Terms:** cancellation fee imposed. **Amenities:** high-speed Internet. **Pool(s):** heated indoor. **Activities:** whirlpool, exercise room. **Guest Services:** valet and coin laundry.

WHERE TO EAT

CLAY POT CAFE
204/726-9467

American. Family Dining. $7-$15 **AAA Inspector Notes:** This unassuming little diner serves up a simple menu throughout the day. Quite a variety of sandwiches is offered along with soups, burgers, salads and comfort food dinner options. For a twist order from the sushi menu. **Address:** 2604 Victoria Ave R7B 0M8 **Location:** Jct Trans-Canada Hwy 1 and 10 (18th St), 3.1 mi (5 km) s, then 0.5 mi (0.8 km) w. [B] [L] [D]

DOUBLE HAPPINESS RESTAURANT
204/728-6388

Chinese. Casual Dining. $6-$12 **AAA Inspector Notes:** Go where the locals go when they get a craving for Chinese food. A simple buffet is offered for lunch and dinner, but they also offer an à la carte menu. **Bar:** full bar. **Address:** 608 Rosser Ave R7A 0K7 **Location:** Between 6th and 7th sts. **Parking:** street only. [L] [D]

ECHO RESTAURANT & WINE BAR
204/728-5775

American. Casual Dining. $10-$33 **AAA Inspector Notes:** Find casual and contemporary décor at this high-energy dining room where the upbeat music can get a bit loud. A sample of appetizers such as Asian lettuce wraps, nachos or spinach dip and honey lime shrimp salad to start is followed by entrées like roast chicken and baby back ribs in a variety of sauces or Certified Angus beef steaks, gourmet thin-crust pizzas and pasta dishes. A feature menu is offered, which includes salad and dessert. **Bar:** full bar. **Address:** 3130 Victoria Ave R7B 0N2 **Location:** Jct Trans-Canada Hwy 1 and 10 (18th St), 3.1 mi (5 km) s, then 1.1 mi (1.8 km) w; in Royal Oak Inn & Suites. [B] [L] [D] CALL

THE GREEN OLIVE
204/726-0207

Canadian. Casual Dining. $8-$28 **AAA Inspector Notes:** From the name alone, one would expect to find Italian fare at this restaurant but the menu also is made up of good Canadian foods, including ribs, steaks and pasta. The desserts are made in-house. **Bar:** full bar. **Address:** 612 Rosser Ave R7A 0K7 **Location:** Between 6th and 7th sts; downtown. **Parking:** street only. [L] [D]

LADY OF THE LAKE CAFE & PUB
204/726-8785

Canadian. Casual Dining. $9-$29 **AAA Inspector Notes:** This distinctive combination of a 50s-style diner, a modern pub and a 7,000-square-foot gift shop is a little quirky but interesting. The menu is multi-faceted with an emphasis on local and organic products and a host to "gourmet comfort" foods that are as tasty as they are healthy. The pub features live jazz most nights and more high-energy entertainment on Friday and Saturday. **Bar:** full bar. **Address:** 135-B 17th St N R7A 1G6 **Location:** Just e on Maple Ave from jct Hwy 10 (18th St). [L] [D] CALL

MARINO'S PIZZA
204/578-5555

Pizza. Casual Dining. $10-$16 **AAA Inspector Notes:** Although this simply decorated spot is best known for its fabulous house made pizza, you can also satisfy your cravings in a number of other ways. Oven roasted wings with a good selection of gourmet flavors, fresh salads, assorted subs, chicken cacciatore and traditional pastas are just some of the ways. **Bar:** beer & wine. **Address:** 441 10th St R7A 4G3 **Location:** Just n of Victoria Ave. [D] CALL

MUM'S FAMILY RESTAURANT
204/717-6867

American. Family Dining. $8-$20 **AAA Inspector Notes:** The restaurant has modest décor and overlooks the tennis courts, golf course and river. A simply prepared comfort-food menu that all will recognize is offered with soup, salads, sandwiches, burgers and other entrées like liver and onions, country-fried steak, battered haddock, veal cutlets with mushroom gravy, salmon, ribs and steak. In the mornings pirogies stand out on the nice selection of breakfast offerings. **Bar:** full bar. **Reservations:** suggested. **Address:** 3500 McDonald Ave R7B 0B9 **Location:** From Victoria Ave, 0.6 mi (1 km) n, then just w; at Wheat City Golf Course. [B] [L] [D]

MUM'S FAMILY RESTAURANT
204/725-0888

American. Family Dining. $8-$20 **AAA Inspector Notes:** This tiny eatery has a basic décor and offers a variety of simply prepared comfort food that all will recognize. Offered are soup, salads, sandwiches, burgers and other entrées like liver and onions, country fried steak, battered haddock, veal cutlets with mushroom gravy, salmon, ribs and steak. Pirogies stand out on the selection of breakfast offerings. **Bar:** full bar. **Address:** 505 24th St R7B 1X6 **Location:** Just e of Hwy 10 (18th St) on Victoria Ave. [B] [L] [D]

REMINGTON'S SEAFOOD & STEAKHOUSE
204/571-3838

Steak. Casual Dining. $12-$58 **AAA Inspector Notes:** Located on the second level, this open, contemporary dining room serves up Canadian Prime beef using their 1,600-degree, down-draft broiler as well as a good variety of seafood. Also offered are tasty appetizers and soups as well as chicken, veal, lamb and pasta choices. Service is competent and friendly. The lounge offers daily specials and happy hour. Parking is accessed via Princess Avenue. **Bar:** full bar. **Reservations:** suggested. **Address:** 800 Rosser Ave R7A 6N5 **Location:** Jct 8th St; in The Town Center; downtown. **Parking:** on-site and street. [L] [D] CALL

CARBERRY (G-3) pop. 1,669, elev. 369m/1,210'

The forests and sand dunes of nearby Spruce Woods Provincial Park *(see attraction listing)* inspired many of the works of artist, naturalist and writer Ernest Thompson Seton, including his stories "The Trail of the Sandhill Stag" and "Wild Animals I Have Known." He was appointed naturalist to the Manitoba government in 1892. A small highway park 15 kilometres (9 mi.) east of Carberry on Hwy. 1 has been dedicated to Seton.

Carberry Municipal Offices: 316 4th Ave., P.O. Box 130, Carberry, MB, Canada R0K 0H0. **Phone:** (204) 834-6600.

CARBERRY PLAINS MUSEUM AND GINGER-BREAD HOUSE, 520 James White Way, contains pioneer artifacts relating to the area, including period clothing, pictures and furniture as well as displays of original 19th-century art, a schoolroom, doll case, sports display, a church, a store and a kitchen. Military memorabilia from World Wars I and II also are displayed. The gingerbread house, built in 1901, is decorated in 1930s-style. **Time:** Allow 30 minutes minimum. **Hours:** Daily 1-6, June-Sept. **Cost:** $5; $3 (students with ID); free (ages 0-4); $10 (family). **Phone:** (204) 834-6609, or (204) 834-2439 in the off-season.

THE SETON CENTRE, 116 Main St., features artwork and photographs depicting the life and philosophies of writer, artist, naturalist and early environmentalist Ernest Thompson Seton. **Time:** Allow 30 minutes minimum. **Hours:** Mon.-Sat. 9-5, June-Aug.; by appointment rest of year. **Cost:** Donations. **Phone:** (204) 834-2509 June-Aug., or (204) 834-2056 rest of year.

SPRUCE WOODS PROVINCIAL PARK is 25 km (16 mi.) s. on Hwy. 5. The 26,950-hectare (66,593-acre) park, a mosaic of geographic features, includes deciduous forests, creeping sand dunes, white spruce-covered sand hills and mixed grass prairie. The park is bisected by the Assiniboine River as it winds its way east.

The desertlike area known as Spirit Sands was formed by an ancient river delta which left behind a 5-kilometre (3-mi.) tract of open sand dunes that tower 30 metres (98 ft.) above the surrounding prairie. The eerie blue-green pond color of Devil's Punch Bowl, near the Spirit Sands, can be observed from several viewpoints; the bowl-shaped depression was caused by the currents of an underground stream.

An 8.6-kilometre (5.1-mi.) self-guiding trail leads through the dunes to the Punch Bowl, and a 4-kilometre (2.5-mi.) trail meanders through the Spirit Sands. Both trail entrances are located just north of the Assiniboine River off Hwy. 5. Interpretive signs along the trails provide insight into the cultural and natural surroundings.

Spruce Woods is home to the western plains hognose snake; the northern prairie skink, Manitoba's only lizard; wapiti (elk); white-tailed deer; coyotes; and pin cushion and prickly pear cacti.

Interpretive programs about park resources and natural and cultural history are offered. Family events, campfire and amphitheater programs and guided hikes are offered weekends May through September. *See Recreation Areas Chart.* Comfortable walking shoes, a hat and drinking water are recommended. **Time:** Allow 2 hours minimum. **Hours:** Park open daily 24 hours. **Cost:** One-day pass $4 per private vehicle. Annual pass $30. **Phone:** (204) 827-8850 May-Sept., or (204) 834-8800 rest of year. 🅰 🍴 🚫 🐾 ⛱

Spirit Sands Wagon Outfitters, 27 km (17 mi.) s.e. on Hwy. 5 in Spruce Woods Provincial Park, offers 90-minute covered wagon rides through the Spirit Sands and Devil's Punch Bowl, providing views of sand dunes, cactuses, rare snakes and lizards, rolling grasslands and marshes. **Hours:** Trips depart daily at noon and 2, mid-May through June 30; daily, July 1-Labour Day (phone for times). **Cost:** $14; $8 (ages 3-16). **Phone:** (204) 827-2800 for wagon office, or (204) 526-2764 off-season.

CHURCHILL (A-4) pop. 813, elev. 29m/100'
• Hotels p. 456 • Restaurants p. 456

Churchill, on the shore of Hudson Bay, is Canada's northernmost subarctic sea port. It also is the site of the Hudson's Bay Co.'s Prince of Wales Fort National Historic Site *(see attraction listing),* a partially restored ruin across from Churchill and Cape Merry Battery at the mouth of the Churchill River. Built over a period of 40 years during the 1700s to hold as many as 400 soldiers, the impressive stone fortress housed only 39 untrained men when three French warships mounted a surprise attack in 1782. The fort's governor wisely surrendered without engaging in battle.

After spending 3 unsuccessful days trying to demolish the 12-metre-thick (40-ft.) outer walls, the French abandoned the fort; it was never occupied again. The site is accessible by boat July through August (weather and tides permitting).

The area around Churchill holds an attraction for two giant mammals: the polar bear and the beluga whale. In fact the Churchill region is said to have the greatest concentration of accessible polar bears in the world. Having spent the winter hunting on the frozen bay, the bears come to shore south of Churchill as the ice melts, scatter along the coast and up to 50 kilometres (31 mi.) inland, and then return to the ice in autumn when the bay refreezes. Beluga whales are often sighted off the coast of Cape Merry during July and August.

Other natural features include flowers, arctic plant life, various wildlife and some 200 species of birds, which nest or pass through Churchill on their annual migrations. An excellent spot for bird-watching is Bird Cove, on the coast 16 kilometres (9 mi.) east of Churchill. The aurora borealis (northern lights) seen from Churchill during the fall and winter months are among the most brilliant in the world.

Churchill can be reached only by train or airplane. Via Rail Canada trains run from Winnipeg and Thompson to Churchill; phone (888) 842-7245. Calm Air offers flights from Winnipeg to Churchill; phone (800) 839-2256.

The Parks Canada Visitor Reception Centre offers information, interpretive displays and programs, historical exhibits and videotaped presentations June through November; by appointment rest of year. Phone (204) 675-8863.

Churchill Chamber of Commerce: 211 Kelsey Blvd., P.O. Box 176, Churchill, MB, Canada R0B 0E0. **Phone:** (204) 675-2022 or (888) 389-2327.

CAPE MERRY NATIONAL HISTORIC SITE, accessible via the Cape Merry Centennial Pkwy., 3 km (1.9 mi.) w. to the e. shore of the Churchill River, is marked by a stone cannon battery built in 1746 to complement the defenses of the Prince of Wales Fort. An original cannon and powder magazine remain. A cairn commemorating Capt. Jens Munk, the first European to enter the Churchill River in 1619, is displayed.

The cape offers views of harbor activity as well as whales, waterfowl and the Prince of Wales Fort. **Time:** Allow 30 minutes minimum. **Hours:** Daily 24 hours. Parks Canada offers guided tours June-Aug. **Cost:** Free. **Phone:** (204) 675-8863.

ESKIMO MUSEUM, 242 La Verendrye Ave., contains exhibits that depict the history and culture of the northern region of Canada. Founded in 1944 by Roman Catholic missionaries, it pays tribute to the creativity and beliefs of the Canadian Inuits. Highlights of the museum are Inuit carvings in bone, ivory, stone and antler as well as wildlife specimens, artifacts and tools dating from 1700 B.C. **Hours:** Mon. 1-5, Tues.-Sat. 9-noon and 1-5, June-Nov.; Mon.-Sat. 1-4:30, rest of year. Closed major holidays. **Cost:** Donations. **Phone:** (204) 675-2030.

FRONTIERS NORTH'S TUNDRA BUGGY ADVENTURE is at 124 Kelsey Blvd. Specially designed vehicles called Tundra Buggies carry guests on full-day fall tours across the tundra to view polar bears in the Churchill Wildlife Management Area. Half- and full-day summer wildlife and nature tours, also on Tundra Buggies, venture along area shorelines. Multiday beluga whale-watching and ecological boat tours off the coast of Cape Merry also are offered; phone for information.

Hours: Full-day Tundra Buggy tours are offered most days, early Oct. to mid-Nov. Half-day and full-day summer wildlife and nature tours are available Tues., Thurs. and Sat., early July-late Sept. **Cost:** Tundra Buggy fare early Oct. to mid-Oct. $299; $219 (ages 0-11). Tundra Buggy fare mid-Oct. to mid-Nov. $399; $299 (ages 0-11). Half-day summer wildlife and nature tour fare $119; $89 (ages 0-11). Full-day summer wildlife and nature tour fare $169; $129 (ages 0-11). Fares may vary; phone ahead to confirm. Reservations are required. **Phone:** (204) 675-5180 or (800) 663-9832.

NORTH STAR TOURS office is at 12 Hearne St. but guests are picked up from their hotel. Guides conduct historical, cultural and wilderness adventure and birding tours of the Churchill area by school bus covering such topics as Fort Churchill, the Hudson's Bay Co., geology, and polar bears and other wildlife. During summer beluga whale sightings are the highlight, and polar bear season runs October 1 to mid-November.

Time: Allow 6 hours minimum. **Hours:** Daily 9-3, mid-June to mid-Nov. (weather permitting). **Cost:** Fare Oct. 1 to mid-Nov. $100; free (ages 1-12). Fare mid-June through Sept. 30 $75; free (ages 1-12). **Phone:** (204) 675-2356 or (800) 665-0690.

PRINCE OF WALES FORT NATIONAL HISTORIC SITE, at the mouth of the Churchill River, is accessible by boat only. A huge stone fortress built 1731-71 by the Hudson's Bay Co., the fort fell to the French without incident in 1782. Independent whale-watching boat tours, including those offered by Sea North Tours Ltd. *(see attraction listing)* and Lazy Bear Lodge, usually include the fort on their itineraries.

Time: Allow 2 hours minimum. **Hours:** Access is possible on the changing tides 6 hours daily, July-Aug. (weather permitting). **Cost:** Boat fare (site admission included) $99; $49.50 (ages 0-11). **Phone:** (204) 675-8863 for Parks Canada historic site information, (204) 675-2195, (204) 675-2969 for the Lazy Bear Lodge, (866) 687-2327 for the Lazy Bear Lodge, or (888) 348-7591 for Sea North Tours information.

SEA NORTH TOURS LTD., 153 Kelsey Blvd., offers boat tours to Prince of Wales Fort National Historic Site *(see attraction listing)* in craft ranging in size up to the 30-passenger *Sea North II.* This vessel is equipped with stereo hydrophones so that passengers can listen to the sounds made by the beluga whales that swim within feet of the boat. Tours also offer chances of sighting polar bears, ice formations and indigenous birds. Kayak tours and snorkeling also are available.

Time: Allow 3 hours minimum. **Hours:** Daily dawn-dusk (times may vary depending on tides), mid-June to late Aug. **Cost:** $105; $52.50 (ages 0-11). **Phone:** (204) 675-2195 or (888) 348-7591.

YORK FACTORY NATIONAL HISTORIC SITE is 250 km (150 mi.) s.e. near the mouth of the Hayes River; access to the site is limited to charter plane or boat. The site was established by the Hudson's Bay Co. as part of a series of fur trading posts. The 1821 depot is the oldest wooden structure still standing on permafrost. Self-guiding tours of the site feature reconstructed buildings containing area artifacts.

Visitors should contact Parks Canada for transportation and safety information. Facilities at the site are limited; camping is not permitted. **Time:** Allow 4 hours minimum. **Hours:** Daily 8-5, June 15-Sept. 1 (weather permitting). **Cost:** Free. **Phone:** (204) 675-8863.

POLAR INN & SUITES (204)675-8878

▼▼ ▼▼ **Motel** $129-$255 **Address:** 153 Kelsey Blvd R0B 0E0 **Location:** Just n at Franklin St; center. **Facility:** 26 units, some efficiencies and kitchens. 1 story, interior corridors. **Parking:** winter plug-ins. **Guest Services:** coin laundry.

🛗 📶 ✕ 🗡 🛢 💷 / SOME UNITS 🖼

THE TUNDRA INN (204)675-8831

▼▼ ▼▼ **Hotel** $121-$220 **Address:** 34 Franklin St R0B 0E0 **Location:** Just n on Kelsey Blvd, then just e; center. Located in a commercial area. **Facility:** 31 units. 2 stories (no elevator), interior corridors. **Parking:** winter plug-ins. **Terms:** 30 day cancellation notice-fee imposed. **Amenities:** high-speed Internet. **Dining:** The Tundra Inn Pub & Dining Room, see separate listing. **Guest Services:** complimentary laundry.

🍽 🍸 CALL ⚡M 🛗 📶 ✕ 🗡 🛢 💷

BEAR COUNTRY INN 204/675-8299

[fyi] Not evaluated. **Address:** 126 Kelsey Blvd R0B 0E0 **Location:** Just n of center. Facilities, services, and décor characterize an economy property.

CHURCHILL MOTEL 204/675-8853

[fyi] Not evaluated. **Address:** 152 Kelsey Blvd R0B 0E0 **Location:** Just n at Franklin St; center. Facilities, services, and décor characterize an economy property.

SEAPORT HOTEL 204/675-8807

[fyi] Not evaluated. **Address:** 299 Kelsey Blvd R0B 0E0 **Location:** Just s at Munick St; center. Facilities, services, and décor characterize a mid-scale property.

WHERE TO EAT

GYPSY RESTAURANT & BAKERY 204/675-2322

▼▼ American. Family Dining. $6-$19 **AAA Inspector Notes:** This incredibly popular eatery features an extensive selection of fresh baked goods, sandwiches, soup, salad, pizza and pierogi. It is the place for to-go lunches. The service is polite. **Bar:** full bar. **Address:** 253 Kelsey Blvd R0B 0E0 **Location:** Just s at Thompson St; center.

[B] [L] [D]

THE REEF RESTAURANT & DINING ROOM 204/675-2577

▼▼ ▼▼ American. Casual Dining. $8-$24 **AAA Inspector Notes:** Choose from a casual coffee shop or a fine dining room serving both lunch and dinner. Sample the poached Arctic char, Angus strap-loin steak or baby back ribs. There is also lighter fare available such as burgers and clubhouse sandwiches which includes a choice of soup or salad. **Bar:** full bar. **Address:** 299 Kelsey Blvd R0B 0E0 **Location:** Just s at Munick St; center; in Seaport Hotel. [L] [D]

THE TUNDRA INN PUB & DINING ROOM 204/675-8831

▼▼ ▼▼ Canadian. Casual Dining. $12-$25 **AAA Inspector Notes:** The bill of fare at this simply decorated restaurant features northern fish and game incorporated in a pub style menu. Well prepared elk meatloaf, venison bangers, caribou and Guinness pot pie or Arctic char with wild rice risotto are examples of what to expect on the menu. **Bar:** full bar. **Reservations:** suggested. **Address:** 23 Franklin St R0B 0E0 **Location:** Just n on Kelsey Blvd, then just e; center; in The Tundra Inn. [D] CALL ⚡M

COOKS CREEK (G-5) elev. 238m/780'

COOK'S CREEK HERITAGE MUSEUM, jct. Hwy. 212 and Sapton Rd., houses artifacts pertaining to the life of the early settlers from Poland, Ukraine and other eastern European countries. Highlights include religious artifacts, folk art, clothing, a blacksmith shop, pioneer houses furnished in period and farm machines. **Time:** Allow 1 hour minimum. **Hours:** Thurs.-Tues. 10-5, mid-May through Aug. 31. **Cost:** $4; $2 (ages 0-18). **Phone:** (204) 444-4448.

IMMACULATE CONCEPTION CHURCH AND THE GROTTO OF OUR LADY OF LOURDES is 3 km (1.9 mi.) n. on Hwy. 212 (Cooks Creek Rd.) from jct. Hwy. 213 (Garvin Rd.). The Ukrainian Catholic church, built by Father Philip Ruh 1930-52, features onion domes and the Icon of Our Lady of Perpetual Help, a replica of the Miraculous Icon in Rome. The grotto next to the church is a replica of the original Grotto of Lourdes in France.

Guided tours are available by appointment. **Time:** Allow 1 hour minimum. **Hours:** Sat.-Sun. and holidays noon-6, May-Sept. **Cost:** $2. **Phone:** (204) 444-2478.

DAUPHIN (F-2) pop. 8,251, elev. 293m/960'

Dauphin (DAW-fin) lies in a fertile farming valley between Duck Mountain Provincial Park *(see Recreation Areas Chart)* and Riding Mountain National Park *(see place listing p. 463)*. Lake Dauphin, 15 kilometres (9 mi.) east of Dauphin, is a popular place for watersports and offers camping, fishing and wildlife tours.

Parkland Recreation Complex, 200 1st Ave. S.E., includes two arenas, a playground, a curling rink and an aquatic center with an indoor wave pool and waterslide; phone (204) 622-3150.

In late June, more than 14,000 country music fans flock to Dauphin's Countryfest, a 4-day music festival held at Selo Ukraina, a heritage village 12 kilometres (7.5 mi.) south of Dauphin near Riding Mountain National Park.

The nation's rich Ukrainian culture and heritage are celebrated in early August at Selo Ukraina during 🌾 Canada's National Ukrainian Festival, a 3-day event featuring Ukrainian music, food and dance.

Dauphin Economic Development & Tourism: 100 Main St. S., Dauphin, MB, Canada R7N 1K3. **Phone:** (204) 622-3216 or (877) 566-5669.

FORT DAUPHIN MUSEUM, 140 Jackson St., is surrounded by a wooden palisade suggestive of an 18th-century fur trading fort of the North West Co. A trapper's cabin, schoolhouse, church, blacksmith shop, trading post and pioneer house inside the fort are furnished in the style of the early settlers. Archeological, fur trade and pioneer artifacts also are featured.

Time: Allow 1 hour minimum. **Hours:** Daily 9-5, July-Aug.; Mon.-Fri. 9-5, May-June and in Sept.; by appointment rest of year. **Cost:** $4; $3 (students with ID); free (ages 0-11 with adult). **Phone:** (204) 638-6630.

ELKHORN (G-1) pop. 471, elev. 526m/1,700'

THE MANITOBA ANTIQUE AUTOMOBILE MUSEUM is on Hwy. 1W. The museum displays some 100 vintage automobiles dating from 1908 to the mid-1960s; several are in operating condition. Also exhibited are steam engines, gas tractors and other farm machinery as well as aboriginal, household and pioneer artifacts. **Time:** Allow 1 hour minimum. **Hours:** Daily 9-6, May-Sept. **Cost:** $7.50; $2 (ages 5-16). **Phone:** (204) 845-2604, or (204) 845-2161 Oct.-Apr.

EMERSON (H-4) pop. 671

Emerson was named after American poet Ralph Waldo Emerson. When Manitoba became a province in 1870, this town on the border of the United States and Canada was the site of the province's first customs house. The original log buildings still stand just north of the Customs Port of Entry.

In 1874 the North West Mounted Police, later renamed the Royal Canadian Mounted Police, organized at Fort Dufferin, thus beginning their career of maintaining law and order in the untamed western areas of Canada. A 5-metre (15-ft.) bronze statue of a North West Mounted Police Officer and his horse is located next to the Tourist Information Centre on Hwy. 75. The statue is a tribute to the members of the force who made the historic "Trek West" from Emerson to Fort Macleod, Alberta.

The Boundary Commission Trail provides 3 kilometres (1.9 mi.) of hiking along the Red River north to the Historic Fort Dufferin Site. At the fort are the remains of old buildings, grave sites and a memorial to the North West Mounted Police.

Town of Emerson: 104 Church St., P.O. Box 340, Emerson, MB, Canada R0A 0L0. **Phone:** (204) 373-2002.

FALCON LAKE (G-6) pop. 277,
elev. 305m/1,001'

As it winds its way across the country, the Trans Canada Trail enters Manitoba from Ontario at West Hawk Lake in Whiteshell Provincial Park (see attraction listing), crossing the park diagonally as it heads westward to Pinawa. Incorporating many existing trails and utilizing abandoned railway lines, the trail offers hikers a diverse sampling of the province's topography.

WHITESHELL PROVINCIAL PARK is accessible via an especially scenic stretch of Hwy. 1E. The park's two districts encompass both wilderness and developed resort areas, more than 200 lakes and 12 rivers.

Alfred Hole Goose Sanctuary, east of Rennie on Hwy. 44, is a nesting ground for giant Canada geese, which can be seen from the interpretive center. Believed extinct 1930-60, the birds can be seen at close range from the interpretive center. The center contains exhibits and information about Alf Hole's legacy and the biology of Canada geese. Rocks found throughout the park are part of the Precambrian Shield, the oldest geological formation in the world. See Recreation Areas Chart.

Among the rivers in the park is the Winnipeg River with numerous falls and rapids. West Hawk Lake, near the Ontario border, is one of the deepest lakes in Manitoba. It is thought that the lake was formed by a meteor more than 100 million years ago.

Near Betula Lake are the Bannock Point Petroforms-ceremonial Anishinabe boulder mosaics of snakes, turtles and geometric shapes. Along with its beauty and tranquility, the park is popular during the summer for interpretive programs, swimming, scuba diving, canoeing, lawn bowling, tennis, miniature golf, horseshoes, horseback riding, sailing, hiking and golfing; in winter it provides ample opportunities for cross-country and downhill skiing, snowmobiling and snowshoeing.

At the Fish Hatchery Interpretive Center, on PR 312 between West Hawk Lake and Caddy Lake, visitors can learn about the fish farming process and see large water tanks filled with thousands of fish.

Hours: Park open daily 24 hours. The Fish Hatchery Interpretive Center is open daily 10-6, June 1-Labour Day. One-hour tours of the center are given daily at 11 and 2. **Cost:** One-day pass $4 per private vehicle. Annual pass $30. **Phone:** (204) 369-3157 for Park Interpreters Office. 🅰 🍴 🎌 🐟 ⛲

Whiteshell Natural History Museum is deep within Whiteshell Provincial Park near Seven Sisters Falls on PR 307 at Nutimik Lake, opposite the boat launch. Mounted animals within the log cabin museum depict the wildlife residing within the provincial park. Other exhibits include displays about the boreal forest, first peoples, wild rice, sturgeon and the Winnipeg River.

Time: Allow 30 minutes minimum. **Hours:** Daily 10:30-6, Victoria Day weekend-Labour Day weekend. **Cost:** One-day pass $4 per private vehicle. **Phone:** (204) 369-3157. ⛲

RECREATIONAL ACTIVITIES
Horseback Riding
- **Falcon Beach Riding Stables and Guest Ranch** is off Hwy. 1 Falcon Lake exit. **Hours:** Horseback rides offered daily 9-5, July-Aug.; by appointment rest of year. **Phone:** (204) 349-2410, or (877) 949-2410 in Canada.

FLIN FLON (B-2) pop. 5,363, elev. 304m/1,000'
• Hotels p. 458 • Restaurants p. 458

Flin Flon was founded in 1915 when Tom Creighton, one of six prospectors, discovered an ore body which led to the development of Flin Flon as a mining town.

The community owes its name to Josiah Flintabbatey Flonatin, the major character of "The Sunless City," a dime novel found in the area by the discoverers of the mineral deposits. Off Hwy. 10 is a humorous 7.5-metre (25-ft.) statue of Flintabbatey Flonatin ("Flinty" for short) designed by the American cartoonist Al Capp, of "L'il Abner" fame. A boardwalk around Ross Lake, a walking trail and a park also remember the city's namesake; the park features a smaller statue of Flinty.

The Flin Flon Station Museum, north on Hwy. 10A, is open daily 10-8 seasonally and displays artifacts collected from mining, transportation and cultural sources; phone (204) 687-2946. Bordering

Saskatchewan, Flin Flon is the northern terminus of the Manitoba stretch of scenic Hwy. 10.

Flin Flon and District Chamber of Commerce: 235-35 Main St., Flin Flon, MB, Canada R8A 1J7. **Phone:** (204) 687-4518.

VICTORIA INN NORTH   204/687-7555

♦♦ **Hotel** $140-$190 **Address:** 160 Hwy 10A N R8A 0C6 **Location:** Jct Hwy 10 and 10A, 0.6 mi (1 km) nw (eastern approach to city). Located in a commercial area. **Facility:** 93 units. 3 stories (no elevator), interior corridors. **Parking:** winter plug-ins. **Dining:** The Kelsey Dining Room, see separate listing. **Pool(s):** heated indoor. **Activities:** whirlpool, exercise room. **Guest Services:** coin laundry.

🛎 🍴 CALL 🅜 � BIZ 🛜 ✖ 🔒 🖵 / SOME UNITS FEE 🐾

WHERE TO EAT

THE KELSEY DINING ROOM   204/687-7555

♦♦ American. Family Dining. $8-$29 **AAA Inspector Notes:** Friendly, efficient service and generous portions keep locals and visitors returning to this restaurant. The menu is varied and offers such selections as steak, chicken, fish and pasta. Booth and table seating are available. **Bar:** full bar. **Address:** 160 Hwy 10A N R8A 0C6 **Location:** Jct Hwy 10 and 10A, 0.6 mi (1 km) nw (eastern approach to city); in Victoria Inn North. B L D CALL 🅜

GARDENTON (H-5) elev. 298m/979'

Some of the earliest Ukrainian settlers in Manitoba came to Gardenton in 1896. St. Michael's Ukrainian Orthodox Historical Church, 4 kilometres (2.5 mi.) west, is purportedly North America's first Ukrainian Orthodox church; the church was built 1897-99. Lithographed icons from St. Petersburg, Moscow and Kiev ornament the sanctuary. A pilgrimage is held in summer. Phone (204) 425-3501 for an appointment to tour the church.

The Ukrainian Museum contains articles of clothing and hand tools depicting life in the late 1800s and early 1900s, a one-room schoolhouse and a thatched roof house. Also in the area is a tall-grass prairie. For further information about the museum phone (204) 425-3072 in summer, or (204) 425-3501 rest of year.

GILBERT PLAINS (F-2) pop. 811

WASYL NEGRYCH PIONEER HOMESTEAD is 17.3 km (10.8 mi.) n. on PR 274, then 3.2 km (2 mi.) e. on Negrych Rd. (gravel). The homestead's 10 log buildings, built in 1899, are said to be the province's most complete set of period farmyard buildings and the oldest Ukrainian-style house in Manitoba. The buildings reflect the architectural style of the Carpathian Mountain region. **Time:** Allow 1 hour minimum. **Hours:** Daily 10-5, July-Aug. **Cost:** $5; $3 (students with ID); free (ages 0-5). **Phone:** (204) 548-2326. 🎟

GIMLI (G-4) pop. 5,845, elev. 220m/723'

Established in 1875, Gimli was the site of Canada's first permanent Icelandic settlement, the largest outside Iceland. The town's name, derived from

Norse mythology, means "home of the gods." A Viking statue designed by Gissur Eliasson and the oldest Icelandic cemetery in Canada testify to Gimli's Nordic heritage. Gimli is located on the western shore of Lake Winnipeg, one of the largest freshwater lakes in the world.

Lake Winnipeg Visitor Centre: 108-84 1st Ave., Gimli, MB, Canada R0C 1B0. **Phone:** (204) 642-7974.

[SAVE] **NEW ICELAND HERITAGE MUSEUM** is at 94 1st Ave. Displayed in two buildings are exhibits that focus on the area's Icelandic roots, the fishing industry and Lake Winnipeg's natural history. Multimedia exhibits at the Waterfront Centre examine area history, while displays at the visitor center feature the fishing industry and the lake's natural history.

Time: Allow 30 minutes minimum. **Hours:** Waterfront Centre daily 10-4, Victoria Day weekend-Labour Day; Mon.-Fri. 10-4, Sat.-Sun. 1-4, rest of year. Visitor center daily 10-6, Victoria Day weekend-Labour Day. **Cost:** $6; $5 (ages 55+ and students with ID); free (ages 0-6); $15 (family). **Phone:** (204) 642-4001. 🎟

LAKEVIEW RESORT & CONFERENCE CENTRE
                                      (204)642-8565

Hotel
$92-$285

Address: 10 Centre St R0C 1B0 **Location:** Hwy 9, 1 mi (1.6 km) e. **Facility:** 99 units, some two bedrooms, efficiencies and kitchens. 3 stories, interior corridors. **Parking:** winter plug-ins. **Terms:** cancellation fee imposed. **Pool(s):** heated outdoor, heated indoor. **Activities:** sauna, whirlpool, ice skating, tobogganing, exercise room. **Fee:** game room. **Guest Services:** coin laundry. **Free Special Amenities:** local telephone calls and high-speed Internet.

SAVE ECO 🍴 🍷 CALL 🅜 � BIZ 🛜 ✖ 🔒 🖵 / SOME UNITS 📷

WHERE TO EAT

MASK RESTAURANT   204/642-4727

♦♦ Italian. Casual Dining. $9-$30 **AAA Inspector Notes:** This cute and quirky little place has casual and more formal dining rooms and a covered patio. Prepared with fresh ingredients and herbs, delicious and creative salads, pizzas and freshly made thin-crust pizzas figure predominantly on the menu along with a few sandwiches and more substantial entrées. Pickerel shows up in a lot of items. The finer dining room fills up fast, so make a reservation if you want a more elegant experience. A breakfast menu and lighter lunch menu are offered. **Bar:** full bar. **Reservations:** suggested. **Address:** 129 7th Ave R0C 1B0 **Location:** Jct Hwy 9 (7th Ave) and Centre St, just s. B L D

GLENBORO (H-3) pop. 645, elev. 375m/1,230'

Glenboro is known as the gateway to Spruce Woods Provincial Park *(see Carberry p. 454)* and the Manitoba Desert. At the junction of hwys. 2 and 5 in Camel Park stands Sara the Camel, a 7-metre-high (24-ft.) symbol of the Spirit Sands. The Glenboro Walking Tour takes visitors on a self-guiding stroll which points out many of the sights. Brochures are available at the village office; phone (204) 827-2083.

Slightly northwest of Glenboro on Hwy. 2 is what is purported to be the last cable river ferry in southern Manitoba; phone (204) 827-2252.

GRANDVIEW (F-2) pop. 859, elev. 434m/1,425'

WATSON CROSSLEY COMMUNITY MUSEUM is on the w. side of town at the sports grounds on Railway Ave. The museum displays regional pioneer items including automobiles, horse-drawn equipment, tractors, farm machinery and other artifacts. A restored 1896 homesteader's cabin, a pioneer church with a free-standing bell tower, a rural schoolhouse and a three-story 1918 pioneer house are furnished in their respective periods.

Time: Allow 2 hours minimum. **Hours:** Daily 10-5, late June-early Sept.; by appointment rest of year. **Cost:** $4; $3 (ages 13-17). **Phone:** (204) 546-2040 late June-early Sept., (204) 546-2764 rest of year or (204) 546-2661.

HADASHVILLE (H-5) elev. 297m/975'

SANDILANDS FOREST CENTRE, about 2 km (1.2 mi.) s. of jct. hwys. 1 and 11, tells visitors about forest conservation, reforestation and fire prevention. A train car used 1919-74 to promote the nationwide planting of trees is shown, an electronic display tests tree species knowledge and a museum has area plants and animals. The Old Beaver Dam Trail, reached by a suspension bridge over the Whitemouth River, penetrates aspen parkland and a boreal forest.

Guided tours of the center are available. **Time:** Allow 1 hour minimum. **Hours:** Thurs.-Mon. 10-5, July-Aug.; by appointment, May-June. Phone ahead to confirm schedule. **Cost:** Donations. Guided tours $3. Reservations are required for guided tours. **Phone:** (204) 426-5374.

HEADINGLEY pop. 3,215

RECREATIONAL ACTIVITIES
Tubing
- **Adrenaline Adventures,** off Hwy. 100 at 600 Caron Rd., offers snow tubing, cable snowboarding and other activities in winter. In summer, cable wakeboarding and a ropes course with ziplines are offered. **Hours:** Open daily at noon; closing times vary. Phone ahead to confirm schedule. **Phone:** (204) 800-2060 or (855) 266-9222.

HECLA ISLAND (E-4) elev. 210m/690'

HECLA/GRINDSTONE PROVINCIAL PARK, 165 km (103 mi.) n. of Winnipeg, or 54 km (34 mi.) n. of Riverton, on Hwy. 8, is comprised of several islands in Lake Winnipeg, the largest of which is Hecla Island. The original settlers were Icelanders displaced from their homeland in 1876, fleeing poverty and Danish rule. Guided walks through the restored

buildings of Hecla Village—a church, school, community hall, period house, dockside fish station, a tool display and a partially completed boarding house—are offered. *See Recreation Areas Chart.*

Interpretive programs also are available, as are camping facilities, cabins, hiking trails, picnic areas, bicycling, fishing and swimming. For further information contact the Department of Conservation, P.O. Box 70, Riverton, MB, Canada R0C 2R0. **Hours:** Daily 24 hours. **Cost:** One-day pass $4 per private vehicle. Annual pass $30. **Phone:** (204) 279-2032 May-Sept. or (204) 378-2261. 🅰 🗙 🎋

Grassy Narrows Marsh and Wildlife Viewing Tower, at Hecla/Grindstone Provincial Park, offers wildlife viewing from trails and boardwalks along the marsh as well as from towers along the trails. Some trails are designated bicycling trails. The marsh, a nesting area for Canada geese and other waterfowl, is named after the Narrows, a channel between Hecla Island and the mainland. The tower was built for viewing moose as they feed in the marsh. **Note:** Visitors should bring drinking water and wear comfortable walking shoes. **Hours:** Daily 24 hours. **Cost:** One-day pass $4 per private vehicle. Annual pass $30. **Phone:** (204) 279-2032 May-Sept., or (204) 378-2261 rest of year.

Hecla Fish Station, at Hecla/Grindstone Provincial Park, is in an old ice house, or "fish station." The site provides a look at the commercial fishing industry of Lake Winnipeg through artifacts, wall plaques and a small museum. During June and September visitors may view fishermen bringing in the day's catch. **Hours:** Daily 11:30-4:30, June 10-Aug. 30. **Cost:** Free. **Phone:** (204) 279-2032.

Hecla Island Heritage Home Museum, at Hecla/Grindstone Provincial Park, depicts the lifestyle of an Icelandic family from the 1920s to the 1940s. The restored 1928 house is furnished in period with items donated by descendants of the original owners and by other islanders. Walking tours are available. **Hours:** Wed.-Sun. 10-4, June 26-Sept. 2. **Cost:** Donations. **Phone:** (204) 279-2032 or (204) 279-2056.

INGLIS (F-1)

INGLIS GRAIN ELEVATORS NATIONAL HISTORIC SITE is along Railway Ave. These five vintage grain elevators, once a common sight on western Canadian prairies, have been restored and are now the last remaining row of standard wooden grain elevators in Canada. Dating to the 1920s, similar rows of elevators, built by grain companies and agricultural cooperatives, once stood along rail lines in most small Canadian communities.

An interpretive center in the Paterson elevator explains the importance of these structures to the nation's agricultural history. Exhibits and displays complement a video presentation, which shows how the elevators operated, transporting wheat into storage bins. A walking tour of the grounds provides further insights into the development of Canada's grain industry.

Time: Allow 1 hour minimum. **Hours:** Wed.-Sun. 10-5, July-Aug.; otherwise by appointment. **Cost:** $5; $3 (students with ID); free (ages 0-5). **Phone:** (204) 564-2243. 🎫

▼ INTERNATIONAL PEACE GARDEN (F-1)

On scenic Hwy. 10 and on US 281, the International Peace Garden consists of 1,451 acres (586 hectares) in Manitoba and an adjoining 888 acres (360 hectares) in North Dakota. Set among the lakes and streams of the wooded Turtle Mountains, the botanical garden and park commemorates the friendship between these two countries on the longest unfortified border in the world.

Points of interest include the 120-foot Peace Tower, which represents people from the four corners of the world coming together for the common purpose of peace; the Peace Chapel, which includes quotations etched in limestone walls; more than 150,000 flowering annuals in the formal gardens that line the boundary; a floral clock; the Carillon Bell Tower, which chimes every 15 minutes; and the 9/11 Memorial, constructed of steel salvaged from the ruins of the World Trade Center, commemorating the tragic events of Sept. 11, 2001.

The Interpretive Centre and Conservatory houses a retail store, internet café, small prairie lands library and a conservatory with more than 2,000 cacti. The North American Game Warden Museum is dedicated to officers who died in the line of duty.

Facilities include campgrounds, hiking and bicycling trails and picnic areas. Self-guiding walking and driving tours are available. Flowers are in full bloom mid-July to early September (weather permitting).

The International Music Camp Summer School of Fine Arts is held at the garden June through July. The Legion Athletic Camp, held July through August, attracts coaches and athletes from many countries.

After leaving the garden all visitors are required to go through customs (U.S. and Canadian customs stations are a short distance from the entrance gate). Allow 2 hours minimum to visit the site. The garden is open daily 24 hours, and the entrance gate is staffed daily 9-7, late May to mid-Sept; Game Warden Museum daily 10-5. Daily vehicle permit $10; pedestrian permit $5; season permit $25. Game Warden Museum admission is free. Phone (204) 534-2510 in Canada, (701) 263-4390 in the United States, or (888) 432-6733.

KILLARNEY (H-2) pop. 3,233, elev. 495m/1,625'

The area's resemblance to Ireland's Killarney Lakes prompted John Sidney O'Brien to change the name of the town of Oak Lake to Killarney. Green

fire engines and a replica of the Blarney Stone are further evidence of the town's Irish heritage.

Killarney and District Chamber of Commerce: P.O. Box 809, Killarney, MB, Canada R0K 1G0. **Phone:** (204) 523-4202.

J.A.V. DAVID MUSEUM, 414 Williams Ave., displays Indian and pioneer artifacts, local memorabilia, an archive, quilts and collections of birds, butterflies and animals. Also featured are an early 1900s schoolroom, a Ninette Sanitorium display, a post office display and a country store. **Time:** Allow 1 hour minimum. **Hours:** Tues.-Sat. 10-noon and 1-5, July-Aug.; by appointment rest of year. Closed major holidays. **Cost:** $2; $1 (students); free (ages 0-10); $5 (family). **Phone:** (204) 523-7325.

LA RIVIÈRE (H-3) pop. 174

ARCHIBALD HISTORICAL MUSEUM is 3 km (2 mi.) e. on Hwy. 3, then 6 km (4 mi.) n. on a dirt road, following signs. The museum consists of buildings moved to the site from neighboring areas. Two homes lived in by social activist and author Nellie McClung in the late 19th- and early 20th centuries are included, both furnished in period, as are the mansard-roofed former CPR train station (with a 1913 wooden caboose in front), a house with tin siding and a three-story barn with a country store, tools, buggies, household artifacts and tractors.

Native artifacts and vintage cars, trucks and gas pumps also can be seen. **Time:** Allow 1 hour minimum. **Hours:** Fri.-Tues. noon-8, mid-May through Labour Day. Phone ahead to confirm schedule. **Cost:** $6; $2 (ages 5-11). **Phone:** (204) 242-2825. 🎫

LOCKPORT (G-4) pop. 754, elev. 313m/1,000'

At Lockport Provincial Heritage Park *(see attraction listing)*, on Hwy. 44 just east of the Lockport bridge, is St. Andrews Lock and Dam. This rare structure on Canada's flat prairies was completed in 1910 to allow access and permit navigation on the Red River from Lake Winnipeg to the city of Winnipeg; it is purportedly the only lock and dam of its kind still standing in North America. Picnic sites and footpaths overlook the dam.

LOCKPORT PROVINCIAL HERITAGE PARK is on Hwy. 44 just e. of the Lockport Bridge. Archeological digs at the park have established the site as the location where Manitoba's aboriginal "first farmers" worked the land along the banks of the Red River. In addition to a display about the St. Andrews Lock and Dam, the park also has a fish ladder and a large colony of white pelicans.

A .7-kilometre (.4-mi.) trail along the river has interpretive signs explaining the resources that brought native peoples to the area. **Hours:** Daily dawn-dusk, mid-May to mid-Oct. **Cost:** Free. **Phone:** (204) 785-5080. 🎫

ST. ANDREW'S CHURCH is 2 km (1.2 mi.) s. on Hwy. 9, then just e. on St. Andrews Rd. (Hwy. 410) to 374 River Rd. (Hwy. 238). Designed by its first rector 1844-49, this stone Gothic-Revival Anglican church is the oldest house of worship in continuous use in western Canada. It retains many of its original fixtures. The church's cemetery is adjacent. **Time:** Allow 30 minutes minimum. **Hours:** Tours by appointment, mid-May through Labour Day. **Cost:** Donations. **Phone:** (204) 334-5700.

St. Andrew's Rectory National Historic Site is 2 km (1.2 mi.) s. on Hwy. 9, then just e. on St. Andrews Rd. (Hwy. 410) to 374 River Rd. (Hwy. 238), across from St. Andrew's Church. The exterior of the two-story stone building can be viewed by visitors. It was constructed in 1854 for the church's rectors and represents Red River architecture. **Hours:** Grounds daily dawn-dusk. **Cost:** Donations. **Phone:** (204) 334-5700.

MINNEDOSA (G-2) pop. 2,587

A walking trail surrounds the fenced-in Bison Park on Hwy. 262 (Beach Road). The Little Saskatchewan River runs beside the animal viewing area, which is open dawn to dusk May through October. Visitors are not permitted to feed the bison.

Minnedosa Lake and Beach offers ample summer and winter recreational options *(see Recreation Areas Chart)*.

Minnedosa Area Community Development Office 39 Main St. S., Minnedosa, MB R0J 1E0. **Phone:** (204) 867-3885 or (866) 577-2968.

Self-guiding tours: The Minnedosa Area Community Development Office has brochures about local self-guiding tours. One guides visitors along Main Street to see the 12 Founders Parks, each with historical aesthetic touches and a plaque detailing a town founder. Another brochure showcases the town's historic stone buildings.

MINNEDOSA HERITAGE VILLAGE is on 3rd Ave. N.E., just e. of Main St. The village highlights are three furnished buildings: the 1904 Hunterville Church, the 1910 Cadurcis Home and the 1910 Havelock School. The grounds also feature a restored blacksmith shop, log house, cabin and barn as well as a windmill and waterwheel. Manitoba's second electrical power plant, built in 1920, contains local historical displays. Catch-and-release fishing is permitted at a stocked trout pond. **Hours:** Daily 1-8, July 1-Labour Day. **Cost:** $3; $6 (family). Cash only. **Phone:** (204) 867-2027. 🅰

RECREATIONAL ACTIVITIES
Skiing and Snowboarding
• **Ski Valley** is 8 km (5 mi.) n. off Hwy. 10. **Hours:** Sat.-Sun. 9-4:30, Mon.-Fri. hours vary, early Dec.-late Mar. **Phone:** (204) 867-3509.

MORDEN (H-4) pop. 7,812, elev. 302m/990'

Named after the area's first settler, Alvey Morden, the town grew almost overnight when the Canadian Pacific Railroad arrived in 1882. Located near the Boundary Commission-NWMP Trail in the Boundary Trail Heritage Region, Morden has a progressive industrial and business sector. Abundant recreational activities at Lake Minnewasta *(see Recreation Areas Chart)* and Colert Beach include camping, swimming, fishing, water skiing, canoeing, sailing, bicycling and hiking in the summer. Winter activities include cross-country skiing, snowmobiling and ice fishing.

A mural on the corner of Stephen and Nelson streets is a re-creation of one of the earliest known photographs taken in the area. The scene depicts the supply train for Her Majesty's British North American Boundary Commission at Dead Horse Creek in June 1873.

Another mural, at the corner of Stephen and 7th streets, remembers the visit of Canada's first prime minister, Sir John A. MacDonald, to the town on July 15, 1886. The depiction features Sir John speaking from the rear of his railcar and Philip Locke presenting him with a bouquet of prairie flowers; a version of an Indian war dance also is depicted.

A third mural, at 306 N. Railway St., depicts the original uniform of the North West Mounted Police and provides a history of the force, now known as the Royal Canadian Mounted Police.

Morden and District Chamber of Commerce: 311 N. Railway St., Morden, MB, Canada R6M 1S9. **Phone:** (204) 822-5630.

Self-guiding tours: Heritage Series Brochures, available at the chamber of commerce, describe self-guiding walking tours of Morden's turn-of-the-20th-century homes and buildings.

CANADIAN FOSSIL DISCOVERY CENTRE is in the lower level of the Access Event Centre at 111-B Gilmour St. Fossil displays chronicle regional paleontology and geology. Marine reptile fossils, such as mosasaurs and plesiosaurs, date from 80 million years ago when the Western Interior Seaway covered much of North America. A highlight of the exhibits is Bruce, a 43-foot mosasaur and said to be the largest discovered in Canada. The process of finding, excavating and displaying the fossils also is depicted. Fossil Dig Adventure Tours offer a chance to excavate fossils at a site nearby.

Time: Allow 1 hour minimum. **Hours:** Daily 10-5, May-Aug.; 1-5, rest of year. Closed Christmas. **Cost:** $6; $3 (ages 5-17); $12 (family, two adults and up to three children). A fee is charged for Fossil Dig. Reservations are recommended 1 week in advance for fossil dig. **Phone:** (204) 822-3406.

MORRIS (H-4) pop. 1,797, elev. 236m/775'

Two rival fur-trading companies—the North West Co. and the Hudson's Bay Co.—set up shop on the Morris River in 1801. Not until 1874 did a permanent settlement take hold; incorporation took place in 1883. Both the town and the river on which it grew were named for Alexander Morris, the second lieutenant governor of Manitoba during the 1870s.

Morris Town Office: 1-380 Stampede Grounds, Box 28, Morris, MB, Canada R0G 1K0. **Phone:** (204) 746-2531.

MORRIS & DISTRICT CENTENNIAL MUSEUM, on Main St. at jct. hwys. 75 and 23, consists of two buildings. The main building is the original Carleton School, which contains pioneer-era displays of farm tools and a laundry and dairy section. The second building contains five rooms featuring furniture and artifacts from the turn of the 20th century. A mural depicts the history of the Red River Valley. **Hours:** Daily noon-5, June-Sept. **Cost:** Donations. **Phone:** (204) 746-2169.

NEEPAWA (G-3) pop. 3,629, elev. 400m/1,300'

Neepawa, whose name derives from a native word for plenty, is a service center for the surrounding grain and livestock farms on the fertile plains northwest of Winnipeg. This community of tree-lined streets, well-known as the birthplace of author Margaret Laurence, offers many pleasant diversions for residents and travelers alike, including Riverbend Park, a fitness trail and camping area.

The city calls itself the World Lily Capital. This claim is bolstered by the annual ▼ Neepawa Lily Festival held over three days in late July. More than 2,000 varieties of lilies are grown in the Neepawa area, and the community celebrates their beauty with live entertainment, music, street vendors and food kiosks, a quilt show, a parade, tours by bus and horse-drawn vehicles and a photography contest.

Neepawa and District Chamber of Commerce: 282 Hamilton St., P.O. Box 726, Neepawa, MB, Canada R0J 1H0. **Phone:** (204) 476-5292.

BEAUTIFUL PLAINS MUSEUM, 91 Hamilton St. W., is housed in a former CNR station. The museum features several rooms of historical items. A children's room contains antique toys and books, and a military room has uniforms and pictures of local residents involved in World Wars I and II. Other rooms include items dedicated to nature, stores, Masonic lodges, sports and vintage clothing. An extensive doll collection also is displayed.

Time: Allow 30 minutes minimum. **Hours:** Mon.-Sat. 9-5, Sun. 1-5, July 1-early Sept.; Mon.-Fri. 9-5, May-June. **Cost:** Donations. **Phone:** (204) 476-3896.

MARGARET LAURENCE HOME, 312 First Ave., contains photographs, memorabilia, autographed books and research materials of the award-winning Canadian author, born here in 1926. **Tours:** Guided tours are available. **Hours:** Daily 10-5, mid-May through Sept. 30; by appointment rest of year. **Cost:** $5; $2 (students ages 15+); free (ages 0-14). **Phone:** (204) 476-3612.

PINAWA (G-5) pop. 1,444, elev. 282m/925'

Named "Pinnawak," meaning calm waters, by the aboriginal people, Pinawa was first settled by families who operated one of the earliest hydroelectric power dams built between Sault Ste. Marie, Ontario, and the Rockies. The townsite was abandoned in 1951, and the historic site is now Pinawa Dam Provincial Heritage Park. The new Pinawa was built in 1963 when the Federal Crown Corp., Atomic Energy of Canada Limited (AECL) built its research center near the old townsite.

PORTAGE LA PRAIRIE (G-3) pop. 12,996, elev. 332m/1,100'

The city's name is derived from the prairie portage between the Red and Assiniboine rivers and Lake Manitoba. In the heart of the city at Crescent Road and Royal Road S. is Island Park. Surrounded by horseshoe-shaped Crescent Lake, this scenic park has a deer sanctuary, a large captive flock of Canada geese and offers opportunities for other bird-watching. Park features include playground areas, exhibition grounds, seasonal harness racing, a golf course, an arboretum, tennis courts, picnic areas and bicycling and hiking trails.

Portage la Prairie City Hall, built in 1898, was designed by one of Canada's foremost architects, Thomas Fuller.

Portage and District Chamber of Commerce: 11 Second St. N.E., Portage la Prairie, MB, Canada R1N 1R8. **Phone:** (204) 857-7778.

FORT LA REINE MUSEUM, PIONEER VILLAGE AND TOURIST BUREAU is at jct. hwys. 26 and 1A E. The central museum includes pioneer household articles and implements, a log fort, school, doctor's office, trading post, furnished homestead and church as well as railway, farming and military displays. Canadian railway official Sir William Van Horne's business car also is displayed. A tourist bureau is available.

Time: Allow 1 hour minimum. **Hours:** Mon.-Sat. 9-6, Sun. noon-6, mid-May to mid-Sept. **Cost:** $8; $6 (ages 60+); $3 (ages 6-12). **Phone:** (204) 857-3259.

CANAD INNS DESTINATION CENTRE PORTAGE LA PRAIRIE   (204)857-9745

▼▼ ◆◆
Hotel
$104-$255

Address: 2401 Saskatchewan Ave W R1N 3L5 **Location:** Jct Hwy 1A and 24th St W. Located in a commercial area. **Facility:** 92 units. 2 stories, interior corridors. **Parking:** winter plug-ins. **Amenities:** *Some:* high-speed Internet. **Dining:** 2 restaurants. **Pool(s):** heated indoor. **Activities:** whirlpool, waterslide, volleyball. **Guest Services:** valet laundry. **Free Special Amenities:** newspaper and high-speed Internet.

SUPER 8

 Hotel $99-$104 **Address:** 2668 Hwy 1A W R1N 3B2 **Location:** On Hwy 1A, 0.9 mi (1.5 km) w. Located in a commercial area. **Facility:** 58 units. 2 stories (no elevator), interior corridors. **Parking:** winter plug-ins. **Amenities:** *Some:* high-speed Internet. **Pool(s):** heated indoor. **Activities:** whirlpool, waterslide. **Guest Services:** coin laundry.

CALL    / SOME UNITS FEE

WHERE TO EAT

BILL'S STICKY FINGERS   204/857-9999

American
Casual Dining
$6-$25

AAA Inspector Notes: This comfortable, casual, older restaurant offers a wide-ranging menu that includes ribs, chicken, steak, lasagna, gyros and pizza, as well as daily specials. The service is friendly and prompt. **Bar:** full bar. **Address:** 210 Saskatchewan Ave E R1N 0K9 **Location:** Just w of Main St.

L   D   LATE   CALL

GARDEN GATE GRILL AND BAKERY   204/856-0540

American. Family Dining. $6-$16 **AAA Inspector Notes:** This rather nondescript restaurant stands out amidst the town's many chain restaurants by serving up a little bit of everything and a whole lot of friendly, small-town service. Everything from soups and sandwiches to burgers and steaks can be found on the menu. **Bar:** full bar. **Address:** 2380 Sissons Dr R1N 0G5 **Location:** Jct Hwy 1A and 24th St W.   L   D

RIDING MOUNTAIN NATIONAL PARK (F-1)

Elevations in the park range from 230 metres (755 ft.) at Henderson Creek in the northeastern area to 756 metres (2,480 ft.) at Bald Hill in the eastern side of the park. Refer to CAA/AAA maps for additional elevation information.

Accessible from the north and south via scenic Hwy. 10, or from the east via Hwy. 19, Riding Mountain National Park lies on the plateau of the Manitoba escarpment, 197 kilometres (123 mi.) north of the U.S. border and 259 kilometres (162 mi.) northwest of Winnipeg. The park also encompasses the historic resort town of Wasagaming on Clear Lake, which offers the amenities of a resort destination. The park's 2,978-square-kilometre (1,150-sq.-mi.) area is blanketed with forests, lakes and meadows. It was officially dedicated in 1933 and is home to elk, moose, deer, bears and a wide variety of birds and vegetation. Waterfowl and beavers populate the waterways, and a herd of bison grazes in a large enclosure near Lake Audy. Driving hwys. 10 and 19 as well as Lake Audy Road offer scenic views and opportunities to spot wildlife. Self-guiding bison tour brochures are available at various park facilities.

During the Depression of the 1930s, the Depression Relief Program created jobs for the unemployed, 1,200 of whom were put to work constructing buildings for the park 1934-35. As is the case with much of the architecture found in the country's national parks, the style widely used was a rustic design that incorporated local materials. Perhaps the most eye-catching of their projects here is the East Gate Complex on Hwy. 19, which includes

a registration building, two staff buildings and an overhead entrance sign. (Northern and southern complexes had been built but no longer exist.)

Another major international event the following decade further influenced the site's development, when World War II changed the site's focus from recreation to a source of attaining fuelwood. During the war the park was used as a minimum security POW camp, housing German prisoners from North Africa to cut cordwood. When the prisoners were released in late 1945, the function of the park turned once again to recreation.

General Information and Activities

Although the park is open year-round, complete facilities are available only from mid-May to mid-October. Recreational activities available within the park include bicycling, boating, camping, tennis, golfing, lawn bowling, swimming, hiking, fishing, canoeing, sailing, horseback riding, swimming, skateboarding, ice-skating, cross-country skiing and snowshoeing. Snowmobiling is permitted on Clear Lake and around the park's perimeter. Clear Lake has a beach and boat launches, and scuba diving is possible; divers must register with the park. More than 400 kilometres (250 mi.) of hiking, bicycling and horseback trails lead to lakes, meadows and evergreen forests. Bicycle and boat rentals are available. The park has more than a dozen picnic sites.

Note: Except for in Wasagaming, water must be boiled for all uses. Swimming areas are unsupervised; lifeguards are not available. Due to the presence of a parasite in most of the bodies of water in the park, developing swimmer's itch is a concern; take proper precautions. Camping permits and fishing licenses are required.

Several forms of recreation can be pursued nearby. Guides and outfitters offer horseback riding and wagon excursions along with other wilderness activities. *See Recreation Areas Chart.*

ADMISSION is $7.80; $6.55 (ages 65+); $3.90 (ages 6-16); free (ages 0-5); $19.60 (family, up to seven people). Annual pass $39.20; $34.30 (ages 65+); $19.60 (ages 6-16); $98.10 (family).

PETS are allowed in the park. Dogs must be leashed at all times.

ADDRESS inquiries to Visitor Information, Riding Mountain National Park, Wasagaming, MB, Canada R0J 2H0; phone (204) 848-7275 or (204) 848-7272.

VISITOR INFORMATION CENTRE OF WASAGAMING is on the s. shore of Clear Lake. The center maintains exhibits and displays about the natural and human history of the area. Interpretive programs include nature walks, campfires, theater programs and guided hikes. **Hours:** Daily 9:30-8, Victoria Day weekend-early Sept. **Cost:** Free. **Phone:** (204) 848-7275 or (204) 848-7272.

RUSSELL pop. 1,669

THE RUSSELL INN HOTEL & CONFERENCE CENTRE
(204)773-2186
◆◆ ◆◆ **Hotel** $100-$196 **Address:** Hwy 16 R0J 1W0 **Location:** 0.8 mi (1.2 km) se on Hwy 16 and 83. Located in a commercial area. **Facility:** 96 units. 1 story, interior/exterior corridors. **Parking:** winter plug-ins. **Terms:** check-in 4 pm, 2 night minimum stay - seasonal and/or weekends, 14 day cancellation notice-fee imposed. **Dining:** Russell Inn Dining Room, see separate listing. **Pool(s):** heated indoor. **Activities:** whirlpool, waterslide, playground, limited exercise equipment. *Fee:* game room. **Guest Services:** coin laundry.

〔⬚ symbols〕 / SOME UNITS

WHERE TO EAT

RUSSELL INN DINING ROOM   204/773-7507
◆◆ ◆◆ American. Family Dining. $8-$23 **AAA Inspector Notes:** This popular local dining room offers generous portions and efficient service in a family atmosphere. The varied menu includes such items as pasta, seafood, chicken and ribs, as well as veal, steaks and quesadillas. Some light meals are also available. **Bar:** full bar. **Address:** Hwy 16 R0J 1W0 **Location:** 0.8 mi (1.2 km) se on Hwy 16 and 83; in The Russell Inn Hotel & Conference Centre.

[B] [L] [D] CALL〔⬚〕

SCANTERBURY

SOUTH BEACH CASINO & RESORT   (204)766-2100
◆◆◆ ◆◆◆
Hotel
$85-$209
Address: One Ocean Dr R0E 1W0 **Location:** On Rt 59, just s of town. **Facility:** Reminiscent of South Beach, the hotel boasts distinctive Art Deco décor; a buffet-style restaurant, ballroom, live entertainment and gambling are offered. 95 units. 6 stories, interior corridors. **Parking:** winter plug-ins. **Amenities:** high-speed Internet. **Pool(s):** heated indoor. **Guest Services:** valet laundry. **Free Special Amenities:** newspaper and high-speed Internet.

〔⬚ symbols〕 / SOME UNITS

SELKIRK (G-5) pop. 9,834, elev. 231m/800'

Selkirk's name honors Lord Selkirk, the Scottish philanthropist whose 1803 settlement in the Red River Valley to the south laid the foundation for Winnipeg. During the late 19th- and early 20th centuries, Selkirk's position on the Red River made it a base for trade and communication with the more isolated settlements around Lake Winnipeg.

Chuck the Channel Catfish, a 9-metre (30-ft.) fiberglass statue, greets visitors on Main Street. The oversize catfish is an apt representation of the live version: Catfish weighing more than 9 kilograms (20 lbs.) abound in the Red River between Selkirk and Lockport.

St. Peter's Dynevor Church, 6.5 kilometres (4 mi.) northeast off Hwy. 59, was built in 1853. The original church, erected in 1836, was the center for Anglican missionary work among the Saulteaux Indians.

Red River North Tourism: 18 Main St., 2nd floor, Selkirk, MB, Canada R1A 1P5. **Phone:** (204) 482-2022 or (800) 894-2621.

⬚GEM **LOWER FORT GARRY NATIONAL HISTORIC SITE,** 5 km (3 mi.) s. on Hwy. 9, is purportedly the oldest intact stone fur-trading post in North America. Farm produce constituted the majority of trade that went on between the locals and the Hudson's Bay Co. The 19th-century buildings have been restored and are furnished as they might have been in their early days. Costumed staff members perform tasks and reenact events that recreate the early 1850s atmosphere of the fort in its heyday. In the 1870s the site served other purposes, including as a training base for the North-West Mounted Police.

The grounds contain an impressive collection of early stone buildings; an exhibit showcases the historic architectural styles. The Visitor Reception Centre offers exhibits about the fort's history. Special events are held occasionally throughout the season and September through December.

Time: Allow 2 hours minimum. **Hours:** Daily 9-5, mid-May through Labour Day. Guided tours depart at 11 and 1. **Cost:** $7.80; $6.55 (ages 65+); $3.90 (ages 6-16); $19.60 (family, up to two adults and five children). **Phone:** (204) 785-6050 or (888) 773-8888. 〔⬚ symbols〕

MARINE MUSEUM OF MANITOBA, at the entrance to Selkirk Park at Eveline St. and Queen Ave., reflects Selkirk's nautical past through displays of outboard motors, tools used for early 1900s shipbuilding, two lighthouses and six restored ships. The 1897 passenger steamship SS *Keenora* houses nautical artifacts and photographs. Other displays include early 1900s underwater diving and a graphite exhibit representing the species of fish caught in Lake Winnipeg and the Red River.

Also displayed are the 1942 *Chickama II;* the 1944 MS *Northland Lady Canadian;* the CGS *Bradbury,* an ice-breaker steam vessel built in 1915; the MS *Peguis II,* a lake and river tug built in 1955; the *Joe Simpson,* a freighter built in 1963; and the 1952 *Jackie S.,* the last all wood, white fish (gas boat) to sail Lake Winnipeg. **Time:** Allow 1 hour minimum. **Hours:** Mon.-Fri. 9-5, Sat.-Sun. and holidays 10-6, mid-May through Labour Day. **Cost:** $6.50; $5 (ages 66+); $3 (ages 6-17). **Phone:** (204) 482-7761.

SHILO (G-2)

THE ROYAL REGIMENT OF CANADIAN ARTILLERY MUSEUM is on the Canadian Forces Base via Hwy. 340. One of the largest military museums in Canada, this indoor-outdoor museum exhibits more than 10,000 articles of dress, technical instruments, ammunition, small arms, guns and World War II vehicles. Among the more than 150 pieces of major military equipment dating to 1796 are German, Russian and French guns.

Guided tours are available by appointment. **Time:** Allow 1 hour minimum. **Hours:** Daily 10-5, Victoria Day-Labour Day; Mon.-Fri. 10-5, rest of year. Closed holidays. **Cost:** $5; $3 (senior citizens and students with ID); free (ages 0-5). **Phone:** (204) 765-3000, ext. 3570.

SOURIS (H-2) pop. 1,837, elev. 396m/1,300'

The free-swinging 177-metre (581-ft.) footbridge built in 1904 over the Souris (SIR-iss) River is considered the second longest free-suspension footbridge in Canada. The bridge was reconstructed after being destroyed by a flood in 1976. Victoria Park has more than 6 kilometres (4 mi.) of walking trails, a viewing tower and a bird sanctuary. **Note:** Serious flooding in 2011 resulted in damage to the swinging footbridge, walking trails and bird sanctuary; phone (204) 483-5213 for updates.

Rockhounding in nearby agate pits yields agate, dendrite, jasper, petrified wood and epidote; the area offers one of the largest varieties of semiprecious stones found in North America. Permits are required and cost $14 per private vehicle. Contact the Rock Shop, 8 First St. S., Souris, MB, Canada R0K 2C0; phone (204) 483-2561.

HILLCREST MUSEUM, Crescent Ave. and Sowden St. next to the swinging bridge, is a restored late 19th-century residence furnished with settler artifacts and antiques. Highlights include an agricultural display with a covered wagon, tractor and farm tools as well as a printing press, a collection of more than 5,000 butterflies and a caboose. **Time:** Allow 30 minutes minimum. **Hours:** Daily 10-5, July 1-Labour Day. **Cost:** $3; $2 (ages 0-16). **Phone:** (204) 483-2008.

STEINBACH (H-5) pop. 13,524, elev. 261m/900'

SAVE **MENNONITE HERITAGE VILLAGE,** 3 km (1.9 mi.) n. on Hwy. 12, centers on a replica of a Mennonite village with more than 20 completely furnished buildings that were moved to the site. On the 16-hectare (40-acre) grounds are a fruit garden, stock pens, a steam engine, gas tractors and other machinery. The village windmill is said to be the only one of its kind in Canada. A museum displays antiques and manuscripts.

Time: Allow 1 hour minimum. **Hours:** Mon.-Sat. 10-6, Sun. noon-6, July-Aug.; Mon.-Sat. 10-5, Sun. noon-5, May-June and in Sept.; Mon.-Fri. 10-4 or by appointment, rest of year. **Cost:** $10; $7 (ages 13-22 and 66+); $2 (ages 6-12); $25 (family). **Phone:** (204) 326-9661.

DAYS INN   (204)320-9200

▼▼ ▼▼ **Hotel** $110-$120 **Address:** 75 Hwy 12 N R5G 1T3 **Location:** 0.5 mi (0.8 km) n of jct Hwy 52. Located in a commercial area. **Facility:** 49 units. 3 stories, interior corridors. **Parking:** winter plug-ins. **Pool(s):** heated indoor. **Activities:** whirlpool, waterslide, exercise room. **Guest Services:** valet and coin laundry.

CALL ⒮Ⓜ ⊃ [BIZ] 🛜 ✕ 🛏 ▣ ▯
/ SOME UNITS FEE 🐕

STONEWALL (G-4) pop. 4,536

Nobody knows for sure if Stonewall was named after founding father S.J. "Stonewall" Jackson or the limestone ridge on which the town is built. The name fits well, though, since limestone quarrying sustained the area's economy from the early 1880s until

1967. Stonewall's past is captured through the old stone buildings dotting its streets.

Town of Stonewall: 293 Main St., Box 250, Stonewall, MB, Canada R0C 2Z0. **Phone:** (204) 467-7979.

SAVE **OAK HAMMOCK MARSH INTERPRETIVE CENTRE** is 13 km (8 mi.) e. on Hwy. 67, then 4 km (2.5 mi.) n. on Hwy. 220. This 3,600-hectare (9,000-acre) restored prairie wetland is home to more than 295 species of birds, 25 species of mammals and thousands of other plant and animal species. Scores of migrating birds and waterfowl can be seen in the spring and fall.

The area is a remnant of the historic St. Andrews Bog that once covered much of southern Manitoba's Interlake area. Hikers can explore 30 kilometres (19 mi.) of trails over a system of boardwalks and dikes. The interpretive center has displays, films and interpretive programs.

The center was designed to educate visitors about the important role wetland environments play in the Earth's ecology. There are daily marsh canoe excursions spring through fall and snowshoe walkabouts in the winter. **Time:** Allow 2 hours minimum. **Hours:** Area open daily 24 hours. Interpretive center open daily 10-8, Sept.-Oct.; 10-4:30, rest of year. Closed Christmas. **Cost:** Interpretive center (includes guided tour of the center and the wetlands) $6; $5 (ages 56+); $4 (ages 3-17); $20 (family). **Phone:** (204) 467-3300 or (800) 665-3825. 🍴 🎣

STONEWALL QUARRY PARK, on the n. end of Main St., commemorates the important role limestone played in the town's development. The Quarry Park Heritage Arts Centre has a museum, video presentations and exhibits; an observation tower affords a panorama of the area. Self-guiding tours around the 30-hectare (75-acre) grounds offer a closer look at kilns, wildlife and fossil deposits in rock. Kinsmen Lake has a sandy beach and swimming; tobogganing is a winter option. *See Recreation Areas Chart.*

Tours: Guided tours are available. **Time:** Allow 1 hour minimum. **Hours:** Daily 11-5, May 1-Labour Day. Hours vary rest of year; phone ahead. **Cost:** Heritage Arts Centre $6; $4 (ages 66+ and students and children); $20 (family). Lake area swimming $6.25; $5.25 (ages 60+ and students); free (ages 0-2). Reservations are required for guided tours. **Phone:** (204) 467-7980. 🅰 🍴 🎣

SWAN RIVER (D-2) pop. 3,907, elev. 340m/1,116'
• Hotels p. 466

During the last 13 years of the 18th century, control of the Swan River Valley was sought by both the North West Co. and the Hudson's Bay Co. Each company built fur-trading posts in the area, but by

1800 the concentrated trapping generated by the rivalry had depleted the number of fur-bearing animals. The Hudson's Bay Co. abandoned the area until the two companies joined in 1821.

The Swan River Valley, nestled between the Duck and Porcupine mountains, offers fishing, hunting, boating, camping, swimming and picnicking. Scenic Hwy. 10 passes just east of town.

Swan Valley Chamber of Commerce: 1500 Main St., P.O. Box 1540, Swan River, MB, Canada R0L 1Z0. **Phone:** (204) 734-3102.

SWAN VALLEY HISTORICAL MUSEUM, 1.5 km (1 mi.) n. on Hwy. 10, reflects life in Manitoba's pioneer era through artifacts and restored buildings. Highlights include two machine sheds, two log cabins, a CN railroad station, a telephone station, a blacksmith shop, a pioneer store, two churches and a 1900s one-room schoolhouse.

Time: Allow 1 hour minimum. **Hours:** Mon.-Fri. 9-5, Sat.-Sun. and holidays 1-5, May-Sept.; by appointment rest of year. **Cost:** $2; free (ages 0-11). **Phone:** (204) 734-3585 or (204) 734-2713.

SWAN VALLEY SUPER 8   (204)734-7888
ᐯᐯ ᐯᐯ **Hotel** $109-$154 **Address:** 115 Kelsey Tr R0L 1Z0 **Location:** Corner of Hwy 10 and 83. **Facility:** 52 units. 3 stories, interior corridors. **Parking:** winter plug-ins. **Amenities:** high-speed Internet. **Activities:** limited exercise equipment. **Guest Services:** coin laundry.

ⓔ CALL Ⓜ 🛜 🔲 🔲 / SOME UNITS FEE 🐾 🖥

THE PAS (C-2) pop. 5,513, elev. 274m/900'

A riverfront lookout in Devon Park at The Pas (pronounced "the paw") honors travelers of the Saskatchewan River including Henry Kelsey, the first known European to see the northern prairies in 1691. It is rumored that the first wheat on the prairies was planted in the area in 1734.

Christ Church (Anglican), on Edwards Avenue, was founded in 1840 by Henry Budd, the first Native American ordained to the Anglican ministry. The church contains hand-hewn furnishings made by ships' carpenters in 1847. Tours are offered by appointment; phone (204) 623-2119.

SAM WALLER MUSEUM is at 306 Fischer Ave. Housed in what is said to be northern Manitoba's oldest brick edifice, the museum originally was the town's Courthouse and Community building. On display are natural history exhibits, local historical materials and Indian and fur-trading artifacts. The basement features original jail cells and a children's discovery room. Historic walking tours of the downtown and riverfront areas also are offered.

Time: Allow 1 hour minimum. **Hours:** Daily 10-5, July-Aug.; 1-5, rest of year. Historic walking tours by appointment. Closed major holidays. **Cost:** $4; $2 (ages 65+ and students with ID); $7 (family). Admission Wed. by donation. **Phone:** (204) 623-3802.

KIKIWAK INN   204/623-1800
ᐯᐯ ᐯᐯ **Hotel.** Rates not provided. **Address:** Hwy 10 N R0B 2J0 **Location:** On Hwy 10, 0.4 mi (0.6 km) n. Located in a commercial area. **Facility:** 60 units. 3 stories, interior corridors. **Parking:** winter plug-ins. **Amenities:** *Some:* high-speed Internet. **Dining:** Niska Dining Room, see separate listing. **Pool(s):** heated indoor. **Activities:** whirlpool, limited exercise equipment. **Guest Services:** valet laundry.

🔌 🍴 🍽 CALL Ⓜ 🛟 🛜 🔲 🔲
/ SOME UNITS 🐾 🖥

SUPER 8   (204)623-1888
ᐯᐯ ᐯᐯ **Hotel** $115-$135 **Address:** 1717 Gordon Ave R9A 1K3 **Location:** At southern approach to town. Located in a commercial area. **Facility:** 70 units. 2 stories (no elevator), interior corridors. **Parking:** winter plug-ins. **Pool(s):** heated indoor. **Activities:** whirlpool, waterslide. **Guest Services:** coin laundry.

🍴 CALL Ⓜ 🛟 🛜 ✕ 🔲 🔲
/ SOME UNITS FEE 🐾 🖥

WHERE TO EAT

NISKA DINING ROOM   204/623-1800
ᐯᐯ ᐯᐯ American. Family Dining. $10-$23 **AAA Inspector Notes:** The menu lists such choices as pickerel, stir-fried beef, steak, chicken, ribs, pasta and salads. Also offered are heart-healthy choices and dishes recommended for diabetics. Native art is displayed in the dining room. **Bar:** full bar. **Address:** Hwy 10 R0B 2J0 **Location:** On Hwy 10, 0.4 mi (0.6 km) n; in Kikiwak Inn.

Ⓑ Ⓛ Ⓓ CALL Ⓜ

THOMPSON (B-3) pop. 12,829, elev. 206m/675'

Thompson sprang up after the discovery of one of the world's largest nickel deposits and is a major mining, communications, transportation, medical and retailing center.

Lakes and rivers abound in this rugged, picturesque area. Paint Lake Provincial Recreation Park *(see Recreation Areas Chart)* is 32 kilometres (20 mi.) south on Hwy. 6.

Also south of Thompson on Hwy. 6 is the starting point for a 10 kilometre (6-mi.) hiking trail that will take you over a bridge to Kwasitchewan Falls, the highest waterfall in the province. Between Wabowden and Thompson, within Pisew Falls Provincial Park, is Pisew Falls, the second-highest waterfall in Manitoba accessible by road. A 1.3-kilometre (.8-mi.) trail leads from the highway through the dense foliage to a platform overlooking the 12.8-metre (42-ft.) falls. Twelve site plaques describe the flora and fauna of this boreal forest. Picnic facilities are available.

Thompson Spirit Way is a combination gravel and pavement path that offers 16 points of interest. Designed for bicycling or walking, the route starts at the Heritage North Museum and ends at Miles Hart Bridge. Though hiking boots are not required, it is essential to wear comfortable walking shoes. The route stretches for 2 kilometres (1 mi.) and highlights include an 86-foot-tall wolf mural that is said to be the largest lighted mural in the world as well as a restored Norseman floatplane. Display panels share information about the sites and vantage points present scenic views. Official Spirit Way guide books may be purchased from the museum or the chamber of commerce.

Thompson Chamber of Commerce: 79 Selkirk Ave., Thompson, MB, Canada R8N 1M2. **Phone:** (204) 677-4155 or (888) 307-0103.

HERITAGE NORTH MUSEUM, in a log cabin at jct. Princeton Dr. and Mystery Lake Rd., also serves as the tourist information center. Displayed are an assortment of stuffed and mounted animals native to the area, fossils, a mining exhibit, a woolly mammoth tusk found near Thompson, a boreal forest exhibit which includes a caribou-hide tepee, and changing exhibits. A second log building houses a mining exhibit. Archives are available.

Hours: Daily 9-5, July-Aug.; Mon.-Sat. 1-5, rest of year. **Cost:** $3.25; $2 (ages 13-18 and 60+); $1 (ages 6-12). **Phone:** (204) 677-2216.

BEST WESTERN THOMPSON HOTEL & SUITES
(204)778-8887

Hotel
$150-$170

AAA Benefit: Members save up to 20%, plus 10% bonus points with Best Western Rewards®.

Address: 205 Mystery Lake Rd R8N 1Z8 **Location:** Hwy 6 exit Mystery Lake Rd. **Facility:** 80 units, some efficiencies. 4 stories, interior corridors. **Parking:** winter plug-ins. **Amenities:** high-speed Internet, safes. **Activities:** sauna, exercise room. **Guest Services:** valet and coin laundry. **Free Special Amenities:** full breakfast and high-speed Internet.

DAYS INN & SUITES   (204)778-6000

 Hotel $138 **Address:** 21 Thompson Dr N R8N 2B5 **Location:** Just e of Mystery Lake Rd (Hwy 6). Located in a commercial area. **Facility:** 74 units. 2 stories, interior corridors. **Parking:** winter plug-ins. **Terms:** cancellation fee imposed. **Amenities:** high-speed Internet. **Activities:** limited exercise equipment. **Guest Services:** valet and coin laundry.

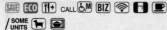

LAKEVIEW INN & SUITES   (204)778-8879

Hotel $120   **Address:** 70 Thompson Dr N R8N 1Y8 **Location:** Just w of Hwy 6. Located in a commercial area. **Facility:** 61 units. 2 stories (no elevator), interior corridors. **Parking:** winter plug-ins. **Terms:** cancellation fee imposed. **Activities:** sauna, whirlpool, limited exercise equipment. **Guest Services:** valet and coin laundry. **Free Special Amenities: continental breakfast and high-speed Internet.**

VIRDEN (G-1) pop. 3,114, elev. 439m/1,440'

About 1,200 oil wells dot the landscape in and around Virden—the richest source of petroleum in Manitoba. The first oil-producing well was sunk in the 1950s in the Rosalee field northwest of Virden.

Many original fieldstone buildings, such as the 1892 St. Mary's Anglican Church at the corner of Queen Street and 9th Avenue, are still in use today. The site of Fort Montagne à la Bosse, built by the North West Co. in 1790, is northeast of Virden on the old Trans-Canada Highway. To help cool things off in the summer, the fairgrounds has a public pool and a waterslide.

Virden Community Chamber of Commerce: 425 6th Ave., P.O. Box 899, Virden, MB, Canada R0M 2C0. **Phone:** (204) 851-1551.

VIRDEN PIONEER HOME MUSEUM INC. is at 390 King St. W. The museum, in a large brick house, is a living memorial to the pioneers who came to the region. Built in 1888, it is furnished with family pieces donated by descendants of the pioneers. **Time:** Allow 30 minutes minimum. **Hours:** Mon.-Sat. 10-6, May-Aug.; by appointment rest of year. **Cost:** $5; $2 (ages 0-16). **Phone:** (204) 748-1659 or (204) 748-3573.

WAPUSK NATIONAL PARK (A-4)

Elevations in the park range from sea level along the Hudson Bay coastal areas to 94 metres (308 ft.) at Silcox Creek. Refer to CAA/AAA maps for additional elevation information.

South and east of Churchill on the shore of Hudson Bay, Wapusk (pronounced to rhyme with tusk) was established in 1996. The park consists of 11,475 square kilometres (7,119 sq. mi.). Translated from the Cree language, Wapusk means "white bear," a fitting name for a park that has an area where polar bears den and produce offspring.

Much of the national park, part of the Hudson Bay and James Bay lowlands, is a flat plain covered by an extensive layer of peat; a layer of permafrost lies underneath. The treeless tundra consists mainly of wetlands—lakes, streams, bogs and rivers.

Polar bears congregate in the northern part of the park near Churchill around October, as they wait for freezing weather and the time when they can return to the ice in search of seals, their main food. The females dig their dens, and their young are born in late November and in December. The area around Churchill (see place listing p. 454) is one of the world's best places for viewing polar bears in their native habitat. Specialized tundra vehicles take visitors for close-up encounters.

The park, along a migratory flyway, also is a popular spring and fall feeding spot for waterfowl and shorebirds, including such rare species as the king eider, Ross' gull and gyrfalcon. Many build their nests here on the coast of Hudson Bay during the summer.

Churchill, in a somewhat remote location in northern Manitoba, can be reached by air and rail from Winnipeg. Since Wapusk is a wilderness park, it has no roads or trails. In order to visit the park, it is necessary to be part of an organized tour group, and several commercial operators provide tours into the park by plane, helicopter or tundra vehicle. The park office can provide a list. Park admission is free. For additional information contact Wapusk National Park, P.O. Box 127, Churchill, MB, Canada R0B 0E0; phone (204) 675-8863.

WARREN (G-4) pop. 798, elev. 248m/815'

V. GROSS' DOLL MUSEUM, on Hwy. 3W, 3 km (1.9 mi.) n. of jct. hwys. 6 and 67, displays some 4,000 dolls, ranging from those of the late 1890s to the present. **Time:** Allow 1 hour, 30 minutes minimum. **Hours:** Sun.-Fri. 10-5, evenings by appointment, May-Oct.; by appointment rest of year. **Cost:** $4; free (ages 0-5). **Phone:** (204) 322-5346.

WINKLER (H-4) pop. 10,670, elev. 271m/890'

PEMBINA THRESHERMEN'S MUSEUM, 5 km (3 mi.) w. on Hwy. 3, features guided tours through displays of agricultural machinery, tools and household items as well as a steam threshing unit and a working sawmill. **Time:** Allow 1 hour minimum. **Hours:** Mon.-Fri. 9-5, Sat.-Sun. and holidays 1-5, May-Sept. **Cost:** $7.50; free (ages 0-11). **Phone:** (204) 325-7497.

DAYS INN & SUITES   (204)325-8888

 Hotel $93-$109 **Address:** 395 Boundary Tr R6W 4B1 **Location:** Main St and Hwy 14; center. Located in a commercial area. **Facility:** 81 units. 3 stories, interior corridors. **Parking:** winter plug-ins. **Amenities:** high-speed Internet. **Pool(s):** heated indoor. **Activities:** whirlpool, waterslide, exercise room. **Guest Services:** coin laundry.

Winnipeg

Then & Now

The real estate agent's cry of "Location!" could have been invented in Winnipeg; the position of Manitoba's capital has determined the city's past and present. Archeological evidence shows that Winnipeg has been an important place of settlement for more than 6,000 years.

The confluence of the Red River, which flows south to north, and the Assiniboine River, whose eastward flowing waters were a main route of Western exploration, led to the founding of fur-trading posts in the early 18th century near the present site of Winnipeg. The fertile lands created by the rivers later drew farmers and other settlers.

Still later, the area's position south of the peaks of the Canadian Shield meant that roads and railroads were forced to converge at Winnipeg, making it the point through which the

eastbound raw materials of the West and the westbound manufactured goods of the East passed. Profiting by the hydroelectric power generated from its rivers, the city emerged in the 20th century as a manufacturing center in its own right.

French Canadian explorer and trader Pierre Gaultier de la Vérendrye founded Fort Rouge at the confluence of the rivers in 1738. This fur-trading post was succeeded by Fort Gibraltar, built by the North West Co. in 1804, and Fort Garry, founded by the Hudson's Bay Co. in 1821. In the same year, Lord Selkirk brought a party of Scottish settlers to these fertile lands, a move that greatly disturbed the trappers and voyageurs who feared their livelihoods would be destroyed.

The small settlement managed to survive, and the shift from trapping and hunting to agriculture began. Because of aggressive Canadian advertising campaigns in Europe and a homestead policy similar to that

being used to settle the plains of the United States, large numbers of immigrants began to flow into the area in the 1860s.

In 1873 the village about a half mile north of Fort Garry was incorporated and named for the Cree Indian words *win* ("muddy") and *nipee* ("water"). The railroad aided Winnipeg's growth still further: In 1876 the city began to ship wheat east, and when the Canadian Pacific Railway connected the coasts in 1885, freight and passengers began to flow through the city in both directions.

The diversity of today's Winnipeg mirrors the many nationalities of the people who settled it, some drawn by agriculture, some by the railroad, some by industry. From countries throughout Great Britain and Europe they came, creating a cultural mix reflected in the city's skyline, which includes the neoclassical splendor of the Manitoba Legislative Building, the century-old buildings of Old Market Square and the rounded spires of the Ukrainian Greek Orthodox Cathedral.

Winnipeg skyline along the Red River

(Continued on p. 470.)

Fast Facts

ABOUT THE CITY

POP: 663,617 ■ ELEV: 229 m/763 ft.

MONEY

SALES TAX: Manitoba's provincial sales tax is 7 percent. A 5 percent Goods and Services Tax (GST) also is levied in Canada on most sales and services. There is no additional local sales tax or tax on hotel/motel rooms or car rentals.

WHOM TO CALL

EMERGENCY: 911

POLICE (non-emergency): (204) 986-6222

TEMPERATURE: (204) 983-2050

HOSPITALS: Concordia Hospital, (204) 667-1560 ■ Grace Hospital, (204) 837-0111 ■ Health Sciences Centre, (204) 787-3661 ■ St. Boniface General Hospital, (204) 233-8563 ■ Seven Oaks General Hospital, (204) 632-7133 ■ Victoria General Hospital, (204) 269-3570.

WHERE TO LOOK AND LISTEN

NEWSPAPERS: Winnipeg has three daily newspapers, the *Winnipeg Free Press*, the *Winnipeg Sun* and *Metro Winnipeg*, all distributed in the morning.

RADIO: The Canadian Broadcasting Corporation (CBC) has both AM (990) and FM (98.3) stations in Winnipeg as well as an AM (1050) station broadcasting in French.

VISITOR INFORMATION

Tourism Winnipeg: 259 Portage Ave., Winnipeg, MB, Canada R3B 2A9. Phone: (204) 943-1970 or (800) 665-0204.
Tourism Winnipeg is open Mon.-Fri. 8:30-4:30. A second branch, at Winnipeg James Armstrong Richardson International Airport, is open daily 8 a.m.-9:45 p.m.; phone (204) 982-7543.

Travel Manitoba's Explore Manitoba Centre at The Forks: 21 Forks Market Rd., Winnipeg, MB, Canada R3C 4T7. Phone: (204) 927-7838 or (800) 665-0040.

Explore Manitoba Centre is staffed with on-site travel counselors daily 9-6. The telephones are manned daily 8:30-4:30. The 24-hour Forks Hot Line, (204) 957-7618, also provides information. The center features dioramas depicting the various regions of the province.

TRANSPORTATION

AIR TRAVEL: Winnipeg James Armstrong Richardson International Airport (YWG) is about 8 kilometres (5 mi.) northwest of downtown off Metro Rte. 90. Daily bus service between the airport and downtown is provided by Winnipeg Transit between 5:50 a.m. and 12:49 a.m. The one-way fare is $2.45; passengers must have exact change. Phone 311 or (877) 311-4974 for information. Major hotels offer limousine service to and from the airport.

RENTAL CARS: Hertz, (800) 263-0600 in Canada, or (800) 654-3080 out of Canada, offers discounts to AAA and CAA members. Winnipeg locations are at Winnipeg James Armstrong Richardson International Airport, 1577 Erin St. and 830 Waverley St.

RAIL SERVICE: The VIA Rail Canada depot is downtown at 123 Main St.; phone (888) 842-7245.

TAXIS: Cab companies include Blueline, (204) 925-8888 ■ Duffy's, (204) 925-0101 ■ and Unicity, (204) 925-3131. Winnipeg rates start at $3.50 plus an average rate of $1.35 per kilometre or $2.02 per mile.

PUBLIC TRANSPORTATION: Winnipeg Transit, the public bus system, serves downtown Winnipeg and its suburbs. Route maps and route information are available by phoning 311 or visiting the Winnipeg Transit website. The average bus fare is $2.45; riders must have exact change.

(Continued from p. 469.)

Evidence has been uncovered through archeological digs that the current site of The Forks was a seasonal meeting place for aboriginal peoples more than 6,000 years ago. Tools, bones, footprints and pottery have been unearthed at the site located at the confluence of the Red and Assiniboine rivers. Still a meeting place, this site has all the expected modern amenities like shopping, dining and entertainment venues as well as a playground, garden, amphitheater and beautiful views. The Assiniboine Riverwalk and the Manitoba Children's Museum are two highlights.

The Golden Boy, sculpted by Georges Gardet of Paris, is a 5.25-metre-tall (17.2-ft.), 1,650-kilogram (3,638-lb.) statue sheathed in 24 karat gold leaf atop the dome of the Legislative Building. In many ways it symbolizes both the past and the future of the residents of Winnipeg. The statue was diverted on its journey from a French foundry during World War I, while the vessel that was carrying it served as a troop transport for 2 years. After crossing the Atlantic many times, the golden immigrant was finally placed where he stands today, one hand holding aloft the torch of progress, the other cradling a symbolic sheaf of wheat. High above the city, he strides toward the increasingly important natural resources of the north, his color echoing the golden hue of the rolling fields of grain that brought the city below both population and prosperity.

Must Do: AAA Editor's Picks

- Roam 7 kilometres of mulch and limestone trails and make your way across floating wetland boardwalks at **FortWhyte Alive**, where you can spot all sorts of critters—from bison to songbirds to prairie dogs—in their natural habitat.
- Salute the province's beloved "Golden Boy" statue with a visit to the **Manitoba Legislative Building**. The 5.25-metre-tall statue, gilded with 23.75-karat gold, stands atop the building's dome with a torch in one hand (representing economic development) and a sheaf of wheat in the other (symbolizing agriculture). Take a guided tour of the building and see if you can identify the hieroglyphic inscriptions and secret number codes said to be hidden in the building's architecture.
- Contemplate sculptures made of caribou antlers and dozens of handmade Inuit stone carvings at the **Winnipeg Art Gallery**, a strikingly designed Modernist building housing one of the world's largest collections of contemporary Inuit art. Browse European and Canadian collections and then head up to the rooftop sculpture garden, where you'll find the upscale **Storm Bistro** and live jazz music on select summer nights.
- Flex your muscles and try lifting a solid gold bar worth more than $600,000 at the interactive coin museum inside the ⤳ **Royal Canadian Mint**, where as many as 20 million Canadian coins roll off the assembly line each day.
- Survey the city skyline and the spot where the Red and Assiniboine rivers meet from a six-story-high viewing platform atop **The Forks Market** at ⤳ **The Forks**, one of the city's most popular gathering places. From this sky-high vantage point, scope out the nearby riverside amphitheater, sculptures, outdoor playground and prairie garden, or opt to explore the area by boat with a narrated ride on **Splash Dash Guided River Tours**.
- Hunt for eclectic treasures and cosmopolitan threads in the Exchange District, a historic neighborhood bursting with hip boutiques and eateries situated 1 block north of the intersection of Portage and Main. For indoor shopping, there are more stores and restaurants off Main Street at **The Forks Market** and in **Johnston Terminal**.
- Chant "GO Jets GO" like a true Jets fan at the **MTS Centre**, where you can cheer on the Peg City's home team during a fast-paced hockey game. Just don't forget to wear your blue and white.
- Stop and smell the dahlias on a stroll through the English Gardens at **Assiniboine Park**, then wander the paths of the **Leo Mol Sculpture Garden**, where bronze statues and a year-round water feature are highlights. If wildlife viewing is more your style, visit **Assiniboine Park Zoo** for a peek at lions, tigers and bison. Be sure to snap a photo with the statue of Winnie the Bear and his owner located just inside the front entrance; the lovable black bear cub was the inspiration for A.A. Milne's character Winnie the Pooh.
- Pack a picnic basket and head to **Kildonan Park** for a stroll along the Red River on a tree-shaded path. Catch a Broadway-caliber musical at the park's outdoor theater, Rainbow Stage, on summer nights, and don't miss the Witch's Hut (think "Hansel and Gretel") at the park's northern end.
- Cross the Esplanade Riel footbridge and step into **St. Boniface**, the French-speaking district where some of Winnipeg's oldest buildings lie. Visit the **Saint Boniface Museum** for a history lesson on Louis Riel and other early Red River settlers and stop by Riel's gravesite (look for the red granite tombstone) in the churchyard of **St. Boniface Basilica** nearby.

Assiniboine Park Zoo

Winnipeg 1-day Itinerary

AAA editors suggest these activities for a great short vacation experience.

Morning

- Kick off your tour of the Peg City with an early start at **Stella's Café**, just across the Assiniboine River in Osborne Village. This casual-yet-trendy eatery serves up yummy homemade breakfast foods all day, with options like heart-shaped waffles, baked eggs and fluffy banana pancakes topped with wild blueberries. You'll want to put in a to-go order for some grilled cinnamon buns, too.

- After breakfast, a walking tour of vibrant and artsy **Osborne Village** is a must. Hunt for chic shoes, vintage threads or secondhand records in the dozens of boutiques along Osborne Street. The Village is a charming mix of old and new, with modern high-rises standing alongside turn-of-the-20th-century stone buildings.

- One of the best ways to get acquainted with Winnipeg is by boat aboard **Splash Dash Guided River Tours**. Relax as your guide shares entertaining stories about city history on a 30-minute sightseeing cruise of the Red and Assiniboine rivers. Tours depart every 15 minutes from the dock at The Forks, but a water taxi can pick you up from any of eight city docks, including one at Osborne Street Bridge at the north end of Osborne Village.

Afternoon

- After your river tour a great place to disembark is ▼ **The Forks**, the popular outdoor gathering spot where the Red and Assiniboine rivers meet. Wander the grounds and make your way to **The Forks Market** and **Johnston Terminal** where you'll find souvenir shops, candy stores, an antique mall and a fresh food market housed in renovated buildings from the railway era. If a sit-down meal is in order, **Beachcombers** and **Muddy Waters Smokehouse** are sure bets for a casual lunch.

- From The Forks, follow the river walk north along the Red River to the Provencher Bridge. Look for the strikingly designed Esplanade Riel footbridge and cross the river to **St. Boniface**, Winnipeg's historic French district. At Tache and Cathedral avenues is the grave of Louis Riel, the Métis leader celebrated as the founder of Manitoba. Nearby is St. Boniface Cathedral. Constructed in 1908 and severely damaged by fire in 1968, the beautiful stone façade of the cathedral is a magnificent photo spot. A stop at the **Saint Boniface Museum** can provide a good overview of local history.

- Back in downtown Winnipeg, spend the rest of the afternoon at ▼ **The Manitoba Museum**. Here you can climb aboard a full-size replica of the "Nonsuch," the British ship whose 1668 voyage to Hudson Bay opened western Canada to commerce. In the Urban Gallery, walk the streets of Winnipeg circa the 1920s in a recreated streetscape, complete with wooden boardwalks and boomtown-era storefronts.

The Manitoba Museum

Evening

- Treat yourself to a fancy meal at one of Winnipeg's fine dining restaurants. **Hy's Steakhouse** near the intersection of Portage Avenue and Main Street serves up perfectly prepared steaks in an upscale atmosphere. **The Current** offers a variety of creative dishes with a fantastic view of The Forks; don't miss the pan-seared Manitoba pickerel and the scallops with vanilla bean and citrus vinaigrette.

- Looking for the nightlife hotspots? When the sun goes down, the place to be is Winnipeg's **Exchange District**, located just north of Portage and Main. The 20-block historic area gets its name from the Winnipeg Grain & Produce Exchange that formed here in the late 1800s. Today the district is chock-full of shops, bars and live music venues known to attract a high-energy nighttime crowd. Find a bench in **Old Market Square** (Bannatyne Avenue and King Street) for prime people-watching or, if you're lucky, watch an outdoor performance on the main stage during summer months.

- If indoor performances are more your style, take in an evening show at the **Royal Manitoba Theatre Centre (MTC) Mainstage**, just off Main Street at 174 Market Ave. The theater presents classics, comedies and modern dramas October through May. Or, reserve seats at Centennial Concert Hall (555 Main St.) for a jaw-dropping performance by the **Royal Winnipeg Ballet**. For schedule information and tickets, phone (204) 942-6537 for the MTC Mainstage or (204) 956-2792 for the Royal Winnipeg Ballet.

Arriving

By Car

Forming a circle around Winnipeg is a perimeter highway. To the north of the Trans-Canada Highway, the major approach from the east and west, this perimeter road is designated Hwy. 101. To the south of the Trans-Canada Highway it is numbered Hwy. 100.

There are three major approaches to the perimeter highway: the Trans-Canada Highway, which approaches from both the east and west, and Hwy. 75, which approaches from the south. To the west of the city the Trans-Canada Highway is posted Hwy. 1W; from the east, Hwy. 1E.

Within the perimeter highway all three major approaches change designation: Hwy. 1W becomes Metro Rte. 85, Hwy. 1E becomes Metro Rte. 135, and Hwy. 75 becomes Metro Rte. 42.

Getting Around

Generally, rush hour in Winnipeg is from 7 to 9 a.m. and 3:30 to 5:30 p.m. As in most cities, stress can be alleviated if driving during rush hour is avoided. If driving during these times, be careful and be patient; the city's speed limit is 50 kilometres per hour (30 mph) unless otherwise posted.

Note the pedestrian crosswalks marked by pavement stripes and illuminated overhead signs. All vehicles must stop if the crosswalk is occupied by a pedestrian or if a pedestrian on the curb indicates an intention to cross. No vehicle may pass another that is stopped or slowing to yield to a pedestrian. Right turns on red are permitted after a stop, unless otherwise posted.

Street System

Winnipeg's streets are laid out in a number of grids, but each is oriented to a different compass direction. Visitors will find it easiest to orient themselves to the major thoroughfares, which have signs carrying the word "Route" and a number. Routes ending in even numbers designate north-south thoroughfares, and those ending in odd numbers designate major east-west arteries.

The primary north-south routes that cross the downtown area are 42, 52 and 62. The major east-west highways include 105, 115, 57 and 85. A good street map will enable drivers to see how the various grids of named streets connect with the main numbered routes.

Parking

Visitors will do best to park in a commercial lot, where rates average $1-$2.50 per hour. Daily rates are about $4 to $10. Parking meters downtown cost $1-$2 per hour, but most carry a 2-hour limit. Some parking in downtown is free in designated metered areas.

Parking is strictly controlled along major downtown streets. Cars parked between signs reading "No Parking Between" from 7 to 9 a.m. and 3:30 to 5:30 p.m. will be towed.

Shopping

The intersection of **Portage Avenue and Main Street** is a good starting point for a shopping excursion. Just one block north of the intersection is the **Exchange District,** a vibrant and historic area filled with more than 40 restaurants and 80 stores including clothing boutiques, vintage shops and toy stores. Portage Avenue is the site of the city's largest department stores. **Portage Place** connects The Bay (The Hudson's Bay Co.) to other department stores with an extensive system of skywalks.

Winnipeg has a historic area where shoppers can browse through merchandise of today amid structures of the past. **The Forks Market** *(see attraction listing p. 478)* is behind Union Station, off Main Street (near Portage and Main). The shops and restaurants are located in an indoor market with more than 80 vendors selling everything from fresh fish and baked goods to arts and crafts items. **Johnston Terminal** *(see attraction listing p. 478),* across from the market, offers specialty boutiques and eateries.

Shopping for Western wear and accessories is possible at such factory outlet stores as **Canada West Boots,** 1250 Fife St., or **MWG Factory Outlet,** 1147 Notre Dame Ave.

More than 125 shops and restaurants can be found at **Osborne Village,** between River and Wardlaw avenues 2 blocks south of the Manitoba Legislative Building.

Travelers in search of a truly representative souvenir may want to examine the native arts and crafts and western wear available at **Winnipeg Outfitters Inc.** at 250 McPhillips St.

The Forks Market

Ice sculpture at Festival du Voyageur

Visitors who like their shopping climate-controlled and under one roof can visit the malls at **Cityplace,** 333 St. Mary Ave. at Hargrave Street; **Garden City,** 2305 McPhillips St., with Sears and Winners as its anchor stores; **Grant Park,** 1120 Grant Ave., with McNally Robinson Booksellers and Zellers; **Kildonan Place,** 1555 Regent Ave. W., with anchors Sears and Zellers; **Polo Park,** 1485 Portage Ave., which has The Bay, Sears and Zellers for anchors; Portage Place, 393 Portage Ave.; or **St. Vital Centre,** 1225 St. Mary's Rd., with The Bay, Sears and Wal-Mart as its anchor stores.

On Saturday mornings June through October, the **St. Norbert Farmers' Market,** 16 kilometres (10 mi.) south at 3514 Pembina Hwy., offers baked goods, fresh produce, flowers, furniture, jewelry and other locally made items from more than 70 vendors.

Big Events

Winnipeg's calendar of events, with more than 170 days of festivals, reflects more than 43 nationalities that have made the city home. The *joie de vivre* spirit of the French voyageurs is revived each February during ▽ **Festival du Voyageur,** a 10-day-long celebration including winter sports, ice-sculpting contests, music and food. With the 18th-century fur trade as its theme, the event takes place in St. Boniface, Winnipeg's French quarter.

The city plays host to the 4-day **Winnipeg International Children's Festival** at **The Forks** in early June. Music, theater, dance and comedy performances are offered as well as hands-on workshops and evening shows.

The 10-day **Jazz Winnipeg Festival** in late June features jazz performers on an outdoor stage in Old Market Square as well as at other indoor venues across the city. The ▽ **Red River Exhibition,** known locally as the "The Ex" is held during mid-and late June. The Ex's many rides, midway activities and games of chance as well as nightly concerts take place at **Red River Exhibition Park** off Perimeter Highway behind Assiniboia Downs. The event also includes a parade, petting zoo and agricultural displays.

Early July brings the 4-day ▽ **Winnipeg Folk Festival** to nearby **Birds Hill Provincial Park,** where more than 200 concerts, children's activities, music workshops and food are highlights. In mid-July is the 10-day **Winnipeg Fringe Festival,** with various independent theater performances in the Exchange District and other locations throughout the city.

Early August brings the 2-week ▽ **Folklorama** multicultural celebration, Winnipeg's largest event and reputedly the largest and longest-running multicultural festival of its kind. The costumes, dances and food of more than 40 cultures are showcased.

Sports & Rec

Devotees of organized sports will find many opportunities to indulge themselves in Winnipeg. Canadians love **hockey,** and those who fancy flying sticks and flashing skates will find the National Hockey League's **Winnipeg Jets** facing off against their opponents downtown at the **MTS Centre** at Donald Street and Portage Avenue.

Football fans can watch the Canadian Football League's **Winnipeg Blue Bombers** play at **Investors Group Field** from June to November; construction of the facility, located at the intersection of University Crescent and Chancellor Matheson Rd., is scheduled to be completed by summer 2013. The American Association of Independent Professional **Baseball's Winnipeg Goldeyes** play at **Shaw Park** at The Forks from May to August.

To obtain additional information and tickets for sports and recreation events listed above, phone (204) 780-3333.

Sports car racing enthusiasts converge at the **Red River Co-op Speedway,** (204) 582-0527, on Hwy. 75, 8 kilometres (5 mi.) south of St. Norbert, from May through October (weather permitting).

Assiniboia Downs, 3975 Portage Ave. at the Perimeter Highway, offers **Thoroughbred racing** early May to mid-September. Simulcast races are offered year-round; phone (204) 885-3330.

Note: Policies concerning admittance of children to pari-mutuel betting facilities vary. Phone for information.

Other spectator sports include minor league hockey, **curling** and **ringette** games, held at municipal skating rinks, and **cricket** played in Assiniboine Park. Ringette, similar to hockey, is a popular women's sport developed in Canada.

There are 33 **golf** courses in the Winnipeg area. Nine-hole public courses include **Crescent Drive,** 781 Crescent Dr., (877) 311-4974, and **Harbour View,** 1867 Springfield Rd., (204) 222-2751. Among the 18-hole public courses are **Kildonan Park,** 2021 Main St., (877) 311-4974; **Tuxedo,** 400 Shaftesbury Blvd., (204) 888-2867; and **Windsor Park,** 10 Rue des Meurons, (877) 311-4974. **John Blumberg,** 4540 Portage Ave., (204) 986-3490, offers both nine- and 18-hole layouts.

Winnipeg has more than 100 **tennis** courts, some lighted for night matches. Many courts are at community centers. Championship matches are held during the summer at various locations throughout the city. **Squash, handball** and **racquetball** players can avail themselves of courts at a number of athletic clubs and local universities. For information contact Sport Manitoba; phone (204) 925-5600.

Fans of **bicycling** and **in-line skating** take to the marked paths in Winnipeg's city parks. Bicycle trails along less-traveled side streets in and around Winnipeg also have been established. **Cross-country skiing, tobogganing** and **ice-skating** facilities are available at Assiniboine, Kildonan and St. Vital parks; facilities for ice-skating also are found at numerous schools and community clubs.

Downhill skiing is available at **Springhill Winter Park Ski Area,** (204) 224-3051, near **Birds Hill Provincial Park** at the junction of Hwy. 59N at the Floodway; and **Stony Mountain Ski Area,** (204) 344-5977, 11 kilometres (6 mi.) north of the Perimeter Highway on Hwy. 7. Birds Hill Provincial Park, (204) 222-9151, also is a site for **snowmobiling** and cross-country skiing.

Swimming can be pursued all year in Winnipeg, where numerous indoor pools include those at four YM-YWCAs; phone (204) 947-3044. The **Pan Am Pool,** 25 Poseidon Bay, is one of the largest indoor bodies of water in Canada and is open all year; phone (877) 311-4974.

Many recreational activities are available at the **Harbour View Recreation Complex** in the northeastern section of Winnipeg in **Kil-Cona Park,** 1867 Springfield Rd. At this 162-hectare (400-acre) park are facilities for **miniature golf, lawn bowling, shuffleboard** and **horseshoes** as well as tennis courts, a golf course and a driving range during the summer. Golf and tennis lessons are available April to October and indoor golf lessons are available year-round. Ice-skating, tobogganing and cross-country skiing are available during the winter. Phone (204) 222-2751.

Performing Arts

Canada's Royal Winnipeg Ballet, Winnipeg Symphony Orchestra and Manitoba Opera perform in Centennial Concert Hall, 555 Main St., opposite City Hall. The oldest company in Canada and the second oldest in North America, Canada's **Royal Winnipeg Ballet** is known for its versatile style and performs an eclectic mix of classical and contemporary ballets. At-home performances are from October

through May. For ticket information phone (204) 956-2792 or (800) 667-4792.

The **Winnipeg Symphony Orchestra** performs September to May and offers classical, contemporary and popular orchestral music; for concert information phone (204) 949-3999. The **Manitoba Opera** performs October through May; phone (204) 942-7479, or (204) 944-8824 for tickets.

Modern dance is presented by **Winnipeg's Contemporary Dancers** from October through April at the **Rachel Browne Theatre,** 211 Bannatyne Ave.; for information phone (204) 452-0229.

Theater lovers can enjoy performances of the classics, comedies and modern dramas at the **Royal Manitoba Theatre Centre (MTC) Mainstage,** 174 Market St., from October to May; for general information or tickets phone (204) 942-6537. The **MTC Warehouse Theatre,** 140 Rupert Ave., (204) 942-6537, features alternative theater performances from November to April. **The Lyric Theatre,** just east of the Pavilion in Assiniboine Park, (204) 927-6000, is an outdoor theater showcasing drama festivals as well as performances by the Royal Winnipeg Ballet, the Winnipeg Symphony Orchestra and other musical groups.

For both adults and young people, the **Prairie Theatre Exchange,** at Portage Place, 393 Portage Ave., (204) 942-7291, or (204) 942-5483 for ticket information, presents a season of modern Canadian plays from October to April. **Rainbow Stage** in Kildonan Park offers musicals in a covered outdoor theater from July through August; phone (204) 989-0888 or (888) 989-0888. **Celebrations Dinner Theatre,** 1824 Pembina Hwy. in the Canad Inns Fort

Serena Sandford, Canada's Royal Winnipeg Ballet

Assiniboine Park

Garry, combines an original, three-act musical comedy with a four-course dinner for a one-stop evening out; phone (204) 982-8282.

The **IMAX Theatre Winnipeg**, at Portage Place, 393 Portage Ave. in downtown Winnipeg, features a five-and-one-half-story-high by 22-metre-wide (72-ft.) screen; phone (204) 956-4629 for information.

A variety of theatrical productions for children of all ages is presented at The Forks by the **Manitoba Theatre for Young People;** for information phone (204) 942-8898.

The French Canadian heritage of St. Boniface, in the heart of the French district, is remembered through the support of the **Centre Culturel Franco-Manitobain** at 340 Provencher Blvd.; phone (204) 233-8972. The center is the home of such cultural groups as **Le Cercle Molière** theater company (Canada's oldest active theater group), the dance group **L'Ensemble Folklorique de la Rivière Rouge,** and the choral groups **L'Alliance Chorale Manitoba** and **La Chorale des Intrépides;** phone (204) 233-8053 for more information.

⚑ ATTRACTIONS

ASSINIBOINE PARK is at jct. Park Blvd. and Corydon Ave.; it also may be accessed from Portage Ave. via a footbridge over the Assiniboine River. The 153-hectare (378-acre) park has a zoo, miniature railway, duck pond, walking and biking paths, a conservatory, sculpture garden, a pavilion, nature playground, Citizens Hall of Fame, gardens, baseball diamonds, soccer fields and an outdoor theater

where concerts are held in summer. Tobogganing, cross-country skiing and ice-skating are available in the winter. Winnipeg's only cricket tournaments are played in the park.

Assiniboine Forest, south of the park off Grant Avenue, is one of the largest urban nature parks in Canada. The 283-hectare (700-acre) forest of aspen and oak is home to more than 39 species of mammals, including deer and foxes, and more than 80 species of birds. The 1-kilometre (.6-mi.) Saginay Trail leads hikers to Eve Werier Pond, where a variety of waterfowl can be seen. **Hours:** The park is open daily 24 hours. Nature Playground daily 8-dusk. **Cost:** Free. **Phone:** (204) 927-6000. ⟨🍽⟩ ⟨✕⟩ ⟨🪑⟩

Assiniboine Park Conservatory, in Assiniboine Park, features indoor gardens, changing floral and plant displays and artwork by local artists. A tropical palm house contains orchids, ferns and banana plants. **Hours:** Daily 9-6, Victoria Day-Labour Day; 9-4, rest of year. **Cost:** Donations. **Phone:** (204) 927-6000 or (877) 927-6006. ⟨🍽⟩

Assiniboine Park Zoo, in Assiniboine Park, has more than 2,000 animals representing 200 different species in naturalistic settings. The zoo specializes in animals found in cooler climates from around the world as well as native North American species. Siberian tigers, snow leopards, two Asian lions, Stellar sea eagles, lynxes, bison, and many other hardy species can be seen outside throughout the year. Large indoor facilities provide warm-weather viewing of many tropical animals. A butterfly garden is open in the summer months.

Hours: Daily 9-6, Easter weekend-Thanksgiving weekend; 10-4, rest of year. Phone ahead for schedule on Nov. 11, Christmas Eve and Dec. 31. Closed Christmas. **Cost:** $5.95; $4.45 (ages 13-17 and 60+); $3.30 (ages 2-12). **Phone:** (204) 927-6000 or (877) 927-6006. ⟨🍽⟩ ⟨🪑⟩

Leo Mol Sculpture Garden, in Assiniboine Park, is said to be the first sculpture garden in North America dedicated to the works of a single artist. The garden and gallery feature bronze sculptures, porcelains, paintings and sketches by the Winnipeg artist. The gardens also are home to the Leo Mol Schoolhouse Studio. A reflecting pool and fountain are located in front of the gallery. **Hours:** Grounds open daily dawn-dusk. Gallery and studio open Tues.-Sun. 10-6, Victoria Day-Labour Day; Sat.-Sun. 11-5, weekend after Labour Day-Sept. 30. **Cost:** Donations. **Phone:** (204) 927-6000.

Pavilion Gallery Museum is in Assiniboine Park at 55 Pavilion Crescent. Housed in a restored 1929 pavilion, the museum contains a permanent collection featuring the work of three prominent artists: Ivan Eyre, Walter J. Phillips and Clarence Tillenius. The Pooh Gallery tells the story of Winnie the Pooh and his connection to Winnipeg. **Time:** Allow 1 hour minimum. **Hours:** Daily 9-6 (also Wed. 6 p.m.-9 p.m.), Victoria Day-Sept. 30; daily 10-5 (also Wed.

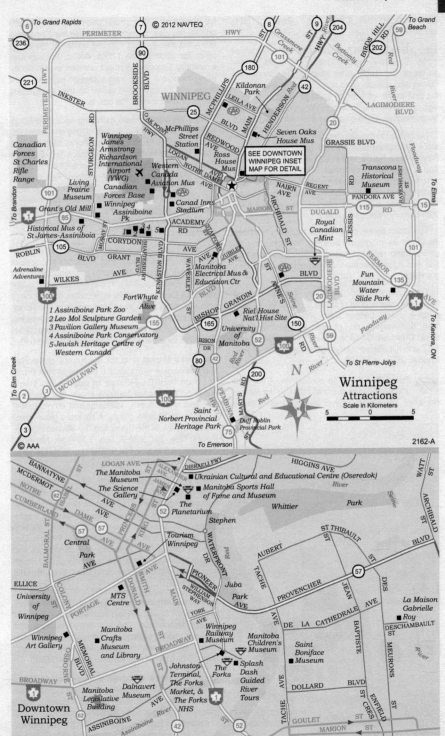

© 2012 NAVTEQ

To Grand Rapids

PERIMETER HWY

WINNIPEG

Winnipeg James Armstrong Richardson International Airport (YWG) Canadian Forces Base

Canadian Forces St Charles Rifle Range

Living Prairie Museum

Grant's Old Mill

Historical Mus of St James-Assiniboia

Adrenaline Adventures

Western Canada Aviation Mus

Winnipeg Assiniboine Pk

Canad Inns Stadium

To Grand Beach

To Elma

To Kenora, ON

McPhillips Street Station

Kildonan Park

Seven Oaks House Mus

SEE DOWNTOWN WINNIPEG INSET MAP FOR DETAIL

Transcona Historical Museum

Ross House Mus

Royal Canadian Mint

Fun Mountain Water Slide Park

Manitoba Electrical Mus & Education Ctr

FortWhyte Alive

Riel House Nat'l Hist Site

University of Manitoba

1 Assiniboine Park Zoo
2 Leo Mol Sculpture Garden
3 Pavilion Gallery Museum
4 Assiniboine Park Conservatory
5 Jewish Heritage Centre of Western Canada

To St Pierre-Jolys

N

Winnipeg Attractions
Scale in Kilometers
5   0   5

To Elm Creek

Saint Norbert Provincial Heritage Park

Duff Roblin Provincial Park

To Emerson

© AAA

2162-A

Downtown Winnipeg

LOGAN AVE

The Manitoba Museum

The Science Gallery

Ukrainian Cultural and Educational Centre (Oseredok)

Manitoba Sports Hall of Fame and Museum

The Planetarium

Whittier Park

Tourism Winnipeg

Stephen

Central Park

University of Winnipeg

Winnipeg Art Gallery

MTS Centre

Manitoba Crafts Museum and Library

Johnston Terminal, The Forks Market, & The Forks NHS

Manitoba Legislative Building

Dalnavert Museum

Juba Park

Winnipeg Railway Museum

The Forks

Splash Dash Guided River Tours

Manitoba Children's Museum

Saint Boniface Museum

La Maison Gabrielle Roy

5-9), rest of year. **Cost:** Free. **Phone:** (204) 927-6000.

DALNAVERT MUSEUM, .5 blk. s. of Broadway at 61 Carlton St., is the former home of Sir Hugh John Macdonald, prominent lawyer and politician and son of John A. Macdonald, the first prime minister of Canada. Built in 1895, it was one of the first houses in Winnipeg to have hot-water heating, electric lighting and indoor plumbing.

Named after the Scottish birthplace of Macdonald's grandmother, the red brick Queen Anne Revival-style house features stained-glass windows and a wraparound verandah. The restored house, which was saved from demolition in 1969, is opulently furnished with Victorian antiques. Guided tours provide a glimpse into the lifestyles of early 20th-century Winnipeg society.

The visitor center at the rear of museum has been designed as a "green" building, incorporating reclaimed and recycled materials during its construction and utilizing geothermal energy to heat and cool the building. **Time:** Allow 1 hour minimum. **Hours:** Guided tours are given Wed.-Fri. 10-5, Sat. 11-6, Sun. noon-4, July 1-Labour Day; Wed.-Fri. 11-4, Sat. 11-6, Sun. noon-4, rest of year. Closed major holidays. **Cost:** $5; $4 (ages 65+); $3 (students ages 5-17 with ID). Rates may vary during special events. **Phone:** (204) 943-2835.

THE FORKS, at the confluence of the Red and Assiniboine rivers at 1-201 Forks Market Rd. at jct. Waterfront Dr., has been a meeting place

Manitoba Children's Museum

for more than 6,000 years, beginning with the aboriginal peoples. By virtue of location the 23-hectare (56-acre) site evolved into the center of the European fur trade in the 1730s. Métis, natives and eventually European settlers created a community along the rivers. More than a century later, the area became a transportation center as the railways laid tracks of steel across the prairie.

Now Winnipeg's main gathering spot, The Forks is a favorite place for shopping, dining and entertainment. Attractions include The Forks Market, The Forks National Historic Site, Johnston Terminal, The Plaza skateboarding park, Manitoba Children's Museum and Variety Heritage Adventure Park for children. The Riverwalk follows the water's edge from the Manitoba Legislature to The Forks through downtown Winnipeg, and the Wall Through Time chronicles area history from glacial Lake Agassiz to the present.

Canoes and "sea cycles" can be rented seasonally at The Forks Historic Port. Concerts and special events take place at The Forks throughout the year *(see Big Events p. 474).* Travel Manitoba's Explore Manitoba Centre provides information about events and attractions throughout Manitoba and The Forks. **Hours:** Hours vary per site. **Cost:** All sites free except for Manitoba Children's Museum. **Phone:** (204) 957-7618 for an events hotline or (800) 665-0040.

The Forks Market is at the confluence of the Red and Assiniboine rivers at 201-1 Forks Market Rd. at jct. Waterfront Dr. Housed in refurbished stable buildings, the market contains shops that offer jewelry and crafts; fresh, specialty and ethnic foods; produce; and baked goods. A six-story glass tower affords a view of the rivers and the downtown area. **Hours:** Mon.-Sat. 9:30-9, Sun. 9:30-6:30, July-Aug.; daily 9:30-6:30 (also Fri. 6:30-9 p.m.), rest of year. **Cost:** Free. **Phone:** (204) 957-7618.

The Forks National Historic Site, at the confluence of the Red and Assiniboine rivers at 201-1 Forks Market Rd., is a 3.5-hectare (9-acre) park that offers an outdoor playground and a riverside amphitheater with a view of historic St. Boniface. Interpretive programs and festivals are held Victoria Day through Labour Day. A variety of guided tours and theatrical presentations are available July through August. **Hours:** Daily 24 hours. **Cost:** Free. **Phone:** (204) 983-6757.

Johnston Terminal, in the heart of The Forks at 25 Forks Market Rd., is a renovated railway cold storage warehouse. The four-story structure now features shops, boutiques and restaurants. **Time:** Allow 1 hour minimum. **Hours:** Mon.-Fri. 10-9, Sat.-Sun. 10-6. **Cost:** Free. **Phone:** (204) 956-5593.

Manitoba Children's Museum, 45 Forks Market Rd., occupies Manitoba's oldest train repair facility. The museum houses a dozen colorful galleries offering a wide variety of educational and fun hands-on activities. Junction 9161 and the Engine House galleries immerse visitors in train history with a 1910 Pullman passenger coach and a 1952 diesel locomotive. A walk through the Illusion Tunnel will test perceptions. Tot Spot caters to little ones. Other areas include Splash Lab, Pop m'Art, Story Line, Tumble Zone, Lasagna Lookout and Milk Machine.

During the holiday season (mid-November to mid-January), visitors can reminisce with a trip to Eaton's Santa's Village, the original holiday display from downtown's Eaton's department store. The setup features 15 scenes from various fairy tales. Special events, public programs and workshops are offered throughout the year.

Time: Allow 1 hour minimum. **Hours:** Daily 9:30-6, July 1-Labour Day; Sun.-Thurs. and holidays 9:30-4:30, Fri.-Sat. 9:30-6, rest of year. Closed Easter, week after Labour Day, Christmas Eve, Christmas and day after Christmas. **Cost:** $10. Children must be accompanied by an adult. **Phone:** (204) 924-4000 or (204) 956-2122. 🎫

FORTWHYTE ALIVE is at 1961 McCreary Rd. A bison herd, deer, foxes, prairie dogs, waterfowl and songbirds can be seen at this 259-hectare (640-acre) nature and recreational center. There also are trails, floating boardwalks, bird-feeding stations, a bison-viewing mound, a family tree house, fishing, boat and canoe rentals, snowshoeing, skating, cross country skiing, a sod house, a tipi encampment and an interpretive center.

"Bison buggies" for touring some areas are available for rent. The interpretive center features the Aquarium of the Prairies, the Honeybee Observation Hive, a burrowing owl and prairie dog exhibit and the Touch Museum. **Time:** Allow 1 hour minimum. **Hours:** Mon.-Fri. 9-5, Sat.-Sun. and holidays 10-5. Schedule varies summer and fall; phone for hours. Evening hours are extended Sept.-Oct. for viewing migrating Canada geese. Closed Christmas. **Cost:** $6; $5 (ages 55+); $4 (ages 3-17 and students with ID); free (ages 0-2). **Phone:** (204) 989-8364. 🍴 ⊗ 🎫

FUN MOUNTAIN WATER SLIDE PARK, off Hwy. 1E on Murdock Rd., offers 10 waterslides, a swimming area, a hot tub, bumper boats, miniature golf, ziplining and locker and changing facilities. **Hours:** Park opens Wed.-Sun. at 10, Mon.-Tues. at noon, mid-June to late Aug. (weather permitting). Closing times vary; phone ahead. **Cost:** $15.99; $12.99 (under 48 inches tall). Combination ticket (includes bumper boats and miniature golf): $19.99; $16.99 (under 48 inches tall). **Phone:** (204) 255-3910. 🍴

GRANT'S OLD MILL is at Portage Ave. and Booth Dr. This operational, reconstructed log flour mill—the original was built in 1829—marks the first use of water power in the Western provinces. **Tours:** Guided tours are available. **Time:** Allow 30 minutes minimum. **Hours:** Daily 10-6, mid-May through Labour Day. **Cost:** Donations. **Phone:** (204) 986-5613.

HISTORICAL MUSEUM OF ST. JAMES-ASSINIBOIA, 3180 Portage Ave., houses a collection of artifacts relating to the history of the St. James-Assiniboia area and a display building of pioneer activities. Guided interpretive tours through the mid-19th-century William Brown Red River Log House offer a glimpse of the pioneer lifestyle. **Time:** Allow 1 hour minimum. **Hours:** Daily 10-4:30, mid-May through Labour Day; by appointment rest of year. **Cost:** Donations. **Phone:** (204) 888-8706.

JEWISH HERITAGE CENTRE OF WESTERN CANADA, 123 Doncaster St., site of the Fort Osborne Barracks, shares the history, experiences, achievements and culture of Jewish people in Western Canada. The Corridor Museum exhibit depicts the settlement of Jews in Western Canada through artifacts, photographs and archival material. The Holocaust Education Centre features items from the Holocaust and stories and artifacts from local survivors.

Time: Allow 30 minutes minimum. **Hours:** Mon.-Thurs. 6 a.m.-10 p.m., Fri. 6 a.m.-7 p.m., Sat. noon-6, Sun. 7-6 (also Sun. 6-7 p.m., Nov.-Mar.). Closed major holidays. **Cost:** Donations. **Phone:** (204) 477-7460 for tours or appointments.

KILDONAN PARK is at 2021 Main St. In its 39 hectares (96 acres) along the Red River the park has some of the province's oldest and largest trees, flower and rock gardens, and a model of the witch's hut from "Hansel and Gretel."

Summer options include swimming; boating; bicycling; walking; in-line skating; and Rainbow Stage, Winnipeg's outdoor theater. Tobogganing, ice-skating and cross-country skiing are winter sports *See Recreation Areas Chart.* **Hours:** Daily 7-dusk. **Cost:** Free. **Phone:** (204) 986-7469. 🍴 ⊗

LA MAISON GABRIELLE ROY, 375 Deschambault St. in St. Boniface, is the birthplace and childhood home of Gabrielle Roy, one of Canada's most famous 20th-century authors, known for her works about the underprivileged and poverty-stricken. The 1905 house contains furnishings and artifacts indicative of the early 20th-century period when the author lived here. Tours are given in English and French.

Time: Allow 30 minutes minimum. **Hours:** Mon.-Fri. 10-5, Sat.-Sun. 1-5, June-Aug.; Wed.-Sun. 1-4, rest of year. Last tour begins 30 minutes before closing. **Cost:** $5; $3 (ages 65+ and students with ID); free (ages 0-5). **Phone:** (204) 231-3853.

LIVING PRAIRIE MUSEUM is at 2795 Ness Ave. This 13-hectare (32-acre) unplowed tract supports more than 160 native plant species and is a remnant of the prairie that once covered much of North America. An interpretive center features displays of plants and animals of the tall grass prairie. Nature talks and hikes are offered, and a self-guiding trail brochure is available. **Time:** Allow 1 hour minimum. **Hours:** Trail open daily dawn-dusk. Interpretive center daily 10-5, July-Aug.; Sun. 10-5, May-June; by appointment rest of year. **Cost:** Donations. **Phone:** (204) 832-0167.

MANITOBA CRAFTS MUSEUM AND LIBRARY, downtown at 183 Kennedy St., has a permanent collection of approximately 9,000 traditional Manitoba crafts, including embroidery, knitting, quilting, weaving, lace, pottery, beadwork and basketry. The library has books, patterns and scrapbooks about many forms of craftwork. **Time:** Allow 30 minutes minimum. **Hours:** Tues.-Sat. 10-4, June-Aug.; Tues.-Wed. 10-4, Sat. noon-4 or by appointment, rest of year. Closed major holidays. **Cost:** Donations. **Phone:** (204) 487-6117.

MANITOBA ELECTRICAL MUSEUM & EDUCATION CENTRE is 1 blk. w. of jct. Pembina Hwy. and Stafford St. at 680 Harrow St. The museum's six galleries tell the story of hydroelectric development in the province beginning in the 1870s.

Themed areas such as The Light Goes On 1882-1900, Energizing Manitoba 1900-1960 and Powering up the Farm 1942-1960 provide an idea of the museum's offerings. A yellow turbine runner from one of the oldest hydroelectric stations in Manitoba is outside the 1931 building. **Tours:** Guided tours are available. **Time:** Allow 1 hour minimum. **Hours:** Mon.-Thurs. 1-4, or by appointment. Closed major holidays. **Cost:** Free. **Phone:** (204) 360-7905.

MANITOBA LEGISLATIVE BUILDING, bordered by Broadway Ave., Kennedy and Osborne sts. and the Assiniboine River, reflects neoclassical design in native Tyndall limestone. The Italian marble grand staircase is guarded at its base by two life-size bronze bison, the emblems of Manitoba.

Atop the dome is Golden Boy by Parisian sculptor Georges Gardet. The torch, in the right hand, points to economic development and progress in the north; the sheaf of wheat in the left arm represents agriculture. This 5.25-metre-tall (17.2-ft.) statue weighs 1,650 kilograms (3,638 lbs.) and is sheathed in 24 karat gold leaf. The statue represents eternal youth and the province's spirit of enterprise. Plots on the site's 12 hectares (30 acres) contain flowers, foliage and ornamental plants.

Hours: Guided tours are conducted daily on the hour 9-4, July 1-Labour Day; by appointment rest of year. Self-guiding tours are available daily 8-8, year-round. **Cost:** Free. **Phone:** (204) 945-5813.

THE MANITOBA MUSEUM, 190 Rupert Ave. at jct. Main St., illustrates the relationship of people and their environment in Manitoba's history through nine permanent galleries. The recently upgraded Earth History Gallery shows geologic and organic evolution, the Arctic/Sub-Arctic Gallery explores Inuit culture and the zone's flora and fauna, and the Boreal Forest Gallery features a diorama of a granite cliff, waterfall, marsh, Cree family and a wandering moose. A bat cave, snake pit and a Ukrainian rye farm can be seen at the Parklands/Mixed Woods Gallery.

Visitors can see a replica of the ketch *Nonsuch;* the ship's 1668 voyage to Hudson Bay opened western Canada to commerce and European settlement. The Hudson's Bay Company Gallery highlights fur trading and early exploration. A teepee and a sod house are part of the Grasslands Gallery, and the Urban Gallery shows a 1920s boom-town Winnipeg.

The museum also houses a planetarium and science gallery. **Time:** Allow 1 hour minimum. **Hours:** Daily 10-5, Victoria Day-Labour Day; Tues.-Fri. 10-4, Sat.-Sun. and holidays 11-5, rest of year. **Cost:** $8; $6.50 (ages 3-17, ages 60+ and students with ID); $28 (family, up to six people with no more than two adults). Combination ticket with The Planetarium and The Science Gallery $19; $13.50 (ages 3-17, ages 60+ and students with ID); $64 (family, up to six people with no more than two adults). **Phone:** (204) 956-2830 or (204) 943-3139.

The Planetarium, on the lower level of The Manitoba Museum at 190 Rupert Ave., presents interactive and multimedia shows about science and our universe. **Time:** Allow 1 hour minimum. **Hours:** Shows are presented daily on the hour 10-5, June-Aug.; Thurs.-Fri. on the hour 10-4 and Sat.-Sun. on the hour 11-5, rest of year. Phone ahead to confirm schedule. **Cost:** $8; $6.50 (ages 3-17, ages 60+ and students with ID); $28 (family, up to six people with no more than two adults). Combination ticket with The Manitoba Museum and The Science Gallery

$19; $13.50 (ages 3-17, ages 60+ and students with ID); $64 (family, up to six people with no more than two adults). **Phone:** (204) 956-2830, or (204) 943-3139 for show times.

The Science Gallery, on the lower level of The Manitoba Museum at 190 Rupert Ave., has more than 100 hands-on exhibits. **Time:** Allow 1 hour minimum. **Hours:** Daily 10-5, June-Aug.; Tues.-Fri. 10-4, Sat.-Sun. and holidays 11-5, rest of year. **Cost:** $8; $6.50 (ages 3-17, ages 60+ and students with ID); $28 (family, up to six people with no more than two adults). Combination ticket with The Manitoba Museum and The Planetarium $19; $13.50 (ages 3-17, ages 60+ and students with ID); $64 (family, up to six people with no more than two adults). **Phone:** (204) 956-2830 or (204) 943-3139.

MANITOBA SPORTS HALL OF FAME AND MUSEUM, on the main floor of the Sport for Life Centre at 145 Pacific Ave., focuses on the province's sports history and legendary athletes and teams with jerseys, trophies and video displays. **Hours:** Tues.-Sat. 10-4, Sun. noon-5. **Cost:** $5; $4 (ages 13-18); $3 (ages 0-12 and 55+). **Phone:** (204) 925-5736.

RIEL HOUSE NATIONAL HISTORIC SITE, 330 River Rd., was the home of the mother of Louis Riel. Although this leader of the Métis and founder of the provisional government of Manitoba never lived in the house, his body lay in state for several days after his execution in 1885. The walkway to the house has signs explaining the history of the Métis and of the Riel family. **Time:** Allow 30 minutes minimum. **Hours:** Daily 10-5 (also Thurs. 5-8), July-Aug.; Mon.-Fri. 10-5, Victoria Day-last Fri. in June. **Cost:** $3.90; $3.40 (ages 65+); $1.90 (ages 6-16); $9.80 (family). **Phone:** (204) 257-1783 or (204) 983-6757.

ROSS HOUSE MUSEUM, 140 Meade St. N. in Joe Zuken Heritage Park, was the first post office in western Canada in 1854. Displays reflect the life of the Ross family, a prominent Métis family, when their home served as the post office. **Time:** Allow 30 minutes minimum. **Hours:** Wed.-Sun. 10-5, June-Aug. First tour begins 30 minutes after opening and last tour begins 30 minutes before closing. **Cost:** Free. **Phone:** (204) 943-3958.

ROYAL CANADIAN MINT is at 520 Lagimodière Blvd. at jct. Trans-Canada Hwy. and Hwy. 59. This high-tech, high-volume manufacturing facility is considered one of the world's most modern mints; its high-speed coining presses can each strike 750 coins per minute. The Winnipeg Plant produces all of the circulation coinage for Canada as well as coinage for more than 75 foreign countries.

The building includes a landscaped interior courtyard and a glass tower overlooking the manufacturing plant. At the mint's interactive museum visitors can lift a gold bar worth more than $600,000.

Tours: Guided tours are available. **Hours:** Daily 9-5, Victoria Day-Labour Day; Tues.-Sat. 9-5, rest of year. Phone ahead to confirm schedule. **Cost:** Museum free. Guided tour (Mon.-Fri.) $6; $3 (ages

Riel House National Historic Site

4-15); $15 (family, two adults and up to four children). Guided tour (Sat.-Sun.) $4.50; $2.25 (ages 4-15); $11.25 (family, two adults and up to four children). Reservations are recommended. **Phone:** (204) 983-6429 or (877) 974-6468.

SAINT BONIFACE MUSEUM, s.e. on Main St. (Hwy. 1), then n. to 494 Taché Ave., was built 1846-51 as the first convent and hospital in western Canada. Displays depict the Red River Settlement and early French and Métis Manitoba; an exhibit is dedicated to Louis Riel, leader of the Red River Resistance. Visitors also can view the nearby ruins of the cathedral as well as the cemetery where Riel is buried.

Tours: Guided tours are available. **Time:** Allow 30 minutes minimum. **Hours:** Mon.-Fri. 9-5, Sat.-Sun. and holidays noon-4. Closed Christmas Eve, Christmas and Dec. 31. **Cost:** $5; $4 (ages 60+, physically impaired and students with ID); free (ages 0-5); $15 (family). Reservations are required for tours. **Phone:** (204) 237-4500.

SAINT NORBERT PROVINCIAL HERITAGE PARK is at 40 Turnbull Dr. at the fork of the Red and La Salle rivers. Near the former village of St. Norbert, this 7-hectare (17-acre) park is rich in history and linked to Manitoba's entry into the Confederation. A restored 19th-century farmhouse and village house are decorated in period.

A walking trail with information about native inhabitants and Manitoba history and a house belonging to a member of Louis Riel's provisional government are available. Fishing is permitted with a valid license. **Tours:** Guided tours are available. **Time:** Allow 1 hour minimum. **Hours:** Daily 10-6,

July-Aug.; Mon.-Fri. 8:30-4:30, Sat.-Sun. 10-6, May-June. **Cost:** Donations. **Phone:** (204) 945-4236, or (204) 945-4375 Sept.-Apr.

SEVEN OAKS HOUSE MUSEUM, 1.5 blks. e. of Main St. off Rupertsland Blvd. and Jones St. in W. Kildonan, is said to be the oldest habitable house in Manitoba. This sturdy building, with its stone foundation, hand-hewn oak timbers, hand-split shingles and buffalo hair-bound plaster, was built 1851-53. The house displays belongings of the original occupants and other period furnishings. **Tours:** Guided tours are available. **Time:** Allow 30 minutes minimum. **Hours:** Daily 10-5, Victoria Day-Labour Day. **Cost:** Donations. **Phone:** (204) 339-7429.

TRANSCONA HISTORICAL MUSEUM is at 141 Regent Ave. W. In a 1925 bank building, the museum explores the origins of Transcona, a railroad town amalgamated into Winnipeg, and the accomplishments of its residents. In addition to displays about the town's railroad heritage, veterans and community leaders, there also are archeology and butterfly exhibits.

Time: Allow 30 minutes minimum. **Hours:** Mon.-Sat. 9-4, June-Aug.; Tues.-Sat. 10-4, rest of year. Closed long holiday weekends. **Cost:** Donations. **Phone:** (204) 222-0423.

UKRAINIAN CULTURAL AND EDUCATIONAL CENTRE (OSEREDOK), 184 Alexander Ave. E., at Main St. and Disraeli Frwy., is dedicated to the preservation of Canadian-Ukrainian culture. Highlights include a museum, an exhibition gallery, a library and archives. Exhibits include a wide range of artifacts, from fine art to farm implements to rare 16th-century maps.

Guided tours are available by appointment. **Time:** Allow 30 minutes minimum. **Hours:** Mon.-Sat. 10-4, Sun. 1-4, July-Aug.; Mon.-Sat. 10-4, rest of year. **Cost:** Donations. **Phone:** (204) 942-0218.

[SAVE] **WESTERN CANADA AVIATION MUSEUM,** in an aircraft hangar off Ellice Ave. at 958 Ferry Rd., displays 24 vintage aircraft. All aspects of aviation are exhibited, from bush planes to commercial airliners to military planes and homemade aircraft. Children can explore the interactive Skyways exhibit. A research library and archives can be seen by appointment.

Guided tours are available by appointment. **Time:** Allow 1 hour minimum. **Hours:** Mon.-Fri. 9:30-4:30, Sat. 10-5, Sun. and holidays noon-5. Closed Jan. 1, Good Friday, Easter, Christmas and day after Christmas. **Cost:** $7.50; $5 (students with ID and senior citizens); $3 (ages 3-12); $18 (family, two adults and three children). **Phone:** (204) 786-5503.

WINNIPEG ART GALLERY is at 300 Memorial Blvd. Nine galleries contain contemporary and historical works by Manitoba, Canadian and international artists. The Inuit art collection is reputed to be the largest public collection of contemporary Inuit art in the world; a small portion of the collection is always on display. Guided tours are offered; phone for scheduled tours and talks.

Time: Allow 1 hour minimum. **Hours:** Tues.-Sun. 11-5 (also Thurs. 5-9). **Cost:** $10; $8 (ages 60+ and students with ID); $25 (family). **Phone:** (204) 786-6641, or (204) 789-1760 for recorded information.

WINNIPEG RAILWAY MUSEUM is at 123 Main St. inside the VIA Rail Station, making it one of only a few North American railroad museums in an active railway station. Highlights on the two sections of 750-foot-long tracks include steam, electric and diesel locomotives, baggage cars, boxcars and cabooses. A 1920 Ford Model T truck and two antique fire trucks also can be seen. Museum exhibits feature a model train display as well as historic items and photos related to the city of Winnipeg, the Canadian National and Canadian Pacific railways and women's roles in railway history.

Time: Allow 45 minutes minimum. **Hours:** Daily 11-4 (also Mon., Thurs. and Sat. 9-11), Mar.-Nov.; Mon., Thurs. and Sat. 9-noon, rest of year. Phone ahead to confirm schedule and for additional hours Dec.-Feb. **Cost:** $5; $3 (ages 6-15); free (ages 0-5). **Phone:** (204) 942-4632.

GAMBLING ESTABLISHMENTS

- **Club Regent** is at 1425 Regent Ave. **Hours:** Mon.-Sat. 10 a.m.-3 a.m., Sun. noon-3 a.m. Closed Good Friday, Easter, Nov. 11, Christmas Eve and Christmas. **Phone:** (204) 957-2500.

- **McPhillips Street Station** is at 484 McPhillips St. **Hours:** Mon.-Sat. 10 a.m.-3 a.m., Sun. noon-3 a.m. Closed Good Friday, Easter, Nov. 11, Christmas Eve and Christmas. **Phone:** (204) 957-2500.

Winnipeg Railway Museum is located in the Via Rail Union Station

Sightseeing

The intersection of Portage Avenue and Main Street, a few blocks from the juncture of Winnipeg's two rivers, has been the major crossroads since the city's earliest days and is a good place to start a sightseeing foray.

Although now part of Winnipeg, the early settlement of St. Boniface has retained its French Canadian identity. A monument honoring the explorer Pierre Gaultier de la Vérendrye is on Taché Avenue opposite St. Boniface Hospital. Also in St. Boniface is the grave of Louis Riel, leader of the Métis and of the provisional government 1869-70. The grave is at Taché and Cathedral avenues in the churchyard of the St. Boniface Basilica.

Boat Tours

SPLASH DASH GUIDED RIVER TOURS departs from the bottom of the river walk at The Forks. The boats provide 30-minute guided historical tours of a section of the Red and Assiniboine rivers. Points of interest are noted along the way. **Time:** Allow 30 minutes minimum. **Hours:** Departures daily every 15 minutes noon-8 p.m. (weather permitting), May 15-Oct. 15. **Cost:** $11; $9 (ages 4-18 and 55+). **Phone:** (204) 783-6633.

Train Tours

Antique rail cars pulled by a vintage locomotive take passengers on 3-hour trips departing from a 1910 station at Inkster Junction, 3 kilometres (1.9 mi.) west of Hwy. 90 off Inkster Boulevard. The Prairie Dog Central Railway makes a stop at a country market in Grosse Isle. The scenic ride operates weekends and holidays, May through September; phone (204) 832-5259.

Walking Tours

Guided walking tours of the 20-block Historic Winnipeg area near Portage Avenue and Main Street in the Exchange District are available June through Labour Day weekend. Departing from Old Market Square at the corner of King St. and Bannetyne Ave., these tours visit many of Manitoba's finest historical buildings; for schedule information phone (204) 942-6716.

Walking tours of the old St. Boniface area are available; phone (204) 233-8343 or (866) 808-8338 for information and reservations.

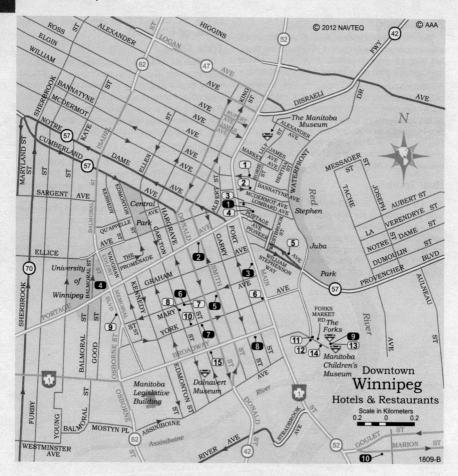

Downtown Winnipeg

This index helps you "spot" where approved hotels and restaurants are located on the corresponding detailed maps. Hotel daily rate range is for comparison only. Restaurant price range is a combination of lunch and/or dinner. Turn to the listing page for more detailed rate and price information and consult display ads for special promotions.

DOWNTOWN WINNIPEG

Map Page		Hotels	Diamond Rated	Rate Range	Page
❶	this page	The Fairmont Winnipeg	▽▽▽	$159-$299	488
❷	this page	**Radisson Hotel Winnipeg Downtown**	▽▽▽	$171-$265 SAVE	489
❸	this page	Humphry Inn & Suites	▽▽▽	$114-$190	489
❹	this page	**Holiday Inn & Suites Winnipeg Downtown**	▽▽▽	$99-$199 SAVE	489
❺	this page	**Place Louis Riel Suite Hotel**	▽▽▽	$120-$300 SAVE	489
❻	this page	Delta Winnipeg	▽▽▽	$99-$399	488
❼	this page	**BEST WESTERN PLUS Charter House Hotel Downtown Winnipeg**	▽▽▽	$140-$150 SAVE	488
❽	this page	The Fort Garry Hotel, Spa & Conference Centre	▽▽▽	$139-$429 SAVE	488
❾	this page	**Inn at the Forks**	▽▽▽	$159-$279 SAVE	489

DOWNTOWN WINNIPEG (cont'd)

Map Page	Hotels (cont'd)	Diamond Rated	Rate Range	Page
10 p. 484	**Norwood Hotel**	◇◇◇	$119-$199 [SAVE]	489

Map Page	Restaurants	Diamond Rated	Cuisine	Price Range	Page
① p. 484	Hermanos Restaurant & Wine Bar	◆◆◆	Latin American	$9-$32	490
② p. 484	Tre Visi Cucina Italiano	◆◆◆	Italian	$12-$29	490
③ p. 484	Hy's Steakhouse	◆◆◆	Steak	$17-$54	490
④ p. 484	**The Velvet Glove**	◇◇◇	Continental	$26-$36	490
⑤ p. 484	Hu's Asian Bistro	◆◆	Asian	$12-$18	490
⑥ p. 484	Ivory Restaurant & Bar	◆◆	Indian	$12-$25	490
⑦ p. 484	Blaze Bistro & Lounge	◆◆	American	$9-$35	489
⑧ p. 484	Ichiban Japanese Steak House & Sushi Bar	◆◆	Japanese	$26-$42	490
⑨ p. 484	Storm Bistro	◆◆	American	$9-$15	490
⑩ p. 484	East India Company Pub & Eatery	◆◆	Indian	$12-$22	489
⑪ p. 484	Sydney's At The Forks	◆◆◆	New American	$14-$55	490
⑫ p. 484	Beachcombers	◆◆	American	$10-$28	489
⑬ p. 484	The Current	◆◆◆	American	$11-$37	489
⑭ p. 484	Muddy Waters Smokehouse	◆◆	Barbecue	$10-$29	490
⑮ p. 484	Amici	◆◆◆	Italian	$12-$38	489

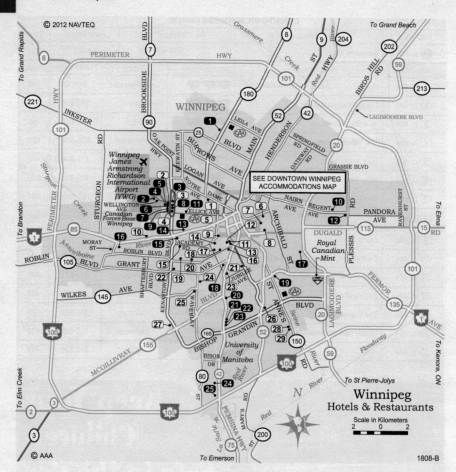

Winnipeg Hotels & Restaurants

© 2012 NAVTEQ

© AAA

1808-B

Map Page	WINNIPEG JAMES ARMSTRONG RICHARDSON INTERNATIONAL AIRPORT	Diamond Rated	Rate Range	Page
7 this page	**Comfort Inn Airport,** 1.4 mi (2.3 km) e of airport	◈◈	$99-$138 SAVE	492
6 this page	Country Inn & Suites By Carlson, 1.2 mi (1.9 km) e of airport	◈◈	$110-$140	492
11 this page	Fairfield Inn & Suites by Marriott, 2.3 mi (3.7 km) e of airport	◈◈◈	$129-$169	492
2 this page	**Four Points by Sheraton Hotel Winnipeg Airport,** at airport	◈◈◈	$130-$150	492
3 this page	Greenwood Inn & Suites, 0.9 mi (1.5 km) e of airport	◈◈◈	$109-$159	492
5 this page	Hilton Suites Winnipeg Airport, 1 mi (1.6 km) e of airport	◈◈◈	$119-$239	492
9 this page	**MainStay Suites Winnipeg,** 1.3 mi (2.1 km) e of airport	◈◈◈	$94-$160 SAVE	493
8 this page	Sandman Hotel & Suites Winnipeg Airport, 0.9 mi (1.5 km) e of airport	◈◈◈	Rates not provided	493
4 this page	**Victoria Inn Hotel & Convention Centre,** 0.8 mi (1.2 km) e of airport	◈◈◈	$134-$174 SAVE	494

✈ **Airport Accommodations**

Winnipeg

This index helps you "spot" where approved hotels and restaurants are located on the corresponding detailed maps. Hotel daily rate range is for comparison only. Restaurant price range is a combination of lunch and/or dinner. Turn to the listing page for more detailed rate and price information and consult display ads for special promotions.

WINNIPEG

Map Page	Hotels	Diamond Rated	Rate Range	Page
1 p. 486	Canad Inns Destination Centre Garden City	🔷🔷🔷	$107-$259 SAVE	491
2 p. 486	Four Points by Sheraton Hotel Winnipeg Airport	🔷🔷🔷	$130-$150 SAVE	492
3 p. 486	Greenwood Inn & Suites	🔷🔷🔷	$109-$159	492
4 p. 486	Victoria Inn Hotel & Convention Centre	🔷🔷🔷	$134-$174 SAVE	494
5 p. 486	Hilton Suites Winnipeg Airport	🔷🔷🔷	$119-$239	492
6 p. 486	Country Inn & Suites By Carlson	🔷🔷	$110-$140	492
7 p. 486	Comfort Inn Airport	🔷🔷	$99-$138 SAVE	492
8 p. 486	Sandman Hotel & Suites Winnipeg Airport	🔷🔷🔷	Rates not provided	493
9 p. 486	MainStay Suites Winnipeg	🔷🔷🔷	$94-$160 SAVE	493
10 p. 486	Canad Inns Destination Centre Club Regent Casino Hotel	🔷🔷🔷	$124-$299 SAVE	491
11 p. 486	Fairfield Inn & Suites by Marriott	🔷🔷🔷	$129-$169	492
12 p. 486	Canad Inns Destination Centre Transcona	🔷🔷	$109-$239 SAVE	491
13 p. 486	Canad Inns Destination Centre Polo Park	🔷🔷🔷	$115-$259 SAVE	491
14 p. 486	Clarion Hotel & Suites	🔷🔷🔷	$143-$250	492
15 p. 486	Ramada Viscount Gort Hotel (See ad p. 493.)	🔷🔷🔷	$120-$170 SAVE	493
16 p. 486	Holiday Inn Winnipeg Airport West	🔷🔷🔷	$126-$139 SAVE	492
17 p. 486	Canad Inns Destination Centre Windsor Park	🔷🔷	$111-$299 SAVE	491
18 p. 486	Quality Inn & Suites	🔷🔷🔷	$90-$300 SAVE	493
19 p. 486	Travelodge Winnipeg	🔷🔷	$116-$130 SAVE	494
20 p. 486	Holiday Inn Winnipeg South	🔷🔷🔷	$139-$179	493
21 p. 486	BEST WESTERN PLUS Pembina Inn & Suites (See ad p. 491.)	🔷🔷🔷	$120-$299 SAVE	490
22 p. 486	Express by Canad Inns	🔷🔷🔷	$103-$142 SAVE	492
23 p. 486	Canad Inns Destination Centre Fort Garry	🔷🔷	$105-$249 SAVE	491
24 p. 486	Four Points by Sheraton Winnipeg South	🔷🔷🔷	$120-$150 SAVE	492
25 p. 486	Comfort Inn South	🔷🔷	$117-$138 SAVE	492

Map Page	Restaurants	Diamond Rated	Cuisine	Price Range	Page
1 p. 486	Ducky's English Style Fish & Chips	🔷	Fish & Chips	$10-$19	496
2 p. 486	Bistro 1800	🔷🔷	American	$9-$38	494
3 p. 486	Chop Steak Fish Bar	🔷🔷🔷	Steak	$18-$39	494
4 p. 486	Hu's Asian Bistro	🔷🔷	Asian	$12-$26	496
5 p. 486	India Palace	🔷🔷	Indian	$11-$21	496
6 p. 486	Resto Gare	🔷🔷🔷	French	$11-$32	497
7 p. 486	Beaujena's	🔷🔷🔷	French	$39-$49	494
8 p. 486	Inferno's Bistro	🔷🔷🔷	French	$11-$24	496
9 p. 486	Restaurant Bistro Dansk	🔷🔷	European	$9-$23	497
10 p. 486	Joe Black Coffee Bar	🔷	Coffee/Tea	$7-$9	496

Map Page	Restaurants (cont'd)	Diamond Rated	Cuisine	Price Range	Page
⑪ p. 486	Buccacino's Cucina Italiana	▼▼	Italian	$10-$25	494
⑫ p. 486	Segovia Tapas Bar & Restaurant	▼▼▼	New Spanish	$20-$35	497
⑬ p. 486	Naru Sushi	▼▼	Japanese	$8-$19	497
⑭ p. 486	529 Wellington	▼▼▼	Steak	$9-$49	494
⑮ p. 486	Fusion Grill	▼▼	Canadian	$10-$33	496
⑯ p. 486	Confusion Corner Bar & Grill	▼▼	American	$11-$32	494
⑰ p. 486	Spuntino Café	▼▼	Italian	$11-$26	497
⑱ p. 486	Fresh Café	▼▼	American	$8-$16	496
⑲ p. 486	Mona Lisa Ristorante	▼▼	Northern Italian	$7-$29	496
⑳ p. 486	Bonfire Bistro	▼▼	Italian	$9-$28	494
㉑ p. 486	Bistro 7 1/4	▼▼▼	New French	$12-$39	494
㉒ p. 486	Stella's Cafe	▼	Breakfast	$8-$15	497
㉓ p. 486	The Round Table Steak House & Pub	▼▼	Steak	$10-$39	497
㉔ p. 486	Wasabi Sabi	▼▼▼	New Sushi	$20-$35	497
㉕ p. 486	Bellissimo Restaurant & Lounge	▼▼	Italian	$9-$26	494
㉖ p. 486	Maxime's Restaurant & Lounge	▼▼	Continental	$11-$23	496
㉗ p. 486	Clay Oven	▼▼	Indian	$12-$26	494
㉘ p. 486	Diana's Gourmet Pizzeria	▼▼	Pizza	$14-$25	496
㉙ p. 486	La Fiesta Cafecito	▼▼	Salvadoran	$8-$19	496

DOWNTOWN WINNIPEG
• Hotels & Restaurants map & index p. 484

BEST WESTERN PLUS CHARTER HOUSE HOTEL DOWNTOWN WINNIPEG (204)942-0101 **7**

Hotel
$140-$150

 AAA Benefit: Members save up to 20%, plus 10% bonus points with Best Western Rewards®.

Address: 330 York Ave R3C 0N9 **Location:** Between Hargrave and Donald sts. Located in business district. **Facility:** 87 units. 5 stories, interior corridors. **Parking:** on-site (fee), winter plug-ins. **Amenities:** high-speed Internet. **Dining:** 2 restaurants. **Activities:** exercise room. **Guest Services:** valet and coin laundry, area transportation-bus & train stations. **Free Special Amenities: local telephone calls and high-speed Internet.**

🅢🅐🆅🅔 ⓔⓒⓞ ✈ 🍴 🍸 CALL 🄶Ⓜ 🛎 BIZ 🛜 ✖ 📹
📱 📠 🖥

DELTA WINNIPEG (204)942-0551 **6**

▼▼▼ Hotel $99-$399 **Address:** 350 St. Mary Ave R3C 3J2 **Location:** At Hargrave St. Adjacent to convention center. **Facility:** 393 units, some two bedrooms. 18 stories, interior corridors. **Parking:** on-site (fee) and valet. **Terms:** 7 day cancellation notice-fee imposed. **Amenities:** video games (fee), high-speed Internet. **Dining:** Blaze Bistro & Lounge, see separate listing. **Pool(s):** heated outdoor, heated indoor. **Activities:** sauna, whirlpool. **Guest Services:** valet and coin laundry.

ⓔⓒⓞ 🍴 🍸 CALL 🄶Ⓜ 🛎 BIZ 🛜 ✖
📹 🖥 / SOME UNITS FEE 🐾 📱

Learn the local driving laws at DrivingLaws.AAA.com

THE FAIRMONT WINNIPEG (204)957-1350 **1**

▼▼▼ Hotel $159-$299 **Address:** 2 Lombard Pl R3B 0Y3 **Location:** Just e of Portage Ave and Main St. Located in a commercial area. **Facility:** 340 units. 21 stories, interior corridors. **Parking:** on-site (fee) and valet, winter plug-ins. **Amenities:** high-speed Internet (fee). *Some:* safes. **Dining:** The Velvet Glove, see separate listing. **Pool(s):** heated indoor. **Activities:** whirlpool, steamroom, exercise room. *Fee:* massage. **Guest Services:** valet laundry.

ⓔⓒⓞ 🍴 🍸 CALL 🄶Ⓜ 🛎 BIZ 🛜 🐕 🖥
/ SOME UNITS FEE 🐾

THE FORT GARRY HOTEL, SPA & CONFERENCE CENTRE (204)942-8251 **8**

Historic Hotel
$139-$429

Address: 222 Broadway R3C 0R3 **Location:** Just w of Main St. **Facility:** Built in the Chicago block-style tradition, this impressive hotel boasts gracious appointments; rooms range from small to spacious. 246 units. 10 stories, interior corridors. **Parking:** on-site (fee) and valet, winter plug-ins. **Terms:** cancellation fee imposed. **Amenities:** video games (fee). *Some:* safes. **Dining:** 2 restaurants, entertainment. **Pool(s):** heated indoor. **Activities:** sauna, whirlpool, steamroom, jogging, exercise room, spa. **Guest Services:** valet laundry. **Free Special Amenities: full breakfast and local telephone calls.**

🅢🅐🆅🅔 🍴 🍸 CALL 🄶Ⓜ 🛎 BIZ 🛜 ✖ 📹
/ SOME UNITS 📱 📠

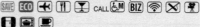

THE **FORT** GARRY

The Fort Garry Hotel, Spa & Conference Centre celebrates 100 years of memories.

(See map & index p. 484.)

HOLIDAY INN & SUITES WINNIPEG DOWNTOWN
(204)786-7011

Hotel
$99-$199

Address: 360 Colony St R3B 2P3 **Location:** Corner of Portage Ave. **Facility:** 140 units. 6 stories, 11 stories, interior corridors. **Parking:** on-site (fee), winter plug-ins. **Terms:** cancellation fee imposed. **Amenities:** video games (fee), high-speed Internet. **Dining:** 2 restaurants. **Pool(s):** heated indoor. **Activities:** whirlpool, exercise room. **Guest Services:** valet and coin laundry.

SAVE ▯ ▯ ▯ CALL ▯M ▯ BIZ ▯ ▯ ▯ ▯ /SOME UNITS ▯ ▯

HUMPHRY INN & SUITES
(204)942-4222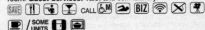

Hotel $114-$190 **Address:** 260 Main St R3C 1A9 **Location:** Corner of St. Mary Ave. Located in business district. **Facility:** 128 units. 6 stories, interior corridors. **Parking:** winter plug-ins. **Terms:** cancellation fee imposed. **Amenities:** high-speed Internet. **Pool(s):** heated indoor. **Activities:** whirlpool, steamroom, exercise room. **Guest Services:** valet and coin laundry.

▯▯ CALL ▯M ▯ BIZ ▯ ▯ ▯ ▯ ▯

INN AT THE FORKS
(204)942-6555

Hotel
$159-$279

Address: 75 Forks Market Rd R3C 0A2 **Location:** At the Forks. Located in a park and entertainment area. **Facility:** 117 units. 5 stories, interior corridors. **Parking:** on-site (fee) and valet, winter plug-ins. **Amenities:** video games (fee), high-speed Internet, safes. **Dining:** The Current, see separate listing. **Activities:** exercise room, spa. **Guest Services:** valet laundry, area transportation-downtown. **Free Special Amenities:** local telephone calls and high-speed Internet.

SAVE ECO ▯ ▯ CALL ▯M BIZ ▯ ▯ ▯ /SOME UNITS ▯ ▯

NORWOOD HOTEL
(204)233-4475

Hotel
$119-$199

Address: 112 Marion St R2H 0T1 **Location:** On Rt 115, just e of St. Mary's Rd. Located in a commercial area. **Facility:** 52 units. 5 stories, interior corridors. **Parking:** winter plug-ins. **Terms:** cancellation fee imposed. **Amenities:** Some: high-speed Internet. **Guest Services:** valet laundry. **Free Special Amenities:** local telephone calls and high-speed Internet.

SAVE ECO ▯ ▯ CALL ▯M FEE ▯ BIZ ▯ ▯ ▯ /SOME UNITS ▯ ▯

 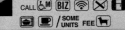

RADISSON HOTEL WINNIPEG DOWNTOWN
(204)956-0410

Hotel
$171-$265

Address: 288 Portage Ave R3C 0B8 **Location:** At Smith St. Located in a commercial area. **Facility:** 263 units. 29 stories, interior corridors. **Parking:** on-site and valet, winter plug-ins. **Terms:** cancellation fee imposed. **Amenities:** high-speed Internet. **Activities:** saunas, exercise room. **Guest Services:** valet and coin laundry, area transportation-within 1.2 mi.

SAVE ECO ▯ ▯ ▯ CALL ▯M BIZ ▯ ▯ ▯ ▯ ▯ /SOME FEE ▯ ▯

WHERE TO EAT

AMICI
204/943-4997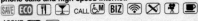

▯▯ Italian. Casual Dining. $12-$38 **AAA Inspector Notes:** You'll find that while Amici offers fine dining in contemporary surroundings, casual dining and more reasonable pricing can be found downstairs at the Bombolini Wine Bar. The innovative menu features dishes with complex preparation and creative presentation. **Bar:** full bar. **Reservations:** suggested. **Address:** 326 Broadway R3C 0S5 **Location:** At Hargrave St. **Parking:** street only.

L D

BEACHCOMBERS
204/948-0020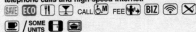

▯▯ American. Casual Dining. $10-$28 **AAA Inspector Notes:** Guests can enjoy the very good menu at this casual restaurant. Offerings include daily-made soups and breads, fresh salad, classic and distinctive sandwiches, creative pasta, tender chicken and veal dishes, mouthwatering ribs, sizzling steaks and succulent seafood. Located in a bustling market, it also has outdoor seating. **Bar:** full bar. **Address:** 162-1 Forks Market Rd R3C 4L8 **Location:** Behind Via Rail's Union Station; in Forks Market.

L D CALL ▯M

BLAZE BISTRO & LOUNGE
204/944-7259

▯▯▯ American. Casual Dining. $9-$35 **AAA Inspector Notes:** This bistro offers an inviting atmosphere with oil paintings that truly depict the prairies. The menu has some tempting items that many will be familiar with and also has some items featuring the local fish or game. **Bar:** full bar. **Reservations:** suggested. **Address:** 350 St. Mary Ave R3C 3J2 **Location:** At Hargrave St; in Delta Winnipeg.

B L D CALL ▯M

THE CURRENT
204/944-2445

▯▯▯ American. Casual Dining. $11-$37 **AAA Inspector Notes:** Large windows in the rear section of the brightly colored dining room of this eatery allow guests to overlook the interesting Forks Market area. Start with wild scallops with vanilla bean and citrus vinaigrette, followed by peppered Manitoba pork tenderloin with brandy Bing cherry jus and sweet potato puree. For dessert try profiteroles and yummy homemade ice cream with warm chocolate sauce. The lunch menu is a little more casual. **Bar:** full bar. **Reservations:** suggested. **Address:** 75 Forks Market Rd R3C 0A2 **Location:** At the Forks; in Inn at the Forks. **Parking:** on-site and valet.

B L D CALL ▯M

EAST INDIA COMPANY PUB & EATERY
204/947-3097

▯▯ Indian. Casual Dining. $12-$22 **AAA Inspector Notes:** Decorated in brightly colored Indian murals and carved wood, the dining room of this eatery is home to a large selection of traditional Indian fare, which guests will find on an extensive lunch and dinner buffet. Biryanis, masalas, curries and vegetarian options and can be ordered off the menu as well. Classic naan bread always is a hit, but more adventurous diners should try the garlic- or cheese-flavored naan. **Bar:** full bar. **Reservations:** suggested. **Address:** 349 York Ave R3C 3S9 **Location:** Jct Carlton St. **Parking:** on-site and street.

L D

(See map & index p. 484.)

HERMANOS RESTAURANT & WINE BAR 204/947-5434 ①
▼▼▼▼ Latin American. Casual Dining. $9-$32 **AAA Inspector Notes:** This lively spot in the historic exchange district has a hip and open design with the original lime brick and wood features accented with bright orange hues and huge photos of South American scenes. The menu references Argentina, Peru, Uruguay and Brazil and promotes a shared dining experience with appealing soups, salads, tapas and sandwiches at lunch and the addition of Latin-style steak entrées at dinner. Weekend nights get even more action packed with the addition of live music. **Bar:** full bar. **Reservations:** suggested. **Address:** 179A Bannatyne Ave R3B 0R4 **Location:** Just e of Main St via McDermott Ave; center. **Parking:** street only.
Ⓛ Ⓓ CALL ♿Ⓜ

HU'S ASIAN BISTRO 204/982-7426 ⑤
▼▼ ▼▼ Asian. Casual Dining. $12-$18 **AAA Inspector Notes:** Opt for any one of the many Asian dishes-Chinese, Thai and Vietnamese-on the menu at this trendy urban bistro. Extremely popular, the place can get noisy when it is packed full, which tends to happen often, especially game nights during baseball season. Outdoor patio seating is available. Closed for lunch on Saturday. **Bar:** full bar. **Reservations:** suggested. **Address:** 1 Portage Ave E R3B 3N3 **Location:** Corner of Waterfront Dr and Pioneer Ave; at CanWest Global Park. Ⓛ Ⓓ

HY'S STEAKHOUSE 204/942-1000 ③
▼▼▼▼ Steak. Fine Dining. $17-$54 **AAA Inspector Notes:** The rich and sophisticated interior, with dark paneling, sweeping drapery and fine artwork, reminds you of an exclusive private club, however, the atmosphere is very hospitable. Knowledgeable servers provide superior service, including some tableside preparations. The focus is on hearty cuts of fine beef, although there are some fine seafood options as well. A very good wine list also offers a few good by-the-glass choices. **Bar:** full bar. **Reservations:** suggested. **Address:** 1 Lombard Pl R3B 0X3 **Location:** Jct Main St and Portage Ave; in Richardson Building, Main Floor. Ⓛ Ⓓ CALL ♿Ⓜ

ICHIBAN JAPANESE STEAK HOUSE & SUSHI BAR
204/925-7400 ⑧
▼▼ ▼▼ Japanese. Casual Dining. $26-$42 **AAA Inspector Notes:** Ichiban features a sushi bar and teppan-style cooking, where your meal is prepared in an entertaining manner at your table. Offerings also include North American dishes of steak, chicken and seafood. The server staff is pleasant, cordial and attentive. Before leaving, the staff will happily validate parking after 5:30 pm for the Delta Parkade, accessible from St. Mary Ave. **Bar:** full bar. **Reservations:** suggested. **Address:** 189 Carlton St R3C 3H7 **Location:** Corner of St. Mary Ave. **Parking:** street only. Ⓓ

IVORY RESTAURANT & BAR 204/944-1600 ⑥
▼▼ ▼▼ Indian. Casual Dining. $12-$25 **AAA Inspector Notes:** An East Indian treat, this restaurant offers diners the option of choices from a nicely developed menu or from the buffet line, which is a showcase for high-quality, well-presented, hot and cold dishes. Food is delightfully seasoned and reflects the diner's preference for spiciness. The decor blends art gallery and bistro styles. Closed for lunch Saturday and Sunday. **Bar:** full bar. **Reservations:** suggested. **Address:** 200 Main St R3C 4V9 **Location:** Between St. Mary and York aves. Ⓛ Ⓓ

MOXIE'S CLASSIC GRILL 204/926-5757
▼▼ ▼▼ American. Casual Dining. $11-$29 **AAA Inspector Notes:** This sleek, funky and popular restaurant presents an extensive menu of creatively prepared dishes, including pizza, pasta, rice, noodles, signature salads and burgers. Other menus include one for children and one for Sunday brunch. Lending to the upbeat, stylish decor are dark wood appointments and river rock fireplaces. **Address:** 300 Portage Ave R3C 5S4 **Location:** Between Hargrave St and Donald Ave. **Parking:** street only. Ⓛ Ⓓ LATE CALL ♿Ⓜ

MUDDY WATERS SMOKEHOUSE 204/947-6653 ⑭
▼▼ ▼▼ Barbecue Burgers. Casual Dining. $10-$29 **AAA Inspector Notes:** This casual spot is famous for their wings. With nearly twenty flavors in wet sauce or dry rub style, the choices include spicy Caesar, Montreal spice, Old Bay seasoning and Caribbean jerk as well as all the traditional favorites. Other menu highlights include salads, chowder, burgers, pulled pork and chicken sandwiches, ribs and chicken. Combos come with in-house fries, coleslaw, beans and bacon-corn mix. The patio overlooking the plaza and the river beside at The Forks is mighty popular. **Bar:** full bar. **Address:** 15 Forks Market Rd R3C 0A2 **Location:** Behind Via Rail's Union Station; in Forks Market; beside Travel Manitoba. **Parking:** street only.
Ⓛ Ⓓ

STORM BISTRO 204/948-0085 ⑨
▼▼ ▼▼ American. Casual Dining. $9-$15 **AAA Inspector Notes:** Located on the top floor of the Winnipeg Art Gallery, an enticing lunch menu is offered. During warmer weather days the large outdoor patio opens to where a number of unique sculptures enhance the scenery. **Bar:** full bar. **Reservations:** suggested. **Address:** 300 Memorial Blvd R3C 1V1 **Location:** Just s of Portage Ave. **Parking:** street only.
Ⓛ CALL ♿Ⓜ

SYDNEY'S AT THE FORKS 204/942-6075 ⑪
▼▼▼▼ New American. Fine Dining. $14-$55 **AAA Inspector Notes:** The chef at this beautifully appointed eatery offers a highly creative, monthly-changing, five course menu with top-notch ingredients. Everything was delightful from the mini corn muffins with black bean and salsa, to the roasted aubergine, to the palate-cleansing watermelon sorbet, to the maple bourbon salmon, and ending with a chocolate tangerine terrine with pistachio shortbread. The portions are sized just right. Service is professional. An a la carte lunch is offered Tuesday through Friday. **Bar:** full bar. **Reservations:** suggested. **Address:** 215 One Forks Market Rd R3C 4L9 **Location:** In Forks Market, Second Level. Ⓛ Ⓓ CALL ♿Ⓜ

TRE VISI CUCINA ITALIANO 204/949-9032 ②
▼▼▼▼ Italian. Casual Dining. $12-$29 **AAA Inspector Notes:** Original art pieces can be found at this comfortable, tiny restaurant where a well-prepared, delicious and traditional classic Italian menu is offered with all the favorites. A scrumptious dessert menu features a fabulous zabaglione con frutti di bosco (a warm creamy egg yolk with Marsala wine custard over fresh berries). Professional and knowledgeable servers are clad in crisp white butchers aprons and rush to meet the needs of the guests. Closed for lunch on Saturday. **Bar:** full bar. **Reservations:** suggested. **Address:** 173 McDermot Ave R3B 0S1 **Location:** Just e of Main St. **Parking:** street only.
Ⓛ Ⓓ CALL ♿Ⓜ

THE VELVET GLOVE 204/957-1350 ④
▼▼ ▼▼
Continental
Fine Dining
$26-$36
AAA Inspector Notes: This elegant, adult-oriented, fine dining restaurant has been serving Winnipeg since 1971. Known for their special preparation of Winnipeg pickerel and rack of lamb, most evenings feature a three-course dinner special including a number of Lifestyle Cuisine items that contribute to optimal health and wellness. The restaurant is ocean friendly and recommended by the Vancouver Aquarium for its support of sustainable fishing practices. **Bar:** full bar. **Reservations:** suggested. **Address:** 2 Lombard Pl R3B 0Y3 **Location:** Just e of Portage Ave and Main St; in The Fairmont Winnipeg. **Parking:** on-site and valet.
Menu on AAA.com Ⓑ Ⓛ Ⓓ CALL ♿Ⓜ

WINNIPEG (F-3)
• **Restaurants p. 494**
• **Hotels & Restaurants map & index p. 486**

(See map & index p. 486.)

CANAD INNS DESTINATION CENTRE CLUB REGENT CASINO HOTEL

(204)667-5560

Hotel
$124-$299

Address: 1415 Regent Ave W R2C 3B2 **Location:** 1.1 mi (1.8 km) e of Lagimodiere Blvd (Hwy 20) at Plessis Rd. **Facility:** With direct access to an adjacent casino, this property offers large, well-appointed guest units that are perfect for business or leisure travelers. 146 units. 6 stories, interior corridors. **Parking:** winter plug-ins. **Amenities:** high-speed Internet. **Dining:** 3 restaurants. **Pool(s):** heated indoor. **Activities:** whirlpool, exercise room. **Guest Services:** valet laundry. **Free Special Amenities:** newspaper and high-speed Internet.

CANAD INNS DESTINATION CENTRE FORT GARRY

(204)261-7450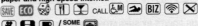

Hotel
$105-$249

Address: 1824 Pembina Hwy R3T 2G2 **Location:** Just n of Bishop Grandin Blvd. **Facility:** 106 units, some two bedrooms. 2 stories, interior corridors. **Parking:** winter plug-ins. **Amenities:** high-speed Internet. *Some:* video games. **Pool(s):** heated indoor. **Activities:** whirlpool, waterslide. **Guest Services:** valet laundry. **Free Special Amenities:** newspaper and high-speed Internet.

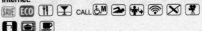

CANAD INNS DESTINATION CENTRE GARDEN CITY

(204)633-0024

Hotel
$107-$259

Address: 2100 McPhillips St R2V 3T9 **Location:** At Jefferson Ave. Located in a commercial area. **Facility:** 72 units, some two bedrooms. 3 stories, interior corridors. **Parking:** winter plug-ins. **Dining:** 2 restaurants, nightclub. **Pool(s):** heated indoor. **Activities:** whirlpool, waterslide. **Guest Services:** valet laundry. **Free Special Amenities:** newspaper and high-speed Internet.

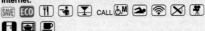

CANAD INNS DESTINATION CENTRE POLO PARK

(204)775-8791

Hotel
$115-$259

Address: 1405 St. Matthews Ave R3G 0K5 **Location:** Just e of St James St. Opposite Canad Inns Stadium. **Facility:** 107 units. 6 stories, interior corridors. **Parking:** winter plug-ins. **Amenities:** video games (fee), high-speed Internet. **Activities:** whirlpool, waterslide, exercise room. **Guest Services:** valet laundry, area transportation-within 2 mi. **Free Special Amenities:** newspaper and high-speed Internet.

CANAD INNS DESTINATION CENTRE TRANSCONA

(204)224-1681

Hotel
$109-$239

Address: 826 Regent Ave W R2C 3A8 **Location:** 1.1 mi (1.8 km) e of Lagimodiere Blvd (Hwy 20) at Plessis Rd. **Facility:** 50 units, some two bedrooms. 2 stories, interior corridors. **Parking:** winter plug-ins. **Dining:** nightclub. **Pool(s):** heated indoor. **Activities:** whirlpool, waterslide. **Guest Services:** valet laundry. **Free Special Amenities:** newspaper and high-speed Internet.

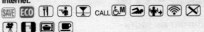

CANAD INNS DESTINATION CENTRE WINDSOR PARK

(204)253-2641

Hotel
$111-$299

Address: 1034 Elizabeth Rd R2J 1B3 **Location:** Jct s of Maginot St and w of Lagimodiere Blvd. Located in a residential/commercial area. **Facility:** 54 units, some two bedrooms. 2 stories (no elevator), interior corridors. **Parking:** winter plug-ins. **Dining:** nightclub. **Pool(s):** heated indoor. **Activities:** whirlpool, waterslide. **Guest Services:** valet laundry. **Free Special Amenities:** newspaper and high-speed Internet.

Visit your AAA/CAA Travel office to book a AAA Vacations® Disney package

▼ See AAA listing p. 490 ▼

(See map & index p. 486.)

CLARION HOTEL & SUITES (204)774-5110 **14**

▼▼▼◈ **Hotel** $143-$250 **Address:** 1445 Portage Ave R3G 3P4 **Location:** Jct Empress St. Located in a commercial area. **Facility:** 139 units. 6 stories, interior corridors. **Parking:** on-site and valet, winter plug-ins. **Terms:** cancellation fee imposed. **Amenities:** video games (fee), high-speed Internet. *Some:* safes. **Pool(s):** heated indoor. **Activities:** whirlpool, steamroom, waterslide, exercise room, spa. **Guest Services:** valet laundry.

COMFORT INN AIRPORT (204)783-5627 **7**

▼▼▼
Motel
$99-$138

Address: 1770 Sargent Ave R3H 0C8 **Location:** At King Edward St. Located in a commercial area. **Facility:** 81 units. 2 stories (no elevator), interior corridors. **Parking:** winter plug-ins. **Terms:** cancellation fee imposed. **Amenities:** high-speed Internet. **Guest Services:** valet laundry.

COMFORT INN SOUTH (204)269-7390 **25**

▼▼▼
Motel
$117-$138

Address: 3109 Pembina Hwy R3T 4R6 **Location:** Just n of jct Perimeter Hwy 100 and 75. Located in a residential/commercial area. **Facility:** 85 units. 2 stories (no elevator), interior corridors. **Parking:** winter plug-ins. **Terms:** cancellation fee imposed. **Guest Services:** valet laundry.

COUNTRY INN & SUITES BY CARLSON (204)783-6900 **6**

▼◈ ▼◈ **Hotel** $110-$140 **Address:** 730 King Edward St R3H 1B4 **Location:** Just s of Wellington Ave. Located in a commercial area. **Facility:** 75 units. 3 stories, interior corridors. **Parking:** winter plug-ins. **Terms:** 4 day cancellation notice-fee imposed. **Activities:** exercise room. **Guest Services:** valet and coin laundry.

EXPRESS BY CANAD INNS (204)269-6955 **22**

▼◈ ▼◈
Motel
$103-$142

Address: 1792 Pembina Hwy R3T 2G2 **Location:** Just n of Bishop Grandin Blvd. **Facility:** 36 units. 2 stories (no elevator), interior corridors. **Parking:** winter plug-ins. **Dining:** nightclub. **Free Special Amenities:** newspaper and high-speed Internet.

FAIRFIELD INN & SUITES BY MARRIOTT (204)783-7900 **11**

▼▼▼ **Hotel** $129-$169 **Address:** 1301 Ellice Ave R3G 1T7 **Location:** Between Empress and Strathcona sts. **Facility:** 126 units. 6 stories, interior corridors. **Parking:** winter plug-ins. **Pool(s):** heated indoor. **Activities:** whirlpool, exercise room. **Guest Services:** valet and coin laundry.

AAA Benefit: AAA hotel discounts of 5% or more.

FOUR POINTS BY SHERATON HOTEL WINNIPEG AIRPORT (204)775-5222 **2**

▼▼▼
Hotel
$130-$150

FOUR POINTS BY SHERATON

AAA Benefit: Members get up to 20% off, plus Starwood Preferred Guest® bonuses.

Address: 1999 Wellington Ave R3H 1H5 **Location:** At Winnipeg James Armstrong Richardson International Airport. **Facility:** 149 units. 7 stories, interior corridors. **Parking:** on-site (fee), winter plug-ins. **Terms:** cancellation fee imposed. **Amenities:** high-speed Internet. **Activities:** exercise room. **Guest Services:** valet laundry. **Free Special Amenities:** local telephone calls and newspaper.

FOUR POINTS BY SHERATON WINNIPEG SOUTH (204)275-7711 **24**

▼▼▼
Hotel
$120-$150

FOUR POINTS BY SHERATON

AAA Benefit: Members get up to 20% off, plus Starwood Preferred Guest® bonuses.

Address: 2935 Pembina Hwy R3T 2H5 **Location:** Jct Perimeter Hwy 100 and 75, 0.7 mi (1.1 km) n. **Facility:** 76 units. 4 stories, interior corridors. **Parking:** winter plug-ins. **Terms:** cancellation fee imposed. **Amenities:** high-speed Internet. **Pool(s):** heated indoor. **Activities:** whirlpool, exercise room. **Guest Services:** valet laundry. **Free Special Amenities:** local telephone calls and high-speed Internet.

GREENWOOD INN & SUITES (204)775-9889 **3**

▼▼▼◈ **Hotel** $109-$159 **Address:** 1715 Wellington Ave R3H 0G1 **Location:** At Century St. Located in a commercial area. **Facility:** 213 units. 6 stories, interior corridors. **Parking:** winter plug-ins. **Amenities:** high-speed Internet. **Pool(s):** heated indoor. **Activities:** whirlpool, steamroom, exercise room. **Guest Services:** valet laundry.

HILTON SUITES WINNIPEG AIRPORT (204)783-1700 **5**

▼▼▼◈ **Hotel** $119-$239 **Address:** 1800 Wellington Ave R3H 1B2 **Location:** At Berry St. Located in a commercial area. **Facility:** 160 units. 5 stories, interior corridors. **Parking:** on-site (fee), winter plug-ins. **Terms:** 1-7 night minimum stay, cancellation fee imposed. **Amenities:** *Some:* high-speed Internet. **Dining:** Bistro 1800, see separate listing. **Pool(s):** heated outdoor, heated indoor. **Activities:** sauna, whirlpool, exercise room. **Guest Services:** valet laundry.

AAA Benefit: Members save 5% or more!

HOLIDAY INN WINNIPEG AIRPORT WEST (204)885-4478 **16**

▼▼▼
Hotel
$126-$139

Address: 2520 Portage Ave R3J 3T6 **Location:** Just e of Moray St. Located in a residential/commercial area. **Facility:** 226 units, some kitchens. 15 stories, interior corridors. **Parking:** winter plug-ins. **Amenities:** video games (fee). **Pool(s):** heated indoor. **Activities:** whirlpool, exercise room. *Fee:* game room. **Guest Services:** valet and coin laundry, area transportation-Polo Park Mall.

(See map & index p. 486.)

HOLIDAY INN WINNIPEG SOUTH (204)452-4747 **20**

▽▽▽▽ **Hotel** $139-$179 **Address:** 1330 Pembina Hwy R3T 2B4 **Location:** At McGillivray Blvd. Located in a commercial area. **Facility:** 170 units. 11 stories, interior corridors. **Parking:** winter plug-ins. **Terms:** cancellation fee imposed. **Pool(s):** heated indoor. **Activities:** whirlpool, exercise room. **Guest Services:** valet and coin laundry.

ECO 🏊 🍽 🛎 🍸 CALL 🔒M 🏊 BIZ 📶 🎬
🖥 🖨 / SOME UNITS FEE 🐾 FEE 📺

QUALITY INN & SUITES (204)453-8247 **18**

▽▽▽▽ **Address:** 635 Pembina Hwy R3M 2L4 **Location:** Jct s of Grant Ave. **Facility:** 69 units, some efficiencies. 4 stories, interior corridors. **Parking:** winter plug-ins. **Terms:** cancellation fee imposed. **Activities:** exercise room. **Guest Services:** valet and coin laundry. **Free Special Amenities: full breakfast and high-speed Internet.**

Hotel $90-$300

SAVE 🍽 🍸 BIZ 📶 🖥 🖨
/ SOME UNITS FEE 🐾 FEE 📺

MAINSTAY SUITES WINNIPEG (204)594-0500 **9**

▽▽▽▽ **Address:** 670 King Edward St R3H 0P2 **Location:** Between Sargent and Ellice aves. Located in a commercial area. **Facility:** 100 efficiencies. 4 stories, interior corridors. **Parking:** winter plug-ins. **Amenities:** high-speed Internet. **Activities:** sauna, whirlpool, exercise room. **Guest Services:** valet and coin laundry. **Free Special Amenities: full breakfast and high-speed Internet.**

Extended Stay Hotel $94-$160

SAVE 🏊 🍽 CALL 🔒M BIZ
📶 ✕ 🖥 🖨 🖥
/ SOME UNITS FEE 🐾

MainStay Suites
BY CHOICE HOTELS

Guest rooms feature full kitchens, 37″ LCD TVs, sofabeds, full hot breakfast & free airport shuttle.

Learn about inspections and Diamond Ratings at AAA.com/Diamonds

---

RAMADA VISCOUNT GORT HOTEL (204)775-0451 **15**

▽▽▽▽ **Address:** 1670 Portage Ave R3J 0C9 **Location:** Jct Rt 90. Located in a commercial area. **Facility:** 135 units. 4-6 stories, interior corridors. **Parking:** winter plug-ins. **Amenities:** video games (fee). **Pool(s):** heated indoor. **Activities:** whirlpool, waterslide, exercise room. **Guest Services:** valet laundry, area transportation-Health Science Center, bus & train stations. **Free Special Amenities: room upgrade (subject to availability with advance reservations) and airport transportation.** *(See ad this page.)*

Hotel $120-$170

SAVE 🏊 🍽 🍸 CALL 🔒M
🏊 BIZ 📶 ✕ 🎬 🖥 🖨
/ SOME UNITS FEE 🐾 📺

SANDMAN HOTEL & SUITES WINNIPEG AIRPORT
204/775-7263 **8**

▽▽▽▽ **Hotel.** Rates not provided. **Address:** 1750 Sargent Ave R3H 0C7 **Location:** Between King Edward and Century sts. Located in a commercial area. **Facility:** 210 units. 4 stories, interior corridors. **Parking:** winter plug-ins. **Amenities:** high-speed Internet. **Dining:** Chop Steak Fish Bar, see separate listing. **Pool(s):** heated indoor. **Activities:** whirlpool, exercise room. **Guest Services:** valet laundry.

ECO 🏊 🍽 🛎 🍸 CALL 🔒M 🏊 BIZ 📶 🎬
🖨 / SOME UNITS FEE 🐾 🖥 📺

▼ See AAA listing this page ▼

(See map & index p. 486.)

TRAVELODGE WINNIPEG   (204)255-6000 **19**

Hotel
$116-$130

Address: 20 Alpine Ave R2M 0Y5 **Location:** Just e of jct Fermor Ave and St. Anne's Rd. Located in a residential/commercial area. **Facility:** 53 units. 2 stories (no elevator), interior corridors. **Parking:** winter plug-ins. **Dining:** nightclub. **Pool(s):** heated indoor. **Activities:** sauna, whirlpool, limited exercise equipment. **Fee:** game room. **Guest Services:** coin laundry. **Free Special Amenities:** local telephone calls and high-speed Internet.

VICTORIA INN HOTEL & CONVENTION CENTRE
(204)786-4801 **4**

Hotel
$134-$174

Address: 1808 Wellington Ave R3H 0G3 **Location:** At Berry St. Located in a commercial area. **Facility:** 260 units. 5 stories, interior corridors. **Parking:** winter plug-ins. **Terms:** cancellation fee imposed. **Amenities:** video games (fee), high-speed Internet. **Some:** safes. **Pool(s):** heated indoor. **Activities:** whirlpool, waterslide, exercise room. **Guest Services:** valet and coin laundry. **Free Special Amenities:** local telephone calls and high-speed Internet.

WHERE TO EAT

529 WELLINGTON   204/487-8325 **14**
Steak. Casual Dining. $9-$49 **AAA Inspector Notes:** This restaurant encourages patrons to think big: big steaks, that is. Also huge on quality are lobster and jumbo prawns. Only Canadian Prime certified Alberta beef is served. Service matches the detailed old dining rooms, which are paneled in rich wood and fitting of a grand old mansion. **Bar:** full bar. **Reservations:** suggested. **Address:** 529 Wellington Crescent R3M 0A5 **Location:** Just s of Academy Rd. [L] [D]

BEAUJENA'S   204/233-4841 **7**
French. Fine Dining. $39-$49 **AAA Inspector Notes:** This intimate restaurant is a hidden gem within a quiet residential area. Vibrant colors and rich, gauzy fabrics create an inviting spot where guests can enjoy French-flavored cuisine with local Manitoban ingredients. Each month the restaurant offers a distinctive, five- or seven-course menu, which will be a delightful surprise every time. An optional wine pairing is offered to enhance your overall enjoyment. **Bar:** full bar. **Reservations:** suggested. **Address:** 302 Hamel Ave R2H 0K9 **Location:** Jct Provencher Blvd and St. Jean Baptiste St. **Parking:** no self-parking. [D]

BELLISSIMO RESTAURANT & LOUNGE   204/489-0495 **25**
Italian. Casual Dining. $9-$26 **AAA Inspector Notes:** This small and sophisticated dining room is very popular with locals. Find classic fare prepared with fresh and local ingredients where possible and the kitchen prepares almost everything from scratch. A good choice of appetizers and salads to start followed by gourmet pastas and pizzas and more complex entrées and wonderful in-house desserts combined with helpful servers make for a nice evening out. Lunch is simpler with the addition of sandwiches. **Bar:** full bar. **Reservations:** suggested. **Address:** 877 Waverly St, #1 R3T 5V3 **Location:** Just s of Taylor Ave; in small strip mall.
[L] [D] CALL

BISTRO 1800   204/783-1700 **2**
American. Casual Dining. $9-$38 **AAA Inspector Notes:** Convenient to the airport, this is an excellent spot for a good meal in a relaxing and quiet setting. **Bar:** full bar. **Address:** 1800 Wellington Ave R3H 1B2 **Location:** At Berry St; in Hilton Suites Winnipeg Airport. [B] [L] [D] CALL

BISTRO 7 1/4   204/777-2525 **21**
New French. Casual Dining. $12-$39 **AAA Inspector Notes:** The constantly evolving menu at this hugely popular spot has roots in French bistro cuisine but with creative twists and a good dose of Canadian ingredients. Mussels are a specialty, done several ways like with beer, bacon and cheddar, and there is a strong tapas representation, including artisan cheeses and charcuterie. Veal and foie gras sliders on brioche buns with sea salt; grilled octopus with chorizo and orange or Yukon arctic char, red beet hash and pistachio pistou are sample menu items. **Bar:** full bar. **Reservations:** suggested. **Address:** 725 Osborne St R3L 2C1 **Location:** Jct Trans-Canada Hwy 1 (Broadway), 1.8 mi (3 km) s. **Parking:** street only. [L] [D]

BONFIRE BISTRO   204/487-4440 **20**
Italian. Casual Dining. $9-$28 **AAA Inspector Notes:** Diners can expect comfortable, simple decor and a friendly atmosphere at this bistro. Management and staff are focused on creating well-prepared dishes. Among choices are wonderful thin-crust gourmet pizza made in a wood-fired oven, assorted pasta creations and varied daily specials posted on a blackboard. They can only accommodate groups of six or less and are closed for lunch on Sunday and on Saturday during the summer months. **Bar:** beer & wine. **Address:** 1433 Corydon Ave R3N 0J2 **Location:** At Waterloo St.
[L] [D]

BUCCACINO'S CUCINA ITALIANA   204/452-8251 **11**
Italian. Casual Dining. $10-$25 **AAA Inspector Notes:** Get together with friends for some great Italian food at this traditional, yet not trendy, eatery. An excellent menu runs the full gamut from appetizers, salads, soups, pasta, pizza, entrées and desserts all offering their own little twists. For a lighter lunch they add sandwiches but lose the appetizers and entrées. The value priced, straightforward all-you-can-eat Sunday brunch is fast becoming a local favorite. The parking lot is on the other side of Osborne Street behind Vita Health. **Bar:** full bar. **Reservations:** suggested, weekends. **Address:** 155 Osborne St R3L 1Y7 **Location:** Jct Trans-Canada Hwy 1 (Broadway), 0.6 mi (1 km) s. **Parking:** street only. [L] [D]

CHEZ CORA   204/928-1200
American. Family Dining. $8-$13 **AAA Inspector Notes:** Eggs, omelets, waffles, crepes (sorry, no American-style pancakes here), French toast, fruit platters and all the breakfast meats--that's the specialty here, all day. However, at lunchtime the menu lists a selection of soups, salads, quiches, sandwiches and a dish called the grilled panini crepe. **Address:** 840 Waverley St R3T 5Z7 **Location:** Jct Wilkes Ave. [B] [L] CALL

CHOP STEAK FISH BAR   204/788-2015 **3**
Steak Seafood. Casual Dining. $18-$39 **AAA Inspector Notes:** High ceilings, dark subdued colors, plush velours and earthy woods contrasting with modern glass light fixtures all contribute to the casually chic decor at this modern steakhouse. A recent addition to the city's restaurant scene, Chop offers the choicest cuts of certified Angus beef and the freshest fish and seafood. **Bar:** full bar. **Reservations:** suggested. **Address:** 1750 Sargent Ave R3H 0C7 **Location:** Between King Edward and Century sts; in Sandman Hotel & Suites Winnipeg Airport. [D]

CLAY OVEN   204/888-2529 **27**
Indian. Casual Dining. $12-$26 **AAA Inspector Notes:** A display case of pastries and desserts is the first thing diners see upon entering this casual spot. Judging by the bright and modern decor, it may not be apparent that this is an East Indian establishment. A good selection of typical cuisine is offered in this combined take-away or dine-in restaurant. Some items are freshly prepared and some are served from the chafing dishes on display. There also is a separate lounge area. **Bar:** full bar. **Address:** 1600 Kenaston Common, #240 R3P 0Y4 **Location:** Just n of McGillivray Blvd; in Kenaston Common Shopping Plaza. [L] [D] CALL

CONFUSION CORNER BAR & GRILL   204/284-6666 **16**
American. Casual Dining. $11-$32 **AAA Inspector Notes:** Located at the hub of a major traffic nightmare, this casual spot offers a respite from the confusion outside. Diners can relax in the cozy space and enjoy a range of fresh menu items with intriguing twists including pork lumpia rolls with tangy chili sauce; a drunken steak sandwich; and mojo chicken marinated in brown sugar, chili, lime, cilantro and mint topped with pineapple salsa. A sports lounge and seasonal rooftop patio are available along with a limited lunch menu and weekend brunch. **Bar:** full bar. **Reservations:** suggested. **Address:** 500 Corydon Ave R3L 0P1 **Location:** Jct Trans-Canada Hwy 1 (Broadway), 0.7 mi (1.2 km) s on Osborne St, just se on Pembina Hwy, then just e. [L] [D] [LATE] CALL

We Do Everything But Jump On The Beds

AAA backs the Diamond Ratings with expert, in-person evaluations – whether the hotel or restaurant is no-frills, moderate or upscale.

▶ AAA/CAA inspections are unannounced to ensure our experience is comparable to yours.

▶ Only hotels and restaurants that meet AAA standards and member expectations are Approved.

▶ The Diamond Rating, from One to Five, describes the type of experience you can expect.

 Learn more at AAA.com/Diamonds

(See map & index p. 486.)

DIANA'S GOURMET PIZZERIA   204/954-7858   (28)
▽▽▽ Pizza. Casual Dining. $14-$25 **AAA Inspector Notes:** The "sweet 'n' spicy divine swine," made with dry-cured pepperoni, fresh hand-cut pineapple, barbecued pulled pork and a splash of hot sauce is just one of the inspired pizzas made with first-rate ingredients at this popular venue. You also can craft your own version of fabulous with a choice of dough, thickness, cheese and sauce, then top it off with an amazing range of regular, gourmet and premium toppings. **Bar:** beer & wine. **Address:** 730R St. Anne's Rd R2N 0A2 **Location:** 1.1 mi (1.8 km) n of Perimeter Hwy 100; in Southglen Shopping Centre. [L] [D] CALL [&M]

DUCKY'S ENGLISH STYLE FISH & CHIPS   204/772-5600   (1)
▽ Fish & Chips. Casual Dining. $10-$19 **AAA Inspector Notes:** Sociable owners at this little spot serve up crispy fish and chips made from fresh halibut, cod and other market fish. Everything is made from scratch including the secret recipe coleslaw and tartar sauce which is very fresh and tasty. Ice cream and cakes are available if you still have room. The décor is very simple with cozy booths and an eclectic collection of memorabilia. **Bar:** full bar. **Address:** 884 Notre Dame Ave R3E 0M7 **Location:** Just e of Arlington St. **Parking:** street only. [L] [D] [D] [火]

EARLS RESTAURANT
▽▽ ▽▽ American. Casual Dining. $11-$29 **AAA Inspector Notes:** Offering an experience that falls between fast food and fine dining, the fun, relaxed restaurant prepares great food at a great price. Choices range from juicy burgers, hearty sandwiches, fresh salads, wings and pizza to full entrees of steak, chops and seafood. Made-from-scratch soups and assorted breads, as well as a nice choice of wines and beers, round out the offerings. This is a fitting spot for impromptu get-togethers and festive occasions. **Bar:** full bar.
[L] [D] [LATE] CALL [&M]
For additional information, visit AAA.com
LOCATIONS:
Address: 2005 Pembina Hwy R3T 5W7 **Location:** Jct Bishop Grandin Blvd, just s. **Phone:** 204/275-1250
Address: 1455 Portage Ave R3G 0W4 **Location:** Jct Empress St; southeast corner of Polo Park Shopping Center parking lot. **Phone:** 204/975-1845

FRESH CAFÉ   204/221-5775   (18)
▽▽ ▽▽ American. Casual Dining. $8-$16 **AAA Inspector Notes:** From the cheery sunlit decor right down to the delectable desserts, everything here is fresh. With an emphasis on natural, organic and local foods, this little jewel-of-a-daytime eatery offers day-long breakfasts, lunch and a juice bar. While the dining room is on the second level, take advantage of a nice sunny day and dine on the large, street-side outdoor terrace. **Bar:** beer & wine. **Address:** 775 Corydon Ave R3M 0W5 **Location:** Between Cockburn and Arbuthnot sts; in Corydon Village. **Parking:** street only. [B] [L]

FUSION GRILL   204/489-6963   (15)
▽▽ ▽▽ Canadian. Casual Dining. $10-$33 **AAA Inspector Notes:** The comfortable little Fusion Grill affords a wonderful opportunity to experience fine Canadian food. Supporting Manitoba producers, the eatery offers the freshest ingredients. The list of Canadian wines is notable. **Bar:** full bar. **Reservations:** suggested. **Address:** 550 Academy Rd R3N 0E3 **Location:** Just e of jct Kenaston Blvd. **Parking:** street only. [L] [D]

HU'S ASIAN BISTRO   204/779-7041   (4)
▽▽ ▽▽ Asian. Casual Dining. $12-$26 **AAA Inspector Notes:** You'll find a trendy and chic décor at this hip establishment. From the many modern style Asian dishes — Chinese, Thai, Japanese, Indonesian and Vietnamese — you will find a good variety of appetizers, soups, salads, curries, noodle and rice dishes along with steak, seafood and chicken entrées. Closed for lunch on Saturday and Sunday. **Bar:** full bar. **Reservations:** suggested. **Address:** 1747 Ellice Ave R3H 1A6 **Location:** Corner of King Edward St.
[L] [D] CALL [&M]

INDIA PALACE   204/774-6061   (5)
▽▽ ▽▽ Indian. Casual Dining. $11-$21 **AAA Inspector Notes:** Diners can enjoy the fresh, flavorful cuisine at this restaurant, where the tandoori chicken is exceptional. The menu is so extensive that it will satisfy the most discerning tastes. A lunch and dinner buffet is available daily. **Bar:** full bar. **Reservations:** suggested. **Address:** 770 Ellice Ave R3G 0B8 **Location:** Corner of Simcoe St. **Parking:** street only. [L] [D]

INFERNO'S BISTRO   204/262-7400   (8)
▽▽ ▽▽ ▽▽ French. Casual Dining. $11-$24 **AAA Inspector Notes:** Well loved by locals, this bistro is spread over two floors and also the patio in season. The menu has some Canadian touches and is extensive so it will be difficult to make up your mind. Appetizers of buffalo frog legs, Pernod prawns or pâté followed by mussels and frites about five different ways, salmon with fresh sorrel and champagne sauce, and duck with orange sauce are just some of the many choices. Colorful art work and lighting decorates the space and often there is live music. **Bar:** full bar. **Reservations:** suggested. **Address:** 312 rue Des Meurons St R2H 2N5 **Location:** Between rue Goulet and rue Marion sts. [L] [D] CALL [&M]

JOE BLACK COFFEE BAR   204/415-1660   (10)
▽ Coffee/Tea. Quick Serve. $7-$9 **AAA Inspector Notes:** This trendy neighborhood spot makes soups, salads and tasty fresh sandwiches, panini and wraps to order. Fabulous dessert treats sourced from the Chocolate Zen Bakery are a great accompaniment to that daily cup of Joe. **Address:** 2037 Portage Ave R3K 0K6 **Location:** Corner of Overdale St. **Parking:** street only.
[B] [L] [D] CALL [&M]

JOEY RESTAURANTS   204/477-5639
▽▽ ▽▽ American. Casual Dining. $13-$33 **AAA Inspector Notes:** The cuisine blends Mediterranean and Asian cooking styles and emphasizes finger foods for sharing. Those who aren't big fans of tapas can consider full meal offerings centered on steaks and chops. **Bar:** full bar. **Address:** 1550 Kenaston Blvd R3P 0Y4 **Location:** On Rt 90; just n of McGillivray Blvd. [L] [D] [LATE]

KELSEY'S   204/668-6689
▽▽ ▽▽ ▽▽ American. Casual Dining. $10-$24 **AAA Inspector Notes:** A fun, relaxed atmosphere and tasty menu of casual fare make the restaurant a popular favorite with locals. Diners might start a meal with some tempting appetizers, such as wings, loaded potato skins or nachos, and follow them with an old-time favorite, such as a burger, wrap, pizza or pasta dish. For a heartier meal, it's hard to beat pork back ribs or a steak. The diverse menu has broad appeal. **Bar:** full bar. **Address:** 1582 Regent Ave W R2C 3B4 **Location:** Just e of jct Lagimodiere Blvd. [L] [D] CALL [&M]

LA FIESTA CAFECITO   204/257-7108   (29)
▽▽ ▽▽ Salvadoran. Casual Dining. $8-$19 **AAA Inspector Notes:** This little family-run restaurant offers true Salvadoran cuisine and the friendliest service. A delicious blend of new and traditional Latin American dishes is served up in a pretty, festively colored dining room. Two must-try items include pupusas and corn tamale. **Bar:** full bar. **Reservations:** suggested. **Address:** 730 St. Anne's Rd, Unit M R2N 0A2 **Location:** Just n of Perimeter Hwy; in South Glen Mall. [D]

MAXIME'S RESTAURANT & LOUNGE   204/257-1521   (26)
▽▽ ▽▽ Continental. Casual Dining. $11-$23 **AAA Inspector Notes:** This restaurant is a favorite with locals. The menu features pasta, Greek specialties, steak, chicken and seafood entrées, which are served in large portions. The service is polite, professional and efficient, and the décor is upscale. **Bar:** full bar. **Address:** 1131 St. Mary's Rd R2M 3T9 **Location:** Just n of Bishop Grandin Blvd. [B] [L] [D] CALL [&M]

MONA LISA RISTORANTE   204/488-3687   (19)
▽▽ ▽▽ Northern Italian. Casual Dining. $7-$29 **AAA Inspector Notes:** This is a warm and inviting dining room where you can enjoy a huge selection of appetizers and salads, delicious house-made pastas and pizza with some gluten-free options, as well as traditional chicken, veal and fish dishes. It's a must to try the Italian-style sushi rolls they have concocted, which are like nothing you have ever tried and tasty to boot. On the lounge side, they feature an Enomatic Wine System at lunch offer an deli-style express-lunch counter as well as restaurant service. **Bar:** full bar. **Reservations:** suggested. **Address:** 1697 Corydon Ave R3N 0J9 **Location:** Corner of Renfrew St. **Parking:** street only. [L] [D] CALL [&M]

(See map & index p. 486.)

NARU SUSHI 204/888-0028 13

♦♦♦ Japanese. Casual Dining. $8-$19 AAA Inspector Notes: Servers at this casual-style Japanese restaurant are quite knowledgeable and eager to guide patrons through the menu. The food is served in smaller, tapas-style portions, which provides diners an excellent opportunity of sampling a variety of dishes with friends. Free parking is available across the street, behind the Urban Barn. Bar: full bar. Address: 159 Osborne St R3L 1Y7 Location: Between Stradbrook and Wardlaw aves; in Osborne Village. Parking: on-site and street. L D

RESTAURANT BISTRO DANSK 204/775-5662 9

♦♦ European. Casual Dining. $9-$23 AAA Inspector Notes: What started as a popular Danish restaurant in the '70s has, over the years, morphed into a well frequented restaurant serving much-loved Eastern European fare. Although many Danish favorites--such as frikadeller and marinated herring--continue to appear on the menu, many regulars now come for the tender schnitzels and mouthwatering chicken paprika. A decent variety of European wines and beers is available to complement any dish. Bar: full bar. Address: 63 Sherbrook St R3C 2B2 Location: Corner of Wolseley Ave. Parking: street only. L D

RESTO GARE 204/237-7072 6

♦♦♦ French. Casual Dining. $11-$32 AAA Inspector Notes: Attentive, knowledgeable service is just part of the package at this renovated 1913 Canadian Northern station with a rail car. A distinguished decor offers original wood timbers and sweeping rich red drapery. A creative, traditional menu utilizes high quality and local ingredients. Escargot casserole is just one of the starters, while other highlights include artisan cheese, grilled bison with truffle whipped potatoes and crepes St. Jacques along with daily foie gras and fresh fish specials. Bar: full bar. Reservations: suggested. Address: 630 Des Meurons St R2H 2P9 Location: Just s of Old Provencher Blvd; east of downtown. L D CALL M

THE ROUND TABLE STEAK HOUSE & PUB
204/453-3631 23

♦♦ Steak. Casual Dining. $10-$39 AAA Inspector Notes: You'll enjoy the casual atmosphere at this restaurant, which has an English-manor décor that includes glowing fireplaces. The house specialty is prime rib, and the menu also offers a very good variety of steak, seafood, chicken and pasta dishes. Bar: full bar. Reservations: suggested. Address: 800 Pembina Hwy R3M 2M7 Location: Just s of Taylor St. L D CALL M

ROYAL FORK BUFFET RESTAURANT 204/668-1960

♦ Comfort Food. Cafeteria. $11-$15 AAA Inspector Notes: The Royal Fork features buffet-style dining with a wide variety of freshly made choices, including sugar-free desserts. Families can be fed for an excellent value. Dinner prices are in effect starting at 4 pm Monday through Saturday and all day on Sunday and major holidays. Address: 900-1615 Regent Ave W R2C 5C6 Location: Jct Lagimodiere Blvd (Metro Rt 20) and Regent Ave W; in Kildonan Crossing Shopping Centre. L D CALL M

SEGOVIA TAPAS BAR & RESTAURANT 204/477-6500 12

♦♦♦ New Spanish Small Plates. Casual Dining. $20-$35 AAA Inspector Notes: This small and trendy popular spot has great contemporary versions of traditional Spanish tapas. No need for a particular order but you could start off with olives in orange and thyme or some charcuterie with a glass of sherry. Next could be the likes of rabbit with Manchego cheese polenta and Serrano ham chips or smoked sturgeon with confit potatoes and poached trout roe. You can keep going but save room for one of the great desserts even if it is just a date with maple mascarpone cheese. Bar: full bar. Address: 484 Stradbrook Ave R3L 0J9 Location: Just e of Osborne St, access by River Ave. Parking: on-site and street. D CALL M

SPUNTINO CAFÉ 204/475-4447 17

♦♦ Italian. Casual Dining. $11-$26 AAA Inspector Notes: This delightful little café features wonderful pasta dishes, veal and some seafood, which are accompanied by fresh bread that is prepared in-house. Desserts are not to be ignored. Closed for lunch on Sunday. Bar: full bar. Reservations: suggested. Address: 926 Grosvenor Ave R3M 0N4 Location: Jct Stafford St. Parking: street only. L D CALL M

STELLA'S CAFE 204/453-8562 22

♦ Breakfast. Casual Dining. $8-$15 AAA Inspector Notes: Start the day with homemade breads and pastries or one of Stella's many signature omelets-this is an all-day breakfast place-and then take advantage of some fabulous area shopping. Diners should get here early on weekend mornings to avoid waiting in line. Free parking is available behind the Urban Barn. Bar: beer & wine. Address: 166 Osborne St R3L 1Y8 Location: Corner of Wardlaw Ave; in Osborne Village. B L D

WASABI SABI 204/415-7938 24

♦♦♦ New Sushi. Casual Dining. $20-$35 AAA Inspector Notes: This Japanese restaurant is as untraditional as it gets with the ultra modern design and equally cool dishes. There is a great choice of quality fish for your regular sushi and sashimi. Where they really get creative is with rolls and other appetizers or hot dishes which have pronounced and balanced flavors. It's best to come with friends because you will have a hard time choosing otherwise and one of the sure things to start with would be the tuna or king crab shooter. One word-Yum! Bar: full bar. Reservations: suggested, weekends. Address: 1360 Taylor Ave, #3 R3M 3Z1 Location: Jct Waverly St; in Piazza di Nardi strip mall. L D CALL M

DELICIOUS VEGETARIAN RESTAURANT 204/477-1530

fyi Not evaluated. Features a Chinese menu of all meat-free dishes such as tofu in peanut sauce. Address: 1467 Pembina Way R3T 2C5

NICOLINO'S RESTAURANT 204/269-5004

fyi Not evaluated. Great stop before or after watching the CFL Blue Bombers football team play. Try the bison spring rolls, they have been a favorite for over 20 years. Address: 4-2077 Pembina Hwy R3T 5J9

Arctic hares, Nunavut

Northwest Territories and Nunavut

Take a journey into northern Canada and you may be surprised at your options for enjoyment.

Residents joke that the four seasons in the Northwest Territories and Nunavut—June, July, August and winter—are a bit unlike seasons in the rest of the world. The absence of a "real" spring or fall leaves busy summers and extra-long winters.

Arrive in June, July or August and you can dip your toes in the Arctic Ocean and marvel at the wildflower-dotted tundra under a midnight sun.

Or visit during the 6 months of winter and you can choose from activities involving snow and ice: snowmobiling, building an igloo, ice fishing, riding on a paw-powered sled or driving on an "ice highway," made of hard-packed snow piled on frozen lakes.

Celebrate the end of a long, dark winter by living it up at Inuvik's Sunrise Festival—held in January in honor of the sun's appearance after months of hiding.

Ice formations, Baffin Island, Nunavut

Canada's Newest Territory

On April Fools' Day, 1999, in the eastern Northwest Territories, Inuit people celebrated the birth of Nunavut, Canada's newest territory.

Twenty-four years after a separation was proposed, Nunavut (meaning "our land" in the Inuktitut language) officially seceded from the Northwest Territories to form its own territory. A new line on the Canadian map allows its approximately 29,474 residents—85 percent of whom are Inuit—the chance to govern their homeland.

Nunavut is a giant chunk of arctic earth stretching so far northeast it almost tickles the shores of Greenland, and yet it contains only one road within its nearly 2 million square kilometres (772,204 sq. mi.). Above the tree line it's a place where animals outnumber humans; where brightly colored rhododendron, yellow buttercups and mountain avens sprinkle treeless tundra; and where it may be easier to hook a trout for dinner than pick up a burger at a drive-thru.

Despite the recent division of Nunavut and Northwest Territories, the two still share similar features. During summer above the Arctic Circle, days have no end. A shining sun never dips below the horizon, and the sky is

illuminated 24 hours a day. In winter the opposite occurs as days and nights melt together under a cold, dark sky.

Picture a black sky pin-pricked with stars surrounding a full, glowing moon, its light sprawling across wide, snow-covered tundra and frozen lakes. On such a clear winter night the flat, stark-white landscape glistens.

Bright Lights, Small Cities

The northern lights, or "aurora borealis," painting the winter sky are no less impressive. A faint glow slightly above the horizon serves as the show's opening act. When the lights rise, they resemble curtains in shades of red, lavender and green. Feather-shaped and stretching across the night sky, the lights ripple to form watercolor waves.

In the Northwest Territories you'll have a good chance to catch this dazzling display October through March. A spot void of city lights is best; try giant Great Slave Lake near Yellowknife. Frozen in winter, this fifth largest freshwater lake in North America provides a fine view of the vivid night sky.

Then visit Yellowknife, on the lake's north arm. Once glittering with gold, this former 1930s mining camp now flaunts its colorful past in Old Town, where shops and quaint neighborhoods nestle against the shore.

West of the city is Nahanni National Park Reserve, where Virginia Falls plummets 90 metres (295 ft.) into South Nahanni River. The falls, arguably more spectacular than Niagara, form a pool of eddies and perilous rapids surrounded by cliffs taller than Toronto's CN Tower.

Recreation

Welcome to the top of the world. The vast Northwest Territories and Nunavut boast an area filled with wild rivers, icy seas, lofty mountains and Arctic tundra. Summer days, typically June through August, are long and surprisingly mild. Hikers can check out a variety of topography, from steep mountain trails to frozen tundra. The Canol Heritage Trail, en route to the Yukon, offers some challenging terrain.

Snowmobiling, snowshoeing, dog sledding and cross-country skiing are a way of life that can extend into May—the warmer air and long days make this the perfect time for such outdoor pursuits. Many outfitters offer snowmobile tours or flights to remote areas to observe the spectacular northern lights. Hint: The best time for viewing this brilliant display is October through March.

Travel anywhere in the territories can include aircraft, boat, automobile, snowmobile, Inuit qomatiq (sled) and even dogsled. Of

the Northwest Territories' five national parks, only Wood Buffalo can be reached by road. Nahanni's rugged beauty is accessible solely by air. One of the newest parks, Tuktut Nogait, is a hiker's paradise where float planes begin landing on the Homaday River in mid-June.

Water challenges come in varying degrees of difficulty. Arctic rivers can offer the ultimate thrill if explored cautiously. Sea kayakers can flow beside towering icebergs, while the many rivers stemming off the Mackenzie are a canoeist's dream. Paddlers will be dazzled by the breathtaking scenery on the Nahanni. Hoist your sails on Great Slave Lake, or if you are brave enough, scuba dive in the frigid waters.

Cold northern waters yield excellent fishing. Plenty of spots are full of prize catches, from the feisty arctic char to the fierce northern pike. Some of the area's waters are ranked the best in the world for angling, including Great Slave, Great Bear and Murky lakes and the Stark and Snowdrift rivers.

The land's beauty, combined with unspoiled wilderness and vast game selections, makes hunting a rewarding experience. And for those who like to shoot with a camera, wildlife viewing also is rewarding. Bird-watchers flock to the Mackenzie River delta, one of the world's biggest nesting grounds.

Alexandra Falls, Enterprise, Northwest Territories

Historic Timeline

1576	Sir Martin Frobisher, searching for the Northwest Passage to the Orient, arrives.
1763	The Treaty of Paris grants Canada to the British.
1771	Hudson's Bay Co. explorer-trader Samuel Hearne arrives at Great Slave Lake.
1789	Alexander Mackenzie leads an expedition along a westward-flowing river, unearthing another route to the Arctic Ocean.
1850	Capt. Robert John Le Mesurier McClure discovers the Northwest Passage.
1870	Hudson's Bay Co. cedes the region to Canada.
1920	Oil is discovered at Norman Wells.
1934	Gold is discovered at Yellowknife on Great Slave Lake.
1978	A Soviet nuclear-powered satellite crashes into the Great Slave Lake area; debris is spread over 124,000 square kilometres.
1993	The Nunavut Land Claims Agreement, under which the Inuit gain the power to govern their own territory, is passed.
1999	Northwest Territories divides into two territories; the eastern, Inuit-governed territory becomes Nunavut.

What To Pack

Temperature Averages Maximum/Minimum (Celsius)	JANUARY	FEBRUARY	MARCH	APRIL	MAY	JUNE	JULY	AUGUST	SEPTEMBER	OCTOBER	NOVEMBER	DECEMBER
Fort Liard	-20 / -28	-8 / -19	-2 / -15	9 / -4	15 / 2	21 / 8	23 / 11	21 / 9	15 / 3	3 / -4	-8 / -15	-15 / -23
Fort Smith	-19 / -28	-14 / -25	-5 / -19	6 / -6	15 / 1	20 / 7	22 / 10	20 / 8	13 / 2	4 / -3	-7 / -15	-16 / -25
Iqaluit, Nunavut	-7 / -22	-8 / -24	-1 / -19	14 / -3	30 / 18	43 / 32	52 / 38	50 / 38	40 / 31	28 / 18	16 / 1	3 / -15
Inuvik	-24 / -33	-23 / -33	-18 / -30	-8 / -20	4 / -6	16 / 4	19 / 8	16 / 5	7 / -1	-5 / -12	-17 / -26	-21 / -31
Tulita	-24 / -30	-21 / -27	-13 / -24	0 / -10	11 / -1	20 / 7	22 / 10	19 / 11	11 / 4	-1 / -2	-15 / -15	-21 / -24
Yellowknife	-24 / -32	-19 / -29	-13 / -24	-1 / -12	10 / -1	18 / 8	21 / 12	18 / 10	10 / 3	1 / -4	-11 / -19	-20 / -28

From the records of The Weather Channel Interactive, Inc.

Good Facts To Know

ABOUT THE TERRITORIES

POPULATION: Northwest Territories 41,462. Nunavut 31,906.

AREA: Northwest Territories 1,140,835 sq km (440,479 sq mi.); ranks 3rd. Nunavut 1,932,255 sq km (746,048 sq mi.); ranks 1st.

CAPITAL: Yellowknife, Northwest Territories; Iqaluit, Nunavut.

HIGHEST POINT: 2,762 m (9,062 ft.), Cirque of the Unclimbables Mountain in Nahanni National Park Reserve.

LOWEST POINT: Sea level, Beaufort Sea.

TIME ZONE(S): Mountain/Central/Eastern/Atlantic. DST.

REGULATIONS

TEEN DRIVING LAWS: Minimum age for an unrestricted driver's license is 17. Phone (867) 873-7406 for more information about Northwest Territories driver's license regulations.

SEAT BELT/CHILD RESTRAINT LAWS: Seat belts required for driver and all passengers 18 kilograms (40 lbs.) and over; children under 18 kilograms (40 lbs.) required to be in a child restraint.

HELMETS FOR MOTORCYCLISTS: Required for all riders.

RADAR DETECTORS: Not permitted.

MOVE OVER LAW: A driver must reduce his speed to half the posted speed limit when passing a stopped emergency or law enforcement vehicle with lights flashing.

FIREARMS LAWS: By federal law, all nonresidents entering Canada with a firearm must declare their weapon in writing and pay a fee of $25 (Canadian).

ALCOHOL CONSUMPTION: Legal age 19.

HOLIDAYS

HOLIDAYS: Jan. 1 ▪ Good Friday ▪ Easter Monday ▪ Victoria Day, May 24 (if a Mon.) or the closest prior Mon. ▪ Aboriginal Day, June 21 ▪ Canada Day, July 1 ▪ Nunavut Day, July 9 ▪ Civic Holiday, Aug. (1st Mon.) ▪ Labour Day, Sept. (1st Mon.) ▪ Thanksgiving, Oct. (2nd Mon.) ▪ Remembrance Day, Nov. 11 ▪ Christmas, Dec. 25 ▪ Boxing Day, Dec. 26.

MONEY

TAXES: The Northwest Territories and Nunavut have no territorial sales tax. However, a 5 percent Goods and Service Tax (GST) is levied.

VISITOR INFORMATION

INFORMATION CENTERS: Territorial welcome centers in the Northwest Territories include an office on Hwy. 1 at the Alberta border (on the 60th parallel) near Enterprise ▪ Dempster/Delta Visitor Information Centre at Km-post 77 on Hwy. 8 near Fort McPherson ▪ the Western Arctic Regional Visitor Information Centre at the termination of the Dempster Hwy. in Inuvik ▪ the Northern Frontier Visitor Centre in Yellowknife.

In Nunavut the Unikkaarvik Visitor Centre is in Iqaluit.

FURTHER INFORMATION FOR VISITORS:
Northwest Territories Tourism
P.O. Box 610
Yellowknife, NT X1A 2N5
Canada
(867) 873-7200
(800) 661-0788

Nunavut Tourism
P.O. Box 1450
IQALUIT, NUNAVUT, NU X0A 0H0
Canada
(866) 686-2888

FISHING AND HUNTING REGULATIONS:
Northwest Territories Environment and Natural Resources
P.O. Box 2668
Yellowknife, NT X1A 2P9
Canada
(867) 873-7184

FERRY AND ROAD INFORMATION:
Northwest Territories
(800) 661-0750

Northwest Territories and Nunavut Annual Events

Please call ahead to confirm event details.

JANUARY

- Kole Crook Fiddle Association Jamboree Fort Simpson 867-874-6880
- Banff Mountain Film Festival World Tour / Yellowknife 867-873-2474
- Sunrise Festival / Inuvik 867-777-8632

FEBRUARY

- Yellowknife Heritage Week Yellowknife 867-920-5693
- NWT Ski Day / Yellowknife 867-446-6721
- Cabin Fever Music Festival Yellowknife 867-920-4041

MARCH

- Snowking Winter Festival Yellowknife 867-920-4944
- DIAVIK 150 Canadian Championship Dog Derby Yellowknife 867-445-7223
- Kamba Winter Carnival Hay River 867-874-4617

APRIL

- Muskrat Jamboree / Inuvik 867-777-2737
- Northwestel Yellowknife Ski Loppet / Yellowknife 867-669-9754
- Top of the World Ski Loppet Inuvik 867-777-2303

MAY

- BioBlitz at Wood Buffalo National Park / Fort Smith 867-872-7960
- StoryNorth and the Storytellers of Canada - Conteurs du Canada Conference / Yellowknife 867-873-4950
- Freezin' for a Reason Polar Plunge / Yellowknife 867-445-7245

JUNE

- Open Sky Festival Fort Simpson 867-695-3004
- Aboriginal Day Yellowknife 867-446-1060
- Yellowknife Solstice Festival / Yellowknife 867-766-3865

JULY

- Folk on the Rocks Music Festival / Yellowknife 867-920-7806
- Canadian North Midnight Golf Classic / Yellowknife 867-873-4323
- Great Northern Arts Festival Inuvik 867-777-8601

AUGUST

- South Slave Friendship Festival / Fort Smith 867-872-3378
- Yellowknife Marathon Yellowknife 867-873-2834
- End of the Road Music Festival / Inuvik 867-678-5426

SEPTEMBER

- Culture Days / Inuvik 867-678-2028
- Aklavik Dizzy Daze Aklavik 867-978-2351
- Thrills in the Hills Yellowknife 867-446-6721

OCTOBER

- Chillsapalooza Youth Halloween Party / Inuvik 867-777-8618
- Postal Precision Shooting Competition / Hay River 780-874-6984
- Star-Gazing Night Hay River 867-874-3872

NOVEMBER

- Geoscience Forum Yellowknife 867-873-5281
- Santa Claus Parade Yellowknife 867-920-5676
- Great Northern Arts Festival Christmas Craft Fair / Inuvik 867-777-8638

DECEMBER

- Santa Claus Parade Inuvik 867-979-5617
- New Year's Eve Celebrations / Hay River 867-874-6522
- New Year's Eve Fireworks Yellowknife 867-920-5676

King eider duck, Nunavut

Inuit stone sculpture by
Eddie Lee

Inukshuk, Hay River,
Northwest Territories

Wood Buffalo National Park, Northwest Territories

Caribou antlers, Northwest Territories

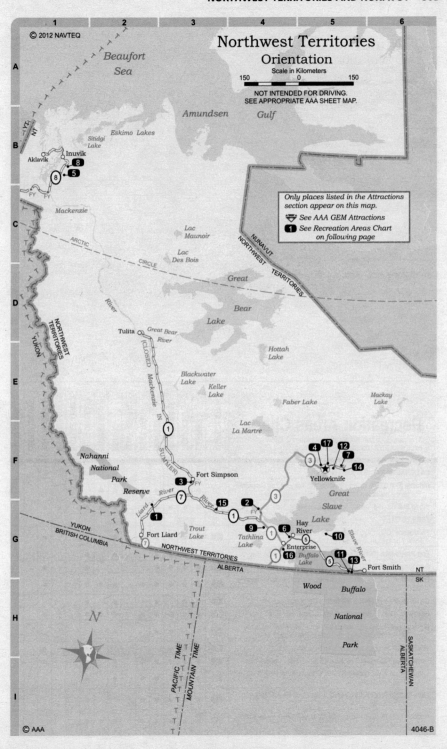

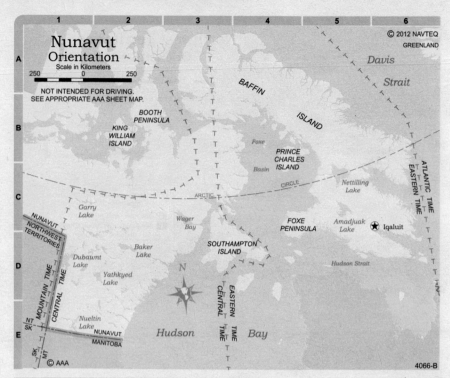

Recreation Areas Chart

The map location numerals in column 2 show an area's location on the preceding map.

	MAP LOCATION	CAMPING	PICNICKING	HIKING TRAILS	BOATING	BOAT RAMP	BOAT RENTAL	FISHING	SWIMMING	PETS ON LEASH	BICYCLE TRAILS	WINTER SPORTS	VISITOR CENTER	LODGE/CABINS	FOOD SERVICE
NATIONAL PARKS *(See place listings.)*															
Nahanni (F-1) 30,000 square kilometres 145 km w. of Fort Simpson. The park is not accessible by road; no motor boats allowed.		•	•	•	•	•		•	•						
Wood Buffalo (H-5) 44,807 square kilometres on Hwy. 5.		•	•	•	•			•	•	•			•	•	
TERRITORIAL															
Blackstone (G-2) 1,430 hectares 166 km s. of Fort Simpson on Hwy. 7 or 115 km n. of Fort Liard on Hwy. 7.	❶	•	•	•	•	•		•	•	•			•		
Fort Providence (G-4) 10 hectares at Fort Providence on Hwy. 3.	❷	•	•	•	•	•		•		•			•		
Fort Simpson (F-3) 18 hectares in Fort Simpson on Hwy. 1.	❸	•	•	•	•	•		•		•				•	
Fred Henne (F-5) 500 hectares on Hwy. 3 across from Yellowknife airport. Sailing. *(See Yellowknife p. 512.)*	❹	•	•	•	•	•		•	•	•			•		
Gwich'in Reserve (B-1) 8,800 hectares s. of Inuvik on Hwy. 8.	❺	•	•	•	•			•		•					
Hay River (G-4) 11 hectares on Vale Island in Hay River.	❻	•	•	•	•	•		•	•	•			•		
Hidden Lake (F-5) 1,950 hectares 45 km e. of Yellowknife along Hwy. 4. Scenic. Canoeing; golf; interpretive displays.	❼	•		•	•			•	•	•					
Jak (B-1) 49 hectares s. of Inuvik on Hwy. 8.	❽	•	•	•						•					
Lady Evelyn Falls (G-4) 5 hectares 6.5 km off Hwy. 1 near Kakisa.	❾	•	•	•	•	•		•		•					
Little Buffalo River Crossing (G-5) 33 hectares off Hwy. 6, 30 km w. of Fort Resolution.	❿	•	•		•	•		•		•					
Little Buffalo River Falls (G-5) 33 hectares off Hwy. 5, 50 km n.w. of Fort Smith.	⓫	•	•		•			•		•					
Prelude Lake (F-5) 95 hectares 29 km w. of Yellowknife on Hwy. 4. *(See Yellowknife p. 512.)*	⓬	•	•	•	•	•		•	•	•					

Recreation Areas Chart

The map location numerals in column 2 show an area's location on the preceding map.

	MAP LOCATION	CAMPING	PICNICKING	HIKING TRAILS	BOATING	BOAT RAMP	BOAT RENTAL	FISHING	SWIMMING	PETS ON LEASH	BICYCLE TRAILS	WINTER SPORTS	VISITOR CENTER	LODGE/CABINS	FOOD SERVICE
Queen Elizabeth (G-5) 38 hectares off Hwy. 5 in Fort Smith.	13	•	•	•				•		•	•		•		
Reid Lake (F-5) 68 hectares 60 km e. of Yellowknife on Hwy. 4.	14	•	•	•	•	•	•	•	•	•					
Sambaa Deh Falls (G-3) 575 hectares s. of Fort Simpson on Hwy. 1.	15	•	•	•						•				•	
Twin Falls Gorge (G-4) 673 hectares at Km-post 75 on Hwy. 1.	16	•	•	•	•					•				•	
Yellowknife River (F-5) 2 hectares 9 km. e. of Yellowknife on Hwy. 4.	17		•		•	•	•	•		•					

AKLAVIK (B-1) pop. 633

Aklavik, which means "the place of the Barrenland grizzly," was founded in 1912 as the Mackenzie River delta outpost of Hudson's Bay Co. A thriving company base in addition to a trading and trapping center, the town became the administrative center of the Western Arctic region.

However, since the community rested in the middle of the largest delta in Canada, it faced constant change as the powerful Mackenzie River built up new land and flooded the old. These conditions prevented the construction of major roads and airstrips. As a result, the newer town of Inuvik *(see place listing p. 509)* absorbed Aklavik's administrative role. There are no roads into Aklavik; it is accessible by air from Inuvik or by ice roads during winter.

Many Aklavik residents refuse to move. The descendants of the early traders and trappers work on oil rigs in the Beaufort Sea or trap muskrat in the delta, which is rich in wildlife. A museum, the original company store and restored log cabins serve as reminders of the past.

Just off Main Street is a tree stump in which Albert Johnson, the suspected "Mad Trapper of Rat River," carved his initials. The town also contains his grave. Johnson, who allegedly killed prospectors and trappers for the gold in their teeth, was shot in 1932 after one of the most intensive manhunts in Canadian history. Whether he actually was the "mad trapper" has been a subject explored in both books and film.

BAFFIN ISLAND, NUNAVUT (A-4)

High in Nunavut's Eastern Arctic is Baffin Island, the homeland of the Inuit. It is a land of majestic fiords, icebergs, bountiful wildlife and the midnight sun, which shines until 3 a.m. from March to June. Although Baffin Island is not accessible by car, Iqaluit *(see place listing p. 510)*, Nunavut's capital city, is served by two airlines.

Qaummaarviit Territorial Park, 12 kilometres (7 mi.) west of Iqaluit, can be reached by boat in summer or by dogsled and snowmobile in spring. An easy-to-follow trail links the island's ruins with signs depicting aspects of prehistoric life and culture.

Auyuittuq National Park, 28 kilometres (17 mi.) from Pangnirtung, is accessible by dogsled, snowmobile or boat. The park is notable for its fiords and glaciated valleys and mountains and for being the first national park established above the Arctic Circle. Polar bears, arctic foxes, caribou, seals, walruses, whales and narwhals inhabit the region.

Included in the approximately 40 bird species spotted in the park are the rare gyrfalcon and whistling swan. Remains of the 1,000-year-old Thule Eskimo culture have been found in Cumberland Sound. Hikers and mountain campers traversing Auyuittuq's Akshayuk Pass—commonly known as the "Pang Pass"—will find challenging trails, abundant wildlife and spectacular scenery.

Quttinirpaaq National Park (formerly known as Ellesmere Island National Park Reserve) is the most northerly land mass in Canada and contains 2,604-metre (8,544-ft.) Mount Barbeau, the highest mountain in eastern North America, and Lake Hazen, one of the largest lakes north of the Arctic Circle. The reserve is primarily a polar desert encompassing 39,500 square kilometres (15,250 sq. mi.) of mountain ranges, glaciers, ice shelves and fiords. Remains of buildings from European expeditions can be found on the rocky terrain. Outfitters in Grise Fiord, Iqaluit and Resolute Bay can arrange trips into the park.

Katannilik Territorial Park, between Kimmirut and Iqaluit, is rich with wildlife and unique flora. River tours, hiking and northern survival challenge even the hardiest adventurers. Information can be obtained from Nunavut Tourism; phone (866) 686-2888.

In spring and summer licensed guides from Angmarlik Visitor Centre lead expeditions into Kekerten Territorial Park, 50 kilometres (32 mi.) south of Pangnirtung; phone (867) 473-8737. Visitors can see remains of whale lookouts, blubber vats, whalers' houses and Inuit homes. A self-guiding trail connects dozens of ruins.

In the northeasternmost part of Baffin Island is Sirmilik National Park, approximately 22,200 square kilometres (8,572 sq. mi.) of rugged mountains, glaciers, ice fields, ocean fiords and coastal lowlands. In fact Sirmilik translates to "the place of glaciers." Pond Inlet, the closest community to the park, is 25 kilometres (16 mi.) south. Travel to the park—by boat, dogsled or snowmobile (depending on the season)—can be arranged through outfitters in Pond Inlet or Arctic Bay.

The park is accessible year-round, except in October and November when the ice freezes up and in July during ice break up. Popular with mountain climbers, Sirmilik is also a haven for bird-watchers. Colonies of seabirds, including thick-billed murres, black-legged kittiwakes and greater snow geese, inhabit Bylot Island. For additional information contact the park office in Pond Inlet; phone (867) 899-8092.

BAKER LAKE (D-2)

INUIT HERITAGE CENTRE is in the n.w. corner of town. The center preserves Inuit culture, representing nine separate Inuit groups, and displays a variety of traditional handmade items including costumes and accessories as well as caribou skin kayaks. Historic artifacts on loan from other institutions are on display. Baker Lake is known for its Inuit art, examples of which are exhibited within the center. **Hours:** The center is open throughout the year. Phone ahead to confirm schedule. **Cost:** Free. **Phone:** (867) 793-2598.

ENTERPRISE (G-4) pop. 87

Enterprise is the first Northwest Territories community encountered by travelers heading north on

Mackenzie Hwy. A major service center for commercial traffic, the town is best known for its spectacular view of Hay River Gorge near the local Esso station.

Scenic 33-metre (108-ft.) Alexandra Falls and 15-metre (50-ft.) Louise Falls in Twin Falls Gorge Territorial Park *(see Recreation Areas Chart)* are about 9 kilometres (6 mi.) south on Mackenzie Hwy. Camping and picnicking are permitted.

FORT LIARD (G-2) pop. 536

Fort Liard is in the Territories' southwest corner. Nearby archeological digs have revealed strata showing 9,000 years of human occupancy. Prior to 1807 Northwest Co. founded a post that was taken over by Hudson's Bay Co. in 1821 when the companies merged. An earnest fur trade continues.

The opening of Liard Hwy. in the early 1980s put the quiet village on the map. The community is characterized by lush growth and a relatively mild climate, despite its northern location. Bird-watchers will find many songbirds during spring and summer. A small lakefront campground is nearby.

Boat launching is possible on the Petitot River or the Liard River, where visitors can see interesting rock formations and fish for pickerel at the rivers' mouth. Fort Liard is a good jumping-off point for exploring the surrounding mountains or Nahanni National Park Reserve *(see place listing p. 510)*. Chartered flights and a forestry office are available in town.

FORT SIMPSON (F-3) pop. 1,238

Established in 1804 at the fork of the Mackenzie and Liard rivers, Fort Simpson is the oldest continuously occupied trading post in the Mackenzie River Valley. Once a district headquarters for Hudson's Bay Co., the town developed into a center of river trade. Originally Fort of the Forks, the town was renamed to honor Thomas Simpson, first governor of the merged Northwest and Hudson's Bay companies.

Fort Simpson has always been a gathering place for people. It serves as a center for territorial government administration and oil and mining exploration. It also serves as a departure point for air, raft and canoe trips into Nahanni National Park Reserve *(see place listing p. 510)*. A visitor center offers interpretive films, historical walking tours and a native crafts display; phone (867) 695-3182.

The Village of Fort Simpson Tourist Information Centre: P.O. Box 438, Fort Simpson, NT, Canada X0E 0N0. **Phone:** (867) 695-3182.

FORT SMITH (G-5) pop. 2,093

Initially a link in a strategic chain of 19th-century trading posts along the Mackenzie portage route to the Arctic, Fort Smith became an autonomous town in 1966. It is regional headquarters for the government of the Northwest Territories and contains several governmental offices. The town also is the site of the Thebacha Campus of Aurora College. Nearby Wood Buffalo National Park *(see place listing p. 511)* is home to one of the largest buffalo herds in the world.

Fort Smith Visitor Information Centre: 149 McDougal Rd., P.O. Box 147, Fort Smith, NT, Canada X0E 0P0. **Phone:** (867) 872-3065 or (867) 872-8400.

NORTHERN LIFE MUSEUM is at 110 King St. The museum examines area history through collections of native artifacts, tools, crafts, manuscripts and paintings. Exhibits cover the history of the fur trade, aboriginal culture and the unique aspects of transportation in the north. Traveling exhibits from other Canadian museums are occasionally featured. **Hours:** Mon.-Fri. 9-5, Sat.-Sun. 10-5, late June-late Aug.; Mon.-Fri. 9-5, rest of year. **Cost:** Donations. **Phone:** (867) 872-2859.

HAY RIVER (G-4) pop. 3,606

Recent archeological finds show that the Slavey Dene have used the area around Hay River for thousands of years, but the first buildings did not appear until 1868 when Hudson's Bay Co. established a trading post. The town's strategic location prompts its occasional reference as the "Hub of the North."

Hay River is the southernmost port of the Mackenzie River system. During the 5-month shipping season barges, fishing boats and Coast Guard craft clog the protected river channels. The town serves as headquarters of the Great Slave Lake commercial fishing industry, which supplies the demand for Great Slave Lake whitefish. Dene Cultural Institute, on the Hay River Dene Reserve, is open for tours mid-May to mid-September. A visitor center on Mackenzie Hwy. is open 9-9, mid-May to mid-September; phone (867) 874-3180.

Hay River Chamber of Commerce: 10K Gagnier St., Hay River, NT, Canada X0E 1G1. **Phone:** (867) 874-2565.

INUVIK (B-1) pop. 3,463

Inuvik, meaning "place of man," was erected in 1958 to replace nearby Aklavik *(see place listing p. 508)*, which appeared to be sinking into the Mackenzie River delta. The town boomed in the 1970s as the center of the Beaufort Sea oil exploration, which since has shifted to other areas. As well as being the communications, commerce and government center for the Western Arctic, the town was the site of a Canadian Forces station until 1986.

Accessible via Dempster Hwy., Inuvik is one of the northernmost points on the North American continent that can be reached by public road. During June and most of July there are 24 hours of daylight. The town also serves as a departure point for plane trips to the Arctic Ocean and the Mackenzie River delta system.

Western Arctic Regional Visitor Centre: 278 Mac-Kenzie Rd., P.O. Box 1160, Bag Service #1, Inuvik, NT, Canada X0E 0T0. **Phone:** (867) 777-4727.

IQALUIT, NUNAVUT (C-6) pop. 6,699

In 1576 British explorer Martin Frobisher arrived at Iqaluit's bay in present-day Nunavut and assumed that he had discovered the Northwest Passage. A discovery he had believed to be gold proved to be iron pyrite, or "fools gold." The Baffin Island town honored his memory in its name—Frobisher Bay—until 1987, when its name officially was changed back to the traditional Inuit name, Iqaluit (ih-KA-loo-it), which means "place of many fish."

Iqaluit, now the capital of Nunavut, began as a small trading post. During the 19th century European and American whalers frequented the bay waters hoping to supply their home ports with whalebone for women's corsets and blubber for lamp oil. Hiking opportunities are plentiful on the outskirts of town or through the nearby mountains. Inaccessible by car, Iqaluit can be reached by air from Calgary and Edmonton via Yellowknife, Winnipeg via Rankin Inlet, Montréal and Ottawa.

With the construction of the Distant Early Warning (DEW) Line in 1954, the town became an important defense site and a major refueling station for both commercial and military aircraft. Iqaluit is the largest community in Nunavut and the educational, administrative, transportation and economic center for the Baffin region. A focal point for Inuit art, the town boasts numerous galleries.

In 1971 the Astro Hill Complex, which includes retail stores, a hotel, movie theater, high-rise apartments, offices and a swimming pool, was completed using modular precast concrete units. Of architectural interest at the time, the complex was designed to withstand northern climatic extremes.

A kilometre northwest of Iqaluit is Sylvia Grinnell Territorial Park on the Sylvia Grinnell River. Visitors to the park can enjoy a picnic with a view of gentle waterfalls and can survey the tundra scenery from a platform overlooking the river. For more information, phone Iqaluit's Unikkaarvik Visitor Centre at (867) 979-4636.

Nunavut Tourism: P.O. Box 1450, Iqaluit, NU, Canada X0A 0H0. **Phone:** (866) 686-2888.

NUNATTA SUNAKKUTAANGIT is at 212 Sinaa. The museum's name translates to "things of the land." Exhibits of various art forms and artifacts, housed in a renovated Hudson's Bay Co. warehouse, focus on the Inuit culture of the Baffin region through displays. **Hours:** Daily 1-5, June-Aug.; Tues.-Sun. 1-5, rest of year. Closed July 1, Nov. 11 and Christmas. **Cost:** Donations. **Phone:** (867) 979-5537.

NAHANNI NATIONAL PARK RESERVE
(F-1)

Elevations in the park range from 1,853 metres (6,079 ft.) at the South Nahanni River to 2,762 metres (9,062 ft.) in the Cirque of the Unclimbables in the park's northwest corner. Refer to CAA/AAA maps for additional elevation information.

About 145 kilometres (90 mi.) west of Fort Simpson and accessible only by air, the park uses Fort Liard and Fort Simpson in the Territories, Muncho Lake in British Columbia, and Watson Lake and Whitehorse in the Yukon as its major supply and jumping-off points. Steeped in myth, mystery and adventure, Nahanni National Park Reserve covers more than 30,000 square kilometres (11,583 sq. mi.) of wilderness in the South Nahanni country.

Liard Highway, linking Fort Nelson and Fort Simpson (see place listing p. 509), passes Blackstone Territorial Park, east of Nahanni National Park Reserve, providing access to Liard River and Nahanni Butte, 30 kilometres (19 mi.) upriver.

A land of rivers, ragged peaks, more than 30 species of mammals and a waterfall twice the height of Niagara Falls, Nahanni National Park Reserve was created in 1972. It was placed on the UNESCO (United Nations Educational, Scientific and Cultural Organization) World Heritage list 6 years later and cited as an "exceptional natural site forming part of the heritage of mankind."

In the early 1900s the area received a reputation for myth and adventure. Gold prospectors, drawn by rumors of placer deposits, began to arrive. When the decapitated bodies of the two MacLeod brothers were found, stories of huge mountain men proliferated.

Although no real mountain men ever were seen, the park remains a place of rugged beauty with little development, including accommodations for visitors. Those who come to raft and canoe on the rivers and hike the forests, alpine tundra and canyons of Nahanni will find it a bracing experience. Travel by water is an excellent way to enjoy the park; however, it can be dangerous and should be attempted only by those experienced in canoeing and rafting. Reservations are required for river trips. Due to the trips' popularity, reservations should be made well in advance; phone the park office for information.

Less experienced river travelers should hire a licensed outfitter for guided river trips down the South Nahanni River. Tours pass Virginia Falls, where the South Nahanni River plunges more than 90 metres (295 ft.); the Gate, a 90-degree river bend below 213-metre (700-ft.) vertical cliffs; and hot springs such as those at First Canyon and Rabbitkettle. Visitors to Rabbitkettle **must** register at the warden's cabin and have park staff accompany them to the springs. Daytime air trips to Virginia Falls should be prearranged through an air charter company in Fort

Simpson, Fort Liard, Watson Lake, Whitehorse or Muncho Lake.

Fishing for arctic grayling, lake and bull trout and northern pike is permitted with a national park fishing license (annual pass $34.30), which can be obtained at the Fort Simpson Administration Office or at the warden's cabin at Rabbitkettle Lake. All national park regulations apply. Firearms are not permitted.

Wildlife species include moose, beavers, woodland caribou, Dall sheep, grizzly and black bears, white-tailed deer and mountain goats. Visitors should take particular care when traveling in areas where they are likely to encounter bears.

The park is open year-round. The park administration office at Fort Simpson is open daily 8-noon and 1-5, June-Sept.; Mon.-Fri. 8:30-noon and 1-5, rest of year. Overnight visitors and those planning river rafting or canoe trips must register before entering the park and upon leaving.

One-day admission to the park is $24.50 per person. For route information, park regulations, weather conditions and park activities write to the Superintendent, Nahanni National Park Reserve, P.O. Box 348, Fort Simpson, NT, Canada X0E 0N0; phone (867) 695-7750. *See Recreation Areas Chart.*

TULITA (D-2) pop. 478

Because of the lack of roads on the frontier, most towns were founded along rivers. Originally called Fort Norman, Tulita was established in 1810 when Northwest Co. built a trading post at the confluence of the Great Bear and Mackenzie rivers. The town's name means "where two rivers meet."

Later years brought additional industries. In 1920 pitchblende—the chief ore-mineral source of uranium—was discovered, and the early 1980s brought the construction of the Wells-Zama oil pipeline.

Tulita is accessible via air service from Norman Wells. No all-weather roads lead into the community, but a winter road—open from late January to mid-March—connects Tulita to surrounding communities. Nearby is one of the Northwest Territories' oldest Anglican churches, built of squared logs in the 1860s. The restored church can be visited.

About 20 kilometres (12 mi.) away is a bed of low-grade coal that has been burning for centuries. Although the fire likely was ignited by lightning, Dene legend attributes it to a giant's campfire. During the summer the surface of the bed sometimes rises and the coals are exposed. Firefighters' attempts to extinguish the smoldering coals have failed.

Hamlet Office: P.O. Box 91, Tulita, NT, Canada X0E 0K0. **Phone:** (867) 588-4471.

WOOD BUFFALO NATIONAL PARK (H-5)

Elevations in the park range from 183 metres (600 ft.) at the Little Buffalo River to 945 metres (3,100 ft.) in the Caribou Mountains. Refer to CAA/AAA maps for additional elevation information.

Accessible by Hwy. 5, which connects with Mackenzie Hwy. at Hay River, Wood Buffalo National Park is the second largest park in the world. Covering about the same area as the states of Maryland and New Jersey combined, the national park straddles the border between the Northwest Territories and Alberta.

This vast subarctic wilderness contains such remarkable geological features as the Salt Plains, Alberta Plateau, the deltas and lowlands of the Peace River and Athabasca River, and extensive gypsum karst formations. The park was established in 1922 to protect one of the world's largest free-roaming herds of wood bison; approximately 5,000 of these animals now live there. Moose, caribou, muskrats, beavers and black bears are among other park residents.

The Peace Athabasca Delta is an important stopover for North America's four major waterfowl flyways. A large variety of waterfowl as well as hawks, eagles and pelicans, are present for part of the year. The northeastern corner of the park is one of the last nesting grounds in the world for the endangered whooping crane. Some of the park's lakes and rivers contain pike, pickerel, trout, whitefish and goldeye. Wildflowers and berries abound in the rolling meadows.

The 508-kilometre (316-mi.) Fort Chipewyan Winter Road is open mid-December to mid-March (weather permitting). The road runs from Fort McMurray, Alberta, to Fort Smith; part of the road is formed by ice. To check road conditions between Fort Chipewyan and Fort Smith, phone the park office or (867) 872-7962 for recorded information. To check road conditions between Fort Chipewyan and Fort McMurray, phone the Regional Municipality of Wood Buffalo at (780) 697-3600.

Visitors can see such magnificent snow-covered scenery as boreal forest, lakes and wide-open meadows. Before departure travelers should contact the park office for a list of driving regulations and recommended travel supplies.

Boating, picnicking and camping are permitted at Pine Lake. The park has hiking trails, which can be used for snowshoeing and cross-country skiing in winter. Contact the park for information about guided nature hikes and other interpretive events.

The park is open year-round; however, campgrounds and facilities are open Victoria Day weekend through Labour Day. The Fort Smith Visitor

Reception Centre at 149 McDougal Rd. is open Mon.-Fri. 9-noon and 1-5, Sat.-Sun. 1-5, mid-June through Labour Day; Mon.-Fri. 9-noon and 1-5, rest of year. Phone (867) 872-7960, or TTY (867) 872-7961. The Fort Chipewyan Visitor Reception Centre on MacKenzie Avenue is open Mon.-Fri. 8:30-noon and 1-5, year-round. Hours may vary; phone ahead. Phone (780) 697-3662.

Admission to the park is free. For route information, road conditions or details about park activities contact the Superintendent, Wood Buffalo National Park, P.O. Box 750, Fort Smith, NT, Canada X0E 0P0; phone (867) 872-7900. *See Recreation Areas Chart.*

YELLOWKNIFE (F-5) pop. 19,234

Although the Dene hunted the Yellowknife region for thousands of years and Europeans explored it in 1771, a permanent settlement was not established until the discovery of gold in 1934. Taking the name of the copper knives carried by the Chipewyan Indians, the town is now the capital of the Northwest Territories and the site of a functioning gold mine and a booming diamond industry.

In 1967 Yellowknife replaced Ottawa as the seat of government for the Northwest Territories. Tours of the Legislative Assembly are available Mon.-Fri. at 10:30, 1:30 and 3:30, Sun. at 1:30, June-Aug.; Mon.-Fri. at 10:30, rest of year. Phone (867) 669-2200. On the northern shore of Great Slave Lake, this "metropolis" of the north lies less than 500 kilometres (311 mi.) from the Arctic Circle and is an excellent place to shop for Northern arts.

The city's historic Old Town retains the gold rush excitement of the 1930s with quaint restaurants, art galleries, shops, and boat, kayak, canoe and yacht rentals. Planes are available for sightseeing and fishing trips. The visitor center on 49th Street can provide information about rentals and excursions. The visitor center also is the starting point for guided tours of the Capital Park area, conducted in July and August.

Best viewed October through March, the aurora borealis, or northern lights, is produced when atomic particles from outside the atmosphere strike and excite atoms within the upper atmosphere. The lights sweep mysteriously across the clear night sky as luminescent curtains of red, green, pink and purple light in patterns called rayed bands. Guided viewing trips are available.

The scenic 71-kilometre (44-mi.) Ingraham Trail (Hwy. 4) to Tibbitt Lake allows year-round access to several chains of lakes and streams. Seven boat launches and two campgrounds lie along the road. Prelude Nature Trail runs 3 kilometres (1.8 mi.) from Prelude Lake Territorial Park *(see Recreation Areas Chart)* through the wilderness to several lookout points, while another trail leads to Cameron Falls.

Prospector's Trail is in Fred Henne Territorial Park *(see Recreation Areas Chart)*, west near Long Lake. The 4-kilometre (2.5-mi.) loop points out the region's

varied geological features and is of interest to rock hounds; sturdy footwear and insect repellent are necessary. Other hiking trails lead from Ingraham Trail; information and brochures are available at the visitor center.

Easily accessible area lakes include Prosperous Lake, Pontoon Lake, Prelude Lake, Reid Lake and Tibbitt Lake. Walsh Lake has good trout fishing, but is accessible only by going through Reid Lake.

The scenic portion of Hwy. 3 runs north from Mackenzie Bison Sanctuary to Edzo, then parallels the northern shore of Great Slave Lake. Driving anywhere in the area, or throughout the Northwest Territories, demands that a vehicle be in top mechanical condition.

Northern Frontier Regional Visitor Center: #4 4807 49th St., Yellowknife, NT, Canada X1A 3T5. **Phone:** (867) 873-4262 or (877) 881-4262.

Self-guiding tours: The visitor center provides brochures for a walking tour of Old Town and New Town.

BECK'S KENNELS DOGSLED TOURS is at 124 Curry Dr. Beck's Kennels offers traditional dogsled rides. During the 5-hour Aurora Viewing Tour, visitors enjoy views of the aurora borealis, or northern lights. Other tours are offered. **Note:** Though spare winter gear is provided, visitors should dress appropriately for cold outdoor weather. **Time:** Allow 30 minutes minimum. **Hours:** Daily 8 a.m.-3 a.m. Nov. 1-May 1; by appointment in summer. **Cost:** Aurora Viewing Tour $100. Prices vary for other tours. **Phone:** (867) 873-5603.

THE PRINCE OF WALES NORTHERN HERITAGE CENTRE is .4 km (.25 mi.) w. on Hwy. 4 at 4750 48th St. The center preserves area history through exhibits depicting aspects of Dene and Inuit cultures. Displays pertain to geology, archeology, exploration, fur trading, transportation, aviation and bush pilots, natural history, artwork and handicrafts. **Hours:** Daily 10:30-5:30, June-Aug.; Mon.-Fri. 10:30-5, Sat.-Sun. noon-5, rest of year. Closed Jan. 1 and Christmas. **Cost:** Donations. **Phone:** (867) 873-7551.

CHATEAU NOVA HOTEL & SUITES   (867)873-9700

Hotel
$149-$199

Address: 4401 50th Ave X1A 2N2 **Location:** Downtown. **Facility:** 80 units, some efficiencies and kitchens. 4 stories, interior corridors. **Parking:** winter plug-ins. **Terms:** cancellation fee imposed. **Activities:** steamroom, exercise room. **Free Special Amenities:** local telephone calls and high-speed Internet.

SAVE ⊞ ▯▮ ▾ BIZ 📶 ✕ ▯ / SOME UNITS FEE 🛏 🔲 🗄

COAST FRASER TOWER   867/873-8700

▼▼▼ Hotel. Rates not provided. **Address:** 5303 52nd St X1A 1V1 **Location:** Corner of 52nd St and 53rd Ave. **Facility:** 58 kitchen units, some two bedrooms. 10 stories, interior corridors. **Parking:** winter plug-ins. **Amenities:** *Some:* high-speed Internet, safes. **Activities:** steamroom, exercise room. **Guest Services:** coin laundry.

ECO BIZ 📶 ✗ 🔲 🗄 ▯ / SOME UNITS FEE 🛏

THE EXPLORER HOTEL   (867)873-3531
▼▼▼ **Hotel** $149-$199 **Address:** 4825 49th Ave X1A 2R3 **Location:** Downtown. **Facility:** 187 units. 8 stories, interior corridors. **Parking:** winter plug-ins. **Terms:** check-in 4 pm. **Dining:** Trader's Grill, see separate listing. **Activities:** exercise room. **Guest Services:** valet laundry.

SUPER 8 YELLOWKNIFE   (867)669-8888
▼▼ **Motel** $179-$182 **Address:** 308 Old Airport Rd X1A 3G3 **Location:** 1.2 mi (2 km) s on Franklin Ave, 0.6 mi (1 km) w; in Wal-Mart Plaza. **Facility:** 66 units. 4 stories, interior corridors. **Parking:** winter plug-ins. **Terms:** cancellation fee imposed. **Activities:** exercise room. **Guest Services:** coin laundry.

WHERE TO EAT

THE BLACK KNIGHT PUB   867-920-4041
▼▼ American. Casual Dining. $8-$24 **AAA Inspector Notes:** The bustling Scottish pub, geared for those 19 and older, is packed at mealtimes. Diners will find classic Old World fare, like Guinness steak and kidney pie, fish and chips, shepherd's pie and bangers and mash. Lots of burgers (including caribou), steaks and sandwiches finish off the menu, and there's a huge Scottish "whisky" selection. Classic, pub-style decor includes dark wood accents, bar towels, beer mats, a suit of armor and an old sword encased on the wall. **Bar:** full bar. **Address:** 4910 49th St X1A 2N8 **Location:** Downtown. **Parking:** street only. [L] [D] [Ⱥ]

BULLOCK'S BISTRO   867/873-3474
▼▼ Regional Canadian. Casual Dining. $15-$43 **AAA Inspector Notes:** Ask locals for a place to eat, and this seafood joint is usually mentioned. Casual service includes guests being asked to grab a drink from the cooler. The menu features freshly caught northern fish like Arctic char, lake trout, northern pike, pickerel and Great Slave cod as well as dishes with caribou, musk ox and buffalo. Fish chowder and musk ox or caribou stew are specialties. Service can be slow, but a rustic décor provides things to view—walls are covered with snapshots and a caribou head. **Bar:** beer & wine. **Address:** 3534 Weaver Dr X1A 2H2 **Location:** 1 mi (1.6 km) ne on Franklin Ave, then just n; in Old Town. [L] [D] [Ⱥ]

FUEGO INTERNATIONAL CUISINE   867/873-3750
▼▼▼ American. Casual Dining. $14-$54 **AAA Inspector Notes:** Intimate mood lighting at this casual spot sets the scene with illuminated local photographs on the walls and a flaming logo on the back wall. The seasonal menu is creative utilizing top quality ingredients including fresh fish from Great Slave Lake, such game meat as elk and buffalo, AAA Angus beef and other interesting meats including ostrich and wild boar. Friendly and knowledgeable servers always are willing to assist with menu choices. **Bar:** full bar. **Reservations:** suggested. **Address:** 4915 50th St X1A 1S1 **Location:** Just nw of 50th Ave; center. **Parking:** street only. [L] [D]

LE FROLIC BISTRO/BAR   867/669-9852
▼▼ French. Casual Dining. $15-$40 **AAA Inspector Notes:** Creative, colorful and regionally inspired cuisine with a French twist is on the menu at this bustling bistro. Locals frequent the restaurant after work and on weekends for its casual, relaxed environment. Guests can mingle with the locals and sample such appetizers as escargot and entrees ranging from venison to Arctic char. All the desserts are made in house. **Bar:** full bar. **Address:** 5019 49th St X1A 2N6 **Location:** Downtown. **Parking:** street only. [L] [D]

TRADER'S GRILL   867/873-3531
▼▼▼ American. Casual Dining. $10-$42 **AAA Inspector Notes:** The fine seasonal menu features such northern fish as Arctic char and halibut, and game meats including musk ox and caribou along with Canadian AAA grade steaks. Great starters include creamy seafood chowder and duck confit ravioli. Other entrées feature veal purse stuffed with spinach spaetzle with a Guinness glace and tandoori lamb rack. The desserts are works of art. Lunch offerings are of a lighter nature with a variety of soups, salads, sandwiches and pasta. **Bar:** full bar. **Reservations:** suggested. **Address:** 4825 49th Ave X1A 2R2 **Location:** Downtown; in The Explorer Hotel. [B] [L] [D] CALL [Ⱥ]

WILDCAT CAFE   867/873-4004
[fyi] **Regional Canadian Casual Dining** $12-$2 Under major renovation, scheduled to be completed July 2012. **Last rated:** ▼ AAA **Inspector Notes:** *Historic.* This historic café is a popular spot at meal times, both with locals and tourists. One of the city's original buildings, the small log cabin has large picnic tables inside, and guests who can't find their own are invited to partake in a city tradition and join another party's table. Among offerings of regional cuisine are musk-ox stew and awesome milkshakes. **Bar:** full bar. **Address:** 3904 Wiley Rd X1A 2N6 **Location:** In Old Town. [B] [L] [D] [Ⱥ]

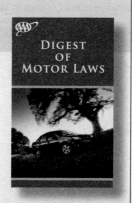

Golden prairie, Maple Creek

Saskatchewan

A visit to Saskatchewan is a perfect escape from the hustle and bustle.

Named after the Plains Cree term *ki-siskatchewan*, meaning "the river that flows swiftly," Saskatchewan boasts more than just a great river with an unusual name.

Along country roads, you'll encounter prairies, mountains, grasslands and even sand dunes. While approximately half the province is covered in pine, white spruce and other trees, a good portion is blanketed with fields of wheat.

Look for signs marked with a barn symbol; they designate bed and breakfast inns and vacation farms, where you can take part in milking cows and enjoy homemade berry preserves or baked goods.

Take a dip into one of more than 100,000 freshwater lakes, including those nestled among resorts and golf courses with rolling fairways in the Qu'Appelle Valley.

Enjoy berry preserves at a bed and breakfast inn

For history, head to towns that preserve the origin of the Mounted Police, the heritage of Métis culture or the rough-and-tumble cowboy lifestyle.

Or visit the Beaver Lodge Cabin on Ajawaan Lake in Prince Albert National Park, residence of naturalist author Grey Owl, who coined the popular belief that "you belong to nature, not it to you."

Colors of the Province

The hues of Saskatchewan's palette were determined both with and without man's help. Painted by nature and the history of the plains, vibrant gold, green and red figure prominently in the province's scheme.

Shimmering fields of grain glint gold in the sunlight. The plains stretch to the horizon in a never-ending series of undulating waves, interrupted only by an occasional silo. More than 50 percent of Canada's wheat crop comes from this land. Proof of the grain's economic importance to the province is the three golden wheat sheaves on its coat of arms. Saskatchewan's flag provides further evidence; its lower half, a solid band of gold, represents the grain fields dominating the province's southern portion.

Color Regina green—the city has more than 350,000 trees. A particularly verdant section of town is Wascana Centre, a 930-hectare urban park that's the heart of Saskatchewan's capital. Lining the rambling shoreline of Wascana Lake, the center is home to cultural and educational institutions and the architecturally impressive Legislative Building, the seat of provincial government.

Prince Albert National Park contributes to the emerald color scheme with nearly 1 million acres of spruce, evergreens and grassland.

The Royal Canadian Mounted Police are immediately recognizable by their scarlet tunics. In fact, the route they took in 1874 to establish law and order in western Canada is retraced along Hwy. 13, the Red Coat Trail.

Regina is home to the RCMP Heritage Centre, the RCMP's only training academy. Watch the cadets drill at the Sergeant Major's Parade, usually held Monday, Wednesday and Friday at 12:45 p.m. In July and early August, the province's colors are displayed in the Sunset Retreat Ceremony. The golden glow cast by the setting sun seems a fitting background as the crimson-clad cadets proudly march against the backdrop of lush greenery bordering the parade grounds.

Recreation

Contrary to popular belief, Saskatchewan is not all prairie. Even in the southern half, where farming is predominant, lakes and parks overflow with recreational options.

Choose from more than 100,000 lakes, rivers and streams for freshwater fishing. While northern pike, rainbow trout and walleye will take your bait throughout the province, head for northern waters to land trophy-size lake trout, Arctic grayling and other sport fish.

Lake Diefenbaker, south of Outlook, is a favorite destination for walleye or northern pike. The Canadian Shield, in the northern third of the province, is a safe bet for anglers; almost 40 percent of its area consists of H_2O. Try Lac la Ronge for trout. Outfitters will fly you to more remote northern fishing lakes.

Tumbling east to west across the province north of the 55th parallel, the Churchill River provides some of North America's best white-water canoeing. Experience white-water rafting on the Clearwater River.

If the rush of white-water action is too intense, paddle your boat along calmer waters. The Bagwa Canoe Route, in Prince Albert National Park, travels through several pristine lakes. Dip your oars in late May through September, when the lakes are warmest.

For the ultimate in calm, head to Little Manitou Lake, near the resort community of Manitou Beach. The lake is believed to have curative powers; its high concentration of minerals makes sinking impossible.

In colder weather, go cross-country skiing on groomed and marked trails. Prince Albert National Park has about 150 kilometres (93 mi.) of trails. Moose Mountain Provincial Park, north of Carlyle, adds another 50 kilometres (30 mi.). Thousands of kilometres of groomed trails link towns and parks along Canada's version of Route 66, a cross-country snowmobile route. Put-in points include Nipawin, North Battleford and Yorkton. Trail permits are mandatory; phone Tourism Saskatchewan, (877) 237-2273, for a provincial snowmobile trail map.

When warm weather returns, everyone flocks to Prince Albert National Park. Loop trails Boundary Bog, Mud Creek and Treebeard traverse fairly level terrain and put you in touch with some of Mother Nature's creations—a black spruce and tamarack bog; sightings of beavers and great blue herons; and forests of aspens and balsam firs.

Another popular summer playground is the Qu'Appelle Valley, a broad swath of land in southern Saskatchewan bordered by rolling hills. A chain of lakes and three provincial parks are the setting for resort villages where guests enjoy boating, water skiing and swimming.

The Royal Canadian Mounted Police

Historic Timeline

1690	Henry Kelsey, an English fur trader, explores Saskatchewan.
1774	The Hudson's Bay Company builds Saskatchewan's first permanent settlement.
1870	Canada acquires present-day Saskatchewan as part of the Northwest Territories.
1873	The massacre of a band of Assiniboine First Nations by U.S. wolf-hunters prompts the creation of the Mounted Police.
1885	Louis Riel leads the Métis tribe's battle for land rights in the Northwest Rebellion.
1905	Saskatchewan becomes a province.
1936	Wheat fields turn to dust as drought compounds the ravages of the Great Depression.
1962	Saskatchewan establishes the first public health insurance program in North America.
1979	John Diefenbaker, Canada's 13th prime minister, is buried at the University of Saskatchewan.
1994	An almost complete tyrannosaurus rex skeleton is unearthed near Eastend.
2001	Prince Charles makes his first royal visit to Saskatchewan.

What To Pack

Temperature Averages Maximum/Minimum (Celsius)	JANUARY	FEBRUARY	MARCH	APRIL	MAY	JUNE	JULY	AUGUST	SEPTEMBER	OCTOBER	NOVEMBER	DECEMBER
Maple Creek	-2 / -14	1 / -12	7 / -6	14 / 0	20 / 5	25 / 9	29 / 12	28 / 11	22 / 5	14 / -1	5 / -7	0 / -13
Meadow Lake	-10 / -19	-7 / -17	-1 / -10	10 / -2	17 / 4	21 / 8	23 / 11	22 / 9	16 / 4	9 / -2	-2 / -11	-8 / -17
Prince Albert	-14 / -26	-9 / -22	-3 / -16	9 / -4	18 / 3	22 / 8	24 / 11	23 / 9	16 / 3	9 / -3	-3 / -13	-12 / -22
Regina	-11 / -22	-8 / -18	-1 / -12	10 / -3	18 / 4	23 / 9	26 / 12	26 / 11	18 / 4	12 / -2	0 / -11	-9 / -19
Saskatoon	-13 / -23	-9 / -19	-2 / -13	10 / -2	18 / 4	23 / 9	25 / 12	24 / 10	17 / 4	11 / -2	-2 / -11	-10 / -19
Yorkton	-13 / -23	-9 / -21	-3 / -14	8 / -3	17 / 3	22 / 9	24 / 11	24 / 9	17 / 4	10 / -2	-2 / -11	-11 / -20

From the records of The Weather Channel Interactive, Inc.

Good Facts To Know

ABOUT THE PROVINCE

POPULATION: 1,033,381.

AREA: 651,036 sq km (251,365 sq mi.); ranks 7th.

CAPITAL: Regina.

HIGHEST POINT: 1,392 m (4,566 ft.), Cypress Hills.

LOWEST POINT: 65 m/213 ft., Lake Athabasca.

TIME ZONE(S): Central and Mountain.

GAMBLING

MINIMUM AGE FOR GAMBLING: 19.

REGULATIONS

TEEN DRIVING LAWS: Teens who have had a license less than 6 months may transport no more than one non-family member. Other passengers must be family members, all of whom must have a seat belt. The minimum age for an unrestricted license is 17 years, 6 months. Phone (800) 667-8015 for more information about Saskatchewan's driver's license regulations.

SEAT BELT/CHILD RESTRAINT LAWS: Seat belts are required for the driver and all passengers ages 16 and over. Children under age 16 and weighing more than 18 kilograms (40 lbs.) are required to wear a seat belt; child restraints are required for children weighing less than 18 kilograms.

CELL PHONE RESTRICTIONS: All drivers are prohibited from using handheld cell phones and text messaging while driving.

HELMETS FOR MOTORCYCLISTS: Required for all riders.

RADAR DETECTORS: Permitted.

MOVE OVER LAW: Motorists may not driver greater than 60 kph (37 mph) while passing highway workers or equipment, stopped emergency vehicles with flashing emergency lights, and stopped tow trucks with flashing amber lights.

FIREARMS LAWS: By federal law, all nonresidents entering Canada with a firearm must declare their weapon in writing and pay a fee of $25 (Canadian). Contact the Canadian Firearms Centre at (800) 731-4000 for additional information or to receive a declaration form.

ALCOHOL CONSUMPTION: Legal age 19.

HOLIDAYS

HOLIDAYS: Jan. 1 ■ Family Day, Feb. (3rd Mon.) ■ Good Friday ■ Victoria Day, May 24 (if a Mon.) or the closest prior Mon. ■ Canada Day, July 1 ■ Saskatchewan Day, Aug. (1st Mon.) ■ Labour Day, Sept. (1st Mon.) ■ Thanksgiving, Oct. (2nd Mon.) ■ Remembrance Day, Nov. 11 ■ Christmas, Dec. 25 ■ Boxing Day, Dec. 26.

MONEY

TAXES: The federal Goods and Service Tax is 5 percent. Saskatchewan's provincial sales tax also is 5 percent.

VISITOR INFORMATION

INFORMATION CENTERS: Provincial welcome centers are along Hwy. 1 east of Fleming ■ at 1922 Park St. in Regina ■ near Maple Creek on Hwy. 1 ■ Hwy. 16 at Langenburg and Lloydminster ■ and Hwy. 39 at North Portal. All information centers are open daily mid-May to early September except the center in Regina, which is open Mon.-Fri. 8-5.

FURTHER INFORMATION FOR VISITORS:
Tourism Saskatchewan
189-1621 Albert St.
Regina, SK S4P 2S5
Canada
(306) 787-9600
(877) 237-2273

FISHING AND HUNTING REGULATIONS:
Ministry of Environment
3211 Albert St.
Regina, SK S4S 5W6
Canada
(306) 787-2314
(800) 567-4224 (in Canada)

Saskatchewan Annual Events

Please call ahead to confirm event details.

JANUARY

- Western Canadian Crop Production Show Saskatoon 306-931-7149
- Lieutenant Governor's New Year's Day Levee / Regina 306-787-4063
- January Jamboree North Battleford 306-445-8033

FEBRUARY

- Canadian Challenge International Sled Dog Race Prince Albert 306-763-1539
- Prince Albert Winter Festival Prince Albert 306-764-7595
- Saskatoon Blues Festival Saskatoon 306-345-9587

MARCH

- Spring Home Show Regina 306-546-5224
- Gardenscape the Outdoor Living Show / Saskatoon 306-931-7149
- Thunder Creek Model Railroad Club Model Train Show / Moose Jaw 306-693-5989

APRIL

- Cinergie Francophone Film Festival of Saskatoon Saskatoon 306-653-7440
- First Nations Spring Celebration Pow Wow Regina 306-790-5950
- Svoboda Ukrainian Dance Festival / North Battleford 306-446-3454

MAY

- Vesna Festival / Saskatoon 306-652-7717
- Regina Highland Games Regina 306-789-6516
- Cathedral Village Arts Festival / Regina 306-569-8744

JUNE

- Mosaic: A Festival of Cultures / Regina 306-757-5990
- Humboldt Summer Sizzler and Rodeo / Humboldt 306-682-3444
- SaskTel Saskatchewan Jazz Festival / Saskatoon 306-652-1421

JULY

- Lloydminster Colonial Days Fair / Lloydminster 306-825-5571
- Saskatchewan Festival of Words / Moose Jaw 306-691-0557
- Shakespeare on the Saskatchewan Festival Saskatoon 306-653-2300

AUGUST

- Queen City Exhibition Regina 306-781-9200
- Saskatoon Folkfest Saskatoon 306-931-0100
- The Saskatoon EX Saskatoon 888-931-9333

SEPTEMBER

- Maple Creek Cowboy Poetry Gathering, and Western Art and Cowboy Gear Show / Maple Creek 306-662-8997
- Goose Festival / Kindersley 306-463-2320
- Metis Fall Festival Prince Albert 306-763-2086

OCTOBER

- Wildlife Art Competition, Show and Sale / Saskatoon 306-382-3155
- Haunted Ghost Town Moose Jaw 306-692-7798
- Thanksgiving Pow Wow Prince Albert 306-764-4751

NOVEMBER

- Yorkton Grain Miller's Harvest Showdown Yorkton 306-783-4800
- Lloydminster Stockade Roundup / Lloydminster 306-825-5571
- Canadian Western Agribition Regina 306-565-0565

DECEMBER

- Sundog Arts and Entertainment Faire Saskatoon 306-384-7364
- Carlyle's Dickens Village Festival / Carlyle 306-453-2363
- Enchanted Forest Holiday Light Tour / Saskatoon 306-655-8881

Great Sand Hills, near Maple Creek

Batoche National Historic Site, Batoche

Colorful town mural, Moose Jaw

Western Development Museum's Heritage Farm and Village, North Battleford

Golden field of wheat

Index: Great Experience for Members

AAA editor's picks of exceptional note

RCMP Heritage
Centre

Wanuskewin Heritage
Park

Royal Saskatchewan
Museum

Prince Albert National
Park

Saskatchewan
Atlas Section

ROADS/HIGHWAYS
- INTERSTATE
- CONTROLLED ACCESS
- CONTROLLED ACCESS TOLL
- TOLL ROAD
- PRIMARY DIVIDED
- PRIMARY UNDIVIDED
- SECONDARY DIVIDED
- SECONDARY UNDIVIDED
- LOCAL DIVIDED
- LOCAL UNDIVIDED
- UNPAVED ROAD
- UNDER CONSTRUCTION
- TUNNEL
- PEDESTRIAN ONLY
- AUTO FERRY
- PASSENGER FERRY
- SCENIC BYWAY
- DISTANCE BETWEEN MARKERS
- EXIT NUMBER-FREE/TOLL
- INTERCHANGE FULL/PARTIAL
- WELCOME CENTER
- REST AREA/ SERVICE CENTER

ROAD SHIELDS
- INTERSTATE/BUSINESS
- U.S./STATE/COUNTY
- FOREST/INDIAN
- TRANS- CANADA
- PROVINCIAL AUTOROUTE
- MEXICO
- HISTORIC ROUTE 66
- VT 41 REFERENCE PAGE INDICATOR

BOUNDARIES
- INTERNATIONAL
- STATE
- COUNTY
- TIME ZONE
- CONTINENTAL DIVIDE

POINTS OF INTEREST
- TOWN
- NATIONAL CAPITAL
- STATE/PROVINCIAL CAPITAL
- AAA/CAA CLUB LOCATION
- FEATURE OF INTEREST
- COLLEGE/UNIVERSITY
- CAMPGROUND INFORMATION PROVIDED BY WOODALL'S®
- CUSTOMS STATION
- HISTORIC
- LIGHTHOUSE
- MONUMENT/MEMORIAL
- STATE/PROVINCIAL PARK
- NATIONAL WILDLIFE REFUGE
- SKI AREA
- SPORTS COMPLEX
- DAM

AREAS OF INTEREST
- INDIAN
- MILITARY
- PARK
- FOREST
- GRASSLANDS
- HISTORIC
- INT'L/REGIONAL AIRPORT
- INCORPORATED CITY

CITIES/TOWNS are color-coded by size, showing where to find AAA Approved and Diamond rated lodgings or restaurants listed in the AAA TourBook guides and on AAA.com:
- ● Red - major destinations and capitals; many listings
- ● Black - destinations; some listings
- ● Gray - no listings

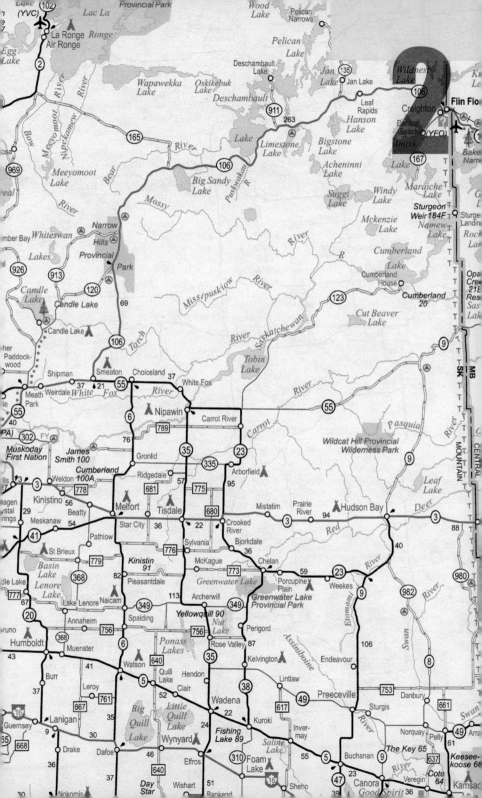

Saskatchewan
Orientation
NOT INTENDED FOR DRIVING.
SEE APPROPRIATE AAA SHEET MAP.
Scale in Kilometers

Only places listed in the Attractions section appear on this map.

See AAA GEM Attractions

See Recreation Areas Chart on following page

Recreation Areas Chart

The map location numerals in column 2 show an area's location on the preceding map.

	MAP LOCATION	CAMPING	PICNICKING	HIKING TRAILS	BOATING	BOAT RAMP	BOAT RENTAL	FISHING	SWIMMING	PETS ON LEASH	BICYCLE TRAILS	WINTER SPORTS	VISITOR CENTER	LODGE/CABINS	FOOD SERVICE
NATIONAL PARKS (See place listings.)															
Grasslands (F-3) 906 square kilometres.		•	•	•					•			•			
Prince Albert (B-3) 3,875 square kilometres. Horse rental.		•	•	•	•	•	•	•	•	•	•	•	•	•	•
PROVINCIAL															
The Battlefords (C-2) 600 hectares 4.75 km n. of Cochin off Hwy. 4. Cross-country skiing; golf.	1	•	•	•	•	•	•	•	•	•			•	•	•
Blackstrap (D-3) 530 hectares 8 km e. of Dundurn via Hwy. 211. Cross-country and downhill skiing; sailboard rental.	2	•	•	•	•	•		•	•	•	•	•	•		
Buffalo Pound (E-4) 1,930 hectares 19 km n. of Moose Jaw on Hwy. 2, then 13 km e. on Hwy. 202. Cross-country and downhill skiing; tennis; pool.	3	•	•	•	•	•		•	•	•	•	•	•		
Candle Lake (C-4) 1,270 hectares 60 km n.e. of Prince Albert on hwys. 55 and 120. Cross-country skiing.	4	•	•	•	•	•	•	•	•	•			•	•	•
Clearwater River 224,040 hectares 50 km n.e. of La Loche on Hwy. 955 (north of area shown on map). Canoeing.		•	•	•				•		•					

Recreation Areas Chart

The map location numerals in column 2 show an area's location on the preceding map.

	MAP LOCATION	CAMPING	PICNICKING	HIKING TRAILS	BOATING	BOAT RAMP	BOAT RENTAL	FISHING	SWIMMING	PETS ON LEASH	BICYCLE TRAILS	WINTER SPORTS	VISITOR CENTER	LODGE/CABINS	FOOD SERVICE
Crooked Lake (E-5) 190 hectares 30 km n. of Broadview on Hwy. 605. Golf.	5	•	•		•	•	•	•	•	•		•		•	•
Cypress Hills (F-2) 20,451 hectares 30 km s. of Maple Creek on Hwy. 21. Historic. Canoeing, cross-country skiing, golf, kayaking, sailing, windsurfing; interpretive programs. *(See Elkwater, Alberta, p. 142.)*	6	•	•	•	•	•	•	•	•	•		•	•	•	•
Danielson (E-3) 2,910 hectares on n. end of Lake Diefenbaker via hwys. 44, 45 or 219.	7	•	•		•	•	•	•	•	•			•		•
Douglas (E-3) 4,430 hectares 11 km s.e. of Elbow on Hwy. 19. Houseboat rental.	8	•	•		•	•	•	•	•	•				•	•
Duck Mountain (D-5) 26,160 hectares 25 km e. of Kamsack on Hwy. 57. Cross-country and downhill skiing, golf, tennis; horse rental.	9	•	•	•	•	•	•	•	•	•		•		•	•
Echo Valley (E-4) 640 hectares 8 km w. of Fort Qu'Appelle off Hwy. 10. Cross-country skiing; horse rental.	10	•	•	•	•	•	•	•	•	•		•		•	•
Good Spirit Lake (D-5) 1,900 hectares 24 km n.e. of Springside via Hwy. 47. Cross-country skiing, tennis.	11	•	•	•	•	•	•	•	•	•		•		•	•
Greenwater Lake (D-5) 20,720 hectares 38 km n. of Kelvington on Hwy. 38. Cross-country skiing, golf, tennis.	12	•	•	•	•	•	•	•	•	•		•	•	•	•
Katepwa Point (E-4) 8 hectares 10 km s.e. of Lebret on Hwy. 56.	13		•		•	•	•	•	•					•	
Lac la Ronge (A-4) 344,470 hectares 48.25 km n. of La Ronge on Hwy. 102. Cross-country skiing; houseboat rental.	14	•	•	•	•	•	•	•	•	•		•		•	•
Makwa Lake (B-2) 2,560 hectares n.w. of Loon Lake off Hwy. 26. Cross-country skiing; horse rental.	15	•	•	•	•	•	•	•	•	•		•		•	•
Meadow Lake (B-2) 156,970 hectares 5 km n. of Goodsoil via Hwy. 26. Cross-country skiing, tennis; horse rental, sailboat rental.	16	•	•	•	•	•	•	•	•	•		•		•	•
Moose Mountain (F-5) 40,060 hectares 22.5 km n. of Carlyle on Hwy. 9. Cross-country skiing, golf (18 holes), tennis; horse rental.	17	•	•	•	•	•	•	•	•	•		•		•	•
Narrow Hills (C-4) 53,610 hectares 64.25 km n. of Smeaton on Hwy. 106. Canoeing, cross-country skiing, snowmobiling; playground.	18	•	•	•	•	•	•	•	•	•		•		•	•
Pike Lake (D-3) 500 hectares 30.5 km s. of Saskatoon on Hwy. 60. Golf, tennis; pool. Ten horsepower limit for boats.	19	•	•	•	•	•	•	•	•	•		•			•
Rowan's Ravine (E-4) 270 hectares 22.5 km w. of Bulyea on Hwy. 220.	20	•	•	•	•	•	•	•	•	•		•		•	•
Saskatchewan Landing (E-2) 5,600 hectares 45 km n. of Swift Current via Hwy. 4. Horse rental, windsurfing rental.	21	•	•	•	•	•	•	•	•	•		•	•		
OTHER															
Bright Sand Lake (C-2) 648 hectares 27 km e. of St. Walburg off Hwy. 26 on a gravel road. Bird-watching, canoeing, cross-country skiing, golf, miniature golf, mountain biking, snowmobiling; beach, canoe rental, nature trails with interpretive signs, playground.	22	•	•	•	•	•	•	•	•	•	•	•	•	•	•
Dunnet (F-4) 50 hectares 7 km s. of Avonlea on Hwy. 334. Cross-country skiing, ice fishing, snowmobiling.	23	•	•	•	•	•		•	•	•		•			•
Kipabiskau (D-4) 16 hectares 35 km s.w. of Tisdale off Hwy. 3 or Hwy. 35. Cross-country skiing, ice fishing, snowmobiling; beach, canoe and kayak rental, nature trails, playground.	24	•	•	•	•	•	•	•	•	•		•		•	•
Last Mountain Lake (E-4) 65 hectares 20 km n.w. of Govan off Hwy. 20 on a gravel road. Bird-watching, ice fishing; pool. *(See Simpson p. 559.)*	25	•	•					•	•	•		•		•	•
Macklin Lake (D-2) 154 hectares .4 km s. of Macklin on Hwy. 31. Golf; beach, playground, wildlife preserve.	26	•	•	•	•	•		•	•	•					
Nipawin and District (C-4) 121 hectares 3 km n.w. of Nipawin on Hwy. 55. Cross-country skiing, golf, snowmobiling; petting zoo, playground, spray pool.	27	•	•	•	•	•	•	•	•	•		•	•		•
Pasquia (C-5) 65 hectares 12 km n. of Arborfield on Hwy. 23. Cross-country and downhill skiing, golf; Andy Jamault nature trail to the Pasquia paleontological site, pool.	28	•	•	•				•	•	•	•	•			•

Recreation Areas Chart

The map location numerals in column 2 show an area's location on the preceding map.

	MAP LOCATION	CAMPING	PICNICKING	HIKING TRAILS	BOATING	BOAT RAMP	BOAT RENTAL	FISHING	SWIMMING	PETS ON LEASH	BICYCLE TRAILS	WINTER SPORTS	VISITOR CENTER	LODGE/CABINS	FOOD SERVICE
Redberry Lake (D-3) 5,600 hectares 12.8 km e. of Hafford on Hwy. 40. Cross-country skiing, golf.	29	•	•	•	•	•	•	•	•	•		•	•	•	•
St. Brieux (D-4) 65 hectares 1 km w. of St. Brieux on Hwy. 368. Historic. Cross-country skiing, golf, miniature golf; beach, playground.	30	•	•	•	•		•	•	•	•	•	•			•
Whitesand (E-5) 49 hectares 9 km n.e. of Theodore off Hwy. 16. Golf, miniature golf; playground.	31	•	•	•	•	•	•		•		•	•			•

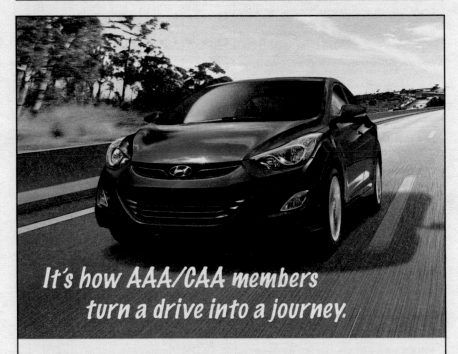

ABERNETHY (E-5) pop. 196

In 1882, about 2 decades before he began his distinguished career in Canadian politics, William Richard Motherwell arrived in southeastern Saskatchewan from his Ontario birthplace and acquired a 64-hectare (160-acre) homestead grant near Abernethy. He farmed the land using several techniques of scientific agriculture then considered revolutionary.

Motherwell was later instrumental in launching the Territorial Grain Growers Association. His knowledge of the land groomed him for later roles as Saskatchewan's minister of agriculture 1905-18 and federal minister of agriculture during the 1920s.

MOTHERWELL HOMESTEAD NATIONAL HISTORIC SITE is 9 km (5 mi.) s. of jct. hwys. 10 and 22. The site commemorates William Richard Motherwell and his contributions to Canadian agriculture. Motherwell's farmstead, including 3 hectares (8 acres) of landscaped grounds, Ontarian-style barn and six-bedroom fieldstone house, have been restored to the pre-World War I era. **Time:** Allow 1 hour minimum. **Hours:** Daily 9-5, Victoria Day-Labour Day. Phone ahead to confirm schedule. **Cost:** Free. **Phone:** (306) 333-2116.

ASSINIBOIA (F-3) pop. 2,418

Assiniboia is an Ojibwa word meaning "one who cooks with stones." Southeast of town off Hwy. 2 is St. Victor Petroglyphs Provincial Historic Park, the site of a sandstone cliff etched with prehistoric First Nations carvings. The carvings at the top of the cliff depict human faces, footprints and animal tracks. Since they have faded with time, the designs are best seen late in the afternoon or on a cloudy day. There is a picnic site near the base of the cliff that is open June 1 through Labour Day. Phone (306) 694-3659 for more information.

The Prince of Wales Cultural and Recreation Centre, 201 3rd Ave. W., was built through volunteer effort; Charles, Prince of Wales turned the sod for the groundbreaking during a visit to Saskatchewan. It houses an auditorium where performing arts, trade shows and other events take place, and the Assiniboia & District Public Library, which presents monthly displays featuring the work of local artists in the Kay Cristo Room. The grounds feature xeriscaping, landscaping with plants that require little water. For information phone (306) 642-3634.

The Visitor Information Centre is in the Prentice Safari Collection Building that holds a collection of 24 mounted animals hunted during three 1970s safaris.

ASSINIBOIA AND DISTRICT MUSEUM is at 506 3rd Ave. W. The museum depicts the growth of Assiniboia from 1912 to the present. A guided tour includes exhibits such as a collection of antique cars dating from 1916-64 as well as vintage heavy farm equipment. **Time:** Allow 30 minutes minimum. **Hours:** Daily 9-4, July-Aug.; Mon.-Fri. 9-noon and

1-4, rest of year. Closed major holidays. **Cost:** $5; $3 (ages 13-18). **Phone:** (306) 642-5353, or (306) 642-3615 after hours. 🅐

SHURNIAK ART GALLERY is at 122 3rd Ave. W. The gallery, which houses the private collection of international businessman William Shurniak, features paintings and sculptures by Canadian artists as well as art, furniture and rugs from China, Southeast Asia and Australia. Included in the collection are pieces by the Canadian artists known as the Group of Seven. **Hours:** Tues.-Sat. 10-4:30, Sun. 1-5, Apr.-Dec.; Tues.-Sat. 10-4:30, rest of year. Closed holiday weekends. **Cost:** Donations. **Phone:** (306) 642-5292. 🍴

BATOCHE (C-3)

Having had their lands in Manitoba's Red River Valley divided and bought out from under them by swelling numbers of homesteaders, the Métis—a people of mixed First Nations and French heritage—migrated to the area around Batoche, in the valley of the South Saskatchewan River, about 1870. Building a settlement along the riverbank, they farmed and hunted, but conflict arose with the Canadian government, which was bent on settling the country's western reaches. Although the Métis set up a provisional government to give voice to their concerns and petitioned for rights to the land, their requests were ignored.

Batoche National Historic Site *(see attraction listing)* chronicles the history behind the events that led to armed conflict in 1885. It also presents the culture and traditions of Métis descendants who continue to prosper in Saskatchewan today.

BATOCHE NATIONAL HISTORIC SITE is w. on Hwy. 225. The decisive battle of the Northwest Rebellion/Métis Resistance of 1885 was fought at this site, which covers 1,080 hectares (1,650 acres). Features include the ruins of a Batoche village, the St. Antoine de Padoue church, a rectory and a Visitor Reception Centre with an audiovisual presentation. There are interpretive signs and costumed interpreters at key locations throughout the park.

Hours: Daily 9-5, Victoria Day weekend to mid-Sept. **Cost:** $7.80; $6.55 (ages 65+); $3.90 (ages 6-16); $19.60 (family). **Phone:** (306) 423-6227 or (306) 423-6228.

BATTLEFORD (C-2) pop. 4,065

Once capital of the Northwest Territories, Battleford is one of Saskatchewan's oldest communities. As soon as the Canadian Pacific Railway began construction, citizens made plans for their town to become a western metropolis. But the railroad took a more southerly route, and in 1883 the capital was moved to Regina.

Battleford's hopes revived in 1905 when the Canadian Northern Railway proposed a westward route, but the line was built north of town on the other side of the Saskatchewan River, spawning the new town of North Battleford *(see place listing p. 540)*. Battleford and its sister city have continued to grow as the province's vast northwest region has become more developed.

FORT BATTLEFORD NATIONAL HISTORIC SITE is 2 km (1.2 mi.) off Hwy. 4. The North West Mounted Police district headquarters was established here in 1876 to enforce law and order. The fort became the site of armed confrontations between the First Nations and federal troops in 1885. Five buildings have been preserved; various illustrative exhibits are featured. Costumed staff members provide interpretive information. Historic weapons demonstrations are given, and historic trails also are on site.

Time: Allow 1 hour, 30 minutes minimum. Hours: Daily 9-5, Victoria Day weekend-Labour Day. Tours are offered hourly beginning at 9:15. Phone ahead to confirm schedule. Cost: $7.80; $6.55 (ages 65+); $3.90 (ages 6-16); $19.60 (family). Rates may vary; phone ahead. Phone: (306) 937-2621. 🏕

FRED LIGHT MUSEUM is at jct. hwys. 4 and 40, just e. on 22nd St., then just s. to 11 20th St. E. Housed in the 1914 St. Vital School, the museum contains a general store, turn-of-the-20th-century furniture, a schoolroom, farm tools, and uniforms from the 1885 Rebellion and World Wars I and II. A firearm collection has more than 300 variety of rifles and pistols dating from 1645. A replica of the Battleford Fire Hall, in operation from 1905-1912 before being destroyed by fire, is on site. Time: Allow 1 hour minimum. Hours: Daily 9-8, Victoria Day weekend-Labour Day weekend; by appointment rest of year. Cost: Donations. Cash only. Phone: (306) 937-7111. 🏕

BIGGAR (D-2) pop. 2,161

Named after W.H. Biggar, General Counsel for the Grand Trunk Pacific Railroad, Biggar was incorporated as a village in 1909 and as a town in 1911. In 1910 the GTPR established a divisional point. A construction boom resulted, and so did an increase in population. The town became one of the home terminals where train crews changed: The station was one of the largest in the West. During the years that followed the population remained stable, and it wasn't until the 1950s that Biggar experienced renewed growth.

The name Sandra Schmirler is synonymous with Biggar. A three-time world curling champion (1993, 1994 and 1997) and 1998 Olympic gold medalist for the sport of curling, Schmirler was born and schooled in Biggar. Sandra Schmirler Olympic Gold Park was opened in her honor in 2000.

BIGGAR MUSEUM AND GALLERY is at 105 3rd Ave. W. Highlighting the story of settlement in Biggar, the museum features two outdoor murals; a plesiosaur diorama; the Earl of Saskesk exhibit; replicas of a CN railway station, the Hanson buck and

a silent film theater; and a Ku Klux Klan exhibit. Also included is an art gallery. Changing exhibits are presented regularly in the museum and art gallery. Time: Allow 30 minutes minimum. Hours: Tues.-Sat. 1-5, Victoria Day weekend-Sept. 30; Mon.-Fri. 1-5, rest of year. Closed major holidays. Cost: Donations. Phone: (306) 948-3451.

BROADVIEW (E-5) pop. 574

Broadview began as a division point on the Canadian Pacific Railway. A marker in a park on the west side of town marks the location of the original tracks laid in 1882.

Broadview Chamber of Commerce: P.O. Box 119, Broadview, SK, Canada S0G 0K0. Phone: (306) 696-2533.

BROADVIEW MUSEUM is 1 blk. s. of Hwy. 1 on N. Front St. A First Nations log house, an 1897 rural school and a Canadian Pacific Railroad station and caboose are displayed at the museum. Exhibits include First Nations and pioneer artifacts, old photographs, maps of early homesteads and trails, and taxidermied goat Sergeant Bill, who was the town's mascot during World War I. Hours: Fri.-Sun. noon-5, June-Aug. Cost: Donations. Phone: (306) 696-3244.

CARLYLE (F-5) pop. 1,441

North of Carlyle is Moose Mountain Provincial Park *(see Recreation Areas Chart)*, which began as a resort beach on Lake Kenosee in 1906. The park is home to herds of moose and elk and is a nesting place for geese and other birds. There also are more than 450 beaver lodges.

Recreational facilities include an 18-hole golf course, hiking and equestrian trails, riding stables, a clubhouse and a swimming beach. Across from the entrance is Kenosee Superslide, a water park.

CANNINGTON MANOR PROVINCIAL HISTORIC PARK is e. on Hwy. 13 to Grid Rd. 603, then 2 km (1.2 mi.) n. on gravel roads. The village of Cannington Manor, founded in 1882, was an attempt to duplicate the upper-middle-class English way of life, including cricket matches and fox hunts. The museum and seven buildings contain antiques, artifacts and farming implements used by the settlers.

Guides in period costumes demonstrate activities typical of the settlement in the last 2 decades of the 19th century. Hours: Wed.-Mon. 10-5, Victoria Day-Labour Day. Cost: $4; $1 (students with ID); free (ages 0-5); $9 (family). Phone: (306) 577-2600 or (306) 739-5251. 🏕

CARLYLE RUSTY RELIC MUSEUM AND TOURIST INFORMATION CENTRE is at Railway Ave. and 3rd St. W. Housed in the former Canadian National Railway Station, the museum features historical items from the area. Thirteen rooms contain such exhibits as a dentistry collection, farm equipment, World War II military uniforms, medical equipment, a restored kitchen and photographs.

A restored one-room schoolhouse and a tourist information center also are on the grounds. **Time:** Allow 1 hour minimum. **Hours:** Tues.-Sat. 10-5, June 1-Labour Day. **Cost:** Donations. **Phone:** (306) 453-2266.

GAMBLING ESTABLISHMENTS

- **Bear Claw Casino** is on Hwy. 9. **Hours:** Mon.-Thurs. 9 a.m.-1 a.m., Fri.-Sat. 9 a.m.-2 a.m., Sun. 10 a.m.-midnight. Closed Christmas Eve and Christmas. **Phone:** (306) 577-4577.

CHAPLIN (E-3) pop. 218, elev. 674m/2,214'

CHAPLIN NATURE CENTRE is at the western approach to town via Hwy. 1. The center is in the midst of the Chaplin Lake area, which encompasses some 6,000 hectares (15,000 acres) of inland saline water. More than 30 species of shorebirds, some endangered, either rest and refuel here during migratory journeys or nest and raise their young in the summer, feasting on brine shrimp that teem in the salty, shallow water.

Guided bus tours are available; binoculars are provided. **Time:** Allow 1 hour, 30 minutes minimum. **Hours:** Daily 9-5, Victoria Day weekend-Labour Day. **Cost:** Center displays free. Guided tour $15. Reservations are recommended. **Phone:** (306) 395-2770.

CLAYBANK (F-4) pop. 25

CLAYBANK BRICK PLANT NATIONAL HISTORIC SITE is 1 km (.6 mi.) e. on Hwy. 339. This plant is said to be North America's most intact early 20th-century brick factory and was active 1914-89. Visitors may tour the large site, which comprises more

than 20 structures. The plant also is open on special event days to afford visitors an opportunity to see the brick-making process.

Time: Allow 1 hour minimum. **Hours:** Tours daily at 11, 1:30, 3 and 4, July-Aug.; by appointment rest of year. **Cost:** $8; $6 (senior citizens); $5 (ages 6-16); $20 (family). **Phone:** (306) 868-4474.
🍴 🎡

CORONACH (F-4) pop. 711

POPLAR RIVER POWER STATION AND STRIP MINE is 10 km (6 mi.) s.e. Bus tours lasting 2.5 hours depart from the information center at jct. Centre St. and Railway Ave. (Hwy. 18). Guides provide interpretive explanations during a walking tour of the power plant and the bus tour of the strip-mining site. Durable clothing and flat-heeled shoes are recommended. **Hours:** Tours are given daily at 9:30 and 1, Mar.-Dec. (weather permitting). **Cost:** Free. **Phone:** (306) 267-2078, or (306) 267-2157 Sat.-Sun.

CRAVEN (E-4) pop. 234

Last Mountain House Provincial Historic Park, 8 kilometres (5 mi.) north of town on Hwy. 20, preserves the site of a fur-trade outpost that operated 1869-71. Park interpreters offer guided tours of the site's three reconstructed buildings Thurs.-Sun. 10-5, July 1-Labour Day; phone (306) 725-5200, (306) 787-0731 or (306) 731-4409 for guided tours on weekends.

CUT KNIFE (C-2) pop. 517

In 1885 Cut Knife was the site of several First Nations uprisings that were inspired by the Métis rebellion *(see Batoche p. 529)*. The Battle of Cut Knife

Hill, between the Cree tribe led by Chief Pound-maker and the North West Mounted Police under Col. W.D. Otter, ended in the retreat of the Mounties to Battleford.

Poundmaker, who stopped his warriors from pursuing and ambushing Otter's troops, later surrendered to the authorities to help restore peace between the First Nations and settlers. A national historic plaque and a framework of tepee poles mark the chief's grave at the Poundmaker Reserve.

Dominating Cut Knife's horizon is the massive tomahawk in Tomahawk Park. The handle is a pipe 17 metres (57 ft.) long and weighs 3,928 kilograms (8,660 lbs.).

Cut Knife Chamber of Commerce: P.O. Box 504, Cut Knife, SK, Canada S0M 0N0. **Phone:** (306) 398-2363.

CLAYTON McLAIN MEMORIAL MUSEUM is 3 blks. w. on Hill Ave. in Tomahawk Park. First Nations artifacts, local historical records and articles used by early settlers are exhibited at the museum, which also includes several buildings depicting an early pioneer settlement. A trout pond is on the grounds. **Time:** Allow 1 hour minimum. **Hours:** Wed.-Sun. 9-5, Mon.-Tues. by appointment, July-Aug.; by appointment rest of year. **Cost:** $2; $1 (ages 0-11); $5 (family). **Phone:** (306) 398-2345.

DUCK LAKE (C-3) pop. 577

The town of Duck Lake lies between the North Saskatchewan and South Saskatchewan rivers. The actual lake is a few kilometres west of town. A nearby cairn marks the site of the Battle of Duck Lake, in which the Métis First Nations defeated the North West Mounted Police on Mar. 26, 1885.

DUCK LAKE REGIONAL INTERPRETIVE CENTRE is at the jct. of hwys. 11 and 212. The center focuses on the historical contributions made by First Nations, Métis and pioneer populations in the area's development. A museum features collections ranging from traditional clothing to tools used in buffalo hunts. The history and cultures of the area are presented in a 15-minute video, and a tower provides panoramic views.

Time: Allow 30 minutes minimum. **Hours:** Daily 10-5:30, Victoria Day weekend-Labour Day weekend. **Cost:** $4.50; $3.50 (senior citizens); $2.50 (students with ID); free (ages 0-5); $12 (family). **Phone:** (306) 467-2057 or (866) 467-2057.

FORT CARLTON PROVINCIAL HISTORIC PARK is 26 km (16 mi.) w. on Hwy. 212. The fort that played a part in the settlement of north-central Saskatchewan has been reconstructed at the site, which features three tepees depicting the Plains Cree culture as it existed 1860-70. A replica of the Hudson's Bay Store is a museum of fur-trading history. The visitor center is a reconstruction of the 1879 home of the trading post overseer.

Time: Allow 30 minutes minimum. **Hours:** Daily 10-6, Victoria Day-Labour Day. **Cost:** $4; $1 (ages 6-17); free (ages 66+); $9 (family). **Phone:** (306) 467-5205. [▲]

EASTEND (F-2) pop. 527

EASTEND MUSEUM-CULTURAL CENTRE is downtown at 306 Redcoat Dr. Items of local interest are displayed, including early settler, business and First Nations artifacts and a collection of dinosaur bones found in the area. Adjoining the museum is a rancher's restored log house dating from around 1911. **Time:** Allow 30 minutes minimum. **Hours:** Daily 10-5:30, Victoria Day-Labour Day; by appointment rest of year. **Cost:** $5; $3 (students ages 13-18 with ID); free (ages 0-11); $10 (family). **Phone:** (306) 295-3375.

T.REX DISCOVERY CENTRE is at 1 T-rex Dr. In partnership with the Royal Saskatchewan Museum, the center houses fossils and replicas of dinosaurs, a 98-seat theater and interpretive displays. Educational activities also are offered. A nearly complete T-rex skeleton was discovered in the area in 1991.

Tours: Guided tours are available. **Time:** Allow 1 hour minimum. **Hours:** Daily 9-7, Jul.-Aug.; 9-5 rest of year. **Cost:** $8.95; $8.45 (ages 65+); $6 (ages 6-17); $26.50 (family). **Phone:** (306) 295-4009.

ELBOW (E-3) pop. 314

ELBOW MUSEUM is at 239 Saskatchewan St. The area's history is depicted from 1905 to the present. Items displayed include arrowheads, photographs and maps. A replica of a sod house, furnished in pioneer style, also is on-site. The house reflects the ingenuity of early settlers in surviving the harsh environment with a scarcity of building materials. **Time:** Allow 30 minutes minimum. **Hours:** Daily 1-5, July-Aug.; by appointment rest of year. **Cost:** Donations. **Phone:** (306) 854-2277.

ESTEVAN (F-5) pop. 11,054, elev. 570m/1,870'

Estevan, founded in 1892 just north of the Souris River, is one of Saskatchewan's major centers for coal and oil. The sun shines an average of 2,540 hours annually, making the town among the sunniest spots in Canada.

Southeast of town off Hwy. 39 is Roche Percée, a group of strangely eroded rock formations that were once venerated by local First Nations. Although most of the animals and initials carved on the rocks can no longer be seen, the site is still supposedly visited by spirits whose murmurs can be heard when the wind blows.

On Hwy. 39 at 118 4th St. is the Estevan Art Gallery & Museum. The facility provides information about local events and also presents changing exhibitions and occasional interpretive programs or tours; phone (306) 634-7644.

The Wood End Building, next to the center, was the 1893 barracks for the North West Mounted Police and contains artifacts that relate to the organization's early days. Also nearby is Eli Mandel Heritage Park, which contains an oil field display.

Tours to Shand Power Station and Prairie Mines and Royalty can be arranged June through August through the Estevan Tourism Booth; phone (306) 634-6044.

Tourism Estevan: 322 4th St., Estevan, SK, Canada S4A 0T8. **Phone:** (306) 634-2828.

BOUNDARY DAM POWER STATION is 5 km (3 mi.) w. on Hwy. 18. This power station, which contains one of the largest lignite-burning plants in Canada, utilizes southeast Saskatchewan's vast coal reserves to produce more kilowatts than any other dam in the province. Swimming and boating are permitted. **Time:** Allow 2 hours minimum. **Hours:** Guided tours are given Tues.-Sat. at 9 and 1, June-Aug. Phone ahead to confirm schedule. **Cost:** Free. **Phone:** (306) 421-2028.

RECREATIONAL ACTIVITIES
Recreational Complex
• **RM of Estevan Aquatic Center** is at 701 Souris Ave. **Hours:** Mon.-Fri. 6 a.m.-9:30 p.m., Sat. 9 a.m.-9:30 p.m., Sun. noon-9:30. **Phone:** (306) 634-1888.

BEST WESTERN PLUS ESTEVAN INN & SUITES
306/634-7447

 Hotel $153-$170 **AAA Benefit:** Members save up to 20%, plus 10% bonus points with Best Western Rewards®.
Address: 92 King St S4A 2T5 **Location:** Hwy 39, 1 mi (1.6 km) n at Kensington Ave. **Facility:** 94 units, some efficiencies and kitchens. 4 stories, interior corridors. **Parking:** winter plug-ins. **Terms:** cancellation fee imposed. **Amenities:** high-speed Internet. **Pool(s):** heated indoor. **Activities:** whirlpool, exercise room. **Guest Services:** valet and coin laundry. **Free Special Amenities: expanded continental breakfast and local telephone calls.**
[SAVE] [YI+] [⇄] [BIZ] [📶] [🛏] [🖥] [💻] /SOME UNITS FEE [🐾]

DAYS INN (306)634-6456
🔷🔷🔷 **Hotel** $122-$150 **Address:** 1305 9th St S4A 1J1 **Location:** Jct Hwy 39, just n on 13th Ave; center. **Facility:** 75 units. 3 stories, interior corridors. **Parking:** winter plug-ins. **Amenities:** high-speed Internet. **Dining:** 2 restaurants. **Activities:** exercise room. **Guest Services:** coin laundry.
[YI] [Y] CALL [&M] [BIZ] [📶] [🛏] [💻] /SOME UNITS [🖥]

MOTEL 6 ESTEVAN 306/634-8666
🔷🔷 Hotel Rates not provided **Address:** 88 King St E S4A 2A4 **Location:** Hwy 39, 1 mi (1.7 km) n at Kensington Ave,then just e. **Facility:** 68 units, some efficiencies. 3 stories, interior corridors. **Parking:** winter plug-ins. **Amenities:** high-speed Internet. **Guest Services:** coin laundry.
[SAVE] [YI+] CALL [&M] [📶] [🛏] [🖥] /SOME UNITS [🐾]

SUPER 8 (306)634-8585
🔷🔷 Hotel $125-$140 **Address:** 134 2nd Ave S4A 2W6 **Location:** Just n of jct Hwy 39. Next to Tim Horton's. **Facility:** 70 units. 3 stories, interior corridors. **Parking:** winter plug-ins. **Amenities:** high-speed Internet. **Activities:** whirlpool, exercise room. **Guest Services:** valet and coin laundry.
[YI+] [BIZ] [✕] [🛏] [🖥] [💻]

EDDIE'S NEIGHBOURHOOD GRILL & BAR 306/634-5656
🔷🔷 American. Casual Dining. $9-$32 **AAA Inspector Notes:** This popular, casual restaurant provides efficient, friendly service in a pleasant atmosphere. The menu offers a good variety. Patio seating can be requested in season. **Bar:** full bar. **Address:** 122 4th St S4A 0T4 **Location:** Just e of jct Hwy 39 E and 2nd Ave.
[L] [D]

ESTON (E-2) pop. 1,031, elev. 682m/2,240'

Founded in 1916, Eston is a major grain center; more than one million bushels of grain are produced annually.

PRAIRIE WEST HISTORICAL CENTRE is at 946 2nd St. S.E. The restored 1910 Evans house contains more than 3,000 artifacts that include period furnishings and photographs, agricultural displays, a homesteader shack and the Heritage Art Gallery. A pioneer schoolroom is depicted at the Lovedale school. A wildflower garden is on the grounds. **Time:** Allow 30 minutes minimum. **Hours:** Mon.-Sat. 9-noon and 1-5, Sun. 1-5, July-Aug.; daily 1:30-4:30, day after Victoria Day weekend-June 30; by appointment rest of year. **Cost:** Free. **Phone:** (306) 962-3772.

FORT QU'APPELLE (E-4) pop. 2,034

With the 1874 signing of Treaty Number IV, representatives of the Cree and Saulteaux First Nations gave away their legal right to vast tracts of southern Saskatchewan; near the center of Fort Qu'Appelle (kwah-PELL) a cairn marks the site of the signing. The fort for which the town is named was built in 1864 mainly for use as a trading post.

Fort Qu'Appelle is on the Qu'Appelle River in a broad valley of lush farmland. The area is known for the wide variety of berries growing on the moist, north-facing slopes. The dry, south-facing slopes are carpeted with wildflowers. Several kinds of hawks soar above this peaceful valley, and pelicans, herons, ducks and geese nest in the marshes. Near Fort Qu'Appelle the river widens into a chain of lakes.

The river's unusual name is the French translation of the Cree word *catabuysepu*, or "the river that calls." According to First Nations legend, the river was haunted by a spirit that could be heard crying as it moved up and down the water.

Also taking its name from this Cree expression is nearby Katepwa Point Provincial Park, a lakeside recreation area offering day-use facilities. Another provincial park, Echo Valley, is west of town. *See Recreation Areas Chart.*

Fort Qu'Appelle Chamber of Commerce: P.O. Box 1273, Fort Qu'Appelle, SK, Canada S0G 1S0.

FISH CULTURE STATION is 6 km (4 mi.) w. on Hwy. 210. The station raises such fish as northern pike, whitefish, walleye, sturgeon and rainbow, brown, lake, tiger and brook trout through their life cycle from the egg stage to adult, then distributes them to various lakes and rivers to bolster fish populations. **Tours:** Guided tours are available. **Time:** Allow 30 minutes minimum. **Hours:** Daily 9-noon and 1-4, May 1-Sept. 3. **Cost:** Free. **Phone:** (306) 332-3200.

FORT QU'APPELLE MUSEUM is at Bay Ave. and 3rd St. A small log building remaining from the original 1864 Hudson's Bay Co. trading post adjoins a modern structure displaying relics of the past, First Nations crafts and a model of Fort Qu'Appelle. **Hours:** Daily 1-5, June 1-Labour Day; other times by appointment. **Cost:** $2; $1 (children); $5 (family). **Phone:** (306) 332-6033.

GRASSLANDS NATIONAL PARK (F-3)

Elevations in the park range from 747 metres (2,450 ft.) at the Frenchman River to 998 metres (3,275 ft.) at Horse Creek. Refer to CAA/AAA maps for additional elevation information.

Grasslands National Park encompasses the grasslands in two separate blocks between Val Marie and Killdeer in the southern part of the province. When completed, the park will preserve 900 square kilometres (350 sq. mi.) of Saskatchewan's original mixed-grass prairie, including such topographic features as buttes, badlands and coulees. Among the wildlife species found in the park are black-tailed prairie dogs, golden eagles, rattlesnakes, short-horned lizards, pronghorn antelopes, mule deer and most recently, reintroduced plains bison.

These grasslands also claim a rich history. The first recorded discovery of dinosaur remains in western Canada was made in the badlands in 1875. Proof of early habitation includes remnants of tepee rings, ranch buildings, corrals and old homestead shacks.

Ranching operations exist in the area, and some of the proposed parkland is still under private ownership. Before entering the park, visitors are invited to contact or stop at the visitor center located in Val Marie, which offers park information, maps and permits as well as interpretive programs, guided hikes and special events. Park open year-round. Visitor center daily 8-5, Victoria Day weekend-Labour Day weekend; 8-noon and 1-4:30, Apr. 1-day before Victoria Day weekend and day after Labour Day weekend-Oct. 31. Write Grasslands National Park, P.O. Box 150, Val Marie, SK, Canada S0N 2T0; phone (306) 298-2257. *See Recreation Areas Chart.*

GRAVELBOURG (F-3) pop. 1,116

CATHÉDRALE NOTRE-DAME DE L'ASSOMPTION is at 1st Ave. and Main St. The 1918 Cathedral of Our Lady of the Assumption is noted for the beauty of its interior murals, painted 1921-29 by founding pastor Monsignor Charles Maillard, as well as its

stained-glass windows. Bilingual guides provide information about the church in both French and English on a narrated tour. **Hours:** Open daily 9-6, June-Aug.; by appointment rest of year. **Cost:** $10. Guided tour $15; free (ages 0-9). **Phone:** (306) 648-2332 to schedule a guided tour.

GRENFELL (E-5) pop. 1,049

Grenfell is about 124 kilometres (77 mi.) east of Regina at the junction of Hwys. 1 and 47. Hwy. 47 north from town leads to scenic Hwy. 247, which runs east along the northern shores of Crooked and Round lakes to the junction with Hwy. 9; from there, Hwy. 9 offers another scenic stretch of roadway south to Whitewood.

GRENFELL MUSEUM, Wolseley Ave. and Stella St. Adare, is the former home of the editor/publisher of Grenfell's first newspaper. Furnished in period, the 1904 house contains a history room, a square grand piano, a rope bed, a brass bed, a wood-burning kitchen range, an icebox, a hand-operated vacuum cleaner and a dining table set with china. A separate building houses antiques, pioneer artifacts and military displays. **Time:** Allow 2 hours minimum. **Hours:** Fri.-Sun. 2-8, early July-Aug. 31; other times by appointment. **Cost:** Donations. **Phone:** (306) 697-2839.

HERSCHEL (D-2) pop. 39

ANCIENT ECHOES INTERPRETIVE CENTRE, on 1st Ave., depicts the area's natural and native history and explores the areas of paleontology and prairie grasslands ecology. Exhibits include fossils, aboriginal artifacts and examples of taxidermy. An art installation tells about the disappearance and resurgence of the buffalo, and Canadian art is on display. Visitors may take a guided tour, using their own vehicle, to 1,800-year-old petroglyphs located 3.2 kilometres (2 mi.) away. At the destination, a hiking trail reveals glacial ravines, freshwater springs and a variety of flora and fauna. A video of the ravines is available for viewing.

Time: Allow 1 hour, 30 minutes minimum. **Hours:** Daily 9-5, May 15-Sept. 1; by appointment rest of year. **Cost:** $12; $10 (ages 5-12 and 65+). Reservations are required for archeological site tours. **Phone:** (306) 377-2045, or (306) 377-2125 Sept. 2-May 14. [🍴] [⛲]

HUMBOLDT (D-4) pop. 5,678

Humboldt is on Hwy. 5 about 111 kilometres (69 mi.) east of Saskatoon; the drive takes about 90 minutes. Named for author, explorer and scientist Baron Friedrich Heinrich Alexander von Humboldt, the town reveals its German heritage through architecture, festivals, downtown murals and folk art, a cottage industry. Annual events include Polkafest, celebrated the last weekend in May; the Summer Sizzler & Rodeo, held the last weekend in June; and Oktoberfest, which takes place the last Saturday in October.

HUMBOLDT AND DISTRICT MUSEUM AND GALLERY

is at Main St. and Sixth Ave. Housed in a restored, early 20th-century post office (a national historic site), the museum features a Humboldt Telegraph Station exhibit, a Sports Hall of Fame and local history displays. It also showcases the work of regional artists. **Time:** Allow 30 minutes minimum. **Hours:** Tues.-Sat. 10-5, Sun. 1-5, July-Aug.; Tues.-Sat. 1-5, rest of year. **Cost:** Donations. **Phone:** (306) 682-5226.

INDIAN HEAD (E-4) pop. 1,815

AESB AGRO FORESTRY DEVELOPMENT CENTRE is 1.6 km (1 mi.) s. of jct. hwys. 1 and 56. A short, self-guiding nature trail and picnic areas are part of the Prairie Farm Rehabilitation Administration (PFRA). **Hours:** Outdoor areas open daily dawn-dusk. **Cost:** Free. **Phone:** (306) 695-2284.

INDIAN HEAD MUSEUM is at 610 Otterloo St. Housed in an old fire hall, this museum displays an extensive collection of artifacts dating back to the district's pioneer beginnings. Also on the grounds is an 1883 cottage that farm laborers lived in, as well as a 1926 school. A 1952 Pontiac in mint condition resides in a replicated 1930s village garage. A large assortment of farm machinery also is on display.

Guided tours are available by appointment. **Time:** Allow 1 hour minimum. **Hours:** Daily 1-4, July-Aug.; by appointment rest of year. **Cost:** $2; 50c (ages 12-19). **Phone:** (306) 695-2234.

KAMSACK (D-5) pop. 1,825

KAMSACK POWERHOUSE MUSEUM is 1.5 km (1 mi.) w. of Hwy. 5 to the Riverside Golf Course, following signs. Housed in a 1914 power plant, the museum features a 1914 generator, old farm equipment, household artifacts, a printing press, vintage clothing and replicas of an early 1900s doctor's office, hospital room, kitchen, bedroom, school and barbershop. **Hours:** Daily 1-5, June 1-Labour Day; by appointment rest of year. **Cost:** $3; free (ages 0-12). **Phone:** (306) 542-4415.

KINDERSLEY (D-2) pop. 4,678

Kindersley is a popular stop for bird-watchers. The surrounding region annually attracts thousands of migrating geese, more than 10 species of ducks, and a few whistling swans and whooping cranes. Kindersley celebrates the annual Goose Festival in September.

Kindersley Chamber of Commerce: 605 Main St., Box 1537, Kindersley, SK, Canada S0L 1S0. **Phone:** (306) 463-2320.

KINDERSLEY PLAINS MUSEUM is 1 km (.6 mi.) e. on Hwy. 7 to 903 11th Ave. Geological displays, First Nations artifacts and farming and military items are featured. **Tours:** Guided tours are available. **Time:** Allow 30 minutes minimum. **Hours:** Daily 10-6 (also Wed.-Sun. 6-8), May 13-Aug. 31. **Cost:** $5; $4 (ages 7-18); $10 (family). **Phone:** (306) 463-6620.

NOVA INN   306/463-4687
▼▼ ▼▼ **Hotel.** Rates not provided. **Address:** 100 12th Ave NW S0L 1S0 **Location:** Jct of Hwy 7 and 21. **Facility:** 43 units. 2 stories (no elevator), interior/exterior corridors. **Parking:** winter plug-ins. **Activities:** sauna.

KINISTINO (C-4) pop. 743

One of the oldest purely agricultural settlements in the province, Kinistino takes its name from *kinistineaux,* meaning "they who were the first to arrive." The allusion refers to the Cree First Nations, who lived in the area before the arrival of homesteaders.

KINISTINO DISTRICT PIONEER MUSEUM is on Main St. The museum displays pioneer and aboriginal artifacts. **Time:** Allow 30 minutes minimum. **Hours:** Mon., Wed. and Fri. 1-7, July-Aug. **Cost:** Donations. **Phone:** (306) 864-2838.

LASHBURN (C-2) pop. 967, elev. 623m/2,047'

LASHBURN CENTENNIAL MUSEUM is at 96 Main St. Housed in a 1906 general store which closed in 1972, the museum pays homage to English immigrants called the Barr Colonists with a comprehensive collection that includes a series of quilt blocks and period pieces. Visitors may see the kitchen, dining room and bathrooms in the furnished apartments on the second floor where the store's owners and families resided. Another room replicates a pharmacy and hospital. A veterans gallery honors those who served in the military from the Boer War through the Korean War. Down the street is a one-room country school in use 1908-1949. A warehouse has a trapper's cabin and a blacksmith's shop as well as historic artifacts. **Hours:** Mon.-Fri. 10-4:30, July-Aug.; Sat.-Sun. by appointment, rest of year. **Cost:** Donations. Cash only. **Phone:** (306) 285-4125 or (306) 285-3533.

LLOYDMINSTER—See Alberta p. 169.

MANITOU BEACH (D-4) pop. 257

The resort community of Manitou Beach is on the shore of Little Manitou Lake. The mineral waters of this lake were believed by the First Nations people to possess curative powers, and the sick of the tribe were brought for treatment long before Europeans knew of the land. Akin to the Dead Sea, the 19-kilometre-long (12-mi.) lake is three times saltier than the ocean and perfectly buoyant, allowing swimmers to float effortlessly. The village has a nine-hole golf course, spa hotel, convention center, mini-mall, tennis courts, drive-in movie theater, cross-country ski trails, an indoor heated mineral pool and a 234-site, full-service campground.

Along the lake lies Camp Easter Seal, which provides summer recreation for the physically impaired;

visitors are welcome. At the east end of town on Hwy. 365 is Danceland, a dance hall with a 464-square-metre (5,000-sq.-ft.) maple hardwood dance floor. On Friday and Saturday evenings couples take to the floor for old-fashioned ballroom and rousing square dancing to live music; gospel shows take place on Sunday. For tourism information phone (866) 756-6665.

MAPLE CREEK (F-2) pop. 2,176

The town of Maple Creek was named by 22 Canadian Pacific Railway workers who spent the winter of 1882 on the banks of Maple Creek. Livestock, grain, tourism, natural gas and oil development provide the area with a stable economy. Maple Creek also has a golf course and campgrounds.

South of town on Hwy. 21 is Cypress Hills Interprovincial Park *(see attraction listing in Alberta p. 142 and the Recreation Areas Chart)*. The lofty hills are characterized by forest-covered buttes, plateaus and ridges interspersed with large areas of ranchland.

The Great Sand Hills region is located about 70 kilometres (44 mi.) north of Maple Creek via Hwy. 21. Occupying approximately 190,000 hectares (469,500 acres), this area in southwestern Saskatchewan is characterized by fragile native grasslands and open sand dunes, the largest some 25 metres (82 ft.) high. The dunes are fringed by small clumps of aspen, birch and willow trees, rose bushes, sagebrush and choke cherry. Subjected to strong winds blowing from the northwest, the dunes are moving east at a rate of almost 4 metres (13 ft.) per year.

Maple Creek Visitor Centre: 114 Jasper St., P.O. Box 428, Maple Creek, SK, Canada S0N 1N0. **Phone:** (306) 662-4005.

FORT WALSH NATIONAL HISTORIC SITE is 55 km (34 mi.) s.w. on Hwy. 271. The site preserves an early North West Mounted Police fort. Reconstructed period buildings house exhibits of original post artifacts. Tours include trips to the site of the 1873 Cypress Hills massacre and the fort. Visitors also can bird-watch, walk a self-guiding nature trail and participate in geocaching. A bus trip around the park includes an interpretive commentary.

Time: Allow 2 hours minimum. **Hours:** Daily 9:30-5:30, Victoria Day weekend-Labour Day. Phone ahead to confirm schedule. **Cost:** $9.80; $8.30 (ages 65+); $4.90 (ages 6-16); $22 (family). Rates may vary; phone ahead. **Phone:** (306) 662-3590.

THE JASPER CULTURAL AND HISTORICAL CENTRE is at 311 Jasper St. Several rooms of historical displays and art are housed in a 1913 two-story brick school building. Exhibits include ranching, railroad, rodeo and school memorabilia. **Time:** Allow 30 minutes minimum. **Hours:** Mon.-Fri. 9-5, Sat.-Sun. and holidays 1-5, May-Aug. **Cost:** $7.50; $5 (students with ID); $2.50 (ages 6-12); $15 (family). **Phone:** (306) 662-2434.

OLDTIMER'S MUSEUM is at 218 Jasper St. The museum contains collections of photographs, artifacts and archival material relating to the First Nations people, the North West Mounted Police, ranching and early settlement. **Hours:** Mon.-Sat. 9-5:30, Sun. 1-4, Victoria Day weekend-Labour Day. **Cost:** $5; $4 (students with ID); $2 (ages 0-11). **Phone:** (306) 662-2474.

WINERIES

- **Cypress Hills Vineyard & Winery** is 20 km (12 mi.) s.w. on Hwy. 271. **Hours:** Mon.-Sat. 10-5:30, Sun. noon-5:30, mid-June through Aug. 31; Tues.-Sat. 10:30-5, Sun. noon-5:30, mid-May to mid-June. Hours vary Sept.-Dec.; phone ahead. **Phone:** (306) 662-4100.

MEADOW LAKE (B-2) pop. 5,045

Meadow Lake functions as a retail, service and distribution center for northwestern Saskatchewan's major industries as well as a shopping destination for communities in the region. Pastimes include fishing and hunting for big game, ducks and geese as well as snowmobiling, cross-country skiing and other recreational activities.

With 25 sparkling lakes, Meadow Lake Provincial Park *(see Recreation Areas Chart)* is a haven for fishing, swimming, boating and camping. The park offers hiking trails, beaches, interpretive and recreational programs, cabins, a miniature golf course and a 179-kilometre (111-mi.) canoe route stretching along the Waterhen and Beaver rivers. The town's recreational facilities include the Lions Regional Campground and RV Park, an aquatic center and an 18-hole golf course.

Of historical interest is Steele Narrows Provincial Historic Park, 72 kilometres (45 mi.) southwest via hwys. 304 and 26. The last armed conflict on Canadian soil occurred between Big Bear and his band of Cree First Nations and Maj. Sam Steele of the North West Mounted Police. The defeat of Big Bear on June 3, 1885, was the end of the Métis and First Nations rebellion that began in March 1885 *(see Batoche p. 529)*.

Meadow Lake & District Chamber of Commerce: P.O. Box 1168, Meadow Lake, SK, Canada S9X 1Y8. **Phone:** (306) 236-4447.

MEADOW LAKE & DISTRICT INFORMATION CENTRE & MUSEUM is at Hwy. 4 and 9th Ave. W. Local pioneer artifacts and antiques are displayed. **Hours:** Mon.-Sat. 8-6, Sun. noon-6, Victoria Day-Labour Day; by appointment rest of year. **Cost:** Donations. **Phone:** (306) 236-3622.

MELFORT (C-4) pop. 5,576, elev. 457m/1,500'

Known as the City of Northern Lights due to the visibility of the aurora borealis in the night sky for much of the year, Melfort is in the Carrot River Valley, an area known for its fertile black loam. Agriculture has been the major industry in the area since the days of early settlement in the late 19th century. Melfort was incorporated as a village in 1903, as a town in 1907 and as the province's twelfth city on Sept. 2, 1980.

Melfort & District Chamber of Commerce: Box 2002, Melfort, SK, Canada S0E 1A0. **Phone:** (306) 752-4636.

MELFORT & DISTRICT MUSEUM is at 401 Melfort St. W. Historic buildings include a 1912 power house, reconstructed log farmhouse, general store and post office, barbershop, schoolhouse, blacksmith shop and real estate office. The museum also features farm machinery, equipment and tools used in the development of the local agricultural industry.

Tours: Guided tours are available. **Time:** Allow 1 hour minimum. **Hours:** Mon.-Fri. 9-noon and 1-5, mid-May to early Sept. Closed major holidays. **Cost:** $4; $3 (ages 12-17); $2 (ages 6-11); $12 (family). **Phone:** (306) 752-5870.

MELVILLE (E-5) pop. 4,517, elev. 555m/1,820'

Situated on the east-west main line of the Canadian National Railway and also on an important north-south line of that company, Melville is known as "The Rail Centre." It came to provincial prominence when it was selected as a major railway service center early in the 20th century. The railway is still the city's largest employer, and its facilities are essential in marketing agricultural products as well as potash from nearby Esterhazy.

Melville & District Chamber of Commerce: P.O. Box 429, Melville, SK, Canada S0A 2P0. **Phone:** (306) 728-4177.

MELVILLE HERITAGE MUSEUM is at 100 Heritage Dr. Formerly the Luther Academy, the restored 1913 building now houses this regional museum. Exhibits include artifacts from various churches and denominations; sports, recreation and railway exhibits; military memorabilia; and more than 100 original photographs depicting Melville's early 20th-century progress. The oldest artifact, a German pulpit Bible, dates to 1721. A chapel and library are here as well.

Tours: Guided tours are available. **Time:** Allow 1 hour minimum. **Hours:** Daily 10-4, mid-May to late Aug.; by appointment rest of year. **Cost:** $3; free (ages 0-12). **Phone:** (306) 728-2070.

MOOSE JAW (E-4) pop. 33,274, elev. 542m/1,778'
• Hotels p. 538 • Restaurants p. 539

Moose Jaw's unusual name is probably derived from the big bend in Moose Jaw Creek. The First Nations called this creek *moosichappishannissippi,* or "the creek that bends like a moose's jaw." Another popular theory is that an early traveler through the area fixed his cart wheel with a moose's jawbone found in the vicinity. Today's visitors are greeted by "Mac," a 9-metre-tall (30-ft.) statue said to be the world's largest moose.

During Prohibition in the United States Moose Jaw was the home of an industrious band of bootleggers and American gangsters, earning the town the nickname "Little Chicago of the Prairies." Moose Jaw is an important western Canadian industrial city, and hard spring wheat also is grown in the area. The Canadian Forces base just south of the city is home to one of Canada's busiest airports and headquarters of the Snowbirds, the Canadian armed forces aerobatic team.

Downtown's roaming ambassadors provide a wealth of information as well as brochures to visitors. The Murals of Moose Jaw, painted on several downtown buildings, are a collection of more than 50 scenes depicting the town's history. The Moose Jaw Trolley Company provides a tour of the murals and heritage buildings *(see attraction listing 538).* The Yvette Moore Gallery, downtown at 76 Fairford St. W., exhibits the work of local artist Yvette Moore, whose paintings also can be seen in Moose Jaw hotels; phone (306) 693-7600 or (888) 793-7600.

A historic landmark south of town is Hwy. 2, once part of the Powder River Trail used by freighters and ranchers to reach Denver before the advent of the railroad. About 42 kilometres (26 mi.) north on Hwy. 2 is Buffalo Pound Provincial Park *(see Recreation Areas Chart),* where 350 hectares (865 acres) are set aside as grazing land for a herd of buffaloes.

Wakamow Valley, in Moose Jaw, is a recreational development that includes Plaxton's Lake, North River Park, Kiwanis River Park, Kinsmen Wellesley Park, Connor Park, McCaig Gardens, Ecological Zone and the Devonian Trail, a pedestrian and bicycle trail system. Visitors can enjoy picnicking, camping, bird-watching, hiking, jogging and bicycling.

Moose Jaw Chamber of Commerce: 88 Saskatchewan St. E., Box 1359, Moose Jaw, SK, Canada S6H 4R3. **Phone:** (306) 692-6414.

Self-guiding tours: Brochures outlining a self-guiding tour of some of downtown Moose Jaw's most significant historic sites are available at the Moose Jaw Art Museum and National Exhibits in Crescent Park *(see attraction listing).*

CRESCENT PARK is at Fairford and Athabasca sts. An outdoor swimming pool, war memorial gardens and recreational facilities are contained on 11 hectares (27 acres). Free entertainment is presented Wednesday evenings July through August. The Moose Jaw Art Museum and National Exhibits, next to the public library, displays historical items of local, regional and national interest.

Hours: Museum open Tues.-Sun. noon-5. Closed Good Friday, Easter and Dec. 25. Outdoor pool open daily 1-4 and 7-8:30, June 1-Labour Day. **Cost:** Museum free. Admission to pool $5.90; $4.90 (ages 13-17); $3.30 (ages 3-12); $12.50 (family). **Phone:** (306) 692-4471, or (306) 694-4500 for the pool.

MOOSE JAW TROLLEY COMPANY tours depart from the Tourism Moose Jaw Visitor Centre at jct. Hwy. 1 and Thatcher Dr. E. Visitors are led on a guided tour of the city's quaint streets and can experience its rich history while riding on board a replicated electric streetcar that originally operated 1911-32. Ghost tours also are offered.

Time: Allow 1 hour minimum. **Hours:** Tours depart daily at 1, 2:15 and 3:30 (weather permitting), July-Aug. Schedule varies May-June, phone ahead to confirm. Ghost tours are given Fri.-Sat. at 9:45 and 11 p.m. **Cost:** $12; $10 (ages 65+ and students grades 9-12 with ID); $6 (students grades K-8); free (ages 0-4); $35 (family, two adults and four children). Ghost tour $15. **Phone:** (306) 693-8537 or (306) 693-8097.

SUKANEN SHIP, PIONEER VILLAGE AND MUSEUM is 13 km (8 mi.) s. on Hwy. 2. The large, unfinished ship was built by Tom Sukanen, a Finnish settler who had planned to sail the boat home to his native country by way of the South Saskatchewan River, Hudson Bay, Greenland and Iceland. A village preserves an old post office, blacksmith shop, school, church, railroad station, a general store and the Diefenbaker homestead as well as a collection of antique tractors, trucks and cars.

Hours: Mon.-Sat. 9-5, Sun. noon-6, mid-May to mid-Sept. **Cost:** $6; $5 (students with ID and ages 66+); $3 (ages 6-12). **Phone:** (306) 693-7315.

TUNNELS OF MOOSE JAW is at 18 N. Main St. Two themed 50-minute tours take visitors under the streets of Moose Jaw. Miss Fanny and Gus are the guides for the Chicago Connection tour, which explores gangster Al Capone's bootlegging operation and the tunnels he is said to have used to escape American authorities. The Passage to Fortune tour depicts the story of early Chinese immigrants who came to build the Canadian Pacific Railway and their footsteps through adversity and persecution to eventual success.

Hours: Guided tours are offered daily 10-7 (also Fri.-Sat. 7-8), July-Aug.; Mon.-Fri. 10-4:30, Sat. 10-5:30, Sun. noon-4:30, rest of year. Hours may vary; phone ahead to confirm schedule. Closed Christmas. **Cost:** Individual tour fare $14; $11 (ages 66+); $10.50 (ages 13-17); $7.50 (ages 5-12). Combination ticket $23; $19 (ages 66+); $18 (ages 13-17); $12 (ages 5-12). Reservations are recommended. **Phone:** (306) 693-5261.

SAVE **WESTERN DEVELOPMENT MUSEUM'S HISTORY OF TRANSPORTATION** is at 50 Diefenbaker Dr. Displays illustrate air, water, rail and land transportation. The museum also houses an observatory. The Snowbird Gallery contains aircraft and memorabilia from the Canadian armed forces aerobatic team. Trips aboard the Short Line, a miniature steam locomotive, are available on weekends.

Note: The miniature locomotive may not be operational; phone ahead for information. **Time:** Allow 1 hour minimum. **Hours:** Museum open Tues.-Sun. 9-5, Apr.-Dec.; Tues.-Sun. 9-5, rest of year. Train rides Sat.-Sun., Victoria Day-Labour Day (weather permitting). Closed Jan. 1, Christmas and day after Christmas. Phone ahead to confirm schedule. **Cost:** Museum $9; $8 (ages 65+); $6.25 (students with ID); $2.50 (ages 6-12); $20 (family). Train rides $2. **Phone:** (306) 693-5989. 🎟

GAMBLING ESTABLISHMENTS

• **Casino Moose Jaw** is at 21 Fairford St. E. **Hours:** Sun.-Thurs. 9 a.m.-2 a.m., Fri.-Sat. 9 a.m.-3 a.m. Closed Christmas. **Phone:** (306) 694-3888.

RECREATIONAL ACTIVITIES
Recreational Complex

• **Kinsmen Sportsplex** is at 855 McDonald St. W. **Hours:** Mon.-Fri. 3:30-5 and 7-9; Sat.-Sun. 1-4 and 7-9. Closed Jan. 1, Good Friday and Dec. 25. **Phone:** (306) 694-4483.

COMFORT INN (306)692-2100

♦♦♦ **Hotel** $120-$145 **Address:** 155 Thatcher Dr W S6J 1M1 **Location:** 0.8 mi (1.2 km) s on Hwy 2 from jct Trans-Canada Hwy 1, then just w. Located in a commercial area. **Facility:** 60 units. 3 stories, interior corridors. **Parking:** winter plug-ins. **Terms:** cancellation fee imposed. **Amenities:** high-speed Internet. **Activities:** limited exercise equipment. **Guest Services:** valet and coin laundry.

🍴 BIZ 📶 🖥 💳 / SOME UNITS FEE 🐕 🛗

HERITAGE INN MOOSE JAW (306)693-7550

♦♦ **Hotel** $127-$252 **Address:** 1590 Main St N S6J 1L3 **Location:** On Hwy 2, 0.9 mi (1.4 km) s of jct Trans-Canada Hwy 1. **Facility:** 103 units, some two bedrooms. 2 stories (no elevator), interior corridors. **Parking:** winter plug-ins. **Terms:** cancellation fee imposed. **Amenities:** Some: high-speed Internet. **Dining:** nightclub. **Pool(s):** heated indoor. **Activities:** whirlpool. **Guest Services:** valet laundry.

🍴 🍸 ♨ BIZ 📶 ✕ 💳 / SOME UNITS FEE 🐕 🖥 🛗

PRAIRIE OASIS MOTEL (306)692-4894

♦♦ **Extended Stay Motel** $89-$99 **Address:** 955 Thatcher Dr E S6H 4N9 **Location:** Just s of jct Trans-Canada Hwy 1. Next to Prairie Oasis Tourist Complex. **Facility:** 40 units, some efficiencies. 1 story, exterior corridors. **Parking:** winter plug-ins. **Terms:** check-in 4 pm. **Amenities:** high-speed Internet. **Pool(s):** heated indoor. **Activities:** whirlpool, waterslide. **Fee:** miniature golf. **Guest Services:** coin laundry. 🍴 ♨ 📶 🖥 💳 / SOME UNITS 🛗

SUPER 8-MOOSE JAW (306)692-8888

♦♦ **Hotel** $115-$135 **Address:** 1706 Main St N S6J 1L4 **Location:** On Hwy 2, 0.7 mi (1.1 km) s of jct Trans-Canada Hwy 1. **Facility:** 60 units. 3 stories, interior corridors. **Parking:** winter plug-ins. **Amenities:** high-speed Internet. **Guest Services:** valet and coin laundry.

ECO 🍴 📶 🖥 💳 / SOME UNITS FEE 🐕 🛗

TEMPLE GARDENS MINERAL SPA RESORT (306)694-5055

♦♦♦ **Hotel** $155-$435 **Address:** 24 Fairford St E S6H 0C7 **Location:** Just e of Main St (Hwy 2); center. Next to Crescent Park. **Facility:** Nicely furnished rooms are housed in the original building and a newer facility across the street, which is connected by an enclosed skywalk. 179 units. 5 stories, interior corridors. **Parking:** on-site (fee), winter plug-ins. **Terms:** check-in 4 pm, cancellation fee imposed. **Amenities:** Some: high-speed Internet. **Dining:** Harwood's, see separate listing. **Activities:** steamroom, rental bicycles, exercise room, spa. **Guest Services:** valet laundry.

ECO ♿ 🍴 ♨ BIZ 📶 ✕ 👤 🖥 💳

WHERE TO EAT

CORDOVA BISTRO   306/693-7100
◆◆ Italian. Casual Dining. $15-$25 **AAA Inspector Notes:** This traditional Italian restaurant features all the classic dishes which are well prepared with tasty sauces. Set in a series of small dining rooms, the smart décor features pretty bottles of fruits and vinegars, wine bottles and ceramic pots. Service is congenial and brisk. Open for lunch Wednesday through Friday. **Bar:** full bar. **Reservations:** suggested. **Address:** 361 Main St N S6H 0W2 **Location:** Just e on Fairford St; downtown. **Parking:** street only. (D)

HARWOOD'S   306/693-7778
◆◆ American. Casual Dining. $9-$38 **AAA Inspector Notes:** Known for its high-quality cuts of beef, the restaurant is a popular spot with locals. **Bar:** full bar. **Reservations:** suggested. **Address:** 24 Fairford St E S6H 0C7 **Location:** Just e of Main St (Hwy 2); center; in Temple Gardens Mineral Spa Resort. **Parking:** on-site (fee). (B) (L) (D)

HICKORY SMOKEHOUSE & GRILL   306/693-3905
◆◆ American. Casual Dining. $8-$26 **AAA Inspector Notes:** Just as the name implies, the juicy chicken and ribs at this grill are smoked in-house and served with a choice of sauces including their own chipotle sauce. Also on the menu are a host of other items including soups, salads, burgers, sandwiches and steak. The atmosphere is casual and diners have a choice of sitting at one of the plentiful banquette seats or at one of the scattered tables. **Bar:** full bar. **Reservations:** suggested. **Address:** 622 Main St N S6H 3K4 **Location:** On Hwy 2, 1.7 mi (2.8 km) s of jct Trans-Canada Hwy 1. **Parking:** street only.
(L) (D) CALL &M

HOUSTON PIZZA   306/693-3934
◆◆ American. Casual Dining. $9-$26 **AAA Inspector Notes:** A nice spot for couples or families, this restaurant presents a menu of steaks, spaghetti, lasagna, ribs, barbecue chicken, seafood, stir-fry and salads, as well as yummy pizza. Servers are prompt. **Bar:** full bar. **Reservations:** suggested. **Address:** 117 Main St N S6H 0V9 **Location:** Just s of High St; 2 mi (3.2 km) s of Trans-Canada Hwy 1. **Parking:** street only. (L) (D)

OVERSEAS RESTAURANT   306/692-2828
◆ Asian. Family Dining. $8-$15 **AAA Inspector Notes:** A simple decor can be found at this eatery along with a variety of classic Chinese, Thai and Malaysian dishes along its fairly extensive buffet. **Bar:** full bar. **Address:** 438 Main St N S6H 3K2 **Location:** On Hwy 2, 1.9 mi (3 km) s of jct Trans-Canada Hwy 1. **Parking:** on-site (fee).
(L) (D) CALL &M

MORSE (E-3) pop. 240

MORSE MUSEUM & CULTURAL CENTRE is at 410 McKenzie St. Housed in a brick school built in 1912, the exhibits focus on the town's development from the time of the early settlers to the 1970s. The displays include nine themed rooms, a Victorian-style parlor and an art gallery featuring works by local, regional and provincial artists. Tea is served at the end of the guided tour.

Time: Allow 1 hour minimum. **Hours:** Mon.-Sat. 9-5, May-July; Mon.-Fri. 9-5, Aug.-Oct. Closed major holidays. **Cost:** Donations. **Phone:** (306) 629-3230.

MUENSTER (D-4) pop. 422

ST. PETER'S ABBEY is 1 km (.6 mi.) e. off Muenster access rd. on Hwy. 5. A self-guiding walking tour of the abbey complex enables visitors to learn about monastic life. Brochures are available at Severin Hall. Sts. Peter and Paul Church, recreational facilities, a farm, gardens, an orchard, trails, print shop,

workshops, a cemetery and a greenhouse are points of interest. The tour includes St. Peter's College, where the first two years of university courses are offered. **Time:** Allow 1 hour minimum. **Hours:** Daily 8-dusk. **Cost:** Free. **Phone:** (306) 682-1777.

ST. PETER'S CATHEDRAL is 1 km (.6 mi.) n. of Hwy. 5 on the Muenster access rd. The cathedral's walls and ceiling are lined with paintings by Berthold von Imhoff, who created the 80 life-size figures as a gift to the abbot of St. Peter's Abbey. **Time:** Allow 30 minutes minimum. **Hours:** Daily 9-9, May-Oct.; by appointment rest of year. **Cost:** Free. **Phone:** (306) 682-1777 or (306) 682-1789.

NIPAWIN (C-4) pop. 4,265

The Nipawin Hydroelectric Station, northwest of town, uses water impounded in Codette Lake by the Francois-Finlay Dam to generate 1.1 billion kilowatt hours of electricity annually. Guided tours of the facility are conducted by the chamber of commerce on Fridays, June through August; phone ahead to confirm tour availability. SaskPower also conducts tours, but requires 2 weeks' advance notice; phone (306) 862-3148.

Nipawin & District Chamber of Commerce: Box 177, Nipawin, SK, Canada S0E 1E0. **Phone:** (306) 862-5252.

LIVING FORESTRY MUSEUM is just w. on Hwy. 35N. The museum contains rotating exhibits that describe the history of the area. Several historic buildings have been relocated to the vicinity, including a sawmill, schoolhouse, shingle mill, church and the 1924 Hornseth House. Demonstrations of the saw and shingle mills and a steam engine are provided during the summer months. **Time:** Allow 1 hour minimum. **Hours:** Daily 9:30-4:30, May-Aug. **Cost:** $3; free (ages 0-12). **Phone:** (306) 862-9299.

NOKOMIS (D-4) pop. 397

First named Blakemore and then Blaikie by railroad officials, Nokomis began as the junction of the Old Grand Trunk Railway and the Canadian Provincial Railway. Arriving from England, Mrs. Thomas Halstead, the town's postmistress, was intrigued by the West and the romantic domain of the First Nations and chose the name Nokomis, from Henry Wadsworth Longfellow's poem "Hiawatha," for the young town.

NOKOMIS AND DISTRICT MUSEUM is at 3rd Ave. and Queen St. Housed in the former railway station, the museum features re-creations of a post office, schoolhouse, dentist's office, hospital room with equipment, hardware store, a garage with a 1930 Chevrolet and a church. Photographs, vintage clothing and antiques are displayed. Junction City 1907, behind the museum, is a replica of a small town. **Time:** Allow 1 hour minimum. **Hours:** Daily 10-5, June 1-Labour Day. **Cost:** $2; $5 (family). **Phone:** (306) 528-2979.

NORTH BATTLEFORD (C-2) pop. 13,888

On the bank of the North Saskatchewan River, North Battleford is a gateway to the province's northwest parkland area. Agriculture is the backbone of the area's economy, with farms producing cereal grains, oil seeds and hay crops as well as cattle, hogs, poultry and bison. Forestry, manufacturing and heavy crude oil development also are important industries.

The Battlefords Provincial Park *(see Recreation Areas Chart)* is approximately 42 kilometres (26 mi.) north off Hwy. 4 and offers fishing, water skiing, boating and hiking trails. Cross-country skiing and ice fishing are popular winter activities at the park.

Battlefords Chamber of Commerce: Hwys. 16 and 40E, P.O. Box 1000, North Battleford, SK, Canada S9A 3E6. **Phone:** (306) 445-6226.

ALLEN SAPP GALLERY is at 1 Railway Ave. This award-winning public gallery features powerful and sensitive images of the Northern Plains Cree by renowned Cree artist Allen Sapp. Sapp's works capture the life and history of the Cree at the turn of the 20th century. Other exhibits include large-screen videos and historical artifacts.

Hours: Daily 11-5, June-Sept.; Wed.-Sun. 1-5, rest of year. **Cost:** Donations. **Phone:** (306) 445-1760.

THE CHAPEL GALLERY is at 891 99th St., just e. of S. Railway Ave., at the s. end of the Don Ross Centre. Formerly a chapel, the building was converted to an art gallery in 1986. The collection includes local, regional and provincial works; exhibits change regularly. **Tours:** Guided tours are available. **Time:** Allow 30 minutes minimum. **Hours:** Daily 1-5, June-Aug.; Wed.-Sun. 1-5, rest of year. Closed Jan. 1 and Christmas. **Cost:** Donations. **Phone:** (306) 445-1757.

WESTERN DEVELOPMENT MUSEUM'S HERITAGE FARM AND VILLAGE is at jct. hwys. 16 and 40. The story of agriculture and pioneer life is the focus of the museum, which preserves a 1920s pioneer village and features the exhibit Winning the Prairie Gamble. A working farm offers demonstrations of early agricultural equipment and techniques.

Time: Allow 2 hours minimum. **Hours:** Daily 9-5, Apr.-Dec.; Tues.-Sun. 9-5, rest of year. Closed provincial holidays Oct.-May. **Cost:** (good for 2 consecutive days) $8.50; $7.50 (ages 65+); $5.75 (students with ID); $2 (ages 6-12); $18.50 (family). **Phone:** (306) 445-8033.

GAMBLING ESTABLISHMENTS

- **Gold Eagle Casino** is at 11902 Railway Ave. E. **Hours:** Thurs.-Sat. 9 a.m.-4 a.m., Sun.-Wed. 9 a.m.-3 a.m. Closed Christmas Eve and Christmas. **Phone:** (306) 446-3833 or (877) 446-3833.

GOLD EAGLE LODGE (306)446-8877

Hotel
$135-$285

Address: 12004 Railway Ave E S9A 3W3 **Location:** Jct Hwy 46 and 16 (Yellowhead Hwy), just w. **Facility:** 112 units, some kitchens. 4 stories, interior corridors. **Parking:** winter plug-ins. **Terms:** check-in 4 pm, 3 day cancellation notice. **Amenities:** high-speed Internet. **Pool(s):** heated indoor. **Activities:** sauna, whirlpools, steamroom, exercise room. **Guest Services:** coin laundry. **Free Special Amenities: continental breakfast and use of on-premises laundry facilities.**

SUPER 8 (306)446-8888

Hotel $95-$125 **Address:** 1006 Hwy 16 Bypass S9A 3W2 **Location:** 0.3 mi (0.5 km) nw of jct Hwy 16 (Yellowhead Hwy). **Facility:** 72 units. 2-3 stories, interior corridors. **Parking:** winter plug-ins. **Terms:** check-in 4 pm, cancellation fee imposed. **Amenities:** high-speed Internet. **Guest Services:** valet laundry.

TROPICAL INN 306/446-4700

Hotel. Rates not provided. **Address:** 1001 Hwy 16 Bypass S9A 3W2 **Location:** Corner of Battleford Rd. **Facility:** 119 units, some two bedrooms. 2 stories, interior corridors. **Parking:** winter plug-ins. **Terms:** check-in 4 pm. **Amenities:** video games (fee). Some: high-speed Internet. **Pool(s):** heated indoor. **Activities:** sauna, whirlpool, waterslide. **Guest Services:** valet laundry.

> **WHERE TO EAT**

KIHIW RESTAURANT 306/486-3833

American. Family Dining. $9-$21 **AAA Inspector Notes:** Separated from the bustle of the busy casino, this open dining room features some lovely pieces of Aboriginal art dominated by a large bronze eagle sculpture and a waterfall. The familiar comfort food menu includes appetizers, soups, salads, sandwiches and such entrées as lasagna, fish and chips, roast chicken, steak, meatloaf and a turkey dinner. **Bar:** full bar. **Address:** 11902 Railway Ave S9A 3K7 **Location:** Jct Hwy 46 and 16 (Yellowhead Hwy), just w; in Gold Eagle Casino.

PORTA BELLA 306/937-3785

American. Casual Dining. $10-$28 **AAA Inspector Notes:** This casual restaurant is popular among locals and offers loads of choices from the huge menu. Choose from salads, mix and match pasta, steak, ribs, rainbow trout and tuna steak as well as more casual fare including burgers, wraps and quesadillas. **Bar:** full bar. **Address:** 2491 99th St S9A 3W8 **Location:** Jct Hwy 4 (100th St) and Territorial Dr, 0.5 mi (0.8 km) n, just w on Sandpiper Rd, then just s.

OUTLOOK (D-3) pop. 2,204

Agriculture has traditionally sustained Outlook, where such crops as corn, potatoes, vegetables and sunflowers are grown. The town came upon its name in an unusual way. As two Canadian Pacific Railway officials stood quietly on the edge of an expansive valley, intensely watching the raging South Saskatchewan River gushing below them, the silence was broken when one uttered the words, "What a wonderful outlook!"

Outlook and District Regional Park, located along the South Saskatchewan River on the west edge of town, covers 40 hectares (100 acres) and features a golf course, swimming pool, campgrounds and hiking trails. Nature enthusiasts will especially appreciate the many species of birds as well as the venerable elm trees. Phone (306) 867-8846.

A large salt and pepper shaker collection is the highlight of the Outlook & District Heritage Museum, in the center of town at 100 Railway Ave. E. Skytrail, just northwest of the center of town following signs, is one of Canada's longest pedestrian bridges, spanning the South Saskatchewan River 46 metres (150 ft.) above the water and running for a distance of 914 metres (3,000 ft.). Side rails and a safe walking surface allow users to focus their attention on the views.

The South Saskatchewan River Project, on the South Saskatchewan and Qu'Appelle rivers, consists of two dams. Gardiner Dam, midway between Elbow and Outlook, is 5 kilometres (3 mi.) long, 64 metres (210 ft.) high and 1,615 metres (5,300 ft.) wide at its base. The impounded water forms Lake Diefenbaker, about 225 kilometres (140 mi.) long, up to 5 kilometres (3 mi.) wide and 56 metres (184 ft.) deep. The second, smaller structure is Qu'Appelle Dam. A visitor center at Gardiner Dam is open Victoria Day weekend-Labour Day; phone (306) 857-5500.

Town of Outlook: 400 Saskatchewan Ave., Box 518, Outlook, SK, Canada S0L 2N0. **Phone:** (306) 867-8663.

PONTEIX (F-3) pop. 605

NOTUKEU HERITAGE MUSEUM is at 110 Railway Ave. An extensive collection of First Nations artifacts, including arrowheads, is displayed. Guided tours are available in French or English. **Time:** Allow 30 minutes minimum. **Hours:** Mon.-Fri. 9-noon and 1-5, Sat.-Sun. by appointment. Closed major holidays. **Cost:** $5 (per couple); $3 (ages 13+); $2 (ages 8-12); $10 (family). **Phone:** (306) 625-3340.

PRINCE ALBERT (C-3) pop. 35,129
• Hotels p. 542 • Restaurants p. 542

The gateway to Saskatchewan's north country, Prince Albert is one of the province's oldest communities. Trapper Peter Pond built a trading post on the north side of the North Saskatchewan River in 1776. Credited with founding the town, the Rev. James Nisbet settled on the south shore in 1866.

The log Presbyterian church that Nisbet built that year is now in Kinsmen Park. A blockhouse next to the church dates from the Northwest Rebellion/Métis Resistance of 1885. The Prince Albert Historical Museum (see attraction listing) occupies the site of the church built by Nisbet.

Prince Albert Tourism & Convention Bureau: 3700 2nd Ave. W., Prince Albert, SK, Canada S6W 1A2. **Phone:** (306) 953-4386.

ART GALLERY OF PRINCE ALBERT is at 142 12th St. W., at jct. Hwy. 2N. The spacious gallery area displays paintings and other works, with a focus on contemporary art. Temporary exhibitions also are presented. **Time:** Allow 30 minutes

minimum. **Hours:** Mon.-Fri. 10-6; Sat.-Sun. noon-5. Closed major holidays. **Cost:** Free. **Phone:** (306) 763-7080.

DIEFENBAKER HOUSE MUSEUM is at 246 19th St. W. The 1947-75 home of the Right Honourable John G. Diefenbaker contains furniture and other possessions of the prime minister of Canada 1957-63. **Time:** Allow 30 minutes minimum. **Hours:** Daily 9-5, Victoria Day-Aug. 31. **Cost:** Donations. **Phone:** (306) 953-4863.

EVOLUTION OF EDUCATION MUSEUM is at the corner of Marquis Rd. and Hwy. 2 at 3700 2nd Ave. W. The one-room, 1920 schoolhouse was designed to provide maximum warmth and light, with all large windows on the building's east side and desks facing south. Exhibits relate to area education and include pencil boxes, Dick and Jane readers and chalk clamps once used to draw lines on a blackboard.

An interpreter is available to answer questions; a visitor information center also is in the building. **Time:** Allow 30 minutes minimum. **Hours:** Daily 9-5, Victoria Day weekend-Aug. 31; by appointment rest of year. **Cost:** Free. **Phone:** (306) 763-3506.

LITTLE RED RIVER PARK is at the confluence of the North Saskatchewan and Little Red rivers on Hwy. 55. A scenic drive follows the north bank of the North Saskatchewan River. Winter sports are available. Swimming in the river is not recommended. **Cost:** Free.

PRINCE ALBERT HISTORICAL MUSEUM is at 10 River St. E. at Central Ave. The museum is housed in an old fire hall that overlooks the North Saskatchewan River. Featured is the first fire engine pumper used in the territory. Other displays include First Nations, fur trade and pioneer artifacts as well as a table and benches carved by the Rev. James Nisbet. A tearoom provides a view of the river. **Time:** Allow 1 hour minimum. **Hours:** Daily 9-5, Victoria Day-Aug. 31. **Cost:** $2; $1 (ages 6-12). **Phone:** (306) 764-2992.

ROTARY MUSEUM OF POLICE AND CORRECTIONS is at the corner of Marquis Rd. and Hwy. 2 at 3700 2nd Ave. W. Displays pertain to the Royal Canadian Mounted Police, local police, provincial police and corrections services. Exhibits include corporal punishment items, police uniforms and weapons. The museum is in a landscaped park with a visitor center; an interpreter is available to answer questions. **Time:** Allow 30 minutes minimum. **Hours:** Daily 9-5, Victoria Day weekend-Aug. 31; by appointment rest of year. **Cost:** Free. **Phone:** (306) 922-3313.

GAMBLING ESTABLISHMENTS

• **Northern Lights Casino** is at 44 Marquis Rd. **Hours:** Daily 9 a.m.-4 a.m. Closed Christmas. **Phone:** (306) 764-4777.

BEST WESTERN MARQUIS INN & SUITES

(306)922-9595

Hotel
$115

 AAA Benefit: Members save up to 20%, plus 10% bonus points with Best Western Rewards®.

Address: 602 36th St E S6V 7P2 **Location:** Jct Hwy 3 (6th Ave E) and Marquis Rd. **Facility:** 77 units. 2 stories, interior corridors. **Parking:** winter plug-ins. **Terms:** check-in 4 pm. **Amenities:** high-speed Internet, safes. **Activities:** exercise room. **Guest Services:** valet laundry. **Free Special Amenities:** full breakfast and high-speed Internet.

COMFORT INN

(306)763-4466

 Hotel $144-$188 **Address:** 3863 2nd Ave W S6W 1A1 **Location:** 1.6 mi (2.6 km) s on Hwy 2. **Facility:** 62 units. 2 stories (no elevator), interior corridors. **Parking:** winter plug-ins. **Terms:** cancellation fee imposed. **Guest Services:** valet laundry.

DAYS INN PRINCE ALBERT

(306)763-8988

 Hotel $120-$130 **Address:** 150 34th St W S6V 8E9 **Location:** On Hwy 2; jct Marquis Rd. Located in a commercial area. **Facility:** 80 units. 4 stories, interior corridors. **Parking:** winter plug-ins. **Amenities:** high-speed Internet. **Pool(s):** heated indoor. **Activities:** whirlpool, waterslide, exercise room. **Guest Services:** valet and coin laundry.

HOLIDAY INN EXPRESS HOTEL & SUITES

306/922-6988

Hotel. Rates not provided. **Address:** 3580 2nd Ave W S6V 5G2 **Location:** Jct Hwy 2 and Marquis Dr, just n. **Facility:** 75 units. 4 stories, interior corridors. **Parking:** winter plug-ins. **Amenities:** high-speed Internet. **Pool(s):** heated indoor. **Activities:** whirlpool, exercise room. **Guest Services:** valet and coin laundry.

RAMADA PRINCE ALBERT

(306)922-1333

Hotel
$120-$150

Address: 3245 2nd Ave W S6V 5G1 **Location:** 1.2 mi (2 km) s on Hwy 2. **Facility:** 66 units. 3 stories, interior corridors. **Parking:** winter plug-ins. **Terms:** check-in 4 pm, cancellation fee imposed. **Amenities:** Some: high-speed Internet, safes. **Dining:** Soprano's, see separate listing. **Activities:** exercise room. **Guest Services:** valet laundry. **Free Special Amenities:** continental breakfast and newspaper.

SUPER 8

(306)953-0088

 Hotel $124-$129 **Address:** 4444 2nd Ave W S6V 5R7 **Location:** 1.7 mi (2.7 km) s on Hwy 2. **Facility:** 58 units. 3 stories, interior corridors. **Parking:** winter plug-ins. **Activities:** exercise room. **Guest Services:** valet and coin laundry.

TRAVELODGE PRINCE ALBERT

(306)764-6441

 Hotel $116-$140 **Address:** 3551 2nd Ave W S6V 5G1 **Location:** 1.4 mi (2.2 km) s on Hwy 2. **Facility:** 80 units. 2 stories (no elevator), interior corridors. **Parking:** winter plug-ins. **Amenities:** high-speed Internet. **Activities:** exercise room. **Guest Services:** valet laundry.

WHERE TO EAT

AMY'S ON SECOND

306/763-1515

American. Casual Dining. $10-$33 AAA Inspector Notes: Nestled into a warm, intimate setting to enjoy homemade cuisine and regional specialties prepared using fresh ingredients. Try the wild rice soup, rack of lamb, Saskatchewan pickerel and cheesecake. **Bar:** full bar. **Reservations:** suggested. **Address:** 2990 2nd Ave W S6V 7E9 **Location:** 0.9 mi (1.4 km) s on Hwy 2.

SHANANIGAN'S COFFEE & DESSERT BAR

306/764-2647

American Coffee/Tea Desserts. Quick Serve. $9-$18 AAA Inspector Notes: Located in an old house filled with a variety of local art for sale, this popular spot is best known for its superb selection of cakes, pies, pastries, squares, cookies and other desserts. But they also offer daily soups, sandwiches, wraps, pot pies, stir-fry, pasta and other entrées. A fine selection of teas and coffee are available. In the summer months guests can enjoy their meal on the outside patio. **Bar:** full bar. **Address:** 2144 6th Ave W S6V 5K6 **Location:** Hwy 2, 0.4 mi (0.6 km) w on 22nd St W; in residential area. **Parking:** street only.

SMITTY'S

306/764-5627

American. Family Dining. $10-$20 AAA Inspector Notes: The family-oriented restaurant satisfies patrons with its ever-popular all-day breakfast items, as well as tasty and wholesome soups and salads at lunchtime. A relaxed mood characterizes the dining space. **Bar:** full bar. **Address:** 2995 2nd Ave W, #20 S6V 5V5 **Location:** Hwy 2; in South Hill Mall.

SOPRANO'S

306/922-1333

American. Casual Dining. $11-$28 AAA Inspector Notes: One of the finer dining spots in the city, this small striking room offers a traditional AAA Angus beef steak menu but also includes a variety or entrées including pickerel, halibut, salmon, chicken, lamb and pork. The lunch menu is scaled back a bit and includes such items as shepherd's pie, stir-fry and a soup and sandwich bar. Service is easy going and practical. Closed for lunch on Saturday and Sunday. **Bar:** full bar. **Reservations:** suggested. **Address:** 3245 2nd Ave W S6V 5G1 **Location:** 1.2 mi (2 km) s on Hwy 2; in Ramada Prince Albert.

SPICY PEPPERCORN

306/763-7755

Chinese. Casual Dining. $8-$16 AAA Inspector Notes: This simply decorated tiny spot dishes up a good variety of tasty Chinese stir-fries as well as soups, ribs, sizzling plates, hot pots and noodle dishes. Also on the menu are some Vietnamese items like spring rolls, curry, satays and lemongrass chicken with rice or vermicelli. **Address:** 3590 6th Ave E S6V 7S5 **Location:** Jct Hwy 3 (6th Ave E) and Marquis Rd, just n.

VENICE HOUSE

306/764-6555

Greek. Family Dining. $8-$50 AAA Inspector Notes: A casual, family-dining experience awaits you at the restaurant. The menu offers steak, pizza, spaghetti and seafood dishes, but the house specialty is Greek-style ribs. The very relaxed atmosphere is quite comfortable and appealing. A lighter senior menu is offered. **Bar:** full bar. **Address:** 1498 Central Ave S6V 4W5 **Location:** Jct 15th St and Central Ave. **Parking:** on-site and street.

ZORBA'S FAMILY RESTAURANT

306/764-2700

International. Family Dining. $7-$36 AAA Inspector Notes: This popular spot offers up a little bit of all your classic favorites from Italian pasta and entrées, to Greek souvlaki and mezedaki to steaks, seafood, burgers, fish and chips and pizza. Service is efficient and friendly. **Bar:** full bar. **Address:** 1401 2nd Ave W S6V 5B3 **Location:** Jct Hwy 2 and 302 (15th St W).

▼ PRINCE ALBERT NATIONAL PARK (B-3)

Elevations in the park range from 488 metres (1,600 ft.) on the western side of the park to 724 metres (2,375 ft.) on the southern side of the park. Refer to CAA/AAA maps for additional elevation information.

The main entrance to Prince Albert National Park is 81 kilometres (50 mi.) north of the city of Prince Albert via hwys. 2 and 264.

The park covers 3,875 square kilometres (1,496 sq. mi.) of wilderness in central Saskatchewan. Its lakes, ponds, streams, bogs and rolling hills are a legacy of the glacial epoch. Notable are Sandy, Waskesiu, Kingsmere, Namekus, Crean and the Hanging Heart lakes. There also are several hundred smaller lakes and ponds and many sand beaches.

Heavy growths of conifers and several species of hardwoods surround the lakes, along with numerous shrubs and wildflowers. Fall foliage is especially colorful. Such wild animals as elk, deer, moose and bears are plentiful. A herd of bison roams the southwest corner of the park.

Early morning and evening provide the best chances of seeing wildlife along park roads, especially the Narrows and Kingsmere roads along Waskesiu Lake. Although some animals may seem tame, they are wild and should be observed only from a safe distance.

The park also preserves the legacy of Grey Owl. Born as Archibald Stansfeld Belaney, this controversial Englishman arrived in Canada in 1905. Adopted by the Ojibwa First Nations and later married into the tribe, Grey Owl turned his love of nature to the re-establishment of the region's beaver population, which had been decimated by hunters and trappers. For 7 years he lived at Beaver Lodge on Ajawaan Lake, where he continued his restoration and conservation efforts.

General Information and Activities

Although the park is open throughout the year, complete facilities are provided Victoria Day-Labour Day only. Information is available from the information bureau in the Waskesiu Lake Visitor Services Centre, 8 kilometres (5 mi.) from the park's main gate on Hwy. 264.

Roads traverse the park and lead to Waskesiu, Namekus, Sandy and the Hanging Heart lakes and to the Kingsmere River. Although no roads lead directly to Kingsmere and Crean lakes, access is possible by boat. A light railway with handcars assists in portaging around the unnavigable stretch of the Kingsmere River.

There are more than 100 kilometres (60 mi.) of hiking trails traversing the park. Some are suitable for day walks, while others require an overnight stop. Pamphlets outlining self-guiding tours are available for the Mud Creek and Boundary Bog nature trails. From the boat dock on the north shore of

Kingsmere Lake a 3-kilometre (1.9-mi.) trail leads to the home and grave of Grey Owl.

Park facilities include boat launching and berthing areas at the Hanging Heart Lakes, the Narrows and the main marina on Waskesiu Lake. Boats, canoes and outboard motors can be rented at all three marinas; paddle-wheeler tours are offered daily in summer. There are bicycle rentals, tennis and volleyball courts and bowling greens at the Waskesiu Lake Visitor Services Centre.

Waskesiu Lake's 18-hole golf course ranks among the finest in Canada. A 150-kilometre (93-mi.) network of groomed cross-country ski trails is open in winter. Snowshoeing and ice fishing also are permitted. Fishing licenses are required and can be obtained at the park information center, park entrances and campground offices.

Park naturalists offer a free summer interpretive program that includes car caravans on park roadways and special daily events. Interpretive programs are regularly presented at the outdoor theaters at the Narrows and Beaver Glen campgrounds.

At the Waskesiu Lake Visitor Services Centre is the Park Nature Centre, which has natural history exhibits, a bookstore and a theater; the nature center is open in July and August. *See Recreation Areas Chart.*

ADMISSION to the park is $7.80 (per day); $6.80 (ages 66+); $3.90 (ages 6-16); $19.60 (per day per group of up to seven adults).

PETS (dogs and cats) are permitted in the park as long as they are on leashes.

ADDRESS inquiries to the Superintendent, Prince Albert National Park, P.O. Box 100, Waskesiu Lake, SK, Canada S0J 2Y0; phone (306) 663-4522.

REGINA (E-4) pop. 193,100, elev. 578m/1,896'
• Hotels p. 549 • Restaurants p. 550
• Hotels & Restaurants map & index p. 547

First Nations people once used the banks of Wascana Creek for drying buffalo meat and cleaning and stretching the hides. Thus the area became known as *Oscana*, a Cree word meaning "pile of bones." In 1882 the Canadian Pacific Railway completed its track across the plains, and the settlement of Pile-O-Bones sprang up at the rail terminal on Wascana Creek.

The seat of government of the Northwest Territories and the headquarters of the North West Mounted Police were established the same year. A few years later Princess Louise, the wife of Canada's governor-general, renamed the city Regina (Latin for queen) to honor her mother, Queen Victoria. In 1905 Saskatchewan became a province, with Regina as its capital.

In the heart of downtown is City Centre, the site of such buildings as the municipal government offices and the public library. The Prairie History Room, which documents local history, and the

(See map & index p. 547.)

Dunlop Art Gallery, which displays works by regional artists, are both housed in the library. A glockenspiel chimes at the corner of 12th Avenue and Scarth Street in tribute to the city's ethnic vitality.

The Globe Theatre in the old City Hall is the home of Regina's professional acting company. Another restored building is Union Station, a transportation hub in the early years of rail travel that is now occupied by Casino Regina. Guided historical tours explore parts of a tunnel system that once stretched beneath downtown streets and also offer a behind-the-scenes look at casino operations; under 19 are not permitted. For ticket information phone (800) 555-3189.

At the Regina Floral Conservatory, 1450B 4th Ave., seasonal floral displays blend with a waterfall and luxuriant foliage in a small greenhouse; phone (306) 781-4769.

Following Wascana Creek for about 8 kilometres (5 mi.) is the Devonian Pathway, a paved bicycle trail that passes through six city parks and is used for jogging and walking as well as other activities; in winter it is groomed and lighted for cross-country skiing. The Condie Nature Refuge, just north of the city on Hwy. 11, offers nature trails that afford views of the refuge's grassland and marsh animals. For spectators the No. 1 sport is summer football, played by the Canadian Football League's Saskatchewan Roughriders at Mosaic Stadium at Taylor Field.

Regina Convention and Visitors Bureau: 1925 Rose St., Regina, SK, Canada S4P 3H1. **Phone:** (306) 789-5099 or (800) 661-5099.

Shopping areas: Regina's major shopping mall is Cornwall Centre, 2101 11th Ave. It has 87 stores, including The Bay and Sears. The specialty shops and eateries of Scarth Street Mall, downtown between 11th and 12th avenues, line a pedestrian-only street. The Cathedral Village shopping district, another downtown cluster of shops, is centered around 13th Avenue from Albert to Argyle streets and from Saskatchewan Drive to College Avenue.

GOVERNMENT HOUSE MUSEUM AND HERITAGE PROPERTY is at 4607 Dewdney Ave. This Italianate-style mansion was the home of the lieutenant governors of the Northwest Territories 1891-1905 and the lieutenant governors of Saskatchewan 1905-45. From 1945 to the mid-1970s the house served as a rest home for World War II veterans and as an adult education center.

Flanked by 2.5 hectares (6 acres) of gardens and orchards, the official residence has been restored to its Victorian elegance. Docents dressed in period conduct guided tours of the house. An interpretive center has hands-on exhibits and depicts the history of the province.

Time: Allow 1 hour minimum. **Hours:** Daily 9-5, May 14-Sept. 3; Tues.-Sun. 9-4, in winter. Closed Good Friday and Dec. 25. **Cost:** Free. **Phone:** (306) 787-5773.

HOLY ROSARY CATHEDRAL is at 3125 13th Ave., just w. of jct. Cameron St. This Cruciform/Romanesque structure, built in 1912, features 43 stained-glass windows installed in 1951 by French artisan Andre Rault, who designed windows for more than 50 other Canadian churches. Their artistry is best appreciated on a sunny day. A Casavant pipe organ, known for its exceptional sound quality, plays during Sunday services.

Guided tours are available; reservations are required 2 weeks in advance. **Time:** Allow 30 minutes minimum. **Hours:** Tues.-Fri. 9-1. The cathedral is kept locked for security purposes. Phone ahead to confirm schedule. **Cost:** Donations. **Phone:** (306) 565-0909.

REGINA PLAINS MUSEUM, on the second floor at 1835 Scarth St., features Saskatchewan artist Jacqueline Berting's sculpture "The Glass Wheatfield," consisting of 14,000 waist-high stalks of wheat made of hand-crafted glass. Also on display is a mural by aboriginal artist Sherry Farrell Racette. Rotating exhibitions focus on the city's history. **Hours:** Tues.-Fri. 10-4; Mon. 1-4. **Cost:** Donations. **Phone:** (306) 780-9435.

RCMP HERITAGE CENTRE is on Dewdney Ave. at the entrance to the RCMP Academy, "Depot" Division. The center tells the story of the Royal Canadian Mounted Police (RCMP), created by an act of Parliament in 1873 to maintain law and order on the Canadian frontier and pave the way for westward settlement. Stretching the length of the main exhibition hall, the sculptural procession "March of the Mounties" anchors the core exhibit areas; graphics trace Canada's geography from west to east and depict the historical evolution of the RCMP from its inception to the present day.

Interactive educational exhibits include Maintaining Law and Order in the West, which chronicles the force's late 19th-century efforts to suppress the whiskey trade, establish amicable relations with Native tribes and ensure the safety of settlers and rail workers; Serving All of Canada, an overview of the RCMP's 20th-century evolution; and Cracking the Case, a hands-on look at the high-tech side of contemporary policing. The 27-minute multimedia presentation "Tour of Duty" is shown in the center's SGI CANADA Theatre.

Time: Allow 2 hours minimum. **Hours:** Mon.-Fri. 9-5, Sat.-Sun. noon-5, day after Victoria Day-Labour Day; Mon.-Fri. 9-6, rest of year. A colorful Sergeant Major's Parade is usually held Mon., Wed. and Fri. at 12:45 p.m. (except on national holidays). Sunset Retreat Ceremonies are held Tues. at 6:30 p.m., July 1 to mid-Aug. Closed Jan. 1, Good Friday and Christmas. **Cost:** $12; $10 (ages 13-17 and 65+); $6 (ages 6-12); $35 (family, two adults and up to five children). **Phone:** (306) 522-7333 or (866) 567-7267. *(See ad p. 545.)*

ST. PAUL'S CATHEDRAL is at 1861 McIntyre St. This Gothic Revival-style church was said to be the oldest in Regina; its cornerstone was laid in 1894. A columbarium (housing the ashes of the deceased)

(See map & index p. 547.)

and museum are located under the church and are open by appointment; the museum houses books and artifacts dating to the 1600s. **Tours:** Guided tours are available. **Time:** Allow 30 minutes minimum. **Hours:** Mon.-Fri. 9-4. **Cost:** Donations. Reservations are required for guided tours. **Phone:** (306) 522-6439.

SASKATCHEWAN SPORTS HALL OF FAME is at 2205 Victoria Ave. Photographs, trophies, records and other memorabilia represent noted athletes and teams from Saskatchewan. **Hours:** Mon.-Fri. 9-5, Sat.-Sun. 1-5, Victoria Day weekend -Labour Day weekend; Mon.-Fri. 9-5, rest of year. Closed major holidays. **Cost:** Free. **Phone:** (306) 780-9232.

WASCANA CENTRE surrounds Wascana Lake. The 930-hectare (2,300-acre) park is the center of recreational and cultural activity in Regina and includes the Conexus Centre of the Arts, a performing arts venue. Wascana Place is both a departure point for sightseeing tours and a reservation office for special events. Ferry boat rides to the Willow Island picnic area are available. Wascana Waterfowl Park and Speakers' Corner also are in the area.

Hours: Wascana Place Mon.-Fri. 8-4:30. **Phone:** (306) 522-3661 daily 5-9 p.m. for reservation information.

Legislative Building (Capitol) is off Albert St. in Wascana Centre. Surrounded by 67 hectares (165 acres) of landscaped grounds, the imposing landmark is the seat of provincial government. Completed in 1912, the building reflects the architecture of the English Renaissance and Louis XIV of France.

The building houses several art galleries, including the Cumberland Gallery, a showcase for works of the Native Heritage Foundation of Canada. More than 34 different types of marble adorn the interior. On the east side of the building is Trafalgar Fountain, which was in London's Trafalgar Square 1845-1939.

Guided tours of the building are offered. Tours in French are available. **Time:** Allow 30 minutes minimum. **Hours:** Daily 8 a.m.-8:30 p.m., Victoria Day-Labour Day; 8-4:30, rest of year. Guided tours are given daily on the half-hour, Victoria Day-Labour Day; on the hour, rest of year. Closed Jan. 1, Good Friday and Dec. 25. **Cost:** Free. **Phone:** (306) 787-5358.

MacKenzie Art Gallery is in the T.C. Douglas Building at the s.w. corner of Wascana Centre at Albert St. and 23rd Ave. A major exhibition center for Saskatchewan, it contains permanent and changing exhibits of Canadian and international art. **Tours:** Guided tours are available. **Time:** Allow 1 hour minimum. **Hours:** Mon.- Fri. 10-5:30 (also Fri. 5:30-9 p.m.), Sat.-Sun. and holidays noon-5:30. **Cost:** Donations. **Phone:** (306) 584-4250.

Royal Saskatchewan Museum is at College Ave. and Albert St. in Wascana Centre. The Earth Sciences Gallery focuses on the geological and paleontological evolution of Saskatchewan and includes Canada's only resident robotic dinosaur. The Paleo Pit features hands-on exhibits. The First Nations Gallery portrays the culture and heritage of the province's aboriginal population through artwork and artifacts.

The Life Sciences Gallery explores Saskatchewan's natural history and current environmental issues. Exhibits depict life in a beaver pond, a Costa Rican rain forest and human actions that are disturbing the global ecosystem. **Time:** Allow 1 hour

▼ See AAA listing p. 544 ▼

The tradition lives here.

RCMPHERITAGECENTRE.COM

(See map & index p. 547.)

minimum. **Hours:** Daily 9:30-5. Closed Christmas. **Cost:** Donations. **Phone:** (306) 787-2815.

SAVE **Saskatchewan Science Centre** is on Winnipeg St. at Wascana Dr. in Wascana Centre. The Powerhouse of Discovery houses more than 100 permanent hands-on science exhibits and features live stage shows and demonstrations. Visitors who want to test their physical skills can tackle one of the tallest climbing walls in Canada. The 165-seat Kramer IMAX Theatre uses a five-story screen and four-way sound system to present science and nature films in a giant format.

Time: Allow 2 hours minimum. **Hours:** Mon.-Fri. 9-6; Sat.-Sun. and statutory holidays 10-6. Hours for IMAX films vary. Phone ahead to confirm schedule. **Cost:** $9; $8 (ages 13-17); $7 (ages 6-12 and 60+); $5 (ages 3-5). IMAX shows $9; $8 (ages 13-17); $7 (ages 6-12 and 60+); $5 (ages 3-5). Combination tickets are available. **Phone:** (306) 522-4629, or (800) 667-6300 in Canada. ⓣ

GAMBLING ESTABLISHMENTS

• **Casino Regina** is at 1880 Saskatchewan Dr. **Hours:** Daily 9 a.m.-4 a.m. Closed Christmas Eve and Christmas. **Phone:** (306) 565-3000 or (800) 555-3189.

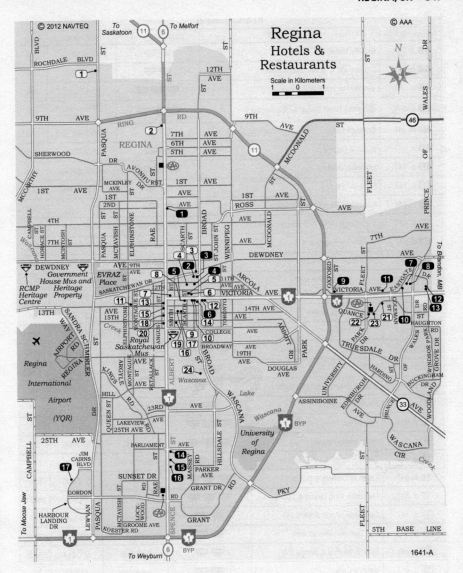

© 2012 NAVTEQ   © AAA

Regina Hotels & Restaurants

Scale in Kilometers

1641-A

Regina

This index helps you "spot" where approved hotels and restaurants are located on the corresponding detailed maps. Hotel daily rate range is for comparison only. Restaurant price range is a combination of lunch and/or dinner. Turn to the listing page for more detailed rate and price information and consult display ads for special promotions.

REGINA

Map Page	Hotels	Diamond Rated	Rate Range	Page
1 this page	BEST WESTERN Seven Oaks Inn	▼▼▼	$150 SAVE	549
2 this page	Delta Regina	▼▼▼	$165-$230	549
3 this page	Wingate by Wyndham	▼▼▼	$119-$199	550
4 this page	Holiday Inn Express Hotel & Suites Regina	▼▼▼	$120-$180	549
5 this page	Radisson Plaza Hotel Saskatchewan (See ad p. 550.)	▼▼▼	$140-$290 SAVE	550

REGINA (cont'd)

Map Page	Hotels (cont'd)	Diamond Rated	Rate Range	Page
6 p. 547	**Quality Hotel**	◊◊	$119-$159 SAVE	549
7 p. 547	Country Inn & Suites By Carlson	◊◊	$115-$199	549
8 p. 547	Holiday Inn Hotel & Suites	◊◊◊	$140-$200	549
9 p. 547	Sandman Hotel Suites & Spa Regina	◊◊◊	Rates not provided	550
10 p. 547	Comfort Inn	◊◊	$136-$148 SAVE	549
11 p. 547	Super 8 Regina	◊◊	$115-$125	550
12 p. 547	HomeSuites Hotel	◊◊◊	$155-$170	549
13 p. 547	Days Inn Regina	◊◊	$128-$153	549
14 p. 547	**Executive Royal Hotel Regina**	◊◊	$122 SAVE	549
15 p. 547	Travelodge Hotel & Conference Centre	◊◊◊	$134-$459	550
16 p. 547	Holiday Inn Express & Suites	◊◊◊	$139-$159	549
17 p. 547	Days Inn-Regina Airport West	◊◊◊	$130-$150	549

Map Page	Restaurants	Diamond Rated	Cuisine	Price Range	Page
1 p. 547	Silver's Steakhouse	◊◊◊	Steak	$15-$47	552
2 p. 547	Luiggi's Pasta House	◊◊	Italian	$11-$27	551
3 p. 547	The Last Spike	◊◊	American	$10-$20	551
4 p. 547	Beer Bros. Bakery & Cuisine	◊◊◊	American	$12-$30	550
5 p. 547	Michi	◊◊	Japanese	$7-$16	552
6 p. 547	Siam Authentic Thai Restaurant	◊◊	Thai	$8-$16	552
7 p. 547	Fresh & Sweet	◊	American	$10-$12	551
8 p. 547	The Dining Room	◊◊◊	American	$13-$39	551
9 p. 547	Golf's Steak House	◊◊◊	Steak	$10-$50	551
10 p. 547	Crave Kitchen & Wine Bar	◊◊	International	$12-$29	551
11 p. 547	Creek In Cathedral Bistro	◊◊◊	American	$12-$30	551
12 p. 547	Memories Fine Dining & Lounge	◊◊◊	International	$9-$35	552
13 p. 547	Cathedral Village Freehouse	◊◊	American	$9-$24	550
14 p. 547	The Diplomat Steakhouse	◊◊	Steak	$10-$50	551
15 p. 547	Slow Brew Pub & Sports Bar	◊◊	American	$10-$14	552
16 p. 547	Henry's Cafe	◊◊	American	$7-$12	551
17 p. 547	Tangerine the food bar	◊	American	$8-$15	552
18 p. 547	La Bodega Tapas Bar & Grill	◊◊◊	Mediterranean	$11-$30	551
19 p. 547	Fireside Bistro	◊◊	American	$7-$32	551
20 p. 547	The Fainting Goat Restaurant	◊◊	Mediterranean	$8-$24	551
21 p. 547	Houston Pizza	◊◊	American	$10-$26	551
22 p. 547	Smokin' Okies BBQ	◊	Barbecue	$9-$23	552
23 p. 547	Mediterranean Bistro	◊◊◊	Continental	$12-$36	552
24 p. 547	The Willow on Wascana	◊◊◊	Regional Canadian	$12-$39	552

(See map & index p. 547.)

BEST WESTERN SEVEN OAKS INN

(306)757-0121 **1**

Hotel
$150

AAA Benefit: Members save up to 20%, plus 10% bonus points with Best Western Rewards®.

Address: 777 Albert St S4R 2P6 **Location:** On Hwy 6; jct 2nd Ave. Located in a commercial area. **Facility:** 157 units. 3 stories, interior corridors. **Parking:** winter plug-ins. **Terms:** cancellation fee imposed. **Dining:** Ricky's All Day Grill, see separate listing. **Pool(s):** heated indoor. **Activities:** sauna, whirlpool, waterslide, exercise room. **Guest Services:** valet and coin laundry. **Free Special Amenities:** local telephone calls and airport transportation.

- Free Airport Shuttle
- Free High Speed Internet
- Swimming Pool w/Water-Slide
- Free Newspaper Daily

COMFORT INN

(306)789-5522 **10**

Hotel
$136-$148

Address: 3221 E Eastgate Dr S4Z 1A4 **Location:** Trans-Canada Hwy 1, 1.3 mi (2 km) e of Ring Rd; at eastern approach to city. Opposite a shopping center and Eastgate Park. **Facility:** 99 units. 2 stories (no elevator), interior corridors. **Parking:** winter plug-ins. **Terms:** cancellation fee imposed. **Guest Services:** valet laundry.

COUNTRY INN & SUITES BY CARLSON

(306)789-9117 **7**

Hotel $115-$199 **Address:** 3321 Eastgate Bay S4Z 1A4 **Location:** Trans-Canada Hwy 1, 1.2 mi (2 km) e of Ring Rd; at eastern approach to city. Opposite a shopping center. **Facility:** 76 units. 3 stories, interior corridors. **Parking:** winter plug-ins. **Terms:** 3 day cancellation notice. **Amenities:** Some: high-speed Internet. **Activities:** exercise room. **Guest Services:** valet and coin laundry.

DAYS INN REGINA

(306)522-3297 **13**

Hotel $128-$153 **Address:** 3875 Eastgate Dr E S4Z 1A4 **Location:** Jct Ring Rd, 1.5 mi (2.4 km) e on Trans-Canada Hwy 1, just n; at eastern approach to city. Located in a commercial area. **Facility:** 129 units, some efficiencies. 3-4 stories, interior corridors. **Parking:** winter plug-ins. **Terms:** check-in 4 pm, cancellation fee imposed. **Amenities:** Some: high-speed Internet. **Pool(s):** heated indoor. **Activities:** whirlpools, waterslide, exercise room. **Guest Services:** valet and coin laundry.

DAYS INN-REGINA AIRPORT WEST

(306)584-3297 **17**

Hotel $130-$150 **Address:** 4899 Harbour Landing Dr S4N 0B7 **Location:** Trans-Canada Hwy 1 exit 80, just n on Lewvan Dr. **Facility:** 99 units. 4 stories, interior corridors. **Parking:** winter plug-ins. **Terms:** check-in 4 pm. **Amenities:** high-speed Internet. **Pool(s):** heated indoor. **Activities:** whirlpool, waterslide, exercise room. **Guest Services:** valet and coin laundry.

DELTA REGINA

(306)525-5255 **2**

Hotel $165-$230 **Address:** 1919 Saskatchewan Dr S4P 4H2 **Location:** At Rose St; center. Across from Casino Regina. **Facility:** 274 units. 25 stories, interior corridors. **Parking:** on-site (fee), winter plug-ins. **Pool(s):** heated indoor. **Activities:** whirlpool, waterslide, exercise room, spa. **Guest Services:** valet laundry.

EXECUTIVE ROYAL HOTEL REGINA

(306)586-6755 **14**

Hotel
$122

Address: 4025 Albert St S S4S 3R6 **Location:** On Hwy 6, 1.2 mi (2 km) n of jct Trans-Canada Hwy 1. **Facility:** 105 units. 5 stories, interior corridors. **Parking:** winter plug-ins. **Terms:** cancellation fee imposed. **Activities:** exercise room. **Guest Services:** valet and coin laundry. **Free Special Amenities:** local telephone calls and high-speed Internet.

HOLIDAY INN EXPRESS & SUITES

(306)789-5888 **16**

Hotel $139-$159 **Address:** 4255 Albert St S4S 3R6 **Location:** On Hwy 6, 1 mi (1.6 km) n of jct Trans-Canada Hwy 1. **Facility:** 102 units. 4 stories, interior corridors. **Parking:** winter plug-ins. **Amenities:** high-speed Internet. **Pool(s):** heated indoor. **Activities:** whirlpool, exercise room. **Guest Services:** valet and coin laundry.

HOLIDAY INN EXPRESS HOTEL & SUITES REGINA

(306)569-4600 **4**

Hotel $120-$180 **Address:** 1907 11th Ave S4P 0J2 **Location:** Corner of Rose St; center. Located near Casino Regina. **Facility:** 78 units. 5 stories, interior corridors. **Parking:** on-site (fee), winter plug-ins. **Terms:** cancellation fee imposed. **Activities:** exercise room. **Guest Services:** valet laundry.

HOLIDAY INN HOTEL & SUITES

(306)789-3883 **8**

Hotel $140-$200 **Address:** 1800 Prince of Wales Dr S4Z 1A4 **Location:** Jct Ring Rd, 1.3 mi (2.1 km) n on Trans-Canada Hwy 1, just n. Opposite a shopping center. **Facility:** 120 units. 4 stories, interior corridors. **Parking:** winter plug-ins. **Terms:** 2 night minimum stay - seasonal and/or weekends. **Amenities:** high-speed Internet. Some: video games (fee). **Pool(s):** heated indoor. **Activities:** whirlpool, waterslide, exercise room. **Guest Services:** valet and coin laundry.

HOMESUITES HOTEL

(306)522-4434 **12**

Extended Stay Hotel $155-$170 **Address:** 3841 Eastgate Dr S4Z 1A5 **Location:** Jct Ring Rd, 1.5 mi (2.4 km) e on Trans-Canada Hwy 1, just n; at eastern approach to city. **Facility:** 60 units, some efficiencies and kitchens. 4 stories, interior corridors. **Parking:** winter plug-ins. **Terms:** check-in 4 pm, resort fee. **Amenities:** high-speed Internet. Some: safes. **Activities:** exercise room. **Guest Services:** valet and coin laundry.

QUALITY HOTEL

(306)569-4656 **6**

Hotel
$119-$159

Address: 1717 Victoria Ave S4P 0P9 **Location:** Just e of Broad St; downtown. **Facility:** 126 units. 7 stories, interior corridors. **Parking:** winter plug-ins. **Terms:** cancellation fee imposed. **Amenities:** video games (fee). **Dining:** Memories Fine Dining & Lounge, see separate listing. **Activities:** sauna, exercise room. **Guest Services:** valet and coin laundry.

(See map & index p. 547.)

RADISSON PLAZA HOTEL SASKATCHEWAN
(306)522-7691 **5**

Hotel
$140-$290

Address: 2125 Victoria Ave S4P 0S3 **Location:** At Scarth St; center. Opposite Victoria Park. **Facility:** 224 units. 10 stories, interior corridors. **Parking:** on-site (fee) and valet, winter plug-ins. **Amenities:** video games (fee), high-speed Internet. *Some:* safes. **Dining:** The Dining Room, see separate listing. **Activities:** whirlpool, steamroom, spa. **Guest Services:** valet laundry, area transportation (fee) within city limits. *(See ad this page.)*

[SAVE] [ECO] FEE 🔌 🍴 🔧 🍸
🛁 [BIZ] 📶 🎥 ✕ 🛎 📠
📺 /SOME UNITS FEE 🐾

SANDMAN HOTEL SUITES & SPA REGINA
306/757-2444 **9**

Hotel. Rates not provided. **Address:** 1800 Victoria Ave E S4N 7K3 **Location:** On Trans-Canada Hwy 1; at eastern approach to city. Located in a commercial area. **Facility:** 132 units. 4 stories, interior corridors. **Terms:** check-in 4 pm. **Amenities:** high-speed Internet. **Dining:** Moxie's Classic Grill, see separate listing. **Pool(s):** heated indoor. **Activities:** whirlpool, exercise room, spa. **Guest Services:** valet laundry.

[ECO] 🍴 🍸 CALL 📞M 🛁 [BIZ] 📶 🛎 📠 📺
/SOME UNITS FEE 🐾

SUPER 8 REGINA
(306)789-8833 **11**

Hotel $115-$125 **Address:** 2730 Victoria Ave E S4N 6M5 **Location:** On Trans-Canada Hwy 1, 1 mi (1.6 km) e of Ring Rd; at eastern approach to city. Opposite a shopping center. **Facility:** 60 units. 3 stories (no elevator), interior corridors. **Parking:** winter plug-ins. **Amenities:** video games (fee). **Guest Services:** valet laundry.

🍴 [BIZ] 📶 🎥 🛎 📺 /SOME UNITS FEE 🐾

Be a better driver.
Keep your mind on the road.

TRAVELODGE HOTEL & CONFERENCE CENTRE
(306)586-3443 **15**

Hotel $134-$459 **Address:** 4177 Albert St S S4S 3R6 **Location:** On Hwy 6, 1 mi (1.6 km) n of jct Trans-Canada Hwy 1. **Facility:** 200 units. 4 stories, interior corridors. **Parking:** winter plug-ins. **Terms:** check-in 4 pm, cancellation fee imposed. **Amenities:** high-speed Internet. **Pool(s):** heated indoor. **Activities:** whirlpool, waterslide, exercise room. **Guest Services:** valet laundry.

[ECO] 🍴 🍸 🛁 [BIZ] 📶 ✕ 🎥 🛎 📠 📺

WINGATE BY WYNDHAM
(306)584-7400 **3**

Hotel $119-$199 **Address:** 1700 Broad St S4P 1X4 **Location:** Corner of Saskatchewan Dr; center. Across from Casino Regina. **Facility:** 118 units. 7 stories, interior corridors. **Parking:** on-site (fee), winter plug-ins. **Terms:** cancellation fee imposed. **Amenities:** high-speed Internet, safes. **Activities:** exercise room. **Guest Services:** valet laundry.

[ECO] 🍴 CALL 📞M [BIZ] 📶 ✕ 🎥 🛎 📠 📺
/SOME UNITS FEE 🐾

WHERE TO EAT

BEER BROS. BAKERY & CUISINE
306/586-2337 **4**

American. Casual Dining. $12-$30 **AAA Inspector Notes:** The creative menu at this casual spot incorporates beer into nearly every menu item. Highlights include smoked cheddar and ale soup, dried fruit spinach salad, chicken glazed in pumpkin ale and brown ale braised AAA Angus beef short ribs. The chef creates a specialty pierogi for the beerogies and sausage entrée. Choose to dine in the main dining room, with stained glass and modern tapestries, or in the beer parlor. The huge selection of beer changes based on availability. Wine also is offered. **Bar:** full bar. **Reservations:** suggested. **Address:** 1801A Scarth St S4P 2G9 **Location:** Between 11th and 12th aves; downtown. **Parking:** street only.

[L] [D] CALL 📞M

CATHEDRAL VILLAGE FREEHOUSE
306/359-1661 **13**

American. Gastropub. $9-$24 **AAA Inspector Notes:** The young and young at heart appreciate the sometimes boisterous atmosphere at this upscale tavern. Servers are friendly. The menu lists an interesting mix of dishes, including ribs, steak, burritos, tandoori chicken stir fry, soups, salads, sandwiches and pizza cooked in a wood-fired oven. The patio is open seasonally. **Bar:** full bar. **Address:** 2062 Albert St S4P 2T7 **Location:** On Hwy 6; jct 13th Ave. **Parking:** on-site and street.

[L] [D] [LATE]

▼ See AAA listing this page ▼

(See map & index p. 547.)

CRAVE KITCHEN & WINE BAR   306/525-8777   10
International. Casual Dining. $12-$29 **AAA Inspector Notes:** Located in one of Regina's oldest clubs, the modern restaurant and lounge offers tempting tapas and a number of delicious entrées. Popular with the downtown crowd, at times the eatery can be loud and jovial. **Bar:** full bar. **Address:** 1925 Victoria Ave S4P 0R3 **Location:** Victoria Ave and Broad St; center of downtown. **Parking:** street only. L D

CREEK IN CATHEDRAL BISTRO   306/352-4448   11
American. Casual Dining. $12-$30 **AAA Inspector Notes:** Located in a residential area close to downtown, this charming bistro has a tasteful decor with local artwork adorning the walls and friendly, capable servers. Market-fresh ingredients are used to whip up a variety of creatively prepared and artfully presented dishes with hints of global flavors. **Bar:** full bar. **Reservations:** suggested. **Address:** 3414 13th Ave S4T 1P7 **Location:** Just e of Elphinstone St. **Parking:** street only. L D

THE DINING ROOM   306/337-4311   8
American. Fine Dining. $13-$39 **AAA Inspector Notes:** Guests will find an upscale Victorian décor which provides for intimate dining here. The chef at this restaurant prepares an interesting menu with some locally sourced ingredients and a good selection of desserts. The breakfast buffet and Sunday brunch are popular, as well as the afternoon tea served on weekends. **Bar:** full bar. **Reservations:** suggested, required for Sunday brunch. **Address:** 2125 Victoria Ave S4P 0S3 **Location:** At Scarth St; center; in Radisson Plaza Hotel Saskatchewan. B L D

THE DIPLOMAT STEAKHOUSE   306/359-3366   14
Steak. Casual Dining. $10-$50 **AAA Inspector Notes:** On the menu at this establishment is wonderful steak, filet mignon, coq au vin and seafood, as well as an impressive choice of wine and cognac. Elegant surroundings and knowledgeable servers are characteristic. Closed for lunch Saturday and Sunday. **Bar:** full bar. **Reservations:** suggested, weekends. **Address:** 2032 Broad St S4P 1Y3 **Location:** Just s of jct Broad St and Victoria Ave.
L D

EARLS RESTAURANT
American. Casual Dining. $11-$29 **AAA Inspector Notes:** Offering an experience that falls between fast food and fine dining, the fun, relaxed restaurant prepares great food at a great price. Choices range from juicy burgers, hearty sandwiches, fresh salads, wings and pizza to full entrees of steak, chops and seafood. Made-from-scratch soups and assorted breads, round out the offerings. This is a fitting spot for impromptu get-togethers and festive occasions. **Bar:** full bar.
L D LATE

For additional information, visit AAA.com

LOCATIONS:
Address: 2606 28th Ave S4S 6P3 **Location:** Jct Albert St S. **Phone:** 306/584-7733

Address: 1875 Victoria Ave E S4N 6E6 **Location:** On Trans-Canada Hwy 1, just e of Ring Rd; at eastern approach to city. **Phone:** 306/949-4955

THE FAINTING GOAT RESTAURANT   306/352-4628   20
Mediterranean. Casual Dining. $8-$24 **AAA Inspector Notes:** This family-operated spot, bright with color and local art, is dedicated to providing a memorable meal. Using the freshest local meats, vegetables and grains, the chefs put their own innovative stamp on Mediterranean cuisine. An interesting selection of soups, salads, appetizers, naan pizza, entrées and desserts are offered. A sample menu might include samosas with wild mushrooms and beets, followed by lamb crepes with couscous and chermoula cream and for dessert a delicious crema Catalan. **Bar:** full bar. **Reservations:** suggested. **Address:** 2330 Albert St S4P 2V7 **Location:** Jct Victoria Ave, 0.4 mi (0.6 km) s. **Parking:** street only.
L D LATE CALL &M

FIRESIDE BISTRO   306/761-2305   19
American. Casual Dining. $7-$32 **AAA Inspector Notes:** In a house built around 1912, the dining room has been updated with some attractive and modern appointments. Some of the creative menu choices include appetizers like Cajun prairie dumplings and coconut shrimp martini. Also offered are a few chicken entrées, including blackened breast with blue cheese sauce, as well as a variety of steaks with delicious sauces, some fish dishes and a nice range of pasta. A cozy lounge and a seasonal outdoor patio are available. **Bar:** full bar. **Reservations:** suggested. **Address:** 2305 Smith St S4P 2P7 **Location:** 3 blks s of Victoria Ave, just e of Hwy 6 (Albert St). **Parking:** street only. L D

FRESH & SWEET   306/751-2233   7
American. Casual Dining. $10-$12 **AAA Inspector Notes:** A feast for the senses is found at this bright and open café where fantastical flavors of homemade gelato, cupcakes, candy apples and other delicious sweets are found. Gourmet panini and wraps are very flavorful and in some cases downright messy like the butter chicken wrap. Breakfast also is very creative with a great range of waffles including the caramel apple pie or Dijon chicken waffles. **Address:** 2500 Victoria Ave S4S 4M2 **Location:** Corner of McIntyre St; center. **Parking:** street only. B L CALL &M

GOLF'S STEAK HOUSE   306/525-5808   9
Steak. Fine Dining. $10-$50 **AAA Inspector Notes:** This restaurant features hearty portions of tasty AAA Angus Pride steak and prime rib, as well as seafood, chicken and rack of lamb. The menu includes a good variety. Professional service and traditional formal decor characterize the restaurant, which signifies when it is open for business by lighting the torch out front. Closed for lunch on Saturday and Sunday. **Bar:** full bar. **Reservations:** suggested. **Address:** 1945 Victoria Ave S4P 0R3 **Location:** Corner of Victoria Ave and Hamilton St. L D

HENRY'S CAFE   306/791-7889   16
American. Casual Dining. $7-$12 **AAA Inspector Notes:** At this cheery café you'll find it hard to make up your mind between the many soups like wicked Thai chicken or lobster bisque, daily quiche choices, enticing salads, pasta or quirky sandwiches like the yummy turkey club made with signature garlic toast. Combos and add-ons help make the decision easier, but you must save room for the cheesecakes, pies and cakes. Set in a nifty boutique complex, you can work off a few calories browsing the art gallery or looking for that perfect gift or outfit. **Bar:** beer & wine. **Reservations:** suggested. **Address:** 2175 Smith St S4P 2P3 **Location:** Jct Hwy 6 (Albert St) and 14th Ave, just e. **Parking:** on-site and street. B L

HOUSTON PIZZA   306/585-6888   21
American. Casual Dining. $10-$26 **AAA Inspector Notes:** Whether dining with someone special or bringing along the whole family, this spot is a good choice for steak, spaghetti, lasagna, ribs, barbecue chicken, seafood, stir-fry and salads, as well as yummy pizza. Servers are prompt. **Bar:** full bar. **Address:** 2815 Quance St S4V 3B7 **Location:** Trans-Canada Hwy 1, just e of Ring Rd, then just s; at Coleman Cres. L D CALL &M

LA BODEGA TAPAS BAR & GRILL   306/546-3660   18
Mediterranean. Casual Dining. $11-$30 **AAA Inspector Notes:** Those who enjoy a variety of taste sensations surely will be pleased with the varied tapas menu. The atmosphere is cozy in the dining room and on the seasonal patio. **Bar:** full bar. **Address:** 2228 Albert St S4P 2V2 **Location:** Just n of jct 15th Ave. **Parking:** street only. L D LATE

THE LAST SPIKE   306/781-7000   3
American. Casual Dining. $10-$20 **AAA Inspector Notes:** In the old Regina train station, this restaurant has one dining room section in a rail passenger car where reservations are required. The menu centers on simple, filling fare along the lines of ribs, chicken and fish and chips. **Bar:** full bar. **Address:** 1880 Saskatchewan Dr S4P 0A8 **Location:** Center; in Casino Regina. **Parking:** on-site (fee). B L D

LUIGGI'S PASTA HOUSE   306/949-7427   2
Italian. Family Dining. $11-$27 **AAA Inspector Notes:** Located in a small strip mall, this family-oriented eatery can be spotted by the antique truck on the roof. Italian food is what it is all about in the colorful and lively atmosphere where large cheese figures hang from the ceiling. Efficient servers dish up hearty portions of traditional dishes. **Bar:** full bar. **Reservations:** suggested. **Address:** 470 Albert St N S4R 3C1 **Location:** Corner of 9th Ave, just s of Ring Rd.
L D

(See map & index p. 547.)

MEDITERRANEAN BISTRO 306/757-1666 (23)
▼▼▼ Continental. Casual Dining. $12-$36 **AAA Inspector Notes:** This casual yet upscale bistro/market uses fresh products and offers a good variety of carefully prepared and creatively presented fish, chicken, red meat and pasta dishes. Service is professional and friendly. **Bar:** full bar. **Reservations:** suggested. **Address:** 2589 Quance St S4V 2Y7 **Location:** Trans-Canada Hwy 1, just se of jct Fleet St; at eastern approach to city. [L] [D]

MEMORIES FINE DINING & LOUNGE 306/522-1999 (12)
▼▼▼ International. Fine Dining. $9-$35 **AAA Inspector Notes:** This long established restaurant has a decor dating from the late eighties with dark wood accents and cozy semi-private booths. A diverse and delicious menu awaits with a predominance of such Greek dishes as souvlaki and chicken Hellas along with French Coquille St. Jacques and Chateaubriand, Asian duck, Indian samosas, steak and seafood. Proficient service includes tableside Caesar salad and specialty coffees. A perfect place for a special night out with tastes to suit any palate. **Bar:** full bar. **Reservations:** suggested. **Address:** 1717 Victoria Ave S4P 0P9 **Location:** Just e of Broad St; downtown; in Quality Hotel. [B] [L] [D] CALL [&][M]

MICHI 306/565-0141 (5)
▼▼ Japanese. Casual Dining. $7-$16 **AAA Inspector Notes:** The décor, although pleasant, is not the draw here—it is the sushi. Since opening its doors in 2003, this restaurant's five chefs (all from Japan) have been serving authentic Japanese cuisine. Extremely well-made sushi is on the menu as well as a good variety of appetizers, salads, tempura, donburi rice bowls, udon noodles and teriyaki items. **Bar:** full bar. **Address:** 1943 Scarth St S4P 2H1 **Location:** Just n of Victoria Ave; center. **Parking:** street only. [L] [D]

MOXIE'S CLASSIC GRILL 306/781-5655
▼▼ Canadian. Casual Dining. $11-$29 **AAA Inspector Notes:** This sleek, funky and popular restaurant presents an extensive menu of creatively prepared dishes, including pizza, pasta, rice, noodles, signature salads and burgers. Other menus include one for children and one for Sunday brunch. Lending to the upbeat, stylish decor are dark wood appointments and river rock fireplaces. **Bar:** full bar. **Address:** 1800A Victoria Ave S4N 7K3 **Location:** On Trans-Canada Hwy 1, just e of Ring Rd; at eastern approach to city; in Sandman Hotel Suites & Spa Regina. [L] [D] [LATE]

RICKY'S ALL DAY GRILL 306/775-3000
▼▼ American. Casual Dining. $12-$27 **AAA Inspector Notes:** The comfortable eatery, which employs friendly servers, presents a varied menu that includes pasta dishes, wraps, omelets, stir-fry preparations and burgers. Portions are generous. Children's and senior selections are offered. Guests can request seating in a booth or at a table. **Bar:** full bar. **Address:** 777 Albert St S4R 2P6 **Location:** On Hwy 6; jct 2nd Ave; in BEST WESTERN Seven Oaks Inn. [B] [L] [D]

SIAM AUTHENTIC THAI RESTAURANT 306/352-8424 (6)
▼▼ Thai. Casual Dining. $8-$16 **AAA Inspector Notes:** Tightly packed tables are necessary to fill the demand for this super popular restaurant. Simple, smart and modern Thai décor sets the mood for the flavorful food. Some of the many choices include favorites like pad thai and curries. Be sure to try some of the appetizers such as the tasty crispy shrimp crepes. A lunch buffet is offered during the week. Service is pretty limited and there sometimes are delays but it is worth the wait. **Bar:** beer & wine. **Address:** 1946 Hamilton St S4P 2C4 **Location:** Center; just n of Victoria Ave. **Parking:** street only. [L] [D]

SILVER'S STEAKHOUSE 306/775-5888 (1)
▼▼▼ Steak. Casual Dining. $15-$47 **AAA Inspector Notes:** This contemporary steakhouse is warm and inviting with partitioned sections and inviting booths. They proudly offer Certified Angus 28-day aged beef served with a potato and vegetables along with soup or salad. The menu also offers pasta, lobster, crab legs as well as their signature entrées including Diefenbaker trout with leek and tomato cream sauce and chicken Marsala with a mushroom reduction. **Reservations:** suggested. **Address:** 1060 Pasqua St N S4X 4B3 **Location:** Hwy 11 exit Pasqua St, 0.9 mi (1.5 km) s. [D] CALL [&][M]

SLOW BREW PUB & SPORTS BAR 306/751-0000 (15)
▼▼▼ American. Gastropub. $10-$14 **AAA Inspector Notes:** This casual spot has an upgraded pub menu and ingredients sourced from local suppliers and vendors so diners can be certain of a tasty meal whether it is fried artisan bread with smoked paprika mayonnaise, chipotle Caesar salad, hand-crafted gourmet pizza or the slow burger. Enjoy local sports on the TVs and listen to a variety of happening music while eating or sipping on one of tasty fresh brews made at this pub which also are available for take-out. Sorry, no minors allowed. **Bar:** full bar. **Reservations:** suggested. **Address:** 2124 Albert St S4P 2T9 **Location:** Jct Victoria Ave, just s; in strip mall. [L] [D] CALL [&][M]

SMOKIN' OKIES BBQ 306/347-2800 (22)
▼ Barbecue. Quick Serve. $9-$23 **AAA Inspector Notes:** Everything is made from scratch from the slow-smoked brisket, pulled pork and ribs to side dishes of corn bread, coleslaw and baked beans. Also on the menu is catfish, burgers and hot dogs. Service is simple as you just place your order at the counter and they bring your food over to the table. Whatever you do, you need to save space in the tummy for the Southern pecan squares which look ordinary but taste unbelievable. **Bar:** full bar. **Address:** 2547 Quance St E S4V 2X7 **Location:** Trans-Canada Hwy 1, just s on University Park Dr; in strip mall. [L] [D] CALL [&][M]

TANGERINE THE FOOD BAR 306/522-3500 (17)
▼ American. Quick Serve. $8-$15 **AAA Inspector Notes:** This cute little spot is one of the most popular spots in Regina for lunch so you will likely find yourself in a line. While you wait, you can peruse the chalkboard and display cases to make your choice. Everything is prepared in house from the breads, soup, salads, freshly made sandwiches to one of the delectable pies and other desserts. **Address:** 2234 14th Ave S4P 0X8 **Location:** Just e of Albert St. **Parking:** street only. [B] [L] CALL [&][M]

THE WILLOW ON WASCANA 306/585-3663 (24)
▼▼▼ Regional Canadian. Casual Dining. $12-$39 **AAA Inspector Notes:** Here is an opportunity to enjoy a cozy restaurant in a park setting with super river views. Service is skilled and friendly and the menu offers a good variety of beautifully prepared dishes utilizing the finest local and organic ingredients. A patio is available in season. **Bar:** full bar. **Reservations:** suggested. **Address:** 3000 Wascana Dr S4P 3B2 **Location:** Jct S Broad St and Wascana Pkwy; next to marina. [L] [D]

BUSHWAKKER BREWPUB 306/359-7276
(fyi) Not evaluated. This restaurant, located on the first floor of the Strathdee Building, treats patrons to a diverse menu including everything from wild boar burgers to specialty pizzas. They also offer regular and seasonal brews as well as specialty mead. **Address:** 2206 Dewdney Ave S4R 1H2 **Location:** In Old Warehouse District.

ROCANVILLE (E-5) pop. 857

ROCANVILLE AND DISTRICT MUSEUM is at Qu'Appelle Ave. and Saint Albert St. A variety of local artifacts include steam tractors, a train station, blacksmith shop and schoolhouse. **Time:** Allow 2 hours minimum. **Hours:** Wed.-Sun. 10-5, July-Aug.; by appointment rest of year. **Cost:** Donations. **Phone:** (306) 645-2113 or (306) 645-2164.

ROSTHERN (D-3) pop. 1,572

SEAGER WHEELER FARM is 7 km (4 mi.) e. on Hwy. 312, following signs. One of the most noted farmers in Canada, Wheeler won five international wheat championships 1911-18 and was a prominent educator in progressive agricultural techniques. The farm features restored buildings and equipment. Also on the grounds are English flower gardens, orchards, a 24-hectare (60-acre) bird sanctuary, a tearoom and a visitor center with interpretive displays.

Tours: Guided tours are available. **Time:** Allow 1 hour minimum. **Hours:** Wed.-Sun. 9-5 (also Thurs. 7-9 p.m.), May-Aug. **Cost:** $5; free (ages 0-12 when accompanied by an adult). **Phone:** (306) 232-5959. ⛺

ST. BRIEUX (D-4) pop. 590, elev. 547m/1,797'

ST. BRIEUX MUSEUM is at 300 Barbier Dr., the main access road to the village. Originally a Roman Catholic rectory, it displays pioneer tools, furniture, period clothing and other artifacts and memorabilia related to the early 20th-century settlement of the St. Brieux district. **Tours:** Guided tours are available. **Hours:** Wed. and Sun. 1-5, Victoria Day-Aug. 31; by appointment rest of year. **Cost:** Donations. **Phone:** (306) 275-2257.

ST. WALBURG (C-2) pop. 716, elev. 634m/2,083'

IMHOFF GALLERY is 2.5 mi. (4 km) s. on Hwy. 26, then 2.5 mi. (4 km) w. on a gravel road, following signs. Born in Germany, religious artist Berthold Von Imhoff moved to St. Walburg in 1913, residing there until his death in 1939. Imhoff's works adorned more than 100 churches throughout Canada and the United States and he was knighted by the pope in 1937. The artist's original working studio holds many original large canvases, photos and a 20-minute video about his life. Two rooms in the original homestead are filled with antiques, including a sculpture of Custer. Several mounted game heads on display show Imhoff's prowess as a hunter.

Tours: Guided tours are available. **Time:** Allow 1 hour minimum. **Hours:** Daily 10-5, June 1-Labour Day. **Cost:** $8; $5 (students ages 6-18 with ID); free (ages 0-5). **Phone:** (306) 248-3812. ⛺

SASKATOON (D-3) pop. 222,189, elev. 487m/1,598'
• Hotels p. 555 • Restaurants p. 557

Saskatoon was founded in 1882 as a temperance colony under leader John Lake. According to legend a Cree brought Lake a handful of the purple berries that grew in abundance alongside the river. Lake was so taken with the fruit he named his settlement Saskatoon, after *misaskquatoomina*, the First Nations name for the wild berries. Today a slice of Saskatoon pie is a traditional treat recalling the city's past.

Straddling the South Saskatchewan River, Saskatoon is known as "The City of Bridges" because of the seven spans connecting its banks. It also is home to the University of Saskatchewan, which is building a reputation for research and development in science, medicine and agriculture. The Diefenbaker Canada Centre on campus showcases memorabilia of Canada's 13th prime minister.

The Local History Room on the second floor of the Frances Morrison Library, 311-23rd St. E., serves as a research facility for information that focuses on prairie history relating to Saskatoon in particular and western Canada in general. Collections include more than 60,000 historic photographs, thousands of books, pamphlets, maps, artifacts and periodicals. An art gallery is next to the room. Phone (306) 975-7558.

The Saskatchewan Railway Museum, 6 kilometres (4 mi.) west on Hwy. 7, then 2 kilometres (1.2 mi.) south on Hwy. 60, is operated by the Saskatchewan Railroad Historical Association and displays old railroad buildings and artifacts, including locomotives, cabooses and streetcars; phone (306) 382-9855 May through September.

TCU Place—Saskatoon's Art & Convention Centre, 35 22nd St., is home to the Saskatoon Symphony and the site of traveling shows throughout the year. The Meewasin Valley Centre, 402 3rd Ave. S., features interpretive displays pertaining to the area's history. Credit Union Centre features rock concerts, trade shows, and hockey and other sporting events. The facility is on the north side of the city next to hwys. 2 and 16.

The Meewasin Valley Trail, following the South Saskatchewan River through the heart of the city, has bicycle and jogging trails, picnic areas and playgrounds and provides opportunities for cross-country skiing and ice skating. Recreational activities are available at nearby Pike Lake and Blackstrap provincial parks *(see Recreation Areas Chart)*.

Queen Elizabeth Power Station, 3 kilometres (1.9 mi.) south of the junction of 11th Street W. and Avenue H S. at 2211 Spadina Crescent W., is a thermal power station originally named the South Saskatchewan River Generating Station but renamed and commissioned in 1959 by Queen Elizabeth II. Free guided tours are available with 24 hours' advance notice; phone (306) 934-7994.

Racing fans can enjoy horse racing at Marquis Downs, 503 Ruth St., from late May to early September. Races are held Fri.-Sat. 7-10 p.m.; phone (306) 242-6100. Drag racing heats up the Saskatchewan International Raceway, 13 kilometres (8 mi.) s. on Hwy. 11, from early May to mid-September; phone (306) 955-3724. Stock car racing takes place at the Auto Clearing Motor Speedway, north on Hwy. 12, from May through September; phone (306) 956-3212.

Note: Policies concerning admittance of children to pari-mutuel betting facilities vary. Phone for information.

Tourism Saskatoon: 101-202 4th Ave. N., Saskatoon, SK, Canada S7K 0K1. **Phone:** (306) 242-1206 or (800) 567-2444.

Shopping areas: Midtown Plaza, downtown at 1st Avenue and 21st Street, is a two-level mall with more than 130 shops, including anchor stores The Bay and Sears.

BEAVER CREEK CONSERVATION AREA is 13 km (8 mi.) s. on Hwy. 219 (Lorne Ave.). Self-guiding nature trails and interpretive displays are offered.

Time: Allow 2 hours minimum. **Hours:** Mon.-Fri. 9-5; Sat.-Sun. and holidays noon-5. Phone ahead to confirm schedule. **Cost:** Free. **Phone:** (306) 374-2474.

DIEFENBAKER CANADA CENTRE is at 101 Diefenbaker Pl. on the University of Saskatchewan campus. The archives and personal belongings of prime minister John Diefenbaker are housed at the only Prime Ministerial center in Canada; his grave site is on the grounds. The museum also offers changing national and international exhibits about Canadian history, citizenship, leadership, art, politics, science, culture, current affairs and Canada's role in the international community.

Half-hour guided tours are available. **Hours:** Mon.-Fri. 9:30-4:30 (also Thurs. 4:30-8), Sat.-Sun. and holidays noon-4:30. Closed Jan. 1, Good Friday, Nov. 11 and Dec. 25-26. **Cost:** Free. Reservations are recommended. **Phone:** (306) 966-8384.

MENDEL ART GALLERY AND CIVIC CONSERVATORY is at 950 Spadina Crescent E. in a park between Queen and 25th sts. This attractive complex overlooks the South Saskatchewan River. In the art gallery are exhibitions of international, national and regional works, including historical and contemporary art. Visitors may view the display of tropical and native plants in the conservatory.

Programs and activities are presented in combination with each series of exhibitions. **Time:** Allow 30 minutes minimum. **Hours:** Daily 9-9. Complex closes at 5 on Dec. 24 and 31. Closed Christmas. **Cost:** Free. **Phone:** (306) 975-7610.

MUSEUM OF ANTIQUITIES is just e. on College Dr., just n. on Wiggins Rd., then just e. on Campus Dr. to Room 106 College Building, 107 Administration Pl. at the University of Saskatchewan. The museum has replicas of Greek, Roman, Egyptian and Near Eastern sculptures as well as original pieces of art and antiquities and a collection of original Greek, Roman and medieval coins. **Hours:** Mon.-Fri. 9-4; Sat.-Sun. by appointment. Guided tours are available by appointment Tues. at 1, Thurs. at 3. Closed late Dec.-early Jan. **Cost:** Donations. **Phone:** (306) 966-7818.

MUSEUM OF NATURAL SCIENCES, 112-114 Science Pl. at the University of Saskatchewan, offers three floors of scientific exhibits. Featured are three full-scale skeletal replicas of dinosaurs: Tyrannosaurus rex, Stegosaurus and Triceratops. Live aquarium, animal and plant displays demonstrate evolutionary processes. Geological processes are explained through displays of rocks, minerals and meteorites; a geological history of the Earth; and mining information. A working seismograph shows real-time volcanic activity around the world. **Time:** Allow 1 hour minimum. **Hours:** Mon.-Fri. 8 a.m.-9 p.m., Sat. 10-5, Sun. and holidays noon-5. Closed Dec. 25-Jan. 1. **Cost:** Free. **Phone:** (306) 966-5729.

SASKATCHEWAN INDIAN CULTURAL CENTRE is at 305 - 2555 Grasswood Rd. E. The center is dedicated to preserving First Nations cultures in Saskatchewan such as the Woodland, Swampy and Plains Cree; Dene; Nakawe; Dakota; Lakota; and Nakota. Exhibits include historic artifacts as well as contemporary arts and crafts. **Time:** Allow 30 minutes minimum. **Hours:** Mon.-Thurs. 8:30-5, Fri. 8:30-4. Tours are given by appointment. **Cost:** Free. **Phone:** (306) 244-1146 to schedule a guided tour.

SASKATOON FORESTRY FARM PARK AND ZOO is n.e. off Attridge Dr., following signs. Displayed in settings resembling their natural habitats are 350 species of birds and animals native to Saskatchewan and western Canada. The park offers a children's zoo, a reptile and tropical fish display, stocked fishing pond and nature walkways. The Kinsmen Express train provides a tour around the park and zoo.

Time: Allow 1 hour, 30 minutes minimum. **Hours:** Zoo and park open daily 9-9, Apr. 1-Labour Day; 10-4, rest of year. **Cost:** $9.50; $5.75 (ages 6-18); $19 (family). Fishing pond $2; $1 (ages 6-16). **Phone:** (306) 975-3382.

SHEARWATER RIVER CRUISES is off Spadina Crescent opposite Kinsmen Park, at the Mendel Art Gallery dock. See Saskatoon from the river on the riverboat *Prairie Lily*. The 120-passenger vessel is equipped with restrooms, a heated and air-conditioned cabin and a licensed bar. A dinner cruise is available on Friday evening. A captain's brunch tour is available on Sunday.

Hours: One-hour cruises depart daily at 4 and 6:30 (also Sun. at 2), early Apr. to mid-Oct. Boarding begins 30 minutes before departure. Phone ahead to confirm schedule. **Cost:** One-hour cruise fare Sat.-Sun. $20; $18 (ages 6-16 and 61+); $12 (ages 2-5). One-hour cruise fare Mon.-Fri. $20; $18 (ages 61+); $16 (ages 6-16); $10 (ages 2-5). Reservations are required for dinner cruise and captain's brunch cruise. **Phone:** (888) 747-7572.

UKRAINIAN MUSEUM OF CANADA is at 910 Spadina Crescent E. Displays include folk and fine art, domestic and agricultural tools, and documents and photographs of Ukrainian immigrants. One gallery features William Kurelek paintings while another has changing exhibits. **Tours:** Guided tours are available. **Time:** Allow 30 minutes minimum. **Hours:** Tues.-Sat. 10-5, Sun. 1-5. Closed Canadian holidays, Orthodox Christmas (early Jan.) and Good Friday. **Cost:** $4; $3 (ages 60+); $2 (ages 6-16). Reservations are required for guided tours. **Phone:** (306) 244-3800.

WANUSKEWIN HERITAGE PARK is 5 km (3.1 mi.) n. on Hwy. 11, 3 km (1.9 mi.) s. on Warman Rd., then 2 km (1.2 mi.) e. on Penner Rd., following signs. This First Nations park traces more than 6,000 years of area history. The park's interpretive center contains a DVD theater and features state-of-the-art exhibits and art pertaining to Northern Plains culture. Cultural programs include storytelling and children's activities.

Self-guiding trails take visitors through the 360-acre (146-hectare) park's prairie landscape, with interpretive signs explaining past uses of the land. Trails lead to 19 sites representing the Northern Plains peoples, including summer and winter campsites, archeological sites, four bison kill sites, a tipi ring site and a boulder alignment known as a medicine wheel. Visitors also can enjoy watching traditional dance performances.

Tours: Guided tours are available. **Time:** Allow 2 hours minimum. **Hours:** Daily 9-6 (11-6 on statutory holidays), Victoria Day-Labour Day; 9-4:30 (closed statutory holidays), rest of year. Dance performances take place daily at 2. **Cost:** $8.50; $7.50 (ages 65+); $6.50 (students with ID); $4 (children); free (ages 0-5). **Phone:** (306) 931-6767 or (877) 547-6546.

SAVE **WESTERN DEVELOPMENT MUSEUM'S 1910 BOOMTOWN** is at 2610 Lorne Ave. This indoor representation of a typical prairie town features more than 30 buildings. Displays include transportation artifacts and vintage agricultural equipment. **Time:** Allow 2 hours minimum. **Hours:** Daily 9-5, Apr.-Dec.; Tues.-Sun. 9-5, rest of year. Museum closes at 3 on Dec. 24 and 31. Closed Jan. 1, third Mon. in Feb., second Mon. in Oct., Nov. 11 and Dec. 25-26. **Cost:** $9; $8 (ages 65+); $6.25 (students with ID); $2.50 (ages 6-12); $20 (family). **Phone:** (306) 931-1910.

GAMBLING ESTABLISHMENTS

- **Dakota Dunes Casino** is 24 km (15 mi.) s. on Hwy. 219. **Hours:** Sun.-Wed. 9 a.m.-3 a.m., Thurs.-Sat. 9 a.m.-4 a.m., in summer; otherwise varies. **Phone:** (306) 667-6400.

BEST WESTERN HARVEST INN (306)244-5552

Hotel
$129-$138

AAA Benefit:
Members save up to 20%, plus 10% bonus points with Best Western Rewards®.

Address: 1715 Idylwyld Dr N S7L 1B4 **Location:** On Hwy 11 (Idylwyld Dr), 0.4 mi (0.7 km) s of jct Circle Dr. Located in a commercial area. **Facility:** 92 units. 2 stories, interior corridors. **Parking:** winter plug-ins. **Terms:** cancellation fee imposed, resort fee. **Amenities:** high-speed Internet. **Dining:** Ricky's All Day Grill, see separate listing. **Activities:** exercise room. **Guest Services:** valet laundry. **Free Special Amenities:** high-speed Internet and airport transportation.

 Banquet & Meeting Facilities Ricky's All Day Grill & Lounge Cold Beer & Wine Store

BEST WESTERN PLUS BLAIRMORE (306)242-2299

Hotel
$152-$162

AAA Benefit:
Members save up to 20%, plus 10% bonus points with Best Western Rewards®.

Address: 306 Shillington Crescent S7M 1L7 **Location:** Jct Hwy 7 and 14. **Facility:** 100 units. 4 stories, interior corridors. **Parking:** winter plug-ins. **Terms:** check-in 4 pm, cancellation fee imposed. **Amenities:** high-speed Internet. *Some:* safes. **Pool(s):** heated indoor. **Activities:** whirlpool, waterslide, exercise room. **Guest Services:** valet and coin laundry. **Free Special Amenities: full breakfast and high-speed Internet.**

 **Salt Water Pool, Waterslide & Whirlpool Tub Business Centre & Meeting Rooms Free Hot Breakfast**

COLONIAL SQUARE INN & SUITES (306)343-1676

Hotel
$114-$149

Address: 1301 8th St E S7H 0S7 **Location:** 1.5 mi (2.4 km) e of jct Hwy 11 (Idylwyld Dr); 1.4 mi (2.3 km) w of jct Circle Dr. Opposite Cumberland Park. **Facility:** 80 units. 2 stories (no elevator), interior corridors. **Parking:** winter plug-ins. **Terms:** cancellation fee imposed. **Activities:** exercise room. **Guest Services:** valet laundry. **Free Special Amenities: local telephone calls and high-speed Internet.**

COMFORT INN (306)934-1122

Hotel
$124-$180

Address: 2155 Northridge Dr S7L 6X6 **Location:** Just ne of jct Hwy 11 (Idylwyld Dr) and Circle Dr. Located in a commercial area. **Facility:** 80 units. 2 stories (no elevator), interior corridors. **Parking:** winter plug-ins. **Terms:** check-in 4 pm. **Guest Services:** valet laundry.

COUNTRY INN & SUITES BY CARLSON (306)934-3900

Hotel $120-$160 **Address:** 617 Cynthia St S7L 6B7 **Location:** Just w on Circle Dr from jct Hwy 11 (Idylwyld Dr), then just n on Ave CN. Located in a commercial area. **Facility:** 76 units. 3 stories, interior corridors. **Parking:** winter plug-ins. **Activities:** exercise room. **Guest Services:** valet and coin laundry.

Tell Us How We're Doing

If your visit to a TourBook-listed property doesn't meet your expectations, tell us about it.

AAA.com/TourBookComments

DAYS INN-SASKATOON (306)242-3297

Hotel
$155-$197

Address: 2000 Idylwyld Dr N S7L 7M7 **Location:** Just nw of jct Hwy 11 (Idylwyld Dr) and Circle Dr. Located in a commercial area. **Facility:** 101 units. 4 stories, interior corridors. **Parking:** winter plug-ins. **Amenities:** high-speed Internet. *Some:* safes. **Pool(s):** heated indoor. **Activities:** whirlpool, waterslide, exercise room. **Guest Services:** valet and coin laundry. **Free Special Amenities: continental breakfast and high-speed Internet.**

Free: Deluxe Continental Breakfast, WI-FI/High-Speed Internet, Airport Shuttle and Local Calls.

DELTA BESSBOROUGH (306)244-5521

Hotel
$139-$399

Address: 601 Spadina Crescent E S7K 3G8 **Location:** At 21st St E; center. Located beside park and river. **Facility:** This lovely castle on the river has grand public spaces and beautifully appointed rooms with a modern elegance that keep with the historical nature of its 1930s railroad lodging roots. 225 units. 6 stories, interior corridors. **Parking:** on-site (fee) and valet, winter plug-ins. **Terms:** cancellation fee imposed. **Amenities:** video games (fee), high-speed Internet. **Dining:** The Garden Court Cafe, Samurai Japanese Restaurant, see separate listings. **Pool(s):** heated indoor. **Activities:** sauna, whirlpool, steamroom, jogging, spa. **Guest Services:** valet laundry.

FOUR POINTS BY SHERATON SASKATOON

(306)933-9889

Hotel
$125-$199

FOUR POINTS BY SHERATON

AAA Benefit: Members get up to 20% off, plus Starwood Preferred Guest® bonuses.

Address: 103 Stonebridge Blvd S7T 0G3 **Location:** Hwy 11 (Louis Riel Tr) exit Clarence Ave S, just s, then just e. **Facility:** 119 units. 4 stories, interior corridors. **Bath:** shower only. **Parking:** winter plug-ins. **Amenities:** high-speed Internet. **Pool(s):** heated indoor. **Activities:** whirlpool, waterslide, exercise room. **Guest Services:** valet and coin laundry. **Free Special Amenities: newspaper and high-speed Internet.**

HILTON GARDEN INN (306)244-2311

Hotel $149-$209 **Address:** 90 22nd St E S7K 3X6 **Location:** Just e of jct Hwy 11 (Idylwyld Dr); at 1st Ave. Located in a downtown business district. **Facility:** 180 units. 16 stories, interior corridors. **Parking:** on-site (fee). **Terms:**

AAA Benefit: Unparalleled hospitality at a special Member rate.

1-7 night minimum stay, cancellation fee imposed. **Amenities:** high-speed Internet. **Pool(s):** heated indoor. **Activities:** whirlpool, exercise room. **Guest Services:** valet and coin laundry.

HOLIDAY INN EXPRESS HOTEL & SUITES (306)384-8844

Hotel $144-$171 **Address:** 315 Idylwyld Dr N S7L 0Z1 **Location:** On Hwy 11 (Idylwyld Dr), just n of 23rd St. Located in a commercial area. **Facility:** 121 units. 4 stories, interior corridors. **Parking:** winter plug-ins. **Amenities:** high-speed Internet. **Pool(s):** heated indoor. **Activities:** whirlpool, exercise room. **Guest Services:** valet laundry.

MOTEL 6 SASKATOON 306/665-6688

Hotel. Rates not provided. **Address:** 231 Marquis Dr S7R 1B7 **Location:** E of jct Trans-Canada Hwy 16; 0.4 mi (0.7 km) w of Hwy 11 (Idylwyld Dr). Opposite truck stop, close to Credit Union Centre. **Facility:** 67 units, some efficiencies. 3 stories, interior corridors. **Parking:** winter plug-ins. **Amenities:** high-speed Internet. **Pool(s):** heated indoor. **Activities:** whirlpool. **Guest Services:** coin laundry.

RADISSON HOTEL SASKATOON (306)665-3322

Hotel
$169-$249

Address: 405 20th St E S7K 6X6 **Location:** At 4th Ave S; center. Located close to a riverside park. **Facility:** 291 units. 19 stories, interior corridors. **Parking:** on-site (fee) and valet. **Terms:** 3 day cancellation notice, resort fee. **Amenities:** high-speed Internet. **Pool(s):** heated indoor. **Activities:** whirlpool, waterslide, exercise room. **Guest Services:** valet laundry. **Free Special Amenities: local telephone calls and high-speed Internet.**

RAMADA HOTEL & GOLF DOME (306)665-6500

Hotel $109-$179 **Address:** 806 Idylwyld Dr N S7L 0Z6 **Location:** On Hwy 11 (Idylwyld Dr), 2.5 mi (4 km) s of jct Circle Dr. **Facility:** 148 units. 6 stories, interior corridors. **Parking:** winter plug-ins. **Pool(s):** heated indoor. **Activities:** whirlpool. *Fee:* putting green, miniature golf. **Guest Services:** coin laundry.

SANDMAN HOTEL 306/477-4844

Hotel. Rates not provided. **Address:** 310 Circle Dr W S7L 2Y5 **Location:** Just w of Hwy 11 (Idylwyld Dr). Located in a commercial area. **Facility:** 190 units. 4 stories, interior corridors. **Parking:** winter plug-ins. **Terms:** check-in 4 pm. **Amenities:** high-speed Internet. **Dining:** 2 restaurants. **Pool(s):** heated indoor. **Activities:** whirlpool, exercise room. **Guest Services:** valet laundry.

SASKATOON INN HOTEL AND CONFERENCE CENTRE

(306)242-1440

Hotel
$139-$199

Address: 2002 Airport Dr S7L 6M4 **Location:** Jct Hwy 16 (Circle Dr) and 11 (Idylwyld Dr N), 0.6 mi (1 km) sw, then just nw. **Facility:** 250 units. 8 stories, interior corridors. **Parking:** winter plug-ins. **Terms:** check-in 4 pm, cancellation fee imposed. **Amenities:** high-speed Internet. **Pool(s):** heated indoor. **Activities:** whirlpool, exercise room. **Guest Services:** valet laundry. **Free Special Amenities: local telephone calls and high-speed Internet.**

SHERATON CAVALIER SASKATOON HOTEL
(306)652-6770

Hotel
$159-$289

Sheraton

AAA Benefit: Members get up to 20% off, plus Starwood Preferred Guest® bonuses.

Address: 612 Spadina Crescent E S7K 3G9 **Location:** At 21st St E; center. Opposite park and river. **Facility:** 249 units. 8 stories, interior corridors. **Parking:** on-site (fee), winter plug-ins. **Terms:** cancellation fee imposed. **Amenities:** high-speed Internet. **Dining:** Carver's Steakhouse, see separate listing. **Pool(s):** heated indoor. **Activities:** whirlpools, waterslide, exercise room. **Guest Services:** valet laundry.

SAVE ECO 🍴 🍷 🏊 BIZ 📶 ✕ 🛎 ⬛ / SOME UNITS 🐕 🖨

SUPER 8
(306)384-8989

Hotel $127-$132 **Address:** 706 Circle Dr E S7K 3T7 **Location:** 1.3 mi (2 km) e of jct Hwy 11 (Idylwyld Dr). Located in a commercial area. **Facility:** 69 units. 3 stories, interior corridors. **Parking:** winter plug-ins. **Guest Services:** valet laundry.

🍴 CALL 🖨 📶 ✕ 🛏 🖨 💻 / SOME UNITS FEE 🐕

WHERE TO EAT

2ND AVE GRILL
306/244-9899

American. Casual Dining. $11-$36 **AAA Inspector Notes:** In the heart of the downtown business district, this upscale grill offers an inviting atmosphere, with a center curved bar, and attentive, casual service. The varied menu features such items as soups, a good choice of tasty salads and appetizers, pasta, pizza, burgers, steaks, candied trout and duck with raspberry sauce. An enclosed courtyard in the rear offers additional seating. **Bar:** full bar. **Address:** 10-123 2nd Ave S S7K 7E6 **Location:** Just w of jct 22nd St; center. **Parking:** street only. L D CALL 🖨

ALEXANDER'S RESTAURANT & BAR
306/956-7777

International. Casual Dining. $9-$19 **AAA Inspector Notes:** Colorful art adorns the walls at this busy casual spot. Simply prepared, there's a little bit of everything to satisfy any palate from jambalaya to meatloaf, butter chicken, stir-fries, burgers, pastas, gourmet pizza, salmon and steak. They boast the fact that they don't use preservatives. **Bar:** full bar. **Reservations:** required. **Address:** 414 Cumberland Ave N S7N 1M6 **Location:** Just s of College Dr.
L D CALL 🖨

AMIGOS CANTINA
306/652-4912

Tex-Mex. Casual Dining. $10-$17 **AAA Inspector Notes:** Don't be put off by the basic bar décor because this spot has the city at its knees with its fabulous enchiladas, burritos and other Tex-Mex influenced pub food. My enchilada stuffed with chili, cottage cheese and fresh spinach came with delicious BBQ black beans and flavorful rice cooked just right. I can hardly wait to get back and try some more. Kids are allowed in until 8 pm which is when the joint gets hopping for their other famous reason; live local and Canadian bands most nights. **Bar:** full bar. **Address:** 806 Dufferin Ave S7H 2B8 **Location:** Just e of Broadway Ave, then just s. **Parking:** street only.
L D CALL 🖨

BLISS FINE FOOD
306/477-2077

Northern American. Casual Dining. $8-$27 **AAA Inspector Notes:** This modern little spot has a smaller menu that is quite creative and really well prepared. A starter of scallops with cinnamon roasted sweet potato, Creole mustard, beet syrup and bacon roast peanuts, followed by drunken fruit stuffed pork rib chop with Saskatoon berry demi glace and a finale of one of the decadent desserts like peanut butter cheesecake. Lunch is more casual with gourmet salad and sandwich offerings. The staff is knowledgeable and helpful. **Bar:** full bar. **Reservations:** suggested. **Address:** 1002 Broadway Ave S7N 1B9 **Location:** Corner of 9th St E. **Parking:** on-site and street. L D CALL 🖨

CALORIES BAKERY & RESTAURANT
306/665-7991

International. Casual Dining. $13-$32 **AAA Inspector Notes:** This bistro style spot absolutely tantalizes the taste buds from fanciful cocktails made with fresh ingredients and carefully selected wines to food which the chef creates utilizing local producers. Start with rabbit pâté and house relish or heirloom tomatoes with lentil mousse and chèvre cheese. Entrées include daily organic beef and lamb creations along with their chicken with corn three ways. Equally delicious, lunch is simpler. You must save room for the delightful desserts. **Bar:** full bar. **Reservations:** suggested. **Address:** 721 Broadway Ave S7N 1B3 **Location:** Just s of Broadway Bridge. **Parking:** street only. L D CALL 🖨

CARVER'S STEAKHOUSE
306/652-8292

Steak. Casual Dining. $26-$45 **AAA Inspector Notes:** This popular, upscale restaurant serves Caesar salads prepared tableside along with made-to-order, mouthwatering steaks. Delightful appetizers and fine fish and meat entrées are offered along with decadent desserts. **Bar:** full bar. **Reservations:** suggested. **Address:** 612 Spadina Crescent E S7K 3G9 **Location:** At 21st St E; center; in Sheraton Cavalier Saskatoon Hotel. **Parking:** on-site (fee) and valet. D

CHIANTI
306/665-8466

Italian. Casual Dining. $10-$19 **AAA Inspector Notes:** Lining the menu is a good selection of fresh pasta creations, as well as veal, seafood and chicken dishes. Personable servers circulate in an atmosphere that suits families and couples. Located near downtown, the dining room boasts warm red walls and travel posters of Italy. **Bar:** full bar. **Reservations:** suggested. **Address:** 102 Idylwyld Dr N S7L 0Y7 **Location:** Corner of 22nd St E; center.
L D

CHRISTIES IL SECONDO BAKERY PIZZERIA
306/384-0506

Breads/Pastries Pizza. Quick Serve. $8-$18 **AAA Inspector Notes:** Delicious gourmet pizza and panini made with quality ingredients are the focal point at this urban chic bakery along with some scrumptious baked goods and breads. Service is limited to ordering at the counter and picking up your food when your number is called. Seating can get a little tight at the busy times. They are also open for early evening dinner later in the week. **Bar:** beer & wine. **Address:** 802C Broadway Ave S7N 1B6 **Location:** Just w on 10th St E. **Parking:** street only. L D CALL 🖨

EARLS RESTAURANT
306/664-4060

American. Casual Dining. $11-$29 **AAA Inspector Notes:** Offering an experience that falls between fast food and fine dining, the fun, relaxed restaurant prepares great food at a great price. Choices range from juicy burgers, hearty sandwiches, fresh salads, wings and pizza to full entrees of steak, chops and seafood. Made-from-scratch soups and assorted breads, as well as a nice choice of wines and beers, round out the offerings. This is a fitting spot for impromptu get-togethers and festive occasions. **Bar:** full bar. **Address:** 610 2nd Ave N S7K 2C8 **Location:** Jct Queen St. **Parking:** street only. L D LATE

THE GARDEN COURT CAFE
306/683-6912

Regional Canadian. Casual Dining. $14-$28 **AAA Inspector Notes:** It is a bit of a secret that this hotel café gussies up with white linen for dinner and the chef creates a creative and delicious menu produced with most ingredients sourced within 100 miles of Saskatoon. The menu changes up, but examples are pecan-crusted Saskatchewan pickerel with corn and barley pilaf, maple duck breast or wild boar shepherd's pie. The best deal is to get an amuse bouche (bite-size hors d'oeuvre) and an intermezzo course with coffee and a sample of wine. **Bar:** full bar. **Reservations:** suggested. **Address:** 601 Spadina Crescent E S7K 3G8 **Location:** At 21st St E; center; in Delta Bessborough. **Parking:** valet and street only.
B L D CALL 🖨

GENESIS FAMILY RESTAURANT
306/244-5516

Chinese. Casual Dining. $8-$16 **AAA Inspector Notes:** The restaurant features a progressive Chinese menu offering many healthy choices, all made with fresh ingredients. Portions are large, and the diverse and creative menu includes Western dishes. Dim sum is served daily 11 am-2:30 pm. Servers are friendly. **Bar:** full bar. **Address:** 901 22nd St W S7M 0R9 **Location:** 0.6 mi (1 km) w of Hwy 11 (Idylwyld Dr). D

GOLDEN PAGODA BURMESE ASIAN RESTAURANT
306/668-9114

◆◆ Burmese. Casual Dining. $7-$16 **AAA Inspector Notes:** Small and simply decorated with a gold pagoda, this restaurant offers flavorful and plentiful specialties from Burma. Highlights include spiced samosas, pickled green tea salad, specialty soups (including the 12-ingredient soup), spicy ginger lemon grass, coconut shrimp and a variety of curries and noodle dishes. Most come in degrees from 1 to 10. The lunch menu is less extensive but includes some Asian-themed pizza. **Bar:** beer & wine. **Reservations:** suggested. **Address:** 411 2nd Ave N S7K 2C1 **Location:** Jct Trans-Canada Hwy 1 (Circle Dr) and Warman Rd, 1.7 mi (2.9 km) s.

L D CALL 🅼

THE IVY DINING & LOUNGE
306/384-4444

◆◆◆ International. Casual Dining. $10-$34 **AAA Inspector Notes:** This upscale and trendy spot is complemented by proficient service and a creative menu which utilizes high-quality ingredients. Menu highlights include Moroccan lamb with a tagine sauce, gourmet pasta, Arctic char or other fresh fish, osso buco, jambalaya and a AAA Premium steak with a choice of delectable toppings. **Bar:** full bar. **Reservations:** suggested. **Address:** 301 Ontario Ave S7K 1S3 **Location:** Jct Trans-Canada Hwy 1 (Circle Rd) and 11 (Idylwyld Rd), 1.6 mi (2.6 km) s, then just e on 24th St E. **Parking:** street only.

L D CALL 🅼

JAKE'S ON 21ST
306/373-8383

◆◆ ◆◆ American. Casual Dining. $6-$12 **AAA Inspector Notes:** Popular with the downtown crowd, this casual hot spot is great for fresh and quick meals. Tasty soups along with salads, grilled panini, baked wraps, burgers and homemade cakes and squares fill out the menu. Sandwiches and burgers come with your choice of pita chips and dill sauce, soup or a garden or Caesar salad. Simple breakfast items are offered until 11 am. Service is friendly and efficient. **Address:** 307 21st St E S7K 0C1 **Location:** Jct Trans-Canada Hwy 1 (Circle Dr) and Warman Rd, 2.2 mi (3.6 km) s, then just e; center. **Parking:** street only.

B L

KEOS THAI & LAO CUISINE
306/652-2533

◆◆ ◆◆ Thai. Casual Dining. $10-$19 **AAA Inspector Notes:** This is a simple little spot with flavorful food. Some interesting soups and salads as well as your usual pad thai, curries and other stir-fry dishes are found on the menu. The owner makes a mouthwatering slightly spicy Lao pork sausage served as an appetizer which I thought paired up nicely with the papaya tum salad. Service can get a bit chaotic but it is worth the wait. **Bar:** full bar. **Address:** 1013 Broadway Ave S7N 1C1 **Location:** 0.6 mi (1 km) s of Broadway Bridge. **Parking:** street only.

L D

LAS PALAPAS RESORT GRILL
306/244-5556

◆◆ ◆◆ Caribbean. Casual Dining. $8-$22 **AAA Inspector Notes:** This little oasis set in the prairie features food and libations from Mexico, Jamaica, Cuba and Latin America. Flavorful and plentiful portions of jerk chicken, curries, pozole, burritos, quesadillas, enchiladas and tacos all are offered with nice little twists. Be sure to try the yummy homemade sweet potato fries. Service is brisk. **Bar:** full bar. **Address:** 910 Victoria Ave S7N 0Z6 **Location:** Jct Hwy 11 (Idylwyld Dr) and 8th St, 0.4 mi (0.6 km) e, then just n. **Parking:** street only.

L D

MOXIE'S CLASSIC GRILL
306/374-9800

◆◆ ◆◆ American. Casual Dining. $12-$33 **AAA Inspector Notes:** This sleek, funky and popular restaurant presents an extensive menu of creatively prepared dishes, including pizza, pasta, rice, noodles, signature salads and burgers. Other menus include one for children and one for Sunday brunch. Lending to the upbeat, stylish decor are dark wood appointments and river rock fireplaces. **Bar:** full bar. **Address:** 3134 8th St E S7H 0W2 **Location:** Jct Circle Dr, just se.

L D LATE

RICKY'S ALL DAY GRILL
306/652-3222

◆◆◆ ◆◆◆
American
Family Dining
$10-$25

AAA Inspector Notes: The comfortable eatery, which employs friendly servers, presents a varied menu that includes pasta dishes, wraps, omelets, stir-fry preparations and burgers. Portions are generous. Children's and senior selections are offered. Guests can request seating in a booth or at a table. **Bar:** full bar. **Address:** 1715 Idylwyld Dr N S7L 1B4 **Location:** On Hwy 11 (Idylwyld Dr), 0.4 mi (0.7 km) s of jct Circle Dr; in BEST WESTERN Harvest Inn.

B L D

ST. TROPEZ BISTRO
306/652-1250

◆◆◆◆ International. Casual Dining. $23-$32 **AAA Inspector Notes:** Lovely exposed brick walls with modern art and lighting set the mood for a great evening out. The well-crafted menu has some global influence and is created using fresh ingredients — some of which come from their roof top garden. Spinach balls or creamy chicken liver pâté would be good to start, followed up with entrées like Saskatoon berry poached salmon, blackened chicken or curried lamb. It would smart to save room for the delicious house desserts. **Bar:** full bar. **Reservations:** suggested. **Address:** 238 2nd Ave S S7K 1K9 **Location:** Just n of 20th St E; center. **Parking:** street only.

D CALL 🅼

SAMURAI JAPANESE RESTAURANT
306/683-6926

◆◆◆ Japanese. Casual Dining. $17-$36 **AAA Inspector Notes:** Finely crafted sushi and authentic tableside Teppanyaki cuisine are featured at this dining room. **Bar:** full bar. **Reservations:** suggested. **Address:** 601 Spadina Crescent E S7K 3G8 **Location:** At 21st St E; center; in Delta Bessborough. **Parking:** on-site (fee).

D

SOULEIO
306/979-8102

◆ Natural/Organic Deli. Quick Serve. $7-$13 **AAA Inspector Notes:** Featuring fabulous gourmet salads, soups, panini and mouthwatering desserts, this casual spot is set inside a warm and inviting organic grocery. Menu items are attractively displayed in showcases and there is an eclectic collection of wine. Orders are placed at the counter guest can collect their meal when their name is called. Family suppers are offered and include a daily special, mixed salad and dressing, a rotating seasonal side and a baguette. **Bar:** wine only. **Address:** 265 3rd Ave S S7K 1M3 **Location:** Between 20th and 21st sts E; center. **Parking:** street only.

L D CALL 🅼

THE SPADINA FREEHOUSE
306/668-1000

◆◆◆ International. Gastropub. $10-$24 **AAA Inspector Notes:** Not really a pub even though they have a great selection of beer, this trendy and popular spot offers an eclectic selection of flavorsome menu items ranging from South American empanadas to tandoori chicken tenders. For an entrée, choose from lovely salads, gourmet sandwiches and such dishes as Kashmiri chicken and fire roasted halibut. A highlight here is the signature birch wood-fired oven pizza. Service is efficient and friendly. **Bar:** full bar. **Reservations:** suggested. **Address:** 608 Spadina Cres E S7K 3G9 **Location:** Jct Hwy 11 (Idylwyld Dr N) and 22nd St E, 0.5 mi (0.9 km) e, then just s; center. **Parking:** street only.

L D LATE CALL 🅼

SUSHIRO
306/665-5557

◆◆ Sushi. Casual Dining. $10-$25 **AAA Inspector Notes:** This is a hip spot with bright fresh design and a bistro feel. The kitchen puts a modern spin on the menu with a great selection of appetizing starters like crab suimeno soup, fresh ceviche, panko-crusted mushroom risotto cakes, acorn squash tempura or spicy octopus salad. The nigiri and sashimi choices are not as abundant as some Japanese restaurants but you cannot deny the quality and the selection of maki sushi is very good. **Bar:** full bar. **Reservations:** suggested. **Address:** 737B Broadway Ave S7N 1B3 **Location:** Just e on 10th St E. **Parking:** street only.

D CALL 🅼

TAJ MAHAL
306/978-2227

◆◆ Indian. Casual Dining. $7-$30 **AAA Inspector Notes:** Chic modern décor with billowing ceiling fabric sets the mood for fine Indian dining. Everything is prepared in house at this family-owned operation down to the grinding of their own spices. You can view the kitchen and tandoor oven cooking through a glass window. The tasty and well prepared menu, while not extensive, has most of the traditional favorites and they seem to take great delight in serving you and assisting with menu choices. **Bar:** full bar. **Reservations:** suggested. **Address:** 157 2nd Ave N, #6 S7K 2A9 **Location:** Just w on 23rd St E; center. **Parking:** street only.

L D CALL 🅼

TRUFFLES BISTRO
306/373-7779

◆◆◆ New Canadian. Casual Dining. $12-$28 **AAA Inspector Notes:** This warm and inviting lengthy room leads to an open kitchen where the delectable menu is prepared. With a leaning toward bistro fare, the chef sources fresh Saskatchewan and Canadian products. Teamwork here ensures diners never lack the delicious house bread or water. Bread, desserts and pastries are made in their own bakery. **Bar:** full bar. **Reservations:** suggested. **Address:** 230 21st St E S7K 0B9 **Location:** Between 2nd and 3rd aves S; center. **Parking:** street only.

L D CALL 🅼

TUSQ RESTAURANT   306/244-8877

▼▼▼ American. Casual Dining. $10-$45 **AAA Inspector Notes:** This stylish fine dining restaurant has an open kitchen concept where a tantalizing range of dishes are created. A sample menu could range from a starter of pan-seared pickerel with pesto cream and fresh pear to such entrées as beef and blue cheese pasta, ginger rack of lamb or smoked apple chicken pasta with stewed bacon and bean cassoulet. Closed for lunch on Saturday and Sunday. **Bar:** full bar. **Reservations:** suggested. **Address:** 416 21st St E S7K 0C2 **Location:** Just e of 4th Ave S; center. **Parking:** street only.

[L] [D]

WECZERIA FOOD & WINE   306/933-9600

Canadian
Casual Dining
$13-S32

AAA Inspector Notes: Expect distinct and delicious flavors in this casual little bistro. Here, innovative Canadian fare is mixed with some French and global influences. The menu is quite small but offerings change often and are marked on chalkboards brought to the table as the chef likes to purchase his product daily from the local markets and producers. Servers are knowledgeable and will gladly help diners choose selections. **Bar:** full bar. **Reservations:** suggested. **Address:** 820 Broadway Ave S7N 0B6 **Location:** Hwy 11 (Louis Riel Tr), just e on 19 St, 0.6 mi (0.9 km) s on Broadway Ave, then just e; south of river. **Parking:** valet and street only.

[L] [D]

SCEPTRE (E-2) pop. 97, elev. 671m/2,200'

GREAT SANDHILLS MUSEUM is on Hwy. 32. Housed in a former school, the museum has rooms depicting early pioneer life in the community, including a boarding house, library, hospital, blacksmith shop, dentist's office, schoolhouse, general store display, barn and church. An interpretive center provides information about the great sandhills. **Time:** Allow 30 minutes minimum. **Hours:** Mon.-Sat. 10-noon and 12:30-4:30, Sun. 1-5, May 15-Sept. 2. **Cost:** $5; $3 (ages 6-18). **Phone:** (306) 623-4345.

SHAUNAVON (F-2) pop. 1,756

GRAND COTEAU HERITAGE AND CULTURAL CENTRE, 2 blks. n. of Third Ave. at 440 Centre St., houses a museum with displays depicting local and natural history. The building also mounts exhibitions of contemporary art and serves as a tourist information center. **Time:** Allow 30 minutes minimum. **Hours:** Mon.-Sat. 9-5 (also Tues. and Thurs. 5-7:30) , May 1-Oct. 1; Tues.-Sat. 1:30-5, rest of year. **Cost:** Free. **Phone:** (306) 297-3882. 🅷

SIMPSON (D-4) pop. 131

LAST MOUNTAIN LAKE SANCTUARY is at the n. end of Last Mountain Lake; access is via a grid road branching off Hwy. 2 (watch for signs). Said to be the oldest bird sanctuary in North America, the wildlife refuge was established in 1887 and covers 1,012 hectares (2,500 acres). The area's favorable habitats and location make it a haven for more than 280 species of birds.

Each year during May and between mid-August and mid-September more than 20,000 sandhill cranes stop at the sanctuary during their seasonal migration. There are two self-guiding nature trails and a self-guiding driving tour. *See Recreation Areas Chart.* **Time:** Allow 1 hour minimum. **Hours:** Sanctuary open daily dawn-dusk. Office open Mon.-Fri. 8-4. **Cost:** Free. **Phone:** (306) 836-2022.

🅰 🗶 🛏 🅷

STOUGHTON pop. 694

POPLAR TREE INN   306/457-3540

▼▼▼ Hotel $108-$149 **Address:** 600 Government Rd S0G 4T0 **Location:** Jct Hwy 33, 47 and 13. **Facility:** 43 units. 3 stories, interior corridors. **Parking:** winter plug-ins. **Terms:** cancellation fee imposed. **Amenities:** high-speed Internet. **Activities:** limited exercise equipment. **Guest Services:** valet laundry.

🍽 CALL 📵 BIZ 📶 🗶 🛏 🖼 🖵

STRASBOURG (E-4) pop. 752

STRASBOURG AND DISTRICT MUSEUM is at Mountain St. and Railway Ave. Nature displays, handicrafts and pioneer artifacts are exhibited. **Hours:** Sat. 10-4, Sun. 1-5, June 2-Aug. 31. **Cost:** Donations. **Phone:** (306) 725-3443.

SWIFT CURRENT (E-3) pop. 15,503
• Hotels p. 560 • Restaurants p. 560

Once the site of transient First Nations and fur trader camps, Swift Current began as a North West Mounted Police encampment on Swift Current Creek in 1874. Soon after, the Canadian Pacific Railway built a depot, and the settlement became the freight terminus for western Canada. From this point goods were hauled by wagon on overland trails; deep ruts can still be seen on the old North Battleford Trail north of Swift Current.

With the turn of the 20th century came the farmers and ranchers whose trades formed the backbone of the city's economy. Oil was discovered in this area in 1952, and in the decades since Swift Current has not only developed into a business hub for the oil, gas and agricultural industries but has become the major health care center for southwestern Saskatchewan.

Swift Current Creek runs through town, and two nearby lakes offer recreational facilities. At Saskatchewan Landing Provincial Park *(see Recreation Areas Chart)*, a plaque marks the spot where pioneers once forded the South Saskatchewan River on their way into the wilds of the northern province. In the park's hills are several First Nations grave sites and tepee rings.

Doc's Heritage Village, 17th Avenue S.E. and S. Railway Street in Kinetic Exhibition Park, has a collection of buildings typical of early 20th-century prairie towns, including a blacksmith shop, church and school. Costumed staff are on hand to answer questions; phone (306) 773-2944.

Tourism Swift Current: 44 Robert St. W., Swift Current, SK, Canada S9H 4M9. **Phone:** (306) 778-9174.

Self-guiding tours: A brochure with details about a walking tour of historic buildings in downtown Swift

Current is available at the Swift Current Museum and from downtown merchants.

ART GALLERY OF SWIFT CURRENT is at 411 Herbert St. E. This public art gallery offers exhibitions of local, provincial and national artwork. Cultural events and festivals are scheduled throughout the year. Guided tours are given upon request. **Hours:** Open Mon.-Thurs. 1-5 and 7-9 p.m., Fri.-Sun. 1-5, Sept.-June; Mon.-Sat. 1-5 (also Mon.-Thurs 7-9 p.m.), rest of year. Closed major holidays and during exhibition changes. Phone ahead to confirm schedule. **Cost:** Free. **Phone:** (306) 778-2736.

SWIFT CURRENT MUSEUM is at 44 Robert St. W. Permanent, interactive and temporary exhibits depict 10,000 years of natural and human history in southwest Saskatchewan. Permanent exhibits include a series of storyboards, artifacts, mounted prairie animals and interactive exhibits. **Tours:** Guided tours are available. **Hours:** Mon.-Fri. 9-5, Sat.-Sun. 1-5, June-Aug.; Mon.-Fri. 9-5, rest of year. Closed major holidays. **Cost:** Donations. Cash only. **Phone:** (306) 778-2775.

GAMBLING ESTABLISHMENTS

- **Living Sky Casino** is at 1401 North Service Rd. E. **Hours:** Daily 9 a.m.-2 a.m. **Phone:** (306) 778-5759.

BEST WESTERN PLUS INN   (306)773-4660

Hotel
$130-$150

AAA Benefit: Members save up to 20%, plus 10% bonus points with Best Western Rewards®.

Address: 105 George St W S9H 0K4 **Location:** Jct Trans-Canada Hwy 1 and Central Ave. **Facility:** 86 units. 2 stories (no elevator), interior corridors. **Parking:** winter plug-ins. **Terms:** check-in 4 pm. **Amenities:** *Some:* high-speed Internet. **Pool(s):** heated indoor. **Activities:** sauna, whirlpools, exercise room. **Guest Services:** valet and coin laundry. **Free Special Amenities: expanded continental breakfast and high-speed Internet.**

COMFORT INN   (306)778-3994

▼▼ **Hotel** $112-$126 **Address:** 1510 S Service Rd E S9H 3X6 **Location:** On south side service road of Trans-Canada Hwy 1, just w of 22nd Ave NE. **Facility:** 74 units. 2 stories (no elevator), interior corridors. **Parking:** winter plug-ins. **Terms:** cancellation fee imposed. **Guest Services:** valet laundry.

GREEN HECTARES BED & BREAKFAST   306/773-7632

▼▼ **Bed & Breakfast** $95-$120 **Address:** Waker Rd S9H 4M7 **Location:** Trans-Canada Hwy 1 exit 22nd Ave NE, just n to Saskatchewan Dr, e to Adams St, then to Waker Rd. Located on a small cattle ranch, close to Cypress Regional Hospital. **Facility:** 6 units. 1 story, interior/exterior corridors. *Bath:* some shared. **Parking:** winter plug-ins. **Activities:** whirlpool, fishing, hiking trails. **Guest Services:** complimentary laundry.

HOLIDAY INN EXPRESS & SUITES   (306)773-8288

▼▼▼ **Hotel** $149-$179 **Address:** 1301 N Service Rd E S9H 3X6 **Location:** Trans-Canada Hwy 1 exit Hwy 4 (Cadillac/Rosetown), 0.6 mi (1 km) w. **Facility:** 103 units. 4 stories, interior corridors. **Parking:** winter plug-ins. **Amenities:** high-speed Internet. **Pool(s):** heated indoor. **Activities:** whirlpool, exercise room. **Guest Services:** valet and coin laundry.

MOTEL 6 SWIFT CURRENT   (306)778-6060

▼▼ ▼▼ **Hotel** $100-$111 **Address:** 1185 5th Ave NE S9H 5N7 **Location:** Trans-Canada Hwy 1, just e of Central Ave N, then just n; just n of N Service Rd. **Facility:** 58 units, some efficiencies. 4 stories, interior corridors. **Parking:** winter plug-ins. **Terms:** check-in 4 pm. **Guest Services:** coin laundry.

SAFARI INN MOTEL   306/773-4608

Motel
$80-$90

Address: 810 S Service Rd E S9H 3T9 **Location:** On south side service road of Trans-Canada Hwy 1, just e of Central Ave. **Facility:** 18 units, some two bedrooms and efficiencies. 1 story, exterior corridors. **Parking:** winter plug-ins. **Terms:** cancellation fee imposed. **Amenities:** high-speed Internet. **Guest Services:** coin laundry. **Free Special Amenities: local telephone calls and high-speed Internet.**

SUPER 8   (306)778-6088

▼▼ ▼▼ **Hotel** $113-$123 **Address:** 405 N Service Rd E S9H 3X6 **Location:** Trans-Canada Hwy 1, just e of Central Ave N. **Facility:** 63 units. 2 stories (no elevator), interior corridors. **Parking:** winter plug-ins. **Pool(s):** heated indoor. **Activities:** whirlpool, exercise room. **Guest Services:** valet and coin laundry.

WHERE TO EAT

AKROPOL FAMILY RESTAURANT   306/773-5454

▼▼ International. Casual Dining. $10-$23 **AAA Inspector Notes:** This popular restaurant has been in the family for more than 45 years and offers a contemporary decor with comfortable semi-private booths as well as open tables. They offer an extensive menu which includes such Greek offerings as gyros and souvlaki as well as salads, pasta, burgers, pizza, steak and fresh fish, including North Saskatchewan pickerel filet which is cooked to perfection. **Bar:** full bar. **Reservations:** suggested. **Address:** 133 Central Ave N S9H 0K9 **Location:** Between Cheadle E and Chaplin E sts; center.

HORIZONS RESTAURANT   306/778-5759

▼▼ American. Casual Dining. $9-$16 **AAA Inspector Notes:** Walk through the casino to get to this bright restaurant which shines with glossy wood floors and tables with metallic leaf insets. Not a complex menu but it is well prepared with quality ingredients and is one of the better spots in town with friendly service. The Saskatchewan fish chowder is a standout, while the Indian bison taco on fry bread is popular. There also is a variety of burgers, sandwiches and other familiar entrées available. Large screen TVs keep up with all the sports action. **Bar:** full bar. **Address:** 1401 N Service Rd E S9H 3X6 **Location:** Trans-Canada Hwy 1 exit Hwy 4 (Cadillac/Rosetown), 0.6 mi (1 km) w; in Living Sky Casino.

MISO HOUSE   306/778-4411

Japanese
Casual Dining
$8-$18

AAA Inspector Notes: At this modern restaurant, guests find a good selection of reasonably priced entrées, many of which include miso soup, rice and kimchee. Couples prefer the sushi boat. **Bar:** beer & wine. **Address:** 285 N Service Rd W S9H 3S8 **Location:** Trans-Canada Hwy 1, 0.4 mi (0.6 km) w of Hwy 4 (Central Ave).

SPRINGS GARDEN   306/773-2021

▼▼ American. Family Dining. $7-$28 **AAA Inspector Notes:** The menu at this casual, contemporary restaurant includes a variety of popular dishes: soup, steak, chicken, seafood, pizza, ribs and Greek specialties. The server staff at this bright and cheerful eatery is friendly, efficient and prompt. **Bar:** full bar. **Reservations:** suggested, Thurs-Sun. **Address:** 1 Springs Dr, Suite 323 S9H 3X6 **Location:** Trans-Canada Hwy 1, on north service road; in Swift Current Shopping Mall.

TNT FAMILY RESTAURANT
306/773-6002

American
Family Dining
$9-$25

AAA Inspector Notes: Slide into a booth at this family-owned and -operated spot which the locals love and prepare to savor such specialties as tender breaded pork cutlets, chicken parmigiana, steaks and barbecue back ribs. In addition they also feature some Greek classics, including spanakopita (spinach pie), souvlaki and chicken steak a la Greek. Gluten-free pizza also is offered. In the evenings it gets more intimate as the lights are dimmed and the candles are lit. **Bar:** full bar. **Address:** 155 N Service Rd W S9H 3X6 **Location:** On north side service road of Trans-Canada Hwy 1, just w of Central Ave N; next to Westwind Motel.
Menu on AAA.com L D

WONG'S KITCHEN
306/773-4636

Chinese. Casual Dining. $11-$30 **AAA Inspector Notes:** One of the best spots in town to visit, this locally popular restaurant features Cantonese-style preparation of its dishes. The menu also offers steak and seafood selections. A smorgasbord is served noon-2 pm each day. The staff is helpful. **Bar:** full bar. **Address:** 320 S Service Rd E S9H 3T6 **Location:** Just e of jct Trans-Canada Hwy 1 and Hwy 4 (Central Ave). L D

TISDALE (C-4) pop. 3,180

This rural community in northeastern Saskatchewan provides easy access to several provincial parks offering recreational activities from fishing and boating in summer to skiing in winter. A roadside attraction, claimed to be the world's largest honeybee, stands on the south side of Hwy. 3 in town.

Greville Jones Wildlife Sanctuary is reached by a gravel access road about 6.4 kilometres (4 mi.) southwest of Tisdale off Hwy. 3, following signs. The site of an old farmstead, it is a pleasant place for a summer picnic or hike along one of several nature trails.

Another scenic route is the Doghide River Trail, a system of walking, cycling and skiing trails that run along several sections of the riverbank. The trail can be accessed from the junction of Hwys. 3 and 35; proceed east .8 kilometre (.5 mi.), then north .5 kilometre (.3 mi.) and turn right into Kinsmen McKay Park.

TISDALE & DISTRICT MUSEUM, HERITAGE CENTRE AND DOGHIDE VILLAGE, at jct. Hwy. 3 and Heritage Rd. at the western approach to town, comprises three main areas. The Station houses a bee farming display, while Doghide Village features the furnished 1920 Pearse House, a log barn and milk house and a fire hall complete with antique water wagon. The Heritage Centre contains the Dagg Collection of vintage automobiles, which range from standard Fords and Chevrolets to such unusual makes as Star, Whippet and Essex.

Tours: Guided tours are available. **Time:** Allow 30 minutes minimum. **Hours:** Mon.-Thurs. 1-6, Victoria Day-Labour Day. **Cost:** $4; $12 (family). **Phone:** (306) 873-4999.

AAA/CAA travel information: Available in print, online and on the go!

UNITY pop. 2,389

PRAIRIE MOON INN & SUITES
306/228-3333

Hotel $116-$152 **Address:** 103 2nd Ave S S0K 4L0 **Location:** Hwy 14, west end of town. **Facility:** 63 units. 3 stories, interior corridors. **Parking:** winter plug-ins. **Terms:** check-in 4 pm. **Amenities:** high-speed Internet. **Activities:** exercise room. **Guest Services:** coin laundry.

🛜 ✖ 📷 🛗 🍽 🖨 / SOME UNITS FEE 🛒

WADENA (D-4) pop. 1,306, elev. 488m/1,600'

WADENA & DISTRICT MUSEUM is at 302 Main St. S. Housed in a 1904 train station, the museum preserves items relating to the history of the pioneers who settled the area in the early 20th century. Exhibits include antique farm equipment, a 1914 farm house, a country schoolhouse, a teacherage, a church, a general store, a blacksmith shop and a Royal Canadian Mounted Police barracks replica. A caboose is adjacent to the station.

Time: Allow 30 minutes minimum. **Hours:** Tues.-Sat. 9-5, Sun. 10-5, mid-May through Labour Day. Closed major holidays. **Cost:** $5; $3 (ages 12-18); $2 (ages 5-11). **Phone:** (306) 338-3454.

WAKAW (D-4) pop. 985

WAKAW HERITAGE MUSEUM is in the center of town at 300 1st St. S. Exhibits include Ukrainian artworks and implements, mementos from both world wars, homestead displays and a wide assortment of items dating from the early to late 1900s. **Time:** Allow 30 minutes minimum. **Hours:** Fri.-Mon. 11-5, July 1-Labour Day. **Cost:** Donations. **Phone:** (306) 233-4223.

John Diefenbaker's Law Office is off 1st St. S. at 3rd Ave. S. The site is a replica of the original office where the 13th prime minister of Canada practiced law 1919-25. Guides are available at the Wakaw Heritage Museum. **Hours:** Fri.-Mon. 1-4, July 1-Labour Day. **Phone:** (306) 233-4223.

WEYBURN (F-4) pop. 10,484
• Hotels p. 562 • Restaurants p. 562

• Hotels p. 562 • Restaurants p. 562

Weyburn's name was coined in 1893 by Scottish railroad workers, who called this marshy area at the headwaters of the Souris River "wee burn." From these humble beginnings the town has grown into a major marketing center for the surrounding agricultural area. Weyburn is the southeastern terminus of scenic Hwy. 39, which continues to Moose Jaw.

The town was immortalized as "Crocus, Saskatchewan" in the works of W.O. Mitchell, who was born and reared in Weyburn and penned the book "Who Has Seen the Wind." A summary of Weyburn's history since its earliest days is depicted on the "Wheel of Progress" at the Weyburn Library. Between the spokes of the brass-rimmed mahogany wheel, which weighs 909 kilograms (2,000 lbs.) and has a diameter of 3.9 metres (13 ft.), are 10 mosaic panels showing highlights of the city's past.

Weyburn Chamber of Commerce: 11 - 3rd St. N.E., Weyburn, SK, Canada S4H 0W1. **Phone:** (306) 842-4738.

SOO LINE HISTORICAL MUSEUM is e. on Hwy. 39 at 411 Industrial Ln. Local pioneer artifacts trace the area's early history. The museum houses more than 5,000 pieces of silver, glass and antique furniture dating 1750-1970. Donated by Charles Wilson, the exhibit is reputed to be one of the country's largest private collections. **Time:** Allow 30 minutes minimum. **Hours:** Mon.-Fri. 9-6, Sat.-Sun. and statutory holidays 11-6, Victoria Day weekend-Labour Day weekend; Mon.-Fri. 1-5, rest of year. **Cost:** $5; $4 (students with ID); $2 (ages 2-11). **Phone:** (306) 842-2922.

WEYBURN HERITAGE VILLAGE is 1 km (.6 mi.) s. from jct. Hwys. 35 and 39, then 1 km (.6 mi.) e. on 10th Ave. S.E. This historical village has been replicated to depict community life from the turn of the 20th century to the 1940s. All the buildings have been restored. Farm machinery is on display and visitors also may view a one-room school, rural municipality office, country church and blacksmith shop.

Tours: Guided tours are available. **Time:** Allow 1 hour minimum. **Hours:** Daily 1-8, May-Aug. **Cost:** $5; $3 (ages 13-17 and 65+); $2 (ages 6-12). **Phone:** (306) 842-6377. 🏠

CANALTA HOTEL   306/842-8000
💎💎💎💎 **Hotel.** Rates not provided. **Address:** 1360 Sims Ave S4H 3N9 **Location:** On Hwy 39, just w of Hwy 35. **Facility:** 67 units. 4 stories, interior/exterior corridors. **Parking:** winter plug-ins. **Amenities:** high-speed Internet. **Activities:** whirlpool, steamroom, exercise room. **Guest Services:** coin laundry, area transportation.

 ECO 🛏️ CALL Ⓜ️ BIZ 📶 ✕ 🛗 🖥️ 💻 / SOME UNITS FEE 🐕

PERFECT INNS & SUITES   (306)842-2691
💎💎 | **Address:** 238 Sims Ave S4H 2J8 **Location:** 0.3 mi (0.5 km) w of jct Hwy 35 and
Motel | 39. Next to McDonalds. **Facility:** 81
$95-$250 | units, some kitchens. 1 story, interior/exterior corridors. **Parking:** winter plug-ins. **Terms:** check-in 4 pm, cancellation fee imposed. **Guest Services:** coin laundry. **Free Special Amenities:** full breakfast and use of on-premises laundry facilities.

SAVE BIZ 📶 🛗 💻 / SOME UNITS FEE 🐕 🖥️

RAMADA INN & SUITES   (306)842-4994
💎💎💎 **Hotel** $139-$219 **Address:** 1420 Sims Ave S4H 3N9 **Location:** On Hwy 39, just w of Hwy 35. **Facility:** 78 units, some efficiencies. 3 stories, interior/exterior corridors. **Parking:** winter plug-ins. **Amenities:** high-speed Internet. **Pool(s):** heated indoor. **Activities:** whirlpool, exercise room. **Guest Services:** coin laundry.

ECO 🛏️ 🛒 BIZ 📶 ✕ 🛗 🖥️ 💻 / SOME UNITS FEE 🐕

 WHERE TO EAT

T & C FAMILY RESTAURANT/DALLAS PIZZA   306/842-2933
💎💎 American. Casual Dining. $7-$25 **AAA Inspector Notes:** This restaurant offers family dining in contemporary and friendly surroundings. The menu features a wide variety of sandwiches, stir-fry, steak, seafood, pizza, souvlaki and Greek ribs. Families, couples and business people alike enjoy this eatery. **Bar:** full bar. **Address:** 72 3rd St NE S4H 0V9 **Location:** Just n of Hwy 39; center. **Parking:** street only. L D

WOLSELEY (E-5) pop. 864

Incorporated in 1898, Wolseley earned the nickname "The Town With the Swinging Bridge" when just such a contraption was built over man-made Fairly Lake in the center of town—itself created by damming Wolf Creek to provide the Canadian Pacific Railway with a badly needed reservoir for its steam engines. The bridge, which connected homes on the north side of the lake with the business section on the south side, has had a checkered history: It was destroyed by a storm in 1954, rebuilt 10 years later, collapsed in 1993 during repairs and reopened again in 2004 thanks to the fund-raising efforts of the Heritage Canada Foundation.

The Romanesque-style Town Hall & Opera House, at the corner of Richmond and Varennes streets, was completed in 1907. The two-tone brick building (brick was imported from Manitoba when the local supply ran out) housed the town's administrative offices, fire hall, library, jail cell and community hall—commonly known as an Opera House—where touring vaudeville, theatrical and opera companies would perform. The building was extensively refurbished in the early 1990s.

Wolseley & District Museum, 101 Blanchard St., has a collection of locally obtained artifacts reflecting life in the area circa 1880-1950. The exhibits, which include medical, real estate and lumber offices as well as clothing from the various eras, are displayed in a two-story 1901 boarding house. The original office of the Beaver Lumber Company, also filled with artifacts, has been moved to the museum site. Phone (306) 698-2360.

WOOD MOUNTAIN (F-3) pop. 25

RODEO RANCH MUSEUM is 8 km (5 mi.) s. on Hwy. 18 in Wood Mountain Regional Park. This museum features exhibits about local ranching, First Nations people and saddle making. An adjacent adobe and log building houses blacksmithing tools. A rodeo is held on the grounds during the second weekend in July.

Time: Allow 1 hour minimum. **Hours:** Daily 10-noon and 1-5, mid-May through Labour Day. **Cost:** $2; $1 (students with ID); free (ages 0-9 with adult). **Phone:** (306) 266-4953 or (306) 266-4205. 🅰️ 🏠

WOOD MOUNTAIN POST PROVINCIAL HISTORIC PARK is 8 km (5 mi.) s. on Hwy. 18. Two buildings are on the site of the North West Mounted Police post that stood 1874-1918; small stumps outline the rest of the post. Inside the buildings are displays about the Mounted Police, Sioux First Nations and local history. An interpretive staff is on duty to answer questions. **Time:** Allow 1 hour minimum. **Hours:** Thurs.-Mon. 10-5, June 1 to mid-Aug. **Cost:** Donations. **Phone:** (306) 266-4322.

YORKTON (E-5) pop. 15,669

In 1882 some 200 settlers from Ontario bought land in the Northwest Territories in what is now southeastern Saskatchewan. They called the community around their trading post York City. In 1890 the railroad arrived in the area 5 kilometres (3 mi.) to the south. The York City colonists relocated to be near the railroad and named the new settlement Yorkton. A plaque marks the site of York City; nearby are millstones from the original colony's gristmill.

Recreation is available at nearby Good Spirit Lake Provincial Park. The park, originally a Hudson's Bay Co. post in the 1880s, is noted for its miles of sandy beaches and fine dunes. *See Recreation Areas Chart.*

Tourism Yorkton Visitor Information Centre: Hwy. 9, Box 460, Yorkton, SK, Canada S3N 2W4. **Phone:** (306) 783-8707.

Self-guiding tours: The Yorkton Heritage Walking Tour affords visitors the opportunity to view gardens and historic buildings. The City Cemetery Walking Tour features the grave sites of many of the city's early pioneers. An art walk highlights art, monuments and murals in the city. Materials outlining each tour are available at the information center.

GODFREY DEAN ART GALLERY is in the Godfrey Dean Cultural Centre at 49 Smith St. E. Assorted art forms are displayed, along with works by contemporary Canadian artists. Exhibits change monthly. **Hours:** Mon.-Fri. 11-5, Sat.-Sun. 1-4. Closed major holidays. **Cost:** Free. **Phone:** (306) 786-2992.

WESTERN DEVELOPMENT MUSEUM – YORKTON is .4 km (.25 mi.) w. on Hwy. 16A. The museum focuses on the cultural roots of the settlers of western Canada. **Time:** Allow 1 hour minimum.

Hours: Tues.-Sun. 9-5. Phone ahead to confirm schedule. **Cost:** $5; $4 (ages 65+); $3 (students with ID); $1 (ages 6-12); $10 (family). **Phone:** (306) 783-8361.

GAMBLING ESTABLISHMENTS

- **Painted Hand Casino** is at 510 Broadway St. W. **Hours:** Wed.-Sat. 9 a.m.-4 a.m., Sun.-Tues. 9 a.m.-3 a.m. Closed Christmas. **Phone:** (306) 786-6777.

BEST WESTERN YORKTON INN (306)783-3297

Hotel
$150-$175

 AAA Benefit: Members save up to 20%, plus 10% bonus points with Best Western Rewards®.

Address: 2 Kelsey Bay S3N 3Z4 **Location:** Just e of jct Hwy 9, 10 and 16 (Yellowhead Hwy). **Facility:** 100 units. 3 stories, interior corridors. **Parking:** winter plug-ins. **Terms:** check-in 4 pm. **Amenities:** high-speed Internet, safes. **Pool(s):** heated indoor. **Activities:** whirlpool, waterslide, exercise room. **Guest Services:** valet and coin laundry. **Free Special Amenities:** expanded continental breakfast and high-speed Internet.

RAMADA YORKTON (306)783-9781

Hotel $119-$149 **Address:** 100 Broadway St E S3N 0K9 **Location:** On Hwy 9, 10, and 16 (Yellowhead Hwy); downtown. **Facility:** 80 units. 2 stories (no elevator), interior corridors. **Parking:** winter plug-ins. **Terms:** cancellation fee imposed. **Pool(s):** heated indoor. **Activities:** sauna, whirlpool, waterslide, exercise room. **Guest Services:** valet and coin laundry.

WHERE TO EAT

YORK HOUSE DINING & LOUNGE 306/782-4333

International. Casual Dining. $12-$30 **AAA Inspector Notes:** One of the finer spots in town, the offerings here include ribs, chicken, prime rib, steak, pizza, pasta and Greek items. Hearty portions are offered and service is efficient and friendly. More casual dining is available in the lounge. Closed for lunch on Saturday. **Reservations:** suggested. **Address:** 12 4th Ave N S3N 1A2 **Location:** Jct Hwy 9, 10 and 16 (Yellowhead Hwy), 0.4 mi (0.6 km) e on Hwy 10A (Broadway St W), then just n.

Signpost near old mining town, Keno

To find gleaming gifts of topaz in out-croppings of rock. To wander trails once trodden by miners and trappers. To cry "Mush!" behind a stalwart team of sturdy Alaskan huskies.

To do any of these is to begin to understand the allure of the endless Yukon.

The roughly triangular territory is a place of majesty and adventure; a lonely wilderness; a rugged, pristine land of splendor and beauty.

Klondike or Bust

"Thick between the flaky slabs, like cheese sandwiches"—this was how prospector George Washington Carmack described the gold he saw glimmering between rocks in Bonanza Creek near Dawson City in 1896.

In 1897 the steamship *Excelsior* arrived in San Francisco carrying a treasure worth more than $500,000; a few days later the *Portland* docked in Seattle with a ton of gold piled on its deck. News of these recently discovered riches spread like wildfire.

Rocky shore of Bennett Lake

Yukon

That winter 100,000 prospectors hopeful of getting rich quick began a long, arduous journey to the Yukon to seek their fortunes. While the rush only lasted about 5 years, history was left in its trampled tracks.

If stampeders survived the trek through Chilkoot Pass—a climb over frozen mountains with heavy backpacks full of supplies—they crossed the border into the Yukon Territory at Bennett Lake.

The lake, surrounded by mighty peaks and woodlands, links to the Yukon River. Most fortune seekers waited out the harsh winter in a crowded tent city. Transients built boats, temporary shelter and a little log church out of timber hewn from the forest. When the lake's ice broke, 7,000 handmade vessels headed across its waters.

Today, those miners' cabins still line Bennett Lake at Carcross, a town full of gold rush history. The 1898 Caribou Hotel, built to welcome gold rushers, is downtown, and graves of early pioneers dot the cemetery.

From Carcross the gold route followed the Yukon River to Miles Canyon, south of Whitehorse. Dangerous currents here caused hundreds of boats to capsize, and licensed guides were a must for piloting would-be miners with smaller vessels through the rocks and whirlpools.

Cheechakos (newcomers) relied upon their own floating devices until stern-wheelers became a popular means of travel. Though boats were specifically designed for the river, many still ran aground or were smashed by rapids or rocks.

The River to Riches

After stopping to relax and dry out in Whitehorse, miners pressed on, traversing Lake Laberge to a stretch of the Yukon called Thirty Mile. Due to swift currents and rocks, it was perhaps the route's most dangerous portion. Historical sites along Thirty Mile include abandoned Northwest Mounted Police posts, grave markers, woodcutters' cabins, telegraph stations, old log buildings and remains of beached paddlewheelers.

More dangerous eddies remained at Five Finger Rapids, outside Carmacks, before exhausted voyagers reached Dawson City.

Downtown Dawson City looks much as it did when prospectors arrived, since codes require that fronts of new buildings be reminiscent of the gold rush era. And old buildings have been restored: Cancan dancing takes place at Diamond Tooth Gertie's Casino and author Jack London's and poet Robert Service's log cabins remain as examples of gold rush housing.

Recreation

Hiking the Chilkoot Trail, Yukon's original inroad, is the best way to understand the challenges faced by gold-rush stampeders. Beginning in Dyea, Alaska, the trail is a 53-kilometre (33-mi.), one-way walk through history that can take 3 to 5 days.

Preparation—proper gear, provisions, permits and registration—is key to this demanding trip through boreal forests, alpine tundra and snow-patched mountains. You must reserve a campsite for each night on the trail through the Trail Centre in Skagway, Alaska. The centre offers maps, safety tips and a few words about bears; phone Parks Canada year-round at (800) 661-0486.

Camping in summer (June to mid-September) is a true wilderness experience. Firewood is free, but you'll have to pump your own water. Government campgrounds are spread throughout the Yukon roughly 81-121 kilometres (50-75 mi.) apart, many beside lakes, rivers or streams where you might hook Arctic graylings for dinner. Of the 10 campgrounds along the Alaska Highway (Hwy. 1), Watson Lake is one of the first as you enter Yukon from British Columbia. Farther west is Congdon Creek, one of Yukon's largest. You can fish, swim and hike at both.

Take scenic Dempster Highway (Hwy. 5) from Dawson City to Rock River Campground, the northernmost public facility. Congratulate yourself: You've crossed the Continental Divide—twice—*and* the Arctic Circle! There's no well water, so get supplies in Dawson City or Eagle Plains (your last chance).

The Klondike Highway (Hwy. 2), open all year, has roadside respites for camping and picnicking. You also can camp just off the Robert Campbell and Silver Trail highways (Hwys. 4 and 11). Travelers can get daily road condition reports from the Department of Highways and Public Works hotline, (877) 456-7623 within the Yukon or (867) 456-7623 outside the Yukon. Watch for wildlife, especially near viewing areas identified with a sign picturing binoculars.

With almost 7 months of winter (October through April), snow skiing is a way of life. Near Whitehorse a chalet and night lighting draw cross-country skiers to Mount McIntyre's trails, while Mount Sima, one of Yukon's largest ski areas, appeals to downhill skiers. Snowboarding is a favorite at Mount Sima as well as on groomed trails around Whitehorse, or over more rugged terrain out of Dawson City, Yukon's snowmobiling capital.

Whitehorse offers kayaking or white-water rafting on the Tatshenshini's Class III and IV rapids, or through Kluane National Park and Reserve on the Alsek, a designated heritage river. Many sections of the Yukon River are easily navigated by canoe.

Snowboarding, Mount Sima

Historic Timeline

1800	The Hudson's Bay Co. sets up trading posts in the Yukon.
1895	Yukon Territory becomes a provisional district of the Northwest Territories.
1898	More than $100 million in gold is mined in the region over a 6-year span beginning just before the turn of the 20th century.
1942	The Alaska Highway is constructed, creating a new overland transportation route.
1953	Yukon's capital is moved from Dawson City to Whitehorse.
1959	At a cost of $1 million, a large fish ladder is built at the Whitehorse Rapids for migrating chinook salmon.
1979	Kluane National Park is declared a Natural World Heritage Site.
1993	The Council for Yukon Indians and the Canadian and Yukon governments agree on final territorial land claim settlements.
1997	Yukon spends $37 million on mining exploration.
1999	Yukon's accord with the Vuntut Gwitchin marks the territory's first recognition of a First Nation tribe as a valid government.
2003	The name of the Yukon Territory is officially changed to Yukon.

What To Pack

Temperature Averages Maximum/Minimum (Celsius)	JANUARY	FEBRUARY	MARCH	APRIL	MAY	JUNE	JULY	AUGUST	SEPTEMBER	OCTOBER	NOVEMBER	DECEMBER
Burwash Landing	-16 / -29	-11 / -26	-3 / -19	4 / -9	12 / -2	17 / 3	19 / 6	17 / 4	11 / -2	2 / -9	-9 / -21	-14 / -26
Dawson City	-21 / -30	-16 / -27	-3 / -20	8 / -8	15 / 1	21 / 6	23 / 8	20 / 5	11 / -1	-1 / -10	-14 / -22	-20 / -29
Faro	0 / -5	1 / -5	5 / -2	11 / 1	14 / 5	18 / 9	19 / 11	18 / 10	14 / 6	9 / 3	3 / -3	0 / -6
Mayo	-22 / -32	-13 / -26	-3 / -18	6 / -6	14 / 1	20 / 7	22 / 8	19 / 6	12 / 1	2 / -7	-13 / -21	-18 / -28
Watson Lake	-19 / -30	-12 / -25	-3 / -18	6 / -7	13 / 0	19 / 6	21 / 8	19 / 7	13 / 2	4 / -5	-11 / -20	-18 / -28
Whitehorse	-14 / -23	-8 / -18	-2 / -13	6 / -6	12 / 0	18 / 5	20 / 7	18 / 6	12 / 2	4 / -3	7 / -14	-12 / -20

From the records of The Weather Channel Interactive, Inc.

Good Facts To Know

ABOUT THE TERRITORY

POPULATION: 33,897.

AREA: 482,443 sq km (186,271 sq mi.); ranks 9th.

CAPITAL: Whitehorse.

HIGHEST POINT: 5,959 m (19,545 ft.), Mount Logan.

LOWEST POINT: Sea level, Beaufort Sea.

TIME ZONE(S): Pacific.

GAMBLING

MINIMUM AGE FOR GAMBLING: 19.

REGULATIONS

TEEN DRIVING LAWS: Driving is not permitted midnight-5 a.m. unless with a qualified co-driver or if a teen has been granted a work exception. A novice driver may not transport more than one passenger under 13 or a combination of passengers including a passenger under 13 and a passenger under 20 unless accompanied by a passenger over 20. Minimum age for an unrestricted driver's license is 17 years, 6 months.

SEAT BELT/CHILD RESTRAINT LAWS: Seat belts are required for driver and all passengers ages 6 and older. Child restraints are required for children under age 6 and under 22 kilograms (48 lbs.).

CELLPHONE RESTRICTIONS: Drivers may not use a cellphone, text or send emails with any kind of hand-held electronic device while driving.

HELMETS FOR MOTORCYCLISTS: Required for all riders.

RADAR DETECTORS: Not permitted.

FIREARMS LAWS: By federal law, all nonresidents entering Canada with a firearm must declare their weapon in writing and pay a fee of $25 (Canadian). Contact the Canadian Firearms Centre at (800) 731-4000 to receive a declaration form or for additional information.

ALCOHOL CONSUMPTION: Legal age 19.

HOLIDAYS

HOLIDAYS: Jan. 1 ▪ Heritage Day, Feb. 25 ▪ Good Friday ▪ Easter Monday ▪ Victoria Day, May 24 or the closest prior Mon. ▪ Canada Day, July 1 ▪ Discovery Day, Aug. (3rd Mon.) ▪ Labour Day, Sept. (1st Mon.) ▪ Thanksgiving, Oct. (2nd Mon.) ▪ Remembrance Day, Nov. 11 ▪ Christmas, Dec. 25 ▪ Boxing Day, Dec. 26.

MONEY

TAXES: Yukon has no territorial sales tax. The federal Goods and Services Tax (GST) is 5 percent.

VISITOR INFORMATION

INFORMATION CENTRES:
Territorial information centres in Beaver Creek; Carcross; Dawson City; Haines Junction; Watson Lake; and Whitehorse are open 12 hours a day, mid-May to mid-Sept., with reduced hours early to mid-May and mid- to late Sept. The Whitehorse Visitor Information Centre also is open Mon.-Fri. 8:30-noon and 1-5, Sat. 10-2, in winter.

ROAD CONDITIONS: Through its Yukon Network the Canadian Broadcasting Corporation reports road conditions on the Alaska Highway and all other Yukon highways. Major participating stations, with their frequencies in kilohertz (kHz), are listed from south to north: Watson Lake, 990; Swift River, 970; Teslin, 940; Whitehorse, 570; Haines Junction, 860; Destruction Bay, 940; Beaver Creek, 690; Carmacks, 990; Mayo, 1230; Elsa, 560; Dawson City, 560; Faro, 105.1 FM; and Ross River, 990.

ROAD CONDITIONS: For changes in Yukon road conditions, phone (867) 456-7623, (877) 456-7623 or 511 within Yukon.

FERRY SCHEDULES AND INFORMATION:
The Department of Highways runs ferries along Dempster Highway and at Dawson City; phone (867) 667-3710.

FURTHER INFORMATION FOR VISITORS:
Department of Tourism & Culture
P.O. Box 2703
Whitehorse, YT Y1A 2C6
Canada
(800) 661-0494

FISHING AND HUNTING REGULATIONS:
Yukon Government Fish and Wildlife Branch
P.O. Box 2703 (V-5)
Whitehorse, YT Y1A 2C6
Canada
(867) 667-5715
(800) 661-0408 in Canada

Yukon Annual Events

Please call ahead to confirm event details.

JANUARY

- New Year's Day
  Snowmobile Poker Run
  Haines Junction
  867-634-2432
- Fulda Challenge
  Whitehorse
  867-633-3755
- Pivot Theatre Festival
  Whitehorse
  867-393-6040

FEBRUARY

- Yukon Quest International
  Sled Dog Race / Whitehorse
  907-452-7954
- Kiki Karnival / Watson Lake
  867-536-7469
- Yukon Sourdough
  Rendezvous / Whitehorse
  867-393-4467

MARCH

- Percy DeWolfe Memorial
  Mail Race / Dawson City
  867-993-5320
- Thaw-Di-Gras Spring
  Carnival / Dawson City
  867-993-5575
- Burning Away the Winter
  Blues / Whitehorse
  867-633-4844

APRIL

- Education Week
  Whitehorse
  867-393-7102
- A Celebration of Swans
  Whitehorse
  867-667-8291
- Rotary Music Festival
  Whitehorse
  867-633-3755

MAY

- Crane and Sheep Viewing
  Festival / Faro
  867-994-2728
- Dawson City International
  Gold Show / Dawson City
  867-993-5274
- May Music Magic
  Whitehorse
  867-667-8044

JUNE

- Aboriginal Day
  Celebrations / Dawson City
  867-993-5385
- Solstice and
  Saint-Jean-Baptiste
  Celebrations / Whitehorse
  867-668-2663, ext. 232
- Kluane Mountain Bluegrass
  Festival / Whitehorse
  867-634-2520

JULY

- Canada Day Festivities
  Watson Lake
  867-536-2246
- Yukon Gold Panning
  Championships
  Dawson City
  867-993-5575
- Pelly Valley Festival / Faro
  867-994-2288

AUGUST

- Fireweed Festival / Faro
  867-994-2375
- Discovery Days
  Watson Lake
  867-536-8020
- Discovery Days Festival
  Dawson City
  867-993-2353

SEPTEMBER

- Terry Fox Run
  Watson Lake
  867-536-8020
- Klondike Trail of '98
  International Road Relay
  Whitehorse
  867-393-8330
- Great Klondike
  International Outhouse
  Race / Dawson City
  867-993-5575

OCTOBER

- Halloween Spooktacular
  Whitehorse
  867-668-8677
- Halloween Bonfire and
  Fireworks / Watson Lake
  867-536-8022
- Halloween Dance
  Watson Lake
  867-536-8022

NOVEMBER

- Official Reception of the
  French-Speaking
  Community / Whitehorse
  867-668-2663, ext. 560
- Cranberry Fair / Whitehorse
  867-393-2389
- Spruce Bog Christmas Craft
  Sale / Whitehorse
  867-633-2416

DECEMBER

- City Lights Festival
  Whitehorse
  867-668-8360
- Christmas Lights Tour
  Whitehorse
  867-668-8394
- TH (Tr'ondek Hwech'in)
  Last Minute Christmas
  Bazaar / Dawson City
  867-993-7100

Gold production, Dawson City

Dall sheep, Kluane National Park and Reserve

Fireweed field

Autumn Cranberry Fair, Whitehorse

Diamond Tooth Gertie's Casino, Dawson City

Index: Great Experience for Members

AAA editor's picks of exceptional note

The SS *Klondike II*
National Historic Site

Yukon Beringia
Interpretive Centre

Yukon River Cruise

Whitehorse (D-2)
The SS *Klondike II* National Historic Site
(See p. 577.)

Yukon Beringia Interpretive Centre
(See p. 578.)
Yukon River Cruise *(See p. 579.)*

Yukon
Orientation

Scale in Kilometers
100   0   100

NOT INTENDED FOR DRIVING.
SEE APPROPRIATE AAA SHEET MAP.

Only places listed in the Attractions
section appear on this map.

▽ See AAA GEM Index
❶ See Recreation Areas Chart
on following page

4029-B   © AAA   © 2012 NAVTEQ

BURWASH LANDING (D-1) pop. 95

In 1904, a year after gold was discovered in Fourth of July Creek, Morley Bones staked a discovery claim on Burwash Creek. Soon after the small community of Burwash sprang up around a trading post. Burwash Landing, with an airstrip and a resort, lies between the Kluane Lake and Kluane Game Sanctuary.

KLUANE MUSEUM OF NATURAL HISTORY is at Historic Mile 1093 on the Alaska Hwy. The museum contains a nature and taxidermy display, handmade indigenous crafts and costumes, a mineral and fossil collection and a large topographical map of the surrounding area. **Time:** Allow 1 hour minimum. **Hours:** Daily 9-7, May 15-Sept. 15. **Cost:** $3.95; $2.95 (ages 61+); free (ages 0-13). **Phone:** (867) 841-5561.

CARCROSS (D-2) pop. 289

Carcross, 74 kilometres (46 mi.) from Whitehorse on the S. Klondike Highway, originally was called Caribou Crossing. The town's current name is a combination of the first syllable of each word. From this settlement George Carmack's party set out on the prospecting trip that began the gold rush of 1898. On July 29, 1900, the railroad's final spike was driven, marking the completion of the White Pass & Yukon Route, which linked Alaska and the Yukon Territory by rail.

Today the White Pass & Yukon Route (see attraction listing in Alaska p. 660) transports passengers between Carcross and Bennett, British Columbia; phone (907) 983-2217 or (800) 343-7373 for schedule and reservations.

Near the town's train depot is the "Duchess," a tiny locomotive that ran the 6.4-kilometre (4-mi.) line from Taku Arm on Tagish Lake to Atlin Lake in the early 1900s. It supposedly was the shortest and most expensive rail trip in the world—one-way fare was $2—and passengers had to sit on their baggage in the cramped compartment.

Recalling the feverish gold rush days is the Caribou Hotel. Regarded as the Yukon's oldest operating hotel, the historic building, which opened in 1898 to accommodate gold seekers heading north, is a Yukon Historic Site. **Note:** The hotel is currently closed for restoration; reopening is scheduled for 2012.

The Carcross Visitor Information Centre is at the Carcross Pavilion, adjacent to the historic White Pass & Yukon Route train depot. The centre provides extensive information about Carcross, one of the Yukon's most picturesque areas; phone (867) 821-4431.

Just north of town along the Klondike Highway lies the Carcross Desert, considered the smallest desert in the world. The 260-hectare (650-acre) area was created by retreating glaciers that left a sandy lake bottom; today winds from Lake Bennett constantly shift the sand, limiting vegetation to such plants as kinnikinnick and lodgepole pine.

CARIBOU CROSSING TRADING POST is 3.2 km (2 mi.) n. on S. Klondike Hwy. to Km-post 109. At this 12-hectare (30-acre) park, visitors can view mounted animals in dioramas representing their natural habitats, explore an outdoor heritage area depicting the region's frontier days and climb to a lookout that provides a view of Lake Bennett, Carcross and surrounding mountains. The park includes a nature trail, petting farm and miniature golf.

Time: Allow 1 hour, 30 minutes minimum. **Hours:** Daily 9-5, mid-May to mid-Sept. **Cost:** $7.25; $5.25 (ages 3-12). Miniature golf tickets $12; $9 (ages 3-12). **Phone:** (867) 821-4055.

CARMACKS (C-2) pop. 503

Carmacks, named for George Washington Carmack, one of the discoverers of gold in the Klondike, was an important stopover point on the Overland Trail that linked Whitehorse and Dawson City before the Klondike Highway was built. Items from early travelers still can be found along the trail near town.

About 22 kilometres (14 mi.) north of Carmacks are the Five Fingers Rapids, which claimed the lives of many prospectors trying to reach Dawson City by way of the Yukon River.

TAGE CHO HUDAN INTERPRETIVE CENTRE is .4 km (.25 mi.) n. on the Klondike Hwy. The culture of the Northern Tutchone people, Yukon's oldest inhabitants, is explored through a collection of traditional tools and dioramas featuring a dugout, moose skin boats and moose skin clothing. Outside displays such as a pole house, a moose skin tanning camp and a winter moose skin home are featured. A garden with medicinal plants and a trail also are onsite.

Tours: Guided tours are available. **Time:** Allow 30 minutes minimum. **Hours:** Mon.-Fri. 9-6, mid-May to mid-Sept. **Cost:** Donations. **Phone:** (867) 863-5831.

DAWSON CITY (C-1) pop. 1,319
• Hotels p. 574 • Restaurants p. 574

Dawson City was the center of the excitement caused by one of the world's most fabulous gold strikes. On Aug. 16, 1896, George Washington Carmack and his companions Skookum Jim and Tagish Charlie made the first strike on Bonanza Creek, a tributary of the Klondike River.

In the summer of 1897 miners from Dawson City arrived in Seattle and San Francisco with nearly $2 million as they carried word of the discovery to the United States, then in the midst of a depression. By the next spring more than 60,000 men and women had passed through Seattle and Alaska's Chilkoot and White passes on their way to the Klondike.

The Dawson settlement, which sprang up at the confluence of the Yukon and Klondike rivers, became a thriving city with some 30,000 inhabitants by the summer of 1898, making it the largest city west of Winnipeg and north of San Francisco.

All the creeks in the area had been staked by the spring of 1899. Hillside and bench claims were made, some yielding rich gold finds in the White Channel gravels. Between 1896 and 1904 Klondike creeks brought in more than $100 million in gold.

This period of Dawson City's history has been preserved by Rex Beach, Jack London, Robert W. Service and others who wrote colorful tales of personal experiences.

It was in Dawson City that London became acquainted with a large dog that he named Buck, a cross between a St. Bernard and a German shepherd that became the prototype for the dog in "Call of the Wild." Daily readings from the works of Jack London are given at a replica of his cabin on Eighth Avenue at Firth Street, part of the Jack London Interpretive Centre (see attraction listing).

A fire destroyed the town center after residents' 1897 Thanksgiving Day celebrations. The Dawson City Firefighters Museum, across from the ferry landing, displays artifacts, early fire extinguishers, gear, and historic vehicles in order to preserve Dawson City's firefighting heritage and is open Mon.-Fri. 11-5, Sat. noon-5, May-Sept.; a gallery showcases pictures and art created for the museum. Phone (867) 993-7407 for more information.

However, many historic buildings—some still in use—do survive from the days when Dawson City was the gold capital of the world. The Midnight Sun and Eldorado hotels conjure memories of a lively past.

Harrington's Store, Princess Street and Third Avenue, has a free photographic exhibit titled "Dawson as They Saw It," open June through September. The post office and other restored buildings can be seen as part of various Parks Canada tours. Tickets for the tours are available at the visitor information centre at Front and King streets.

The summit of Midnight Dome, 7 kilometres (4 mi.) southeast via Front Street, offers a panorama of Dawson City, the Yukon and Klondike rivers and the gold fields. Many Dawson City pioneers are buried in cemeteries on the hillsides flanking the dome.

South on Bonanza Creek Road is the Discovery Claim National Historic Site, the place of the gold discovery that started the great rush (see attraction listing). Panning for gold is possible at several locations along the Klondike Highway: Claim 33, Guggieville RV Park, Dawson City RV Park, Gold Bottom Mines and Eureka Mines.

The Dawson City Visitor Information Centre features exhibits about Klondike history and is open daily 8-8, mid-May to mid-Sept.; 10-6, early to mid-May and mid- to late Sept.

The town celebrates its gold mining heritage during ♥ Discovery Days Festival, a weeklong event held at various locations in mid-August.

Dawson City Visitor Information Centre: Front and King streets, Dawson City, YT, Canada Y0B 1G0. **Phone:** (867) 993-5566.

Self-guiding tours: A brochure describing walking tours of historic sites is available at the visitor information centre.

INSIDER INFO:
Sourdoughs and Cheechakos

To distinguish between the fortune seekers who entered the Yukon Territory during the 1897-98 Klondike Gold Rush, veterans of the '49 California Rush labeled the seasoned arrivals "Sourdoughs" and the greenhorns "Cheechakos" (CHE-cha-kos). Named after the staple bread of the frontier, Sourdoughs were prospectors who had survived a Yukon winter. The term Cheechako came from the Chinook Indian word for "new to come."

Once off the steamer at Skagway, Alaska, these newcomers had to transport thousands of pounds of survival gear—the Northwest Mounted Police wisely required each prospector to bring a year's supply of food—over the precipitous Chilkoot Pass. After that they had to float their unwieldy cargo over the treacherous rapids of the Yukon River.

More obstacles awaited the greenhorns at the gold sites. By the time the Cheechakos arrived, much of the gold field already was depleted or staked. To make things worse, Cheechakos were often directed to the hills by unscrupulous Sourdoughs who knew the gold nuggets tended to settle in creek beds. Nonetheless, some did tap into a channel of an ancient gold-bearing stream on Cheechako Hill.

Those who had survived to see the ice melt were dubbed Sourdoughs; the graveyards of those who had not succeeded dotted the route all the way back to Skagway. As one cynical Sourdough put it: "We were SOUR on the Yukon and didn't have enough DOUGH to get out."

DANOJA ZHO CULTURAL CENTRE is on Front St., across from the Dawson City Visitor Information Centre. Guided tours, exhibits, video presentations, dance performances and hands-on activities give visitors an interesting perspective into the culture of the Tr'ondek Hwech'in First Nations peoples. Displays include archeological artifacts, traditional costumes and reproduction tools. Special events also are featured. **Time:** Allow 30 minutes minimum. **Hours:** Daily 10-6, mid-May to Sept. **Cost:** $6; $2.50 (ages 12-18); free (ages 0-11). **Phone:** (867) 993-6768.

DAWSON CITY MUSEUM is on Fifth Ave. Gold rush items are displayed at the museum, which contains a smithy, a general store, an old miner's cabin, a saloon and Chilkoot Hall. Indigenous artifacts and an outdoor transportation exhibit with locomotives from the Klondike Mines Railway also are featured.

Hours: Daily 10-6, Victoria Day weekend-Labour Day; limited hours in May and day after Labour Day-Sept. 30. **Cost:** $9; $7 (senior citizens and high school students with ID); $5 each for pre-booked parties of 6+; free (ages 0-6); $18 (family, two adults and two children under 18). **Phone:** (867) 993-5291.

DAWSON CITY'S *KLONDIKE SPIRIT* CRUISE departs at Front Street Dock. Two-hour tours downriver of Dawson City take place aboard the *Klondike Spirit*. Passengers have a choice of barrier-free views from the observation deck or main deck as they cruise on the paddlewheeler-style vessel. An evening outing with an option for dinner takes in a few areas north of the city, including the Sternwheeler Graveyard with its decaying watercrafts, Tr'ochëk/Moosehide Village and a cave occupied by one of the local characters before the tour heads south for a scenic segment.

Inquire about 10-person minimum and weather policies. **Tours:** Guided tours are available. **Time:** Allow 2 hours minimum. **Hours:** Dawson City's *Klondike Spirit* departs daily at 6:30, May 24-Sept. 10. Passengers should arrive 30 minutes prior to departure. Phone ahead to confirm schedule. **Cost:** $55; free (ages 0-12). Fare with dinner $79.14; $15 (ages 0-12). Reservations are recommended. **Phone:** (867) 993-5323 or (800) 764-3555. 🎭

DAWSON HISTORICAL COMPLEX NATIONAL HISTORIC SITE comprises more than a dozen restored buildings scattered throughout Dawson City. The structures evoke the time and place of the Klondike Gold Rush of the 1890s. Visitors may explore the richly appointed Palace Grand Theatre; the Commissioner's Residence mansion and gardens; the Robert Service Cabin, where the Bard of the Yukon lived and wrote many of his ballads and poems 1909-12; and Harrington's Store, which displays photographs and letters from the gold rush.

Self-guiding audio tours and guided tours led by costumed site interpreters are available. Tour tickets are available at the visitor information centre. **Hours:** Programs offered daily 9:30-8, late May to mid-Sept. Tour departure times vary. Palace Grand Theatre tours offered daily at 11:30. Commissioner's Residence tours open daily; hours vary. Robert Service Cabin program offered daily at 1. Phone for additional tours and departure times. **Cost:** Self-guiding audio tour and guided tour $6.30; free (children). **Phone:** (867) 993-7200.

DISCOVERY CLAIM NATIONAL HISTORIC SITE is 14.8 km (9.3 mi.) s. on Bonanza Creek Rd. Signs along a walking trail portray the story of gold mining at Bonanza Creek—the site of the 1896 gold discovery which sparked the Klondike Gold Rush. A historical marker at Km-post 17.71 identifies the town of Grand Forks, which had a population of 5,000 during its prime. Interpretive trail brochures are available in the visitors centre. **Hours:** Daily 24 hours. **Cost:** Free. Interpretive trail brochure $2. **Phone:** (867) 993-7200.

DREDGE NO. 4 NATIONAL HISTORIC SITE is 12.3 km (7.8 mi.) s. on Bonanza Creek Rd. This massive eight-story dredging machine rests alongside Bonanza Creek where it sifted millions of dollars worth of gold from 1899 to 1959. The dredge was once the largest wooden-hull mining dredge of its kind in North America.

Note: Due to budget cuts, Parks Canada is adjusting offerings. This may be one of those sites; phone ahead for the latest information. **Phone:** (867) 993-7200.

GRAY LINE YUKON TOURS, 902 Front St., offers a variety of tours by bus, jeep and raft. The Tales of Dawson City bus tour visits historic buildings, museums and Dredge No. 4 National Historic Site *(see attraction listing)*. **Hours:** Tales tour departs daily at 9, late May-early Sept. Schedule varies for other tours. **Cost:** Tales tour $35. Fares vary for other tours. **Phone:** (867) 993-5599 or (800) 544-2206.

JACK LONDON INTERPRETIVE CENTRE, Eighth Ave. and Firth St., features London's food cache and a replica of the cabin, built with some of the original logs, where the author spent time at the beginning of the 1898 Klondike gold rush prior to his writing career.

A separate building houses a well-illustrated photo museum documenting his life in the North and how he integrated experiences from that period into his works. Daily readings from London's works are given at the cabin. Informative talks are given by interpreters twice daily at 12:15 and 3:15. **Time:** Allow 30 minutes minimum. **Hours:** Daily 11-6, June 1 to mid-Aug.; schedule varies in May and mid-Aug. to mid-Sept. **Cost:** $5; free (ages 0-12). **Phone:** (867) 993-6317. 🅰

SS *KENO* NATIONAL HISTORIC SITE is on Front St. between King and Queen sts.; tickets are available at the visitor information centre. Built in 1922, the dry-docked stern-wheeler was once used to transport silver, lead and zinc ore from the mines on the Klondike River. It was one of the last riverboats to run between Dawson City and Whitehorse. Visitors can walk the gangplank and view on-board exhibits highlighting the mining history of the Yukon Territory and the challenges of navigating wild northern rivers.

Note: Due to budget cuts, Parks Canada is adjusting offerings. This may be one of those sites; phone ahead for the latest information. **Time:** Allow 30 minutes minimum. **Hours:** Daily 9:30-1, mid-May through Labour Day; schedule varies late Aug. to mid-Sept. Phone ahead to confirm schedule. **Cost:** $6.30. **Phone:** (867) 993-7200.

TOMBSTONE TERRITORIAL PARK is 71 km (44 mi.) n. of jct. Dempster and Klondike hwys. This park spans an area of more than 2,164 square kilometres (836 sq. mi.) and features a diversity of wildlife and bird species as well as a variety of vegetation. This is a remote park with few established hiking trails, but there are accessible portions off the highway that offer short hikes and challenging backpacking and mountain climbing excursions. The park's arctic tundra environment creates a landscape with spectacular views. The interpretive centre has natural history displays and provides interpretive programs and nature walks.

Note: When traveling to the park have enough gas and spare tires since there are no roadside services available until Eagle Plains, which is 369 kilometres (229 mi.) north of the Klondike Highway. Once in the park, be aware that it is an isolated and potentially hazardous environment. Rough terrain, drastic weather changes and encounters with wildlife are factors to consider. **Time:** Allow 3 hours minimum. **Hours:** Park is open daily 24 hours. Interpretive centre open daily 9-9, mid-June to mid-Sept. Phone ahead to confirm schedule. **Cost:** Free. **Phone:** (867) 667-5648.

GAMBLING ESTABLISHMENTS

- **Diamond Tooth Gertie's Casino** is at Queen St. and Fourth Ave. Entertainment includes cancan and music shows. **Hours:** Daily 7 p.m.-2 a.m., May 12-Sept. 17 (opens at 2 p.m. Sat.-Sun., mid-June through Labour Day). **Phone:** (867) 993-5575.

DAWSON CITY BED & BREAKFAST   867/993-5649

Bed & Breakfast
$140-$165

Address: 451 Craig St Y0B 1G0 **Location:** Just off 7th Ave. **Facility:** You'll see a nice collection of travel artifacts in this B&B's comfortable rooms, complete with plush bathrobes and a separate seating area. Be sure to check out the owner's pet parrot. 4 units. 2 stories (no elevator), interior corridors. **Parking:** winter plug-ins. **Amenities:** high-speed Internet. **Guest Services:** area transportation-bus station & town dock. **Free Special Amenities: full breakfast and high-speed Internet.**

THE ELDORADO HOTEL   (867)993-5451

Motel
$129-$244

Address: 902 3rd Ave Y0B 1G0 **Location:** Jct 3rd Ave and Princess St; downtown. **Facility:** 40 units, some kitchens. 2 stories (no elevator), interior/exterior corridors. **Parking:** winter plug-ins. **Terms:** closed 12/7-2/15, cancellation fee imposed. **Guest Services:** coin laundry. **Free Special Amenities: local telephone calls and room upgrade (subject to availability with advance reservations).**

/ SOME UNITS

KLONDIKE KATE'S CABINS   (867)993-6527

Cabin $145-$195 **Address:** 1102 3rd Ave Y0B 1G0 **Location:** Corner of 3rd Ave and King St. **Facility:** 15 cabins. 1 story, exterior corridors. **Terms:** closed 10/1-4/14, check-in 4 pm, cancellation fee imposed. **Amenities:** high-speed Internet. **Dining:** Klondike Kate's Restaurant, see separate listing. **Guest Services:** valet laundry.

/ SOME UNITS FEE

WESTMARK INN DAWSON CITY   (867)993-5542

Hotel $119-$189 **Address:** 813 5th Ave Y0B 1G0 **Location:** At Harper St. **Facility:** 177 units. 2 stories (no elevator), interior corridors. **Terms:** closed 9/4-5/16, cancellation fee imposed. **Guest Services:** coin laundry.

/ SOME UNITS FEE

YUKON HOTEL   (867)993-5451

Hotel $125-$160 **Address:** 702 Front St Y0B 1G0 **Location:** Corner of Church St. **Facility:** 6 efficiencies. 2 stories (no elevator), interior corridors. **Parking:** winter plug-ins. **Terms:** closed 11/1-5/1, off-site registration, cancellation fee imposed. **Guest Services:** coin laundry.

WHERE TO EAT

THE DRUNKEN GOAT TAVERNA   867/993-5868

Traditional Greek. Casual Dining. $15-$33 **AAA Inspector Notes:** Here you'll enjoy delicious, authentic Greek food created by the owner/chef amid a dining room plastered with a large, scenic mural of Greece covering the walls and ceiling. **Reservations:** suggested. **Address:** 952 2nd Ave Y0B 1G0 **Location:** Center. **Parking:** street only.

KLONDIKE KATE'S RESTAURANT   867/993-6527

Canadian Casual Dining $10-$35

AAA Inspector Notes: *Historic.* Catch a sense of Dawson City's history and the gold rush era at this restaurant located across the street from the theater. The menu features a good variety of appetizers and enticing fish and meat entrées. Rather than dining inside, opt for a seat on the covered heated patio in the summer. Off-season hours and meal openings can vary, so it is a good idea to check with the restaurant. **Bar:** full bar. **Reservations:** suggested. **Address:** 1102 3rd Ave Y0B 1G0 **Location:** Corner of 3rd Ave and King St; in Klondike Kate's Cabins. *Menu on AAA.com*

RIVER WEST BISTRO   867/993-6339

American. Quick Serve. $5-$12 **AAA Inspector Notes:** This small café, simply decorated, features flame broiled burgers (including buffalo), prime rib, lamb, chicken and salmon as well as a variety of fries. A range of soups, pre-made salads, sandwiches and wraps also are offered. For dessert, there are tasty squares, cookies and creme pies. Breakfast is offered as well as an outdoor patio. **Address:** 958 Front St Y0B 1G0 **Location:** Between Princess and Queen sts; center. **Parking:** street only.

SOURDOUGH JOE'S RESTAURANT   867/993-6590

Seafood. Casual Dining. $10-$20 **AAA Inspector Notes:** Dawson City's first lot where Joe Ladue staked not just a claim, but a whole town site, now hosts this simple and rustic eatery boasting their delicious signature fish made with a light and tasty batter in a choice of halibut, cod or Alaskan wild red salmon served with hand-cut chips. Also on the menu are chowder, salad and a variety of burgers including a breaded oyster burger or just plain old beef and chicken. Outside seating is available. **Bar:** beer & wine. **Address:** 902 Front St Y0B 1G0 **Location:** Between Princess and Queen sts. **Parking:** on-site and street.

FARO (C-2) pop. 344, elev. 717m/2,352'

CAMPBELL REGION INTERPRETIVE CENTRE is on Campbell Street. A spruce log building houses a permanent exhibit about the history, geology and wildlife of the Faro area. **Time:** Allow 1 hour minimum. **Hours:** Daily 8-6, June-Aug.; 9-5, May 5-31 and Sept. 1-29. **Cost:** Donations. **Phone:** (867) 994-2288.

IVVAVIK NATIONAL PARK (A-1)

Ivvavik National Park is in the extreme northwestern corner of the Yukon. Virtually untouched by humans, the Arctic wilderness is of great geologic interest; it is one of the few regions in Canada that contains areas never covered by glaciers.

Every spring it becomes the calving grounds of Porcupine caribous that arrive after a long, difficult migration from the south and west. The park provides an important nesting area for North American waterfowl and a home to grizzly, black and polar bears. The only access to the park is by air.

KENO (C-2) elev. 812m/2,667'

In 1919 silver and lead ore were discovered in Keno Hill, and by 1920 Keno became a busy community with cabins, a stable and a hotel. The following year, the city was the center of a thriving mining district. The town's name comes from the popular gambling game played at casinos. Today, Keno is home to artists who are inspired by the area's natural beauty.

No matter the season, outdoor recreational opportunities abound and include hiking, bicycling, cross-country skiing, snowmobiling, fishing and canoeing. The awe-inspiring northern lights may be seen from late August through April. A must-see is the often-photographed signpost at the top of Keno Hill, showing mileage to such cities as London, Paris and Rome. The 1,829-metre (6,000-ft.) hill also plays host to a breathtaking view.

Self-guiding tours: This historic walking tour starts from Tolmie Cabin on Duncan Creek Road and includes the Beer Bottle House, Keno City Mining Museum and All Saints Anglican Church. Brochures are available from the Keno City Mining Museum. Phone (867) 995-3103.

KENO CITY MINING MUSEUM is on Silver Trail Hwy. Housed in a dance hall, the museum depicts the history of the local community and gold and silver mining through exhibits, photographs, equipment and tools. An interpretive centre focuses on the history of alpine wildlife, including wildflowers, birds, butterflies and wild animals; several hiking trails begin at the centre. **Time:** Allow 30 minutes minimum. **Hours:** Daily 10-6, mid-May to Labour Day. **Cost:** $3.50; $2.50 (ages 66+); free (ages 0-12). **Phone:** (867) 995-3103.

KLUANE NATIONAL PARK AND RESERVE (D-1)

Elevations in the park range from 400 metres (1,300 ft.) in the Alsek River to 5,959 metres (19,545 ft.) at Mount Logan. Refer to CAA/AAA maps for additional elevation information.

Kluane (kloo-AH-nee) National Park and Reserve is bounded by the Haines (Hwy. 3) and Alaska (Hwy. 1) highways along its northeastern border. The park covers 22,015 square kilometres (8,500 sq. mi.) of wilderness.

Near its southeastern boundary was the Dalton Trail, a route used during the Klondike Rush of 1898. In 1904 a North West Mounted Police post was established on the south shore of Kluane Lake,

and in 1942 the lake became a meeting place for crews building the Alaska Highway.

During the building of the highway the wilderness area was preserved as the Kluane Game Sanctuary. In 1979 Kluane was declared a World Heritage Site for its impressive topographical features and its massive nonpolar ice fields.

The park is dominated by the Saint Elias Mountains, which run through the park in a southeasterly direction. Mount Logan, Canada's highest peak at 5,959 metres (19,545 ft.), and Mount St. Elias at 5,489 metres (18,008 ft.) dominate the range. The Saint Elias Mountains hold extensive ice fields that date from the last ice age and constitute the largest nonpolar glacier systems in the world.

An extensive network of glaciers, together with the ice fields, covers more than half of the park's area throughout the year. Notable are the Steele Glacier, which moves sporadically at a relatively rapid rate, and the Kaskawulsh and Lowell glaciers, which are flanked by moraines—accumulations of earth and stones carried and deposited by the glaciers. The movement and debris of the glaciers contribute to such park features as sand dunes and dust storms.

The park has a variety of flora. Such coniferous species as white spruce characterize the boreal forest of the river valleys. Lichens, dwarf birch trees and low shrubs distinguish the tundra uplands in the northern section, and colorful Arctic flowers cling to the crevices and ledges of the mountains. In the southeastern section, where the Pacific Ocean's moderating influence is felt in the climate, the vegetation is more luxuriant.

Arctic grayling, lake trout, northern pike and kokanee salmon are found in lakes and streams. Other park species include golden eagles, ptarmigans, Dall sheep, mountain goats, caribou, moose and wolves. Kluane has one of the largest populations of grizzly bears and subspecies of moose in the world.

General Information and Activities

The park is open all year, but access may be limited in the winter, depending on weather conditions. The Kluane National Park and Reserve headquarters, at Km-post 1635 in Haines Junction, is open daily 9-5, mid-May to mid-Sept., and weekdays by appointment, rest of year. The Tachäl Dhäl (Sheep Mountain) Visitor Centre at Km-post 1707 is open daily 9-4, mid-May to early September.

The park primarily is a wilderness area, so there are no roads except on the eastern and northern perimeters, traversed by Hwy. 3 and Hwy. 1, respectively. Hiking is the most popular activity in the park, with approximately 250 kilometres (155 mi.) of hiking trails. Hiking is possible along a few old mining roads, creekside paths and marked trails. Some trails are self-guiding. All overnight hikers must register at one of the information centres or with a park warden before and after hikes.

Mountain climbing should be done only by well-trained climbers, who must obtain a climbing permit and register with the Warden Service before and after climbs.

Other recreational pursuits include fishing, backpacking, boating, cross-country skiing and ice fishing. All anglers within the park must obtain a national park fishing license, available at the park visitor centres and from area stores and lodges. Camping, fishing and picnic facilities are available at Kathleen Lake, 27 kilometres (17 mi.) south of Haines Junction.

During the summer the Kluane National Park and Reserve headquarters sponsors interpretive activities including campfire talks and guided walks. A relief map and an interactive computer touch screen are available. Information about recreational opportunities, sightseeing by small aircraft and other guided tours is available.

ADMISSION to the park is free.

PETS are permitted in the park if kept on a leash, but visitors are advised not to bring them.

ADDRESS inquiries about the park to Kluane National Park and Reserve, P.O. Box 5495, Haines Junction, YT, Canada Y0B 1L0; phone (867) 634-7250.

MAYO (C-2) pop. 226

Mayo lies 53 kilometres (33 mi.) northeast of the Klondike Highway at the confluence of the Stewart and Mayo rivers. Both the town and the river were named for the pioneer prospector and trader Alfred Mayo. In the early 1900s Mayo Landing became a shipping point for the gold and silver that was mined farther north in Elsa.

Mayo Lake to the northeast provides excellent fishing. The summit of nearby 1,890-metre (6,200-ft.) Keno Mountain provides a scenic view of the mining village of Keno. This once bustling community has a mining museum.

Further details about the silver mining towns of Mayo, Elsa and Keno, known collectively as the Silver Trail, are available at the information booth at Stewart Crossing.

BINET HOUSE INTERPRETIVE CENTRE is at jct. Second Ave. and Centre St. The two-story building features exhibits that include a collection of historic photographs, artifacts and a 3-D relief map of the region identifying the location of mineral deposits. **Tours:** Guided tours are available. **Time:** Allow 30 minutes minimum. **Hours:** Daily 10-6, late May to mid-Sept. **Cost:** $2.50; free (ages 0-11). **Phone:** (867) 996-2926. 🏕

TESLIN (D-2) pop. 122

The Nisutlin Bay Bridge, the longest water span on the Alaska Highway, crosses an arm of Teslin Lake at Teslin. The highway parallels the 116-kilometre (72-mi.) lake for about 55 kilometres (34 mi.), providing a scenic drive bordered on both sides by mountains. The area is noted for abundant game, and the fjord-like lake provides excellent fishing. The

economy of the community depends heavily on hunting, fishing and trapping.

Teslin has one of the largest indigenous populations in the Yukon, with many of its residents descended from the coastal Tlingit tribe. The original settlement is reached by a loop road. In the old village are Catholic and Anglican missions as well as a Royal Canadian Mounted Police station.

GEORGE JOHNSTON MUSEUM is 1 km (.6 mi.) w. of the Alaska Hwy. at Km-post 296. George Johnston, a Tlingit Indian, recorded his culture through his camera. A selection of Johnston's work, displays of the Tlingit tribe's rich and colorful history, Tlingit dancing costumes and pioneer items are exhibited. **Hours:** Daily 9-5, mid-May through Labor Day. **Cost:** $5; $4 (ages 60+ and students with ID); $3 (ages 0-12); $15 (family, five members). **Phone:** (867) 390-2550.

TESLIN TLINGIT HERITAGE CENTRE is 4 km (2.5 mi.) w. on Hwy. 1. Totem poles, hand-carved masks, crafts, artifacts and photographs provide insight into the life and culture of the Teslin Tlingit people. **Time:** Allow 30 minutes minimum. **Hours:** Mon.-Sat. 9-5, Sun. 11-5, June-Aug. **Cost:** $4; $3 (ages 55+ and students with ID); $3 (ages 6-17); $15 (family). **Phone:** (867) 390-2070. 🏕

WATSON LAKE (D-3) pop. 802

At Km-post 1016.8 on the Alaska Highway, Watson Lake is an important transportation, distribution and communication center for the southern Yukon. The town was named for Frank Watson, a trapper from England who settled there in 1898.

Watson Lake is known for the signpost collection that was begun by a homesick soldier during construction of the Alaska Highway in 1942. Over the years, tourists have continued adding signs showing the names of their hometowns, and now the collection includes more than 60,000 signs.

From Watson Lake the historic Robert Campbell Highway loops north and west through the wilderness of southeastern Yukon.

NORTHERN LIGHTS CENTRE is at 807 Frank Tr. Images of the aurora borealis are displayed in a planetarium-like dome theater. Narration details the myths and science behind the luminous phenomena. **Time:** Allow 1 hour minimum. **Hours:** Daily 12:30-9:30, mid-May to mid-Sept. **Cost:** $10; $9 (ages 66+ and students with ID); $6 (ages 6-12); $24 (family, two adults and three children). **Phone:** (867) 536-7827.

WATSON LAKE VISITOR INFORMATION CENTRE is at jct. Alaska and Robert Campbell hwys. A DVD presentation explains the history and hardship surrounding the construction of the Alaska Highway. **Time:** Allow 30 minutes minimum. **Hours:** Daily 8-8, mid-May to mid-Sept.; hours may vary, early to mid-May and mid- to late Sept. Phone ahead to confirm schedule. **Cost:** Free. **Phone:** (867) 536-7469.

WHITEHORSE (D-2) pop. 23,276,
elev. 689m/2,260'
• Hotels p. 579 • Restaurants p. 580

Whitehorse began during the Klondike gold rush when thousands of prospectors journeyed by ship to Skagway, Alaska, then climbed the rugged mountain passes to the headwaters of the Yukon River. They constructed nearly anything floatable for the more than 900-kilometre (559-mi.) trip to Dawson City via Whitehorse. Above Whitehorse many prospectors died in the dangerous Whitehorse Rapids.

When stern-wheeler service to Dawson became available, the trip from Whitehorse took 2.5 days; the return trip against the current took 5 days. The first rails of the White Pass & Yukon Route were laid at Skagway in May 1898, and the line to Whitehorse opened in July 1900.

During World War II Canadian and United States Army personnel building the Alaska Highway moved to Whitehorse, which became the capital of the Yukon Territory in 1953.

Evolving into the transportation, communication and distribution center of the Yukon, Whitehorse also became the territorial headquarters of the Royal Canadian Mounted Police as well as the heart of the territorial government and federal departments.

Attractions on a much larger scale include Lake Laberge, the setting for Robert W. Service's "The Cremation of Sam McGee," and the Robert Lowe Suspension Bridge across Miles Canyon.

The Whitehorse Power Dam features one of the world's longest wooden fish ladders; the salmon, running in late July or early August, can be seen from viewing windows. Lake Schwatka, impounded by the power dam, was named after Frederick Schwatka, the first U.S. army lieutenant to navigate the entire length of the Yukon River.

Visible from the Alaska Highway, 24 kilometres (15 mi.) south of Whitehorse, is Marsh Lake Lock, the northernmost lock in the Western Hemisphere. It is used by small craft navigating the upper Yukon River.

Guided tours of the town and surrounding area are available through Gray Line/Yukon (see attraction listing). Several companies provide Yukon River cruises, guided hikes, and canoe, boat and raft trips on area rivers. The Yukon Conservation Society gives guided nature walks in the summer.

The Swan Haven Interpretive Centre, on the shores of M'Clintock Bay, affords bird enthusiasts the opportunity to learn about migratory birds, in particular trumpeter swans. The centre is open Mon.-Fri. 5-9 p.m., Sat.-Sun. noon-7, in April. Phone (867) 667-8291.

Whitehorse Visitor Information Centre, at Second Avenue and Lambert Street, features exhibits and audiovisual presentations about the Yukon. The centre is open daily 8-8, mid-May to mid-Sept.; hours may vary, early to mid-May and mid- to late Sept.; Mon.-Fri. 8:30-noon and 1-5, rest of year. Phone (867) 667-3084.

Whitehorse is the terminus for the 1,000-mile Yukon Quest International Sled Dog Race,

which starts in Fairbanks, Alaska, and takes place over a 2-week period from early to mid-February.

City of Whitehorse Tourism: 3128 Third Ave., Whitehorse, YT, Canada Y1A 1E7. **Phone:** (867) 668-8687. *(See ad p. 578.)*

Self-guiding tours: Guidebooks and audio walking tours are available from the Yukon Historical and Museums Association, 3126 Third Ave., P.O. Box 4357, Whitehorse, YT, Canada Y1A 3T5; phone (867) 667-4704.

FRANTIC FOLLIES is presented in the Village Square room of the Westmark Whitehorse Hotel at 201 Wood St. The Gay '90s vaudeville revue has a cast of professional actors, dancers and musicians and recaptures the spirit and enthusiasm of the Klondike gold rush. The 1.7-hour family-style show includes music, comedy, magic, dancing and the poetry of Robert W. Service, Bard of the Yukon.

Hours: Performances are given Tues.-Sun at 8:30, June-Aug. Phone ahead to confirm schedule. **Cost:** $24; $10 (ages 0-13). **Phone:** (867) 668-2042.

GRAY LINE YUKON WHITEHORSE CITY TOUR leaves from the Westmark Whitehorse Hotel, 201 Wood St. The narrated bus tour acquaints visitors with the city by calling upon such landmarks as the stern-wheeler SS *Klondike II* and the Whitehorse Power Dam. Other places of interest that can be seen include museums, the longest wooden fish ladder in North America and a log skyscraper. **Hours:** Tours depart Sun.-Mon. and Wed.-Fri. at 9:45, June-Aug. **Cost:** Fare $39. **Phone:** (867) 668-3225.

MacBRIDE MUSEUM OF YUKON HISTORY is at 1124 First Ave. The museum offers an in-depth look at the Yukon heritage with exhibits ranging from prehistoric mammals to the 1898 gold rush. Displays include Sam McGee's 1899 cabin, indigenous relics and sample minerals of the territory. On the grounds are an old steam locomotive, a sleigh wagon and a giant nugget of copper weighing about 1,170 kilograms (2,580 lbs.).

Hours: Daily 9:30-5, mid-May through Labour Day; Tues.-Sat. 10-4, Labour Day through mid-May. **Cost:** $10; $9 (ages 60+); $5 (ages 3-17); $25 (family, four members). **Phone:** (867) 667-2709.

OLD LOG CHURCH MUSEUM is at Third Ave. and Elliott St. Built in 1900, the church houses many missionary, Gwitch'in and Inuit items as well as an audiovisual presentation about the history of the Anglican church in the Yukon. **Tours:** Guided tours are available. **Time:** Allow 30 minutes minimum. **Hours:** Daily 10-6, mid-May through Labour Day. **Cost:** $6; $5 (students ages 6-18 with ID and ages 56+); free (ages 0-6); $12 (family, two adults and two children). **Phone:** (867) 668-2555.

THE SS *KLONDIKE II* NATIONAL HISTORIC SITE is next to the river at Second Ave. and Robert Campbell Bridge. One of the largest stern-wheelers on the Yukon River, the

Klondike II ran its route 1937-55. The original *Klondike* struck a reef in 1936; a replacement was built the same year. **Note:** Due to budget cuts, Parks Canada is adjusting offerings. This may be one of those sites; phone ahead for the latest information.

Time: Allow 30 minutes minimum. **Hours:** Daily 10-6, mid-May to mid-Sept. **Cost:** $6; free (ages 0-5). **Phone:** (867) 667-4511.

TAKHINI HOT SPRINGS is 10 km (6 mi.) w. off Klondike Hwy. at Km-post 10. Natural mineral hot spring pools are maintained at 36 degrees C (96.8 degrees F) for year-round swimming. Other activities include horseback riding, hiking, camping, climbing and cross-country skiing. **Hours:** Pool open daily 8 a.m.-11 p.m., mid-June to mid-Aug.; noon-10 p.m., mid-May to mid-June and mid-Aug. to Oct. **Cost:** $10.50; $9 (ages 65+); $8 (ages 13-17); $7 (ages 3-12). **Phone:** (867) 633-2706.

WATERFRONT TROLLEY departs northbound from Rotary Peace Park and southbound from Spook Creek Station. Visitors may ride a restored narrow-gauge 1925 trolley originally from Portugal. The bright yellow car seats 24 passengers and travels along the waterfront in downtown Whitehorse, making stops along the way at Rotary Peace Park, the visitor centre, White Pass Train Depot, Jarvis Street, Shipyards Park and Kishwoot. The conductor provides narration about the history of the waterfront and the White Pass & Yukon Railroad.

Time: Allow 1 hour minimum. **Hours:** Trips depart on the hour 9-6 from Rotary Peace Park and on the half-hour 8:30-5:55 p.m. from Spook Creek Station, mid-May to mid-Sept. **Cost:** Fare $2; free (ages 0-7). **Phone:** (867) 667-6355.

WHITEHORSE FISHWAY is at the end of Nisutlin Dr. via Lewes Blvd. Said to be the longest wooden fish ladder in the world, the fishway enables chinook salmon and other fish to bypass the Whitehorse Rapids Dam during their 3,000-kilometre (1,860-mi.) migration between the Bering Sea and their fresh-water spawning grounds in southern Yukon. Underwater windows provide a close-up view of the migrating fish. **Time:** Allow 30 minutes minimum. **Hours:** Daily 9-9, Aug.; 9-7, July; 10-6, June. **Cost:** Donations. **Phone:** (867) 633-5965.

YUKON ARTS CENTRE is at 80 Range Rd. This art gallery features contemporary revolving exhibits, and the theatre presents concerts, dramas and musicals throughout the year. **Time:** Allow 1 hour minimum. **Hours:** Tues.-Sun. noon-5. Phone ahead for show information and schedules. Closed major holidays. **Cost:** Donations. **Phone:** (867) 667-8574.

GEM YUKON BERINGIA INTERPRETIVE CENTRE is 2 km (1.2 mi.) e. on the Alaska Hwy. to Km-post 1473 (mi. 914) by Whitehorse Airport. An area of the Yukon, Alaska and Siberia never covered by glaciers during the ice age, Beringia is believed

▼ *See AAA listing p. 577* ▼

www.visitwhitehorse.com

Whitehorse

Visit us – corner of 3rd & Wood – for a FREE three-day Visitor Parking Pass & Pin.

YUKON
LARGER THAN LIFE

Contact us for a
FREE Vacation Planner:
tourism@whitehorse.ca
867-668-8687

Whitehorse
THE WILDERNESS CITY

to be the route traveled by the first peoples who entered the Americas from Asia.

Fossils, life-size animal and aborigine exhibits, interactive computer kiosks, and murals and dioramas of Beringia's landscape illustrate the area's history, geographical events and culture, from the ice age to the present. Highlights include fossils of woolly mammoths, scimitar cats, giant beavers, short-faced bears and steppe bison. A diorama depicts the Bluefish Caves, an important North American archeological site.

Hours: Daily 9-6, mid-May to mid-Sept.; Sun.-Mon. noon-5, rest of year. Phone ahead to confirm schedule. **Cost:** $6; $5 (ages 55+); $4 (ages 6-12 and students with ID); $25 (family, yearly pass). Combination ticket with Yukon Transportation Museum $9. **Phone:** (867) 667-8855.

YUKON HISTORICAL AND MUSEUMS ASSOCIATION GUIDED TOURS depart from the Donnenworth House, 3126 Third Ave. Guides in period costume describe the architecture, history and local color of Whitehorse on 1-hour walking tours. Historic structures include the 1901 telegraph office, the log church and rectory, the city fire station, the Klondike Airways building, the Royal Canadian Mounted Police compound, the Mast house and Sam McGee's cabin.

Self-guiding walking tour brochures also are available. **Time:** Allow 1 hour minimum. **Hours:** Tours depart Mon.-Sat. at 9, 11, 1 and 3, June-Aug. **Cost:** $6; free (ages 0-11). Self-guiding walking tour brochure $8.95. **Phone:** (867) 667-4704.

 YUKON RIVER CRUISE docks 3.2 km (2 mi.) s. of downtown at 68 Miles Canyon Rd. Two-hour narrated excursions of the Yukon River through Miles Canyon are offered aboard the MV *Schwatka*. The boat passes the remains of a wooden tramway built to carry freight around the rapids, the site of Canyon City and the ruins of the Camp McCrae laundry, which served 30,000 troops stationed nearby during the construction of the Alaska Highway.

Gray Line/Yukon provides shuttle service to the departure site from downtown hotels. **Hours:** Cruises depart daily at 2 and 4, mid-June to mid-Aug.; at 2, early June to mid-June and mid Aug. to mid-Sept. Hours may vary; phone ahead. Shuttle departs hotels about 30 minutes before cruise time. **Cost:** Cruise fare $30; $15 (ages 6-12). A fee is charged for the shuttle. Fare may vary; phone ahead. **Phone:** (867) 668-4716, or (867) 668-3225 for the shuttle service.

YUKON TRANSPORTATION MUSEUM is off Alaska Hwy. at Km-post 1475.7 by Whitehorse Airport. Exhibits highlight various modes of transportation, including snowshoes, dog sleds, stage coaches, boats, aircraft and military vehicles used during the construction of the Alaska Highway. The *Queen of the Yukon*, the sister plane of Charles A. Lindbergh's *Spirit of St. Louis*, also is displayed.

Time: Allow 30 minutes minimum. **Hours:** Daily 10-6, mid-May through Aug. 31. Phone ahead to confirm schedule. **Cost:** $6; $5 (ages 55+); $4 (ages 13-17 and students with ID); $3 (ages 6-12). Combination ticket with Yukon Beringia Interpretive Centre $9. **Phone:** (867) 668-4792.

YUKON WILDLIFE PRESERVE is 40 km (25 mi.) n. on Takhini Hot Springs Rd. Guided 1-hour interpretive tours depart by bus or on foot from the log gatehouse every two hours. The more than 283-hectare (700-acre) site is home to 10 major species of Northern mammals, including moose, musk ox, mountain goat and caribou. **Time:** Allow 1 hour minimum. **Hours:** Daily 9:30-6, May-Sept. **Cost:** $22; $20 (senior citizens); $12 (ages 6-17); $55 (family, two adults and up to three children). **Phone:** (867) 456-7300.

RECREATIONAL ACTIVITIES

White-water Rafting

- **Tatshenshini Expeditions** is at 101 Jarvis St. **Hours:** Daily 10-6, June through Labour Day. Phone ahead to confirm schedule. **Phone:** (867) 633-2742.

Ziplines

- **WildPlay Yukon** is at 770 Mt. Sima Rd. Other activities also are available. **Hours:** Hours may vary (weather permitting), mid-June to late Sept.; reservations recommended. **Phone:** (867) 668-4557.

BEST WESTERN GOLD RUSH INN   (867)668-4500

Hotel
$140-$175

 AAA Benefit: Members save up to 20%, plus 10% bonus points with Best Western Rewards®.

Address: 411 Main St Y1A 2B6 **Location:** Between 4th and 5th aves; center. **Facility:** 99 units, some two bedrooms and kitchens. 4 stories, interior corridors. **Parking:** winter plug-ins. **Amenities:** *Some:* high-speed Internet. **Activities:** exercise room, spa. **Guest Services:** coin laundry. **Free Special Amenities:** high-speed Internet and airport transportation.

SAVE ECO ✈ 🍸 BIZ 🛜 ✕ 🛏 ⬚ 💻 / SOME UNITS FEE 🐾 🏌

HIGH COUNTRY INN   (867)667-4471

Hotel
$140-$175

Address: 4051 4th Ave Y1A 1H1 **Location:** 0.4 mi (0.6 km) e of Main St. **Facility:** 80 units, some efficiencies. 4 stories, interior corridors. **Parking:** winter plug-ins. **Terms:** 3 day cancellation notice-fee imposed. **Amenities:** *Some:* high-speed Internet. **Activities:** exercise room. **Guest Services:** coin laundry. **Free Special Amenities:** high-speed Internet and airport transportation.

SAVE ECO ✈ 🍴 🍸 BIZ 🛜 ✕ 🛏 ⬚ 💻 / SOME UNITS FEE 🐾 🏌

MIDNIGHT SUN BED & BREAKFAST   (867)667-2255

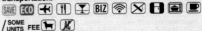 **Bed & Breakfast** $120-$150 **Address:** 6188 6th Ave Y1A 1N8 **Location:** Corner of Cook St. Located in a residential area. **Facility:** 4 units. 3 stories (no elevator), interior corridors. **Parking:** winter plug-ins. **Terms:** check-in 4 pm, 2 night minimum stay - seasonal and/or weekends, 7 day cancellation notice-fee imposed. **Amenities:** *Some:* high-speed Internet. **Guest Services:** coin laundry.

🛜 ✕ 🏌 / SOME UNITS 🛏

TOWN & MOUNTAIN HOTEL

(867)668-7644

Motel
$129-$169

Address: 401 Main St Y1A 2B6 **Location:** Center. Located in downtown area. **Facility:** 30 units. 3 stories (no elevator), interior corridors. **Parking:** on-site and street, winter plug-ins. **Terms:** 3 day cancellation notice-fee imposed. **Amenities:** *Some:* high-speed Internet. **Dining:** nightclub. **Free Special Amenities:** early check-in/late check-out and high-speed Internet.

WESTMARK WHITEHORSE HOTEL & CONFERENCE CENTER

(867)393-9700

Hotel $119-$249 **Address:** 201 Wood St Y1A 2E4 **Location:** At 2nd Ave; center. **Facility:** 180 units. 3 stories, interior corridors. **Parking:** winter plug-ins. **Terms:** cancellation fee imposed. **Amenities:** *Some:* high-speed Internet (fee). **Activities:** exercise room. **Guest Services:** coin laundry.

WHERE TO EAT

ALPINE BAKERY

867/668-6871

Breads/Pastries
Vegetarian
Quick Serve
$8-$15

AAA Inspector Notes: A short walk from the downtown core, this organic bakery/cafe is housed in its own two-story log building and features a hand-crafted, authentic masonry oven. A wide variety of wholesome breads, pastries, pizza, soup, raw foods and sushi-all organic and vegetarian-are offered. Home-made, fair-trade dark chocolates speckled with wild, Yukon cranberries is a specialty. A sunny deck with an organic herb and edible flower garden is in the back. Repeat customers should pre-order favorite breads. **Address:** 411 Alexander St Y1A 2L8 **Location:** Jct 4th Ave. *Menu on AAA.com*

ANTOINETTE'S

867/668-3505

New International. Casual Dining. $17-$30 **AAA Inspector Notes:** The mosaic tile floor at the entry, along with dark red walls, vivid art pieces and tropical tunes, set the tone for a cuisine which is difficult to pigeonhole. The menu is creative and flavorful, and though not strictly Caribbean, it does utilize some elements found in that type of food. Try the halibut in a coconut-tomato curry sauce with fresh lime and spinach. For dessert, the chocolate truffle rum cake is a nice choice. **Bar:** full bar. **Reservations:** suggested. **Address:** 4121 4th Ave Y1A 1H7 **Location:** Corner of Steele St. **Parking:** street only.

BAKED CAFE & BAKERY

867/633-6291

American. Quick Serve. $7-$10 **AAA Inspector Notes:** Primarily an organic bakery, this Main Street mainstay is a popular gathering spot for those looking to enjoy a freshly made soup, quiche, calzones, scones, muffins and cookies while sipping on a locally roasted cup of coffee. **Address:** 108-100 Main St Y1A 2A8 **Location:** Center. **Parking:** street only.

BURNT TOAST

867/393-2605

American. Casual Dining. $11-$26 **AAA Inspector Notes:** At this casual lunch spot, the modern décor is a mix of pine wood and black walls lined with black-and-white photos. The menu is a bit eclectic and lists a good range of appetizers designed for sharing, plus yummy salads. Nice entrée choices include fish tacos, jambalaya, pasta, and fish or meat dishes. The place also is very popular for breakfast, so you may find yourself there more than once. **Bar:** full bar. **Reservations:** suggested, for dinner. **Address:** 2112 2nd Ave Y1A 1B9 **Location:** Just n of Main St. **Parking:** street only.

THE CELLAR STEAKHOUSE AND WINE BAR

867/667-2572

Steak. Casual Dining. $26-$42 **AAA Inspector Notes:** You'll enjoy offerings of prime rib, halibut, Alaskan king crab, steak, salmon, baby back ribs, chicken at this well-appointed, popular restaurant. **Bar:** full bar. **Address:** 101 Main St Y1A 2A7 **Location:** Opposite White Pass Rail Depot; in Edgewater Hotel. **Parking:** on-site and street.

THE CHOCOLATE CLAIM

867/667-2202

American. Quick Serve. $6-$10 **AAA Inspector Notes:** Tucked away on a side street a short distance from the downtown core, this small art gallery-style café offers delicious freshly-made soups, sandwiches, panini and a range of delightful cakes and other desserts. **Address:** 305 Strickland St Y1A 2J9 **Location:** Jct 4th Ave, just e.

CORK AND BULL STEAKHOUSE

867/633-3305

Steak. Casual Dining. $24-$38 **AAA Inspector Notes:** No, this is not a pub! The name is just a play on words since they offer a good selection of wine and great steaks. Old wood beams and brick walls serve as the backdrop for this lively restaurant. So enticing are the appetizers and salads, it will be hard to make up your mind, especially since they include fresh oysters. Aged Angus beef, Australian lamb and wild Alaskan salmon are among the grilled options. You'll also find some pasta dishes. **Bar:** full bar. **Reservations:** suggested. **Address:** 103 Main St Y1A 2A7 **Location:** Just n of 1st Ave; center. **Parking:** street only.

THE DELI

867/667-7583

Deli. Quick Serve. $6-$9 **AAA Inspector Notes:** A short walk from the downtown core, this unassuming little butcher shop offers a wide variety of prepackaged items, such as locally made sausages, pates and baked goods as well as homemade caribou and reindeer hot dogs. Also tempting are traditional delicatessen salads and meats, which the sandwich corner uses in custom-made sandwiches that can be enjoyed on the limited tables inside or at picnic tables at the SS Klondike a few blocks away. **Address:** 203 Hanson St Y1A 1Y3 **Location:** Corner of 2nd Ave. **Parking:** street only.

GIORGIO'S CUCCINA

867/668-4050

Italian. Casual Dining. $17-$38 **AAA Inspector Notes:** This attractive dining room serves up Italian food, including thin crust pizza, fish, seafood, pasta and steak. Many dishes are prepared on a mesquite-flavoring charbroiler. Fresh fruit smoothies and a wide selection of wines round out the menu. **Bar:** full bar. **Address:** 206 Jarvis St Y1A 2H1 **Location:** Between 2nd and 3rd aves; downtown.

KLONDIKE RIB & SALMON BBQ

867/667-7554

Seafood. Casual Dining. $14-$33 **AAA Inspector Notes:** This popular restaurant opens seasonally to serve regional cuisine prepared in memorable and creative manners. On the menu are Arctic char, halibut and salmon, as well as entrée-size salads and pasta dishes. Guests can eat inside, where they might share a table with other diners, or enjoy the midnight sun on the patio. **Bar:** beer & wine. **Address:** 2116 2nd Ave Y1A 2B9 **Location:** Jct Main St; downtown. **Parking:** street only.

SANCHEZ CANTINA

867/668-5858

Mexican. Family Dining. $12-$24 **AAA Inspector Notes:** Cheerfully decorated, this casual restaurant is a special gem highly popular with the locals. Senora Sanchez offers a variety of home-made authentic Mexican dishes, including ceviche, tacos, enchiladas and entrees created with her secret recipes. A seasonal patio also is available. **Bar:** full bar. **Reservations:** suggested. **Address:** 211 Hanson St Y1A 1Y3 **Location:** Corner of 3rd Ave; downtown. **Parking:** street only.

TOKYO SUSHI

867/633-4567

Sushi. Casual Dining. $10-$20 **AAA Inspector Notes:** In the heart of downtown, this is a super sushi spot with simple Japanese décor and an open room. The comprehensive menu selection has a nice range of appetizers, including very tender gyoza, some tasty salads and tempura. Other good choices include classic, well-prepared sushi and sashimi, as well as a variety of rolls and other entrée choices such as udon noodles, donburi rice and teriyaki dishes. The bento boxes are popular at lunch. **Bar:** beer & wine. **Address:** 204B Main St Y1A 2A9 **Location:** Center. **Parking:** street only.

Safety tip: Keep a current AAA/CAA
Road Atlas in every vehicle

Mount McKinley and wild fireweed flowers

Alaska

Natives didn't call this state Alyeska—the Great Land—for nothing. There are approximately 3 million lakes, 3,000 rivers, 1,800 islands and 100,000 glaciers in Alaska's 586,000 square miles of untamed wilderness. And if that isn't enough, nine national parks and preserves and two expansive national forests total about 66 million acres of undisturbed land.

Alaska's diversity is illustrated through its distinct natural features. The state is home to towering Mount McKinley—so high that it's cloaked in clouds most of the time. Long, bright days are typical during the summer solstice, when the sun never completely disappears.

Options for excitement in The Land of the Midnight Sun seem endless. Walk on an ice field and feel the crunch of ice under your boots; peer over chunky glaciers and sweeping mountain ranges from a helicopter; gaze at a sky painted with brilliant northern lights;

Northern lights, Matanuska-Susitna Valley

ride on a boat navigating through blue-green waters packed with bobbing icebergs; marvel at 25-foot-tall sand dunes; or board a bush plane to catch a glimpse of steam from an active volcano.

Tribe members, ingenious at adapting to their variable and sometimes hostile surroundings, made the most of the state's natural offerings, which includes the creatures portrayed in their art. Salmon and orcas are just a couple of animals that appear on totem poles. Used for sustenance, they were often depicted in oral tales; today animals remain the focus of many pictures and the subjects of travelogues. Visitors relish the opportunity to snap a photograph of a moose cow nibbling grass alongside her twins or grizzly cubs wrestling under the protective watch of mama bear.

For many residents Alaska's riches are liquid: The creation of the Trans-Alaska Pipeline made it possible to transport crude oil almost 800 miles from Prudhoe Bay south to Valdez. The pipeline, an amazing engineering feat crossing three mountain ranges and three fault lines, can withstand an earthquake measuring up to 8.5 on the Richter scale as well as temperatures as low as minus 80 F.

Oil isn't Alaska's only rich resource. Discoveries of gold in Fairbanks, Fort Yukon, Juneau, Nome, Skagway and Wrangell lured prospectors from the "Lower 48" to seek their fortune. Visit abandoned gold dredges, camps and mines and imagine the fervor that once pervaded these sites. And there was more money to be made; Russian trappers came in search of valuable sea otter pelts.

But Alaska's native tribes have left the most enduring impact. Traditions of the Aleut, Alutiiq, Athabascan, Cup'ik, Haida, Inupiaq, Tlingit, Tsimpshian and Yup'ik tribes can be appreciated through the acts of proud dancers and storytellers who keep family legacies alive. Artisans create soapstone and whalebone carvings, clothing adorned with intricate beading and baskets made from white birch bark.

And totem poles, Alaska's silent, symbolic sentries, are just one reminder of what makes this land truly great.

Recreation

In the Land of the Midnight Sun, chances for wildlife viewing are as plentiful as snowflakes during winter.

Alaska has one of the largest bald eagle populations in the world. They aren't difficult to spot at the Chilkat Bald Eagle Preserve near Haines; more than 3,500 visit the area to feed from October to February.

Many wildlife cruises headed for the Inside Passage depart from Juneau. Arm yourself with some good binoculars, a camera and a journal to record your sightings. Entries might include descriptions of huge, barking Steller sea lions lounging on top of each other; Dall's porpoises frolicking in a boat's wake; or Sitka black- or white-tailed deer sipping from a stream.

Black bears fish for salmon in Anan Creek near Wrangell Island, and the west coast of Prince of Wales Island (near Ketchikan) is a great spot for watching tufted puffins. It's no "fluke" to see a whale tail; humpbacks often make appearances in Prince William Sound, and wherever there's an iceberg, you can find harbor seals resting upon floating ice chunks.

Day cruises depart from Seward and Whittier to explore Prince William Sound and Kenai Fjords National Park, home to sea mammals galore. Along the Kenai Peninsula, both humpback and beluga whales perform aquatic acrobatics near the Turnagain Arm. Nearby, Dall sheep can be seen grazing atop steep cliffs that grace Cook Inlet.

Looking for bears? The Kodiak National Wildlife Refuge is home to some 2,300 Kodiak bears, and Brooks Camp in Katmai National Park and Preserve safeguards one of the world's largest brown bear populations.

Grizzlies as well as caribou and moose roam the desertlike tundra of Denali National Park and Preserve; take a narrated bus tour

to catch a glimpse. Near the park entrance, forest rangers give a demonstration of sled dogs at work. Even better, hang on tight for a sled ride pulled by Iditarod huskies in Seward.

Many activities in Alaska include a magnificent view: Try rafting in Denali on the Nenana River Gorge or canoeing near Admiralty Island National Monument. Kayakers also enjoy the Sarkar Lake Canoe Route in Tongass National Forest. Winter options include cross-country skiing, dog sledding or snowmobiling on the Twin Ridge or Upper Twin ski trails in Tongass National Forest, or downhill skiing at Mount Alyeska in Girdwood.

Want to stand on a glacier? Hikers in Kenai Fjords National Park follow rangers on nature walks to a nearby ice field. Floatplane or helicopter sightseeing is an excellent way to see glaciers, ice fields, mountain ranges, waterfalls, lakes or stark tundra. Nearly every city has flightseeing tour operators.

A fishing charter from one of various harbors is a good way to hook steelhead, grayling or rainbow trout. Sport fishing yields red snapper or cod—and Resurrection Bay (near Seward), Sitka and Wrangell are home to world-class halibut and salmon.

Native rye grass basket

Historic Timeline

1741	Russian explorer Vitus Bering, sent by Peter the Great to explore the North Pacific, is the first European to set foot on Alaskan soil.
1867	In a deal known as "Seward's Folly," Secretary of State William Seward buys Alaska from Russia for 2 cents per acre.
1880	"Seward's Folly" becomes a gold mine as vast deposits of precious metals are discovered in Juneau and other cities.
1903	A submarine cable links Seattle to Sitka and Sitka to Valdez, increasing communication between Alaska and the world.
1942	Japan attacks Dutch Harbor and consequently occupies the Aleutian Islands for nearly a year during World War II.
1964	A Good Friday earthquake severely damages Anchorage, Valdez, the Northwest Panhandle and Cook Inlet.
1968	Oil is discovered on Prudhoe Bay, spurring the construction of an 800-mile pipeline to transport the oil to Valdez.
1977	Construction of the Trans-Alaska Pipeline is complete.
1989	The *Exxon Valdez* spills some 11 million gallons of crude oil into Prince William Sound.
2004	Mitch Seavey of Seward wins the Iditarod Trail Sled Dog Race on his 11th attempt.
2008	Gov. Sarah Palin is the first woman to be on a Republican presidential ticket after Sen. John McCain names her his running mate.

What To Pack

Temperature Averages Maximum/Minimum (Fahrenheit)	JANUARY	FEBRUARY	MARCH	APRIL	MAY	JUNE	JULY	AUGUST	SEPTEMBER	OCTOBER	NOVEMBER	DECEMBER
Anchorage	22/9	26/12	34/18	44/29	55/39	62/47	65/52	63/49	55/41	40/28	28/16	24/11
Barrow	-8/-20	-10/-22	-7/-20	6/-7	25/15	40/30	47/34	44/34	35/28	19/10	5/-6	-5/-16
Fairbanks	2/-13	10/-10	26/1	44/19	61/35	71/47	73/50	67/45	55/34	32/16	12/-2	5/-9
Juneau	31/21	34/24	39/28	48/33	56/40	62/46	64/49	63/48	56/44	47/38	38/29	33/24
Kotzebue	4/-9	3/-10	7/-8	20/3	38/25	51/39	60/49	57/47	46/37	28/19	13/3	6/-6
Nome	13/-2	14/-2	18/1	27/12	43/31	54/41	59/47	56/45	49/37	34/23	23/11	16/1

From the records of The Weather Channel Interactive, Inc.

Good Facts To Know

ABOUT THE STATE

POPULATION: 626,932.

AREA: 586,412 square miles; ranks 1st.

CAPITAL: Juneau.

HIGHEST POINT: 20,320 ft., Mount McKinley.

LOWEST POINT: Sea level, Pacific Ocean.

TIME ZONE(S): Alaska for most of the state; Hawaii-Aleutian for the extreme western portion of the Aleutian Islands. DST.

REGULATIONS

TEEN DRIVING LAWS: Driving is not permitted 1 a.m.-5 a.m. No passengers under age 21, with the exception of family members, are permitted for the first 6 months. The minimum age for an unrestricted driver's license is 16 years and 6 months.

SEAT BELT/CHILD RESTRAINT LAWS: Seat belts are required for driver and all passengers 16 and older. Children ages 8 through 15 are required to be in a child restraint or seat belt; child restraints are required for children under age 8 unless they are at least 4 feet, 9 inches tall or weigh more than 65 pounds.

CELL PHONE RESTRICTIONS: All drivers are prohibited from text messaging while driving.

HELMETS FOR MOTORCYCLES: Required for drivers under 18 years old and all passengers.

RADAR DETECTORS: Permitted.

MOVE OVER LAW: Driver is required to slow down and vacate the lane nearest stopped police, fire and rescue vehicles and tow trucks using audible or flashing signals.

FIREARMS LAWS: Vary by state and/or county. Contact the Division of State Troopers, Headquarters, 5700 E. Tudor Rd., Dept. P, Anchorage, AK 99507; phone (907) 269-5511.

HOLIDAYS

HOLIDAYS: Jan. 1 ▪ Martin Luther King Jr. Day, Jan. (3rd Mon.) ▪ Presidents Day, Feb. (3rd Mon.) ▪ Seward's Day, Mar. (last Mon.) ▪ Memorial Day, May (last Mon.) ▪ July 4 ▪ Labor Day, Sept. (1st Mon.) ▪ Columbus Day, Oct. (2nd Mon.) ▪ Alaska Day, Oct. 18 ▪ Veterans Day, Nov. 11 ▪ Thanksgiving ▪ Christmas, Dec. 25.

MONEY

TAXES: Alaska does not have a statewide sales tax, but cities and boroughs may levy a sales tax of up to 7 percent, plus special taxes on goods and services. A 10 percent tax is levied on rental cars.

VISITOR INFORMATION

INFORMATION CENTERS: Tourist literature and reports on highway and weather conditions are available at the Log Cabin Visitor Information Center, jct. F St. and 4th Ave. in Anchorage ▪ the Fairbanks Visitor Information Center, 101 Dunkel St. in Fairbanks ▪ the Southeast Alaska Discovery Center, 50 Main St. in Ketchikan ▪ and the Tok Information Center, jct. SR 2 (Alaska Hwy.) and SR 1 in Tok.

FURTHER INFORMATION FOR VISITORS:
Alaska Travel Industry Association
2600 Cordova St., Suite 201
Anchorage, AK 99503
(907) 929-2200

NATIONAL FOREST INFORMATION:
U.S. Forest Service
8510 Menden Hall Loop Rd.
P.O. Box 21628
Juneau, AK 99802
(907) 586-8800
(877) 444-6777 (reservations)
TTY (907) 790-7444

NATIONAL PARK INFORMATION:
Alaska Public Lands Information Center
101 Dunkel St., Suite 110
Fairbanks, AK 99701
(907) 459-3730
(866) 869-6887
TTY (907) 456-0532

FISHING & HUNTING REGULATIONS:
Alaska Department of Fish and Game
1255 W. 8th St.
P.O. Box 115526
Juneau, AK 99811-5526
(907) 465-4180 (Division of Sport Fishing)
(907) 465-4190 (Division of Wildlife Conservation)

ALASKA FERRY INFORMATION:
Alaska Marine Highway
6858 Glacier Hwy.
P.O. Box 112505
Juneau, AK 99811-2505
(907) 465-3941
(800) 642-0066

Alaska Annual Events

Please call ahead to confirm event details.

JANUARY

- Polar Bear Jump Off
  Seward
  907-224-5230
- Anchorage Folk Festival
  Anchorage
  907-278-4118
- Alcan 200 Road Rally
  Haines
  907-766-2051

FEBRUARY

- Homer Winter Carnival
  Homer
  907-235-7740
- World Ice Art
  Championships / Fairbanks
  907-451-8250
- Tent City Festival / Wrangell
  800-367-9745

MARCH

- Wasilla Winterfest Iditarod
  Days / Wasilla
  907-373-2698
- Iditarod Trail Sled Dog
  Race / Anchorage
  907-376-5155
- Chatanika Days
  Fairbanks
  907-389-2164

APRIL

- NYO Games / Anchorage
  907-793-3267
- Alaska Hummingbird
  Festival / Ketchikan
  907-228-6220
- Stikine River Migratory Bird
  Festival / Wrangell
  907-874-2381

MAY

- Kodiak Crab Festival
  Kodiak
  907-486-5557
- Juneau Jazz and Classics
  Juneau
  907-463-3378
- Ketchikan King Salmon
  Derby / Ketchikan
  907-225-2077

JUNE

- Midnight Sun Festival
  Nome
  907-443-6624
- Alaskan Scottish Highland
  Games / Eagle River
  907-770-4967
- Sitka Summer Music
  Festival / Sitka
  907-277-4852

JULY

- Girdwood Forest Fair
  Girdwood
  800-880-3880
- Bear Paw Festival
  Eagle River
  907-694-4702
- Southeast Alaska State Fair
  Haines
  907-766-2476

AUGUST

- Blueberry Arts Festival
  Ketchikan
  907-225-2211
- Tanana Valley State Fair
  Fairbanks
  907-452-3750
- Alaska State Fair / Palmer
  907-745-4827

SEPTEMBER

- Kodiak Rodeo and State
  Fair / Kodiak
  907-487-4440
- Kachemak Bay Wooden
  Boat Festival / Homer
  907-235-2986
- Alaska Airlines Autumn
  Classics / Anchorage
  907-747-6774

OCTOBER

- Kendall Hockey Classic
  Anchorage
  907-279-0618
- Make It Alaskan Festival
  Anchorage
  907-279-0618
- Alaska Day Festival / Sitka
  907-747-5124

NOVEMBER

- Carrs/Safeway Great Alaska
  Basketball Shootout
  Anchorage
  907-786-1293
- Crafts Weekend and
  ReadAlaska Book Fair
  Anchorage
  907-929-9200
- WhaleFest / Sitka
  907-747-5940

DECEMBER

- New Year's Eve Torchlight
  Parade and Fireworks
  Anchorage
  907-754-1111
- Anchorage International
  Film Festival / Anchorage
  907-338-3690
- Colony Christmas / Palmer
  907-745-2880

Cessna and deHavilland
floatplanes, Ketchikan

Bull moose, Alaska Wildlife
Conservation Center

Shooting star wildflower,
Denali National Park and
Preserve

Native Tlingit carving, Juneau

White Pass & Yukon Route, Skagway

Index: Great Experience for Members

AAA editor's picks of exceptional note

Alaska Native Heritage Center

Riverboat Discovery

Alaska SeaLife Center

Kenai Fjords Tours

Make the Most of Your Trip
with AAA eTourBook® Guides

Maximize your travel experience when you take along AAA eTourBook guides for your ereader or smartphone. Each of the more than 100 available digital titles is packed with:

- Destination details
- AAA Approved and Diamond Rated hotel and restaurant listings
- Attraction and event information
- Preplanned itineraries
- Editor's don't-miss picks

Download now at
AAA.com/ebooks

Alaska, Yukon and

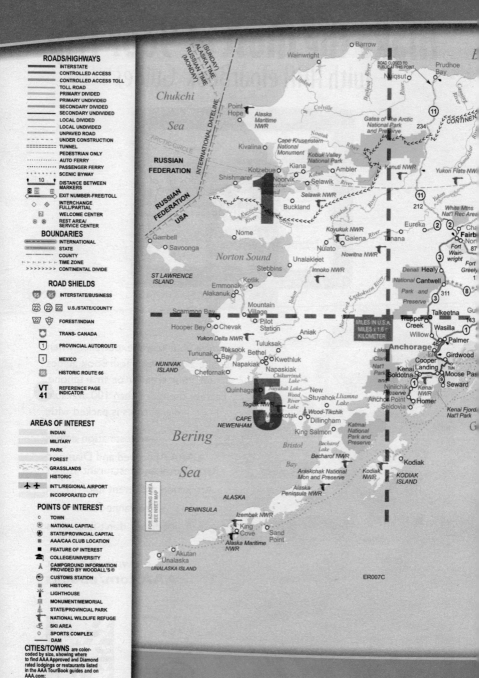

ROADS/HIGHWAYS
- INTERSTATE
- CONTROLLED ACCESS
- CONTROLLED ACCESS TOLL
- TOLL ROAD
- PRIMARY DIVIDED
- PRIMARY UNDIVIDED
- SECONDARY DIVIDED
- SECONDARY UNDIVIDED
- LOCAL DIVIDED
- LOCAL UNDIVIDED
- UNPAVED ROAD
- UNDER CONSTRUCTION
- TUNNEL
- PEDESTRIAN ONLY
- AUTO FERRY
- PASSENGER FERRY
- SCENIC BYWAY
- DISTANCE BETWEEN MARKERS 10
- EXIT NUMBER-FREE/TOLL
- INTERCHANGE FULL/PARTIAL
- WELCOME CENTER
- REST AREA/ SERVICE CENTER

BOUNDARIES
- INTERNATIONAL
- STATE
- COUNTY
- TIME ZONE
- CONTINENTAL DIVIDE

ROAD SHIELDS
- 95 65 INTERSTATE/BUSINESS
- 22 22 22 U.S./STATE/COUNTY
- 127 127 FOREST/INDIAN
- TRANS- CANADA
- 1 PROVINCIAL AUTOROUTE
- 1 MEXICO
- 66 HISTORIC ROUTE 66
- VT 41 REFERENCE PAGE INDICATOR

AREAS OF INTEREST
- INDIAN
- MILITARY
- PARK
- FOREST
- GRASSLANDS
- HISTORIC
- INT'L/REGIONAL AIRPORT
- INCORPORATED CITY

POINTS OF INTEREST
- ○ TOWN
- ⊛ NATIONAL CAPITAL
- ⊛ STATE/PROVINCIAL CAPITAL
- ■ AAA/CAA CLUB LOCATION
- ■ FEATURE OF INTEREST
- ■ COLLEGE/UNIVERSITY
- ⚲ CAMPGROUND INFORMATION PROVIDED BY WOODALL'S®
- ⊛ CUSTOMS STATION
- HISTORIC
- LIGHTHOUSE
- MONUMENT/MEMORIAL
- STATE/PROVINCIAL PARK
- NATIONAL WILDLIFE REFUGE
- SKI AREA
- ○ SPORTS COMPLEX
- DAM

CITIES/TOWNS are color-coded by size, showing where to find AAA Approved and Diamond rated lodgings or restaurants listed in the AAA TourBook guides and on AAA.com:
- ● **Red** - major destinations and capitals; many listings
- ● **Black** - destinations; some listings
- ● **Grey** - no listings

Northwest Territories
Atlas Section

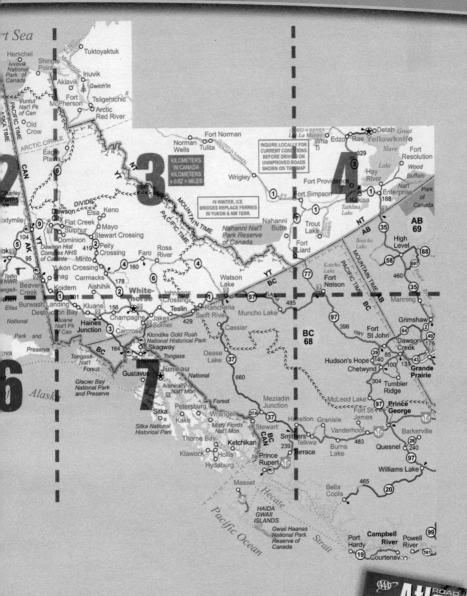

Ufort Sea

Herschel
Ivvavik National Park of Canada
Shingle Point
Tuktoyaktuk
Inuvik
Aklavik
Gwich'in
Fort McPherson
Tsiigehtchic
Arctic Red River

Old Crow
Vuntut Nat'l Pk of Can

2

CAN

PACIFIC TIME / ALASKA TIME

ARCTIC CIRCLE

Charley National
Eagle Plains

DIVIDE

Dawson City
Elsa Keno
Flat Creek
Sulphur
Mayo
Dominion
Stewart Crossing
419
Pelly Crossing
Minto
Yukon Crossing
Shag Carmacks
Koidern
Aishihik
Beaver Creek
Burwash Landing
Destruction Bay
Kluane
156
Champagne
Haines Junction
Carcross
164

YT AK

104
95

Tetlin NWR
Wrangell St. Elias National Park and Preserve

6

Alaska

Glacier Bay National Park and Preserve

Tongass Nat'l Forest

38
Haines
Gustavus
Juneau

Admiralty Is Nat'l Mon

7

Sitka
Sitka National Historical Park

Petersburg
Wrangell
Kake
Misty Fiords Nat'l Mon

Thorne Bay
Klawock
Hollis
Hydaburg
Ketchikan

Masset
Hecate

HAIDA GWAII ISLANDS
Gwaii Haanas National Park Reserve of Canada

Pacific Ocean

Strait

3

Norman Wells
Fort Norman
Tulita
Wrigley

KILOMETERS IN CANADA
KILOMETERS x 0.62 = MILES

IN WINTER, ICE BRIDGES REPLACE FERRIES IN YUKON & NW TERR.

Nahanni Nat'l Park Reserve of Canada

MOUNTAIN TIME / PACIFIC TIME

NT
YT

Ross River
Faro
160
4

Watson Lake
YT BC

Johnsons Crossing
White horse
1
Teslin
Rancheria
Swift River
Cassiar
429

Dease Lake
37

Meziadin Junction

37A
Stewart
BC CAN
37

Hazelton
Granisle
Smithers
Telkwa
239
Terrace
Burns Lake
483

Prince Rupert

Bella Coola
465

Lac La Martre
Wha Ti
Edzo Rae
Detah
Yellowknife
329

INQUIRE LOCALLY FOR CURRENT CONDITIONS BEFORE DRIVING ON UNIMPROVED ROADS SHOWN ON THIS MAP

Nahanni Butte

Fort Providence
Fort Simpson
1
7
Trout Lake
Fort Liard
77
Fort Nelson

Great Slave Lake

Hay River
Kakisa
Tathlina Lake
188

Bistcho Lake

Katcho Lake

97
485

97

398
Fort St John
29
85
Hudson's Hope
140
Chetwynd
100
304
Tumbler Ridge

McLeod Lake
Fort St James
Vanderhoof
16

Muncho Lake

BC 68

MOUNTAIN TIME / AB / BC

Fort Resolution
Wood Buffalo
Fort Enterprise
Nat'l Park of Canada

AB 69

High Level
58
88
460
35

Manning
35

Grimshaw
64
Dawson Creek
49
176
131
Grande Prairie

Prince George
16
Barkerville
26
Quesnel
240
97
Williams Lake
20

4

Port Hardy
19
Courtenay
Campbell River
Powell River
99
101

Use driving maps from the AAA Road Atlas to plan your itinerary and route. Purchase the complete 2013 AAA Road Atlas at participating AAA/CAA offices, retail stores and online booksellers.

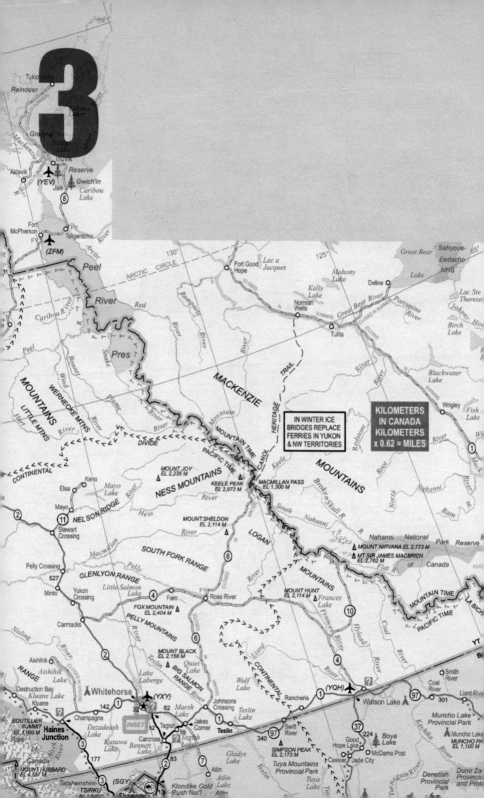

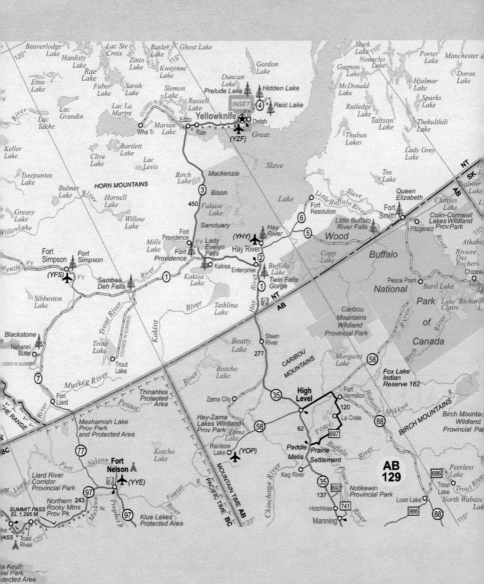

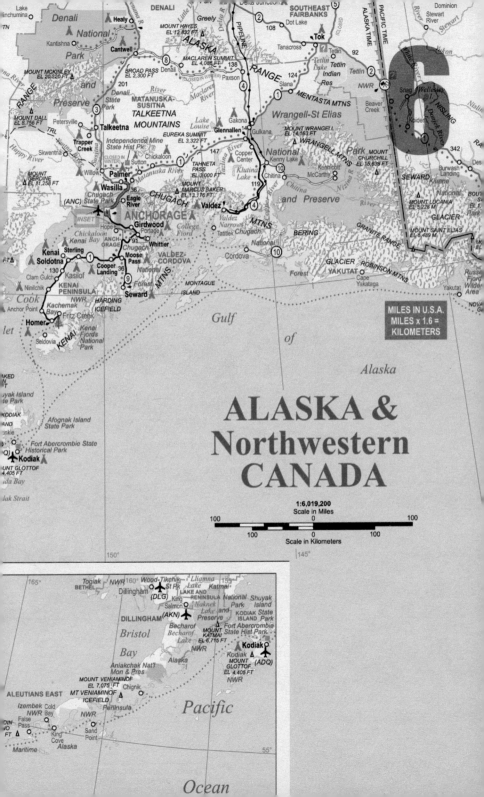

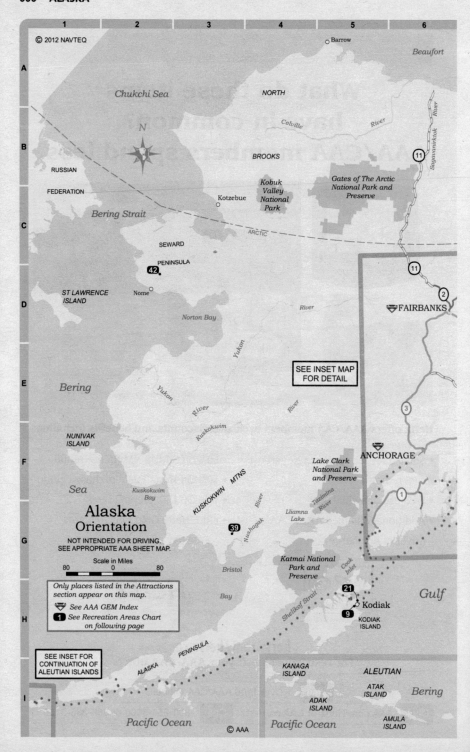

© 2012 NAVTEQ

Barrow

Beaufort

Chukchi Sea

NORTH

N

RUSSIAN

Colville River

BROOKS

FEDERATION

Kobuk
Valley
National
Park

Gates of The Arctic
National Park and
Preserve

Kotzebue

11

Bering Strait

ARCTIC

Sagavanirktok River

SEWARD

11

PENINSULA

42

ST LAWRENCE
ISLAND

Nome

2

Bering

Norton Bay

River

FAIRBANKS

River

Yukon

Yukon

River

SEE INSET MAP
FOR DETAIL

River

3

NUNIVAK
ISLAND

Kuskokwim

ANCHORAGE

Sea

*Kuskokwim
Bay*

Lake Clark
National Park
and Preserve

1

Alaska
Orientation

NOT INTENDED FOR DRIVING.
SEE APPROPRIATE AAA SHEET MAP.

KUSKOKWIN MTNS

River

Tazimina
River

39

Nushagak

Lliamna
Lake

Scale in Miles

80   0   80

Only places listed in the Attractions
section appear on this map.

▽ See AAA GEM Index

1 See Recreation Areas Chart
on following page

Bristol

Katmai National
Park and
Preserve

Cook Inlet

21

Gulf

Bay

Shelikof Strait

9

Kodiak

KODIAK
ISLAND

SEE INSET FOR
CONTINUATION OF
ALEUTIAN ISLANDS

ALASKA

PENINSULA

KANAGA
ISLAND

ALEUTIAN

ATAK
ISLAND

Bering

ADAK
ISLAND

AMULA
ISLAND

Pacific Ocean

© AAA

Pacific Ocean

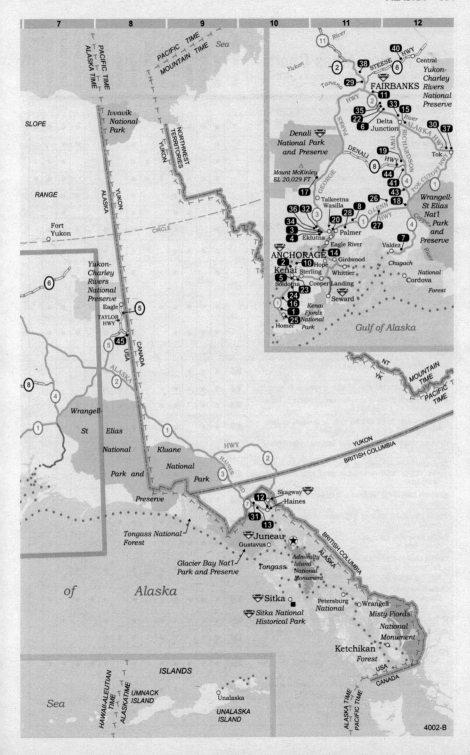

Recreation Areas Chart

The map location numerals in column 2 show an area's location on the preceding map.

	MAP LOCATION	CAMPING	PICNICKING	HIKING TRAILS	BOATING	BOAT RAMP	BOAT RENTAL	FISHING	SWIMMING	PETS ON LEASH	BICYCLE TRAILS	WINTER SPORTS	VISITOR CENTER	LODGE/CABINS	FOOD SERVICE
NATIONAL PARKS AND PRESERVES *(See place listings.)*															
Denali (B-10) 6,028,203 acres. Cross-country skiing, dog mushing, snowmobiling, snowshoeing.		•	•	•				•		•		•	•	•	•
Gates of the Arctic (B-5) 8,500,000 acres. Bird watching.		•		•				•				•	•		
Glacier Bay (G-9) 3,283,168 acres. Bird watching, hunting, kayaking, rafting.		•		•	•	•	•	•		•			•	•	•
Katmai (G-4) 4,159,097 acres. Canoeing, hunting, kayaking.		•	•	•	•	•	•	•					•	•	•
Kenai Fjords (D-11) 600,000 acres. Cross-country skiing, kayaking, snowmobiling.		•	•	•				•		•		•	•	•	•
Kobuk Valley (C-4) 1,710,000 acres. Sand dunes.		•		•	•			•					•		
Lake Clark (F-4) 4,000,000 acres. Bird watching, hunting, kayaking, rafting.		•		•				•		•		•	•	•	•
Wrangell-St. Elias (C-12, F-8) 3,000,000 acres. Hunting, sea kayaking; all-terrain vehicle trails.		•	•	•	•			•		•		•	•	•	•
Yukon-Charley Rivers (A-12, D-7) 500,000 acres. Historic. Hunting.		•		•				•					•		
NATIONAL FORESTS *(See place listings.)*															
Chugach (D-12) 5,500,000 acres in south-central Alaska. Cross-country skiing, hunting, snowboarding, snowmobiling.		•	•	•	•	•		•		•	•	•	•	•	•
Tongass (G-10) 17,000,000 acres in southeastern Alaska. Canoeing, cross-country and downhill skiing, ice skating, kayaking, snowboarding, snowmobiling.		•	•	•	•			•		•		•	•	•	•
STATE															
Anchor River (D-10) 264 acres near Anchor Point on Sterling Hwy., Milepost 157.	**1**	•	•	•				•	•	•					
Bernice Lake (C-10) 152 acres 10 mi. n. of Kenai on N. Kenai Rd.	**2**	•	•		•	•	•	•							
Big Lake (North) (C-10) 19 acres 10 mi. w. of Wasilla on Parks Hwy., then 6 mi. s.w. on Big Lake Rd.	**3**	•	•		•	•		•	•	•					
Big Lake (South) (C-10) 16 acres 10 mi. w. of Wasilla on Parks Hwy., then 4 mi. s.w. on Big Lake Rd. and 2 mi. s.	**4**	•	•		•	•		•	•	•					
Bings Landing (D-10) 126 acres e. of Soldotna on Sterling Hwy., Milepost 79.	**5**	•	•	•	•	•		•		•					
Birch Lake (B-11) 191 acres n.e. of Delta Junction on Richardson Hwy., Milepost 305.5. Ice fishing, jet skiing, water skiing; ice fishing huts.	**6**	•	•		•	•		•	•	•					
Blueberry Lake (C-12) 192 acres e. of Valdez on Richardson Hwy., Milepost 23.	**7**	•	•	•				•	•	•					
Bonnie Lake (C-11) 129 acres e. of Palmer on Glenn Hwy., Milepost 83. Canoeing.	**8**	•			•			•	•	•					
Buskin River (H-5) 168 acres 4 mi. s.e. on Base-Town Rd. in Kodiak. Historic.	**9**	•	•	•				•		•		•			
Captain Cook (C-10) 3,466 acres 24 mi. n. of Kenai on N. Kenai Rd., Milepost 36. Beachcombing, berry picking (in season), bird watching, canoeing, hunting, ice fishing.	**10**	•	•	•	•	•		•	•	•			•		
Chena River (A-12) 254,000 acres 27 mi. e. of Fairbanks on Chena Hot Springs Rd. Canoeing, cross-country skiing, kayaking, rock climbing, snowmobiling.	**11**	•	•	•	•			•		•		•	•	•	
Chilkat (F-10) 9,837 acres 7 mi. s. of Haines on Haines Hwy.	**12**	•						•		•				•	
Chilkoot Lake (G-10) 80 acres 11 mi. n. of Haines on Lutak Rd., Milepost 10.	**13**	•			•	•		•	•						
Chugach (C-11) 495,204 acres just e. of Eagle River on Glenn Hwy. Numerous access points. Rafting; horse rental. *(See Eagle River p. 629.)*	**14**	•	•	•	•	•		•		•	•	•	•		
Clearwater (B-12) 27 acres 11 mi. s.e. of Delta Junction on Alaska Hwy., Milepost 1415, then 8 mi. n.e. on side road.	**15**	•		•	•			•		•					
Deep Creek (D-10) 155 acres near Ninilchik on Sterling Hwy., Milepost 137.3. Bird watching, clam digging.	**16**	•		•	•			•	•						

Recreation Areas Chart

The map location numerals in column 2 show an area's location on the preceding map.

	MAP LOCATION	CAMPING	PICNICKING	HIKING TRAILS	BOATING	BOAT RAMP	BOAT RENTAL	FISHING	SWIMMING	PETS ON LEASH	BICYCLE TRAILS	WINTER SPORTS	VISITOR CENTER	LODGE/CABINS	FOOD SERVICE
Denali (C-10) 325,240 acres n. of Talkeetna on Parks Hwy., Milepost 135-164.	17	•	•	•	•	•	•	•	•	•				•	
Dry Creek (C-12) 372 acres n. of Glennallen on Richardson Hwy., Milepost 117.5.	18	•	•	•				•		•					
Fielding Lake (B-12) 300 acres s. of Delta Junction on Richardson Hwy., Milepost 201.	19	•			•	•		•		•					
Finger Lake (C-11) 47 acres 4 mi. w. of Palmer on Palmer-Wasilla Rd., then 1 mi. n. and .5 mi. w.	20	•	•	•	•	•		•	•	•		•			
Fort Abercrombie (H-5) 183 acres 4.5 mi. s.e. of Kodiak on Miller Point. Historic. *(See Kodiak p. 650.)*	21	•	•	•				•	•	•			•		
Harding Lake (B-11) 169 acres .5 mi. n.e. from Milepost 321 on the Richardson Hwy. Canoeing, jet skiing.	22	•	•	•	•	•		•	•	•		•			
Izaak Walton (D-10) 8 acres e. of Soldotna off Glenn Hwy.	23	•	•		•	•		•		•					
Johnson Lake (D-10) 332 acres 16 mi. s. of Soldotna on Glenn Hwy.	24	•	•		•	•		•		•					
Kachemak Bay (D-10) 368,290 acres near Seldovia, at the end of Sterling Hwy., then by boat or plane across Kachemak Bay. Bird watching, kayaking.	25	•	•	•	•			•		•				•	
Lake Louise (C-11) 90 acres n.w. of Glennallen on Glenn Hwy., Milepost 160.	26	•	•		•	•		•		•					
Little Nelchina (C-11) 22 acres s.e. of Glennallen on Glenn Hwy., Milepost 137.4.	27	•		•	•			•		•					
Long Lake (C-11) 480 acres 7 mi. e. of Sutton on Glenn Hwy.	28	•	•		•	•		•	•	•					
Lower Chatanika River (A-11) 120 acres n.w. of Fairbanks off SR 2, Milepost 9.	29	•	•		•	•		•		•					
Moon Lake (B-12) 22 acres 18 mi. w. of Tok on Alaska Hwy., near Milepost 1332. Water skiing.	30	•	•		•	•		•		•					
Mosquito Lake (G-10) 10 acres 27.5 mi. w. of Haines on Haines Hwy., then 2.5 mi. on Mosquito Lake Rd.	31	•	•		•	•		•	•	•			•		
Nancy Lake (C-10) 22,685 acres 3.5 mi. s. of Willow on Parks Hwy., then 7 mi. w. on side road.	32	•	•		•	•		•		•				•	
Quartz Lake (A-12) 600 acres 2 mi. n.w. of Delta Junction on Alaska Hwy.	33	•	•	•	•	•	•	•	•	•		•			•
Rocky Lake (C-10) 48 acres 28 mi. w. of Palmer via Wasilla off Parks Hwy. at Milepost 3.5 of Big Lake Rd.	34	•	•		•	•		•		•					
Salcha River (B-11) 61 acres s.e. of North Pole on Alaska Hwy., Milepost 323. Canoeing.	35	•			•	•		•		•			•		
South Rolly Lake (C-10) 200 acres just w. of Wasilla off Parks Hwy. at Milepost 6.5 of Nancy Lake Pkwy.	36	•	•		•	•		•	•	•		•			
Tok River (B-12) 9 acres 5 mi. e. of Tok Junction on Alaska Hwy., Milepost 1309.	37	•	•		•	•		•		•					
Upper Chatanika River (A-11) 73 acres n.e. of Fairbanks off Steese Hwy.	38	•	•	•				•	•	•					
Wood-Tikchik (G-3) 1,600,000 acres n. of Dillingham.	39	•		•				•						•	
OTHER															
Cripple Creek (A-12) 5 acres 50 mi. n.e. of Fairbanks on Steese Hwy., Milepost 60.	40	•	•	•				•		•					
Paxson Lake (B-12) 80 acres 10 mi. s. of Paxson on Richardson Hwy., Milepost 175.	41	•	•		•	•		•		•					
Salmon Lake (D-2) 20 acres 40 mi. n. of Nome.	42	•	•		•	•		•		•					
Sourdough (C-12) 140 acres 35 mi. n. of Glennallen on the Richardson Hwy., Milepost 148.	43	•	•		•	•		•		•					
Tangle Lakes (B-12) 100 acres 22 mi. w. of Paxson on Denali Hwy., Milepost 22.	44	•	•		•			•		•					
Walker Fork (D-8) 10 acres 80 mi. n.e. of Tok on Taylor Hwy., Milepost 82.	45	•	•	•				•		•					

ADMIRALTY ISLAND NATIONAL MONUMENT (G-10)

Accessible by floatplane from Juneau and Sitka or via ferries of the Alaska Marine Highway to Angoon, Admiralty Island is part of Tongass National Forest *(see place listing p. 664)*. Between the rocky beaches and high mountain peaks lie a million acres of coastal rain forests, freshwater lakes and streams, alpine meadows and dense thickets of wild currants and other berries.

Alaskan brown bears outnumber human beings, and the greatest concentration of bald eagles in North America nests along the coast. Beavers, martens, minks, river otters, Sitka black-tailed deer and weasels share the island with Vancouver Canada geese and trumpeter and whistling swans. Offshore are harbor seals, sea lions and whales.

Motorboating and sea kayaking are popular in protected saltwater bays, and a canoe portage trail connects nine interior lakes to bays on the east and west shores. Rustic cabins can be reserved, and campsites and open shelters are available on a first-come, first-served basis. Most of the island is a wilderness area; be prepared for rain and follow no-trace camping practices.

For more information write the U.S. Forest Service *(see Fast Facts)*, or phone (907) 586-8800 or TTY (907) 790-7444.

ANCHORAGE (F-6) pop. 291,826, elev. 118'
- Hotels p. 614 • Restaurants p. 618
- Attractions map p. 608
- Hotels & Restaurants map & index p. 611

Anchorage, on a high bluff enfolded by the two branches of Cook Inlet, lies as far west as the Hawaiian Islands and as far north as Helsinki, Finland. The tides in the inlet rise from 30 to 33 feet, and the surrounding mountains loom several thousand feet overhead. The protective mountain barrier and the proximity of the ocean afford Anchorage a surprisingly moderate climate, relative to most of Alaska.

Anchorage is Alaska's largest city and is home to almost half of the state's residents. While not a dazzling metropolis, each summer the city is beautifully decorated with almost 100,000 hanging flower baskets brimming with brightly-colored blooms.

Established in 1915 as the construction headquarters for the Alaska Railroad *(see attraction listing)*, it is the transportation and business center of south-central Alaska and a major winter recreation area. Anchorage's heritage as a road town is recalled by a number of historic buildings, notably the Pioneer Schoolhouse in Ben Crawford Memorial Park and two nearby one-room log cabins. As well, landmarks denote both Russian and American Indian heritage.

▼ See AAA listing p. 609 ▼

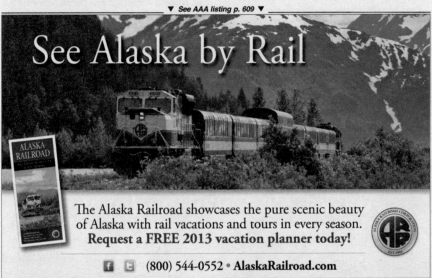

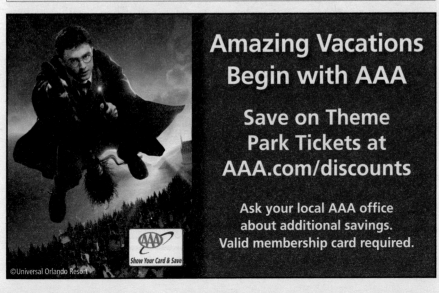

(See map & index p. 611.)

Anchorage suffered from the effects of the 1964 Good Friday earthquake, one of the strongest in history, which destroyed much of downtown. Earthquake Park, at the west end of Northern Lights Boulevard, has a walking trail and interpretive signs that provide information about the massive temblor. The park also provides a stunning vista of Cook Inlet.

The dramatic beauty of the nearby mountains, inlets and glaciers offers an easily accessible sampling of Alaska's natural splendors. Two roads affording beautiful views link to Anchorage; scenic SR 1/9 extends south to Seward, and SR 1 extends north to Glennallen.

From Anchorage visitors also can take various sightseeing tours of the area, including the Kenai Peninsula and places of interest inaccessible by road. Among the more novel sightseeing trips are dog sled tours, which leave from the Alyeska Resort and Ski Area *(see Girdwood p. 636)* December through March. Trolley tours given by Anchorage City Trolley Tours depart daily May through September from the Log Cabin Visitor Information Center at Fourth Avenue and F Street; phone (907) 276-5603 or (888) 917-8687.

The Park Connection offers twice-daily shuttle service from Anchorage to Denali National Park and Preserve and Seward mid-May to mid-September; phone (907) 344-8775 or (800) 266-8625.

One-hour float trips on the Matanuska River depart by van from Anchorage to the launch point. Panning for gold is available an hour from downtown. For a different perspective, try flightseeing—operators can be found at the airport and Lake Hood.

Gray Line of Alaska and Princess Tours offer a float adventure on Eagle River; tours to Barrow, Juneau, Kodiak Island, Kotzebue, Matanuska Valley, Nome, Portage Glacier and Prudhoe Bay; fishing on the Kenai River; cruises on Prince William Sound to Columbia Glacier; and a city tour of Anchorage.

These agencies also offer 2-, 3- and 4-day round trips between Anchorage and Denali National Park and Preserve. The trips include travel in railway cars equipped with glass ceiling panels. These same three companies also offer longer excursions to the interior and cruises up the Inside Passage.

The Alaska Center for the Performing Arts Sydney Laurence Theatre, at 621 W. 6th Ave., presents a 40-minute, large-screen slide show called "AurorA" that displays a series of stunning images of the aurora borealis synchronized to classical music. Shows are offered daily late May through August; tickets are available at the door. Phone (907) 263-2993 to confirm schedule information

Alaska - It's waiting for you.
Potter Marsh, Anchorage

Lodging • Tours • Transportation

Custom vacations to Alaska's most spectacular destinations! Call us or visit our website and see what's waiting for you.

Alaska
TOUR & TRAVEL

1-800-208-0200 | AlaskaTravel.com

Get pet travel tips and enter the photo contest at AAA.com/PetBook

(See map & index p. 611.)

Anchorage serves as the starting line for the 1,049-mile 🐾 Iditarod Trail Sled Dog Race, which begins the first Saturday in March. The actual mileage of the 2013 race is 1,131 miles; however, 1,049 is often used as a symbolic figure because the distance is always more than 1,000 miles, and 49 was added to signify Alaska's rank as the 49th state. Dogs and mushers travel over the Alaska Range and across frozen Norton Bay, arriving in Nome nearly 2 weeks later.

The Bear & Raven Adventure Theater, 315 E St., offers "The Amazing Trail," a 30-minute multimedia presentation relating the history of the Iditarod race as well as interactive sledding, ballooning and fishing exhibits. The theater is open mid-May to mid-September and during the Iditarod; phone (907) 277-4545.

Anchorage Convention and Visitors Bureau: 524 W. Fourth Ave., Anchorage, AK 99501-2212. **Phone:** (907) 276-4118, or (800) 478-1255 to request a visitors guide.

Self-guiding tours: A guide outlining a walking tour and driving tours north and south of the city is available at Log Cabin Visitor Information Center, Fourth Avenue and F Street; phone (907) 257-2363.

26 GLACIER CRUISE BY PHILLIPS CRUISES— see Whittier p. 667.

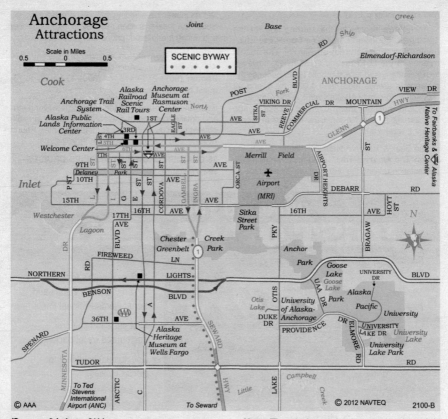

Anchorage Attractions

Scale in Miles

0.5 — 0 — 0.5

SCENIC BYWAY

(See map & index p. 611.)

ALASKA AVIATION HERITAGE MUSEUM, on Lake Hood at 4721 Aircraft Dr., displays 26 vintage aircraft and a flight simulator. Visitors also can observe restorations in progress. Memorabilia and photographs chronicle the history of civilian and military aviation in Alaska; films are shown continuously. **Time:** Allow 30 minutes minimum. **Hours:** Daily 9-5, mid-May to mid-Sept.; Wed.-Sat. 9-5, Sun. noon-5, rest of year. Closed major holidays in winter. **Cost:** $10; $8 (ages 65+ and active military and veterans with ID); $6 (ages 5-12). **Phone:** (907) 248-5325.

ALASKA BOTANICAL GARDEN is 3 mi. e. of New Seward Hwy. on Tudor Rd., then just s. to 4601 Campbell Airstrip Rd. Arctic horticulture is showcased in a 110-acre birch and spruce woodland replete with more than 1,100 varieties of perennials, 150 species of native Alaskan plants as well as herb and alpine rock gardens. The park includes a wildflower walk, a 1-mile interpretive nature trail and a creek where salmon spawn in the summer. The peak blooming season commences in late May and culminates in mid-September, occasionally lasting into October.

Note: Though the garden is open in winter, it is often snow-covered. Guided tours are available. **Time:** Allow 1 hour, 30 minutes minimum. **Hours:** Daily dawn-dusk. **Cost:** $7; $5 (ages 3-18). **Phone:** (907) 770-3692.

ALASKA HERITAGE MUSEUM AT WELLS FARGO, at Northern Lights Blvd. and C St. in the Wells Fargo Bank Building, displays more than 900 Eskimo and other native artifacts, an extensive collection of walrus ivory carvings, traditional clothing and paintings by Alaskan artists. The collection also includes a two-third scale stagecoach from the Gold Rush era. **Time:** Allow 30 minutes minimum. **Hours:** Mon.-Fri. noon-5 in summer; noon-4, rest of year. Closed major holidays. **Cost:** Free. **Phone:** (907) 265-2834.

ALASKA NATIVE HERITAGE CENTER is about 3 mi. e. on Glenn Hwy. to N. Muldoon Rd. exit, then 1 mi. e. on Heritage Center Dr. Situated on 26 wooded acres, the center presents information about the five regional, native groups that inhabit Alaska: the Aleut and Alutiiq; Athabascan; Eyak, Tlingit, Haida and Tsimshian; Inupiaq and St. Lawrence Island Yup'ik; and Yup'ik and Cup'ik cultures.

(See map & index p. 611.)

The main building offers the Gathering Place for storytelling, dance, native games and musical performances as well as a theater for cultural films. The Hall of Cultures exhibit is divided into five areas with changing multimedia displays about the ways of life of native cultures. Artisans create and display their crafts in adjacent studios.

Outside, five village sites surround Lake Tiulana, and site hosts are available to explain each dwelling, aspects of daily life and customs. **Tours:** Guided tours are available. **Time:** Allow 2 hours minimum. **Hours:** Daily 9-5, early May-early Sept. **Cost:** $24.95; $21.15 (ages 62+ and military with ID); $16.95 (ages 7-16); $71.50 (family, two adults and two children). Combination ticket with Anchorage Museum at Rasmuson Center $29.95. **Phone:** (907) 330-8000 or (800) 315-6608. 🍴

ALASKA PUBLIC LANDS INFORMATION CENTER, 605 W. Fourth Ave., offers information about Alaska's state and federal public lands, including forests, parks and refuges. Exhibits include displays about Alaska's native culture, history and wildlife; films and interpretive programs are offered during the summer season. Visitors can plan their own trips with assistance from the staff as well as obtain free brochures and maps. State and federal passes also are available. **Hours:** Daily 9-5, late May to mid-Sept.; Mon.-Fri. 10-5, rest of year. Closed winter holidays. **Cost:** Free. **Phone:** (907) 644-3661, (866) 869-6887 or TTY (907) 271-2738.

ALASKA RAILROAD SCENIC RAIL TOURS departs from 411 W. First Ave. Narrated sightseeing tours on the Denali Star Train are offered northward between Anchorage and Fairbanks with stops at Wasilla, Talkeetna and Denali National Park and Preserve. The Glacier Discovery Train travels south from Anchorage to Whittier following the Turnagain Arm of Cook Inlet. Stops include Girdwood, Portage and Spencer Glacier, a whistle stop where passengers can take a 1.5-mile ranger-guided hike to see the glacier. The Coastal Classic Train runs from Anchorage to Seward and offers a glimpse of wildlife and glaciers.

Domed cars with glass-covered viewing platforms allow for 180-degree views. Special winter routes as well as excursions and connections to air, rail and boat tours are available. **Hours:** Trips depart daily, mid-May through mid-Sept.; trains depart Sat.-Sun., rest of year. Phone ahead to confirm schedule. **Cost:** One-way fares $54-$231 (an extra fee applies for first-class seating). Reservations are required. **Phone:** (907) 265-2494, (800) 544-0552 or TTY (907) 265-2620. *(See ad p. 605.)*

ALASKA ZOO is 7.5 mi. s. on SR 1 (Seward Hwy.), then 2 mi. e. on O'Malley Rd.; a shuttle provides transportation from some local hotels during summer months. The grounds encompass a 25-acre wooded home to arctic, subarctic and Alaskan native animals, including Amur (Siberian) tigers, black

and polar bears, seals, snow leopards, Tibetan yaks and wolves. Visitors may interact with selected animals during the 2-hour Discovery Tour. The Animal Encounter program allows visitors to work with animal handlers as they clean, feed and train the animals.

Time: Allow 1 hour, 30 minutes minimum. **Hours:** Daily 9-9, June-Aug.; 9-6, May and Sept.; 10-5, Mar.-Apr. and Oct.; 10-4, rest of year (weather permitting). Discovery Tour departs daily at 12:15, late May to mid-Sept. Closed Thanksgiving and Christmas. Phone ahead to confirm schedule. **Cost:** $12; $9 (ages 65+ and military with ID); $6 (ages 3-17). Zoo admission and Discovery Tour $25; $15 (ages 3-17). Animal Encounter (does not include zoo admission) $85; $45 (ages 0-11 with paid adult). Reservations are required for Animal Encounter. **Phone:** (907) 346-2133. 🍴 🏕

▼ GEM SAVE ANCHORAGE MUSEUM AT RASMUSON CENTER, 625 C St., has exhibits focusing on the art, history and cultures of Alaska. The Alaska Gallery includes objects dating from prehistoric times through European exploration, Russian settlement, the gold rush era, World War II and statehood. Full-scale dioramas of an Athabascan tent; Yupik Eskimo, Tlingit and Aleut houses; a gold miner's cabin; an early Anchorage house; and Quonset huts (in use during World War II) provide insight to early Alaskan life. The state-of-the-art Smithsonian Arctic Studies Center has multimedia exhibits and displays more than 600 Alaska Native artifacts.

In addition, a display about the Alaska Pipeline features a sample of the 4-foot-tall pipe. "Art of the North" contains drawings and paintings by Alaska's first explorers to current artists. The interactive Imaginarium Discovery Center offers exhibits that explore nature, science and technology, including a marine wildlife area, reptile exhibits and a bubble lab. Other highlights include the Thomas Planetarium and traveling exhibitions.

Time: Allow 1 hour minimum. **Hours:** Daily 9-6, mid-May to mid-Sept.; Tues.-Sat. 10-6, Sun. noon-6, rest of year. Closed Jan. 1, Thanksgiving and Christmas. **Cost:** $12; $9 (ages 65+, military and students with ID); $7 (ages 3-12). Combination ticket with Alaska Native Heritage Center $29.95. **Phone:** (907) 929-9200. 🍴

ANCHORAGE TRAIL SYSTEM, found throughout and near the city, consists of 120 miles of paved trails and 300 miles of unpaved and wilderness trails. The 11-mile Tony Knowles Coastal Trail stretches from downtown and winds along the scenic coastline; Flattop Mountain is a popular 3-mile day hike with spectacular views of the Alaska Range and Anchorage; Williwaw Valley contains a 14-mile-long trail with views of emerald lakes, wildflowers and Dali sheep; Kincaid Park's 43-mile trail meanders throughout 1,400 acres and is popular with runners; and Turnagain Arm Trail is a pleasant

(See map & index p. 611.)

9-mile amble along Turnagain Arm. **Cost:** Free. **Phone:** (907) 276-4118.

MAJOR MARINE TOURS—see Whittier p. 667.

PORTAGE GLACIER RECREATION AREA—see Chugach National Forest p. 623.

RUST'S FLYING SERVICE departs from the south shore of Lake Hood off International Airport Rd. at Anchorage International Airport. The service provides narrated sightseeing tours by seaplane of Denali National Park and Preserve, Knik Glacier, Mount McKinley and Prince William Sound. Tours to Brooks Falls and Redoubt Bay Lodge provide opportunities to view such wildlife as brown bears and marine animals. Glacier landings, river float trips and one-day and three-night fishing trips also are available.

Note: Departures require a minimum of 2 people. Singles are accommodated on a space-available basis. **Time:** Allow 1 hour, 30 minutes minimum. **Hours:** Daily by appointment, mid-May to mid-Sept.; Mon.-Fri. by appointment, rest of year. Closed Jan. 1, Thanksgiving and Christmas. **Cost:** Fare $100-$795. **Phone:** (907) 243-1595, or (800) 544-2299 (not available from Anchorage land lines).

TRANS ARCTIC CIRCLE TREKS AND GLACIER BLUE TOURS—see Fairbanks p. 633.

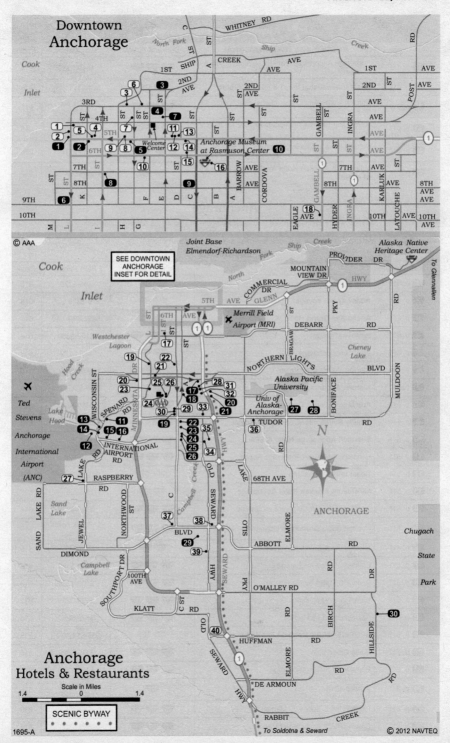

Downtown
Anchorage

Anchorage Museum at Rasmuson Center

Anchorage
Hotels & Restaurants

Scale in Miles

SCENIC BYWAY

1695-A

© 2012 NAVTEQ

✈ Airport Accommodations

Map Page	ANCHORAGE INTERNATIONAL	Diamond Rated	Rate Range	Page
⑭ p. 611	Anchorage Airport Courtyard by Marriott, 1.7 mi e of airport	▼▼▼	$149-$239	614
⑫ p. 611	Coast International Inn, 1.8 mi e of airport	▼▼	$81-$171 SAVE	615
⑮ p. 611	Comfort Suites Anchorage International Airport, 1.6 mi e of airport	▼▼▼	Rates not provided	615
⑪ p. 611	Holiday Inn Express Anchorage Airport, 1.9 mi e of airport	▼▼▼	$89-$289	616
⑯ p. 611	Microtel Inn & Suites by Wyndham, 1.7 mi e of airport	▼▼	$85-$170	616
⑬ p. 611	Millennium Alaskan Hotel Anchorage, 1.8 mi e of airport	▼▼	$129-$299 SAVE	617

Anchorage

This index helps you "spot" where approved hotels and restaurants are located on the corresponding detailed maps. Hotel daily rate range is for comparison only. Restaurant price range is a combination of lunch and/or dinner. Turn to the listing page for more detailed rate and price information and consult display ads for special promotions.

ANCHORAGE

Map Page	Hotels	Diamond Rated	Rate Range	Page
❶ p. 611	Copper Whale Inn	▼▼	$95-$220	615
❷ p. 611	Rodeway Inn Voyager Hotel	▼▼	$79-$229 SAVE	618
❸ p. 611	Anchorage Grand Hotel (See ad p. 614.)	▼▼	$89-$189 SAVE	614
❹ p. 611	Hilton Anchorage	▼▼▼	$100-$350	616
❺ p. 611	Westmark Anchorage	▼▼	$89-$279	618
❻ p. 611	Clarion Suites Downtown	▼▼▼	$89-$259 SAVE	615
❼ p. 611	Historic Anchorage Hotel	▼▼	$159-$269 SAVE	616
❽ p. 611	Anchorage Marriott Downtown	▼▼▼	$110-$320	614
❾ p. 611	Quality Suites near Convention Center	▼▼▼	$89-$229 SAVE	618
❿ p. 611	Sheraton Anchorage Hotel & SPA	▼▼▼	$219-$369 SAVE	618
⓫ p. 611	Holiday Inn Express Anchorage Airport	▼▼▼	$89-$289	616
⓬ p. 611	Coast International Inn	▼▼	$81-$171 SAVE	615
⓭ p. 611	Millennium Alaskan Hotel Anchorage	▼▼	$129-$299 SAVE	617
⓮ p. 611	Anchorage Airport Courtyard by Marriott	▼▼▼	$149-$239	614
⓯ p. 611	Comfort Suites Anchorage International Airport	▼▼▼	Rates not provided	615
⓰ p. 611	Microtel Inn & Suites by Wyndham	▼▼	$85-$170	616
⓱ p. 611	Embassy Suites-Anchorage	▼▼▼	$139-$469	616
⓲ p. 611	SpringHill Suites by Marriott	▼▼▼	$109-$259	618
⓳ p. 611	Hampton Inn-Anchorage	▼▼▼	$109-$289	616
⓴ p. 611	Residence Inn by Marriott	▼▼▼	$129-$269	618
㉑ p. 611	BEST WESTERN Golden Lion Hotel	▼▼	$89-$189 SAVE	615
㉒ p. 611	Hilton Garden Inn	▼▼▼	$119-$329	616
㉓ p. 611	Homewood Suites-Anchorage	▼▼▼	$129-$389	616
㉔ p. 611	Motel 6-4216	▼	Rates not provided	618
㉕ p. 611	Fairfield Inn & Suites by Marriott	▼▼▼	$89-$269	616
㉖ p. 611	Crowne Plaza Anchorage-Midtown	▼▼▼	$99-$309	616

ANCHORAGE (cont'd)

Map Page	Hotels (cont'd)	Diamond Rated	Rate Range	Page
27 p. 611	University Lake SpringHill Suites by Marriott	◆◆◆	$99-$239	618
28 p. 611	Camai Bed & Breakfast	◆◆◆	$60-$159	615
29 p. 611	**Dimond Center Hotel**	◆◆◆	$104-$269 SAVE	616
30 p. 611	**Highland Glen Lodge B&B**	◆◆◆	$89-$189 SAVE	616

Map Page	Restaurants	Diamond Rated	Cuisine	Price Range	Page
1 p. 611	Snow City Cafe	◆◆	American	$8-$16	621
2 p. 611	Simon & Seaforts	◆◆◆	Regional American	$12-$40	621
3 p. 611	Snow Goose Restaurant	◆◆	American	$12-$28	621
4 p. 611	**Crow's Nest Restaurant**	◆◆◆◆	New American	$36-$40	619
5 p. 611	Bangkok Cafe	◆◆	Thai	$10-$15	618
6 p. 611	**Marx Bros. Café**	◆◆◆◆	New American	$35-$40	620
7 p. 611	Sack's Cafe & Restaurant	◆◆◆	International	$10-$34	621
8 p. 611	Orso	◆◆◆	Italian	$19-$36	620
9 p. 611	Glacier Brewhouse	◆◆	American	$9-$34	619
10 p. 611	Humpy's Great Alaskan Ale House	◆◆	American	$10-$45	620
11 p. 611	ginger	◆◆◆	Pacific Northwest	$9-$29	619
12 p. 611	Club Paris	◆◆	Steak	$13-$45	619
13 p. 611	Phyllis's Cafe and Salmon Bake	◆◆	American	$9-$26	620
14 p. 611	Sullivan's Steakhouse	◆◆◆	Steak	$10-$58	621
15 p. 611	Crush Wine Bistro and Cellar	◆◆	Small Plates	$9-$19	619
16 p. 611	Muse	◆◆	Regional Pacific Northwest	$14-$28	620
17 p. 611	Fire Island Rustic Bakeshop	◆	Breads/Pastries	$3-$12	619
18 p. 611	Falafel King	◆	Middle Eastern	$9-$14	619
19 p. 611	Ray's Place	◆◆	Vietnamese	$9-$19	621
20 p. 611	City Diner	◆◆	American	$8-$19	618
21 p. 611	Sweet Basil Cafe	◆	Coffee/Tea	$6-$15	621
22 p. 611	The Greek Corner	◆◆	Greek	$9-$21	620
23 p. 611	Yak and Yeti Himalayan Restaurant	◆◆	Indian	$8-$17	621
24 p. 611	Jens' Restaurant	◆◆◆	Pacific Northwest	$13-$45	620
25 p. 611	Larry's Cocoon	◆◆	Asian	$8-$23	620
26 p. 611	Campobello Bistro	◆◆	Italian	$11-$28	618
27 p. 611	Kincaid Grill	◆◆◆	Regional Alaskan	$30-$36	620
28 p. 611	Kinley's Restaurant & Bar	◆◆◆	Fusion	$11-$32	620
29 p. 611	Pepper Mill	◆◆	American	$10-$40	620
30 p. 611	Sea Galley	◆◆	Seafood	$10-$40	621
31 p. 611	Moose's Tooth Pub & Pizzeria	◆◆	American	$10-$28	620
32 p. 611	Yamato Ya	◆◆	Sushi	$6-$24	621
33 p. 611	Aladdin's	◆◆	Mediterranean	$14-$24	618

Map Page	Restaurants (cont'd)	Diamond Rated	Cuisine	Price Range	Page
㉞ p. 611	The Peanut Farm Sports Bar & Grill	▼▼	American	$10-$28	620
㉟ p. 611	Sourdough Mining Co	▼▼	American	$14-$45	621
㊱ p. 611	Fu Do Chinese Restaurant	▼▼	Chinese	$8-$20	619
㊲ p. 611	Las Margaritas	▼▼	Mexican	$9-$20	620
㊳ p. 611	Sushi Ya Japanese Restaurant	▼▼	Japanese	$8-$23	621
㊴ p. 611	China Lights Oriental Cuisine	▼▼	Asian	$10-$19	618
㊵ p. 611	Southside Bistro	▼▼▼	American	$8-$33	621

ANCHORAGE AIRPORT COURTYARD BY MARRIOTT
(907)245-0322 **14**

▼▼▼▼ **Hotel** $149-$239 **Address:**
4901 Spenard Rd 99517 **Location:** Just
ne of Jewell Lake and International Airport rds. **Facility:** 154 units. 3 stories, interior corridors. **Amenities:** high-speed
Internet. **Pool(s):** heated indoor. **Activities:** sauna, whirlpool, exercise room. **Guest Services:** valet and coin laundry, area
transportation-train station.

AAA Benefit:
AAA hotel discounts
of 5% or more.

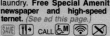

ANCHORAGE GRAND HOTEL (907)929-8888 **3**

Extended Stay
Hotel
$89-$189

Address: 505 W 2nd Ave 99501 **Location:** Corner of 2nd Ave and E St.
Across from Anchorage Market. **Facility:** 31 units, some efficiencies and
kitchens. 5 stories, interior corridors.
Terms: cancellation fee imposed.
Guest Services: valet and coin
laundry. **Free Special Amenities:**
newspaper and high-speed Internet. *(See ad this page.)*

ANCHORAGE MARRIOTT DOWNTOWN (907)279-8000 **8**

▼▼▼▼ **Hotel** $110-$320 **Address:**
820 W 7th Ave 99501 **Location:** Between I and H sts. **Facility:** 392 units. 20
stories, interior corridors. **Parking:** valet
only. **Pool(s):** indoor. **Activities:** whirlpool, exercise room. **Guest
Services:** valet laundry.

AAA Benefit:
AAA hotel discounts
of 5% or more.

ASPEN SUITES HOTEL (907)770-3400

fyi Extended Stay Hotel $129-$139 Too new to rate. **Address:**
100 E Tudor Rd 99503 **Location:** Midtown. **Amenities:** 92 units,
coffeemakers, microwaves, refrigerators, exercise facility. **Terms:**
cancellation fee imposed.

▼ See AAA listing this page ▼

(See map & index p. 611.)

BEST WESTERN GOLDEN LION HOTEL
(907)561-1522 **21**

Hotel
$89-$189

AAA Benefit: Members save up to 20%, plus 10% bonus points with Best Western Rewards®.

Address: 1000 E 36th Ave 99508 **Location:** SR 1 (Seward Hwy) and 36th Ave. **Facility:** 83 units. 3 stories, interior corridors. **Terms:** cancellation fee imposed. **Activities:** exercise room. **Guest Services:** valet and coin laundry. **Free Special Amenities:** local telephone calls and high-speed Internet.

CAMAI BED & BREAKFAST
(907)333-2219 **28**

 Bed & Breakfast $60-$159 **Address:** 3838 Westminster Way 99508 **Location:** SR 1 (Seward Hwy), 2.8 mi e on Benson/Northern Lights Blvd, 0.6 mi s on Wesleyn Dr to Queen Ct, then just e. **Facility:** The home-like B&B is located in a quiet residential area and provides guests with spacious, well-equipped rooms with a comfortable decor. 3 units. 2 stories (no elevator), interior/exterior corridors. **Terms:** 21 day cancellation notice-fee imposed. **Amenities:** high-speed Internet. **Activities:** whirlpool. **Guest Services:** complimentary and valet laundry.

CLARION SUITES DOWNTOWN
(907)222-5005 **6**

Hotel
$89-$259

Address: 1110 W 8th Ave 99501 **Location:** Corner of L St and W 8th Ave. **Facility:** 110 units. 3 stories, interior corridors. **Terms:** 3 day cancellation notice-fee imposed. **Amenities:** safes (fee). **Pool(s):** heated indoor. **Activities:** whirlpool, limited exercise equipment. **Guest Services:** valet and coin laundry, area transportation-train station.

COAST INTERNATIONAL INN
(907)243-2233 **12**

Hotel
$81-$171

Address: 3450 Aviation Ave 99502 **Location:** Jct International Airport Rd, just n on Spenard Rd, then just w. **Facility:** 141 units. 2 stories (no elevator), interior corridors. **Terms:** cancellation fee imposed. **Activities:** sauna, exercise room. **Guest Services:** valet and coin laundry. **Free Special Amenities:** local telephone calls and airport transportation.

The Coast International Inn

Close to Ted Stevens International Airport. Great Location to major attractions and downtown.

COMFORT SUITES ANCHORAGE INTERNATIONAL AIRPORT
907)243-8080 **15**

Hotel. Rates not provided. **Address:** 2919 W International Airport Rd 99502 **Location:** Just e of Spenard Rd, on Frontage Rd. **Facility:** 78 units, some two bedrooms. 3 stories, interior corridors. **Parking:** winter plug-ins. **Pool(s):** heated indoor. **Activities:** whirlpool, exercise room. **Guest Services:** valet and coin laundry.

COPPER WHALE INN
907)258-7999 **1**

Bed & Breakfast $95-$220 **Address:** 440 L St 99501 **Location:** Corner of 5th Ave. Located in a commercial area. **Facility:** 14 units. 2 stories (no elevator), interior corridors. **Bath:** some shared. **Parking:** no self-parking. **Terms:** 7 day cancellation notice-fee imposed. **Activities:** rental bicycles. **Guest Services:** coin laundry.

▼ *See AAA listing p. 667* ▼

Find thousands of places to show your card
and save at AAA.com/discounts

(See map & index p. 611.)

CROWNE PLAZA ANCHORAGE-MIDTOWN
(907)433-4100 **26**

Hotel $99-$309 **Address:** 109 W International Airport Rd 99518 **Location:** Jct C St, just n on A St. **Facility:** 165 units. 6 stories, interior corridors. **Terms:** check-in 4 pm, cancellation fee imposed. **Amenities:** high-speed Internet. **Pool(s):** heated indoor. **Activities:** whirlpool, exercise room. **Guest Services:** valet and coin laundry.

DIMOND CENTER HOTEL
(907)770-5000 **29**

Hotel
$104-$269

Address: 700 E Dimond Blvd 99515 **Location:** SR 1 (Seward Hwy) exit Dimond Blvd, just w, then s on Dimond Center Dr. **Facility:** 109 units. 3 stories, interior corridors. **Terms:** 24 day cancellation notice-fee imposed. **Amenities:** high-speed Internet. **Guest Services:** valet and coin laundry.

EMBASSY SUITES-ANCHORAGE
(907)332-7000 **17**

Hotel $139-$469 **Address:** 600 E Benson Blvd 99503 **Location:** SR 1 (Seward Hwy), just w on Northern Lights Blvd, just s on Denali St, then just e. **Facility:** 169 units, some two bedrooms. 4 stories, interior corridors. **Terms:** 1-7 night minimum stay, cancellation fee imposed. **Amenities:** high-speed Internet (fee). **Pool(s):** heated indoor. **Activities:** whirlpool, exercise room. **Guest Services:** valet and coin laundry, area transportation-within 3 mi.

AAA Benefit: Members save 5% or more!

FAIRFIELD INN & SUITES BY MARRIOTT
(907)222-9000 **25**

Hotel $89-$269 **Address:** 5060 A St 99503 **Location:** Jct C St, just e on International Airport Rd, then just n. **Facility:** 106 units. 4 stories, interior corridors. **Amenities:** high-speed Internet. **Pool(s):** heated indoor. **Activities:** whirlpool, exercise room. **Guest Services:** valet and coin laundry.

AAA Benefit: AAA hotel discounts of 5% or more.

HAMPTON INN-ANCHORAGE
(907)550-7000 **19**

Hotel $109-$289 **Address:** 4301 Credit Union Dr 99503 **Location:** Corner of Tudor Rd and C St. **Facility:** 101 units. 3 stories, interior corridors. **Terms:** 1-7 night minimum stay, cancellation fee imposed. **Pool(s):** heated indoor. **Activities:** whirlpool, exercise room. **Guest Services:** valet and coin laundry, area transportation-within 3 mi & train station.

AAA Benefit: Members save up to 10%!

HIGHLAND GLEN LODGE B&B
(907)336-2312 **30**

Bed & Breakfast
$89-$189

Address: 11651 Hillside Dr 99507 **Location:** SR 1 (Seward Hwy) exit O'Mally Rd, 3.7 mi e, then 0.5 mi s. **Facility:** This lovely Tudor-style home offers guests comfortable accommodations in an attractive country setting; the rooms are spacious and well equipped. 5 units. 2 stories (no elevator), interior corridors. **Terms:** check-in 5 pm, 30 day cancellation notice-fee imposed. **Activities:** whirlpool. **Free Special Amenities:** full breakfast and early check-in/late check-out.

HILTON ANCHORAGE
(907)272-7411 **4**

Hotel $100-$350 **Address:** 500 W 3rd Ave 99501 **Location:** Corner of E St. **Facility:** 606 units. 15-22 stories, interior corridors. **Parking:** valet only. **Terms:** 1-7 night minimum stay, cancellation fee imposed. **Amenities:** safes. *Fee:* video games, high-speed Internet. **Pool(s):** heated indoor. **Activities:** whirlpool, steamrooms, exercise room. **Guest Services:** valet laundry.

AAA Benefit: Members save 5% or more!

HILTON GARDEN INN
(907)729-7000 **22**

Hotel $119-$329 **Address:** 4555 Union Square Dr 99503 **Location:** SR 1 (Seward Hwy) exit Tudor Rd, 0.8 mi w; U-turn at C St, then just s. **Facility:** 125 units. 4 stories, interior corridors. **Terms:** 1-7 night minimum stay, cancellation fee imposed. **Amenities:** high-speed Internet. **Pool(s):** heated indoor. **Activities:** whirlpool, exercise room. **Guest Services:** valet and coin laundry, area transportation-within 3 mi & train station.

AAA Benefit: Unparalleled hospitality at a special Member rate.

HISTORIC ANCHORAGE HOTEL
(907)272-4553 **7**

Historic Hotel
$159-$269

Address: 330 E St 99501 **Location:** Between 3rd and 4th aves. **Facility:** Established in 1916, the hotel still retains that Old World charm yet with modern amenities. The standard rooms are on the compact side and meant for one or two people; the suites are more spacious. 26 units. 3 stories, interior corridors. **Parking:** on-site (fee). **Terms:** 7 day cancellation notice-fee imposed. **Activities:** exercise room. **Guest Services:** valet laundry. **Free Special Amenities:** continental breakfast and high-speed Internet.

HOLIDAY INN EXPRESS ANCHORAGE AIRPORT
(907)248-8848 **11**

Hotel $89-$289 **Address:** 4411 Spenard Rd 99517 **Location:** 0.5 mi ne of Jewell Lake and International Airport rds. **Facility:** 129 units. 3 stories, interior corridors. **Amenities:** video games (fee), high-speed Internet. **Pool(s):** heated indoor. **Activities:** whirlpool, exercise room. **Guest Services:** valet and coin laundry.

HOMEWOOD SUITES-ANCHORAGE
(907)762-7000 **23**

Extended Stay Hotel $129-$389 **Address:** 101 W 48th Ave 99503 **Location:** SR 1 (Seward Hwy) exit Tudor Rd, 0.8 mi w, U-turn at C St, then just s on Union Square Dr. **Facility:** 122 efficiencies, some two bedrooms. 4 stories, interior corridors. **Terms:** 1-7 night minimum stay, cancellation fee imposed. **Amenities:** high-speed Internet. **Pool(s):** heated indoor. **Activities:** whirlpool, basketball, exercise room. **Guest Services:** valet and coin laundry, area transportation-within 3 mi & train station.

AAA Benefit: Contemporary luxury at a special Member rate.

MICROTEL INN & SUITES BY WYNDHAM
(907)245-5002 **16**

Motel $85-$170 **Address:** 5205 Northwood Dr 99517 **Location:** Jct International Airport Rd, just n. **Facility:** 79 units. 3 stories, interior corridors. **Parking:** winter plug-ins. **Terms:** check-in 4 pm. **Amenities:** video games (fee). **Activities:** whirlpools. **Guest Services:** valet and coin laundry.

(See map & index p. 611.)

MILLENNIUM ALASKAN HOTEL ANCHORAGE
(907)243-2300 **13**

Hotel
$129-$299

Address: 4800 Spenard Rd 99517 **Location:** Jct International Airport Rd, just n. **Facility:** 247 units. 4 stories, interior corridors. **Parking:** winter plug-ins. **Terms:** 3 day cancellation notice-fee imposed. **Activities:** sauna, exercise room. **Guest Services:** valet and coin laundry, area transportation-downtown. **Free Special Amenities:** room upgrade (subject to availability with advance reservations) and airport transportation.

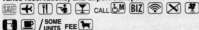

▼ See AAA listing p. 637 ▼

(See map & index p. 611.)

MOTEL 6-4216   907/677-8000 **24**

◇ **Motel.** Rates not provided. **Address:** 5000 A St 99503 **Location:** Jct C St, just n on A St, then just n. **Facility:** 85 units. 3 stories, interior corridors. **Guest Services:** coin laundry.

QUALITY SUITES NEAR CONVENTION CENTER
(907)274-1000 **9**

Hotel
$89-$229

Address: 325 W 8th Ave 99501 **Location:** Corner of C St and W 8th Ave. **Facility:** 110 units. 3 stories, interior corridors. **Terms:** 3 day cancellation notice-fee imposed. **Amenities:** safes (fee). *Some:* high-speed Internet. **Pool(s):** heated indoor. **Activities:** whirlpool, limited exercise equipment. **Guest Services:** valet and coin laundry, area transportation-train station.

RESIDENCE INN BY MARRIOTT   (907)563-9844 **20**

◇◇◇ **Extended Stay Hotel** $129-$269 **Address:** 1025 E 35th Ave 99508 **Location:** Corner of SR 1 (Seward Hwy) and 36th Ave. **Facility:** 148 kitchen units, some two bedrooms. 3 stories, interior corridors. **Amenities:** high-speed Internet. **Pool(s):** heated indoor. **Activities:** whirlpool, sports court, exercise room. **Guest Services:** valet and coin laundry, area transportation-train station.

AAA Benefit: AAA hotel discounts of 5% or more.

RODEWAY INN VOYAGER HOTEL (907)277-9501 **2**

Hotel
$79-$229

Address: 501 K St 99501 **Location:** At K St and 5th Ave; downtown. **Facility:** 40 units. 4 stories, interior corridors. **Parking:** on-site (fee). **Terms:** 3 day cancellation notice-fee imposed. **Amenities:** high-speed Internet. **Guest Services:** valet and coin laundry.

SHERATON ANCHORAGE HOTEL & SPA
(907)276-8700 **10**

Hotel
$219-$369

Sheraton
HOTELS & RESORTS

AAA Benefit: Members get up to 20% off, plus Starwood Preferred Guest® bonuses.

Address: 401 E 6th Ave 99501 **Location:** 6th Ave and Denali St. **Facility:** 370 units. 16 stories, interior corridors. **Parking:** on-site (fee). **Terms:** cancellation fee imposed. **Amenities:** high-speed Internet (fee). **Activities:** exercise room, spa. **Guest Services:** valet laundry, area transportation-downtown.

SPRINGHILL SUITES BY MARRIOTT   (907)562-3247 **18**

◇◇◇ **Hotel** $109-$259 **Address:** 3401 A St 99503 **Location:** Corner of 36th Ave and A St. **Facility:** 101 units. 3 stories, interior corridors. **Amenities:** high-speed Internet. **Pool(s):** heated indoor. **Activities:** whirlpool, limited exercise equipment. **Guest Services:** valet and coin laundry, area transportation-train station.

AAA Benefit: AAA hotel discounts of 5% or more.

UNIVERSITY LAKE SPRINGHILL SUITES BY MARRIOTT
(907)751-6300 **27**

◇◇◇ **Hotel** $99-$239 **Address:** 4050 University Lake Dr 99508 **Location:** SR 1 (New Seward Hwy), 2 mi e on E 36th Ave and Providence Dr, just s on University Dr, then just e. **Facility:** 159 units. 3 stories, interior corridors. **Amenities:** high-speed Internet. **Pool(s):** heated indoor. **Activities:** whirlpool, jogging, exercise room. **Guest Services:** valet and coin laundry, area transportation-train station, hospital & university.

AAA Benefit: AAA hotel discounts of 5% or more.

WESTMARK ANCHORAGE   (907)276-7676 **5**

◇◇ **Hotel** $89-$279 **Address:** 720 W 5th Ave 99501 **Location:** At G St and W 5th Ave; downtown. **Facility:** 200 units. 14 stories, interior corridors. **Parking:** on-site (fee). **Terms:** cancellation fee imposed. **Activities:** exercise room. **Guest Services:** valet laundry.

WHERE TO EAT

ALADDIN'S   907/561-2373 **33**

◇◇ Mediterranean. Casual Dining. $14-$24 **AAA Inspector Notes:** Menu offerings range from Greek and Middle Eastern dishes to Indian and French-influenced fare. Vegetarians and vegans will find selections sharing menu space with lamb, chicken, beef and seafood selections. **Bar:** beer & wine. **Reservations:** suggested. **Address:** 4240 Old Seward Hwy 99503 **Location:** Jct Tudor Rd, just n; in City Center Mall.

BANGKOK CAFE   907/274-2233 **5**

◇◇ Thai. Casual Dining. $10-$15 **AAA Inspector Notes:** Authentic cuisine in an unassuming location. It's a bit hard to find, as it is set back from the street, but it's worth looking for. The tom yum soup is made from scratch and judging from the aroma and wonderful flavors, I would say it is. This small restaurant does a brisk and busy lunch business. **Address:** 930 W 5th Ave 99501 **Location:** Between I and K sts; downtown. **Parking:** street only.

CAMPOBELLO BISTRO   907/563-2040 **26**

◇◇ Italian. Casual Dining. $11-$28 **AAA Inspector Notes:** Hidden in a midtown roadside mall, this simple, pleasant dining room is a perfect place for a casual, yet romantic, meal. Italian cooking features various preparations of homemade pasta while the seafood includes fresh wild Alaskan king salmon. Desserts are all made in-house. **Bar:** beer & wine. **Reservations:** suggested. **Address:** 601 W 36th Ave 99503 **Location:** Jct Arctic Blvd, just e; in Bering Village Shopping Center.

CHINA LIGHTS ORIENTAL CUISINE   907/522-5888 **39**

◇◇ Asian. Casual Dining. $10-$19 **AAA Inspector Notes:** Diners can fill up at this Asian buffet boasting more than 100 dishes from China, Japan, Thailand and Vietnam. An a la carte menu also is available. **Bar:** beer & wine. **Address:** 9220 Old Seward Hwy 99515 **Location:** Just s of E Dimond Blvd.

CITY DINER   907/277-2489 **20**

◇◇ American. Casual Dining. $8-$19 **AAA Inspector Notes:** This slick, shiny-mirrored and glassed '50s-style diner offers all your classic items like meatloaf, chicken-fried steak, burgers, all kinds of sandwiches and a good variety of salads. Soda-fountain milk shakes, dessert pies and cakes finish off the menu. Bustling and popular, the restaurant also caters to the breakfast crowd with great diner breakfasts. **Bar:** beer & wine. **Address:** 3000 Minnesota Dr 99503 **Location:** Corner of Minnesota Dr and W Benson Blvd.

(See map & index p. 611.)

CLUB PARIS 907/277-6332 12

♥♥♥ Steak Seafood. Casual Dining. $13-$45 **AAA Inspector Notes:** Home to the locally renowned 4-inch filet mignon, the restaurant was established in 1957 and is said to be the oldest steakhouse in the city. The dimly lit dining room, with its dark brown vinyl upholstery and padded booths, has an early 1960s loungelike feel, which will certainly bring back memories for some. It's a popular spot, especially during the tourist season. **Bar:** full bar. **Reservations:** suggested. **Address:** 417 W 5th Ave 99501 **Location:** Between D and E sts; downtown. **Parking:** street only. L D ♥

CROW'S NEST RESTAURANT 907/276-6000 4

♥♥♥♥   **AAA Inspector Notes:** Perched high on the 20th floor of the Hotel Captain Cook it affords one of the best panoramic mountain and Cook Inlet views, especially on long summer days, which makes this restaurant and lounge a must visit while in the city. The menu features standard dining fare like rack of lamb, New York steak, lobster tail and pork tenderloin in an Old World dining room featuring lots of wood accent walls and gold and brass trim. **Bar:** full bar. **Reservations:** suggested. **Address:** 939 W 5th Ave 99501 **Location:** Between I and K sts; in The Hotel Captain Cook. **Parking:** on-site and valet. *Menu on AAA.com* D CALL ♥M

New American Fine Dining $36-$40

CRUSH WINE BISTRO AND CELLAR 907/865-9198 15

♥♥ Small Plates. Casual Dining. $9-$19 **AAA Inspector Notes:** Located across the street from the entrance to Nordstrom's department store, this tiny but wonderfully delightful wine bar and tapas restaurant features first-class, by-the-glass wines with a menu featuring very reasonably priced lunch and dinner items that are meant for sharing. **Bar:** beer & wine. **Address:** 343 W 6th St 99501 **Location:** Corner of W 6th Ave and D St. **Parking:** street only. L D CALL ♥M

FALAFEL KING 907/258-4328 18

♥ Middle Eastern Kosher. Quick Serve. $9-$14 **AAA Inspector Notes:** The focus here is on falafels-hand-scooped and cooked to order. The shawarma (an Israeli version of the gyro) utilizes daily-baked pita bread lined with smooth and garlicky hummus. To prevent needless waste, seasoned crackers are made from the unused pita each day. Schnitzel and grilled chicken round out the menu. The authentic baklava is made with a kiss of honey and well worth the indulgence. Ask about weekly specials. This small restaurant has only a few tables and a small deck. **Address:** 930 Gambell St 99501 **Location:** Jct 9th Ave; downtown. L D ♥

FIRE ISLAND RUSTIC BAKESHOP 907/569-0001 17

♥ Breads/Pastries. Quick Serve. $3-$12 **AAA Inspector Notes:** This small family-owned artisan bakery is located in a residential neighborhood. Organic baked goods include crusty traditional breads, excellent sweet and savory pastries, delectable cookies, and other seasonal specialties. Organic coffee from K-Bay Caffe and teas from Summit Spice are offered. There are a few small tables in the bakery. **Address:** 1343 G St 99501 **Location:** 0.5 mi s on L St, just e on W 13th Ave, then just s on G St; jct W 14th Ave. **Parking:** street only. B L

FU DO CHINESE RESTAURANT 907/561-6611 36

♥♥♥ Chinese. Casual Dining. $8-$20 **AAA Inspector Notes:** A good mix of Western-style Mandarin, Cantonese and Szechuan cooking is offered along with a wide variety of lunch combo plates at reasonable prices, while dinner features dishes like crispy duck, orange beef and sesame chicken. The room is brightly decorated in an ornate Chinese style that hasn't changed much in the 25 years they've been in business. **Bar:** full bar. **Address:** 2600 E Tudor Rd 99507 **Location:** Jct Old Seward Hwy, 1 mi e. L D

GINGER 907/929-3680 11

♥♥♥ Pacific Northwest. Fine Dining. $9-$29 **AAA Inspector Notes:** A hot and happening restaurant and bar featuring local ingredients whenever possible. Recommended are the chicken and lettuce hand wraps—stir-fried ground chicken served with crisp fresh lettuce and tasty coconut-curry sauce—and the spicy tuna tower, which includes marinated ahi tuna with avocado with a wonton crisp. A local favorite is the grilled rib-eye with Szechuan pepper crust served with roasted potatoes. **Bar:** full bar. **Reservations:** suggested. **Address:** 425 W 5th Ave 99501 **Location:** Between D and E sts; across from JC Penney. **Parking:** street only. L D CALL ♥M

GLACIER BREWHOUSE 907/274-2739 9

♥♥ American. Gastropub. $9-$34 **AAA Inspector Notes:** With a large stone fireplace as its focal point, the decor blends contemporary, industrial and rustic themes, creating an inviting, yet bustling, room. Large beer-brewing vats producing a number of tasty brews loom behind glass walls. Varied seafood and alder wood-fired rotisserie meat dishes, pizzas, sandwiches, salads and pastas are served in generous portions. Seasonal salmon is the standout, but dinner prime rib, barbecue pork ribs, bread pudding and peanut butter pie are plenty tempting. **Bar:** full bar. **Reservations:** suggested. **Address:** 737 W 5th Ave, Suite 110 99501 **Location:** At H St; downtown. **Parking:** street only. L D CALL ♥M

(See map & index p. 611.)

THE GREEK CORNER   907/276-2820 22

▼▼ ▼▼ Greek. Casual Dining. $9-$21 **AAA Inspector Notes:** Folks might miss the small, family-run restaurant, one of the city's best-kept secrets. The menu lists both Greek and Italian cuisine, and there is something for everyone. Guests are greeted warmly, whether they are there all the time or for their first visit, and the service is friendly. Portions are hearty. The casual, traditional atmosphere is family-friendly. **Bar:** beer & wine. **Address:** 201 E Northern Lights Blvd 99503 **Location:** Between Darrow and Cordoba sts.

L D CALL ⑤M AC

HUMPY'S GREAT ALASKAN ALE HOUSE   907/276-2337 10

▼▼ ▼▼ American. Casual Dining. $10-$45 **AAA Inspector Notes:** With an impressive selection of Alaskan microbrewed beers the casual ale house is a usually packed with locals, especially after work. The menu is pub fare, featuring a variety of sandwiches, burgers and pastas, including dinner entrées of Alaskan halibut and salmon and steak. Patio seating is available in warm spring/summer months. Under 21 years of age allowed from 11 am to 9 pm and must be accompanied by a parent. **Bar:** full bar. **Address:** 610 W 6th Ave 99501 **Location:** Between F and G sts; downtown. **Parking:** street only.

L D LATE

JENS' RESTAURANT   907/561-5367 24

▼▼ ▼▼ Pacific Northwest. Fine Dining. $13-$45 **AAA Inspector Notes:** Proudly serving Danish dishes for lunch and Northwest cuisine by night, this cozy bistro-style restaurant is one of the city's finest. Local artists have featured and their artwork is for sale and displayed on the walls. The monthly changing menu relies on the freshest Alaskan dishes such as halibut, king salmon, local oysters and rock fish, while their pepper steak has been a menu favorite since the restaurant opened in 1988. **Bar:** beer & wine. **Reservations:** suggested. **Address:** 701 W 36th Ave 99503 **Location:** Just e of Arctic Blvd and W 36th Ave; in Olympic Center.

L D CALL ⑤M

KINCAID GRILL   907/243-0507 27

▼▼ ▼▼ ▼▼ Regional Alaskan. Fine Dining. $30-$36 **AAA Inspector Notes:** It's no surprise that locals flock to this popular restaurant featuring warm and inviting décor, with a wonderfully innovative menu that changes with the season. Alaskan seafood is a huge feature and includes half-shell oysters, king crab cakes, steamed clams, fresh-caught Alaskan salmon and local halibut. Meat lovers have not been forgotten with filet mignon and prime New York steak, roast chicken, smoked duck and rack of lamb. Probably one of the finest dining experiences in Anchorage. **Bar:** full bar. **Reservations:** suggested. **Address:** 6700 Jewel Lake Rd 99502 **Location:** Jct Raspberry St.

D CALL ⑤M

KINLEY'S RESTAURANT & BAR   907/644-8953 28

▼▼ ▼▼ ▼▼ Fusion. Casual Dining. $11-$32 **AAA Inspector Notes:** Guests of this popular gathering spot will find an award-winning wine bar and innovative fare sure to tempt the taste buds. A daily fresh sheet menu highlights the day's entrée specials for both lunch and dinner. Try one of the wonderfully distinctive sandwiches such as the crispy onion-crusted chicken breast or the chef's BLT. Substitute the fries with a salad (Caesar, Parisian or house) or the soup de jour. **Bar:** beer & wine. **Address:** 3230 Seward Hwy 99503 **Location:** Jct 36th Ave, just n on SR 1.   L D CALL ⑤M AC

LARRY'S COCOON   907/222-1178 25

▼▼ ▼▼ Asian Fusion. Casual Dining. $8-$23 **AAA Inspector Notes:** This is one of those places that shouldn't be judged from the outside. The nondescript strip mall opens into a pearl of a restaurant, with newer décor and multiple plants. The menu is diverse, with Korean, Thai and Vietnamese specialties. The finesse of the cooks is apparent with upscale presentations. **Address:** 601 W 36th Ave, Suite 8 99503 **Location:** From W 6th Ave, 2 mi s on C St, then just w; in Bering Village Shopping Center.   L D CALL ⑤M AC

LAS MARGARITAS   907/349-4922 37

▼▼ ▼▼ Mexican. Casual Dining. $9-$20 **AAA Inspector Notes:** This restaurant is a little out of the way, but it's worth the drive. The restaurant has a charming and casual country-style ambience, and its cuisine features popular Mexican and Italian specialties, including burritos, spaghetti, pizza, steak and shrimp. Every table gets a basket of fresh-made taco chips and tangy salsa. **Bar:** full bar. **Reservations:** suggested. **Address:** 541 W Dimond Blvd 99515 **Location:** Between Arctic Blvd and C St.   D CALL ⑤M

MARX BROS. CAFÉ   907/278-2133 6

▼▼ ▼▼ ▼▼ ▼▼

New
American
Fine Dining
$35-$40

AAA Inspector Notes: *Historic.* For a truly exquisite meal, look no further than the dining rooms of this renovated 1916 home. Innovative and artistic selections of Alaskan seafood highlight the menu, and the locally renowned Caesar salad is prepared tableside. Choices include not only a wide selection of seafood, such as oysters, salmon and halibut, but also lamb, elk and other meats. Save room for one of the divine desserts. The atmosphere is delightful, and the service friendly and genuine. **Bar:** beer & wine. **Reservations:** required. **Address:** 627 W 3rd Ave 99501 **Location:** Between F and G sts; downtown. **Parking:** street only.   D AC

MOOSE'S TOOTH PUB & PIZZERIA   907/258-2537 31

▼▼ ▼▼ American. Casual Dining. $10-$28 **AAA Inspector Notes:** This rustic hangout with a bustling, casual atmosphere is popular with locals and tourists alike, so expect a long wait as no reservations are accepted. The specialty is gourmet pizzas, and they come with regular or thick crust; red sauce, green sauce or sauceless; assorted meats, steak, chicken, seafood or vegetable toppings; cheeses ranging from mozzarella and provolone to Gorgonzola, Parmesan, cheddar and feta. Also featured are sodas and beers brewed in their own brewery. **Bar:** beer & wine. **Address:** 3300 Old Seward Hwy 99503 **Location:** Old Seward Hwy at 34th St.

L D CALL ⑤M AC

MUSE   907/929-9210 16

▼▼ ▼▼ Regional Pacific Northwest. Casual Dining. $14-$28 **AAA Inspector Notes:** This café at The Anchorage Museum is the perfect setting to enjoy creations from the same folks who bring you the Marx Bros. Café. Guests can enjoy gourmet lighter fare for lunch with the freshest seafood from local waters. Alaskan spot prawn cocktail with homemade tomato jelly or grilled Copper River red salmon are just a few favorites. The lunch menu offers a variety of salads, soups and sandwiches. Dinner is offered Thursday, Friday and Saturday and features several full-plate entrées. **Bar:** full bar. **Address:** 625 C 99501 **Location:** Downtown; in Anchorage Museum at Rasmuson Center. **Parking:** street only.   L CALL ⑤M

ORSO   907/222-3232 8

▼▼ ▼▼ ▼▼ Italian. Casual Dining. $19-$36 **AAA Inspector Notes:** The restaurant features the freshest Alaskan ingredients whenever possible, including steelhead salmon and Alaska king crab, fresh-made pasta and house-made desserts like molten chocolate cake. Parking is at street meters or at one of several downtown parking lots. **Bar:** full bar. **Reservations:** suggested. **Address:** 737 W 5th Ave 99501 **Location:** Between H and G sts. **Parking:** street only.

L D CALL ⑤M

THE PEANUT FARM SPORTS BAR & GRILL
    907/563-3283 34

▼▼ ▼▼ American. Casual Dining. $10-$28 **AAA Inspector Notes:** Sports fanatics will be in heaven as flat-screen TVs dominate the walls, and those lucky enough to get a booth will have their own mini flat-screen TV. This sports bar is the place to be to watch any big game. Menu options include salads, hearty sandwiches, burgers and pizza, while dinner expands into steaks and seafood. A heated outdoor deck overlooks a picturesque wooded creek. **Bar:** full bar. **Address:** 5227 Old Seward Hwy 99518 **Location:** Jct International Airport Rd.   B L D LATE CALL ⑤M

PEPPER MILL   907/561-0800 29

▼▼ ▼▼ American. Casual Dining. $10-$40 **AAA Inspector Notes:** Offering up tasty gourmet pizzas, warm sandwiches and sizzling classic steaks that can be topped off with wide variety of exotic peppers, hence the name Pepper Mill. On warm summer evenings they open their outdoor patio. **Bar:** full bar. **Address:** 4101 Credit Union Dr 99503 **Location:** Jct C and 40th sts.   D CALL ⑤M

PHYLLIS'S CAFE AND SALMON BAKE   907/274-6576 13

▼▼ ▼▼ American. Casual Dining. $9-$26 **AAA Inspector Notes:** The large covered outdoor patio lets guests enjoy the long Alaskan days in the summer months. The menu features a selection of hot and cold appetizers, their ever-popular chowder in a bread bowl, a few steaks and, of course, the fresh Alaska halibut and salmon. The highlight is the selection of really good locally brewed draft beers on tap. **Bar:** beer & wine. **Address:** 436 D St 99501 **Location:** Between 4th and 5th aves. **Parking:** street only.

L D CALL ⑤M AC

(See map & index p. 611.)

RAY'S PLACE 907/279-2932 ⑲
▼▼ Vietnamese. Casual Dining. $9-$19 **AAA Inspector Notes:** In the style of a true family-run restaurant, the owner's pay homage to their deceased dad by naming the restaurant after him. All of the dishes have been passed down through the generations, utilizing the freshest and most authentic ingredients. Since the pho (soups) are made in house, and require extensive labor, you may want to call ahead to see if your favorite is on the menu that day. **Bar:** beer & wine. **Address:** 2412 Spenard Rd 99503 **Location:** 1.3 mi s on C St, 0.5 mi w on W Fireweed Ln, then just s. Ⓛ Ⓓ CALL ♿Ⓜ

SACK'S CAFE & RESTAURANT 907/274-4022 ⑦
▼▼▼ International. Fine Dining. $10-$34 **AAA Inspector Notes:** In a word, this restaurant is delightful. The chic choice's menu draws largely on area ingredients, including fresh salmon, scallops and halibut. Thai and Asian influences are abundant. At lunch, sandwiches and casual fare are at the heart of the offerings; dinner is a bit more complex, with several entrées that change nightly as the season changes. There usually is a jazz musician on Thursdays. **Bar:** beer & wine. **Reservations:** suggested. **Address:** 328 G St 99501 **Location:** Between 3rd and 4th aves; downtown. **Parking:** street only. Ⓛ Ⓓ CALL ♿Ⓜ Ⓚ

SEA GALLEY 907/563-3520 ㉚
▼▼ ▼ Seafood. Casual Dining. $10-$40 **AAA Inspector Notes:** A great place to dine for those in the mood for seafood, this restaurant features a distinct nautical decor complete with fish nets and a wide selection of fresh fish and seafood cooked up in a variety of ways. Dinners include tasty chowder or an all-you-can-eat salad bar. Desserts are a highlight here; a huge display case filled with sweet treats sits near the dining room entrance. **Bar:** full bar. **Address:** 4101 Credit Union Dr 99503 **Location:** Jct C and 40th sts. Ⓛ Ⓓ CALL ♿Ⓜ

SIMON & SEAFORTS 907/274-3502 ②
▼▼▼▼ Regional American. Casual Dining. $12-$40 **AAA Inspector Notes:** This local favorite specializes in fresh, creatively prepared seafood flown in daily from Homer and Black Angus beef aged for 28 days for flavor and tenderness. A wonderful selection of wines by the glass and draft beers is offered. The highlight of this restaurant has to be the view of Cook Inlet, so try for window table. **Bar:** full bar. **Reservations:** suggested. **Address:** 420 L St 99501 **Location:** Between 4th and 5th aves. **Parking:** street only. Ⓛ Ⓓ CALL ♿Ⓜ

SNOW CITY CAFE 907/272-2489 ①
▼▼ American. Casual Dining. $8-$16 **AAA Inspector Notes:** It is all but guaranteed that a line will form on Saturday and Sunday morning at this popular spot, and it is definitely worth the wait. Home to an all-day breakfast, this one has been ranked highly by city residents. The cafe bustles with energy during the breakfast and lunch hours and provides an upbeat atmosphere in which to enjoy hearty, delicious food, organic coffee and trans fat-free cooking. **Bar:** beer & wine. **Address:** 1034 W 4th Ave 99501 **Location:** Jct L St; downtown. **Parking:** street only. Ⓑ Ⓛ CALL ♿Ⓜ Ⓚ

SNOW GOOSE RESTAURANT 907/277-7727 ③
▼▼ ▼ American. Casual Dining. $12-$28 **AAA Inspector Notes:** Those looking for a pint of locally brewed beer should visit this great stop, which also offers views of the Cook Inlet and shipyard. Upstairs is a casual pub-type atmosphere, and downstairs, though still casual, is more of a restaurant. Service can be unpredictable, but the food and view make a visit worthwhile. **Bar:** full bar. **Reservations:** suggested. **Address:** 717 W 3rd Ave 99501 **Location:** Corner of 3rd Ave and G St. **Parking:** on-site and street. Ⓛ Ⓓ CALL ♿Ⓜ

SOURDOUGH MINING CO 907/563-2272 ㉟
▼▼ ▼ American. Family Dining. $14-$45 **AAA Inspector Notes:** A close replica of the mill house at Independence Mine, this restaurant has a tunnel entrance made from mine-blasted rock. Mesquite-smoked ribs and succulent rotisserie chicken, Alaskan seafood, steaks, pot pies, stews and chowders line the menu. Do not pass up the corn fritters, or a trip to the all-you-can-eat ice cream bar, included with each entrée. During the summer, guests can listen to the adventures of Dusty Sourdough and see a gold panning demonstration Tuesday-Sunday at 7:30 pm. **Bar:** full bar. **Reservations:** suggested. **Address:** 5200 Juneau St 99518 **Location:** Just e of jct Old Seward Hwy and International Airport Rd. Ⓛ Ⓓ CALL ♿Ⓜ Ⓚ

SOUTHSIDE BISTRO 907/348-0088 ㊵
▼▼▼▼ American. Casual Dining. $8-$33 **AAA Inspector Notes:** Located in the heart of a southside Anchorage business park, this little strip mall eatery features an upbeat and contemporary decor. The menu features a wide variety of items to suit all tastes with cooking styles that defy classification. Fresh seafood, assorted meat dishes, pasta and thin-crust pizza ooze with flavor and a creative bent. The menu lists additional selections of sandwiches. The wine list focuses mainly on western United States products. **Bar:** beer & wine. **Reservations:** suggested. **Address:** 1320 Huffman Park Dr 99515 **Location:** SR 1 (Seward Hwy) exit Huffman Rd, just w, then just n. Ⓛ Ⓓ CALL ♿Ⓜ Ⓚ

SULLIVAN'S STEAKHOUSE 907/258-2882 ⑭
▼▼▼▼ Steak Seafood. Fine Dining. $10-$58 **AAA Inspector Notes:** Named for John L. Sullivan, heavyweight champion of the world in the 1880s, the upscale steak house prepares a wide selection of steaks, chops and seafood. Decorated with black-and-white photographs of Sullivan, Jack Dempsey and other boxing legends. **Bar:** full bar. **Reservations:** suggested. **Address:** 320 W 5th Ave, Suite 100 99501 **Location:** Corner of 5th Ave and C St. **Parking:** street only. Ⓛ Ⓓ CALL ♿Ⓜ

SUSHI YA JAPANESE RESTAURANT 907/522-2244 ㊳
▼▼ ▼ Japanese Sushi. Casual Dining. $8-$23 **AAA Inspector Notes:** This delightful restaurant features a distinct Japanese decor complete with sushi bar and fine Asian ornamental artifacts throughout. In addition to an outstanding sushi selection, diners can also choose from traditional favorites such as tempura and teriyaki entrees and combination plates. Most entrees include miso soup and a salad. **Bar:** beer & wine. **Address:** 1111 E Dimond Blvd 99515 **Location:** Jct Old Seward Hwy. Ⓛ Ⓓ CALL ♿Ⓜ

SWEET BASIL CAFE 907/274-0070 ㉑
▼ Coffee/Tea. Casual Dining. $6-$15 **AAA Inspector Notes:** Diners who enjoy homemade soups, freshly squeezed juices, large sandwiches and salads and sumptuous desserts might find the casual, bright and cheerful café an appealing spot. Locals and visitors alike frequent this place. The kitchen closes at 4 pm weekdays and 3 pm on Saturday for dine-in only service. **Bar:** beer & wine. **Address:** 1021 W Northern Lights Blvd 99503 **Location:** Jct 10th St and W Northern Lights Blvd. **Parking:** street only. Ⓛ CALL ♿Ⓜ

YAK AND YETI HIMALAYAN RESTAURANT 907/743-8078 ㉓
▼▼ Indian. Casual Dining. $8-$17 **AAA Inspector Notes:** This cozy family-owned and -operated restaurant is in the heart of Spenard. The owners feature some of their favorite dishes from India, Nepal and Tibet. Custom-created spices and authentic ingredients set this restaurant apart. One uniquely Tibetan dish offered, the delicious Lhasa mfomos (steamed beef dumplings), will not be found anywhere else in the state. The restaurant has limited seating and does not accept reservations, except call-ahead seating for parties of five or more. **Address:** 3301 Spenard Rd 99503 **Location:** 1 mi s on L St, just e on W Benson Blvd, then just s. Ⓛ Ⓓ Ⓚ

YAMATO YA 907/561-2128 ㉜
▼▼ ▼ Sushi. Casual Dining. $6-$24 **AAA Inspector Notes:** Excellent sushi and sashimi featuring several creative rolls like the caterpillar roll with fresh-water eel, rice and avocado and the crunch roll with tempura shrimp. Can't decide? Try the sushi and sashimi lunch or dinner boxes with assorted rolls for a chance to try different rolls. All meals come with delicious miso soup and small green salad. **Bar:** beer & wine. **Address:** 3501 Old Seward Hwy 99503 **Location:** Jct 36th St. Ⓛ Ⓓ CALL ♿Ⓜ

BARROW (A-5) pop. 4,212, elev. 2'

The northernmost settlement in Alaska, Barrow is 340 miles north of the Arctic Circle on the edge of the omnipresent Arctic icepack. The sun does not go below the horizon for 82 days from early May to early August or rise above the horizon for 51 days between November and January. The town is reached by daily scheduled flights from Anchorage and Fairbanks. Husky sled dogs still are used, but snowmobiles have become more popular.

Barrow is one of the world's largest Eskimo settlements. Although to some extent the people continue to follow their old traditions, the trend is toward a more modern way of life: The North Slope oil discovery created great wealth in the area.

The Post-Rogers Memorial, at the airport, commemorates the deaths of Will Rogers and his pilot, Wiley Post, who were killed in a 1935 plane crash 12 miles down the coast.

CANTWELL pop. 219

BACKWOODS LODGE   907/768-2232

Motel
S90-S170

Address: Denali Hwy MM 133.8 99729 **Location:** Parks Hwy (Milepost 210), just e. Located in a quiet area. **Facility:** 10 units, some kitchens. 1 story, exterior corridors. **Parking:** winter plug-ins. **Terms:** 10 day cancellation notice-fee imposed. **Free Special Amenities:** local telephone calls. *(See ad this page.)*

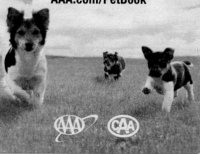
▼ *See AAA listing this page* ▼

CHUGACH NATIONAL FOREST (D-12)

Elevations in the forest range from sea level at the Pacific Ocean at Prince William Sound to 13,176 ft. at Mount Marcus Baker. Refer to AAA maps for additional elevation information.

Extending along the Gulf of Alaska from Cape Suckling to Seward, Chugach (CHEW-gatch) National Forest covers 5,500,000 acres, roughly as large as New Hampshire. It is second in size only to the Tongass National Forest *(see place listing p. 664)* and includes many of the islands and much of the land bordering Prince William Sound and the northeastern portion of the Kenai Peninsula.

Within the 700,000-acre Copper River Delta Wildlife Management Area just east of Cordova is one of the largest concentrations of trumpeter swans in North America. Also in abundance are dusky Canada geese, short-billed dowitchers, red-throated loons and green-winged teal. Prince William Sound has spectacular scenic opportunities with its 3,500 miles of coastline as well as dramatic tidewater glaciers and marine life that includes many species of whales.

Both saltwater and freshwater fishing are available in abundance in the forest. Halibut, red snapper, salmon and crabs are plentiful along the more than 3,500 miles of saltwater shoreline. Popular spots are Resurrection Bay at Seward and in Prince William Sound around Valdez and Cordova. Freshwater lakes and streams provide red salmon, Dolly Varden char and rainbow trout. A sportfishing license is required for all types of fishing within the forest.

For photographers and sport hunters, the forest offers a variety of big game, including black and brown bears, moose and Dall sheep. Hunting is subject to Alaska's fish and game management laws, seasons and bag limits.

Seward Highway offers 127 miles of scenic driving along saltwater bays, ice-blue glaciers and valleys dotted with native wildlife. The highway connects the cities of Anchorage and Seward. Bordering the forest on the northwest is SR 4; its scenic portion extends from Valdez to the junction of SR 10 west of Chitina. Portions of one of the most famous trails, The Historic Iditarod Trail, can be hiked, skied, dog sledded or explored on snowmobile.

In addition to 14 road-accessible campgrounds and 200 miles of hiking trails, the Forest Service operates 40 cabins in remote areas near lakes, bays and streams. Accessible by trail, boat or floatplane, the cabins are equipped with bunks, tables, chairs, wood or oil stoves and outdoor sanitary facilities, but not electricity.

The fee is $35-$45 per night per party. Reservations are required and can be made up to six months in advance. Further information also can be obtained from the Chugach National Forest, 161 E. 1st Ave., #8, Anchorage, AK 99501, phone (907) 743-9500, (877) 444-6777 for reservations or the U.S. Forest Service in Juneau *(see Fast Facts). Also see Recreation Chart.*

ALASKA WILDLIFE CONSERVATION CENTER, Seward Hwy. Milepost 79, is a 140-acre, drive-through wild animal park. Musk oxen, red foxes, lynx, buffaloes, Sitka blacktail deer, caribous, eagles, moose, reindeer, elk and bears may be seen on the drive. **Time:** Allow 30 minutes minimum. **Hours:** Daily 8-8, mid-May to mid-Sept.; daily 10-6, Mar. 1 to mid-May; daily 10-5, mid-Sept. through Jan. 1; Sat.-Sun. 10-5, rest of year. Last admission is 30 minutes before closing. Phone ahead to confirm schedule. **Cost:** $10; $7.50 (ages 4-12, ages 65+ and active military with ID). The maximum fee is $30 per carload. Pets are not permitted. **Phone:** (907) 783-2025.

PORTAGE GLACIER CRUISES depart 1.5 mi. s. of the Begich-Boggs Visitor Center in the Portage Glacier Recreation Area *(see attraction listing).* A 1-hour narrated cruise aboard the MV *Ptarmigan* takes passengers to the face of Portage Glacier. Sections of the glacier "calving" or breaking away into the lake below often can be seen. The 200-passenger ship has a climate-controlled cabin with oversize windows and an open-air observation deck. Shuttle and tour packages from Anchorage also are available.

Inquire about weather policies. **Time:** Allow 1 hour, 30 minutes minimum. **Hours:** Cruises depart daily at 10:30, noon, 1:30, 3 and 4:30, mid-May to mid-Sept. **Cost:** Fare $34; $17 (ages 2-12). **Phone:** (907) 277-5581 or (888) 452-1737.

PORTAGE GLACIER RECREATION AREA is 5.5 mi. e. from Milepost 79 of the Seward-Anchorage Hwy. Large icebergs calve off the face of the glacier into 650-foot-deep Portage Lake. An observation platform and a wayside exhibit are at the entrance to Williwaw Campground. Wayside exhibits also are available at Explorer Glacier. Iceworm safaris are offered. **Tours:** Guided tours are available. **Hours:** The road to and within the area is open all year. **Phone:** (907) 783-3242. 🍴 🛏

Begich-Boggs Visitor Center, off the Seward-Anchorage Hwy. on Portage Valley Rd., contains an observatory, orientation area, exhibit hall and learning center. A 20-minute film titled "Voices from the Ice" is shown every half hour. **Hours:** Daily 9-6, mid-May to mid-Sept.; hours vary rest of year. Phone ahead to confirm schedule. **Cost:** Visitor center and film $5; free (ages 0-15). **Phone:** (907) 783-2326.

COOPER LANDING (D-11) pop. 289
• Hotels p. 624 • Restaurants p. 624

RECREATIONAL ACTIVITIES
Boating
• **Alaska Wildland Adventures** departs for Kenai River trips from the launch site on Sterling Hwy. (SR 1) Milepost 50.1. Other activities are offered. **Hours:** Daily May-Sept. **Phone:** (907) 783-2928 or (800) 334-8730. *(See ad p. 655.)*

KENAI PRINCESS WILDERNESS LODGE   (907)595-1425
▼▼▼▼ **Hotel** $129-$249 **Address:** 17245 Frontier Cir 99572 **Location:** SR 1 (Sterling Hwy) at Milepost 47.8, just n of bridge, then 2.1 mi w. **Facility:** 86 units. 1 story, exterior corridors. **Terms:** closed 9/16-5/22, check-in 3:30 pm, 3 day cancellation notice-fee imposed. **Dining:** Eagle's Crest Dining Room, see separate listing. **Activities:** whirlpool, fishing, hiking trails, horseshoes, shuffleboard, exercise room. **Fee:** charter fishing. **Guest Services:** coin laundry.

🍽 🍸 CALL 🚭M BIZ 📶 ✕ 🎿 💻

WHERE TO EAT

EAGLE'S CREST DINING ROOM   907/595-1425
▼▼ Pacific Northwest. Casual Dining. $12-$30 **AAA Inspector Notes:** Diners will enjoy the rustic lodge ambiance complete with country pine walls and a huge stone fireplace. The main focus of the dining room is, however, the large panoramic windows that offer spectacular views of the mountains on a clear day. Light luncheon fare is featured including lots of salads, sandwiches and local fish and chips, and a more upscale dinner menu is also offered. **Bar:** full bar. **Reservations:** suggested. **Address:** 17245 Frontier Cir 99572 **Location:** SR 1 (Sterling Hwy) at Milepost 47.8, just n of bridge, then 2.1 mi w; in Kenai Princess Wilderness Lodge.

B L D CALL 🚭M 🎿

CORDOVA (D-12) pop. 2,239, elev. 100'

Cordova is located on the eastern shores of Prince William Sound and is surrounded by the Chugach Mountain Range and the Chugach National Forest. The town can be reached by air from Juneau and Anchorage or via the Alaska Marine Highway from Valdez and Whittier. In the early 1900s, Cordova was the terminus of the Copper River Northwest Railroad that carried copper ore from the Kennecott Mines in McCarthy. Today the town's industry focuses on commercial fishing.

Cordova Chamber of Commerce: 404 First St., Cordova, AK 99574. **Phone:** (907) 424-7260.

RECREATIONAL ACTIVITIES
Kayaking
• **Cordova Coastal Outfitters** offers tours departing from #13 Harbor Loop Rd. at the Cordova Harbor. Other activities are offered. **Hours:** Trips depart daily by appointment. **Phone:** (907) 424-7424.

DELTA JUNCTION (B-12) pop. 958

The official northern terminus of the Alaska Highway, Delta Junction is one of the state's strongest agricultural producers. The town offers panoramic views of the Alaska Range as well as the Trans-Alaska Pipeline, the Delta Bison Range and glaciers.

BIG DELTA STATE HISTORICAL PARK AND RIKA'S ROADHOUSE AND LANDING, at Milepost 275 on Richardson Hwy., is a restored 10-acre homestead with a museum, historic cabins, a roadhouse, a garden and livestock and poultry pens. **Tours:** Guided tours are available. **Hours:** Daily 9-5, May 15-Sept. 15. **Cost:** Free. **Phone:** (907) 895-4201. 🍽

DENALI NATIONAL PARK AND PRESERVE (B-10)
• Hotels p. 627 • Restaurants p. 629

Elevations in the park and preserve range from 626 ft. at the northwest corner of the park at Chilcukabena Lake to the 20,320 ft. Mount McKinley. Refer to AAA maps for additional elevation information.

In the interior of Alaska, primitive and wild Denali National Park and Preserve covers 9,419 square miles and offers spectacular views of quiet lakes, snowcapped peaks and varicolored tundra. In addition to 20,320-foot Mount McKinley, the highest peak in North America, the park encompasses 17,400-foot Mount Foraker, 13,220-foot Silverthrone and 11,670-foot Mount Russell.

Mount McKinley, known to the early Athabascan Indians as Denali, "the high one," has two peaks: South Peak, the true summit, and 2 miles away, 19,470-foot North Peak. Most of the mountain is covered by ice and snow all year. Excellent views of Mount McKinley are possible along the park road (weather permitting); clouds hide the summit about 75 percent of the time in summer and 60 percent the rest of the year.

The park's many glaciers originate on the slopes of the Alaska Range. Muldrow Glacier, the largest northward-flowing glacier in Alaska, stretches from between Mount McKinley's twin peaks to within a few miles of the park road; it can be seen from several vantage points.

More than 167 species of birds and 39 kinds of mammals inhabit the park; grizzly bears, moose, Dall sheep, wolves and caribou are some of the larger mammals. Equally varied is the vegetation. The chief conifers are black and white spruce, while dwarf birch grow in thickets on the lower slopes and along the intermountain valleys. Low, boggy meadows are the habitat of stunted, twisted black spruce.

Above the river valleys, forests give way to vast stretches of wet tundra supporting shrubby plants and often underlain by permafrost. Dry alpine tundra blankets the slopes and ridges at the higher elevations.

General Information and Activities

From Anchorage and Fairbanks, the George Parks Highway (SR 3) provides access to the park all year, and SR 8 from Paxson is usually open from early June to mid-October. The park also is accessible from Anchorage or Fairbanks via the Alaska Railroad; there is daily service from late May to mid-September. Trains run northbound to Fairbanks on Saturday and southbound to Anchorage on Sunday the rest of the year. Charter flights are available from principal airports.

Denali Park Road, beginning at SR 3 at the park's eastern boundary, runs about 90 miles westward through the park, terminating at a partly abandoned mining town, Kantishna. Only the first 14.8 miles to

Savage River are paved, and most of the road is narrow with many sharp curves. It is usually open from early June to mid-September. The George Parks Highway (SR 3) runs along the eastern border of the park and offers sweeping views of the park's alpine scenery from Willow to Nenana.

Private vehicles may be used only on the first 14.8 miles of Denali Park Road unless you have a registered campsite at Teklanika Campground. Transportation beyond Savage River or to Sanctuary, Igloo and Wonder Lake campgrounds is provided by shuttle buses that operate to Toklat, Wonder Lake and other points in the park.

Fare for the shuttle varies with destination. Fare to Kantishna $50; $25 (ages 15-17). Fare to Wonder Lake $46; $23 (ages 15-17). Fare to Toklat and Polychrome $26.75; $13.50 (ages 15-17). Fare to Eielson Visitor Center $34; $17 (ages 15-17). Three- and 6-day trip passes are available; prices vary by destination. These fares do not include the park admission fees.

More than half of the shuttle seats can be reserved by telephone and Internet; phone (907) 272-7275 or (800) 622-7275 in advance. The rest of the spaces can be reserved only in person within 2 days of departure; phone (907) 683-9274 for more information. Buses depart approximately every half-hour beginning at 5:15 a.m. from the Wilderness Access Center near the entrance at Milepost 0.75 on Denali Park Road. The bus stops to view wildlife when conditions are safe. Shuttle buses also drop off and pick up passengers along the park road on a space-available basis. The center houses a small theater.

The Denali Visitor Center, Milepost 1.2 on Denali Park Road, has an information desk, exhibits, a 20-minute film, a bookstore and interpretive programs. It is open daily 8-6, late May to mid-September. Only

accessible by shuttle bus, the Eielson Visitor Center, Milepost 66 on Denali Park Road, displays "Seasons of Denali," a quilt by fabric artist Ree Nancarrow. The center is open daily 9-7, early June to mid-September.

The Murie Science and Learning Center, at Milepost 1.4 on Denali Park Road, is dedicated to research and education about America's eight northernmost national parks and offers field seminars and educational programs. It is open daily 9:30-5, mid-May to mid-September; 9-4, rest of year. Phone (907) 683-1269 or (888) 688-1269.

The Talkeetna Ranger Station, Milepost 98 on George Parks Highway (SR 3), also offers interpretive programs and is open daily 8-5:30, mid-April through Labor Day; Mon.-Fri. 8-4:30, rest of year. Phone (907) 733-2231.

To camp outside the established campgrounds, stop at the Wilderness Access Center for a backcountry permit. Reservations for all campgrounds may be made here.

Sled dog demonstrations are given by rangers at the park kennels, Milepost 3 on Denali Park Road. The 40-minute presentations are offered daily at 10, 2 and 4, June through August; phone ahead for availability. Ranger-naturalists also present various lectures, hikes and other activities daily at various campgrounds. Information about activities is available at the park Visitor Center and ranger stations, or pick up a copy of the park's informational newspaper, *Denali Alpenglow*.

Guided and self-guiding hikes are available along several nature trails with trailheads along the paved portion of the park road. Throughout the rest of the park, hiking is generally cross-country. The Spruce Forest Trail loop takes about 15 minutes, while the

▼ *See AAA listing p. 667* ▼

Morino Trail takes 30 minutes to complete. Back-country permits are available from the Backcountry Information Center, adjacent to the Wilderness Access Center. The park offers several ranger-guided hikes. The hikes are free; however, hikers must purchase shuttle bus tickets to reach the various trails that do not originate at the Denali Visitor Center. Fares are $26.75-$50; $13.50-$25 (ages 15-17) depending on the trailhead.

Do not feed or disturb wildlife. Grizzly bears in particular can be dangerous; inquire at the Visitor Center about how to avoid close encounters with grizzlies. Firearms must be declared and made inoperative when you enter the park; hunting and shooting are forbidden.

Most fishing is poor in the park; only streams that are free of glacial silt are good fishing spots. No license is required within the national park; the daily creel limit is 10 fish, only two of which may be lake trout. An Alaska fishing license is required in the national preserve areas. Check at a ranger station for further information.

Temperatures during the park season can vary from 40 to 80 degrees Fahrenheit, with an average of 50 to 54 degrees June through August. Daylight generally lasts for more than 18 hours during the summer months.

Morino Grill, a cafeteria-style restaurant, is next to the Denali Visitor Center. A store near the park entrance contains supplies, but no gas is available; the store is open approximately 7 a.m.-9 p.m. during peak season, shorter hours at other times. A gas station north of the park entrance on George Parks Highway (SR 3) is open in the summer. Food and supplies also are available at Riley Creek campground just inside the park boundaries. *See Recreation Chart.*

ADMISSION , valid for 7 days, is $10 per person; free (ages 0-15).

PETS are permitted in the park only if they are leashed or otherwise physically restrained; they are not allowed on trails, shuttle buses or in the backcountry.

ADDRESS inquiries to the Superintendent, Denali National Park and Preserve, P.O. Box 9, Denali Park, AK 99755; phone (907) 683-2294 or (800) 622-7275 for reservations.

ALASKA CABIN NITE DINNER THEATRE is 1.7 mi. n. of the park entrance on George Parks Hwy. (SR 3) at Milepost 239. The theater presents a 1915-style dinner show that highlights Alaska's gold-mining history. A pre-show dinner is served family-style. **Time:** Allow 2 hours minimum. **Hours:** Shows Mon.-Fri. at 5:30 and 8:30 p.m., mid-May to mid-Sept. Phone ahead to confirm schedule. **Cost:** $63; $31.50 (ages 3-11). Reservations are required. **Phone:** (907) 683-8200, or (800) 276-7234 for reservations. ⏸

DENALI AIR is 10 mi. s. on George Parks Hwy. (SR 3) at Milepost 229.5. Commentary about history, scenery and topography complements an hour-long flight along the Alaska Range and around Mount McKinley. **Time:** Allow 1 hour minimum. **Hours:** Flights depart every even hour daily 8-8 (weather permitting), mid-May to mid-Sept. **Cost:** Fare $350; $175 (ages 2-12). Reservations are recommended. **Phone:** (907) 683-2261.

DENALI BACKCOUNTRY ADVENTURE departs from Denali Cabins, Milepost 229, George Parks Hwy. (SR 3), 9 mi. s. of park entrance. This narrated bus tour travels along the 95-mile Denali Park Road to Denali Backcountry Lodge in Kantishna. Along the route, the guide points out wildlife such as moose and caribou, and makes stops at various times for photography. The complete trip lasts 13 hours and includes either goldpanning or a guided nature walk to Fannie Quigley's historic pioneer cabin. Lunch and snacks are provided.

Allow a full day. **Hours:** Tours depart daily at 6:15 a.m., early June to mid-Sept. **Cost:** Fee $159 (plus $10 park entrance fee). **Phone:** (907) 376-1992 or (877) 233-6254. *(See ad p. 605, p. 628, p. 627.)*

DENALI WILDERNESS SAFARIS, at Milepost 216 on George Parks Hwy. (SR 3), offers 3-hour heated jet boat rides or 2-hour sled dog-pulled cart rides to a camp in the Alaskan "bush" country, where locals share their methods of hunting, prospecting and trapping. Gold panning opportunities are presented. Free transportation is provided from all area hotels. **Hours:** Wilderness trips depart daily at 8, 10, 2 and 6. **Cost:** Boat fare $119; $79 (ages 0-12); free (active military with ID). Dog sled $89; $49 (ages 0-12); free (active military with ID). Fees include a snack. Reservations are recommended. **Phone:** (907) 768-2550.

ERA HELICOPTERS FLIGHTSEEING TOURS, 1 Glacier Way, offers a narrated 2-hour aerial tour (with 50 minutes of actual flight time) of North America's highest mountain, Mount McKinley. A 70-minute glacier landing tour consists of 50 minutes in the air and 20 minutes on the ice. Five-hour heli-hiking excursions also are available. Caribous, moose and Dall sheep can be seen in the valleys. Free transportation is provided from area hotels. **Hours:** Daily 7-7, May-Sept. **Cost:** Tours range from $339-$475. Tours subject to passenger minimums. **Phone:** (907) 683-2574 or (800) 843-1947.

KANTISHNA EXPERIENCE TOUR departs from local hotels. This bus tour takes visitors along the Gold Rush trails once traveled by pioneer Fannie Quigley to Kantishna. An interpretive park ranger explains in detail the region's geology, flora and fauna as well as the history of Kantishna on the 11- to 12-hour tours. The trip is 92 miles each way. Guests may bring binoculars for a better view of such wildlife as moose, caribou and bears.

Note: Guests are advised to dress in layers. The tour is not recommended for the physically impaired.

Time: Allow 11 hours minimum. **Hours:** Trips depart daily 6:40-7:20 a.m. from area hotels, early June to mid-Sept. Phone ahead to confirm schedule. **Cost:** Fare (includes park admission, lunch, beverages and snacks) $169; $79.50 (ages 0-14). Reservations are required. **Phone:** (907) 272-7275 or (800) 622-7275. 🍴

NATURAL HISTORY TOUR, departing from area hotels, takes visitors on a bus tour across sections of the park where they can enjoy views of the Alaska Range from Mount McKinley to Mount Deborah. Driver-guides explain the region's natural history, unusual geological formations and local flora and fauna. A stop at the Wilderness Access Center allows time to view the film "Across Time and Tundra."

Hours: The 5-hour trip departs two times daily, mid-May to mid-Sept. Phone ahead to confirm schedule. **Cost:** Fare (includes park admission and a snack) $76.50; $33.25 (ages 0-14). **Phone:** (907) 272-7275 or (800) 622-7275.

TUNDRA WILDERNESS TOURS picks up visitors at local hotels. Buses travel to Toklat River, making frequent stops en route for photography. Driver-guides explain in detail the region's geology, flora and fauna on the 7- to 8-hour tours. Binoculars are recommended for spotting moose, caribous, bears and other wildlife.

Inquire about weather policies. **Hours:** Trips depart daily 5-9 a.m. and 1:30-3:30 p.m., mid-May to mid-Sept. **Cost:** Fare (includes park admission and a box lunch) $123.25; $56.75 (ages 0-14). Reservations are recommended. **Phone:** (907) 272-7275 or (800) 622-7275.

RECREATIONAL ACTIVITIES
White-water Rafting
- **Alaska Raft Adventures** departs from the McKinley Chalet at Milepost 238 on George Parks Hwy. (SR 3). **Hours:** Trips depart daily at 7:30, 1:30 and 6, mid-May to mid-Sept. **Phone:** (907) 276-7234 or (800) 276-7234.
- **Denali Raft Adventures, Inc.** is .5 mi. n. of the park entrance at Milepost 238.6 on George Parks Hwy. (SR 3). **Hours:** Trips depart daily mid-May to mid-Sept.; check-in times vary depending on trip. **Phone:** (907) 683-2234 or (888) 683-2234.

DENALI BACKCOUNTRY LODGE (907)376-1900

◆◆◆ Cabin $790-$930 **Address:** MM 95 Denali Park Rd 99755 **Location:** End of the 90 mi Denali National Park Rd. **Facility:** 42 cabins. 1-2 stories (no elevator), exterior corridors. **Parking:** no self-parking. **Terms:** closed 9/13-6/3, check-in 7:30 pm, check-out 6 am, 45 day cancellation notice-fee imposed. **Activities:** recreation programs, bicycles, hiking trails. **Guest Services:** area transportation-park entrance & lodge. *(See ad p. 605, p. 628, this page.)*

DENALI BLUFFS HOTEL (907)683-7000

◆◆◆ Hotel $99-$239 **Address:** Milepost 238.4 Parks Hwy 99755 **Location:** Milepost 238.4, on SR 3 (Parks Hwy). **Facility:** 112 units. 2 stories (no elevator), exterior corridors. **Terms:** closed 9/15-5/15, 3 day cancellation notice-fee imposed. **Guest Services:** coin laundry, area transportation-within 5 mi & visitor center.

DENALI CABINS (907)376-1900

◆ Cabin $152-$189 **Address:** Milepost 229 Parks Hwy 99755 **Location:** 11 mi s, Milepost 229 on SR 3 (Parks Hwy). **Facility:** 46 cabins. 1 story, exterior corridors. **Bath:** shower only. **Terms:** closed 9/13-5/31, 45 day cancellation notice-fee imposed. **Activities:** whirlpools. **Guest Services:** area transportation-visitor center & Denali area. *(See ad p. 605, p. 628, this page.)*

DENALI PRINCESS WILDERNESS LODGE   (907)683-2282

 Hotel $99-$299 **Address:** Milepost 238.5 99755 **Location:** Milepost 238.5 on SR 3 (Parks Hwy). **Facility:** 656 units. 2-3 stories (no elevator), interior/exterior corridors. **Terms:** closed 9/24-5/14, cancellation fee imposed. **Dining:** 3 restaurants, also, King Salmon, see separate listing. **Activities:** whirlpools. *Fee:* massage. **Guest Services:** coin laundry, area transportation-train terminal & visitor center.

MCKINLEY CHALET RESORT   907/683-8200

Hotel. Rates not provided. **Address:** Milepost 238.5 Parks Hwy 99755 **Location:** Milepost 238.5 on SR 3 (Parks Hwy). **Facility:** 345 units. 2 stories (no elevator), interior/exterior corridors. **Dining:** 2 restaurants, also, Nenana View Grille, see separate listing. **Activities:** recreation programs. **Guest Services:** coin laundry, area transportation-shops & visitor center.

GRANDE DENALI LODGE   (907)683-5100

Hotel $149-$299 **Address:** Milepost 238.2 Parks Hwy 99755 **Location:** Milepost 238.2 on SR 3 (Parks Hwy) on east side of road, 0.7 mi ne on Grande Dr. Located on a high bluff. **Facility:** 170 units, some cabins. 4 stories, interior/exterior corridors. **Terms:** closed 9/15-5/15, 3 day cancellation notice-fee imposed. **Guest Services:** coin laundry, area transportation-within 5 mi & visitor center.

Contact us about AAA/CAA
Approved properties at
AAA.com/TourBookComments

Where The Wild Things Are.

Nestled 92 miles inside Denali National Park's borders lies Denali Backcountry Lodge. With comfortably appointed cedar cabins, the Lodge offers a guest experience where all activities and meals are included – even the encounters with wildlife!

FEEL AT HOME IN THE ALASKA WILDERNESS

denali backcountry lodge

www.DenaliLodge.com   1.800.808.8068

 alaska denali travel

Alaska - It's waiting for you.
Toughfare Pass, Denali National Park

CUSTOM VACATIONS TO ALASKA'S MOST SPECTACULAR DESTINATIONS!

Alaska TOUR & TRAVEL

Lodging • Tours • Transportation
1-800-208-0200 | AlaskaTravel.com

MCKINLEY CREEKSIDE CABINS (907)683-2277

Cabin
$99-$199

Address: Milepost 224 Parks Hwy 99755 **Location:** 13 mi s; Milepost 224 on SR 3 (Parks Hwy). **Facility:** 32 cabins. 1 story, exterior corridors. *Bath:* shower only. **Terms:** closed 9/17-5/15, check-in 4 pm, 14 day cancellation notice-fee imposed. **Dining:** Creekside Cafe, see separate listing. **Activities:** hiking trails, horseshoes. **Free Special Amenities: high-speed Internet.**

[SAVE] [icons] / SOME UNITS [icons]

CAMP DENALI 907/683-2290

[fyi] Not evaluated. **Address:** Milepost 89 Denali National Park Rd 99755 **Location:** Milepost 89 Denali National Park Rd. Facilities, services, and décor characterize an economy property.

NORTH FACE LODGE 907/683-2290

[fyi] Not evaluated. **Address:** Milepost 89 Denali National Park Rd 99755 **Location:** Milepost 89 Denali National Park Rd. Facilities, services, and décor characterize an economy property.

WHERE TO EAT

CREEKSIDE CAFE 907/683-2277

American. Casual Dining. $8-$23 **AAA Inspector Notes:** Although the décor and service is simple, the café's food is hearty and delicious. You'll find a wide selection of sandwiches and salads, as well as one of the best breakfasts in the park. At the front of the restaurant is a large dessert case featuring selections such as cookies, squares, cinnamon buns and cakes. **Bar:** beer & wine. **Address:** Milepost 224 Parks Hwy 99755 **Location:** 13 mi s; Milepost 224 on SR 3 (Parks Hwy); in McKinley Creekside Cabins. [B] [L] [D] [icon]

KING SALMON 907/683-2282

American. Casual Dining. $12-$40 **AAA Inspector Notes:** A really charming dining room featuring a custom-made hand-blown glass chandelier of a large salmon that dominates the room—it's a real conversation starter. The lunchtime menu is a more casual fare of burgers, sandwiches and salads, while the dinner menu features Alaskan seafood such as fresh halibut, salmon and wonderful crab cakes. **Bar:** full bar. **Reservations:** suggested, for dinner. **Address:** Milepost 238.5 99755 **Location:** Milepost 238.5 on SR 3 (Parks Hwy); in Denali Princess Wilderness Lodge. [B] [L] [D] CALL[icon] [icon]

MORINO GRILL 907/683-9225

American. Quick Serve. $9-$17 **AAA Inspector Notes:** This grill located adjacent to the Denali Visitor Center is comprised of a full-service coffee shop barista station, a grill area in which your selection is made to order featuring grilled panini and a premade pack-and-go station for your picnic lunch in the park. **Bar:** beer & wine. **Address:** Denali Visitor Center 99755 **Location:** Adjacent to Denali Visitor Center. [B] [L] CALL[icon] [icon]

NENANA VIEW GRILLE 907/683-8258

American. Casual Dining. $15-$32 **AAA Inspector Notes:** Stunning mountain views await those who dine in this open-style restaurant. Choose from a wide variety of carefully selected Alaskan fare, such as wild Alaskan salmon, locally caught halibut and rockfish or try the free-range chicken or aged beef. After dinner, unwind and enjoy the views from the lounge. **Bar:** full bar. **Reservations:** suggested. **Address:** Milepost 238.5 Parks Hwy 99755 **Location:** Milepost 238.5 on SR 3 (Parks Hwy); in McKinley Chalet Resort. [D] CALL[icon]

THE PERCH 907/683-2523

Regional American. Casual Dining. $11-$30 **AAA Inspector Notes:** Follow the gravel road up the hill and, as the name suggests, The Perch sits nestled on a side of a mountain, offering wonderful views of the Denali mountain range. The aroma of fresh baked bread and other enticing smells from the open kitchen fills the dining room. The Alaskan salmon and locally caught halibut are the specialties of the house, but if you're not into fish try the caribou medallions or beef rib-eye. There's always something wonderful for dessert, so be sure to ask. **Bar:** full bar. **Reservations:** suggested, for dinner. **Address:** Milepost 224 (Parks Hwy) 99755 **Location:** 13 mi s; Milepost 224, on SR 3 (Parks Hwy), follow signs up hill. [B] [D] [icon]

DENALI STATE PARK

MT. MCKINLEY PRINCESS WILDERNESS LODGE (907)733-2900

Resort Hotel $79-$199 **Address:** Milepost 133.1 99683 **Location:** SR 3 (George Parks Hwy), Milepost 133.1, 1 mi e on Mt. McKinley View Rd. **Facility:** The hotel and some of the guest rooms offer exceptional views of Mt. McKinley when the mountain is not shrouded in clouds. Guest rooms feature a contemporary mountain wilderness motif set in a number of lodges. 460 units. 1-2 stories (no elevator), interior/exterior corridors. **Terms:** closed 9/24-5/14, check-in 3:30 pm, 3 day cancellation notice-fee imposed. **Dining:** 3 restaurants. **Activities:** whirlpools, recreation programs, hiking trails, limited exercise equipment. **Guest Services:** coin laundry, area transportation (fee)-Talkeetna. [icons] CALL[icon] [icons]

DOUGLAS

THE ISLAND PUB 907/364-1595

Pizza. Gastropub. $8-$21 **AAA Inspector Notes:** Well worth the trek across the bridge for gourmet pizza, salads and sandwiches. The pub's menu features fresh ingredients and house-made pizza dough and focaccia bread. **Bar:** full bar. **Address:** 1102 2nd St 99824 **Location:** Jct E St. **Parking:** on-site and street. [L] [D] CALL[icon]

EAGLE (D-8) pop. 86

Eagle was settled in 1897 by 28 miners who named the town after the bald eagles that nested on the nearby bluff. In 1899, the Army established Fort Egbert and within several years, some 37 military buildings were constructed. Founded along the Yukon River near the Canadian border, Eagle is the only planned town of the gold rush.

Eagle Historical Society: P.O. Box 23, Eagle, AK 99738. **Phone:** (907) 547-2325.

EAGLE MUSEUMS are all within 1 sq. mi. of town. Tours depart from the courthouse at First and Berry sts. Visitors can join a walking tour that includes six restored buildings, including Judge James Wickersham's original courthouse, the Army Mule Barn, Redman Lodge, Customs House, St. Paul's Log Church and the Waterwagon Shed. Each building contains memorabilia portraying the small town's history. **Time:** Allow 2 hours minimum. **Hours:** Tours depart Mon.-Sat. at 9 and 1, Sun. at 9 and 2:30, Memorial Day-Labor Day. Phone ahead to confirm schedule. **Cost:** $7; free (ages 0-11). **Phone:** (907) 547-2325.

EAGLE RIVER (C-11)
• Restaurants p. 630

CHUGACH STATE PARK is e. on Glenn Hwy. Wildlife populations flourish within the park's 700 square miles of mountains, rivers, lakes and glaciers, providing many opportunities for viewing moose and beavers as well as the occasional bear or wolf. Major areas are Eklutna Lake, Eagle River, Anchorage Hillside and Turnagain Arm. A number of recreational activities are available. The park's headquarters is in the historic Potter Section House, at Milepost 115 of the Seward Highway. *See Recreation Areas Chart.*

Hours: Headquarters open Mon.-Fri. 10-4:30. **Cost:** Free. **Parking:** $5 at many trailheads. **Phone:** (907) 345-5014. ▲ ⊠ 🐾 🏕

EAGLE RIVER NATURE CENTER is 12 mi. s.e. on Eagle River Rd. to its end at 32750 Eagle River Rd. The center sponsors interpretive programs including guided nature walks along the four trails it maintains. A hands-on area allows visitors to touch antlers, bones, pelts and other collected items. **Time:** Allow 30 minutes minimum. **Hours:** Wed.-Sun. 10-5, May-Sept.; Fri.-Sun. 10-5, rest of year. Guided nature walks depart Wed.-Sun. at 1:30, June-Aug. Closed major holidays. **Cost:** Free. **Parking:** $5. **Phone:** (907) 694-2108.

HAUTE QUARTER GRILL   907/622-4745
▼▼▼ American. Casual Dining. $15-$29 **AAA Inspector Notes:** This ever-popular restaurant offers upscale cuisine in a relaxed, casual atmosphere-dress up or dress down, everyone is welcome! Husband and wife owners offer amazingly fresh food, all locally grown or caught, including Alaska salmon. What keeps people coming back are the rib-eye steak, roasted duck and baby back ribs which always are on the menu. Those with a sweet tooth should see the dessert menu-the servers give a mouth-watering description of the featured dessert of the day. **Bar:** full bar. **Reservations:** suggested. **Address:** 11221 Old Glenn Hwy 99577 **Location:** Jct Glenn Hwy (SR 1) exit Eagle River, just e. Ⓓ CALL Ⓜ Ⓐ

EKLUTNA (C-11)

About 30 miles north of Anchorage, the village of Eklutna has been home to the Dena'ina Athabascan Indians for more than 350 years. In the 1840s, Russian Orthodox missionaries came to convert the natives, and today the village exhibits traits of both Russian and Dena'ina Athabascan cultures.

The circa 1830 St. Nicholas Russian Orthodox Church was reconstructed in the 1970s. Next to the 1830 structure is a newer church; built in the 1960s, the diminutive white building is topped by a cupola, two small onion-shaped domes and two three-bar crosses. The church still holds religious services and also houses Russian icons.

Adjacent to the church, colorfully painted spirit houses adorn gravesites at the Eklutna Cemetery, which dates to the 1650s and remains in use. Built to hold the souls of the deceased, the shapes and colors of the spirit houses denote their family and status. The churches and cemetery are located at the Eklutna Historical Park, Milepost 26 on Glenn Highway, where you can see religious relics and historic artifacts at the Eklutna Village Heritage House. The park is open Mon.-Sat. 10-5, mid-May through Sept. 30. A small admission fee is charged; phone (907) 688-6026 to confirm schedule.

FAIRBANKS (D-6) pop. 31,535, elev. 432'
• Hotels p. 634 • Restaurants p. 635
• Attractions map p. 632

Fairbanks, near the geographical center of Alaska, is a major visitor center and the northern terminus of the Alaska Railroad. The military, transportation and market nucleus of the Alaskan interior, Fairbanks is a supply point for arctic oil operations and a departure point for airlines statewide.

In 1901 Capt. E.T. Barnette founded a trading post where Fairbanks now stands—a riverboat captain refused to ferry him any farther up the Chena River due to the low water level. Gold was discovered nearby a year later, and the first wave of prospectors flooded up the river. The settlement was named for Charles Warren Fairbanks of Indiana, a U.S. senator who later became vice president to Theodore Roosevelt.

The construction of the Alaska Highway and the influx of the military into Fairbanks heralded a second boom. And in 1968 the discovery of oil in Prudhoe Bay, 390 miles north, triggered a third wave of development.

Fairbanks offers a variety of winter sports and other activities, including aurora viewing, cross-country and downhill skiing, curling, ice hockey and dog mushing. The city's geographical location allows the semiprofessional Alaska Goldpanners baseball team to play its ⚾ Midnight Sun Game at 10:30 p.m. on June 21 without using artificial lighting.

The Robert G. White Large Animal Research Station, 2220 Yankovich Rd., is a 134-acre facility offering .25-mile narrated walking tours of its grounds, allowing visitors to observe caribou, musk oxen and reindeer. Tours are conducted June-Aug. Phone (907) 474-7207 or (907) 474-5724.

Local sightseeing tours to Alaska's arctic zone and other remote places are available from Fairbanks. Using railway cars with skylights, ⟨SAVE⟩ Gray Line of Alaska and Princess Tours offer trips between Anchorage and Fairbanks via Denali National Park and Preserve. Canoes for trips on the Chena River can be rented from several outfitters.

Interesting drives include visits to Chena Hot Springs and the town of Ester. Abandoned gold dredges can be seen outside of Fairbanks along the roads to Chatanika and Ester. The Alaska Public Lands Information Center, at the Morris Thompson Cultural and Visitors Center at 101 Dunkel St., has museum exhibits, shows free movies and offers information about public lands and parks; phone (907) 459-3700 or (866) 869-6887, or TTY (907) 456-0532.

Fairbanks Convention and Visitors Bureau: 101 Dunkel St., Suite 111, Fairbanks, AK 99701. **Phone:** (907) 456-5774 or (800) 327-5774. *(See ad p. 631.)*

Self-guiding tours: Information about a historical walking tour is available from the Fairbanks Visitor Information Center, 101 Dunkel St.

FAIRBANKS COMMUNITY MUSEUM is at 410 Cushman St. at jct. 5th St. Housed in the 1935 city hall building, the museum features Deluge: The Flood of '67, an exhibit which relates the story of the disastrous 1967 flood that caused more than $80 million in damage to the area. Antique winter sports equipment, including a still-operable 1962 snowmobile, is displayed. Exhibits highlight the area's gold

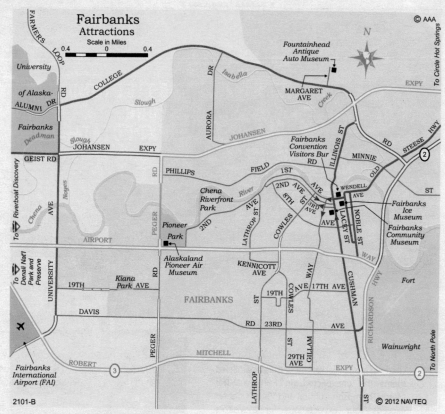

Fairbanks Attractions
Scale in Miles
0.4   0   0.4

2101-B
© 2012 NAVTEQ

rush and dog mushing history and include a replica of a gold panner's home and such mushing equipment as vintage dog sleds.

Time: Allow 30 minutes minimum. **Hours:** Mon.-Fri. 11-7, Sun. 11-3, May-Sept.; Mon.-Fri. 11-3, rest of year. Phone ahead to confirm schedule. **Cost:** Donations. **Phone:** (907) 457-3669.

FAIRBANKS ICE MUSEUM, jct. 2nd Ave. and Lacey St. at 500 2nd Ave., showcases life-size ice sculptures viewable from either inside their glass-fronted display cases, which are kept at a frosty 20 degrees Fahrenheit, or from an indoor theater. The 25-minute multimedia presentation "Freeze Frame" details the harvesting of ice blocks and their evolution into the finished products displayed at Ice Art, an international ice-sculpting competition held each March in Fairbanks. Ice-carving demonstrations are offered during winter, the sculpting season's acme.

Hours: Daily 10-8, May-Sept.; by appointment rest of year. **Cost:** $12; $11 (ages 65+ and military with ID); $6 (ages 6-12). **Phone:** (907) 451-8222.

FOUNTAINHEAD ANTIQUE AUTO MUSEUM is off Johansen Expwy. exit 4 (College Rd.), just w. on College Rd., then .2 mi. n. on Margaret Ave.; the museum is at 212 Wedgewood Dr. on the grounds of the Wedgewood Resort. The museum's collection of more than 70 pristine working condition automobiles, which date from the turn of the 20th century to the late 1930s, includes the only surviving 1920 Argonne; a 1917 Owen-Magnetic M-25 Touring, a gas hybrid; and series of Fords and Packards.

Other exhibits include historical photographs and vintage clothing displays. One-hour guided tours of the vehicles, 55 of which are displayed at any given time, are offered.

Time: Allow 1 hour minimum. **Hours:** Sun.-Fri. 11-10, Sat. 11-6, mid-May to mid-Sept.; Sun. noon-6, rest of year. Phone ahead to confirm schedule. **Cost:** $8; $5 (ages 3-12); $4 (Fountainhead Hotel guests). Guided tour $28. Reservations and a minimum of 2 people are required for guided tours. **Phone:** (907) 450-2100 or (800) 528-4916.

NORTHERN ALASKA TOUR COMPANY departs from the e. ramp of the Fairbanks International Airport. Tours highlight the natural and cultural aspects of Alaska's arctic region. Excursions, which last a full day to multiple days, explore the arctic circle by plane, or bus along the Dalton Highway. Other trips visit the Anaktuvuk Pass, Beaver Village, Brooks Range, Barrow and Nome. Guides offer insight along the route. **Time:** Allow 1 hour minimum. **Hours:** Tours depart daily, mid-May to mid-Sept.;

Mon.-Sat., rest of year. Hours vary by trip. **Cost:** Fare $189-$1,189. Reservations are required. **Phone:** (907) 474-8600 or (800) 474-1986. *(See ad this page.)*

PIONEER PARK is at 2300 Airport Way. The pioneer theme park offers four museums; the Kitty Hensley and Wickersham houses, two restored early 20th-century dwellings; the renovated *S.S. Nenana*, one of the largest wooden sternwheelers ever constructed; Red & Roela's Carousel; and a train that travels and offers unique views of the park. Such activities as miniature golf are provided; bocce courts as well as horseshoe and volleyball areas also are on the premises. A revue show at The Palace Theatre and The Big Stampede show at Pioneer Hall also are offered.

Hours: Park open daily noon-8, Memorial Day-Labor Day. Train trips depart every 15 minutes from noon-7:45. Palace Theater show nightly at 8:15. Big Stampede shows are presented daily at 11:30, 1, 2:30 and 4. **Cost:** Park free. Train ride $2; $1 (ages 4-13). Palace Theater show $19.95; $9 (ages 4-13). Big Stampede show $4; $2 (ages 6-16). A small fee is applicable at several of the attractions and museums. **Phone:** (907) 459-1087. 🍴 🎿

Alaskaland Pioneer Air Museum, in Pioneer Park, is housed in a gold-domed building and offers an aeronautical collection consisting of 14 intact aircraft, including a Stinson SR-5 Junior and a UH-1 Iroquois "Huey" helicopter, as well as a variety of recovered plane wrecks. A large assortment of flight records, newspaper articles, pilot manuscripts and some 500 photographs details the history of solo aviators, early flight and selected airlines. Such items as engines, propellers, model aircraft and memorabilia also are displayed.

Tours: Guided tours are available. **Time:** Allow 1 hour minimum. **Hours:** Daily noon-8, mid-June to mid-Sept. **Cost:** $3; free (ages 0-12); $7 (family of four). **Phone:** (907) 451-0037.

RIVERBOAT DISCOVERY, departing from a pier on Discovery Rd. off Airport Way, provides 3.5-hour trips on the Chena and Tanana rivers aboard the stern-wheeler *Discovery III*. Guides discuss area wildlife, history, anthropology, geology and customs. Views vary from wilderness to elegant houses, and the trip includes a guided walking tour of the Chena Indian village. **Hours:** Trips depart daily at 9 and 2, mid-May to mid-Sept. Phone ahead to confirm schedule. **Cost:** Fare $54.95; $37.95 (ages 3-12). Reservations are required. **Phone:** (907) 479-6673 or (866) 479-6673.

TRANS ARCTIC CIRCLE TREKS AND GLACIER BLUE TOURS is at 3820 University Ave. This tour company offers a variety of guided excursions including day trips to the Arctic Circle and multi-day trips to the Arctic Ocean, Brooks Range, Prudhoe Bay and Point Barrow. Visitors on the 1-day tour can enjoy mountain scenery, a walk through alpine tundra and a hands-on Trans-Alaska Pipeline demonstration. Add-on land and air excursions are available.

Hours: One-day tour departs daily June-Aug.; departs 3-5 days per week in May and Sept. Other tours depart throughout the year. Phone ahead to confirm schedule. **Cost:** Fare for 1-day tour $189. Rates vary according to tour; phone ahead. Reservations are required. **Phone:** (907) 479-5451 or (800) 336-8735.

UNIVERSITY OF ALASKA MUSEUM OF THE NORTH, on the West Ridge of the University of Alaska campus, contains natural and cultural history

▼ *See AAA listing p. 632* ▼

exhibits. The Rose Berry Alaska Art Gallery is dedicated to Alaskan art. Also on display are an extensive gold collection and a steppe bison killed by a lion 36,000 years ago and preserved in the permafrost. "Dynamic Aurora," which explains the northern lights, and "Winter," which documents Alaska's longest season, are 50-minute multimedia presentations offered during summer months.

Time: Allow 30 minutes minimum. **Hours:** Daily 9-7, May 15-Sept. 15; Mon.-Sat. 9-5, rest of year. "Dynamic Aurora" daily at 10, 12:15, 1:45, 3:15 and 5:30. "Winter" daily at 11:30, 2:30 and 4:45, in summer. Closed Jan. 1, Thanksgiving and Christmas. **Cost:** $10; $9 (ages 60+); $5 (ages 7-17). Multimedia shows $5. **Phone:** (907) 474-7505.

Student-guided Walking Tours of the University of Alaska Fairbanks depart from Signers' Hall. Tours of the campus last 1.5 to 2 hours. Comfortable shoes are recommended. Other activities include the Arctic Region Supercomputing tour; the International Arctic Research Center tour; the Geophysical Institute tour; and the Georgeson Botanical Garden tour. **Hours:** Mon.-Fri. at 10, June-Aug. Closed for a few days around the July 4 holiday. **Cost:** Free. Reservations are required. **Phone:** (907) 474-7500 for campus tours, or (800) 478-1823 for all other tours.

A BED AND BREAKFAST INN ON MINNIE STREET
(907)456-1802

Bed & Breakfast $99-$239 **Address:** 345 Minnie St 99701 **Location:** Just n of downtown, follow Cushman St over bridge to Illinois St, 0.5 mi n, then just e. Located in a residential area. **Facility:** 12 units, some kitchens. 2 stories (no elevator), interior/exterior corridors. **Parking:** winter plug-ins. **Terms:** check-in 4 pm, 14 day cancellation notice-fee imposed. **Guest Services:** coin laundry.

ALL SEASONS INN
(907)451-6649

Bed & Breakfast $99-$199 **Address:** 763 7th Ave 99701 **Location:** Just w of Barnette St; downtown. Located in a residential area. **Facility:** 8 units. 2 stories (no elevator), interior corridors. **Parking:** winter plug-ins. **Terms:** 21 day cancellation notice-fee imposed. **Guest Services:** coin laundry.

A TASTE OF ALASKA LODGE
(907)488-7855

Bed & Breakfast $160-$245 **Address:** 551 Eberhardt Rd 99712 **Location:** Jct US 2 (Steese Hwy) and Johansen Expwy, 2.9 mi ne, 5 mi e on Chena Hot Springs Rd, then 0.5 mi s, follow signs. Located in a quiet secluded area. **Facility:** 10 units, some cottages. 2 stories (no elevator), interior/exterior corridors. **Parking:** winter plug-ins. **Terms:** 60 day cancellation notice-fee imposed.

BEST WESTERN PLUS CHENA RIVER LODGE
(907)328-3500

Hotel
$86-$240

AAA Benefit: Members save up to 20%, plus 10% bonus points with Best Western Rewards®.

Address: 1255 Tvsa Way 99709 **Location:** Jct Airport and Sportsman ways, just w on Boat St. **Facility:** 67 units. 3 stories, interior corridors. **Parking:** winter plug-ins. **Terms:** check-in 4 pm, cancellation fee imposed. **Amenities:** high-speed Internet. **Activities:** exercise room. **Guest Services:** coin laundry, area transportation-train station. **Free Special Amenities:** expanded continental breakfast and local telephone calls.

BRIDGEWATER HOTEL
(907)452-6661

Hotel $125-$145 **Address:** 723 1st Ave 99701 **Location:** Just w of Cushman St; downtown. **Facility:** 93 units. 5 stories, interior corridors. **Terms:** closed 9/16-5/14, check-in 4 pm, cancellation fee imposed. **Guest Services:** valet and coin laundry, area transportation-train station.

FAIRBANKS HAMPTON INN & SUITES
(907)451-1502

Hotel $99-$275 **Address:** 433 Harold Bentley Ave 99701 **Location:** Jct SR 2 (Steese Hwy) and Johansen Expwy, then just s at Hunter St. **Facility:** 101 units. 4 stories, interior corridors. **Parking:** winter plug-ins. **Terms:** 1-7 night minimum stay, cancellation fee imposed. **Amenities:** high-speed Internet. **Pool(s):** heated indoor. **Activities:** whirlpool, exercise room. **Guest Services:** valet and coin laundry, area transportation-train station.

AAA Benefit: Members save up to 10%!

FAIRBANKS PRINCESS RIVERSIDE LODGE
(907)455-4477

Hotel $89-$199 **Address:** 4477 Pikes Landing Rd 99709 **Location:** Jct Airport Way and Pikes Landing Rd, just nw. **Facility:** 325 units. 3 stories, interior corridors. **Parking:** winter plug-ins. **Terms:** cancellation fee imposed. **Dining:** 2 restaurants. **Activities:** steamrooms, horseshoes, exercise room. **Guest Services:** coin laundry, area transportation-train station.

HOLIDAY INN EXPRESS
(907)328-1100

Hotel $89-$289 **Address:** 400 Merhar Ave 99701 **Location:** Jct SR 2 (Steese Hwy) and Johansen Expwy, 0.6 mi w, then just s at Hunter St. Across from shopping mall. **Facility:** 114 units. 4 stories, interior corridors. **Parking:** winter plug-ins. **Terms:** cancellation fee imposed. **Amenities:** high-speed Internet. **Pool(s):** heated indoor. **Activities:** whirlpool, exercise room. **Guest Services:** valet and coin laundry.

PIKE'S WATERFRONT LODGE
(907)456-4500

Hotel
$89-$450

Address: 1850 Hoselton Dr 99709 **Location:** Jct Airport Way and Hoselton Dr. **Facility:** 208 units, some cabins. 1-3 stories, interior/exterior corridors. **Parking:** winter plug-ins. **Terms:** cancellation fee imposed. **Dining:** Pike's Landing Restaurant, see separate listing. **Activities:** sauna, steamroom, putting green, exercise room. **Fee:** miniature golf. **Guest Services:** valet and coin laundry, area transportation-train station & riverboat. **Free Special Amenities:** local telephone calls and local transportation.

REGENCY FAIRBANKS HOTEL
(907)459-2700

Hotel $72-$290 **Address:** 95 10th Ave 99701 **Location:** Just w of SR 2 (Steese Hwy). **Facility:** 128 kitchen units, some two bedrooms. 4 stories, interior corridors. **Parking:** winter plug-ins. **Activities:** exercise room. **Guest Services:** valet and coin laundry, area transportation-train station.

RIVER'S EDGE RESORT (907)474-0286

Cottage
$89-$215

Address: 4200 Boat St 99709 **Location:** Airport Way, just n on Sportsman Way, then 0.5 mi w. **Facility:** 94 cottages. 1-2 stories (no elevator), interior/exterior corridors. **Terms:** closed 9/16-5/14, cancellation fee imposed. **Dining:** Chena's Alaskan Grill, see separate listing. **Guest Services:** valet and coin laundry, area transportation-train station. **Free Special Amenities:** high-speed Internet and airport transportation.

Private bath, 2 queen beds, TV, phone, air conditioning, and private patio. Restaurant on site.

SOPHIE STATION HOTEL (907)479-3650

Extended Stay Hotel $120-$235 **Address:** 1717 University Ave S 99709 **Location:** Airport Way, just s. **Facility:** 148 kitchen units. 3 stories, interior corridors. **Parking:** winter plug-ins. **Terms:** check-in 4 pm, cancellation fee imposed. **Amenities:** Some: high-speed Internet. **Activities:** exercise room. **Guest Services:** valet and coin laundry, area transportation-train station.

SPRINGHILL SUITES BY MARRIOTT (907)451-6552

Hotel $99-$199 **Address:** 575 1st Ave 99701 **Location:** Between Cushman and Lacey sts. Across from visitors center. **Facility:** 140 units. 6 stories, interior corridors. **Parking:** winter plug-ins. **Amenities:** high-speed Internet. **Dining:** Lavelle's Bistro, see separate listing. **Pool(s):** heated indoor. **Activities:** whirlpool, exercise room. **Guest Services:** valet and coin laundry, area transportation-train station.

AAA Benefit:
AAA hotel discounts of 5% or more.

WEDGEWOOD RESORT (907)452-1442

Condominium $70-$199 **Address:** 212 Wedgewood Dr 99701 **Location:** Johansen Expwy, 1 mi w on College Rd to Margaret Dr, then just n. **Facility:** On the fringes of a bird sanctuary, this sprawling complex has a variety of rooms ranging from hotel-type standard rooms to condos with full kitchens and separate bedrooms. A must-see is the antique car museum. 463 condominiums. 3 stories (no elevator), interior/exterior corridors. **Parking:** winter plug-ins. **Terms:** check-in 4 pm, cancellation fee imposed. **Guest Services:** valet and coin laundry, area transportation-train station.

WESTMARK FAIRBANKS HOTEL & CONFERENCE CENTER (907)456-7722

Hotel $79-$239 **Address:** 813 Noble St 99701 **Location:** Just n of Airport Way at 10th Ave; just w of SR 2; downtown. **Facility:** 400 units. 4-8 stories, interior corridors. **Parking:** winter plug-ins. **Terms:** cancellation fee imposed. **Activities:** exercise room. **Guest Services:** valet and coin laundry.

Save on theme park tickets
at AAA.com/discounts

WHERE TO EAT

ALASKA COFFEE ROASTING CO 907/457-5282

Coffee/Tea Desserts. Quick Serve. $2-$10 **AAA Inspector Notes:** Known for its huge selection of coffee roasted on the premises this busy coffeehouse also serves a variety of light lunches. You can enjoy vegetable empanadas, wraps and pizzas, and there is a large dessert case to tempt your sweet tooth. You order at the counter and can either get your food to go or linger in the café at one of their many small tables. **Address:** 4001 Geist Rd, Suite 2 99709 **Location:** Just w of University Ave; in West Valley Plaza.

ALASKA SALMON BAKE 907/452-7274

Seafood. Family Dining. $33 **AAA Inspector Notes:** Located in Pioneer Park, this traditional salmon bake offers all-you-can-eat, carved prime rib, deep-fried halibut, grilled salmon and Bering Sea cod with a simple salad bar. Guests pay for a ticket at the counter, then serve themselves at the salad bar, fish barbecue and dessert cabin. Seats can be had at the outdoor picnic tables or inside under a covered area. Open mid-May to mid-September with discounted children's prices. **Bar:** beer & wine. **Address:** 3175 College Rd, #1 99709 **Location:** Airport Way; in Pioneer Park.

CHENA'S ALASKAN GRILL 907/474-3644

American. Casual Dining. $8-$31 **AAA Inspector Notes:** Antiques and other decorative touches are used in creating décor that suggests early 1900s Alaska. The menu emphasizes steaks and seafood, and items are very well prepared and nicely presented. Enjoy the large outdoor deck during the long, warm Alaskan summer season. **Bar:** full bar. **Reservations:** suggested. **Address:** 4200 Boat St 99709 **Location:** Airport Way, just n on Sportsman Way, then 0.5 mi w; in River's Edge Resort.

THE COOKIE JAR RESTAURANT 907/479-8319

American. Casual Dining. $8-$25 **AAA Inspector Notes:** Enjoy leisurely dining in a relaxed and casual atmosphere. The kitchen turns out a variety of selections prepared using fresh ingredients. Much is made on-site and when ordered. Save room for the restaurant's homemade cookies and pastries. **Address:** 1006 Cadillac Ct 99701 **Location:** Jct Johansen Expwy, just n on Danby St.

GAMBARDELLA'S PASTA BELLA 907/457-4992

Italian
Casual Dining
$10-$28

AAA Inspector Notes: Enjoy the fine lasagna and tiramisu at this warm and comfortable restaurant located right downtown. Among other good choices are homemade pizza, bread, cheesecake, espresso and cappuccino. Seating is available on the covered patio during the warm summer season. **Reservations:** suggested. **Address:** 706 2nd Ave 99701 **Location:** Between Barnette and Wickersham sts. **Parking:** on-site and street.

LAVELLE'S BISTRO 907/450-0555

Regional American. Casual Dining. $10-$34 **AAA Inspector Notes:** This busy downtown restaurant features an extensive wine list and a varied menu, from casual entrées like pizza, beer-battered halibut and chips to hearty dinner entrées of king crab legs, salmon, baby back ribs and New York steak. There's always a daily specials sheet, and during the long warm summer evenings the outdoor patio is open. **Bar:** full bar. **Reservations:** suggested. **Address:** 575 1st Ave 99701 **Location:** Between Cushman and Lacey sts; in SpringHill Suites by Marriott.

PIKE'S LANDING RESTAURANT 907/479-6500

American. Casual Dining. $10-$30 **AAA Inspector Notes:** One nice thing about Alaska in the summer is endless nights under the midnight sun, and one of the city's best places to enjoy this is on the patio of the restaurant, which is set along the riverbank. There is a wide selection of pub-style foods like burgers, halibut fish and chips and a great selection of appetizers that go really well with the great selection of locally brewed beers. **Bar:** full bar. **Reservations:** suggested. **Address:** 1850 Hoselton Dr 99709 **Location:** Jct Airport Way and Hoselton Dr; in Pike's Waterfront Lodge.

THE PUMP HOUSE RESTAURANT & SALOON
907/479-8452

American
Casual Dining
$11-$40

AAA Inspector Notes: *Historic.* An authentic former tin pumphouse used in gold-mining operations, the restaurant is listed on the National Register of Historic Places. The decor exudes a warm Victorian mining era charm, and a deck affords a great view of the Chena River. Fresh oysters feature on the menu as well as a variety of Alaskan seafood, steaks and reindeer. **Bar:** full bar. **Reservations:** suggested. **Address:** 796 Chena Pump Rd 99708 **Location:** Jct Parks Hwy and Geist Rd, just e to Chena Pump Rd, then 1.3 mi s. *Menu on AAA.com* L D CALL M

THAI HOUSE RESTAURANT
907/452-6123

Thai. Casual Dining. $9-$20 **AAA Inspector Notes:** This cozy, unassuming downtown spot is very popular with locals. Yellow curry powder, onion, egg, fresh ginger, chili and garlic are a few of the ingredients that bring the cuisine to life. Service is friendly. **Bar:** beer & wine. **Address:** 412 5th Ave 99701 **Location:** Between Lacey and Noble sts; downtown. **Parking:** street only.

L D CALL M

THE TURTLE CLUB
907/457-3883

American. Casual Dining. $21-$37 **AAA Inspector Notes:** Located about 15 minutes outside Fairbanks, this popular restaurant delivers bang for the buck with healthy portions. Menu selections are limited, but diners will find quality products with such specialties as prime rib and seafood. All dinners include a salad bar. Throughout the restaurant, curio cabinets are filled with turtle knick-knacks. The last reservation is taken for 9 pm. **Bar:** full bar. **Reservations:** required. **Address:** 2098 Old Steese Hwy 99712 **Location:** 10 mi n on SR 2 (Steese Hwy), 0.6 mi w on SR 6 (Old Steese Hwy).

D CALL M

WOLF RUN RESTAURANT
907/458-0636

American. Casual Dining. $9-$28 **AAA Inspector Notes:** Known for its decadent desserts, Wolf Run also features a good selection of homemade soups, sandwiches and salads. Dinner entrees include such classics as beef Wellington or chicken Kiev. Originally designed as a private home, the restaurant maintains a coziness with its simple decor. A very popular spot with the locals, this is a great place to sit and linger over a cup of coffee and dessert. **Bar:** beer & wine. **Reservations:** suggested, for dinner. **Address:** 3360 Wolf Run 99709 **Location:** Jct Johansen Expwy and University Ave.

L D CALL M

FORT YUKON (C-7) pop. 583

Just 8 miles north of the Arctic Circle at a point where the Yukon River is almost 3 miles wide, the Athabascan Indian village of Fort Yukon was established as a trading post by the Hudson's Bay Co. in 1847. The village was an important port during the gold rush days, and the post office has remained popular for those who wish to mail from above the Arctic Circle.

Fort Yukon is reached by daily air service from Fairbanks; flight time is approximately 1 hour. Visitors travel here for spectacular viewings of the northern lights and may also see fish wheels in operation and purchase craftwork and fine furs. Temperatures have ranged as high as 100 degrees Fahrenheit in the summer and as low as minus 78 degrees Fahrenheit in winter.

Keep seasonal vehicles travel-ready
with a AAA/CAA Battery Tender®

GATES OF THE ARCTIC NATIONAL PARK AND PRESERVE (B-5)

Elevations in the park and preserve range from 300 ft. along the Kobuk River to 8,510 ft. at Mount Igikpak. Refer to AAA maps for additional elevation information.

Lying north of the Arctic Circle, Gates of the Arctic National Park and Preserve's 8.5 million acres features a raw, austere landscape of sparse vegetation and jagged spires. The rocky spine of the Brooks Range forms the park's backbone, and a boreal forest, or taiga, of spruce, birch and poplar meets the almost treeless tundra that rolls uninterrupted to the Arctic Ocean.

Despite being four times the size of Yellowstone National Park, Gates of the Arctic is a meager larder for the caribou, moose, wolves and bears that roam the park in search of food. Fortunately much of their arctic range is protected, as Gates of the Arctic is joined on either side by Noatak National Preserve and nearby Arctic National Wildlife Refuge.

It was a forester on leave, Bob Marshall, who, in exploring this uncharted region in the late 1930s, christened this land Gates of the Arctic. The term both describes and evokes the grandeur of this wilderness—the soaring immensity of sky and mountains, the burst of wildflowers in summer and the cyclical abundance of wildlife.

But as Marshall remarked, the greatest pleasure is its undeveloped and wild character, which gives the visitor the sense of being the first to visit the tundra foothills or one of the park's nameless peaks. Today a good way to enjoy the park is to follow Marshall's example and hike the park's rugged terrain, which offers challenging backpacking. A popular alternative is to canoe or raft the network of rivers and lakes.

Most visitors use various air charter services from Fairbanks and Bettles Field to reach the park's interior. The Dalton Highway skirts the park's eastern edge and is the only road that approaches the park. Because of Gates of the Arctic's fragile ecology, there are no park facilities, trails or campgrounds within the park. For trip planning assistance and a list of outfitters, guides and air taxi operators, write Gates of the Arctic National Park and Preserve, P.O. Box 30, Bettles, AK 99726; phone (907) 692-5494. *See Recreation Areas Chart.*

GIRDWOOD (C-11) elev. 23'

Initially called Glacier City, Girdwood was established at the turn of the 20th century as a gold mining town. The community prospered until mine closures in the 1930s reduced it to a virtual ghost town. Misfortune struck again when the 1964 Good Friday earthquake caused massive destruction along the coast, forcing residents to move the town 2.5 miles inland to its present location. Today Girdwood thrives as a year-round recreation destination.

Girdwood is on Turnagain Arm, a fjord carved by glaciers and known for its dramatic bore tides, which can be 6 feet high and travel at speeds of up to 15 miles an hour. The town also is located at the base of 3,939-foot Mount Alyeska; a 60-passenger tramway ascends to the 2,300-foot level and offers a panorama of the valley and Turnagain Arm.

RECREATIONAL ACTIVITIES

Skiing

- **Alyeska Resort and Ski Area** is on SR 1 (Seward Hwy.). Other activities are offered. **Hours:** Mid-Nov. to mid-Apr., weather permitting. **Phone:** (907) 754-2111.

THE HOTEL ALYESKA   (907)754-1111

Resort Hotel
$149-$500

Address: 1000 Arlberg Ave 99587 **Location:** SR 1 (Seward Hwy), 3 mi n on Alyeska Blvd, then 1 mi e. Located in a quiet area. **Facility:** A truly stunning mountain setting, as the hotel sits at the base of a large mountain surrounded by seven glaciers. It's an ideal spot for winter skiing or summer mountain hiking. 304 units. 8 stories, interior corridors. **Parking:** on-site and valet. **Terms:** check-in 4 pm, cancellation fee imposed, resort fee. **Amenities:** video games (fee), high-speed Internet, safes. **Dining:** 5 restaurants, also, Sakura Asian Bistro, Seven Glaciers Restaurant, see separate listings. **Pool(s):** heated indoor. **Activities:** sauna, whirlpool, cross country skiing, ice skating, rental bicycles, hiking trails, game room, exercise room, spa. **Fee:** downhill skiing, snowmobiling. **Guest Services:** valet laundry, area transportation-within city. *(See ad p. 617.)*

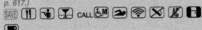

DOUBLE MUSKY INN   907/783-2822

Regional Cajun. Casual Dining. $22-$40 **AAA Inspector Notes:** Guests are sure to enjoy the twist on New Orleans dishes prepared with fresh Alaskan seafood. Many savory delights-such as crab meat-stuffed halibut served with Creole burre blanc or shrimp etouffee-are among locals' favorites. A unique decor comprises Mardi Gras beads and masks surrounding locally made, framed stained-glass create a festive atmosphere. This is a very popular spot and reservations are not accepted, so patrons should be prepared for a wait. **Bar:** full bar. **Address:** Milepost 0.3 (Crow Creek Rd) 99587 **Location:** 1.9 mi n on Alyeska Blvd from SR 1 (Seward Hwy), 0.3 mi w. D CALL M

SAKURA ASIAN BISTRO   907/754-1111

Asian
Sushi
Casual Dining
$12-$35

AAA Inspector Notes: The restaurant makes the most of its cozy space with seating at the sushi bar or family-style at long granite tables. The temptations are endless and include fresh white king salmon, black cod, eel, octopus and king crab presented as sushi, sashimi, nigiri or maki. Bento box meals also are available. And for those who may want their fish cooked, the chef expertly grills your choice for a mouthwatering meal. **Bar:** full bar. **Address:** 1000 Arlberg Ave 99587 **Location:** SR 1 (Seward Hwy), 3 mi n on Alyeska Blvd, then 1 mi e; in The Hotel Alyeska. **Parking:** on-site and valet. D CALL M

SEVEN GLACIERS RESTAURANT   907-754-2237

Regional
American
Fine Dining
$28-$74

AAA Inspector Notes: The unusual mountaintop location is accessible only by an aerial tram from the hotel. The menu centers on creative Alaskan and West Coast preparations of seafood, beef and more exotic game. The wow factor begins the moment the elevator doors open to the Northern Lights display on the reception desk and continues while you dine surrounded by the spectacular panoramic view of the Seven Glaciers. **Bar:** full bar. **Reservations:** suggested. **Address:** 1000 Arlberg Ave 99587 **Location:** SR 1 (Seward Hwy), 3 mi n on Alyeska Blvd, then 1 mi e; in The Hotel Alyeska. **Parking:** on-site and valet. *(See ad p. 617.)* D CALL M

GLACIER BAY NATIONAL PARK AND PRESERVE (G-9)

Elevations in the park and preserve range from sea level at Glacier Bay to 15,320 ft. at Mount Fairweather. Refer to AAA maps for additional elevation information.

Stretching northward from Cross Sound to the Canadian border, Glacier Bay National Park is one of the most scenic spots in Alaska. In this 3,283,168-acre park, blue-white glaciers flow from the snow-clad peaks of the Fairweather Range to fiordlike inlets.

The park features 15,320-foot Mount Fairweather and Glacier Bay. The bay, about 65 miles long and 2.5 to 10 miles wide, was filled with ice 5,000 feet thick as recently as 200 years ago. The park contains some of the world's most impressive tidewater glaciers. Icebergs that crack off, or calve, from the nearly vertical ice cliffs dot the waters of the upper bay. Boaters are likely to encounter numerous harbor seals and an occasional whale.

This spectacular region is accessible only by plane, boat or cruise ship. Alaska Airlines offers flights from Juneau daily June through early September. A 10-mile road connects the park headquarters with the small community of Gustavus, where charter vessels and air and boat service to Juneau are available.

An 8-hour boat tour of the bay departs from Glacier Bay Lodge daily, late May-early Sept. (weather permitting); phone (888) 229-8687.

Due to concern for the endangered humpback whale, permits are required from June through August for private vessels to enter Glacier Bay. An Alaska fishing license is required for fishing. Boaters should contact the National Park Service for current regulations; phone (907) 697-2627. For further information about the park contact the Superintendent, Glacier Bay National Park and Preserve, P.O. Box 140, Gustavus, AK 99826; phone (907) 697-2230. *See Recreation Areas Chart.*

Get more from your membership

with an upgrade to Plus or Premier

GLENNALLEN pop. 483

LAKE LOUISE LODGE　　　　　　　(907)822-3311
▼ **Motel** $95-$150 **Address:** Mile 16.1 Lake Louise Rd 99588 **Location:** Jct US 4 and 1, 31 mi w, 15.5 mi n, then 0.8 mi on gravel road. **Facility:** 7 units. 2 stories (no elevator), interior/exterior corridors. **Parking:** winter plug-ins. **Terms:** check-in 4 pm, 14 day cancellation notice-fee imposed. **Activities:** rental boats, rental canoes, boat dock, fishing.

[icons]

GUSTAVUS pop. 442

ANNIE MAE LODGE　　　　　　　(907)697-2346
▼ ▼ **Country Inn** $135-$230 **Address:** 2 Grandpa's Farm Rd 99826 **Location:** From airport, 3 mi w to Good River Rd, 0.5 mi to Grandpa's Farm Rd. Located in a quiet area. **Facility:** 11 units. 2 stories (no elevator), interior/exterior corridors. *Bath:* some shared. **Terms:** 30 day cancellation notice-fee imposed. **Activities:** fishing, bicycles, hiking trails. **Guest Services:** valet laundry, area transportation.

[icons]

GLACIER BAY LODGE　　　　　　907/697-4000
▼ ▼ **Motel.** Rates not provided. **Address:** 179 Bartlett Cove 99826 **Location:** 9 mi w of airport. **Facility:** 48 units. 2 stories (no elevator), exterior corridors. **Dining:** Fairweather Dining Room, see separate listing. **Activities:** hiking trails. **Guest Services:** coin laundry, area transportation.

[icons]

GLACIER BAY'S BEAR TRACK INN　　　(907)697-3017
▼ ▼ ▼ **Country Inn** $730 **Address:** 255 Rink Creek Rd 99826 **Location:** 7 mi e of airport; at end of Rink Creek Rd. Located in a quiet area. **Facility:** A true log cabin nestled in the wilderness makes staying here a true Alaskan adventure. Guests enjoy lounging in the main room, with a huge stone fireplace, and dining in the large dining hall. 14 units. 2 stories (no elevator), interior corridors. **Terms:** closed 9/6-5/24, 90 day cancellation notice-fee imposed. **Amenities:** high-speed Internet. **Guest Services:** valet laundry, area transportation.

[icons]

WHERE TO EAT

FAIRWEATHER DINING ROOM　　　　907/697-4000
▼ ▼ American. Casual Dining. $10-$30 **AAA Inspector Notes:** This hotel dining room offers both a wonderful view of the inlet and creatively prepared, locally caught seafood, as well as a variety of standards ranging from sandwiches to steaks. **Bar:** full bar. **Address:** 179 Bartlett Cove 99826 **Location:** 9 mi w of airport; in Glacier Bay Lodge. [B] [L] [D] [icons]

HAINES (G-10) pop. 1,713, elev. 66'

Haines lies in a spectacular setting on the Chilkat Peninsula near the northern end of Lynn Canal between the waters of the Inside Passage and the Chilkat River. The Alaska Marine Highway links Haines with Prince Rupert, British Columbia, and Bellingham, Wash., and enables visitors to connect with the Alaska Highway at Haines Junction, Milepost 1016, via SRs 7 and 4. For information about the Alaska Marine Highway phone (907) 465-3941 or (800) 642-0066.

The 40-acre Kroschel Wildlife Center, 27 miles north on scenic Haines Highway, is home to reindeer, wolverines, bears, falcons and other native species. Reservations are required for tours; phone (907) 767-5464.

Nearby, from late October through February the 48,000-acre Chilkat Bald Eagle Preserve, between Mileposts 9 and 31 on Haines Highway, harbors one of the largest congregations of bald eagles in the world. More than 3,500 of the birds gather to feed on the salmon in the Chilkat River; sometimes as many as 30 eagles roost in a tree during this time. Use roadside pull-offs for viewing; stopping on the road is prohibited. Tour information is available at Haines Visitor Center.

Other interesting drives near Haines include Lutak Road, leading to Chilkoot Lake, and Mud Bay Road, which passes Pyramid Harbor and an old cannery with its salmon boats before approaching Chilkat State Park *(see Recreation Chart).* Davidson and Rainbow glaciers also are visible from this route.

Buildings that once comprised Fort William H. Seward, the site of the first permanent Army post in Alaska, have been restored and contain several inns, private residences and galleries. A historic area at the south end of Haines Highway, the fort also contains a replica of a tribal house. The old hospital houses carvers who use traditional Tlingit Indian methods. Phone (907) 766-2234 for fort information.

Fjord Express, (800) 320-0146, and Haines-Skagway Fast Ferry, (907) 766-2100 or (888) 766-2103, provide efficient transportation between Haines, Skagway and Juneau.

Haines Convention & Visitors Bureau: 122 Second Ave., P.O. Box 530, Haines, AK 99827. **Phone:** (907) 766-2234 or (800) 458-3579.

Self-guiding tours: Brochures featuring walking tours of Haines and Fort William H. Seward are available from Haines Visitor Center and Hotel Halsingland.

CHILKAT BALD EAGLE PRESERVE FLOAT TRIPS, on Sawmill Rd., pass through the Bald Eagle Preserve on the Chilkat River and offer views of the Chilkat Mountains and bald eagles in their natural habitat. Transportation to and from the river is provided. Bring warm clothes, binoculars, camera, sunglasses and rain gear. Inquire about weather policies. **Hours:** The 4- to 4.5-hour float trip departs daily, May-Sept. Phone ahead to confirm schedule. **Cost:** Fare $93.90; $65.41 (ages 7-12). Reservations are recommended. **Phone:** (907) 766-2491.

CHILKOOT LAKE TOURS, 1069 Haines Hwy., offers sightseeing and fishing cruises of Chilkoot Lake. Brown bears, bald eagles and spawning salmon often are seen. Inquire about weather policies. **Time:** Allow 3 hours minimum. **Hours:** Tours depart daily, May 1-Sept. 15. Phone ahead to confirm schedule. **Cost:** Fare for sightseeing cruise $90; fishing cruise $115. Reservations are required. **Phone:** (907) 766-2891, or (706) 573-8130 (cellular number).

SHELDON MUSEUM AND CULTURAL CENTER, on Main St. above the boat harbor, allows visitors to experience the art and culture of the Tlingit native people and to learn about the early pioneer history of Haines Mission, the Porcupine gold rush and Fort Seward, a frontier army post. **Time:** Allow 1 hour, 30 minutes minimum. **Hours:** Mon.-Fri. 10-5, Sat.-Sun. 1-4, mid-May to mid-Sept.; Mon.-Sat. 1-4, rest of year. **Cost:** $5; free (ages 0-12). **Phone:** (907) 766-2366.

RECREATIONAL ACTIVITIES
Bicycling

- **Sockeye Cycle Co.,** 24 Portage St., offers rental bikes and guided biking tours. **Hours:** Trips depart daily by appointment. Bike rentals are available Mon.-Sat. 10-5, Apr.-Sept. **Phone:** (907) 766-2869.

CAPTAIN'S CHOICE MOTEL (907)766-3111

Motel
$137-$184

Address: 108 2nd Ave N 99827 **Location:** Jct 2nd Ave and Dalton St. **Facility:** 38 units. 2 stories (no elevator), exterior corridors. **Guest Services:** coin laundry, area transportation-ferry. **Free Special Amenities:** continental breakfast and airport transportation.

WHERE TO EAT

CHILKAT RESTAURANT & BAKERY 907/766-3653

American
Family Dining
$6-$21

AAA Inspector Notes: A few steps away from downtown, this local favorite offers a variety of well-prepared and hearty dishes and features in-house bakery items. The owners are Thai and have a nice selection of authentic dishes. **Address:** 25 5th Ave 99827 **Location:** Jct 5th Ave and Dalton St. **Parking:** on-site and street.

LIGHTHOUSE RESTAURANT 907/766-2442

American
Casual Dining
$8-$30

AAA Inspector Notes: Overlooking the boat harbor marina, guests can dine in a casual setting and watch the ferry and cruise ships come in during season. Fresh seafood is available in season. The rest of the year diners can enjoy great burgers and sandwiches. **Bar:** full bar. **Address:** 101 N Front St 99827 **Location:** Waterfront; next to marina.

HEALY pop. 1,021
• Restaurants p. 640

DENALI DOME HOME BED & BREAKFAST
(907)683-1239

Bed & Breakfast
$110-$200

Address: 137 Healy Spur Rd 99743 **Location:** Jct SR 3 and Healy Spur Rd, 0.5 mi e. Located in a quiet area. **Facility:** In a scenic area just 10 miles from Denali National Park, this dome-shaped B&B offers comfortable guest rooms along with two spacious common areas. Large viewing windows highlight the spring flowers. 7 units. 3 stories (no elevator), interior/exterior corridors. **Parking:** winter plug-ins. **Terms:** check-in 4 pm, 30 day cancellation notice-fee imposed. **Guest Services:** rental car service. **Free Special Amenities:** full breakfast and high-speed Internet.

DENALI LAKEVIEW INN (907)683-4035

Bed & Breakfast
$79-$209

Address: Mile 1.2 Otto Lake Rd 99743 **Location:** SR 3, Milepost 247, 1.2 mi w. **Facility:** 20 units. 2-3 stories (no elevator), interior/exterior corridors. **Terms:** check-in 4 pm, 14 day cancellation notice-fee imposed. **Guest Services:** coin laundry. **Free Special Amenities:** expanded continental breakfast and use of on-premises laundry facilities.

HEALY HEIGHTS FAMILY CABINS (907)683-2639

Cabin $100-$220 **Address:** Hill Top Rd 99743 **Location:** SR 3, Milepost 247, 0.9 mi w on Otto Lake Rd, then 1.5 mi n, follow signs. **Facility:** 6 cabins. 1 story, exterior corridors. **Terms:** closed 9/21-5/14, check-in 4 pm, 15 day cancellation notice-fee imposed.

WHERE TO EAT

BLACK DIAMOND GRILL   907/683-4653

 American. Casual Dining. $10-$36 **AAA Inspector Notes:** This is a casual restaurant with simple décor and surprisingly good food, including salads, sandwiches, burgers, pastas and dinner entrées of Alaskan halibut and salmon, pork, steak and chicken. There's a really good selection of Alaskan draft beers. The dining room's large bay windows have stunning views of huge snowcapped mountains, which is exactly what you'd expect to see in Alaska. **Bar:** beer & wine. **Address:** 1 Mile Otto Lake Rd 99743 **Location:** SR 3, Milepost 247, 0.8 mi w. B L D CALL M

HOMER (D-10) pop. 5,003, elev. 67'

Homer Pennock landed a party of gold and coal prospectors in the schooner *Excelsior* in 1896 and established Homer. Gold was not found, but an abundance of coal was and the settlement remained.

Healthy fishing and tourism industries support Homer's economy. Kachemak Bay, a 30-mile arm of lower Cook Inlet, provides a usually ice-free deepwater harbor for Homer. A small boat harbor has launching facilities and charter boats. Charter planes are available in town for hunting, fishing, wildlife viewing and sightseeing expeditions. Cross-country skiing is popular in winter. The city is linked by daily air service with Anchorage, and by the Alaska Marine Highway with Seward, Kodiak and Seldovia.

Skyline Drive, accessible from West and East Hill roads, follows the rim of the plateau behind the town and offers access to ski slopes and views of the bay, Homer Spit and the Kenai Mountains. Chartered bush flights afford panoramas of the bay, open coal seams and Harding Icefield to the southeast.

Homer Chamber of Commerce: 201 Sterling Hwy., Homer, AK 99603. **Phone:** (907) 235-7740.

ALASKA ISLANDS & OCEAN VISITOR CENTER is at 95 Sterling Hwy. The center presents an overview of the area through interpretive exhibits about Kachemak Bay; local estuaries; research ships; and the seabird and marine inhabitants of the Alaska Maritime National Wildlife Refuge. Outdoor nature trails link the 60-acre site with Bishop's Beach Park on Kachemak Bay. Naturalist-led tours are offered, and a short movie about the Aleutian Islands is shown.

Time: Allow 2 hours minimum. **Hours:** Daily 9-5, Memorial Day-Labor Day; hours are limited and vary rest of year. Closed major holidays. Phone ahead to confirm schedule. **Cost:** Donations. **Phone:** (907) 235-6961.

PRATT MUSEUM is .5 blks. n. of Pioneer Ave. at 3779 Bartlett St. Highlights at the community museum include a botanical garden; a homestead cabin; a marine gallery; fishing boat models; sea birds and marine mammals; a forest trail; an exhibit detailing the impact of the *Exxon Valdez* oil spill; and native artifacts. Alaskan art from the Kenai Peninsula also is exhibited. Remote cameras provide visitors live images of seabirds and local wildlife.

Time: Allow 1 hour minimum. **Hours:** Daily 10-6, mid-May to mid-Sept.; Tues.-Sun. noon-5, Feb. 1 to mid-May and mid-Sept. through Dec. 31. Closed Thanksgiving and Christmas. **Cost:** $8; $6 (ages 66+); $4 (ages 6-18); $25 (family, two adults and children). **Phone:** (907) 235-8635.

RECREATIONAL ACTIVITIES

Fishing

- **Homer Ocean Charters** is at Cannery Row boardwalk on Homer Spit Rd. **Hours:** Trips depart daily by appointment, May-Sept. **Phone:** (907) 235-6212 or (800) 426-6212.

BEST WESTERN PLUS BIDARKA INN   (907)235-8148

 Hotel $79-$219

AAA Benefit: Members save up to 20%, plus 10% bonus points with Best Western Rewards®.

Address: 575 Sterling Hwy 99603 **Location:** Just n of Pioneer Ave on Sterling Hwy (SR 1). **Facility:** 74 units. 2 stories (no elevator), interior/exterior corridors. **Parking:** winter plug-ins. **Terms:** check-in 4 pm, cancellation fee imposed. **Amenities:** *Some:* high-speed Internet. **Activities:** exercise room. **Guest Services:** coin laundry, area transportation-ferry. **Free Special Amenities:** full breakfast and local telephone calls.

SAVE / SOME UNITS FEE

LANDS END RESORT   (907)235-0400

Hotel $90-$500 **Address:** 4786 Homer Spit Rd 99603 **Location:** Oceanfront. 5 mi se; at end of Homer Spit Rd. Adjacent to ferry terminal. **Facility:** 113 units, some two bedrooms and condominiums. 3 stories, interior/exterior corridors. **Terms:** check-in 4 pm, 3 day cancellation notice. **Activities:** sauna, whirlpool, rental bicycles, limited exercise equipment, spa. *Fee:* fishing, charter fishing.

/ SOME UNITS

PIONEER INN   (907)235-5670

Motel $89-$149 **Address:** 244 W Pioneer Ave 99603 **Location:** Jct Sterling Hwy (SR 1), just e. **Facility:** 7 units, some kitchens. 2 stories (no elevator), exterior corridors. **Terms:** 7 day cancellation notice-fee imposed.

WHERE TO EAT

CAFE CUPS   907/235-8330

American. Casual Dining. $9-$35 **AAA Inspector Notes:** Considered to be one of the best places in town, this eclectic restaurant serves up a variety of homemade goods and is well known for its seafood options. There are only about 15 tables at this funky place, which features a mosaic wall around the door. You can choose from salmon, shrimp and other seafood dishes, or try the feature of the day. The servers are efficient and personable. **Bar:** beer & wine. **Reservations:** suggested. **Address:** 162 W Pioneer Ave 99603 **Location:** Jct Sterling Hwy (SR 1), just w. D

CAPTAIN PATTIE'S FISH HOUSE   907/235-5135

Seafood. Casual Dining. $7-$27 **AAA Inspector Notes:** Those who spent the day fishing and cannot wait to eat their catch can bring it in to this restaurant for preparation and cooking. Alaskan art contributes to the simple decor. The ever-changing menu boasts freshly caught fish dishes, along the lines of halibut, scallops and salmon. Early birds can take advantage of specials from 5 pm to 6 pm. On the famous Homer Spit, this spot is distinctive and casual. **Bar:** beer & wine. **Reservations:** suggested. **Address:** 4241 Homer Spit Rd 99603 **Location:** 5 mi along Homer Spit Rd. L D

CARIBOU FAMILY RESTAURANT   907/235-5148

♥♥ American. Family Dining. $7-$20 AAA Inspector Notes: Hearty breakfasts are served all day at this casual eatery, along with other comfort food fare like chili cheeseburgers and patty melts. Seafood, steaks and chicken round out the menu. Homemade cakes and pies cause many guests to linger. Address: 672 East End Rd 99603 Location: Jct Sterling Hwy (SR 1), 0.4 mi e on Lake Rd.

[B] [L] [D] [AC]

DON JOSE'S MEXICAN RESTAURANT & CANTINA
907/235-7963

♥♥ Mexican. Casual Dining. $9-$17 AAA Inspector Notes: This colorful cantina has been part of the Homer community since 1982. The menu includes all the traditional Mexican favorites like enchiladas, burritos, fajitas and chimichangas, along with house specialties like carne asada and coconut shrimp. Bar: full bar. Address: 127 W Pioneer Ave 99603 Location: Jct Sterling Hwy (SR 1), just e.

[L] [D] CALL [&M] [AC]

DUNCAN HOUSE DINER   907/235-5344

♥♥ Breakfast Sandwiches. Family Dining. $7-$16 AAA Inspector Notes: Well worth a visit for the hearty home-style fare and cozy atmosphere, this country diner is known for its all-day breakfast that features hearty portions of freshly cooked fare. It's a great way to start the day. In addition to the breakfast options, a light lunch menu is offered from 11 am. Options there include hearty burgers, sandwiches, fresh soups and entrée salads. The decor is delightful, with a true, rustic Alaskan feel and a homelike touch. Address: 125 E Pioneer Ave 99603 Location: Jct Sterling Hwy (SR 1), just e.

[B] [L] [AC]

FAT OLIVES   907/235-8488

♥♥ Pizza Sandwiches. Casual Dining. $8-$24 AAA Inspector Notes: Wood-fired pizza is the specialty of the house at this casual eatery. Huge sandwiches on house-made Tuscan bread and sizable salads are featured at lunch, and the dinner menu expands to include seafood, lamb and beef as well as other tasty options. A lengthy wine list offers more than 30 wines by the glass. There are no reservations so arrive early or plan to wait for a table. Bar: beer & wine. Address: 376 Ohlson Ln 99603 Location: Jct W Pioneer Ave, just s on Sterling Hwy (SR 1). [L] [D] CALL [&M] [AC]

FRESH SOURDOUGH EXPRESS BAKERY & CAFE
907/235-7571

♦♦ Breads/Pastries. Casual Dining. $6-$25 AAA Inspector Notes: A popular spot with the locals, the Sourdough Express is a warm, inviting place serving up locally produced and some organic fare. Whether you're stopping in for a big breakfast, a sandwich for lunch or an evening bite to eat, you might also be tempted by the display case in the bakery, which features a wide array of delicious desserts. In the summer, outdoor patio dining is available, complete with a small play area for the kids. Bar: beer & wine. Address: 1316 Ocean Dr 99603 Location: 3 mi sw on Sterling Hwy (SR 1), on way to Homer Spit Rd. [B] [L] [D] CALL [&M] [AC]

THE HOMESTEAD RESTAURANT   907/235-8723

♥♥♥ Pacific Northwest. Casual Dining. $19-$34 AAA Inspector Notes: A bit hard to find, the restaurant is located 8 miles down East End Road across from Tesoro gas station. Diners enjoy wonderful views of the Homer Spit in this charming restaurant, which centers its menu on innovative preparations of fresh Alaskan seafood, steaks, duck, chicken and more. Bar: full bar. Reservations: suggested. Address: Mile 8.2 East End Rd 99603 Location: Jct Pioneer Ave and Lake St, 8.2 mi e. [D] CALL [&M] [AC]

TWO SISTERS BAKERY   907/235-2280

♥ Breads/Pastries. Quick Serve. $4-$10 AAA Inspector Notes: For healthy, organic baked goods and light lunches, the three sisters at the Two Sisters Bakery have what it takes. Located in a big house on the outskirts of downtown and near several galleries, the eatery offers giant cinnamon buns, scones, quiches, breakfast granola and, of course, a fine selection of fresh breads. Guests have the option to lounge for a few hours, or take their baked goods to go. Either way, service comes with a smile. Bar: beer & wine. Address: 233 E Bunnell Ave 99603 Location: Sterling Hwy (SR 1), just s at Main St, then just e. [B] [L] [AC]

HOPE (C-11) pop. 192, elev. 32'

RECREATIONAL ACTIVITIES
White-water Rafting
- **Chugach Outdoor Center** departs from Milepost 7.5, Hope Hwy. Other activities are offered. **Hours:** Trips depart daily, May-Sept. **Cost:** Reservations are required. **Phone:** (907) 277-7238 or (866) 277-7238.

JUNEAU (G-10) pop. 31,275, elev. 12'
- **Hotels p. 645** • **Restaurants p. 645**
- **Attractions map p. 642**

Juneau, Alaska's capital city, lies along the beautiful Gastineau Channel at the foot of snowcapped mounts Roberts and Juneau. The borough of Juneau covers 3,108 square miles of towering mountains, islands, saltwater bays, forested valleys and residential flatlands. Its road system extends from Thane, 6 miles southeast of downtown, northwest to Echo Cove at Milepost 40.2 on the Glacier Highway. The city is accessible by air or by sea.

When Joe Juneau and Richard Harris discovered gold in 1880, they started the first rush in American Alaska. At one time the Alaska-Juneau and Treadwell mines were producing about 20,000 tons of ore daily. Not until 1944, when the low price of gold and the high cost of extraction rendered it impractical, did mining operations cease.

The Alaska State Capitol offers free 30-minute tours in summer; the immense building lies between 4th and 5th streets and Main and Seward streets. The State Office Building, one block west of the capitol at 333 Willoughby Ave., contains a century-old totem pole and a Kimball Theatre pipe organ equipped with such accessories as a glockenspiel, sleigh bells and bird whistles. Free concerts are held Friday at noon in the eighth-floor atrium. Also on the eighth floor, a terrace affords panoramas of the harbor and the surrounding mountains.

Impromptu, informal tours of one of the oldest churches in southeastern Alaska are generally available Mon.-Fri. 9-5, mid-May to mid-Sept. Built in 1894, St. Nicholas Russian Orthodox Church is at Fifth and Gold streets; inquire at the church gift shop, or phone (907) 523-0986. The Shrine of St. Therese, near Milepost 23 on the Glacier Highway, is a stone chapel on an island connected to shore by a gravel causeway.

There are many ways to tour Juneau. Nearby hiking trails, which vary in length and difficulty, lead to fishing spots, scenic mountain areas, old mine ruins and points near Mendenhall Glacier. Bus tours circle points of interest in Juneau and visit Mendenhall Glacier and the log Chapel-by-the-Lake at Auke Lake. Tours depart from the cruise ship docks during the summer. Visitors also can charter boats for sightseeing or fishing.

A good way to see the ice field is to take a charter flight. Companies that offer flightseeing tours from Juneau are Alaska Fly 'n' Fish Charters, (907) 790-2120; Alaska Seaplane Service, (907)

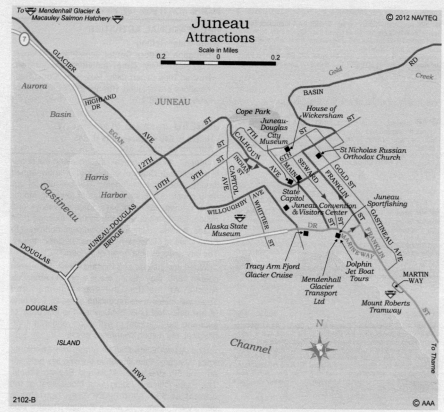

Juneau
Attractions

To Mendenhall Glacier &
Macauley Salmon Hatchery

© 2012 NAVTEQ

Scale in Miles

2102-B

© AAA

789-3331; Ward Air, (907) 789-9150; and Wings of Alaska, (907) 789-0790. Helicopter tours, float trips, gold-panning excursions and several tours of nearby and more distant points of interest are available through [SAVE] Gray Line of Alaska, (907) 586-3773; and Princess Tours, (907) 463-3900.

Salmon bakes are held at Thane Ore House daily in summer. The house is a few miles south of Juneau and free transportation from downtown is available. Admission to the all-you-can-eat feast is $25.95; phone (907) 586-3442.

Juneau Convention and Visitors Bureau: 800 Glacier Ave., Suite 201, Juneau, AK 99801. **Phone:** (907) 586-2201 or (888) 581-2201.

Self-guiding tours: Free walking tour maps of the historical and governmental districts are available at the Juneau Convention and Visitors Bureau.

[GEM] **ALASKA STATE MUSEUM,** w. of Egan Dr. at 395 Whittier St., chronicles the state's history and preserves and exhibits Tlingit and Athabascan Indian, Eskimo and Aleut culture. Wildlife and mining displays, Russian-American historical exhibits and art of Alaska are featured. Highlights include a bald eagle nesting tree.

Guided tours are available in summer. **Time:** Allow 1 hour minimum. **Hours:** Daily 8:30-5:30, mid-May to late Sept.; Tues.-Sat. 10-4, rest of year. Closed Memorial Day, July 4 and Labor Day. **Cost:** Mid-May to mid-Sept. $7; $6 (ages 65+); free (ages 0-18). Rest of year $3; free (ages 0-18 and first Fri. of the month 4:30-7). **Phone:** (907) 465-2901.

DOLPHIN JET BOAT TOURS provides pick-up downtown at the tram parking area. Three-hour tours on a jet boat offer the opportunity to view humpback and killer whales, porpoises, sea lions, seals and eagles. Other tours are available. **Hours:** Tours depart daily at 9, 11, 1, 3 and 5, May-Sept. **Cost:** Fare for departures at 1 and 5 are $110; $90 (ages 2-12). Fare for departures at 9, 11 and 3 are $105; $85 (ages 2-12). **Phone:** (907) 463-3422 or (800) 719-3422.

ERA HELICOPTERS FLIGHTSEEING TOURS depart from the North Douglas Heliport. Narrated, 1-hour tours (with 35 minutes of flight time) offer views of the capital city, abandoned mines and four glaciers in the Juneau Icefield. Highlights include a glacier landing to explore the blue ice. A 95-minute tour (with 35 minutes in the air) visits a dog sled camp near Norris Glacier. **Time:** Allow 2 hours minimum. **Hours:** Daily 8-5, May-Sept. **Cost:** Fare

$286-$499. Flights require a minimum of four passengers. **Phone:** (907) 586-2030 or (800) 843-1947.

FOREST SERVICE INFORMATION CENTER is at 8510 Mendenhall Loop Rd. Trail guides, maps, current conditions and recreation and cabin reservation information about Tongass National Forest and Glacier Bay National Park are available. **Hours:** Mon.-Fri. 8-5. **Cost:** Free. **Phone:** (907) 586-8800.

GLACIER GARDENS RAINFOREST ADVENTURE is at 7600 Glacier Hwy. A motorized shuttle takes passengers up Thunder Mountain through botanical gardens nestled in a lush Alaskan rain forest. Guests travel past streams, ponds, waterfalls and such flora as rhododendrons, Japanese maples and ferns. A scenic overlook at the 580-foot marker offers a spectacular view of the Mendenhall Valley and Chilkat Mountains. **Time:** Allow 1 hour minimum. **Hours:** Daily 9-6, May-Sept. **Cost:** $24.95; $15.95 (ages 6-12). **Phone:** (907) 790-3377.

HOUSE OF WICKERSHAM, 213 Seventh St., was the residence of Judge James Wickersham, noted Alaskan statesman, historian and pioneer judge. Built 1898-99 on "Chicken Ridge," this large Victorian house offers panoramic views of Gastineau Channel. Wherever the judge traveled in Alaska he collected ivory pieces, basketry and carvings, which are on display.

Hours: Sun.-Fri. 10-4, May-Sept. Phone ahead to confirm schedule. **Cost:** Free. **Phone:** (907) 586-9001.

JUNEAU-DOUGLAS CITY MUSEUM is at Fourth and Main sts. Visitors can view exhibits about the area's early gold mining days, Tlingit culture and life in the Juneau-Douglas areas. Special exhibits about the greater Juneau area change annually. A relief map of the city's topography and a video presentation titled "Juneau: City Built on Gold" are other features. Guided 1-hour downtown walking tours or free maps outlining a historic self-guided walking tour are available.

Hours: Mon.-Fri. 9-6, Sat.-Sun. 10-5, May-Sept.; Tues.-Sat. 10-4 and by appointment, rest of year. Guided walking tours depart Tues.-Thurs. at 1:30, mid-May to mid-Sept. Closed July 4, Labor Day and winter holidays. **Cost:** $6; $5 (ages 65+); free (ages 0-12). Guided tour (includes museum admission) $20; $15 (ages 0-12). **Phone:** (907) 586-3572.

LAST CHANCE MINING MUSEUM is just n. on Franklin St., just e. on 6th St., then 2 mi. n.e. following signs to 1001 Basin Rd. The museum is housed in a wood building used during the area's gold mining heydays 1912-1944. Collections feature one of the world's largest air compressors circa 1912, industrial tools, a 3-D map of the ore body and rail cars used to carry workers to the mine and deliver ore to the mill. **Note:** The parking lot and walkways are made of gravel; comfortable walking shoes are recommended. **Time:** Allow 1 hour minimum. **Hours:** Daily 9:30-12:30 and 3:30-6:30, mid-May to mid-Sept. **Cost:** $4; free (ages 0-12). **Phone:** (907) 586-5338.

MACAULAY SALMON HATCHERY is at 2697 Channel Dr. During 10- to 15-minute presentations, tour guides explain hatchery processes, beginning with the imprinting of young salmon to ensure a return at the end of their lifespan and concluding with egg retrieval. In May-June, visitors may observe the juvenile salmon pre-release; from mid-June through October, the returning salmon may be seen in their outdoor holding tanks where they are separated and prepared for egg harvesting. Indoor aquariums contain more than 100 species of southeast Alaska sea life, including anemones, crabs and octopi. Visitors may feel such animals as starfish in touch tanks.

Tours: Guided tours are available. **Time:** Allow 30 minutes minimum. **Hours:** Mon.-Fri. 10-6, Sat.-Sun. 10-5, May-Sept.; by appointment rest of year. **Cost:** $3.25; $1.75 (ages 2-12). **Phone:** (907) 463-4810 or (877) 463-2486.

▼GEM **MENDENHALL GLACIER,** 13 mi. n.w. via SR 7 and Mendenhall Loop Rd., is an impressive river of blue ice, 13 miles long and 1.5 miles wide at its widest point. The glacier is fed by the 1,500-square-mile Juneau Icefield, part of the Tongass National Forest *(see place listing p. 664).*

Trails on either side of the glacial valley afford scenic views. To the east are Mendenhall Lake and Nugget Creek Falls; the west trail ascends above the glacier. Camping and picnic facilities are available at Mendenhall Lake. An easily traversable .5-mile nature trail begins near the visitor center; brochures are available.

The Steep Creek viewing platform near the visitor center parking lot is a good vantage point from which to see spawning sockeye salmon mid-July through mid-September. The salmon run attracts bald eagles and black bears mid-September through November.

Mendenhall Glacier Visitor Center, at the end of Glacial Spur Rd., contains a model depicting glacier dynamics, dioramas and display cases that interpret five evolving ecosystems at the glacier and a naturalistic salmon-filled stream that tumbles over rocks. A film is shown three times every hour during the summer, otherwise by request. Interpretive talks and nature hikes also are offered. **Hours:** Tues.-Sun. 8-7:30, Mon. 11:30-7:30, May-Sept.; Thurs.-Sun. 10-4, rest of year. Closed winter holidays. **Cost:** May-Sept. $3; free (ages 0-15 and rest of year). **Phone:** (907) 789-0097 or (907) 789-6640.

MENDENHALL GLACIER TRANSPORT LTD., departing from the cruise ship dock downtown, provides sightseeing excursions of Juneau by bus. The tour stops at the Chapel by the Lake and Mendenhall Glacier. The company also offers direct round-trip bus transportation from the cruise ship dock to Mendenhall Glacier on its Blue Glacier Express. **Time:** Allow 2 hours, 30 minutes minimum. **Hours:** Tours depart daily at 9:30, 10:30 and 3:30, May-Sept. Blue Glacier Express departs daily every half-hour, 9-6, May-Sept. **Cost:** Tour fare $30. Blue Glacier Express fare $16. **Phone:** (907) 789-5460. *(See ad this page.)*

MOUNT ROBERTS TRAMWAY, 490 S. Franklin St. on the cruise ship dock, offers a 6-minute ride to the 1,800-foot level of Mount Roberts. At the top, visitors can stop at the nature center, see a live bald eagle displayed by the Juneau Raptor Center, take wildlife or nature walks and view the spectacular scenery. "Seeing Daylight," a movie about Alaska's native Tlingit, is presented in the Chilkat Theater. Other tours are available. **Time:** Allow 1 hour, 30 minutes minimum. **Hours:** Tues.-Sun. 8 a.m.-9 p.m., Mon. noon-9, May-Sept. Hours may vary in May and Sept. Phone ahead to confirm schedule. **Cost:** Fare $29; $14.50 (ages 6-12). **Phone:** (907) 463-3412 or (888) 461-8726. 🏧

TAKU LODGE FEAST & FIVE GLACIER SEAPLANE DISCOVERY departs from the wharf near the cruise ship docks. A Wings Airways floatplane takes passengers to a 1923 fishing and hunting lodge in the Taku River Valley for a salmon feast. Aerial views include mountains, Taku Inlet, waterfalls and five glaciers. Walking trails explore the area surrounding the historic lodge, which is across the river from the Hole-in-the-Wall Glacier. **Time:** Allow 3 hours minimum. **Hours:** Trips depart daily, May-Sept. Phone ahead to confirm schedule. **Cost:** Fare $290; $240 (ages 2-11); free (ages 0-1 on lap). Reservations are recommended. **Phone:** (907) 586-6275.

RECREATIONAL ACTIVITIES

Fishing

- **Juneau Sportfishing** offers round-trip transportation from local hotels and ships. Half, full and multiple day tours are available. **Hours:** Trips depart daily. **Phone:** (907) 586-1887.

- **Salmon Guaranteed Charters** is at 4510 Prospect Way. **Hours:** Daily May-Oct. **Phone:** (907) 364-3474.

Skiing

- **Eaglecrest Ski Area** is 12 mi. n.w. off the N. Douglas Hwy. **Hours:** Thurs.-Mon. 9-4, Dec. to mid-April. (also Thurs. 4-9, early Jan. to mid-April). Phone ahead to confirm schedule. **Phone:** (907) 790-2000.

▼ *See AAA listing this page* ▼

ASPEN SUITES HOTELS
907-500-7700

▼▼▼ **Extended Stay Hotel.** Rates not provided. **Address:** 8400 Airport Blvd 99801 **Location:** Just e on Yandukin Dr, just n on Crest St, then just e. **Facility:** 78 kitchen units. 3 stories, interior corridors. **Activities:** exercise room. **Guest Services:** coin laundry.

BIZ 📶 🛢 🖥 🖥

BEST WESTERN COUNTRY LANE INN
(907)789-5005

▼▼▼
Motel
$130-$180

AAA Benefit: Members save up to 20%, plus 10% bonus points with Best Western Rewards®.

Address: 9300 Glacier Hwy 99801 **Location:** Just e off Egan Dr. **Facility:** 55 units, some efficiencies. 2 stories (no elevator), exterior corridors. **Terms:** cancellation fee imposed. **Amenities:** Some: high-speed Internet. **Guest Services:** valet and coin laundry, area transportation-within 10 mi & ferry. **Free Special Amenities: expanded continental breakfast and high-speed Internet.**

SAVE ⊞ 🍴 🛗 BIZ 📶 ✕ 🎬 🛢 🖥 🖥

BEST WESTERN GRANDMA'S FEATHER BED
(907)789-5566

▼▼▼
Country Inn
$140-$180

AAA Benefit: Members save up to 20%, plus 10% bonus points with Best Western Rewards®.

Address: 2358 Mendenhall Loop Rd 99801 **Location:** Just e off Egan Dr. **Facility:** 14 units. 2 stories, interior corridors. **Terms:** cancellation fee imposed. **Amenities:** high-speed Internet. **Guest Services:** valet laundry, area transportation-within 10 mi & ferry. **Free Special Amenities: local telephone calls and high-speed Internet.**

SAVE ⊞ 🍴 🛗 BIZ 📶 ✕ 🛢 🖥 🖥

GOLDBELT HOTEL JUNEAU
907-586-6900

▼▼▼ **Hotel.** Rates not provided. **Address:** 51 Egan Dr 99801 **Location:** Just n of Main St; downtown. **Facility:** 106 units. 7 stories, interior corridors. **Guest Services:** valet laundry.

⊞ 🍴 🍸 BIZ 📶 🎬 🖥 / SOME UNITS 🛢 🖥

PEARSON'S POND LUXURY INN & ADVENTURE SPA
(907)789-3772

▼▼▼▼
Bed & Breakfast
$139-$732

Address: 4541 Sawa Cir 99801 **Location:** From Egan Dr, 3.5 mi n on Mendenhall Loop Rd. Located in a quiet residential area. **Facility:** A placid pond beautifies the property's lovely grounds, which feature gazebos and sitting areas where you can view the Mendenhall Glacier or soak in an outdoor hot tub. Every whim is taken care of. 5 efficiencies. 2 stories (no elevator), interior/exterior corridors. **Terms:** 2 night minimum stay - seasonal, 30 day cancellation notice-fee imposed, resort fee. **Amenities:** high-speed Internet. **Activities:** sauna, whirlpools, paddleboats, boat dock, fishing, bicycles, exercise room. **Fee:** massage. **Guest Services:** complimentary laundry. **Free Special Amenities: expanded continental breakfast and high-speed Internet.**

SAVE BIZ 📶 ✕ 🎬 🧖 ♨ ☎ 🛢 🖥 🖥

THE SILVERBOW INN BAKERY & RESTAURANT
(907)586-4146

▼ **Historic Bed & Breakfast** $99-$219 **Address:** 120 2nd St 99801 **Location:** Jct Main and 2nd sts; downtown. **Facility:** This restored 1914 building has quaint but small guest rooms with cheery, bright décor. In the historic district downtown, the Silverbow Inn is a trendy option. 11 units. 3 stories (no elevator), interior corridors. **Terms:** 7 day cancellation notice-fee imposed. **Dining:** Silverbow Inn & Bakery, see separate listing. **Activities:** whirlpool. **Guest Services:** valet laundry. 🍴 📶 ✕ 🎬

Learn the local driving laws
at DrivingLaws.AAA.com

WESTMARK BARANOF HOTEL
(907)586-2660

▼▼ **Hotel** $125-$239 **Address:** 127 N Franklin St 99801 **Location:** At 2nd and Franklin sts; downtown. **Facility:** 195 units, some efficiencies and kitchens. 9 stories, interior corridors. **Terms:** cancellation fee imposed. **Dining:** The Gold Room, see separate listing. **Activities:** exercise room. **Guest Services:** valet laundry.

🍴 🍸 BIZ 📶 ✕ 🎬 🖥 / SOME UNITS 🐾 🛢 🖥

WHERE TO EAT

THE GOLD ROOM
907-586-2660

▼▼▼▼ Regional American. Fine Dining. $20-$39 **AAA Inspector Notes:** In the Westmark Hotel in an upscale setting, the restaurant has an attentive staff and offers artful presentations of regional delectables such as salmon, halibut, prawns and crab. A large painting on the wall depicts the Gold Rush. **Bar:** full bar. **Reservations:** suggested. **Address:** 127 N Franklin St 99801 **Location:** At 2nd and Franklin sts; downtown; in Westmark Baranof Hotel.

D CALL 🎬 M

THE HANGAR ON THE WHARF
907-586-5018

▼▼▼ Regional American. Casual Dining. $11-$50 **AAA Inspector Notes:** Popular with locals, this vibrant eatery offers no-frills dining. Diners can watch seaplanes take off and land while munching on fried halibut fingers and sipping an Alaskan Brewing Co. amber ale. **Bar:** full bar. **Address:** 2 Marine Way, Suite 106 99801 **Location:** Downtown; on wharf at Sea Plane runway.

L D CALL 🎬 M 🎬

MI CASA RESTAURANT
907-789-3636

▼▼ Mexican. Casual Dining. $16-$20 **AAA Inspector Notes:** Mexican American cuisine features steak and seafood at this restaurant. **Bar:** full bar. **Address:** 9200 Glacier Hwy 99801 **Location:** Just e off Egan Dr; in Juneau Travelodge Hotel.

B L D CALL 🎬 M

OLIVIA'S DE MEXICO
907-586-6870

▼▼ Mexican. Casual Dining. $11-$19 **AAA Inspector Notes:** Wend your way downstairs to this little Mexican cantina in the basement. They have been serving authentic home-style cooking for more than 30 years to loyal locals and tourists alike. Homemade corn tortillas and salsa are presented, and you can enjoy everything from traditional soups, tacos, burritos, enchiladas and tostadas to chile verde and specials with fresh Alaskan halibut or shrimp and finishing off with homemade creamy caramel custard flan. Service is casual and food arrives fast. **Bar:** beer & wine. **Address:** 222 Seward St 99801 **Location:** Between 2nd and 3rd sts; center. **Parking:** on-site (fee).

L D 🎬

PARADISE CAFE
907/586-2253

▼ Sandwiches Desserts. Quick Serve. $3-$9 **AAA Inspector Notes:** Funky décor adds to the appeal of this café. Turkey and Havarti on homemade bread and the curry chicken wrap are a few of the savories. Scrumptious desserts will finish your lunch off nicely. **Address:** 245 Marine Way 99801 **Location:** Downtown; across from cruise ship docks. **Parking:** street only. B L 🎬

SILVERBOW INN & BAKERY
907-586-4146

▼ Deli. Quick Serve. $5-$10 **AAA Inspector Notes:** Silverbow, a restored historical structure with funky decor, is a fun spot where kids are allowed to color on the table covers. Classic and golden oldies films are shown two nights a week, and an adjacent New York-style bakery offers sinful desserts. **Bar:** beer & wine. **Address:** 120 2nd St 99801 **Location:** Jct Main and 2nd sts; downtown; in The Silverbow Inn Bakery & Restaurant. **Parking:** on-site and street.

B L D 🎬

SUWANNA CAFE
907-789-1250

▼ Thai. Quick Serve. $4-$8 **AAA Inspector Notes:** In the atrium of an office building, this family-run restaurant serves food fast, hot and tasty. This is quick serve, order at the cashier and pick up your order to go. There is limited seating. The menu is short, but with choice selections such as pad thai, pa nang and yellow curry dishes. The pork filling in the dumplings is overflowing and delicious! All is made from scratch by the matriarch or one of the many sisters bustling in the kitchen. **Address:** 8800 Glacier Hwy 99801 **Location:** Jct Egan Dr; in Jordan Creek Business Center. L CALL 🎬 M

TIMBERLINE BAR & GRILL   907/463-3412

♦♦♦ American. Casual Dining. $12-$29 **AAA Inspector Notes:** Take a 6-minute cable car ride to the top of Mount Roberts—there's a fee—from which you'll be treated to stunning views of Juneau and the Gastineau Channel below. It also takes you to this restaurant, which would be equally worthy at sea level. The Alaskan alpine experience is sure to be memorable. **Bar:** full bar. **Address:** 490 S Franklin St 99801 **Location:** Downtown; top of Mount Roberts Tramway. [L] [D] CALL [&M] [AC]

TWISTED FISH COMPANY   907/463-5033

♦♦♦ Seafood. Casual Dining. $9-$30 **AAA Inspector Notes:** Alaskan seafood is the specialty at this restaurant, located on the pier near the cruise ship landing areas. Service is quick and friendly, and if it is a sunny day, guests can enjoy dining al fresco. **Bar:** full bar. **Address:** 550 S Franklin St 99801 **Location:** On cruise dock; downtown. [L] [D] CALL [&M] [AC]

ZEPHYR RESTAURANT   907/780-2221

♦♦♦ Mediterranean. Casual Dining. $21-$36 **AAA Inspector Notes:** Alaskan twists on Mediterranean dishes are the standouts here. Daily specials may include freshly caught salmon or halibut. Pastas are made fresh daily. The setting is perfect for that special occasion. **Bar:** beer & wine. **Address:** 200 Seward St 99801 **Location:** Jct Second St; center. **Parking:** street only. [D] CALL [&M]

KATMAI NATIONAL PARK AND PRESERVE (G-4)

Elevations in the park and preserve range from sea level at the Shelikof Strait to 7,606 ft. at Mount Dennison. Refer to AAA maps for additional elevation information.

On the northern portion of the Alaska Peninsula, 4.1-million-acre Katmai National Park and Preserve displays an outstanding example of volcanism. In 1912 one of the greatest volcanic explosions in recorded history turned a nameless green valley into what became known as the Valley of Ten Thousand Smokes. For more than 45 years the eruption was attributed to Mount Katmai, but recent studies indicate that the source was a new volcanic vent called Novarupta, some 6 miles distant.

During or shortly after the eruption, the peak of Mount Katmai collapsed, forming a caldera that subsequently filled with water. Molten material released from Novarupta and surrounding vents flowed down the valley, and thousands of holes from which smoke and gases arose formed as gases and vaporized surface water percolated through the volcanic deposits. These fumaroles, which gave the valley its name, lasted only about 20 years.

Although nearly all of the "smokes" have died out, steam columns from nearby volcanoes sometimes can be seen. By air it is possible to see the jade-green lake in the crater of Mount Katmai and to circle over still-active mounts Trident, Mageik and Martin.

In addition to its superlative scenery—large lakes, rivers, glaciers and active volcanoes—the park is noted for its abundant wildlife. The most prominent mammal is the Alaskan brown bear, the world's largest carnivore, averaging 500 pounds with some reaching 1,200 pounds. It is recommended that visitors maintain at least 50 yards from individual bears

and 100 yards from sows with young. Visitors also should make noises while walking or hiking.

Katmai National Park can be reached only by boat or plane. A boat ramp is at Lake Camp, 10 miles by dirt road from King Salmon. Commercial airlines serve King Salmon, 35 miles from Brooks Camp. Amphibious aircraft make daily scheduled flights between King Salmon and Brooks Camp. Bush planes can be chartered.

Daily 7-hour bus and hiking tours to the Valley of Ten Thousand Smokes begin at Brooks Lodge at 8:30 a.m. Fare $96 (with bag lunch); $88 (no lunch); $51 (one way). Departures require a minimum of 2 people. Other tours are available; for more information phone Katmailand, Inc., (800) 544-0551. For further information about the park contact the Superintendent, Katmai National Park and Preserve, P.O. Box 7, King Salmon, AK 99613; phone (907) 246-3305. *See Recreation Areas Chart.*

KENAI (D-10) pop. 7,100, elev. 86'

Established as Fort St. Nicholas by Russian fur traders in 1791, Kenai (KEEN-eye) is one of the oldest permanent settlements in Alaska. Until 1953 the town grew under a squatters' rights policy. Kenai is the closest settlement to the south-central region's most promising oil-development fields and is the site of major petrochemical plants.

Kenai's Russian Orthodox Church, established in 1894, contains religious and art objects brought from Russia in 1841.

A popular, colorful pastime during the summer months in Kenai is berry picking. Such berries as Alaska blueberries (a smaller version of its common cousin), nagoonberries (reddish purple in color), cloudberries and salmonberries (both peach in color), crowberries (black in color), northern red currants, wild raspberries and cranberries grow on the peninsula.

Kenai Visitors and Convention Bureau: 11471 Kenai Spur Hwy., Kenai, AK 99611. **Phone:** (907) 283-1991.

KENAI NATIONAL WILDLIFE REFUGE—see Soldotna p. 661.

KENAI VISITORS & CULTURAL CENTER, 11471 Kenai Spur Hwy., offers visitor information as well as displays about Kenai's history and culture. Exhibit rooms showcase Dena'ina Athabascan art and artifacts, Russian relics and educational displays describing Alaskan wildlife. The center also hosts traveling and temporary exhibitions of photography, art, crafts, native culture and Alaska history throughout the year.

Time: Allow 30 minutes minimum. **Hours:** Mon.-Fri. 9-6, Sat.-Sun. 10-6, Memorial Day-Labor Day; Mon.-Fri. 9-5, Sat. 11-4, rest of year. **Cost:** $5; $3 (ages 55+); free (ages 0-18 and to all Sept.-Apr.). **Phone:** (907) 283-1991.

ASPEN EXTENDED STAY SUITES   (907)283-2272

▼▼▼▼ **Extended Stay Hotel** $99-$199 **Address:** 10431 Kenai Spur Hwy 99611 **Location:** 0.5 mi e; center; behind McDonald's. **Facility:** 78 efficiencies. 3 stories, interior corridors. **Parking:** winter plug-ins. **Terms:** cancellation fee imposed. **Activities:** exercise room. **Guest Services:** valet and coin laundry.

🛎↑ CALL 🖥M BIZ 🛜 🖥 🖨 💻

HARBORSIDE COTTAGES   (907)283-6162

◆   **Address:** 813 Riverview Dr 99611 **Lo-**
Cottage   **cation:** Just s on Main St, then just e;
$150-$195   center. **Facility:** 5 cottages. 1 story, ex-
                   terior corridors. *Bath:* shower only.
                   Terms: closed 10/2-4/30, check-in 4 pm,
3 night minimum stay - seasonal, 30 day cancellation notice.
Free Special Amenities: early check-in/late check-out and high-speed Internet.

SAVE 🛜 ✕ 🍴 ✆ 🖥 🖨 💻

CHARLOTTE'S   907/283-2777

▼▼ ▼▼ Sandwiches Soup. Quick Serve. $8-$12 **AAA Inspector Notes:** A popular lunch spot, this cozy cafe features a menu of hearty salads and gourmet sandwiches, along with homemade desserts to tempt the sweet tooth. **Address:** 115 S Willow Cir, Suite 102 99611 **Location:** Jct Kenai Spur Hwy, just n. [B] [L] CALL 🖥M 🍴

VERONICA'S   907/283-2725

◆ American. Quick Serve. $6-$15 **AAA Inspector Notes:** *Historic.* This charming bistro is the perfect spot to savor a homemade pastry with an aromatic cup of coffee or tea. Originally built as a private home in 1918, the restaurant serves delicious, specialty homemade items, including sandwiches and creative soups. Live music energizes the place on Friday and Saturday evenings. **Address:** 604 Petersen Way 99611 **Location:** Kenai Spur Hwy, just s on Main St, just w on Overland Ave, then just n on Mission Ave; in historic district. [L] 🍴

KENAI FJORDS NATIONAL PARK (D-11)

Elevations in the park range from sea level at Nuka Bay to 6,400 ft. at a peak on the Harding Icefield. Refer to AAA maps for additional elevation information.

On the southeastern side of the Kenai Peninsula, Kenai Fjords National Park covers more than 600,000 acres. Access to the park is by private vehicle, plane or boat from Seward. Air charters also are available from other communities on the Kenai Peninsula. Scheduled bus service is available between Seward and Anchorage. Several tour companies offer trips to Exit Glacier and boat trips to the fjords.

The park encompasses a coastal mountain range that includes most of Harding Icefield, one of the four largest ice fields in the United States. A remnant of the ice age, it blankets all but the top of the Kenai Mountains. Along the coast is the rugged shoreline of the glacier-carved Kenai Fjords. Seals, porpoises, whales and sea otters are some of the 23 marine mammal species that inhabit the coastal waters.

Exit Glacier is the most accessible of the glaciers that flow from Harding Icefield. Three miles north of Seward via the Seward Highway and Exit Glacier Road, the glacier is reached by a .7-mile trail that begins at the Exit Glacier parking area; guided tours

depart daily at 10, 2 and 4, mid-May to mid-September. A strenuous 8.2-mile round-trip journey from the base of Exit Glacier to Harding Icefield departs from the Exit Glacier Nature Center on Saturdays at 9, July through August. Bald eagles, bears, moose, mountain goats and Steller sea lions inhabit the area.

Picnicking and backcountry camping are permitted; a 12-site walk-in tent campground and three rustic cabins are available. Winter activities at Exit Glacier include skiing, snowmobiling, snowshoeing and dog sledding. Boat and air charters offer access to the coast during the summer.

Both park headquarters and a visitor center are in Seward. Park headquarters is at 500 Adams St., Suite 103, and the visitor center is at 1212 4th Ave. next to the harbormaster's office. The Exit Glacier Nature Center is inside the park at the Exit Glacier parking area. Slide shows, exhibits and information about ranger-conducted activities are available.

The visitor center in Seward is open daily 8:30-7, Memorial Day-Labor Day. The Exit Glacier Nature Center is open daily 9-8, Memorial Day-Labor Day; 9-5, May 15-day before Memorial Day and day after Labor Day to mid-Sept. Admission to Exit Glacier is free. For information write the Superintendent, Kenai Fjords National Park, P.O. Box 1727, Seward, AK 99664; phone (907) 224-7500 or (907) 224-2132 for recorded information. *See Recreation Areas Chart.*

KETCHIKAN (H-12) pop. 8,050

• Hotels p. 649 • Restaurants p. 649

Alaska's southernmost city sits on stilts at the base of the Tongass National Forest *(see place listing p. 664).* On Revillagigedo Island, separated from the mainland by Behm Canal, Ketchikan claims to be the salmon capital of the world. An average annual rainfall of 156 to 162 inches makes it the wettest community in North America. The city's economic base relies on fishing, canning, mineral exploration, tourism and logging and cold-storage operations.

The town is populated with native culture and contains the largest concentration of Tlingit (KLINK-it), Haida (HY-dah), and Tsimshian (SIMP-shee-ane) people in Alaska. This heritage can be seen in the many totem poles that populate the area. Totem poles—tall cedar logs carved with eagles, ravens, wolves, bears, whales and other figures—depict stories or designate clans or lineage, and Ketchikan is reputed to contain the most in the world.

Creek Street is a relic of Ketchikan's rough-and-tumble past. Built on stilts over Ketchikan Creek, the street was once the site of a thriving red-light district. Highlights include art galleries, shops and a museum. The creek is a spawning ground for salmon.

SAVE Gray Line of Alaska, (907) 225-2404, and Princess Tours, (800) 774-6237, are among the companies that offer tours of the city. Ketchikan Visitor Information Center (on the waterfront at the corner of Front and Mission streets) can provide a more complete list; phone (907) 225-6166 or (800) 770-3300. Information about charter aircraft, boats, rental cars, buses and taxis is available at the Visitor Information Center, the airport and the ferry terminal.

Southeast Alaska Discovery Center: 50 Main St., Ketchikan, AK 99901. **Phone:** (907) 228-6220 or TTY (907) 228-6237.

Self-guiding tours: Information about a 2-hour walking tour of downtown is provided at the Ketchikan Visitors Bureau, 131 Front St., Ketchikan, AK 99901; phone (907) 225-6166 or (800) 770-3300.

Shopping areas: The Creek Street boardwalk area in downtown contains a number of specialty shops and boutiques.

ALASKA AMPHIBIOUS TOURS is inside the Ketchikan Visitor Center on the cruise ship dock, booth # 10, 131 Front St. Take a 90-minute historic tour through downtown Ketchikan, passing by Ketchikan Creek and then splashing into the Tongass Narrows waterway, where you can see fishing boats and sea planes in the harbor as well as nearby canneries where bald eagles are known to visit. Passengers ride on an amphibious vehicle which is driven on dry land and becomes a boat in the water. **Time:** Allow 1 hour, 30 minutes minimum. **Hours:** Tours depart daily 7:30-3, May-Sept. Phone ahead to confirm schedule. **Cost:** $40; $25 (ages 3-12). **Phone:** (907) 225-9899 or (866) 341-3825.

BERING SEA CRAB FISHERMEN'S TOUR departs from the Main Cruise Ships dock at the Front St. pier. This 3.5-hour excursion on the waters of the Metlakatla Indian Community is conducted on the *Aleutian Ballad* — a vessel featured in the TV show "Deadliest Catch" — and offers passengers a first-hand look at the king crab fishing industry and its techniques. As the tour proceeds, passengers are regaled with tales of life at sea and educated about the state's fishing history and the variety of fishing vessels used. A heated and sheltered amphitheater allows passengers to observe the ship's crew as it unloads 700-pound crab pots.

Often seen among the ship's catch are such sea creatures as octopi, prawns, sharks and wolf eels; many animals are placed in an on-deck tank for observation and photo opportunities prior to release back into the sea. Such local wildlife as bald eagles, sea lions, seals and humpback whales may be seen during the tour.

Note: Photo ID is required. Prior to boarding, potential passengers should seek to locate a tour representative on the dock at least 30 minutes before the scheduled departure time. Those unable to locate a representative at least 15 minutes prior to departure may proceed to the *Aleutian Ballad* at the Berth 3 Tender Float. Passengers should dress in comfortable and warm layers of clothing. Each passenger should be of sufficient age and capacity to remain in the ship's passenger-designated zones and outside its working areas as well as be able to navigate the ship's aisles and stairs. Limited storage space is available.

Time: Allow 3 hours, 30 minutes minimum. **Hours:** Tours depart once or twice daily (departure times vary), early May to mid-Sept. The schedule is designed to accommodate cruise ship passengers; phone ahead to verify departure times. **Cost:** Fare $159; $99 (ages 5-12). Children ages 0-4 are not permitted on the tour. Reservations are recommended. **Phone:** (360) 642-4935 or (888) 239-3816. 🍴

CLASSIC TOURS picks up passengers at the downtown cruise ship docks or local accommodation. Up to five passengers may ride in a restored 1955 Chevy driven by a retired schoolteacher clad in a poodle skirt and saddle shoes. Two narrated tours focus on the natural and cultural history of Ketchikan. The 2-hour Totem Tour includes visits to Saxman Totem Pole Park and the Creek Street boardwalk area. The 3-hour Totems and Eagles Tour also includes a visit to the rainforest, a bald eagle's nest and a king salmon site (in season). Wildlife viewing is possible. Private tours can be arranged.

Hours: Daily 8-6, early May-Sept. 30. **Cost:** Fare $139 (3-hour tour); $109 (2-hour tour). Fare includes admission to area museums and parks. Reservations are required. **Phone:** (907) 225-3091.

DEER MOUNTAIN TRIBAL HATCHERY AND EAGLE CENTER, .5 mi. n.e. at 1158 Salmon Rd. across the bridge from the Totem Heritage Center, raises king (chinook) and coho (silver) salmon, and steelhead and rainbow trout. Bald eagles also are featured in a landscaped enclosure. **Time:** Allow 30 minutes minimum. **Hours:** Daily 8-4:30, late April to mid-Sept. Hours may vary in Sept. Phone ahead to confirm schedule. **Cost:** Guided tour $12; $5 (ages 0-11). **Phone:** (907) 228-5530.

SAXMAN NATIVE VILLAGE, 2.5 mi. s. on S. Tongass Hwy., is a Tlingit (KLINK-it) Indian village of about 350 residents. The totem park contains 30 totem poles, and master carvers can be seen at work in the carving center. A 2-hour guided tour also includes the Beaver Tribal House, the Old School House and Cape Fox Dancers performances.

Time: Allow 30 minutes minimum. **Hours:** Daily 8-5, mid-May through Sept. 30; hours vary rest of year. Cape Fox Dancers performance schedule varies; phone ahead. **Cost:** $5. Guided tour prices vary; phone ahead for information. **Phone:** (907) 225-4846, ext. 100.

TONGASS HISTORICAL MUSEUM, 629 Dock St. in Ketchikan's Centennial Building, displays pioneer items as well as art and artifacts from northwest cultures. Historical and changing exhibits are offered. **Time:** Allow 30 minutes minimum. **Hours:** Daily 8-5, May-Sept.; Tues.-Fri. 1-5, Sat. 10-4, rest of year. Closed winter holidays. **Cost:** May-Sept. $2; rest of year free. **Phone:** (907) 225-5600.

TOTEM BIGHT STATE HISTORICAL PARK, 10 mi. n. on N. Tongass Hwy., displays 14 poles by Haida and Tlingit clans and a model of a Tlingit clan house. The site is reached by a short trail through a forest from the parking area. A brochure describes typical totem characters and gives insight to the art of totem carving. More totem poles are in Saxman Native Village, 2.5 miles south on S. Tongass Highway. **Time:** Allow 30 minutes minimum. **Hours:** Daily 6 a.m.-10 p.m., May-Sept.; Mon.-Fri. 10-4, rest of year. **Cost:** Free. **Phone:** (907) 247-8574.

TOTEM HERITAGE CENTER, 601 Deermount St., displays original 19th-century totem poles retrieved from native villages and emphasizes traditional Tlingit, Haida and Tsimshian art. **Tours:** Guided tours are available. **Time:** Allow 30 minutes minimum. **Hours:** Daily 8-5, May-Sept.; Mon.-Fri. 1-5, rest of year. Closed winter holidays. **Cost:** May-Sept. $5; rest of year free. **Phone:** (907) 225-5900.

BEST WESTERN PLUS LANDING HOTEL
(907)225-5166

Hotel
$145-$246

AAA Benefit: Members save up to 20%, plus 10% bonus points with Best Western Rewards®.

Address: 3434 Tongass Ave 99901 **Location:** Across from Alaska Marine Hwy ferry terminal. **Facility:** 107 units. 2-4 stories, interior/exterior corridors. **Amenities:** *Some:* high-speed Internet. **Dining:** The Landing, see separate listing. **Activities:** exercise room. **Guest Services:** valet and coin laundry, area transportation-ferry terminal. **Free Special Amenities:** early check-in/late check-out and room upgrade (subject to availability with advance reservations).

CAPE FOX LODGE
(907)225-8001

Hotel
$99-$210

Address: 800 Venetia Way 99901 **Location:** Above Creek St (tramway from Creek St). **Facility:** 72 units. 3 stories, interior/exterior corridors. **Terms:** cancellation fee imposed. **Dining:** Cape Fox Lodge Dining Room & Lodge, see separate listing. **Guest Services:** valet and coin laundry, area transportation-ferry terminal. **Free Special Amenities:** high-speed Internet and airport transportation.

WHERE TO EAT

ANNABELLE'S FAMOUS KEG & CHOWDER HOUSE
907/225-9423

Regional Seafood. Casual Dining. $10-$39 **AAA Inspector Notes:** Located directly across from the cruise ship docks, diners can enjoy freshly caught seasonal seafood such as fresh salmon, clam chowder or halibut cheeks in either an attractive bar or classy dining room. **Bar:** full bar. **Reservations:** suggested. **Address:** 326 Front St 99901 **Location:** Center; across from cruise ship docks; in The Gilmore Hotel. **Parking:** street only.

BAR HARBOR RESTAURANT
907/225-2813

Alaskan. Casual Dining. $9-$26 **AAA Inspector Notes:** All anyone needs to know about this restaurant is they serve fresh local seafood prepared simply so the flavors are the stars. It's extremely popular with the local crowd and has limited seating, so reservations are suggested. **Bar:** beer & wine. **Address:** 2813 Tongass Ave 99901 **Location:** 1 mi s of the Alaska Marine Hwy ferry terminal. **Parking:** street only.

CAPE FOX LODGE DINING ROOM & LODGE
907/225-8001

American. Casual Dining. $10-$28 **AAA Inspector Notes:** Perched 130 feet above Creek Street and high above the busy cruise ship harbor is this eatery with spectacular views of the harbor which are framed by pine boughs just outside the windows. This house by the creek is legendary for celebrating special events. Local seafood anchors the menu, which also includes aged beef, chicken and pasta. **Bar:** full bar. **Reservations:** suggested. **Address:** 800 Venetia Way 99901 **Location:** Above Creek St (tramway from Creek St); in Cape Fox Lodge.

THE LANDING
907/225-5166

American. Casual Dining. $8-$22 **AAA Inspector Notes:** This 1950s-style diner offers an extensive menu of comfort foods as well as some of the best pies in the area. **Bar:** full bar. **Address:** 3434 Tongass Ave 99901 **Location:** Across from Alaska Marine Hwy ferry terminal; in BEST WESTERN PLUS Landing Hotel.

THE NARROWS INN RESTAURANT
907/247-2600

American. Casual Dining. $8-$25 **AAA Inspector Notes:** Named for the Tongass Narrows on whose shores it is located, the restaurant offers casual dining about 1.5 miles north of town. The quiet, rain-forest setting is adjacent to The Narrows Inn. The menu features fresh local seafood as well as pasta, steaks and chops. **Bar:** full bar. **Address:** 4871 N Tongass Hwy 99901 **Location:** 1.6 mi n from Alaska Marine Hwy ferry terminal; 1.2 mi n from Airport ferry terminal.

SALMON FALLS RESORT
907/225-2752

Regional American. Casual Dining. $19-$34 **AAA Inspector Notes:** Overlooking the Clarence Straits and Behm Canal of the Inland Passageway, the restaurant serves fresh Northern-water seafood and grilled steaks. Fourteen miles outside the town of Ketchikan, the facility is surrounded by water and woods. Wide windows offer a panoramic view of the straits. The friendly young staff comes from local communities and can offer exuberant information concerning the surrounding areas. **Bar:** full bar. **Reservations:** suggested. **Address:** 16707 N Tongass Hwy 99901 **Location:** 14.5 mi n from Alaska Marine Hwy ferry terminal; 14.1 mi n from Airport ferry terminal.

KLONDIKE GOLD RUSH NATIONAL HISTORIC PARK—See
Skagway p. 659.

KOBUK VALLEY NATIONAL PARK (C-4)

Elevations in the park range from 100 ft. at the point where the Kobuk River flows out of the southwest corner of the park to 4,700 ft. in the Brooks Range, which forms the park's northern border. Refer to AAA maps for additional elevation information.

Some 25 miles north of the Arctic Circle, Kobuk Valley National Park covers 1,710,000 acres in the heart of the arctic wildlands, where the boreal forest gives way to the frozen tundra. The broad Kobuk Valley is enclosed almost completely by the Baird Mountains to the north and the Waring Mountains to the south. Traversing the valley from east to west, the wide and placid Kobuk River offers good fishing and idyllic float trips. The swifter Salmon River, a designated Wild and Scenic River, flows south from the Baird Mountains.

Preserved within the park are the 25-square-mile Great Kobuk Sand Dunes, the largest active dunes in the Arctic. Created by the grinding action of ancient glaciers, the sand was carried by wind and water to a wide area south of the Kobuk River. The 100-foot dunes are accessible by a difficult hike from the river along Kavet Creek.

Home to seminomadic tribes for more than 12,500 years, the region still supports the native Inupiats; they are granted by law the right to continue subsistence hunting, trapping and other practices. Important to their survival is North America's largest caribou herd, numbering some 500,000. Many can be seen crossing the Kobuk River in September during their migration southward.

Other wildlife common to the region include moose, grizzly and black bears, wolves, red foxes, lynxes, wolverines and martens. Golden eagles can be seen in the northern latitudes; other birds include sandhill cranes, arctic loons, American golden plovers and arctic terns.

The park attracts experienced backpackers, campers and river travelers. Though the park is open year-round, the elements limit most visits to June through September. Fishing is good when the rivers are clear of silt; catches include salmon, pike, arctic char, whitefish and grayling. An Alaska fishing license is required. Hunting is not permitted, but it is legal to carry a firearm for protection from bears.

Access to the region is by daily commercial flights from Anchorage and Fairbanks to Kotzebue *(see place listing p. 651)*, where connections to the villages of Kiana and Ambler can be made. Air taxi service into the park is available from Kotzebue, Kiana and Ambler. There are no facilities, services, trails or campgrounds in the park. Park headquarters is at the Northwest Arctic Heritage Center in Kotzebue and is open Mon.-Fri. 8:30-6:30, Sat. 10:30-6:30, June-Sept.; Tues.-Fri. 9-noon and 1-6, Sat. noon-4, rest of year. The visitor center has museum exhibits and can provide information about the park; phone (907) 442-3890.

Due to its location, the area is subject to harsh weather and high winds. It is advisable to carry protection against hypothermia, mosquitoes and biting flies.

For trip planning assistance and a list of authorized outfitters, guides and air taxi operators, write the Superintendent, Western Arctic National Parklands, P.O. Box 1029, Kotzebue, AK 99752; phone (907) 442-3890. *See Recreation Areas Chart.*

KODIAK (H-5) pop. 6,130

One of the oldest towns in Alaska, Kodiak is on the northeastern tip of Kodiak Island and is home to the Kodiak brown bear. A Russian explorer-trader's quest for sea otter pelts led to the European settlement of the island in 1784. The community was established about 1792 when Alexander Baranov moved his headquarters from the original 1784 settlement at Three Saints Bay, making Kodiak the first capital of Russian America.

Kodiak was nearly destroyed twice; in June 1912, an eruption from Mount Novarupta covered the town with ash. On Good Friday in 1964 an earthquake in south central Alaska created tsunamis that enveloped the islands. Citizens found refuge on nearby Pillar Mountain and returned with the task of rebuilding the city.

Kodiak is a leading commercial fishing port. Several cruise lines dock at the Port of Kodiak for shore excursions. On days when cruise ships are in port, visitors can enjoy performances by the Kodiak Alutiiq Dancers at 11 a.m. at the Kodiak Tribal Council building, 312 W. Marine Way; phone (907) 486-4449. The blue, onion-shaped domes of the Holy Resurrection Russian Orthodox Church recall the days when the Russian Empire in the North Pacific was administered from Kodiak.

Kodiak can be reached by air service from Anchorage or by the Alaska Marine Highway, a passenger/vehicle ferry, from Homer and Seward. Reservations are required well in advance for the ferry; write Alaska Marine Highway, P.O. Box 703, Kodiak, AK 99615, or phone (907) 486-3800 or (800) 642-0066.

Kodiak Island Convention and Visitors Bureau: 100 Marine Way, Suite 200, Kodiak, AK 99615. **Phone:** (907) 486-4782 or (800) 789-4782.

ALUTIIQ MUSEUM is at 215 Mission Rd. in the Alutiiq Center across from Holy Resurrection Russian Orthodox Church. Permanent exhibits tell the 7,500-year history, lifestyle and cultural traditions of the Alutiiq people through archeological artifacts, photographs, petroglyph rubbings, oral histories, videos and art. An interactive kiosk educates visitors about the Alutiiq language. **Tours:** Guided tours are available. **Time:** Allow 1 hour minimum. **Hours:** Mon. and Wed.-Fri. 9-5, Sat.-Sun. 9-3, June-Aug.; Tues.-Fri. 9-5, Sat. noon-4, rest of year. Closed major holidays. Phone ahead to confirm schedule. **Cost:** $5; free (ages 0-16). **Phone:** (907) 486-7004.

BARANOV MUSEUM, in the Erskine House on the harbor front, has collections of early Russian and Alaskan artifacts as well as American household furnishings from the early 20th century. The building, which dates from 1808, was used by Alexander Baranov as a warehouse for storing furs. Original log construction methods can be examined inside. **Time:** Allow 1 hour minimum. **Hours:** Mon.-Sat. 10-4, Memorial Day-Labor Day; Tues.-Sat. 10-3, rest of year. Closed major holidays. **Cost:** $5; free (ages 0-12). **Phone:** (907) 486-5920.

FORT ABERCROMBIE STATE HISTORICAL PARK, 4.5 mi. n.e. on Miller Point, is a World War II fortification. The 183-acre park offers a view of the rocky coastline and nearby islands. Interpretive programs are given, and hiking trails are available. World War II artifacts remain; the visitor center offers natural-history displays and information about Alaska's participation in World War II. Tidal pools are within walking distance of the visitor center. *See Recreation Areas Chart.*

Hours: Park open daily 24 hours. Visitor center daily 8-5, May-Sept. **Cost:** Free. **Phone:** (907) 486-6339.

KODIAK LABORATORY AQUARIUM & TOUCH TANK is at the Kodiak Fisheries Research Center at 301 Research Ct. The 3,500-gallon aquarium displays specimens collected from Kodiak Island's waters, including crabs, mollusks and other invertebrates as well as such echinoderms as anemones, sea cucumbers and starfish. A touch tank allows visitors to interact with selected intertidal organisms.

Time: Allow 30 minutes minimum. **Hours:** Mon.-Sat. 8-4:30 in summer; Mon.-Fri. 8-4:30, rest of year. Closed major holidays. Phone ahead to confirm schedule. **Cost:** Free. **Phone:** (907) 481-1800.

KODIAK NATIONAL WILDLIFE REFUGE occupies the southwestern two-thirds of Kodiak Island and 50,000 acres on Ban Island and the northwestern tip of Afognak Island. The 1,865,000 acres were set aside to preserve the habitat of the Kodiak bear, some of which weigh up to 1,500 pounds. Among other inhabitants are Sitka black-tailed deer, sea lions, sea otters and bald eagles. The refuge is accessible only by plane and boat. Cabins and a number of recreational activities are available. **Cost:** Free. **Phone:** (907) 487-2600 or (888) 408-3514.

Visitor Center, 402 Center Ave., offers displays, interpretive programs, maps and brochures, and a 12-minute film about the refuge. **Time:** Allow 1 hour minimum. **Hours:** Daily 9-5, Memorial Day-Labor Day; Tues.-Sat. 10-5, rest of year. Closed Jan. 1, July 4, Thanksgiving and Christmas. **Cost:** Free. **Phone:** (907) 487-2626 or (888) 592-6942.

KODIAK TOURS depart from the lobby of the Best Western Kodiak Inn. Custom narrated historic tours of the island are tailored to the interests of the visitor. The U.S. Coast Guard Base, Cannery Row, boat harbors, Fisheries Research Center and Pillar Mountain are among the sites. The tour stops to view the island's wildlife and scenery. Half-day tours last 3 hours, while full-day tours last 7 hours.

Inquire about weather policies. **Hours:** Full-day tours depart daily at 9. Half-day tours depart daily at 9 and 1. **Cost:** Full-day fare (includes all attraction admission fees) $100. Half-day fare $60. Reservations are required. **Phone:** (907) 486-3920.

BEST WESTERN KODIAK INN & CONVENTION CENTER
(907)486-5712

Hotel
$105-$206

AAA Benefit: Members save up to 20%, plus 10% bonus points with Best Western Rewards®.

Address: 236 W Rezanof Dr 99615 **Location:** 0.3 mi w of ferry terminal; center. **Facility:** 82 units. 3 stories, interior/exterior corridors. **Amenities:** Some: high-speed Internet. **Dining:** Chart Room Restaurant and Lounge, see separate listing. **Activities:** whirlpool, exercise room. **Guest Services:** coin laundry, area transportation-ferry. **Free Special Amenities:** expanded continental breakfast and high-speed Internet.

COMFORT INN KODIAK　　　　　　　(907)487-2700

Hotel $110-$190 **Address:** 1395 Airport Way 99615 **Location:** Adjacent to Kodiak Airport. **Facility:** 50 units. 2 stories, interior corridors. **Terms:** check-in 4 pm, cancellation fee imposed. **Activities:** limited exercise equipment. **Guest Services:** coin laundry, area transportation-ferry.

WHERE TO EAT

CHART ROOM RESTAURANT AND LOUNGE　　907/486-5712

Regional American. Casual Dining. $10-$30 **AAA Inspector Notes:** Diners enjoy a lovely view from the large panoramic windows of this second-floor restaurant. The luncheon menu has a nice variety of casual fare including fresh chowder, tasty salads, sandwiches, pastas and burgers, as well as the ever-popular halibut and chips. Dinner features an extensive fish and seafood selection that is sure to please. **Bar:** full bar. **Reservations:** suggested. **Address:** 236 W Rezanof Dr 99615 **Location:** 0.3 mi w of ferry terminal; center; in BEST WESTERN Kodiak Inn & Convention Center.

HENRY'S GREAT ALASKAN RESTAURANT　　907/486-8844

American. Casual Dining. $10-$35 **AAA Inspector Notes:** The lengthy menu of burgers, sandwiches, steaks, fresh seafood and pasta draws a crowd at this casual downtown eatery. Specialties include breaded and fried seafood, prime rib and bouillabaisse as well as their famous crawfish pie. **Bar:** full bar. **Address:** 512 Marine Way 99615 **Location:** Just w of ferry terminal; on The Mall.

OLDS RIVER INN　　　　　　　　　　907/486-6040

American. Casual Dining. $11-$32 **AAA Inspector Notes:** In good weather, the drive to this place from town could be spectacular; on a misty day it's still fabulous. Homemade Parmesan crackers with smoked salmon dip or filet mignon are some of the features. The owners are hands-on and very friendly. **Bar:** full bar. **Address:** 32233 Pasagshak Rd 99615 **Location:** From airport, 30 mi s.

KOTZEBUE (C-3) pop. 3,201, elev. 20'

Kotzebue, on the Baldwin Peninsula, sits on glacial moraine on the eastern edge of Kotzebue Sound. It was named after Otto Von Kotzebue, a German sailor exploring for Russia around 1818. Inhabited by the Kikiktagruk Inupiat Eskimos since the early 19th century, the area later became a seasonal trading center for the various Eskimo tribes due to its position at the confluence of the Noatak and Kobuk rivers. Its establishment as a permanent city began in 1899 with a Quaker mission.

Kotzebue is situated 33 miles above the Arctic Circle in the treeless tundra; the sun rises each year in early June and remains above the horizon for only 38 days. A spectacular ice breakup takes place for 2 weeks between mid-May and mid-June.

The second-largest Eskimo village in Alaska, Kotzebue is reached only by daily air service from Anchorage, Nome and Fairbanks. Arrangements for bush plane flights over the surrounding tundra and to the Kobuk River for hunting and fishing expeditions can be made at the airport. Short air and boat excursions to most of the surrounding villages also are available through independent operators. Northwest Arctic Heritage Center, near the airport, is the visitor center for Kobuk Valley National Park *(see place listing p. 649)*. The center has an exhibit hall and also provides information about the surrounding area; phone (907) 442-3890.

LAKE CLARK NATIONAL PARK AND PRESERVE (F-4)

Elevations in the park and preserve range from sea level along Cook Inlet to 10,197 ft. at Mount Redoubt. Refer to AAA maps for additional elevation information.

West of Cook Inlet, Lake Clark National Park and Preserve is an almost 4-million-acre mountainous crossroads where ice and fire meet. The Pacific crust grinds beneath the North American plate, creating the Chigmit Mountains, a jagged array of spires and two steaming volcanoes, Mount Redoubt and Mount Iliamna. Mount Redoubt, the more active, last erupted in March 2009; it continues to emit steam.

Covered by massive ice fields, the seemingly impenetrable Chigmit Mountains are formed by the linkage of two great ranges, the Alaska and the Aleutian. Together the ranges divide the park into distinct areas: the eastern flank's coastal plain bordering Cook Inlet and the lake and tundra region on the western flank. Lake Clark, 50 miles long, juts in from the southwest.

Moisture abounds along the park's coastal area, which is characterized by rocky cliffs along its southern portion, giving way to tidal marshes and grasslands in the north. In contrast to the luxuriant alder thickets and Sitka spruce along Cook Inlet, lakes, boreal forests and rolling tundra highlands distinguish the park's western landscape.

Numerous glacier-fed rivers and creeks are channeled through Lake Clark, creating one of the richest sockeye salmon spawning grounds in the world. The park was created primarily to protect this fruitful breeding area.

Although the park is open all year, most people visit during the peak of the summer season, late June through August. Even in summer months, weather conditions vary in the interior; it is advisable to bring protection against insects as well as clothing for sunny, wet or freezing weather. Visitors should outfit themselves in Kenai, Homer or Anchorage, as the communities closer to the park have limited supplies.

For anglers the rivers and lakes on the park's western side provide a variety of trophy-size fish, including salmon, arctic grayling and trout. A 2- to 3-mile trail to Tanalian Falls and Kontrashibuna Lake is accessible from Port Alsworth, near Lake Clark. The open foothills are ideal for backpacking. River-running also is popular on the Mulchatna, Tlikakila and Chilikadrotna rivers, all federally designated wild and scenic rivers.

As there are no roads in the park, access is almost exclusively by air. Most travelers charter aircraft; the closest airport is south of the park in Iliamna. A 1- to 2-hour flight from Anchorage, Homer or Kenai will provide access to most points within the park and preserve.

The National Park Service facility is at Port Alsworth and contains a visitor center with displays regarding natural history topics; phone (907) 781-2218. The center is open daily 9-5, Memorial Day-Labor Day; Mon.-Fri. 9-4, rest of year. While there are minimal National Park facilities—staffed patrol cabins at Telaquana Lake, Twin Lakes, Crescent Lake and Chinitna Bay—there are a number of private lodges and cabins in the park.

For information about accommodations as well as a list of outfitters and maps, write the Superintendent, Lake Clark National Park and Preserve, 240 W. 5th Ave., Suite 236, Anchorage, AK 99501; phone (907) 644-3626. *See Recreation Areas Chart.*

MISTY FIORDS NATIONAL MONUMENT (H-11)

East of Ketchikan and within the Tongass National Forest *(see place listing p. 664)*, Misty Fiords National Monument covers about 3,580 square miles of wilderness. The area is accessible by float plane from Ketchikan and other communities near the national forest. An information center and cruises to the monument are available in Ketchikan *(see place listing p. 647)*.

Behm Canal, a deep inlet of the Pacific Ocean, leads to the interior of the monument, where rock walls that rise 3,000 feet surround Walker Cove and Rudyerd Bay. Geological features include mineral springs, 237-foot-tall New Eddystone Rock, 3,150-foot-tall Punchbowl Face, lava flows, five major rivers and hundreds of small streams. The region receives more than 120 inches of precipitation each year. Bald eagles, brown and black bears, wolves and mountain goats inhabit the area; whales, porpoises, seals and sea lions can be sighted in Behm Canal or in the ocean nearby.

Recreational activities include backpacking, picnicking, bird watching, hunting, fishing and crabbing. Rustic cabins are available for $25-$45 per day; reservations may be made by calling Reserve America, (877) 444-6777. Four free Adirondack-type shelters are available on a first-come, first-served basis. For further information contact the Southeast Alaska Discovery Center, 50 Main St., Ketchikan, AK 99901; phone (907) 228-6220, or TTY (907) 228-6237.

MOOSE PASS pop. 219

TRAIL LAKE LODGE   907/288-3101

Motel. Rates not provided. **Address:** 33654 Depot Rd 99631 **Location:** US 9 (Seward Hwy) at MM 29.5. **Facility:** 21 units. 1-2 stories (no elevator), exterior corridors. **Bath:** shower only. **Parking:** winter plug-ins. ⊞ ⬚ ⬚ ⬚ ⬚ / SOME UNITS ⬚

NOME (D-2) pop. 3,598, elev. 13'

Placer gold washed from the hillsides to the beaches at Nome lured ~~thousands~~ to the remote shores of the Bering Sea in 1898. At the height of the gold rush, 20,000 people lived in Nome, once the largest settlement in Alaska.

On the Seward Peninsula, Nome is the judicial and commercial center of northwestern Alaska and the main supply point for nearby mining districts and Eskimo villages. The city is accessible daily by plane from Anchorage. Regularly scheduled and charter flights are available to various Eskimo villages.

Cruise ships serve Nome during the summer, and rental cars provide visitors with opportunities for self-guiding trips to nearby villages.

When a diphtheria epidemic threatened the town in 1925, the necessary serum was delivered by dog team. The annual 🐾 Iditarod Trail Sled Dog Race commemorates this emergency mission. The race, which begins in Anchorage *(see place listing p. 605)* the first Saturday in March, encompasses treacherous climbs, river passages and bone-chilling blizzards. Mushers cross the finish line in Nome after traveling roughly 1,112 miles, exhausted but invigorated by cheers from supporters lining the chute on Front Street.

One of the activities during the final week of the race is the Bering Sea Ice Classic, a six-hole golf tournament played on frozen Norton Sound.

The Midnight Sun Folk Fest celebrates the summer solstice, the longest day of the year with almost 24 hours of sunlight. The mid-June festival lasts several days and includes a parade, live music and The Nome River Raft Race.

Nome Convention and Visitors Bureau: 301 Front St., Nome, AK 99762. **Phone:** (907) 443-6555.

INSIDER INFO:
The Last Great Race

To commemorate the 1925 event in which 20 mushers relayed serum to Nome to save children who contracted diphtheria, the first Iditarod Trail Sled Dog Race took place on Mar. 3, 1973.

Beginning in Anchorage and culminating in Nome, the race trail covers some 1,112 miles of rugged terrain, takes between 9-17 days to complete and can reach temperatures of minus 60 F.

In preparation for the great race, the trail is broken and marked with reflector tape, and checkpoints are chosen where teams stop to eat and rest. Since it's not feasible for mushers to carry all of their provisions in their sleds, the bulk of food and supplies is shipped to the checkpoints prior to the race.

To aid in endurance, dogs ingest 5,000 calories or more each day, gobbling such delicacies as moose, caribou or even seal meat. Concern for the dogs' health is strong: Booties are worn for paw protection, and about 25 veterinarians man the checkpoints to examine each dog.

While teams may begin the race with as many as 16 dogs, some drop from the race. "Dropped dogs"—dogs that do not finish the race due to dehydration, flu or fatigue—are carried to the nearest checkpoint and flown back to Anchorage. A musher must finish the race with at least five dogs.

Teams travel at night as well as during the day, and dogs rest about 10-12 hours per 24-hour period. But mushers don't enjoy that luxury: Responsible for feeding and caring for the dogs (including changing their booties every 100 miles), they rarely sleep more than 2 hours per night.

The goal? Nome's Burled Arch on Front Street. At this finish line, teams are greeted by cheering crowds and the sounding of the city's fire siren.

CARRIE M. McLAIN MEMORIAL MUSEUM is at 223 Front St. The museum showcases the history of the Nome gold rush, the lifestyles of Bering Strait Eskimos and the early days of sled dog racing. **Hours:** Mon.-Fri. 10-5:30, Sat.-Sun. 1-5, Memorial Day-Labor Day; Tues.-Fri. noon-5, rest of year. Closed Jan. 1, Thanksgiving and Christmas. Phone ahead to confirm schedule. **Cost:** Donations. **Phone:** (907) 443-6630.

PALMER (C-11) pop. 5,937, elev. 240'
• Restaurants p. 654

The peaks of the Chugach and Talkeetna mountains rise above Palmer, a city surrounded by the lush pastures and dairy and vegetable farms of the fertile Matanuska Valley, where cabbages can grow to weigh more than 70 pounds. A drive to Wasilla *(see place listing p. 666)* provides a good view of the valley and its farms. The Matanuska Agricultural Experimental Farm, 7 miles southwest, is operated by the University of Alaska Fairbanks' School of Natural Resources and Agricultural Sciences and welcomes visitors; phone (907) 746-9495.

Palmer lies near the intersection of the Glenn and George Parks highways (SRs 1 and 3), both of which are scenic highways. An interesting drive is along a narrow, rough, winding road that follows Willow Creek through formerly rich gold areas. The road crosses Hatcher Pass en route to Willow.

The Palmer Museum and Visitor Center, 723 S. Valley Way, contains a historical museum featuring items from the city's pioneer era. The 2-acre Agricultural Showcase Garden is on the center's grounds and features a variety of perennials; phone (907) 745-8878. Garden open daily 24 hours. Visitor Center open daily 9-6, May-Sept.

Mat-Su Convention & Visitors Bureau: Milepost 35.5, George Parks Hwy. (SR 3), 7744 E. Visitors View Ct., Palmer, AK 99645. **Phone:** (907) 746-5000.

INDEPENDENCE MINE STATE HISTORICAL PARK, 19 mi. n. on Hatcher Pass Rd., is a 761-acre park in the 221,000-acre Hatcher Pass region. The park preserves 15 buildings and numerous artifacts from its heyday as a gold boom town in the 1930s and 1940s. The history of the mine is chronicled in a museum and at the visitor center. Walking trails lead visitors past many of the mine camp's buildings, including bunkhouses, warehouses, the commissary and mess halls.

Tours: Guided tours are available. **Hours:** Park open daily. Visitor center open daily 11-6, mid-June to Labor Day. Tours are given daily at 1 and 3. **Cost:** $5 (per private vehicle). Guided tour $6. **Phone:** (907) 745-2827 or (907) 745-3975.

MUSK OX FARM, 2 mi. n. at Milepost 50 on Glenn Hwy., is said to be the only musk ox domestication project in the world. The shaggy creatures are valued for their fine underwool called "qiviut." Eskimos knit the hair, eight times warmer by weight than wool, into hats and scarves. Hands-on exhibits are available. Guided tours offer insight into the animal's history and behavior and allow observation from fenced walkways.

Hours: Daily 10-6, mid-May to mid-Sept. Tours depart every 45 minutes. Last tour begins 1 hour before closing. **Cost:** $11; $9 (ages 65+); $5 (ages 6-17). **Phone:** (907) 745-4151. 🅿️

THE INN CAFE   907/746-6118

♦♦ American. Casual Dining. $7-$10 **AAA Inspector Notes:** Just a short distance from the tourist information center, this small restaurant overflows the lobby of the Inn B&B. Immensely popular with locals, the casual place is well known for its tastily prepared meals. Using a mix of local and seasonal ingredients, the chef/owner creates approachable food, such as daily quiches, light sandwiches and salads strong on flavor. **Address:** 325 E Elmwood Ave 99645 **Location:** 1 mi e of Glenn Hwy (SR 1) along Evergreen Ave (which becomes E Elmwood Ave); in Colony Inn. Ⓛ Ⓚ

PETERSBURG (H-11) pop. 2,948, elev. 28'

Petersburg, at the north end of Mitkof Island, is an Alaska Marine Highway port. In 1897 Norwegian Peter Buschmann decided to build a cannery on Mitkof Island at the head of picturesque Wrangell Narrows. The facility at the north end of Nordic Drive was completed in 1900 and packed 32,750 cases of salmon during its first production year. Now Petersburg Fisheries, the firm is a pioneer in Alaska's expanding bottom-fishing and salmon industries.

Nicknamed "Little Norway," Petersburg boasts brightly painted wooden houses decorated with hand-painted floral designs, a traditional craft called rosemaling.

Among the nearby points of interest is LeConte Glacier, the southernmost of its kind in the northern hemisphere; just south of Petersburg; it can be reached via chartered plane, helicopter or boat. In nearby Frederick Sound whale-watching is popular; the area is home to orca and humpback whales as well as other sea mammals.

Petersburg Visitor Information Center: First and Fram sts., P.O. Box 649, Petersburg, AK 99833. **Phone:** (907) 772-4636 or (866) 484-4700.

CLAUSEN MEMORIAL MUSEUM, 203 Fram St., features exhibits about commercial fishing and canning, a dugout Tlingit Indian canoe, tools and artifacts. A "Fisk" fountain and a 126.5-pound king salmon, said to be a world record catch, also are on display. **Tours:** Guided tours are available. **Hours:** Mon.-Sat. 10-5, May 1-Sept. 4; Tues.-Sat. 10-2, Sept. 5-Dec. 23. Winter hours may vary; phone ahead. Closed major holidays. **Cost:** $3; free (ages 0-11). **Phone:** (907) 772-3598.

SEWARD (D-11) pop. 2,693, elev. 70'
• Hotels p. 656 • Restaurants p. 657

Named for William H. Seward, who negotiated the purchase of Alaska, Seward is an ice-free port in a setting of great beauty. At the northeast end of a bay named Resurrection by Russians who arrived in its waters on Easter, the city is surrounded by lush, tall mountains and ice fields.

Charter boats and planes can be hired for fishing, hunting and sightseeing trips. Seward is the southern terminus of the Seward Highway, a national scenic byway extending north to Anchorage through an alpine terrain of glaciers and lakes. Seward also is the main access point to Kenai Fjords National Park *(see place listing p. 647)*, which includes Exit Glacier, one of the few accessible glaciers.

Seward Community Library, 238 5th Ave., shows a movie about the havoc wreaked by the 1964 Good Friday earthquake. The movie is screened Memorial Day-Labor Day; phone (907) 224-4082 for schedule information.

Seward Chamber of Commerce: 2001 Seward Hwy., Seward, AK 99664. **Phone:** (907) 224-8051.

Self-guiding tours: Information about a walking tour is available at the chamber of commerce's visitor information center, 2001 Seward Hwy.; phone (907) 224-8051 for details.

🔻 🆂🅰🆅🅴 **ALASKA SEALIFE CENTER,** on Seward Hwy. (SR 9) at Milepost 0, is dedicated to understanding and maintaining the integrity of Alaska's marine ecosystem through research, rehabilitation, conservation and public education. Highlights include Steller sea lions, harbor seals, Giant Pacific octopus and a sea bird habitat that allows visitors to get up close to puffins, kittiwakes and other Alaskan avian wonders.

Exhibits also include a jellyfish display, the hands-on Discovery touch pool and the Lifecycles of Pacific Salmon, which examines the life stages of all five species of Pacific salmon. More than 300 of the fish may be observed in 2,200- to 6,000-gallon tanks. Guided behind-the-scenes tours are available, including marine mammal, octopus and puffin encounters. Reservations for behind-the-scenes and encounter tours are recommended.

Time: Allow 1 hour, 30 minutes minimum. **Hours:** Mon.-Thurs. 9-6:30, Fri.-Sun. 8-6:30, mid-May to mid-Sept.; daily 10-5, rest of year. Behind-the-scenes tours depart daily at 10, 1 and 3, mid-May to mid-Sept.; daily at 1, rest of year. Marine mammal encounter tours depart daily at 11 and 3. Under 12 are not permitted on behind-the-scenes tours or marine mammal encounters. Puffin encounter tours depart daily at 11 and 2. Octopus encounter tours depart daily at 1 (under 6 are not permitted). Closed Thanksgiving and Christmas. **Cost:** $20; $15 (ages 12-17 and college students with ID); $10 (ages 4-11). Behind-the-scenes tours $15; $10 (ages 12-17). Marine mammal, puffin and octopus encounter tours $79; $59 (ages 12-17); $39 (ages 6-11). **Phone:** (907) 224-6300, (888) 378-2525 for reservations or (800) 224-2525.

GODWIN GLACIER DOG SLED TOURS offers excursions departing from the Seward Airport off Seward Hwy. Beginning with a helicopter flight to Godwin Glacier, the guided tour includes a 2.5-mile dog sled ride traversing the glacier's ancient snowfield. During the round-trip flight, passengers may spot mountain goats, bears, moose and eagles. Other tours are available. **Time:** Allow 2 hours minimum. **Hours:** Tours depart daily, June-Aug. (weather permitting). **Cost:** Fare $450; $420 (ages 0-12). Reservations are recommended. **Phone:** (907) 224-8239 or (888) 989-8239.

IDIDARIDE SLED DOG TOURS is off Seward Hwy. (SR 9) Milepost 3.6, 1 mi. w. on Exit Glacier Rd., .4 mi. n. on Old Exit Glacier Rd. (gravel road) following signs. An Iditarod champion offers a summer version of a sled dog ride aboard a wheeled sled during a 2-mile trip through Box Canyon. Visitors can tour the dog kennel to socialize with the husky puppies and witness a sled dog training demonstration.

Time: Allow 1 hour, 30 minutes minimum. **Hours:** Tours depart daily at 8:30, 10, 11:45, 1:45, 3:30 and 6, mid-May to mid-Sept. **Cost:** $69; $34.50 (ages 2-11). Reservations are recommended. **Phone:** (907) 224-8607 or (800) 478-3139.

 KENAI FJORDS TOURS depart from the Seward Small Boat Harbor. The company offers glacier and wildlife cruises into the waters that surround Kenai Fjords National Park. Cruises also explore Resurrection Bay and the northwestern fjords, where active tidewater glaciers are a highlight. A variety of marine mammals can be seen; gray whales often are spotted on whale-watching tours. Six- and 8.5-hour Kenai Fjords National Park tours; 9-hour Northwestern Fjords tours; and 3- and 4.5-hour Resurrection Bay wildlife cruises with an all-you-can-eat salmon bake at Fox Island, are available.

Inquire about weather policies. **Hours:** Tours depart daily, mid-May to mid-Sept. Kenai Fjords National Park tours depart at 8, 10 and 11:30. Northwestern Fjords tours depart at 9. Resurrection Bay wildlife cruises depart at noon and 5. Phone ahead to confirm schedule. **Cost:** Park tour $144-$164; $72-$82 (ages 2-11). Fjord tour $174; $87 (ages 2-11). Bay tour $64-$94; $32-$47 (ages 2-11). Reservations are recommended. **Phone:** (907) 224-8068 or (877) 777-4051. *(See ad p. 610.)*

MAJOR MARINE TOURS depart from the Seward Small Boat Harbor, 1 blk. e. of Seward Hwy. Narrated glacier and wildlife sightseeing cruises visit Kenai Fjords National Park. Passengers may spot bald eagles, otters, porpoises, puffins, sea lions and whales.

Inquire about weather policies. Full-day cruise not recommended for infants and toddlers. **Hours:** Cruises depart daily, early May to late Sept. Half-day cruises depart at noon and 6, full-day cruises depart at 10 and 11:30. **Cost:** Half-day fare $69-$79;

▼ See AAA listing p. 623 ▼

$34.50-$39.50 (ages 2-11). Full-day fare $149-$159; $74.50-$79.50 (ages 2-11). Reservations are recommended. **Phone:** (907) 274-7300 or (800) 764-7300. *(See ad p. 610, this page.)*

 SCENIC MOUNTAIN AIR (FLIGHTSEEING) operates wheeled planes from Seward Airport and float planes from Trail Lake in Moose Pass. Sights on the varied tours include Harding Icefield, Kenai Fjords and wildlife. Fly-in fishing tours also are available. **Hours:** Flights depart daily 8 a.m.-7 p.m., early May to mid-Sept. (weather permitting). **Cost:** Fares $129-$379, depending on length of tour. Reservations are recommended. **Phone:** (907) 288-3646 or (800) 478-1449.

SEWARD MUSEUM, 336 Third Ave., is operated by the Resurrection Bay Historical Society and has exhibits about the main events in Seward's history. A collection of native baskets and ivory carvings is displayed. **Hours:** Wed.-Sun. 1-5, early June to early Sept.; otherwise varies. Phone ahead to confirm schedule. **Cost:** $3; 50c (ages 5-18). **Phone:** (907) 224-3902.

RECREATIONAL ACTIVITIES
Kayaking
- **Sunny Cove Sea Kayaking** offers tours departing 2 mi. from downtown at Lowell's Point on Resurrection Bay, and from Seward Small Boat Harbor traveling to Fox Island. Other activities are offered. **Hours:** Daily 7:30-7, May-Sept.; by appointment, rest of year. Closed winter holidays. **Phone:** (907) 224-4426, or (800) 770-9119 for reservations.

BEST WESTERN PLUS EDGEWATER HOTEL
(907)224-2700

Hotel
$129-$289

AAA Benefit: Members save up to 20%, plus 10% bonus points with Best Western Rewards®.

Address: 202 Fifth Ave 99664 **Location:** Just n of Alaska SeaLife Center; downtown. **Facility:** 76 units. 3 stories, interior corridors. **Terms:** closed 10/1-4/30, check-in 4 pm, cancellation fee imposed. **Guest Services:** coin laundry, area transportation-train depot & cruise terminal. **Free Special Amenities:** expanded continental breakfast and local telephone calls.

BOX CANYON CABINS
(907)224-5046

 Cabin $159-$280 **Address:** 31515 Lois Way 99664 **Location:** 3.5 mi n on SR 9 (Seward Hwy), just w on Herman Leirer Rd; 1 mi n on Old Exit Glacier Rd, then just e. **Facility:** 6 cabins. 1 story, exterior corridors. *Bath:* shower only. **Terms:** check-in 4 pm, 45 day cancellation notice-fee imposed. **Guest Services:** coin laundry.

HARBORVIEW INN
(907)224-3217

Motel $79-$309 **Address:** 804 Third Ave 99664 **Location:** Just n of Alaska SeaLife Center; downtown. **Facility:** 39 units, some two bedrooms and kitchens. 2 stories (no elevator), exterior corridors. **Terms:** closed 10/1-4/30, check-in 4 pm, 3 day cancellation notice-fee imposed.

HOLIDAY INN EXPRESS SEWARD HARBOR HOTEL
(907)224-2550

Hotel $79-$289 **Address:** 1412 4th Ave 99664 **Location:** At Small Boat Harbor. **Facility:** 90 units. 3 stories, interior corridors. **Terms:** check-in 4 pm, cancellation fee imposed. **Amenities:** high-speed Internet. **Pool(s):** heated indoor. **Activities:** whirlpool. **Guest Services:** coin laundry.

▼ See AAA listing p. 655 ▼

Experience
Kenai Fjords National Park
- Cruise among wildlife and glaciers.
- Kenai Fjords Park Ranger onboard.
- Dine on Alaska salmon and prime rib.
- Full & half day cruises from Seward.
- AAA members receive 10% off.

Major **MARINE TOURS**
www.majormarine.com
800-764-7300

Visit your AAA/CAA Travel office to book a AAA Vacations® Disney package

HOTEL SEWARD

(907)224-8001

Hotel
$59-$379

Address: 221 Fifth Ave 99664 **Location:** Just n of Alaska SeaLife Center; downtown. **Facility:** 38 units. 2 stories, interior corridors. **Parking:** on-site and street. **Terms:** check-in 4 pm, 3 day cancellation notice-fee imposed. **Activities:** fishing. **Guest Services:** coin laundry, area transportation-train depot & cruise terminal. **Free Special Amenities: high-speed Internet and use of on-premises laundry facilities.**

SEWARD WINDSONG LODGE

907/224-7116

Hotel
Rates not provided

Address: 31772 Herman Leirer Rd 99664 **Location:** 3.5 mi n on SR 9 (Seward Hwy) exit Glacier Rd, 0.5 mi w. **Facility:** 180 units. 2 stories (no elevator), exterior corridors. **Dining:** Resurrection Roadhouse, see separate listing. **Guest Services:** area transportation-downtown & harbor. **Free Special Amenities: local telephone calls and high-speed Internet.**

WHERE TO EAT

CHINOOKS WATERFRONT RESTAURANT   907/224-2207

Seafood
Steak
Casual Dining
$8-$35

AAA Inspector Notes: Diners can enjoy, on a clear day, the spectacular views of the mountains and harbor from the large panoramic windows. A great choice for both family and special occasion dining, the restaurant features two floors of dining with great views from all tables. The view is complemented by the chef's selection of fresh local seafood, pasta and steak selections. **Bar:** full bar. **Address:** 1404 Fourth Ave 99664 **Location:** At Small Boat Harbor. **Parking:** street only.

CHRISTO'S PALACE

907/224-5255

American. Casual Dining. $12-$28 **AAA Inspector Notes:** This popular downtown spot has a little something for everyone on its menu. Pizza is the house specialty but burgers, Mexican fare, pasta, steaks and such fresh Alaskan seafood as king crab legs, salmon and halibut round out the offerings. **Bar:** full bar. **Address:** 133 Fourth Ave 99664 **Location:** Just n of Alaska SeaLife Center; downtown. **Parking:** street only.

ORIENTAL GARDEN

907/224-7677

Chinese. Casual Dining. $10-$18 **AAA Inspector Notes:** This casual restaurant has very authentic Oriental décor complete with Chinese lanterns and a comfortable ambience. A tasty luncheon buffet is featured Monday through Saturday in addition to the full à la carte selections. Chinese and a few Korean dishes are featured here, with some very reasonably priced combination meals being popular choices. **Address:** 313 4th Ave 99664 **Location:** Just n of Alaska SeaLife Center; downtown. **Parking:** street only.

PEKING RESTAURANT

907/224-5444

Chinese. Casual Dining. $7-$15 **AAA Inspector Notes:** This traditional restaurant serves a variety of dishes, including chicken balls and lemon chicken and rice, as well as dishes inspired by the area. For a new twist, try the kung pao halibut, a tasty dish that is sure to please. At lunch you satisfy any hunger at the all-you-can-eat buffet, or order a la carte off the menu. **Bar:** full bar. **Address:** 338 Fourth Ave 99664 **Location:** Downtown. **Parking:** street only.

RESURRECTION ROADHOUSE

907/224-7116

Regional American. Fine Dining. $12-$35 **AAA Inspector Notes:** Continuing the theme of the adjacent lodge, diners will be seated in a dining room with a natural wood decor while enjoying the views of the wooded setting overlooking a glacial stream. The chef's creativity shines when he is handed one of the first king salmon of the season from local waters for your eating pleasure. Expect the freshest seafood and the highest grades of beef, including Kobe, on the menu. The staff has honed in on the varied wine selection in order to offer the best. **Bar:** full bar. **Reservations:** suggested. **Address:** 31772 Herman Leirer Rd 99664 **Location:** 3.5 mi n on SR 9 (Seward Hwy) exit Glacier Rd, 0.5 mi w; in Seward Windsong Lodge.

SALMON BAKE

907/224-2204

Alaskan. Family Dining. $9-$30 **AAA Inspector Notes:** Their motto is "Cheap Beer and Lousy Food," taken tongue-in-cheek, of course! The log cabin-style restaurant is nestled in a wooded area on the outskirts of town, on the way to Exit Glacier. Very family friendly, this is a true Alaskan treat with fresh salmon, halibut and crab cooked a variety of ways and served in a basket with all the trimmings. **Bar:** full bar. **Address:** 1/4 Mile Exit Glacier Road 99664 **Location:** Jct Seward Hwy, just e on Herman Leirer Rd.

SITKA (H-10) pop. 8,881
• Hotels p. 658 • Restaurants p. 658

Surrounded by high peaks and small wooded islands, historic Sitka is accessible by air or the Alaska Marine Highway.

In 1804 Russians led by Alexander Baranov established a settlement on the site of an ancient Tlingit (KLINK-it) village; that settlement became the capital of Russian America. Originally named New Archangel, it was a thriving port of nearly 3,000 when San Francisco was just a mission village. Castle Hill marks the site of Baranov's headquarters and commemorates the 1867 ceremony that transferred ownership of Alaska from Russia to the United States. St. Michael's Cathedral, a restored Russian church with an onion-shaped dome, contains a collection of religious icons and artwork; phone (907) 747-8120.

The colorfully costumed New Archangel Dancers perform Russian dances in the Harrigan Centennial Hall auditorium, 330 Harbor Dr., during summer when large ships are in port; phone (907) 747-5516. Performances by the Sheet'ka Kwaán Naa Kahídi Native Dancers are given at the Tribal Community House on Katlian Street; phone (907) 747-7290.

For cruise ship and ferry passengers, Sitka Tribal Tours offers a short bus tour of Sitka, which includes guide service and round-trip transportation from the port; its native Alaskan guides all live in the Sitka community. The company also offers performances by native dancers as well as walking tours of the town and Sitka National Historical Park; phone (888) 270-8687.

Sitka Convention and Visitors Bureau: P.O. Box 1226, Sitka, AK 99835. **Phone:** (907) 747-5940 or (800) 557-4852.

ALASKA RAPTOR CENTER, .8 mi. e. of Lake St. at 1000 Raptor Way, is home to more than 20 "raptors in residence," including bald and golden eagles, hawks, falcons and owls. The

17-acre rehabilitation center, surrounded by muskeg, mountains and the Indian River, provides medical treatment to more than 100 eagles and other birds of prey each year. A stage presentation, a videotape, live demonstrations of birds in flight training and a .25-mile nature trail are available.

Raptors unable to be released into the wild help educate visitors and travel to schools nationwide to raise awareness of wild birds and their habitats. Feathers, bones, photographs and a national map indicating where birds have been released are displayed. Visitors can view raptors in their natural habitats outside the center as well as in the clinic's treatment room and recuperation areas.

Tours: Guided tours are available. **Time:** Allow 1 hour, 30 minutes minimum. **Hours:** Daily 8-4, May-Sept. **Cost:** $12; $6 (ages 0-12). **Phone:** (907) 747-8662 or (800) 643-9425.

SHELDON JACKSON MUSEUM is at 104 College Dr. Housed in one of the first concrete structures built in Alaska, it is reputed to be the oldest continuing museum in Alaska. Displays of Eskimo, Aleut and Northwest Coast and Athabaskan Indian artifacts include pelts, sleds, kayaks, ceremonial masks, and tools and utensils of wood, bone and ivory.

Time: Allow 30 minutes minimum. **Hours:** Daily 9-5, mid-May to mid-Sept.; Tues.-Sat. 10-4, rest of year. Closed major holidays. **Cost:** mid-May to mid-Sept. $5; $4 (ages 65+); free (ages 0-18); rest of year $3; free (ages 0-18). **Phone:** (907) 747-8981.

SITKA HISTORICAL SOCIETY AND MUSEUM is at 330 Harbor Dr. in the Harrigan Centennial Building. The museum features exhibits depicting the history of Sitka, including the area's earliest inhabitants and the legacy of World War II. Displays illustrate the lifestyles of the Tlingit along with the town's Russian, Finish, Asian and American settlers. An 8-square-foot diorama shows Sitka as it appeared in 1867, the year Alaska was transferred to the United States from Russia.

Time: Allow 30 minutes minimum. **Hours:** Mon.-Fri. 9-5, Sat.-Sun. 10-4, early May-late Sept.; Tues.-Sat. 10-4, rest of year. Phone ahead to confirm schedule. **Cost:** $2; free (ages 0-18). **Phone:** (907) 747-6455.

ALASKA OCEAN VIEW BED AND BREAKFAST INN
(907)747-8310
Bed & Breakfast $99-$249 **Address:** 1101 Edgecumbe Dr 99835 **Location:** 1 mi n on Halibut Point Rd, just e on Kashevaroff St, then just s. Located in a residential area. **Facility:** 3 units. 2 stories (no elevator), interior corridors. **Terms:** cancellation fee imposed. **Activities:** whirlpool, horseshoes.

SHEE ATIKA TOTEM SQUARE INN (907)747-3693

Hotel
$149-$229

Address: 201 Katlian St 99835 **Location:** In Totem Square Complex near Municipal Office. **Facility:** 68 units, some kitchens. 4 stories, interior corridors. **Terms:** cancellation fee imposed. **Amenities:** high-speed Internet. **Activities:** exercise room. **Guest Services:** coin laundry, area transportation-within 3 mi. **Free Special Amenities: high-speed Internet and airport transportation.**

SUPER 8-SITKA (907)747-8804

Hotel $99-$139 **Address:** 404 Sawmill Creek Rd 99835 **Location:** Just e from corner of Lake St and Halibut Point/Sawmill Creek Rd; center. **Facility:** 35 units. 2 stories (no elevator), interior corridors. **Amenities:** high-speed Internet, safes. **Activities:** whirlpool. **Guest Services:** coin laundry.

WESTMARK SITKA (907)747-6241

Hotel $99-$299 **Address:** 330 Seward St 99835 **Location:** Center. **Facility:** 105 units, some kitchens. 4 stories, interior corridors. **Terms:** cancellation fee imposed. **Dining:** Raven Dining Room, see separate listing. **Activities:** exercise room. **Guest Services:** valet and coin laundry.

WILD STRAWBERRY LODGE FISHING RESORT
907/747-3232
Resort Motel $75-$195 **Address:** 724 Siginaka Way 99835 **Location:** 1 mi n on Halibut Point Rd, just w on Katlian (only traffic light on island). Located at Thomsen Harbor. **Facility:** This is not your typical fishing lodge, as the owners encourage males and females of all ages to try their hand at catching "the big one." The owners and staff are very family oriented and welcoming. 12 units, some two bedrooms, kitchens and houses. 1 story, interior/exterior corridors. **Terms:** cancellation fee imposed. **Amenities:** Some: high-speed Internet. **Activities:** Fee: charter fishing. **Guest Services:** complimentary laundry, area transportation-ferry terminal, town & local attractions.

WHERE TO EAT

CHANNEL CLUB 907/747-7440
Regional American. Fine Dining. $18-$42 **AAA Inspector Notes:** A Sitka tradition since 1956, this restaurant's owners completely rebuilt the establishment in 2008. It retained many of its original, best-loved menu offerings, so guests will still find signature cuts of organic meats and some signature salads. Highlights include delicious seafood plucked fresh from Sitka's waters, salads using organic ingredients and decadent desserts. Every seat in the restaurant has a view of the bay, and a complimentary shuttle is available. **Bar:** full bar. **Reservations:** suggested. **Address:** 2906 Halibut Point Rd 99835 **Location:** 2.9 mi n on Halibut Point Rd from 4-way stop; 3.4 mi s of Alaska Marine Hwy ferry terminal.

KENNY'S ROMA AMERICAN & ITALIAN RESTAURANT
907/966-4600
Italian. Casual Dining. $9-$23 **AAA Inspector Notes:** In a convenient location downtown, this restaurant is open all day long and features burgers, sandwiches, hot subs, specialty pizza and some oven baked pasta. **Bar:** beer & wine. **Address:** 327 Seward St 99835 **Location:** Center; across from Westmark Sitka.

LARKSPUR CAFE 907/966-2326
American. Casual Dining. $8-$16 **AAA Inspector Notes:** Organic and some gluten-free offerings are featured at this coffee house/café. Local seafood is always on the menu. **Bar:** beer & wine. **Address:** 2 Lincoln St, Suite 1A 99835 **Location:** Center. **Parking:** on-site and street.

LITTLE TOKYO
907/747-5699

◆ Sushi. Casual Dining. $8-$15 **AAA Inspector Notes:** This small restaurant with a sushi bar sits just a short walk from the marina. Diners can watch chefs prepare their sushi and sashimi, or they can order from the standard menu. **Bar:** beer & wine. **Address:** 315 Lincoln St 99835 **Location:** Between Lake and Maksoutoff sts; downtown. **Parking:** street only. [L] [D] [K]

LUDVIG'S BISTRO
907/966-3663

◆◆◆ Mediterranean. Casual Dining. $20-$33 **AAA Inspector Notes:** A popular choice with locals and visitors alike, this small restaurant with limited seating serves a variety of Mediterranean fare prepared with regional influences. Reservations are recommended. **Bar:** beer & wine. **Reservations:** required. **Address:** 256 Katlian St 99835 **Location:** Center; 0.3 mi n of Totem Square. **Parking:** street only. [D]

RAVEN DINING ROOM
907/747-6241

◆◆ American. Casual Dining. $12-$50 **AAA Inspector Notes:** This casual restaurant has long served as the training kitchen for chefs who later go on to work on the cruise ships that the restaurant overlooks. Diners can expect standard items ranging from sandwiches to steak as well as creative touches to locally caught and seasonal seafood. **Bar:** full bar. **Reservations:** suggested. **Address:** 330 Seward St 99835 **Location:** Center; in Westmark Sitka. **Parking:** on-site and street. [B] [L] [D] CALL 🅂🅼 [K]

VAN WINKLE & SONS
907/747-7652

◆◆◆ American. Casual Dining. $10-$30 **AAA Inspector Notes:** Tasty regional cuisine awaits at this popular eatery. Alaskan art adorns the walls, and guests can gaze at the water while dining. Located upstairs in a small shopping mall near the bridge, the restaurant's view of the bay is spectacular and the food well prepared. **Bar:** full bar. **Reservations:** suggested, in summer. **Address:** 205 Harbor Dr 99835 **Location:** Downtown; across from Crescent Harbor, just before O'Connell Bridge. [L] [D] CALL 🅂🅼

◈ SITKA NATIONAL HISTORICAL PARK (H-10)

Near downtown Sitka on Lincoln Street, this urban park commemorates the Battle of Sitka, fought in 1804 between the Kiksadi Tlingit Indians and the fur hunters and Aleut natives of the Russian-American Co. The battle marked the last major resistance by Alaskan natives to European domination. The 113-acre park preserves the Tlingit fort site, the battlefield and the 1842 Russian Bishop's House.

A fine collection of Tlingit (KLINK-it) and Haida (HY-dah) totem poles, some more than a century old, is displayed along a 2-mile trail through the park's temperate rain forest and coastal intertidal area. During August and September visitors may view salmon spawning in the Indian River.

The visitor center contains exhibits and audiovisual presentations about the area's Tlingit Indian heritage as well as its Russian legacy. Within the visitor center skilled native artisans demonstrate traditional crafts at the Southeast Alaska Indian Cultural Center, which is open daily.

Park open daily 6 a.m.-10 p.m., May-Sept.; 8-7, rest of year. Visitor center open daily 8-5, May-Sept.; Mon.-Sat. 8-5, rest of year. Closed winter holidays. Park and visitor center free. Address inquiries to the Superintendent, Sitka National Historical Park, 103 Monastery St., Sitka, AK 99835; phone (907) 747-0110.

THE RUSSIAN BISHOP'S HOUSE, 501 Lincoln St. across from Crescent Harbor, is a two-story log structure completed in 1842. It is one of the last surviving colonial Russian buildings in North America. Restored to its 1853 appearance, the building reflects the influence of the Russian Orthodox Church and the traders of the Russian-American Co., who made Sitka the capital of colonial Russian America.

Time: Allow 30 minutes minimum. **Hours:** Daily and holidays 8:30-5, mid-May to late Sept.; by appointment rest of year. **Cost:** $4; free (ages 0-15). **Phone:** (907) 747-0110.

SKAGWAY (F-10) pop. 920, elev. 2'
• Hotels p. 660 • Restaurants p. 661

During the icy winter of 1897-98 hordes of enthusiastic would-be prospectors who had heard of the Klondike gold strike swarmed ashore at Dyea. They assembled their gear and began the trek over treacherous mountains and down raging rivers to the Klondike. Within 3 months of the first gold strike, the settlement at Skagway grew from one cabin into a thriving city of more than 20,000 people. But the gold rush ended suddenly, and those who had come to Skagway moved on.

The notorious outlaw Jefferson R. "Soapy" Smith and Frank Reid, who represented the outraged citizenry, shot it out in a battle that cost both men their lives. Gold Rush Cemetery, 1.5 miles from town, contains the graves of both "Soapy" Smith and Frank Reid.

A stop on many summer cruises along the Inside Passage, Skagway is the northern terminus of the Alaska Marine Highway. Sightseeing opportunities include visits to Reid Falls and flower gardens; tours of the city and the harbor; flightseeing tours to Glacier Bay, gold rush trails and the Juneau Ice Cap; bus excursions to Dyea and Carcross, Yukon; and hiking trips to AB Mountain and the Dewey Lakes.

[SAVE] Gray Line of Alaska offers historical points-of-interest tours daily; phone (907) 983-2241 or (800) 452-1737.

Skagway Convention & Visitors Bureau: P.O. Box 1029, Skagway, AK 99840. **Phone:** (907) 983-2854 or (888) 762-1898.

THE DAYS OF '98 SHOW WITH SOAPY SMITH, presented at Eagles' Hall, 6th Ave. and Broadway, includes a stage show with original songs, a cancan line, a historic shoot-out and mock gambling. **Hours:** Mock gambling nightly at 7. Stage shows daily at 10:30, 12:30, 2:30 and 8, mid-May to mid-Sept. On days without multiple cruise ships in port, some showtimes may not be offered. Also, some Sundays are dark. Phoning ahead to confirm schedule is highly recommended. **Cost:** Daytime shows $20; $10 (ages 3-12). Evening show $22; $11 (ages 3-12). **Phone:** (907) 983-2545.

JEWELL GARDENS & GLASSWORKS is 1.5 mi. n. on Klondike Hwy. Once the site of a late 19th-century vegetable farm known best for its rhubarb, the gardens feature such spectacular flowers as begonias, delphiniums, lilacs, nasturtiums and poppies. The mountains along the Lynn Canal serve as a backdrop to the site, which also is home to organic herb and vegetable gardens and a greenhouse. At the glassblowing theater, visitors may observe daily demonstrations.

Time: Allow 3 hours minimum. **Hours:** Daily 9-5, early May-late Sept. **Cost:** $12; $6 (ages 0-12). **Phone:** (907) 983-2111. 🍴 🍽

KLONDIKE GOLD RUSH NATIONAL HISTORICAL PARK includes the Skagway Historic District and Chilkoot and White Pass trails, over which each prospector was required to haul nearly a ton of supplies during the gold rush of 1897-98. It was during this stampede that Skagway's population boomed from 5 to more than 10,000.

The park visitor center is in the original White Pass and Yukon Route Railroad Depot, one of Alaska's oldest. At Broadway and Second Avenue, it contains exhibits and interpretive programs about the era. Two films are shown: an orientation film about the gold rush, and a film about hiking the Chilkoot Trail. Walking tours led by a park ranger explore the Skagway Historic District, where many restored buildings represent a colorful history. The Chilkoot Trail Center provides information about day hikes and backpacking on the Chilkoot Trail.

Hours: Visitor center Mon.-Fri. 7:30 a.m.-7 p.m., Sat.-Sun. 8-6, early May-late Sept. Visitor center exhibits daily 7:30 a.m.-6 p.m., early May-late Sept.; 8-5, rest of year. Orientation film is shown on the hour at 8, 9 and 11-5, early May-late Sept. Walking tours depart the visitor center daily on the hour 9-11 and 2-3, early May-late Sept. Trail center daily 8-5, June-Labor Day weekend. **Cost:** Visitor center (including exhibits), walking tours and trail center free. Fees apply and reservations are recommended for Chilkoot Trail backpacking. **Phone:** (907) 983-2921 for the visitor center, (907) 983-9234 for trail information June-Aug., or (800) 661-0486 for trail information rest of year.

SKAGWAY MUSEUM is at Seventh Ave. and Spring St. in the McCabe College Building. Displays pertain to Alaskan history and native cultures, including a Tlingit war canoe, photographs, documents, gold rush relics and native artifacts. **Hours:** Mon.-Fri. 9-5, Sat. 10-5, Sun. 1-4, May-Sept.; hours vary rest of year. **Cost:** $2; $1 (senior citizens and students with ID); free (ages 0-12). **Phone:** (907) 983-2420.

WHITE PASS & YUKON ROUTE is at Second Ave. and Spring St. A vintage train chugs across mountain rivers and chasms during fully narrated narrow-gauge rides. The rail line was built in 1898 to carry people and supplies to the Klondike gold rush. Passengers travel round-trip in a period parlor car to the summit of White Pass or Fraser Meadows, past granite gulches, cascading waterfalls and spectacular scenery. A narrator tells the story of the stampede north into the gold fields through some of the most rugged terrain in the United States and Canada.

The 3-hour White Pass summit excursion rises from tidewater elevations to 2,865 feet in 20 miles. The 4-hour summit excursion to Fraser Meadows rises from tidewater elevation to 3,000 feet in 26 miles. One-way excursions to Lake Bennett and Fraser, British Columbia as well as to Carcross, Yukon also are available.

Hours: Ticket office open daily 7:30-4:30, May-Sept. White Pass excursions depart daily at 8:15 and 12:45, also Tues.-Wed. at 4:30 (weather permitting), late May-early Sept. Fraser Meadows excursions depart Fri. and Mon. at noon, mid-May to mid-Sept. Phone ahead to confirm schedule. **Cost:** White Pass fare $113; $56.50 (ages 3-12). Fraser Meadows fare $155; $77.50 (ages 3-12). Reservations are required. **Phone:** (800) 343-7373. *(See ad this page.)*

WHERE TO EAT

BOMBAY CURRY   907/983-2400

W Indian. Casual Dining. $8-$18 **AAA Inspector Notes:** This small, family-run diner offers an extensive buffet for lunch or individual combination plates. The Indian music lends an authentic feel to the simple decor. The focus is on traditional curries made with lamb and chicken, while specialties include goat and Alaskan seafood. Delicious naan and paratha breads are baked in the tandoori oven. Appetizers include mushrooms or prawns in a garlic curry sauce. A refreshing mango lassi is a good meal ender. **Address:** 302 5th Ave 99840 **Location:** Downtown. **Parking:** street only.
(L) (D) (K)

BONANZA BAR & GRILL   907/983-6214

W American. Casual Dining. $9-$16 **AAA Inspector Notes:** Open seasonally, this sports bar can be loud and boisterous and is a popular spot for those looking for a wide selection of bar favorites. **Bar:** full bar. **Address:** 3rd Ave & Spring St 99840 **Location:** Jct 3rd and Broadway sts; downtown; in Westmark Inn Skagway. **Parking:** street only. (L) (D) CALL (M) (K)

STARFIRE   907/983-3663

WW Thai. Casual Dining. $13-$19 **AAA Inspector Notes:** Just off Main Street, this casual setting features an American chef trained in Thailand, so the twist is American. The spices are perfectly authentic, so diners should specify the heat level. **Bar:** beer & wine. **Address:** 4th Ave & Spring St 99840 **Location:** Jct 4th Ave and Spring St. **Parking:** street only. (L) (D) CALL (M) (K)

SWEET TOOTH CAFE   907/983-2405

W American. Family Dining. $7-$15 **AAA Inspector Notes:** A local favorite, this casual Victorian-style restaurant offers few surprises but is well regarded for its nicely-prepared breakfasts and lunches. **Address:** 315 Broadway St 99840 **Location:** Jct 3rd St; downtown. **Parking:** street only. (B) (L) (K)

SOLDOTNA (D-10) pop. 4,163

Soldotna's location on the Kenai Peninsula at the junction of Sterling and Kenai Spur highways has ensured its steady growth since homesteading began in 1947. World War II veterans were among the first homesteaders; they were given a 90-day preference right in choosing and filing for land.

The area is rich with opportunities for year-round recreation—hiking, fishing, camping, canoeing and ice fishing are favored activities. Nearby Kenai River yields record catches of salmon and rainbow trout.

Soldotna Chamber of Commerce and Visitor Information Center: 44790 Sterling Hwy., Soldotna, AK 99669. **Phone:** (907) 262-9814.

KENAI NATIONAL WILDLIFE REFUGE, with its headquarters in Soldotna, covers about 1,920,000 acres. The refuge was established in 1941 by President Franklin D. Roosevelt to preserve the area's large moose population. Other wildlife include Dall sheep, coyotes, black bears and bald eagles. Fishing and hunting are subject to state and federal regulations. Boat ramps, trails and camping are available. **Hours:** The refuge is open all year, except when roads are impassable. **Phone:** (907) 262-7021 or TTY (907) 260-2803.

Visitor Center, 1 mi. s.e. of the Kenai River Bridge on Ski Hill Rd., exhibits wildlife dioramas and presents films. **Hours:** Mon.-Fri. 8-4:30, Sat.-Sun. 9-5, June 1-Labor Day; Mon.-Fri. 8-4:30, Sat. 10-5, rest of year. Phone ahead to confirm schedule. **Cost:** Free.

ASPEN HOTEL-SOLDOTNA   (907)260-7736

WWW Hotel $99-$199 **Address:** 326 Binkley Cir 99669 **Location:** Sterling Hwy (SR 1); center. **Facility:** 63 units, some two bedrooms and efficiencies. 2 stories, interior corridors. **Parking:** winter plug-ins. **Terms:** cancellation fee imposed. **Pool(s):** heated indoor. **Activities:** whirlpool, limited exercise equipment. **Guest Services:** valet and coin laundry.

BEST WESTERN KING SALMON MOTEL   (907)262-5857

WWW
Motel
$89-$199

AAA Benefit: Members save up to 20%, plus 10% bonus points with Best Western Rewards®.

Address: 35546A Kenai Spur Hwy 99669 **Location:** Jct Sterling Hwy (SR 1), 1 mi w. **Facility:** 47 units. 2 stories (no elevator), exterior corridors. **Parking:** winter plug-ins. **Terms:** check-in 4 pm, 7 day cancellation notice-fee imposed. **Amenities:** high-speed Internet. **Guest Services:** coin laundry. **Free Special Amenities:** full breakfast and local telephone calls.

ORCA LODGE   (907)262-5649

W Cottage $175-$300 **Address:** 44250 Oehler Dr 99669 **Location:** Sterling Hwy (SR 1) at Milepost 96.5, 0.8 mi e on Funny River Rd, just n. **Facility:** 6 cabins. 1 story, exterior corridors. **Terms:** closed 10/1-4/30, 30 day cancellation notice-fee imposed. **Activities:** fishing. **Fee:** charter fishing.

WHERE TO EAT

BUCKETS SPORTS GRILL   907/262-7220

WW American. Casual Dining. $10-$20 **AAA Inspector Notes:** This isn't the fanciest restaurant in town but it is the place to watch sports on the big screen while enjoying a cold one with friends. The menu is chock-full of tasty bar munchies like ribs and wings, not to mention awesome burgers and fries. Halibut, chicken, pasta dishes and salads ensure there will be something to satisfy everyone. **Bar:** full bar. **Address:** 43960 Sterling Hwy (SR 1) 99669 **Location:** Jct Kenai Spur Hwy, just n. (B) (L) (D) (K)

CHINA SEA RESTAURANT   907/262-5033

W Chinese. Casual Dining. $8-$15 **AAA Inspector Notes:** A local favorite for the all-day all-you-can-eat Chinese buffet, this restaurant offers a nice mix of casual fare in a relaxed setting. The buffet includes a tasty salad bar; a choice of soups; and mixed Chinese fare, including noodles, stir-fry, sweet and sour pork, chicken wings and rice. **Address:** 44539 Sterling Hwy, Suite 210 99669 **Location:** Sterling Hwy (SR 1); in the Blazy Soldotna Mall, 2nd Floor. (L) (D)

FINE THYME CAFE AT RIVER CITY BOOKS   907/262-6620

W Sandwiches Soup. Quick Serve. $8-$11 **AAA Inspector Notes:** Tucked in the back of a bookstore, the restaurant is one of the city's best-kept secrets. A limited menu lists a choice of sandwiches, wraps, soups and often a quiche of the day. Guests are welcomed to linger over a cup of coffee, then browse the bookstore. **Address:** 43977 Sterling Hwy 99669 **Location:** Jct Sterling Hwy (SR 1) and Kenai Spur Hwy, on east side of intersection; in Cornerstone Marketplace. (L) (K)

FROSO'S FAMILY DINING   907/262-7797

WW American. Casual Dining. $9-$26 **AAA Inspector Notes:** This family-oriented restaurant has a distinct Greek influence in its decor and menu selections. Guests enjoy the comfortable booths and ornate chandeliers that adorn the ceilings. The extensive menu includes fine steak and seafood options, freshly made pizza and pasta dishes, and a full Mexican section. All entrées include soup or salad, or for an additional charge, diners can indulge in the salad bar. **Bar:** full bar. **Address:** 35433 Kenai Spur Hwy 99669 **Location:** Jct Sterling Hwy (SR 1), 0.7 mi w. (L) (D) CALL (M) (K)

STERLING (D-10) pop. 5,617, elev. 198'

RECREATIONAL ACTIVITIES
Fishing
- **Great Alaska International Adventure,** 33881 Sterling Hwy. Other activities are offered. **Hours:** Trips are offered mid-May to late Sept. **Phone:** (907) 262-4515, mid-Apr. to late Sept., or (800) 544-2261, rest of year.

SUZIE'S CAFE   907/260-5751

◆◆◆◆ American. Family Dining. $7-$14 **AAA Inspector Notes:** Ask anyone in Sterling for a great, inexpensive place to eat, and this place will be mentioned again and again. The diner-style eatery is conveniently located on the highway so guests can stop to enjoy huge burgers, fish and chips, sandwiches and salads. Breakfast is available on weekends, and service is prompt and attentive. **Address:** 38515 Barbara St 99672 **Location:** Milepost 83, Sterling Hwy (SR 1). Ⓛ Ⓓ Ⓚ

TALKEETNA (C-11) pop. 876, elev. 355'

Situated at the confluence of the Talkeetna, Susitna and Chulitna rivers, Talkeetna takes its name from the Tanaina Indian word for "river of plenty." The village was an important supply station for gold prospectors from the late 1800s to 1940, but is now a popular staging area for outdoors enthusiasts.

Self-guiding tours: A map of a downtown walking tour is available at Talkeetna Historical Society Museum (see attraction listing) and the visitor center next to Village Park on Main Street.

K-2 AVIATION is at Talkeetna State Airport off Talkeetna Spur Rd. Flightseeing tours of varying types and lengths include the 1-hour McKinley Experience, which offers views of Mount McKinley and Ruth Glacier; the 75-minute McKinley Climber & Summit Tour to the mountain's summit; the McKinley Flyer Tour, which lasts 75 minutes and offers views of the mountain range's south side; and the 90-minute Denali Grand Tour, which encircles the mountain and offers views of Kahiltna and Ruth glaciers. Glacier landings are available for an additional fee.

Note: A fuel surcharge of 5 percent is added to the cost of each trip. **Hours:** Daily 7 a.m.-9 p.m., mid-May to late-Sept.; Mon.-Fri. 8:30-4, rest of year (weather permitting). **Cost:** McKinley Climber & Summit Tour fare $310. Denali Grand Tour fare $310; $385 (with glacier landing). McKinley Flyer Tour fare $265; $340 (with glacier landing). McKinley Experience fare $205; $280 (with glacier landing). Reservations are recommended. **Phone:** (907) 733-2291 or (800) 764-2291.

MAHAY'S RIVERBOAT SERVICE departs from Milepost 14 on Talkeetna Spur Rd. The company offers three excursions: a 2-hour, 20-mile Wilderness Jetboat Adventure; a 3.5-hour, 50-mile three-river tour on the Chulitna, Susitna and Talkeetna rivers; and a 5-hour Devil's Canyon tour. Tours offer a leisurely .25-mile nature walk to a native Indian encampment and a view into the lives of turn-of-the-century trappers.

Time: Allow 2 hours minimum. **Hours:** Office open daily 7 a.m.-9 p.m., mid-May to mid-Sept. Wilderness Jetboat Adventure departs daily at 8:45, noon, 2:30 and 6:30, mid-May to mid-Sept. Three-river tour departs daily at 3:30, mid-May to mid-Sept. Canyon tour departs daily at 9:30, mid-May to mid-Sept. **Cost:** Wilderness Jetboat Adventure $65; $49 (ages 0-12). Three-river tour $110; $82.50 (ages 0-12). Canyon tour $155; $116 (ages 0-12). **Phone:** (907) 733-2223 or (800) 736-2210.

MUSEUM OF NORTHERN ADVENTURE, on Main St. across from the post office, recounts the eras, lore and natural history of northern Alaska through dioramas, life-size wax figures, sound effects, photographs and newspaper articles. A trophy room contains big game and other wildlife taxidermy. **Time:** Allow 30 minutes minimum. **Hours:** Daily 10-6, mid-May to mid-Sept. **Cost:** $2; $1 (ages 65+); free (ages 0-12). **Phone:** (907) 733-3999.

TALKEETNA AERO SERVICES/FLY DENALI departs from Talkeetna State Airport, off Talkeetna Spur Rd., and Healy River Airport near Denali National Park and Preserve. Passengers are treated to views of Mt. McKinley, Denali National Park and Preserve or the Kahiltna Glacier from 20,000 feet as well as glacier landings on Mt. McKinley. Flights from Anchorage and Talkeetna to Denali National Park and Preserve are available. **Time:** Allow 2 hours minimum. **Hours:** Daily 7 a.m.-8 p.m., mid-May to mid-Sept.; 9-5, rest of year (weather permitting). **Cost:** Fare $250-$449 (depending on tour). **Phone:** (907) 733-2899 or (888) 733-2899.

TALKEETNA AIR TAXI, at Talkeetna State Airport off Talkeetna Spur Rd., offers three flightseeing tours: a 1-hour South Face McKinley Tour, with views of Ruth Gorge; a 75-minute McKinley Base Camp Tour, which circles over Kahiltna Glacier; and a 90-minute Grand Denali Tour, which offers views of active gold mines, Kahiltna base camp and Wickersham Wall. Other activities such as mountain climbing, glacier landings and support and wilderness tours also are offered.

Hours: Daily 7 a.m.-10 p.m., May-Sept.; 9-4, rest of year (weather permitting). Phone ahead to confirm schedule. **Cost:** South Face McKinley Tour fare May-Sept. $195; $270 (with glacier landing). McKinley Base Camp Tour fare May-Sept. $250; $325 (with glacier landing). Grand Denali Tour fare May-Sept. $290; $365 (with glacier landing). Call ahead for winter rates. Reservations are recommended. **Phone:** (907) 733-2218 or (800) 533-2219.

TALKEETNA HISTORICAL SOCIETY MUSEUM, in five buildings at the corner of First Alley and Village Airstrip Rd., displays a wealth of local history memorabilia within re-creations of a log cabin, a one-room schoolhouse, a railroad depot and section house. Of interest is a large-scale model of Mount McKinley and the surrounding area. **Time:** Allow 30 minutes minimum. **Hours:** Daily 10-6, May-Sept.; by appointment rest of year. Phone ahead to confirm schedule. **Cost:** $3; free (ages 0-12). **Phone:** (907) 733-2487.

TALKEETNA ALASKAN LODGE   (907)733-9500

Hotel

$189-$599

Address: 23601 S Talkeetna Spur Rd 99676 **Location:** 3.5 mi s of Talkeetna. **Facility:** 211 units. 3 stories, interior/exterior corridors. **Terms:** closed 9/18-5/14, 15 day cancellation notice-fee imposed. **Dining:** Foraker Dining Room, see separate listing. **Activities:** hiking trails, limited exercise equipment. **Guest Services:** coin laundry, area transportation-train depot & town. **Free Special Amenities:** local telephone calls.

WHERE TO EAT

FORAKER DINING ROOM   907/733-9500

Italian. Casual Dining. $11-$24 **AAA Inspector Notes:** Every table offers wonderful views of the distant snowcapped mountains and North America's tallest mountain, Mt. McKinley. The menu is Italian with an "Alaskan flare." Try the duck marsala; it's pan seared with a Brussels sprout hash. Or how about Kobe meatballs with aged Parmesan cheese? Also excellent is the osso buco featuring Berkshire pork shank. Something a little lighter is the mushroom lasagna. Try one of their fine wine selections, either by the glass or the bottle. **Bar:** full bar. **Reservations:** suggested. **Address:** 23601 S Talkeetna Spur Rd 99676 **Location:** 3.5 mi s of Talkeetna; in Talkeetna Alaskan Lodge.

TALKEETNA ROADHOUSE   907/733-1351

Coffee/Tea. Casual Dining. $6-$15 **AAA Inspector Notes:** *Historic.* The food is simple and the decor basic, but the atmosphere and desserts are unforgettable. A stop is not complete without a visit to this historic roadhouse. The dessert case is stocked with fresh, homemade goodies, ranging from huge hiker cookies to pies to the ultimate cinnamon bun. Guests seat themselves as they walk in the door and are entertained by the banter of the staff. This is the place to come for morning breakfasts. **Bar:** beer & wine. **Address:** 13550 E Main St 99676 **Location:** Downtown; in historic district.

WILD FLOWER CAFE   907/733-2695

American. Casual Dining. $13-$35 **AAA Inspector Notes:** This cute little café is located in the heart of historic Talkeetna. For lunch try the delicious Alaskan halibut sandwich with house mayo, a fresh green salad, pizza or burger. Dinner entrées include fresh stuffed halibut and grilled salmon. Grab one of the deck tables and watch all the tourists invade the street. **Bar:** beer & wine. **Address:** 13578 E Main St 99676 **Location:** Downtown; in historic district. **Parking:** street only.

TOK (B-12) pop. 1,258
• Hotels p. 664 • Restaurants p. 664

On the Alaska Highway 93 miles from the Canadian border, Tok is a trade center for nearby Athabascan villages. Some claim that Tok's name derives from the native word meaning "peace crossing"; others say Tok was the name of a survey crew's dog.

A center for dog breeding, training and mushing, Tok claims the title "Dog Capital of Alaska."

Tok Chamber of Commerce: P.O. Box 389, Tok, AK 99780. **Phone:** (907) 883-5775.

ALASKA PUBLIC LANDS INFORMATION CENTER, Milepost 1314 on Alaska Hwy., includes displays, state and federal information, a trip planning room and interpretive programs. **Hours:** Mon.-Fri. 8-6, Memorial Day-Labor Day; Mon.-Fri. 8-4:30, rest of year. **Cost:** Free. **Phone:** (907) 883-5666 or (907) 883-5667.

TETLIN NATIONAL WILDLIFE REFUGE is in e. central Alaska, directly s. of the Alaska Hwy. and n. of Wrangell-St. Elias National Park and Preserve; the visitor center is at Milepost 1229 on Alaska Hwy. The gateway to Alaska, the refuge occupies 730,000 acres along a major bird migration corridor. At least 115 of the 186 bird species stay to nest. Black and

grizzly bears, moose, wolves and caribou are year-round residents. A visitor center, containing an observation deck and wildlife exhibit, is built in a log trapper's cabin style with a sod roof.

Recreational activities include bird-watching, canoeing, fishing, hiking and hunting. The refuge operates three cabins and two seasonal, public campgrounds. **Hours:** Refuge open daily 24 hours. Visitor center open daily 8-4:30, May 15-Sept. 15. **Cost:** Free. **Phone:** (907) 883-5312. ⬛

CLEFT OF THE ROCK BED & BREAKFAST   (907)883-4219

⬛⬛ **Bed & Breakfast** $110-$165 **Address:** 0.5 Sundog Tr 99780 **Location:** Jct SR 1 and 2 (Alaskan Hwy), 2.5 mi w on SR 2 (Alaskan Hwy) to Sundog Tr, then 0.5 mi n. **Facility:** 8 units, some cabins. 1-2 stories (no elevator), interior/exterior corridors. *Bath:* some shared. **Terms:** 3 day cancellation notice-fee imposed. **Activities:** horseback riding, basketball.

⬛⬛⬛⬛⬛⬛/SOME UNITS FEE⬛⬛

WESTMARK INN TOK   (907)883-5174

⬛⬛ **Motel** $99-$199 **Address:** Jct Alaska & Glenn Hwys 99780 **Location:** On SR 1; jct SR 2 (Alaskan Hwy). **Facility:** 93 units. 2 stories (no elevator), exterior corridors. **Terms:** closed 9/4-5/17, cancellation fee imposed. **Guest Services:** coin laundry.

⬛⬛CALL⬛⬛⬛⬛⬛/SOME UNITS⬛

WHERE TO EAT

FAST EDDY'S RESTAURANT   907/883-4411

⬛⬛ American. Family Dining. $7-$32 **AAA Inspector Notes:** Specializing in gourmet burgers, sandwiches and hoagies made with fresh baked-daily buns and handmade pizzas. Also featured are steak, ribs and seafood platters accompanied by a salad bar. The key word is "fast." Meals are served with remarkable speed. It's really the only place in town to eat. **Bar:** beer & wine. **Address:** 1313 Alaska Hwy 99780 **Location:** Jct SR 1 and 2 (Alaskan Hwy), 1 mi e on SR 2 (Alaskan Hwy). B L D CALL⬛⬛

TONGASS NATIONAL FOREST (G-10)

Elevations in the forest range from sea level at the Pacific Ocean to 10,290 ft. at Mount Ratz. Refer to AAA maps for additional elevation information.

In southeastern Alaska, Tongass National Forest covers about 17 million acres, making it the largest national forest. In 1907 Teddy Roosevelt created the forest, taking the name from the "Tongass" clan of Tlingit Indians that lived along the southern edge of the forest's present-day boundaries. It boasts more than 5 million acres of preserved wilderness, including Misty Fiords National Monument *(see place listing p. 652)* and Admiralty Island National Monument *(see place listing p. 604).*

Consisting mostly of islands, the forest also includes a mountainous mainland strip deeply cleft by rock-walled fiords, bays, inlets and channels with glaciers, ice fields and waterfalls. The abundant wildlife includes trumpeter swans, bald eagles and Alaskan brown (grizzly) and black bears. Licenses are required for hunting and fishing.

The largest island within the National Forest and one of the largest islands in the United States is Prince of Wales Island. Long inlets and deep bays mark its 1,000-mile coastline, while U-shaped valleys and low

mountains rising up to 3,800 feet distinguish its interior. Thanks to a moist climate, a dense forest of spruce and hemlock blankets the landscape.

One of the most interesting features of the island is its caves, including El Capitan, a large limestone cave system with 11,000 feet of mapped passages. Grizzly bear bones more than 12,000 years old have been found inside. The Forest Service provides free 2-hour tours of El Capitan from mid-May to early September; reservations are required. Access to the cave entrance is via a steep 1,300-foot-long trail and visitors need to bring their own equipment for the tour, including flashlights and sturdy footgear. The underground temperature is a constant 40 degrees Fahrenheit. Phone (907) 828-3304 for information and reservations.

The Forest Service provides cabins at several locations within Tongass National Forest. Many rental cabins are near lakes and streams or high in alpine meadows. Although a few can be reached by boat or trail, most are accessible only by charter plane from Craig, Hoonah, Juneau, Ketchikan, Petersburg, Sitka, Wrangell and Yakutat. Charter planes seating two to five people cost about $325-$550 an hour.

A $25-$45 per-party, per-night fee is charged for cabins. There is a 7-night limit May through September; a 10-night limit the rest of the year. Cabin permits are necessary and can be requested up to 180 days prior to use; full payment is required at the time the reservation is made. Forest information centers with exhibits, films and cabin reservation information are in Juneau *(see place listing p. 641),* Ketchikan *(see place listing p. 647)* and Petersburg *(see place listing p. 654).*

For further information write Southeast Alaska Discovery Center, 50 Main St., Ketchikan, AK 99901; phone (907) 228-6220, TTY (907) 228-6237, or (877) 444-6777 for camping and cabin reservations. *See Recreation Areas Chart.*

MENDENHALL GLACIER—see Juneau p. 643.

TRAPPER CREEK pop. 481

GATE CREEK CABINS   (907)733-1393

⬛⬛ **Cottage** $150-$590 **Address:** Mile 10.5 Petersville Rd 99683 **Location:** Milepost 114 (Parks Hwy), 10.5 mi w at Petersville Rd. **Facility:** 8 cottages. 1-2 stories (no elevator), exterior corridors. **Parking:** winter plug-ins. **Terms:** check-in 4 pm, 2 night minimum stay - seasonal and/or weekends, 10 day cancellation notice. **Activities:** canoeing, paddleboats, bicycles, playground. *Fee:* snowmobiling.

⬛⬛⬛⬛⬛⬛/SOME UNITS FEE⬛

TRAPPER CREEK INN & RV PARK   (907)733-2302

⬛ **Motel** $99-$139 **Address:** Mile 114.6 Parks Hwy 99683 **Location:** George Parks Hwy (SR 3), Milepost 114. **Facility:** 4 units, some two bedrooms, three bedrooms and kitchens. 3 stories (no elevator), exterior corridors. **Parking:** winter plug-ins. **Terms:** 10 day cancellation notice. **Guest Services:** coin laundry.

⬛⬛⬛⬛⬛⬛⬛⬛⬛/SOME UNITS FEE⬛

VALDEZ (C-12) pop. 3,976, elev. 15'
• Hotels p. 666 • Restaurants p. 666

Called the "Switzerland of Alaska," Valdez (val-DEEZ) is ringed by snowcapped mountains. As the northernmost ice-free port, the town was established in 1898 as an outfitting point for miners taking the hazardous pack trail over Valdez Glacier to the northern gold fields.

In addition to the gold rush, Valdez's rich history includes the 5-minute, 9.2-magnitude Good Friday earthquake in 1964; construction of the Trans-Alaska Pipeline and Marine Terminal in the 1970s; and the 1989 *Exxon Valdez* oil spill and cleanup.

Access into Valdez is by scheduled air service, ferry or via the scenic Richardson Highway. Near Milepost 16 are Bridal Veil and Horsetail falls and the Historic 1899 Trans-Alaska Military Trail & Wagon Road. Thompson Pass, Milepost 26, offers a spectacular view of the Chugach Mountains, valley rivers and historic Keystone Canyon. At Milepost 29 is Worthington Glacier State Park, which has walking trails.

Nearby glaciers in Prince William Sound include Mears, Shoup and Columbia, the second largest tidewater glacier in North America.

Valdez Convention and Visitors Bureau: 104 Chenega St., Valdez, AK 99686. **Phone:** (907) 835-4636.

MAXINE & JESSE WHITNEY MUSEUM is on the grounds of Prince William Sound Community College at 303 Lowe St. The museum's collection of Alaskan native art, artifacts, beadwork, dolls and furs comprises one of the largest of its kind. Its pieces were collected over more than 50 years of travel to Alaskan villages by Jesse Whitney and wife Maxine after the couple moved to Alaska in 1947. The Paul Kulik History of Transportation Collection features to-scale vehicle models made of Eskimo ivory and that interpret the state's aviation history.

Time: Allow 30 minutes minimum. **Hours:** Daily 9-7, May-Sept.; Mon.-Fri. 10-5, rest of year. Closed major holidays. **Cost:** Free. **Phone:** (907) 834-1690.

STAN STEPHENS GLACIER & WILDLIFE CRUISES departs from 112 N. Harbor Dr., 3 blks. e. of jct. Richardson Hwy. and Meals St. The outfit offers 7- and 9-hour narrated sightseeing cruises on Prince William Sound to Columbia and Meares glaciers. Along the way, guests might glimpse bald eagles, Dall's porpoises, black bears, sea otters, Steller sea lions, puffins, mountain goats and humpback, minke and orca whales. A narrator details area history and information about the Trans-Alaska Pipeline. A light meal is included.

Hours: Columbia Glacier trips depart daily at noon, mid-May to mid-Sept. Meares Glacier trips depart daily at 10, early June through Aug. 31. Meares Glacier trips not available on some days. Phone ahead to confirm schedule. **Cost:** Fare $120-$155; $60-$77 (ages 3-12). Reservations are recommended. **Phone:** (907) 835-4731 or (866) 867-1297. *(See ad this page.)*

VALDEZ MUSEUM & HISTORICAL ARCHIVE is at 217 Egan Dr. The museum documents the complete history of Valdez. Interpretive exhibits explain the impact of the gold rush, the 1964 earthquake, the construction of the Trans-Alaska Pipeline and the 1989 *Exxon Valdez* oil spill. The Remembering Old Valdez exhibit, 436 S. Hazelet Ave., focuses on the years 1957-67. A 1907 Ahrens fire truck and a Fresnel lighthouse lens also are featured.

Time: Allow 30 minutes minimum. **Hours:** Museum daily 9-5, mid-May to mid-Sept.; Tues.-Sun. noon-5, rest of year. Remembering Old Valdez daily 9-5, mid-May to mid-Sept.; by appointment rest of year. **Cost:** $7; $6 (ages 60+); $5 (ages 14-17). **Phone:** (907) 835-2764.

WORTHINGTON GLACIER, about 30 mi. e. on the Richardson Hwy., is Alaska's most accessible glacier. Milepost 28.7 provides an excellent viewpoint; a road leads to the glacier. The Moraine Trail leads to a viewing platform.

RECREATIONAL ACTIVITIES
Kayaking
• **Anadyr Adventures** departs from 225 N. Harbor Dr. **Hours:** Daily 9-5, mid-Apr. to mid-Sept.;

▼ See AAA listing this page ▼

phone ahead for specific excursion times and dates. **Phone:** (907) 835-2814.

BEST WESTERN VALDEZ HARBOR INN (907)835-3434

Hotel
$100-$180

AAA Benefit: Members save up to 20%, plus 10% bonus points with Best Western Rewards®.

Address: 100 N Harbor Dr 99686 **Location:** Just s at Meals Ave. Located at small boat harbor. **Facility:** 88 units. 2 stories (no elevator), interior corridors. **Terms:** cancellation fee imposed. **Amenities:** *Some:* high-speed Internet. **Dining:** Off the Hook Grill, see separate listing. **Activities:** exercise room. **Guest Services:** coin laundry, area transportation-ferry. **Free Special Amenities: expanded continental breakfast and high-speed Internet.**

WHERE TO EAT

ALASKA HALIBUT HOUSE 907/835-2788

Fish & Chips. Quick Serve. $7-$15 **AAA Inspector Notes:** This restaurant located just steps from the harbor features fresh seafood, primarily halibut and salmon, prepared breaded and deep-fried. **Address:** 208 Meals Ave 99686 **Location:** Just n.

L D

FU KUNG 907/835-5255

Chinese Sushi. Casual Dining. $9-$26 **AAA Inspector Notes:** This local favorite features sushi, Thai, Mandarin and Cantonese specialties. Chinese ginger halibut and Thai red curry seafood hot pot are sublime. Patrons dine on burl wood tables set in a nice atmosphere. **Bar:** beer & wine. **Address:** 207 Kobuk St (Box 263) 99686 **Location:** Richardson Hwy, just s on Meals Ave, then just e.

L D

MIKE'S PALACE 907/835-2365

Regional International. Casual Dining. $9-$27 **AAA Inspector Notes:** This simple eatery offers a menu of Italian, Greek and Mexican selections as well as some sandwiches, steaks and seafood. As you'd expect, the service is informal. **Bar:** full bar. **Address:** 205 N Harbor Dr 99686 **Location:** Just s; in small boat harbor. L D

OFF THE HOOK GRILL 907/835-8114

International Fusion. Casual Dining. $12-$30 **AAA Inspector Notes:** A wall of windows, with a stunning view of the mountains and harbor, is the perfect setting to enjoy more upscale fare from the same folks who run T.H.C. (The Harbor Cafe). The menu is eclectic with fusions of Latin American, Japanese and Italian fare. The freshest of seafood is joined with flavors usually found on international plates. Scallops sprinkled with Parmesan cheese and baked in a wine-lemon sauce pays homage to the owner's Peruvian background. **Bar:** full bar. **Address:** 100 N Harbor Dr 99686 **Location:** Just s at Meals Ave; in BEST WESTERN Valdez Harbor Inn.

L D

T.H.C. (THE HARBOR CAFE) 907/835-4776

Regional International. Quick Serve. $9-$19 **AAA Inspector Notes:** Anyone in town will tell you that the T.H.C. (The Harbor Café) is the place to grab a quick lunch. The gourmet burgers are huge, the crisp salads are served in large bowls with homemade dressing, the seafood is succulent and the chowder is steaming fresh. This is quick serve so guests order and pick up their food from the window and then head either to the limited-seating dining room or to the deck overlooking the harbor. **Address:** 255 N Harbor Dr 99686 **Location:** In small boat harbor. **Parking:** street only. L

WASILLA (C-11) pop. 7,831

Founded in 1917 with the construction of the Alaska Railroad, the community of Wasilla is contiguous to the junction of SRs 1 and 3, both of which are scenic highways, and rests in the Matanuska-Susitna Valley. The area's name originates from that of a respected Indian chief and has varying interpretations; some believe the word is defined as "breath of air" in the Dena'ina Athabascan Indian dialect, while others attribute it to a variation of the Russian word for the name William, "Vasili."

Gold miners from nearby Knik and Willow Creek flocked to Wasilla in the early 1900s due to its proximity to the gold fields and newly constructed railroad. With the advent of Anchorage in 1915 and Wasilla's founding two years later, Knik and other neighboring communities were rapidly abandoned. Mining in Wasilla played an integral role through much of World War II and the mid-20th century; a handful of the area's mines, which once numbered more than 50, remain active to this day.

The Dorothy G. Page Museum, 323 N. Main St., contains historical artifacts and relates the heritage of Wasilla, Knik and Willow Creek. The museum is open year-round; phone (907) 373-9071. Adjoining the museum is the Old Wasilla Town Site, which preserves Wasilla's first school, two log cabins, a post office, a smithy and the town's first public bath.

In August 2008, former Alaska Gov. Sarah Palin, who served two terms as mayor of Wasilla 1996-2002, was chosen by Arizona Sen. John McCain as his running mate in the November presidential election. Her GOP nomination set several precedents as Palin became the first Alaskan and only the second woman—and the first woman as a Republican—to appear on a major party's presidential ticket.

Greater Wasilla Chamber of Commerce: 415 E. Railroad Ave., Wasilla, AK 99654. **Phone:** (907) 376-1299.

MUSEUM OF ALASKA TRANSPORTATION AND INDUSTRY, Milepost 47 on George Parks Hwy. (SR 3), displays various items relating to Alaska's transportation and industrial history. Fifteen acres of outdoor exhibits include aircraft, boats, tractors, dog sleds, snowmobiles, farm implements, railroad cars, fire trucks, antique automobiles and memorabilia from early railroading days. Also featured are aviation photographs, vintage farm equipment and engines.

Hours: Daily 10-5, mid-May to Labor Day. **Cost:** $8; $5 (ages 3-17 and 65+); free (active military with ID); $18 (family). **Phone:** (907) 376-1211.

AGATE INN (907)373-2290

Hotel $139-$375 **Address:** 4725 Begich Cir 99654 **Location:** 0.9 mi n of jct SR 3 (George Parks Hwy) and Seward Meridian Rd, 0.8 mi e, just s, then just e. **Facility:** 13 units, some two bedrooms, three bedrooms, kitchens and houses. 2 stories (no elevator), interior/exterior corridors. **Parking:** winter plug-ins. **Terms:** check-in 4 pm, 14 day cancellation notice-fee imposed. **Amenities:** high-speed Internet. **Activities:** horseshoes. **Guest Services:** coin laundry.

BEST WESTERN LAKE LUCILLE INN   (907)373-1776

Hotel
$99-$199

AAA Benefit: Members save up to 20%, plus 10% bonus points with Best Western Rewards®.

Address: 1300 W Lake Lucille Dr 99654 **Location:** SR 3 (George Parks Hwy), just w on Hallea Ln; center. **Facility:** 54 units. 2 stories (no elevator), interior corridors. **Terms:** cancellation fee imposed. **Amenities:** *Some:* high-speed Internet. **Activities:** sauna, whirlpool, boat dock, exercise room. **Guest Services:** coin laundry. **Free Special Amenities:** expanded continental breakfast and high-speed Internet.** (See ad p. 615, p. 625.)

SAVE CALL (GM) 🖧 ✕ 🐾 🖥 💻
/SOME UNITS FEE 🐾

WHERE TO EAT

EVANGELO'S RESTAURANT   907/376-1212

▼▼ Italian. Casual Dining. $8-$35 **AAA Inspector Notes:** This open, airy, elegant restaurant has some lovely windows overlooking the scenery while still maintaining some privacy nooks. One of the most popular restaurants in town, it features a mainly Italian menu with a touch of Greek. Pastas, pizzas, steaks, seafood and a variety of sandwiches and calzones are standard fare. **Bar:** full bar. **Address:** 2530 E Parks Hwy 99654 **Location:** 1.2 mi n of jct Parks Hwy and Fairview Loop exit. [D] CALL (GM)

WHITTIER (D-11) pop. 220

Nearly surrounded by mountains and perched at the edge of beautiful Prince William Sound, Whittier remained relatively isolated until June 2000 when a 2.5-mile railroad tunnel was converted to accommodate automobile traffic. The unusual Anton Anderson Memorial Tunnel is a single-lane combination highway and railway that enables cars and trains to take turns passing through the tunnel.

Because the tunnel has only one lane, the direction of traffic alternates, ceasing altogether while trains travel through.

Phone (877) 611-2586 for the tunnel's traffic schedule. Tunnel information also is broadcast by radio on 530 AM in Whittier and 1610 AM in Portage and Bear Valley. A toll of $12 per car is charged at the tunnel's western entrance; toll increases with size of vehicle.

26 GLACIER CRUISE BY PHILLIPS CRUISES departs from the port of Whittier. Cruises explore the calm, protected waters of Prince William Sound. Passengers aboard the company's high-speed catamaran can see tidewater glaciers plus an array of wildlife on this 4.5-hour tour.

Hours: Cruises depart daily at 12:30, May-Sept. **Cost:** Fare (includes onboard lunch) $139; $79 (ages 2-11). Bus or rail service is offered from Anchorage at an additional cost. Reservations are recommended. **Phone:** (907) 276-8023 or (800) 544-0529.

MAJOR MARINE TOURS depart from the marina day-cruise dock. A 4.5-hour sightseeing cruise narrated by a Chugach forest ranger takes passengers to see spectacular 1,700-foot-tall active tidewater glaciers and picturesque waterfalls in Prince William Sound. Eagles, otters and shorebirds may be spotted.

Inquire about weather policies. **Time:** Allow 5 hours minimum. **Hours:** Departures daily at 12:45, mid-May to mid-Sept. **Cost:** Fare $119; $59.50 (ages 2-11). Onboard lunch available at an additional cost. Reservations are recommended. **Phone:** (907) 274-7300 or (800) 764-7300. *(See ad p. 610, this page.)* 🍴

▼ *See AAA listing this page* ▼

PRINCE WILLIAM SOUND CRUISES AND TOURS, departing from the foot of Pier 1 at the Whittier Boat Harbor, offers a 6-hour Wilderness Explorer Glacier Cruise that plies the calm waters of Prince William Sound, passes glaciers in Esther Passage, Harriman Fjord and Barry Arm, and stops at a working fish hatchery. The trip includes lunch and opportunities for spotting wildlife. **Time:** Allow 6 hours minimum. **Hours:** Departs daily at 11, mid-May to mid-Sept. **Cost:** Fare $144; $72 (ages 2-11). Reservations are recommended. **Phone:** (907) 472-2410 or (800) 922-1297. *(See ad p. 610.)*

RECREATIONAL ACTIVITIES

Kayaking

- **Alaska Sea Kayakers** depart from the Whittier Boat Harbor. **Hours:** Daily 8-7, May-Sept. **Phone:** (907) 472-2534 or (877) 472-2534.

WRANGELL (H-11) pop. 2,369, elev. 37'

Petroglyphs pecked into shale rock and elaborately carved totem poles, cedar monuments of the Stikine (STIK-een) and Tlingit (KLINK-it) Indians, are interesting aspects of Wrangell. Although European and American explorers visited the area in the late 1700s, Russians began trading here by 1811 and established a redoubt in Wrangell in 1834. The only Alaskan town to have existed under Russian, British and American rule, it also survived three gold rushes in 1861, 1872 and 1898, when the lure of riches brought an onslaught of miners and settlers.

Petroglyphs can be seen on a beach at the north end of Wrangell Island. Of undetermined age, some carvings face the water, others the shore or sky. They are best viewed at low tide. Nearby Anan Creek allows the opportunity to observe sea lions and seals and watch black bear fish for salmon.

Other attractions include the nine totem poles (some are replicas carved by the Civilian Conservation Corps in the late 1930s) on Shakes Island in Wrangell Harbor, as well as the four totem poles in Kiksadi Totem Park at Front and Episcopal streets. Artifacts are displayed in Chief Shakes Tribal House, also on the island. A large concentration of bald eagles gather in Wrangell from January to mid-April waiting for smelt to run up the Stikine River.

Wrangell Chamber of Commerce: 224 Front St., P.O. Box 49, Wrangell, AK 99929. **Phone:** (907) 874-3901.

WRANGELL MUSEUM is at 296 Campbell Dr. The collection describes the colorful history of the Wrangell area. Of note are four beautiful Tlingit houseposts—carved in the 1700s, they are believed to be the oldest in existence. A variety of displays detail early Russian and English settlement and the city's role in the 1861 Stikine gold rush. Spruceroot and cedarbark baskets, beadwork, stone tools and other artifacts crafted by Alaskan natives are shown.

Time: Allow 30 minutes minimum. **Hours:** Mon.-Fri. 10-5, Sat. 8-5, May-Sept.; Tues.-Sat. 1-5, rest of

year. Closed major holidays. Phone ahead to confirm schedule. **Cost:** $5; $3 (ages 60+); $2 (ages 6-12); $12 (family). **Phone:** (907) 874-3770.

WRANGELL-ST. ELIAS NATIONAL PARK AND PRESERVE (C-12, F-8)

Elevations in the park and preserve range from sea level at the Gulf of Alaska to 18,008 ft. at Mount St. Elias. Refer to AAA maps for additional elevation information.

In south central Alaska bordering Canada's Yukon, Wrangell-St. Elias National Park and Preserve is the country's largest national park. It is a place of overpowering dimensions, embracing an area larger than Massachusetts, Rhode Island and Connecticut combined; glaciers five times the size of Manhattan; and nine of the 16 highest peaks in North America.

In this 13-million-acre park, the collision of two continental plates has produced some of the world's highest coastal ranges. Forming a barrier along the Gulf of Alaska are the Chugach Mountains, and paralleling them to the north are the Wrangell Mountains.

Between these two ranges are the St. Elias Mountains, extending like the stem of the letter "Y" into Canada's Kluane National Park. Atop these towering peaks are ice fields so immense that they act as a natural cooling system, affecting areas as far south as Chicago and the Central Plains.

As imposing as its ice fields are, it was another commodity traded by the Ahtna Dene or "people of the Copper River" that caught the world's attention. These and other tribes forged tools of locally mined copper. The first person of European descent to verify the source of the copper trading was Lt. Henry Allen, who in 1885 explored much of Alaska's interior.

Fifteen years later two miners discovered the malachite cliffs above the Kennicott Glacier, which became one of the world's richest sources of copper. The subsequent founding of the Kennicott Mine became one of the most significant events in Alaska's history: The great wealth and development it spawned affected not only Alaska but the entire nation. Currently the ruined mine, a 14-story mill building and a few historic structures are all that remain of this immense enterprise, preserved as the Kennecott Mines National Historic Landmark. Free ranger-guided tours of the grounds are offered daily, Memorial Day-Labor Day. St. Elias Alpine Guides offers two-hour guided tours of the mill building daily at 9:30, 1:30 and 3:30, late May to mid-Sept.; the cost is $25 per person. The Kennecott Visitor Center is open daily 9-5:30, Memorial Day-Labor Day; phone (907) 822-7476 for ranger-guided tour information. Phone (907) 345-9048 for mill building tour information, or inquire in-person at the visitor center.

Legacies of the Kennecott Mine and the Yukon gold fields are some of the area's roads, which provide limited access to the park. One of Alaska's oldest roadways is the Richardson Highway, which was completed in 1919 and was the first all-Alaska route to the Yukon gold fields. Both the Richardson and Glenn highways follow the curve of the park's western boundary and offer several spectacular views of 12,010-foot Mount Drum, 14,163-foot Mount Wrangell and 16,237-foot Mount Sanford.

Two other roads penetrate the park's interior—the Chitina-McCarthy and the Nabesna. Both of these gravel roads offer good views of the mountains and are convenient jumping-off places for hiking and river-running. The 60-mile McCarthy Road follows an abandoned railroad bed. Visitors should allow a minimum of 3 hours to drive between Chitina and McCarthy. Before using either of these routes, check with the ranger stations in Slana and Chitina.

The park's headquarters and visitor center, 3 miles north of Copper Center on Richardson Highway at Milepost 106.8, provides trip-planning assistance and information about park activities. Fishing, hiking, rafting and wildlife- viewing, especially of the park's large population of Dall sheep, are just some of the activities pursued in the park; phone (907) 822-7250.

On the southeastern edge of the park and accessible only by sea is Hubbard Glacier on Disenchantment Bay. In 1986 this vast, active tidewater glacier advanced so quickly that for several months it blocked the entrance to Russell Fjord behind a dam of ice, briefly turning it into a lake.

For more information write the Superintendent, Wrangell-St. Elias National Park and Preserve, P.O. Box 439, Copper Center, AK 99573; phone (907) 822-5234. *See Recreation Areas Chart.*

YUKON-CHARLEY RIVERS NATIONAL PRESERVE (A-12, D-7)

Elevations in the preserve range from 600 ft. on the Yukon River where it leaves the preserve near Circle to 6,435 ft. in the Cirque Lakes area on the Charley River drainage. Refer to AAA maps for additional elevation information.

Near the Canadian border in east central Alaska, more than 140 miles of the Yukon River and the entire watershed of the Charley River are encompassed within the 2.5 million acres of the Yukon-Charley Rivers National Preserve. John McPhee remarked in his book "Coming into the Country" that New Jersey could easily fit into this vast emptiness between Eagle and Circle.

Although only 10 year-round residents now live within the preserve's boundaries, it was not always so sparsely populated. During the gold rush, the Yukon—a summer waterway and winter highway—was thronged with people who briefly transformed such communities as Circle and Dawson City, Canada into the "Paris of the North." This rough-and-tumble gold rush region was the grist of Robert Service's poetry and Jack London's stories.

Now quiet has returned, and where riverboats once departed from Eagle, river runners make the 5- to 7-day float down the river to Circle. One of the pleasures of this trip is the opportunity to see Peregrine falcons, a threatened species that makes its home in the bluffs along the river. Hikers can catch a glimpse of caribou and Dall sheep in the preserve's upland regions and moose in the lowlands.

The Taylor and Steese highways are the primary summer access routes to the national preserve, terminating respectively in Eagle and Circle just outside the preserve's boundaries. The scenic portion of the Taylor Highway from Chicken to Eagle runs through mountains, rolling tundra and river valleys. Most people, however, reach the park by boat or float on the Yukon River and its tributaries.

The preserve has no roads and no established trails or maintained public airstrips. Seven public-use cabins are available on a first-come, first-served basis. Food service, basic supplies, lodgings and charter boat and air service are available during the summer months in nearby Eagle and Circle. A list of authorized guides can be obtained from the preserve headquarters and visitor center in Eagle.

In addition, the Bureau of Land Management administers Fort Egbert and a campground in Eagle. The park visitor center is open daily 8-5, mid-May through Labor Day; Mon.-Fri. 8-5, rest of year. The center can be contacted at P.O. Box 167, Eagle, AK 99738; phone (907) 547-2233. For more information write the Superintendent, Yukon-Charley Rivers National Preserve, 4175 Geist Rd., Fairbanks, AK 99707-4718. *See Recreation Areas Chart.*

NEW!
Disney's Art of Animation **Resort**

©Disney/Pixar

Disneyland® **Resort Hotel**

ENJOY A MAGICAL DISNEY VACATION

What's the best way to experience all the enchantment of a vacation to the *Walt Disney World*® Resort in Florida or the *Disneyland*® Resort in California? How do you squeeze the most magic out of the Theme Parks and the whimsically themed *Disney Resort* hotels? And how can you enjoy great savings and exclusive benefits not available anywhere else? By booking a *AAA Vacations*® package from AAA Travel, of course!

DISNEYLAND® RESORT, CALIFORNIA

- Stay just steps away from the magic at a *Disneyland*® Resort Hotel.

- **Now open!**
  Get ready to be floored—cruise into the amazing new Cars Land at *Disney California Adventure*® Park.

WALT DISNEY WORLD RESORT, FLORIDA

- Stay in the middle of the magic at a *Walt Disney World* Resort hotel.

- **Now open!**
  New *Fantasyland*®—immersing you in Disney stories like never before at the *Magic Kingdom*®.

©Disney WDWSALES-12-22964

New *Fantasyland*

Artist Rendering

©Disney/Pixar

Cars Land

WITH ENCHANTING AAA BENEFITS!

LET AAA BE YOUR GUIDE...

With a *AAA Vacations®* package, you can create the Disney vacation that fits your family, your taste and your budget. And not only will your AAA Travel professional help put everything (like accommodations, tickets and flights) together, you'll also get to enjoy great Disney benefits on top of the exclusive AAA benefits and savings once you get there! Then all you need to do is relax and have fun.

READY TO START MAKING MAGIC?
Then contact your **AAA Travel professional** today!

Disney Parks

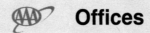 **Offices**

Cities with main offices are listed in **BOLD TYPE** and toll-free member service numbers in *ITALIC TYPE*.
All are closed Saturdays, Sundays and holidays unless otherwise indicated.
The addresses, phone numbers and hours for any AAA/CAA office are subject to change.
The type of service provided is designated below the name of the city where the office is located:

✛ Auto travel services, including books and maps, and on-demand TripTik ® routings.
● Auto travel services, including selected books and maps, and on-demand TripTik ® routings.
■ Books/maps only, no marked maps or on-demand TripTik ® routings.
▲ Travel Agency Services, cruise, tour, air, car and rail reservations; domestic and international hotel reservations; passport photo services; international and domestic travel guides and maps; travel money products; and International Driving Permits. In addition, assistance with travel related insurance products including trip cancellation, travel accident, lost luggage, trip delay and assistance products.
❂ Insurance services provided. If only this icon appears, only insurance services are provided at that office.
◖ Car Care Plus Facility provides car care services.
▣ Electric vehicle charging station on premises.

AAA NATIONAL OFFICE: 1000 AAA DRIVE, HEATHROW, FLORIDA 32746-5063, (407) 444-7000

ALASKA

ANCHORAGE—AAA MOUNTAINWEST, 3565 ARCTIC BLVD STE D5, 99503. WEEKDAYS (M-F) 8:30-5:30. (907) 344-4310, *(800) 391-4222.* ✛ ▲ ❂

ALBERTA

CALGARY—ALBERTA MOTOR ASSOCIATION, #100 530 8TH AVE SW, T2P 3S8. WEEKDAYS (M-F) 9:00-5:00. (403) 262-2345, *(800) 642-3810.* ● ▲ ❂

CALGARY—ALBERTA MOTOR ASSOCIATION, #600 85 SHAWVILLE BLVD SE, T2Y 3W5. WEEKDAYS (M-F) 9:00-6:00, SAT 9:00-5:00. (403) 254-2447, *(800) 642-3810.* ● ▲ ❂

CALGARY—ALBERTA MOTOR ASSOCIATION, 220 CROWFOOT CRES NW, T3G 3N5. WEEKDAYS (M-F) 9:00-6:00, SAT 9:00-5:00. (403) 239-6644, *(800) 642-3810.* ● ▲ ❂

CALGARY—ALBERTA MOTOR ASSOCIATION, 3650 20 AVE NE, T1Y 6E8. WEEKDAYS (M-F) 9:00-6:00, SAT 9:00-5:00. (403) 590-0001, *(800) 642-3810.* ● ▲ ❂

CALGARY—ALBERTA MOTOR ASSOCIATION, 4700 17TH AVE SW, T3E 0E3. WEEKDAYS (M-F) 9:00-6:00, SAT 9:00-5:00. (403) 240-5300, *(800) 642-3810.* ● ▲ ❂

CALGARY—ALBERTA MOTOR ASSOCIATION, 524-10816 MACLEOD TRL SE, T2J 5N8. WEEKDAYS (M-F) 9:00-6:00, SAT 9:00-5:00. (403) 278-3530, *(800) 642-3810.* ● ▲ ❂

CAMROSE—ALBERTA MOTOR ASSOCIATION, 6702 48 AVE, T4V 4S3. WEEKDAYS (M-F) 9:00-5:30, SAT 9:00-2:00. (780) 672-3391, *(800) 642-3810.* ● ▲ ❂

EDMONTON—ALBERTA MOTOR ASSOCIATION, 10310 GA MACDONALD AVE NW, T6J 6R7. WEEKDAYS (M-F) 9:00-6:00, SAT 9:00-5:00. (780) 430-5555 ● ▲

EDMONTON—ALBERTA MOTOR ASSOCIATION, 11220 109 ST NW, T5G 2T6. WEEKDAYS (M-F) 9:00-6:00, SAT 9:00-5:00. (780) 474-8601, *(800) 642-3810.* ✛ ▲ ❂

EDMONTON—ALBERTA MOTOR ASSOCIATION, 5040 MANNING DR NW, T5A 5B4. WEEKDAYS (M-F) 9:00-6:00, SAT 9:00-5:00. (780) 473-3112, *(800) 642-3810.* ● ▲ ❂

EDMONTON—ALBERTA MOTOR ASSOCIATION, 9938 170 ST, T5T 6G7. WEEKDAYS (M-F) 9:00-6:00, SAT 9:00-5:00. (780) 484-1221, *(800) 642-3810.* ● ▲ ❂

FORT MCMURRAY—ALBERTA MOTOR ASSOCIATION, 4 HOSPITAL ST, T9H 5E4. WEEKDAYS (M-F) 9:00-5:30. (780) 743-2433, *(800) 642-3810.* ● ▲ ❂

GRANDE PRAIRIE—ALBERTA MOTOR ASSOCIATION, 11401 99 ST, T8V 2H6. WEEKDAYS (M-F) 9:00-5:30, SAT 9:00-2:00. (780) 532-4421, *(800) 642-3810.* ● ▲ ❂

LETHBRIDGE—ALBERTA MOTOR ASSOCIATION, 120 SCENIC DR S, T1J 4R4. WEEKDAYS (M-F) 9:00-5:30, SAT 9:00-2:00. (403) 328-1181, *(800) 642-3810.* ● ▲ ❂

MEDICINE HAT—ALBERTA MOTOR ASSOCIATION, 2710 13 AVE SE, T1A 3P8. WEEKDAYS (M-F) 9:00-5:30, SAT 9:00-2:00. (403) 527-1166, *(800) 642-3810.* ● ▲ ❂

RED DEER—ALBERTA MOTOR ASSOCIATION, 141 2004 50TH AVE, T4R 3A2. WEEKDAYS (M-F) 9:00-5:30, SAT 9:00-2:00. (403) 342-6633 ✛ ▲ ❂

RED DEER—ALBERTA MOTOR ASSOCIATION, 2965 BREMNER AVE, T4R 1S2. WEEKDAYS (M-F) 9:00-5:30, SAT 9:00-2:00. (403) 342-6632, *(800) 642-3810.* ❂

SHERWOOD PARK—ALBERTA MOTOR ASSOCIATION, #19 101 BREMNER DR, T8H 0M5. WEEKDAYS (M-F) 9:00-6:00, SAT 9:00-5:00. (780) 467-7945 ● ▲ ❂

SHERWOOD PARK—ALBERTA MOTOR ASSOCIATION, 236-222 BASELINE VILLAGE, T8H 1S8. WEEKDAYS (M-F) 9:00-6:00, SAT 9:00-6:00. (780) 467-8520 ❂

ST. ALBERT—ALBERTA MOTOR ASSOCIATION, 200 665 ST ALBERT TRL, T8N 3L3. WEEKDAYS (M-F) 9:00-6:00, SAT 9:00-5:00. (780) 418-8900, *(800) 642-3810.* ✛ ▲ ❂

BRITISH COLUMBIA

ABBOTSFORD—CAA BRITISH COLUMBIA, 33338 S FRASER WAY, V2S 2B4. WEEKDAYS (M-F) 9:00-5:30, SAT 9:00-5:00. (604) 870-3850, *(800) 663-1956.* ✛ ❂

BURNABY—CAA BRITISH COLUMBIA, 4567 CANADA WAY, V5G 4T1. WEEKDAYS (M-F) 9:00-5:30, SAT 9:00-5:00. (604) 268-5500, *(800) 663-1956.* ✛ ❂

CHILLIWACK—CAA BRITISH COLUMBIA, #190-45428 LUCKAKUCK WAY, V2R 3S9. WEEKDAYS (M-F) 9:00-6:00, SAT 9:00-5:00. (604) 824-2720, *(800) 663-1956.* ✛ ❂

COQUITLAM—CAA BRITISH COLUMBIA, 50-2773 BARNET HWY, V3B 1C2. WEEKDAYS (M-F) 9:00-5:30, SAT 9:00-5:00. (604) 268-5750, *(800) 663-1956.* ✛ ❂

COURTENAY—CAA BRITISH COLUMBIA, 17-1599 CLIFFE AVE, V9N 2K6. WEEKDAYS (M-F) 9:00-5:30, SAT 9:00-5:00. (250) 703-2328, *(800) 663-1956.* ✛ ❂

DELTA—CAA BRITISH COLUMBIA, SCOTT 72 CTR 7343-120 ST, V4C 6P5. WEEKDAYS (M-F) 9:00-6:00, SAT 9:00-5:00. (604) 268-5900, *(800) 663-1956.* ✛ ❂

KAMLOOPS—CAA BRITISH COLUMBIA, 400-500 NOTRE DAME DR, V2C 6T6. WEEKDAYS (M-F) 9:00-6:00, SAT 9:00-5:00. (250) 852-4600, *(800) 663-1956.* ✛ ❂

KELOWNA—CAA BRITISH COLUMBIA, #18-1470 HARVEY AVE, V1Y 9K8. WEEKDAYS (M-F) 9:00-6:00, SAT 9:00-5:00. (250) 870-4900, *(800) 663-1956.* ✛ ❂

LANGLEY—CAA BRITISH COLUMBIA, 10 - 20190 LANGLEY BYP, V3A 9J9. WEEKDAYS (M-F) 9:00-6:00, SAT 9:00-5:00. (604) 268-5950, *(800) 663-1956.* ✚ ❂

MAPLE RIDGE—CAA BRITISH COLUMBIA, #500 20395 LOUGHEED HWY, V2X 2P9. WEEKDAYS (M-F) 9:00-6:00, SAT 9:00-5:00. (604) 205-1200, *(800) 633-1956.* ✚

NANAIMO—CAA BRITISH COLUMBIA, METRAL PL-6581 AULDS RD, V9T 6J6. WEEKDAYS (M-F) 9:00-6:00, SAT 9:00-5:00. (250) 390-7700, *(800) 663-1956.* ✚ ❂

NELSON—CAA BRITISH COLUMBIA, 596 BAKER ST, V1L 4H9. WEEKDAYS (M-F) 9:00-5:00, SAT 9:00-5:00. (250) 505-1720, *(800) 663-1956.* ✚ ❂

NEW WESTMINSTER—CAA BRITISH COLUMBIA, 501 SIXTH ST, V3L 3B9. WEEKDAYS (M-F) 9:00-5:30, SAT 9:00-5:00. (604) 268-5700, *(800) 663-1956.* ✚

NORTH VANCOUVER—CAA BRITISH COLUMBIA, 1527 LONSDALE AVE, V7M 2J2. WEEKDAYS (M-F) 9:00-6:00, SAT 9:00-5:00. (604) 205-1050, *(800) 663-1956.* ✚ ❂

PENTICTON—CAA BRITISH COLUMBIA, 100-2100 MAIN ST, V2A 5H7. WEEKDAYS (M-F) 9:00-5:30, SAT 9:00-5:00. (250) 487-2450, *(800) 663-1956.* ✚ ❂

PRINCE GEORGE—CAA BRITISH COLUMBIA, 100 - 2324 FERRY AVE, V2N 0B1. WEEKDAYS (M-F) 9:00-6:00, SAT 9:00-5:00. (250) 649-2399, *(800) 663-1956.* ✚ ❂

RICHMOND—CAA BRITISH COLUMBIA, #618-5300 NO 3 RD, V6X 2X9. WEEKDAYS (M-F) 9:00-6:00, SAT 9:00-5:00. (604) 268-5850, *(800) 663-1956.* ✚ ❂

SURREY—CAA BRITISH COLUMBIA, #C4-15285 101 AVE, V3R 9V8. WEEKDAYS (M-F) 9:00-6:00, SAT 9:00-5:00. (604) 205-1000, *(800) 663-1956.* ✚ ❂

SURREY—CAA BRITISH COLUMBIA, 130 2655 KING GEORGE BLVD, V4P 1H7. WEEKDAYS (M-F) 9:00-6:00, SAT 9:00-5:00. (604) 205-1150, *(800) 663-1956.* ✚ ❂

VANCOUVER—CAA BRITISH COLUMBIA, 2347 W 41ST AVE, V6M 2A3. WEEKDAYS (M-F) 9:00-6:00, SAT 9:00-5:00. (604) 268-5800, *(800) 663-1956.* ✚ ❂

VANCOUVER—CAA BRITISH COLUMBIA, 999 W BROADWAY, V5Z 1K5. WEEKDAYS (M-F) 9:00-6:00, SAT 9:00-5:00. (604) 268-5600, *(800) 663-1956.* ✚ ❂

VERNON—CAA BRITISH COLUMBIA, #520 4400 32ND ST, V1T 9H2. WEEKDAYS (M-F) 9:00-6:00, SAT 9:00-5:00. (250) 550-2400, *(800) 663-1956.* ✚ ❂

VICTORIA—CAA BRITISH COLUMBIA, #120-777 ROYAL OAK DR, V8X 4V1. WEEKDAYS (M-F) 8:30-5:30, SAT 9:00-5:00. (250) 704-1750, *(800) 663-1956.* ✚ ❂

VICTORIA—CAA BRITISH COLUMBIA, 1262 QUADRA ST, V8W 2K7. WEEKDAYS (M-F) 9:00-6:00, SAT 9:00-5:00. (250) 414-8320, *(800) 663-1956.* ✚ ❂

VICTORIA—CAA BRITISH COLUMBIA, 169 2401C MILLSTREAM RD, V9B 3R5. WEEKDAYS (M-F) 9:00-5:30, SAT 9:00-5:00. (250) 391-3250, *(800) 663-1956.* ✚ ❂

WEST VANCOUVER—CAA BRITISH COLUMBIA, 608 PARK ROYAL N, V7T 1H9. WEEKDAYS (M-F) 9:00-6:00, SAT 9:00-5:00. (604) 268-5650, *(800) 663-1956.* ✚ ❂

WESTBANK—CAA BRITISH COLUMBIA, 301 3550 CARRINGTON RD, V4T 2Z1. WEEKDAYS (M-F) 9:00-6:00, SAT 9:00-5:00. (250) 707-4800, *(800) 663-1956.* ✚ ❂

MANITOBA

ALTONA—CAA MANITOBA, 61 2ND AVE NE, R0G 0B0. WEEKDAYS (M-F) 9:00-5:00, SAT 9:00-1:00. (204) 324-8474 ● ▲ ❂

BRANDON—CAA MANITOBA, 305 - 18TH ST N, R7A 6Z2. WEEKDAYS (M-F) 9:00-5:00, THU 9:00-8:00, SAT 9:00-4:00. (204) 571-4111, *(877) 222-1321.* ✚ ▲ ❂

WINNIPEG—CAA MANITOBA, 2211 MCPHILLIPS ST UNIT C, R2V 3M5. WEEKDAYS (M-F) 9:00-6:00, SAT 9:00-4:00. (204) 262-6223, *(800) 222-4357.* ● ▲ ❂

WINNIPEG—CAA MANITOBA, 501 ST ANNES RD, R2M 3E5. WEEKDAYS (M-F) 9:00-6:00, SAT 9:00-4:00. (204) 262-6201, *(800) 222-4357.* ● ▲ ❂

WINNIPEG—CAA MANITOBA, 870 EMPRESS ST, R3G 3H3. WEEKDAYS (M-F) 9:00-6:00, SAT 9:00-4:00. (204) 262-6100, *(800) 222-4357.* ✚ ▲ ❂

SASKATCHEWAN

ESTEVAN—CAA SASKATCHEWAN, 1340-400 KING ST, S4A 2B4. WEEKDAYS (M-F) 9:00-5:30, SAT 9:00-5:30. (306) 637-2185, *(800) 564-6222.* ✚ ▲ ❂

MOOSE JAW—CAA SASKATCHEWAN, 80 CARIBOU ST W, S6H 2J6. WEEKDAYS (M-F) 9:00-5:30, SAT 9:00-5:30. (306) 693-5195, *(800) 564-6222.* ✚ ▲ ❂

NORTH BATTLEFORD—CAA SASKATCHEWAN, 2002-100TH ST, S9A 0X5. WEEKDAYS (M-F) 9:00-5:30, SAT 9:00-5:30. (306) 445-9451, *(800) 564-6222.* ✚ ▲ ❂

PRINCE ALBERT—CAA SASKATCHEWAN, #29 2995 2ND AVE W, S6V 5V5. WEEKDAYS (M-F) 9:00-5:30, SAT 9:00-5:30. (306) 764-6818, *(800) 564-6222.* ✚ ▲ ❂

REGINA—CAA SASKATCHEWAN, 1501 4TH AVE, S4R 8P9. WEEKDAYS (M-F) 8:00-5:00, SAT 9:00-6:00 (SALES ONLY). (306) 791-9500 ◖

REGINA—CAA SASKATCHEWAN, 200 ALBERT ST, S4R 2N4. WEEKDAYS (M-F) 9:00-5:30, SAT 9:00-5:30. (306) 791-4337, *(800) 564-6222.* ✚ ▲ ❂

REGINA—CAA SASKATCHEWAN, 2510 E QUANCE ST, S4V 2X5. WEEKDAYS (M-F) 9:00-5:30, SAT 9:00-5:30. (306) 791-4323, *(800) 564-6222.* ✚ ▲ ❂

REGINA—CAA SASKATCHEWAN, 4528 ALBERT ST, S4S 6B4. WEEKDAYS (M-F) 9:00-5:30, SAT 9:00-5:30. (306) 791-4322, *(800) 564-6222.* ✚ ▲ ❂

SASKATOON—CAA SASKATCHEWAN, 150 - 1ST AVE S, S7K 1K2. WEEKDAYS (M-F) 9:00-5:30, SAT 9:00-5:30. (306) 668-3737, *(800) 564-6222.* ✚ ▲ ❂

SASKATOON—CAA SASKATCHEWAN, 2112 MILLAR AVE, S7K 6P4. WEEKDAYS (M-F) 8:00-5:00, SAT 9:00-6:00 (SALES ONLY). (306) 668-3768 ◖

SASKATOON—CAA SASKATCHEWAN, 3110 8TH ST E #1, S7H 0W2. WEEKDAYS (M-F) 9:00-5:30, SAT 9:00-5:30. (306) 668-3770, *(800) 564-6222.* ✚ ▲ ❂

SWIFT CURRENT—CAA SASKATCHEWAN, 15 DUFFERIN ST W, S9H 5A1. WEEKDAYS (M-F) 9:00-5:30, SAT 9:00-5:30. (306) 773-3193, *(800) 564-6222.* ✚ ▲ ❂

WEYBURN—CAA SASKATCHEWAN, 110 SOURIS AVE, S4H 2Z8. WEEKDAYS (M-F) 9:00-5:30, SAT 9:00-5:30. (306) 842-6651, *(800) 564-6222.* ✚ ▲ ❂

YORKTON—CAA SASKATCHEWAN, 159 BROADWAY ST E, S3N 3K6. WEEKDAYS (M-F) 9:00-5:30, SAT 9:00-5:30. (306) 783-6536, *(800) 564-6222.* ✚ ▲ ❂

Metric Equivalents Chart

TEMPERATURE

To convert Fahrenheit to Celsius, subtract 32 from the Fahrenheit temperature, multiply by 5 and divide by 9. To convert Celsius to Fahrenheit, multiply by 9, divide by 5 and add 32.

ACRES

1 acre = 0.4 hectare (ha)   1 hectare = 2.47 acres

MILES AND KILOMETRES

Note: A kilometre is approximately 5/8 or 0.6 of a mile. To convert kilometres to miles multiply by 0.6.

Miles/Kilometres		Kilometres/Miles	
15	24.1	30	18.6
20	32.2	35	21.7
25	40.2	40	24.8
30	48.3	45	27.9
35	56.3	50	31.0
40	64.4	55	34.1
45	72.4	60	37.2
50	80.5	65	40.3
55	88.5	70	43.4
60	96.6	75	46.6
65	104.6	80	49.7
70	112.7	85	52.8
75	120.7	90	55.9
80	128.7	95	59.0
85	136.8	100	62.1
90	144.8	105	65.2
95	152.9	110	68.3
100	160.9	115	71.4

Celsius °		Fahrenheit °
100	BOILING	212
37		100
35		95
32		90
29		85
27		80
24		75
21		70
18		65
16		60
13		55
10		50
7		45
4		40
2		35
0	FREEZING	32
-4		25
-7		20
-9		15
-12		10
-15		5
-18		0
-21		-5
-24		-10
-27		-15

LINEAR MEASURE

Customary	Metric
1 inch = 2.54 centimetres	1 centimetre = 0.4 inches
1 foot = 30 centimetres	1 metre = 3.3 feet
1 yard = 0.91 metres	1 metre = 1.09 yards
1 mile = 1.6 kilometres	1 kilometre = .62 miles

WEIGHT

If You Know:	Multiply By:	To Find:
Ounces	28	Grams
Pounds	0.45	Kilograms
Grams	0.035	Ounces
Kilograms	2.2	Pounds

LIQUID MEASURE

Customary	Metric
1 fluid ounce = 30 millilitres	1 millilitre = .03 fluid ounces
1 cup = .24 litres	1 litre = 2.1 pints
1 pint = .47 litres	1 litre = 1.06 quarts
1 quart = .95 litres	1 litre = .26 gallons
1 gallon = 3.8 litres	

PRESSURE

Air pressure in automobile tires is expressed in kilopascals. Multiply pound-force per square inch (psi) by 6.89 to find kilopascals (kPa).

24 psi = 165 kPa	28 psi = 193 kPa
26 psi = 179 kPa	30 psi = 207 kPa

GALLON AND LITRES

Gallons/Litres				Litres/Gallons			
5	19.0	12	45.6	10	2.6	40	10.4
6	22.8	14	53.2	15	3.9	50	13.0
7	26.6	16	60.8	20	5.2	60	15.6
8	30.4	18	68.4	25	6.5	70	18.2
9	34.2	20	76.0	30	7.8	80	20.8
10	38.0	25	95.0	35	9.1	90	23.4

Explore. Excite. Experience.

Get the travel information that turns vacations into extraordinary experiences.

- Descriptive destination details
- Suggested itineraries
- Don't-miss things to see and do
- Insider tips from AAA travel experts
- AAA inspector comments and consumer reviews
- Member rates and convenient hotel booking

 Explore AAA.com and CAA.ca today.

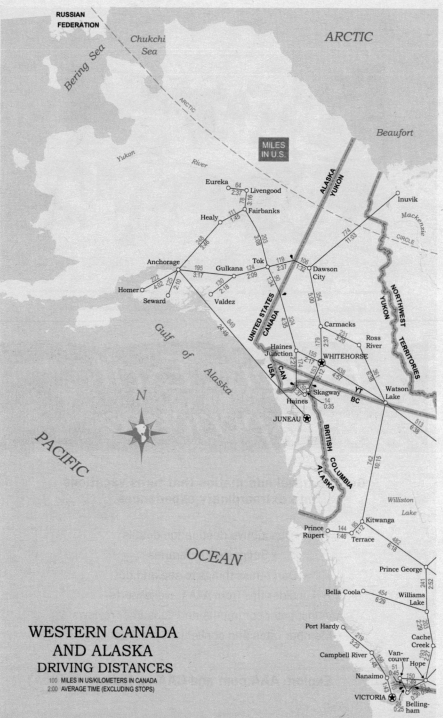

RUSSIAN
FEDERATION

*Chukchi
Sea*

Bering Sea

ARCTIC

Beaufort

ALASKA / YUKON

MILES
IN U.S.

Yukon   *River*

ARCTIC

CIRCLE

Mackenzie

Inuvik

Eureka — 64 / 2:37 — Livengood
78 / 3:16
Healy — 111 / 1:45 — Fairbanks

774 / 11:03

NORTHWEST

Anchorage — 195 / 3:17 — Gulkana — 124 / 2:09 — Tok — 119 / 2:37 — 106 / 1:32 — Dawson City

248 / 3:46
308
203

Homer — 222 / 4:02 — 125 / 2:10
Seward

130 / 2:18
Valdez

98 / 1:59

YUKON

TERRITORIES

324 / 4:35

354
5:00

Carmacks
231 / 3:20
Ross River

849 / 24:49

UNITED STATES
CANADA

179 / 2:37

361 / 6:38

Haines Junction
155 / 2:27
174 / 2:17
155 / 1:55
WHITEHORSE
439 / 4:57
Watson Lake

USA
CAN
YT
BC

112
35 / 0:55
Skagway
14 / 0:35
Haines

513 / 6:38

JUNEAU

BRITISH COLUMBIA

ALASKA

742 / 10:15

*Williston
Lake*

Prince Rupert — 144 / 1:46 — 95 / 1:12 — Kitwanga
Terrace — 482 / 6:18

Prince George

241 / 2:52

Bella Coola — 454 / 6:29 — Williams Lake

226
203

Port Hardy — 219 / 3:23 — Campbell River — 147 / 1:48 — Nanaimo
51 / 0:45
Vancouver
Hope
150 / 1:49
193 / 2:27

Cache Creek

VICTORIA — 71 / 1:43 — 24 / 0:25 — Bellingham

PACIFIC

OCEAN

Gulf
of
Alaska

N

WESTERN CANADA
AND ALASKA
DRIVING DISTANCES

100 MILES IN US/KILOMETERS IN CANADA
2:00 AVERAGE TIME (EXCLUDING STOPS)

© AAA

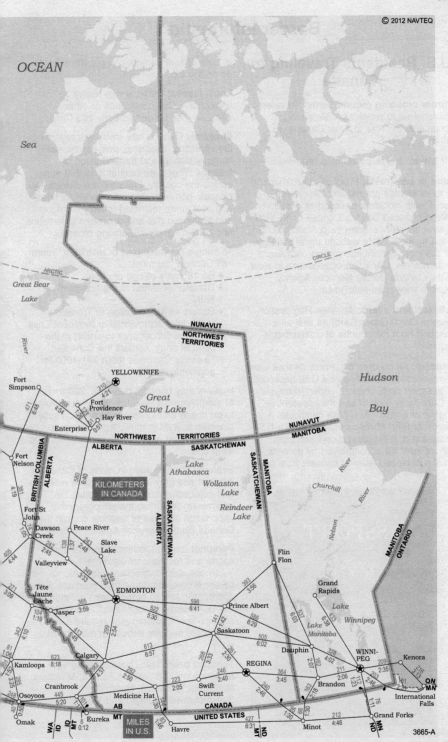

3665-A

Border Information

U.S. Residents Traveling to Canada

Border crossing requirements: Travelers are required to present proper travel documents in order to enter Canada and return to the U.S.

Air travel: A U.S. passport is required.

Land or sea travel: Proof of citizenship and proof of identity are required. Approved documents include a passport or passport card, Enhanced Driver's License or NEXUS trusted traveler program card. Visit the U.S. Department of State website travel.state.gov for the most current information on these requirements. Canadian citizens should refer to the Canada Border Services Agency website www.cbsa-asfc.gc.ca.

U.S. resident aliens: An Alien Registration Receipt Card (Green Card) as well as a passport from the country of citizenship is required.

Children: All children must provide their own travel documents. In lieu of a U.S. passport or passport card, children under 16 traveling to Canada by land or sea may present an original or copy of their birth certificate, a Report of Birth Abroad obtained from a U.S. consulate or a Naturalization Certificate. Minors must be accompanied by parents, or have a notarized letter of consent from one or both absent parents giving permission to go on the trip.

Legal Issues: Persons with felony convictions, DUI convictions or other offenses may be denied entry into Canada.

Firearms: Canada has strict laws regarding the importing, exporting, possession, use, storage, display and transportation of firearms. These are federal laws that apply across the country. Firearms are divided into classes: non-restricted (most ordinary rifles and shotguns); restricted (mainly handguns) and prohibited (full and converted automatics and certain handguns, among others).

To bring a non-restricted or restricted firearm into Canada you must:
- Be 18 years of age or older
- Declare firearm(s) at the first point of entry
- Obtain an Authorization to Transport (ATT) from a provincial or territorial Chief Firearms Officer prior to arrival at the point of entry; contact the Canadian Firearms Centre at (800) 731-4000 for additional details.

Hunters may bring in, duty-free, 200 rounds of ammunition; a valid license or declaration to purchase ammunition is required. Those planning to hunt in multiple provinces or territories must obtain a hunting license from each one.

Firearms are forbidden in many of Canada's national and provincial parks, game reserves and adjacent areas. For additional information regarding the temporary importation and use of firearms consult the Canada Border Services Agency website.

Personal items: Clothing, personal items, sports and recreational equipment, automobiles, snowmobiles, cameras, personal computers and food products appropriate for the purpose and duration of the visit may be brought into Canada duty and tax-free. Customs may require a refundable security deposit at the time of entry.

Tobacco products: Those meeting age requirements (18 years in Alberta, Manitoba, Northwest Territories, Nunavut, Saskatchewan, Quebec and Yukon; 19 years in other provinces) may bring in up to 50 cigars, 200 cigarettes, 200 grams of tobacco and 200 tobacco sticks.

Alcohol: Those meeting age requirements (18 years in Alberta, Manitoba and Quebec; 19 years in other provinces and territories) may bring in limited alcoholic beverages: 40 ounces of liquor, 1.6 quarts of wine or 9 quarts of beer or ale (equivalent to 24 12-ounce bottles or cans).

- Amounts exceeding the allowable quantities are subject to federal duty and taxes, and provincial/territorial liquor fees.
- Provincial fees are paid at customs at the time of entry in all provinces and Yukon.
- It is illegal to bring more than the allowable alcohol quantity into the Northwest Territories or Nunavut.

Purchases: Articles purchased at Canadian duty-free shops are subject to U.S. Customs exemptions and restrictions; those purchased at U.S. duty-free shops before entering Canada are subject to duty if brought back into the United States.

Prescription drugs: Persons requiring medication while visiting Canada are permitted to bring it for their own use. Medication should be in the original packaging with a label listing the drug and its intended use. Bring a copy of the prescription and the prescribing doctor's phone number.

Gifts: Items not exceeding $60 (CAN) in value (excluding tobacco, alcoholic beverages and advertising matter) taken into or mailed to Canada are allowed free entry. Gifts valued at more than $60 are subject to regular duty and taxes on the excess amount.

Pets: You must have a certificate for a dog or cat 3 months and older. It must clearly describe the animal, declare that the animal is currently vaccinated against rabies and include a licensed veterinarian signature.

- Collar tags are not sufficient proof of immunization.
- Be sure the vaccination does not expire while traveling in Canada.
- The certificate is also required to bring the animal back into the U.S.

Exemptions: Service animals; healthy puppies and kittens under 3 months old with a health certificate signed by a licensed veterinarian indicating that the animal is too young to vaccinate.

Vehicles
- Vehicles entering Canada for leisure travel, including trailers not exceeding 8 feet 6 inches (2.6 m) in width, are generally subject to quick and routine entry procedures.
- To temporarily leave or store a car, trailer or other goods in Canada if you must leave the country, you must pay an import duty and taxes or present a valid permit. Canadian Customs officials issue vehicle permits at the point of entry.
- You are required to carry your vehicle registration document when traveling in Canada.
- If driving a car other than your own, you must have written permission from the owner.
- If driving a rented car, you must provide a copy of the rental contract.
- A valid U.S. driver's license is valid in Canada.
- In all Canadian provinces and territories except Alberta, British Columbia and Saskatchewan, it is illegal to use radar detectors, even if unplugged.
- Seat belt use is required for the driver and all passengers.

Financial Responsibility Laws in Canada: When an accident involves death, injury or property damage, Canadian provinces and territories require evidence of financial responsibility.

U.S. motorists should check with their insurance company regarding whether they are required to obtain and carry a yellow Non-Resident Inter-Province Motor Vehicle Liability Insurance Card (accepted as evidence of financial responsibility throughout Canada). Those not carrying proper proof may be subject to a substantial fine. If renting a vehicle, check with the rental car company.

U.S. Residents Returning to the U.S.

U.S. citizens returning to the U.S. from Canada by air must have a valid passport. Those returning by land or sea are required to present the appropriate travel documents outlined above.

Every individual seeking entry into the United States—foreign visitors, U.S. citizens or lawful permanent residents—must be inspected at the point of entry. Random searches may be conducted by U.S. Customs and Border Protection agents.

U.S. Exemptions for a Stay in Canada of 48 Hours or More

- Each individual may bring back tax- and duty-free articles not exceeding $800 in retail value.
- Any amount over the $800 exemption is subject to duty.
- The exemption is allowed once every 30 days.
- A family (related persons living in the same household) may combine purchases to avoid exceeding individual exemption limits.
- Exemptions are based on fair retail value (keep receipts of all purchases as proof).
- Exemptions apply to articles acquired only for personal or household use or as gifts and not intended for sale.
- The exemption may include 100 cigars, 200 cigarettes and 1 liter of liquor per person over age 21 (state liquor laws are enforced).
- All articles must accompany you on your return.

U.S. Exemptions for a Stay in Canada Less Than 48 Hours

- Each individual may bring back tax- and duty-free articles not exceeding $200 in retail value.
- The exemption may include no more than 50 cigarettes, 10 cigars, 5 fluid ounces (150 milliliters) of alcoholic beverage or 150 milliliters of perfume containing alcohol.
- A family may not combine purchases.
- If purchases exceed the $200 exemption, you forfeit the exemption and all purchases become subject to duty.
- All articles must be declared and accompany you upon return.

Gifts

- Gifts up to $100 fair retail value may be sent to friends or relatives in the United States provided no recipient receives more than one gift per day (gifts do not have to be included in the $800 exemption).
- Gifts of tobacco products, alcoholic beverages or perfume containing alcohol valued at more than $5 retail are excluded from this provision.
- Mark the contents, retail value and "Unsolicited Gift" on the outside of the package.

Prohibited: Narcotics and dangerous drugs, drug paraphernalia, obscene articles and publications, seditious or treasonable matter, lottery tickets, hazardous items (fireworks, dangerous toys, toxic or poisonous substances) and switchblade knives. Also prohibited are any goods originating in embargoed countries.

Canadian Residents Traveling to the U.S.

Canadian citizens entering the U.S. by air must have a valid passport. Canadian citizens entering the U.S. by land or sea are required to present the appropriate travel documents; refer to the Canada Border Services Agency website www.cbsa-asfc.gc.ca for the most current information on these requirements.

If traveling to the United States with a minor, carry documentation proving your custodial rights. A person under age 18 traveling to the United States alone or with only one parent or another adult must carry certified documentation proving that the trip is permitted by both parents.

U.S. Customs permits Canadian residents to bring—duty-free for personal use and not intended for sale—the following: clothing, personal items and equipment appropriate to the trip, up to 200 cigarettes, 50 cigars or 2 kilograms of tobacco, and 1 liter of alcoholic beverage.

Canadian Residents Returning to Canada

Canadian residents may bring back, free of duty and taxes, goods valued up to $400

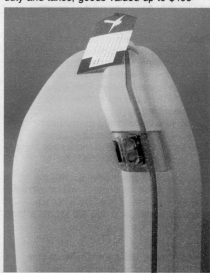

(CAN) any number of times a year, provided the visit to the United States is 48 hours or more and all goods accompany the purchaser (a written declaration may be required).

You may claim a $50 (CAN) exemption on goods, excluding alcoholic beverages and tobacco products, if returning after an absence of less than 48 hours and not using any other exemption. If bringing back more than $50 worth of goods, the regular duty and tax rate is levied on the entire value. This exemption may apply any number of times in a year. No tobacco or alcohol may be brought back if returning from a visit of less than 48 hours.

If returning after 7 days or more (not counting the departure day from Canada)

you may claim up to a $750 (CAN) exemption. Goods other than alcohol and tobacco products need not accompany you (a written declaration may be required).

Permitted within the $400 and $750 exemptions: up to 50 cigars, 200 cigarettes, 200 tobacco sticks and 6.4 ounces of tobacco, and up to 40 ounces of liquor or 1.6 quarts of wine or 9 quarts of beer or ale (the equivalent of 24 12-ounce bottles or cans). You must meet the minimum age requirement of the province or territory entered to claim alcohol or tobacco products.

While AAA makes every effort to provide accurate and complete information, AAA makes no warranty, express or implied, and assumes no legal liability or responsibility for the accuracy or completeness of any information contained herein.

Points of Interest Index

Attractions appear at the top of each category
and offer a Great Experience for Members®.

Index Legend

CHILDREN'S ACTIVITIES

EVENTS & FESTIVALS

HISTORIC SITES & EXHIBITS

OUTDOORS & SCIENCE

SHOPPING

SPORTS & RECREATION

TOURS & SIGHTSEEING

Photo Credits

Page numbers are in bold type. Picture credit abbreviations are as follows:
- (i) numeric sequence from top to bottom, left to right ▪ (AAA) AAA Travel library.

- (Cover) Stanley Park, Vancouver, BC / © William Manning / Alamy
- **7** © Monashee Frantz / age fotostock
- **13** © Adivin / iStockphoto
- **18** (i) © Dan Merkel / Panoramic Images
- **18** (ii) © ESP-Photo / age fotostock
- **19** © Scott Dimond / age fotostock
- **20** (i) Courtesy of Wikimedia Commons
- **20** (ii) Courtesy of Wikimedia Commons
- **23** (i) © age fotostock / Robert Harding
- **23** (ii) © Ilene MacDonald / Alamy
- **23** (iii) © Rolf Hicker Photography / Alamy
- **23** (iv) © Helge Schulz / age fotostock
- **23** (v) © Design Pics / SuperStock
- **24** (i) © All Canada Photos / Alamy
- **24** (ii) © Danita Delimont / Alamy
- **24** (iii) © Tibor Bognar / Alamy
- **24** (iv) © Michael Wheatley / age fotostock
- **53** © Dan Bannister / awl-images
- **56** © Thompson Paul / age fotostock
- **57** © Rosanne Tackaberry / Alamy
- **58** © Rolf Hicker Photography / Alamy
- **59** © Rachid Dahnoun / Auro / age fotostock
- **60** © Design Pics Inc. / Alamy
- **108** © Design Pics Inc. / Alamy
- **111** © Michael Wheatley / Alamy
- **112** © Tibor Bognar / Alamy
- **113** © Andrew Bain / Alamy
- **114** © Paul Heinrich / Alamy
- **115** © Fancy / Alamy
- **118** © Barrett & MacKay / age fotostock
- **190** (i) © Steven Lindner / Panoramic Images
- **190** (ii) © All Canada Photos / Alamy
- **191** © Gus Curtis / Alamy
- **192** (i) Courtesy of Wikimedia Commons
- **192** (ii) © Jennifer Mackenzie / Alamy
- **195** (i) © Dennis Frates / Alamy
- **195** (ii) © Chuck Haney / DanitaDelimont.com
- **195** (iii) © Don Johnston / Alamy
- **195** (iv) © Grandmaison Photography
- **195** (v) © Grandmaison Photography
- **196** (i) © nagelestock.com / Alamy
- **196** (ii) © John E Marriott / Alamy
- **196** (iii) © Gunter Marx / IN / Alamy
- **196** (iv) © Alex Law / Britannia Mine Museum
- **342** © Michael Wheatley / age fotostock
- **345** Published with permission from AAA Executive Editor Bill Wood
- **346** © PhotoBliss / Alamy
- **347** © Chris Cheadle / Alamy
- **348** © Realimage / Alamy
- **349** © Christian Kober / age fotostock
- **350** © David Buzzard / Alamy
- **351** © Gunter Marx / Alamy
- **352** © All Canada Photos / Alamy
- **358** © GerryRousseau / Alamy
- **360** © PhotoBliss / Alamy
- **396** © Ron Niebrugge / Alamy
- **399** © SuperStock / Alamy

(cont'd)

(cont'd)

Keep Your Children Safe in the Car

AAA and the timeless characters of best-selling children's author Richard Scarry have partnered to promote child passenger safety. Visit **AAA.com/SafeSeats4Kids** for car seat guidelines, and go to **SeatCheck.org** or call **866-SEAT-CHECK (732-8243)** for installation information.
In Canada, visit the Child Safety section of Transport Canada's website at **tc.gc.ca.**
Remember, car seats save lives!

We Do Everything But Jump On The Beds

AAA backs the Diamond Ratings with expert, in-person evaluations – whether the hotel or restaurant is no-frills, moderate or upscale.

▶ AAA/CAA inspections are unannounced to ensure our experience is comparable to yours.

▶ Only hotels and restaurants that meet AAA standards and member expectations are Approved.

▶ The Diamond Rating, from One to Five, describes the type of experience you can expect.

 Learn more at AAA.com/Diamonds

AAA Travel Information

AAA delivers reliable travel information just the way you want it.

In Print

Get printed TourBook® guides at AAA and CAA offices.

Online

Access robust travel information and planning tools like TripTik® Travel Planner at AAA.com and CAA.ca.

On The Go

Download eTourBook® guides for ereaders and smartphones at AAA.com/ebooks and get the multi-featured AAA or CAA app from the iTunes Store or Google Play.